WORDSPELLER

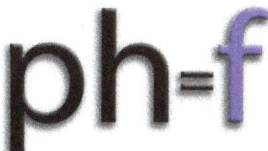

Phonetic Dictionary

American English 2-Color Edition

- Cross-references your word with other words which may sound similar or are spelled similarly (is it petal or pedal or peddle?)

- Provides suffix endings associated with your word and spells them out for you (funny, funnies, funnier, funniest, and so on)

- Provides prefixes with definitions that can be associated with your word (unable, enable, disable, and so on)

- Includes selected commonly used proper nouns (no people or place names)

Diane M. Frank

Summary: Over 70,000 entries of commonly used American English words with multiple misspellings per word based upon their phonetic sound. Brief definitions allow for quickly ascertaining the proper word you wish to use. Extensive cross-referencing allows for words that are either similar in meaning and/or spelling.

All available prefixes are defined. Each correctly spelled word lists all potential suffix endings leaving no guesswork as to how to spell the future and past tense of a word. Use this reference tool as a bridge to go from the sound of your word to a standard dictionary if further comprehension is needed.

Misspelled words are printed in a second color to allow differentiation between a properly spelled word and a misspelled word.

Proper nouns are not listed unless they are common in everyday communication. Proper nouns which are included in this resource tool; days of the week, months of the year, common medical and legal terms, common plants, animals and others which can be cross-referenced with a word which may not be a proper noun.

Notice of Rights

All rights reserved. No part of this book may be reproduced, digitized, stored in a retrieval system or transmitted in any form or by any means, without the prior written permission of the publisher.

Notice of Liability

The author and publisher have made every effort to ensure the accuracy of the information herein. However, the information contained in this book is sold without warranty, either expressed or implied. Neither the author, co-author, publisher, dealers or distributors will be held liable for any mistakes.

Authored by Diane M. Frank
Co-authored by Gabrielle M. Purcell
Consultant Editor by Jeremy Sarka
Cover Design by Martian Source Productions
Publisher i.m.Press

Copyright © May, 2015 by i.m.Press
PO Box 412, Rainier, Washington 98576, USA

Library of Congress Cataloging-in-Publication Data
Library of Congress Control Number: 2015939314

Wordspeller Phonetic Dictionary; American English 2-Color Edition
> **Summary:** Over 70,000 entries of commonly used American English words can be located by how their phonetic sounds. Very brief definitions intended to help you quickly locate your word to bridge you to a standard dictionary. Most proper nouns are not listed unless employed in everyday use (ie. months, days, animals, legal, medical). Extensive cross-referencing allows for words that are either similar in meaning and/or spelling. Defined Prefixes as well as all available Suffix endings for root words are easily located. Use this reference tool as a bridge to go from the sound of your word to a standard dictionary. Misspelled words are printed in a second color to allow differentiation from correctly spelled words.

www.phoneticdictionary.com
www.wordspeller.net
www.americanwordspeller.com

ISBN 978-0-9830381-4-6

Manufactured in the United States of America

1st Edition

AUTHOR'S WORD

The reasons for creating a dictionary which locates your word by the "way it sounds" are multitudinous. Earning a degree in Communications was not without careful thought and examination. Having witnessed unnecessary embarrassment, the marginalization of many peoples of all types, unfounded pompous arrogance and flaming egos exposes the English language for what it is, a throne. A throne that can seat only a small number of butts. It has been over 200 years, longer than any other country in the world can boast, since a mandate to simplify the language in some form or fashion was brought forth and executed. As every American well knows, mastery of the written language ensures the survival of economic hierarchy. And why this particular language should prevail, despite all the thousands of practical and phonetically matching alphabets of the world, is quite a conundrum and a bit sad since it is the least worthy of such power and rule. Logic would suggest modifying this language to be more user-friendly since communication is primary for everyone.

People of all ages, of all walks of life, from every corner of the globe have been or will be marginalized by this English language at some point in time. Ranging from 'forgetting' the spelling of a word as we dawn into our senior years or suffer head injuries ensuring us of re-learning our own native language all over again. Whether coming into American English via another country or being in your first 6 years of elementary schooling warrants a useful communication tool. Last but not least and more importantly, our friends, neighbors and loved ones who may be experiencing some varying degree of dyslexia, dyspraxia or any of the innumerable afflictions we fondly refer to as 'learning disabilities' that affect over 1/5th of the people in the United States deserve a tool designed with all of them in mind.

Over 50% of populations in all countries are abstract and/or picture thinkers. Words take on lesser meaning when written than when spoken inviting a chasm in communication. The author of this book of reference sees absolutely no reason why communication should be challenged on any level, at any time and for any reason. If American leaders have no intention of leveling the playing field by overhauling the English language so that all people have fair access to a language that is logical and phonetic, then the release of this dictionary should help fill that void where compassion displaces humility.

And while we're at it, let's have a little discussion about...
Dialects, Annunciation and Pronunciation

Perhaps, in my opinion, there is more emphasis placed upon the problems with spelling as it relates to the 'speller' and their perceived disabilities, when, in actuality, more emphasis could be placed upon annunciation or pronunciation by those who speak the English language.

As a child learning EFL (English as a First Language) or a traveler new to this country learning ESL (English as a Second Language) there lies one common trait...hearing the language for the first time on American soil. When it comes to spelling English there are a number of issues facing the speller such as; hearing difficulties (tones, accents, dialects), sight difficulties (irregular neuronet firing, eye muscle control). These challenges are compounded by someone who speaks the language without articulating, pronouncing or annunciating correctly.

Dialects within the United States alone ranges from hundreds to thousands (depending upon whom is citing the study). It's very challenging to take a spelling test with a new teacher who has a strong southern drawl or to grow up in one region of the country where entire letters are dropped from words, letters such as 'r', 't', 'g' and 'd'. In some regions letters are even added that do not belong to a proper English word such as the letters 'r' or 't' or 'd'. Words such as 'something' turn into 'sumthen' and 'children' into 'chilren'. Some people in parts of the country 'warsh' their clothes. Some English speakers may not use the proper tense of a word and interrelate 'forget' with 'forgot' and 'drank' with 'drunk'.

Confusion goes even further with a new speller when, upon hearing a word taken out of context, may experience the inability to grasp and differentiate how to spell the word. Words spoken and not articulated give rise to synonymous sounding words such as 'petal, pedal and peddle' or 'procession', 'precession' and 'precision'.

It behooves us all to ease off on the pressure we place upon those who are challenged with spelling the written word and take responsibility for how we articulate our speech and stop 'warshing our clothes'!

Diane M. Frank

FOREWORD

"Its a damn poor mind that can think of only one way to spell a word."

Andrew Jackson

The literal meaning of the word *dyslexia* – from its Greek roots – is "difficulty with words". And with over 50% of the world experiencing this in varying degrees, we will discuss dyslexia generally and specifically since it is the primary motivation for the creation of this work.

Dr. Maryanne Wolfe, author of *Proust and the Squid: The Story and Science of the Reading Brain*, explains, "the more you know about a word, the faster you can read it." Dr. Virginia Berninger, of the University of Washington, has demonstrated that reading fluency is enhanced for dyslexic students through instruction that focuses on the interrelation between the three "forms" shared by each word: the meaning of the word, its visual appearance, and its sound.

Ronald Davis, author of *The Gift of Dyslexia* (and a man who mastered his autism), builds his program for dyslexia correction upon the insight that word mastery is essential to reading development, using only two essential materials: clay and a dictionary. Students use clay to create three-dimensional models of the meaning of each word, as well as the letters that spell the word. The modeling is needed because dyslexic individuals think mostly in pictures, unable to think with words unless they have mental pictures to go along with them.

But here is where dyslexics encounter their biggest barrier: spelling. The most persistent and pervasive symptom of dyslexia is an orthographic barrier; they have difficulty remembering the conventional spelling of phonetically irregular words. Many educators focus on intensive teaching of phonics, as this provides one avenue for decoding many of the simpler words encountered by beginning readers. English is not a phonetic language, but rather a polyglot and amalgam of words drawn from different languages, often retaining spellings that reflect histories and pronunciations long forgotten.

Through brain scans, Dr. Sally Shaywitz of Yale University has shown that dyslexic readers typically underutilize the "visual word form area" of the brain – the part of the visual cortex believed to be involved in instantaneous recognition of whole words. This is the part of the brain that probably stores a picture of the right letters arranged in the right order, the part that is engaged when you choose the correct spelling because it just *looks* right to you.

It isn't that dyslexic writers are unable to spell a word; with their creative problem-solving strengths, they can easily spell the same word half a dozen different ways. As Andrew Jackson once said, "its a damn poor mind that can think of only one way to spell a word." The problem is in figuring out which spelling is the one that everyone else will use and understand...

If you can't spell a word, you cannot find it in a dictionary.

This is where the most powerful tool – the dictionary – is also the most inaccessible. Because if we err in guessing the first 2 or 3 letters of the word, we will never find it.

And here is where *Wordspeller & Phonetic Dictionary* becomes indispensible – it provides the key to the door that opens the dictionary. This dictionary is the key to independence: it provides the correct spelling and all possible definitions and use of each word. It is where all those phonetic decoding skills emphasized by well-meaning primary school teachers can finally be brought to fruition: *krecher* may not be a word, but it *is* a spelling, albeit an incorrect one. In a regular dictionary, it leads us to the Kremlin, which is not where we wanted to go. But *Wordspeller & Phonetic Dictionary* gives us the answer in exactly the place we have gone to find it: "creature."

Suname leads to tsunami. *Fanomanen* takes us to phenomenon. *Ekselerate* turns into accelerate. And pretty soon, the world of words is ours for the taking. If we already know the meaning of the word, that is all that is needed. The correct spelling is there, in a form that we can copy and use.

If our trip to the dictionary is also a search for meaning, or etymology, or information as to usage, or a set of synonyms, then this *Wordspeller & Phonetic Dictionary* has opened the door for us. By providing the spelling we need, we can access the larger dictionary or thesaurus which can provide us with whatever information we seek.

This reference book should be in every school library, in every classroom, and at home on every student's desk. It is the key to independence for every learner.

-Abigail Marshall, Author of *The Everything Parent's Guide to Children with Dyslexia* and *When Your Child Has ... Dyslexia*. She also manages the *Dyslexia the Gift* site www.dyslexia.com

INTRODUCTION

This American English edition of the *Wordspeller & Phonetic Dictionary* is primarily designed to allow the user to locate their word by the way it sounds (phonetically). As a resource tool, it empowers the user to not only locate their word within seconds...but as a *phonetic* dictionary qualifies it as suitable for ESL, dyslexics and EFL. This reference book (unlike any dictionary ever created) also performs the following functions:

Cross-referencing...

- *emigrant* or *immigrant*?
- *gym* or *gem*?
- *marry* or *merry*?
- *scene* or *seen* or *seine*?
- *pedal* or *petal* or *peddle*?
- *carrot* or *karat* or *caret* or *carat*?

Learn how to spell the word correctly the first time you hear it...

korts, spelled phonetically could lend to words such as:
quartz
courts
quarts
chords
cords

bol, spelled phonetically could be...
ball
bowl
bawl
bull

All these words, as well as thousands of others are cross-referenced extensively throughout this phonetic dictionary.

Wordspeller *provides short, concise definitions* to enable the user to quickly identify which word they wish to spell correctly. This lends the user the ability to then consult a standard dictionary for further comprehension of the word if desired.

Misspellings often involve transposing letters which are most commonly misinterpreted in hearing such as:

t	with	d	au	with	ow
b	with	p	ch	with	sh
ph	with	f	ou	with	ow
kn	with	n	th	with	f
qu	with	kw	c	with	s

Another advantage of the Wordspeller is *providing suffix endings for over 70,000 commonly used words to include legal, medical and slang.* Over 12 notable standard dictionaries were required to retrieve every conceivable suffix ending for each word. No single dictionary performs this added feature. As well, the Wordspeller & Phonetic Dictionary has provided *all known 'proper' prefix's as well as their definitions.*

HOW TO USE THIS DICTIONARY
METHODOLOGY: for misspelled words + root words

RULE #1: If you have a difficult time using this dictionary, refer back to these rules!

RULE #2: Simply look up the word by the way it SOUNDS...not the way it should/would/could be spelled.

RULE #3: Look up the **root** word. The root word is the word without suffixes added:

Example of a misspelled word in this dictionary:

baged, bag(gged) / back(ed)

baged, is the misspelled word

= bag(gged) is "bagged" spelled properly ~ bag is the root word to look up in the dictionary to make certain this is the word you want

= back(ed) is "backed" spelled properly ~ back is the root word to look up in the dictionary to make certain this is the word you want

Example:

beder, better / bid(dder) / bitter / bet(ttor)

beder, is the misspelled word

= better is spelled properly

= bid(dder) "bidder" spelled properly~ bid is the root word to look up in the dictionary to make certain this is the word you want

= bitter is spelled properly

= bet(ttor) "bettor" spelled properly~ bet is the root word to look up in the dictionary to make certain this is the word you want

Example:

eksploratory, explore(ratory)

eksploratory is the misspelled word

= explore(ratory) "exploratory" spelled properly ~ explore is the root word to locate in the dictionary to make certain this is the word you want

METHODOLOGY: for properly spelled words

RULE #1:   If you have a difficult time using this dictionary, refer back to these rules!

RULE #2:   Simply look up the word the way it SOUNDS...not the way it should/would/could be spelled.

RULE #3:   Suffixes (endings for words which describe past, present, future tense) how to:

A.)   The asterisk (*) means to add an "s" to the end of the word.

Example:
receptionist,* = receptionist + 's' = receptionists

B.)   Go back into the latter part of the root word for a letter that matches the beginning letter of the suffix ending.

Example:
paralysis,ytic,yze,yzed,zying,yzation,yzer = **paral**y**tic, paral**y**ze, paral**y**zed, paral**y**zing, paral**y**zation, paral**y**zer**

C.)   The suffix ending for the word is either added onto the end of the last letter or from a letter towards the end of the word.

Examples:

~ **call,***lled,lling,ller
= **cal**l**ed, cal**l**ing, cal**l**er**
(Double 'll' is listed to assure you that there are two 'll's)

~ **reckless**,ssly,ssness
= **reckles**s**ly, reckles**s**ness**
(Double 'ss' is listed to assure you that there are two 'ss')

~ **balance,***ed,cing
= **balance**s**, balance**d**, balan**c**ing**
(Asterisk (*) means "just add an 's)

~ **nag**,gged,gging,ggingly
= **na**g**ged, na**g**ging, na**g**ginly**
(Double 'gg' is listed to assure you that there are two 'gg's)

~ **immaculate**,ely,eness,acy
= **immaculat**e**ly, immaculat**e**ness, immaculac**y

~ **adapt,***ted,ting,tive,tively,tation,table,tability
= **adapt**s**, adapt**ed**, adapt**ing**, adapt**ive**, adapt**ively**, adapt**ation**, adapt**able**, adapt**ability

RULE #4:   DE...If your word begins with a prefix such as 'de', simply remove the first 2 letters - 'de' then look up the remainder of the word (the root word).
  Example: deice, *'de'* means "AWAY FROM/DOWN FROM" then look up the root word 'ice'.

RULE #5:   UN... If your word begins with a prefix such as 'un', simply remove the first 2 letters - 'in' then look up the remainder of the word (the root word).
  Example: unfavorable, *'un'* means "NOT/REVERSAL" then look up the root word 'favorable'.

ix

a, PREFIX INDICATING 'TO/TOWARDS/ AT' MOST OFTEN MODIFIES THE WORD
ab, PREFIX INDICATING 'FROM/AWAY FROM' MOST OFTEN MODIFIES THE WORD
aback, SURPRISED
abak, aback
abal, able
abalishen, abolition
abalone, A MOLLUSK
abanden, abandon
abandon,*,ned,ning,nment, LEFT ALL ALONE
abaration, aberration
abart, apart
abate,*,ed,ting,table,ement,ements, SUBSIDE/REDUCE/DECREASE
abatizing, appetizing
abaut, about
abawt, about
abazet, opposite
abbey,*, A MONASTERY
abbreveashen, abbreviate(tion)
abbreviate,*,ed,ting,tion,tor,tory, SHORTEN/CONDENSE
abcent, absent
abcerd, absurd
abcint, absent
abcurd, absurd
abdicate,*,ed,ting,tion,tor,able, RELINQUISH
abdikate, abdicate
abdikeit, abdicate
abdiman, abdomen
abdomen,minal,minally, STOMACH AREA
abducate, abdicate
abduct,*,ted,ting,tee,tion,tor, KIDNAP
abdukate, abdicate
abdukt, abduct
abdumen, abdomen
abe, abbey
abed, abet
abedeinse, obedience
abedeint, obedient
abedience, obedience
abel, able / apple / appeal
abelete, ability
abelishen, abolition
abelone, abalone
abeluty, ability
aberant, aberrant

aberegene, aborigine
aberigine, aborigine
aberition, aberration
aberrant,tly,nce,ncy, DEVIATE/STRAY AWAY FROM
aberration,*,nal, DEVIATE FROM THE STANDARD/NORM
abes, abyss
abet,*,tted,tting,tment, BACK UP/ ENCOURAGE/APPROVE
abetchuery, obituary
abeting, abet(tting)
abezit, opposite
abide,*,ed,er,ding,dingly,dance, STAY, WITHSTAND
abidid, abide(d)
abil, able / apple
ability,ties, CAPACITY "prefixes: dis/in"
abilone, abalone
abirant, aberrant
abirition, aberration
abis, abyss
abitchuery, obituary
abituary, obituary
abius, abuse
abl, able / apple
able,ly,bility, CAPABLE "prefixes: dis/en/ un"
ableb, ad-lib
ablederate, obliterate
ableveus, oblivious
ablib, ad-lib
abliveon, oblivion
abliveus, oblivious
abnormal,lly,lity, NOT TYPICAL/ NATURAL
abnormil, abnormal
abnormul, abnormal
aboard, GET ONTO SOMETHING SUCH AS VESSEL/TRAIN/ORGANIZATION (or see about)
abof, above
abol, able / apple
abolesh, abolish
abolish,hes,hed,hing,her,hment,hable, ition, END, TERMINATE
abolishon, abolition
abolition,nist, DESIRES TO END/ TERMINATE SOMETHING
abomanable, abominable
abominable,ly,eness, HORRID
abominuble, abominable
aborant, aberrant

aborchen, abortion
aborchun, abortion
abord, aboard / abort
aboregini, aborigine
aboreginul, aborigine(nal)
aborigine,*,nal, INDIGINEOUS, NATIVE
aborijinul, aborigine(nal)
aborshun, abortion
abort,*,ted,ting,tion, STOP/QUIT ACTION (or see aboard)
abortion,*, CANCEL PROJECT/ PREGNANCY
about, APPROXIMATELY
above, OVER
abowt, about
abpropreate, appropriate
abproximat, approximate
abpruval, approve(val)
abral, apriljanuary
abrasive,ely,eness, ROUGH, SCOURING
abredg, abridge
abreg, abridge
abrehenshun, apprehension
abrel, april
abreveashen, abbreviate(tion)
abreveat, abbreviate
abreveation, abbreviate(tion)
abreviate, abbreviate
abridge,*,ed,ging,er, SHORTEN LENGTH BY CONDENSING/REWRITING
abridged, SHORTEN LENGTH BY CONDENSING/REWRITING
abrig, abridge
abrihenshun, apprehension
abrikot, apricot
abril, april
abroad, LEFT HOME TO GO OVERSEAS
abrod, abroad
abrol, april
abropt, abrupt
abrowtch, approach
abruhensev, apprehensive
abruhenshun, apprehension
abrul, april
abrupt,tly,tness, SUDDEN
abscess,sses,ssed,ssing,ssion, INFECTION IN THE BONE
absence,*, NOT PRESENT, UNAVAILABLE (or see absent(s))
absens, absence / absent(s)
absent,tly,tee,teeism, INTENTIONALLY UNAVAILABLE (or see absence)
abserd, absurd

abserdity, absurd(ity)
abserdly, absurd(ly)
abses, abscess
absilute, absolute
absilutly, absolute(ly)
absins, absence / absent(s)
absint, absent
absintee, absent(ee)
absird, absurd
absirdety, absurd(ity)
absirdly, absurd(ly)
absolute,tely,tion,tism, DEFINITELY
absolve,*,ed,ving,vable,er,lution, FORGIVEN, RELEASED
absorb,*,bed,bing,bingly,bable,ber, bance,bent,rption,rptive,rptivity, COLLECT/ GATHER "prefixes: non"
absorbshen, absorption
absorbtef, absorptive
absorbtion, absorption
absorption, ACCUMULATE/HOLD/ GATHER
absorptive,vity,ion, ACCUMULATES/ HOLDS/GATHERS
absorshen, absorption
absortef, absorptive
absortion, absorption
absortive, absorptive
abstain,*,ned,ning,nment,ner,tinence, DENY, REFRAIN
abstane, abstain
abstinent,nce,tly, VOLUNTARILY DENY/ REFRAIN
abstract,*,ted,ting,tedly,tedness,tion, tionist, APART FROM, THEORETICAL
abstrakt, abstract
abstunent, abstinent
absulootly, absolute(ly)
absulution, absolve(lution)
absunt, absent
absurd,dly,dity,dities,dness, CRAZY
absurdety, absurd(ity)
abtetude, aptitude
abtitude, aptitude
abtumin, abdomen
abuf, above
abul, able
abulishen, abolition
abulone, abalone
abundance,*,nt,ntly, PLENTY
abundince, abundance
abundint, abundance(nt)
aburant, aberrant
aburation, aberration
aburegene, aborigine
aburijene, aborigine
aburition, aberration
abuse,*,sed,sing,sive,siveness, TREAT WRONGLY "prefixes: dis"
abusef, abuse(sive)
abusif, abuse(sive)
abutizing, appetizing
abuve, above
abuze, abuse
abuzet, opposite
aby, abbey
abyss,smal,smally,ssal, CHASM, GREAT DEPTH EITHER PHYSICAL/ EMOTIONAL
abzaulv, absolve
abzdanent, abstinent
abzent, absent
abzilute, absolute
abzint, absent
abzolv, absolve
abzorb, absorb
abzuloot, absolute
abzulute, absolute
abzulution, absolve(lution)
ac, PREFIX INDICATING 'TO/TOWARDS/ AT' MOST OFTEN MODIFIES THE WORD
academic,*,mism,micism,mia,mician, mical,mically, SCHOOLING
academy,mies, SPECIAL SCHOOL
acadume, academy
acamadasions, accomodations
acampany, accompany
accadintul, accident(al)
accedental, accident(al)
accel,*,lled,lerate, ABBREVIATION OF 'ACCELERATE' (or see excel)
accelarate, accelerate
accelerate,*,ed,ting,tion,tor, QUICKEN, FORCE TO GO/MOVE, GAS PEDAL
accelirate, accelerate
accent,*, TONES IN SPEECH, HIGHLIGHTS
accentuate,*,ted,ting,tion, TO EMPHASIZE
accepshen, except(ion)
accept,*,ted,ting,tingly,tance,table, tably,tability,tation, APPROVE (or see except) "prefixes: un"
acceptinse, accept(ance)
acceshen, accession
accesorize, accessory(rize)
access,sses,ssed,ssing,ssible,ssibility, ssion, ENTER "prefixes: in"
accession,*,ned,ning, ENTER "prefixes: de"
accessory,ries,rize,rizing, ADDITIONAL
accident,*,tal,tally, INVOLUNTARILY
acclaim,amatory,amation, LOUD APPROVAL/APPLAUSE (or see acclimate)
acclimate,*,ed,ting,tion,tize,tized,tizing, tization, BECOME ACCUSTOMED TO (or see acclaim(ation))
accomadate, accommodate
accomadation, accommodate(tion)
accomedate, accommodate
accomedashen, accommodate(tion)
accomidation, accommodate(tion)
accommodate,*,ting,tion,tive, ASSIST "prefixes: un"
accomodate, accommodate
accomodation, accommodate(tion)
accompany,nies,nied,nying,niment,nist, GOES ALONG WITH "prefixes: un"
accompeny, accompany
accomplice,*, PARTICIPATED IN A CRIME
accomplish,hes,hed,hing,hment,hable, her, GOAL/IDEA ACHIEVED
accomudation, accommodate(tion)
accord,*,ded,ding,dingly,dance,dant, dantly, GIVE, GRANT TO, IN HARMONY WITH "prefixes: dis"
account,*,ted,ting,tant,tancy,table, tability, RESPONSIBLE/LIABLE FOR "prefixes: un"
accredit,*,ted,ting,table,tation,tive, RESPONSIBLE/LIABLE FOR "prefixes: un"
accrue,*,ual,ed,uing, TO STORE/SAVE UP "prefixes: non/un"
accuate, acuate
accudental, accident(al)
accuiesent, acquiesce(nt)
accumulate,*,ted,ting,tion,tive,tively, tor, GATHER/GROW "prefixes: bio"
accupuncture, acupuncture
accurate,ely,eness,acy, CORRECT "prefixes: in"
accuse,*,ed,sing,singly,satory,satorial, satorially,sative,sation,er, CHARGE OR IMPLY
accustom,med, FAMILIAR, HABITUAL "prefixes: un"

ace,*,ed, A SCORE IN GAME, ON DIE(DICE), TO WIN
acebt, except / accept
acedik, acetic / acidic / ascetic
acempany, accompany
acer, acre
acerens, occur(rrence)
aceshun, accession
acetic,tous, PROPERTIES OF VINEGAR, SOUR (or see ascetic/acidic)
acetify,fies,fied,fying,fier,fication, OF ACETIC, CONVERT TO ACID/VINEGAR (or see acidify)
acewmulate, accumulate
ache,*,ed,hing,hy,hiness, HURT
acheeve, achieve
acheve, achieve
achieve,*,ed,ving,vment,vable,vably, vability, GAIN "prefixes: over/un/under"
achin, action
achual, actual
acid,*,dic,dity,dly,dulate,dulated, dulating,dulation,dulent,dulous, dulously, CHEMICAL COMPOUND
acidemic, academic
acidental, accident(al)
acidic, CHEMICAL BALANCE, OF ACID (or see acetic/ascetic)
acidify,fies,fied,fying,fiable,fication,fier, CONVERT TO ACID (or see acetify) "prefixes: de"
aciuponcsher, acupuncture
ack, ache
ackawnt, account
acklimation, acclimate(tion) / acclaim(amation)
acknowledge,*,ed,ging,ement,gable,er, RECOGNIZE
ackomplish, accomplish
ackord, accord
ackownt, account
ackraget, aggregate
ackred, acrid
ackret, acrid
acks, ax / ache(s) / ask
acksderminate, exterminate
ackseal, axis(ial)
ackses, access / ax(es) / axis
ackseshen, accession
acksesory, accessory
acksglood, exclude
acksul, axil / axle
ackuiesent, acquiesce(nt)

ackumulate, accumulate
ackustumed, accustom(ed)
aclemate, acclimate
aclimate, acclimate
aclimation, acclimate(tion) / acclaim(amation)
acne, AFFLICTION OF THE SKIN
acnolege, acknowledge
acomadashen, accommodate(tion)
acomblesh, accomplish
acomedate, accommodate
acomidate, accommodate
acomidation, accommodate(tion)
acompany, accompany
acompined, accompany(nied)
acomplise, accomplice
acomplish, accomplish
acompuny, accompany
acomudashen, accommodate(tion)
acomudate, accommodate
acord, accord
acordant, accord(ant)
acount, account
acoustic,*,cal,cally, OF SOUND
acquaint,*,ted,ting,tance, ASSOCIATE WITH "prefixes: un"
acquaintance,*,eship, FAMILIAR
acquiesce,*,ed,cing,ence,ent,ently, AGREE/ALLOW IN A HUMBLE/PASSIVE WAY
acquire,*,red,ring,rement,rable,er, OBTAIN
acquisition,*,ned,ning,nist, ACQUIRED
acquisitive,ely,eness, READILY ACQUIRES
acquit,*,tted,tting,ttal,ttance,ttances, tter, ABSOLVES, FREED
acquittal,*, ABSOLVES, FREE OF JUDGEMENT
acqwaentense, acquaintance
acqwantinse, acquaintance
acrabats, acrobat(s)
acrad, acrid
acraget, aggregate
acravat, aggravate
acre,*,eage, AMOUNT OF LAND
acred, acrid
acreget, aggregate
acrevat, aggravate
acrid,dity,dly, BITTER/CAUSTIC SMELL "prefixes: sub"
acriget, aggregate
acrit, acrid
acrivat, aggravate

acro, PREFIX INDICATING 'END/BEGINNING/HEIGHT' MOST OFTEN MODIFIES THE WORD
acrobat,*,tic,tics, INVOLVES VARIOUS CONFIGURATIONS
acroget, aggregate
acronym,*, INITIALS, FIRST LETTER OF WORDS
across, OVER
acrovat, aggravate
acruget, aggregate
acruvat, aggravate
acseal, axis(ial)
acsebt, except / accept
acsecute, execute
acsel, excel / accel / axle
acselurashen, accelerate(tion)
acsent, accent
acsentric, eccentric
acsepshen, except(ion)
acsept, accept / except
acses, access / excess
acsesurize, accessory(rize)
acshan, action
acshen, action
acshin, action
acshooul, actual
acshual, actual
acshuated, acuate(d)
acshun, action
acsis, access / ax(es) / axis
acsisory, accessory
acsite, excite
acsiul, axis(ial)
acskershin, excursion
acspereanse, experience
act,*,ted,ting,tor, ACTION "prefixes: over/re/retro/under"
actaf, active
actef, active
actevate, activate
acteve, active
actin, action
action,*,nable,nably, DOING, MOVEMENT "prefixes: in/re"
activate,*,ed,ting,tion, START "prefixes: de/in"
active,ely,vity,veness,vate,vation,tor, vist,vism, MOVING, CAUSE TO ACT "prefixes: bio/in/over/pro/re/retro"
actovate, activate
actseed, exceed
actual,lly,lity,lization,lize, REAL

actuate,*,ted,ting,tion, INITIATE/BEGIN ACTIVITY "prefixes: de/un"
actule, actual
actuvate, activate
actuve, active
acudemic, academic
acuemulate, accumulate
acuesativ, acquisitive
acuiesant, acquiesce(nt)
acuisativ, acquisitive
acuital, acquittal
acult, occult
acumpany, accompany
acumpened, accompany(nied)
acumulate, accumulate
acupansy, occupancy
acupuncture,*,rist, TREATMENT FOR HEALING BODY
acurate, accurate
acurens, occur(rrence)
acurit, accurate
acuse, accuse
acustic, acoustic
acustumed, accustom(ed)
acute,ely,eness, SHARP
acwatic, aquatic
acwaynt, acquaint
acwayntense, acquaintance
acwazition, acquisition
acweesent, acquiesce(nt)
acwifalent, equivalent
acwire, acquire
acwit, acquit
acwuzeshun, acquisition
acwyre, acquire
ad, PREFIX INDICATING 'TO/TOWARDS' MOST OFTEN MODIFIES THE WORD, SHORT FOR ADVERTISEMENT (or see at/add/aid)
adacity, audacity
adakit, etiquette
adalesint, adolescent
adam, atom
adamant,tly,tine, RELENTLESS, NOT PENETRABLE, A METAL
adamently, adamant(ly)
adamize, atom(ize)
adapt,*,ted,ting,tive,tively,tation,table, tableness,tability,ter,tor, ADJUST (or see adept) "prefixes: pre/retro"
adasity, audacity
adatif, additive
add,*,dded,dding,ddable,dditive, ddition,dditional,dditionally, ddendum, INCREASE, PLUS, MORE THAN BEFORE
addendum,*, SOMETHING ADDED
addict,*,ted,ting,tion,tive, HABITUAL/ OBSESSIVE USE
additive,*, MORE, AN INCREASE, ADDITIONALLY
address,sses,ssed,ssing,ssee, ROUTE/ LOCATION OF "prefixes: re"
adebt, adapt / adept
adec, attic / addict
adecuasi, adequacy
adecuat, adequate
adek, attic / addict
adekt, addict
adekuasi, adequacy
adekuat, adequate
adelesinse, adolescence
ademant, adamant
adement, adamant
ademize, atom(ize)
ademunt, adamant
adenaficashun, identification
adendum, addendum
adept,tly,tness, SKILLFUL (or see adapt)
adequace, adequacy
adequacy,cies, ABILITY
adequate,ely,eness, SUFFICIENT "prefixes: in"
adequise, adequacy
adequot, adequate
ader, adhere
adeshen, edition / add(ition)
adetif, additive
adetion, edition / add(ition)
adetude, attitude
adewlation, adulate(tion)
adgetate, agitate
adgitate, agitate
adgrenalin, adrenaline
adgudekashen, adjudicate(tion)
adgunct, adjunct
adgust, adjust
adhear, adhere
adhere,*,ed,ring,ent,ently,ence,esion, esive, STICKS TO
adhesion, STICKS TO
adhesive,*,eness, STICKS TO
adible, audible
adic, attic / addict
adict, addict
adicuasi, adequacy
adieu,*, GOOD-BYE
adik, attic / addict
adikit, etiquette
adikshen, addict(ion)
adikt, addict
adimant, adamant
adimdum, addendum
adimunt, adamant
adindum, addendum
adinefecashin, identification
adiquacy, adequacy
adiquase, adequacy
adiquit, adequate
adiquot, adequate
adishen, edition / add(ition)
aditev, additive
adition, edition / add(ition)
aditiv, additive
aditude, attitude
adiu, adieu
adjacent,tly, NEAR "prefixes: non"
adjasent, adjacent
adjasint, adjacent
adje, etch / edge
adjective,*,val,vally, WORD THAT MODIFIES A NOUN
adjewdikashen, adjudicate(tion)
adjewlation, adulate(tion)
adjitate, agitate
adjoin,*,ned,ning,nt,nts, TO JOIN/ UNITE
adjourn,*,ned,ning,nment, DELAY
adjudicate,*,ed,ting,tion,tor,tive, JUDGE
adjudikashen, adjudicate(tion)
adjulation, adulate(tion)
adjunct,*,tive,tly,tion, JOINS/ ACCOMPANIES
adjust,*,ted,ting,table,tment, CHANGE TO NEW CIRCUMSTANCE
adleb, ad-lib
adlesense, adolescence
adlesinse, adolescence
ad-lib,*,bbed,bbing, SPONTANEOUS PREPARATION
admenaster, administer
admenastrashen, administrate(tion)
admenester, administer
admenister, administer
admenistration, administrate(tion)
admenustrashen, administrate(tion)
admeshun, admission
admet, admit
admichin, admission
admichun, admission
admided, admit(tted)

adminaster, administer
administer,*,red,ring, SUPERVISE, DISPENSE
administrate,*,ed,ting,tion,tive,tively,tor, ONE WHO SUPERVISES
admire,*,er,ring,rable,rably,ration, CHERISH
admisable, admissible
admisef, admission(ive)
admishun, admission
admisible, admissible
admissible,ly,bility, ALLOWABLE "prefixes: in"
admission,*,ive, ENTRANCE, ADMIT TO
admisuf, admission(ive)
admit,*,tted,tting,ttance,ttedly, ALLOW "prefixes: non"
admited, admit(tted)
admizable, admissible
admizible, admissible
admonish,hes,hed,hing,her,hment,ition, itions,itory, WARN/ADVISE/DIRECT AGAINST
admyre, admire
ado, adieu
adobiografe, autobiography
adobt, adopt
adobyografy, autobiography
adograf, autograph
adolecense, adolescence
adolescence,nt, OF YOUTH
adolescent,*, YOUTH
adolesense, adolescence
adolesinse, adolescence
adolesint, adolescent
adolt, adult
adom, atom
adomadik, automatic
adoment, adamant
adometer, odometer
adomider, odometer
adomint, adamant
adomize, atom(ize)
adomobil, automobile
adoo, adieu
adoor, adore
adopt,*,ted,ting,tion,tive,table, ACQUIRE "prefixes: un"
adore,*,ed,ring,ringly,rable,rably, rability,rableness,ration, WORSHIP
adorn,*,ned,ning,nment, ENHANCE
adranalin, adrenaline
adrenaline, HORMONE
adrenulen, adrenaline

adress, address
adrift, MOVE/FLOAT WITHOUT DIRECTION
adroit,tly,tness, NIMBLE, SKILLFUL
adsedura, etcetera
adsetera, etcetera
adshe, etch / edge
adt, eight / ate
adu, adieu
adukit, etiquette
adulate,*,ed,ting,tor,tory,tion, EXCESSIVE PRAISE/COMPLIMENT
adulesinse, adolescence
adulesint, adolescent
adult,*, FULLY MATURE PHYSICALLY
adulterate,*,ed,ting,tion,ant,tor, DEBASE OR ALTER "prefixes: un"
adultery,rous,rously,rer, SEX WITH OTHERS WHEN MARRIED
adum, atom
adumant, adamant
adumint, adamant
adumize, atom(ize)
aduquacy, adequacy
adutif, additive
adutude, attitude
advance,*,ed,cing,ement, PROGRESS "prefixes: under"
advans, advance
advanse, advance
advantage,*,ed,ging,eous,eously, BENEFIT, BETTER CHANCE "prefixes: dis"
advantech, advantage
advantig, advantage
advantuge, advantage
advecate, advocate
advekate, advocate
advencher, adventure
advent,*, EXPECTED/IMPORTANT ARRIVAL
adventure,*,er,rous,rously,esome,ess, EXPLORATION "prefixes: mis"
adverb,*,bial, OF VERBS
advercity, adverse(sity)
advers, adverse
adversarie, adversary
adversary,ries,rial, OPPONENT
adverse,ely,eness,sity,sities,sary,saries, sarial,sative,satively, OPPOSE (or see averse)
adversly, adverse(ly)

advert,*,ted,ting,tence, CHANGE DIRECTION/ATTENTION TOWARDS (or see avert) "prefixes: in"
advertise,*,ed,sing,ement, DECLARE
advertize, advertise
advicate, advocate
advice, RECOMMEND (or see advise)
advikete, advocate
advincher, adventure
advinshure, adventure
advinture, adventure
advirb, adverb
advirsare, adversary
advirse, adverse
advirsere, adversary
advise,*,ed,sing,edly,edness,ement,sor, ser,sory,sable,sably,sability, INFORM (or see advice) "prefixes: in/un"
advize, advise / advice
advizuble, advise(sable)
advocate,*,ed,ting,tory,acy,tion,tor, SUPPORTER
advukate, advocate
advurb, adverb
advurcity, adverse(sity)
advurs, adverse
advursary, adversary
advursle, adverse(ly)
advursudy, adverse(sity)
advurtise, advertise
adyewlation, adulate(tion)
ael, ail
aem, aim
aemeable, amiable
aenckshes, anxious
aengwish, anguish
aenjul, angel
aenkre, angry
aenkshes, anxious
aent, aunt / ant
aenus, anus
aenxiatee, anxiety
aepaloge, apology
aerial, BY AIRCRAFT
aero, PREFIX INDICATING 'AIR' MOST OFTEN MODIFIES THE WORD
aerobic,*, OXYGEN EXERCISE
aerodynamic,*,cal,cally, AIR MOTION
aerosol,*, COMPRESSED CONTENTS IN A CAN
aesthetic,*,cal,cally, PLEASING TO THE EYES
aet, eight / ate

af, PREFIX INDICATING 'TO/TOWARDS' MOST OFTEN MODIFIES THE WORD
afadavit, affidavit
afair, affair
afale, avail
afare, affair
afder, after
afeador, aviator
afeator, aviator
afect, effect / affect
afectation, affect(ation)
afection, affection
afed, aphid
afedavit, affidavit
afekshin, affection
afekt, effect / affect
afektashin, affect(ation)
afektation, affect(ation)
afektion, affection
afeleat, affiliate
afemanit, effeminate
afend, offend
afenity, affinity
afens, offense
afensef, offense(sive)
afensif, offense(sive)
afer, affair / ever
afermative, affirm(ative)
afes, office
afeser, office(r)
afeshent, efficient
afeshul, official
afet, aphid
afeus, effuse
afews, effuse
affadavit, affidavit
affair,*, INTERACTION/BUSINESS
affare, affair
affecient, efficient
affect,*,ted,ting,ter,tation,tive, CAUSE SOMETHING TO HAPPEN, TRYING TO IMPRESS, PRETENTIOUS (or see effect) "prefixes: dis/un"
affection,*,nate,nately,nateness, TO EXPRESS FONDNESS
affenity, affinity
affidavit,*, LEGALLY BINDING STATEMENT
affiliate,*,ed,ting,tion, ASSOCIATED WITH "prefixes: dis/un"
affinity,tive, ATTRACTION
affirm,*,med,ming,mative,mation, SUPPORT WITH APPROVAL "prefixes: dis/un"

afflict,*,ted,tion,ter,tively, DISTRESS
affluence,*,nt,ntly, ABUNDANCE
affluent,tly, ABUNDANCE
afford,*,ded,dable,dability,dance, SPARE "prefixes: un"
affront,*,ted,ting, CONFRONT
affus, effuse
afid, aphid
afileat, affiliate
afimanit, effeminate
afinity, affinity
afinse, offense
afinsef, offense(sive)
afirm, affirm
afis, office
afiser, office(r)
afishensy, efficiency
afishent, efficient
afishinsy, efficiency
afishul, official
afishuly, official(lly)
afit, aphid
aflict, afflict
aflikt, afflict
afloat, FLOATING
aflot, afloat
afluense, affluence
afluent, affluent
afluinse, affluence
afoot, ABOUT TO HAPPEN, IN PROGRESS
aford, afford
aforduble, afford(able)
afore, PREFIX INDICATING 'BEFORE' MOST OFTEN MODIFIES THE WORD
afortuble, afford(able)
afot, afoot / aphid
afraid, FEARFUL
afrayed, afraid
afrebaudy, every(body)
afrewar, every(where)
afront, affront
afrunt, affront
aften, often
after, PREFIX INDICATING "AFTER" MOST OFTEN MODIFIES THE WORD FOLLOWING
aftur, after
afud, aphid
afudavit, affidavit
afurmative, affirm(ative)
afus, office / effuse
afuser, office(r)
afut, afoot

ag, PREFIX INDICATING 'SOIL/FIELD' MOST OFTEN MODIFIES THE WORD
again, REPEAT
against, TOWARD, FACING, OPPOSITE OF FLOW
agany, agony
agasent, adjacent
agasint, adjacent
agd, age(d)
age,*,ed,ging,eless, MEASURE OF TIME "prefixes: over/under"
agen, again / age(ging)
agency,cies, OF BUSINESS, OPERATION OF POWER
agenda,*, SCHEDULE/FORMAT/PLAN
agene, agony
agenst, against
agent,*,ncy,ncies, CATALYST, INTRODUCED TO PERFORM A TASK "prefixes: re"
agenta, agenda
ageny, agony
agern, adjourn
agetat, agitate
agetiv, adjective
agewdicate, adjudicate
aggravate,*,ed,ting,tingly,tion, AGITATE
aggravation, AGITATE
aggregate,*,ed,ting,ely,tion,tive,tor, FORM TOGETHER, UNITE "prefixes: dis"
aggresef, aggressive
aggresefly, aggressive(ly)
aggreshen, aggression
aggresive, aggressive
aggression,*, OFFENSIVE/ROUGH/ FORCEFUL
aggressive,ely,eness,ssor, AGGRAVATE/ AGITATE "prefixes: un"
aggressor,*, ONE WHO AGGRAVATES/ AGITATES
aggretion, aggression
agile,lity,eness, LIMBER, FLEXIBLE
aginda, agenda
aginst, against
aginsy, agency
agint, agent
aginy, agony
agirn, adjourn
agitate,*,ed,ting,tor,tion,tive,edly, AROUSE, AGGRAVATE, AGGRESSIVE STIMULATION
ago, PAST
agony,nies,nize,nized,nizing, SUFFER

agorn, adjourn
agrabat, acrobat
agravashen, aggravation
agravate, aggravate
agravation, aggravation
agrecultsher, agriculture
agree,*,eed,eeing,eement,eeable,
    eeably, CONSENT TO "prefixes: dis"
agregate, aggregate
agrekulcher, agriculture
agrenalin, adrenaline
agresef, aggressive
agreshen, aggression
agresif, aggressive
agresifle, aggressive(ly)
agresion, aggression
agresiv, aggressive
agresor, aggressor
agression, aggression
agressive, aggressive
agretion, aggression
agrevat, aggravate
agri, agree
agribat, acrobat
agricultcher, agriculture
agriculture,*,ral,rist,ralist,ralism,
    ralization, FARMING
agriget, aggregate
agrikultcher, agriculture
agrivate, aggravate
agrobat, acrobat
agrovat, aggravate
agrubat, acrobat
agruget, aggregate
agruvashen, aggravation
agruvat, aggravate
agruvation, aggravation
agsberament, experiment
agsblane, explain
agsebt, except / accept
agsecutive, executive
agseed, exceed
agsept, except / accept
agsersize, exercise / exorcise
agsert, exert
agspel, expel
agsplan, explain
agsplisit, explicit
agsrem, extreme
agstend, extend
agstenshen, extension
agstenuate, extenuate
agstereor, exterior
agsternal, external

agstinkt, extinct
agstradite, extradite
agstrakt, extract
agstreem, extreme
agstrordenair, extraordinaire
agstrordinery, extraordinary
agsturnal, external
agucolture, agriculture
agudecate, adjudicate
agudikate, adjudicate
agul, agile
agunct, adjunct
agune, agony
agunt, agent
aguny, agony
agust, august
agustible, adjust(able)
agutate, agitate
agutev, adjective
agzemt, exempt
ahead, COMING UP
ahed, ahead
ahod, ahold
ahold, TAKE NOTICE, MAKE CONTACT,
    GAIN CONTROL
ahpotment, appointment
aid,*,ded,ding, HELP
ail,*,led,ling,lment, SICK/NOT WELL (or
    see ale/aisle)
aile, aisle
aim,*,med,ming,mless,mlessly,
    mlessness, FOCUS ON A POINT,
    DIRECT ATTENTION
ainches, anxious
ainckshes, anxious
ainkshus, anxious
air,*,red,ring,rless, SPACE, A GAS/AURA
    (or see are/heir/err) "prefixes: un"
airborne, OFF THE GROUND
airea, area
airloom, heirloom
airobic, aerobic
airodynamic, aerodynamic
airoganse, arrogance
airport,*, AIRCRAFT BASE
aisle,*,ed, PASSAGEWAY
ait, eight / ate
aiz, eye(s) / ice
aj, age / edge
ajar, WHEN A DOOR IS NOT CLOSED ALL
    THE WAY
ajasent, adjacent
ajasint, adjacent
ajative, adjective

ajaur, ajar
aje, age
ajenda, agenda
ajensy, agency
ajent, agent
ajern, adjourn
ajetate, agitate
ajewdicat, adjudicate
ajewdikashen, adjudicate(tion)
ajil, agile
ajilety, agile(lity)
ajinda, agenda
ajinsy, agency
ajint, agent
ajitate, agitate
ajodikate, adjudicate
ajor, ajar
ajorn, adjourn
ajourn, adjourn
ajrenalin, adrenaline
ajudikate, adjudicate
ajul, agile
ajunct, adjunct
ajunt, agent
ajurn, adjourn
ajust, adjust
ajustible, adjust(able)
ajutev, adjective
ak, ache
akademe, academy
akademic, academic
akadume, academy
akamidate, accommodate
akashenul, occasion(al)
akaumplish, accomplish
akawnt, account
akcelaration, accelerate(tion)
akchen, action
akchuel, actual
akchun, action
akedemik, academic
aker, acre
akerens, occur(rrence)
akewmulate, accumulate
akewpunksher, acupuncture
akews, accuse
akewsashen, accuse(sation)
akidemic, academic
akiuponcsher, acupuncture
akiut, acquit
aklemate, acclimate
aklimation, acclimate(tion) /
    acclaim(amation)
aklumate, acclimate

aknaulig, acknowledge	aksedent, accident	akspres, express
akne, acne	akseed, exceed	akspreshen, express(ion)
aknolege, acknowledge	aksel, excel / accel / axle	aksquse, excuse
akod, echo(ed)	akselarashen, accelerate(tion)	akst, ax(ed) / ask(ed)
akomedashen, accommodate(tion)	akselarate, accelerate	akstereor, exterior
akomidate, accommodate	akselaratur, accelerate(tor)	akstinkt, extinct
akomidation, accommodate(tion)	akseld, excel(lled) / accel(lled)	aksturnal, external
akomodate, accommodate	akselerate, accelerate	aksudentul, accident(al)
akompaned, accompany(nied)	akselirashen, accelerate(tion)	aksul, axil / axle
akompeny, accompany	akseluratur, accelerate(tor)	aksulens, excel(lled) / accel(lled)
akomplis, accomplice	aksent, accent	aksus, axis / ax(es)
akomplish, accomplish	aksentric, eccentric	akt, act / ache(d)
akomudate, accommodate	aksentuate, accentuate	akter, act(or)
akonume, economy	aksepshen, except(ion)	aktevate, activate
akord, accord	aksept, accept / except	akteve, active
akordant, accord(ant)	akseptense, accept(ance)	aktir, act(or)
akorinse, occur(rrence)	akseptid, accept(ed)	aktivate, activate
akount, account	akseptinse, accept(ance)	aktive, active
akr, acre	akses, access / ax(es) / axis / ask(s)	aktober, october
akrabat, acrobat	aksesares, accessory(ries)	aktovate, activate
akrabatek, acrobat(ic)	aksesarize, accessory(rize)	aktuate, acuate
akrad, acrid	aksesd, access(ed)	aktur, act(or)
akragate, aggregate	aksesible, access(ible)	aktuvate, activate
akranem, acronym	aksesirize, accessory(rize)	aktuve, active
akrat, acrid	aksesory, accessory	akuazition, acquisition
akrebat, acrobat	aksesuble, access(ible)	akudemic, academic
akred, acrid	aksesurize, accessory(rize)	akuiesent, acquiesce(nt)
akree, agree	aksglude, exclude	akult, occult
akregate, aggregate	aksglute, exclude	akumpany, accompany
akrenem, acronym	akshen, action	akumulate, accumulate
akret, acrid	akshin, action	akupansy, occupancy
akrevat, aggravate	akshual, actual	akupunksher, acupuncture
akribat, acrobat	akshuat, actuate	akur, occur / acre
akrid, acrid	akshuated, acuate(d)	akurense, occur(rrence)
akrigate, aggregate	akshuel, actual	akuret, accurate
akrinem, acronym	akshun, action	akurints, occur(rrence)
akrit, acrid	aksident, accident	akusashen, accuse(sation)
akrivat, aggravate	aksidentul, accident(al)	akuse, accuse
akrobat, acrobat	aksil, axle	akustik, acoustic
akrogate, aggregate	aksint, accent	akustumed, accustom(ed)
akronem, acronym	aksintuate, accentuate	akute, acute
akross, across	aksis, ax(es) / axis / access	akwa, aqua
akrovat, aggravate	aksisory, accessory	akwaent, acquaint
akrugat, aggregate	aksite, excite	akwantense, acquaintance
akruget, aggregate	aksitment, excite(ment)	akwashin, equation
akrunem, acronym	akskeus, excuse	akwasition, acquisition
akruvat, aggravate	akskusis, excuse(s)	akwate, equate
aks, ax / ache(s) / ask / ask(ed) / ax(ed)	aksle, axil / axle	akwater, equator
aksald, excel(lled) / accel(lled)	aksol, axil / axle	akwatic, aquatic
akschange, exchange	aksorsize, exercise / exorcise	akwaynt, acquaint
aksd, ax(ed) / ask(ed)	akspensif, expense(sive)	akwayntinse, acquaintance
aksderminate, exterminate	akspinsif, expense(sive)	akwazeshin, acquisition
aksdurminate, exterminate	aksplan, explain	akwefer, aquifer
akseal, axis(ial)	aksplisit, explicit	akwesishun, acquisition

akwet, acquit
akwezishun, acquisition
akwinox, equinox
akwipment, equipment
akwire, acquire
akwit, acquit
akwitment, equipment
akwivulense, equivalent(ncy)
akwivulint, equivalent
akwoduct, aqueduct
akwufir, aquifer
akwuzishen, acquisition
akyerit, accurate
akzamen, examine
akzenshuate, accentuate
akzent, accent
akzinshuate, accentuate
akzint, accent
al, PREFIX INDICATING 'TO/TOWARDS' MOST OFTEN MODIFIES THE WORD (or see ail/ale/all/awl)
alabi, alibi
alactrishun, electrician
alagator, alligator
alagible, eligible
alakwens, eloquence
alakwent, eloquent
alaquens, eloquence
alarm,*,med,ming,mingly,mist, ALERT
alasteck, elastic
alastick, elastic
alastreus, illustrious
alau, allow
alaven, eleven
albem, album
albow, elbow
album,*, MEDIA COLLECTION
alcohol,lic,lism, CHEMICAL
alcove,*, NOOK
alder,*, A TREE (or see altar/alter)
aldir, alder / altar / alter
aldur, alder / altar / alter
ale,*, A BREWED DRINK (or see ail/all/alley/awl)
alean, alien
aleas, alias
alebi, alibi
aleby, alibi
alecate, allocate
alech, allege
alechens, allegiance
aleckt, elect
alecktrek, electric
alederite, illiterate

aledge, allege
alee, alley
alef, olive
aleg, allege
alegal, illegal
alegatur, alligator
alege, allege
alegens, allegiance / elegance
alegins, allegiance
alein, alien
aleinashen, alien(ation)
aleinate, alien(ate)
alej, allege
alejanse, allegiance
alejens, allegiance
alejins, allegiance
alekate, allocate
alekshen, elect(ion)
alekt, elect
alektrician, electrician
alektrik, electric
alektrishen, electrician
alekwens, eloquence
alekwent, eloquent
alemenade, eliminate
alemony, alimony
aleon, alien
alequence, eloquence
alequent, eloquent
alerche, allergy
alerchic, allergic
alerge, allergy
alerges, allergy(gies)
alergic, allergic
alert,*,ted,ting,tness, NOTIFY, SHARPLY AWARE
alesit, elicit / illicit
alet, elite
aletist, elite(tist)
aleun, alien
aleunashen, alien(ation)
aleunate, alien(ate)
aleus, alias
alev, olive
aleveate, alleviate
aleven, eleven
aleviate, alleviate
alevin, eleven
alevinth, eleven(th)
alevon, eleven
aley, alley
alf, elf
alfabedikul, alphabet(ical)
alfabet, alphabet

alfibetize, alphabet(ize)
alfubedikul, alphabet(ical)
alfubutize, alphabet(ize)
algae, WATER ORGANISM
algebra,aic,aically, TYPE OF MATH
algubra, algebra
ali, ally / alley
alians, alliance
alias,ses, ANOTHER NAME
alibi,*, EXCUSE
alicate, allocate
alid, ally(lied)
aliderate, illiterate
alien,*,nate,nation,nable, FOREIGNER (or see alliance) "prefixes: in/un"
alienashen, alien(ation)
alif, olive
aligater, alligator
align,*,ned,ning,nment, STRAIGHTEN "prefixes: re"
alikate, allocate
alike, SIMILAR
alikwens, eloquence
alikwent, eloquent
alimenate, eliminate
alimony, MONETARY ALLOWANCE AFTER DIVORCE
aline, align
alinment, align(ment)
aliquence, eloquence
aliquent, eloquent
alirt, alert
alis, ally(lies)
alisit, elicit / illicit
aliterate, illiterate
alitest, elite(tist)
aliunate, alien(ate)
alive, NOT DEAD, HAS SPIRIT
alja, algae
aljebra, algebra
aljibra, algebra
alk, elk
alkali,ine,inity,loid, CHEMICAL BALANCE
alkohol, alcohol
alkove, alcove
alkuhol, alcohol
all, EVERYTHING (or see ail/ale/awl) "prefixes: over"
allege,*,ed,ging,edly, ASSERT
allegiance,*,nt, LOYALTY
allelo, PREFIX INDICATING 'OTHER/ALTERNATE' MOST OFTEN MODIFIES THE WORD
allergic, SENSITIVE/REACTION TO

allergy,gies,genic,gic, SENSITIVE/REACTION TO
alleviate,*,ed,ting,tion,tive,tory, RELIEVE
alley,*,yway, PASSAGEWAY (or see ally)
alli, ally / alley
alliance,*,cing, JOIN "prefixes: mis/pro"
alligator,*, LARGE REPTILE
allocate,*,ed,ting,tion,table,tor, ASSIGN
allow,*,wed,wing,wable,wance, PERMIT "prefixes: dis/un"
allowance,*, PERMITTED, ALLOTTED
alloy,*, METALS TOGETHER
alltogether, altogether
allude,*,ed,ding,usion,usive, CASUALLY MAKE REFERENCE TO (or see elude)
allure,*,ed,ring,ement,ringly, TEMPT
allusion,*,ive, TO MENTION INDIRECTLY/CASUALLY (or see illusion)
allusive, TO MENTION INDIRECTLY/CASUALLY (or see elusive/illusive)
ally,llies,llied,llying,lliance, UNITED (or see alley)
almanac,*, BOOK WITH INFORMATION AS IT RELATES TO SPACE/STARS
alminak, almanac
almonak, almanac
almost, CLOSE
almozt, almost
almunak, almanac
alof, aloof
alokate, allocate
alone, NO ONE, NOTHING ELSE
aloof,fly,fness, RESERVED/DISINTERESTED COMPOSURE
aloore, allure
aloosuf, allusive / elusive / illusive
alop, elope
aloquence, eloquence
aloquent, eloquent
alosiv, allusive / elusive / illusive
alow, allow
alowins, allowance
alowy, alloy
aloy, alloy
alphabet,*,tic,tical,tize,tizes,tized,tizing, tization,tizer, SET OF SYMBOLS/LETTERS TO FORM WORDS
alphebetical, alphabet(ical)
alphubedikul, alphabet(ical)
already, BY THIS TIME
also, INCLUDED, ALONG WITH

alt, PREFIX INDICATING 'HIGH' MOST OFTEN MODIFIES THE WORD
altamatum, ultimatum
altar,*, PLATFORM FOR WORSHIP (or see alter/alder)
altematum, ultimatum
alter,*,red,ring,ration, TO SLIGHTLY CHANGE/MODIFY (or see alder/altar) "prefixes: in"
alterashen, alter(ation)
alternate,*,ed,ting,ely,tely,tion,tive, tively, TO GO BACK AND FORTH BETWEEN, ROTATE "prefixes: sub"
alternative,*,ely, CHOICES/OPTIONS
alternutiv, alternative
altetude, altitude
although, EVEN THOUGH
alti, PREFIX INDICATING 'HIGH' MOST OFTEN MODIFIES THE WORD
altimatum, ultimatum
altir, alder / altar / alter
altirashen, alter(ation)
altiration, alter(ation)
altird, alter(ed)
altirnetly, alternate(ly)
altirnitef, alternative
altirnutiv, alternative
altitude,*, HEIGHT
alto, PREFIX INDICATING 'HIGH' MOST OFTEN MODIFIES THE WORD
altogether, IN ONE PLACE
altumatum, ultimatum
altur, alder / altar / alter
alturashen, alter(ation)
alturation, alter(ation)
alturd, alter(ed)
alturnetly, alternate(ly)
alturnutiv, alternative
altwogether, altogether
aluby, alibi
alucate, allocate
alude, elude
aluf, aloof
alufent, elephant
alugable, eligible
alujen, illusion / allusion
alukate, allocate
alukwens, eloquence
alukwent, eloquent
alumenum, aluminum
aluminate, illuminate
aluminum, A METAL
alumony, alimony
alumunum, aluminum

aluquence, eloquence
aluquent, eloquent
alure, allure
alurgik, allergic
alurjik, allergic
alurt, alert
alusif, allusive / elusive / illusive
alusion, allusion / illusion
alusov, allusive / elusive / illusive
alustrious, illustrious
aluv, olive
always, FOREVER (or see aim)
alwaz, always
aly, ally
alyan, alien
alyke, alike
am, PRESENT TENSE OF "BE/BEING" (or see aim)
amachur, amateur
amaculet, immaculate
amagen, imagine
amagenation, imagine(nation)
amakewlit, immaculate
amakulit, immaculate
amasher, amateur
amateur,*,rish,rishly, NONPROFESSIONAL
amatur, amateur
amaunt, amount
amawntuble, amount(able)
amaze,*,ed,edly,zing,zingly,ement, IMPRESS
ambaquety, ambiguity
ambechis, ambitious
ambegedy, ambiguity
ambegues, ambiguous
ambekyues, ambiguous
ambeshun, ambition
ambeshusnes, ambitious(ness)
ambetious, ambitious
ambi, PREFIX INDICATING 'BOTH/AROUND' MOST OFTEN MODIFIES THE WORD
ambichen, ambition
ambiches, ambitious
ambiguity,ties, TWO OR MORE WAYS AN EXPRESSION COULD BE INTERPRETED
ambiguous,sly,sness, TWO OR MORE WAYS AN EXPRESSION COULD BE INTERPRETED "prefixes: un"
ambiquety, ambiguity
ambishisnes, ambitious(ness)
ambishun, ambition

ambishus, ambitious
ambishusnes, ambitious(ness)
ambition,*, DESIRE TO ACHIEVE A GOAL
ambitious,sly,sness, STRIVING DILIGENTLY TOWARDS A GOAL
amblanse, ambulance
amblins, ambulance
ambolanse, ambulance
amboosh, ambush
amboshd, ambush(ed)
ambuguedy, ambiguity
ambulance,*,atory,atories, RESCUE VEHICLE
ambulence, ambulance
ambush,hes,hed,her, ENTRAP
ambushd, ambush(ed)
ambutashen, amputate(tion)
ame, aim
ameable, amiable
ameba, amoeba
amechur, amateur
amedeat, immediate
ameds, emit / omit
ameible, amiable(ly)
amekibul, amicable
amekuble, amicable
amend,*,ded,ding,dment,dable,datory, REPAIR
amense, immense
amensurabl, immensurablee
amenus, ominous
amepa, amoeba
amerchen, immerse(sion)
amergensee, emergency
amerse, immerse / emersed
amershen, immerse(sion)
amertize, amortize
ameshen, omission / emission
ameteut, immediate
amethist, amethyst
amethyst,*, PURPLE QUARTZ
ameuble, amiable / amiable(ly)
amewsd, amuse(d)
amewsmint, amuse(ment)
amiable,eness,ly,bility, GOOD-NATURED
amicable,ly,bility, FRIENDLY
amichur, amateur
amikable, amicable
amikuble, amicable
amind, amend
amindment, amend(ment)
aminse, immense
aminsurable, immensurable

aminus, ominous
amirchen, immerse(sion)
amirse, immerse / emersed
amirshen, immerse(sion)
amishen, omission / emission
amit, emit / omit
amithist, amethyst
amitz, emit / omit
amiuble, amiable(ly)
ammonea, ammonia
ammonia,aic, A GAS
ammurshen, immerse(sion)
amne, omni
amnevore, omnivore
amnivore, omnivore
amochure, amateur
amoeba,*,bic, ANIMAL
among,gst, IN THE MIDST OF, WITH OTHERS
amonia, ammonia
amonkst, among(st)
amonya, ammonia
amortize,*,zable,tization, IN LOAN CALCULATION
amount,*,ted,ting, SUM
amownt, amount
ampakuety, ambiguity
ampegues, ambiguous
ampekuedy, ambiguity
ampel, ample
ampetate, amputate
ampeutashen, amputate(tion)
ampewtation, amputate(tion)
amphi, PREFIX INDICATING 'BOTH/AROUND' MOST OFTEN MODIFIES THE WORD
ampigewus, ambiguous
ampil, ample
ampition, ambition
amplafikashen, amplify(fication)
ample,er,est,eness, ENOUGH, PLENTY
amplefy, amplify
amplifucation, amplify(fication)
amplify,fies,fied,fier,ying,fiable,fication, MAGNIFY SOUND "prefixes: pre"
amplufikashen, amplify(fication)
amplufy, amplify
ampol, ample
amportant, important
ampukuety, ambiguity
ampul, ample
amputashen, amputate(tion)
amputate,*,ed,ting,tion,tee, REMOVE LIMB FROM MAIN TORSO

amrold, emerald
amruld, emerald
amune, immune
amunety, immune(nity)
amung, among
amunity, immune(nity)
amunkst, among(st)
amunxt, among(st)
amurchen, immerse(sion)
amurgensee, emergency
amurse, immerse / emersed
amurshen, immerse(sion)
amuse,*,ed,sing,ement, ENTERTAIN
amuthist, amethyst
amuze, amuse
amuzment, amuse(ment)
amythest, amethyst
an, PREFIX INDICATING 'TO/TOWARDS' MOST OFTEN MODIFIES THE WORD
ana, PREFIX INDICATING 'UP/BACK/AGAIN' MOST OFTEN MODIFIES THE WORD
anadot, anecdote
anagma, enigma / enema
anal,lly, NEAR/INVOLVING THE ANUS (or see annul)
analesis, analysis
analidek, analytic
analigy, analogy
analitek, analytic
analize, analyze
analog,gous,gously, TYPE OF WAVE/SOUND
analogy,gies,gous,gously, LIKENESS
analysis,ses, BREAKDOWN TO STUDY
analyst,*, PERSON WHO STUDIES DETAILS
analytic,*,cal,cally, PERSON WHO STUDIES DETAILS
analyze,*,ed,zing,er,zable,zation, STRICT EXAMINATION/STUDY "prefixes: un"
anamashen, animate(tion)
anamation, animate(tion)
anamulistik, animal(istic)
anarchy,hies,hism,hist,histic,hic,hical,hically, NO GOVERNMENT/CAPITALISM
anarkey, anarchy
anasthesia, anesthesia
anatomy,mic,mical,mically, COMPLETE STRUCTURE OF A BODY
anaumely, anomaly
anauns, announce

anbroder, embroider
ancestor,*,ry,tral,trally, LINEAGE
anchor,*,red,ring,rage,rages, STABILITY, BOAT HOLD
ancient,*,tness,tly, OLD, GREAT IN AGE
anckshes, anxious
ancorij, encourage / anchor(age)
ancshes, anxious
ancsiuty, anxiety
and, WORD USED AS A CONJUNCTION, THIS PLUS THAT, ALSO, INCLUDING (or see ant/aunt/end)
andanger, endanger
andefir, endeavor
andevur, endeavor
andlis, endless
andure, endure
ane, any
anebody, anybody
anebreated, inebriate(d)
anecdote,*,tal, STORY (or see antidote)
anedot, anecdote / antidote
anedotul, anecdote(tal)
anegma, enigma / enema
anekdote, anecdote
anekwitable, inequitable
anel, anal / annul
anelidek, analytic
anelog, analog
anelyze, analyze
anemal, animal
anemashen, animate(tion)
anemate, animate
anemation, animate(tion)
aneme, enemy
anemea, anemia
anemek, anemic
anemia, BLOOD HAS A DEFICIENCY/ NEED (or see enema/enigma)
anemic,cally, BLOOD HAS A DEFICIENCY/NEED
anemul, animal
anemulestik, animal(istic)
anequitable, inequitable
aneresm, aneurysm
anerism, aneurysm
anerjetek, energetic
anes, anus
aneshil, initial
anesthesia,iologist,iology, AN ANESTHETIC
anesthetic,*,cally,ist,ize, PAIN KILLER
anesthetist,*, ONE WHO ADMINISTERS ANESTHESIA

anesthetize,*,ed,zing,zation, TO DULL PAIN WITH DRUG
anesthezia, anesthesia
anesthutize, anesthetize
aneurysm,* , WEAK BLOOD VESSEL WALL AT BASE OF BRAIN
anew, FRESH/NEW START
anewity, annuity
anewol, annual
anezthetic, anesthetic
anforse, enforce
angaje, engage
angchus, anxious
angel,*,lic,lical,lically, SPIRITUAL BEING (or see angle)
angelek, angel(ic)
anger,*,red,ring,gry,grily, MAD
angil, angel / angle
angir, anger
angle,*,ed,ling,er, SLANT/TILT/ PERSPECTIVE IN DEGREES (or see angel)
angrafe, engrave
angrave, engrave
angre, angry
angrele, angrily
angreust, angry(riest)
angri, angry
angrily, OF ANGER
angry,rier,riest, EMOTION OF IRRITATED DISAPPOINTMENT
angryest, angry(riest)
angshes, anxious
angshus, anxious
angsiute, anxiety
anguish,hed,hing, SORROW
angul, angle / angel
angwish, anguish
angziute, anxiety
anialate, annihilate
anibreated, inebriate(d)
anidot, anecdote / antidote
anidotul, anecdote(tal)
anikdote, anecdote / antidote
anil, anal / annul
anilate, annihilate
anilidek, analytic
anilize, analyze
anilog, analog
anilyze, analyze
animal,*,listic,lise,lism,list,lity, NOT HUMAN
animashen, animate(tion)

animate,*,ed,ting,tion,tic,to,tor, LIVELY, AS IF REAL "prefixes: in"
animea, anemia / enema
animec, anemic
animic, anemic
animul, animal
animulistek, animal(istic)
aniresm, aneurysm
anis, anus
anishal, initial
anisthedek, anesthetic
anisthetic, anesthetic
anisthezia, anesthesia
anitiate, initiate
aniulate, annihilate
anjekshen, inject(ion)
anjel, angel
anjelik, angel(ic)
anjil, angel
anjoiment, enjoy(ment)
anjul, angel
ankches, anxious
ankchus, anxious
anker, anchor
ankor, anchor
ankoreg, encourage / anchor(age)
ankreust, angry(riest)
ankry, angry
ankshis, anxious
ankshus, anxious
anksiuty, anxiety
ankulent, inoculate(ant)
ankureg, anchor(age)
ankurig, encourage / anchor(age)
anlarje, enlarge
anliten, enlighten
anmal, animal
annihilate,*,ed,ting,tion,tor, DESTROY
announce,*,ed,cing,ement,er, DECLARE
annoy,*,yed,ying,yance, IRRITATE
annoyents, annoy(ance)
annual,*,lly,lize, YEARLY "prefixes: bi/ semi"
annuely, annual(lly)
annuity,ties, ANNUAL STIPEND/ PAYMENT
annul,lment, VOID, REVOKE (or see anal)
anoed, annoy(ed)
anoent, anoint
anof, enough
anogreashen, inaugurate(tion)
anogreation, inaugurate(tion)

anoint,*,ted,ting,tment, TO SELECT/ CONSECRATE
anolidek, analytic
anomale, anomaly
anomaly,lies,lous,lously,listic, NOT NORMAL, IRREGULAR
anomile, anomaly
anomulus, anomaly(lous)
anonemous, anonymous
anonemusly, anonymous(ly)
anonimous, anonymous
anonimusly, anonymous(ly)
anonseate, enunciate
anonymity, REMAINS UNKNOWN
anonymous,sly,sness,mity, NOT KNOWN
anoqulent, inoculate(ant)
anoresm, aneurysm
anorgee, energy
anorgetek, energetic
anorkey, anarchy
anormus, enormous
another, ADDITIONAL
anothir, another
anough, enough
anounse, announce
anowe, annoy
anownse, announce
anoy, annoy
anoyance, annoy(ance)
anoyd, annoy(ed)
anportant, important
anrich, enrich
anrol, enroll
anrold, enroll(ed)
anser, answer
anseruble, answer(able)
ansestor, ancestor
anshent, ancient
anshunt, ancient
ansiklopedea, encyclopedia
ansir, answer
ansistor, ancestor
ansur, answer
ansuruble, answer(able)
answer,*,red,ring,rable,rably, SOLUTION "prefixes: un"
ant,*, SMALL SIX-LEGGED INSECT (or see and/ante/anti/aunt)
antagonize,*,ed,ist,istic,istically, ENEMY/OPPOSITION
ante, PREFIX INDICATING 'BEFORE/ PRECEDING' MOST OFTEN MODIFIES THE WORD, POKER EXPRESSION, TO PRECEDE/COME BEFORE (or see anti/aunt(ie))
antebiotik, antibiotic
antecepate, anticipate
antefreeze, antifreeze
antehistamene, antihistamine
anteke, antique
antekwity, antique(uity)
antelope,*, MAMMAL
antena, antenna
antenna, DEVICE TO ATTRACT SIGNALS/ FREQUENCY
anterior,*,rity,rly, BEFORE, IN FRONT OF, TOWARDS THE FRONT (or see interior)
antesapashen, anticipate(tion)
antesepate, anticipate
antesupation, anticipate(tion)
anthem,*, SONG
anthim, anthem
anthrapology, anthropology
anthripology, anthropology
anthropology,*gical, STUDY OF HUMANITY
anti, OPPOSE/DISAGREE, PREFIX INDICATING 'AGAINST' MOST OFTEN MODIFIES THE WORD (or see aunt(ie)/ante)
antibiotic,*,cally, MANMADE CHEMICAL
anticepate, anticipate
anticipate,*,ed,ting,tion,tive,tory, EXPECT
antidote,*,tal, USED TO REVERSE EFFECTS OF POISON (or see anecdote)
antifreeze, SUBSTANCE TO PREVENT FREEZING
antihistamine, INACTIVATES HISTAMINE
antikwedy, antique(uity)
antilope, antelope
antina, antenna
antique,*,ed,ely,uity,uate,uated, ANCIENT
antiquedy, antique(uity)
antireor, anterior / interior
antisapashen, anticipate(tion)
antisupation, anticipate(tion)
antonym,*,mic,mous, WORDS WITH OPPOSITE MEANINGS
antorse, endorse / indoor(s)
antser, answer
antulope, antelope

anu, anew
anual, annual
anuale, annual(lly)
anudot, anecdote
anuel, annual
anuety, annuity
anuile, annual(lly)
anuity, annuity
anul, annul
anulidek, analytic
anulise, analyze
anulyze, analyze
anumashen, animate(tion)
anumate, animate
anumation, animate(tion)
anumel, animal
anumilestik, animal(istic)
anunseate, enunciate
anuresm, aneurysm
anurgee, energy
anurjetek, energetic
anus, LOWER ORIFICE
anustheshu, anesthesia
anusthetik, anesthetic
anuther, another
anuzthetek, anesthetic
anvilope, envelope
anvirunmint, environment
anvy, envy
anwritch, enrich
anxiety,ties,ious,iously,iousness, UNEASINESS
anxious,iously,iousness, UNEASINESS
any,ybody,yhow,ymore,yone,ything, yway,ywhere,ytime, SOME AT RANDOM, A PORTION OF
anybody,y's, ANY PERSON
anyerism, aneurysm
anyual, annual
anyurism, aneurysm
aoch, ouch
ap, PREFIX INDICATING 'TO/TOWARDS' MOST OFTEN MODIFIES THE WORD
apademic, epidemic
apal, apple / appall
apaloge, apology
aparatus, apparatus
apareshun, apparition
aparint, apparent
aparition, apparition
apart, MAKE INTO SEPARATE PIECES
apartment,*, ROOMS IN DWELLING
apartmint, apartment
apasenter, epicenter

apasom, opossum
apathetic,cal,cally, INDIFFERENT, NO EMOTION
apathy,hetic, INDIFFERENT, NO EMOTION
apatight, appetite
apatit, appetite
apatizer, appetizer
apatizing, appetizing
apauled, appall(lled)
apaustrufe, apostrophe
apdoman, abdomen
apdukt, abduct
apduman, abdomen
apeal, appeal
apearance, appearance
apecal, apical
apecl, apical
apeel, appeal
apekal, apical
apel, apple / appeal / appall
apendektumy, appendectomy
apenyun, opinion
apera, opera
aperal, apparel
aperant, apparent
aperatus, apparatus
apereshen, apparition
aperil, apparel
aperint, apparent
aperishen, apparition
aperition, apparition
aperul, apparel
aperunt, apparent
apesode, episode
apethetik, apathetic
apetight, appetite
apetit, appetite
apetizer, appetizer
aphed, aphid
aphid,*, INSECT
apical,lly, APEX, TIP/TOP OF "prefixes: sub"
apidemic, epidemic
apikal, apical
apil, apple / able / appeal
apindectemy, appendectomy
apineun, opinion
apinyun, opinion
apiol, appeal
apirans, appearance
apirens, appearance
apiretion, apparition
apithetik, apathetic

apitite, appetite
apitizer, appetizer
aplakashen, application
aplaud, applaud
aplauz, applause
aple, apple
aplecable, applicable
aplecant, applicant
aplecation, application
aplecator, applicator
aplefeus, oblivious
aplekant, applicant
aplekashen, application
aplekator, applicator
aplekuble, applicable
apli, apply
aplianse, appliance
aplicable, applicable
aplicant, applicant
aplicator, applicator
aplid, apply(lied)
apliderate, obliterate
aplifeus, oblivious
aplikashen, application
aplikation, application
aplikator, applicator
aplikuble, applicable
apliveon, oblivion
aplod, applaud
aplos, applause
aplukant, applicant
aplukashen, application
aplukation, application
aplukator, applicator
aply, apply
apodimic, epidemic
apoent, appoint
apoentment, appointment
apoint, appoint
apointment, appointment
apol, apple / able / appall
apold, appall(lled)
apolegize, apology(gize)
apoligize, apology(gize)
apology,gies,gize,gizes,gized,gizing, getic,getically, ASK FORGIVENESS
apolstery, upholstery
apoluge, apology
apolugize, apology(gize)
aponent, opponent
aponit, opponent
apose, oppose
apostrophe,*, SYMBOL IN ENGLISH LANGUAGE

aposum, opossum
apotizing, appetizing
apotment, appointment
apoynt, appoint
apoze, oppose
appal, apple / appall
appall,*,lled,lling,llingly, DISMAYED, SHOCKED, HORRIFIED
apparatus,ses, EQUIPMENT
apparel, CLOTHING
apparent,tly,tness, CLEAR
apparition,*, SPIRIT
appatite, appetite
appatizer, appetizer
appeal,*,led,ling,lingly,lable, CALL FOR MERCY, VIEW FAVORABLY "prefixes: un"
appear,*,red,ring,rance, BECOME VISIBLE "prefixes: dis"
appearance,*, BECOME VISIBLE
appel, appeal / apple
appendectomy,mies, REMOVE APPENDIX FROM BODY
apper, appear
apperal, apparel
apperent, apparent
appetite,*,tive,izing,izer, DESIRE, A HUNGER, A FOOD
appetizer,*, FOOD BEFORE A MEAL
appetizing,gly,zer, DESIRE, A HUNGER, A FOOD
applaud,*,ded,ding,use, USE HANDS TO CLAP
applause, ACCLAIM, USE HANDS TO CLAP
apple,*, FRUIT
appliance,*, SPECIALIZED TOOL/ MACHINE TO PERFORM SPECIFIC TASKS
applicable,eness,ly, RELEVANT, USEFUL "prefixes: in"
applicant,*, CANDIDATE FOR EMPLOYMENT
applicate,*,ed,ting,tion,tor,ant, PUT TO USE, APPLY
application,*, FORM TO APPLY FOR WORK "prefixes: dis"
applicator,*,ting, USED TO APPLY SOMETHING
apply,lies,lied,lying,lier,liable,liableness, licate,lication,licator,licatory, licative,licatively,licable,licably, licability, PUT ON, RELEVANT TO "prefixes: mis/pre/un"

appoint,*,ted,ting,tee,tment, ASSIGN, DESIGNATE "prefixes: dis"
appointment,*, AN ASSIGNED TIME "prefixes: dis"
apprahenshun, apprehension
appraisal,*,ser,sement, EVALUATION
appraise,*,ed,sing,sable,ement,er,sal, EVALUATION
apprapo, apropos
appreciate,*,ed,ting,tion,tory,tive,able, GRATEFUL "prefixes: in/un"
apprehend,*,ded,ding,nsive,nsively, nsiveness,nsion,nsible, TO SEIZE, BE CAUTIOUS "prefixes: mis"
apprehension,*, CAUTIOUS, HESITANT "prefixes: mis"
apprehensive,ely,eness,ion,ible, CAUTIOUS "prefixes: mis"
apprentice,*,ed,cing,eship, LEARNER/IN TRAINING
appresif, oppress(ive)
appripo, apropos
approach,hes,hed,hing,hable,hability, hableness,hably, ADVANCE TOWARDS, NEARING "prefixes: in/un"
appropo, apropos
appropriate,*,ted,ting,ely,eness, PROPER TO, BELONGS ALONG WITH, IN CHARACTER WITH "prefixes: in/mis/non"
approve,*,ed,ving,val,vable,vingly, ACCEPTANCE/COMMENDATION "prefixes: dis"
approximate,ed,ely,ting,tion, AROUND/SOMEWHAT
apprupo, apropos
apracot, apricot
aprahenshun, apprehension
apraisal, appraisal
apraise, appraise
apral, april
aprapo, apropos
aprase, appraise
aprased, appraise(d)
aprasing, appraise(sing)
aprazul, appraisal
apreciate, appreciate
aprehend, apprehend
aprehenshun, apprehension
aprehensive, apprehensive
aprehind, apprehend
aprekot, apricot
aprel, april

apren, apron
aprentis, apprentice
apres, oppress
apresheate, appreciate
apreshen, oppress(ion)
apresif, oppress(ive)
aprhenshun, apprehension
apricot,*, FRUIT
aprikot, apricot
april, A MONTH OF THE YEAR (ENGLISH)
aprin, apron
aprintise, apprentice
apripo, apropos
aproach, approach
aproch, approach
aprol, april
apron,*, CLOTHING PROTECTOR
apropos, SUITABLE IN A PARTICULAR SITUATION/TIME
apropreate, appropriate
apropriate, appropriate
aprotch, approach
aproval, approve(val)
aproxemat, approximate
aproxemation, approximate(tion)
aproximate, approximate
aproxumation, approximate(tion)
apruful, approve(val)
apruhensev, apprehensive
aprul, april
aprupo, apropos
apruvel, approve(val)
apsalutly, absolute(ly)
apsens, absence / absent(s)
apsent, absent
apsentee, absent(ee)
apserd, absurd
apserdle, absurd(ly)
apshen, option
apsiloot, absolute
apsins, absence / absent(s)
apsintee, absent(ee)
apsird, absurd
apsoloot, absolute
apsolute, absolute
apsolution, absolve(lution)
apsolv, absolve
apsorb, absorb
apstane, abstain
apstinent, abstinent
apstract, abstract
apstrukshen, abstract(ion) / obstruct(ion)

apstunent, abstinent
apsulootly, absolute(ly)
apsulute, absolute
apsulutly, absolute(ly)
apsurd, absurd
apsurdly, absurd(ly)
aptetood, aptitude
aptetude, aptitude
aptikate, abdicate
aptimen, abdomen
aptitewd, aptitude
aptitude,*, TENDENCY TOWARDS, AFFINITY FOR
aptomen, abdomen
aptumen, abdomen
apul, apple
aputhetik, apathetic
aputit, appetite
aputizer, appetizer
apuzit, opposite
apzaulv, absolve
apzolv, absolve
apzorb, absorb
aqaint, acquaint
aqefir, aquifer
aqire, acquire
aqiuponcsher, acupuncture
aqiut, acquit
aqua,atic,atics,ueous, WATER, TO DO WITH WATER, A COLOR "prefixes: non/sub"
aquaduct, aqueduct
aquaent, acquaint
aquafer, aquifer
aquaint, acquaint
aquareum, aquarium
aquarium,*, FISH CONTAINER
aquatic,*, IN WATER "prefixes: non/semi/sub"
aqueduct,*, WATER CHANNEL
aquefer, aquifer
aquiesent, acquiesce(nt)
aquifer,*,rous, PROVIDES WATER
aquipd, equip(pped)
aquivalint, equivalent
aqute, acute
aqwazitun, acquisition
aqwiesent, acquiesce(nt)
aqwire, acquire
aqwit, acquit
aqwuzishen, acquisition
ar, are / heir / air / our / hour
ara, array / aura

arachnid,*,noid, WINGLESS ANTHROPODS
aradekate, eradicate
aradic, erratic / erotic
aradikashen, eradicate(tion)
aradikate, eradicate
araign, arraign
araignment, arraign(ment)
arainment, arraign(ment)
arakned, arachnid
arangment, arrange(ment)
aranj, arrange
aranment, arraign(ment)
arase, erase
araser, eraser
arashinal, irrational
aratic, erratic
araudik, erotic
aray, array
arayn, arraign
araze, erase
arazer, eraser
arbeder, arbiter
arbeter, arbiter
arbetrate, arbitrate
arbiter,*,tral, ONE WHO MAKES DETERMINATION
arbitrary,rily,riness, RANDOM DETERMINATION
arbitrate,*,ed,ting,tion,tor, TO DETERMINE
arborne, airborne
arbutrashen, arbitrate(tion)
arbutrate, arbitrate
arc,*, PART OF A CURVE (or see ark/arch)
arcade,*,dia, OF GAMES OR ARCHED PASSAGEWAY
arcaek, archaic
arch,hes,hed,hing, A CURVED BEND, PREFIX INDICATING 'CHIEF/BEGINNING' MOST OFTEN MODIFIES THE WORD (or see ark/arc) "prefixes: over"
archaek, archaic
archaic, OLD-FASHIONED, ANCIENT
archeology,gist,gical, STUDY OF PEOPLE
archer,*,ry, ONE WHO USES BOWS AND ARROWS
archetekt, architect
archir, archer
architect,*,ture,tural, BUILDER
archive,*,ed,ving,val,vist, PLACE OF PUBLIC RECORDS "prefixes: un"

archur, archer
archure, archer(y)
arckiology, archeology
arctic, NORTH POLE "prefixes: sub"
ardefishal, artificial
ardekle, article
ardent,tly, PASSIONATE
ardery, artery
ardest, artist
ardewous, arduous
ardgewus, arduous
ardifishel, artificial
ardikle, article
ardint, ardent
ardiry, artery
ardist, artist
ardjewous, arduous
ardufishul, artificial
ardukle, article
arduous,sly,sness, DIFFICULT
ardury, artery
are, TO BE, IS (or see air/heir/hour/our)
area,*,al, RANGE OF CONCEPT/EVENT/OPERATION
arear, arrear
ared, arid
aregate, irrigate
aregenashen, originate(tion)
aregeno, oregano
aregenul, origin(al)
arejenul, origin(al)
arekshin, erect(ion)
arekt, erect
aren't, CONTRACTION OF THE WORDS 'ARE NOT'
arena,*, ENCLOSED SPACE
arend, errand
areplasible, irreplaceable
areprochible, irreproachable
arer, error / arrear
arest, arrest
arestokrat, aristocrat
arethmatic, arithmetic
areu, area
areul, aerial
arezt, arrest
argeumint, argument
argew, argue
argkeumint, argument
argue,*,ed,uing,uable,uably, DEBATE, DISCUSS "prefixes: in/un"
argument,*,tation,tative,tum, DEBATE, DISCUSS
arguous, arduous

arguwus, arduous
aria, area
arid,dity, PARCHED "prefixes: semi"
arie, awry
arife, arrive
ariful, arrival
arigate, irrigate
arigenashen, originate(tion)
ariginul, origin(al)
arijinul, origin(al)
arind, errand
arint, aren't
ariplasible, irreplaceable
arir, error
arisol, aerosol
aristocrat,*,tic,acy, WEALTHY UPPER CLASS
arithmetic,cal,cally,cian, MATH
arivd, arrive(d)
arive, arrive
arivul, arrival
arjuwus, arduous
ark,*, BOX/CHEST/CUPBOARD/BOAT(or see arc/arch)
arkade, arcade
arkaek, archaic
arkaik, archaic
arkeoligy, archeology
arketekt, architect
arkeu, argue
arkiology, archeology
arkitect, architect
arkiteksher, architect(ure)
arkive, archive
arktic, arctic
arku, argue
arkumint, argument
arkutekshur, architect(ure)
arkyve, archive
arloom, heirloom
arm,*,med,ming,mament, APPENDAGE ON UPPER TORSO, TO TAKE UP WEAPONS "prefixes: dis/un/under"
armature,*, DEVICE OR STRUCTURE/SUPPORT
arme, army
armes, army(mies)
armicher, armature
armonica, harmonica
armor,red,ry,ries,rer, BODY PROTECTION, COVERING, MILITARY/WEAPONS "prefixes: un"
armucher, armature
armur, armor

army,mies, MANY BODIES
arn, iron
arnamint, ornament
arnge, orange
arnje, orange
arnt, aren't
arnument, ornament
aro, arrow
aroara, aurora
arobek, aerobic
arobik, aerobic
arochun, erosion
arode, erode
arodik, erotic
arodynamic, aerodynamic
aroganse, arrogance
arogate, irrigate
arogent, arrogance(nt)
arogint, arrogance(nt)
aroma,*,atic,atize, ODOR, SMELL
aromadek, aroma(tic)
arond, errand
aronic, ironic
aror, error
arora, aurora
arosef, erosive
aroshin, erosion
arosive, erosive
around, HERE AND THERE
arouse,*,ed,sing,sal, AWAKEN/ STIMULATE/ACTIVATE
arouzel, arouse(sal)
arow, arrow
arownd, around
arowsul, arouse(sal)
arowze, arouse
arport, airport
arraign,*,ned,ning,nment, ANSWER INDICTMENT
arrange,*,ed,ging,ement,er, ADJUST, SITUATE "prefixes: dis/un"
arranment, arraign(ment)
array,*,yed, ORDER "prefixes: dis"
arrear,*,rage, PAST DUE
arrest,*,ted,ting,tingly, SUSPEND, CAPTURE
arrival,*, BE AT DESTINATION
arrive,*,ed,ving,val, PRESENT AT DESTINATION
arrogance,nt,ntly, OVERLY SELF-IMPORTANT
arrow,*, SHAFT WITH POINT
arrowgance, arrogance
arsen, arson

arson,*,nist, MALICIOUS/INTENTIONAL BURNING
arsunest, arson(ist)
art,*,tist,tistry,tsy,ty,tistic,tistical, tistically,tisan,tful,tfully,tfulness, tless, tlessly,tlessness,tiness, METHOD OF EXPRESSION "prefixes: in/non"
arteculate, articulate
artefishel, artificial
artekewlate, articulate
artekulashen, articulate(tion)
artekulate, articulate
artelury, artillery
artereal, arterial
arterial,*, PATH FOR FLOW
artery,ries,ric, CHANNEL FOR TRANSPORTATION
artesdik, artist(ic)
artest, artist
artestek, artist(ic)
arthridek, arthritis(ic)
arthridis, arthritis
arthritis,ic, INFLAMMATION
arthudox, orthodox
article,*, PART, ONE OF SEVERAL
articulate,*,ed,ting,tion,tely,eness, INTEGRATE, SPECIFIC "prefixes: dis/in"
artificial,lly, SIMULATED, NOT REAL
artifishul, artificial
artik, arctic
artikel, article
artikewlate, articulate
artikulashen, articulate(tion)
artikulate, articulate
artillery, FOR WEAPONS
artireal, arterial
artiry, artery
artisdik, artist(ic)
artist,*,tistic,tistically, SKILLED "prefixes: in/un"
artistek, artist(ic)
artsh, arch
artsher, archer
artucle, article
artufishul, artificial
artury, artery
arubshen, erupt(ion) / irrupt(ion)
arubt, erupt / irrupt
arubtif, erupt(ive) / irrupt(ive)
arugate, irrigate
arupshen, erupt(ion) / irrupt(ion)
arupt, erupt / irrupt

aruptif, erupt(ive) / irrupt(ive)
aruption, erupt(ion) / irrupt(ion)
arye, awry
aryve, arrive
as, WORD USED TO COMPARE, PREFIX INDICATING 'TO/TOWARDS' MOST OFTEN MODIFIES THE WORD (or see ace)
asaeal, assail
asaee, essay
asail, assail
asalt, assault
asasen, assassin
asault, assault
asay, essay
asbekt, aspect
asberashun, aspirate(tion)
asberegus, asparagus
asbeshulee, especially
asbestos, TYPE OF FIBER
asbir, aspire
asburin, aspirin
ascape, escape
ascend,*,ded,ding,dable,dance,dancy, dence,dency,dant,der,nsion,nsional, DOMINANT, RISING ABOVE, GO UP (or see assent/ascent)
ascendant,*,nce, DOMINANT, RISE ABOVE OTHERS
ascension,*,nal, TO GO UP
ascent,*,nsion, MOTION UPWARDS (or see assent/ascend)
ascertain,*,ned,ning,nable,nably,ner, nment, MAKE SURE "prefixes: un"
ascetic,cal,cally,cism, STRICT, SEVERE, EXCESSIVE (or see acetic/acidic)
ascind, ascend / ascent / assent
ascrow, escrow
asd, ask(ed) / ax(ed) / ace(d) / acid
asdeem, esteem
asdonesh, astonish
ased, ask(ed) / ax(ed) / acid / ace(d)
asedek, acetic / acidic / ascetic
asemble, assemble / assemble(ly)
asemetric, asymmetric
asemewlate, assimilate
asemulate, assimilate
asend, ascend / ascent / assent
asendent, ascendant
asense, essence
asenshil, essential
asent, ascend / ascent / assent
asential, essential
asershen, assert(ion)

asert, assert
asertane, ascertain
asertif, assert(ive)
asertion, assert(ion)
ases, assess / access / ace(s)
aseshun, accession
asesible, access(ible)
asesment, assessment
asest, assist
asesuble, access(ible)
aset, acid / asset
asetic, acetic / acidic / ascetic
asexual, NOT SEXUAL
asfalt, asphalt
asfault, asphalt
asfikseate, asphyxiate
asfixiate, asphyxiate
asfolt, asphalt
ashamed,dly, TOUCHED BY SHAME, NOT PROUD "prefixes: un"
ashamt, ashamed
asheeve, achieve
asher, assure
ashirense, assure(rance)
ashtarik, asterisk
ashuranse, assure(rance)
asid, acid / aside
aside, SEPARATE FROM
asidic, acetic / acidic / ascetic
asiduous, assiduous
asign, assign
asignment, assignment
asijuous, assiduous
asilum, asylum
asim, awesome
asimble, assemble
asimetric, asymmetric
asimetry, asymmetry
asimilate, assimilate
asimulate, assimilate
asind, ascend
asindent, ascendant
asine, assign
asinment, assignment
asinse, essence
asinshul, essential
asint, ascend / ascent / assent
asirshen, assert(ion)
asirt, assert
asirtane, ascertain
asirtev, assert(ive)
asist, assist
asitic, acetic / acidic / ascetic

ask,*,ked,king, DORMANT STATE "prefixes: un"
askalador, escalator
askalater, escalator
askap, escape
askort, escort
askrow, escrow
askt, ask(ed) / ax(ed)
askulader, escalator
asleep, DORMANT STATE
asmu, asthma
asocheate, associate
asociate, associate
asolt, assault
asorded, assorted
asordment, assortment
asorted, assorted
asortment, assortment
asosheate, associate
asoshiate, associate
asparagus, VEGETABLE
aspect,*, OUTLOOK
aspekt, aspect
asperagus, asparagus
asperashun, aspirate(tion)
asperation, aspirate(tion)
asperen, aspirin
asperugus, asparagus
aspeshilee, especially
aspeshulee, especially
aspestus, asbestos
asphalt, MINERAL PITCH
asphixiate, asphyxiate
asphyxiate,*,ed,ting,tion, OF BREATHING
aspirashun, aspirate(tion)
aspirate,*,ed,ting,tor,tion,tional, AMBITION, OF BREATHING "prefixes: un"
aspire,*,ed,ring,er,rate,rant,ration, GOAL, DESIRE "prefixes: un"
aspirin,*, PAIN RELIEVER
asprashun, aspirate(tion)
aspren, aspirin
aspurashun, aspirate(tion)
aspuration, aspirate(tion)
aspuren, aspirin
assail,lable,lant, IMPACT UPON "prefixes: un"
assasin, assassin
assassin,*,nate,nation, TO MURDER, A MURDERER
assault,*,ted,ting, ATTACK WITH INTENT TO HARM

assemble,*,ed,ling,lage,ly, PUT TOGETHER "prefixes: dis/un"
assent,ted,ting,ter,tor,tingly,tive,tively, tiveness, AGREEMENT (or see ascent)
assert,*,ted,ting,tion,table,ter,tive, tively,tiveness, INSIST
assess,sses,ssed,ssing,ssment,ssable, EXAMINE, EVALUATE "prefixes: non"
assessment,*, APPRAISAL, EVALUATION
asset,*, POSSESS SOMETHING VALUABLE
assiduous,sly, DILIGENT
assign,*,ned,ning,nment, APPORTION
assignment,*, ASSIGNED WORK
assimetric, asymmetric
assimilate,*,ed,ting,tion, MAKE INTO, BECOME LIKE
assint, assent
assist,*,ted,ting,tant,tance, HELP
associate,*,ed,ting,tion,tive, CONNECTION TO "prefixes: dis/non"
assorted,ting,tment, VARIOUS TYPES
assortment, VARIOUS TYPES
assume,*,ed,ming,mingly,mer,mable, mption,mptive, SUPPOSE A FACT "prefixes: un"
assumption,*,ive, TAKE FOR GRANTED
assure,*,ed,rance,rances, CERTAINTY "prefixes: re"
assymetric, asymmetric
ast, ask / ask(ed) / ax(ed)
asteem, esteem
astemate, estimate
asterik, asterisk
asterisk, LITTLE TEXT STAR
asteroed, asteroid
asteroid,*, PERTAINING TO STAR
asthetik, aesthetic
asthma,atic,atical,atically, DIFFICULTY BREATHING
asthmu, asthma
astimate, estimate
astonesh, astonish
astonish,hes,hed,hing,hment, SURPRISE/IMPRESS
astragen, estrogen
astral,ly, STELLAR "prefixes: sub"
astrawneme, astronomy
astrek, asterisk
astrengent, astringent
astrenjint, astringent
astrenot, astronaut

astres, estrus
astrik, asterisk
astringent,*,ncy,tly, ACRID "prefixes: sub"
astrinot, astronaut
astris, estrus
astroed, asteroid
astrol, astral
astrolegy, astrology
astrology,ger,gic,gical,gically,gist, PREDICT THE FUTURE WITH THE STARS
astronaut,*, PERSON OF SPACE FLIGHT
astroneme, astronomy
astronomic,mical,mically, NUMEROUS/ GREAT PROPORTION
astronomy,mer,mers, OBSERVE CELESTIAL BODIES "prefixes: bio"
astronot, astronaut
astronume, astronomy
astroyd, asteroid
astrugen, estrogen
astrul, astral
astrunot, astronaut
astumate, estimate
astural, astral
asturik, asterisk
asturisk, asterisk
asum, awesome / assume
asumetric, asymmetric
asumpshen, assumption
asumption, assumption
asunse, essence
asurans, assure(rance)
asurants, assure(rance)
asurshen, assert(ion)
asurtif, assert(ive)
asylom, asylum
asylum, REFUGE FOR DESTITUTE
asymetric, asymmetric
asymmetric,cal,ry,ries, OFF-BALANCE
asymmetry,ries, OFF-BALANCE
at, A PREPOSITION EXPRESSING LOCATION OR SOMETHING IN PARTICULAR, PREFIX INDICATING 'TO/TOWARDS' MOST OFTEN MODIFIES THE WORD (or see ate/ eight/add)
atach, attach
atack, attack
ataen, attain
atain, attain
atak, attack
atament, adamant

atamint, adamant
atane, attain
atatch, attach
atcheeve, achieve
ate, PAST TENSE FOR THE WORD 'EAT' (or see eight/add) "prefixes: over"
atec, attic / addict
ated, add(ed)
atek, attic / addict
atekwase, adequacy
atembt, attempt
atemobel, automobile
atempt, attempt
atemt, attempt
atenchin, attention
atend, attend
atendens, attend(ance)
atendent, attend(ant)
atenshin, attention
atentef, attentive
atention, attention
atentive, attentive
atequasy, adequacy
ateqwit, adequate
aternal, eternal
aterney, attorney
atest, attest
atesy, odyssey
atetif, additive
atetude, attitude
atgasent, adjacent
atgasint, adjacent
atgern, adjourn
atgewdikate, adjudicate
atgust, adjust
athear, adhere
atheist,ism,tic,tical,tically, DISBELIEF IN A GOD
athek, ethic
athere, adhere
athesif, adhesive
athic, ethic
athiest, atheist
athik, ethic
athleat, athlete
athlete,*,tic,tics,tically, SPORTS TRAINED, ATHLETE "prefixes: deca"
athletic,*,tically, SPORTS TRAINED, ATHLETE
athnek, ethnic
athnuk, ethnic
athorety, authority
athrek, ether(ic)
athuk, ethic

atic, attic / addict
atid, add(ed)
atikit, etiquette
atikwit, adequate
atikwuse, adequacy
atimant, adamant
atimint, adamant
atimt, attempt
atinchon, attention
atind, attend
atinshun, attention
atipecle, atypical
atipikul, atypical
atiquit, adequate
atiquot, adequate
atire, attire
atisum, autism
atitif, additive
atitude, attitude
atmechen, admission
atmedid, admit(tted)
atmenester, administer
atmenustrashen, administrate(tion)
atmeshen, admission
atmesphere, atmosphere
atmichen, admission
atmided, admit(tted)
atminaster, administer
atminastrashin, administrate(tion)
atminuster, administer
atminustrashen, administrate(tion)
atmird, admire(d)
atmire, admire
atmisef, admission(ive)
atmisfeer, atmosphere
atmishun, admission
atmisphere, atmosphere
atmisuble, admissible
atmit, admit
atmonish, admonish
atmosfear, atmosphere
atmosphere,ric,rical,rically, AROUND A PLANET "prefixes: sub"
atmusfeer, atmosphere
atmusphere, atmosphere
atmyre, admire
atobiografy, autobiography
atograf, autograph
atolesense, adolescence
atolesint, adolescent
atom,*,mic,mically,mize,mizer, PARTICLES OF ELEMENT "prefixes: non/sub"
atomadik, automatic

atomatik, automatic
atomobel, automobile
atonal,*,lity,listic,lly, CANNOT HEAR TRUE TONES
atone,*,eable,nable,ement, MAKE UP FOR, AMEND
atonime, autonomy
atonome, autonomy
atorney, attorney
atracshun, attraction
atract, attract
atraction, attraction
atrakshun, attraction
atrakt, attract
atraktif, attract(ive)
atrebute, attribute
atrefee, atrophy
atrenulen, adrenaline
atress, address
atreum, atrium
atribute, attribute
atriem, atrium
atrifee, atrophy
atriss, address
atrium,*, GLASS ROOM
atrocious,sly,sness, OUTRAGEOUS
atrocity,ties, OUTRAGEOUS
atrocius, atrocious
atrofee, atrophy
atrophy,hies,hied,hic, DEGENERATE
atrosety, atrocity
atroshus, atrocious
atrufee, atrophy
atsetera, etcetera
atsheve, achieve
attach,hes,hed,hing,hment, FASTEN "prefixes: un"
attack,*,ked,king,ker, ASSAIL
attain,*,ned,ning,nability,nable, nableness,nment, GAIN "prefixes: un"
attempt,*,ted,ting, TRY TO ACCOMPLISH
attemt, attempt
attenchon, attention
attend,*,ded,ding,dingly,dance,dant, der, ACCOMPANY, GO TO "prefixes: un"
attention,ive, FOCUS ON "prefixes: in"
attentive,ively,eness, FOCUS ON "prefixes: in"
attest,*,ted,ting,tation,tations, BEAR WITNESS TO THE TRUTH, CAN BE CERTIFIED TO BE CORRECT

attic,*, IN THE ROOF (or see addict)
attichon, attention
attinchon, attention
attire,*,ed,ring, APPAREL
attitude,*,dinal, MENTAL POSTURE
attorney,*, REPRESENTATIVE OF LAW
attotode, attitude
attract,*,ted,ting,tive,tively, TO DRAW TOWARDS "prefixes: un"
attraction,*, DRAWN TOWARDS
attribute,*,ed,ting,tion, TO CREDIT "prefixes: de"
atukit, etiquette
atulesense, adolescence
atum, atom / autumn
atument, adamant
aturnal, eternal
aturney, attorney
atutif, additive
atutode, attitude
atvacate, advocate
atvanse, advance
atvantech, advantage
atvanteg, advantage
atvantuge, advantage
atvencher, adventure
atvenshure, adventure
atverb, adverb
atverse, adverse
atversery, adversary
atvertize, advertise
atvincher, adventure
atvinsher, adventure
atvirb, adverb
atvirsary, adversary
atvirse, adverse
atvise, advice / advise
atvisuble, advise(sable)
atvize, advise / advice
atvokate, advocate
atvukate, advocate
atvurb, adverb
atvurcity, adverse(sity)
atvursle, adverse(ly)
atvurtize, advertise
atypical, IRREGULAR
aubazit, opposite
aubligate, obligate
aubozit, opposite
aubrebul, operable
aubtemal, optimal
aubuzit, opposite
aucalate, osculate / oscillate
auch, ouch

aucilate, osculate / oscillate
aucshen, auction
auction,*,ning,neer,neering, SELL BY BID
aud, odd / ought / out
audacity, WILLING/DARING TO DEAL WITH DIFFICULT ISSUE/ SITUATION
audamate, automate
audamotive, automotive
audasity, audacity
audeance, audience
audeble, audible
audej, outage
audem, autumn
audeo, audio
auder, otter / outer / odd(er)
audeshun, audition
audet, audit
audetorium, auditorium
audety, odd(ity)
audfit, outfit
audgo, outgo
audiance, audience
audible,ly,bility,eness, WELL HEARD "prefixes: in/sub"
audience,*, GROUP WHO OBSERVES
audimotive, automotive
auding, outing
audio, HEAR
audir, otter / outer
audishun, audition
audit,*,ted,ting,tor,tory, UNDER EXAMINATION
audition,*,ned,ning, SUBMIT TO EXAMINATION "prefixes: sub"
auditorium,*, FOR PUBLIC AUDIENCE
audity, odd(ity)
audlau, outlaw
audle, odd(ly)
audlieng, outlying
audline, outline
audlook, outlook
audobiography, autobiography
audomotive, automotive
audpost, outpost
audraje, outrage
audrit, outright
audside, outside
audskirt, outskirt
audsmart, outsmart
audstanding, outstand(ing)
audwerd, outward
audwet, outwit
auel, owl

auer, our / hour / oar
auful, awful
auger,*, TOOL TO BORE SOMETHING
augir, auger
augment,*,ted,ting,tation, INCREASE SIZE "prefixes: bio"
augre, auger
august, A MONTH OF THE YEAR (ENGLISH)
auil, owl
aukshun, auction
auksidize, oxide(dize)
auktober, october
aukward, awkward
aul, owl / all / awl
auldir, alder / altar / alter
aulfubet, alphabet
aulso, also
aultamatum, ultimatum
aultematum, ultimatum
aulter, alter / altar
aulternate, alternate
aultirnetly, alternate(ly)
aultogethur, altogether
aultumatum, ultimatum
aulturnate, alternate
aulways, always
auneng, awning
auns, ounce / own(s)
aunt,*,tie, SISTER OF MOTHER/FATHER (or see ant)
auntefrese, antifreeze
auperuble, operable
aupewlent, opulent
aupiruble, operable
aupizit, opposite
aupoyntmint, appointment
aupshen, option
auptemal, optimal
auptimize, optimize
auptumistic, optimist(ic)
aupulent, opulent
aupuset, opposite
aur, hour / our / oar
aura,*,al,ric, LIGHT FIELD
aurajin, origin
aurekel, auricle / oracle
auri, awry
aurickle, auricle / oracle
auricle,*,cular, OF THE EAR (or see oracle)
aurikel, auricle / oracle
aurk, arc / ark

aurle, hour(ly)
aurmer, armor
auroara, aurora
aurora,*,al, RADIANT EMISSION
aurthodox, orthodox
ausalate, osculate / oscillate
auselate, osculate / oscillate
ausem, awesome
ausilate, osculate / oscillate
ausim, awesome
auspicious,sly,sness, FAVORABLE "prefixes: in"
auspishus, auspicious
auspitious, auspicious
austere,ely, HARSH
ausulate, osculate / oscillate
ausum, awesome
aut, out / ought
autej, outage
autem, autumn
autemate, automate
autemobel, automobile
auteo, audio
auter, otter / outer
autfit, outfit
autgo, outgo
authentic,cally,city,cate,cation,cator, VALID, NOT FICTITIOUS OR FAKE "prefixes: in"
auther, author
authintik, authentic
authir, author
author,*,red,ring, CREATOR/ ORIGINATOR
authoretarian, authoritarian
authoritarian, DICTATORIAL
authority,ties,tative,tatively, EXERCISES COMMAND
autim, autumn
autimate, automate
autimotive, automotive
auting, outing
autio, audio
autir, otter / outer
autism,stic, BRAIN FIRING MALADY
autlaw, outlaw
autlet, outlet
autlieng, outlying
autline, outline
autlook, outlook
autluk, outlook
autly, odd((ly)

auto, PREFIX INDICATING 'OF OR BY ONESELF' MOST OFTEN MODIFIES THE WORD
autobiografy, autobiography
autobiography,hies,her,hical,hically, WRITTEN BY ONESELF "prefixes: semi"
autobyografy, autobiography
autograf, autograph
autograph,*,hed,hing,her,hic,hics,hical, hically, AUTHOR'S SIGNATURE
automadik, automatic
automate,*,ed,ting,ticity,tion,tism, SELF-CONTROLLING, PERFORMS THRU PROGRAMMING
automatic,*,cally, SELF-CONTROLLING, PERFORMS THRU PROGRAMMING "prefixes: semi"
automobel, automobile
automobile,*, PERSONAL TRANSPORTATION
automotive, ASSOCIATED WITH VEHICLES
autoname, autonomy
autonime, autonomy
autonomy,mous,mist, INDEPENDENCE "prefixes: semi"
autopsy,*, POST-MORTEM EXAMINATION
autpost, outpost
autput, output
autragus, outrage(ous)
autraje, outrage
autrite, outright
autset, outset
autside, outside
autskurt, outskirt
autsmart, outsmart
autstanding, outstand(ing)
autumate, automate
autumn, FALL SEASON
autwerd, outward
autwet, outwit
autwit, outwit
autwurd, outward
auxilery, auxiliary
auxiliary,ries, HELP OR AID
avacado, avocado
avacodo, avocado
avacuate, evacuate
avade, evade
avaeleble, available
avail,*,led,ling,lable, READY TO USE/ HELP "prefixes: un"

available,bly,bility, READY TO USE/HELP "prefixes: bio/un"
avaire, aviary
avakuate, evacuate
avalable, available
avalanche,*,ed, COME DOWN/ DESCEND WITH GREAT ACCUMULATION
avale, avail
avalible, available
avaluade, evaluate
avaluashen, evaluate(tion)
avaluate, evaluate
avanew, avenue
avantig, advantage
avantij, advantage
avaperation, evaporate(tion)
avaporashen, evaporate(tion)
avarage, average
avaredge, average
avasef, evasive
avashen, evasion
avashun, aviation
avasive, evasive
avate, evade
avau, avow
aveador, aviator
aveashin, aviation
aveation, aviation
avecado, avocado
avedent, evident
aveere, aviary
avekado, avocado
avekshin, evict(ion)
avekt, evict
avelanch, avalanche
avenchur, adventure
avendful, eventful
avenew, avenue
avenge,*,ed,ging,er, INFLICT PAIN/ HARM IN RETALIATION
avenje, avenge
avenshuale, event(ually)
avent, event
aventful, eventful
aventshur, adventure
avenue,*, WAY TO PERFORM, STREET/ ROAD
aver, ever
average,*,ed,ging, IN BETWEEN
averb, adverb
avere, aviary
averege, average
averije, average

aversarie, adversary
averse,ely,eness,sion,sions,sive,sively, siveness, AGAINST/OPPOSE (or see adverse)
avert,*,ted,ting,table,tible,rsion,rsive, GO OFF COURSE, CHANGE DIRECTION/ATTENTION AWAY FROM (or see advert/overt)
avertise, advertise
averyen, ovary(rian)
aviador, aviator
aviary,ries, PLACE TO KEEP BIRDS
aviashun, aviation
aviation,tor, FLYING TRANSPORTATION
aviator,*, ONE WHO PILOTS AIR SHIPS
avicado, avocado
avicate, advocate
avidens, evidence
avident, evident
aviere, aviary
avikado, avocado
avikd, evict
avikshen, evict(ion)
avikt, evict
avikted, evict(ed)
avilanch, avalanche
avincher, adventure
avindful, eventful
avinew, avenue
avinge, avenge
avinje, avenge
avint, event
avintful, eventful
avinu, avenue
avirage, average
avirej, average
avirse, averse / adverse
avirsere, adversary
avirtize, advertise
avocado,*, EDIBLE FRUIT
avocate, advocate
avoed, avoid
avoid,*,ded,ding,dance,dable,dably, STAY CLEAR OF, PURPOSELY STAY AWAY FROM "prefixes: un"
avokodo, avocado
avolve, evolve
avow,*,wed,wing,wable,wably,wedly, STATE THAT IT'S TRUTH "prefixes: dis"
avoyd, avoid
avrag, average
avrebaudy, every(body)
avrebode, every(body)

avree, every
avrege, average
avridge, average
avrige, average
avucate, advocate
avukodo, avocado
avulanch, avalanche
avundful, eventful
avurb, adverb
avurij, average
avurse, averse / adverse
avurt, avert / advert / overt
avurtize, advertise
awa, away
await,*,ted,ting, TO EXPECT
awake,*,en,ening,king, FROM SLEEP
award,*,ded,ding, A PRIZE
aware,eness, CAUTIOUS, ALERT "prefixes: un"
awate, await
away, SOMEWHERE ELSE
awayt, await
awbuzit, opposite
awcshen, auction
awd, odd / ought / out
awdacity, audacity
awdamate, automate
awdamotive, automotive
awdasety, audacity
awdeanse, audience
awdeble, audible
awdege, outage
awdeje, outage
awdeo, audio
awder, outer / otter
awdet, audit
awdete, odd(ity)
awdetoreum, auditorium
awdfet, outfit
awdgo, outgo
awdible, audible
awdij, outage
awdimotive, automotive
awding, outing
awdir, outer / otter
awdishun, audition
awdit, audit
awdition, audition
awditorium, auditorium
awdity, odd(ity)
awdlet, outlet
awdlieng, outlying
awdline, outline
awdlook, outlook

awdrit, outright
awdside, outside
awdskirt, outskirt
awdsmart, outsmart
awdstanding, outstand(ing)
awdur, outer / otter
awdwet, outwit
awdwurd, outward
awe,*,ed,wing, TAKEN ABACK, STUNNED
awel, owl
awer, our / hour
awesome,ely,eness, IMPRESSIVE
awfil, awful
awful,lly,lness, DREADFUL
awger, auger
awgest, august
awgir, auger
awgist, august
awgment, augment
awgmint, augment
awgre, auger
awgur, auger
awgus, august
awgust, august
awhile, FOR SOME TIME NOW
awil, awhile
awkewpie, occupy
awksedize, oxide(dize)
awksegin, oxygen
awkshun, auction
awkupy, occupy
awkward,dly,dness, BUNGLING OR EMBARRASSING
awl,*, TOOL FOR SEWING LEATHER (or see owl/all)
awlso, also
awning,*, ROOF OVERHANG
aword, award
awpazit, opposite
awperuble, operable
awposit, opposite
awpuzit, opposite
awr, our / hour
awreginal, origin(al)
awrekt, erect
awrickle, auricle
awrie, awry
awrikle, auricle
awroara, aurora
awrode, erode
awrora, aurora
awru, aura
awry, OFF COURSE

awselate, osculate / oscillate
awsem, awesome
awsilate, osculate / oscillate
awsome, awesome
awspeshus, auspicious
awspitious, auspicious
awstear, austere
awsteer, austere
awsulate, osculate / oscillate
awsum, awesome
awt, out / ought
awtem, autumn
awter, otter / outer
awtesm, autism
awtfit, outfit
awtgo, outgo
awthentik, authentic
awthintik, authentic
awthir, author
awthority, authority
awtim, autumn
awting, outing
awtir, otter / outer
awtism, autism
awtitorium, auditorium
awtizm, autism
awtlaw, outlaw
awtlet, outlet
awtlieng, outlying
awtline, outline
awtlook, outlook
awtluk, outlook
awtlying, outlying
awtobiografy, autobiography
awtopse, autopsy
awtpost, outpost
awtput, output
awtrage, outrage
awtragus, outrage(ous)
awtraje, outrage
awtrite, outright
awtset, outset
awtside, outside
awtskurt, outskirt
awtsmart, outsmart
awtstanding, outstand(ing)
awtum, autumn
awtur, outer / otter
awtward, outward
awtwerd, outward
awtwit, outwit
awtwurd, outward
awul, owl
awur, our / hour

ax,xes,xed,xing, TOOL WITH A SHARP BLADE FOR CHOPPING WOOD (or see ache(s)/axis/ask)
axcebt, except / accept
axcedent, accident
axceed, exceed
axcelerate, accelerate
axchange, exchange
axchoole, actual
axcident, accident
axclude, exclude
axcurshin, excursion
axderminate, exterminate
axdurminate, exterminate
axebt, except / accept
axecutive, executive
axent, accent
axepshen, except(ion)
axeptinse, accept(ance)
axesory, accessory
axess, access
axeul, axis(ial)
axglood, exclude
axicute, execute
axil,*, ANGLE BETWEEN STEM/BRANCH (or see axle)
axint, accent
axis,xes,ial,ially, A PIVOTAL POINT ON WHICH SOMETHING IS CENTERED (or see ax(es)) "prefixes: bi"
axkerjen, excursion
axklude, exclude
axkuze, excuse
axle,*, ROD WITH TWO WHEELS ATTACHED(or see axil)
axol, axil / axle
axplan, explain
axsedintal, accident(al)
axseed, exceed
axselense, excellent
axseluratur, accelerate(tor)
axsenshuate, accentuate
axsent, accent
axsentuate, accentuate
axsept, accept / except
axseptense, accept(ance)
axseptinse, accept(ance)
axses, access / ax(es) / axis
axsesares, accessory(ries)
axsesori, accessory
axsesurize, accessory(rize)
axshule, actual
axshun, action
axsident, accident

axsidental, accident(al)
axsidint, accident
axsint, accent
axsintuate, accentuate
axst, ax(ed) / ask(ed)
axsudentul, accident(al)
axterminate, exterminate
axturminate, exterminate
axturnal, external
axual, actual
axuated, acuate(d)
axukute, execute
axul, axil / axle
axule, actual
azbekt, aspect
azberigus, asparagus
azbestus, asbestos
azburashun, aspirate(tion)
azdragen, estrogen
azemulate, assimilate
azendent, ascendant
azertane, ascertain
azfalt, asphalt
azfault, asphalt
azfikseate, asphyxiate
azfolt, asphalt
azide, aside
azilum, asylum
azinment, assignment
azinshul, essential
azma, asthma
azmu, asthma
azpekt, aspect
azpir, aspire
azpren, aspirin
azspect, aspect
azteem, esteem
azthma, asthma
aztonesh, astonish
aztral, astral
aztranaut, astronaut
aztrawneme, astronomy
aztrengent, astringent
aztringent, astringent
aztroid, asteroid
aztrol, astral
aztrolegy, astrology
aztronume, astronomy
aztrul, astral
aztrunot, astronaut
azumshin, assumption
azurtane, ascertain
b, be / bee
ba, bay

babby, baby
babe, TERM OF ENDEARMENT
babesit, babysit
baby,bies,bied,bying, CHILD UNDER THE AGE OF ONE YEAR
babysit,*,tter,tting,babysat, WATCH OTHERS CHILDREN
bacen, bacon / bake(king) / basin
bach, back / batch / badge / bash / bake / bog / balk / baulk
bachelor,*, UNMARRIED MAN
bacher, badger
bachful, bashful
bachiler, bachelor
bachin, back(ing) / bake(king) / batch(ing) / bacon
bachuler, bachelor
bacin, bacon
back,*,ked,king,ker, GO TO THE PREVIOUS/PAST, IN THE REAR OF (or see bake) "prefixes: un"
backward,*,dness, IN REVERSE
backwurd, backward
bacon, SALTED HOG MEAT/FAT
bacos, because
bacteri, PREFIX INDICATING 'BACTERIA' MOST OFTEN MODIFIES THE WORD
bacteria,al,ium, MICROSCOPIC ORGANISM "prefixes: non"
bactirea, bacteria
bactireul, bacteria(l)
bactiria, bacteria
bacuerd, backward
bad,dly,dness, NOT GOOD (or see bat/bade)
badare, battery
badchelor, bachelor
badder, batter
bade, PAST TENSE FOR THE WORD 'BID' (or see bat/bad)
badel, battle
bader, batter
badery, battery
badge,*, INSIGNIA (or see batch)
badger,*,red,ring, TO HECKLE SOMEONE, AN ANIMAL
badiry, battery
badje, badge
badjur, badger
badle, battle
badol, battle
badore, battery
badre, battery
badshelor, bachelor

badul, battle
baduly, body(dily)
badur, batter
badury, battery
bae, bay
baege, beige
baej, beige
bael, bail / bale
baenkwit, banquet
baet, bait / bate
bafal, befall
bafileon, pavilion
bafol, befall
bag,*,gged,gging,gger,ggy,ggier,ggiest, A CONTAINER TO HOLD ITEMS (or see back/beige/batch/badge)
bagage, baggage
bagd, bag(gged) / back(ed)
bage, badge / beige / baggy
baged, bag(gged) / back(ed)
bagege, baggage
bageje, baggage
bagel,*, ROLL WITH A HOLE
bagener, begin(nner)
bager, bag(gger) / badger
baggage, LUGGAGE
baggy,ggies,gily,giness, LOOSE, SAGGY
bagige, baggage
bagil, bagel
baginer, begin(nner)
bagir, badger / bag(gger)
bagle, bagel
baguj, baggage
bagul, bagel
bagur, bag(gger) / badger
bahaf, behave
bahaver, behavior
bahavior, behavior
bahind, behind
baige, beige
baije, beige
bail,*,led,ler, LIBERATE, REMOVE FROM (or see bale/bowel)
bailef, bailiff
bailif, bailiff
bailiff,*, CIVIL OFFICER OR FUNCTIONARY
bainquet, banquet
bair, bear / bare
bait,*,ted,ting, LURING TO CATCH (or see bate/bite)
baj, badge / beige / batch
bajer, badger
bak, back / bake / balk / baulk

bakd, bake(d) / back(ed)
bake,*,ed,king,er, COOK FOOD IN AN OVEN (or see back) "prefixes: un"
bakeeny, bikini
baken, bacon
bakene, bikini
bakery,ries, WHERE PASTRIES ARE BAKED
bakin, bacon
bakini, bikini
bakiry, bakery
bakose, because
bakry, bakery
bakt, bake(d) / back(ed)
bakterea, bacteria
baktereul, bacteria(l)
baktirea, bacteria
bakuj, baggage
bakwerd, backward
bakwurd, backward
bal, ball / bale / bail / bawl
bala, ballet
balad, ballad / ballade
balance,*,ed,cing, EQUILIBRIUM, CENTERED "prefixes: un"
balarena, ballerina
balat, ballot / ballad / ballade
balay, ballet
balcene, balcony
balcony,nies, PORCH ABOVE THE FIRST STORY ON A BUILDING
balcuny, balcony
bald,ding,dness, LOOSING HAIR (or see bold/ball(ed)/bale(d)/bail(ed))
bale,*,ed,ling,er, TO BUNDLE (or see bail)
baled, bale(d) / bail(ed) / ballad / ballade
baleef, belief
baleeve, believe
balef, bailiff
baleger, beleaguer
balens, balance
balerena, ballerina
balestic, ballistic
balet, ballet / ballot / ballad / ballade
baleve, believe
balevuble, believe(vable)
balid, ballad / ballade
balif, bailiff
balins, balance
balirena, ballerina
balit, ballot / ballet

balk,*,ked,king,ker,kingly, ALSO 'BAULK', EXPRESS UNWILLINGNESS TO DO SOMETHING, HINDER/ PREVENT (or see bulk/baulk) "prefixes: un"
balkeny, balcony
balkune, balcony
ball,*,lled,lling, ROUND OBJECT FOR THROWING/SPORTS, A FORMAL DANCE STYLE (or see bawl/bail/bale)
ballad,*,dic,dist,dry, SIMPLE SONG/ POEM (or see ballade)
ballade,*, SPECIFIC STYLE OF POEM/ MUSICAL PIECE (or see ballad)
balled, ballad / ballade / ball(ed)
ballerena, ballerina
ballerina,*, FEMALE DANCER
ballet,*, CLASSICAL DANCE (or see ballot)
ballid, ballad / ballade
ballistic,*, PROJECTILE IN AIR
balloon,*,ned,ning, FULL OF AIR
ballot,*,ted,ting,ter, OF VOTING
balm,*, OINTMENT FROM PLANTS
balme, balmy
balmy,mier,miest,mily,miness, OF WARM/MILD CLIMATE
balo, below / bellow / billow
balonee, bologna / baloney
baloney, NONSENSE, MEAT (or see bologna)
balong, belong
baloom, bloom
baloon, balloon
balot, ballot / ballet
balow, below / billow / bellow
bals, bowel(s) / ball(s) / bale(s) / bail(s)
baluf, bailiff
balume, bloom
balune, balloon
balunse, balance
balurena, ballerina
banana,*, EDIBLE FRUIT
band,*,ded,ding, COLLECTION OF PERFORMING MUSICIANS, TO BE GROUPED/BOUND TOGETHER "prefixes: contra/multi"
bandage,*,ed,ging, FOR REPAIRING WOUNDS
bandry, boundary
baneeth, beneath
baner, banner
banesh, banish

banevulense, benevolence
banign, benign
banine, benign
banir, banner
banish,hes,hed,hing,hment, CONDEMNED TO EXILE
bank,*,ked,king,ker, BUSINESS THAT STORES GOODS/CASH, SMALL BERM/HILL "prefixes: under"
bankrupsee, bankrupt(cy)
bankrupt,tcy,tcies, BROKE TO THE BANK, CAN'T PAY
bankwit, banquet
banner,*, TYPE OF SIGN
banquet,*, FEAST WITH FRIENDS
banquit, banquet
bantry, boundary / pantry
banur, banner
baptesm, baptism
baptism,*,mal,ize, REBIRTHING RITUAL
baptize,*,ed,zing, REBIRTHING RITUAL
baptizm, baptism
bar,*,rred,rring, LONG/FLAT SECTION/ COUNTER (or see bare/bear)
bara, barrette / beret
barack, barrack
barbarian,*,ic, UNCIVILIZED PERSON
barbecue,*,ed,uing, GRILLED MEAT
barbekew, barbecue
barbeku, barbecue
barber,*, CUTS HAIR
barberean, barbarian
barberian, barbarian
barbetchuet, barbiturate
barbichuit, barbiturate
barbique, barbecue
barbir, barber
barbitchuet, barbiturate
barbiturate,*, SEDATIVE DRUG "prefixes: non"
barbur, barber
barc, bark
barder, barter
bardur, barter
bare,*,ed,ring,rren, WITHOUT COVER (or see bear/berry/bury)
bareave, bereave
bareck, barrack
bareeve, bereave
bareft, bereft
barel, barrel
baren, barren
bareng, bearing / bar(rring) / bare(ring)
barestur, barrister

baret, barrette / beret
baretone, baritone
bareur, barrier
bargain,*,ned,ning, AFFORDABLE DEAL
barge,*,ed,ging, FLAT-BOTTOM BOAT, BEHAVE LIKE A BOAT
bergen, bargain
bargun, bargain
bargund, bargain(ed)
baricade, barricade
barier, barrier
barikade, barricade
baril, barrel
barin, barren
baring, bearing / bare(ring) / bar(rring)
barister, barrister
barit, barrette / beret
baritone,*, DEEP TONE
barje, barge
bark,*,ked,king,ker, SOUND FROM A DOG, COVER ON TREES "prefixes: de"
barn,*, LARGE STRUCTURE FOR FARM ANIMALS (or see born/barren)
baro, PREFIX INDICATING 'PRESSURE/WEIGHT' MOST OFTEN MODIFIES THE WORD (or see barrow/borrow)
baroge, barrage
baroje, barrage
barol, barrel
barometer,*,tric, INSTRUMENT MEASURING PRESSURE
baromiter, barometer
baron, barren
baroque, TYPE OF MUSIC, WILD, UNUSUAL
barow, borrow / burrow / borough
barrack,*, LODGE FOR MANY PEOPLE
barrage,*,ed,ging, ALL AT ONCE
barrel,*,led,ling, DRUM OR GREAT SPEED
barren,nly,nness, UNFERTILE
barrette,*, CLASP (or see beret)
barricade,*,ded,ding, BLOCK AGAINST
barrier,*, OBSTRUCTION
barring, EXCEPTING, REFUSAL (or see bear(ing)/bar(ing))
barrister,*, LAWYER
barrow, CASTRATED HOG (or see borrow)
bartender,*, TENDS BAR
barter,*,red,ring, TRADE
bartinder, bartender
bartur, barter

baruton, baritone
bary, berry / bury
bas, base / bass
basball, baseball
basboll, baseball
base,*,ed,sing,eless, A FOUNDATION, FORM IN BASEBALL (or see bass) "prefixes: de"
baseach, beseech
baseball, SPORT
baseech, beseech
basek, basic
basekly, basic(ally)
basel, basil
basement,*, UNDER HOUSE
basen, basin
bases, basis / base(s)
baset, basset
bash,hes,hed,hing, A PARTY, TO SMASH/DESTROY SOMETHING, INSULT SOMEONE
bashfel, bashful
bashful, SHY
basi, PREFIX INDICATING 'BOTTOM/BASE' MOST OFTEN MODIFIES THE WORD
basic,*,cally, FUNDAMENTAL
baside, beside
basik, basic
basikly, basic(ally)
basil, HERB
basin,*, SHAPED LIKE BOWL
basis, ON WHICH IT STANDS (or see base(s))
basit, basset
basket,*, WOVEN CONTAINER
baskit, basket
baskut, basket
basmant, basement
basmint, basement
baso, PREFIX INDICATING 'BOTTOM/BASE' MOST OFTEN MODIFIES THE WORD
basoon, bassoon
bass,sses,ssist, A FISH, STRINGED INSTRUMENT, LEVEL OF SOUND TONE/FREQUENCY (or see base)
basset, DOG, HOUND
bassoon, HORN
basuk, basic
basul, basil
basun, basin / bassoon
basurk, berserk
basus, basis / base(s)

basut, basset
bat,*,tted,tting,tter, STUFFING, TOOL USED IN BASEBALL, TO HIT (or see bate/bait)
batch,hes,hed,hing, INCREMENTS/CERTAIN AMOUNTS OF SOMETHING AT A TIME (or see badge/botch)
batcheler, bachelor
batchuler, bachelor
bate,*,ed,ting, DECREASE, HOLD BACK (or see bait)
batel, battle
baten, batten
batenshul, potential
bater, batter
batery, battery
bath,*,hroom, A PLACE TO WASH, TO IMMERSE IN LIQUID (or see bathe)
bathe,*,ed,hing,ers, TO WASH UP, IMMERSE IN LIQUID (or see bath)
batil, bottle / battle
batin, batten
batinshul, potential
batiry, battery
batle, battle
batom, bottom
baton,*, WAND
batore, battery
batre, battery
batrothed, betrothed
batshelor, bachelor
batshiler, bachelor
batten, SECURE/STRENGTHEN, WOOD STRIPS (or see bat(tting))
batter,*,red,ring, FRYING MIXTURE, BASEBALL PLAYER, TO BE ATTACKED
battery,ries, APPLIES TO MILITARY, MECHANICAL, ELECTRICAL, BASEBALL
battle,*,ed,ling, FIGHT BETWEEN TWO FORCES
batul, battle
batur, batter
batury, battery
batween, between
bauch, botch
bauchulism, botulism
baul, ball / bawl / bail / bale / bowel
baulk,*,ked,king,ker,kingly, ALSO 'BALK', EXPRESS UNWILLINGNESS TO DO SOMETHING, HINDER/PREVENT (or see bulk/balk) "prefixes: un"

baulm, balm
baulme, balmy
bauls, bowel(s) / bawl(s) / ball(s)
baund, bound
baundre, boundary
bauns, bounce / bound(s)
baunse, bounce(cy) / buoyant(ncy)
baunti, bounty
bauntiful, bountiful
bauntre, boundary
baurk, bark
baush, botch
baut, bought / bout
bautel, bottle
bavileon, pavilion
bawdil, bottle
bawildre, bewilder
bawl,*,led,ling,ler, WEEP, SHOUT AT (or see ball)
bawls, bawl(s) / bowel(s) / ball(s)
bawnd, bound
bawnse, bounce / bound(s)
bawntee, bounty
bawntiful, bountiful
bay,*, RELATES TO WINDOW, BARN, DOG HOWLING, SHIP HOSPITAL, AIRCRAFT, SHRUB, OCEAN INLET
bayle, bail / bale
bayond, beyond
bayou, OUTLET OF WATER
bayu, bayou
bazaar,*, SALE OF ARTICLES (or see bizarre)
bazel, basil
bazen, basin
bazil, basil
bazin, basin
bazul, basil
bazurk, berserk
bazzar, bizarre / bazaar
be, A VERB EXPRESSING PRESENT TENSE, A PREFIX INDICATING 'COMPLETELY/INTENSELY' MOST OFTEN MODIFIES THE WORD (or see bee)
beach,hes,hed,hing, SHORELINE (or see beech)
beacon,*, SIGNAL (or see beckon)
bead,*,ded,ding, ROUNDED FORM/ OBJECT (or see beat/beet)
beafy, beef(y)
beagle,*, DOG
beagul, beagle
beak,*, BIRD BILL

beaker,*, VESSEL
beam,*,med,ming, TO SHINE, LINEAR SUPPORT
bean,*, VEGETABLE, TO HURT (or see been/bin)
bear,*,ring,rish,rishly, ANIMAL, PUT PRESSURE ON/AGAINST (or see bare/beer/bearing) "prefixes: over"
bearable, TOLERABLE "prefixes: un"
beard,*,ded, MALE FACIAL HAIR
bearing,*, SUPPORTS, PRESSURE, MACHINE PART, HEADING (or see bare(ring))
beast,*,tly,tliness, ANIMA
beat,*,ting,ten,ter, THRASH/STRIKE/HIT (or see beet) "prefixes: un/up"
beau,*, BOYFRIEND (or see bow/bough)
beauru, bureau
beautician,*, HAIRDRESSER
beautiful,lly, EYE PLEASER
beautishun, beautician
beauty,ties,tify,tiful,tifully,tious,teously, teousness,tification, PLEASING TO THE SENSES, GMP
beaver,*, ANIMAL
bebleografy, bibliography
became, PAST TENSE FOR THE WORD 'BECOME'
because, THE REASON FOR
becin, beckon / beacon / bacon
becken, beckon / beacon / bacon
beckon,*,ned,ning, TO SUMMON/CALL FORTH, ENTICE TO COME (or see beacon/bacon)
beckun, beckon/beacon/bacon
become,*,ming,came, GOING TO BE (or see became) "prefixes: un"
becon, beckon / beacon / bacon
becos, because
becum, become
becun, beckon / beacon / bacon
becus, because
becuz, because
bed,*,dded,dding, SOMETHING TO SLEEP/ LIE DOWN UPON (or see bead/bet/bit/beat)
beded, bet(tted) / bed(dded) / bead(ed)
beder, better / bid(dder) / bitter / bet(ttor)
bedid, bet(tted) / bed(dded)
bedil, beetle
bedir, better / bid(dder) / bitter / bet(ttor)
bedol, beetle

bedraggled, MUSSED UP
bedragled, bedraggled
bedraguled, bedraggled
bedridden, CONFINED TO BED
bedriden, bedridden
bedritin, bedridden
bedrothed, betrothed
bedspread,*, BED COVER
bedspred, bedspread
bedud, bet(tted) / bed(dded)
bedul, beetle
bedur, better / bid(dder) / bitter / bet(ttor)
bedwritin, bedridden
bee,*, FURRY INSECT (or see be)
beech, TREE (or see beach)
beedil, beetle
beedul, beetle
beef,fy,finess,fed,fing, FLESHY, MEAT FROM BOVINE, TO COMPLAIN
beek, beak
beeker, beaker
beekin, beacon
beem, beam
been, PAST TENSE FOR THE WORD 'BE' (or see bean)
beeng, being
beer,*, FERMENTED BREW (or see bear)
beerd, beard
beest, beast
beestro, bistro
beet,*, A VEGETABLE (or see beat)
beetle,*, BUG
beetul, beetle
beever, beaver
befall, OCCUR
befol, befall
before, PREVIOUS
befour, before
befrend, befriend
befriend,*,ded, MAKE FRIENDS WITH
befrind, befriend
beg,*,gged,gging, PLEAD (or see big/ beach)
began, PAST TENSE FOR THE WORD 'BEGIN'
begar, beggar
begen, begin
begenir, begin(nner)
beger, beggar
beggar,*,ry,rly,rliness, ONE WHO BEGS
beggir, beggar
beggur, beggar
begil, beagle / bagel

begin,*,nner,nning,gan, TO START
beginer, begin(nner)
begir, beggar
begle, beagle / bagel
begot, bigot
begul, beagle / bagel
begur, beggar
begut, bigot
begutre, bigot(ry)
behaf, behalf
behalf, ON THE PART OF
behave,*,ed,ving,vior, ACT IN A PARTICULAR WAY "prefixes: mis"
behaveor, behavior
behavior,*,ral,rism,rist,ristic, MANNERISMS, ATTITUDE
behavyur, behavior
behind, TO THE BACK
behoof, behoove
behoove,*,ed,ving, TO BE PROPER
behufe, behoove
behuve, behoove
beige, COLOR
being,*, EXISTS
bekame, became
beken, beckon / beacon / bacon
beker, beaker
bekin, beckon / beacon / bacon
bekit, bigot
bekom, become
bekon, beckon / beacon / bacon
bekos, because
bekum, become
bekur, beaker
bekus, because
bekut, bigot
bekuz, because
beladed, belated
beladid, belated
belated,dly, OVERDUE
belatide, belated
beld, build / bill(ed) / built
bele, belly
beleaguer, BLOCK, SIEGE
belegarant, belligerent
beleger, beleaguer
beleon, billion
belerds, billiards
belevuble, believe(vable)
beli, belly
belief,*, FAITH, HOPE "prefixes: dis/mis/un"
believe,*,ed,ving,vable,vably,vability, FAITH, HOPE "prefixes: dis/mis/un"

believeable, believe(vable)
beligerent, belligerent
belise, police
belittle,*,ed,ling,ement, TO INSULT
belle, belly
belligerent,tly,nce,ncy, WAR-LIKE AGGRESSIVENESS
bellow,*,wed,wing, DEEP ROAR, INSTRUMENT (or see below/billow)
belly,llies, ABDOMEN "prefixes: under"
belo, bellow / below / billow
belonee, bologna / baloney
belong,*,ging,gings, HAVE RIGHTS TO
beloon, balloon
below, BENEATH, LOWER (or see bellow/billow)
belt,*,ted,ting, STRAP TO WEAR AROUND THE WAIST, PUNCH/HIT SOMETHING (or see built) "prefixes: un"
belurds, billiards
belyon, billion
belyunar, billion(aire)
bemt, beam(ed)
ben, been / bin / bean
benafactor, benefactor
benaficial, beneficial
benaficiary, beneficiary
benafishiary, beneficiary
benafishul, beneficial
benafit, benefit
benansa, bonanza
benanu, banana
bench,hes,hed,hing, RELATES TO LAW, GEOLOGY, SPORTS "prefixes: un"
bend,*,ding,nt, CROOK/ANGLE (or see bent/bind) "prefixes: un"
bended, bent
bendid, bent
bene, PREFIX INDICATING 'GOOD/ WELL' MOST OFTEN MODIFIES THE WORD
beneath, UNDER, LOWER
beneeth, beneath
benefactor,*,tion, CONTRIBUTOR
beneficial,lly, HELPFUL "prefixes: un"
beneficiary,ries, ONE WHO BENEFITS FROM
benefishiery, beneficiary
benefishul, beneficial
benefit,*,ted,ting, TO SERVE "prefixes: dis"
benevolance, benevolence
benevolence,nt, BIG HEARTED, KIND

benevolent,ntly, BIG HEARTED, KIND
benevulense, benevolence
benge, binge
benifactor, benefactor
benificial, beneficial
benifisheary, beneficiary
benifishul, beneficial
benifit, benefit
benign,nity,nities,nly, KINDLY
benine, benign
benje, binge
bent, PAST TENSE FOR THE WORD" BEND" "prefixes: un"
bented, bent
benufactor, benefactor
benuficial, beneficial
benuficiary, beneficiary
benufisheary, beneficiary
benufishul, beneficial
benufit, benefit
beond, beyond
ber, burr / bear / bare / beer
berbin, bourbon
berch, birch
berd, bird / beard
berden, burden
berdinsum, burden(some)
bere, berry / bury / bare / bear
bereave,*,ed,ving,ement, ANGUISH OVER LOSS
bereble, bearable
berecade, barricade
bereft, LACKING/ LOSS/ DEPRIVED
berek, barrack
berekade, barricade
berel, barrel
beren, barren
bereng, bearing / bare(ring)
berer, bear(er) / barrier
berestur, barrister
beret,*, CLOTH CAP (or see barrette)
beretone, baritone
bereul, burial
bereur, barrier
bergendy, burgundy
bergler, burglar
bergundy, burgundy
beri, bury / berry
berial, burial
berible, bearable
bericade, barricade
berick, barrack
berier, barrier
berikade, barricade

beril, barrel
berin, barren
bering, bearing / bar(ing) / bar(rring)
berister, barrister
beristur, barrister
beritone, baritone
beriv, bereave
berkler, burglar
berlap, burlap
berlesk, burlesque
berly, burly
berm,*,med, SLOPED SOIL
bern, burn
bernt, burnt
bero, barrow / burrow / burro / borough
berog, barrage
beroj, barrage
berol, barrel
beron, barren
berow, barrow / borrow
berp, burp
berry,rries, FRUIT (or see bury)
bersaverense, persevere(rance)
bersd, burst
bersding, burst(ing)
berserk, VIOLENT FRENZY
berst, burst
berth,*, PLACE TO SETTLE INTO/SLEEP (or see birth)
berthday, birthday
beruble, bearable
berubul, bearable
berukad, barricade
berul, barrel
beruton, baritone
bery, berry / bury
berzd, burst
berzding, burst(ing)
bes, bee(s) / best
besanes, business
besar, bizarre / bazaar
besd, best / beast
bese, busy
beseach, beseech
beseech,her,hingly, IMPLORE
besely, busy(sily)
besenes, business
beserk, berserk
besi, busy
beside,*, ALONGSIDE, AS WELL AS
besines, business
besirk, berserk
besk, bisque

besket, biscuit
besque, bisque
best, PAST TENSE FOR THE WORD 'BETTER' (or see beast)
bestro, bistro
besurk, berserk
besy, busy
bet,*,tted,tting,ttor, PLACE A WAGER WITH HOPE OF WINNING SOMETHING (or see beet/beat/bed)
beted, bet(tted) / bed(dded)
beter, better / bid(dder) / bitter / bet(ttor)
betid, bet(tted) / bed(dded)
betir, better / bid(dder) / bitter / bet(ttor)
beton, baton
betor, better / bid(dder) / bitter / bet(ttor)
betray,*,yal,yer, VIOLATION OF TRUST
betrothed, ENGAGEMENT TO SOMEONE
better,red,ring,rment, MORE SUPERIOR (or see bet(ttor))
betud, bet(tted) / bed(dded)
between, IN THE MIDDLE OF HERE AND THERE
beudeful, beautiful
beudiful, beautiful
beudy, beauty
beugl, bugle
beurd, beard
beuro, bureau
beurocrasy, bureaucracy
beurocrat, bureaucrat
beut, butte
beuteshun, beautician
beutiful, beautiful
beuty, beauty
bevarige, beverage
bevel,*,led,ling, INCLINED SURFACE
beverage,*, FLAVORED LIQUID TO DRINK
bevil, bevel
bevir, beaver
bevirage, beverage
bevle, bevel
bevol, bevel
bevrag, beverage
bevrech, beverage
bevrig, beverage
bevul, bevel
bevur, beaver

beware, CAUTION
bewere, beware
bewhere, beware
bewhove, behoove
bewilder,*,red,ring,ringly,rment, CONFUSE
bewt, butte
bewte, beauty
bewteful, beautiful
bewteshin, beautician
bewyon, bouillon
beyeng, being
beyond, OUT OF REACH
beyut, butte
bezar, bizarre / bazaar
bezd, best / beast
beze, busy
bezenes, business
bezerk, berserk
bezi, busy
beznes, business
bezt, best / beast
bezunes, business
bezzar, bizarre / bazaar / buzz(er)
bi, PREFIX INDICATING 'TWO/TWICE' MOST OFTEN MODIFIES THE WORD (or see by/bye/bee)
biadic, biotic
biagrafik, biography(hic)
bialegy, biology
bianeal, biennial / biannual
bianel, biennial / biannual
biannual, TWICE A YEAR (or see biennial)
bianuel, biannual
bianyual, biannual
bias, PREFERENCE TOWARDS/FOR "prefixes: un"
biatic, biotic
biaudec, biotic
biaugrafe, biography
biaulugy, biology
biautec, biotic
bibleografy, bibliography
bibleogrufy, bibliography
biblio, PREFIX INDICATING 'BOOK' MOST OFTEN MODIFIES THE WORD
bibliography,hies,hic,hical, LIST OF PRINTED MATERIAL
bic, bike / beak
bicame, became
bicas, because
bicentenial, bicentennial

bicentennial,*, TWO HUNDRED YEAR MARK
biceps, MUSCLES
bicker,*,red,ring, ARGUE (or see bike(r))
bicom, become
bicon, beacon
bicos, because
bicus, because
bicycle,*,ed,ling,list, TWO-WHEEL TRANSPORTATION
bid,*,dder,dding, TO TELL, BE TOLD, BID FAREWELL, WAGER SOMETHING TO GAIN SOMETHING ELSE (or see bite(r)/bitter/bit/bed/bide/bead) "prefixes: over/under"
bidder, bitter / bid(der) / bite(r)
bide,*,ed,ding, WAIT, WITHSTAND (or see bid/bite) "prefixes: un"
bider, bite(r) / bid(dder) / bitter
bidragled, bedraggled
bidraguled, bedraggled
bidtrothed, betrothed
bieng, buy(ing)
bienial, biennial / biannual
biennial, TWO YEARS (or see biannual)
bifal, befall
bifocals, TWO-PART LENS
bifocul, bifocals
bifokul, bifocals
bifol, befall
bifor, before
bifour, before
bifrend, befriend
big,gger,ggest,ggy, LARGE (or see beg)
bigan, began / begin
bigetry, bigot(ry)
bigot,ted,try, NARROW-MINDED "prefixes: un"
bigutry, bigot(ry)
bihaf, behave / behalf
bihalf, behave / behalf
bihav, behave / behalf
bihind, behind
bikame, became
bike,*,ed,king,er, WHEEL TRANSPORTATION "prefixes: retro"
bikeeny, bikini
bikeim, became
biker,*, RIDES MOTORCYCLE (or see bicker/beaker)
bikini,*, TWO-PIECE BATHING SUIT
bikose, because
bikum, become
bikur, bicker / biker

bikus, because
bikut, bigot
bilak, black
bilanear, bilinear
bilards, billiards
bilateral, BOTH SIDES
bilatirul, bilateral
bild, build / bill(ed) / built
bile, FLUID MADE BY THE LIVER (or see bill)
biled, build / bill(ed) / built
bileef, belief
bileeve, believe
bileger, beleaguer
bilenear, bilinear
bilengual, bilingual
bilengwul, bilingual
bileon, billion
bilerds, billiards
bileve, believe
bilevuble, believe(vable)
biliards, billiards
bilinear, TWO LINES
bilingual, SPEAKS TWO LANGUAGES
bilingwal, bilingual
bilion, billion
bilitol, belittle
bill,*,lled,lling, TOTAL COSTS (or see bile) "prefixes: over/pre"
billiards, POOL GAME
billion,*,nth,naire, ONE THOUSAND MILLION
billow,*,wed,wing, OF WIND (or see below/bellow)
bilo, billow / below / bellow
bilonee, baloney / bologna
bilong, belong
bilow, below / billow / bellow
bilt, built / build
bilurds, billiards
bilyon, billion
bilyunar, billion(aire)
bimonthly, TWICE A MONTH
bimunthly, bimonthly
bin,*,nned,nning, COMPARTMENT FOR STORAGE, PREFIX INDICATING 'TWO/TWICE' MOST OFTEN MODIFIES THE WORD (or see been/bean)
binanu, banana
binanzu, bonanza
binary,ries, UNITS OF TWO
binch, binge / bench

bind,*,bound,ding,dingly,der, HOLD THINGS TOGETHER "prefixes: multi/un"
bineeth, beneath
binefacter, benefactor
binery, binary
binevilance, benevolence
binevulense, benevolence
bing, being / binge
binge,*,ed,ging, SPREE
binign, benign
binine, benign
binith, beneath
binje, binge
binocular,*, DEVICE THAT MAGNIFIES FOR BOTH EYES
binokuler, binocular
binomeal, binomial
binomial,*, HAS TWO NAMES/TERMS
binoquler, binocular
bint, bent
binufakter, benefactor
binufishal, beneficial
binufishary, beneficiary
binufit, benefit
binury, binary
bio, PREFIX INDICATING 'LIFE' MOST OFTEN MODIFIES THE WORD
biocide,dal, CIVILIZATION CHOKING OFF IT'S OWN LIFE SUPPLY
biodagradable, biodegradable
biodec, biotic
biodegradable, ELEMENTS EASILY BREAKS DOWN
biofisics, biophysics
biofizecs, biophysics
biografee, biography
biography,hies,hic,hical, STORY OF PEOPLE'S HISTORY "prefixes: auto"
biogrufee, biography
biology,gical,gically,gist, STUDY OF LIFE "prefixes: exo/pre"
biophisics, biophysics
biophysics, STUDY OF LIFE
biopsy,sies, STUDY OF TISSUE
biorethum, biorhythm
biorhythm, BIOLOGICAL RHYTHM
biorithum, biorhythm
biorythm, biorhythm
bios, bias
biosfeare, biosphere
bioside, biocide
biosphere, ALL THAT SUPPORTS LIFE ON EARTH

biotic,*, ABOUT LIVE ORGANISMS "prefixes: pre/pro/sym"
bipadle, bipedal
bipardesan, bipartisan
bipardisan, bipartisan
bipartisan, TWO SIDES SHARING SAME PURPOSE
bipedal, ANIMAL THAT USES TWO LEGS/ARMS
bipedle, bipedal
bipedul, bipedal
bipetle, bipedal
bir, burr / beer
birben, bourbon
birch, A TREE
bird,*, ANIMAL WITH WINGS/ FEATHERS (or see beard)
birden, burden
birdensum, burden(some)
birdinsum, burden(some)
biret, barrette / beret
birglur, burglar
birgundy, burgundy
birkler, burglar
birlesk, burlesque
birlup, burlap
birm, berm
birn, burn
birnt, burnt
biro, burro / burrow / borough
birometer, barometer
birp, burp
birsd, burst
birsding, burst(ing)
birst, burst
birth,*,hed,hing, PHYSICAL BODY BECOMES VISIBLE (or see berth) "prefixes: re"
birthday,*, DATE OF BIRTH
birzd, burst
birzding, burst(ing)
bis, PREFIX INDICATING 'TWO/TWICE' MOST OFTEN MODIFIES THE WORD
bisar, bizarre / bazaar
biscuit,*, NORMALLY GOES WITH GRAVY, A SOFT ROLL
biscut, biscuit
bise, busy
biseach, beseech
biseech, beseech
bisekul, bicycle
bisenteneal, bicentennial
biseps, biceps
bisi, busy

bisicle, bicycle
biside, beside
bisikul, bicycle
bisintineal, bicentennial
bisk, bisque
biskit, biscuit
biskut, biscuit
bisness, business
bisnis, business
bisnus, business
bisque, OF SPORTS, A SOUP
bistro, NIGHTCLUB
bisurk, berserk
bisy, busy
bit,*, TINY INCREMENTS OF SOMETHING, TOOL FOR DRILLING, PAST TENSE FOR THE WORD 'BITE' (or see bite/bid/bead/beat/beet)
bite,*,ting,ter, USE OF MOUTH AS A TOOL(or see bit) "prefixes: non/over/under"
biter, bitter / bid(dder) / bite(r)
biton, baton
bitray, betray
bitrothed, betrothed
bitter,*,rer,rest,red,ring,rly,rness, UNPLEASANT/HARSH, ALCOHOLIC BREW (or see bid(dder)/bite(r))
bitur, bitter / bid(dder) / bite(r)
bitween, between
bius, bias
biusfere, biosphere
biusphere, biosphere
biwar, beware
biwelder, bewilder
biwilder, bewilder
biyopse, biopsy
biyorethum, biorhythm
biyou, bayou
biyu, bayou
biyus, bias
bizar, bizarre / bazaar
bizarre,ely,eness, PECULIAR (or see bazaar)
bizee, busy
bizenes, business
bizerk, berserk
biznes, business
bizurk, berserk
bizzar, bizarre / bazaar
black,*,ken,kened,ker,kest, COLOR
bladder, HOLDS URINE/LIQUIDS
blade,*, USED TO SLICE/CUT
bladur, bladder

blaenkit, blanket
blair, blare
blak, black
blam, blame
blame,*,ed,ming,mable,eful,eless, elessly,eness, WHAT/WHO IS RESPONSIBLE
bland,der,dest,dly,dness, EXPRESSIVELY FLAT
blank, NOTHING
blanket,*,ted,ting, COVER
blankit, blanket
blanquet, blanket
blare,*,ed,ring, SOUND LOUDLY
blasa, plaza
blase, blaze
blasem, blossom
blasfemus, blasphemy(mous)
blasfemy, blasphemy
blasma, plasma
blasphemy,mous, SPEAK BADLY OF SOMEONE
blast,*,ted,ting, BURSTING FORCE/ RUSH, PREFIX INDICATING "GERM/ BUD" MOST OFTEN MODIFIES THE WORD, BURSTING FORCE/RUSH
blastek, plastic
blastik, plastic
blasto, PREFIX INDICATING "GERM/ BUD" MOST OFTEN MODIFIES THE WORD, BURSTING FORCE/RUSH
blatebus, platypus
blater, bladder
blatibus, platypus
blaus, blouse
blawse, blouse
blaze,*,ed,zing,er, FLAME, HORSE MARK, PROCLAIM, SPORT COAT
blazu, plaza
blea, plea
bleach,es,hed,hing, TO MAKE WHITE "prefixes: un"
bleachers, SEATS FOR SPECTATORS
bleak,kish,kly,kness, PALLID, DESOLATE, STARK
bled, PAST TENSE FOR THE WORD 'BLEED'
bleech, bleach
bleechers, bleachers
bleed,*,der,ding, LOOSE BLOOD, ALLOW RELEASE OF FLUID
bleef, belief
bleek, bleak
blek, bleak

blemish,hes,hed,hing,her, DEFECT ON A SURFACE
blemp, blimp
blend,*,ded,ding,der, MIX
blenk, blink
bler, blur / blare
blerb, blurb
bles, bless / bliss
bless,ssess,ssed,ssing, FAVOR UPON (or see bliss) "prefixes: un"
blester, blister
blew, TO DO WITH AIR, PAST TENSE FOR THE WORD 'BLOW' (or see blue)
blezurd, blizzard
blight,*, DESTROYED BY ORGANISM (or see plight)
blimp,*, HELIUM BALLOON
blind,*,ded,ding,ders, WITHOUT SIGHT, WINDOW COVERING (or see blend)
blink,*,ked,king,ker, TO OPEN/CLOSE/OPEN "prefixes: un"
blinker,*, TURN INDICATORS ON VEHICLES
blir, blur
blirb, blurb
blire, blur(rry)
blis, bliss
blisful, bliss(ful)
bliss,ssful,ssfully,ssfulness, EXTREMELY HAPPY (or see bless)
blister,*,red,ring, SORE
blisurd, blizzard
blite, blight
blizzard,*, VIOLENT STORM
blo, blow / below
bloan, blown
bloat,*,ted,ting, SWELL (or see blot)
block,*,ked,king,kage, IN PATHWAY "prefixes: un"
blockade,*,ed,ding, OBSTRUCT TRAVEL
blod, blood / bloat / blown
blog,*,gged,gging,gger, COMPUTER INTERNET TERM (or see block)
blok, block / blog
blokade, blockade
blon, blown / blonde
blonde,*, A COLOR
blone, blown / blonde
blont, blonde / blown
blood,*,ded,dy,dily,dless,diness, BODY FLUID CARRYING NUTRIENTS
blooish, blue(uish)
bloom,*,med,ming, OPEN UP

blosim, blossom
blossom,*,med,ming, FLOURISH
blosum, blossom
blot,*,tted,tting,tter, SPOT, STAIN (or see bloat/blood)
blouse,es, WOMAN'S SHIRT
blouze, blouse
blow,*,wing,lew,wn, FORCEFUL AIR CURRENT (or see below)
blown, TO DO WITH AIR, PAST TENSE FOR THE WORD 'BLOW' "prefixes: over"
blowse, blouse
blowt, bloat
blu, blue / blew
blubber,*,red,ring,ry,rer, WHALE FAT, SOBBING
blubur, blubber
blud, blood
blue,*,uish,uing, COLOR (or see blew)
bluesh, blue(uish)
bluff,*,ffed,ffing,ffer, A CLIFF, TO PRETEND/FAKE
blume, bloom
blunder,*,red,ring, BUNGLES
blunt,*,tly,tness, DULL
bluper, blubber
blupir, blubber
blur,*,rred,rring,rry, INDISTINCT/FUZZY
blurb,*,bed,bing, SHORT DESCRIPTION
blush,hes,hed,hing, PHYSICAL RESPONSE IN THE CHEEKS, TYPE OF WINE "prefixes: un"
blut, blood
bluty, blood(y)
bo, bough / bow / beau
boar,*, SWINE, PIG (or see bore)
board,*,ded,ding, MILLED WOOD, FURNISH WITH FOOD (or see bore(d)) "prefixes: over/pre"
boast,*,ted,ting,tful,tfully, TO BRAG, COMPLIMENT
boat,*,ting,ter, VESSEL IN WATER
bob,*,bbed,bbing, TO MOVE UP AND DOWN (or see bobbin/bop)
bobbin,*, SEWING TOOL (or see bop(pping))
bobd, bop(pped) / bob(bbed)
boben, bobbin / bob(bbing)
bobin, bobbin / bob(bbing)
bobt, bop(pped) / bob(bbed)
bochulism, botulism
bock, box / bog
bocks, box

bocs, box
bodchulism, botulism
boddle, bottle
bode,*, PAST TENSE FOR THE WORD 'BIDE', TO WAIT (or see body/bought)
bodeese, bodice / body
bodel, bottle
bodely, body(dily)
bodem, bottom
bodes, body(dies) / bodice
bodice, WOMAN'S GARMENT FOR UPPER TORSO
bodim, bottom
bodis, body(dies) / bodice
bodjulism, botulism
bodle, bottle
bodul, bottle
bodulism, botulism
bodum, bottom
body,dies,dily, THE PHYSICAL FORM WHICH HOUSES A SPIRIT/LIFE (or see bodice) "prefixes: under"
boe, boy / buoy
boee, boy / buoy
boel, boil
boence, bounce(cy) / buoyant(ncy)
boensy, buoyant(ncy)
boent, buoyant
boes, boy(s)
boesdrus, boisterous
boestures, boisterous
boeul, boil
boeunse, buoyant(ncy)
bofalou, buffalo
bofer, buffer
bog,*,gged,gging,ggy,gginess, SOGGY/SPONGY/WET SOIL AREA/GROUND, SLOW DOWN, A LAVATORY (or see balk/baulk)
boi, boy / buoy
boiant, buoyant
boient, buoyant
boil,*,led,ling,ler, BRING LIQUID TO STEAM TEMPERATURE
boince, buoyant(ncy)
boisdrus, boisterous
boisterous,sly,sness, ROWDY
boiunse, buoyant(ncy)
boiunt, buoyant
bojwaze, bourgeois(ie)
bok, book / poke / bog / baulk / balk
boka, bouquet
bokol, buckle

boks, box
bol, ball / bowl / bawl / bull
bolb, bulb
bolbus, bulb(ous)
bold,der,dest,dly,dness, BRAVE, STANDS OUT (or see bolt) "prefixes: semi"
bolder, boulder / bold(er)
bole, bowl / ball / bawl / bully
bolef, belief
boletin, bulletin
boletle, belittle
boleve, believe
bolidel, belittle
boligerant, belligerent
bolistic, ballistic
bolit, bullet
boliten, bulletin
bolivard, boulevard
bolk, bulk / baulk / balk
boll, bowl / ball / bawl
bollion, bullion / bouillon
bolm, balm
bolme, balmy
bolmy, balmy
bologna, MIXTURE OF MEAT TYPES (or see baloney)
bolonee, baloney / bologna
bolster,*,red,ring, SUPPORT
bolt,*,ted,ting, SECURES, THREADED ROD WITH HEAD (or see bold) "prefixes: un"
bolter, boulder / bold(er)
bolyon, bullion / bouillon
bom, balm / bomb
bomb,*,bed,bing,ber, EXPLOSIVE DEVICE
bomirang, boomerang
bon, bone
bona fide, GENUINE
bonafide, SPELLED AS TWO WORDS "BONA FIDE", GENUINE
bonanza, BONUS DEAL
bond,*,ded,ding,dage,dable,der, TO JOIN/ATTACH TO, TIE UP "prefixes: non"
bondry, boundary
bone,*,ed,ning,ny,nier,niest,niness, SKELETAL
bonefide, bona fide
boneon, bunyon / bunion
bones, bone(s) / bunny(nnies) / bonus
bonifide, bona fide
bonion, bunyon / bunion

bonis, bonus / bunny(nnies)
bonsy, bounce(cy) / buoyant(ncy)
bonufide, bona fide
bonus,ses, EXTRA, ADDITIONAL, MORE
bony, bone(y)
bonyen, bunyon / bunion
bonyon, bunion / bunyon
book,*,ked,king,kish,kishly,kishness,kie, BOUND PAPER WITH A COVER, TO RESERVE A PLACE "prefixes: over"
bookie,*, BOOKS BETS
booky, bookie
boomerang,*,ged,ging, ARTICLE FOR SPORT
boomurang, boomerang
boose, booze / buzz
boost,*,ted,ting,ter, TO LIFT (or see boast/bust)
boosum, bosom
boot,*, OVER ANKLE SHOE (or see butte) "prefixes: re"
booteek, boutique
booth,*, PRIVATE STALL/AREA
bootshur, butcher
booy, buoy
booyon, bouillon / bullion
booze, HARD LIQUOR (or see buzz)
bop,*,pped,pping,pper, TO HIT/WHACK (or see bob)
boped, bop(pped) / bob(bbed)
bopt, bop(pped) / bob(bbed)
boquet, bouquet
bor, boar / bore / bar
borbon, bourbon
borc, bark
bord, board / bore(d)
bordem, boredom
border,*,red,ring, TO LIMIT
bordim, boredom
bordor, border
bordum, boredom
bordur, border
bore,*,ed,ring,ringly, PIERCE/ PUNCTURE/DRILL, LACKS INTEREST, PAST TENSE FOR THE WORD 'BEAR' (or see boar) "prefixes: re"
boredom, DOLDRUMS, LACK OF INTEREST
boren, borne / born
boret, barrette / beret
borin, borne / born
born, BROUGHT INTO EXISTENCE (or see borne/barn) "prefixes: in/re/un"

borne, SUFFIX MEANING TO BE CARRIED/MOVED BY A PARTICULAR THING (or see born/barn)
boro, PREFIX INDICATING 'BORON' MOST OFTEN MODIFIES THE WORD (or see borrow/borough)
borot, borrow(ed)
borough,*, SELF-GOVERNING TOWN (or see burrow/burro/borrow)
borow, borrow/ burrow/ borough
borrow,*,wed,wing,wer, LOAN (or see burrow)
bort, bore(d) / board
borter, border
bortur, border
bos, boss / bus
bose, bough(s) / bow(s) / bossy
bosed, boss(ed)
boseness, boss(iness)
boserd, buzzard
boshel, bushel
bosiness, boss(iness)
bosom,*,med,my,mier,miest, WOMEN'S BREASTS
boss,sses,ssed,ssing,ssy,ssily,ssiness, COMMAND/ORDER SOMEONE TO DO SOMETHING, ONE IN CHARGE "prefixes: under"
bossom, bosom
bossy,siness, DOMINEERING
bost, boast / boss(ed) / boost
bosy, bossy
bot, but / butt / boat / bought
botany,nic,nical,nist, OF PLANTS
botch,hes,hed,hing, MESS SOMETHING UP, SLANG WORD IN WRESTLING, A BAND
botcher, butcher
botchulism, botulism
bote, boat / bought
boteek, boutique
botel, bottle
botem, bottom
botes, body(dies) / bodice
both, TWO TOGETHER (or see booth)
bother,*,red,ring,rsome, ANNOY "prefixes: un"
botil, bottle
botim, bottom
botiney, botany
botle, bottle
botler, butler / bottle(r)
botn, button
botni, botany

botok, buttock
botom, bottom
boton, button
botshulism, botulism
bottle,*,ed,ling,er, GLASS CONTAINER
bottom,*,med,ming,mless,mlessness, BASE
botul, bottle
botulism, FOOD POISONING
botum, bottom
boty, body
bou, beau / bow
bough,*, BUNCHED FLOWERS, TREE BRANCHES, PART OF A SHIP (or see bow/beau)
bought, PURCHASED, PAST TENSE FOR THE WORD 'BUY' (or see bout) "prefixes: over"
bouillon, BROTH (or see bullion)
boulder,*, LARGE ROCK (or see bold)
boulevard,*, AVENUE
boulion, bouillon / bullion
bouls, bowel(s) / bowl(s)
bounce,*,ed,cing,cy,er, REBOUND, UP/DOWN ACTION (or see buoyant(nce))
bound,*,ded,ding,dless,dlessly, dlessness, TO HOLD, JUMP, DESTINY "prefixes: in/out/re/un"
boundary,ries, A LIMIT/BORDERLINE
bounse, bounce / buoyant(ncy)
bounsy, bounce(y)
bountiful,lly,lness, PLENTIFUL
bounty,ties,tiful,tifully,tifulness,teous, teously,teousness, PAYMENT/REWARD FOR CAPTURE, PLENTY, ABUNDANCE
bouquet, BUNCH OF FLOWERS
bourbon, WHISKEY
bourgeois,sis, PROPERTY-OWNING UPPER MIDDLE CLASS
bout,*, A SPELL OF, TEMPORARY EXPERIENCE (or see boat)
boutique,*, WOMEN'S CLOTHING
bouwls, bowel(s)
bouyant, buoyant
bouynce, buoyant(ncy)
bow,*,wed,wing, BEND, HAIR ORNAMENT, TOOL USED WITH INSTRUMENT/ARROW (or see bough/beau) "prefixes: un"
bowel,*, INTESTINES OF ANYTHING
bowkay, bouquet

bowl,*,led,ling,ler, ROUND VESSEL, GAME OF BALLS WITH PINS (or see ball/bawl)
bowlder, boulder / bold(er)
bownce, bounce / bounce(cy)
bownd, bound
bowndee, bounty
bowndeful, bountiful
bowndery, boundary
bowndury, boundary
bowndy, bounty
bownse, bounce / bound(s)
bownsee, bounce(cy)
bowntee, bounty
bownteful, bountiful
bownts, bounce / bound(s)
bowt, bout
bowteek, boutique
box,xes,xed,xing,xer,xy, SQUARE SHAPED CONTAINER, SPORT "prefixes: un"
boy,*,yish,yishly, YOUNG MALE (or see buoy)
boyanse, buoyant(ncy)
boyant, buoyant
boyent, buoyant
boyint, buoyant
boyle, boil
boysdrus, boisterous
boysterus, boisterous
boyunse, buoyant(ncy)
boyunt, buoyant
bra,*, WOMEN'S UNDERGARMENT
brace,*,ced,cing, SUPPORT (or see brass/braise) "prefixes: un"
bracelet,*, WRIST ORNAMENT
bracket,*,ting, FIXTURE TO ATTACH TO, TO ENCLOSE WITHIN
bracoli, broccoli
brad,*, VERY SMALL NAILS (or see brat/braid)
brael, brail / braille
braen, brain
braes, brace / braise
braf, brave
brag,*,gged,gging,ggart, TO BOAST/PRAISE
bragert, braggart
braggart,*, ONE WHO BOASTS
bragirt, braggart
braid,*,ded,ding, TO INTERTWINE TOGETHER
brail, OF BOATS, BIRD, FISH (or see braille)

braille, TEXT FOR THE BLIND (or see brail)
brain,*,nless,nlessly,nlessness,ny, THINKING PART/MASS IN THE SKULL
braise,*,ed,sing, TO BROWN MEAT THEN COVER TO COOK (or see brace)
brakale, broccoli
brake,*,ed,king,er, TO STOP, HOLD BACK (or see break)
braket, bracket
brakible, breakable
brakit, bracket
brakle, broccoli
brakoli, broccoli
brakuble, breakable
bral, brail / braille / brawl
bran,*, A GRAIN YOU EAT (or see brain/brawn/brown/brand)
brand,*,ded,ding, A NAME THAT SIGNIFIES OWNERSHIP "prefixes: mis/un"
brane, brain
brankeal, bronchial
braquet, bracket
bras, brace / brass / braise / bra(s)
braslet, bracelet
brass,ssy,ssier,ssiest,ssily,ssiness, METAL, MILITARY OFFICERS (or see brace/braise)
brat,*,tty,ttish, SOMEONE WHO IS AGGRAVATING/IRRITATING (or see braid/brad)
brathren, brethren
brau, bra / brow
braucoli, broccoli
braud, broad
braukali, broccoli
braukle, broccoli
braun, brown / brawn
braus, browse / brow(s)
brave,*,ed,ving,er,ely,est,ery,eness, COURAGEOUS
braw, bra
brawkley, broccoli
brawl,*, LOUD FIGHT
brawn, MUSCLES (or see brown)
brawnkeul, bronchial
brawnkitis, bronchitis
brawnze, bronze
brayed, braid
brayel, brail / braille
braz, braise / brace / bra(s)

breach,hes,hed,hing, BREAK CONTRACT/AGREEMENT
bread,ded,ding,dth, BAKED DOUGH (or see bred/breed)
breadth, THE EXTENT/DISTANCE/ BROADNESS (or see breath)
break,*,king,kage,ker,roke, COME APART (or see brake)
breakable, CAN COME APART "prefixes: un"
breakuble, breakable
breast,*,ted, BOSOM
breath,hes,hed,hing,hless,hlessly,her, INHALE, EXHALE AIR (or see breadth)
brec, brick
brech, breach
bred, PAST TENSE FOR THE WORD 'BREED', HAVING MATED (or see bread/breed/barrette) "prefixes: in/ under"
breed,*,ding,der,red, TO MATE FOR PROCREATION, A CLASSIFICATION/ TYPE (or see bred/bread) "prefixes: in/un"
breef, brief
breeng, bring
breenk, brink
breeth, breath
breeve, bereave
breeze,*,ed,zing,zily,zy, GENTLE WIND
bref, brief
brege, bridge
breif, brief
brej, bridge
brek, brick / break
breluns, brilliance
brelyans, brilliance
brem, brim
breng, bring
brenk, brink
brese, breeze
brest, breast
bret, barrette / beret / breed / bread / bred
breth, breath / breadth
brethless, breath(less)
brethlis, breath(less)
brethren, PLURAL FOR BROTHER
brethrin, brethren
brew,*,wed,wing, A DRINK CONCOCTION
breze, breeze

bribe,*,ed,bing,ery, REWARD FOR CORRUPTION
brick,*,ked,king, CLAY BLOCK
brid, bride / bright / bread
bride,*,dal, FEMALE GETTING MARRIED
bridegroom,*, MALE GETTING MARRIED
bridesmaid,*, ATTENDS BRIDE
bridge,*,ed,ging,eable,eless, LINK FOR TRAVEL "prefixes: under"
bridgroom, bridegroom
bridgrum, bridegroom
bridle,*,ed,ling, FOR RESTRAINT (or see brittle) "prefixes: un"
bridmade, bridesmaid
bridol, bridle / brittle
bridsmaid, bridesmaid
bridul, bridle / brittle
brief,*,fed,fing, SHORT/SWEET/TO THE POINT, UNDERWEAR
brig, bridge
bright,*,ter,test,tly,tness, STRONG LIGHT ENERGY
brij, bridge
brik, brick
brileans, brilliance
briliance, brilliance
brilliance,nt, INTENSE LIGHT ENERGY
brilliant,ntly, INTENSE LIGHT ENERGY
brim,*,mmed,mming, THE EDGE/RIM OF SOMETHING
bring,*,ging,rought, BEAR FORTH "prefixes: up"
brink, NEAR THE EDGE
brit, bright / bride
britesmade, bridesmaid
britle, bridle / brittle
brittle,eness, CRISP (or see bridle)
britul, bridle / brittle
brn, burn/ barn
bro,*, SHORT FOR BROTHER (or see bra)
broad,*,dly,den,dness, AS IN WIDTH OR BREADTH
broadcast,*,ted,ting,ter, ANNOUNCE, SCATTER
broccoli , VEGETABLE (same as brocoli)
brochere, brochure
brochure,*, PAMPHLET
brocoli, VEGETABLE (same as broccoli)
brocolli, broccoli
brod, broad / brought / brood
brodkast, broadcast
broeel, broil

broel, broil
broil,*,led,ling,ler, WAY TO COOK
brok, broke
brokali, broccoli
broke,en, PAST TENSE FOR THE WORD 'BREAK', NO MONEY "prefixes: un"
brokle, broccoli
brokley, broccoli
brokule, broccoli
brol, brawl
bron, brawn / brown
brona, prana / piranha
bronceal, bronchial
bronch, PREFIX INDICATING 'BRONCHIAL' MOST OFTEN MODIFIES THE WORD
broncheul, bronchial
bronchi, PREFIX INDICATING 'BRONCHIAL' MOST OFTEN MODIFIES THE WORD
bronchial,lly, OF THE AIR/BREATHING PASSAGES
bronchitis, BREATHING PROBLEM
broncho, PREFIX INDICATING 'BRONCHIAL' MOST OFTEN MODIFIES THE WORD
bronckial, bronchial
bronkeul, bronchial
bronkites, bronchitis
bronse, bronze
bronze,ed,zing, METALLIC
brood,*,ding,dingly, CONCERNING OFFSPRING IN A GROUP, TO GRIEVE, BIRD SITTING ON EGGS
broodel, brutal
brook,*, STREAM
broom,*, FOR SWEEPING
broonet, brunet
brootal, brutal
brootle, brutal
bropane, propane
brosh, brush
brosher, brochure
broshur, brochure
brot, brought / broad
broth, SOUP
brother,*,rly, MALE SIBLING
brought, PAST TENSE FOR THE WORD "BRING"
broun, brown / brawn
brow,*, ABOVE EYES (or see browse)
browl, brawl
brown,*,ned,ning,ner,nest, COLOR (or see brawn)

browse,*,ed,sing,er, GLANCE/PERUSE/ CASUALLY GO THROUGH (or see brow(s))
broyl, broil
brud, brood
brudel, brutal
brue, brew
bruise,*,ed,sing,er, A BLOW TO, DAMAGED TISSUE
bruke, brook
brume, broom
brunet, DARK COLOR
brunkitis, bronchitis
brunnet, brunet
bruro, bureau
bruse, bruise
brush,hes,hed,hing, ENCOUNTER, HAIR TOOL, BUSHES "prefixes: under"
brutal,lly,lize,lization,lity, SAVAGE
bruther, brother
brutil, brutal
bruz, bruise
brydgroom, bridegroom
brydle, bridle / brittle
brydsmade, bridesmaid
bryt, bright
buanse, bounce(cy)
bubble,*,ed,ling,er,ly, AIR, GAS GLOBULES
bubil, bubble
buble, bubble
bucame, became
bucher, butcher
buchur, butcher
buck,*,ked,king, UNSEAT RIDER, MALE DEER, DOLLAR
bucket,*, A CONTAINER
buckil, buckle
buckit, bucket
buckle,*,ed,ling, TOOL TO SECURE SOMETHING, TO FOLD UNDER PRESSURE
bud,*,dded,dding, READY TO OPEN, FULL OF FUTURE POTENTIAL (or see butt/butte/but) "prefixes: de/dis"
budder, butter
buddy,ddies,ddied,ddying, SOMEONE YOU BEFRIEND, TRAVEL ALONGSIDE (or see beauty)
bude, buddy / beauty
budeful, beautiful
buden, button
buder, butter
budge,*,ed,ging, TO MOVE

budget,*,ted,ting,ter,tary, RATION A SPECIFIC AMOUNT FOR EXPENDITURES
budi, buddy / beauty
budiful, beautiful
budin, button
budj, budge
budler, butler
budok, buttock
budres, buttress
budris, buttress
budrothed, betrothed
buduk, buttock
budy, buddy / beauty
buee, buoy
bufa, buffet
bufal, befall
bufalo, buffalo
bufer, buffer
buff,*,ffed,ffing,ffer, A COLOR, NUDE, MASCULINE/MUSCULAR, TO POLISH WITH CLOTH "prefixes: re"
buffalo,*, ANIMAL
buffer,*,red,ring, ABSORBS SHOCK, POLISHES
buffet,*, SELF-SERVE RESTAURANT
bufilo, buffalo
bufir, buffer
bufol, befall
bufrend, befriend
bufulo, buffalo
bufur, buffer
bug,*,gged,gging,ggy,ggier,ggiest, gginess,gger, ERROR IN DEVICE, AN INSECT, TO IRRITATE SOMEONE/ SOMETHING, SPY DEVICE (or see budge) "prefixes: de"
buge, budge / buggy
bugel, bugle
bugener, begin(nner)
buget, budget
buggy,ggies, LIGHTWEIGHT CARRIAGE FOR MANY PURPOSES
bugil, bugle
bugin, begin
bugit, budget
bugle,*, INSTRUMENT
bugul, bugle
bugwazee, bourgeois(ie)
bugy, buggy
buhaf, behave
buhind, behind
build,*,der,ding,dable,lt, CONSTRUCT (or see built) "prefixes: over/re/up"

built, PAST TENSE FOR THE WORD 'BUILD'
buj, budge
bujet, budget
bujit, budget
bujwau, bourgeois
bujwazee, bourgeois(ie)
buk, buck / book / bug
bukame, became
bukaus, because
buke, bookie
bukel, buckle
bukene, bikini
buket, bucket
bukie, bookie
bukil, buckle
bukit, bucket
bukos, because
bul, bull
bulated, belated
bulaten, bulletin
bulatide, belated
bulavard, boulevard
bulb,*,bous, OF PLANTS, GLASS GLOBES WITH FILAMENTS
bulbus, bulb(ous)
bulch, bulge
bulck, bulk
bule, bully
buledul, belittle
buleef, belief
buleeve, believe
bulef, belief
buleger, beleaguer
bulegirant, belligerent
buleon, bullion / bouillon
bulese, police
bulet, bullet
buletin, bulletin
bulevard, boulevard
buleve, believe
bulevuble, believe(vable)
bulge,*,ed,ging, SWELL OUT
bulian, bouillon
buligerant, belligerent
bulijurent, belligerent
bulion, bullion / bouillon
bulistic, ballistic
bulit, bullet
bulitel, belittle
buliten, bulletin
bulivard, boulevard
bulje, bulge

bulk,ky,kiness,kier,kiest, MASS OF SOMETHING
bull,*, MALE ANIMAL
bullet,*, PROJECTILE
bulletin,*, DOCUMENT
bullion, OF GOLD (or see bouillon)
bully,llies,llied,llying, INTIMIDATOR
bullyon, bouillon / bullion
bulo, blow / below
bulonee, baloney / bologna
bulong, belong
buloon, balloon
bulow, below / bellow / billow
bulp, bulb
bulune, balloon
buluvard, boulevard
buly, bully
bulyon, bullion / bouillon
bumbelbee, bumblebee
bumblebee,*, BIG BEE
bumer, bummer
bumerang, boomerang
bumir, bummer
bummer, OF QUARRY, NOT HAPPY
bumur, bummer
bumurang, boomerang
bunana, banana
bunansa, bonanza
bunch,hes,hed,hing, MORE THAN A FEW IN THE GROUP
bundle,*,ed,ling,er, TO GROUP/BIND TOGETHER "prefixes: un"
bune, bunny
buneeth, beneath
buneon, bunion / bunyon
bunes, bunny(nnies) / bonus
buneun, bunyon / bunion
bunevilance, benevolence
bungil, bungle
bungle,*,ed,ling,ler, MESS UP, SPOIL, WRECK
bunie, bunny
bunine, benign
bunion,*, SWELLING ON BIG TOE, ALSO SPELLED "BUNYON"
bunis, bunny(nnies)
bunny,nies, RABBIT
bunsh, bunch
buny, bunny
bunyon,*, SWELLING ON BIG TOE, ALSO SPELLED "BUNION"
bunyun, bunion / bunyon
buond, beyond
buorgeoise, bourgeois(ie)

buownse, bounce(cy)
buoy,*, FLOATING DEVICE
buoyant,ncy, TO FLOAT
bur, burr
bura, barrette / beret
buracracy, bureaucracy
buracrat, bureaucrat
burakracy, bureaucracy
burau, bureau
buraukracy, bureaucracy
burave, brave
burbon, bourbon
burch, birch
burd, bird
burden,*,ned,ning,nsome, HEAVY LOAD "prefixes: dis/over/un"
burdensum, burden(some)
burdin, burden
burdinsum, burden(some)
burdon, burden
bureal, burial
bureau,*, A DRESSER, GOVERNMENT DEPARTMENT
bureaucracy,cies,at, GOVERNMENT ADMINISTRATION
bureaucrat,*, AGENTS OF GOVERNMENT ADMINISTRATION
bureeve, bereave
bureft, bereft
buret, barrette / beret
bureve, bereave
burgendy, burgundy
burgeois, bourgeois
burglar,*,ry,ries,rize,rizes,rized,rizing, ROBBER/THIEF
burglir, burglar
burgundy, A COLOR, A WINE
burial,*, BURYING DECEASED
burileans, brilliance
buring, bring
burite, bright
burkler, burglar
burlap, WOVEN HEMP/JUTE
burlee, burly
burlesk, burlesque
burlesque,er, MOCKERY
burlip, burlap
burly, BIG MUSCULAR BODY
burm, berm
burn,*,ned,ning,nable,nt, SCORCH "prefixes: un"
burnt, BEEN BURNED, PAST TENSE FOR THE WORD 'BURN'

buro, burro / burrow / borough / bureau
burocrasy, bureaucracy
burocrat, bureaucrat
burog, barrage
burokracy, bureaucracy
burokrat, bureaucrat
buromiter, barometer
burow, burro / burrow / borough / bureau
burp,*,ped,ping, BELCH
burr,*,rred,rring, PRICKLY SEED, ROUGH EDGES, EXPRESSION FOR BEING COLD "prefixes: de"
burro,*, DONKEY (or see burrow/ borough)
burrow,*,wed,wing, LODGE INTO HOLE (or see burro/borough)
bursd, burst
burst,*,ting,ter, ERUPT
burth, berth / birth
burthday, birthday
bury,ries,ried,rying, PUT IN GROUND (or see berry) "prefixes: un"
bus,sses,ssed,ssing, LARGE VEHICLE TO TRANSPORT MANY PASSENGERS, CARRIER OF INFORMATION
busar, bizarre / bazaar
busd, bust / boost / bus(ssed)
busdid, bust(ed) / burst
busech, beseech
buseech, beseech
busel, bustle
busem, bosom
buserd, buzzard
buses, bus(sses)
bushel,*, MEASUREMENT OF AMOUNT
bushil, bushel
bushwaze, bourgeois(ie)
busi, busy
buside, beside
busil, bustle
busim, bosom
business,sses, A SERVICE
busle, bustle
busness, business
busniss, business
bust,*,ted,ting,ty,tier,tiest, HEAD AND SHOULDERS, WOMEN'S BREASTS, CAUGHT RED-HANDED (or see boost/burst/bus(ssed))
busted, burst / bust(ed)
bustle,*,ed,ling, HURRIES ABOUT, FOR SKIRTS

busul, bustle
busum, bosom
busurk, berserk
busy,sies,sier,siest, ENGROSSED
but, A PREPOSITION MEANING "EXCEPT/ONLY/DIFFERENCE" (or see butte/bud/boot)
butcher,*,red,ring, CUT UP
bute, boot / but / butt / butte
buted, butt(ed) / bud(dded)
buteek, boutique
buteful, beautiful
buten, button
butenchul, potential
buter, butter
buth, booth
buti, buddy / beauty
butid, butt(ed) / bud(dded)
butiful, beautiful
butike, boutique
butin, button
butinchul, potential
butir, butter
butishun, beautician
butler,*, MALE SERVANT
butlur, butler
butok, buttock
buton, baton / button
butra, betray
butres, buttress
butris, buttress
butrothed, betrothed
buts, butt(s) / bud(s) / boot(s)
butsher, butcher
butshir, butcher
butt,*,tted,tting, REAR END/BOTTOM OF SOMETHING, FORCE UPON (or see bud/but/butte)
butte,*, HILL/MOUNTAIN WITH FLAT TOP (or see but/butt)
butter,red,ring,ry, CHURNED FROM MILK
buttock,*, RUMP
button,*,ned,ning, FIXTURE FOR CLOTHING "prefixes: un"
buttress, TO STRENGTHEN
butuk, buttock
butween, between
buty, buddy / beauty
buvileon, pavilion
buware, beware
buwee, buoy
buwelder, bewilder
buwildre, bewilder

buwro, bureau
buwte, beauty
buy,*,ying,yer,bought, TO PURCHASE (or see bye/by/bi)
buyent, buoyant
buyint, buoyant
buyond, beyond
buzar, bizarre / bazaar / buzz(er)
buzd, buzz(ed) / bust / bus(ssed)
buzded, bust(ed)
buze, booze / buzz
buzer, buzz(er) / bizarre / bazaar
buzerd, buzzard
buzerk, berserk
buzir, buzz(er) / bizarre / bazaar
buzor, buzz(er) / bizarre / bazaar
buzted, bust(ed) / burst
buzum, bosom
buzurk, berserk
buzz,zzes,zzed,zzing,zzer, A SOUND, DEVICE WHICH MAKES SOUND
buzzar, bizarre / bazaar / buzz(er)
buzzard,*, CARNIVOROUS BIRD
buzzer, buzz(er) / bizarre / bazaar
by, ALONGSIDE, PREFIX INDICATING 'NEAR/SECONDARY' MOST OFTEN MODIFIES THE WORD (or see bye/bi/buy)
bye, AS IN GOOD-BYE (or see by/bi/buy)
byeneul, biennial / biannual
byker, bike(r)
bysenteneal, bicentennial
byu, bayou
c, see / sea
cabach, cabbage
cabage, cabbage
cabaret, TYPE OF MUSICAL SHOW
cabbage,*, VEGETABLE
cabdive, captive
cabduve, captive
cabech, cabbage
cabel, cable
caben, cabin
caberay, cabaret
cabich, cabbage
cabichulate, capitulate
cabige, cabbage
cabin,*, RUSTIC STRUCTURE
cabinet,*,try, STORAGE WITH DOORS, POLITICAL ADVISORY
cabiret, cabaret
cabitate, capitate
cabitch, cabbage

cable,*,ed,ling, WIRE ROPE, CONNECTION
cabnet, cabinet
cabnit, cabinet
caboose, LAST CAR ON A TRAIN
cabsel, capsule
cabshure, capture
cabten, captain
cabture, capture
cabtuve, captive
cabul, cable
cabus, caboose
cac, PREFIX INDICATING 'HARSH/BAD' MOST OFTEN MODIFIES THE WORD (or see cake/caulk/cock)
cach, catch / cache / cash
cache,*,ed,hing, PLACE TO HIDE ITEMS IN (or see cash/catch)
cacher, catcher / cashier
cachup, ketchup / catsup
cachwul, casual
cackle,*,ed,ling, SHRILL SOUND/LAUGH
caco, PREFIX INDICATING 'HARSH/ BAD' MOST OFTEN MODIFIES THE WORD
cacol, cackle
cacoon, cocoon
cactis, cactus
cactus,ses,ti, DESERT PLANT
cacun, cocoon
cadagory, category
cadal, cattle
cadaver,*,ric, LIFELESS BODY
caddie, caddy
caddy,ddie,ddies, PERSON WHO CARRIES CLUBS IN GOLF, BOX
cadech, cottage
cadecism, catechism
cadee, caddy
cadegerize, categorize
cadegory, category
cadekism, catechism
cadence, MARCHING RHYTHM
cader, cater
caderact, cataract
cadet,*, TRAINING FOR SERVICE
cadi, caddy
cadigorize, categorize
cadigory, category
cadikism, catechism
cadil, cattle
cadilist, catalyst
cadilog, catalog
cadinse, cadence
cadl, cattle

cadle, cattle
cadol, cattle
cadugorize, categorize
cadugory, category
cadul, cattle
cadulist, catalyst
cadulize, catalyst(yze)
cadulog, catalog
cadur, cater
caduract, cataract
caf, calf / cave / cough
cafa, cafe
cafanated, caffeine(nated)
cafe,*, SMALL RESTAURANT (or see coffee/calf)
cafeene, caffeine
cafene, caffeine
cafeteria,*, SELF-SERVE RESTAURANT
caffeine,nate,nated,nation,nism, ALSO SPELLED 'CAFFEIN', STIMULANT, DIURETIC "prefixes: de/under"
cafin, caffeine
cafiteria, cafeteria
cafs, calves / cave(s)
cafunated, caffeine(nated)
cafutirea, cafeteria
cage,*,ed,ging, FOR CONFINEMENT
cagwal, casual
cahoot,*, IN PARTNERSHIP
cahute, cahoot
cainker, canker / chancre
cairfree, carefree
cairful, careful
caje, cage
cajewul, casual
cajole,*,ed,ling, COAX
cajuol, casual
cajwul, casual
cak, caulk / calk / cake / cock
cakd, cake(d)
cake,*,ed,king,ey, BAKED SWEET DOUGH, RESEMBLES CAKE
cakel, cackle
cakt, cake(d)
caktis, cactus
caktus, cactus
caky, khaki
cal, call / cowl / kale
calaberate, collaborate
calabrate, calibrate
caladeral, collateral
calag, collage / college
calametous, calamity(tous)
calamity,ties,tous,tously, DISASTER

calander, calendar / calender / colander
calanize, colony(nize)
calany, colony
calapse, collapse
calas, callous / callus
calasthenics, calisthenics
calastomy, colostomy
calasul, colossal
calateral, collateral
calaug, collage
calcefy, calcify
calcify,fies,fied,fying,fication,fier, BECOME RIGID, LIME/CALCIUM DEPOSIT "prefixes: de"
calcilate, calculate
calcilus, calculus
calcium, ELEMENT ON EARTH
calcufy, calcify
calculate,*,ed,ting,tingly,tion,tor, TO MENTALLY/MATHEMATICALLY ESTIMATE/FIGURE "prefixes: in/mis/un"
calculus,li,ses, REFERENCE TO MATH, ORGAN STONE "prefixes: pre"
cale, kale
calebrate, calibrate
calech, college
caleflower, cauliflower
caleg, colleague / college
calegen, collision
caleget, collegiate
calek, colic
calendar,*,red,ring,rize,dric,drical, REGISTER OF MONTHS/DAYS OF THE YEAR (or see calender/colander)
calender,*,red,ring,rer, PRESS/ROLLER FOR PAPER/CLOTH (or see calendar/colander)
calendula, MEDICINAL FLOWER
caler, collar / call(er)
cales, callous / callus
calesthenics, calisthenics
calf,lves,lved,lving, YOUNG BOVINE, BIRTHING OF BOVINE, LOWER PORTION OF LEG
caliber,*,bre, OF MEASUREMENT, DIAMETER (or see caliper) "prefixes: sub"
calibrate,*,ed,ting,tion,tor, SET/DETERMINE MEASUREMENT/SIZE
calibre, caliber
calide, collide
calidiscope, kaleidoscope

califlower, cauliflower
calig, college
caligen, collision
caligent, collegiate
calinder, calendar / calender / colander
calindula, calendula
caliper,*,lliper, INSTRUMENT FOR MEASURING (or see caliber)
calire, calorie
calis, callous / callus
calision, collision
calisthenics, EXERCISES
calk, DEVICE FOR SHOES (or see caulk)
calkilate, calculate
calkulus, calculus
call,*,lled,lling,ller, ATTEMPT TO CONTACT/INVITE SOMEONE TO ANSWER/RESPOND (or see cowl) "prefixes: mis"
calleague, colleague
callous,llus,ses,sed,sly,sness, HARDENED/ROUGH AREA ON SKIN/PLANT, INSENSITIVE BEHAVIOR (also spelled callus)
callus,ses,sed,sing,sity,llose, HARDENED/ROUGH AREA ON SKIN/PLANT, INSENSITIVE BEHAVIOR (also spelled callous)
calm,mes,med,ming,mly,mative,mness, TO SOOTHE (or see come)
calobrate, calibrate
calokweul, colloquial
caloquial, colloquial
calorie,*,ric,rically,rific, UNIT OF MEASUREMENT FOR FOOD
calorize,*,ed,zing, PROCESS USED IN METALLURGY
calos, callous / callus
calostemy, colostomy
calosthenics, calisthenics
calous, callous / callus
calsefy, calcify
calseum, calcium
caluber, caliber
calubrate, calibrate
calunder, colander
caluper, caliper
calur, collar / call(er)
calury, calorie
calus, callous / callus
calusthenics, calisthenics
calves,ed,ving, PLURAL FOR THE WORD 'CALF', YOUNG BOVINE, BIRTHING BOVINE

camb, camp
came, PAST TENSE FOR THE WORD 'COME', CHANNEL USED FOR MANUFACTURING "prefixes: over"
camel,*, ANIMAL
camend, commend
camendible, commendable
camenduble, commendable
camera,*, TAKES PHOTOS
camfor, camphor
camind, commend
caminduble, commendable
camins, commence
camitee, committee
camofloje, camouflage
camouflage,*,ed,ging, DISGUISED
camp,*,ped,ping,per, STAY OVERNIGHT/ OUTDOORS IN WILDERNESS "prefixes: en"
campaign,*,ned,ning,ner, ACTION TO INFLUENCE
campane, campaign
camphor,ric, FROM TREES, MEDICINAL
campis, campus
campus,ses, SCHOOL GROUNDS
camra, camera
camuflodge, camouflage
camul, camel
camune, commune
camunicate, communicate
camunity, community
camute, commute
can,*,nned,nning,nner,nnery, ABLE TO, TIN VESSEL (or see cane)
can't, CONTRACTION OF THE WORDS 'CAN NOT' (or see cent/ sand/ can(nned)/con(nned))
canabis, cannabis
canabol, cannibal
canabus, cannabis
canal,*, WHERE FLUIDS FLOW
canalop, cantaloupe
canan, canon / canyon
canapi, canopy
canare, cannery / canary
canary,ries, A YELLOW BIRD (or see cannery)
cancel,*,led,ling,lable,ler,llation, DELETE,RENDER NULL/VOID
cancellation,*, DELETE, ELIMINATE, INVALIDATE
cancer,rous, DISEASE
cancl, cancel
cancr, cancer

cancur, chancre / canker
candedate, candidate
candid,dly,dness, TO BE FRANK/ TRUTHFUL
candidate,*,acy,acies, SEEKS OFFICE
candle,*,ed,ling, WAX WITH WICK
candudite, candidate
candul, candle
candy,dies,died, WEET TREAT
cane,*,ned, STICK OF WOOD/SUGAR
canebulize, cannibal(ize)
canelop, cantaloupe
caneon, canyon
canere, cannery / canary
canery, cannery / canary
canesis, kinesis
cangaroo, kangaroo
cangruis, congruous
canibal, cannibal
canibis, cannabis
canikcanik, kinnikinnick
canin, cannon / canine
canine,*, DOG
canion, canyon
canipe, canopy
caniry, cannery / canary
canister,*, CONTAINER
canker,*,rous, DISEASE, SORE (or see chancre)
cannabis, A USEFUL PLANT
cannery,ries, PLACE WHICH CANS FOOD (or see canary)
cannibal,*,lism,listic,lize, EATS FLESH OF ITS OWN SPECIES
cannon,*, WEAPON
canon, cannon
canopy,pies,pied,ying, COVERING FOR SHELTER
canosieur, connoisseur
canseld, cancel(lled)
canser, cancer
cansil, cancel
cansilashen, cancellation
cansir, cancer
cansl, cancel
cansr, cancer
cansul, cancel
cansulation, cancellation
cansuld, cancel(lled)
cantaloupe,*,pe,pes, EDIBLE FRUIT
cantankerous,sly,sness, RESISTANT, DIFFICULT
canted, candid
canteen,*, CONTAINER FOR LIQUIDS

cantelope, cantaloupe
cantena, cantina
canter,*, SPEED OF HORSE
cantidit, candidate
cantiguis, contiguous
cantilope, cantaloupe
cantina,*, SALOON, BAG FOR SADDLE
cantul, candle
cantulope, cantaloupe
cantur, canter
canty, candy
canubelize, cannibal(ize)
canubil, cannibal
canubis, cannabis
canulop, cantaloupe
canupe, canopy
canuster, canister
canvas,ses, WOVEN HEMP/NATURAL FIBERS (or see canvass)
canvass,sser, TO SOLICIT (or see canvas)
canves, canvas / canvass
canvis, canvas / canvass
canvus, canvass / canvas
canyon,*, DEEP VALLEY
cap,*,pped,pping,pful, TOP, HAT, TO LIMIT (or see cape) "prefixes: re/ un"
capability,ties, CAPACITY, ABILITY, SKILL
capable,eness,ly,bility,bilities, CAPACITY, ABILITY, SKILL "prefixes: in"
capacity,ties, STATUS OF, AMOUNT "prefixes: over"
capadol, capital / capitol
capalery, capillary
capasety, capacity
capatol, capital / capitol
capatulism, capitalism
capcher, capture
capchun, caption
capchur, capture
capdivate, captivate
capdof, captive
capduvate, captivate
cape,*,ped, CLOAK, GARMENT, LAND FORM (or see cap)
capebilety, capability
capechulate, capitulate
capedal, capital
capedalism, capitalism
capedul, capital / capitol
capedulism, capitalism
capelary, capillary
capetate, capitate

capetul, capital / capitol
capetulate, capitulate
capetulesm, capitalism
capichulate, capitulate
capidal, capital
capidalism, capitalism
capillary,ries, OF THE BODY
capital,*,list,lists,listically,lize,lizable, lizes,lized,lizing,lization,lly,lism, LARGE, MAIN, TOP (or see capitol) "prefixes: under"
capitalism, PRIVATE/FREE ENTERPRISE
capitate,*,ed,ting,tion,tions,tive, COUNTING/TAXING BY HEADS, HEAD OF SOMETHING
capitol, CENTER OF GOVERNMENT (or see capital)
capitulate,*,ed,ting,ant,tion,tions,tor, tory, CONSENT/GIVE IN/YIELD "prefixes: re"
capol, couple
capshun, caption
capshur, capture
capsile, capsule
capsize,*,ed,zing, OVERTURN A BOAT
capsulate,*,ed,ting,tion,tor, MATERIAL BEING CONTAINED "prefixes: de/en/in"
capsule,*,ed,ling,lar,late,lize,lized,lizing, CONTAINED MATERIAL, COMPACT FORM WITH PROTECTIVE EXTERIOR
captain,*, ONE WHO COMMANDS
captin, captain
caption,*,ned,nless, HEADING OR TITLE
captivate,*,ed,ting, CHARMED, HELD UNWILLFULLY
captive,*,vity,vation,vator, CONTROLLED/HELD AGAINST ONE'S WILL
captun, captain
capture,*,ed,ring,er, TAKE BY FORCE "prefixes: re"
captuvate, captivate
captuve, captive
capubility, capability
capuble, capable
capudul, capital / capitol
capudulesm, capitalism
capulary, capillary
caput, kaput
caputate, capitate
car,*,rful, AUTOMOBILE (or see care)
caracter, character
carakter, character

caramel,*,lize,lizes,lized,lizing,lization, CANDY, HEAT PROCESS
caraoke, karaoke
carat,*, MILLIGRAMS (or see caret/carrot/karat)
carate, karate
carauti, karate
caravan,*,ned,ning,ner, GROUP OF VEHICLES/TRAVELERS
carbarator, carburetor
carbender, carpenter
carberator, carburetor
carbin, carbon
carbinete, carbonate
carbirater, carburetor
carbon,*,nize,nator, FORMS ORGANIC COMPOUNDS
carbonate,*,ed,ting,tion, SALT OR GAS "prefixes: bi/de"
carbunete, carbonate
carburetor,*, HEART OF COMBUSTIBLE ENGINE
carcass,sses, EXTERNAL REMAINS OF ANYTHING
carcino, PREFIX INDICATING 'CANCER' MOST OFTEN MODIFIES THE WORD
carcinogen,*,nic,nicity,nesis, CANCER CAUSING
carcus, carcass
card,*,ded,ding, STIFF PAPER, ASKED FOR I.D. (or see cart)
cardboard, THICK PAPER
cardeac, cardiac
cardenul, cardinal
cardi, PREFIX INDICATING "HEART" MOST OFTEN MODIFIES THE WORD
cardiac, OF THE HEART
cardilege, cartilage
cardin, carton
cardinal,*, A BIRD, RANK IN CATHOLIC CHURCH
cardio, PREFIX INDICATING 'HEART' MOST OFTEN MODIFIES THE WORD
cardulege, cartilage
care,*,ed,ring,ringly,eful,efully,efulness, eless,elessness, CONCERN OVER (or see carry) "prefixes: multi/un"
careboo, caribou
carebral, cerebral
carebrul, cerebral
carech, carriage
carecter, character
caredge, carriage
caredor, corridor

careen,*,ned,ning, LEAN TO ONE SIDE
career,*, PROFESSION
carefree, WITHOUT CARE
careful,lly,lness, WITH CARE
carege, carriage
carekter, character
careless,ssly,ssness, NOT WITH CARE
caremel, caramel
careoke, karaoke
carer, career
cares, care(s) / caress
caress,sses,ssed,ssing,ssingly,ssive, ssively, PET/STROKE SMOOTHLY/GENTLY
caret,*, PROOFREADING MARK (or see carrot/carat/karat)
careur, carrier
carful, careful
cargo,oes,os, FREIGHT ON VESSEL
cariage, carriage
carib, carob
caribou, reindeer
caricature,*,ed,ring,rist, EXAGGERATED IMITATION
carich, carriage
caricter, character
carie, carry
carier, carrier
carige, carriage
carikter, character
carioke, karaoke
carir, career
carisma, charisma
carit, carat / caret / carrot / karat
carivan, caravan
carkis, carcass
carkus, carcass
carlis, careless
carma, karma
carmel, caramel
carmil, caramel
carmu, karma
carmul, caramel
carn, care(ring) / carton
carnashun, carnation
carnation,*, FLOWER
carnival,*, TRAVELING AMUSEMENT SHOW
carnivore,*,rous, EATS FLESH
carnuvil, carnival
carnuvore, carnivore
carob, LOCUST BEAN RESEMBLING CHOCOLATE
caroberate, corroborate

carode, corrode
carogan, corrode(osion)
carogate, corrugate(d)
carogen, corrode(osion)
carogin, corrode(osion)
carojen, corrode(osion)
carojin, corrode(osion)
carojun, corrode(osion)
caroke, karaoke
carol,*,led,ling, SONGS
caroner, coroner
carosef, corrode(osive)
carosel, carousel
carosene, kerosene
caroshen, corrode(osion)
carot, carat / caret / carrot / karat
caroty, karate
carouse,*,ed,sing, UNDESIRABLE DRUNKEN BEHAVIOR
carousel,*, MERRY-GO-ROUND
carpenter,*,try, BUILDS WITH WOOD
carpet,*,ted,ting, SOFT FLOOR COVERING
carpinder, carpenter
carpinter, carpenter
carpit, carpet
carriage,*, PULLED FOUR-WHEELED CART, OF CARRYING "prefixes: mis/under"
carrier,*, ONE WHO TRANSPORTS (or see career)
carrot,*, VEGETABLE (or see carat/caret/karat)
carry,rries,rried,rrying,rrier,rriage, rriages, TO TRANSPORT "prefixes: mis"
carsenagen, carcinogen
carsinugen, carcinogen
cart,*,ted,ting, VEHICLE FOR TRANSPORT
cartilage, SOFT BONE IN THE BODY "prefixes: sub"
cartin, carton
cartleg, cartilage
cartn, carton
cartnul, cardinal
carton,*, PAPER BOX
cartoon,*,ning,nist, ANIMATED CARICATURES
cartrege, cartridge
cartridge,*, REFILLABLE/REPLACEABLE CONTAINER
cartrige, cartridge
cartulige, cartilage

cartun, carton / cartoon
carubtion, corrupt(ion)
carubu, caribou
carudge, carriage
carupd, corrupt
carupshen, corrupt(ion)
carupt, corrupt
carusel, carousel
carusen, kerosene
carut, carat / caret / carrot / karat
carve,*,ed,ving,er, TO SHAPE WITH KNIFE
cary, carry
casadilla, quesadilla
casal, castle / cause(sal)
casc, cask
cascade,*,ed,ding, LIKE A WATERFALL
cascara, TREE
case,*,ed,sing, CERTAIN NUMBER OF ITEMS CONTAINED TOGETHER (too many definitions, please see standard dictionary) "prefixes: en/upper"
casedilla, quesadilla
caseng, casing
caseno, casino
caserole, casserole
casete, cassette
cash,hed,hing, MONETARY/MONEY (or see cache)
cashere, cashier
cashew,*, NUT
cashier,*, HANDLES MONEY
cashmere, GOAT WOOL
cashon, caution
cashos, cautious
cashu, cashew
cashual, casual
cashuol, casual
cashwul, casual
casil, castle
casing,*, COVERING OR SUPPORT
casino,*, FOR GAMBLING
casirole, casserole
casiroll, casserole
cask,*, KEG FOR LIQUIDS
caskade, cascade
caskeid, cascade
caskera, cascara
casket,*, COFFIN
caskit, casket
casmic, cosmic
casol, castle

casserole,*, MIXTURE OF FOOD INTO ONE DISH
cassette,*, AUDIO CARTRIDGE
cast,*,ting,ter, TO THROW AWAY FROM (or see caste) "prefixes: mis/over/re/up"
caste,*, A SOCIAL CLASS OF PEOPLE (or see cast)
caster,*, ON/FOR FURNITURE, FISHING, MOLD MAKER, CONDIMENT STAND
castle,*,ed, FORTRESS
castrate,*,ed,ting,tion, REMOVE REPRODUCTIVE ORGANS
castum, costume
casual,lly,lness, BY CHANCE, RELAXED
casudilla, quesadilla
casul, castle
caswal, casual
cat,*, ANIMAL, PREFIX INDICATING "APART/DOWN" MOST OFTEN MODIFIES THE WORD
cata, PREFIX INDICATING "APART/DOWN" MOST OFTEN MODIFIES THE WORD
catal, cattle
catalog,*,ged,ging, LIST IN ORDER
catalyst,*,ysis,ytic,yze,yzes,yzed,yzing, yzer, STIMULUS "prefixes: bio"
catapult,*,ted,ting, TO BE HURLED
cataract,*, EYE DISEASE OR WATERFALL
catastrophe,*,hic, DISASTER
catch,hes,hing,her,aught, CAPTURE (or see cache)
catcher,*, BASEBALL FIELD POSITION
catchup, ketchup / catsup
catech, cottage
catechism, TEACHING OF CHRISTIAN PRINCIPLES
catecism, catechism
categorize,*,ed,zing,zable,zation, ASSIGN TO SPECIFIC AREA/RANGE "prefixes: un/mis"
category,ries,ric,rical,rically,ricalness, rize,rizes,rized,rizing,rizable, rization, SPECIFIC AREA/RANGE "prefixes: mis/un"
catekisom, catechism
catelog, catalog
catepiler, caterpillar
catepult, catapult
cater,*,red,ring, PROVIDE FOR
cateract, cataract
caterpillar,*, WORM

cath, PREFIX INDICATING 'APART/DOWN' MOST OFTEN MODIFIES THE WORD
catichisom, catechism
catigorize, categorize
catigory, category
catikisom, catechism
catilist, catalyst
catilog, catalog
catl, cattle
catle, cattle
catol, cattle
catsup, ketchup
cattle, DOMESTIC BEEF, BOVINE
catugorize, categorize
catugory, category
catukism, catechism
catulist, catalyst
catulize, catalyst(yze)
catulog, catalog
catupiler, caterpillar
catupult, catapult
caturact, cataract
cau, cow
cauc, caulk
cauchis, cautious / caucus
caucus,ses, NOMINATION PARTY
caught, PAST TENSE FOR THE WORD 'CATCH', OBTAINED (or see cot)
caul, call / cowl
caulagen, collision / collagen
caulam, column
cauliflower, VEGETABLE
caulk,*,ked,king, FILL SEAMS/JOINTS (or see calk)
caulm, calm
caulom, column
caum, calm / come
cauncil, council
caunsel, council
caunt, count
caunter, counter
caunti, county
caunvex, convex
cause,*,ed,sing,sal,sality,salities,sation, BRING ABOUT "prefixes: retro"
caushes, cautious
caushesly, cautious(ly)
caushus, cautious
causmic, cosmic
caustic,cal,cally,city, CORROSIVE CHEMICAL "prefixes: en"
caut, caught / cot

caution,*,ned,ning,nary,ous, BEWARE, BE CAREFUL "prefixes: pre"
cautious,sly,sness, PREPARED FOR DANGER "prefixes: in"
cava, kava
cavalry,ries, MOUNTED SOLDIERS
cave,*,ed,ving, HOLE IN THE EARTH
cavern,*,nous, HOLLOW IN EARTH
cavety, cavity
cavilry, cavalry
cavirn, cavern
cavitate,*,ed,ting,tion, HOLLOWED OUT AREAS/BUBBLES
cavity,ties,tate,tation,tational, HOLLOWED OUT AREA, DECAYED TOOTH
cavs, calves / cave(s)
cavu, kava
cavulry, cavalry
cavurn, cavern
cawcus, caucus
cawl, call / cowl
cawshesly, cautious(ly)
cawshis, cautious
cawshun, caution
cawt, caught / cot
cawtion, caution
cayan, cayenne
cayenne, HOT PEPPER
cayning, canine
cazual, casual
ce, see / sea
cease,ses,ed,sing,eless,elessly, STOP (or see sea(s)/seize/see(s)) "prefixes: sur/un"
cechup, ketchup / catsup
ceel, keel
cegar, cigar
ceiling,*, OVERHEAD IN ROOM (or see seal)
cel, cell / seal / sell
celabent, celibate
celabet, celibate
celafane, cellophane
celar, cellar / sell(er) / seal(er)
celary, celery
celebrate,*,ed,ting,tion,tive,tory,ant, REJOICE
celebrity,ties, PERSON WELL EXPOSED TO THE PUBLIC
celer, cellar / sell(er) / seal(er)
celery, VEGETABLE
celestial,*,lly, SPIRITUAL, NOT PHYSICAL ON THIS PLANE "prefixes: sub"

celibate,acy,tarian, ABSENT FROM SEXUAL ACTIVITY "prefixes: un"
celibet, celibate
celibrate, celebrate
celinder, cylinder
celing, ceiling / seal(ing)
celir, cellar / sell(er) / seal(er)
cell,*,llular,llularly,llularity, OF STRUCTURES/SCIENCE (or see sell/sail/keel) "prefixes: intra/multi/sub/uni"
cellar,*, STORAGE UNDERGROUND (or see sell)
cellophane, PLASTIC WRAP
cellular,rly,rity, OF COMMUNICATIONS OR SCIENCE "prefixes: intra/multi/non/sub/uni"
cellulite, FAT POCKETS IN THE BODY
cellulose,sic, CARBOHYDRATE "prefixes: non"
celofane, cellophane
celophane, cellophane
celseus, celsius
celsius, METHOD OF REPORTING TEMPERATURE
celt,*,tic, TOOL, GROUP OF PEOPLE, LANGUAGE
celubasy, celibate(acy)
celubet, celibate
celubit, celibate
celubrate, celebrate
celular, cellular
celulite, cellulite
celulose, cellulose
celur, cellar / sell(er) / seal(er)
cem, seem / seam
cematari, cemetery
cement,ted,ter,tum,tation,tatory,tless, COMBINATION OF MATERIALS WHICH HARDENS, CONCRETE
cemest, chemist
cemetery,ries,tarial, GRAVEYARD
cemist, chemist
cemiteri, cemetery
cempothe, sympathy
cems, seem(s) / seam(s)
cemutary, cemetery
cenameter, centimeter
cendral, central
cendrulize, centralize
cenik, cynic
cenikal, cynical
cenima, cinema
cense, since / sense / cent(s) / scent(s)

censeer, sincere
censhury, century
censor,*,red,ring,rship,rable,rious, riously,riousness,sure, CONTROL INFORMATION (or see sensor/censure) "prefixes: pre"
censure,rable,er, SEVERE/OFFICIAL CRITICISM/STATEMENT (or see censor/sensor)
census, SURVEY (or see sense(s))
cent,*, PREFIX INDICATING 'HUNDRED/HUNDREDTH' MOST OFTEN MODIFIES THE WORD, MONETARY (or see scent/sent)
centennial,*,lly, HUNDREDTH YEAR ANNIVERSARY "prefixes: bi"
center,*,red,ring, THE MIDDLE "prefixes: con/re"
centi, PREFIX INDICATING 'HUNDRED/HUNDREDTH' MOST OFTEN MODIFIES THE WORD
centigrade,*, WAY OF REPORTING TEMPERATURE
centiment, sentiment
centimeter,*, MORE THAN 0.39 OF AN INCH
centinial, centennial
centipede,*, POISONOUS BUG
central,lly,lity,lism,lize, FOCUS BETWEEN TWO OR MORE "prefixes: non"
centralize,*,ed,zing,zation, LOCATE CONVENIENTLY IN THE CENTER/MIDDLE "prefixes: de/non"
centri, PREFIX INDICATING 'CENTER' MOST OFTEN MODIFIES THE WORD (or see sentry)
centric,cal,cally,city, AT OR NEAR CENTER "prefixes: exo"
centro, PREFIX INDICATING 'CENTER' MOST OFTEN MODIFIES THE WORD
centrul, central
centry, sentry / centri
centugrade, centigrade
centumeter, centimeter
centupede, centipede
century,ries, YEAR MARK
cenverdable, convertible
ceptic, septic
cer, care
ceramic,*, CLAY-FIRING METHOD
cerashen, serrate(tion)
cerat, carat / caret / carrot / karat / serrate

ceration, serrate(tion)
cerb, curb
cercimscribe, circumscribe
cercle, circle
cercol, circle
cerculate, circulate
cercumcise, circumcise
cercumfurens, circumference
cercumscribe, circumscribe
cercumstance, circumstance
cerdafy, certify
cerdenle, certain(ly)
cerdenly, certain(ly)
cerdify, certify
cerdle, curdle
cerdufy, certify
cere, care / carry
cereal, EDIBLE GRAIN (or see surreal)
cerebr, PREFIX INDICATING 'BRAIN' MOST OFTEN MODIFIES THE WORD
cerebral,lly, IN/OF THE BRAIN "prefixes: intra"
cerebro, PREFIX INDICATING 'BRAIN' MOST OFTEN MODIFIES THE WORD
ceremony,nies,nial,nially,nious, FORMAL GROUP GATHERING "prefixes: un"
ceret, carat / caret / carrot / karat
cereul, cereal / surreal
cereur, carrier
cerf, curve / surf
cerfew, curfew
cerfue, curfew
ceri, carry
cerial, cereal / serial
cericewlum, curriculum
cericuture, caricature
cerikachur, caricature
cerikulum, curriculum
cerimony, ceremony
cerin, serene
cerisel, carousel
cerit, carat / caret / carrot / karat
ceriul, cereal / serial
cerivan, caravan
cerkemscribe, circumscribe
cerklar, circular
cerkle, circle
cerkomferinse, circumference
cerkul, circle
cerkumsize, circumcise
cerkus, circus
cerl, curl
cernal, colonel

cernil, colonel / kernel
cerogun, corrode(osion)
cerol, carol
cerosene, kerosene
cerot, carat / caret / carrot / karat
cerpent, serpent
cersanthemum, chrysanthemum
cerse, curse
cersif, cursive
cersog, corsage
certain,nly,nty,nties,nness, KNOW FOR SURE "prefixes: un"
certale, curtail
certan, curtain
certatude, certitude
certeficashen, certificate(tion)
certeficate, certificate
certen, certain
certifi, certify
certificasion, certificate(tion)
certificate,*,ed,ting,tion, VALIDATION FOR LEARNING
certify,fies,fied,fying,fier,fiable,fiably, ficated,fication, MAKE CERTAIN, A LEGAL DOCUMENT "prefixes: de/re"
certin, certain
certinly, certain(ly)
certitude,*, FEELING THAT SOMETHING IS CERTAIN "prefixes: in"
certsy, curtsy
certufi, certify
certul, curdle
certunle, certain(ly)
certunly, certain(ly)
certutude, certitude
cerunsy, currency
cerunt, currant / current
cerus, cirrus / scirrhus
cerusel, carousel
cerut, carat / caret / carrot / karat
ceruvan, caravan
cerv, curve / serve
cervant, servant
cervis, service
cervitud, servitude
cervix,xes,ical, OF THE NECK
cervuchure, curvature
cery, curry / carry
ces, see(s) / sea(s) / seize / cease
cesami, sesame
ceshel, seashell
ceshon, session
cest, cyst / zest

cesta, siesta
cesturn, cistern
ceven, seven
cevendi, seventy
ceventieth, seventieth
ceventin, seventeen
ceventy, seventy
cevin, seven
cevon, seven
cevontin, seventeen
cevul, civil
cevulization, civil(ization)
cevun, seven
cew, cue
cewth, couth
cez, see(s) / sea(s) / seize / cease
cfood, seafood
cfud, seafood
chacra, chakra
chader, chatter
chado, shadow
chaf, chafe / chaff
chafd, shaft / chafe(d) / chaff(ed)
chafe,*,ed,fing, ANNOYED/IRRITATED, RUBBED UNTIL SORE (or see shaft/chaff)
chaff,*,ffed,ffing,ffer,ffy, TO TEASE/JOKE WITH SOMEONE (or see chafe)
chafs, chafe(s) / chaff(s)
chaft, shaft / chafe(d) / chaff(ed)
chain,*,ned,ning, LINKS PUT/HOOKED TOGETHER "prefixes: en/un"
chair,*,red,ring, FURNITURE, HEAD OF MEETINGS/ORGANIZATION
chak, chalk / choke / shock / chock
chakra,*, CENTERS IN BODY
chalant,tly,nce, OVERLY CONCERNED/ANXIOUS "prefixes: non"
chalenge, challenge
chalinge, challenge
chalk,*,ked,king,ky, LIMESTONE
challenge,*,ed,ging,gable,er, TEST OF SKILLS
chalons, chalant(nce)
chalont, chalant
champagne, EFFERVESCENT WINE
champane, champagne
champeon, champion
champion,*,ned,ning,nship, WINS CONTEST OF SKILL
chanal, channel
chance,*,ed, A GAMBLE

chancre,*,rous, ULCERATION ON THE SKIN (or see canker)
chandelier,*, LAMP WITH MANY ARMS FOR BULBS
chandulere, chandelier
chane, chain
chanel, channel
change,*,ed,ging,gable, TRANSFORM "prefixes: un"
chanil, channel
channel,*,led,ling,ler,lize, AVENUE TO RECEIVE "prefixes: re"
channelize,*,zed,zing,zation, TO CHANNEL/DIRECT "prefixes: de/re"
chanse, chance / chant(s)
chant,*,ted,ting,tingly, RECITE/REPEAT WORDS IN VERBAL RHYTHM (or see chain(ed))
chanul, channel
chaos,otic, APPEARS TO US TO BE DISORGANIZED
chap,*,pped,pping, DRY/ROUGH SKIN, LEATHER PART
chapel,*, FOR RITUALS
chaplain,*, PERFORMS RITUAL SERVICES
chaplan, chaplain
chapter,*, SECTION OF PRINT, COLLEGE OR SCHOOL
chapul, chapel
char,*,rred,rring, TO BURN/BLACKEN, CHORES (or see chair/chore/share)
character,*,ristic,ristically,rize,rization, PERSONALITY/QUALITIES
charade,*, PANTOMINE GAME
charcoal,*,led, ORGANIC SUBSTANCE IN EARTH
charder, charter
chare, chair / cherry / sherry / share
charecter, character
charge,*,ed,er,ging,eable, APPLY TOWARDS CREDIT, CREATE POWER, ENERGIZE, APPLY FORCE "prefixes: dis/over/re/sur/under"
charguble, charge(able)
chari, cherry / sherry
charidy, charity
charisma,atic, INSPIRATIONAL QUALITY
charitable,ly, GIVING
charity,ties,table, GIVING UNCONDITIONALLY
charj, charge
charjuble, charge(able)
charjur, charge(r)

charkol, charcoal
charm,*,med,ming,mingly,mer, ALLUREMENT, LUCKY OBJECT
chart,*,ted,ting, PLOT OUT "prefixes: un"
charter,*,red,ring, CONTRACT, OUTLINE "prefixes: un"
charutable, charitable
chary, cherry / sherry
chas, chase / chaste
chasd, chaste / chase(d)
chase,*,ed,sing,er, PURSUE TO CAPTURE (or see chaste)
chasem, chasm
chasim, chasm
chasm,*,mic, DEEP VOID
chassis, FRAME OF VEHICLE
chaste,er,est,ely,eness, SIMPLE, PLAIN, FAITHFUL (or see chase(d))
chasum, chasm
chasy, chassis
chater, chatter / shatter
chatter,*,red,ring, TALK TOO MUCH ABOUT UNINTERESTING TOPICS
chauffeur,*, DESIGNATED DRIVER
chauk, chalk / choke / shock / chock
chaukra, chakra
chaumein, chowmein
chaurkol, charcoal
chauvinist,*,tic, TERM FOR MEN WHO TREAT WOMEN AS LESSERS/UNEQUAL
chayos, chaos
chazm, chasm
chazum, chasm
cheap,per,pest,ply,pens, LOW COST (or see chip)
cheat,*,ted,ting,ter, DISHONEST ACQUISITION
check,*,ked,king,ker,kers,kered, BANK DRAFT, A MARK, TO MAKE CERTAIN, A GAME "prefixes: re/un"
cheef, chief
cheep, cheap
cheer,*,red,ring,ringly,rer,rful,rfully, rfulness,ry,rily,riness,rless, HAPPY/JOYFUL/ENCOURAGEMENT/SHOUTING/TOASTING
cheese, CURDLED MILK
cheet, cheat
chef,*, HEAD COOK (or see sheaf)
chek, check / cheek
chekan, chicken
chekurs, check(ers)

cheldren, children
chelenge, challenge
chelons, chalant(nce)
chelont, chalant
chelren, children
chemest, chemist
chemical,*, OF CHEMISTRY "prefixes: bio"
chemist,*, SCIENTIST WHO STUDIES PROPERTIES OF MATTER "prefixes: bio"
chemistry, MOTHER OF SCIENCE, STUDY OF MATTER "prefixes: bio"
chemney, chimney
chemotherapy, RADIATION TREATMENT
chemucal, chemical
chemustry, chemistry
chen, chin
chep, cheap / sheep
chepd, chip(pped) / ship(pped)
cheped, chip(pped) / ship(pped)
cher, share / chair / cheer
cherch, church
chere, cherry / sherry / cheer(y)
cheretable, charitable
cherety, charity
cheridy, charity
cheritable, charitable
cherity, charity
cherle, sure(ly)
chern, churn
cherry,rries, LITTLE RED FRUIT (or see sherry)
chery, cherry / sherry
chese, cheese
chest, schist
chevolry, chivalry
chevulry, chivalry
chew,*,wed,wing,wable, GRIND WITH TEETH
chewt, shute / chute
cheys, chase
cheyst, chaste
chic, STYLISH
chick,*, YOUNG BIRD, GIRL
chicken,*, FOWL, BIRD
chicory, HERB
chief,*,tain, HIGHEST AUTHORITY
chif, chief
chik, chick
chiken, chicken
chikury, chicory

child,*,dren,dish,dishly,dishness,dly, dlike,PERSON UNDER AGE 18
children,PEOPLE UNDER AGE 18
chilons, chalant(nce)
chilont, chalant
chilostomy, colostomy
chilren, children
chimest, chemist
chimist, chemist
chimney,*, SMOKE STACK
chimotherapy, chemotherapy
chimukul, chemical
chin,*, POINT OF JAW (or see shin/shine)
chip,*,pped,pping,pper, THIN SLICE/WEDGE OF SOMETHING (or see ship/cheap) "prefixes: bio"
chiped, chip(pped) / ship(pped)
chirch, church
chirle, sure(ly)
chiro, PREFIX INDICATING 'HAND' MOST OFTEN MODIFIES THE WORD
chiropractor,tic, REALIGNS BONES OF BODY FOR HEALTH
chirtch, church
chis, cheese
chisel,*,led,ling, TOOL FOR FORMING SHAPES
chist, schist
chivalry,rous, COURTEOUS AND HELPFUL GENTLEMAN
chizt, schist
chizul, chisel
chlor, PREFIX INDICATING 'GREEN/CHLORINE' MOST OFTEN MODIFIES THE WORD
chlorene, chlorine
chlorine,nate,idize, CHEMICAL IRRITANT
chloro, PREFIX INDICATING 'GREEN/CHLORINE' MOST OFTEN MODIFIES THE WORD
chock,*,ked,king, TO BLOCK/SECURE/BRACE (or see choke/chalk/shock)
chocklat, chocolate
choclat, chocolate
chocolate,*,ty,tier,tiest, FROM CACAO NUT
choice,*, SELECTION "prefixes: pro-"
choir,*, SINGING GROUP
chok, chalk / choke / shock / chock
choke,*,ed,king,kingly,er, RESTRICTED SUPPLY OF AIR/MOVEMENT(or see chalk/shock/chock)

choklat, chocolate
choklut, chocolate
chokra, chakra
chol, PREFIX INDICATING 'BILE/GALLBLADDER' MOST OFTEN MODIFIES THE WORD
chole, PREFIX INDICATING 'BILE/GALLBLADDER' MOST OFTEN MODIFIES THE WORD
cholesterol, NATURALLY PRESENT IN THE BODY
cholk, chalk
cholons, chalant(nce)
cholont, chalant
cholostemy, colostomy
choo, chew / shoe
choose,*,sing,er,sy,sier,siest,sily,siness, hose, PICK ONE OVER THE OTHER (or see chew(s)/chose)
chop,*,pped,pping,pper,ppy,ppier, pppiest,ppily,ppiness, HACK/CUT INTO PIECES, SUDDEN CHANGE IN DIRECTION (or see shop)
chopeng, chop(pping) / shop(pping)
chor, chore / shore / char
choral, OF A CHOIR (or see coral/corral/chorale)
chorale, A HYMN OF SIMPLE TUNE (or see choral/corral/coral)
chorcol, charcoal
chord,*, OF MUSICAL NOTES (or see cord/short)
chore,*, SMALL TASKS (or see shore)
chorkol, charcoal
chorn, shorn
chorus, A UNION OF PERFORMERS (or see course)
chorz, chore(s) / shard(s)
chose,en, HAVING SELECTED, PAST TENSE FOR THE WORD 'CHOOSE' (or see choose)
choyse, choice
chrapnul, shrapnel
christmas, A RELIGIOUS HOLIDAY
chrom, PREFIX INDICATING 'COLOR/CHROMIUM' MOST OFTEN MODIFIES THE WORD (or see chrome)
chrome,ed,ming, METALLIC
chromizone, chromosome
chromo, PREFIX INDICATING 'COLOR/CHROMIUM' MOST OFTEN MODIFIES THE WORD
chromosome,*, DNA STRAND

chronalogical, chronology(gical)
chronic,cally,city, CONTINUOUS
chronicle,*,ed,ling, LIST OF FACTS
chronk, shrunk
chrono, PREFIX INDICATING 'TIME' MOST OFTEN MODIFIES THE WORD
chronology,gical,lgically, ORGANIZE BY DATES
chronulogical, chronology(gical)
chrud, shrewd / truth
chrunk, shrunk
chrys, PREFIX INDICATING 'GOLD' MOST OFTEN MODIFIES THE WORD
chrysanthemum,*, FLOWER
chryso, PREFIX INDICATING 'GOLD' MOST OFTEN MODIFIES THE WORD
chu, chew
chue, chew
chugar, sugar
chugur, sugar
chulons, chalant(nce)
chulont, chalant
churade, charade
chural, choral / coral / corral / chorale
church,hes,hy, FOR RELIGIOUS PURPOSES
churle, sure(ly)
churn,*,ned,ning, FAT, MILK SEPARATION
chus, chew(s) / choose / shoe(s)
chuse, chew(s) / choose / choose(sy) / shoe(s)
chute,*,ed,ting, RAPID/STEEP DESCENT (or see shoot/shut)
cianide, cyanide
ciburnetiks, cybernetics
ciclist, cyclist
cid, kid / kite
cider, STRONG JUICE
cidur, cider
cigar,*, ROLLED TOBACCO
cigarette,*, OF TOBACCO
cilinder, cylinder
cilinoid, solenoid
cilosal, colossal
cimbeosis, symbiosis
cimbol, cymbal / symbol
cimen, semen
ciment, cement
cimist, chemist
cimpathetic, sympathetic
cimpathy, sympathy

cinch,hes,hed,hing, FIRM GRIP ON, EASILY ACHIEVED, FOR CERTAIN (or see singe)
cinda, kind of
cinder,*, CHARRED SUBSTANCE (or see send)
cinduf, kind of
cine, PREFIX INDICATING 'MOTION PICTURE' MOST OFTEN MODIFIES THE WORD
cinema,*,atic, MOTION PICTURE
cinery, canary / cannery
cing, zing / sing
cinima, cinema
cinnamon, SPICE FROM TREE BARK
cinsestently, consistent(ly)
cinsistency, consistence(cy)
cinspirusy, conspiracy
cinstrucshen, construction
cint, can't / cent / scent / sent
cintential, centennial
cinverdable, convertible
cip, zip / sip
circle,*,ed,ling, ROUND FIGURE/SHAPE "prefixes: semi"
circompherence, circumference
circuit,*,try, MAKES THE ROUNDS, GOES AROUND, NETWORK
circular,*, GOES AROUND IN THE SHAPE OF A CIRCLE "prefixes: semi"
circulate,*,ed,ting,tion, FLOWING/ MOVING "prefixes: un"
circum, PREFIX INDICATING 'AROUND' MOST OFTEN MODIFIES THE WORD
circumcise,*,ed,sing,sion,er, REMOVAL OF FORESKIN ON PENIS "prefixes: un"
circumference, DISTANCE/LINE AROUND A CIRCLE
circumscribe,*,ed,bing,bable,er, SET NARROW LIMITS, ENCIRCLE "prefixes: un"
circumstance,*,ntial,ntiate, INCIDENT
circus,ses, ENTERTAINING PERFORMANCE IN TENTS
cireol, cereal / serial
cirial, cereal / serial
cirios, serious
ciris, series
cirius, serious
cirkemscribe, circumscribe
cirkumscribe, circumscribe
cirkumsize, circumcise
cirnel, colonel / kernel

ciroberate, corroborate
cirogun, corrode(osion)
cirrus, CLOUD TYPE/SHAPE (or see scirrhus)
cirsanthemum, chrysanthemum
cirten, certain
cirteus, courteous
cirus, cirrus / scirrhus
cirvature, curvature
cis, PREFIX INDICATING 'ON THIS SIDE' MOST OFTEN MODIFIES THE WORD
cist, COFFIN OF THE STONE AGE (or see cyst/kiss(ed))
citashun, citation
cistern,*,nal, CONTAINER/COLLECTOR FOR LIQUID/WATER
citation,*, A SUMMONS
cite,*,ed,ting,tation,tations, OFFICIALLY CALL FORTH (or see site)
citizen,*,nry,nship, MEMBER OF, WITH PRIVILEDGES
citres, citrus
citric, ACID FROM FRUIT
citrus, FRUIT
citusin, citizen
city,ties, METROPOLIS
ciunide, cyanide
civic, CITIZENSHIP
civil,lly,lize,lizes,lized,lizing,lization, lizations, OF STATE OR COMMUNITY "prefixes: in/un"
civilean, civilian
civilian,*, NOT MILITARY CITIZENS
civul, civil
civulization, civil(ization)
ciyen, cayenne
cla, claw
clad,*,ding, WEARING ON BODY, COVERED WITH "prefixes: un"
clae, clay
claim,*,med,ming,mer,mant,mable, ASSERT POSSESSION OF (or see clamor/climb) "prefixes: re/de"
claimant,*, TAKE POSSESSION OF
clairvoyance,nt, THOSE WHO CHANNEL INFORMATION
clam,*,mmed,mming, SHELLFISH (or see claim)
clamable, claim(able)
clament, claimant
clamor,*,red,ring,rer, SUDDEN/LOUD/ INSISTENT NOISE (or see claim(er))
clamp,*,ped,ping, PINCH TOGETHER
clams, claim(s) / clam(s)

clan, BODIES OF LIKE-MINDED INDIVIDUALS
clandestine,ely,eness, WITH DECEPTION IN MIND
clandustine, clandestine
clap,*,pped,pping,pt, SOUND, GONORRHEA
clarical, clerical
clarify,fies, GIVE SPECIFIC MEANING TO
clarity, MAKE CLEAR
clarvoyants, clairvoyance
claset, closet
clash,hes,hed,hing, COLLIDE, LOUD SOUND
clasha, cliche
clasic, classic
clasify, classify
clasp,*,ped,ping, HOLD "prefixes: en/un"
class,sses,ssed,ssing,ssy, GROUPED TOGETHER DUE TO SIMILARITIES "prefixes: un/under"
classic,*,cal,cally, WITHSTOOD TEST OF TIME "prefixes: neo/semi"
classify,fies,fied,fying,fication,fiable, ABLE TO PLACE INTO A GROUP "prefixes: de/non/un"
clasuc, classic
clauc, clock / cloak
claud, cloud
clauged, clog(gged) / cloak / clock(ed)
clause,*,sal, STIPULATION (or see claw(s))
claustrophobia, FEAR OF COZY/TIGHT PLACES
claustrophobic, FEAR OF COZY/TIGHT PLACES
claw,*,wed,wing, HOOKED, FINGERLIKE (or see clause)
clawn, clown
clawsit, closet
clawzet, closet
clay, SOIL FROM EARTH
clean,*,ned,ning,ner,nly,liness, UNSOILED "prefixes: un"
cleanse,*,sed,sing,er, MAKE CLEAN
cleanser, CHEMICALS USED TO CLEAN
clear,*,red,ring,rance, FREE OF OBSTRUCTION
clearance,*, TO CLEAR OF
cleat,*, FOR TRACTION, STRENGTH
clebtomaniac, kleptomania(c)
clecha, cliche
cleche, cliche

cleck, click / clique
cleen, clean
cleer, clear
cleerance, clearance
cleff, cliff
clek, click / clique
clen, clean
clench,hes,hed,hing, TO HOLD/GRASP TIGHTLY (or see clinch)
cleng, cling
clenik, clinic
clens, cleanse / clean(s)
clenser, cleanser
clenz, cleanse / clean(s)
clenzr, cleanser
clep, clip
cleptomaniac, kleptomania(c)
clepur, clipper
cler, clear
clerady, clarity
clerchi, clergy
clerd, clear(ed)
cleredy, clarity
clereng, clear(ing)
clerense, clearance
clerety, clarity
clergy,gies, ORDAINED BY CHRISTIANS
clerical, OFFICE WORKER
cleridi, clarity
clering, clear(ing)
clerity, clarity
clerk,*,kly, PERFORMS GENERAL DUTIES
clerle, clear(ly)
clert, clear(ed)
clervoyanse, clairvoyance
clesha, cliche
clet, cleat
cletoras, clitoris
clever,rly,rness, INGENIOUS
clew, clue
cliant, client
clibtomaniac, kleptomania(c)
cliche,*, STEREOTYPICAL PHRASE
click,*,ked,king,ker, SNAPPING NOISE, FIT WELL TOGETHER (or see clique)
clics, click(s) / clique(s)
client,*,tele, CUSTOMER
cliff,*, STEEP ROCK FACE
clik, click / clique
clim, climb
climate,*,tic,tize,tized,tizing,tization, WEATHER OR ATMOSPHERIC CONDITION "prefixes: ac/bio"

climax,xes,xed,xing,actic, GREATEST HEIGHT
climb,*,bed,bing,bable, MOMENTUM UPWARDS,GO UP (or see claim)
clims, climb(s)
climute, climate
clinch,hes,hed,hing,her, TO RESOLVE, FASTEN/HOLD (or see clench)
cling,*,clung,ging,gy,gingly,ger, ATTACH TIGHTLY TO
clinic,*,cal,cally, PLACE FOR EXAMINATION "prefixes: sub"
clinser, cleanser
clip,*,pped,pping,pper, CUT OFF OR OUT, A TACKLE
clipper,*, CUTTING TOOL
cliptomaniac, kleptomania(c)
clipur, clipper
clique,*,uish,ey, A SELECT GROUP
clirans, clearance
clirge, clergy
clirk, clerk
clisha, cliche
clishe, cliche
clitoris,ral, POINT FOR FEMININE AROUSAL
cloak,*,ked,king, A GARMET, TO CONCEAL/DIGUISE (or see clock) "prefixes: un"
clob, club
clobber,*,red,ring, TO BEAT UP
clober, clobber
cloc, cloak / clock
cloch, clutch / clock
clock,*,ked,king, KEEP TIME (or see cloak)
cloder, clutter
clodur, clutter
clofe, clove
clofur, clover
clog,*,gged,gging, STOPPED/BACKED UP (or see cloak/clock(ed)) "prefixes: un"
cloger, closure
cloister,*,red,ring, OF BUILDINGS, TO ENCLOSE
clojer, closure
clok, clock / cloak
cloked, clog(gged) / cloak / clock(ed)
clomp, clump
clomsi, clumsy
clone,*,ed,ning, REPLICAS (or see clown/cologne)
clos, clothes / claw(s) / close / clause

closder, cluster
close,*,ed,sing,ely,er,est, SHUT DOWN, NEAR TO (or see clause/clothes) "prefixes: en/ex/re/un"
closet,*,ted,ting, SMALL PRIVATE SPACE
closher, closure
closir, close(r) / closure
closline, clothesline
closter, cluster
closturfobeu, claustrophobia
closur, close(r) / closure
closure,*, CONCEAL, SHUT DOWN (or see close(r))
clot,*,tted,tting, LUMP, MASS OF MATTER
cloted, clot(tted)
cloter, clutter
cloth,*,he,hes,hed,hing, WOVEN FIBERS INTO MATERIAL, USED FORCLOTHING (or see close)
clothes, OUTER/UNDER GARMENTS FOR THE BODY (or see close/cloth(es)) "prefixes: under"
clothesline,*, LINE FOR HANGING GARMENTS/CLOTHES ON
cloths, clothes / cloth(es)
clothsline, clothesline
clotur, clutter
cloud,*,dy,ded,ding,diness, SMOKE, WATER PARTICLES, OBSCURES VISION "prefixes: over"
cloun, clown / clone / cologne
clout, INFLUENCE, TO STRIKE (or see cloud)
clove,*, OF A PLANT, FORM OF MEASUREMENT
clover,*, HERBAL PLANT
clow, claw
clowd, cloud
clown,*,ned,ning,nish, FUNNY, GOOFY, NOT NORMAL, SOMETIMES RIDICULOUS/OBNOXIOUS
clows, clothes / claw(s) / close / clause
clowsit, closet
clowt, clout
cloyster, cloister
cloz, clothes / claw(s) / close / clause
clozer, close(r) / closure
clozir, close(r) / closure
clozline, clothesline
clozur, close(r) / closure
club,*,bbed,bbing, GROUP MEMBERSHIP, AN INSTRUMENT USED AS A WEAPON

cluch, clutch
cluder, clutter
clue,*,ed,eless,elessness, HINT
clump,*,ped,ping,py, COLLECTION OF/ INTO A MASS
clumsy,sily,siness, AWKWARDLY DONE
clumze, clumsy
clurgy, clergy
cluster,*,red,ring,ry, GROUPINGS TOGETHER "prefixes: non"
clutch,hes,hed,hing, USED TO CHANGE GEARS IN TRANSMISSION, GRASP FIRMLY, GROUP OF EGGS "prefixes: de"
cluter, clutter
clutorus, clitoris
clutter, CONFUSING SIGHT OR NOISE "prefixes: un"
co, PREFIX INDICATING 'WITH/ TOGETHER' MOST OFTEN MODIFIES THE WORD
co-op, COMMUNITY-OWNED BUSINESS, A COOPERATIVE (or see coop/coup)
coach,hes,hed,hing, TO GUIDE OTHERS (or see couch)
coagulate,*,ed,ting,tion, TO THICKEN, FORM CLOTS
coal,*, ORGANIC SUBSTANCE IN THE EARTH
coalition,*,nal,nist, VOLUNTARY GATHERING OF PEOPLE FOR A CAUSE
coar, core / corp
coarse,er,est,ely,eness, HARSH, ABRASIVE, ROUGH (or see course)
coast,*,ted,ting, BETWEEN LAND AND WATER, TO BE MOVING WITHOUT PROPULSION (or see cost) "prefixes: bi/intra"
coaster,*, TO SET DRINKS ON
coat,*,ted,ting, OUTER GARMENT FOR WARMTH "prefixes: over/sur/ under"
coax,xes,xed,xing, TO PERSUADE/ INFLUENCE
cob,*, TUBULAR IN SHAPE
cobalt, CHEMICAL, BLUE COLORING
cobi, cubby
cobolt, cobalt
cobra,*, SNAKE
cobweb,*, SPIDER'S WEB
coc, caulk / cock
cocaine, NARCOTIC DRUG
cocane, cocaine

coch, coach
cocher, kosher
coches, cautious
cochus, cautious
cock,*,ky, A ROOSTER, OF MASCULINE SUGGESTION (or see cook)
cockroach,hes, INFESTATING INSECT
cocktail,*, ALCOHOLIC BEVERAGES
cocoa, FROM THE CACAO SEED
coconut,*, FRUIT
cocoon,*, HOME SPUN BY LARVAE
coctale, cocktail
cocun, cocoon
cocunut, coconut
cocus, caucus
cod,*, FISH, A POD, A PENINSULA (or see code/caught/could/cold)
code,*,ded,ding, LANGUAGE "prefixes: en"
codeine, DRUG FROM OPIUM
coden, cotton / codeine
codich, cottage
codien, codeine
codin, cotton / codeine
codol, cuddle
coduge, cottage
coed,*, BOTH SEXES
coel, coil
coelate, collate
coen, coin
coencident, coincident
coenside, coincide
coensident, coincident
coerce,*,ed,cing,cible,cion,cive,civeness, cively, FORCE INTO COMPLIANCE "prefixes: in/non"
coersment, coerce(ment)
cof, cough / cuff
cofe, cove / coffee / cough
cofen, coffin / cough(ing)
cofert, covert / cover(ed)
coffee, BEVERAGE (or see cove)
coffin,*, BOX FOR TRANSPORT, CASKET
cofi, coffee
cofin, coffin / cough(ing)
cofy, coffee
cognative, cognitive
cogneshun, cognition
cognezant, cognizant
cognisant, cognizant
cognition,nal,ive, PERCEPTIVE/AWARE (or see cognizant) "prefixes: pre/ retro"

cognitive,ely,vism,ion, COME TO KNOW THROUGH PERCEPTION/REASONING "prefixes: pre/retro"
cognizant,nce,able,ably,nce,ition, PERCEPTIVE/AWARE
cognutev, cognitive
cohabitate,*,ed,ting,tion, DWELL/LIVE TOGETHER
cohabutate, cohabitate
coherent,nce,ncy, WORKS CONSISTENTLY/PREDICTABLY "prefixes: in/non"
coherse, coerce
cohersive, coerce(cive)
cohersment, coerce(ment)
cohesive,ely,eness,ion, BONDS TOGETHER
cohesuf, cohesive
cohort,*, CO-PARTNER
cohurse, coerce
cohursive, coerce(cive)
coil,*,led,ling, SPIRAL SHAPE "prefixes: un"
coin,*,ned,nage, METAL USED FOR MONEY
coincide,*,ed,ding,ence,ent, TO HAPPEN/OCCUPY AT SAME TIME
coincident,nce,tal,tally, CHANCE HAPPENING "prefixes: un"
coircment, coerce(ment)
cok, cook / cock
cokane, cocaine
cokes, coax
cokie, cookie
cokroch, cockroach
coktale, cocktail
col, PREFIX INDICATING 'INTESTINES' MOST OFTEN MODIFIES THE WORD (or see call/cowl/coal)
colaborate, collaborate
colach, collage
coladerul, collateral
colage, collage
colamedy, calamity
colander,*, STRAINER
colani, colony
colanize, colony(nize)
colanoid, solenoid
colaps, collapse
colapse, collapse
colapsuble, collapse(sible)
colar, color / collar / call(er)
colash, collage / college
colastomy, colostomy

colasul, colossal
colate, collate
colcher, culture
cold,der,dest,dly, OPPOSITE OF HOT (or see colt)
coldesak, cul-de-sac
coldslaw, coleslaw
cole, coal / call
coleage, colleague
colech, college
colechat, collegiate
colecshon, collection
colect, collect
colection, colleciton
colector, collect(or)
coleg, colleague / college
colegen, collision / collagen
coleget, collegiate
colegiate, collegiate
colekshin, collection
colem, column
colen, colon
colenise, colonize
colenoid, solenoid
coleny, colony
coler, color / cooler / collar
colesh, college
coleshon, collision / coalition
coleshun, collision / coalition
coleslaw, CABBAGE SALAD
colic, PAIN CAUSED BY ACID IN THE INTESTINES
colich, college
colide, collide
coliflower, cauliflower
colig, college / colleague
coligen, collision / collagen
colijin, collision
colim, column
colinary, culinary
colinoid, solenoid
coliny, colony
colk, calk / caulk
collaborate,*,ed,ting,tion,tive,tively, COOPERATE
collage,*, MIXED MEDIA ART
collagen,*,nic,nous, FIBROUS PROTEIN FOUND IN BONE/TISSUE
collander, colander
collapsable, collapse(sible)
collapse,*,ed,sing,sable, BREAK DOWN
collar,*,red,rless, RIM ON SHIRT, BELT FOR NECK
collard greens, VEGETABLE

collate,*,ed,ting,tion, MERGE, COMPARE
collateral,lly,lize, USED TO GUARANTEE/SECURE A LOAN
colleague,*, ASSOCIATE
collect,*,ted,ting,tion,tive,tor, GATHER "prefixes: non/re"
collection,*, ACT OF GATHERING THINGS "prefixes: re"
college,*, HIGHER EDUCATION
collegiate, OF COLLEGE AND/OR STUDENTS
collide,*,ed,ding,ision, RUN INTO
collision,*, ACT OF RUNNING INTO
colloquia,al, PLURAL FOR COLLOQUIUM, STYLE/ADVENT OF WRITING OR SPEAKING
colloquial,lity,lly,lness,lism,ium,iums, STYLE/ADVENT OF WRITING OR SPEAKING
colloquium,*, MEETING/CONFERENCE OF SPEAKERS ON SPECIFIC TOPIC
colm, calm
colmenate, culminate
colminate, culminate
colo, PREFIX INDICATING 'INTESTINES' MOST OFTEN MODIFIES THE WORD
coloch, collage / college
colog, collage / college
cologne,*, TOILET WATER (or see colon)
colokweul, colloquial
colon, INTESTINES, PUNCTUATION IN TEXT (or see cologne) "prefixes: semi"
coloneal, colonial
colonel,*, U.S. MILITARY OFFICER (or see kernel)
colonial,list,lism, FIRST EUROPEANS TO AMERICA "prefixes: neo"
colonize,*,ed,zing,zation, FIRST SETTLERS "prefixes: de"
colony,nies,nize, ACCUMULATION OF SIMILAR PEOPLES
color,*,red,ring,rful,rless,rlessly, rlessness,ration,rant,rize,rizes, rized, rizing,rization, HUES OF LIGHT SPECTRUM "prefixes: bi/de/un/uni"
colossal, GREAT MAGNITUDE
colostomy,mies, INVOLVES INTESTINES/ANUS
colpret, culprit
colsla, coleslaw
colt,*, THE YOUNG OF SOME IN ANIMAL KINGDOM (or see cold)

coltevate, culminate
coltivate, cultivate
coltsfoot, USEFUL HERB
coltuvate, cultivate
coluge, college
column,*,ned,nar,nist, VERTICAL PILLARS OR ROWS, WRITTEN ARTICLE
colun, colon
colunise, colonize
coluny, colony
colurd, collard greens
colvert, culvert
com, PREFIX INDICATING 'WITH/TOGETHER' MOST OFTEN MODIFIES THE WORD (or see come/comb)
coma,*,atose, UNCONSCIOUSNESS (or see comma) "prefixes: semi"
comand, command
comander, commander
comasery, commissary
comb,*,bed,bing, TOOL FOR HAIR (or see come)
combat,*,ted,ting,tant,tive, OPPOSE
combensashen, compensation
comber, cumber
combersome, cumber(some)
combination,*,tive,able, UNIFY "prefixes: re"
combine,*,ed,ning,nation, BRING TOGETHER, FARM MACHINE
combrahensiv, comprehensive
combunashen, combination
combunation, combination
combustchen, combustion
combustible,*,bility,eness,ion,ive, POTENTIAL TO IGNITE INTO FLAMES
combustion,ive, CHEMICAL REACTION, FIRE/OXYGEN
come,*,ming,came, RESPOND, GO TOWARDS (or see comb/cum) "prefixes: over/up"
comec, comic
comedeun, comedian
comedian,*, AMUSING ENTERTAINER
comedy,dies,dic, HUMOROUS ACCOUNTS
comemorate, commemorate
comence, commence
comend, commend
comendable, commendable
comendation, commendation
comenduble, commendable
comens, commence

comensirate, commensurate
comensurate, commensurate
coment, comment
comentative, commentate(tive)
comentator, commentator
coments, commence / comment(s)
comerbund, cummerbund
comerce, commerce
comercial, commercial
comerse, commerce
comershul, commercial
comesary, commisary
comeshen, commission
comeshener, commissioner
comet,*, SPACE MATTER AND ICE AT HIGH SPEED (or see commit)
comete, committee
cometion, commission
cometioner, commissioner
cometment, commitment
comewn, commune
comfert, comfort
comfort,*,ted,ting,ter, RELIEF, CALM, PLEASANT "prefixes: dis"
comfortable,ly, RELIEF, CALM, PLEASANT "prefixes: un"
comfurter, comfort(er)
comic,*,cal,cally,cality,calness, FUNNY, HUMOROUS
comidian, comedian
comidore, commodore
comidy, comedy
comimurate, commemorate
comin, common
comind, commend
comindation, commendation
cominduble, commendable
comins, commence
cominsirate, commensurate
comint, comment
comintator, commentator
comirse, commerce
comirshul, commercial
comisary, commissary
comishen, commission
comishener, commissioner
comisioner, commissioner
comissary, commissary
comission, commission
comit, comet / commit
comitee, committee
comition, commission
comitioner, commissioner
comitment, commitment

comittee, committee
comity, comedy
comma,*, PUNCTUATION (or see coma)
command,*,ded,ding,der, DOMINATING, DIRECTING
commander,*, DOMINANCE, MILITARY
commemorate,*,ed,ting,tion,tive, HONORING SOMEONE OR SOMETHING OF THE PAST
commence,*,ed,cing,ement, TO BEGIN "prefixes: re"
commend,*,ded,ding,dable,dation, SERIES OF CIRCLES WITH SAME CENTER POINT "prefixes: re"
commendable,*,eness,ly,ation, PRAISEWORTHY
commendation,*, PRAISE "prefixes: re"
commensurable,bility,bly,ate, SHARE THE SAME MEASURABLE QUALITIES "prefixes: in"
commensurate,ely,tion,able, EQUAL/CORRESPONDS TO "prefixes: in"
comment,*,ted,ting,tate,tary,taries, tative,tation,tator, MAKE REMARKS, GIVE OPINION
commentate,*,ed,ting,tion,tive,tor,ary, aries, TO COMMENT UPON
commentator,*,tate, ONE WHO GIVES OPINIONS/REMARKS
commerce, EXCHANGING WARES OR GOODS
commercial,*,lize,lization, ADVERTISEMENTS, ABOUT TRADE "prefixes: non/un"
commisary, commissary
commision, commission
commissary,ries, MILITARY STORE
commission,*,ned,ning, ALOTTED SUM/PERCENT, DELEGATE "prefixes: de"
commissioner,*, POSITION OF AUTHORITY
commit,*,tted,ttedly,tting,tment,ttable, tter, RELEGATE, ENTRUST "prefixes: non/over/un"
commitee, committee
commitment,*, OBLIGATED, ENTRUSTED TO SOMEONE OR SOMETHING
committee,*, SELECTED GROUP TO DO WORK "prefixes: sub"
commodity,ties, OBJECT FOR TRADE
commodore,*, MILITARY OFFICER
common,*,nly,ner,nest,nness, FAMILIAR "prefixes: un"

communal,*, OF COMMUNITY
commune,*, COLLECTION OF PEOPLE WITH SIMILAR IDEAS/VALUES
communicable, PASSED ON, ABLE TO COMMUNICATE "prefixes: in"
communicate,*,ed,ting,tion,tive,tively, tiveness,able, EXCHANGE INFORMATION "prefixes: ex/in/non/un"
communion,*, CHRISTIAN RITUAL
communism, TYPE OF GOVERNMENT
communist,*,tic, ADVOCATE OF COMMUNISM
community,ties, ASSOCIATION OF SIMILAR PEOPLES
commute,*,ed,ting,table, INTERCHANGE, DISTANCE TRAVEL, MATHEMATICAL EXPRESSION, REDUCE/REPLACE "prefixes: in/non"
comodity, commodity
comodore, commodore
comon, common
compact,*,ted,ting,tion, SMALLEST DIMENSION POSSIBLE "prefixes: sub"
compalshen, compulsion
compaltion, compulsion
companeon, companion
companion,*,nship, MATE/PARTNER
company,nies, ASSOCIATION OF INDIVIDUALS "prefixes: intra"
comparable,ly,eness,bility, SIMILAR, ALIKE "prefixes: in"
compare,*,ed,ring,arative,aratively, rable,rably,rison, PARALLEL EXAMINATION "prefixes: in"
comparetive, compare(rative)
comparison,*, ENGAGING EXAMINATION
compartment,*,tal,tally,talize,talized, talizing, SECTIONED SEPARATELY "prefixes: non"
compashinet, compassionate
compasionate, compassionate
compass,ses, DIRECTION FINDER "prefixes: en"
compassion,nate,nless, TAKE PITY ON
compassionate,ely,eness, TAKE PITY ON
compatible,bility,bilities, AGREEABLE "prefixes: bio/in/non"
compedidor, competitor
compeditor, competitor

compel,*,lled,lling,llingly,llingness, DRIVEN TO, AN URGING/DESIRE
compelation, compellation
compellation,*, NAME, DENOMINATION
compensate,*,ed,ting,tion,tory, MAKE UP FOR "prefixes: over"
compensation, MAKE UP FOR "prefixes: de"
compeny, company
comper, compare
comperable, comparable
comperative, compare(rative)
compereson, comparison
comperison, comparison
compersome, cumber(some)
comperuble, comparable
compes, compass
compete,*,ed,ting,tition,titive,titively, titiveness,titor, BE BETTER THAN
competent,nce,ncy, BEING ADEQUATE "prefixes: in"
competishen, competition
competition,*, MATCH FOR SKILL TESTING
competitor,*, ONE WHO COMPETES
compilashun, compellation
compile,*,ed,ling,lation, BRING/ PUT TOGETHER
compinsate, compensate
compitance, competent(nce)
compiut, compute
compiuter, computer
compizishen, composition
complacence,cy,cies,nt,ntly, HAPPY WITH SELF (or see complaisance)
complain,*,ned,ning,nt,ner, FIND FAULT
complaisance,nt, DESIRE TO PLEASE, CIVIL (or see complacence)
complasens, complacence / complaisance
complekate, complicate
compleks, complex
complekshin, complexion
complement,*,tal,tary,tarily,tarity, tarities,tation, WHEN ADDED MAKES COMPLETE (or see compliment)
compleshin, completion
complete,*,ed,ting,tly, CONCLUDE, FINISH "prefixes: in"
completion, CONCLUDE/FINISH

complex,xes,xity, COMBINATION OF INTERCONNECTED PARTS
complexion,*,ned, SKIN PHYSICAL CHARACTERISTIC
compli, comply
compliant,tly,nce,ncy, CONFORM/ AGREE TO "prefixes: in/non"
complicashin, complication
complicate,*,ed,ting,tion, MORE TO CONSIDER "prefixes: un"
complication,*, ADDITIONAL INVOLVEMENT/ CONSIDERATION
complient, compliant
complikashun, complication
complikat, complicate
compliment,*,ted,ting,tary, PRAISE, EXPRESS ADMIRATION (or see complement)
complishon, completion
complokeit, complicate
comploqueit, complicate
complucashun, complication
complukate, complicate
complument, complement / compliment
comply,lies,ying,liance,liant, CONFORM
compolshon, compulsion
compoltion, compulsion
component,*, PHASE/PART OF SOMETHING "prefixes: sub"
compose,*,ed,sing,er, TO FORM "prefixes: de/dis/re"
composite,*, PARTS OF THE WHOLE
composition,*,nal,nally, IDENTIFY/ ARRANGE PARTS OF THE WHOLE
compost,*,ted,ting, RECYCLING ORGANIC MATTER
composure, CENTERED STATE OF MIND
compound,*,ded,ding, ADDITIONAL PARTS, TO ADD TO THE WHOLE
compownd, compound
compoze, compose
comprable, comparable
compramise, compromise
compreble, comparable
comprehend,*,ded,ding,nsion,nsive, nsible, GRASP, UNDERSTAND "prefixes: in"
comprehenshun, comprehension
comprehensible,bility,eness, ABLE TO GRASP/UNDERSTAND "prefixes: in"
comprehension,ive,ible, UNDERSTAND/ GRASP "prefixes: in"

comprehensive,ely, UNDERSTAND/ GRASP "prefixes: in"
comprehinsive, comprehensive
compreshun, compression
compress,ses,sed,sing,sible,sibility,ssive, ssion, COMPACT, CONDENSE "prefixes: de/in"
compression,nal, REDUCING VOLUME
compressor,*, MACHINE THAT CONDENSES/REDUCES
compretion, compression
compromise,*,ed,sing, OUTCOME IMPERFECT, AGREE FOR THE SAKE OF BEING AGREEABLE "prefixes: un"
compruble, comparable
compruhensive, comprehensive
comprumize, compromise
comptroller,*, CONTROLLER OF FINANCES
compuder, computer
compulashun, compellation
compulsary, compulsory
compulsev, compulsive
compulshun, compulsion
compulsion,*,ive, IRRESISTIBLE URGE TO ACT
compulsive,ely,eness,ion,sory, GIVEN TO ACT ON URGES
compulsory,rily, REINFORCED FACT
compultion, compulsion
compusition, composition
computashun, computation
computation,*,nal,ive,ively, TO RECKON/ESTIMATE
compute,*,ed,ting,table, FIGURE DATA, ESTIMATE
computer,*,rize,rized,rization, ELECTRONIC DATA PROCESSOR "prefixes: bio"
computishen, competition
compuzishen, composition
comrade,*,ely,ery,eship, CLOSE ASSOCIATES
comtroler, comptroller
comudoor, commodore
comunal, communal
comune, commune / common
comunecuble, communicable
comunete, community
comunicable, communicable
comunicate, communicate
comunion, communion
comunism, communism

comunist, communist
comunity, community
comurse, commerce
comurshal, commercial
comusery, commissary
comutable, commute(table)
comute, commute
con,*,nned,nning, TO TRICK, PREFIX INDICATING 'WITH/TOGETHER' MOST OFTEN MODIFIES THE WORD (or see cone)
conaseur, connoisseur
conasure, connoisseur
conc, conch / konk
concaf, concave
concaquently, consequent(ly)
concarge, concierge
concave,*,ed,ving,ely,eness,vity,vities, OF INWARD CURVES "prefixes: bi"
conceairg, concierge
conceal,*,led,ling,lment, TO HIDE FROM SIGHT
concede,*,ed,ding, YIELD (or see conceit)
conceit,ted, VAIN (or see concede)
conceivable,bility,eness,ly, ABILITY TO UNDERTAND, IMAGINE "prefixes: in"
conceive,*,ed,ving,vable,vably,vability, vableness, A THOUGHT WHICH BECOMES "prefixes: mis"
concent, consent
concentrate,*,ed,ting,tion, FOCUS, CONDENSE "prefixes: de"
concentric,cally,city, SERIES OF CIRCLES WITH SAME CENTER POINT
concept,*,tive,tively, IDEA/PLAN
conception,nal, MOMENT OF CREATION "prefixes: mis/pre"
conceptual,lism,lize,lly,lization,lizer, THOUGHTS BECOMING
concequence, consequence
concerg, concierge
concern,*,ned,ning,nment, WORRIED ABOUT NEGATIVE OUTCOME, INTEREST IN "prefixes: non/un"
concert,*,ted,ting, PLAN/WORK/ACT TOGETHER IN MUSIC/THEATER "prefixes: pre"
concervashon, conservation
concesion, concession
concession,*, TO PART WITH SOME CONTROL, SELL UNDER AUTHORITY
conch,hes, A SHELL, OF DOME

conchas, conscious
concheinchus, conscientious
conches, conscious / conch(es)
conchis, conscious / conch(es)
conchos, conscious / conch(es)
conchus, conscious / conch(es)
concierge, OVERSEES GATES/ ENTRYWAYS
concint, consent
concise,ely,eness, TO THE POINT WITH FEW WORDS
concistensy, consistent(ncy)
concistent, consistent
conclewsive, conclusive
conclude,*,ed,ding,usion,usive, WRAP-UP, SUMMARIZED ENDING
conclugen, conclusion
conclusion,*, FINALIZE, END
conclusive,ely,eness, FINALIZE, END "prefixes: in"
conclution, conclusion
concoct,*,ted,ting, PUTTING TOGETHER IDEAS
concrete,ely,eness, HARDENED GRAVEL MIXTURE
concussion,*,ssive, INJURY FROM IMPACT
concution, concussion
condemn,*,ned,ning,nation, STEP TOWARDS ELIMINATION
condensashen, condensation
condensation,*, GAS REDUCED TO LIQUID
condense,*,ed,er,sing,sable,sation, REDUCE
condescend,ding,dingly, TALK DOWN TO SOMEONE, TREAT AS AN INFERIOR
condesend, condescend
condewit, conduit
condimeneum, condominium
condiment,*, SPICES, SAUCES
condinsashen, condensation
condinsation, condensation
condisend, condescend
condishen, condition
condition,*,ned,ning,nal, TO FORCE INTO ANOTHER FORM, RESTRUCTURE "prefixes: bi/de/pre/un"
condolence,*, SYMPATHY FOR SOMEONE'S PAIN
condom,*, COVER FOR PENIS
condomeneum, condominium

condominium,*, FORM OF APARTMENTS
condone,*,ed,ning, FORGIVE
conduct,*,ted,ting,tion,tive,tor, ESCORT, TRANSPORT, BEHAVIOR "prefixes: mis"
conductor,*,rial,rship, TRANSMITS, LEADS, GUIDES "prefixes: semi"
conduit, CHANNEL FOR ENERGY, FLUIDS, ETC.
condukter, conductor
condum, condom
condument, condiment
condunsation, condensation
cone,*, GEOMETRIC SHAPE OF MANY THINGS
conect, connect
conekshen, connection
conesur, connoisseur
conexshon, connection
confadant, confidant / confident
confection,*,nary,nery,ner, A DESSERT
confedant, confidant / confident
confederate,*,acy,tion, UNITED ALLIANCE
confedont, confidant
confeduret, confederate
confedy, confetti
confekshen, confection
conference,*, MEETING FOR DISCUSSION
confermation, confirmation
confesion, confession
confess,sses,ssed,ssing,ssion,ssor, DISCLOSE INFORMATION, ADMIT FACTS
confession,*,nal, ADMIT INVOLVEMENT
confetion, confession
confetti, PARTY MATERIAL
confety, confetti
confidant,*, TRUSTED PERSON (or see confident)
confide,*,ed,ding, SHARE THOUGHTS WITH SOMEONE
confidence,nt,ntial, TRUST
confidenshul, confidential
confident,tly,tial, TRUST
confidential,lly,lity,lness, PRIVATE/ SECRET
confidont, confidant
configerashun, configuration
configuration,*, ARRANGEMENT OF PARTS

confine,*,ed,ning,nment, RESTRICTED, IMPRISONED "prefixes: un"
confinement, BEING RESTRICTED, IMPRISONED
confinment, confinement
confirents, conference
confirm,*,med,ming,mation,mative, TO VALIDATE "prefixes: dis"
confirmation,*,ive, ACT OF VALIDATION
conflict,*,ted,ting, GOES AGAINST
conform,*,med,ming,mer,mist,mity, mism,mance, TO TAKE ON ANOTHER FORM "prefixes: dis/non/ un"
confrens, conference
confrins, conference
confront,*,ted,ting,tation,tational, FACE, ENCOUNTER
confudant, confidant / confident
confudense, confidence
confujen, confusion
confuranse, conference
confurmashun, confirmation
confuse,*,ed,sing, DISORDER, OFF-CENTER
confusion, STATE OF DISORDER, OFF-CENTER
congectivitis, conjunction(ivitis)
conger, conjure
congest,*,ed,ting,tible,tive,tion, TOO MUCH WITHIN A SMALL SPACE/ PLACE "prefixes: de"
congestun, congest(ion)
conglomerate,*,ed,ting,tion, GATHERED INTO MASS
congradulashen, congratulation
congratulate,*,ed,ting,tion, WISH ONE WELL, COMPLIMENT
congratulation,*, EXPRESS WISHING ONE WELL, COMPLIMENT
congregate,*,ed,ting,tion, GATHERING, ASSEMBLY
congregation,*,nal, TO GATHER, ASSEMBLY
congress,ssional,ssionally, LEGISLATIVE ASSEMBLY TO PROMOTE A GROUPS INTERESTS
congrewedy, congruent(uity)
congrewes, congruous
congrewint, congruent
congrewity, congruent(uity)
congrigate, congregate
congris, congress
congruedy, congruent(uity)

congruent,nce,ncy,ntly,uity,uties, AGREEMENT, CONSISTENCE(CY) "prefixes: in/non"
congrugashun, congregation
congrugate, congregate
congruous,sly,sness, AGREEMENT, CONSISTENCE(CY) "prefixes: in"
conifer,*, TREE GROUP
coning, cunning / con(nning)
conjesten, congest(ion)
conjugal,lity,lly, RELATION WITH PARTNER/MATE
conjugate,*,ed,ting,tion,tive, RELATION WITH PARTNER/MATE
conjunctavitis, conjunction(ivitis)
conjunction,*,nal,nally,ivitis, UNIFICATION, BRING TOGETHER
conjunkshen, conjunction
conjure,*,ed,ring, CREATE/ CONSPIRE
conkaf, concave
conkafety, concave(vity)
conkavudy, concave(vity)
conker, conquer
conklude, conclude
conkrete, concrete
conkur, conquer
conkushen, concussion
conkwest, conquest
connasure, connoisseur
connect,*,ted,ting,tive,tivity,tion, BOND, ASSOCIATE, BRING TOGETHER "prefixes: dis/un"
connection,*, ACT OF BRINGING TOGETHER, LINK, BOND
conniseur, connoisseur
connoisseur,*, SPECIALIZES, TRAINED, WELL-VERSED IN SOMETHING SUCH AS THE FINE ARTS
conoseur, connoisseur
conosieur, connoisseur
conosure, connoisseur
conphert, comfort
conquer,*,red,ring, OBTAIN BY FORCE
conquest,*, WIN BY WILL
consacrashen, consecrate(tion)
consacrate, consecrate
consacration, consecrate(tion)
consalidate, consolidate
consaquently, consequent(ly)
conscientious,sly,sness, WITH UNSELFISH MOTIVES
conscious,sly,sness, AWARE OF PHYSICAL REALITY "prefixes: non/ semi/sub/un"

consdatute, constitute
conseal, conceal
consecrate,*,ed,ting,tive,tor,tory,tion, tive, MAKE SACRED/HOLY "prefixes: de"
consecutive,ely,eness, DIRECTLY FOLLOWING ANOTHER "prefixes: in"
consedarashen, considerate(tion)
conseduration, considerate(tion)
conseed, conceit / concede
conseet, conceit / concede
conseevable, conceivable
conseeve, conceive
conseinshus, conscientious
conseintious, conscientious
consekcutive, consecutive
consekwential, consequent(ial)
consekwently, consequent(ly)
consel, conceal / council / counsel
consemate, consummate
consensus,ual,ually, AGREEMENT, MUTUAL CONSENT
consent,*,ted,ting, YIELD OR COMPLY
consentrate, concentrate
consentric, concentric
consepshun, conception
consept, concept
conseption, conception
conseptual, conceptual
consequence,*,nt, REACTION TO AN ACTION "prefixes: in"
consequent,*,tly,ntial,ntially,ntiality, ntialness,ntialist,ntialism, REACTION TO AN ACTION "prefixes: in"
consern, concern
consert, concert
conservation,nist,nism, TO PRESERVE/ PROTECT
conservative,*,ely,eness,vism, PRACTICES RESTRAINT "prefixes: neo/semi"
conservator,*,ry,ries,rial,rship, PROTECTOR/GUARDIAN
conservatory,ries, A SCHOOL OF MUSIC, GREENHOUSE
conserve,*,ed,ving,vatist,vative,vator, vatize,vation, TO PRESERVE/ PROTECT/RESTRAIN
conseshun, concession
consestintly, consistent(ly)
conset, conceit / concede
consetion, concession

consev, conceive
consevable, conceivable
conseve, conceive
conshas, conscious
conshus, conscious
consider,*,red,ring,rable,rate, ENGAGE IN THOUGHT "prefixes: in/un"
considerate,ely,eness,ation, ENGAGE IN THOUGHT "prefixes: in"
consierge, concierge
consignment,*, GIVING SOMEONE A PERCENT FOR SELLING YOUR WARES
consikwense, consequence
consil, conceal / council
consilation, consolation
consimate, consummate
consinent, consonant
consinment, consignment
consintrate, concentrate
consintric, concentric
consiquence, consequence
consirvation, conservation
consirvator, conservator
consirvatory, conservatory
consirve, conserve
consise, concise
consist,*,ted,ting,tence,tent, COMPOSED OF
consistence,cy,cies, HOW FLUID, VISCOUS "prefixes: in"
consistency, consistence(cy)
consistent,tly, COMPOSED OF "prefixes: in"
consolation,*, TO OFFER SOLACE/ SUPPORT FOR EFFORT (or see constellation)
console,*,ed,ling,lable,latory,er,lingly, SOOTHE, OFFER SUPPORT, CABINET FOR ELECTRONICS (or see counsel/ council) "prefixes: dis/in"
consolidate,*,ed,ting,tion, PUT ALL TOGETHER
consonant,*, LETTERS IN ENGLISH WORDS THAT AREN'T VOWELS
consoom, consume
conspearusy, conspiracy
conspicuous,sly,sness, OBVIOUS, STRIKING "prefixes: in"
conspikuos, conspicuous
conspikyous, conspicuous
conspiracy,cies, A GROUP OF PEOPLE PLOTTING AN EVENT TO USPSET STATUS QUO

constancy, DILIGENT/REPEATEDLY CONSISTENT
constant,*,tly,ncy, UNIFORM, UNCHANGING "prefixes: in"
constatushen, constitution
constatute, constitute
constellation,*, NAME FOR GROUPED CELESTIAL STARS (or see consolation)
constense, constancy
constetute, constitute
constilashen, constellation
constilation, constellation
constint, constant
constipashen, constipation
constipation, RESTRICTED BOWEL MOVEMENT
constitushen, constitution
constitute,*,ed,ting,tion, SET-UP/ CREATE/ESTABLISH "prefix: re"
constitution,*,nal, WRITTEN RULES/ PRINCIPLES/ REGULATIONS "prefixes: un"
constrict,*,ted,ting,tion,tive, PREVENT FROM PROPER MOVEMENT
construct,*,ted,ting,tive,tively,tion, tional,tionally, MOLD/FORM/ CREATE "prefixes: de/re"
construction,nal,nally, BUILDING/ FORMING "prefixes: mis/re"
constulashen, constellation
constulation, constellation
constupashen, constipation
consucrat, consecrate
consukwenshul, consequent(ial)
consukwently, consequent(ly)
consukwinse, consequence
consulashen, consolation
consulation, consolation
consult,*,ted,ting,tant,tation,table, tative,tatively,ter, COMMUNICATE WITH SOMEONE WHO IS SEEKING ADVICE
consultashen, consult(ation)
consumate, consummate
consume,*,ed,er,erism,ming,mable, mption,mptive, DECOMPOSE OR DESTROY, INGEST, MAKE USE OF
consummate,*,ed,ting, COMPLETE, FULFILL
consumpshen, consumption
consumption,ive, USED, DIGESTED, DECOMPOSED
consumshen, consumption

consunent, consonant
consuquential, consequent(ial)
consurt, concert
consurvation, conservation
consurvator, conservator
consurvatory, conservatory
consurve, conserve
contact,*,ted,ting, TOUCHING, ASSOCIATION WITH
contagious,sly,sness, SPREAD TO OTHERS
contain,*,ned,ning,ner,nment, HOLD WITHIN
contaminate,*,ed,ting,ant,tion, SOMETHING INCLUDED WHICH DOESN'T BELONG AT ALL "prefixes: de"
conteguis, contiguous
contemplate,*,ed,ting,tion,tive,tively, tiveness, TO OBSERVE THOROUGHLY
contemporary,ries,riness, REFLECTIVE OF CURRENT TIMES "prefixes: non"
contempt,tible,tibleness,tibly,tuous, tuously, THE STATE OF BEING DISHONORED/DISRESPECTED
contend,*,ded,ding,der, CHOOSE OR FORCED TO DEAL WITH, FACE OFF
content,*,ted,tedly,tedness,tment, THAT WHICH IS CONTAINED WITHIN, SATISFIED "prefixes: dis"
contenual, continue(ual)
contenuense, continuance
contenuisly, continue(uously)
contenule, continue(ual)
contest,*,ted, DISPUTE, FOR SUPERIORITY "prefixes: in"
context,ture, INTERWOVEN MEANING IN TEXT
contiguis, contiguous
contiguous,sly,sness, NEIGHBORING/ SHARING A BORDER
contimplate, contemplate
contimporary, contemporary
continent,*,tal, LAND MASS "prefixes: intra/sub"
continet, continent
contingent,*,nce,ncy,ncies, MAY HAPPEN IF...
contint, content
continuance, POSTPONEMENT TO CONTINUE AT A FUTURE DATE
continuants, continuance

continue,*,ed,uing,ual,ually,uation, uouse,uously,uousness,uity, KEEP GOING "prefixes: dis"
contorshenist, contortionist
contortionist,*, FLEXIBLE ACTS WITH THE BODY
contour,*,red,ring, THE SHAPE/FORM OF OUTLINE
contra, PREFIX INDICATING 'AGAINST' MOST OFTEN MODIFIES THE WORD
contraception,ive, FOR PREVENTION OF PREGNANCY
contract,*,ted,ting,tor,tual,tive,tion, tional,tionary, WRITTEN OBLIGATION OF SERVICE "prefixes: non/sub"
contraction,*,nal,nary, MUSCLES TIGHTENING, COMBINATION OF WORDS
contradict,*,ted,ting,tion,tory, CONTRARY/OPPOSE/DENY
contrak, contract
contrakshen, contraction
contrary,ries,rily,riness,rian,riety,rieties, PROVE OPPOSITE, DENY "prefixes: sub"
contrast,*,ted,ting,tingly,tive,tively, tiveness,table,tably, COMPARING DIFFERENCES
contraversy, controversy
contravert, controvert
contravertible, controvert(ible)
contrebute, contribute
contrery, contrary
contribute,*,ed,ting,tion,tive,tory, GIVE, LEND
contrition, AMENDING SIN WITH PRAYER
contro, PREFIX INDICATING 'AGAINST' MOST OFTEN MODIFIES THE WORD
control,*,lled,lling,ller,llable,llably, llability, ATTEMPT TO GAIN ORDER "prefixes: bio/in/sub/un"
controversy,sies,sial, DIFFERENCE IN OPINION, DEBATE
controvert,*,ted,ting,ter,tible,tibly, DEBATE STRONGLY AGAINST "prefixes: in"
contrudik, contradict
contrusepshun, contraception
contumplate, contemplate
contunent, continent
conture, contour
conufir, conifer

conva, convey
convalescence,nt, RECOVERING HEALTH
convay, convey
convayer, convey(or)
convelesents, convalescence
convene,*,ed,ning, CALL TO APPEAR, MEET
convenient,nce,nces, EASE OF FACILITIES, COMFORT "prefixes: in"
convense, convince
convention,*,nal, PEOPLE GATHERING, AN ASSEMBLY "prefixes: non/un"
convenyant, convenient
convenyut, convenient
conversashen, conversation
conversation,*,nal,nally,nalist, COMMUNICATING THOUGHTS
converse,es,sing,sant, EXCHANGE INFORMATION, MADE OPPOSITE/ REVERSE
conversion,*, CHANGED IN ONE FORM OR ANOTHER "prefixes: bio"
convert,*,ted,ting,ter,rsion, OF CHANGE, TRANSFORM "prefixes: in"
convertible,*,bility, CHANGE FROM ONE FORM TO ANOTHER, VEHICLE WITH REMOVABLE ROOF
convex,xes,xed,xedly,xedness,xing,xly, xity,xities, CURVING OUTWARD "prefixes: bi/sub"
convey,*,yed,ying,yable,yance,yances, yancing,yor, TRANSFER OF PEOPLE/ ITEMS/MEANING/EXPRESSION "prefix: re"
convicshen, convict(ion)
convict,*,ted,ting,tion, HAVING BEEN FOUND GUILTY/AT FAULT
convilesense, convalescence
convince,*,ed,cing, TO PERSUADE SOMEONE TO YOUR OPINION "prefixes: in"
convinshon, convention
convintion, convention
convirsation, conversation
convirse, converse
convirt, convert
convulesense, convalescence
convulesent, convalescent
convulgin, convulsion
convulshen, convulsion
convulsion,*,sive,sively, INTENSE MUSCLE CONTRACTION

convurgin, conversion
convursashen, conversation
convursation, conversation
convurtable, convertible
coocoo, cuckoo
cood, could
coodent, couldn't
cooger, cougar
cook,*,ked,king, PREPARE FOOD "prefixes: pre"
cookie,*, SWEET CAKE TREAT
cool,*,led,ling,lingly,lly,lness,ler, BETWEEN WARM/COLD TEMPERATURE, EXPRESSION OF APPRECIATION "prefixes: pre/sub/un/under"
cooler,*, COLD CONTAINER FOR FOOD
coop,*,ped, SMALL CAGE FOR SMALL ANIMALS (or see co-op/coup)
cooperate,*,ed,ting,tion,tive, UNITE TO PRODUCE
coordinate,*,ed,ting,ely,eness,tive,tion,tor, ORGANIZE FOR DESIRED RESULTS, LINE SYSTEM "prefixes: in/un"
cooth, couth
cop,*,pped,pping,pper, SLANG FOR "POLICE", RUN OUT OF ENERGY (or see co-op/coup/coop/cope/copy)
copbord, cupboard
cope,*,ed,ping, TO DEAL WITH STRESS, SHAPE/MATCH (or see co-op/coup/coop/copy)
coper, copper
copeur, copy(pier)
copi, copy
copitchulate, capitulate
copler, coupler
copol, couple
copper,*,ry, METAL
copulate,*,ed,ted,tion, PHYSICAL SEXUAL UNITY
copur, copper
coputr, computer
copy,pies,pied,ying, TO REPRODUCE
copyuter, computer
cor, TO TRICK, PREFIX INDICATING 'WITH/TOGETHER' MOST OFTEN MODIFIES THE WORD (or see core/car)
coraborate, corroborate
coragated, corrugate(d)
coral, OCEAN REEF ANIMALS
corc, cork

corchal, cordial
cord,*, STRANDS WOVEN/TWISTED TOGETHER (or see chord/quart(s)/quartz)
cordaroy, corduroy
cordial,lity,lness,lly, GRACIOUS, KIND, A LIQUEUR
cordinate, coordinate
cordunate, coordinate
corduroy, RIBBED MATERIAL
core,*,ed,ring, THE CENTER OF (or see corp)
corect, correct
coredor, corridor
corelate, correlate
cores, core(s) / chorus / caress
corespond, correspond
corgul, cordial
coridor, corridor
corigate, corrugate
corilate, correlate
coriner, coroner
corinery, coronary
coris, chorus / course
corispond, correspond
corjil, cordial
cork,*,ked, BARK FROM A TREE (or see quark) "prefixes: un"
corn,*, GRAIN, ON TOE
cornacopia, cornucopia
cornea,al, PART OF EYE
corner,*,red,ring, WHERE WALLS OR LINES MEET, NO WAY OUT
cornia, cornea
cornikopea, cornucopia
cornol, colonel
cornucopia, HORN OF PLENTY
coroborate, corroborate
corode, corrode
corogan, corrode(osion)
corogen, corrode(osion)
corogin, corrode(osion)
corojin, corrode(osion)
coronary,ries, HEART ARTERIES
coroner,*, INVESTIGATES SUSPICIOUS DEATHS
coropt, corrupt
corosef, corrode(osive)
coroud, corrode
corp,*, NUMBER OF PEOPLE WORKING TOGETHER (or see core)
corparul, corporal
corpirate, corporate
corporal, OF THE PHYSICAL BODY

corporate,tion,ely, UNITE MANY INTO ONE "prefixes: in/non"
corpret, corporate
corpse,*, DEAD BODY
corpural, corporal
corpurate, corporate
corral,*, FENCED ENCLOSURE FOR ANIMALS (or see coral)
correct,*,ted,ting,tly,tion,tional,table, tible,tness,tor, TO SET RIGHT/STRAIGHT "prefixes: in/over"
correlate,*,ed,ting,tion, IF ONE... THEN THE OTHER
correspond,*,ded,ding,dence, SIMILAR/RELATED TO, COMMUNICATE WITH
corridor,*, NARROW PASSAGE
corroborate,*,ed,ting,tion,tive,tively,tor,tory, CAN BACK UP THE TRUTH WITH EVIDENCE
corrode,*,ed,ding,osion,osive,dant,dible,dibility, CHEMICAL EROSION, EATEN AWAY
corrugate,*,ed,ting, ALTERNATING BENDS, FORMS
corrupt,*,ted,ting,tion,tible,tibly,tibility,tibleness,tness, TO NEGATIVELY STEER OFF COURSE "prefixes: in"
cors, course / coarse / core(s)
corsage,*, FLOWERS TO WEAR, BODICE
corse, course / coarse / core(s)
corsog, corsage
corsoge, corsage
cort, cord / court / quart
cort-marshul, court-martial
corteks, cortex
cortex,xes,tices,tical,tically, INTERNAL ORGAN'S PROTECTIVE LAYER "prefixes: sub"
corts, cord(s) / court(s) / quart(s)
corudoor, corridor
corugate, corrugate
corul, choral / coral / corral / chorale
corulate, correlate
corunary, coronary
coruner, coroner
corupt, corrupt
coruspond, correspond
cos, cause / cuss
cosdodian, custodian
cosdum, costume
cosee, cozy
coshen, caution
cosher, kosher
coshis, cautious

coshun, caution
cosin, cousin
cosmic,cally, NOT OF THIS PHYSICAL PLANE
cosmopolitan, BELONGS TO THE WORLD, NO ATTACHMENT
cosmos, UNIVERSAL HARMONY
cospid, cuspid
cost,*,ting,tly, EXPENSE (or see coast/cause(d))
costard, custard
costem, custom
coster, coaster
costic, caustic
costodian, custodian
costom, custom / costume
costomer, customer
costomize, custom(ize)
costoom, costume
costume,*, GARMENTS TO SUIT A CHARACTER TYPE
cosy, cozy
cot,*, FOLDING BED (or see caught/coat/cut)
cotage, cottage
cotej, cottage
coten, cotton
cotn, cotton
coton, cotton
cottage,*, SMALL DWELLING
cotton, PLANT WHICH CLOTH IS PRODUCED FROM
cotuge, cottage
couc, caulk
couch,hes,hed,hing, FURNITURE, PUT-DOWN (or see coach)
coud, code / could
coued, coed
couers, coerce
couf, cough / cove
cougar,*, ANIMAL
cough,*,hed,hing, FORCEFULLY EXPEL AIR FROM LUNGS
cought, caught / cot / cough(ed)
could, PAST TENSE FOR THE WORD 'CAN'
could've, CONTRACTION OF THE WORDS 'COULD HAVE'
couldn't, CONTRACTION OF THE WORDS 'COULD NOT'
coulishun, coalition
coun, cone

council,*, A GROUP MEETING TO DISCUSS/MAKE DECISIONS (or see counsel/console)
counsel,*,led,ling,lor, GIVES ADVISE, PROVIDES INFORMATION (or see console/council)
counside, coincide
count,*,ted,ting,table,tless, ADD THE NUMBER OF THINGS "prefixes: dis/mis/re-/un"
counter,*,red,ring,ract, PREFIX INDICATING 'AGAINST' MOST OFTEN MODIFIES THE WORD, SURFACE FOR SERVING, SOMETHING THAT COUNTS, OPPOSING MOVE "prefixes: en"
country,ries, OUT OF THE CITY, COLLECTION OF STATES, NATION OF PEOPLE "prefixes: up"
county,ties, A GEOGRAPHICAL AREA
coup, QUICK/SUCCESSFUL MOVE (or see coop)
couple,*,ed,ling,er, PARTNERS, BRING TWO TOGETHER "prefixes: un"
coupler,*,ling, DEVICE FOR CONNECTING
coupon,*, REDEEM FOR CASH VALUE
coupurate, cooperate
courage,eous,eously,eousness, BRAVE IN FACING DANGER "prefixes: dis/en"
courier,*, MESSENGER
cours, course / coerce
course,*, PATH, IDEA, CONCEPT TO FOLLOW (or see coarse) "prefixes: dis/re"
coursive, coerce(cive)
coursment, coerce(ment)
court,*,ted,ting, ENCLOSED AREA, HALL/CHAMBER FOR SPORTS/CIVIC ACTIVITIES FOLLOW (or see quart)
court-martial,led,ling, MILITARY TRIAL
courteous,sly,sness, POLITE
courtesy,sies, POLITE BEHAVIOR "prefixes: dis"
cousin,*, KINSHIP, RELATIVE
cout, caught / cot / coat
couth, SOPHISTICATED "prefixes: un"
cova, kava
cove,*,ed,ving, NOOK, CAVE (or see coffee)
covenant,*, AGREEMENT, CONTRACT TO KEEP PROMISE "prefixes: un"

cover,*,red,ring,rage, TO HIDE/PROTECT "prefixes: dis/re/un/under"
coverage, ACT OF HIDING OR BEING PROTECTED
covert,tly,tness, UNDER COVER, DISGUISED, SHELTERED
covet, DESIRE WITHOUT REGARDS TO CONSEQUENCE
covrach, coverage
covunent, covenant
covurt, covert
cow,*, THE FEMININE OF VARIOUS SPECIES, BOVINE
coward,*,dly,dliness,dice, CANNOT BRAVELY FACE DANGER
cowch, couch
cowculus, calculus
cowerd, coward
cowkulate, calculate
cowl,*,ling, A HOOD (or see call)
cownder, counter
cownsul, council / counsel / console
cownt, count
cowntur, counter
cownty, county
cowurd, coward
coxs, coax
coyol, coil
coz, cause
cozmic, cosmic
cozmopoletin, cosmopolitan
cozmos, cosmos
cozy,zies,zily,ziness, COMFORTABLE, CONTENT, SNUG
crab,*, CRUSTACEAN, HARD SHELLED OCEAN ANIMAL
crachin, creation / crash(ing)
crack,*,ked,king, TO SPLIT APART, SLANG FOR A SERIOUSLY ADDICTIVE DRUG, A SOUND
cracker,*, YEASTLESS BISCUIT, FIREWORKS
crackle,*,ed,ling, SOUND, GLAZE ON POTTERY
cracol, crackle
crader, crater / creator
cradible, credible
cradle,*,ed,ling, BED FOR INFANT, HOLD IN ARMS, TOOL
cradul, cradle
crafe, crave
craft,*,ted,ting,ter,tily,tiness, KILL USING HANDS, VESSEL FOR TRAVEL

crain, crane
craink, crank
crak, crack
crakel, crackle
craker, cracker
cral, crawl
cram,*,mmed,mming, FORCE INTO A SPACE
cramp,*,ped,ping, CONFINES, MUSCLE CONTRACTIONS
crampt, cramp(ed)
cranberry,ries, EDIBLE BERRY
crane,*,ed,ning, A MACHINE, TO STRETCH OUT
craneum, cranium
crani, PREFIX INDICATING 'SKULL' MOST OFTEN MODIFIES THE WORD
cranio, PREFIX INDICATING 'SKULL' MOST OFTEN MODIFIES THE WORD
cranium,*,ia,ial, SKULL "prefixes: endo/intra"
crank,*,ked,king,ky, TOOL, SOMEONE IRRITABLE
cranny,nies, CREVICE, NOOK, CRACK
crany, cranny
craon, crayon
crap,*,pped,pping,ppy, GAME OF DICE, TIRED OUT (or see crepe)
crape, crepe / crap(ppy)
crase, crazy
crash,hes,hed,hing, SOUND, TO RUN INTO, OFF OF SOMETHING
crass,sness, COARSE, THICK, DENSE
crate,*,ed,ting, BOX, BOX UP
crater,*,red,ring, BOWL-SHAPED DEPRESSION, CONCAVE (or see creator)
crauch, crouch
craud, crowd
craul, crawl
craun, crown
craunec, chronic
craunekl, chronicle
crave,*,ed,ving, TO YEARN, DESIRE HEAVILY
crawl,*,led,ling, ON HANDS AND KNEES, MOVE SLOWLY, CROUCHED POSITION
crayon,*, WAX PENCIL
crazy,zier,ziest,zily,ziness, INSANE, INFATUATED
creachin, creation
creader, creator
creak,*,ked,king, NOISE (or see creek)

creal, creel
cream,my,mily,miness, FROM MILK, TO WHIP ON SOMEONE (or see creme)
creap, creep
creapy, creep(y)
crease,*,ed,sing, MAKE FOLDED LINES, MARK IN "prefixes: in"
creashun, creation
creasul, creosol
create, *,ed,ting,tive,tively,tiveness,tion,tivity, TO TURN THOUGHT INTO REALITY "prefixes: mis/pro/re"
createf, creative
creation,*,nist, ACT OF CREATING
creative,ely,eness,ion,vity, IMAGINE/ CREATE SOMETHING UNUSUAL "prefixes: un"
creator,*, ONE WHO TURNS THOUGHT INTO PHYSICAL REALITY
creature,*,ely, SOMETHING OTHER THAN HUMAN, ANIMATE, INANIMATE
creb, crib
crebeg, cribbage
crec, creek / creak
crecher, creature
crechor, creature
credable, credible
crededer, creditor
credenchol, credential
credential,*,led, TO VALIDATE CONFIDENCE, ASSURE OF AUTHENTICITY "prefixes: un"
creder, critter
credible,ly,bility,eness, WORTHY/ BELIEVABLE "prefixes: in"
credibul, credible
credider, creditor
credinshul, credential
credisize, criticize
credit,*,ted,ting,table,tor, RECORD OF HANDLING OTHER'S MONEY/ SPENDING/EARNINGS, ACCOUNT TO BORROW AGAINST "prefixes: ac/dis/un"
creditor,*, ONE WHOM MONEY IS OWED TO
creduble, credible
creducal, critical
creecher, creature
creek,*, SMALL STREAM/TRIBUTARY (or see creak)
creel, FISH BASKET, OF SEWING MACHINES

creen, careen
creenkul, crinkle
creep,*,rept,ping,py,per, SOMETHING WHICH CAUSES FEARFUL SENSATION, TO SNEAK UP
creisote, creosote
creke, creak / creek
crekit, cricket
cremate,*,ed,ting,tion,tor,torium, BURN A BODY TO ASH
creme, LIKE CREAM (or see cream)
cremenul, criminal
cremson, crimson
creng, cringe
crenium, cranium
crenj, cringe
crenkle, crinkle
creosol, BLACK, FROM TAR AND RESIN (or see creosote)
creosote, FROM WOOD TAR USED FOR PRESERVATIVE/ANTISEPTIC (or see creosol)
crep, creep / crepe
crepe,*, THIN PAPER, FABRIC (or see creep)
creple, cripple
crept, PAST TENSE FOR THE WORD "CREEP"
creptic, cryptic
crepy, creep(y)
crescendo,*,di, GRADUAL/GROWING/ INCREASING
crescent,*, SHAPE OF QUARTER MOON
crescross, crisscross
crese, crease
cresendo, crescendo
cresent, crescent / croissant
cresmas, christmas
cresmus, christmas
crest,*,ted,ting, TOP/CROWN/PEAK
cresunt, crescent / croissant
cretable, credible
creteek, critique
creteke, critique
cretible, credible
cretik, critic
cretir, critter / creator
cretisize, criticize
creusol, creosol
creusote, creosote
crevasse,*,ed,sing, FISSURE OF GLACIER/RIVER (or see crevice)
crevice,*, CRACK/FISSURE (or see crevasse)

crevus, crevasse crevice
crew,*, GANG/BODY OF PEOPLE (or see cruise) "prefixes: un"
crewd, crude
crews, cruise / crew(s)
crewsade, crusade
crewshul, crucial
crewsufix, crucifix
crewton, crouton
criasol, creosol
criasot, creosote
crib,*,bbed,bbing,bbage, ENCLOSURE/ CONTAINER, CHEAT SHEET
cribach, cribbage
cribage, cribbage
cribbage, GAME, CARDS
cribd, crib(bbed)
cribeg, cribbage
cric, creek / creak
crichur, creature
cricket,*, INSECT
crid, cried
cridenshols, credential(s)
cridentials, credential(s)
crider, critter
cridik, critic
criducal, critical
cridusize, criticize
cried, PAST TENSE FOR THE WORD "CRY"
cries, PAST TENSE FOR THE WORD "CRY"
crik, creek / creak
criket, cricket
crim, crime / cream / creme
crime,*, ACT AGAINST MAN'S LAWS
crimenal, criminal
criminal,*,lly, ONE WHO VIOLATED MAN'S LAWS
crimson, COLOR
cringe,*,ed,ging, RECOIL IN POSTURE, RETRACT
crinj, cringe
crinkle,*,ed,ling, NOISE, CRUMPLE
criple, cripple
cripol, cripple
cripple,*,ed,ling,ler, LAME, DISABLE
criptic, cryptic
criquet, cricket / croquet
crisanthemom, chrysanthemum
criscross, crisscross
crisis,ses, TURNING POINT IN LIFE
crismas, christmas
crismus, christmas

crisont, croissant
crisp,ply,piness,py, BRITTLE, FRESH
crisscross,sses,ssed,ssing, TWO LINES THAT INTERSECT TO FORM AN "X"
cristal, crystal
cristashen, crustacean
cristl, crystal
cristolize, crystal(ize)
criter, critter
critic,*,cal,cize,cism,ique, ONE WHO PASSES JUDGEMENT
critical,cally,calness, BEING JUDGEMENTAL "prefixes: sub/un"
criticize,*,ed,zing,ism, TO PROVIDE PERSONAL JUDGEMENT
critique,*,ed,uing, PROVIDE WRITTEN OPINION
critir, critter
critter,*, NON-HUMAN CREATURE
criz, cries
croak,*,ked,king, FROG SOUND, TO DIE
croan, crone
croch, crutch
crochet,*,ted,ting, KNIT WITH NEEDLE
crock,*,kery, KETTLE, POT, DEROGATORY RESPONSE (or see croak)
crocodile,*, LARGE BROWN REPTILE
crocus, FLOWER
croissant,*, FRENCH PASTRY
crok, crock / croak
crokedile, crocodile
croket, croquet / croquette
crokudile, crocodile
crol, crawl
crom, crumb
crombl, crumble
crompl, crumple
cronalogical, chronology(gical)
cronch, crunch
crone,*, AGED WOMAN WITH WISDOM
cronec, chronic
cronecal, chronicle
cronological, chronology(gical)
cronuc, chronic
cronucl, chronicle
crony,nies, FRIENDS, BUDDIES
crook,*,ked,kedly,kedness,kery, DISHONORABLE PERSON, A BEND/ HOOK "or see croak"
croose, cruise / crew(s)
crop,*,pped,pping, YIELD IN FIELD, SUDDEN APPEARANCE "prefixes: over"

croquet, GAME (or see croquette)
croquette, PREPARED FOOD (or see croquet)
cros, cross / crow(s)
crosant, croissant
croshay, crochet
cross,sses,ssed,ssing, TWO LINES PERFORMING INTERSECTION "prefixes: un"
crost, cross(ed) / crust
crostashen, crustacean
crotch,hless, WHERE LEGS MEET THE TORSO, FORK OF SOMETHING
crouch,hes,hed,hing, HUDDLE, SQUAT, CRINGE
croud, crowd
croun, crown / crone
crouton, SMALL TOAST
crow,*,wed,wing, BOAST, ROOSTER SOUND
crowch, crouch
crowd,*,ded,ding, BODIES CLOSE TOGETHER "prefixes: over"
crowkus, crocus
crown,*,ned,ning, PEAK, CREST, TOP, HEAD ADORNMENT "prefixes: un"
crowshay, crochet
crowtch, crouch
cru, crew
cruc, crook
cruch, crutch
crucial, UPMOST IMPORTANCE
crucifix,xion, PERTAINING TO CHRISTIAN CROSS
crucs, crux
crude,er,est,ely,eness, NEED FURTHER DEVELOPMENT
crudenshul, credential
crudinshuls, credential(s)
crue, crew
cruise,*,ed,sing,er, MOVE ABOUT IN CAR/BOAT FOR PLEASURE (or see crew)
cruke, crook
cruks, crux
crumb,*,ble, TINY BITS OF SOMETHING
crumble,*,ed,ling,ly, FALL APART IN PIECES
crumple,*,ed,ling, WRINKLE, SQUEEZE OR FORM CREASES
crunch,hes,hed,hing,hy,hiness, TO BREAK, WRINKLE
crupt, corrupt

crusade,*,ed,ding,er, MOVEMENT WITH ASSERTIVE INTENT
cruse, cruise / crew(s)
crusendo, crescendo
crush,hes,hed,hing,her,hable, TO SMASH
crushul, crucial
crust,*,ty,ted,tal,tless, PASTRY LINING, PLANETARY GEOLOGY "prefixes: en"
crustacean,*,eous, WATER ANIMAL, ANTHROPOD
crutch,hes, TOOL FOR SUPPORT
cruteek, critique
cruteke, critique
cruton, crouton
crux,xes, TROUBLE, CROSS
cry,ries,ried,ying, VERBAL SOUND, EMOTIONAL RELEASE
cryptic,cally,calness, CODES TO CONCEAL OR HIDE
crysis, crisis
crystal,*,llize,llized,llizing,llizability, llizable,llization,llizer,lline, llinity, llite, OF OR LIKE CLEAR QUARTZ ROCK
cshel, seashell
cu, cue
cuadrent, quadrant
cuagmayer, quagmire
cuaint, quaint
cuak, quake
cual, quail
cualify, qualify
cuality, quality
cuam, qualm
cuandry, quandary
cuantify, quantify
cuantity, quantity
cuarel, quarrel
cuarentin, quarantine
cuark, quake
cuasar, quasar
cuasi, quasi
cuazar, quasar
cubby,bies, SMALL, SNUG SPACE
cube,*,ed,bic,bicle,bicles, SHAPE WHERE ALL SIDES ARE THE SAME, MATHEMATICAL EXPRESSION (or see cubby)
cubek, cubic
cubekle, cubicle
cubic, OF A CUBE, MATHEMATICAL EXPRESSION

cubicle,*, AREA SECTIONED OFF, SMALL SPACE
cubird, cupboard
cuburd, cupboard
cubuse, caboose
cuc, cook
cuce, cook / kook(y) / cookie
cuci, kook(y) / cookie
cuckoo,*,oed,oing, BIRD, CRAZY
cucu, cuckoo
cucumber,*, VEGETABLE
cucune, cocoon
cud, WHAT A COW CHEWS (or see could/cue(d)/cute)
cudaver, cadaver
cuddle,*,ed,ling,er,ly, HOLD SNUGGLY
cudent, couldn't
cudet, cadet
cudev, could've
cudint, couldn't
cudle, cuddle
cudov, could've
cudv, could've
cue,*,ed,uing, SIGNAL/SIGN, SOMETHING WHICH DISTINGUISHES "prefixes: mis"
cueic, quake / quick
cueint, quaint
cueisar, quasar
cueizar, quasar
cuek, quake
cuel, quail
cuen, queen
cuepon, coupon
cuerc, quirk
cueshten, question
cuf, cuff
cufer, cover
cuferege, coverage
cuff,*,fed,fing, FIST BLOW, ON SLEEVES, ON CREDIT, RESTRAINT FOR WRISTS/ANKLES
cuger, cougar
cugole, cajole
cuil, quill
cuilt, quilt
cuin, queen
cuintuplet, quintuplet
cuir, queer
cuirk, quirk
cuisine, FINE COOKING
cuit, quit / quite
cuiver, quiver
cuk, cook / cock / kook

cuke, cook / cookie / kook
cuki, kook(y) / cookie
cukoon, cocoon
cuku, cuckoo
cukumber, cucumber
cul, cool
cul-de-sac,*, BULB SHAPE AT END OF STREET WITH EXIT/ENTRANCE BEING THE SAME
culagen, collision / collagen
culamity, calamity
culander, colander
culapse, collapse
culejet, collegiate
culekshun, collection
culekt, collect
culektur, collect(or)
culenary, culinary
culendjula, calendula
culer, color / cooler
culide, collide
culidescope, kaleidoscope
culigen, collision
culinary, ART OF FOOD PREPARATION
culindula, calendula
culishun, collision
culition, collision
cull,*,lled,lling,ller, TO SEPARATE OUT FROM OTHERS, CHOOSE, GLEAN (or see cool)
culmenate, culminate
culminate,*,ed,ting,tion, CLIMAX/ GREAT HEIGHT
culoge, collage
culokweul, colloquial
culone, cologne / colon
culoneul, colonial
culoquial, colloquial
culor, color
culostimy, colostomy
culosul, colossal
culprit,*, ONE WHO COMMITTED AN OFFENSE
culsher, culture
cult, GROUP OF PEOPLE WITH FIRM RELIGIOUS BELIEFS
cultavashen, cultivate(tion)
cultivashen, cultivate(tion)
cultivate,*,ed,ting,tion, DEVELOP/ FACILITATE GROWTH OF SOMETHING
cultsher, culture

culture,*,ral,rally, ESSENCE OF A GROUP/SOCIETY, NURTURING "prefixes: ac/bi/en/sub"
culvert,*, A DRAIN
cum, WITH/TOGETHER, A SECRETION (or see come)
cum laude, METHOD OF COMPARING GRADUATES AGAINST ONE ANOTHER
cumaletive, cumulative
cumand, command
cumander, commander
cumber,*,red,ring,rsome,rsomely, rsomeness, BULKY/AWKWARD TO HANDLE/MANAGE "prefixes: en"
cumberbun, cummerbund
cumbine, combine
cumbuschen, combustion
cumbustible, combustible
cumedean, comedian
cumemorate, commemorate
cumenduble, commendable
cumenserite, commensurate
cuments, commence
cumerbund, cummerbund
cumershal, commercial
cumewtable, commute(table)
cumfert, comfort
cumfertible, comfortable
cuminduble, commendable
cumishen, commission
cumishioner, commissioner
cumitee, committee
cumitment, commitment
cumlota, cum laude
cummerbund,*, BAND FOR WAIST WORN WITH FORMALS
cumnee, company
cumodity, commodity
cumpartment, compartment
cumpashun, compassion
cumpashunet, compassionate
cumpass, compass
cumpatuble, compatible
cumpedidor, competitor
cumpel, compel
cumpeny, company
cumperible, comparable
cumperison, comparison
cumpersome, cumber(some)
cumpete, compete
cumpetitor, competitor
cumpient, compliant
cumpile, compile

cumplane, complain
cumplasens, complacence / complaisance
cumplecshun, complexion
cumpleks, complex
cumpleshun, completion
cumplete, complete
cumplians, compliant(nce)
cumply, comply
cumponent, component
cumpose, compose
cumposier, composure
cumposit, composite
cumpownd, compound
cumpreshun, compression
cumpresor, compressor
cumpress, compress
cumpuder, computer
cumpulsery, compulsory
cumpulshun, compulsion
cumpulsuve, compulsive
cumpute, compute
cumputer, computer
cumulative,ely,eness, ACCUMULATION/ COLLECTS
cumunal, communal
cumunikable, communicable
cumunyon, communion
cumutable, commute(table)
cunal, canal
cunclude, conclude
cunclusive, conclusive
cunclution, conclusion
cuncoct, concoct
cundem, condemn
cundense, condense
cundinse, condense
cundishen, condition
cundition, condition
cundolense, condolence
cundone, condone
cundukt, conduct
cunekshen, connection
cunekt, connect
cunfecshin, confection
cunferm, confirm
cunfeshun, confession
cunfess, confess
cunfetion, confetion
cunfetty, confetti
cunfide, confide
cunfiguration, configuration
cunfine, confine
cunfinment, confinement

cunfirm, confirm
cunflict, conflict
cunform, conform
cunfront, confront
cunfugin, confusion
cunfuse, confuse
cunfusion, confusion
cunglomurete, conglomerate
cungradulashen, congratulation
cungratshulate, congratulate
cungruint, congruent
cungunctavitis, conjunction(ivitis)
cuning, cunning
cunjest, congest
cunjested, congest(ed)
cunjestion, congest(ion)
cunjunctivitis, conjunction(ivitis)
cunjunkshen, conjunction
cunklusev, conclusive
cunklusion, conclusion
cunkokt, concoct
cunkushun, concussion
cunning,gly,gness, CRAFTY, SKILLFUL
cunsederashen, considerate(tion)
cunseed, concede
cunseel, conceal
cunseet, conceit
cunseeve, conceive
cunseevuble, conceivable
cunsent, consent
cunsentric, concentric
cunsepshual, conceptual
cunsepshun, conception
cunseption, conception
cunservutive, conservative
cunsiduration, considerate(tion)
cunsinment, consignment
cunsise, concise
cunsist, consist
cunsistency, consistence(cy)
cunsiter, consider
cunsole, console
cunsoludate, consolidate
cunsoom, consume
cunsoul, console
cunspikuos, conspicuous
cunstrict, constrict
cunstrucshen, construction
cunstruct, construct
cunsult, consult
cunsurn, concern
cuntamunate, contaminate
cuntane, contain
cunteguis, contiguous

cuntemporary, contemporary
cuntemt, contempt
cuntend, contend
cuntent, content
cuntenuense, continuance
cuntest, contest
cuntiguis, contiguous
cuntrakshen, contraction
cuntree, country
cuntrery, contrary
cuntrishen, contrition
cuntrol, control
cunvay, convey
cunvekt, convict
cunvence, convince
cunvene, convene
cunvenshen, convention
cunvenyent, convenient
cunverdable, convertible
cunvergin, conversion
cunvershen, conversion
cunvert, convert
cunvertable, convertible
cunvulgin, convulsion
cunvulshen, convulsion
cuoda, quota
cuonatative, quantitative
cuorum, quorum
cuoshent, quotient
cuot, quote
cuota, quota
cup,*,pped,pping, VESSEL/SHAPE LIKE SMALL BOWL (or see coop/coup)
cupal, couple
cupasity, capacity
cupboard,*, CABINET IN KITCHEN
cupcake,*, SMALL CAKE
cupe, coop
cupil, couple
cupitchulate, capitulate
cupler, coupler
cupon, coupon
cupul, couple
cupyuter, computer
curabirate, corroborate
curable,bility,eness,ly, CAN BE CURED "prefixes: in"
curach, courage
curader, curator
curage, courage
cural, corral
curamic, ceramic
curant, currant / current

curator,*, APPOINTED BY COURT, OVERSEER "prefixes: pro"
curb,*,bed,bing, FOR RESTRAINT, TO PROTECT SOMETHING
curcle, circle
curcumsize, circumcise
curd,*, USED TO MAKE CHEESE (or see cure(d))
curdesy, courtesy
curdeus, courteous
curdisy, courtesy
curdle,*,ed,ling, COAGULATING
cure,*,ed,ring,rative,rable, GET BACK TO EQUILIBRIUM/HEALTHY STATE (or see curry)
cureen, careen
cureer, career
curege, courage
curekt, correct
curekulum, curriculum
curency, currency
curensy, currency
curent, currant / current
cureosedy, curiosity
cureosity, curiosity
cures, cure(s) / care(s) / caress
curess, caress
cureur, courier
cureus, curious
cureusol, creosol
curf, curve
curfew,*, A TIME TO BE OFF THE STREETS
curfu, curfew
curi, curry
curiculum, curriculum
curier, courier
curige, courage
curiosity,ties, ACT OF BEING CURIOUS
curious,sly,sness, INQUISITIVE, QUESTIONING "prefixes: in"
curl,*,led,ling,ler,ly, A TWIST, LOOP, RINGLET "prefixes: un"
curnol, colonel / kernel
curnul, colonel / kernel
curoberate, corroborate
curoborate, corroborate
curode, corrode
curogen, corrode(osion)
curogun, corrode(osion)
curojin, corrode(osion)
curosef, corrode(osive)
curoshen, corrode(osion)
curotion, corrode(osion)

curoty, karate
curowse, carouse
currant, FRUIT, BERRY (or see current)
currency,cies, MONEY
current,*,tly,tness, AS OF NOW IN TIME, FLOWING, HOW WATER/AIR CARRIES ITSELF (or see currant) "prefixes: in/re/under"
curriculum,*,lar, LEARNING COURSES
curry,rried,rric, SPICE
cursash, corsage
curse,ed,sing,edness, SWEAR
cursive,ely, FLOWING HAND WRITING
curtail,lment, SHORTEN
curtain,*, TEMPORARY DIVIDER, CLOTH PROTECTION
curtale, curtail
curten, curtain
curtesy, courtesy
curteus, courteous
curtsy,sies,sied,ying, FEMALE BOW TO AUDIENCE
curtul, curdle
curuge, courage
curvature,*, PROFILE OF SHAPE
curve,*,ed,ving,vature, BEND WITH NO ANGLES "prefixes: in/up/re"
curvechure, curvature
cury, curry
cus, cuss
cusen, cousin
cuset, cassette
cushen, cushion
cushion,*,ned,ning, PADDING TO SOFTEN, FORM OF PROTECTION
cusin, cousin
cusp,*,pid,pidate,pidated,pidation, INTERSECTION OF TWO ARCS/ CURVES/POINTS
cuspid,*,dal,dated, TOOTH "prefixes: bi"
cuss,sses,ssed,ssing,ssedly,ssedness, sser, TO CURSE
custard,*, DESSERTS
custedy, custody
custodian,*,al,nship, GUARDIAN
custody,dies,dial,dian, UNDER CARE OF GUARDIAN, IMPRISONED
custom,*,mable,mize, TRADITION, HABIT "prefixes: ac"
customary,ries,rily,riness, ROUTINE, TRADITIONALLY
customer,*, CLIENT, PURCHASER

customize,*,ed,zing,zation, INDIVIDUAL SHAPE/DESIGN FOR DESIRED RESULTS
cut,*,tter,tting, CAUSE SEPARATION (or see cud/cute) "prefixes: in/over/un/under/upper"
cutastrufe, catastrophe
cute,er,test,tie, APPEALING TO THE EYE, SHREWD
cutev, could've
cuth, couth
cuticle,*, AROUND NAILS AND CELLS
cutlary, cutlery
cutlery, CUTTING TOOL, KNIVES
cutov, could've
cutukle, cuticle
cutv, could've
cuvenent, covenant
cuver, cover
cuvit, covet
cuvridge, coverage
cuwiat, quiet
cuzen, cousin
cuzn, cousin
cwuzene, cuisine
cyanide, ELEMENT FOR POISON/EXTRACTING GOLD
cybernetics, STUDY OF COMMUNICATIONS SYSTEMS
cyborg,*, HUMAN MODIFIED INTO PARTIAL ROBOT
cycle,*,ed,ling, REPEATING INTERVALS, A COURSE OF EVENTS, REVOLUTIONS "prefixes: bi/en/re"
cyclist,*, THOSE WHO RIDE TWO-WHEELED BIKES
cyclone,*,nic,nal,nically, CONICAL SHAPED WIND STORM
cylanoid, solenoid
cylinder,*,dric,drical,dricality,drically, GEOMETRIC SHAPE WHICH MAY BE MOBILE OR STATIONERY
cymbal,*,list, MUSICAL INSTRUMENT (or see symbol)
cympathetic, sympathetic
cympathy, sympathy
cynic,*,cal,cally,calness,cism, DISBELIEVER
cynical,lly,lness, BEING A DISBELIEVER
cyst,tic, SACK OF FLUID "prefixes: en"
cyt, PREFIX INDICATING 'CELL' MOST OFTEN MODIFIES THE WORD
cyto, PREFIX INDICATING 'CELL' MOST OFTEN MODIFIES THE WORD

czar,*, RULER OF PEOPLE
da, day / they
dab,*,bbed,bbing,bber, BLOT/DIP/BARELY TOUCH
dabate, debate
dabble,*,ed,ling,er, PARTICIPATE WITHOUT SERIOUS COMMITMENT
dabekable, despicable
dabelatate, debilitate
dabilutate, debilitate
dable, dabble
dabre, debris
dacend, descend / dissent / descent / decent
daciduous, deciduous
dacind, descend / dissent / descent / decent
daclare, declare
dacree, decree
dacrepit, decrepit
dacury, daiquiri
dad,*,ddy,ddies, TERM FOR 'FATHER' (or see that/date/they'd)
dada, data
dadu, data
dadukt, deduct
dadur, daughter
daduse, deduce
dae, day
daedy, deity
dafalt, default
dafeet, defeat
dafenative, definitive
dafensable, defensible
dafense, defense
dafeshansy, deficiency
daffy,ffily,ffiness, BEING SILLY
dafiants, defiance
dafide, divide
dafie, defy / daffy
dafiense, defiance
dafinative, definitive
dafindant, defendant
dafine, define
dafinse, defense
dafinsible, defensible
dafisable, divisible
dafishantsy, deficiency
dafishensy, deficiency
dafishent, deficient
dafisubilety, divisible(bility)
dafoleate, defoliate
daform, deform
dafraust, defrost

dafray, defray
dafrod, defraud
dafumation, defamation
dafunkt, defunct
dafur, defer
dafuze, diffuse
dafy, defy / daffy
dagavoo, dejavu
dager, dagger
dagger,*, SHARP INSTRUMENT
dagree, degree
dai, die / day / dye
daidy, deity
daily,lies, EVERY DAY (or see dally/dale)
dainty,tily,tiness, FRAGILE, DELICATE
daiquiri,*, MIXED RUM DRINK
dair, dare
dairy,ries, WHERE MILK IS
dairyar, derriere
daisy,sies, A FLOWER
daity, deity
dajavu, dejavu
dakary, daiquiri
daklare, declare
dakline, decline
dakorate, decorate(tion)
dakrate, decorate(tion)
dakree, decree
dakrepit, decrepit
dakury, daiquiri
dal, dale / dowel / doll / dole / they'll
dalar, dollar
dalay, delay
dale,*, VALLEY (or see daily/dalles/dell/dolly)
daleburite, deliberate
dalectable, delectable
dalema, dilemma
dalenkwent, delinquent
dalenquent, delinquent
daler, dollar
dalereus, delirious
daleshus, delicious
dalete, delete
dalfan, dolphin
dali, dolly
daliberate, deliberate
dalima, dilemma
dalinquent, delinquent
dalishus, delicious
dalite, delight / daylight
daliver, deliver
dalles, SHALLOW RIVER ROCK BOTTOM WITH RAPIDS (or see dowel/doll)

dally,llies,llied,llying, TO DABBLE IN, NOT SERIOUS (or see dale/daily/dolly)
daloot, dilute
dalugen, delusion / dilute(tion)
daluks, deluxe
dalushen, delusion / dilute(tion)
dalute, dilute
daluxe, deluxe
daly, daily / dally / dale
dam,*,mmed,mming, BARRIER AGAINST WATER (or see damn)
damage,*,ed,ging, TO HARM/ALTER NEGATIVELY
damand, demand
dameg, damage
damenish, diminish
dameno, domino
damenor, demeanor
damenshen, dimension
damented, demented
damention, dimension
damenyen, dominion
damestic, domestic
damig, damage
daminish, diminish
damino, domino
daminyun, dominion
damize, demise
damn,ned,ning,nable,nation, EXPRESSION OF FRUSTRATION (or see dam)
damolish, demolish
damonik, demon(ic)
damp,per,pest, MOIST "prefixes: un"
dampen,*,ned,ning,ner, TO MOISTEN
damper,*, CONTROLS FLOW
dampin, dampen
dampun, dampen
dampur, damper
damsel,*, YOUNG WOMAN
damsul, damsel
damug, damage
damzul, damsel
dan, then / than
danc, dank
dance,*,ed,cing,er, TO BODILY MOVE TO MUSIC
dancher, danger
dandreff, dandruff
dandruff, FLAKEY SKIN ON SCALP
danger,*,rous,rously,rousness, BEWARE OF IMMINENT HARM "prefixes: en"
dangle,*,er,ling,ly, TO SWING FREELY

dangul, dangle
danjur, danger
dank,kly,kness, UNPLEASANTLY DAMP
danominashun, denomination
danote, denote
danse, dance
dante, dainty
danty, dainty
daoderant, deoderant
daoderize, deodorize
daparsher, departure
dapart, depart
department, department
daparture, departure
dapend, depend
dapikt, depict
dapind, depend
dapindant, dependant / dependent
dapindence, dependence
dapleshin, depletion
daplete, deplete
daploma, diploma
daplomacy, diplomacy
daplorable, deplorable
daplore, deplore
daport, deport
dapose, depose
daposit, deposit
dapresheate, depreciate
dapreshen, depression
dapress, depress
daprive, deprive
darbe, darby
darbies, HANDCUFFS
darby,bies, PLASTERER'S TOOL
darc, dark
dare,*,ed,ring,ringly,ringness, HAVE COURAGE TO CHALLENGE (or see dairy)
dareair, derriere
darear, derriere
darect, direct
darection, direction
darectory, directory
darekshun, direction
darektory, directory
darelik, derelict
darevutive, derivative
darier, derriere
darivadev, derivative
darivative, derivative
darive, derive

dark,*,ker,kest,ken,kened,kness, OPPOSITE OF LIGHT "prefixes: semi"
darling,*,gly,gness, SOMEONE ENDEARING/ BELOVED
darn, TO SEW, SHORT FOR "OH, TOO BAD..."
dart,*,ted,ting, OF SPORT, MOVE WITH QUICK SPEED
darulik, derelict
dary, dairy
das, day(s) / daze / that(s)
dasal, dazzle
dasbikable, despicable
dasbite, despite
dasblay, display
dasburse, disperse / disburse
dascrepshun, description
dasdrakt, distract
dasdruction, destruction
dasdrust, distrust
dase, daisy / daze
dasease, decease / disease
daseet, deceit
daseeve, deceive
dasegin, decision
dasel, dazzle
dasember, december
dasenagrate, disintegrate
dasend, descend / dissent / descent / decent
dasendent, descendant
dasenshen, dissension/ descension
dasent, dissent / descent / decent / descend
dasentugrate, disintegrate
daservise, disservice
dasesd, decease(d) / disease(d)
dasese, decease / disease
daset, deceit
dasetful, deceit(ful)
daseve, deceive
dash,hes,hed,hing, SMALL AMOUNT OF, QUICKLY IN SHORT TIME, TEXT TYPE
dasidewus, deciduous
dasifur, decipher
dasigen, decision
dasijen, decision
dasile, docile
dasimbur, december
dasinagrate, disintegrate
dasind, descend / dissent / descent / decent
dasinshen, dissension/ descension

dasinshent, dissent(ient)
dasint, dissent / descent / decent / descend
dasipher, decipher
dasiple, disciple
daskreptef, descriptive
daskripshen, description
daskwalefy, disqualify
dasmiss, dismiss
dasosheate, dissociate
daspare, despair
daspekable, despicable
daspense, dispense
daspensible, dispensable
dasperse, disperse / disburse
daspikable, despicable
daspite, despite
daspize, despise
dasplay, display
daspondent, despondent
daspose, dispose
daspute, dispute
dasrebutuble, disreputable
dasrobe, disrobe
dastardly,dliness, COWARDLY
dasteengwish, distinguish
dastengwesh, distinguish
dastenkt, distinct
dastill, distill
dastingwish, distinguish
dastirdly, dastardly
dastort, distort
dastract, distract
dastress, distress
dastroy, destroy
dasturb, disturb
dasturdly, dastardly
dasul, dazzle
dasy, daisy
dat, date / that / dot
data, FACTS, INFORMATION
dataunt, detente
date,*,ed,ting, TIME REFERENCE, A SOCIAL OUTING WITH ANOTHER, A FRUIT "prefixes: up"
datective, detective
datekt, detect
datektif, detective
datektor, detector
datenshin, detention
dater, daughter
daterant, deterrent
datereate, deteriorate
daterent, deterrent

datereorate, deteriorate
datergent, detergent
daterminent, determine(nt)
datont, detente
datu, data
daturgent, detergent
daturjent, detergent
daturmen, determine
daturmenashen, determination
daturmenint, determine(nt)
daubt, doubt
dauder, daughter
daug, dog
daughter,*, FEMALE BORN/LEGALLY ENDOWED TO MOTHER/FATHER
daul, dowel / doll
daule, dolly
daulfen, dolphin
daulur, dollar
daun, don't / daunt / don(nned) / dawn(ed) / down
daunt,*,ted,ting,ter,tingly,tless,tlessly, tlessness, MAKE SOMEONE FEEL DISCOURAGED/UNSURE (or see don't/don(nned)/dawn(ed)) "prefixes: un"
daus, douse / dowse
dausil, docile
daut, doubt
dauter, daughter
dautful, doubt(ful)
dav, they've
davegen, division
davejin, division
davelop, develop
daversidy, diversity
daversudy, diversity
davert, divert
davesubility, divisible(bility)
davide, divide
davigen, division
davine, divine
davisable, divisible
davision, division
davize, device
davoid, devoid
davorse, divorce
davoshen, devotion
davout, devout
davurt, divert
davurzade, diversity
dawn,*,ned,ning, MORNING DAYBREAK (or see don/down)
dawrekt, direct

daws, douse / dowse
day,*, SUNRISE TO SUNRISE (or see daze)
dayede, deity
dayity, deity
dayjavue, dejavu
daylight, LIGHT IN THE DAY
daytont, detente
daze,ed, NOT OF CLEAR THINKING, CONFUSED (or see daisy/day(s))
dazeese, disease / daisy(s)
dazel, dazzle
dazzle,*,ed,ling, INFLUENCE BY UNUSUAL MEASURES
dcline, decline
ddukt, deduct
de, PREFIX INDICATING 'AWAY FROM/ DOWN FROM/REVERSE/ NEGATIVE' MOST OFTEN MODIFIES THE WORD (or see the/thee/they)
deacon,*,ness,nry,nries, OFFICIAL OF A CHURCH "prefixes: sub"
deactivate,*,ed,ting,tion,tor, STOP ACTION, DISSOLVE
deactovate, deactivate
dead,dly,dlier,dliest,den,dens,dened, dening,dener, PAST TENSE FOR THE WORD 'DIE', NO LONGER ALIVE/ FUNCTIONAL (or see deed/did) "prefixes: un"
deaden,*,ner,ning,ner, TO SEEM DEAD, NUMB (or see did(n't))
deadleist, dead(liest)
deaf,fen,fening,feningly,fness,fly, LOSS OF THE ABILITY TO HEAR
deakon, deacon
deaktevat, deactivate
deaktuvate, deactivate
deal,*,ler,ling,dealt, ARRANGEMENT BETWEEN PEOPLE, DO IN CARD GAME (or see dell/dill)
dealed, dealt
dealt, PAST TENSE FOR THE WORD "DEAL"
deam, deem
dean,*, HEAD OF FORMAL GROUP (or see den)
deanky, dinky
deap, deep
dear,rly,rness,rie, HEARTFELT (or see deer)
death,hless,hly, WHEN THE SPIRIT LEAVES THE BODY
debach, debauch

debasition, deposition
debate,*,ed,ting, ARGUE FACTS
debauch,hes,hed,hing,hment,hery, heries, CORRUPT, CHANGED FROM ORIGINAL DIRECTION
debauchury, debauch(ery)
debazishen, deposition
debelatate, debilitate
debelutat, debilitate
debenar, debonair
deber, deburr
debet, debit
debilitate,*,ed,ting,tion,tive, NOT UP TO PAR, WEAKEN
debinar, debonair
debir, deburr
debisition, deposition
debit,*,ted,ting, A DEBT OWING
debizeshen, deposition
debloma, diploma
deblomusy, diplomacy
debo, depot
deboch, debauch
debochury, debauch(ery)
debonair, CHARMING, LIKABLE, AIR OF CLASS
deboner, debonair
debosition, deposition
debotch, debauch
debozeshen, deposition
debozishen, deposition
debre, debris / deburr
debri, debris
debrief,*,fed,fing,fings, REPORT IN AFTER MISSION/EVENT
debris, GARBAGE, RUBBISH
debry, debris
debt,*,tor, IN THE STATE OF OWING TO ANOTHER
debth, depth
debtor, ONE WHO OWES ANOTHER (or see detour/deter)
debude, deputy
debunair, debonair
debunar, debonair
debunk,*,ked,king,ker, MAKE UNTRUE, PROVE FALSE
deburr,*,rred,rring, REMOVE BURRS/ ROUGH EDGES
debut,*,ted,ting, FIRST SHOWING TO THE PUBLIC (or see debit)
debutize, deputize
debuty, deputy

dec, PREFIX INDICATING "TEN" MOST OFTEN MODIFIES THE WORD (or see deck)
deca, PREFIX INDICATING "TEN" MOST OFTEN MODIFIES THE WORD (or see deck)
decade,*, TEN YEARS (or see decay(ed))
decadence,ncy, ON THE DECLINE/ DETERIORATE
decadent,tly, ON THE DECLINE/ DETERIORATE
decal,*, IMAGE OF PICTURE OR WORDS
decanter,*, VESSEL FOR STORAGE
decapitate,*,ed,ting,tion,tor, LOSS OF HEAD
decarate, decorate(tion)
decate, decade / decay(ed)
decay,*,yed,ying, DETERIORATE, CHANGE FROM ONE FORM TO ANOTHER
decease,*,ed, TO PASS AWAY, DEPART FROM THIS PHYSICAL REALITY (or see disease) "prefixes: pre"
decedent,*, PAST TENSE FOR THE WORD 'DECEASED' (or see decadent)
deceit,tful,tfully,tfulness, TO PURPOSELY MISLEAD
deceive,*,ed,ving,vingly,vable,vably, vableness,vability, TO PURPOSELY MISLEAD "prefixes: un"
decelerate,*,ed,ting,tion,tor, TO DECREASE SPEED
december, A MONTH OF THE YEAR (ENGLISH)
decency,cies, WHAT'S PROPER
decend, descend / decent
decension, descension
decent,tly,tness, RESPECTABLE (or see descent/ dissent)
decentralize,*,ed,zing,zation, TAKE FROM A FEW AND GIVE TO MANY, TO SHARE AROUND
deception,*,ive,ively,iveness, THE ACT OF PURPOSELY MISLEADING "prefixes: un"
deceptive,ely,eness, THE ACT OF PURPOSELY MISLEADING
decerate, decorate
dech, ditch
dechevled, dishevel(ed)
dechonary, dictionary
deci, PREFIX INDICATING "TENTH" MOST OFTEN MODIFIES THE WORD

decibel,*, MEASUREMENT OF SOUND WAVES
decide,*,ed,ding,edly,er,ision, FORM A CONCLUSION, PICK AN OPTION "prefixes: un"
deciduous, SHEDS ITS LEAVES IN THE FALL "prefixes: in"
decifur, decipher
decimal,*,lize,lized,lizing, A POINT TO SEPARATE NUMBERS
decimate,*,ed,ting, TO DESTROY, KILL ONE IN TEN
decimber, december
decind, descend / dissent / descent / decent
decint, descent / decent / dissent / descend
decintralize, decentralize
decipher,*,red,ring,rable,rer,rment, TO DECODE "prefixes: in"
decision,*,ive,ively,iveness, FINAL CONCLUSION "prefixes: in"
deck,*,ked,king, OUTDOOR FLOOR
deckorus, decorous
deckrotive, decorative
deckstarety, dexterity
decksterity, dexterity
deckstrus, dexterous
declaration,*,ive,tory, ANNOUNCEMENT, MAKE A STATEMENT
declare,*,ed,ring,rable,edly,ration, rations,rative,rator,ratory, ratorily, TO STATE/ANNOUNCE "prefixes: un"
decleration, declaration
decline,*,ed,ning,nation, DOWNWARD BEND/SLOPE
decode,*,ed,ding,dable,er, DECAY, TO TRANSFORM TO BASIC ELEMENTS
decompose,*,ed,sing,sition, DECAY, TO TRANSFORM TO BASIC ELEMENTS
decon, deacon
decorashun, decoration
decorate,*,ed,ting,tor,tion,tive, ADORN, ORNAMENTAL "prefixes: re"
decoration, ADORNMENT, ORNAMENTAL
decorative,ely,eness, ADORNMENT, ORNAMENTAL
decorous,sly,sness, COMPATIBLE/ APPROPRIATE, DIGNIFIED "prefixes: in"

decorum, COMPATIBLE/APPROPRIATE, MATCHES "prefixes: in"
decoy,*, A FAKE TO FOOL OR MISLEAD
decradive, decorative
decrative, decorative
decrease,*,ed,sing, BECOME LESS THAN THE ORIGINAL "prefixes: non"
decree,*,eed,eeing,eeable, JUDICIAL/AUTHORITATIVE DECISION
decrepit,tly,tude,tate,tated,tating, tation,tness, WEAK/WORN/WASTED
decrese, decrease
decritive, decorative
decrous, decorous
decrutive, decorative
decsterity, dexterity
decudens, decadence
decudent, decedent / decadent
decumpose, decompose
decurate, decorate(tion)
ded, dead / deed / did
dedakashun, dedication
dedakate, dedicate
dedar, debtor
deden, didn't / den / deaden
dedicate,*,ed,ting,tion,tory,tive, APPROPRIATE, DEVOTE
dedication,*,nal, APPROPRIATE, DEVOTE
dedin, deaden
dedinate, detonate
dedir, debtor
dedle, dead(ly)
dedleist, dead(liest)
dedleur, dead(lier)
dedly, dead(ly)
dedlyest, dead(liest)
dednate, detonate
dedo, ditto
dedonate, detonate
dedor, debtor
dedriment, detriment
dedrument, detriment
deduce,*,ed,cing, DRAW CONCLUSION FROM EVIDENCE
deduct,*,ted,ting,tible,tibilty,tion,tive, SUBTRACT, TAKE AWAY "prefixes: non"
dedukashun, dedication
dedukate, dedicate
dedun, deaden

deed,*,ded, AN ACT/CONTRACT/AGREEMENT (or see dead) "prefixes: mis"
deel, deal
deeled, dealt
deem,*,med, JUDGED/BELIEVED/THOUGHT
deen, dean / den
deenge, dinghy / dingy
deenky, dinky
deep,per,pest,ply,pen,penly,pened, pness, BEYOND THE SURFACE, GREAT IN DIMENSION
deer, ANIMAL (or see dear)
def, deaf / thief
deface,*,ed,cing,eable,ement,er, ALTER THE FACE/FRONT OF
defakate, defecate
defalt, default
defamation,tory, INTENT TO INJURE ANOTHER'S CHARACTER
defame,*,ed,ming,mation,matory,er, INTENT TO INJURE ANOTHER'S CHARACTER
defanishun, definition
defanit, definite
defasit, deficit
defastate, devastate
default,*,ted,ting,ter, LEGALLY FAILING TO ANSWER, FAIL AN AGREEMENT
defeat,*,ted,ting,tism,tist, OVERCOME, OVERTHROW
defecate,*,ed,ting,tion,tor, CLEAR THE BOWELS
defechant, deficient
defect,*,ted,ting,tion,tor,tive, NOT USEFUL AS INTENDED, MARRED "prefixes: in"
defective,ely,eness, NOT USEFUL AS INTENDED
defector,*, ABANDON NATIVE STATE/COUNTRY
defecult, difficult
defekate, defecate
defekt, defect
defektive, defective
defektor, defector
defemation, defamation
defend,*,ded,ding, PROTECT
defendant,*, ONE WHO DEFENDS/PROTECTS AGAINST
defenet, definite
defenetly, definite(ly)
defenishun, definition

defense,*,sive,eless,elessly,elessness, PROTECT AGAINST ATTACK
defensible,eness,bility,ly, ABLE TO DEFEND "prefixes: in"
defenutef, definitive
defer,*,rred,rring,rrable,rence,rent,rrer, rential,rral,rment, DELAY, POSTPONE, YIELD TO ANOTHER (or see differ)
deferens, difference
deferensheate, differentiate
deferent, different
deferentiate, differentiate
defesit, deficit
defews, diffuse
defi, defy
defiance,nt,ntly, CHALLENGE, RESIST, OPPOSE
deficate, defecate
deficiency,cies, SHORT OF EXPECTATIONS/NEEDS, NOT ENOUGH
deficient,tly,ncy, LESS THAN EXPECTED/NEEDED
deficit,*, OWE MORE THAN WHAT'S AVAILABLE
deficult, difficult
defide, divide
defients, defiance
defikate, defecate
defimation, defamation
defind, defend
defindant, defendant
define,*,ed,ning, SET BOUNDARIES/RULES/BORDERS "prefixes: in/re"
defineshun, definition
definet, definite
definetion, definition
definetly, definite(ly)
definite,ely,eness,tive, FOR SURE, ABSOLUTELY
definition,*,nal, STATEMENT DESCRIBING BOUNDARIES/RULES/BORDERS
definitive,ely,eness, FOR CERTAIN, FINAL
definute, definite
defir, defer / differ
defishant, deficient
defishantsy, deficiency
defisit, deficit
defistate, devastate
deflashun, deflate(tion)

deflate,*,ed,ting,tion,tionary,tionist, REMOVE VOLUME/FULLNESS, REDUCE
deflect,*,ted,ting,tive,tor,tion, RICHOCHET OFF/ALTER COURSE/ DIRECTION OF SOMETHING
defoleate, defoliate
defoliate,*,ed,ting,tion,tor, LOSS OF LEAVES FROM PLANT
deforestation,*, REMOVE TREES FROM FOREST
deforistashun, deforestation
deform,*,med,ming,mation,medly, medness,mity, OF UNUSUAL/ ABNORMAL FORM
deforustashin, deforestation
defostate, devastate
defraud,*,ded,ding,der,dation,dment, ROB OF RIGHTS/PROPERTY
defraust, defrost
defray,*,yed,ying,yer,yal,yment,yable, MONETARY COMPENSATION/ ARRANGEMENT
defrense, difference
defrent, different
defrint, different
defrod, defraud
defrost,*,ted,ting,ter, REMOVE FROST/ICE
defruns, difference
defukate, defecate
defumashun, defamation
defunct, NO LONGER IN USE
defuneshun, definition
defunetle, definite(ly)
defunishun, definition
defunit, definite
defur, defer / differ
defurinse, difference
defurns, difference
defuse, diffuse
defusit, deficit
defustate, devastate
defuze, diffuse
defy,fies,fied,ying,fier, TO RESIST/DARE/CHALLENGE
deg, dig
degekt, deject
degenerate,*,ed,ting,tive,acy,ely,eness, BECOME LESS, OPPOSITE OF GETTING BETTER
deginerate, degenerate
degit, digit
degradashen, degrade(dation)

degrade,*,ed,ding,dable,dability,dation, LOWER/BREAK DOWN IN RANK/ STANDARDS/GRADE "prefixes: bio"
degree,*, MEASUREMENT OF STANDARD/ANGLES, SUM OF
degression,ive, LOWERING, DECREASING (or see digress(ion))
degrudashen, degrade(dation)
dehidrate, dehydrate
dehumanize,*,ed,zing,zation, REMOVE HEALTHY HUMAN CHARACTERISTICS
dehumidify,fies,fied,fying,fier,fication, REMOVE MOISTURE FROM THE AIR
dehydrate,*,ed,ting,tion,tor, REMOVE MOISTURE FROM
deity,ties, SUPREME BEING
dejavu, TWO WORDS (deja vu), SEEN BEFORE
deject,*,ted,ting,tedly,tedness,tion, DISPIRIT, DISCOURAGE
dejenurate, degenerate
dejinurate, degenerate
dejit, digit
dek, deck
deka, PREFIX INDICATING "TEN" MOST OFTEN MODIFIES THE WORD (or see deck)
dekad, decay(ed) / decade
dekadins, decadence
dekadint, decedent / decadent
dekal, decal
dekantur, decanter
dekaputate, decapitate
dekay, decay
deken, deacon
dekerashun, decoration
dekerate, decorate
dekin, deacon
deklare, declare
dekleration, declaration
dekline, decline
deklurashun, declaration
dekodable, decode(dable)
dekode, decode
dekompose, decompose
dekon, deacon
dekorashun, decoration
dekorate, decorate(tion) / decorate
dekorative, decorative
dekorus, decorous
dekoy, decoy
dekradashen, degrade(dation)
dekratev, decorate(tion) / decorative

dekrative, decorative
dekree, decree
dekrepit, decrepit
dekrese, decrease
dekrous, decorous
dekrudev, decorative
dekrus, decorous
dekrutive, decorative
deksderady, dexterity
deksdrus, dexterous
dekshunare, dictionary
deksterudy, dexterity
dekstrus, dexterous
dektion, diction
dekudens, decadence
dekudent, decedent / decadent
dekumpose, decompose
dekun, deacon
dekurashun, decoration
dekurater, decorate(tor)
del, deal / dell / dill
delacatesen, delicatessen
delacit, delicate
delacusy, delicacy
delagation, delegation
delakatesen, delicatessen
delaket, delicate
delay,*,yed,ying,yer, DETAIN, HINDER, PROLONG
deld, dealt
dele, deli
deleburant, deliberate
delecacy, delicacy
delectable,*,eness,bility,ly, HIGHLY PLEASURABLE
deled, dealt
delegate,*,ed,ting,tion,tor,ee,able, APPOINT AS REPRESENTATIVE, ENTRUST "prefixes: non"
delegation,*, TO DELEGATE, ASSEMBLY OF PEOPLE "prefixes: non"
delenkwent, delinquent
delenquent, delinquent
deler, deal(er)
delereus, delirious
delete,*,ed,ting,tion, REMOVE/UNDO "prefixes: un"
deleverens, deliverance
delf, delve
deli,*, A DELICATESSEN, STORE WITH VARIETY OF PREPARED FOODS/ MEATS

deliberate,*,ed,ting,eness,ely,tion, PURPOSEFUL, CAREFULLY THOUGHT OUT "prefixes: un"
deliburate, deliberate
delicacy,cies, OF REFINED QUALITY IN TASTE "prefixes: in"
delicate,*,ely,eness, FRAGILE, FINE QUALITY, CHOICE "prefixes: in"
delicatessen,*, STORE WITH VARIETY OF PREPARED FOODS/MEATS
delicious,sly,sness, EXQUISITE TASTE, HAPPY TO TASTE BUDS
deligation, delegation
delight,*,ted,ting,tful,tedly,tfully, tfulness, PROVIDE GREAT SATISFACTION (or see daylight)
delikatesen, delicatessen
deliket, delicate
delinquent,tly,ncy,ncies, FAILURE TO SATISFY AGREEMENT ON TIME
deliquet, delicate
delir, deal(er)
delirious,sly,sness, IRRATIONAL BEHAVIOR
delishus, delicious
delite, delight / daylight
deliver,*,red,ring,ry,rable,rability,rer, rance, TO SEND/PRESENT ITEMS SUCH AS GOODS/THOUGHTS/ ARTICLES
deliverance,*, TO BE RESCUED, AN ANNOUNCEMENT
dell, A HOLLOW/VALLEY (or see deal/ dill)
deloot, dilute
delor, deal(er)
delt, dealt
delugashun, delegation
delugen, delusion / dilute(tion)
delukatesen, delicatessen
delukit, delicate
deluks, deluxe
delukusy, delicacy
delur, deal(er)
delusion,nal, PAST TENSE FOR THE WORD "DELUDE", BEING MISLED, HAVING FALSE IMPRESSION
delute, dilute
deluxe, FINEST QUALITY
delve,*,ed,ving, TO BURY/DIG INTO
dem, deem / dim / them / they
demacrasy, democracy
demacrat, democrat

demagogue,*,guery,gic,gical, LEADER WHO USES POPULAR EMOTIONS
demagrafy, demography
demakratic, democratic
demalishun, demolition
demand,*,ded,ding, COMMAND/INSIST ON FULFILLMENT OF DESIRES "prefixes: un"
demarcation,*, SETTING BOUNDARIES, ESTABLISHING GUIDELINES
demarkashun, demarcation
demble, dimple
demean,*,ned,ning, HUMILIATE
demeanor, CONCERNING BEHAVIOR/ CONDUCT "prefixes: mis"
demenor, demeanor
demented, CRAZY, UNPOPULAR BEHAVIOR/THOUGHTS
demer, dimmer
demestek, domestic
demi, PREFIX INDICATING "HALF/ PARTLY" MOST OFTEN MODIFIES THE WORD
demigog, demagogue
demikrat, democrat
demilaturise, demilitarize
demilitarize,*,ed,zing,zation, REMOVE MILITARY
demiluturise, demilitarize
demin, demon
deminstrate, demonstrate
demir, dimmer
demise,ed,sing, TRANSFER, PASSED FROM THIS REALITY
demobilize,*,ed,zing,zation, DISARM, DISBAND
democracy,cies, BY AND FOR ALL PEOPLE
democrat,*, ONE IN PARTY WHO WORKS FOR SOCIAL EQUALITY FOR ALL
democratic,ize,ization, PROCESS OF WORKING TOWARDS SOCIAL EQUALITY FOR ALL "prefixes: un"
demography,hic,hical,hically, STATISTICS/RECORDS OF PUBLIC VITAL INFORMATION
demokrasy, democracy
demokrat, democrat
demokratic, democratic
demokruse, democracy
demolish,hes,hed,hing,ition, DESTROY, RUIN

demolition,*,nist, ACT OF DESTROYING/ RUINING
demon,*,nic,niac,niacal,nically,nization, nize,nizes,nized,nizing, nization, nism, MAKE OR APPEAR EVIL
demonek, demon(ic)
demonstrate,*,ed,ting,tion,tive, HOW TO, EXPLAIN CLEARLY/ DELIBERATELY "prefixes: in/un"
demple, dimple
demugog, demagogue
demuleshin, demolition
demun, demon
demunstrashen, demonstrate(tion)
demunstrate, demonstrate
demur, dimmer
den,*, CONCEALED HIDEOUT,COZY/ TUCKED AWAY PLACE (or see then)
denacher, denature
denaturalize,es,ed,zing,zation, REMOVE CITIZENSHIP OR NATURE OF
denature,*,ed,ring,rant,ration, ROB OF NATURAL COMPOSURE
dencher, denture
dendr, PREFIX INDICATING "TREE" MOST OFTEN MODIFIES THE WORD
dendri, PREFIX INDICATING "TREE" MOST OFTEN MODIFIES THE WORD
dendrite,*, PATHWAYS OF NEURONS CARRYING IMPULSES IN THE BRAIN
deng, ding
denge, dingy / dinghy
dengle, dangle
deni, deny
deniable,lity,ly, REFUSE AS TRUTH, DISAVOW
denial,*, REFUSE, DENY
denil, denial
denim,*, HEAVY COTTON FABRIC
denir, dinner
deniul, denial
denje, dingy
denky, dinky
denomenator, denominator
denomination,*,nal,nally,nalism,ive,tor, SPECIES OF THE WHOLE, SEPARATE BUT SAME
denominator,*, OF FRACTIONS
denote,*,ed,ting,tive,table,tation,tive, tative, DESIGNATED, SYMBOLIZES
dense,er,est,ely,eness,sity, THICK/ COMPACT, CLOSE TOGETHER
density,ties, DEGREE OF MASS/ CONCENTRATION

dent,*, AN IMPRESSION OR HOLLOW, PREFIX INDICATING "TOOTH" MOST OFTEN MODIFIES THE WORD (or see didn't)
dental,*, OF TEETH
denti, PREFIX INDICATING "TOOTH" MOST OFTEN MODIFIES THE WORD
dentist,*,try, DOCTOR FOR TEETH
denture,*,rist, ARTICIFIAL TEETH
denum, denim
denur, dinner
deny,nies,nied,ying,nial, NOT ADMIT, WON'T CLAIM "prefixes: un"
deoderant, deodorant
deoderint, deodorant
deoderize, deodorize
deodorant, HIDES ODOR/SMELLS
deodorize,*,ed,zing,zation,er, REMOVE ODOR/SMELL
deoksidize, deoxidize
deoksudize, deoxidize
deoxidize,*,ed,zing, REMOVE OXYGEN
dep, deep / dip
deparcher, depart(ure)
deparjur, depart(ure)
deparsher, depart(ure)
depart,*,ted,ting,ture, GO AWAY FROM
departer, depart(ure)
department,*,tal,talize,talizes,talized, talizing, SECTIONS OF THE WHOLE, A SUBSET
departure,*, TO GO AWAY FROM, LEAVE
depazeshen, deposition
depazishen, deposition
depend,*,ded,ding,dable,dably,dability, dant,dent,dance, RELY ON "prefixes: in/un"
dependant,*, RELATIONSHIP TO OTHER THINGS (or see dependent) "prefixes: in"
dependence,cy,cies, TO NEED/RELY UPON "prefixes: in"
dependent,*,tly,nce, SUPPORTED BY OTHERS "prefixes: in"
deper, dipper
depewtise, deputize
depict,*,ted,ting,tion, SHAPE/FORM/ CREATE IMAGE
depir, dipper
deplete,*,ed,ting,tive,table,tability,tion, USE TO THE END, RUNNING OUT OF
depletion, THE ACT OF RUNNING OUT OF

deploma, diploma
deplomacy, diplomacy
deplomat, diplomat
deplorable,ly,bility,eness, LAMENT
deplore,*,ed,ring,ringly,rable, LAMENT
deploy,*,yed,ying,yable,yer,yment, PREPARE TO BE USED/MAKE USE OF "prefixes: re"
depo, depot
depoortashen, deportation
depor, deep(er)
deporcher, depart(ure)
deport,*,ted,ting,tment,tation,tee,table, BE EXPELLED, SENT FROM COUNTRY
deportation, ACT OF SENDING FROM THE COUNTRY
deportee,*, ONE WHO WAS DEPORTED FROM COUNTRY
depose,*,ed,sing,sal,er,sable,sition, WRITE OR SPEAK UNDER OATH
deposit,*,ted,ting,tor,tory,tories, PLACE SOMETHING OF VALUE INTO SAFEKEEPING "prefixes: non"
deposition,*, STATEMENT UNDER OATH
depot,*, LOADING/UNLOADING STATION FOR TRANSPORT
depravashen, deprivation
depravation, deprivation
depreciate,*,ed,ting,able,tion,tive, tingly, ESTIMATE OF LOWER VALUE
depresheate, depreciate
depreshen, depression
depresion, depression
depress,sses,ssed,ssing,ssion, LOWER IN ELEVATION, LOW IN HOPE/FAITH
depression,*, A LOW POINT
deprivation, LACK OF ACCESS TO
deprive,*,ed,ving,vable,val,vation,er, PREVENT FROM HAVING ACCESS TO
depruvashen, deprivation
depth,*, A MEASURE DOWNWARDS OR INTO
depude, deputy
depudize, deputize
depur, dipper
depusishen, deposition
deputize,*,ed,zing, APPOINT AS DEPUTY
deputy,ties,tize,tizes,tized,tizing, AGENT OF THE LAW
depuzishen, deposition
der, dear / deer / dare / there / they're

derable, durable
deracenate, deracinate
deracinate,*,ed,ting,tion, UPROOT, REMOVE FROM NATIVE LAND/ CULTURE/ENVIRONMENT
deralik, derelict
derasenate, deracinate
derashen, duration
derasinate, deracinate
deration, duration
derdee, dirty
dere, dairy
derear, derriere
derekshen, direction
derektury, directory
derelict,*,tion, SOMEONE/ SOMETHING LEFT WITHOUT A GUIDE
deress, duress
derevative, derivative
derfor, therefore / therefor
deri, dairy
derible, durable
deric, derrick
derier, derriere
derik, derrick
derilect, derelict
dering, during / dare(ring)
derivative,*,ely,ion,ional, ROOT/ ORIGIN OF
derive,*,ed,ving,vable,vative,vatively, vation,vational, FROM THE ORIGINAL, DESCENDED FROM
derma, PREFIX INDICATING "SKIN" MOST OFTEN MODIFIES THE WORD
dermal,atitis,mis, CONCERNS THE SKIN "prefixes: endo/intra/sub"
dermat, PREFIX INDICATING "SKIN" MOST OFTEN MODIFIES THE WORD
dermato, PREFIX INDICATING "SKIN" MOST OFTEN MODIFIES THE WORD
dermes, dermal(mis)
dermititus, dermal(atitis)
dermle, dermal
dermotidus, dermal(atitis)
dermul, dermal
dermus, dermal(mis)
dermutidis, dermal(atitis)
derrick,*, TOWERLIKE EQUIPMENT WITH A CENTRAL POST
derriere,*, REAR END, GLUTEUS MAXIMUS MUSCLES
dert, dirt
derty, dirty
deruble, durable

derulik, derelict
dery, dairy
des, this / these / ditch
desabelity, disability
desable, disable
desacord, disaccord
desacrate, desecrate
desadisfacshen, dissatisfy(faction)
desadvantage, disadvantage
desafect, disaffect
desagre, disagree
desakord, disaccord
desalinate,*,ed,ting,tion,tor,nize,nizes, nized,nizing,nization, REMOVE SALT FROM
desalow, disallow
desalugen, disillusion
desalunate, desalinate
desapashen, dissipate(tion)
desapate, dissipate
desaplen, discipline
desapoint, disappoint
desaprove, disapprove
desaray, disarray
desarm, disarm
desarmament, disarmament
desaster, disaster
desatisfaction, dissatisfy(faction)
desavantage, disadvantage
desbaleef, disbelief / disbelieve
desband, disband
desbar, disbar / despair
desbaret, desperate
desbatch, dispatch
desbekable, despicable
desberit, desperate
desbicable, despicable
desbikable, despicable
desbiret, desperate
desbite, despite
desblay, display
desbondent, despondent
desboret, desperate
desbot, despot
desbozul, disposal
desbulef, disbelief / disbelieve
desburet, desperate
desburse, disperse / disburse
desbute, dispute
desbuzishun, disposition
desc, desk / disk / disc
descard, discard
descend,*,ded,ding,dible,dable,nt,nsion, STEP DOWN FROM, DOWNWARD
(or see descent/decent) "prefixes: con/un"
descendant,*,dent, PREVIOUS/PRIOR TO THE CURRENT GENERATION, IN RELATION TO
descension,nal, GO DOWN/INTO, SINK/FALL (or see dissension)
descent,*,nsion, PAST TENSE FOR THE WORD "DESCEND", A STEP DOWN (or see decent/descend)
descerech, discourage
descharge, discharge
desclose, disclose
descontenue, discontinue
descord, discord
descors, discourse
descotek, discotheque
descover, discover
descredit, discredit
descremenate, discriminate
descrepensy, discrepancy
descrete, discreet / discrete
descretion, discretion
describe,*,ed,bing,bable,er,iptively, iptiveness,iptivist,iptivism, EXPLAIN DETAILS OF SOMETHING
descripshen, description
description,*,ive, PROVIDE DETAILS, EXPLAIN
descriptive,*,ely,eness,vist,vism, PROVIDE DETAILS, EXPLAIN
descumfert, discomfort
descurech, discourage
descushen, discussion
descust, disgust
descuver, discover
desdanation, destination
desdane, disdain
desdany, destiny
desdaste, distaste
desdent, distant
desdeny, destiny
desdination, destination
desdinduble, distend(sible)
desdindubleshen, distend(nsion)
desdindubletion, distend(nsion)
desdint, distant
desdiny, destiny
desditute, destitute
desdort, distort
desdrabute, distribute
desdrakt, distract
desdrot, distraught
desdruckshen, destruction
desdruktion, destruction
desdrust, distrust
desdunashun, destination
desduny, destiny
desdurb, disturb
desdutute, destitute
desease, disease
deseble, decibel
desecragate, desegregate
desecragation, desegregate(tion)
desecrate,*,ed,ting,er,tor,tion, TO TREAT WHAT'S SACRED TO OTHERS AS UNSACRED
desecrogate, desegregate
desecrogation, desegregate(tion)
desee, dizzy
deseese, decease / disease
deseet, deceit
desefect, disaffect
desegon, decision
desegregate,*,ed,ting,tion,tionist, UNDO RACIAL SEGREGATION
desegrigate, desegregate
desegrugate, desegregate
deselarate, decelerate
deselurate, decelerate
desemate, decimate
desember, december
desemul, decimal
desencion, descension
desend, descend / descent / dissent / decent
desendent, descendant
desenherit, disinherit
desensee, decency
desent, decent / descent
desenter, dissent(er)
desentient, dissent(ient)
desentralise, decentralize
desepshun, deception
deseption, deception
deseptive, deceptive
desern, discern
desert,*,ted,ting,ter,tification,tion, LAND LACKING LUSH VEGETATION, TO LEAVE WITHOUT PERMISSION (or see dessert) "prefixes: non/semi/un"
deserter,*, SOMEONE WHO LEAVES/ABANDONS WITHOUT PERMISSION
deserve,*,ed,ving,edly,er, REWARD/PUNISHMENT FOR ACT/THOUGHT/DEED "prefixes: un"
deservise, disservice

desesd, decease(d) / disease(d)
deset, deceit
desetful, deceit(ful)
deseve, deceive
desfegure, disfigure
desfigure, disfigure
desfunction, dysfunction
desfunkshen, dysfunction
desgard, discard
desgarge, discharge
desgise, disguise
desgoint, disjoint
desgrase, disgrace
desgrechun, discretion
desgretion, discretion
desgruntle, disgruntle
desgruntled, disgruntle(d)
desgurag, discourage
desgus, discus / discuss
desgust, disgust / discuss(ed)
desguys, disguise
desh, dish
desharden, dishearten
desharten, dishearten
deshevel, dishevel
desheveld, dishevel(ed)
deshonest, dishonest
deshonor, dishonor
deshonorable, dishonorable
desibal, decibel
desible, decibel
desicrate, desecrate
desid, decide
desidewus, deciduous
desifer, decipher
design,*,ned,ning,nable,nedly,ner, CREATION OF A MODEL, OUTLINE/ PLAN FOR SOMETHING "prefixes: re/un"
designate,*,ed,ting,tion,tive,tory,tor, TO ASSIGN/APPOINT "prefixes: re"
designer,*, ONE WHO CREATES DESIGNS
desijen, decision
desijues, deciduous
desil, diesel
desilat, desolate
desimal, decimal
desimanate, disseminate
desimate, decimate
desimbark, disembark
desimber, december
desincy, decency
desind, descend

desine, design
desiner, designer
desinfect, disinfect
desingage, disengage
desinsee, decency
desinshen, dissension / descension
desint, decent / descent
desintary, dysentery
desintegrate, disintegrate
desinter, dissent(er) / dissent
desintient, dissent(ient)
desintion, dissension / descension
desintralise, decentralize
desinugrate, disintegrate
desipher, decipher
desipul, disciple
desirable,*,bility,eness,ly, LIKE TO HAVE
desire,*,ed,ring,rous,rously,rousness, rable,rability,rableness,rably, A WISH/ WANT/COMPULSION FOR "prefixes: un"
desirtashen, dissertation
desiruble, desirable
desis, disease / decease
desisd, disease(d) / decease(d)
desisev, decision(ive)
desjoint, disjoint
desk,*, FURNITURE (or see disc/disk)
deskard, discard
deskerdeus, discourteous
deskerege, discourage
desklame, disclaim
deskonekt, disconnect
deskontenue, discontinue
deskord, discord
deskordeus, discourteous
deskors, discourse
deskover, discover
deskredit, discredit
deskremenate, discriminate
deskrepdef, descriptive
deskrepincy, discrepancy
deskribe, describe
deskripshen, description
deskunekt, disconnect
deskurdeus, discourteous
deskurege, discourage
deskus, discus / discuss
deskushun, discussion
deskust, disgust / discuss(ed)
deskuver, discover
deskwalefy, disqualify
desl, diesel
desleksea, dyslexia

deslexia, dyslexia
deslocate, dislocate
desloch, dislodge
deslodge, dislodge
deslog, dislodge
deslokate, dislocate
desmantul, dismantle
desmanul, dismantle
desmay, dismay
desmember, dismember
desmimbur, dismember
desmiss, dismiss
desmount, dismount
desmownt, dismount
desmul, dismal
desobay, disobey
desobedeanse, disobedience
desocheate, dissociate
desociate, dissociate
desolate,ed,ely,eness,tion,er, DESERTED, EMPTY OF
desolenate, desalinate
desolushen, dissolute(tion)
desolute, dissolute
desolve, dissolve
deson, disown
desonent, dissonant
desoner, dishonor
desonerible, dishonorable
desonest, dishonest
desonins, dissonant(nce)
desont, decent / descent
desorder, disorder
desorderly, disorderly
desoreint, disorient
desosheate, dissociate
desown, disown
despair,*,red,ring,ringly, DEEPLY TROUBLED, HOPELESS
desparashin, desperation
despare, despair
desparedy, disparity
despatch, dispatch
despense, dispense
despensible, dispensable
desperashun, desperation
desperate,ely,eness,ado,tion, OF FEELING FRANTIC, GIVEN TO HOPELESSNESS
desperation, BEYOND REGARD FOR HOPE
desperit, desperate
desperity, disparity
desperse, disperse / disburse

despicable,eness,ly,bility, BEING WORTHLESS/ NO GOOD
despikable, despicable
despinse, dispense
despinsuble, dispensable
despise,*,ed,sing,sable,sal,sableness, edness,ement,er, VERY LOW OPINION OF, STRONG DISLIKE "prefixes: un"
despit, despite
despite,ed,ting,eful,efully,eous,eously, IN SPITE OF, INSULT, MALICE, ILL INTENT
desplas, displace
desplased, displace(d)
desplay, display
desplejur, displease(sure)
desplesed, displease(d)
desplesher, displease(sure)
despond,*,ded,ding,dingly,dency,dent, SEVERELY DISPIRITED/DEPRESSED/ HOPELESS
despondent,ncy,tly, SEVERELY DISPIRITED/DEPRESSED
desposal, disposal
desposeshun, disposition
desposition, disposition
despositive, dispositive
desposuble, disposable
despot,*,tic,tical,tically,tism, ABUSIVE/ TYRANNICAL USE OF POWER
despraporshen, disproportion
desproportion, disproportion
despurashin, desperation
despurit, desperate
despusishun, disposition
despute, dispute
desputuble, dispute(table)
despuzition, disposition
desqualify, disqualify
desqwalefy, disqualify
desregard, disregard
desrepare, disrepair
desreputable, disreputable
desrespect, disrespect
desrespkt, disrespect
desrobe, disrobe
desrobt, disrupt
desropt, disrupt
desrubshen, disruption
desrubt, disrupt
desrupshen, disruption
desrupt, disrupt
desruption, disruption

dessapate, dissipate
dessapation, dissipate(tion)
dessatisfaction, dissatisfy(faction)
dessemble, dissemble
dessenter, dissent(er)
dessert,*, A TASTY SWEET DISH FOLLOWING MAIN COURSE (or see desert)
dessertation, dissertation
dessimble, dissemble
dessinter, dissent(er)
dessirtashen, dissertation
dessociate, dissociate
dessolute, dissolute
dessolution, dissolute(tion)
destanashin, destination
destanation, destination
destance, distance
destane, disdain
destany, destiny
destaste, distaste
destemper, distemper
desten, distend / destine
destenation, destination
desteni, destiny
destenkt, distinct
destense, distance
destenshen, distend(nsion)
destent, distant
destention, distend(nsion)
desterb, disturb
destill, distill
destimper, distemper
destinachen, destination
destination,*, ARRIVAL POINT "prefixes: pre"
destinct, distinct
destinduble, distend(sible)
destine,*,ned,ning,ny,nation, FATE, PREORDAINED, SPECIFIC OUTCOME (or see destiny) "prefixes: pre"
destint, distant
destiny,nies, FATE, OVERALL ARRIVAL POINT
destitute,*,eness,tion, WITHOUT POSSESSION OF, HOMELESS
destort, distort
destrabute, distribute
destract, distract
destraught, distraught
destrekt, district
destrikt, district
destrot, distraught

destroy,*,yed,ying,yable,yer, OBLITERATE/RUIN/DEMOLISH
destruct,*,ted,ting,tible,tibility,tion,tive, tor, DESTROY A MISSILE AFTER LAUNCH "prefixes: in/non"
destruction, ACT OF RUINING/ DEMOLISHING
destructive,ely,eness,vity, OBLITERATE/ RUIN/DEMOLISH
destrukshen, destruction
destruktive, destructive
destruktof, destructive
destrust, distrust
destulashen, distill(ation)
destunashin, destination
destuny, destiny
destutute, destitute
desuade, dissuade
desubel, decibel
desubilety, disability
desucrate, desecrate
desufect, disaffect
desugree, disagree
desukrate, desecrate
desul, diesel
desulit, desolate
desulooshen, dissolute(tion)
desuloot, dissolute
desulow, disallow
desumal, decimal
desumate, decimate
desumbark, disembark
desunt, decent / descent
desupashen, dissipate(tion)
desupate, dissipate
desupeer, disappear
desupoent, disappoint
desuprove, disapprove
desurn, discern
desurt, desert / dessert
desurtashen, dissertation
desurve, deserve
deswade, dissuade
det, debt
detach,hes,hed,hedly,hedness,hing, ment,hable,hably,her, PULL AWAY FROM, SEPARATE "prefixes: semi"
detachment,*, DISCONNECTED, SEPARATE FROM THE WHOLE
detail,*,led,ling,ler, EXACT PARTICULARS
detain,*,ned,ning,nable,nment,nee, TO KEEP FROM GOING, HOLD BACK, DELAY

detakashun, dedication
detakate, dedicate
detale, detail
detane, detain
detauks, detox
detch, ditch
detect,*,ted,ting,table,tably,tability,tion, tor, UNCOVER, SENSE, DISCOVER
detective,*, ONE WHO UNCOVERS FACTS, DISCOVERS
detector,*, A DEVICE WHICH SENSES/ DISCOVERS
detekt, detect
detektif, detective
detektur, detector
deten, deaden
detenate, detonate
detenshen, detention
detente,*, CEASE-FIRE, LESSENING OF TENSIONS BETWEEN WARRING PEOPLE
detention,*, FORCED CONFINEMENT
deter,*,rred,rring,rrable,rrability,rment, rrent,rrence, ATTEMPT TO RESTRAIN FROM (or see detour/ debtor)
deterant, deterrent
detereate, deteriorate
deterent, deterrent
detergent,*, CHEMICAL CLEANSER
deteriorate,*,ed,ting,tion,tive, LOOSE FORM/FUNCTION
determenent, determine(nt)
determination,*, DECIDED, DECISION, STRONG DESIRE FOR ACCOMPLISHMENT
determine,*,ed,ning,nism,nist,nistic, nistically,nedly,nedness,ner,nant, nate, nation,native,natively,nable, THINK OUT, PLAN A COURSE OF ACTION "prefixes: in/non/pre"
deterrent,nce, PAST TENSE FOR "DETER", USED TO PREVENT/ RESTRAIN
detest,*,ted,ting,table,tably,tability, tableness,tation,ter, EXTREME DISLIKE, DISAGREE WITH
deteur, detour / debtor / deter
deth, death
deticashun, dedication
deticate, dedicate
detikashun, dedication
detikate, dedicate
detin, deaden

detinate, detonate
detinshun, detention
detir, debtor / detour / deter
detirmenedly, determine(dly)
detirmenent, determine(nt)
detly, dead(ly)
detnate, detonate
deto, ditto
detoks, detox
detoksefy, detoxify
detoksuficashen, detoxify(fication)
detonate,*,ed,ting,table,tion,tive,tor, CAUSE TO EXPLODE
detont, detente
detor, debtor / detour / deter
detour,*,red,ring, STEER FROM PRIMARY PATH/ROAD
detox,xes,xed,xing,xify,xicate,xication, xicant, SLANG FOR "DETOXIFY", ELIMINATE CHEMICALS FROM THE BODY
detoxicate,*,ed,ting,tion, DETOXIFY, REMOVE IMPURITIES
detoxify,fies,fied,fying,fication, REMOVE IMPURITIES FROM BODY
detract,*,ted,ting,tion,tive,tively,tor, TAKES AWAY FROM
detrament, detriment
detriment,*,tal,tally, COULD HARM, NEGATIVE INPUT
detrument, detriment
dets, debt(s)
detukashun, dedication
detukate, dedicate
detunate, detonate
detur, deter / detour / debtor
deture, detour / debtor / deter
deturgent, detergent
deturmen, determine
deturmenashen, determination
deturmenent, determine(nt)
deturmenism, determine(nism)
deturminent, determine(nt)
deuce,*,ed,edly, TWO DOTS ON DICE, GAMBLING EXPRESSION (or see duce)
deva, ENTITY OF GOOD SPIRITS (or see diva)
devadend, dividend
devastate,*,ed,ting,tive,tion,tor, TOTAL DISARRAY/CHAOTIC ARRANGEMENT,UNRECOGNIZABLE
devaulv, devolve
deveanse, deviance

deveant, deviant
deveashen, deviation
deveat, deviate
deveation, deviation
deveents, deviance
devegen, division
devel, devil
develop,*,ped,ping,pment,pmental, pmentally,per, GATHERING OF THOUGHTS AND PLANS TOGETHER INTO ON "prefixes: re/under"
deverse, diverse
devershen, diversion
devestate, devastate
deveunse, deviance
deveunt, deviant
deviance,cy, UNACCEPTABLE BEHAVIOR
deviant,*,ate, THOSE WHO DISPLAY UNACCEPTABLE BEHAVIOR
deviate,*,ed,ting,tingly,tion,ance,ant, TO STEER OFF THE PATH "prefixes: un"
deviation,*,nism,nist, TO DEVIATE, BE DEVIANT
device, SOMETHING DESIGNED TO BE USED AS A TOOL/AID (or see devise)
devide, divide
devidend, dividend
devil,*,led,ling,lish,lishness,lishly,lment, lry, FOOD PROCESS, MAN'S CREATION OF A BEING TO BE FEARED
devine, divine
devious,sly,sness, NOT TRUTHFUL, EVASIVE IN TRUTH/DIRECTION
devise,*,ed,sing,sable,er, OF WILLS/ PROPERTY, TO CREATE (or see device)
devisible, divisible
devistate, devastate
devize, devise / device
devoid,dness, ABSENCE OF, EMPTY
devol, devil
devolve,*,ed,ving,ement,lution,lutionist, DOWNWARD, DEGENERATE, DETERIORATE
devorse, divorce
devoshen, devotion
devostate, devastate
devote,*,ed,edly,edness,ting,tion,tional, tee, DEDICATED, LOYAL COMMITMENT
devotion,*,nal,nally, DEDICATED, LOYAL

devour,*,red,ring,ringly,rer, EARNEST TO RELIGION
devout,tly,tness, DEEPLY DEVOTED
devoyd, devoid
devu, deva / diva
devudend, dividend
devul, devil
devulg, divulge
devulution, devolve(lution)
devursity, diversity
devurt, divert
devustate, devastate
dew,*,wed,wing,wy, MOISTURE THAT COLLECTS INTO DROPS (or see do/due/doe)
dewal, dual / duel
dewdle, doodle
dewet, duet
dewing, doing
dewl, duel / dual
dewo, duo
dewplecity, duplicity
dewplekate, duplicate
dewplex, duplex
dewse, duce / deuce / due(s)
dewsh, douche
dex, deck(s) / dig(s)
dexshen, diction
dexshunery, dictionary
dexsteridy, dexterity
dexterity,ties, SHARP/QUICK MENTAL/PHYSICAL SKILL
dextero, PREFIX INDICATING "RIGHT" MOST OFTEN MODIFIES THE WORD
dexterous,sly,sness, OF DEXTERITY
dextr, PREFIX INDICATING "RIGHT" MOST OFTEN MODIFIES THE WORD
dextro, PREFIX INDICATING "RIGHT" MOST OFTEN MODIFIES THE WORD
dextrus, dexterous
dez, these
dezal, diesel
dezapashen, dissipate(tion)
dezapate, dissipate
dezapeer, disappear
dezaster, disaster
dezbot, despot
deze, dizzy
dezeez, disease
dezenteant, dissent(ient)
dezert, desert / dessert
dezerve, deserve
dezignate, designate
dezine, design

deziner, designer
dezinteant, dissent(ient)
dezirable, desirable
dezire, desire
dezklose, disclose
dezl, diesel
dezmay, dismay
dezmul, dismal
dezolve, dissolve
dezordurly, disorderly
dezposuble, disposable
dezrepare, disrepair
dezugnate, designate
dezul, diesel
dezurt, desert / dessert
dezurtashen, dissertation
dezurve, deserve
dfraust, defrost
dfrost, defrost
dfroust, defrost
di, PREFIX INDICATING "FROM/AWAY/NEGATIVE" MOST OFTEN MODIFIES THE WORD
dia, PREFIX INDICATING "ACROSS/THROUGH" MOST OFTEN MODIFIES THE WORD
diabalekle, diabolical
diabedik, diabetic
diabetes, IMBALANCE IN GLUCOSE LEVELS
diabetic, SOMEONE WITH GLUCOSE IMBALANCE
diabolic,cal,ize,izes,ized,izing,ism, OF BEING/SEEMING EVIL/CRUEL, OF THE DEVIL
diabolical,lly,lness, OF BEING DIABOLIC, EVIL
diacdavate, deactivate
diactevate, deactivate
diafram, diaphragm
diagenul, diagonal
diagnose,*,ed,sing,sable,sis,stic,stically,stician, TO STUDY THE NATURE OF A PROBLEM
diagnosis, OPINION ON THE NATURE OF A PROBLEM
diagnul, diagonal
diagnule, diagonal(lly)
diagonal,lly, OPPOSITE/CATTY CORNER FROM
diagram,*,mmed,mming,mmatic,mmatical,mmatically,mmable, DRAWING "prefixes: mis/un"
diahrea, diarrhea

dial,*,led,ling,ler, FACE OF WATCH, PLACE A PHONE CALL "prefixes: mis/re"
dialasis, dialysis
dialect,*,tal,tally,tic,tician,ticism,tical,tically, THE WAY THE LANGUAGE IS SPOKEN
dialogue,*,ed,uing,gist,gistic,gize,gizes,gized,gizing, VERBAL COMMUNICATION BETWEEN ENTITIES
dialysis,ytic,ytically,lyze,lyzes,lyzed,lyzing,lyzable,lyzability,lyzation, CLEANSE THE BLOOD OF WASTES, SEPARATE SUBSTANCES BY DIFFUSION
diameter,*,ric,rical,trically,tral, STRAIGHT LINE THROUGH THE CENTER OF A CIRCULAR SHAPE LEAVING EQUAL PARTS "prefixes: semi"
diamider, diameter
diamond,*, CUT STONE INTO GEM/SHAPE/PATTERN
diaper,*,red, ABSORBENT PANTS FOR FLUIDS
diaphragm,*,matic,matically, A DIVISION BETWEEN TWO THINGS, CONTRACEPTIVE DEVICE
diarea, diarrhea
diaretik, diuretic
diarrhea,al,hoea,hoeic, VERY LIQUID FECAL EXCREMENT
diary,ries,rist,rize,rizes,rized,rizing, LOG/JOURNAL OF THOUGHTS EACH DAY
diatery, dietary
dibach, debauch
dibate, debate
dibauch, debauch
dibelutate, debilitate
diber, dipper / diaper
dibiletate, debilitate
diblomu, diploma
diblomusy, diplomacy
dibochury, debauch(ery)
dibs, SLANG FOR LAYING A CLAIM, SMALL MONETARY PARTICIPATION
dibur, dipper / diaper
dic, thick / dike / dyke
dical, decal
dicanter, decanter
dicapitate, decapitate
dicaudame, dichotomy

dicay, decay
dice,*,ed,cing,ey, PLURAL FOR "DIE", TWO CUBES WITH VARIETY OF DOTS, TO CHOP UP (or see dicey)
dicelerate, decelerate
dicember, december
dicensy, decency
dicentrolize, decentralize
dicet, deceit
diceve, deceive
dicey,cier,eist, IFFY/RISKY WITH ELEMENT OF DANGER
dich, ditch / dish
diches, ditch(es)
dicheveled, dishevel(ed)
dichotomy,mies,mic,mous,mously,mize, mizes,mized,mizing,mization, SEPARATION/DIVISION INTO TWO PARTS
dichroic,cism, DIFFERENT COLORS FROM DIFFERENT ANGLES
dicker,*,red,ring, RALLY TO STRIKE A DEAL
diclain, decline
dicler, declare
dicompos, decompose
dicon, deacon
dicotomy, dichotomy
dicoy, decoy
dicreped, decrepit
dicrepit, decrepit
dicroek, dichroic
dicshen, diction
dicshunairy, dictionary
dictate,*,ed,ting,tor,tory,torial, COMMAND/RULE/GIVE ORDERS
dictation, TO WRITE OR TYPE WHAT SOMEONE IS SAYING
dictatorial,lly,lness, OPPRESSIVE, AUTHORITARIAN
diction, A WAY OF SPEAKING, ENUNCIATION "prefixes: retro"
dictionary,ries, WORDS WITH DEFINITIONS ARRANGED ALPHABETICALLY
did,does, PAST TENSE FOR THE WORD "DO"(or see dead/died) "prefixes: un"
diden, didn't / deaden
didn't, CONTRACTION OF THE WORDS 'DID NOT' (or see dent/deaden)
dido, ditto
didukt, deduct
diduse, deduce

die,*,ed,dying,dead, TO BE DEAD/ CEASE TO BE ALIVE, AN ENGRAVED STAMP, A PUNCHED OUT TEMPLATE, CUBE USED FOR GAMING (or see dye)
died, PAST TENSE FOR THE WORD "DIE" (or see dye(d))
diegnosus, diagnosis
dielekt, dialect
diere, diary
dierrhea, diarrhea
diesel,*,led,ling, TYPE OF ENGINE/FUEL "prefixes: bio"
diet,*,ted,ting,tary,taries,tetic,tetically, tician, SPECIFIC FOOD/BEVERAGE
dietary,ries, A SYSTEM OF FOOD FOR TYPES OF PEOPLE
dif, PREFIX INDICATING "FROM/AWAY/ NEGATIVE" MOST OFTEN MODIFIES THE WORD (or see thief)
difadend, dividend
difalt, default
difase, deface
difault, default
dife, dive
difechant, deficient
difechensi, deficiency
difeet, defeat
difekult, difficult
difend, defend
difenitive, definitive
difense, defense
difensible, defensible
difensive, defense(sive)
difer, defer / differ
diferens, difference
diferense, difference
diferensheate, differentiate
diferent, different
diferentiate, differentiate
diferently, different(ly)
diferintiate, differentiate
difeshensy, deficiency
difet, defeat
difews, diffuse
differ,*,red,ring,rent,rence,rential, TO NOT BE ALIKE
differantly, different(ly)
difference,*, QUALITIES NOT ALIKE "prefixes: in"
different,tly,tness,tial, NOT THE SAME "prefixes: in"
differential,*, RATE DIFFERENCE/ VARIANCE

differentiate,*,ed,ting,tion, TO OUTLINE DIFFERENCES, BIOLOGY TERM "prefixes: un"
difficult,ty,ties, NOT EASY TO PERFORM
diffuse,*,ed,sing,ely,eness,er,sive,sible, sibility, ELIMINATE FOCUS BY SPREADING OUT, TO END PRESSURE
difichant, deficient
difichensy, deficiency
dificult, difficult
difiense, defiance
difikult, difficult
difine, define
difir, defer / differ
difishant, deficient
difishensy, deficiency
diflact, deflect
diflate, deflate
difoleate, defoliate
difor, differ / defer
diforensheate, differentiate
diforent, different
diform, deform
diformed, deform(ed)
difraud, defraud
difraust, defrost
difray, defray
difrense, difference
difrent, different
difrod, defraud
difrost, defrost
difucult, difficult
difukult, difficult
difunkt, defunct
difur, defer / differ
difurense, difference
difurensheate, differentiate
difurent, different
difurently, different(ly)
difurinsheate, differentiate
difurintly, different(ly)
difuse, diffuse
dify, defy
dig,*,dug,gging,gger, TO GO BELOW/ BEYOND THE SURFACE
digesgen, digestion
digest,*,ted,ting,tible,tibility,tibleness, tive,tively,tiveness,tion, CONSUME, PROCESS, SUMMARIZATIONS "prefixes: pre/un"
digestev, digest(tive)
digestif, digest(tive)
digestion, CONSUME AND PROCESS

digestuf, digest(tive)
digestyon, digestion
diget, digit
digit,*,tize,tization,tal,tally,talize, talization, COUNTING/MEASURING
dignafid, dignified
dignafied, dignified
dignified, STATELY IN FIGURE OR FORM, HONORABLE
dignify,fies,fied,fying, EXPRESS HONOR FOR
dignity,ties,tary, WORTHY OF RESPECT, HONOR "prefixes: in"
dignosis, diagnosis
dignufied, dignified
digrade, degrade
digree, degree
digress,sses,ssed,ssing,ssion,ssional, ssionary,ssive,ssively,ssiveness, WANDER AWAY FROM, DEPART FROM MAIN TOPIC/SUBJECT (or see degression)
dijest, digest
dijestev, digest(tive)
dijeston, digestion
dijet, digit
dika, decay
dikad, decay(ed)
dikanter, decanter
dikautumy, dichotomy
dikdutoreal, dictatorial
dike,*,ed,king,er, ALSO SPELLED "DYKE", A BARRIER/CAUSEWAY/PASSAGE
diker, dicker
diklar, declare
diklin, decline
dikotumy, dichotomy
dikrepit, decrepit
dikroic, dichroic
dikshen, diction
dikshenare, dictionary
dikshun, diction
dikshunare, dictionary
diksterity, dexterity
diktashen, dictation
diktate, dictate
diktater, dictate(tor)
diktation, dictation
diktatur, dictate(tor)
diktion, diction
diktionery, dictionary
diktutoreal, dictatorial
dil, dial / dill / deal
dilagense, diligence

dilajense, diligence
dilate,*,ed,ting,tion,tability,table,tably, tingly,tive, EXPAND/SWELL/BROADEN
dilatont, dilettante
dilay, delay
dilectable, delectable
diledaly, dillydally
dilekt, dialect
dilema, dilemma
dilemma,*,atic, NOT A SITUATION OF CHOICE
dilenkwent, delinquent
dilenquent, delinquent
dilereus, delirious
dileshos, delicious
dilete, delete
diletont, dilettante
dilettante,*,tish,tism, A DABBLER FOR AMUSEMENT
dilidaly, dillydally
diligence,nt,ntly, STEADY PERSEVERANCE, CONSTANT
dilikt, dialect
dilinquent, delinquent
dilirious, delirious
dilishos, delicious
diliver, deliver
dill, AN HERB (or see dial/deal)
dilledaly, dillydally
dillydally,llies,yied,ying, SHOULD BE SEPARATED INTO 2 WORDS "DILLY DALLY", TO WASTE TIME
diloot, dilute
diluchen, delusion / dilute(tion)
dilucs, deluxe
dilugen, delusion / dilute(tion)
dilugense, diligence
dilugent, diligence(nt)
dilujents, diligence
diluks, deluxe
dilur, deal(er)
dilushen, delusion/ dilute(tion)
dilute,*,ed,ting,eness,tion,tive,er, WEAKEN THE STRENGTH OF
dilutont, dilettante
diluxe, deluxe
dim,*,mmed,mming,mly,mness,mmer, mmest, BETWEEN BRIGHT AND DARK, NOT CLEAR/BRIGHT (or see dime)
dimagog, demagogue
dimand, demand
dimaugraphy, demography

dimaulesh, demolish
dimble, dimple
dime,*, A COIN (or see dim)
dimean, demean
dimeanor, demeanor
dimen, demean
dimend, diamond
dimenor, demeanor
dimension,*,nless,nal,nally,nality,nless, MORE THAN ONE LAYER "prefixes: multi"
dimentchen, dimension
dimented, demented
dimer, dimmer
dimestek, domestic
diminish,hes,hed,hing,hingly,hment, TO LESSEN/MAKE SMALLER
dimis, demise
dimize, demise
dimmer,*, LESSEN BRIGHTNESS
dimobalize, demobilize
dimocrat, democrat
dimografy, demography
dimokresy, democracy
dimolish, demolish
dimolishin, demolition
dimon, demon / diamond
dimond, diamond
dimonek, demon(ic)
dimple,*,ed,ling,ly, A DEPRESSION INTO SURFACE, INDENTATION
dimukratic, democratic
dimulishun, demolition
dimunstrate, demonstrate
dimur, dimmer
din, den / dine / dean / didn't
dinamek, dynamic
dinamic, dynamic
dinamination, denomination
dinamite, dynamite
dinasor, dinosaur
dinasty, dynasty
dinaumenation, denomination
dincher, denture
dindrite, dendrite
dine,*,ed,ning,er, TO EAT
diner,*, PLACE TO EAT (or see dinner)
dinesor, dinosaur
dinet, dinette
dinette, DINING ROOM/PLACE NEAR KITCHEN TO EAT
ding,*,ged,ging, BELL SOUNDS, INDENTATIONS/MARKS
dingee, dinghy / dingy

dinger,*, HOME RUN BASEBALL
dinghy,hies, SMALL BOAT/VESSEL ON WATER (or see dingy)
dingy,gier,giest,giness,gily, DIM/MURKY, NOT VIBRANT (or see dinghy/dinky)
dinial, denial
dinie, deny
dinil, denial
dinisor, dinosaur
dinje, dingy
dinky,kier,kiest, SMALL/TINY
dinner,*, EVENING MEAL (or see diner)
dinomenashin, denomination
dinomenator, denominator
dinominashan, denomination
dinominator, denominator
dinomite, dynamite
dinosaur,*, PREHISTORIC CREATURES
dinostea, dynasty
dinote, denote
dinse, dense
dinsity, density
dint, dent / didn't / dine(d)
dintal, dental
dintist, dentist
dinture, denture
dinumite, dynamite
dinur, diner / dinner
dinusor, dinosaur
dinusty, dynasty
dioderant, deodorant
dioreu, diarrhea
dip,*,pper,pped,pping, SLIGHTLY IMMERSE/DECLINE/GO INTO
diparcher, departure
diparsher, departure
dipart, depart
dipartment, department
diparture, departure
dipect, depict
dipend, depend
dipendant, dependant / dependent
dipendence, dependence
diper, diaper / dipper
diplechen, depletion
dipleshin, depletion
diplete, deplete
diploma,*, DOCUMENT FOR COMPLETION OF COURSE/SCHOOL
diplomacy, SKILLFUL NEGOTIATIONS
diplomat,*,tic,tics,tically,acy,tist, PERSON WHO PERFORMS TACTFUL NEGOTIATIONS "prefixes: non/un"
diplorable, deplorable

diplore, deplore
dipo, depot
diporcher, depart(ure)
diport, deport
diportashon, deportation
diportee, deportee
dipose, depose
diposeshon, deposition
diposit, deposit
dipozishen, deposition
dipper,*, SPOON WITH HANDLE, A BIRD (or see diaper)
dipres, depress
dipresheate, depreciate
dipreshen, depression
dipresion, depression
diprive, deprive
dipur, diaper / dipper
dirashen, duration
dirdee, dirty
dire,ely,eness, EXTREME, DISASTROUS
direct,*,ted,ting,tly,tness,tor,tion,tive, torate,torship,tory, AIM FOR/WITH, OF COMMANDS "prefixes: in/mis/multi/non/re/sub/un"
direction,*,nal,nality,nless, WAVE/SIGNALS IN SPACE "prefixes: in/multi/non/uni"
directive,*,eness, A DIRECTION/INDICATOR/GUIDE
directory,ries, BOOK WITH ALPHABETICAL LISTINGS "prefixes: sub"
direkshen, direction
direktory, directory
direng, during
diress, duress
dirivative, derivative
dirive, derive
dirmal, dermal
dirmas, dermal(mis)
dirmatites, dermal(atitis)
dirmle, dermal
dirmul, dermal
dirmus, dermal(mis)
dirmutidus, dermal(atitis)
dirmutitis, dermal(atitis)
dirt,ty,ties,tied,tying,tier,tiest,tily,tiness, SOILED, SOIL (earth)
dirty,tied,tier,tiest,ying,tily,tiness, UNCLEAN
dis, PREFIX INDICATING "NOT/OPPOSITE/LACK OF" MOST OFTEN MODIFIES THE WORD (or see this/dice/die(s)/dye(s))

disabelity, disability
disability,ties, UNABLE TO PERFORM AT NECESSARY CAPACITY
disable,*,ed,ling,ement,bility, UNABLE TO PERFORM, DISCONNECT
disaccord,*,ded,ding, NOT IN HARMONY/AGGREEMENT
disadisfaction, dissatisfy(faction)
disadvantage,*,ed,ging,eous,eously, eousness, A DIFFICULTY/CHALLENGE IN ACCOMPLISHING SUCCESS/GOAL
disaffect,*,ted,ting,tedly,tion, NEGATIVELY AFFECT SOMEONE CONCERNING ANOTHER
disagree,*,eed,eeing,eement,eeable, eeably,eeability,eeableness, NOT AGREE WITH
disakree, disagree
disalanate, desalinate
disallow,*,wed,wing,wance,wable, NOT ALLOWED
disalow, disallow
disalugen, disillusion
disalusion, disillusion
disalute, dissolute
disalution, dissolute(tion)
disambiguate,*,ed,ting,tion, EXPRESSION OPEN TO MISINTERPRETATION, CONFUSING
disanens, dissonant(nce)
disanent, dissonant
disapate, dissipate
disapation, dissipate(tion)
disaper, disappear
disaplen, discipline
disappear,*,red,ring,rance, VANISH FROM SIGHT
disappoint,*,ted,tedly,ting,tingly,tment, HOPES NOT REALIZED
disapprove,*,ed,ving,vingly,val, DOESN'T CARE FOR/APPROVE OF
disaray, disarray
disarm,*,med,ming,mament,mer, REMOVE POWER/WEAPONS
disarmament,*, ACT OF DISARMING
disarray,*,yed,ying, DISORDERED/JUMBLED
disassociate, dissociate
disaster,*,rous,rously,rousness, MISFORTUNE, CALAMITY, EXTENSIVE DAMAGE

disatation, dissertation
disatisfaction, dissatisfy(faction)
disavantage, disadvantage
disbaleef, disbelief / disbelieve
disband,*,ded,ding,dment, DISMISSED FROM GROUP OR MILITARY
disbar,rred,rring, REMOVED FROM LEGAL COURT OR PRACTICE (or see despair)
disbatch, dispatch
disbecable, despicable
disbekable, despicable
disbelief,*,eve, DOESN'T BELIEVE TO BE TRUE
disbelieve,*,ed,ving,vingly,er, DOESN'T BELIEVE TO BE TRUE
disberse, disperse / disburse
disbicable, despicable
disbikable, despicable
disbileef, disbelief / disbelieve
disbite, despite
disblay, display
disblese, displease
disbolef, disbelief / disbelieve
disbondent, despondent
disbose, dispose
disbozishun, disposition
disbozul, disposal
disbraporshen, disproportion
disbuleef, disbelief / disbelieve
disburse,*,ed,sing,sable,ement,er, FUND, PAY OUT MONEY (or see disperse)
disbusishun, disposition
disbute, dispute
disbuzishun, disposition
disc,*, COMPUTER/MUSIC STORAGE DEVICES, SECTIONS IN THE SPINE, BRAKE PARTS (or see disk)
discard,*,ded,ding, TO RID OF/THROW AWAY
discension, dissension / descension
discerach, discourage
discern,*,ned,ning,nible,nibleness,nibly,nment, PERCEIVE ONE FROM ANOTHER, SEE A DIFFERENCE "prefixes: in"
discharge,*,ed,ging,eable,er, TO RELEASE FROM
discinshen, dissension / descension
disciple,*, ONE WHO FOLLOWS A TEACHER
discipline,*,ed,ning,nable,nary,narian, er,nal, CONTROL/TRAIN TO PERFORM SPECIFICALLY "prefixes: in"
disclaim,*,med,ming,mer, NOT LAY CLAIM TO, DISOWN/DENY RESPONSIBILITY OF
disclose,*,ed,sing,sure,ser, REVEAL/ MAKE KNOWN "prefixes: un"
discombobulate,*,ed,ting,tion, DISTURB, PERPLEX
discomfort,*,ted,ting,tingly,table, UNCOMFORTABLE, UNHAPPY
disconnect,*,ted,ting,tion,tedly,tedness, BE REMOVED FROM CONNECTION WITH
discontinue,*,ed,uing,uation,uity,uities, uance,uous,uously, uousness,uity, unities,er, ABANDON, CEASE, STOP THE USE OF
discord,dance,dancy,dancies,dant, dantly, NOT IN HARMONY WITH, DISAGREE WITH
discotek, discotheque
discotheque,*, NIGHTCLUB WITH MUSIC
discount,*,ted,ting, MAKE LESS, REDUCE PRICE OF
discourage,*,ed,ging,ement,gingly,er, LESSEN HOPES OF ACCOMPLISHING
discourse,*,ed,sing,er, REVEAL/MAKE KNOWN
discourteous,sies,sly,sness, NOT POLITE/COURTEOUS
discover,*,red,ring,rer,ry,ries,rable, TO FIND, REALIZE "prefixes: un"
discownt, discount
discredit,*,ted,ting,table,tably,tor, GIVE NO CREDIT TO, DISBELIEF
discreet,tly,tness, GUARDED, CAREFUL, SUBTLE (or see discrete) "prefixes: in"
discremenate, discriminate
discrepancy,cies,nt,ntly, DIFFERENCE BETWEEN
discrepant,ntly,ncy, DIFFERENCE BETWEEN THINGS
discrepchen, description
discreptef, descriptive
discreption, description
discrete,ely,eness,tion, SEPARATE PARTS, DISTINCT/FINITE (or see discreet) "prefixes: in"
discretion,nary,narily, MAKE YOUR OWN DECISION/JUDGEMENT, BEING DISCREET "prefixes: in"
discribe, describe
discriminate,*,ed,ting,nation,nable, nably,nability,nant,nately, native, nator,natory,natorily, USING DIFFERENCE AGAINST, CHOOSE ONE OVER ANOTHER "prefixes: in"
discripchen, description
discripshen, description
discumbobulate, discombobulate
discumfert, discomfort
discunect, disconnect
discuntenue, discontinue
discurage, discourage
discurech, discourage
discus,ses, USED FOR THROWING (or see discuss)
discuss,sses,ssed,ssing,ssable,ssant,sser, ssion, CONVERSATION TO EXAMINE SUBJECT (or see discus)
discussion,*, ACT OF CONVERSATION TO EXAMINE SUBJECT
discust, disgust
discuver, discover
disdain,*,ned,ning,nful,nfully,nfulness, SCORN, CONTEMPT FOR, REJECT
disdend, distend
disdendible, distend(sible)
disdendshen, distend(nsion)
disdendtion, distend(nsion)
disdent, distant
disderb, disturb
disdinduble, distend(sible)
disdort, distort
disdrabushen, distribute(tion)
disdrabute, distribute
disdrakt, distract
disdrebute, distribute
disdress, distress
disdrot, distraught
disdrubute, distribute
disdruckshen, destruction
disdruktion, destruction
disdrust, distrust
disdulashen, distill(ation)
disdurb, disturb
dise, dice / dizzy / dicey
disease,*,ed,sing, BLOCK OF ENERGY ALLOWING TISSUE BREAKDOWN VIA MINUTE ORGANISMS
disecragate, desegregate
disecragation, desegregate(tion)
disecrogate, desegregate
disecrogation, desegregate(tion)
disect, dissect

diseese, decease / disease
diseet, deceit
diseeve, deceive
disefect, disaffect
disefectant, disinfect(ant)
disegragate, desegregate
disegragation, desegregate(tion)
disegrogate, desegregate
disegrogation, desegregate(tion)
disekt, dissect
diselarate, decelerate
diselooshen, dissolute(tion)
diseloot, dissolute
disembar, december
disembark,*,ked,king,kation,kment, MOVE FROM SHIP TO SHORE
disemble, dissemble
disembowel,*,led,ling,lment, REMOVE ORGANS/INTESTINES
disembur, december
diseminate, disseminate
disenagrate, disintegrate
disenchan, descension / dissension
disend, descend / decent / descent / dissent
disendant, descendant
disenfect, disinfect
disengage,*,ed,ging,ement, SET FREE FROM BEING ATTACHED
disenherit, disinherit
disenshent, dissent(ient)
disenshin, dissension / descension
disenshun, dissension / descension
disent, dissent / decent / descend / descent
disentagrate, disintegrate
disentary, dysentery
disenter, dissent(er)
disentient, dissent(ient)
disention, dissension / descension
disentralize, decentralize
disepchen, deception
diseplen, discipline
disepoint, disappoint
diseption, deception
diseray, disarray
disern, discern
disert, dessert / desert
disertation, dissertation
diserv, deserve
diservice, disservice
disesd, decease(d) / disease(d)
diset, deceit
disetful, deceit(ful)

diseve, deceive
disfigure,*,ed,ring,ration,ement, CAUSING UNSIGHTLY APPEARANCE
disfoncshon, disfunction
disfunction, dysfunction
disfunkshon, dysfunction
disgarge, discharge
disgise, disguise
disgoint, disjoint
disgrace,*,ed,cing,eful,efully,efulness, er, SHAME, DISHONOR
disgrechen, discretion
disgretion, discretion
disgrundeld, disgruntle(d)
disgruntle,*,ed,ling,ement, NOT CONTENTED, UNGRATIFIED
disguise,*,ed,sing,sable,er, MASK TRUE IDENTITY "prefixes: un"
disgurag, discourage
disgus, discuss / discus
disgust,*,ted,ting,tingly,tingness, REPUGNANT, AWFUL (or see discuss(ed))
dish,hes,hed,hing, SHALLOW PLATE/ BOWL/VESSEL, TO SERVE IT UP (or see ditch)
disharten, dishearten
dishaveled, dishevel(ed)
dishearten,*,ned,ning,nment, LOOSE SPIRIT/HOPE/COURAGE
dishevel,*,led,ling,lment, MESSED UP, UNTIDY
dishonest,ty,tly,ties, BEING DECEITFUL, NOT HONEST
dishonor,*,red,ring,rable,rably, rableness, NOT TREATED RESPECTFULLY, SHAMEFUL
dishonorable,ly,eness, UNRESPECTABLE, NOT HONORABLE
disi, dizzy
disidvantege, disadvantage
disifer, decipher
disillusion,ned,nment,ive, NO LONGER UNDER ILLUSION, KNOWING
disilushen, disillusion
disimanate, disseminate
disimbark, disembark
disimbul, dissemble
disimbur, december
disin, design
disiner, designer
disinfect,*,ted,ting,tant,tion,tor, CLEANSE AWAY UNWANTED MICROORGANISMS

disingage, disengage
disinherit,*,ted,ting,tance, REMOVED FROM A WRITTEN WILL
disint, descend / decent
disintegrate,*,ed,ting,tion,tor,able,tive, TO FALL APART
disintery, dysentery
disintient, dissent(ient)
disiplen, discipline
disipul, disciple
disir, desire
disirable, desirable
disis, decease
disisev, decision(ive)
disiv, deceive
disjoint,*,ted,ting,tedly,tedness, DISLOCATE, ALTER UNITY/ MOVEMENT
disk,*, FLAT/CIRCULAR, FLOWER HEAD, STEEL BLADE (or see disc/desk)
diskard, discard
diskeruge, discourage
disklame, disclaim
disklose, disclose
diskomfurt, discomfort
diskonect, disconnect
diskontenue, discontinue
diskord, discord
diskors, discourse
diskotek, discotheque
diskover, discover
diskownt, discount
diskredit, discredit
diskrepincy, discrepancy
diskreshun, discretion
diskrete, discreet / discrete
diskribe, describe
diskripshen, description
diskumbobulate, discombobulate
diskumfert, discomfort
diskunekt, disconnect
diskuntenue, discontinue
diskurdeus, discourteous
diskurege, discourage
diskus, discus / discuss
diskust, disgust / discuss(ed)
diskuver, discover
diskwalefy, disqualify
diskwolify, disqualify
dislecsea, dyslexia
disleksea, dyslexia
dislexia, dyslexia
dislocate,*,ed,ting,tion, MOVE FROM ORIGINAL PLACE

disloch, dislodge
dislodge,*,ed,ging,gment, MOVE FROM FIXED POSITION
dislog, dislodge
dismal,lly,llness, DEPRESSING/GLOOMY
dismanle, dismantle
dismantle,*,ed,ling,ement,er, REMOVE, TAKE APART
dismanul, dismantle
dismay,*,yed,ying,yingly, DISTRESS, DREAD, DISILLUSIONED
dismbark, disembark
dismember,*,red,ring,rment, DESTROY/ REMOVE ALL PARTS OF THE WHOLE
dismiss,sses,ssed,ssing,ssal,ssion,ssive, ssively,ssiveness,ssible, PERMIT TO LEAVE, REMOVE, DISCHARGE "prefixes: non/pre/re"
dismount,*,ted,ting,table, REMOVE FROM POSITION
dismownt, dismount
dismul, dismal
disoba, disobey
disobdeinse, disobedience
disobedience,nt,ntly, REFUSE TO BE CONTROLLED
disobey,*,yed,ying,edient,ediently, edience, BEYOND CONTROL
disociate, dissociate
disolfe, dissolve
disolve, dissolve
dison, disown
disonance, dissonant(nce)
disonent, dissonant
disoner, dishonor
disonerible, dishonorable
disoninse, dissonant(nce)
disonist, dishonest
disonurable, dishonorable
disorder,*,red,ring,rly,redness, NOT ORGANIZED
disorderly,liness, NOT PROPER ORDER
disoreint, disorient
disorient,*,ted,ting,tate,tates,tated, tating,tation, LOSS OF PERCEPTION, CONFUSED
disosheate, dissociate
disown,*,ned,ning, RELEASE OWNERSHIP OF
dispair, despair
dispar, despair
disparity,ties, GAP BETWEEN, INEQUALITY
disparody, disparity

disparty, disparity
dispatch,hes,hed,hing,her, SEND SOMEONE OUT
dispekable, despicable
dispensable,bility,eness, CAN BE DISCARDED "prefixes: in"
dispense,*,ed,sing,er,sable,sability, sableness,sary, TO DISTRIBUTE "prefixes: un"
disper, despair
disperse,*,ed,sing,sion,sive,sively, siveness,er,sal, SCATTER INTO VARIOUS DIRECTIONS (or see disburse)
disperudy, disparity
dispeutible, dispute(table)
dispewt, dispute
dispikuble, despicable
dispinsable, dispensable
dispite, despite
dispize, despise
displace,*,ed,cing,eable,ement,er, NOT IN PLACE OR POSITION NORMALLY FOUND
display,*,yed,ying, ON SHOW, EXHIBITION
displease,*,ed,sing,sure, NOT TO SOMEONE'S SATISFACTION
displejur, displease(sure)
displese, displease
displesher, displease(sure)
dispondent, despondent
disposable,*,bility,eness, CAN DISCARD/THROW AWAY
disposal,able, PLACE/WAY TO DISCARD ITEMS
dispose,*,ed,sing,sal,sable,er, TO RID OF, ORGANIZE "prefixes: in/pre/un"
disposition,nal, ATTITUDE, INCLINATION "prefixes: in"
dispositive, FINAL SETTLEMENT OF COURT CASE
dispraporshen, disproportion
disproportion,nal,nate,nately,nally, nateness,nation, NOT IN RELATION TO ITSELF OR ITS SURROUNDINGS
disput, dispute
dispute,*,ed,ting,table,tably,tability, tableness,tant, DEBATE "prefixes: in/un"
disputuble, dispute(table)
disqard, discard

disqualify,fies,fied,ying,fication,fiable, fier, DISBAR, REMOVE FROM COMPETITION
disregard,*,ded,ding, PAY NO NOTICE OF OR ATTENTION TO
disrepair, NEED TO BE FIXED
disreputable,eness,bility,ly, OF POOR REPUTATION/CHARACTER
disrespect,*,ted,ting,table,tful,tfully, tfulness, SHOW NO HONOR/ RESPECT
disrobe,*,ed,bing, UNDRESS, REMOVE GARMENTS
disrupt,*,ted,ting,tion,tive,tiveness, tively, INTERRUPT, CAUSE CHAOS
disruption, INTERRUPT, CAUSE CHAOS
dissalute, dissolute
dissalution, dissolute(tion)
dissanence, dissonant(nce)
dissanent, dissonant
dissapate, dissipate
dissapation, dissipate(tion)
dissatation, dissertation
dissatisfy,fies,fied,fying,faction,factory, UNHAPPY WITH OUTCOME
dissect,*,ted,ting,tion,tible,tor, CRITICALLY EXAMINE, TAKE APART
dissemble,*,ed,ling,lingly,lance, HIDING TRUE FEELINGS/FACTS
disseminate,*,ed,ting,tion,tive,tor, TO PASS ON, SPREAD
dissend, descend/ descent/ dissent
dissension,*, INTENSE DIFFERENCE/ DISAGREEMENT IN OPINION (or see descension)
dissent,*,ted,ting,ter,tience,tiency,tient, tiently,nsion, WILL NOT BEND TOWARDS MAJOR AUTHORITY (or see descent)
dissertation,*,nal,nist, WRITTEN/ FORMAL PAPER FOR DEGREE
disservice, UNWANTED SERVICE
dissipate,*,ed,edly,edness,ting,tive,tor, tion, DISAPPEARS, GOES AWAY
dissociate,*,ed,ting,tion,able,tive, STOP ASSOCIATING WITH "prefixes: un"
dissolute,ely,eness,tion, DISMEMBER, DISINTEGRATE, TERMINATE
dissolve,*,ed,ving,vable,ent,er,luble, lubility,lubleness, BREAK AWAY TO NOTHING, DISAPPEAR
dissonance, dissonant(nce)
dissonant,tly,nce,ncies, LACK OF COMPLETION/CONSISTENCY

dissosheate, dissociate
dissuade,*,ed,ding,dable,er,asion,sive, sively,siveness, SWAY SOMEONE AWAY FROM INTENDED IDEA/PATH
distalashen, distill(ation)
distance,*,ed,cing,nt, TIME/SPACE IN BETWEEN
distane, disdain
distanst, distance(d)
distant,tly, REMOVED IN MIND OR BODY FROM THIS PLACE OR TIME
distaste,eful,efully,efulness, DOESN'T LIKE THE WAY IT APPEALS TO THE SENSES
disteengwish, distinguish
distemper, CONTAGIOUS DISEASE IN ANIMALS, OF PAINTING
distence, distance
distend,*,ded,ding,nsibility,sible,nsion, SWELLING FROM INTERNAL PRESSURE
distengwish, distinguish
distenkt, distinct
distent, distant
disterb, disturb
distill,*,lled,lling,llation,llate,llable, llatory,ller,llery,lleries, SEPARATION, CONDENSATION OF LIQUID
distimper, distemper
distinct,tly,tness,tion,tive,tively, tiveness, CONTRAST, DISTINGUISHED, DIFFERENT "prefixes: in"
distinguish,hed,hes,hing,hable,hably, her, DIFFERENCE/ UNIQUENESS "prefixes: contra/in/un"
distort,*,ted,ting,tion,tional,tnary,tive, ter, WARP/TWIST/CONFUSE FROM NATURAL/PROPER FORM
distrabushen, distribute(tion)
distrabute, distribute
distract,*,ted,ting,tingly,tion,tive,tibility, tible,tor, DEVIATE FROM ORIGINAL FOCUS/INTENT
distrat, distraught
distraught,tly, EXTREME STRESS
distrekt, district
distress,sses,ssed,ssing,ssingly,ssful, GREAT NEED, PAIN OR GRIEF
distribute,*,ed,ting,tion,tional,tive, tively,tal,tor, TO SPREAD AROUND, PASS ALONG "prefixes: re/un"
district,*, SPECIFIC AREA OF TERRITORY/LAND "prefixes: re/sub"

distrocshen, destruction
distroct, destruct
distroctive, destructive
distrot, distraught
distroy, destroy
distruction, destruction
distructive, destructive
distrukshen, destruction
distruktof, destructive
distrust,*,ted,ting,tful, NOT TRUST OR HAVE CONFIDENCE IN
distulashen, distill(ation)
distunst, distance(d)
disturb,*,bed,bing,bingly,bance,bances, ber, TO MAKE IRREGULAR, INTERRUPT "prefixes: un"
disuade, dissuade
disubiluty, disability
disufectant, disinfect(ant)
disugre, disagree
disugree, disagree
disulow, disallow
disulugen, disillusion
disulushen, dissolute(tion)
disulute, dissolute
disumbark, disembark
disuneins, dissonant(nce)
disunent, dissonant
disupate, dissipate
disupation, dissipate(tion)
disupeer, disappear
disuplen, discipline
disupoint, disappoint
disuprove, disapprove
disuray, disarray
disurn, discern
disurvuse, disservice
diswade, dissuade
dit, died / diet / dye(d) / did
ditach, detach
ditan, detain
ditch,hes,hed,hing, A GULLEY IN THE EARTH, SKIP OUT OF SCHOOL, LEAVE SOMEONE
ditect, detect
ditective, detective
ditector, detector
ditekt, detect
ditektur, detector
ditel, detail
ditenshon, detention
diterent, deterrent
ditereorate, deteriorate
diteriorate, deteriorate

ditermenint, determine(nt)
ditermin, determine
ditermination, determination
ditest, detest
dito, ditto
ditocs, detox
ditox, detox
ditrakt, detract
ditto,*, COPY, DUPLICATE, SAME BACK TO YOU
ditur, deter
diturgent, detergent
diturmenism, determine(nism)
diubolikul, diabolical
diufram, diaphragm
diugnose, diagnose
diugram, diagram
diul, dial
diulekt, dialect
diulog, dialogue
diure, diary
diurea, diarrhea
diuretek, diuretic
diuretic,*, INCREASES THE ELIMINATION OF LIQUID
diureuh, diarrhea
diutery, dietary
diva, GODDESS (or see deva)
divadend, dividend
divaulv, devolve
divaut, devout / devote
dive,*,ving,er,dove, TO PLUNGE HEAD- FIRST INTO ANYTHING
divelop, develop
diverse,ely,sify,sifies,sified,sifying, sifability,sifiable,sification,sion, eness, sifier,rt,sity, A VARIETY, OTHER THAN THE NORM
diversion,*,nal,nary,nist, CHANGE COURSE/DIRECTION
diversity,ties, TO BE DIFFERENT "prefixes: bio"
divert,*,ted,ting,tingly,rse,rsion,rsity, CHANGE COURSE/DIRECTION
divians, deviance
divide,*,ed,ding,ision,isive,er,isor, SEPARATE, CREATE PARTS "prefixes: sub"
dividend,*, A NUMBER THAT CAN BE DIVIDED BY ANOTHER NUMBER
divient, deviant
divine,ely,eness,nity, OF A HIGH DEGREE, SUPREME, ABOVE

AVERAGE (or see define) "prefixes: semi"
divise, device / devise
divisible,bility,ly, CAN BE DIVIDED "prefixes: in/multi"
division,*,nal, SEPARATE PARTS WITHIN THE WHOLE "prefixes: multi/sub"
divize, devise
divoed, devoid
divoid, devoid
divolve, devolve
divorce,*,ed,cing,eable,ee, FORMAL DIVISION/SEPARATION FROM
divoshen, devotion
divout, devout
divoution, devotion
divu, diva / deva
divudend, dividend
divulge,*,ed,ging,ence, REVEAL A SECRET/FACT
divurse, diverse
divurshen, diversion
divursity, diversity
divurt, divert
dixtarety, dexterity
diyul, dial
dizalujen, disillusion
dizapashen, dissipate(tion)
dizapate, dissipate
dizastur, disaster
dizatation, dissertation
dizbondent, despondent
dize, dizzy
dizeez, disease
dizembark, disembark
dizemunate, disseminate
dizenteant, dissent(ient)
dizi, dizzy
dizinfect, disinfect
dizmantul, dismantle
dizmul, dismal
dizobay, disobey
dizolve, dissolve
dizorder, disorder
dizordurly, disorderly
dizposuble, disposable
dizrepare, disrepair
dizrespekt, disrespect
dizumbark, disembark
dizupashe, dissipate(tion)
dizupate, dissipate
dizuray, disarray
dizzy,zier,ziest,zily,zied,zying, FUZZY, DISORIENTED, UNFOCUSED

do,oing,oes,one,oable,did, THE ACT OF (or see dew/due/doe/dough) "prefixes: over/un/under"
doal, dual / duel
dob, dub
dobal, double
dobil, double
dobl, double
dobul, double
doc, dock / duck / dose
docd, dock(ed) / duct / duck(ed)
docenchen, descension / dissension
docend, descend / dissent / descent / decent
docent, descend / dissent / descent / decent
doch, dodge
docile,ely,lity, OF RECEPTIVE/ACCEPTABLE ATTITUDE, ABLE TO CONFORM
docinchen, descension / dissension
docind, descend / dissent / descent / decent
docint, descend / dissent / descent / decent
dock,*,ked,king,ker, TYPE OF HERB BEHAVIOR, LOADING PLATFORM FOR VESSELS, TO REMOVE "prefixes: un"
docma, dogma
docmadek, dogmatic
doct, dock(ed) / duct / duck(ed)
doctor,*,red,ring,rly,ral,rate, ONE WHO REPAIRS BODILY INJURY "prefixes: pre"
doctrenul, doctrine(nal)
doctrine,*,nal,nality,nally,naire, DOGMATIC TEACHING OF BELIEFS/VALUES "prefixes: in"
document,*,ted,ting,tary,tation,tal, talist,table,ter, PAPERS WHICH STATE EVIDENCE
documentary,ries,rily, FACTS FOR PUBLIC VIEWING "prefixes: semi"
dodad, doodad
dodch, dodge
doder, daughter
doderize, deodorize
dodge,*,ed,ging,er, MOVES ASIDE, SHIFTS FROM PREDICTED POSITION (or see dog)
dodil, doodle
dodul, doodle
dodurent, deodorant

doe,*, FEMALE OF SHEEP/GOAT/DEER/RABBIT/ANTELOPE (or see do/dough)
doel, duel / dual
doeng, doing
does, A TENSE OF THE WORD 'DO', DOING CURRENTLY (or see due(s)/doe(s)/dose/douse)
doesn't, CONTRACTION OF THE WORDS 'DOES NOT'
doet, duet
dofesubelity, divisible(bility)
dofisable, divisible
dofol, duffle
dog,*,ggy,ggies, IN CANIS ANIMAL FAMILY (or see dodge) "prefixes: under"
doge, dodge / dog
dogma,*,atize,atizes,atized,atizing, atism,atist,atic,atically, PRINCIPLES/TRUTHS DECIDED BY AUTHORITY
dogmadek, dogmatic
dogmatic,*,cally, BELIEVE YOUR PRINCIPLES ARE THE TRUTH
dogmutized, dogma(tized)
doil, duel / dual
doing,one, CURRENTLY IN THE ACT OF
doje, dodge
dok, dock
dokewment, document
dokma, dogma
dokter, doctor
doktren, doctrine
dokument, document
dol, doll / dole / dual / duel / dull
dolar, dollar
dolcimer, dulcimer
dole,*,ed,ling,eful, DEAL/HAND/GIVE OUT PORTIONS OF SOMETHING (or see dolly)
doler, dollar
dolfen, dolphin
dolfin, dolphin
dolir, dollar
doll,*,lled,lling,lly,llish,llishly,llishness, A TOY, CUTE LOOKING, GET DRESSED UP (or see dole/dodge)
dollar,*, U.S. MONEY/BILL
dolly,lies, OBJECT WITH WHEELS FOR MOVING THINGS, TOOL FOR VARIOUS TRADES, A DOLL
dolphin,*, LIVES IN WATER, CETACEAN
dolsemer, dulcimer
dolsumer, dulcimer

dom, dome / doom / dumb
domain,*,anial, TERRITORY/ PROPERTY WITH BOUNDARIES "prefixes: sub"
domane, domain
domanet, dominant
domasile, domicile
dome,*,ed,ming, HALF CIRCLE/180O (or see dumb/doom) "prefixes: semi"
domenate, dominate
domeneer, domineer
domenint, dominant
domenion, dominion
domeno, domino
domenyen, dominion
domestic,*,cally,cate,cated,cating, cation,cator,cable,city,cities, cize, FORCED TO CONFORM TO HUMAN USE "prefixes: semi"
domi, dummy
domicile,*,ed,ling,liary,liate,liation, HOME/RESIDENCE
dominance,cy, AUTHORITY, RULE "prefixes: pre"
dominant,tly,nce, AUTHORITY, RULE "prefixes: pre"
dominate,*,ed,ting,tion,tive,tor,ant, POWER OVER, OVERRULER "prefixes: pre/sub"
domineer,*,red,ring,ringly, EXCESSIVE RULE OVER OTHERS
dominion,*,ium, CONTROL OVER TERRITORY, OWNERSHIP OF
dominish, diminish
domino,oes, MASQUERADE COSTUME, GAME
domnate, dominate
domonent, dominant
domosile, domicile
domplin, dumpling
domunate, dominate
domunent, dominant
domunet, dominant
domusile, domicile
don,*,nned,nning, TO PUT ON, ADDED TO NAME (or see dawn/done)
don't, CONTRACTION FOR WORDS "DO NOT" (or see daunt/don(nned)/ dawn(ed))
donate,*,ed,ting,tion,tor,tive, A GIFT, PERHAPS WITH STRINGS ATTACHED
donc, dunk
dond, don't / daunt / don(nned) / dawn(ed)

done, PAST TENSE FOR THE WORD "DO", TASK/JOB COMPLETED "prefixes: re/under"
doner, donor
dong, dung
dongari, dungaree
dongen, dungeon
dongeri, dungaree
donjen, dungeon
donk, dunk
donkey,*, AN ANIMAL
donor,*,rship, SOMEONE WHO GIVES SOMETHING AWAY
dont, don't / daunt / don(nned) / dawn(ed)
donur, donor
donut, doughnut
dooal, duel / dual
dood, dude
doodad,*, GADGET, DECORATION
doode, duty
doodle,*,ed,ling,er, IDLY SKETCH, DRAW
doom,*,med,ming,msday, THE END OF
doon, dune
doop, dupe
dooplicity, duplicity
door,*,rless, OBJECT WHICH SEPARATES TWO SIDES WHEN CLOSED
doose, duce / deuce / due(s)
doosh, douche
doote, duty
dooz, due(s)
dope,*,ed,ping,er,ey, SLANG FOR DRUGS, NOT SMART
doplex, duplex
doplicate, duplicate
doplicity, duplicity
dor, door
dorivative, derive(vative)
dorive, derive
dormant,ncy, ASLEEP
dormatory, dormitory
dormet, dormant
dormetory, dormitory
dormit, dormant
dormitory,ries, A LARGE PLACE WITH MANY ROOMS FOR SLEEPING/ LIVING
dormut, dormant
dormutory, dormitory
dorsal,lly, ON THE BACK
dorsil, dorsal

dorsul, dorsal
dos, does / doze / doe(s) / dose / due(s) / dowse / those
dosable, disable
dosach, dosage
dosage,*, AMOUNT OF DRUG
dosbekable, despicable
dosberse, disperse / disburse
dosbikable, despicable
dosblased, displace(d)
dosblay, display
dosbose, dispose
doscremenate, discriminate
doscrete, discreet / discrete
dosderb, disturb
dosdrakt, distract
dosdrebute, distribute
dosdress, distress
dosdrust, distrust
dosdurb, disturb
dose,*,ed,sing,sage,sages, SPECIFIC AMOUNT OF SOMETHING (or see doze/due(s)) "prefixes: over"
dosech, dosage
dosege, dosage
dosej, dosage
dosemanate, disseminate
dosembar, december
dosend, descend / dissent / descent / decent
dosent, doesn't / descend / dissent / descent / decent
dosenugrate, disintegrate
doser, dozer
dosfigyer, disfigure
dosgreshun, discretion
dosgruntle, disgruntle
dosh, douche
dosich, dosage
dosige, dosage
dosij, dosage
dosil, docile
dosimbur, december
dosimer, dulcimer
dosin, dozen
dosind, descend / dissent / descent / decent
dosint, descend / dissent / descent / decent
dosk, dusk
doskrete, discreet / discrete
dospinse, dispense
dosplaced, displace(d)
dosplay, display

dosplease, displease
dospose, dispose
dosposuble, disposable
dospozul, disposal
dosputuble, dispute(table)
dosqualify, disqualify
dosreputuble, disreputable
dosrupshen, disruption
dosrupt, disrupt
dost, dust
dostengwish, distinguish
dosterb, disturb
dostingwish, distinguish
dostract, distract
dostress, distress
dostrust, distrust
dosuj, dosage
dosul, docile
dot,*,tted,tting, ROUND SPOTS (or see dote)
dote,*,ed,ting,tingly, TO WATCH OVER, OVERSEE CLOSELY (or see dot/doubt)
doted, dot(tted) / dote(d)
doter, daughter
dotir, daughter
dotur, daughter
dou, doe / dough
double,*,ed,ling,eness,ly,er, TWICE AS MANY AS THE ORIGINAL "prefixes: re"
doubt,*,ted,ting,table,tingly,tful,tfully, tless,tlessly, NOT COMPLETELY BELIEVABLE "prefixes: re/un"
douche,*,ed,hing, INTRODUCING FLUID INTO CAVITY OF BODY
dough,hy,hier,hiest,hiness, PASTY/ TACKY MIXTURE, MONEY
doughnut,*, ROUND PASTRY WITH HOLE
doul, dual / duel / dowel / dole
douls, dowel(s)
doun, down
doup, dope
dous, dose / douse / those / thus
douse,*,ed,sing,er, SMOTHER, PUT OUT, EXTINQUISH, SEEKS WATER, ALSO SPELLED 'DOUSE' (or see dowse)
dout, doubt / dote
dove,*, PAST TENSE FOR THE WORD "DIVE", A BIRD
dovegin, division
dovesubelity, divisible(bility)
dovesubl, divisible

dovine, divine
dovisability, divisible(bility)
dovorse, divorce
dow, dough / doe
dowel,*,led,ling, USED LIKE A NAIL/PIN/ SCREW
dowen, doing
dowl, dowel
down, OPPOSITE OF UP, FEATHERS OF A FOWL
downut, doughnut
dows, douse / dowse / dowel(s)
dowse,*,ed,sing,er, SMOTHER, PUT OUT, EXTINGUISH, SEEKS WATER, ALSO SPELLED 'DOUSE' (or see douse)
dowt, doubt
dowtful, doubt(full)
doz, doze / does / dose
doze,*,ed,zing,er,zy,zily,ziness, SLEEP LIGHTLY (or see dose)
dozen, TWELVE OF SOMETHING
dozent, doesn't
dozer,*, HEAVY EQUIPMENT WHICH MOVES EARTHEN MATERIAL
drad, dread
draft,*,ted,ting,ter,tier,tiest,ty,tily, tiness, A LIGHT BREEZE, TO PULL/ DRAW FROM "prefixes: in/over/up"
drag,*,gged,gging,ggingly, SLIDE/PULL WITH DIFFICULTY, PULLING WITHOUT LIFTING, MEN IN WOMEN'S CLOTHING
dragen, dragon
dragenfly, dragonfly
dragin, dragon
draginfly, dragonfly
dragon,*,nish, MYTHICAL ANIMAL
dragonfly,lies, INSECT
draid, dried
draier, drier
draiest, driest
draik, drake
drain,*,ned,ning,nage, FLUID/ENERGY FLOWING AWAY FROM, OUTLET "prefixes: under"
drake,*, INSECT FOR BAIT, MALE IN DUCK FAMILY
drama,*,atic,atical,atically,atize,aturgy, atist, GIVEN TO THEATER/PLAYS/ CHARACTER ROLES "prefixes: over/ melo"

dramatize,*,ed,zing,zation, GIVEN TO THEATER/PLAYS/ CHARACTER ROLES "prefixes: over"
dran, drawn / drain
drank, PAST TENSE FOR THE WORD "DRINK"
draot, drought
drape,*,ed,ping,ery,eries, HANGING CLOTH USED TO VEIL SOMETHING FROM SIGHT OR TO ENHANCE
drapir, dropper
drapur, dropper
dras, dress
drastic,cally, SEVERELY
drau, draw
draught, U.K. WORD FOR DRAFT (or see drought)
draul, droll / drawl
draun, drawn / drown
drauper, dropper
drause, drowsy
draut, drought
draw,*,wing,wn,rew,wable, TO BRING FORTH FROM OUT OF SIGHT, BRING TOWARDS "prefixes: over/un"
drawin, drawn
drawl,*,led,ling,ler,lingly, TO DRAG VOWELS OUT SLOWLY IN SPEAKING (or see droll)
drawn, PAST TENSE FOR THE WORD "DRAW" (or see drown) "prefixes: in/over"
drawnd, drown(ed)
drawpur, dropper
drawt, drought
dread,*,ded,ding,dful,dfully,dfulness, COMPLETE APPREHENSION IN FACING A SITUATION
dream,*,med,ming,mless,mlessly, mlessness,mful,mfully, mfulness, mily, my,mt, IMAGINE, THINK, ENVISION "prefixes: un"
dreary,rily,riness, GLOOMY
drebul, dribble
drebuld, dribble(d)
drech, dredge
dred, dread
dredge,*,ed,ging,er, TO GATHER OBJECTS UP FROM THE BOTTOM OF A BODY OF WATER WITH TOOLS/ MACHINERY
dreem, dream
dreft, drift
dreg, dredge

dreid, dried
drej, dredge
drel, drill
drem, dream
drench,hes,hed,hing,her, SOAKING WET
drenk, drink
drenker, drinker
drep, drip
drere, dreary
drery, dreary
dres, dress
dreser, dresser
dress,sses,sser,ssing,ssage, TO PUT ON CLOTHING "prefixes: re/un/under"
dresser, ONE WHO HELPS OTHERS DRESS IN COSTUMES, A CABINET WITH DRAWERS
dresur, dresser
drew, PAST TENSE FOR THE WORD "DRAW" "prefixes: over"
drewl, drool
drewp, droop
drezur, dresser
dri, dry
dribble,*,ed,ling,er, SMALL OR SHORT AMOUNT OF ANYTHING
dribul, dribble
drid, dried
dried, PAST TENSE FOR THE WORD "DRY"
drier, MORE DRY
driest, MOST" DRY
drift,*,ted,ting,tingly,tless,ty,ter, AMBLES ABOUT/AROUND/AWAY WITH EASE
drill,*,lled,lling,llable,ller, TO BORE, MAKE OPENINGS
drinch, drench
drink,*,king,rank,ker,kable,kability,runk, TO TAKE IN LIQUIDS
drinker,*, ONE WHO OVER INDULGES IN ALCOHOL
drip,*,pped,pping,ppy,pless, FALLING DROPS OF FLUID
drire, dreary
dris, dry(ries)
driur, drier / dryer
drive,*,ving,en,rove,er, TO MOVE/ PUSH/RIDE SOMETHING ALONG "prefixes: over"
drizzle,*,ed,ling,ly, VARIETY OF RAINFALL
dro, draw
drofe, drove

drog, drug
drol, drawl / droll
droll,ller,llest,llness,lly, ODDLY HUMOROUS (or see drawl)
droma, drama
dron, drone/ drawn / drown
dronc, drunk
drone,*,ed,ning,ningly,er, SINGLE TONE SOUND, A BEE, INCAPABLE OF FREE WILL/THOUGHT, REMOTE COMBAT VEHICLE
drool,*,led,ling,lingly,ler, SALIVA COMING FROM MOUTH
droop,*,ped,ping,pingly,py, TO LAY FORWARD LAZILY, SLUMP
drop,*,pped,pping,ppings,pper, LIQUID FALLING IN BLOBS, LET SOMETHING GO
droper, dropper
dropir, dropper
dropper,*,rful, AN INSTRUMENT WHICH ALLOWS A DROP AT A TIME
dropur, dropper
drought,*,ty, LONG PERIODS OF TIME WITHOUT WATER (or see draught)
droun, drown / drone
drouse, drowsy
drout, drought
drouze, drowsy
drove,*, PAST TENSE FOR THE WORD "DRIVE", MANY OF SOMETHING
drow, draw
drown,*,ned,ning, INTAKE OF WATER WHICH MAY KILL (or see drawn)
drowsy,sily,siness, NEARING SLEEP
drowt, drought
droz, draw(s)
dru, drew / true
druch, drudge
druchary, drudge(ry)
drudge,*,ed,ging,ery,eries,gingly, MENIAL/DULL WORK
druel, drool
drug,*,gged,gging,ggy, CHEMICALS (or see drudge)
drugd, drug(gged) / drudge(d)
druge, drudge / drug
druj, drudge
drujary, drudge(ry)
druk, drug
drul, drool
drum,*,mmed,mming,mmer, PERCUSSION INSTRUMENT, A LURING SOUND OR ACTION

drumd, drum(mmed)
drumer, drum(mmer)
drunk,*,ken,ker,kest,kard, PAST TENSE FOR THE WORD "DRINK", SOMEONE WHO DRINKS TOO MUCH ALCOHOL
drupe, droop
drus, dress
dry,ries,ried,ying,yable,yer,yest,iest, yable,yness,yly, TO REMOVE MOISTURE "prefixes: semi"
dryd, dried
dryer, APPLIANCE THAT DRIES CLOTHES (or see dry(rier))
dryest, driest
dryur, drier / dryer
du, dew / due / do
duable, do(able) / due(able)
dual,lity,lly,lism, TWO WORKING THE SAME, DOUBLE (or see duel) "prefixes: non"
duarf, dwarf
duarfs, dwarf(rves)
duat, duet
dub,*,bbed,bbing,bber, TITLE/NAME BESTOWED ON YOU BY ANOTHER, SOUND RECORDING
dubate, debate
dubilutate, debilitate
duble, double
dublikate, duplicate
dubol, double
dubry, debris
dubul, double
ducanter, decanter
duce,*, TWO, PEACE, LEAVING, LATER, STREET GANG (or see deuce)
ducenchen, descension / dissension
ducend, descend / dissent / descent / decent
ducent, dissent / descent / decent / descend
duch, douche
ducinchen, descension / dissension
ducind, descend / dissent / descent / decent
ducint, dissent / descent / decent / descend
duck,*,ked,king,ker,ky, TO STOOP/ TUCK/DIVE, FOWL/BIRD (or see duct)
ducline, decline

duct,*,ted,ting,tless,tal, CABLE/CHANNEL FOR VARIOUS THINGS, TAPE (or see duck(ed))
dud,*, DOESN'T WORK, CLOTHES (or see dude)
dudad, doodad
dude,*, TOURIST ON A RANCH, INFORMAL REFERENCE TO ANOTHER PERSON (or see duty)
dudi, duty
dudil, doodle
dudol, doodle
dudy, duty
due,*, OUTSTANDING DEBT, DATE IT IS PAYABLE UPON (or see dew/do) "prefixes: en/over/un"
dueble, do(able) / due(able)
duel,*,ling,list,ler, DISPUTE/FIGHT BETWEEN TWO PEOPLE/ FACTIONS (or see dual/dwell)
duen, doing
dueng, doing
duet,*,tist, TWO VOICES/INSTRUMENTS PERFORMING TOGETHER
duf, dove
dufalt, default
dufase, deface
dufeet, defeat
dufel, duffel
dufenative, definitive
dufendant, defendant
dufense, defense
dufensible, defensible
duffel, CANVAS/WOOL MATERIAL
duffil, duffel
duffle, duffel
dufianse, defiance
dufide, divide
dufil, duffel
dufinative, definitive
dufine, define
dufishant, deficient
dufishensy, deficiency
dufle, duffel
dufol, duffel
dufray, defray
dufrost, defrost
duful, duffel
dufunkt, defunct
dufy, defy
dugrade, degrade
dugree, degree
duible, do(able) / due(able)
duil, dual / duel

duin, doing
duing, doing
duk, duck / duke / duct
duka, decay
dukanter, decanter
dukd, duck(ed) / duct / duke(d)
duke,*,edom, FISTS, POSITION UNDER THAT OF PRINCE (or see duck/duct)
dukline, decline
dukrepit, decrepit
dukt, duck(ed) / duct / duke(d)
dul, dual / duel / dull
dulay, delay
dulcimer,*, STRINGED INSTRUMENT
dulectable, delectable
dulema, dilemma
dulereus, delirious
dulete, delete
dulever, deliver
duliburate, deliberate
dulicacy, delicacy
dulimu, dilemma
dulishus, delicious
dulite, delight / daylight
duliver, deliver
dull,*,lled,lling,ller,llest,llish,llness,lly, llard, WITHOUT SHINE/ ATTRACTIVENESS, BORING (or see duel/dual)
dulsemur, dulcimer
dulsimer, dulcimer
dulujen, delusion / dilute(tion)
duluxe, deluxe
dum, doom / dumb
dumand, demand
dumb,*,ber,best,bing,bly,bness,mmy, CANNOT SPEAK, NOT TOO BRIGHT, MANNEQUIN
dumbling, dumpling
dume, dummy / doom
dumean, demean
dumeener, demeanor
dumenish, diminish
dumenshen, dimension
dumention, dimension
dumenyen, dominion
dumer, dumb(er)
dumes, dummy(mies)
dumesdek, domestic
dumest, dumb(est)
dumestic, domestic
dumie, dummy
duminish, diminish
duminted, demented

dumir, dumb(er)
dumist, dumb(est)
dumize, demise
dummy,mmies,mmied,mmying, ONE BEING MANIPULATED INTO ACTION/MOTION, A MANNEQUIN/ PUPPET
dumonik, demon(ic)
dumor, dumb(er)
dump,*,ped,ping,per,py,pily,piness,pier, piest, TO HEAVILY FALL, BE DROPPED
dumpling,*, DOUGHBALLS EATEN IN SAUCE
dumur, dumb(er)
dumy, dummy
dun, done / dune
dunce,*, DERAGATORY TERM FOR SLOW LEARNER
dune,*, MOUND/HILL OF SAND
dung,*,ged,ging,gy, MANURE (or see dunk)
dungaree,*, HEAVY COTTON CLOTHING
dungeon,*, PRISON CELL, CASTLE BASEMENT
dungeree, dungaree
dunguree, dungaree
dunie, deny
dunjen, dungeon
dunk,*,ked,king, TO DIP INTO (or see dung)
dunomenator, denominator
dunomunashin, denomination
dunote, denote
duns, dunce / dune(s)
duo,uet, A PAIR
duol, dual / duel
duorf, dwarf
duorfs, dwarf(rves)
duparsher, departure
dupart, depart
dupartment, department
duparture, departure
dupe,*,ed,ping, TO TRICK/DECEIVE
dupend, depend
dupendant, dependant / dependent
dupendence, dependence
dupikt, depict
dupind, depend
duplacate, duplicate
dupleshin, depletion
duplete, deplete
duplex,xes,xity, TWO WORKING IDENTICALLY, SIDE-BY-SIDE

duplicate,*,ed,ting,tion,tor,able,ability,tely,tive, COPY OF THE ORIGINAL "prefixes: in/re"
duplicity,tous, TWO-FACED, MISLEADING
duplokate, duplicate
duploma, diploma
duplomusy, diplomacy
duplorable, deplorable
duplore, deplore
dupose, depose
dupozishen, deposition
dupozit, deposit
dupresheate, depreciate
duprive, deprive
durable,*,bility,eness,ly, USEFUL MANY TIMES "prefixes: non"
durachon, duration
durashen, duration
duration, FROM NOW UNTIL...
durdee, dirty
durebul, durable
durect, direct
durection, direction
durectory, directory
durekshun, direction
durekt, direct
durektory, directory
dureng, during
dureshon, duration
duress, UNDER STRESS, RESTRAINED FROM FREEDOM
duretion, duration
durible, durable
during, AT THE SAME TIME
durivadive, derivative
durivative, derivative
durive, derive
durmatites, dermal(atitis)
durt, dirt
durty, dirty
dus, does / due(s) / deuce
dusabiludy, disability
dusable, disable
dusaster, disaster
dusbite, despite
dusblay, display
dusbose, dispose
dusbute, dispute
duscrete, discreet / discrete
duscretion, discretion
duscuss, discuss
dusdane, disdain
dusdent, distend

dusdention, distend(nsion)
dusdentshen, distend(nsion)
dusderb, disturb
dusdort, distort
dusdrakt, distract
dusdrebute, distribute
duse, does / due(s) / deuce
duseese, decease / disease
duseft, deceive(d)
dusember, december
dusemble, dissemble
dusembul, dissemble
dusemunate, disseminate
dusenagrate, disintegrate
dusenchen, descension / dissension
dusend, descend / dissent / descent / decent
dusendent, descendant
dusenshen, dissension / descension
dusent, dissent / descent / decent / descend
duses, decease / disease / deuce(s)
dusest, decease(d) / disease(d)
duset, deceit
dusetful, deceit(ful)
dusev, deceive
dusevd, deceive(d)
duseze, disease
dusfegure, disfigure
dusgard, discard
dusgise, disguise
dusgrase, disgrace
dush, douche
dushevul, dishevel
dusidewus, deciduous
dusimanate, disseminate
dusimbul, dissemble
dusimbur, december
dusin, dozen
dusinagrate, disintegrate
dusindent, descendant
dusinshun, dissension/ descension
dusint, doesn't
dusipul, disciple
dusk,ky,kily,kiness, END OF DAY BEFORE NIGHTFALL
duskremanate, discriminate
duskrepensy, discrepancy
duskrete, discreet / discrete
duskribe, describe
duskripshen, description
duskust, disgust
duskuver, discover
duskwolify, disqualify

duslocate, dislocate
dusloge, dislodge
dusmanul, dismantle
dusmay, dismay
dusmiss, dismiss
dusmownt, dismount
dusolfe, dissolve
dusoreant, disorient
duspensible, dispensable
duspeut, dispute
duspinse, dispense
duspite, despite
dusplay, display
dusplease, displease
duspose, dispose
dusposil, disposal
dusposuble, disposable
dusregard, disregard
dusrobe, disrobe
dust,*,ted,ting,ty,tless,tily,tiness,ter, TINY PARTICLES OF MATTER
dustane, disdain
duste, dust(y)
dusteengwish, distinguish
dustendible, distend(sible)
dustenkt, distinct
dusterb, disturb
dustill, distill
dustingwish, distinguish
dustintible, distend(sible)
dustort, distort
dustract, distract
dustress, distress
dustroy, destroy
dustrukshen, destruction
duswrubshen, disruption
duswrubt, disrupt
dute, duty
dutektur, detector
dutenshin, detention
dutereate, deteriorate
dutereorate, deteriorate
duterint, deterrent
dutermin, determine
duterminashen, determination
duti, duty
duturgent, detergent
duty,ties,tiful,tifully,tifulness,teous, OBLIGATION, RESPONSIBILITY, NECESSARY "prefixes: un"
duv, dove
duvejin, division
duvelup, develop
duversity, diversity

duvesubelity, divisible(bility)
duvide, divide
duvigen, division
duvigin, division
duvijen, division
duvine, divine
duvise, device
duvisubil, divisible
duvize, device
duvoid, devoid
duvorse, divorce
duvoshen, devotion
duvursedy, diversity
duwen, doing
dux, duck(s) / duct / duke(s)
duz, due(s) / does
duzaster, disaster
duzen, dozen
duzent, doesn't
duzeze, disease
duzin, dozen
duzint, doesn't
duzolve, dissolve
duzoreint, disorient
dwarf,*,fed,fing,fish,fishly,fishness,fism, rves, STUNTED FROM FULL GROWTH "prefixes: semi"
dwarves, MORE THAN ONE DWARF (or see dwarf)
dwell,*,lled,lling,ller,lt, DELAY, LINGER
dwendle, dwindle
dwindle,*,ed,ling,er, SHRINK, DEGENERATE, SHRIVEL
dworf, dwarf
dyagnol, diagonal
dyagnose, diagnose
dyalekt, dialect
dyameter, diameter
dyatery, dietary
dye,*,ed,eing,er,yable, STAIN/COLOR/PIGMENTS TO APPLY (or see die/di) "prefixes: over"
dyet, diet
dyetery, dietary
dyignose, diagnose
dying, TOWARDS DEATH, TRANSFORMATION "prefixes: un"
dyke,*, MASCULINE LESBIAN (or see dike)
dylate, dilate
dynamic,*,ism,ist,istic,cal,cally, MOTION OF HIGH ENERGY "prefixes: bio"
dynamite,tic,er, EXPLOSIVES

dynasty,ties, STRING OF HEREDITARY RULERS
dypur, diaper / dipper
dyre, dire
dys, PREFIX INDICATING "BAD" MOST OFTEN MODIFIES THE WORD (or see die(s)/dice)
dysekt, dissect
dysentery,ric, INFECTIOUS DISEASE
dysfunction,*,nal, NOT ACTING WITHIN IDEAL LIMITS
dyslexia,ic, TIMING IN CORRPUS CALLOSUM NEURON SIGNALS WHICH AFFECTS COMMUNICATION BETWEEN BRAIN HEMISPHERES
dyufram, diaphragm
dyul, dial
dyulog, dialogue
dyureuh, diarrhea
each, ONE APIECE, TREATED INDIVIDUALLY
eager,rly,rness, MOTIVATED, VERY INTERESTED
eagle,*, BIRD
ear,*, GROWTH ON HEAD TO HEAR WITH
earing, earring
early,lier,liest,liness, PRIOR TO ORIGINAL TIME
earn,*,ned,ner,ning, REWARD FOR SERVICE/LABOR (or see urn) "prefixes: non/un"
earnest,*,tly,tness, SINCERE FEELINGS, EFFORT, MONEY TRANSACTION TO HOLD CONTRACT
earring,*, EAR ADORNMENT
earth,*,hed,hing,hen,hly,hlier,hliest, OUR PLANET "prefixes: un"
ease,*,ed,sing,eful,efully,efulness,sy, ABLE TO PERFORM WITHOUT STRAIN (or see easy) "prefixes: dis/un"
easel,*, TRIPOD TO HOLD WORKBOARDS, ETC.
easement,*, LEGAL USE/RIGHTS TO SOMETHING, TO HELP MAKE EASIER
easily, NO DIFFICULTY
east,tern,ternly,tward,terly,terlies, terner,ting,tings, COMPASS DIRECTION
easy,sier,siest,sily,siness, NOT DIFFICULT/HARD (or see ease) "prefixes: un"

eat,*,ting,ten,tery,table,tables,ter, edible, TO INGEST "prefixes: over"
eaves, OVERHANG OF A BUILDING
eaze, ease / easy
eb, ebb
ebademik, epidemic
ebasode, episode
ebb,*,bbed,bbing, TO FALL/SINK/RECEDE
ebdikate, abdicate
ebdumin, abdomen
ebedemek, epidemic
eberigenie, aborigine
ebide, abide
ebirijeny, aborigine
ebiss, abyss
ebnormul, abnormal
ebolish, abolish
ebomenable, abominable
ebominable, abominable
ebony, BLACK WOOD
ebord, aboard / abort
ebort, abort / aboard
ebowt, about
ebreveate, abbreviate
ebrod, abroad
ebsolv, absolve
ebstain, abstain
ebundinse, abundance
ebune, ebony
ebuve, above
ecademic, academic
eccentric,*,cally,city,cities, ODD, NOT OF THE NORM
ech, each / etch / edge / itch
echd, itch(ed) / etch(ed)
echo,oes,oed,oing,oingly, REPETITIVE SOUNDS BOUNCING BACK TOWARDS ORIGINATOR "prefixes: re"
echu, issue
echud, issue(d)
eckbrest, express(ed)
ecksderminate, exterminate
ecksdensible, extensible
eckdravert, extrovert
ecksdreem, extreme
eckspedeant, expedient
ecksplikuble, explicable
ecksploit, exploit
eckstensev, extensive
eckstensibly, extensible(ly)
ecksterminate, exterminate
ecksturminate, exterminate

eckuivocal, equivocal
eckwalibreum, equilibrium
eckwunimity, equanimity
eclectic,cally,cism, COMPILATION OF OTHERS WORK/VARIOUS SOURCES
eclektic, eclectic
eclepse, eclipse
eclipse,*,ed,sing,ptic, SHADOW CAST BY PLANETARY BODIES BLOCKING ANOTHER PLANETARY BODY
ecnolege, acknowledge
eco, PREFIX INDICATING "ECOLOGY" MOST OFTEN MODIFIES THE WORD (or see echo)
ecoli, A BACTERIA, PROPERLY SPELLED 'E COLI'
ecology,gical,gically,gist, SCIENCE ON ORGANISMS IN THE ENVIRONMENT
ecolugy, ecology
economy,mies,mic,mics,mical,mically, mize,mism,mist, GOODS AND MONEY "prefixes: dis/non/un"
econumy, economy
ecosfere, ecosphere
ecosistem, ecosystem
ecosphere, BREATHABLE AREA FOR LIFE
ecosystem,*, ORGANISMS INTERACTING TO CREATE ENVIRONMENT
ecquit, acquit
ecsclimashin, exclamation
ecsebt, except / accept
ecselerate, accelerate
ecsempt, exempt
ecsepshen, except(ion)
ecsite, excite
ecsklumashen, exclamation
ecspekt, expect
ecstasy,sies,atic,atically, JUBILANT, IN BLISS
ecsteengwish, extinguish
ecstradite, extradite
ecstrakt, extract
ecstuse, ecstasy
ecto, PREFIX INDICATING "OUTSIDE" MOST OFTEN MODIFIES THE WORD
ecute, acute
ecwanemity, equanimity
ecwashin, equation
ecwatic, aquatic
ecwilebreum, equilibrium
eczema,atous, SKIN IRRITATION FROM BACTERIA
eczima, eczema

ed, eat / eight / ate
edable, edible
edabt, adapt
edakit, etiquette
edapd, adapt
edapt, adapt
edatur, editor
edch, etch / edge / itch
eddy,ddies,ddied,ying, CIRCULAR MOVING CURRENT IN WATER/AIR
ede, eddy
edel, it'll
edelescense, adolescence
edelt, adult
edendum, addendum
edeology, ideology
edeosy, idiocy
edept, adept
edeshen, edition / add(ition)
edet, edit
edetur, editor
edeusy, idiocy
edeut, idiot
edge,*,ed,ging,gy,gier,giest,giness,er, POINT OF ANGLE WHERE ONE ANGLE DROPS OFF AT
edgust, adjust
edhere, adhere
edible,*,lity,eness, CAN BE SAFELY EATEN "prefixes: in"
edikit, etiquette
edikshen, addict(ion)
edil, it'll
edindum, addendum
ediosy, idiocy
edishen, edition / add(ition)
edit,*,ted,ting,tor,tion, MAKE READY FOR PUBLICATION "prefixes: in/un"
edition,*, ONE OUT OF A SET OF A PUBLISHED VOLUME (or see add(ition))
editor,*,rial,rially,rialist,rialize,rializes, rialized,rializing, DIRECTOR/ PREPARER OF WRITTEN MATERIAL
editur, editor
edj, etch / edge / itch
edjust, adjust
edmechen, admission
edmichen, admission
edmire, admire
edmishun, admission
edmit, admit
edmonish, admonish
edobt, adopt

edolt, adult
edoo, adieu
edopt, adopt
edore, adore
edorn, adorn
edrenulin, adrenaline
edres, address
edroit, adroit
edsedura, etcetera
edself, itself
edsh, etch / edge / itch
edu, adieu
eduble, edible
educate,*,ed,ting,tion,tional,tive,tor, INSTRUCT "prefixes: in/un"
edukit, etiquette
edul, it'll
edulescense, adolescence
edult, adult
edut, edit
edvantij, advantage
edverse, adverse
edvirse, adverse
edvise, advise / advice
edvurse, adverse
edy, eddy
edzetera, etcetera
eel,*, OCEAN FISH
eet, eat / yet
ef, if / eve
efact, effect / affect
efadent, evident
efaire, affair
efakt, effect / affect
efal, evil
efalushin, evolution
efan, even
efar, ever
efare, affair
efect, effect / affect
efegy, effigy
efekt, effect / affect
efektive, effect(ive) / affect(ive)
efeminate, effeminate
efeminit, effeminate
efen, even
efening, evening
efenity, affinity
efer, ever / affair
efert, effort
eferves, effervesce
efervesant, effervescent
efervescent, effervescent
efeus, effuse

efews, effuse
effect,*,ted,ting,tive,tively,tiveness,tual, tually,tualness,tuate, tuation, RESULT, FULFILLMENT ACCOMPLISHMENT (or see affect) "prefixes: in"
effeminate,acy,acies,ely,eness, OF FEMININE PERSUASION
effervesce,*,ed,cing,ence,ent,ently, GASEOUS BUBBLES, HAPPY FEELINGS
effervescent,tly,nce, GASEOUS BUBBLES, STRONG FEELINGS
efficacy,city,cious,ciously,ciousness, TO BE EFFECTIVE "prefixes: in"
efficiency,cies,nt, PRODUCE WELL IN SHORT PERIOD OF TIME, TYPE OF LIVING QUARTERS
efficient,tly,ncy, PRODUCE EFFECTIVELY IN SHORT PERIOD OF TIME "prefixes: in"
effigy,gies, SOMETHING CONSTRUCTED IN HUMAN LIKENESS
effort,*,tless,tlessly,tlessness, ATTEMPT TO PRODUCE, SHOW SKILLS/ TALENTS
effuse,*,ed,sing,sion,sive,sively,siveness, EXPRESS/FLOW/SPREAD FREELY
efichent, efficient
eficiency, efficiency
efident, evident
efigy, effigy
efil, evil
efilushen, evolution
efin, even
efinity, affinity
efir, ever
efirves, effervesce
efirvesant, effervescent
efishensy, efficiency
efishent, efficient
efisiancy, efficiency
efl, evil
eflikt, afflict
eflot, afloat
efluinse, affluence
efning, evening
efodent, evident
efogy, effigy
efol, evil
efolushin, evolution
efolve, evolve
efon, even
efoot, afoot

efor, ever
eford, afford
efort, effort
efrad, afraid
efrebote, every(body)
efreda, every(day)
efree, every
efrething, every(thing)
efrewer, every(where)
efrewun, every(one)
efriwun, every(one)
efront, affront
efrunt, affront
efryday, every(day)
efudent, evident
efugy, effigy
eful, evil
efulushun, evolution
efur, ever
efurt, effort
efurves, effervesce
efurvesant, effervescent
efuse, effuse
efut, afoot
eg, edge / egg / etch / itch
egajurate, exaggerate
egalatarian, egalitarian
egalitarian,*,nism, EQUALITY OF ALL PEOPLES
egalutarean, egalitarian
egekt, eject
egemplify, exemplify
egenst, against
eger, eager
egern, adjourn
egg,*,gged,gging,ggy, PRODUCED BY FOWL/BIRD/REPTILES
eginst, against
egle, eagle
egneranse, ignorant(nce)
egneshin, ignition
egneus, igneous
egnide, ignite
egnishin, ignition
egnite, ignite
egnor, ignore
egnorants, ignorant(nce)
egnurant, ignorant
ego,*,oism,oist,otistic,oistical,oistically, otist,otism,ocentric, PART OF US THAT IS SELF-SERVING/FEARFUL (or see echo)
egotist,tic,tical,tically, CENTERED ON SELF

egotistic,cal,cally, CENTERED ON ONESELF
egre, agree
egresiv, aggressive
egsabishen, exhibit(ion)
egsadera, etcetera
egsagurate, exaggerate
egsajurate, exaggerate
egsakt, exact
egsam, exam
egsample, example
egsaspurate, exasperate
egsastshin, exhaust(ion)
egsbarenshal, experiential
egsbereanse, experience
egsberenshal, experiential
egsberimentashen, experiment(ation)
egsbire, expire
egsblan, explain
egsblekuble, explicable
egsblod, explode
egsblor, explore
egsbloshen, explosion
egsbort, export
egsboz, expose
egsbres, express
egsburenshal, experiential
egsburt, expert
egscavate, excavate
egsclusive, exclusive
egsdensible, extensible
egsdra, extra
egsdradite, extradite
egsdrakt, extract
egsdreem, extreme
egsdrordinare, extraordinaire
egsdrordinary, extraordinary
egsduse, ecstasy
egsebit, exhibit
egsebt, except / accept
egsecutive, executive
egsedira, etcetera
egseed, exceed
egsemplify, exemplify
egsempt, exempt
egsemshen, exempt(ion)
egsepshen, except(ion)
egsept, except / accept
egsersize, exercise / exorcise
egsert, exert
egsesif, excess(ive) / access(ive)
egsest, exist
egsetara, etcetera
egsglumashen, exclamation

egshale, exhale
egsibeshen, exhibit(ion)
egsibit, exhibit
egsilarate, exhilarate / accelerate
egsile, exile
egsima, eczema
egsimplify, exemplify
egsimt, exempt
egsist, exist
egsistens, exist(ence)
egsit, exit
egskershun, excursion
egskurshen, excursion
egskuvate, excavate
egsorsize, exercise / exorcise
egsost, exhaust
egsostshen, exhaust(ion)
egsotic, exotic
egspadishen, expedition
egspand, expand
egspans, expanse / expense
egspect, expect
egspedient, expedient
egspeedeint, expedient
egspel, expel
egspense, expense
egsperament, experiment
egspereanse, experience
egspinse, expense
egspirashen, expire(ration)
egspire, expire
egsplanashen, explanation
egsplanatory, explanatory
egsplane, explain
egsplecable, explicable
egsplesit, explicit
egsplod, explode
egsplor, explore
egsplorashen, explore(ration)
egsploratory, explore(ratory)
egsploshen, explosion
egsplosive, explosive
egsplunashen, explanation
egsport, export
egsportashen, export(ation)
egspos, expose
egspres, express
egspurashen, expire(ration)
egspurt, expert
egsqwizit, exquisite
egstend, extend
egstengwish, extinguish
egstenkt, extinct
egstensev, extensive

egstenshen, extension
egstenuate, extenuate
egstereor, exterior
egsternul, external
egstinkt, extinct
egstinsev, extensive
egstra, extra
egstradite, extradite
egstrakt, extract
egstravert, extrovert
egstrem, extreme
egstremly, extreme(ly)
egstrordinare, extraordinaire
egstrordinary, extraordinary
egsturnal, external
egsubishen, exhibit(ion)
egsulent, excellent
egsurshen, exert(ion)
egsurt, exert
egszemt, exempt
egukate, educate
egul, eagle
egur, eager
egzajurate, exaggerate
egzakt, exact
egzam, exam
egzample, example
egzema, eczema
egzershin, exert(ion)
egzile, exile
egzilurate, exhilarate / accelerate
egzima, eczema
egzimpt, exempt
egzimt, exempt
egzist, exist
egzit, exit
egzotek, exotic
egzurshen, exert(ion)
egzursize, exercise / exorcise
egzurtion, exert(ion)
ehed, ahead
eight,*,teen,teenth,tieth,ty, ENGLISH NUMBER (or see ate)
eighteen,nth,nths, ENGLISH NUMBER
eil, aisle
eir, air / heir / err
eit, eight / ate
ej, edge / etch / itch
ejakt, eject
eject,*,ted,ting,tion,table,tive,tor,tors, FORCED TO LEAVE/BE EXPELLED
ejekt, eject
ejenda, agenda
ejern, adjourn

ejorn, adjourn
ejrenalin, adrenaline
ejukate, educate
ejusduble, adjust(able)
ejust, adjust
ekademe, academy
ekadume, academy
ekaunemity, equanimity
ekcept, accept / except
ekcesori, accessory
ekchange, exchange
eklektic, eclectic
eklipse, eclipse
ekliptik, eclipse(ptic)
eknolege, acknowledge
eknor, ignore
eknurint, ignorant
eko, echo / ego
ekod, echo(ed)
ekology, ecology
ekolugy, ecology
ekonimy, economy
ekonume, economy
ekosestum, ecosystem
ekosfere, ecosphere
ekosistem, ecosystem
ekosphere, ecosphere
eksadra, etcetera
eksagerashen, exaggerate(tion)
eksajurashen, exaggerate(tion)
eksakute, execute
eksalant, excellent
eksalins, excel(llence)
eksam, exam
eksamen, examine
eksamenashen, examine(nation)
eksamin, examine
eksaminashen, examine(nation)
eksample, example
eksapurashen, exasperate(tion)
eksaqute, execute
eksated, exit(ed)
eksbarenshal, experiential
eksbedeant, expedient
eksberament, experiment
eksberenshal, experiential
eksbire, expire
eksbirenshal, experiential
eksblan, explain
eksblanashen, explanation
eksblanatory, explanatory
eksbleckable, explicable
eksblinashen, explanation
eksblod, explode

eksblor, explore
eksblorashen, explore(ration)
eksbloshen, explosion
eksbloytashen, exploit(ation)
eksbortashen, export(ation)
eksbos, expose
eksbres, express
eksburashen, expire(ration)
eksburenshal, experiential
eksburt, expert
ekscalate, escalate / escalade
ekscerjen, excursion
ekschange, exchange
eksclemashin, exclamation
eksclusive, exclusive
ekscurshin, excursion
ekscuse, excuse
eksdansev, extensive
eksdensible, extensible
eksderminate, exterminate
eksdra, extra
eksdradite, extradite
eksdrakt, extract
eksdravert, extrovert
eksdreem, extreme
eksdrem, extreme
eksdremly, extreme(ly)
eksdrivurt, extrovert
eksdrordinare, extraordinaire / extraordinary
eksdurminate, exterminate
eksebit, exhibit
eksebt, except / accept
eksecutive, executive
eksedra, etcetera
eksekute, execute
eksel, excel / accel
ekselarashen, accelerate(tion)
ekseld, excel(lled) / accel(lled)
ekselense, excellent
ekselerashen, accelerate(tion)
ekselerate, accelerate
ekselurashen, accelerate(tion)
ekseluratur, accelerate(tor)
eksemplify, exemplify
eksentrek, eccentric
eksentrik, eccentric
eksepshen, except(ion)
ekseptense, accept(ance)
ekserpt, excerpt
eksert, exert
ekses, excess / access
eksesif, excess(ive) / access(ive)
eksesis, excess(es) / access(es)

eksesori, accessory
eksetera, etcetera
eksfoleate, exfoliate
eksglud, exclude
eksglumashen, exclamation
eksglut, exclude
ekshale, exhale
eksibishen, exhibit(ion)
eksibit, exhibit
eksilarat, exhilarate / accelerate
eksile, exile
eksilens, excel(llence)
eksimplify, exemplify
eksimpt, exempt
eksimshen, exempt(ion)
eksinshuate, accentuate
eksintrik, eccentric
eksirpt, excerpt
eksistens, exist(ence)
eksit, exit / excite
eksitment, excite(ment)
ekskalate, escalate / escalade
eksklumashen, exclamation
ekskurshen, excursion
ekskuse, excuse
ekskuvaded, excavate(d)
ekskuvashen, excavate(tion)
ekskuvate, excavate
ekskwisit, exquisite
ekslusef, exclusive
eksolent, excellent
eksorbeint, exorbitant
eksorbident, exorbitant
eksorsize, exercise / exorcise
ekspadishen, expedition
ekspand, expand
ekspans, expanse / expense
ekspedishen, expedition
ekspekt, expect
ekspektashen, expect(tation)
ekspektent, expect(ant)
ekspel, expel
ekspend, expend
ekspense, expense
ekspensef, expense(sive)
eksperament, experiment
ekspereanse, experience
eksperenshal, experiential
ekspert, expert
ekspinse, expense
ekspire, expire
ekspirenshal, experiential
eksplan, explain
eksplanashen, explanation

eksplanatory, explanatory
eksplecable, explicable
eksplicit, explicit
eksplisit, explicit
eksplisitly, explicit(ly)
eksplod, explode
eksploet, exploit
eksploit, exploit
eksplor, explore
eksplorashen, explore(ration)
eksploratory, explore(ratory)
eksploshen, explosion
eksplosive, explosive
eksployt, exploit
eksplunashen, explanation
eksport, export
eksportashen, export(ation)
ekspos, expose
eksprenshal, experiential
ekspres, express
ekspurenshal, experiential
eksqus, excuse
ekstansive, extensive
ekstend, extend
ekstengwish, extinguish
ekstensebly, extensible(ly)
ekstensev, extensive
ekstenshen, extension
ekstenuate, extenuate
ekstenzable, extensible
ekstereur, exterior
ekstind, extend
ekstinkt, extinct
ekstinsebly, extensible(ly)
ekstinsev, extensive
ekstra, extra
ekstradite, extradite
ekstrakt, extract
ekstravert, extrovert
ekstrem, extreme
ekstremly, extreme(ly)
ekstrivurt, extrovert
ekstrordinare, extraordinaire
ekstrordinary, extraordinary
ekstruvert, extrovert
eksturnal, external
ekstuse, ecstasy
eksubishen, exhibit(ion)
eksulant, excellent
eksulashen, exhale(lation)
eksulins, excellent(nce)
eksuqushen, execute(tion)
eksurpt, excerpt
eksurshen, exert(ion)

eksursize, exercise / exorcise
eksurt, exert
eksuvashen, excavate(tion)
ekuate, equate
ekute, acute
ekwabil, equable
ekwable, equable
ekwade, equity
ekwader, equator
ekwal, equal
ekwalebreum, equilibrium
ekwalete, equality
ekwaliz, equal(ize)
ekwanimety, equanimity
ekwanimity, equanimity
ekwashun, equation
ekwate, equate / equity
ekwatur, equator
ekwaul, equal
ekwauzition, acquisition
ekwebul, equable
ekwel, equal
ekwelebreum, equilibrium
ekwenox, equinox
ekwevalent, equivalent
ekwevokul, equivocal
ekwil, equal
ekwinoks, equinox
ekwip, equip
ekwipment, equipment
ekwit, acquit
ekwity, equity
ekwivokate, equivocate
ekwivulent, equivalent
ekwolity, equality
ekwoliz, equal(ize)
ekwotek, aquatic
ekwuble, equable
ekwude, equity
ekwul, equal
ekwulebrium, equilibrium
ekwuliz, equal(ize)
ekwunimity, equanimity
ekwunox, equinox
ekwuzition, acquisition
el, eel / ail / ill / ale
elagint, elegant
elakwens, eloquence
elakwense, eloquence
elakwent, eloquent
elamentary, elementary
elaquence, eloquence
elaquens, eloquence
elaquent, eloquent

elarm, alarm
elastic,*,cally,city,cize,cizes,cized,cizing, STRETCHES OUT/ SHRINKS BACK "prefixes: in"
elastrate, illustrate
elate,*,ed,ting,tion, RAISED MOOD/ SPIRIT
elavashen, elevate(tion)
elavater, elevate(r)
elbow,*,wed,wing, JOINT IN THE ARM
elbum, album
elchuhol, alcohol
elder,*,est,rly,liness,rship, ONE WHO HAS LIVED MORE YEARS THAN OTHERS (or see alder)
eldur, elder
ele, alley
elect,*,ted,ting,tion,tions,table,tive, tively,tiveness,tor,toral, torally, torate,tioneer,tioneers,tioneered, tioneering, TO MAKE A CHOICE "prefixes: un"
elective,*,ely,eness, OPTION TO CHOOSE
elector,*,ral,rally,rate, VOTERS
electric,cal,cals,cally,city,ify,ro,cian, FREQUENCY/ENERGY EXISTING IN ALL PARTICLES "prefixes: bio"
electrician,*, PEOPLE WHO WORK WITH WIRES/ELECTRICITY
electrishun, electrician
electro, PREFIX INDICATING "ELECTRIC" MOST OFTEN MODIFIES THE WORD
electron,*,nic,nics,nically, A CHARGED PARTICLE
eledge, allege
elefint, elephant
elegable, eligible
elegance, BEAUTIFUL/CLASSY "prefixes: in"
eleganse, allegiance / elegance
elegant,tly,nce, BEAUTIFUL/CLASSY "prefixes: in"
elege, allege
elegible, eligible
elegul, illegal
elejense, allegiance / elegance
elekt, elect
elektev, elective
elektric, electric
elektrician, electrician
elektrishen, electrician
elekul, illegal
elekwens, eloquence

elekwent, eloquent
elemanate, eliminate
element,*,tal,tally,tary, BASIC, FUNDAMENTAL "prefixes: retro"
elementary,rily,riness, FIRST AND BASIC
elephant,*, AN ANIMAL
eleptic, elliptic
elere, allure
elergik, allergic
elert, alert
elet, elite
eletist, elite(tist)
elevashen, elevate(tion)
elevate,*,ed,ting,tion,tional,tor, RAISE HORIZONTAL LEVEL
eleveate, alleviate
eleven,nth,nths, AN ENGLISH NUMBER
elevin, eleven
elevinth, eleven(th)
elf,elves,fin,fish, IMAGINARY ENTITIES
elfs, elf(lves)
elgebra, algebra
elianse, alliance
elicit,*,ted,ting,tation,tor, PROVOKE/ DRAW RESPONSE (or see illicit)
eliderate, illiterate
elifent, elephant
eligable, eligible
eligent, elegant
eligible,*,bly,bility,bilities, POTENTIAL TO BE CHOSEN "prefixes: in"
elikwens, eloquence
elikwent, eloquent
elimenate, eliminate
eliminate,*,ed,ting,tion,tive,tor,tory, GET RID OF, DISPOSE
elimony, alimony
eline, align
elipse, ellipse
elipsus, ellipsis
eliptic, elliptic
eliquence, eloquence
eliquent, eloquent
eliset, elicit / illicit
elisit, elicit / illicit
elistrate, illustrate
elite,*,tist,tism, GROUP OF THOSE WHO BELIEVE THEY ARE THE BEST OF THEIR KIND/CATEGORY
eliturate, illiterate
elivashen, elevate(tion)
elive, alive
elk, IN THE DEER FAMILY
ellipse,sis, GEOMETRIC SHAPE

ellipsis, SYMBOL USED IN PLACE OF A WORD (...)
elliptic,cal,cally,city,cities, OVAL SHAPE, TO BE CONCISE "prefixes: semi"
ellisit, elicit / illicit
elliterate, illiterate
ellustrious, illustrious
elnes, ill(ness)
elogekul, illogical
elogicul, illogical
elongate,*,ed,ting,tion, TO LENGTHEN, MAKE LONGER
elood, elude
eloor, allure
eloosuf, allusive / elusive / illusive
eloot, elude
elope,*,ed,ping, GO AWAY TO BE WED WITHOUT NOTIFICATION
eloquence,*, TASTEFULLY/PERSUASIVELY COMMUNICATED
eloquent,tly,tness,nce, STRIKING/MOVING EXPRESSION "prefixes: in"
elorm, alarm
elostrious, illustrious
elovate, elevate
eloy, alloy
else,*, NOT WHO/WHAT/WHERE INTENDED OR EXPECTED
elsewhere, SOMEWHERE OTHER THAN WHERE EXPECTED TO BE
elso, also
eltetude, altitude
eltitude, altitude
elucidate,*,ed,ting,tion,tive,tor,tory, useness,usion, MAKE CLEAR/UNDERSTANDABLE, EXPLAIN
elude,*,ed,ding,usive,usion, GET AWAY, NOT BE PERCEIVED/DEFINED (or see allude)
elufint, elephant
elugable, eligible
elugant, elegant
elugens, elegant(nce) / elegance
elugent, elegant
elugint, elegant
elukwens, eloquence
elukwent, eloquent
elumenade, illuminate
elumentary, elementary
elumenum, aluminum
eluminate, illuminate
elumintry, elementary
eluminum, aluminum
elumony, alimony

eluquence, eloquence
eluquent, eloquent
elure, allure
elurgik, allergic
elurjik, allergic
elurt, alert
elushun, illusion / allusion
elusive,ely,eness,sory, GET AWAY, NOT BE PERCEIVED (or see allusive/illusive)
elustrate, illustrate
elustrious, illustrious
eluvashen, elevate(tion)
eluvate, elevate
em, PREFIX INDICATING "INTO/ON/PUT INTO" MOST OFTEN MODIFIES THE WORD (or see am/them)
emachure, amateur
emaculet, immaculate
emage, image
emagenashen, imagine(ation)
emagrant, immigrant / emigrant
emagrashen, immigrate(tion)
emagrate, immigrate
emagrunt, immigrant / emigrant
emagunashen, imagine(ation)
emaj, image
emajinashen, imagine(nation)
emakewlit, immaculate
emakulit, immaculate
emanate,*,ed,ting,tion,tional,tionist,tive, EMITS, GIVES OFF, SENDS OUT
emancipate,*,ed,ting,tion, FREE FROM BONDAGE
emanens, eminence / imminence / immanence
emanent, eminent / imminent / immanent
emanit, eminent / imminent / immanent
emansepade, emancipate
emansipate, emancipate
ematashin, imitate(tion)
ematate, imitate
ematation, imitate(tion)
ematerial, immaterial
emature, immature
embankment,*, A BURM/MOUND
embargo,oes, RESTRICT FROM PORTS
embaris, embarrass
embark,*,ked,king, PREPARING TO TAKE A JOURNEY "prefixes: dis"

embarrass,sses,ssed,ssing,ssingly,ssment, UNDESIRABLY EXPOSED "prefixes: dis"
embassy,sies, SAFE PLACE WITHIN ANOTHER COUNTRY
embaudes, embody(dies)
embed,*,dded,dding, SINK INTO UNTIL FLUSH
ember,*, SPARK/COAL FROM FIREWOOD
emberis, embarrass
embilukil, umbilical
embishun, ambition
emblem,*, A SYMBOL OR FIGURE
emblie, imply
emblum, emblem
embody,dies,died,dying,diment,diments, OF A VISIBLE FORM, TANGIBLE, PARTS INTO A WHOLE "prefixes: dis"
emboss,sses,ssed,ssing,sser,ssment, IMPRINT INTO
embostur, imposter
emboudes, embody(dies)
embrace,*,ed,cing,eable,ement,er, TO HOLD DEAR
embrase, embrace
embreo, embryo
embroeder, embroider
embroider,*,red,ring,rer,ry,ries, STITCH WITH NEEDLE/THREAD
embrufe, improve
embrufment, improve(ment)
embryo,*,onic,onical,onically,ology,ologist,otic, SOMETHING GROWING INSIDE BEFORE IT EMERGES "prefixes: pre"
embtee, empty
embulense, ambulance
embur, ember
embush, ambush
embuzishun, impose(sition)
emcompruble, incomparable
emcumblete, incomplete
emeable, amiable
emedeat, immediate
emej, image
emenate, emanate
emend, amend
emense, immense
emensurable, immensurable
emerald, A COLOR, A GEMSTONE
emerchen, immerse(sion)

emerge,*,ed,ging,ence,ent,ency,encies, COME FROM WITHIN, ERUPT, COME INTO BEING
emergency,cies, TO BE DEALT WITH IMMEDIATELY
emerjensee, emergency
emersable, immersible
emersed, PLANT PARTS ABOVE WATER (or see immerse(d))
emershen, immerse(sion)
emeshen, emission / omission
emeterial, immaterial
emfadek, emphatic
emfasis, emphasis / emphasize
emfusis, emphasis / emphasize
emigrant,*, FOREIGNER FROM ANOTHER COUNTRY (or see immigrant)
emigrate,*,ed,ting,tion, LEAVE A COUNTRY TO GO TO ANOTHER (or see immigrate)
emigrunt, immigrant / emigrant
emij, image
eminate, emanate
emind, amend
eminence,cy, FORMAL RANK/POSITION (or see imminence/immanence)
eminens, eminence / imminence / immanence
eminent,tly,nce, SOMEONE WHO ACHIEVES BEYOND OTHERS (or see eminence/imminence/immanence) "prefixes: pre"
eminse, immense
eminsurable, immensurable
emirchen, immerse(sion)
emirge, emerge
emirsable, immersible
emirshen, immerse(sion)
emission,*, SOMETHING DISCHARGED, PUT INTO CIRCULATION (or see omission)
emit,*,tted,tting,tter, DISCHARGE, PUT OUT A FREQUENCY (or see omit)
emitate, imitate
emitation, imitate(tion)
emiterial, immaterial
emmagrate, immigrate / emigrate
emmensurable, immensurable
emmershen, immerse(sion)
emminsurable, immensurable
emmirsible, immersible
emmobile, immobile
emmpresion, impression

emmpressive, impressive
emmurshen, immerse(sion)
emobile, immobile
emochun, emotion
emograte, immigrate / emigrate
emonate, emanate
emonens, eminence / imminence / immanence
emonent, eminent / imminent / immanent
emonia, ammonia
emople, immobile
emoral, immoral
emordul, immortal
emortal, immortal
emortalety, immortal(ity)
emorul, immoral
emoshin, emotion
emoterial, immaterial
emotion,*,nal,nally,nality,nless,nalize, nalizes,nalized,nalizing,ive,ivism, REACTION CAUSED BY CHEMICALS RELEASED BY WHAT WE ARE THINKING "prefixes: non/un"
emownt, amount
empachuis, impetuous
empact, impact
empairm, empower
empar, empower
emparasist, empirical(cist)
empare, impair
emparetive, imperative
emparical, empirical
emparment, empower(ment)
emparor, emperor
empathy, ABILITY TO UNDERSTAND/ FEEL ANOTHER PERSON'S EXPERIENCE/FEELINGS
empaurment, empower(ment)
empeach, impeach
empecable, impeccable
empechuis, impetuous
empede, impede
empeed, impede
empekuble, impeccable
emperative, imperative
emperfect, imperfect
emperor,*, RULER OF PEOPLE/LAND
empersenate, impersonate
empersonal, impersonal
empersonashen, impersonate(tion)
empersonate, impersonate
empetchuis, impetuous

emphasis,ize, PLACE GREAT IMPORTANCE IN/UPON "prefixes: de-/over"
emphasize,*,ed,zing,is, PLACE GREAT IMPORTANCE IN/UPON "prefixes: de-/over"
emphatic,cally, PLACE GREAT IMPORTANCE IN/UPON
emphisis, emphasis / emphasize
empire,*, REGION OF PEOPLE/LAND RULED BY AN EMPEROR
empirer, emperor
empirfect, imperfect
empirical,lly,cism,cist,cists,rics, RELIES ONLY ON OBSERVATION/ EXPERIMENT
empirsonal, impersonal
emplament, implement
emplant, implant
emplicate, implicate
emplication, implicate(tion)
emploe, employee / employ
emploer, employer
employ,*,yed,ying,yable,yability,yer, yee,yeement, USE SOMETHING/ SOMEONE TO COMPLETE A TASK WHICH MAY/MAY NOT INVOLVE MONEY (or see employee) "prefixes: sub/un"
employee,*, SOMEONE WHO IS LEGALLY HIRED AND WORKS FOR PAY (or see employ) "prefixes: non/ under"
employer,*, SOMEONE WHO PAYS SOMEONE ELSE TO WORK "prefixes: non"
employment,*, BEING HIRED TO WORK "prefixes: un"
emplucashen, implicate(tion)
emplucate, implicate
emplument, implement
emply, imply
empofuresh, impoverish
empolite, impolite
empolse, impulse
emport, import
emportant, important
emportashen, import(ation)
emportins, important(nce)
empose, impose
emposible, impossible
emposter, imposter
emposuble, impossible
empound, impound

empour, empower
empourtens, important(nce)
empourtent, important
empoverish, impoverish
empower,*,red,ring,ment, TEACH/ PROVIDE SOMEONE WITH ABILITY TO DO THINGS FOR THEMSELVES "prefixes: dis"
empoze, impose
empraktecul, impractical
emprapuble, improbable
emprasev, impressive
emprashen, impression
emprasise, imprecise
empravize, improvise
emprechen, impression
emprecise, imprecise
empregnable, impregnable
empregnate, impregnate
empregnuble, impregnable
emprent, imprint
empres, empress / impress
empresef, impressive
empreshen, impression
empresif, impressive
empresise, imprecise
empresive, impressive
empresont, imprison(ed)
empress,sses, FEMALE RULER OF EMPIRE (or see impress)
empretion, impression
emprint, imprint
emprison, imprison
emprobable, improbable
empromptu, impromptu
empromtu, impromptu
empropable, improbable
emproper, improper
emprove, improve
emprovement, improve(ment)
emprovisation, improvise(sation)
emprovize, improvise
emprovusashen, improvise(sation)
emprufe, improve
emprus, empress / impress
empruve, improve
empruvize, improvise
emptee, empty
empty,ties,tied,tying,tier,tiest,tily,tiness, REMOVE CONTENTS FROM SOMETHING "prefixes: non"
empulite, impolite
empulse, impulse
empulsef, impulse(sive)

empulsive, impulse(sive)
empurfect, imperfect
empurfekt, imperfect
empuror, emperor
empursenate, impersonate
empursonal, impersonal
emput, input
emputate, amputate
empuzishen, impose(sition)
emruld, emerald
emte, empty
emug, image
emugrant, immigrant / emigrant
emugrashen, immigrate(tion) / emigrate(tion)
emugrate, immigrate
emuj, image
emulate,*,ed,ting,tion,tive,tively,tor, lous,lously,lousness, STRIVE TO LIVE UP TO
emune, immune
emunens, eminence / imminence/ immanence
emunety, immune(nity)
emunezashen, immunize(zation)
emunise, immunize
emurg, emerge
emurgensee, emergency
emursable, immersible
emurse, immerse / emersed
emutashin, imitate(tion)
emutate, imitate
emuterial, immaterial
emuze, amuse
en, PREFIX INDICATING "INTO/ON/PUT INTO" MOST OFTEN MODIFIES THE WORD (or see prefix in/un/inn)
enabiledy, inability
enability, inability
enabishen, inhibit(ion)
enable,*,ed,ling,ement,er, EMPOWER/ AID SOMEONE/SOMETHING TO PERFORM MORE EFFICIENTLY (or see unable) "prefixes: dis"
enabul, enable / unable
enaccessible, inaccessible
enact,*,ted,ting,tment,table,tor,tive, TO PERFORM/MAKE INTO (or see inactive)
enaction, inaction
enacuracy, inaccurate(acy)
enacurate, inaccurate
enadekwit, inadequate
enadequate, inadequate

enadikwit, inadequate
enadmisable, inadmissible
enadukwit, inadequate
enadverdent, inadvertent
enadvirdent, inadvertent
enadvisable, inadvisable
enagerashen, inaugurate(tion)
enaksesible, inaccessible
enakshen, inaction
enakt, enact
enaktif, inactive / enact(ive)
enakurite, inaccurate
enalegy, analogy
enalesis, analysis
enaleuble, inalienable
enalienable, inalienable
enaligy, analogy
enaliuble, inalienable
enalugy, analogy
enamel,*,led,ling,ler,list, PAINT, A PROTECTIVE COATING
enamoly, anomaly
enanemit, inanimate
enanimate, inanimate
enapal, enable / unable
enappreciative, inappreciative
enapproachable, inapproachable
enappropriate, inappropriate
enaprochible, inapproachable
enapropriate, inappropriate
enapul, enable / unable
enaquerisy, inaccurate(acy)
enaqulashen, inoculate(tion)
enaqulate, inoculate
enaqurite, inaccurate
enarferins, interfere(nce)
enarkey, anarchy
enarup, interrupt
enasinse, innocence
enate, innate
enatequit, inadequate
enatible, inaudible
enatmisable, inadmissible
enatvirdent, inadvertent
enatvisable, inadvisable
enatvurtent, inadvertent
enaudible, inaudible
enauf, enough
enaugurate, inaugurate
enaukulate, inoculate
enaumily, anomaly
enavadif, innovate(tive)
enbankment, embankment
enbark, embark

enbasee, embassy
enbed, embed
enberis, embarrass
enblem, emblem
enboard, inboard
enbord, inboard
enboss, emboss
enbrase, embrace
enbroder, embroider
encamp,*,ped,ping,pment, BE IN/ OF A CAMP
encandescent, incandescent
encantashen, incantation
encantation, incantation
encapable, incapable
encapacitate, incapacitate
encapacity, incapacity
encapsulate,*,ed,ting,tion, SURROUND, ENCLOSE
encapuble, incapable
encarnate, incarnate
encarsurate, incarcerate
encase,*,ed,sing,ement, ENCLOSE/ SURROUND WITH A COVER
encast, encase(d)
encendiary, incendiary
encenerate, incinerate
encentive, incentive
enception, incept(ion)
encereg, encourage / anchor(age)
encesant, incessant
encesint, incessant
encesunt, incessant
ench, inch
enchant,*,ted,ting,tment, DELIGHT, FASCINATE "prefixes: dis"
enchenyewus, ingenuous
enchor, anchor
enchur, ensure / insure
encindeary, incendiary
encircle,*,ed,ling,ement, SURROUND WITH A CIRCLE
encisor, incise(sor)
encite, incite / inside
encitment, incite(ment)
encize, incise
enclanation, incline(nation)
encline, incline
enclood, include
enclose,*,ed,sing,sable,sure, SURROUND/KEEP IN
encloser, enclose(sure)
enclosment, enclose(ment)
enclude, include

enclunashen, incline(nation)
enclusef, inclusive
enclusion, inclusion
encogneto, incognito
encoherent, incoherent
encokneto, incognito
encombatent, incompetent
encomber, encumber
encome, income
encommodious, incommode(dious)
encomode, incommode
encomodious, incommode(dious)
encomoteous, incommode(dious)
encomparable, incomparable
encompass,sses,ssed,ssing, ITEMS WITHIN A CIRCLE
encompatible, incompatible
encompetent, incompetent
encomplete, incomplete
encompruble, incomparable
enconclusef, inconclusive
enconclusive, inconclusive
enconsiderate, inconsiderate
enconsistent, inconsistent
enconvenient, inconvenient
encoragable, incorrigible
encore,*,ed,ring, ASKED TO PERFORM MORE BY AN AUDIENCE
encorect, incorrect
encorij, encourage / anchor(age)
encorporate, incorporate
encorrect, incorrect
encounter,*,red,ring, TO EMBARK UPON SOMETHING/SOMEONE
encourage,*,ed,ging,gingly,ement, INSTILL FAITH/HOPE
encrease, increase
encredible, incredible
encremenate, incriminate
encrement, increment
encriminate, incriminate
encroach,hes,hed,hing,hingly,hment, her, NEARLY TRESPASSING
encrust,*,ted,ting,tation, FORM A THICK COVER/EXTERIOR
encubate, incubate
encumbent, incumbent
encumber,*,red,ring,brance,brances, brancer, TO BE A WEIGHT/BURDEN, TO HAMPER
encumode, incommode
encumpatable, incompatible
encumplete, incomplete
encunklusif, inconclusive

encunsestant, inconsistent
encunveneunt, inconvenient
encupasitate, incapacitate
encupasity, incapacitate
encur, incur
encurable, incurable
encuragable, incorrigible
encurej, encourage / anchor(age)
encurekt, incorrect
encurig, encourage / anchor(age)
encyclopedia,*, REFERENCE SOURCE THAT DEFINES/EXPLAINS THINGS THAT ARE NOUNS
encyst,*,ted,ting,tation,tment, WITHIN A CYST (or see insist)
end,*,ded,ding, NO MORE, OVER (or see and) "prefixes: un/up"
endakashen, indicate(tion)
endaluble, indelible
endanger,*,red,ring,rment, IN HARM'S WAY, NEEDS PROTECTION
endangurment, endanger(ment)
endanjer, endanger
endapendense, independent(nce)
endasishen, indecision
endau, endow
endaument, endow(ment)
endavigual, individual
endear,*,red,ring,ringly,rment, VERY FOND OF
endeavor,*,red,ring,rer, SET ABOUT THE TASK TO DO SOMETHING
endebted, indebted
endecashen, indicate(tion)
endecision, indecision
endecisive, indecisive
endecks, index
endeed, indeed
endefanete, indefinite
endefinite, indefinite
endefir, endeavor
endefur, endeavor
endefurent, indifferent
endego, indigo
endelible, indelible
endelluble, indelible
endemafy, indemnify
endemic,*,cally,city,ism, CONFINED/ LIVING IN ONE GROUP/AREA
endemnafy, indemnify
endent, indent
endentashen, indent(ation)
endependense, independent(nce)
endependent, independent

ender, inter / enter
enderfere, interfere
endermetant, intermittent
endesent, indecent
endeted, indebted
endever, endeavor
endex, index
endicashen, indicate(tion)
endicate, indicate
endifrent, indifferent
endigo, indigo
endirmedent, intermittent
endirmetant, intermittent
endisisuf, indecisive
endite, indict
endless,ssly,ssness, WILL NEVER STOP
endlis, endless
endo, PREFIX INDICATING "INSIDE" MOST OFTEN MODIFIES THE WORD
endocrine,nology,nologic,nological, nologist, OF THE GLANDS IN THE BODY
endoer, endure
endoose, induce
endormetant, intermittent
endors, indoor(s)
endorse,*,ed,sing,ement, TO SUPPORT/ AFFIRM IN WRITING (or see indoor(s))
endostry, industry
endoument, endow(ment)
endow,*,wed,wing,wment, PROVIDE SOMEONE SOMETHING THEY WANT/NEED "prefixes: dis"
endrukit, intricate
enduce, induce
enduckshen, induct(ion)
enducktor, induct(or)
enduction, induct(ion)
endukren, endocrine
endukshen, induct(ion)
endukt, induct
enduktor, induct(or)
endulge, indulge
endulgense, indulge(nce)
endupendent, independent
endur, inter / enter / endure
endure,*,ed,ring,rance,rable,rably, PUT UP WITH/TOLERATE "prefixes: un"
endurmedeate, intermediate
enduse, induce
enduseshin, indecision
endustreul, industrial
endustry, industry

enduztreal, industrial
ene, any
enebody, anybody
eneckwitable, inequitable
eneduble, inedible
eneg, inning
enegma, enigma / enema
enekwetable, inequitable
enekwity, inequity
enema,*, RECTAL CLEANSING (or see anemia/enigma)
enemik, anemic
enemut, intimate
enemy,mies, A FOE, NOT FRIENDS WITH
eneng, inning
enept, inept
enequitable, inequitable
enequity, inequity
ener, inner
eneract, interact
enerchange, interchange
enercom, intercom
enerconnect, interconnect
enercors, intercourse
enerelate, interrelate
energetic,cally, TO HAVE LOTS OF ENERGY "prefixes: bio"
energy,gies,gize,gizes,gizing,gizer, gization,getic,getically, HAVING ENOUGH POWER TO DO SOMETHING "prefixes: de-"
enerject, interject
enerjetek, energetic
enerkorse, intercourse
enerlude, interlude
enermedeary, intermediary
enermingle, intermingle
enermission, intermission
enermost, innermost
enernashenul, international
enernet, internet
enersculastic, interscholastic
enersect, intersect
enersection, intersection
enersekshen, intersection
enersperse, intersperse
enerstate, interstate
enert, inert
enervene, intervene
enervue, interview
enervul, interval
enerwoven, interwoven
enescapable, inescapable

enesense, innocence
enesheation, initiate(tion)
enesthezia, anesthesia
eneviduble, inevitable
enevitable, inevitable
enexpensive, inexpensive
enexperience, inexperience
enfachuashen, infatuate(tion)
enfachuate, infatuate
enfadik, emphatic
enfallible, infallible
enfaltrate, infiltrate
enfaluble, infallible
enfansy, infant(ncy)
enfant, infant
enfantry, infantry
enfasiz, emphasis / emphasize
enfatchuashen, infatuate(tion)
enfatik, emphatic
enfatuate, infatuate
enfecshus, infect(ious)
enfect, infect
enfekshen, infect(ion)
enfekt, infect
enfeltrate, infiltrate
enfenativly, infinite(tively)
enfentre, infantry
enfereorety, inferior(ity)
enferior, inferior
enfermashen, information
enfermation, information
enfesiz, emphasis / emphasize
enfestructure, infrastructure
enfeureate, infuriate
enfiltrate, infiltrate
enfinetly, infinite(ly)
enfinite, infinite
enfirmary, infirmary
enfirmashen, information
enfirmation, inform(ation)
enfisiz, emphasis / emphasize
enfistructure, infrastructure
enfite, invite
enfitengly, invite(ingly)
enflagingly, unflagging(ly)
enflame, inflame
enflamitory, inflame(mmatory)
enflammation, inflammation
enflammatory, inflame(mmatory)
enflamutory, inflame(mmatory)
enflapable, unflappable
enflashen, inflate(tion)
enflate, inflate
enflection, inflection

enfleksuble, inflexible
enflemashen, inflammation
enflewanse, influence
enflexchen, inflection
enflexible, inflexible
enflextion, inflection
enflicked, inflict
enflict, inflict
enflimation, inflammation
enfluence, influence
enfluensable, influence(able)
enflumation, inflammation
enforce,*,ed,cing,ement,eable,cability, er, SUPPORT, TO BACK "prefixes: un"
enform, inform
enformal, informal
enformant, informant
enformation, inform(ation)
enfraction, infraction
enfrakshen, infraction
enfrared, infrared
enfrastructure, infrastructure
enfrekwent, infrequent
enfrenj, infringe
enfrequent, infrequent
enfringe, infringe
enfrured, infrared
enfugen, infuse(sion)
enfujen, infuse(sion)
enfultrate, infiltrate
enfunsy, infant(ncy)
enfunt, infant
enfuntre, infantry
enfuriate, infuriate
enfurmashen, inform(ation)
enfurmery, infirmary
enfuse, infuse
enfushen, infuse(sion)
enfusiz, emphasis / emphasize
enfustrukture, infrastructure
engage,*,ed,ging,gingly,ement,er, TO PUT INTO MOTION, DIRECT ATTENTION "prefixes: dis"
enganly, ungainly
enge, inch
engect, inject
engection, inject(ion)
engekshen, inject(ion)
engelate, ungulate
engen, engine
engeneer, engineer
engenious, ingenious
engenuity, ingenuity

engenuous, ingenuous
engenyus, ingenious
enger, injure / anger
engest, ingest
enget, ingot
engilate, ungulate
engine,*, MACHINE/DEVICE USED FOR POWER/PROPELLING
engineer,*,red,ring, PUT ITEMS TOGETHER TO BECOME SOMETHING ELSE "prefixes: bio"
enginuety, ingenuity
engoement, enjoy(ment)
engoeuble, enjoy(able)
engoiment, enjoy(ment)
engolf, engulf
engot, ingot
engoy, enjoy
engoyuble, enjoy(able)
engrain, ingrain
engrave,*,ed,ving,er, TO MARK/CARVE TEXT/SYMBOLS INTO SOMETHING
engredient, ingredient
enguish, anguish
engulate, ungulate
engulf,*,fed,fing, TAKE IN, OVERCOME
engun, engine
enguneer, engineer
engury, injure(ry)
engustes, injustice
engut, ingot
enhabetent, inhabit(ant)
enhabit, inhabit
enhabitency, inhabit(ancy)
enhalant, inhalant
enhalation, inhale(lation)
enhale, inhale
enhance,*,ed,cing,ement,cive,er, MAKE MORE APPEALING
enharent, inherent
enharet, inherit
enharitance, inherit(ance)
enharmonic,*,ed,cing,ement,cive,er, MUSICAL NOTATION/FREQUENCY (or see inharmonic)
enhebit, inhibit
enhelashen, inhale(lation)
enherent, inherent
enherit, inherit
enheritance, inherit(ance)
enhewmane, inhumane
enhibishen, inhibit(ion)
enhibit, inhibit
enhosbatalety, inhospitable(ality)

enhosbitable, inhospitable
enhubishen, inhibit(ion)
enhulashen, inhale(lation)
enhumane, inhumane
eni, any
enialate, annihilate
enibishen, inhibit(ion)
enibode, anybody
enielate, annihilate
enig, inning
enigma,*,atic,atical,atically, NOT EXPLAINABLE, NOT UNDERSTOOD (or see enema/anemia)
enigrate, integrate
enima, enema / anemia
enime, enemy
enimut, intimate
enindashen, inundate(tion)
enindate, inundate
ening, inning
enipropreut, inappropriate
eniquality, inequality
enir, inner / inter
enircom, intercom
enircors, intercourse
enirelate, interrelate
enirgetek, energetic
enirgy, energy
enirlude, interlude
enirmission, intermission
enirnet, internet
enirsculastic, interscholastic
enirsection, intersection
enirtwine, intertwine
enirupt, interrupt
enirvene, intervene
enirview, interview
enirvue, interview
enishiashen, initiate(tion)
enishul, initial
enisthezia, anesthesia
enitial, initial
enitiate, initiate
enitiation, initiate(tion)
eniulate, annihilate
enje, inch
enjecshen, inject(ion)
enjekt, inject
enjelate, ungulate
enjen, engine
enjeneer, engineer
enjenuedy, ingenuity
enjenuity, ingenuity
enjenuous, ingenuous

enjenyewus, ingenuous
enjest, ingest
enjin, engine
enjineer, engineer
enjoement, enjoy(ment)
enjoy,*,yed,ying,yment,yable,yably, yableness, APPRECIATE "prefixes: pre"
enjoyuble, enjoy(able)
enjulate, ungulate
enjuner, engineer
enjure, injure
enjustice, injustice
enk, ink
enkabuble, incapable
enkamped, encamp(ed)
enkampment, encamp(ment)
enkapacity, incapacity
enkapasitate, incapacitate
enkapasity, incapacitate
enkapuble, incapable
enkarserade, incarcerate
enkase, encase
enker, anchor / incur
enkerej, encourage / anchor(age)
enkewbate, incubate
enkipacity, incapacity
enklin, incline
enkling, inkling
enklood, include
enklose, enclose
enkloshur, enclose(sure)
enkloze, enclose
enklud, include
enklunashen, incline(nation)
enklusev, inclusive
enklushen, inclusion
enkogneto, incognito
enkomber, encumber
enkomodeus, incommode(dious)
enkompus, encompass
enkomputent, incompetent
enkonsistent, inconsistent
enkore, encore
enkoreg, encourage / anchor(age)
enkoreguble, incorrigible
enkorpurate, incorporate
enkownter, encounter
enkreduble, incredible
enkredulus, incredulous
enkreese, increase
enkremunate, incriminate
enkroch, encroach
enkrument, increment

enkrust, encrust
enkum, income
enkumbent, incumbent
enkumber, encumber
enkumodeus, incommode(dious)
enkumpatuble, incompatible
enkumpus, encompass
enkunsiduret, inconsiderate
enkunsistent, inconsistent
enkunvenyunt, inconvenient
enkupacity, incapacity
enkupasedy, incapacity
enkupasitate, incapacitate
enkurable, incurable
enkurekt, incorrect
enkwesishun, inquisition
enkwire, inquire / inquire(ry)
enkwisative, inquisitive
enkwisition, inquisition
enland, inland
enlarge,*,ed,ging,ement,er, MAKE BIGGER/ GREATER
enlargment, enlarge(ment)
enlarje, enlarge
enlaw, in-law
enles, unless
enlest, enlist
enlet, inlet
enlighten,*,ned,ning,nment, ACHIEVE GREATER KNOWLEDGE
enlist,*,ted,ting,tment,ter, SIGN-UP, JOIN SOMETHING
enliten, enlighten
enlund, inland
enmachure, immature
enmade, inmate
enmate, inmate
enmature, immature
ennacurate, inaccurate
enner, inner
ennuendo, innuendo
enoardinent, inordinate
enoberative, inoperable(ative)
enocence, innocence
enocreate, inaugurate
enoculate, inoculate
enoculation, inoculate(tion)
enodible, inaudible
enof, enough
enogreashen, inaugurate(tion)
enogreate, inaugurate
enogurate, inaugurate
enokewlate, inoculate
enokulation, inoculate(tion)

enomoly, anomaly
enonimus, anonymous
enonseade, enunciate
enoperable, inoperable
enopertune, inopportune
enopurative, inoperable(ative)
enopurtunity, inopportune(nity)
enoqulent, inoculate(ant)
enorcors, intercourse
enordenate, inordinate
enordunet, inordinate
enorgetek, energetic
enorgy, energy
enormis, enormous
enormous,sly,sness, GIGANTIC/ BIGGEST
enormus, enormous
enorpherans, interfere(nce)
enorsect, intersect
enosent, innocence(nt)
enotable, inaudible
enouf, enough
enough, TIME TO STOP
enovadef, innovate(tive)
enovate, innovate
enovative, innovate(tive)
enowe, annoy
enownse, announce
enoy, annoy
enoyens, annoy(ance)
enpare, impair
enpatient, inpatient
enpecable, impeccable
enpech, impeach
enpersonate, impersonate
enpli, imply
enpolite, impolite
enpolse, impulse
enportant, important
enpose, impose
enposibul, impossible
enposter, imposter
enposuble, impossible
enpound, impound
enpoverish, impoverish
enpownd, impound
enpractical, impractical
enprasise, imprecise
enpration, impression
enpravize, improvise
enprecise, imprecise
enpregnable, impregnable
enpregnate, impregnate
enpres, impress

enpreshen, impression
enpresidented, (un)precedent(ed)
enpresise, imprecise
enpresive, impressive
enpreson, imprison
enpressed, impress(sed)
enprint, imprint
enprison, imprison
enprobuble, improbable
enpromptu, impromptu
enpromtu, impromptu
enpropable, improbable
enproper, improper
enprove, improve
enprovement, improve(ment)
enprovisation, improvise(sation)
enprovise, improvise
enprovusashen, improvise(sation)
enprufe, improve
enpruve, improve
enpruvize, improvise
enpulite, impolite
enpulse, impulse
enpulsef, impulse(sive)
enpulsive, impulse(sive)
enput, input
enqubate, incubate
enquesidev, inquisitive
enquire, SEE WORD "INQUIRE"
enquisadev, inquisitive
enquisition, inquisition
enquisitive, inquisitive
enquizeshen, inquisition
enrage,*,ed,ging,ement, GREAT ANGER/ RAGE
enraj, enrage
enrech, enrich
enrich,hes,hed,hing,hment, MAKE BETTER/FINER
enrjekshen, interject(ion)
enrol, enroll
enroll,*,led,ling,lment,llee, JOIN, ENLIST
enrolment, enroll(ment)
enroot, enroute
enroute, OR "EN ROUTE", IN THE PROCESS OF TRAVELING TO/ TOWARDS
enrut, enroute
ensabordinate, insubordinate
ensadent, incident
ensafishent, insufficient
ensakure, insecure
ensakuredy, insecure(rity)
ensakurity, insecure(rity)

ensalate, insulate
ensane, insane
ensanetashen, insanitary(ation)
ensanety, insane(nity)
ensanidy, insane(nity)
ensanitary, insanitary
ensanitashen, insanitary(ation)
ensasheat, insatiate
ensasheuble, insatiable
ensatiable, insatiable
ensatiate, insatiate
ensaulvent, insolvent
ensbarashen, inspire(ration)
ensbekable, unspeakable
ensboken, unspoken
enscribe, inscribe
enscription, inscription
enseam, inseam
ensebordinate, insubordinate
ensect, insect
ensecticide, insecticide
ensecure, insecure
ensedent, incident
ensedius, insidious
ensegnea, insignia
ensegnifukent, insignificant
ensejen, incision
ensekt, insect
ensektaside, insecticide
enselashen, insulate(tion)
ensem, inseam
ensemanation, inseminate(tion)
enseminate, inseminate
ensen, ensign
ensenarate, incinerate
ensendiary, incendiary
ensense, incense
ensenseer, insincere
ensensible, insensible
ensensitive, insensitive
ensentive, incentive
ensentuf, incentive
ensenuashen, insinuate(tion)
ensenuate, insinuate
ensepshen, incept(ion)
ensept, incept
enserekshen, insurrection
ensermowntible, insurmountable
ensershen, insert(ion)
ensert, insert
ensesint, incessant
ensest, incest / insist / encyst
ensh, inch
ensher, ensure / insure

enshiranse, insure(rance)
enshree, entry / entree
enshure, insure
enshurence, insure(rance)
enside, inside / insight / incite
ensident, incident
ensidious, insidious
ensidnea, insignia
ensigen, incision
ensight, insight / incite / inside
ensightation, incite(tation)
ensightment, incite(ment)
ensign,*, MILITARY RANK
ensignia, insignia
ensignificant, insignificant
ensiklopedia, encyclopedia
ensikure, insecure
ensikuredy, insecure(rity)
ensilate, insulate
ensilin, insulin
ensim, enzyme / inseam
ensimanashen, inseminate(tion)
ensimanate, inseminate
ensin, ensign
ensinarate, incinerate
ensincere, insincere
ensinsative, insensitive
ensinse, incense
ensinsuble, insensible
ensinuashen, insinuate(tion)
ensinuate, insinuate
ensirection, insurrection
ensishen, incision
ensisor, incise(sor)
ensist, insist
ensistent, insist(ent)
ensitation, incite(tation)
ensite, inside / insight / incite
ensiteful, insight(ful)
ensitement, incite(ment)
ensiteus, insidious
ensition, incision
ensize, incise
enskribe, inscribe
enskripshen, inscription
ensoluble, insoluble
ensolvable, insolvable
ensolvent, insolvent
ensomnia, insomnia
ensovent, insolvent
ensoyuble, insoluble
ensparashen, inspire(ration)
enspecshen, inspect(ion)
enspect, inspect

enspection, inspect(ion)
enspekable, unspeakable
enspekshen, inspect(ion)
enspekt, inspect
enspire, inspire
enspoken, unspoken
enspuration, inspire(ration)
enstall, install
enstalment, install(ment)
enstance, instance
enstant, instant
enstantaneous, instantaneous
enstatute, institute
enstatution, institute(tion)
enstaulment, install(ment)
ensted, instead
enstenked, instinct
enstense, instance
enstetushen, institute(tion)
enstigate, instigate
enstill, instill
enstinct, instinct
enstinse, instance
enstintaneusly, instantaneous(ly)
enstitute, institute
enstol, install
enstolashen, install(ation)
enstolment, install(ment)
enstrament, instrument
enstriment, instrument
enstrucshen, instruct(ion)
enstruct, instruct
enstruction, instruct(ion)
enstrukt, instruct
enstrument, instrument
enstrumental, instrument(al)
enstugate, instigate
enstunt, instant
enstuntly, instant(ly)
ensubordinate, insubordinate
ensucure, insecure
ensue,*,ed,uing, CLOSELY FOLLOW
ensufishent, insufficient
ensugnifakent, insignificant
ensulate, insulate
ensulation, insulate(tion)
ensulin, insulin
ensult, insult
ensunseer, insincere
ensure,*,ed,ring, GUARANTEE/
 PROMISE (or see insure)
ensurkle, encircle
ensurmountable, insurmountable
ensurrection, insurrection

ensurshen, insert(ion)
ensurt, insert
ensyklopedia, encyclopedia
ensym, enzyme
ent, end / and
entacate, indicate
entact, intact
entaferance, interfere(rance)
entager, integer
entagral, integral
entagrate, integrate
entail,*,led,ling,lment, RESTRICTIONS
 TO OWNERSHIP "prefixes: dis"
entak, intact / intake
entale, entail
entalect, intellect
entalectual, intellect(ual)
entamet, intimate
entangible, intangible
entangle,*,ed,ling,ement, GET MIXED
 UP IN "prefixes: dis/un"
entanjuble, intangible
entareor, anterior / interior
entarmedeate, intermediate
entatee, entity
enteger, integer
entegral, integral
entegrate, integrate
entegrity, integrity
entegrude, integrity
entekashen, indicate(tion)
entelagents, intelligent(nce)
entelijuble, intelligible
entellect, intellect
entelugeble, intelligible
entelugint, intelligent
entenation, intonate(tion)
entend, intend
entense, intense
entenshin, intent(ion)
entensity, intense(sity)
entensuve, intense(sive)
entent, intent
enter,*,red,ring,rable,rance, GO INTO,
 PREFIX INDICATING "INTESTINE"
 MOST OFTEN MODIFIES THE WORD
 "prefixes: re"
enteract, interact
entercede, intercede
entercept, intercept
enterchange, interchange
entercom, intercom
enterconnect, interconnect
entercourse, intercourse

enterd, enter(ed)
entereor, anterior / interior
enterferans, interfere(nce)
enterfere, interfere
enterference, interfere(rance)
entergekshen, interject(ion)
enterim, interim
enterior, anterior / interior
enterject, interject
enterlock, interlock
enterlude, interlude
entermediary, intermediary
entermediate, intermediate
entermetant, intermittent
entermingle, intermingle
entermission, intermission
entern, intern
enternal, internal
enternational, international
enternet, internet
entero, PREFIX INDICATING
 "INTESTINE" MOST OFTEN
 MODIFIES THE WORD
enterog, entourage
enterogate, interrogate
enterpreneur, entrepreneur
enterpret, interpret
enterpretation, interpretation
enterprise,*,sing,singly, USE AMBITION
 TO TAKE ON RISKS
enterrelate, interrelate
enterrogate, interrogate
enterrupt, interrupt
enterscholastic, interscholastic
entersept, intercept
entersperse, intersperse
enterstate, interstate
entertain,*,ned,ning,nment,ner,
 AMUSE/ENGAGE SOMEONE
entertaner, entertain(er)
entertanment, entertain(ment)
entertwine, intertwine
enterupt, interrupt
enterval, interval
entervene, intervene
enterview, interview
enterwoven, interwoven
entestine, intestine
entety, entity
entever, endeavor
enthooseastik, enthuse(siastic)
enthrall,*,led,ling, OVERWHELMED
 WITH AWE
enthrol, enthrall

enthuse,ed,siasm,siastic,siastically, HAVE INTEREST/ENERGY FOR "prefixes: over/un"
enthuseastek, enthuse(siastic)
enthuziazm, enthuse(siasm)
entice,*,ed,cing,ement,er, APPEAL TO, ALLURE, SUCCUMB TO
entid, end(ed)
entidle, entitle
entiger, integer
entigo, indigo
entigral, integral
entigration, integrate(tion)
entil, until
entilect, intellect
entimadate, intimidate
entimate, intimate
entimidate, intimidate
entina, antenna
entinse, intense
entinsive, intense(sive)
entint, intent
entintion, intent(ion)
entire,ely,ety, COMPLETE, THE WHOLE THING
entirest, interest
entirferans, interfere(nce)
entirle, entire(ly)
entirmediate, intermediate
entirmitant, intermittent
entirnet, internet
entirpreneur, entrepreneur
entirprize, enterprise
entirprutashen, interpretation
entirty, entire(ty)
entisepate, anticipate
entitle,*,ed,ling,ement, RIGHTS, AUTHORITY TO
entity,ties, A BEING WITH HUMAN FORM "prefixes: non"
entlis, endless
ento, into
entoishen, intuit(ion)
entolerable, intolerable
entonate, intonate
entor, enter
entouet, intuit(ive)
entourage,*, GROUP WHO TRAVELS WITH IMPORTANT/FAMOUS PEOPLE
entowment, endow(ment)
entoxicate, intoxicate
entra, entree
entraduction, introduce(ction)

entraduse, introduce
entrakit, intricate
entramural, intramural
entrance,ed,cing, PLACE/WAY TO GET IN
entranet, intranet
entrapreneur, entrepreneur
entraspect, introspect
entravenous, intravenous
entray, entree
entree,*, A MEAL, FOOD SERVING (or see entry)
entrege, intrigue
entrense, entrance
entrensic, intrinsic
entrepreneur,*,rial,rialism,rism,rship, ONE WHO RISKS FINANCING A NEW BUSINESS/ ENTERPRISE
entres, entry(ries) / entree(s)
entrest, interest
entri, entry / entree
entricate, intricate
entrigue, intrigue
entrinsic, intrinsic
entroduce, introduce
entrospect, introspect
entrost, interest / entrust
entrovert, introvert
entrude, intrude
entrudukshen, introduce(ction)
entruduse, introduce
entrugen, instrusion
entrumural, intramural
entrunse, entrance
entrupreneur, entrepreneur
entrusef, intrusive
entrushen, intrusion
entrust,*,ted,ting, LEAVE THE CARE OF SOMETHING/ SOMEONE TO ANOTHER (or see interest)
entry,ries,rant, OPENING GOING IN, ENTER INTO (or see entree) "prefixes: re/sub"
entuative, intuit(ive)
entueshen, intuit(ion)
entuetion, intuit(ion)
entufere, interfere
entuger, integer
entugrate, integrate
entuishen, intuit(ion)
entuit, intuit(ive) / intuit
entuition, intuit(ion)
entunate, intonate
entur, enter

enturact, interact
enturauj, entourage
enturem, interim
enturlock, interlock
enturmediate, intermediate
enturmetant, intermittent
enturn, intern
enturnal, internal
enturnalize, internal(ize)
enturpreneur, entrepreneur
enturpret, interpret
enturprise, enterprise
entursept, intercept
enturtane, entertain
enturtaner, entertain(er)
enturtanment, entertain(ment)
entutes, entity(ties)
entwoishen, intuit(ion)
entwoit, intuit(ive)
entyre, entire
enubelidy, inability
enubishen, inhibit(ion)
enuendo, innuendo
enuf, enough
enuindo, innuendo
enume, enemy
enunciate,*,ed,ting,tion,tive,tively,tor, SPEAK CLEARLY/SPECIFICALLY
enundate, inundate
enunseate, enunciate
enupresheative, inappreciative
enuprochible, inapproachable
enupropreut, inappropriate
enur, inner
enuract, interact
enurcom, intercom
enurelate, interrelate
enurferins, interfere(nce)
enurgee, energy
enurgekshen, interject(ion)
enurim, interim
enurjetek, energetic
enurlude, interlude
enurmediary, intermediary
enurmingle, intermingle
enurmission, intermission
enurmost, innermost
enurnet, internet
enursculastic, interscholastic
enursecshen, intersection
enursperse, intersperse
enurt, inert
enurupt, interrupt
enurval, interval

enurvene, intervene
enurview, interview
enurvue, interview
enurwoven, interwoven
enuscapuble, inescapable
enusense, innocence
enusent, innocence(nt)
enuther, another
enuvate, innovate
envachinate, invaginate
envade, invade
envaginate, invaginate
envagination, invaginate(tion)
envajunate, invaginate
envalid, invalid
envalope, envelope
envaluable, invaluable
envasef, invasive
envashen, invasion
envashenation, invaginate(tion)
envasion, invasion
envatashen, invitation
envate, invade
envaulve, involve
enve, envy
enved, envy(vied)
envelope,*,ed,ping,ement, ENCLOSE/WRAP TO PROTECT SOMETHING
envensable, invincible
envenshen, invent(ion)
envent, invent
enventory, inventory
enverdebrae, invertebrate
envereably, invariable(ly)
enverse, inverse
enversion, inversion
enversive, inverse(sive)
envert, invert
envertebrate, invertebrate
enves, envy(vies)
envest, invest
envestagashen, investigate(tion)
envestigate, investigate
envestmant, invest(ment)
envetashen, invitation
enveuble, enviable
enveus, envious
enviable,ly, SOMEONE WISHING THEY HAD
enviding, invite(ingly)
envigorate, invigorate
envilope, envelope
envincible, invincible
envintory, inventory

enviornmental, environment(al)
envious,sly,sness, BEING JEALOUS
envirdebate, invertebrate
environment,*,tal,tally,talist,talism, EXTERIOR SURROUNDINGS
envirs, inverse
envirsion, inversion
envirsive, inverse(sive)
envirtebrate, invertebrate
envisability, invisible(bility)
envisible, invisible
envitashen, invitation
envitation, invitation
envitingly, invite(ingly)
envizable, invisible
envoice, invoice
envoluntary, involuntary
envolve, involve
envoyse, invoice
envulid, invalid
envurdabrae, invertebrate
envurt, invert
envy,vies,vied,vying,vyingly,vious,viously,viousness,viable, WANT SOMETHING THAT SOMEONE ELSE HAS "prefixes: un"
enward, inward
enword, inward
enwrech, enrich
enwrich, enrich
enwroll, enroll
eny, any
enzerkle, encircle
enzide, inside
enzyme,*,matic,mic,mically,mology, CHEMICAL ACTION CREATED BY CELLS "prefixes: endo/exo/non/pro"
ep, PREFIX INDICATING "OVER/NEAR" MOST OFTEN MODIFIES THE WORD
epademic, epidemic
epareshin, apparition
eparition, apparition
epart, apart
epartmint, apartment
epasenter, epicenter
epasode, episode
epazode, episode
epeal, appeal
epeel, appeal
eperatus, apparatus
eperinse, appearance
eperint, apparent
eperul, apparel

epi, PREFIX INDICATING "OVER/NEAR" MOST OFTEN MODIFIES THE WORD
epicenter,*, CENTRAL SPOT OF EARTHQUAKE
epidemic,*, MANY LIVES AT RISK IN AN AREA
episode,*, PARTS OF AN ONGOING SHOW
epizode, episode
epliense, appliance
eplod, applaud
eply, apply
epodemec, epidemic
epoint, appoint
epointment, appointment
epoynt, appoint
epoyntment, appointment
eprasal, appraisal
epreciate, appreciate
eprentis, apprentice
epresheate, appreciate
eprintise, apprentice
epruvel, approve(val)
epsolv, absolve
epsorb, absorb
epstane, abstain
epsurd, absurd
eptikate, abdicate
epusode, episode
epzolv, absolve
epzorb, absorb
epzurd, absurd
eqaul, equal
eqaulity, equality
eqaunimity, equanimity
eqauzition, acquisition
eqivocate, equivocate
equable,ly,bility,eness, IS EQUAL TO, SAME IN VALUE, UNIFORM "prefixes: in"
equal,*,led,ling,lly,able,lize,lizes,lized,lizing,lizer,lization, SAME AS, EQUIVALENT, UNIFORM "prefixes: un"
equalibrium, equilibrium
equality,ties,tarian,tarianism, OF BEING THE SAME, EQUIVALENT "prefixes: in"
equanemity, equanimity
equanimity,ties,mous, OF EVEN TEMPERAMENT
equate,*,ed,ting,tion,table,tability, COMPARE/BALANCE/MAKE UNIFORM "prefixes: un"

equation,*,nal,nally, BALANCE OF BOTH SIDES
equator,*,rial,rially, ONE OF TWO HALVES OF A PLANET/STAR "prefixes: sub"
equel, equal
equelebreum, equilibrium
equevocal, equivocal
equi, PREFIX INDICATING "EQUAL" MOST OFTEN MODIFIES THE WORD
equifocal, equivocal
equifocate, equivocate
equil, equal
equilibrium,*, BALANCE, STABILITY "prefixes: dis/non"
equinox,xes, WHEN DAY/NIGHT ARE IN EQUAL PARTS
equip,*,pped,pping,pper,pment, TO MAKE READY FOR A TASK, EVENT
equipment, ARTICLES/IMPLEMENTS TO PERFORM WORK
equity,ties,tize,tizes,tized,tizing,tization, HOW MUCH YOU OWN, JUSTICE/ RIGHTS "prefixes: in"
equivalent,tly,nce,ncy, THE SAME AS, EQUAL "prefixes: non"
equivilense, equivalent(ncy)
equivocal,lity,lly,lness,ate, EQUAL ENOUGH TO LEAD TO MISINTERPRETATION, SUSPICION, DOUBT "prefixes: un"
equivocate,*,ed,ting,tingly,tor,tory,tion, tions, EQUAL ENOUGH TO LEAD TO MISINTERPRETATION, SUSPICION, DOUBT
eqwanemity, equanimity
eqwanimity, equanimity
eqwareum, aquarium
eqwashin, equation
eqwel, equal
eqwerium, aquarium
er, PREFIX INDICATING EMPHASIS ON THE ACTIVITY/DOING OF A VERB (or see ear/err/air/heir)
erabrochuble, irreproachable
eracer, eraser
eradeate, irradiate
eradesent, iridescent
eradiate, irradiate
eradic, erratic / erotic
eradicate,*,ed,ting,tion,tive,able,ably, tor, ELIMINATE, DISPOSE "prefixes: in/un"
eradukashen, eradicate(tion)

eragardles, irregardless
eragashen, irrigate(tion)
eragate, irrigate
eragation, irrigate(tion)
eraguardless, irregardless
erain, arraign
erakned, arachnid
eran, arraign
erand, errand
erange, arrange
erangment, arrange(ment)
eranment, arraign(ment)
erant, errant
eraplasible, irreplaceable
eraprochuble, irreproachable
erasbonsuble, irresponsible
erasbonzible, irresponsible
erase,*,ed,sing,er,sable, ELIMINATE COMPLETELY
eraser,*, RUBBER/FELT PAD FOR REMOVING INK
erashinul, irrational
erashunal, irrational
erasistible, irresistible
erasol, aerosol
eraspective, irrespective
eraspektif, irrespective
erasponsuble, irresponsible
erasponzuble, irresponsible
eratant, irritant
eratashen, irritate(tion)
eratate, irritate
eratible, irritable
eratic, erratic / erotic
erational, irrational
eratrevible, irretrievable
eraudik, erotic
eravokable, irrevocable
eray, array
erayn, arraign
erazestuble, irresistible
erazistuble, irresistible
erb, herb
erbal, herb(al)
erbashis, herb(aceous)
erbel, herb(al)
erbivore, herbivore
erborne, airborne
erbul, herb(al)
erbulism, herb(alism)
erbulist, herb(alist)
erchen, urchin
erchin, urchin
erea, area

erebrochuble, irreproachable
erect,*,ted,ting,tion,tile,table,tly,tness, tor, SET STRAIGHT UP, RAISE
ered, arid
eredesent, iridescent
ereer, arrear
eregardles, irregardless
eregashen, irrigate(tion)
eregate, irrigate
eregation, irrigate(tion)
eregeno, oregano
eregewler, irregular
eregler, irregular
erekshen, erect(ion)
erelavense, irrelevant(nce)
erelavent, irrelevant
ereluvense, irrelevant(nce)
ereluvint, irrelevant
erena, arena
ereng, earring
erent, errant
ereperuble, irreparable
erepirable, irreparable
ereprochible, irreproachable
erepruble, irreparable
erepurable, irreparable
erer, error
eresistible, irresistible
erespective, irrespective
erest, arrest
erestokrat, aristocrat
eretant, irritant
eretashen, irritate(tion)
eretat, irritate
eretibul, irritable
eretrevible, irretrievable
eretrievable, irretrievable
ereu, area
ereul, aerial
erevocable, irrevocable
erg, urge
ergense, urge(ncy)
ergent, urge(nt)
erginsy, urge(ncy)
ergint, urge(nt)
eri, awry
eribrochuble, irreproachable
erid, arid
eridesent, iridescent
erift, arrive(d)
eriful, arrival
erigardles, irregardless
erigashen, irrigate(tion)
erigate, irrigate

erigation, irrigate(tion)
eriguardless, irregardless
erind, errand
ering, earring / err(ing)
eriplasible, irreplaceable
eriproachable, irreproachable
erir, error
erisbonsuble, irresponsible
erisistible, irresistible
erisol, aerosol
erispective, irrespective
erispektif, irrespective
erisponsuble, irresponsible
eristocrat, aristocrat
eritant, irritant
eritate, irritate
erithmatic, arithmetic
eritrevuble, irretrievable
erive, arrive
erivokuble, irrevocable
erivul, arrival
erizisduble, irresistible
erj, urge
erjense, urge(nce) / urge(ncy)
erjinse, urge(nce) / urge(ncy)
erjint, urge(nt)
erk, irk
erle, early
erloom, heirloom
erly, early
ern, earn / urn
ernest, earnest
ero, arrow
erobik, aerobic
erochun, erosion
erode,*,ed,ding,osion,osive,dible,
    dibility,osible, WEAR, WASH AWAY
    "prefixes: non/un"
erodik, erotic
erodynamic, aerodynamic
eroganse, arrogance
erogate, irrigate
erogint, arrogance(nt)
eroma, aroma
eromadek, aroma(tic)
erond, errand
eronic, ironic
eror, error
erosbonsuble, irresponsible
erosef, erosive
erosion,nal,nally, WEARING, WASHING
    AWAY
erosive,eness,vity, WEARS/WASHES
    AWAY

erosponsuble, irresponsible
erote, erode
erotic,ca,cally,cize,cism,tology,tological,
    tologist, SEXUAL AROUSAL/
    SENSATION
erport, airport
err,*,rred,rring,rrancy, SHORT FOR
    ERROR, TO MAKE A MISTAKE (or
    see ear/air/heir) "prefixes: un"
erradiate, irradiate
errand,*, TRAVEL TO PERFORM A TASK
errant,tly,try, TO WANDER "prefixes:
    in"
erratate, irritate
erratic,cally,cism, SUDDEN/
    UNPREDICTABLE MOVEMENTS OR
    THOUGHTS
errogate, irrigate
error,*, NOT CORRECT
ershen, urchin
ertearial, arterial
erth, earth
erubt, erupt / irrupt
erubtif, erupt(ive) / irrupt(ive)
erubtion, erupt(ion) / irrupt(ion)
erugardles, irregardless
erugashen, irrigate(tion)
erugate, irrigate
erugation, irrigate(tion)
eruguardless, irregardless
erunt, errant
eruplasuble, irreplaceable
eruprochuble, irreproachable
erupshen, erupt(ion) / irrupt(ion)
erupt,*,ted,ting,tion,tive,tively,tible,
    FORMING BULGE WHICH OPENS/
    BURSTS (or see irrupt)
eruptif, erupt(ive) / irrupt(ive)
erur, error
erusbonsuble, irresponsible
erusistible, irresistible
erusol, aerosol
eruspective, irrespective
eruspektif, irrespective
erusponsuble, irresponsible
erutant, irritant
erutashen, irritate(tion)
erutate, irritate
erutible, irritable
erutrevible, irretrievable
erutuble, irritable
eruvokuble, irrevocable
eruzistuble, irresistible
es, is / ease

esa, essay
esael, assail
esail, assail
esalt, assault
esanse, essence
esasen, assassin
esault, assault
esay, essay
esbeshulee, especially
escalade,*,er, TO SCALE WALL WITH
    LADDERS (or see escalator)
escalate,*,ed,ting,tor,tory,tion, TO RISE
    (or see escalade) "prefixes: de-"
escalator,*, A CONVEYOR WHICH
    CARRIES/MOVES ITEMS/PEOPLE
escapade,*, AN ADVENTURE WITHOUT
    PERMISSION
escape,*,ed,ping,pable,er,pist,pism,pee,
    pees,pology,pologist, TO GET AWAY
    FROM WITHOUT PERMISSION
    "prefixes: in"
escort,*,ted,ting, SOMEONE WHO
    ACCOMPANIES TO ASSIST
escrow,*,wed,wing, MONEY RETAINED
    BY THIRD PARTY
esculator, escalator
esdeem, esteem
ese, ease / easy
esedik, acetic / acidic / ascetic
esemble, assemble
esemulate, assimilate
esence, essence
esend, ascend / isn't
esenshul, essential
esent, ascend / ascent / assent / isn't
esential, essential
esert, assert
esesmint, assessment
esfikseat, asphyxiate
esfixeat, asphyxiate
eshamed, ashamed
esherance, assure(rance)
eshew, issue
eshu, issue
eshurance, assure(rance)
eside, aside
esidik, acetic / acidic / ascetic
esidjewus, assiduous
esiguous, assiduous
esil, easel
esilum, asylum
esily, easily
esimble, assemble
esimelate, assimilate

esimetric, asymmetric
esind, ascend
esindant, ascendant
esine, assign
esinment, assignment
esinse, essence
esinshul, essential
esint, isn't / ascend / ascent / assent
esirt, assert
esist, assist
eskapade, escapade
eskape, escape
eskort, escort
eskplinashen, explanation
eskrow, escrow
eskulate, escalate / escalade
eskulater, escalator
eskupade, escapade
esm, ism
esment, easement
esmint, easement
esnt, isn't
esofigus, esophagus
esolt, assault
esophagus,gi,geal, TUBE IN THE THROAT
esordment, assortment
esorted, assorted
esortment, assortment
esosheate, associate
esoshiate, associate
esoteric,ca,cally,cism, KNOWLEDGE GAINED BY A FEW
especially, PARTICULARLY, MOST CERTAINLY
esperugus, asparagus
espeshulee, especially
espir, aspire
essay,*,yed,ying,yist,yistic, WRITE ABOUT A SPECIFIC POINT/THING
essence,*, THE AMBIANCE OR BASIC SENSE OF THE OVERALL
essential,*,lly,tiality,tialness, MUST HAVE, MOST IMPORTANT "prefixes: in/non/un"
est, east
estableshment, establish(ment)
establish,es,ed,hing,hment,her, hmentarian, TO CREATE A BASIS, BEGINNING "prefixes: dis/non"
estamashen, estimate(tion)
esteem,*,med,ming, BEST REGARDS FOR, ADMIRE "prefixes: dis"
esteengwish, extinguish

estem, esteem
estemut, estimate
estern, east(ern)
estimashen, estimate(tion)
estimate,*,ed,ting,tion,able,ably, ableness,tive,tor, TO APPROXIMATE BASED ON KNOWLEDGE "prefixes: in/over/under"
estirle, east(erly)
estonesh, astonish
estragen, estrogen
estrawlegy, astrology
estrengent, astringent
estringent, astringent
estris, estrus
estrogen, A HORMONE CREATED BY FEMALES BEGINNING AT PUBERTY
estrolugy, astrology
estronume, astronomy
estrugen, estrogen
estrus,rum,ual, WHEN CONCEPTION IS POSSIBLE
estumashen, estimate(tion)
estumit, estimate
esturle, east(erly)
esue, issue
esuense, issue(uance)
esuinse, issue(uance)
esul, easel
esume, assume
esunse, essence
esunt, isn't
esylum, asylum
et, eat / eight / ate
etable, edible
etach, attach
etack, attack
etaen, attain
etak, attack
etalek, italic
etane, attain
etatch, attach
etcetera, MORE OF THE SAME
etch,hes,hed,hing,her, CARVE INTO (or see edge/itch)
ete, eddy
etempt, attempt
etemt, attempt
etenchin, attention
etend, attend
etenshin, attention
etenshun, attention
eternal,lly,nity,nities,lity,lize,lizes,lized, lizing, FOREVER

eteusy, idiocy
eteut, idiot
ether,ric, ALL THINGS AROUND AND BEYOND THE EARTH
ethic,*,cal,cally,cality,calness,cist, JUDGEMENT OF CONDUCT/ BEHAVIOR "prefixes: bio/un"
ethnac, ethnic
ethnic,*,cally,city,cities,nology,nologist, nologic,nologically, GROUP OF PEOPLE WITH THE SAME LANGUAGE, TRAITS
ethnuk, ethnic
ethrik, ether(ic)
ethuk, ethic
etikit, etiquette
etimt, attempt
etinchon, attention
etinshun, attention
etiquette, RULES OF PROPER BEHAVIOR
etire, attire
etmonish, admonish
etrakshun, attraction
etrakt, attract
etroshus, atrocious
ets, it's / eat(s)
etself, itself
etsetara, etcetera
etsulf, itself
eturnal, eternal
eturney, attorney
eu, PREFIX INDICATING "GOOD" MOST OFTEN MODIFIES THE WORD
eucalyptus, A TREE
euforia, euphoria
eul, eel
eunaform, uniform
euphoria,ant,ic,ically, FEELS JOYFUL/ UNREAL
euraneum, uranium
eurinery, urinary
eutopea, utopia
evacuate,*,ed,ting,tion,tive,tor, TO EMPTY FROM A PLACE
evade,*,ed,ding,asion,evasive,er, TO NOT BE/THINK/BEHAVE AS EXPECTED
evadins, evidence
evakuashen, evacuate(tion)
evakuate, evacuate
evale, evil(lly)
evaluashen, evaluate(tion)

evaluate,*,ed,ting,tion,tive, TO STUDY/REVIEW FOR FINAL OPINION/JUDGEMENT
evalushen, evolution
evalutionery, evolution(ary)
evan, even
evanly, even(ly)
evaperate, evaporate
evaperation, evaporate(tion)
evaporate,*,ed,ting,tion, LIQUID/SOLID CONVERTED INTO GAS
evapurashen, evaporate(tion)
evapurate, evaporate
evarewer, every(where)
evasef, evasive
evashen, evasive
evasion, TO NOT BE/THINK/BEHAVE AS EXPECTED
evasive,ely,eness, TO NOT BE/THINK/BEHAVE AS EXPECTED
evate, evade
eve, THE EVENING, A PERIOD OF TIME BEFORE AN EVENT
evedins, evidence
evekshin, evict(ion)
evekt, evict
even,*,ed,ning,nly,nness, LEVEL WITH "prefixes: un"
evendful, eventful
evening,*, AFTER 6 O'CLOCK P.M.
evenshuele, event(ually)
event,*,tual,tually,tful,tfully,tfullness, SOMETHING OUT OF THE ORDINARY, WILL HAPPEN IN THE FUTURE "prefixes: un"
eventful,lly,lness, SOMETHING OUT OF THE ORDINARY
eventualy, event(ually)
ever,rmore, AT ANY TIME "prefixes: for"
everewar, every(where)
everves, effervesce
evervesent, effervescent
every,ybody,yday,yone,ything,ywhere, ALL
eves, eaves
evict,*,ted,ting,tion,tee, TO FORCIBLY REMOVE
evidence,*,ed,cing,nt, PROOF OF TRUTH "prefixes: in"
evidens, evidence
evident,tly,tial,tially,tiality,tiary,tialism, nce, PROOF OF BEING SEEN, UNDERSTOOD, TRUTH "prefixes: in"
evikshen, evict(ion)

eviktion, evict(ion)
evil,*,lly,lness, OPPOSITE OF LOVE, THREATENING
evilutionary, evolution(ary)
evin, even
evindful, eventful
evinly, even(ly)
evinshuale, event(ually)
evint, event
evintualy, event(ually)
evir, ever
evl, evil
evneng, evening
evning, evening
evoke,*,ed,king,ocable,ocator,er, MAKE HAPPEN, CREATE REACTION
evol, evil
evolushenary, evolution(ary)
evolution,*,nal,nally,nary,narily,nist, nism, THE ACT OF EVOLVING
evolvd, evolve(d)
evolve,*,ed,ving,lution, ADAPT, GAIN WISDOM, TRANSFORM
evon, even
evoneng, evening
evor, ever
evow, avow
evre, every
evrebode, every(body)
evreda, every(day)
evretheng, every(thing)
evrewer, every(where)
evrewun, every(one)
evriwun, every(one)
evry, every
evryday, every(day)
evrywere, every(where)
evs, eaves
evudens, evidence
evudins, evidence
evudintly, evident(ly)
evul, evil
evule, evil(lly)
evulushin, evolution
evuneng, evening
evunle, even(ly)
ew, ewe / you / yew
eway, away
ewe,*, FEMALE SHEEP (or see you/yew)
ewrekt, erect
ex, PREFIX INDICATING "FORMER/OUTSIDE/EXTERNAL" MOST OFTEN MODIFIES THE WORD

exact,ted,ting,tingly,tingness,tly,tness, table,tor, SPECIFIC "prefixes: in"
exagerate, exaggerate
exageration, exaggerate(tion)
exaggerate,*,ted,tedly,ting,tingly,tive, tion,tor, STRETCH/ELONGATE THE TRUE FORM
exajurashen, exaggerate(tion)
exakude, execute
exakushen, execute(tion)
exale, exhale
exam,*,mine, A TEST/EVALUATION
examenashen, examine(nation)
examine,*,ed,ning,nation,nable,ee,er, CLOSELY/CAREFULLY OBSERVE
example,*,ed,ling, SIMILAR TO, USED TO DESCRIBE "prefixes: un"
exampul, example
examunashen, examine(nation)
exaqushen, execute(tion)
exasperate,*,ed,edly,ting,tingly,tion, GREATLY ANNOY/IRRITATE
exaspiration, exasperate(tion)
exaspurate, exasperate
exaustshen, exhaust(ion)
exbarenshal, experiential
exbedeant, expedient
exberenshal, experiential
exbirenshal, experiential
exblanashen, explanation
exblanatory, explanatory
exblikuble, explicable
exblode, explode
exbloetashen, exploit(ation)
exblor, explore
exbloshen, explosion
exbloshun, explosion
exblosive, explosive
exblunashen, explanation
exborashen, expire(ration)
exbort, export
exbortashen, export(ation)
exbos, expose
exbress, express
exburashen, expire(ration)
exburenshal, experiential
excalate, escalate / escalade
excavate,*,ed,ting,tion,tor, DIG FOR SOMETHING "prefixes: un"
exceed,*,ded,ding,dingly,dance, EXCEL, DO MORE THAN EXPECTED
excel,*,lled,lling,llence,llency,llent, PERFORM BETTER THAN NORMAL/

AVERAGE (or see accel) "prefixes: un"
excelaration, accelerate(tion)
excellent,tly, OUTSTANDING
excelurashen, accelerate(tion)
exceluration, accelerate(tion)
excenshuate, accentuate
excentuate, accentuate
excepshen, except(ion)
except,*,ted,ting,tion,tional,tionalism, tionality,tionalities,tionalness, tionable, tive, THIS BUT NOT THAT, EXTRACT FROM (or see accept) "prefixes: un"
excerpt,*,ted,ting,tible,tion,tor, A SMALL PART OF THE WRITTEN WHOLE
excesorize, accessory(rize)
excesory, accessory
excess,sses,ssive,ssively,ssiveness, MORE THAN ENOUGH (or see access)
exchange,*,ed,ging,eable,eability,er, TO TRADE
excinshuate, accentuate
excite,*,ed,ting,ement,table,tability, tableness, AROUSE, FEEL TINGLY INSIDE "prefixes: un"
excksbedeant, expedient
exclamation,*,nal, DISPLAY OF FORCE/ ENTHUSIASM/WILLFULLNESS, PUNCTUATION, EXCLAMATION POINT
excloot, exclude
exclude,*,ded,ding,usive,usively, usiveness,usivity,usion,usions, usionary, NOT INCLUDED AS PART OF SOMETHING OR GROUP
exclusive,ely,eness, SPECIAL, UNLIKE ANY OTHER
excrow, escrow
excuisit, exquisite
exculate, escalate / escalade
excursion,*,nist,ive,ively,iveness, A SHORT TRIP, CHEAP FARE
excuse,*,ed,sing,sable,sably,sableness, er, REASONS FOR A PROBLEM BEING "prefixes: in/un"
excuvashen, excavate(tion)
excuvation, excavate(tion)
exdansev, extensive
exdensible, extensible
exdensive, extensive
exdensubly, extensible(ly)

exderminate, exterminate
exdinsev, extensive
exdravert, extrovert
exdruvirt, extrovert
exdurminate, exterminate
execute,*,ed,ting,tion,tor, CARRY OUT/ ENFORCE/ENACT A PLAN, TO KILL FOR RELIGIOUS/POLITICAL REASONS
executive,*,ely, PERSON WITH POSITION/POWER TO CREATE/ ENACT WITHIN AN ORGANIZATION
exelarate, exhilarate / accelerate
exema, eczema
exemplify,fies,fied,fying,fiable,fication, fier, MAKE CLEAR OR CONVINCING
exempt,ted,ting,tion,tible, SET FREE, EXCUSE FROM DUTY/TAXES/RULES/ LEGAL HOLDINGS
exemshen, exempt(ion)
exepshen, except(ion)
exequtef, executive
exercise,*,ed,sing,sable,er, MENTAL/ PHYSICAL ACTIVITY FOR IMPROVEMENT (or see exorcise)
exert,*,ted,ting,tion, PUT FORTH POWER/ENERGY
exest, exist
exfoliate,*,ed,ting,tion,tive,ant,tor, LAYERS LIFTING OFF
exglusef, exclusive
exhale,*,ed,ling,lation, TO BREATH OUT
exhaust,*,ted,ting,tion,tive,tively, tiveness,ter,tible,tibility, RUN OUT OF, DISCHARGE, FUMES FROM A MOTOR "prefixes: in"
exhaustein, exhaust(ion)
exhibit,*,ted,ting,tion,tioner,tory,tor, tive,tively,tionist,tionism, ON SHOW
exhilarate,*,ed,ting,tingly,tion,tive,tor, REFRESHING, EXCITING (or see accelerate)
exhilation, exhale(lation)
exhostion, exhaust(ion)
exhostshen, exhaust(ion)
exhulation, exhale(lation)
exibit, exhibit
exicute, execute
exicution, execute(tion)
exikude, execute
exikushen, execute(tion)
exikut, execute
exile,*,ed,ling,lic, TO REMOVE/BE REMOVED FROM YOUR COUNTRY

exilurate, exhilarate
exima, eczema
eximplify, exemplify
exirsize, exercise / exorcise
exirtion, exert(ion)
exist,*,ted,ting,tence,tent,tential, tentially,tialism, OF FORM, AN ENTITY "prefixes: in/pre"
exit,*,ted,ting, TO LEAVE FROM
exitment, excite(ment)
exkalate, escalate / escalade
exkergen, excursion
exkerjen, excursion
exkeus, excuse
exklumashen, exclamation
exkro, escrow
exkulate, escalate / escalade
exkurgen, excursion
exkurshun, excursion
exkuze, excuse
exlant, excellent
exo, PREFIX INDICATING "OUTSIDE/ EXTERNAL" MOST OFTEN MODIFIES THE WORD
exorbeant, exorbitant
exorbetant, exorbitant
exorbiant, exorbitant
exorbitant,tly, WAY TOO MUCH, RIDICULOUS AMOUNT
exorcise,*,ed,sing,ism,ist, BANISH/ EXPEL SPIRITS (or see exercise)
exost, exhaust
exostshen, exhaust(ion)
exotic,*,cally, MYSTERIOUS/DIFFERENT/ STRANGE
expadishen, expedition
expadition, expedition
expand,*,ded,ding,der,dable,dability, nse, TO EXTEND BEYOND WHAT IS
expanse,*,sive,sively,siveness,sivity, sion,sionary,sible,sionism, EXTEND BEYOND WHAT IS (or see expense)
exparential, experiential
expect,*,ted,tedly,ting,tation,tant, tantly,table,tably,tedness,tancy, tancies, WANT/WISH SOMETHING TO HAPPEN "prefixes: un"
expedient,*,tly,ncy,ncies, HASTEN THE PROCESS BUT MAY COMPROMISE INTEGRITY "prefixes: in"
expedition,*,nary,ous,ously,ousness, JOURNEY TO GATHER INFORMATION

expel,*,lled,lling,llable,llant,llee,ller, FORCE OUT/AWAY FROM
expend,*,ded,ding,dable,dability,diture, PAY OUT
expense,*,ed,sing,sive,sively,siveness, REQUIRES TIME AND/OR MONEY (or see expanse) "prefixes: in"
experential, experiential
experience,*,ed,cing,ntial,ntially, SKILL/KNOWLEDGE ABOUT "prefixes: in/un"
experiential,lly, GAIN KNOWLEDGE/WISDOM THROUGH EXPERIENCE
experiment,*,ted,ting,tation,tal,tally, talism,ter, TRY SOMETHING NEW
expert,*,tly,tness,tise, SPECIALIZES IN, GREAT DEAL OF EXPERIENCE "prefixes: in"
expire,*,ed,ring,ration,ratory,ry, DETERIORATE, RUN OUT OF TIME
expirential, experiential
explain,*,ned,ning,anation,nable,ner, anatory,anatorily, LIST THE FACTS ABOUT SOMETHING
explanation, PROVIDE DETAILS/REASONS FOR/ABOUT
explanatory,rily, AIDS/SERVES TO EXPLAIN SOMETHING "prefixes: un"
explenashen, explanation
explicable,ly, CAN BE EXPLAINED "prefixes: in"
explicit,*,tly,tness, SPECIFIC, EXACT, FACTUAL "prefixes: in"
explikable, explicable
explinashen, explanation
explode,*,ed,ding,osion,osive, SUDDEN POWERFUL FORCE OUT "prefixes: un"
exploit,*,ted,ting,tate,tation,tative, TAKE UNFAIR ADVANTAGE OF FOR SELFISH GAIN "prefixes: non/under"
explore,*,ed,ring,ration,ratory, SEARCH BEYOND WHAT IS KNOWN
explosion, INTENSE FORCE/BLAST
explosive,ely,eness, INTENSIVE ACTION/REACTION "prefixes: un"
exploytation, exploit(ation)
explunashen, explanation
expodeshen, expedition
exporashen, expire(ration)
export,*,ted,ting,tation,table,tability, ter, SHIP GOODS OUT OF THE COUNTRY "prefixes: re"

expose,*,ed,sing,sure,sal,sition,sitive, sitory,sition,sitor,er, LET IT OUT/BE SEEN "prefixes: non/over/under"
exposhur, expose(sure)
expreshun, express(ion)
express,sses,ssed,ssing,ssion,ssional, ssionless,ssible,ssive,ssively, ssiveness, ssivity,ssionism,sser, TO VERBALIZE/ACT OUT WHAT ONE THINKS, GET THERE FASTER "prefixes: in/un"
expurashen, expire(ration)
expuration, expire(ration)
expurential, experiential
exquisite,ely,eness, PERFECTLY BEAUTIFUL
exqwisit, exquisite
exsalins, excel(llence)
exsdensive, extensive
exseed, exceed
exsel, excel / accel
exselarashen, accelerate(tion)
exselaratur, accelerate(tor)
exseld, excel(lled) / accel(lled)
exselens, excel(llence)
exselent, excellent
exselerashen, accelerate(tion)
exselurashen, accelerate(tion)
exselurate, accelerate
exseluratur, accelerate(tor)
exsenshuate, accentuate
exsentrik, eccentric
exserpd, excerpt
exsersize, exercise / exorcise
exses, excess / access
exsesif, excess(ive) / access(ive)
exsesis, excess(es) / access(es)
exsesory, accessory
exshange, exchange
exsibition, exhibit(ion)
exsilent, excellent
exsilurate, exhilarate / accelerate
exsintrik, eccentric
exsirped, excerpt
exsistens, exist(ence)
exsitment, excite(ment)
exskalate, escalate / escalade
exskavate, excavate
exskuvashen, excavate(tion)
exsost, exhaust
exspedient, expedient
exspektashen, expect(ation)
exspektent, expect(ant)
exspel, expel

exspense, expense
exsplod, explode
exsploshen, explosion
exsplosive, explosive
exstase, ecstasy
exstend, extend
exstengwish, extinguish
exstenshen, extension
exstinsibly, extensible(ly)
exstract, extract
exstradite, extradite
exstrakt, extract
exstravert, extrovert
exstrem, extreme
exstremly, extreme(ly)
exstrivurt, extrovert
exstrordenary, extraordinary
exstusee, ecstasy
exsubishen, exhibit(ion)
exsulens, excel(llence)
exsulent, excellent
exsuqushen, execute(tion)
exsurpt, excerpt
exteenkt, extinct
extend,*,ded,ding,nsion,nsive,nsively, nsiveness,dable,dability,dible,nsible, STRETCH/ADD BEYOND WHAT EXISTS "prefixes: over/pre"
extenquish, extinguish
extensible,bility,bly, ABLE TO STRETCH BEYOND WHAT EXISTS "prefixes: in"
extension,*,ive, STRETCH/ADD BEYOND WHAT EXISTS
extensive,ely,eness,ible, STRETCH/ADD BEYOND WHAT EXISTS
extenuate,*,ed,ting,tingly,tion,tive,tor, tory, LESSEN A MISTAKE BY PROVIDING GOOD EXCUSE
exterior,*,rity,rize,rizes,rized,rizing, rization, OUTSIDE LAYER
exterminate,*,ed,ting,tion,tive,tor,tory, able, COMPLETELY GET RID OF
external,lly,lism,lity,lize,lizes,lized,lizing, lization, OUTSIDE OF SOMETHING OR SOMEONE
extinct,tion,tive, DOES NOT EXIST ANY LONGER
extinguish,hes,hed,hing,hable,hment, her, TO PUT OUT, END "prefixes: in"
extra,*, PREFIX INDICATING "OUTSIDE/BEYOND" MOST OFTEN MODIFIES THE WORD, MORE OF THE SAME
extract,*,ted,ting,tion,table,tive,tively, tor, TAKE/DRAW FROM

extradite,*,ed,ting,tion, RELEASE FROM ONE LEGAL AUTHORITY TO ANOTHER
extraneous,sly,sness, EXTRA, FROM OUTSIDE OF, NOT NECESSARY
extraordinaire,*,ry, OVER AND ABOVE, EXCELLENT
extraordinary,rily,riness, OVER AND ABOVE, EXCELLENT
extravurt, extrovert
extreme,*,ely,eness,mity,mities,mism, OF THE GREATEST/MOST
extro, PREFIX INDICATING "OUTSIDE/BEYOND" MOST OFTEN MODIFIES THE WORD
extrovert,*,ted,tly, OUTGOING, GREGARIOUS
exturminate, exterminate
exuated, acuate(d)
exukushen, execute(tion)
exuqushen, execute(tion)
exuqute, execute
exursize, exercise / exorcise
exurt, exert
exurtion, exert(ion)
exzamen, examine
exzema, eczema
eye,*,ed,ying, ORGAN OF SIGHT (or see I)
eyebrow,*, HAIR AROUND TOP OF EYES
eyelash,hes, HAIR ON EYELIDS
ez, ease / easy
ezale, easily
ezay, essay
ezbeshulee, especially
ezdragen, estrogen
eze, easy / ease
ezel, easel
ezinshil, essential
ezkort, escort
ezment, easement
ezoteric, esoteric
ezperagus, asparagus
ezsperugus, asparagus
eztablush, establish
ezteem, esteem
eztimate, estimate
eztonish, astonish
eztrawlegy, astrology
eztrogin, estrogen
eztrus, estrus
ezul, easel
ezule, easily
fabewlus, fabulous

fabewlusly, fabulous(ly)
fable,*, MYTH/LEGEND/STORY
fabrecation, fabricate(tion)
fabrek, fabric
fabrekashin, fabricate(tion)
fabrekate, fabricate
fabric,*,cate,cation,cator, THREADS WOVEN TOGETHER "prefixes: bio"
fabricate,*,ed,ting,tion,tor, TO CREATE, CHANGE FROM ONE MATERIAL FORM TO ANOTHER "prefixes: pre"
fabrukashen, fabricate(tion)
fabrukate, fabricate
fabuare, february
fabul, fable
fabules, fabulous / fable(s)
fabulis, fabulous
fabulous,sly,sness, EXCELLENT, WONDERFUL
fabulus, fabulous
fabulusly, fabulous(ly)
fac, face / fake / phase / faze
facade,*, FALSE FRONT, PHONY
facalty, faculty
face,*,ed,cing,cial,cially,cable,eable, EXTERIOR FRONT, ON FRONT OF HEAD (or see phase) "prefixes: re/sur"
facechus, facetious
facelity, facility
facelty, faculty
facen, fasten / face(cing) / fake(king)
faceshus, facetious
facest, fascist
facet,*,tious, ONE PLANE/FACE/SIDE AMONG MANY (or see faucet) "prefixes: multi"
facetious,sly,sness, NOT SERIOUS, BEING AMUSING
facha, fascia
fachel, facial
fachen, fashion
fachest, fascist
fachinuble, fashion(able)
fachism, fascism
fachist, fascist
fachul, facial
fachun, fashion
fachunible, fashion(able)
facial,*,lly,list, HAVING TO DO WITH THE FACE
facilitate,*,ed,ting,tion,tive,tor, HELP/ENABLE SUCCESS

facility,ties, PLACE PROVIDING SERVICES
facin, fasten / face(cing) / fake(king)
facinate, fascinate
facishus, facetious
facism, fascism
facit, facet / faucet
facitious, facetious
facshun, faction
fact,*,tual,tually,tuality,tualness, tualism, FOR REAL, TRUE (or see fake(d)/ fax/face(d)) "prefixes: contra"
faction,*,nal,nally,nalism, OF MATH, PART OF A LARGER GROUP
faculty,ties,tative,tatively, SKILL OR ABILITY, TEACHING STAFF
fad,*, CURRENT STYLE (or see fade/fate)
fadar, father / fodder
fadaret, federate
fade,*,ed,ding,eless, LOSS OF COLOR/MEMORY/SUBSTANCE (or see fate) "prefixes: pre"
fadel, fatal
fadelity, fidelity
fadul, fatal
faen, feign
faer, fair / fire
faes, phase
fafret, favorite
fag,*,gged,ggot,ggoting, BUNDLE OF STICKS, CIGARETTE, DERAGATORY REMARK
fagism, fascism
fahrenheit, OF THERMOMETERS/TEMPERATURE
fail,*,led,ling,lingly,lure, NOT SUCCEED(or see fall) "prefixes: un"
fain, feign / vain / vein / vane / fine
faint,*,ted,ting,tly,tness,ter, LOOSE OXYGEN TO BRAIN CAUSING COLLAPSE, NOT CLEAR
fair,*,red,ring,rly,rness, PLACE OF ACTIVITY, IN BETWEEN GOOD AND BAD (or see fare) "prefixes: un"
fairenhite, fahrenheit
fairwel, farewell
fairy,ries, TINY ENTITIES WITH WINGS SEEN ONLY TO A FEW (or see ferry)
fais, phase
faith,*,hful,hfully,hless,hlessly, hlessness, HAVING A BELIEF OR HOPE "prefixes: multi/un"

faiz, phase
fajism, fascism
fak, fake
fakchinul, faction(al)
fakd, fact / fake(d)
fake,*,ed,king,er, PHONY OR ILLUSION
fakelty, faculty
fakilty, faculty
fakshen, faction
fakshunil, faction(al)
fakt, fact / fake(d)
faktionul, faction(al)
fakulty, faculty
fal, fail / fall / fowl / foul
falacy, fallacy
falanthropist, philanthropy(pist)
fald, fault / fail(ed)
falek, phalli(c)
falese, fallacy
falfill, fulfill
falic, phalli(c)
falicity, felicity
falise, fallacy
fall,*,llen,lling,fell, A SEASON, COME DOWN (or see fail)
fallacy,cies, NOT TRUE, UNFOUNDED
fallow,wness, AGRICULTURE EXPRESSION, NOT ACTIVE (or see follow)
fallsefy, falsify
fallsify, falsify
falo, follow / fallow
faloer, follow(er)
falose, fallacy
falosify, philosophy
falou, follow / fallow
falow, follow / fallow
falowir, follow(er)
false,ely,eness,sies,sify,sity,sifier,shood, NOT TRUE
falsify,fies,fied,fying,fiable,fiability, fication,fier, PRETEND/FEIGN TO BE TRUTHFUL
falt, fault / fail(ed)
falter,*,red,ring,ringly,rer, LOOSE FOOTING/CONFIDENCE (or see fault) "prefixes: un"
faluse, fallacy
faly, folly
fam, fame
famas, famous
famaslee, famous(ly)
famblee, family

fame,*,ed,ming,mous, REKNOWN, RECOGNIZED, PUBLIC REPUTATION "prefixes: de/in"
famelur, familiar
famen, famine
fames, famous
fameslee, famous(ly)
familiar,rly,rity, EXPERIENCE WITH, A KNOWING "prefixes: over/un"
family,lies,lial, GROUP OF PEOPLE RELATED IN SOME WAY "prefixes: multi/sub"
famine,*,ish, SEVERE LACK OF FOOD OVER TIME
famis, famous
famislee, famous(ly)
famlee, family
famous,sly,sness, WIDELY KNOWN "prefixes: in"
famus, famous
famuslee, famous(ly)
fan,*,nned,nning,nner,nny, MOTION TO CREATE BREEZE/LIFT, SPREAD OUT (or see feign)
fana, fauna
fanadek, phonetic / fanatic
fanatic,*,cal,cally,cism, EXTREME/ IRRATIONAL ENTHUSIASM, HIGHLY MOTIVATED IN BELIEF/BEHAVIOR (or see phonetic)
fancy,cier,ciest,ciful,cifully,cifulness, DECORATIVE, PLAYFUL, LIGHT
fane, feign / fan(ny)
fanedik, phonetic / fanatic
fanesh, finish
fanetic, phonetic / fanatic
fang,*,ged,ging, TOOTH IN SNAKE/ CANINE/SPIDER "prefixes: de"
fangeprint, fingerprint
fangernail, fingernail
fangur, finger
fanic, phonic
fanomanen, phenomenon
fanomena, phenomenon
fanomenul, phenomenal
fanominul, phenomenal
fansee, fancy
fant, faint
fantaja, fantasy(sia)
fantastic,cal,cally,cality,calness, ABSOLUTELY GREAT
fantastikul, fantastic(al)

fantasy,sies,sia,size,sizes,sized,sizing, sist, DREAMY IDEA OF A FUTURE EVENT
fantem, phantom
fantesy, fantasy
fantisy, fantasy
fantum, phantom
fantusy, fantasy
faond, found
faprecate, fabricate
faprek, fabric
faprekashin, fabricate(tion)
faprukashen, fabricate(tion)
fapulus, fabulous
far,rther,rthest, QUITE A DISTANCE AWAY (or see for/fare/fair/fire)
farce, SATIRE, NON-FACTUAL, COMICAL
fare,*,ed,ring, COST FOR TRANSPORTATION, PRESENT CONDITION (or see fair/fire/fairy)
farenhite, fahrenheit
fares, ferry(ries) / fairy(ries)
farest, far(thest)
farewell,*, GOOD-BYE
farit, ferret
farm,*,med,ming,mable,mer, LAND WHERE ANIMALS/CROPS ARE RAISED/GROWN "prefixes: un"
farmaceutical, pharmaceutic(al)
farmasist, pharmacist
farmasutical, pharmaceutic(al)
farmir, farm(er)
farmisist, pharmacist
farmosutekul, pharmaceutic(al)
farmusutekul, pharmaceutic(al)
faro, pharaoh
farotious, ferocious
fars, farce / fair(s)
farsighted,dness, ABLE TO SEE FARTHER AWAY BETTER THAN CLOSE UP
farsited, farsighted
farther,hest,rmost, EXCEEDS CURRENT PHYSICAL DIMENSION/DEPTH (or see further)
farthist, farther(hist)
farthur, farther
farwell, farewell
fary, ferry / fairy
fas, phase / face / faze
fasa, fascia
fascanate, fascinate
fascia,ae,as,al, ROOFLINE ADDENDUM, BIOLOGY/ANATOMY TERM

fascinate,*,ed,edly,ting,tingly,tion,tor, CAPTIVATES INTEREST/ATTENTION
fascism,st,stic, CENTRALIZED OPPRESSIVE CONTROL
fascist,*,tic,sm, PERSON WHO SUPPORTS OPPRESSIVE/ AUTHORITARIAN CONTROL
fasd, face(d) / fast / phase(d) / faze(d)
fasea, fascia
fasechus, facetious
fasecian, physician
fased, face(d) / fast / phase(d)
fasek, physique / physic
fasel, fossil
faselisd, fossil(ized)
faselitashen, facilitate(tion)
faselitation, facilitate(tion)
faselity, facility
faselutate, facilitate
fasen, fasten / face(cing)
fasenate, fascinate
fasener, fastener
faseque, physique
faseshan, physician
faseshis, facetious
faseshus, facetious
fasesm, fascism
faset, facet / faucet
fasetious, facetious
fasfate, phosphate
fasha, fascia
fashel, facial
fashen, fashion
fashenuble, fashion(able)
fashest, fascist
fashil, facial
fashin, fashion
fashinuble, fashion(able)
fashion,*,ned,ning,nable,nably,nability, nableness,ner, CLOTHING STYLES WITHIN A CERTAIN TIMEFRAME "prefixes: un"
fashism, fascism
fashist, fascist
fashul, facial
fashun, fashion
fashunebul, fashion(able)
fasia, fascia
fasichus, facetious
fasician, physician
fasik, physic / physique
fasil, fossil
fasilatashen, facilitate(tion)
fasilatat, facilitate

fasilatation, facilitate(tion)
fasilety, facility
fasilitate, facilitate
fasility, facility
fasin, fasten / face(cing)
fasinate, fascinate
fasiner, fastener
fasing, face(cing) / phase(ing)
fasique, physique
fasishus, facetious
fasism, fascism
fasit, facet / faucet
fasitious, facetious
fasner, fastener
fasnir, fastener
fasnor, fastener
fasnur, fastener
fast,*,ted,ting,ter,test,tness,tnesses, RATE OF SPEED, TO NOT EAT FOOD, REMAIN FIXED/SECURE
fasten,*,ned,ning,ner, ADHERE, CLOSE, SECURE "prefixes: un"
fastener,*, BUTTONS, ZIPPERS, SNAPS, CLOSURE
fasul, fossil
fasunate, fascinate
fat,*,tter,ttest,tten,ttening,tteningly,tty, tness,tso, LAYER OF FOOD STORE IN MOST LIVING THINGS (or see fad/ fade/fate/fought) "prefixes: non"
fatal,*,lly,lity,lities,list,lism, LIFE THREATENING
fate,*,ed,eful,efully,efulness, THE BELIEF THAT EVENTS ARE PRE-PLANNED
fateg, fatigue
fatek, fatigue
fath, faith
father,*, MALE PARENT, NAME FOR A PRIEST
fathom,*,med,ming,mless,mable, MEASUREMENT FOR THE OCEAN DEPTH, DEEP TO UNDERSTAND "prefixes: un"
fathur, feather / father
fatia, fascia
fatig, fatigue
fatigue,*,ed,uing,gable, EXHAUSTION, WEARY, MILITARY CLOTHING "prefixes: inde"
faucet,*, PLUMBING DEVICE FOR WATER/LIQUIDS
fauculize, focal(ize)
faukalize, focal(ize)

faul, foul / fowl / fall
faulsefy, falsify
faulsify, falsify
fault,*,ted,ting,tier,tiest,ty,tless,tlessly, tily,tiness, SOMETHING/SOMEONE TO BLAME, A PROBLEM, TECTONIC EXPRESSION (or see falter)
faulter, falter
faun,*, HALF GOAT HALF HUMAN (or see fawn)
fauna, ANIMALS OF A REGION
faund, found
faundashen, foundation
faundation, foundation
faundry, foundry
faunic, phonic
faunt, found
fauntry, foundry
fausefy, falsify
fausel, fossil
fausfate, phosphate
fausify, falsify
fausit, faucet
fausphate, phosphate
fauster, foster
fausul, fossil
faut, fought
faux, FALSE/IMITATION/FAKE/ ARTIFICIAL
fauxpas, ALSO FAUX PAS, A BLUNDER
faveret, favorite
favor,*,red,ring,rable,rably,rableness, rite,rer, PREFERENCE FOR "prefixes: dis/un"
favorite,*,tism, PREFERENCE FOR
fawcet, faucet
fawdur, fodder
fawel, foul / fowl
fawl, foul / fowl
fawlust, foul(est)
fawn,*, BABY DEER (or see faun)
fawnd, fond / found
fawndashen, foundation
fawnt, font / found
fawntry, foundry
fawsefy, falsify
fawsel, fossil
fawsify, falsify
fawsilized, fossil(ized)
fawsul, fossil
fawt, fought
fawul, foul / fowl
fax,xes,xed,xing, SEND A LETTER BY PHONE (or see fact(s))

faze,*,ed,zing, SEND A LETTER BY PHONE (or see phase)
fazek, physique
fazeshan, physician
fe, fee
feable, feeble
fear,*,red,ring,rful,rfully,rfulness,rless, rlessly,rlessness,rsome,rsomely, rsomeness, AFRAID, POWERLESS
feasent, pheasant
feasible,eness,ly,bility, QUESTION/ STUDY ABILITY TO ACCOMPLISH/ ACHIEVE "prefixes: de/inde/un"
feast,*,ted,ting, GREAT AMOUNT OF FOOD
feasta, fiesta
feasubilety, feasible(bility)
feasuble, feasible
feat,*, PERFORM WITH UNUSUAL ABILITY (or see feet)
feather,*,red,ring,ry, BIRD CLOTHES, A DECORATIVE EFFECT
feature,*,ed,ring,eless, SPECIAL "prefixes: dis/multi/un"
feb, fib
febal, feeble
february, A MONTH OF THE YEAR (ENGLISH)
febuare, february
febul, feeble
febwuare, february
fecechus, facetious
fecer, figure
feces, EXCREMENT, WASTE PRODUCT, BODILY DISCHARGE (or see face(s))
feceshis, facetious
fecetious, facetious
fech, fetch
fecher, feature
fechet, fidget
fecility, facility
feckle, fickle
fecsher, fixture
fecster, fixture
fed, PAST TENSE FOR THE WORD "FEED"
fedality, fidelity
fedar, fetter / feed(er) / feather
fedarashen, federation
fedaration, federation
fedarul, federal
fedder, fetter / feed(er)
feder, fetter / feed(er) / feather

federal,*,lly,list,lize,lizes,lized,lizing,lism, ation,ative, NATIONAL GOVERNMENT "prefixes: con"
federate,*,ed,ting,tion,tive, GROUPS JOINED UNDER ONE UNIT/ UMBRELLA
federation,*,ive, GROUP OF PEOPLE FORMING IN UNION, UNITED
fedir, fetter / feed(er) / feather
fedirate, federate
fediration, federation
fedish, fetish
fedle, fiddle
fedler, fiddle(r)
fedral, federal
fedrol, federal
fedul, fiddle
fedulize, fertile(lize)
fedur, fetter / feed(er) / feather
fedurashen, federation
fedurate, federate
fee,*, COST FOR/TO DO SOMETHING
feeble,er,est,eness,ly, WEAK, LACKS STRENGTH "prefixes: en"
feebul, feeble
feecher, feature
feed,*,ding,der,fed, GIVE FOOD TO (or see feet) "prefixes: under"
feel,*,ling,lings,felt,ler, USE OF TOUCH/ EMOTIONS TO SENSE ENVIRONMENT "prefixes: un"
feeld, field
feer, fear
feest, feast
feesta, fiesta
feet, MORE THAN ONE FOOT (or see feat)
fefer, fever
feferish, fever(ish)
fefir, fever
fefiresh, fever(ish)
fefor, fever
feftee, fifty
fefteen, fifteen
feften, fifteen
fefth, fifth
feftinth, fifteen(th)
feftis, fifty(ties)
fefty, fifty
fefur, fever
fefurish, fever(ish)
feg, fig
fegen, fission / fusion
feger, figure

fegit, fidget
fegmint, figment
feianse, fiance'
feign,*,ned,ning, TO PRETEND/COPY
feild, field
fein, feign
feis, phase
feiz, phase
fejin, fission / fusion
fejit, fidget
fejon, fission / fusion
fekle, fickle
fekment, figment
feks, fix
feksher, fixture
fekshun, fiction
fekst, fix(ed)
fekster, fixture
feksus, fix(es)
fekul, fickle
fekur, figure
fel, feel / fell / fill / full
felade, fillet
feladendron, philodendron
felanthrepy, philanthropy
felanthropist, philanthropy(pist)
felay, fillet
feld, felt / field / fill(ed) / fell(ed)
feldration, filtrate(ion)
feldur, filter / field(er)
fele, fillet / filly
felicity,ties,tous,tously,tousness,tate, tates,tated,tation,tator, HAPPINES WITH PERFECTION "prefixes: in"
feline,*,ely,eness,nity, OF CATS
fell,lled,lling,ller, PAST TENSE FOR THE WORD "FALL", CUT DOWN TREE (or see fill/feel)
felm, film
felosofy, philosophy
felt, PAST TENSE FOR THE WORD "FEEL", CRUSHED WOOL/COTTON (or see field)
felter, filter
felth, filth
felthe, filthy
feltration, filtrate(ion)
feludindron, philodendron
felurmonek, philharmonic
female,*,eness, THE FEMININE, LIFE GIVER
femanen, feminine
femanist, feminist
femelear, familiar

feminine,nity,ely,eness,nism,ist,ize,izes, ized,izing,ization,mme, THE COMPLIMENT OF MASCULINE "prefixes: de"
feminist,*,tic, A PERSON WHO SUPPORTS WOMEN'S EQUALITY WITH MEN
femunin, feminine
femunist, feminist
fen, fin
fence,*,ed,cing,eless,er, OUTSIDE BARRIER/WALL, A SPORT
fench, finch
fender,*, PART OF A BICYCLE/VEHICLE, A SCREEN, A GUITAR
fenedic, phonetic / fanatic
fenesh, finish
fenetick, phonetic / fanatic
fenger, finger
fengernail, fingernail
fengerprint, fingerprint
fengur, finger
fenish, finish
fenker, finger
fenkerprint, fingerprint
fenkur, finger
fennel, EDIBLE HERB
fenomanen, phenomenon
fenomena, phenomenon
fenominul, phenomenal
fense, fence
fensh, finch
fentur, fender
feonsa, fiance'
fepel, feeble
fepol, feeble
fepuary, february
fepul, feeble
fepuwary, february
fer, fear / for / fir / fur / far / fair / fare
ferbed, forbid
ferbedin, forbid(dden)
ferbid, forbid
ferdelize, fertile(lize)
ferdul, fertile
ferdulizashen, fertile(lization)
fere, ferry / fairy / furry
ferefur, forever
ferenhite, fahrenheit
feres, ferry(ries) / fairy(ries)
feret, ferret
ferever, forever
fergave, forgave
fergetful, forget(ful)

fergif, forgive
fergifness, forgive(ness)
fergit, forget
fergitful, forget(ful)
fergive, forgive
fergivnes, forgive(ness)
fergot, forgot
fergoten, forgot(tten)
feriner, foreign(er)
ferius, furious
ferkets, forget(s)
ferkiv, forgive
ferlough, furlough
ferlow, furlough
ferm, firm
fermaledy, formal(ity)
fermality, formal(ity)
fermashen, formation
fermation, formation
ferment,*,ted,ting,table,tability,tation, tative, MOVING TOWARDS FERMENTATION
fermentation,nal, ENZYMATIC/ CELLULAR REACTION
fern,*, A PLANT
fernachur, furniture
fernecher, furniture
fernes, furnace
fernis, furnace
fernish, furnish
ferniture, furniture
fernus, furnace
fernush, furnish
fero, pharaoh / furrow
ferochusle, ferocious(ly)
ferocious,sly,sness, FIERCE, INTENSE
feroshusle, ferocious(ly)
ferotious, ferocious
ferow, furrow / pharaoh
ferr, PREFIX INDICATING "IRON" MOST OFTEN MODIFIES THE WORD
ferret,*, MEMBER OF THE WEASEL FAMILY
ferri, PREFIX INDICATING "IRON" MOST OFTEN MODIFIES THE WORD
ferro, PREFIX INDICATING "IRON" MOST OFTEN MODIFIES THE WORD
ferroso, PREFIX INDICATING "IRON" MOST OFTEN MODIFIES THE WORD
ferry,rries,rried,rrying, BOAT THAT CROSSES WATER CARRYING THINGS (or see fairy/furry)
fers, fierce / fear(s) / first
fersake, forsake

fersakin, forsake(n)
fersd, first
ferse, fierce
fersest, fierce(st)
fersly, fierce(ly)
fersnis, fierce(ness)
ferst, first
ferther, farther / further
ferthur, farther / further
fertile,lity,ely,eness,lize, ABLE/READY TO PRODUCE, PREPARE FOR PRODUCTION "prefixes: in/inter"
fertilize,*,ed,er,zing,zation, USED TO ENHANCE PRODUCTION
fertulize, fertilize
ferut, ferret
ferwal, farewell
ferwel, farewell
fery, ferry / fairy / furry
ferys, ferry(ries) / fairy(ries)
ferzd, first
ferzt, first
fesabilety, feasible(bility)
fesable, feasible
fesasist, physicist
fescal, fiscal
fesdev, festive
feseble, feasible
fesechus, facetious
fesekl, physical
fesekly, physical(lly)
feseks, physics
fesent, pheasant
feseologe, physiology
feseshus, facetious
fesetious, facetious
fesh, fish
feshen, fission / fusion
fesible, feasible
fesical, physical
fesichus, facetious
fesics, physics
fesik, physique
fesikle, physical
fesilatashen, facilitate(tion)
fesilaty, facility
fesint, pheasant
fesiologe, physiology
fesiology, physiology
fesishen, physician
fesishus, facetious
fesitious, facetious
feskal, fiscal
fesode, facade

fest, fist
festaful, festive(val)
festive,ely,eness,val,vity,vities, A CELEBRATION
festofil, festive(val)
fesubility, feasible(bility)
fesuble, feasible
fesunt, pheasant
fesusist, physics(cist)
fet, feet / feat / feed / fed
fetarashen, federation
fetaration, federation
fetch,hes,hed,hing, TO GET AND BRING BACK
feteg, fatigue
feter, fetter / feed(er)
feth, fifth
fethar, feather
fethur, feather
fetir, fetter / feed(er)
fetirashen, federation
fetish,hes,hism,hist, OBSESSION FOR SOMETHING
fetler, fiddle(r)
fetter,*,red,ring, TO SHACKLE/ RESTRAIN "prefixes: un"
feturation, federation
feture, feature
feu, few
feucher, future
feud,*,ding,dal,dalism,dality,dalize, datory, A LONGSTANDING QUARREL/FIGHT
feugen, fusion / fission
feul, fuel
feuld, field
feum, fume
feumegat, fumigate
feumigate, fumigate
feumugation, fumigate(tion)
feuree, fury / furry
feurius, furious
feus, fuse
feushen, fusion / fission
feut, feud
fever,*,red,ring,rish, BODY TEMPERATURE TOO HIGH
fevir, fever
fevirish, fever(ish)
fevur, fever
fevurish, fever(ish)
few, MORE THAN TWO
fewchur, future
fewd, feud

fewgen, fusion / fission
fewgitive, fugitive
fewmigashen, fumigate(tion)
fewmigate, fumigate
fewmigation, fumigate(tion)
fewnarul, funeral
fewreus, furious
fews, fuse
fewton, futon
fewul, fuel
fex, fix
fext, fix(ed)
feyuree, fury
fezability, feasible(bility)
fezable, feasible
fezacul, physical
fezakle, physical
fezakul, physical
fezalogical, physiology(gical)
fezasest, physics(cist)
fezek, physique
fezekle, physical
fezeks, physics
fezent, pheasant
fezeology, physiology
fezeshan, physician
fezik, physique
fezikol, physical
feziks, physics
fezint, pheasant
fezubelity, feasible(bility)
fezuble, feasible
fezucul, physical
fezuks, physics
fezukul, physical
fezulogically, physiology(gically)
fezunt, pheasant
fezusist, physics(cist)
fi, fee
fiance', HUMAN TO BE MARRIED
fiar, fire
fib,*,bber,bbing, TO TELL A LIE
fiber,*,brous, PLANT MATERIAL (or see fib(bber)/fever) "prefixes: multi"
fibre, fiber
fibrous,sly,sness, TEXTURE IS THREAD-LIKE "prefixes: multi"
fibur, fiber
fichar, feature
fichen, fish(ing) / fusion / fission
ficher, feature
fichet, fidget
fichur, feature

fickle,er,est,eness, WILL LIKELY CHANGE PERSPECTIVE/PREFERENCE
ficshan, fiction
ficshen, fiction
ficsher, fixture
ficshon, fiction
ficster, fixture
fiction,nal,nalize,nalizes,nalized,nalizing, nalization,tious,tiously,tiousness, ive,ively, STORIES/BOOKS ABOUT MADE UP CHARACTERS "prefixes: non"
fiddle,*,er,ling, AN INSTRUMENT
fidelity, FAITHFUL "prefixes: in"
fider, fight(er) / fit(tter)
fidget,*,ted,ting,tingly,ty,tiness, AN INSTRUMENT
fidir, fight(er) / fit(tter)
fidle, fiddle
fidlur, fiddle(r)
fidol, fiddle
fidor, fight(er) / fit(tter)
fidul, fiddle
fidur, fight(er) / fit(tter)
field,*,der,ding, LAND WITH FEW IF NO TREES "prefixes: in/sub/up"
fierce,er,est,ely,eness, DANGEROUS, THREATENING
fiesta,*, CELEBRATION
fife, five
fiflth, filth
fifteen,nth, NUMBER
fiftees, fifty(ties)
fiften, fifteen
fiftenth, fifteen(th)
fiftes, fifty(ties)
fifth,*, ONE-FIFTH OF FIVE PARTS
fifty,ties,tieth, A NUMBER
fig,*, A FRUIT
figen, fission
figer, figure
figerene, figurine
figet, fidget
fight,*,ter,ting,fought, STRUGGLE, BATTLE BETWEEN "prefixes: in"
figit, fidget
figment,*, IMAGINARY
figure,*,ed,ring,ral,rant,ration,rative, ratively,rativeness,rine, SHAPE/ FORM OF SOMETHING, NUMBERS "prefixes: con/dis/pre"
figurine,*, SHAPE/FORM OF SOMETHING
fijen, fission / fusion

fijet, fidget
fijon, fission / fusion
fikchen, fiction
fiker, figure
fikle, fickle
fikment, figment
fiks, fix / fig(s)
fikshin, fiction
fikshur, fixture
fikster, fixture
fiksus, fix(es)
fikt, fix(ed)
fikul, fickle
fikur, figure
fil, fill / fell / file / feel
fila, fillet
filadendron, philodendron
filanthrepy, philanthropy
filanthropist, philanthropy(pist)
filarmonek, philharmonic
filasofical, philosophy(hical)
fild, file(d) / field / fill(ed)
fildration, filtrate(ion)
fildur, filter
file,*,ed,ling,er, TO ORGANIZE, TOOL TO GRIND, FORM A LINE (or see fill/fillet/filly) "prefixes: inter/pre"
filermonek, philharmonic
filet, fillet
filhermonic, philharmonic
filings, file(lings) / feel(ings)
fill,*,lled,lling,ller, MAKE OPPOSITE OF EMPTY (or see file/fell)
fillet,*,ted,ting, ALSO FILET, BONES REMOVED FROM FISH/ANIMALS
filly,llies, YOUNG FEMALE HORSE
film,*,med,ming,mation,my,mily, miness,mer, A COATING, A MOVING PICTURE "prefixes: bio"
filodendron, philodendron
filosofy, philosophy
filosophy, philosophy
filt, file(d) / field / fill(ed)
filter,*,red,ring,rless,rable,trable,trate, rer, USED TO SEPARATE/SORT "prefixes: bio"
filth,hy, DIRTIEST OF THE DIRTY, NASTY
filthy,hier,hiest, DIRTIEST OF THE DIRTY, NASTY
filtrate,*,ed,ting,tation, TO SEPARATE/STRAIN
filudendron, philodendron
filurmonic, philharmonic
fily, filly

fimanist, feminist
fimilear, familiar
fin,*,nned,nning, EXTRUSION FOR WEAVING THROUGH AIR/WATER (or see fine)
final,*,lly,le,list,lize,lizes,lized,lizing, lization,lizer, THE END, THE LAST "prefixes: semi"
finance,*,ed,cing,cial,cials,cially,eable, cier, ABOUT MONEY
finants, finance
finch,hes, A BIRD
find,*,der,ding,found, REVEAL THE UNSEEN/UNKNOWN
findur, fender / find(er)
fine,*,er,est,ed,ning,ely,eness, THIN, VERY NICE, MONETARY PUNISHMENT (or see fin)
finedik, phonetic / fanatic
finel, final / fennel
finely, fine(ly) / final(lly)
fines, finesse / fine(s) / fine(st)
finesh, finish
finesse,*, HANDLE WITH SKILL/CONTROL/DELICATELY (or see fine(st))
finetic, phonetic / fanatic
finger,*,red,ring, ON THE HAND, USE THE HAND, EXTRUSION
fingernail,*, ON THE FINGER
fingerprint,*,ted,ting, ON THE FINGER
finight, finite
finish,es,hed,hing,her, TO COMPLETE "prefixes: semi/un "
finite,ely,eness, LIMITED
finker, finger
finkerprint, fingerprint
finle, final / fennel
finol, final / fennel
finomanen, phenomenon
finomena, phenomenon
finominul, phenomenal
finse, fence
finsh, finch
fintur, fender
finul, final / fennel
finuly, final(lly)
fionsa, fiance'
fiper, fiber
fipur, fiber
fir,*, AN EVERGREEN TREE (or see fire/fur/for/fear)
firbed, forbid
firbedin, forbid(dden)

firbiten, forbid(dden)
firdul, fertile
firdulize, fertilize
fire,*,ed,ring,er, CHEMICAL REACTION THAT BURNS, TAKE JOB AWAY, EMOTIONAL (or see far/furry) "prefixes: mis/retro"
firefur, forever
firevur, forever
firgave, forgave
firgefnis, forgive(ness)
firget, forget
firgetful, forget(ful)
firgitful, forget(ful)
firgive, forgive
firgot, forgot
firgoten, forgot(tten)
firketing, forget(tting)
firkets, forget(s)
firkiteng, forget(tting)
firkiv, forgive
firlow, furlough
firm,*,med,ming,mly,mness,mer,mest, BETWEEN SOFT/HARD, CAPITALIST GROUP
firmaledy, formal(ity)
firmality, formal(ity)
firmashen, formation
firmation, formation
firment, ferment
firn, fern
firnus, furnace
firochusle, ferocious(ly)
firoshis, ferocious
firoshusle, ferocious(ly)
firow, furrow
firs, fir(s) / fire(s) / first / fierce
firsaken, forsake(n)
first,*,tly, BEFORE ALL
firtalize, fertilize
firtul, fertile
firy, furry
firzd, first
fisasist, physicist
fiscal,lly, REFERRING TO MONEY
fisealugist, physiology(gist)
fisecal, physical
fisek, physic / physique
fiseks, physics
fiselity, facility
fiseolagekul, physiology(gical)
fiseolochi, physiology
fiseologist, physiology(gist)
fiseology, physiology

fiseshan, physician
fisesist, physicist
fish,hed,hing,hy,her,hery,heries, VERTEBRATE IN WATER, CATCH FISH IN WATER
fishun, fission / fish(ing) / fusion
fisic, physic / physique
fisical, physical
fisician, physician
fisics, physics
fisicul, physical
fisik, physique
fisiolochi, physiology
fisiologest, physiology(gist)
fision, fission / fusion
fisique, physique
fisisest, physicist
fisishan, physician
fisishen, physician
fiskul, fiscal
fisode, facade
fisokul, physical
fisologically, physiology(gically)
fisots, facade(s)
fission,nable, USE HEAT TO SPLIT AN ATOMS NUCLEUS (or see fusion)
fist,*,ted,ting, CLOSED HAND, AN EXPRESSION (or see feast)
fit,*,tted,tting,ttingly,ttingness,tter, ttest,tful,tfully,tfulness,tness, SOMETHING THAT WEARS WELL, EMOTIONAL OUTBURST (or see fight/feat/feet) "prefixes: mis/retro/un"
fite, fight
fiteg, fatigue
fiter, fight(er) / fit(tter)
fith, fifth
fitlur, fiddle(r)
fitur, fight(er) / fit(tter) / feature
fiud, feud
five,*,er, AN ENGLISH NUMBER
fiver, fever
fix,xes,xed,xer,xing,xate,xates,xated, xating,xation,xative,xatives, xable, INTENSE FOCUS, TO REPAIR "prefixes: un"
fixture,*, PERMANENTLY FASTENED
fizalogical, physiology(gical)
fizasist, physicist
fizek, physique
fizeolagekul, physiology(gical)
fizeolagist, physiology(gist)
fizeological, physiology(gical)

fizeology, physiology
fizeshan, physician
fizesist, physicist
fizicol, physical
fizik, physique
fiziks, physics
fiziologest, physiology(gist)
fiziological, physiology(gical)
fizisest, physics(cist)
fizocol, physical
fizological, physiology(gical)
fizukle, physical
fizulogically, physiology(gically)
flabides, phlebitis
flabites, phlebitis
flabodumy, phlebotomy
flabotimest, phlebotomy(mist)
flack, flake
flader, flatter / fillet
fladery, flatter(y)
flafur, flavor
flag,*,gged,gging,gger, MATERIAL WITH A SYMBOL, WAVE SOMEONE OVER, TAG SOMEONE "prefixes: re"
flail,*,led,ling, THRASH ABOUT, A TOOL FOR THRASHING GRAIN
flain, flat(tten)
flair,*, APTITUDE/KNACK FOR, DEMEANOR(or see flare)
flake,*,ed,king,er,ky,kier,kiest,kily, kiness, THIN LAYER, NOT RELIABLE
flal, flail
flamable, flammable
flame,*,ed,ming,mer, TIP OF FIRE, SUDDEN ERUPTION
flamingo,*, A BIRD, DANCE
flammable,*,bility, CAN CATCH ON FIRE "prefixes: in"
flanel, flannel
flank,*,ked,king,ker, THE REAR, SIDES
flannel,*, COTTON MATERIAL
flap,*,pped,pping,pper,ppy, WAVE ABOUT, REMOVABLE COVER
flare,*,ed,ring, SHOOTING LIGHT, TO SPREAD OUT (or see flair)
flash,hes,hed,hing,her, LIGHTS FOR A BRIEF MOMENT, TATTOO LINGO
flat,*,tten,tter,tters,ttest,ttens,ttened, ttening,ttener, THIN, HORIZONTAL, OFF KEY
flatter,*,ry, PRAISE THAT'S NOT SINCERE/SERIOUS "prefixes: un"
flatur, flat(tter) / flatter
flau, flaw / flow

flaunder, flounder
flaur, flower / flour / floor
flaus, floss / flaw(s)
flavor,*,red,ring,rful,rless, PERCEIVED BY TASTEBUDS ON THE TONGUE
flaw,*,wed,wless,wlessly,wlessness, NOT RIGHT (or see flow)
flawer, flour / flower
flawnder, flounder
fle, flea / flee
flea,*, A TINY BUG (or see flee)
flebant, flippant
flebidis, phlebitis
flebitis, phlebitis
flebodumy, phlebotomy
fleck,*,ked,king, BITS/PIECES/FLAKES OF SOMETHING (or see flex)
flecks, fleck(s) / flex
flecs, flex / fleck(s)
fled, PAST TENSE FOR THE WORD "FLEE" (or see fleet/flee(d))
flee,*,eed,eeing,led,eer, RUN AWAY (or see flea)
fleece,es,ed,cing,cy,er, SHEEP COAT, COAT MATERIAL
fleet,*,ted,ter,ting,tingly,ter,test, tingness,tly,tness, GROUP OF BOATS, MOVE SWIFTLY, QUICKLY
flegm, phlegm
fleks, flex / fleck(s)
flem, phlegm
flemingo, flamingo
flemsy, flimsy
flench, flinch
fleng, fling
flent, flint
flep, flip
flepant, flippant
fleper, flipper
fler, flare / flair
flert, flirt
flery, flurry
flese, fleece / flea(s)
flesh,hy,hier,hiest,hiness,hly,hlier,hliest, hliness, SOFT/FIRM PARTS OF FRUIT/ANIMALS
flete, fleet
flew, PAST TENSE FOR THE WORD "FLY" (or see flu/flue) "prefixes: over"
flewent, fluent
flewid, fluid
flex,xes,xed,xing,xible,xibly,xibility, xibleness, TO BEND, TEMPORARILY

BEND (or see fleck(s)) "prefixes: re/retro"
fli, fly / flea / flee
fliar, flier / fly(er)
flibent, flippant
flibidis, phlebitis
flibitis, phlebitis
flibodumy, phlebotomy
flibotimest, phlebotomy(mist)
flick,*,ker,king,kered,kering,keringly, SNAP, CANDLE FLAME ACTION
flid, flew / flight
flier,*, A PIECE OF PAPER WITH INFORMATION TO BE CIRCULATED (or see fly(er))
flight,*,ty,tless, TO TRAVEL THROUGH THE AIR "prefixes: over"
flik, flick
flim, phlegm
flimengo, flamingo
flimsy,sier,siest,siness, LIGHTWEIGHT, DELICATE
flinch,hes,hed,hing,hingly,her, TO JERK "prefixes: un"
fling,*,ging,lung,ger, THROW/CAST AWAY, A CAREFREE TIME
flint,*,ty,tiness, USED TO START FIRE
flip,*,pped,pping,pper, ALTERNATING SIDES WHILE IN THE AIR
fliper, flipper
flippant,tly,tness, NOT TREAT SERIOUSLY
flipper,*, MOVEABLE EXTRUSION ON ANIMALS FOR MOVEMENT, MANMADE FOOT PADDLES
flirt,*,ted,ting,tation,tatious,tatiously, tatiousness,ty,tier,tiest,tily,tiness, TEASING/TOYING WITH
flit,*,tted,tting,tter,tters,ttered,ttering, DART IN/OUT (or see flight)
fliur, flier / fly(er)
flo, flow
float,*,ted,ting,ter,table,tability, STAYS ON TOP OF LIQUID/AIR, BUOYANT
flock,*,ked,king, GROUP TOGETHER
flod, flood / float
floder, flutter / float(er)
floent, fluent
flof, fluff
flok, flock
flone, flown
flong, flung
flood,*,ded,ding,dable,der, TOO MUCH WATER

flooint, fluent
flook, fluke
floor,*,red,ring,rage, A SURFACE TO WALK ON "prefixes: sub/under"
flooride, fluoride
floot, flute
flop,*,pped,pping,ppy,ppier,ppiest,ppily, ppiness, FALL FLAT DOWN, LOOSE
flor, floor / flour / flower
floral,*,lly, FLOWERS
florescent,nce, FLOWERING (or see fluorescent) "prefixes: in"
floresh, flourish
florid, fluoride
florish, flourish
florist,*, WORKS WITH FLOWERS
flosh, flush
floss,sses,ssed,ssing,sser, WAY TO CLEAN BETWEEN TEETH
floster, fluster
flot, float / flood
floter, flutter / float(er)
flounder,*,red,ring, FISH, STRUGGLE FOR PROPER STANCE
flour,red,ring,ry,rier,riest, GRINDING GRAIN TO POWDER (or see flower)
flourescent, fluorescent / florescent
flouride, fluoride
flourish,hes,hed,hing, GROW HEALTHY AND STRONG
flow,*,wed,wing,wingly, STEADILY MOVING ALONG, MOVEMENT "prefixes: in/over/under"
flower,*,red,ring,ry,rer,orescent, orescence, PLANT, PART OF PLANT WHICH PREPARES THE SEED (or see flour) "prefixes: de"
flown, PAST TENSE FOR THE WORD "FLY"
flownder, flounder
flu, A VIRUS (or see flew/flue)
flubotemist, phlebotomy(mist)
flubotemy, phlebotomy
fluc, fluke
flucks, flux
flucshuate, fluctuate
fluctuate,*,ed,ting,tion,ant, MOVE BACK AND FORTH IN DEGREES
flud, flood
fludder, flutter
fluder, flutter
flue,*, CHIMNEY PIPE (or see flew/flu)
flued, fluid
fluent,tly,ncy, CONSISTENTLY CORRECT

fluff,*,fed,fing,fy,ffier,ffiest,ffily,ffiness, LIGHTEN UP BY SHAKING
fluid,*,dal,dally,dity,dly,dness,dic,dize, dizes,dized,dizing,dization,dizer, LIQUID STATE "prefixes: semi"
fluke,*,ky,kily,kiness, UNUSUAL OCCURANCE, PART OF A FISH, PART OF ANCHOR
fluks, flux
flumengo, flamingo
flung, PAST TENSE FOR THE WORD "FLING" (or see flunk)
flunk,*,ked,king,ker, TO FAIL
flunt, fluent
fluo, PREFIX INDICATING "FLOURINE" MOST OFTEN MODIFIES THE WORD
fluor, PREFIX INDICATING "FLOURINE" MOST OFTEN MODIFIES THE WORD
fluorescent,nce, ILLUMINATING LIGHT (or see florescent)
fluoride,date,dates,dated,dating,dation, GAS, CHEMICAL ADDED TO WATER CONSIDERED POISONOUS
fluoro, PREFIX INDICATING "FLOURINE" MOST OFTEN MODIFIES THE WORD
fluresent, florescent / fluorescent
fluresh, flourish
flurid, flouride
flurish, flourish
flurry,rries,rried,rrying, SPORADIC, FAST SNOW/BEHAVIOR
flurt, flirt
flury, flurry
flush,hes,hed,hing,hable,her, RID OF SOMETHING
fluster,*,red,ring, CONFUSED, NERVOUS
flute,*,ed,ting,tist, AN INSTRUMENT/DESIGN
fluter, flutter
flutter,*,red,ring, BACK AND FORTH OR UP AND DOWN VIGOROUSLY
flux,xes,xed,xing,xion, OF/PROMOTES FLUIDITY/FLOW "prefixes: re"
fly,lies,lew,ying,yer, AIRBORNE, INSECT (or see flier) "prefixes: over"
fo, foe / faux / for
foal,*,led,ling, YOUNG ANIMAL
foalt, foal(ed)
foam,*,med,ming,my, ENCASED POCKETS OF AIR
fobea, phobia
fobia, phobia

focal,lly,lize,lizes,lized,lizing,lization, KEEP ON FOCUS WITH EYES/ MENTALLY/ EMOTIONALLY "prefixes: bi"
foceshes, facetious
foceshis, facetious
foch, fudge
focis, focus
focks, fox
focle, focal
foculize, focal(ize) / focal
focus,ses,sed,sing,sable,ser, CONCENTRATE ONLY ON ONE THING OR THOUGHT, HAVE NO THOUGHTS "prefixes: re/un"
fod, food
fodagraf, photo(graph)
fodar, fodder
fodasenthesis, photosynthesis
fodasinthesis, photosynthesis
fodch, fudge
fodder,*, FOOD FOR CATTLE
fodegraf, photo(graph)
foder, fodder
fodigraf, photo(graph)
fodir, fodder
fodisinthasis, photosynthesis
fodo, photo
fodograf, photo(graph)
fodon, photon / futon
fodosinthesis, photosynthesis
fodugraf, photo(graph)
fodur, fodder
fodusinthesis, photosynthesis
foe,*, AN ADVERSARY (or see faux)
foel, foil / foal
foeul, foil
fog,*,gged,gger,gging,ggy, A MISTY CLOUD "prefixes: de"
foil,*,led,ling,ler, THIN SHEETS OF METAL, TRICKED
fok, folk / fog
fokes, focus
fokis, focus
fokle, focal
foklize, focal(ize)
foks, folk(s) / fox
fokul, focal
fokulize, focal(ize)
fokus, focus
fol, foal / fool / full / fall
folanthrapy, philanthropy
fold,*,ded,der,ding,dable, BEND/ CREASE OVER (or see foal(ed)/ fool(ed)/fault) "prefixes: en/inter/ over/multi/un"
folder,*, FOLDED SHEET TO HOLD PAPERS
foldur, folder
foleashun, foliate(tion)
foleate, foliate
folecity, felicity
foleg, foliage
folesee, fallacy
folesh, fool(ish)
folfill, fulfill
foliage,ed,aceous,ate,ation, ABOUT PLANTS
foliate,*,ed,ting,tion, THIN SHEETS, CONCERNS LEAVES "prefixes: bi/de/ multi/uni"
folicity, felicity
folig, foliage
folish, fool(ish)
folk,*,ksy, STYLE OF MUSIC, THE PARENTS/PEOPLE
folksee, folk(sy)
follow,*,wed,wing,wer, ONE BEHIND ANOTHER (or see fallow)
folly,llies, FOOLISH
folo, follow / fallow
foloer, follow(er)
folowir, follow(er)
fols, false / foal(s) / fall(s)
folsefy, falsify
folsify, falsify
folt, foal(ed) / fold
folter, folder
foltur, folder
foly, folly
folze, false
fombal, fumble
fombl, fumble
fombul, fumble
fome, foam / foam(y)
fomileur, familiar
fomy, foam(y)
fon, fun / phone / fawn / faun
fona, fauna
fonadik, phonetic / fanatic
fonagraf, phonograph
fonatek, phonetic / fanatic
foncshin, function
fond,der,dest,dly,ness, ATTRACTED TO (or see font/phone(d))
fondamental, fundamental
fondle,*,ed,ling, AFFECTIONATE TOUCHING WITH HANDS
fondumentle, fundamental
fone, phone / funny / phony
fonec, phonic
fonedik, phonetic / fanatic
fonegraf, phonograph
fonek, phonic
fonel, funnel
fonemic, phoneme(mic)
fonetic, phonetic / fanatic
fongas, fungus
fongus, fungus
foni, funny / phony
fonic, phonic
fonigraf, phonograph
fonik, phonic
fonil, funnel
fonimic, phoneme(mic)
fonkshen, function
font,*,tal, SIZE/STYLE OF LETTERS, BASIN (or see fond)
fontementul, fundamental
fonugraf, phonograph
fonul, funnel
food,*, WHAT IS CHEWED/ SWALLOWED FOR SUSTENANCE
fool,*,led,ling,lingly,lish,lishly,lishness, lery, DOESN'T COMPREHEND THE SITUATION
foome, fume
foonrul, funeral
foot,ting,tings,tage,tless,tling,ter, ATTACHED TO LEG, FIRM SPOT, U.S. MEASUREMENT OF LENGTH "prefixes: under"
footon, futon
fophade, phosphate
for, PREFIX INDICATING "AWAY/OFF/ EXTREMELY" MOST OFTEN MODIFIES THE WORD, ALSO MEANS, GIVE TOWARDS, BELONGS TO (or see fore/four/far)
forach, forage
forage,*,ed,ging,er, TO SEARCH FOR
foram, forum
foran, foreign
foraner, foreign(er)
forasdry, forest(ry)
forast, forest
forastir, forest(er)
forbedin, forbid(dden)
forbet, forbid
forbetin, forbid(dden)
forbid,*,dden,dding,ddingly,ddingness, ddance,dder,bade, NOT ALLOWED

forbiten, forbid(dden)
force,*,ed,cing,eless,eful,efully,efulness, cible,cibly,cibility,cibleness,er, A PUSH OR PULL WITH INTENSE ENERGY "prefixes: en/un"
forceps, MEDICAL INSTRUMENT
forchanet, fortunate
forchen, fortune
forchun, fortune
forchunet, fortunate
forchunitly, fortunate(ly)
fordafid, fortify(fied)
forde, forty
fordeath, fortieth
fordeen, fourteen
fordefication, fortification
fordefid, fortify(fied)
fordefy, fortify
fordeith, forty(tieth)
fordi, forty
fordifid, fortify(fied)
fordify, fortify
fordle, fertile
fordufecashen, fortification
fordufid, fortify(fied)
fordufy, fortify
fordulizashen, fertilize(zation)
fordulize, fertilize
fordyeth, fortieth
fore, PREFIX INDICATING "BEFORE/IN FRONT" MOST OFTEN MODIFIES THE WORD, FRONT OF A VESSEL (or see four/for)
foreg, forage
forego,es,one,oing,oer, PRECEDE, GO BEFORE
foregone, PAST TENSE FOR THE WORD "FOREGO"
foreign,ner,ners, NOT FAMILIAR, FROM ANOTHER PLACE
forein, foreign
forem, forum
foren, foreign
forenir, foreign(er)
foresaw, PAST TENSE FOR THE WORD WORD 'FORESEE'
foresdashen, forest(ation)
foresdry, forest(ry)
foresee,*,saw,een,eeing,eeable,eeably, eer, TO KNOW BEFORE IT HAPPENS/ YOU SEE IT
foresent, florescent / fluorescent

foreside, LAND ALONG THE OCEAN, THE FRONT OF SOMETHING (or see foresight)
foresight,*,ted,tedly,tedness, KNOW/ THINK BEFOREHAND (or see farsighted)
foresite, foresight
forest,*,ted,tal,tial,tation,ter,try, LAND MADE UP OF WILD ANIMALS/ PLANTS, LARGE/HEAVILY WOODED/ TREED AREA "prefixes: dis/re"
forestashen, forest(ation)
foresteul, forest(ial)
forestur, forest(er)
foretuety, fortuity
forever, ON AND ON WITHOUT END
foreword,*, INTRODUCTORY WRITING (or see forward)
forfat, forfeit
forfeit,*,ted,ting,ture, FORCED TO LET GO OF
forfut, forfeit
forg, fork / forge / forage
forgave, PAST TENSE FOR THE WORD "FORGIVE"
forge,*,ed,ging,eable,eability,er,ery, eries, FAKE COPY, SOFTEN METAL BY FIRE (or see forage)
forget,*,tting,got,gotten,tter,tful,tfully, tfulness,ttable, CHOOSE TO OR CANNOT REMEMBER "prefixes: un"
forgifnes, forgive(ness)
forgit, forget
forgitful, forget(ful)
forgive,*,en,ving,eness,gave,vable, vably,er, GIVEN MERCY, PARDON, EXCUSED "prefixes: un"
forgo, forego / foregone
forgon, foregone
forgot,tten, PAST TENSE FOR THE WORD "FORGET"
forgoten, forgot(tten)
forige, forage / forge
forim, forum
forin, foreign
foriner, foreign(er)
forisdashen, forest(ation)
forisdry, forest(ry)
forist, forest
foristation, forest(ation)
foristir, forest(er)
foristry, forest(ry)
forje, forge / forage

fork,*,ked,king, TOOL FOR EATING/ WORKING, SPLIT IN THE PATH
forketing, forget(tting)
forkit, forget
forkiv, forgive
forlow, furlough
form,*,med,ming,mation,mational, mative,matively,mable,mless,mer, SHAPED BY FORCE OR INTENT "prefixes: con/multi/pre/re/-re/un"
formad, format
formaded, format(tted)
formader, format(tter)
formal,*,lly,lity,lities,lize,lization,lizer, PROPER, DONE WITH CERTAIN RULES,DRESS-UP OCCASION "prefixes: in/semi"
formalesation, formal(ization)
formalidy, formal(ity)
formalise, formal(ize)
formaluzashen, formal(ization)
formaly, formal(lly) / former(ly)
formashen, formation
format,*,tted,tting,tter,tion,tive,tively, SPECIFIC PROTOCOL/DESIGN/ SHAPE/ STRUCTURE MOST OFTEN USED "prefixes: un"
formated, format(tted)
formatef,format(ive)
formater, format(tter)
formatif,format(ive)
formation,*,nal, MADE/ENCOURAGED INTO A SHAPE "prefixes: re"
formativly, format(ively)
formd, form(ed)
formel, formal
formelize, formal(ize)
formely, formal(lly)
former,*,rly, PREVIOUSLY, USED TO BE
formetive,format(ive)
formewla, formula
formewlashen, formula(tion)
formil, formal
formily, formal(lly) / former(ly)
formir, former
formirly, former(ly) / formal(lly)
formitevly, format(ively)
formitive,format(ive)
formle, formal
formolezashen, formal(ization)
formolize, formal(ize)
formotev,format(ive)
formotivly, format(ively)
formt, form(ed)

formul, formal
formula,*,ate,ates,ated,ating,ation,aic, aically,arize,arizes,arized,arizing, arizer, lism, SPECIFIC MIXTURE OF MOLECULES
formulashen, formula(tion)
formule, formal(lly)
formulisashen, formal(ization)
formulise, formal(ize)
formulu, formula
formuluzashen, formal(ization)
formuly, formal(lly)
formur, former
formurly, former(ly)
formutef, format(ive)
formutivly, format(ively)
forogt, forage(d)
foroshus, ferocious
fors, force / four(s) / farce
forsake,*,en,king,sook, ABANDON, QUIT
forsakin, forsake(n)
forsau, foresaw
forsaw, foresaw
forseable, foresee(able)
forsee, foresee
forseps, forceps
forseuble, foresee(able)
forshen, fortune
forside, foreside / foresight
forsite, foresight / foreside
fort,*,tify,tress, A STRUCTURE OR AREA TO BE PROTECTED
fortafid, fortify(fied)
fortchunetly, fortunate(ly)
forte, forty
forteen, fourteen
forteenth, fourteenth
forteeth, forty(tieth)
forteficashen, fortification
fortefid, fortify(fied)
fortefy, fortify
fortens, fourteen(s)
forteuth, forty(tieth)
fortewnit, fortunate
forth,hright, MOVEMENT FORWARD (or see fourth)
fortieth,*, AN ENGLISH NUMBER
fortification,*, PROTECTING AN AREA/ STRUCTURE, TO STRENGTHEN/ IMPROVE UPON
fortifid, fortify(fied)

fortify,fies,fied,fying,fyingly,fiable,fier, fication, STRENGTHEN/ADD/ IMPROVE UPON "prefixes: un"
fortifyed, fortify(fied)
fortinth, fourteenth
fortoety, fortuity
fortufecation, fortification
fortufid, fortify(fied)
fortufy, fortify
fortuity,ties,tous,tously,tousness, SELF-CREATED OPPORTUNITY
fortunate,ely,eness, SELF-CREATED OPPORTUNITY
fortune,*, GREAT WEALTH "prefixes: mis"
fortunetly, fortunate(ly)
fortunit, fortunate
fortunitly, fortunate(ly)
forty,ties,tieth,tyish, AN ENGLISH NUMBER
fortyeth, forty(tieth)
foruge, forage
forujt, forage(d)
forum,*, GROUP OF PEOPLE IN DISCUSSION
forun, foreign
foruner, foreign(er)
forusdashen, forest(ation)
forusdry, forest(ry)
forust, forest
forustashen, forest(ation)
foruster, forest(er)
forustre, forest(ry)
forward,*,ded,ding,dly,dness, GO AHEAD, BE FRANK (or see foreword)
forwurd, forward / foreword
fos, foe(s) / faux / fuss
fosal, fossil
fosder, foster
fosdur, foster
fosechus, facetious
fosefy, falsify
fosel, fossil
foselisd, fossil(ized)
foset, faucet
fosfade, phosphate
fosfate, phosphate
fosiches, facetious
fosify, falsify
fosil, fossil
fosilisd, fossil(ized)
fosphate, phosphate

fossil,*,lize,lized,lizing,lizable,lization, ssorial, CARBON MATTER TURNED TO STONE "prefixes: sub"
foster,*,red,ring,rage, PLACEBO PARENT
fosul, fossil
fosulisd, fossil(ized)
fosulzd, fossil(ized)
fosut, faucet
fot, foot / food / fought
fotagraf, photo(graph)
fotar, fodder
fotasinthesis, photosynthesis
fotegraf, photo(graph)
foter, fodder
fother, father
fotigraf, photo(graph)
fotigue, fatigue
fotir, fodder
foto, photo
fotograf, photo(graph)
foton, photon / futon
fotosinthesis, photosynthesis
fotugraf, photo(graph)
fotur, fodder
fotusinthesis, photosynthesis
fought, PAST TENSE FOR THE WORD "FIGHT"
foul,*,led,ling,ler,lest,lly,lness, OFFENSIVE, OUTSIDE OF THE RULES (or see fowl)
found,ded,der,ding, PAST TENSE FOR THE WORD "FIND", ONE WHO DISCOVERED/LOCATED FIRST, INITIAL DATE OF DISCOVERY "prefixes: un"
foundashen, foundation
foundation,*,nal,nally,nalist,nalism, BASE/BASIS FOR A BUILDING/ CORPORATION/ BUSINESS/ FRIENDSHIP
foundry,ries, WHERE METAL IS MELTED
fountain,*, STATUE OR STRUCTURE SHOOTING WATER
fountin, fountain
four,*,rth,rteen, AN ENGLISH NUMBER (or see fore/for)
fourest, forest
fourever, forever
fourfit, forfeit
fourgave, forgave
fourget, forget
fourgive, forgive
fourgot, forgot

fourmadur, format(tter)
fourmalize, formal(ize)
fourmashin, formation
fourmer, former
fourmul, formal
fours, force / four(s)
foursau, foresaw
foursaw, foresaw
fourseable, foresee(able)
foursee, foresee
fourteen,*,nth, AN ENGLISH NUMBER
fourteenth,*, AN ENGLISH NUMBER, ONE OF 14
fourth,*,hly, AN ENGLISH NUMBER, ONE TO FOUR PARTS (or see forth)
fourtinth, fourteenth
fourtuety, fortuity
fourwurd, forward
fow, foe / faux
fowel, foul / fowl
fowks, fox
fowl,*,ler,ling, WILD BIRD (or see foul/foal)
fowlest, foul(est)
fowlust, foul(est)
fownd, found
fowndashun, foundation
fowndation, foundation
fowndre, foundry
fownt, found
fowntin, fountain
fowt, fought
fowul, foul / fowl
fox,xes,xed,xing,xy,xier,xiest,xiness, A FURRY ANIMAL
foyel, foil
foyl, foil
foz, fuzz / foe(s)
fozdur, foster
fozel, fossil
fozter, foster
fra, fray
fracshan, fraction
fracshenal, fraction(al)
fracsher, fracture
fracshun, fraction
fracshur, fracture
fraction,*,nal,nally,nalize,nalizes, nalized,nalizing,nalization,nary,nate, nates, nated,nating,nation,nator, nary, PART OF THE WHOLE (or see friction/fracture)
fractioneal, fraction(al)

fracture,*,ed,ring,rable, A BREAK, BROKEN (or see fraction)
frad, afraid / fray(ed) / freight
fraded, freight(ed)
frader, freighter
fradewlent, fraud(ulent)
fradewlently, fraud(ulently)
frael, frail
fraeltee, frail(ty)
fragelidy, fragile(lity)
fraghted, freight(ed)
fragile,ely,lity, DELICATE
fragise, franchise
fragment,*,ted,ting,tal,tary,tarily,tize, tizes,tized,tizing,tation, PIECE OF THE WHOLE
fragmint, fragment
fragmintashen, fragment(ation)
fragmintul, fragment(al)
fragrance,*,cy,nt, A SMELL, AROMA
fragrant,*,tly,nce,nces, A SMELL, AROMA
fragrinse, fragrance
fragrint, fragrant
fragul, fragile
fraight, freight
fraighter, freighter
frail,ler,lest,lty,lties, VERY DELICATE
frailtee, frail(ty)
frait, freight
frajilety, fragile(lity)
frajiludy, fragile(lity)
frajul, fragile
frakchen, fraction
frakment, fragment
frakmentashen, fragment(ation)
frakmentul, fragment(al)
frakmint, fragment
frakmintul, fragment(al)
frakshenul, fraction(al)
frakshin, fraction
frakshur, fracture
fraktionul, fraction(al)
frakul, freckle
frale, frail
fralest, frail(est)
fralic, frolic
fraluc, frolic
frame,*,ed,ming,mable,er, STRUCTURE TO ENCASE SOMETHING, CRIMINAL ACT "prefixes: sub/under"
framur, frame(r)
franc,*, FRENCH MONEY (or see frank)

franchise,*,ee,ement,er, MEMBERSHIP OF SPORTS TEAMS/ BUSINESS "prefixes: disen/en"
frandikly, frantic(ally)
frank,*,ker,kest,kly,kness, HONEST, OPEN EXPRESSION, HOT DOGS (or see franc)
frankist, frank(est)
frankle, frank(ly)
franshise, franchise
frantek, frantic
frantekly, frantic(ally)
frantic,cally, ANXIOUS, DISORDER, WILDLY RUNNING ABOUT
frantikly, frantic(ally)
frash, fresh
frate, freight / fray(ed)
frater, freighter
fraternal,*,lly,lism, BROTHERS, MALE FRIENDSHIP
fraternity,ties, MEN'S SOCIAL/SOCIETY "prefixes: con"
fraternize,*,ed,zing,zation,er, INAPPROPRIATE RELATIONSHIP "prefixes: non"
fratid, freight(ed)
fraud,*,dly,dulent,dulently,dulence, TRICKING/CHEATING
fraul, frail
frauler, frail(er)
fraulist, frail(est)
fraultee, frail(ty)
fraun, frown
frauns, frown(s)
frawd, fraud
frawdly, fraud(ly)
frawn, frown
fraxshen, fraction
fray,*,yed,ying, MATERIAL THAT UNRAVELS, A BRAWL, SITUATION THAT IS STRESSFUL OR EXCITING
fre, free / fray
freak,*,ked,king,ky,kier,kiest,kily,kiness, kish, SHOCKING/ODD, UNUSUAL
freaze, freeze
frech, fridge
freched, frigid
frechen, fresh(en)
frecher, fresh(er)
frechnur, fresh(ener)
frechun, fresh(en)
freckle,*,ed,ling,ly, BEAUTY SPOT ON SKIN
frecol, freckle

frection, friction
fred, free(d) / fret / afraid
fredom, freedom
fredum, freedom
free,*,eed,eeing,eer,eest,eely,eeness, eedom, LIBERTY
freedom,*, TO HAVE LIBERTY
freekwensee, frequency
freekwint, frequent
freekwintly, frequent(ly)
freeky, freak(y)
freese, freeze
freetim, freedom
freetum, freedom
freeze,*,roze,zing,er,zable, LIQUID TO SOLID, WATER AT 32° F, 0° C "prefixes: re/sub/un"
freg, fridge
freged, frigid
freghted, freight(ed)
fregit, frigid
freight,*,ted,ting,ter, GOODS BEING TRANSPORTED
freighter,*, SHIP CARRYING CARGO
freigter, freighter
freiht, freight
freit, freight / fright
freitor, freight
frej, fridge
frejid, frigid
frek, freak
frekal, freckle
frekol, freckle
frekqint, frequent
frekqintly, frequent(ly)
frekshen, friction
frekul, freckle
frekwensee, frequency
frekwent, frequent
frekwently, frequent(ly)
freky, freak(y)
frel, frail
frely, free(ly)
fren, french / fringe
french, A NATIONALITY (or see fringe)
frend, friend
frendle, friend(ly)
frendleist, friend(liest)
frendlenes, friend(liness)
frendleur, friend(lier)
frenge, french / fringe
frense, frenzy
frent, friend
frentleist, friend(liest)

frentleur, friend(lier)
frently, friend(ly)
frenzy,zies,zied, CHAOTIC EXCITEMENT
frequency,cies,nt, DISTANCE/NUMBER OF TIMES BETWEEN WAVE PEAKS, NUMBER OF OCCURENCES
frequent,*,ted,ting,tly,tness,ntation,ter, ncy, HOW OFTEN "prefixes: un"
freqwensee, frequency
freqwint, frequent
freqwintly, frequent(ly)
fres, freeze / free(s) / frizz
frese, freeze / frizz(y)
fresh,her,hest,hen,hens,hened,hening, hener,hly,hness, PEAK CONDITION "prefixes: re"
freshenur, fresh(ener)
freshin, fresh(en)
freshir, fresh(er)
freshnur, fresh(ener)
freshon, fresh(en)
freshur, fresh(er)
frestrate, frustrate
fret,*,tted,tting,tless, PART OF A CLOCK/STRINGED INSTRUMENT, TO WORRY, BE ERODED/CORRODED (or see afraid/free(d))
fretem, freedom
freter, freighter
fretum, freedom
frevalus, frivolous
frevolus, frivolous
frewgul, frugal
frewktose, fructose
frez, freeze / frizz / free(s)
freze, frizz(y) / freeze / free(s)
fri, fry / free
frich, fridge
friched, frigid
frichid, frigid
fricshen, friction
friction,nal,nless, RESISTANCE BETWEEN TWO THINGS (or see fraction)
frid, fried / fright
frida, friday
friday,*, A DAY OF THE WEEK (ENGLISH)
friden, frighten
fridgarator, refrigerate(tor)
fridge,*, SLANG FOR REFRIGERATOR
fridy, friday
fried, PAST TENSE FOR THE WORD "FRY", COOK IN SKILLET "prefixes: re"

friend,*,dly,dlier,dliest,dliness, FRIENDSHIP, MUTUAL INTEREST/ ADMIRATION "prefixes: un"
frier, fry(er)
fries,ed, COOK IN SKILLET, GET TOO HOT, POTATOES DEEP FRIED
frig, fridge
frigarador, refrigerate(tor)
friged, frigid
frigerator, refrigerate(tor)
friget, frigid
fright,ten,tener,tens,tened,tening,tful, tfully,tfulness, SUDDEN FEAR
frighten,*,ned,ning, TO SUDDENLY SCARE SOMEONE
frigid,dly,dness,dity, STIFF/COLD
frigirator, refrigerate(tor)
frigit, frigid
frij, fridge
frijik, frigid
frikshen, friction
frikshenles, friction(less)
frikshenul, friction(al)
friktion, friction
friktional, friction(al)
frin, friend
frinch, french / fringe
frind, friend
frindleist, friend(liest)
frindlenes, friend(liness)
frindleur, friend(lier)
frindly, friend(ly)
fringe,*,ed,ging, DECORATIVE EDGE, ON THE OUTSIDE EDGE (or see french)
frinsy, frenzy
frint, friend
frintleist, friend(liest)
frintleur, friend(lier)
frintly, friend(ly)
frinzy, frenzy
fris, fries / frizz
frisy, frizz(y)
frit, fried / fright
friten, frighten
frivalus, frivolous
frivolous,sly,sness,lity, SILLY, NOT SERIOUS
frivulus, frivolous
friz, frizz / freeze / fries
frize, frizz(y) / fries
frizy, frizz(y)
frizz,zzes,zzed,zzing,zzier,zziest,zzy, zziness,zzily,zzliness,zzle, KINKY/ WAVY (or see freeze/fries)

frock, frog
frod, fraud
frodewlint, fraud(ulent)
frodewlintly, fraud(ulently)
frodth, froth
frodulent, fraud(ulent)
frodulently, fraud(ulently)
frog,*,gged,ggy, AN AMPHIBIAN
frogle, frugal
frogy, frog(ggy)
frojewlint, fraud(ulent)
frojewlintly, fraud(ulently)
frojiledy, fragile(lity)
frojulent, fraud(ulent)
frojulently, fraud(ulently)
frok, frog
frolek, frolic
frolic,*,cked,cking, PLAY LIGHTHEARTED, ROMP HAPPILY
froluc, frolic
from, WHERE IT WAS BEFORE
frond, front
frondeer, frontier
front,*,ted,ting, OUTSIDE FACING, GIVE IN ADVANCE
frontal,lly, IN/AT THE FRONT OF "prefix: pre"
fronteer, frontier
frontid, front(ed)
frontier,*, FRINGE OR EDGE OF A PLACE OR IN INFORMATION
frontle, frontal
froogle, frugal
frooishen, fruition
froot, fruit
fros, froze
frosd, frost / froze
frosdee, frost(y)
frosen, froze(n)
frosin, froze(n)
frost,*,ted,ting,ty,tier,tiest,tless,tily, tiness, COATING OF SOMETHING ON OBJECT, ICE, ICING ON CAKES (or see froze)
froth,*,hed,hing,hy,hier,hiest,hily, hiness, FOAM
frous, froze
frousen, frozen
frouzen, frozen
frowd, fraud
frown,*,ned,ning,ningly,ner, MOUTH TURNED DOWN, DOESN'T APPROVE
frozd, frost / froze

froze,en, PAST TENSE FOR THE WORD "FREEZE"
frozen, PAST TENSE FOR THE WORD "FREEZE" "prefixes: un"
fructose, NATURAL SUGAR
frude, fruit
frueshin, fruition
frug, frog
frugal,lly,lity,lities,lness, VERY LITTLE WASTE
frugelidy, fragile(lity)
frugiledy, fragile(lity)
frugle, frugal
fruishin, fruition
fruit,*,ted,ting,ty,tiness,tful,tfully, tfulness,tless, SEED BEARING PART PRODUCED BY FEMALE PLANTS "prefixes: un"
fruition, A REALIZATION/REWARD FOR EFFORT/ACCOMPLISHMENT
frujilety, fragile(lity)
frujiludy, fragile(lity)
fruktose, fructose
frum, from
frund, front
frundeer, frontier
frundle, frontal
frunt, front
frunteer, frontier
fruntle, frontal
frushtrate, frustrate
frustrate,*,ed,ting,tingly,ter,tion,tive, SHAKEN BY LACK OF KNOWLEDGE OR INFORMATION "prefixes: re"
frut, fruit
frute, fruit(y)
fry,ries,ried,ying,yer, COOK IN SKILLET, GET TOO HOT, GET IN TROUBLE
fryd, friday / fried
fryday, friday
fu, few
fuceshes, facetious
fuch, fudge
fucher, future
fucishas, facetious
fud, feud / food / foot
fudaledy, fidelity
fudch, fudge
fudelity, fidelity
fudge,*,ed,ging, CHOCOLATE DESSERT, EXAGGERATE THE TRUTH
fudon, futon
fued, feud

fuel,*,led,ling,ler, USED TO POWER THINGS "prefixes: bio/re"
fug, fudge
fugative, fugitive
fugitive,*, RUNAWAY, ROAMS
fugt, fudge(d)
fuil, fuel
fuj, fudge
fujative, fugitive
ful, fool / full / fuel
fula, fillet
fulanthrapist, philanthropy(pist)
fulanthrapy, philanthropy
fulate, fillet
fulay, fillet
fuld, fool(ed) / fuel(ed)
fule, fuel / fool / full / full(lly)
fuled, fool(ed) / fuel(ed)
fuler, full(er)
fulesh, fool(ish)
fulesity, felicity
fulest, full(est)
fulfill,*,lled,lling,llment,ller, CONTENT, HAVE WHAT WAS WANTED "prefixes: un"
fulir, full(er)
fulish, fool(ish)
fulisity, felicity
fulist, full(est)
full,ler,lest,lly,llness, HOLDING THE MOST IT CAN HOLD
fulor, full(er)
fulosofy, philosophy
fulur, full(er)
fulust, full(est)
fuly, full(y)
fum, fume
fumbel, fumble
fumbil, fumble
fumble,*,ed,ling,er, DROP SOMETHING ACCIDENTALLY, DROP A BALL DURING PLAY
fumbol, fumble
fume,*,ed,ming,mingly,my,migate, EMIT STEAM/GAS/SMOKE, SMELL
fumegashen, fumigate(tion)
fumegate, fumigate
fumegation, fumigate(tion)
fumelear, familiar
fumigashen, fumigate(tion)
fumigate,*,ed,ting,tion,ant, TO FLOOD/ OVERWHELM WITH SMOKE/GAS
fumpl, fumble
fumugation, fumigate(tion)

fun,nny,nnier,nniest, HAPPINESS, PLAYFUL (or see fund(s))
funal, funnel
funarul, funeral
funcshenul, function(al)
funcshin, function
function,*,ned,ning,nal,nally,nalist, nality,nalities,nalism,nary,nalize, nalizes,nalization, SERVE, HAVE OPERATIONAL, PERFORM "prefixes: inter/multi/neo/over/pre"
functionul, function(al)
functshen, function
fund,*,ded,ding,der, PUT MONEY TOWARDS, HOLDS MONEY FOR PURPOSE "prefixes: re/un"
fundamental,*,lly,lism, NECESSARY
fundemintol, fundamental
fundumintel, fundamental
fundur, fund(er)
fune, funny
funedic, phonetic / fanatic
funeir, fun(nnier)
funeist, fun(nniest)
funel, funnel
funeor, fun(nnier)
funeral,*, EVENT HONORING THE DEAD
funes, finesse / fun(nnies)
funetic, phonetic / fanatic
funeur, fun(nnier)
fungis, fungus
fungus, NOT A PLANT BUT IS LIVING AND GROWS
funie, funny
funies, fun(nnies)
funiest, fun(nniest)
funil, funnel
funior, fun(nnier)
funiral, funeral
funkshenul, function(al)
funkshin, function
funkshunal, function(al)
funkus, fungus
funle, funnel
funnel,*,led,ling, CONE SHAPE WITH HOLE IN MIDDLE
funnil, funnel
funny,nnies,nnier,nniest,nniness, CREATES SMILE/LAUGHTER, HUMOR "prefixes: un"
funol, funnel
funomenal, phenomenal
funominul, phenomenal
funrul, funeral

funs, fund(s)
funt, fund
funtamental, fundamental
funy, funny
funyer, fun(nnier)
funyest, fun(nniest)
funyur, fun(nnier)
fur,*,rred,rring,rry,rless, HAIR ON ANIMAL (or see for/fury) "prefixes: under"
furbed, forbid
furbedin, forbid(dden)
furbet, forbid
furbid, forbid
furbiten, forbid(dden)
furdal, fertile
furdalize, fertilize
furdil, fertile
furdulizashen, fertilize(zation)
furdulize, fertilize
fure, fury / furry
furefir, forever
furefur, forever
furesteul, forest(ial)
fureus, furious
furever, forever
furgave, forgave
furgefnis, forgive(ness)
furget, forget
furgetful, forget(ful)
furgitful, forget(ful)
furgive, forgive
furgivnes, forgive(ness)
furgot, forgot
furgotin, forgot(tten)
furious,sly,sness, BEYOND ANGRY
furket, forget
furketing, forget(tting)
furkiv, forgive
furlough,*, A LEAVE OF ABSENCE
furlow, furlough
furm, firm
furmaledy, formal(ity)
furmality, formal(ity)
furmashen, formation
furment, ferment
furn, fern
furnace,*, HEATER
furnacher, furniture
furnature, furniture
furnish,hes,hed,hing,hings, PLACE FURNITURE INTO A ROOM "prefixes: un"

furniture, OBJECTS/ARTICLES PLACED IN A ROOM FOR COMFORT
furnusher, furniture
furochusle, ferocious(ly)
furod, furrow(ed)
furoshus, ferocious
furoshusle, ferocious(ly)
furot, furrow(ed)
furotious, ferocious
furow, furrow
furrow,*,wed,wing, A TRENCH IN THE SOIL, WRINKLE IN BROW
furry,rrier,rriest, HAIRY (or see fury)
fursake, forsake
fursaken, forsake(n)
furst, first
furtal, fertile
further,red,ring,est, MORE THAN FAR (or see farther)
furtile, fertile
furtulize, fertile(lize)
fury,ries,rious, RAGE (or see furry)
furzd, first
fuse,*,ed,sing,sible, ITEM WHICH PROTECTS FROM FIRE HAZARD, USED TO IGNITE EXPLOSIVES, MELT ITEMS TOGETHER (or see fuss/fuzz) "prefixes: inter"
fusechus, facetious
fuseir, fuss(ier) / fuzz(ier)
fuseist, fuss(iest) / fuzz(iest)
fusek, physique
fuselitate, facilitate
fuselitation, facilitate(tion)
fuselity, facility
fuseur, fuss(ier) / fuzz(ier)
fushen, fusion / fission
fusher, future
fusiches, facetious
fusilatate, facilitate
fusilatation, facilitate(tion)
fusines, fuss(iness) / fuzz(iness)
fusion,nism, BLEND/COMBINE, SCIENTIFIC TERM (or see fission) "prefixes: in"
fusod, facade
fuss,sses,ssed,ssing,ssy,ssily,ssiness, TO FOCUS ON MINOR DETAILS (or see fuse/fuzz)
fusy, fuss(y) / fuzz(y)
fut, food / foot / feud
futaledy, fidelity
futch, fudge
futeg, fatigue

futon,*, A CUSHION/MATTRESS WITH HEAVY COTTON BATTING (or see photon)
futsher, future
future,*,rity,ristic,ristically,rless, rlessness,rism, A TIME AFTER NOW
fuz, fuzz / fuse / fuss
fuzd, fuse(d) / fuss(ed)
fuze, fuse/ fuss(y) / fuzz(y)
fuzed, fuse(d) / fuss(ed)
fuzeir, fuss(ier) / fuzz(ier)
fuzek, physique
fuzines, fuss(iness) / fuzz(iness)
fuzt, fuse(d) / fuss(ed)
fuzyest, fuss(iest) / fuzz(iest)
fuzynes, fuss(iness) / fuzz(iness)
fuzz,zzy,zzes,zzed,zzing,zzies,zzier,zziest,zziness, FUR/ OTHER MATERIAL, BLURRY TO THE EYES (or see fuse/fuss)
fuzzyness, fuss(ines) / fuzz(iness)
fynite, finite
gab,*,bbed,bbing,bby,bbier,bbiest, TALKING JUST TO BE TALKING (or see jab)
gabe, gab(bby)
gaber, jabber
gach, gauge
gack, jack
gad, jade / gate
gader, gather / gaiter
gadget,*, AN ITEM USED AS A TOOL
gaend, gain(ed)
gaf, golf / gave
gafel, gavel
gaful, gavel
gag,*,gged,gging, NEARLY CHOKE, TO KEEP SOMEONE FROM SPEAKING (or see gauge/jag)
gagd, gag(gged) / guage(d) / jag(gged)
gagels, goggles
gaget, gadget
gail, jail / gale
gain,*,ned,ning,nful,nfully, BENEFIT, IMPROVE
gait,*, DISTANCE BETWEEN FOOTSTEPS (or see gate)
gaiter,*, WRAP FOR LEGS BELOW THE KNEE, SLANG FOR ALLIGATOR
gaje, gauge
gajit, gadget
gak, jack
gakass, jackass
gakd, jack(ed)

gal,*, REFERENCE TO A FEMALE (or see gall/gale/jail)
galactic,cally, THE MILKY WAY, GALAXY "prefixes: inter"
galan, gallon
galant, gallant
galashes, galoshes
galaxy,xies, PLANETS/STARS WITHIN A SYSTEM
gale,*, STRONG WINDS (or see gal/galley/jail)
galeksy, galaxy
galen, gallon
galent, gallant
galep, gallop
galery, gallery
galexy, galaxy
galey, galley / jelly
galf, golf
gali, galley / jelly
galin, gallon
galip, gallop
galiry, gallery
gall,*,lled,lling, TO UNNERVE/IRRITATE/ANNOY/RUB SOMEONE/ SOMETHING THE WRONG WAY, A GROWTH (or see gal)
gallant,*,ted,ting,tly,try, COURAGEOUS, STATELY, AMOROUS, IN REFERENCE TO MALES
gallen, gallon
gallery,ries,ria, SHOWPLACE FOR ART
galley,*, KITCHEN IN A VESSEL, ANCIENT BOAT
gallon,*, U.S.MEASURE FOR LIQUID
gallop,*,ped,ping, GAIT OF A HORSE OR ANIMAL BEING RIDDEN
gallows, STRUCTURE FROM WHICH PEOPLE WERE HUNG TO DEATH
gallun, gallon
galon, gallon
galop, gallop
galory, gallery
galoshes, RUBBER BOOTS
galows, gallows
galre, gallery
galun, gallon
galup, gallop
galury, gallery
galy, july / jelly
gam, jam / jamb / game
gamble,*,ed,ling,er, BET MONEY ON NUMBERS
game,*,ming,er, COMPETITION TO WIN

gamet, gamut
gamut, FULL SCALE OF MUSICAL NOTES, THE WHOLE RANGE OF THINGS
gander,*, MALE GOOSE
gane, gain
ganedic, genetic
ganeuary, may
gang,*,ged,ging, GROUP OF PEOPLE/ THINGS WITH COMMONALITY
ganitor, janitor
gant, gain(ed) / chant
gantlet, gauntlet
ganuary, january
gap,*,pped,pping,ppy,pper, A SPACE, BREAK IN CONTINUITY (or see gape/gob)
gape,ped,ping,pingly, NORMALLY CONCERNS THE MOUTH OPENING WIDE (or see gap/gob)
gar, jar
garage,*,ed,ging, STRUCTURE INTENDED FOR VEHICLES
garantee, guarantee
garbage, TRASH
gard, guard
garden,*,ned,ning,ner, GROWING PLANTS
gardeun, guardian
gardian, guardian
garela, gorilla / guerilla
garentee, guarantee
gargen, jargon
gargle,*,ed,ling, RINSE THE THROAT WITH LIQUID
gargoele, gargoyle
gargoyle,*, CARVED GOTHIC FIGURES
garila, gorilla / guerilla
garland,*, PLANT ITEMS WOVEN TOGETHER
garlic,cky, EDIBLE BULB FROM PLANT
garment,*, CLOTHING "prefixes: under"
garner,*,red,ring,nish, GATHER/GAIN SOMETHING
garnish,hes,hed,hing,hment,hee,iture, DECORATION FOR FOOD/DRINK, TO PORTION OUT
gart, guard
garteun, guardian
gas,ses,ssed,ssing,seous,seousness,sify, sifies,sified,sifying,sification, NOT LIQUID OR SOLID, PETROLEUM PRODUCT
gasoline, USED TO POWER MOTORS
gasp,*,ped,ping, STRUGGLE FOR AIR

gastr, PREFIX INDICATING "STOMACH" MOST OFTEN MODIFIES THE WORD
gastro, PREFIX INDICATING "STOMACH" MOST OFTEN MODIFIES THE WORD
gasture, gesture
gasuntite, gesundheit
gate,*,ted,ting, CLOSURE TO MONITOR EXIT/ENTRANCE
gater, alligator / gaiter
gather,*,red,ring, COLLECT TOGETHER
gator, alligator / gaiter
gaudy,dier,diest,dily,diness, OUTRAGEOUS STYLE NAMED AFTER FAMOUS ARCHITECT IN BARCELONA
gauge,*,ed,ging,eable,eably,er, INSTRUMENT FOR MEASURING THINGS SUCH AS PRESSURE "prefixes: en/mis/multi/re" (or see gouge)
gauly, jolly / golly
gaunt,tly,tness, HAGGARD/THIN, LACKING AVERAGE VOLUME/SIZE (or see jaunt)
gauntlet,*, CHALLENGE
gaurantee, guarantee
gaus, gauze
gauze,zily,zy, CLOTH FOR BANDAGES
gava, java
gave, PAST TENSE FOR THE WORD "GIVE"
gavel,*, WOODEN HAMMER USED IN COURTROOMS
gaw, jaw
gawalk, jaywalk
gawn, gown
gawok, jaywalk
gawul, jowl
gay,*,yly, BRIGHT, HAPPY, HOMOSEXUAL (or see guy)
gaywalk, jaywalk
gaywok, jaywalk
gaz, jazz / gaze / guaze
gaze,*,ed,zing,er, A LONG LOOK AT (or see gauze)
gazuntite, gesundheit
ge, PREFIX INDICATING "EARTH" MOST OFTEN MODIFIES THE WORD
geagrafee, geography
gear,*,red,ring, INTERLOCKING NOTCHED RINGS WHICH DRIVE MACHINES
geburish, gibber(ish)
ged, get

gedo, ghetto
geeneol, genial
geens, jean(s) / gene(s)
geese, MORE THAN ONE GOOSE
gef, give
geffy, jiffy
geft, gift
geg, gig / jig
gegle, giggle / jiggle
geit, gait / gate
gel,*,lled,lling,llable, SEMI-SOFT/FIRM SUBSTANCE (or see jello/jail/gal)
gelatin,*,nous, LIKE JELLO
geld, guild / guilt / jell(ed)
gele, jelly
geletin, gelatin
geli, july / jelly
gelt, guilt / jilt / jell(ed) / guild
gelty, guilt(y)
gelus, jealous
gelutin, gelatin
gely, july / jelly
gem,*, STONE, JEWEL (or see gym)
gemek, gimmick
gemik, gimmick
gemmy, jimmy
gemnaseum, gymnasium
gemnast, gymnast
gen, gene / jean
genacide, genocide
genarate, generate
genaration, generation
genarulize, general(ize)
genarus, generous
genasis, genesis
gender,*,rless, CLASSIFICATION BY SEX "prefixes: en"
gendr, gender
gene,*, STRING OF CHROMOSOMES (or see jean)
genedic, genetic
genepig, guineapig
general,*,lly,lity,lities,lize,lizes,lized, lizing,lizable,lizability,lization, ENCOMPASSES MANY THINGS, A MILITARY OFFICER "prefixes: over"
generate,*,ed,ting,tion,tive,tively, tiveness,tor, CREATE, PRODUCE
generation,*,nal, PEOPLE BORN IN GROUPS AT SAME TIME "prefixes: inter/multi"
generator,*, MACHINE THAT CREATES AC ENERGY

generic,*,cally, GENERAL NAME BRAND/CLASSIFICATION
generous,sly,sness,osity,osities, GIVE AWAY WHAT CAN BE SPARED "prefixes: multi"
genesis, BEGINNING OF TIME/ EVENT "prefixes: bio"
genetic,*,cal,cally,cist,trix, STUDY OF GENES AND ASSOCIATED PARTICLES "prefixes: bio"
geneul, genial
geneus, genius
genial,lly,lity,lness, WELCOMING, DOESN'T APPEAR JUDGEMENTAL
genie,*, MAGIC ENTITY IN A BOTTLE
geniral, general
genirus, generous
genises, genesis
genital,*,lia,lly, EXTERNAL REPRODUCTIVE ORGANS
genius,ses,sness, CAPABLE OF DEEP THINKING
genjur, ginger
genle, gentle
genocide,dal,dally, KILLING CERTAIN PEOPLES SYSTEMATICALLY
genome,*,mic, STUDY OF HUMAN GENES AND ALL ASSOCIATED INTERACTIONS
genre',*, DIFFERENT STYLES/MEDIUM, EXPRESSION FOR ART, MUSIC "prefixes: sub"
genrul, general
gentle,er,est,tility,eness, KIND IN BEHAVIOR/DISPOSITION, NON-THREATENING
gentul, gentle
genucide, genocide
genuine,ely,eness, TRUTHFUL, REAL
genurul, general
genurus, generous
genus,nera, METHOD TO ORGANIZE PLANTS AND ANIMALS "prefixes: sub"
genyus, genius
geo, PREFIX INDICATING "EARTH" MOST OFTEN MODIFIES THE WORD
geography,hies,hic,hical,hically, ophysicist, THE STUDY OF EVERYTHING ON THE SURFACE OF THE EARTH "prefixes: bio"
geology,gies,gic,gical,gist,ophysicist, STUDY OF THE EARTH'S CRUST

geometry,ries,ric,rical,rically,rize,rizes,
   rized,rizing,rization,rician, VARIOUS
   SHAPES/SYMBOLS/ LINES/ANGLES
gep, gyp
gepardy, jeopardy
gepsee, gypsy
gepsum, gypsum
gerantee, guarantee
gerbil,*, A SMALL RODENT
gere, gear / jury
geresdikshen, jurisdiction
gergul, gurgle
gerila, gorilla / guerilla
gerk, jerk
gerky, jerky
gerl, girl
gerlfrend, girlfriend
germ,*,minate, BACTERIA
germinate,*,ed,ting,tion,tive,tor, SEED
   BEGINNING TO GROW
gernal, journal
gernalist, journal(ist)
gerne, journey / gurney
gernulest, journal(ist)
gerny, gurney / journey
gerter, girder
gerth, girth
gerunte, guarantee
gerur, juror
gery, jury
gesd, guest / guess(ed) / jest
gese, geese / guess
gesoontite, gesundheit
gess, guess
gest, jest / just / guest / guess(ed)
gesture,*,ed,ring, BODILY MOTIONS
gesundheit, WISHING GOOD HEALTH
   TO SOMEONE WHO SNEEZED
   (German)
gesuntite, gesundheit
get,*,got,tta,tten,tter,tting, TO TAKE IN,
   HAVE IT (or see jet)
gete, jetty
geter, jitter
geto, ghetto
getsam, jetsam
gety, jetty
gev, give
gewdeshal, judicial
gewdishes, judicious
gewel, jewel
gewly, july
gewn, june / goon
gews, juice

geyser,*, WATER WHICH SHOOTS UP
   FROM A HOLE IN THE EARTH
ghetto,*, A SECTION OF LAND WHERE
   OVERCROWDING IS A RESULT OF
   DISCRIMINATION
ghost,*,tly, SPIRITS WHICH PROVE TO
   EXIST BUT ARE INVISIBLE TO US
gi, guy
giant,*, HUGE, ENORMOUS
gib, jib / jibe
gibber,*,red,ring,rish,rer, LANGUAGE/
   WORDS THAT DO NOT MAKE SENSE
   (or see jibe)
gibe,*,ed,bing,bingly, COMMENT MADE
   TO PROVOKE NEGATIVE FEELINGS
   IN ANOTHER (or see jibe)
giberish, gibber(ish)
gid, get / guide
giddy,ddier,ddiest,ddily,ddiness,
   JOYFUL, EXTREMELY EXCITED,
   FRIVOLOUS (or see jibe)
gide, guide
gidense, guidance
gif, give
giffy, jiffy
gift,*,ted,ting, TO GIVE SOMETHING
   WITHOUT EXPECTATIONS OF
   RETURN
gig,*, ARRANGEMENT FOR MUSICAL
   PERFORMANCE (or see jig)
giga, PREFIX INDICATING "ONE
   BILLIONTH" MOST OFTEN MODIFIES
   THE WORD
gigantic,cally,ism, INCREDIBLY HUGE,
   ENORMOUS
gigger, jigger
giggle,*,ed,ling,lly,er, STYLE OF
   LAUGHING (or see jiggle)
gigle, giggle
gigol, giggle
gigsaw, jigsaw
gilatnus, gelatin(ous)
gild, guild / guilt / jell(ed)
gildy, guilt(y)
giloshes, galoshes
gilt, guild / guilt / jell(ed)
gilty, guilt(y)
gily, july / jelly
gim, gem / gym
gimik, gimmick
gimmick,*,ky, TRICK, ATTENTION
   GETTER
gimmy, jimmy
gimnaseum, gymnasium

gimnast, gymnast
ginacologist, gynecology(gist)
ginarashin, generation
ginarate, generate
ginarator, generator
ginarulize, general(ize)
ginarus, generous
ginasis, genesis
gindur, gender
gine pig, guineapig
ginecologist, gynecology(gist)
ginerik, generic
ginetic, genetic(s)
ginger,*,red,ring,ry,rly, EDIBLE PLANT,
   TO BE CAUTIOUS
gingle, jingle
ginks, jinx
ginokologist, gynecology(gist)
ginrul, general
ginter, gender
ginucalugist, gynecology(gist)
ginucide, genocide
ginucologist, gynecology(gist)
ginuen, genuine
ginul, gentle
ginurulize, general(ize)
ginus, genus
ginuses, genesis
giologee, geology
giometry, geometry
gip, gyp
gipsee, gypsy
gipsum, gypsum
girate, gyrate
girble, gerbil
gird,*,ded,ding,der, PHYSICALLY
   PROTECT YOURSELF, PHYSICAL
   PROTECTION BY GIRDLE/BELT/
   STRAPS "prefixes: under"
girder,*, BEAM USED FOR HORIZONTAL
   BRACING IN BUILDINGS
girgul, gurgle
girl,*,ly, YOUNG FEMALE PERSON
girlfriend,*, A GIRL WHO IS ALSO A
   FRIEND
girm, germ
girmanate, germinate
girnalist, journal(ist)
girney, gurney / journey
girnul, journal
girth,*, WIDTH OF SOMETHING ACROSS,
   CIRCUMFERENCE
giry, jury
giser, geyser

gisuntite, gesundheit
git, get
gito, ghetto
gitter, jitter
give,*,ving,gave,en, PROVIDE/GIFT/ PRESENT SOMETHING (or see jive) "prefixes: mis"
gizer, geyser
gizuntite, gesundheit
glachal, glacial
glachel, glacial
glachil, glacial
glachol, glacial
glacial,*,ally,ate,ates,ated,ating,ation, ICE, FROZEN WATER, FROM THE WORD 'GLACIER' "prefixes: en/ inter/sub"
glacier,*,red,ial, ICE, FROZEN WATER AROUND MOUNTAIN
glad,dder,ddest,dly, PLEASED
glair, glare
glamour,rous,rously,rousness,orize, orizes,orized,orizing,orization,orizer, ALLURING, BEWITCHING
glance,*,ed,cing, A QUICK LOOK
gland,*,dule,dular,dulous,dulously,dless, ORGANS IN THE BODY "prefixes: multi"
glare,*,ed,ring,ringly,ringness, A SHARP LOOK WITH THE EYES, INTENSE LIGHT
glas, glass / glaze
glaser, glacier / glaze(r)
glashal, glacial
glashel, glacial
glasher, glacier
glashil, glacial
glashol, glacial
glass,sses,ssed,ssy,ssful,ssier,ssiest,ssily, ssiness, HARD/FLAT/FRAGILE SUBSTANCE MADE WITH MIXTURE OF MINERALS/CHEMICALS
glaze,*,ed,zing,er, A COATING OF SUBSTANCE ON SOMETHING "prefixes: multi/over/under"
glazr, glaze(r)
gleam,*,med,ming,my,mier,miest, A BRIEF MOMENT IN APPEARANCE
glech, glitch
gleder, glitter
gledur, glitter
glee,*,eful,efully,efulness, WITH JOY, EXUBERANCE "prefixes: un"
gleful, glee(ful)

glemmer, glimmer
glempse, glimpse
glent, glint
glesen, glisten
glesten, glisten
gletch, glitch
gleu, glue
glew, glue
glich, glitch
glide,*,ed,ding,er, TO MOVE SMOOTHLY WITHOUT RESISTANCE
glider, glide(r) / glitter
glimer, glimmer
glimmer,*,red,ring, A DIM LIGHT
glimpse,*,ed,sing, SLIGHT GLANCE, SEE BRIEFLY
glint,*,ted,ting, A TWINKLE, SPARKLE
glisen, glisten
glisten,*,ned,ning, TO REFLECT LIGHT, SHINY
glitch,hes,hy, MONKEYWRENCH IN THE PLANS, PROBLEM IN THE OPERATION OF
glite, glide
gliter, glitter / glide(r)
glitter,*,red,ring,ringly,ry, SHINY SPECKS, FLECKS OF LIGHT (or see glider)
gliture, glitter / glide(r)
glo, glow
gloat,*,ted,ting,tingly,ter, OVERLY PROUD OF AN ACCOMPLISHMENT
global,lly,lize,lizes,lized,lizing,lization, lism,lizer, INCORPORATES THE GLOBE, INCLUDES THE WORLD
globe,*,ed,bing,boid, THE SHAPE AND PICTURE OF THE WORLD
globel, global
globul, global
glof, glove
glofs, glove(s)
glomp,*,ped,ping, MANY THINGS WHICH GRAB/STICK, AFFECTIONATE POUNCE/HUG
gloo, glue
gloom,*,med,ming,my,mily,miness, DULL SENSE OF FEAR
glorify,fies,fied,fying,fication,fier,ious, WORSHIP
glorufy, glorify
glory,ries,rify,rious,riously,riousness, IN HONOR, PRAISE "prefixes: in"
glosery, glossary

gloss,sses,ssed,ssing,ssy,ssier,ssiest,ssily, ssiness, SHINE UP "prefixes: semi"
glossary,ries, AREA IN SOME BOOKS WITH DEFINITIONS
glote, gloat / glow(ed)
glove,*,ed,ving,eless, COVERING FOR HANDS
glow,*,wed,wing,wingly,wer, TO BE LITE FROM WITHIN, INTERNAL LIGHT
gluco, PREFIX INDICATING "SUGAR" MOST OFTEN MODIFIES THE WORD
glucose, SUGAR, SYRUP
glue,*,ed,uing,ey,uily,uiness, TYPE OF LIQUID USED TO STICK THINGS TOGETHER, STUCK TO SOMETHING "prefixes: un"
gluecose, glucose
glufs, glove(s)
glukose, glucose
glum,mly,mness,mmer,mmest, DISAPPOINT, NEGATIVE PERSPECTIVE, APPEARS TO BE NO SOLUTION, SULLEN (or see gloom)
glumy, glum(mmy) / gloom(y)
glutinous,sly, STICKS TOGETHER, LIKE GLUE
gluvs, glove(s)
glyco, PREFIX INDICATING "SUGAR" MOST OFTEN MODIFIES THE WORD
gnat,*,tty,tier,tiest, TINY FLY
gnaw,*,wed,wing, MOUTH OR CHEW ON SOMETHING GENTLY
gnome,*, A SMALL HUMAN ENTITY WHICH ONLY SOME PEOPLE CAN SEE
go,oes,oing,one, READY, SET, MOVE/ MOBILIZE TO ANOTHER PLACE "prefixes: in/under"
goad,*,ded,ding, TO PROD/POKE/ FORCE SOMETHING/SOMEONE TO REACT (or see goat)
goal,*,lie, SOMETHING TO ACHIEVE/GO FOR, ATTEMPT TO REACH
goalie,*, SOMEONE WHO DEFENDS AGAINST SOMEONE WHO WANTS TO MAKE POINTS IN A GAME
goat,*, AN ANIMAL
goatee,*, A BEARD SHAVED TO A POINT
gob,*,ed, A CLUMP/LUMP OF WAY TOO MUCH OF SOMETHING
gobble,*,ed,ling,er, TO EAT VERY QUICKLY
goble, gobble

goblet,*, A DRINKING VESSEL
goblin,*, AN ENTITY ONLY SOME PEOPLE CAN SEE
gobul, gobble
god,*, REFERENCE TO A SUPREME BEING (or see good/got/goad) "prefixes: un"
goddess,sses, FEMALE ENTITY WHO CO-CREATES
gode, gaudy
goden, gotten
goen, join
goent, joint / join(ed)
goes, FORM OF "GO", IS MOVING TO ANOTHER SPACE/ATTITUDE/LEVEL
goest, joist
gof, golf
gofener, governor
gofer, gopher / golf(er)
gofeul, jovial
gofur, gopher
gog, jog
gogels, goggles
goger, jog(gger)
goggles, SAFETY EYE PROTECTION
gogils, goggles
gogir, jog(gger)
goguls, goggles
gogur, jog(gger)
goin, join
goint, joint / join(ed)
goke, joke / jockey
goky, jockey
gol, goal
golaktik, galactic
gold,den, A PRECIOUS METAL
golden,nly,nness, THE COLOR OF GOLD
goldun, golden
gole, goal / goalie / golly / jolly
golf,*,fed,fing,fer, A SPORT
golie, goal / goalie / golly / jolly
golly, VERBAL EXPRESSION OF SURPRISE (or see goalie/jolly)
goloshes, galoshes
golt, jolt / gold
golten, golden
goly, jolly / golly / goalie
gon, gone / going
gondes, jaundice
gone,er, PAST TENSE FOR THE WORD "GO", ALREADY LEFT
goner,*, SOMEONE WHO IS GONE OR IN TROUBLE
gong,*, A MUSICAL INSTRUMENT

gonir, gone(r)
gont, jaunt / gaunt / join(ed)
gontlet, gauntlet
gonur, gone(r)
good,*,dy,dly,dness, ACCEPTABLE
good-bye,*, FAREWELL, EXPRESSION FOR LEAVING
goods, STUFF, STUFF FOR SALE
gooly, july
goon,*, THUG, A DERAGATORY NAME FOR SOMEONE
goose,geese, A FEMALE BIRD, SQUEEZE SOMEONE (or see juice)
goot, jute
gopher,*, A RODENT, SOMEONE WHO GOES TO PICK UP SOMETHING
gor, jar
gord, gourd / guard
gorela, gorilla / guerilla
gorge,*,ed,ging,er, TO STUFF, GEOLOGICAL FORMATION "prefixes: dis/en"
gorgeous,sly,sness, SOMETHING VERY ATTRACTIV
gorgis, gorgeous
gorgus, gorgeous
gorilla,*, A MAMMAL (or see guerilla)
gorj, gorge
gorjus, gorgeous
gorlend, garland
gorlic, garlic
gorma, gourmet
gorment, garment
gorner, garner
gornish, garnish
gos, goes / gauze
gosep, gossip
gosepd, gossip(ed)
gosip, gossip
gospel,*, PARTS OF THE BIBLE
gossip,*,ped,ping,per,pry,py, WORDS SAID ABOUT SOMEONE WHO ISN'T AROUND TO HEAR
gost, ghost
gosup, gossip
got,tten, PAST TENSE FOR THE WORD "GET", ACQUIRED SOMETHING DIDN'T HAVE BEFORE (or see goat/god/jot)
gote, goat / goatee / gaudy
goten, gotten
goth,hic,hically,hicism, DARK FORM OF SELF EXPRESSION, MEDIEVAL THEME

gothec, goth(ic)
gotin, gotten
gotten, PAST TENSE FOR THE WORD "GET/GOT"
goty, gaudy
gouge,*,ed,ging, MAKE HOLES OR GROOVES INTO
goun, gown
gourd,*, FRUIT FROM A PLANT
gourmet,*, ONE WHO UNDERSTANDS FINE FOODS
goverment, government
govern,*,ned,ning,nable,nance,ness,nment,nor, CONTROLLING ENTITIES WHO UPHOLD, CREATE RULES "prefixes: un"
government,*,tal,tally,talize, GROUP OF PEOPLE WHO RULE, UPHOLDS RULES FOR A PEOPLE "prefixes: inter"
governor,*,ness,rate, STATE ELECTED POLITICIAN
goveul, jovial
govirment, government
govnur, governor
gowge, gouge
gown,*, FULL LENGTH DRESS, ROBE
gownse, jounce
gowul, jowl
goy, joy
goyful, joy(ful)
goyn, join
goynd, joint / join(ed)
goynt, joint / join(ed)
goyus, joy(us)
goz, goes / gauze / jaw(s)
gra, gray
grab,*,bbed,bbing,bby,bbable,bber, TAKE ROUGHLY/QUICKLY
grabel, gravel / grapple
grabetate, gravitate
grable, grapple / gravel
grabuling, gravel(ing) / grapple(ling)
grace,*,ed,cing,eful,efully,efulness,cious,ciously,ciousness, ELEGANCE (or see graze) "prefixes: dis/un"
grachuashen, graduate(tion)
grachus, gracious
gracious,sly,sness, PERFORM ELEGANTLY "prefixes: un"
grad,*, SHORT FOR 'GRADUATE' (or see grade/grate/great) "prefixes: under"

grade,*,ed,ding,er,dient, LEVEL IN LEARNING, DEGREES, STEPS (or see grate/great/grad) "prefixes: de/inter/multi/retro/sub/up"
gradeant, grade(dient)
gradetude, gratitude
gradful, grateful
gradguashen, graduate(tion)
gradiant, grade(dient)
gradify, gratify
graditude, gratitude
gradjual, gradual
gradjuate, graduate
gradle, great(ly)
gradly, great(ly)
gradual,lly,lness,lism, MOVEMENT A BIT AT A TIME
graduate,*,ed,ting,tion, CEREMONY CELEBRATING COMPLETION, MOVE UP TO THE NEXT LEVEL "prefixes: under"
graf, graph
grafe, grave
grafek, graphic
graffiti,to, PICTURES/WORDS PLACED/PAINTED IN PUBLIC PLACES WITHOUT PERMISSION
grafic, graphic
grafite, graphite / graffiti / gravity
grafity, gravity / graffiti
graft,*,ted,ting,ter, TO ATTACH PART OF A LIVE THING TO PART OF ANOTHER LIVE THING "prefixes: en"
grafudy, gravity
grafux, graphic
gragereus, gregarious
graguashen, graduate(tion)
graguate, graduate
grain,*,ned,ner,nless,ny,nery,anul, EDIBLE PLANT/SEED, WOOD TEXTURE, BASIC CHARACTERISTIC "prefixes: en/multi"
grainery,ries, GRAIN STOREHOUSE
grainual, granule
grajeashen, graduate(tion)
grajual, gradual
grajuashen, graduate(tion)
grajuate, graduate
gram,*, MEASURE OF WEIGHT "prefixes: deca"
gramatical, grammatical
grammar,*,atical,rian,atology, WORDS AND THE WAY THEY ARE USED BY PEOPLE

grammatical,lly,lity,lness, WORDS AND THE WAY THEY ARE USED BY PEOPLE "prefixes: un"
gran, grain
grand,der,dest,dly,dness,deur,diose, OF GREAT STATURE, IMMENSE, BEST THERE IS (or see grant)
grandeos, grandiose
grandiose,ely,eness,sity, IMPRESSIVE STATURE
grandure, grand(eur) / grand(er)
granery, grainery
granet, granite
granite, IGNEOUS ROCK
granola, DRIED GRAIN AND FRUIT MIXED TOGETHER
grant,*,ted,ting,tee,tor, GIVE WHAT WAS ASKED FOR
granual, granule
granule,*,lar,larity,larly,late,lates,lated,lating,lation,lative,lator, VERY SMALL MASS OF SOMETHING "prefixes: multi"
granut, granite
grape,*, FRUIT OF THE VINE
grapefruit,*, CITRUS FRUIT
grapevine,*, VINE OF A FRUIT
grapfruit, grapefruit
grapfrut, grapefruit
graph,*,hed,hing,her,hic, TO PLOT ON, SHOWS CHANGES IN NUMBERS
graphic,*,cal,cally,cness,cacy, VISUAL ART BY PEOPLE OR COMPUTER
graphite, TYPE OF ROCK
grapple,*,ed,ling,er, TO STRUGGLE/WRESTLE WITH
grapul, grapple / gravel
grapvine, grapevine
grase, grace / graze
grashis, gracious
grasp,*,ped,ping,pable, GET A FIRM HOLD OF SOMETHING "prefixes: un"
grass,sses,ssed,ssing,ssy,ssier,ssiest,ssiness, PLANT
grat, great / grate / grade
grate,*,ed,ting,er, FABRICATED METAL/STEEL, KITCHEN DEVICE, SOMETHING IRRITATING(or see great/grade)
grateant, grade(dient)
grateful,lly,llness, APPRECIATE "prefixes: un"
gratetude, gratitude

gratiant, grade(dient)
gratify,fies,fied,fying,fication,itude,tuity, FULFILLING, PLEASURABLE
gratitude,*, APPRECIATION "prefixes: in"
gratle, great(ly)
gratly, great(ly)
gratshuation, graduate(tion)
gratuate, graduate
gratuity,ties,tous,tously,tousness, TIP/MONEY FOR SERVICE
graul, growl
grave,*,er,est,ely,eness,en, WHERE SOMETHING IS BURIED, SERIOUS SITUATION
gravedy, gravity
gravel,*,led,ling,lly, SMALL ROCKS
gravitate,*,ed,ting,tive,tion, BEING DRAWN BY A FORCE
gravitation,nal,nally, THE ACT OF BEING AFFECTED BY GRAVITY
gravity,tate,tative,tation, POWERFUL FORCE KEEPING THINGS FROM FLOATING INTO SPACE
gravul, gravel
gravy,vies, THICK SAUCE
grawl, growl
grawnd, ground
gray,*,yer,ying, COLOR, FROM AGING
graze,*,ed,zing,er, HOW HERD ANIMALS EAT (or see grace)
grease,*,ed,sing,er,sy,sier,siest,eless,sily,siness, FROM ANIMAL FAT, LUBRICANT FOR MOVING MACHINE PARTS
great,*,ter,test,tly,tness, HIGH ON THE SCALE OF IMPRESSIVE (or see grate)
greater, great(er) / grate(r)
greatful, grateful
gred, grid / greed
gredy, grit(tty) / greed(y)
greed,dy,dier,diest,dily,diness, TAKE MORE THAN NEED
greef, grief
green,*,ner,nest, COLOR, PLANTS
greese, grease
greet,*,ted,ting, TO WELCOME
greeve, grieve
greeze, grease
grefiti, graffiti
gregarious,sly,sness, PREFERS TO LIVE IN SOCIAL ENVIRONMENT WITH LIKE KIND
grell, grill

grem, grim / grime
grematical, grammatical
gren, grin / green
grenola, granola
grep, grip
greshus, gracious
gret, grit / greet / greed
grety, grit(tty) / greed(y)
grew, PAST TENSE FOR THE WORD "GROW"
grewsome, gruesome
greze, grease
grid,*, PERPENDICULAR LINES
griddle,*,ed,ling,er, FLAT COOKING UTENSIL
gride, grit(tty)
gridul, griddle
grief,eve, DEEP SADNESS (or see grieve)
grieve,*,ed,ving,vant,vance,vances, gous,gously,gousness, MOURNING A LOSS
grifete, graffiti
grigarious, gregarious
grill,*,lled,lling,ller, COOK ON METAL GRID OVER COALS
grim,mmer,mmest,mly,mness, STUBBORN, VIRTUALLY UNCHANGABLE (or see grime)
grime,*,ed,ming,my, DIRT/GREASE/ SOOT (or see grimy)
grimy,mier,miest,mily,miness, DIRT/GREASE/SOOT
grin,*,ned,ning, SMILE BROADLY (or see green)
grind,*,ded,ding,round,der, TO MILL/CHOP/SMASH/PULVERIZE (or see grin(nned))
grinola, granola
grip,*,pped,pping,pper, FIRMLY GRASP, HAND HOLD (or see gripe)
gripe,*,ed,ping,er, VERBALLY COMPLAINING TO SOME OTHER THAN THE INTENDED RECIPIENT (or see grip)
grit,*,tted,tting,tty,ttier,ttiest,ttily, ttiness, TINY GRANULES OF VARIETY OF MATERIAL, GROUND CORN
grital, griddle
gritle, griddle
grity, grit(tty)
gro, grow
groan,*,ned,ning, MOAN FROM PAIN
grocery,ries, FOOD, NON-FOODS BOUGHT FROM STORE

grof, gruff / grove
groggy,gier,giest,ggily,gginess, NOT QUITE AWAKE, STUPOR
grone, groan
groof, groove
groom,*,med,ming,mer, MALE GETTING MARRIED, TO CLEAN THE BODY
groove,*,ed,ving,vy,vier,viest,vily,viness, LONG INDENTATION IN SOMETHING, GET IN-STEP TO BE COOL
grope,*,ed,ping,per, TO AIMLESSLY ATTEMPT TO GRASP WITH HAND (or see group)
grosery, grocery
grosry, grocery
gross,sses,ssed,ssing,sser,ssest,ssly, ssness, SUM BEFORE EXPENDITURES, MEASUREMENT OF WEIGHT, DISTASTEFUL, REPULSIVE "prefixes: en"
grotesk, grotesque
grotesque,ely,eness, UGLY, DESPICABLE
groth, growth
grouch,hes,hy,hier,hiest,hily,hiness, UNREASONABLY IRRITATED
groul, growl
groun, groan / grown
ground,*,ded,ding,der,dless,dlessly, dlessness, THE EARTH, FEET PLANTED SOLIDLY, BE ON THE EARTH'S SURFACE "prefixes: over/under"
group,*,ped,ping,per,pable,pie, TO PUT SIMILAR OBJECT, THINGS, PEOPLE TOGETHER "prefixes: re/semi/sub/un"
grouse,*, GAME BIRD (or see gross)
grout,*,ted,ting,ter, MORTAR FOR STONE/TILE
grove,*, A FIELD WHERE TREES WITH EDIBLE FRUIT IS GROWN
grow,*,wing,rew,wn,wth, GET BIGGER/TALLER "prefixes: in/over/under"
growch, grouch
growl,*,led,ling,ler, VERBAL WARNING COMING FROM DEEP IN THE THROAT
grown, PAST TENSE FOR THE WORD "GROW" (or see groan) "prefixes: in/over/under"
grownd, ground
grows, grow(s) / grouse / gross

growth,*, COMPARE SIZE OR AMOUNT OF SOMETHING GROWING "prefixes: in/inter/over/up"
groz, gross / grow(s) / grouse
grub,*,bbed,bbing,bber,bby,bbier, bbiest,bbily,bbiness, SLANG FOR FOOD, DIRTY AND MESSY
grudge,*,ed,ging,gingly,eless,er, WILL NOT FORGIVE SOMEONE "prefixes: un"
gruel,*,ling, RUNNY/SLOPPY BOWL OF FOOD
grueling,gly, HARD AND TEDIOUS
gruesome,ely,eness, AWFUL
gruf, groove
grufede, graffiti
gruff,ffer,ffest,ffly,ffiness, RUDE AND ROUGH
grufiti, graffiti
grug, grudge
grugarious, gregarious
gruj, grudge
grumatical, grammatical
grumble,*,ed,ling, LOW/IRRITABLE MUMBLING, STOMACH SOUNDS WHEN HUNGRY
grundled, grunt(led)
grunola, granola
grunt,*,ted,ting,tingly,tled, ANNOYED VERBAL RESPONSE, LOW-RANK WORKER "prefixes: dis"
grupe, group
grusome, gruesome
guady, gaudy
guage, gauge
guantlet, gauntlet
guarantee,*,eed,eeing,tor, BACK UP A CLAIM, WITHOUT A DOUBT
guard,*,ded,ding,dian, PROTECT AGAINST INVADER "prefixes: un"
guardian,*,nship, PROTECTOR
guaze, gauze
gubalee, jubilee
gubelashen, jubilant(ation)
gubilation, jubilant(ation)
gud, good / gut
gud-by, good-bye
guder, gutter
guderal, guttural
gudge, judge
gudishal, judicial
gudishes, judicious
gudo, judo
guds, goods / gut(s)

guel, jewel
guerilla,*, PEOPLE WHO HIDE WHEN FIGHTING (or see gorilla)
guess,sses,ssed,ssing,sser, TAKE A GAMBLE AT THE PROPER ANSWER, DON'T KNOW ANSWER
guest,*, STAYING TEMPORARILY AT A PLACE THAT IS NOT YOURS (or see guess(ed))
gufener, governor
gufner, governor
gug, jug / judge
guggle, juggle
gugul, juggle
guidance, RECEIVE DIRECTION
guide,*,ded,ding,dance, SHOW THE WAY "prefixes: mis"
guil, jewel
guild,*, COOPERATIVE GROUP OF PEOPLE WITH A PARTICULAR INTEREST
guilt,ty,tier,tiest,tily,tiness, BEING OR FEELING RESPONSIBLE FOR AN ACTION
guineapig,*, TWO WORDS 'GUINEA PIG', A RODENT
gul, gull / jewel / joule
gulactic, galactic
gulaktek, galactic
gulatnus, gelatin(ous)
guleble, gull(ible)
gull,*,llery,lled,lling,llible,llibility,llibly, TYPE OF BIRD, TO BE TRICKED/DECEIVED
guloshes, galoshes
gulp,*,ped,ping,pingly,per, TAKE IN A LARGE MOUTHFUL
guly, july
gum,*,mmed,mming,my,mmier,mmiest,mmily,miness, SOMETHING CHEWABLE, RUBBERY, FROM A TREE
gumble, jumble
gump, jump
gun,*,nned,nning,nner, A FIRING WEAPON, TO STEP ON THE ACCELERATOR, TO SHOOT SOMEONE (or see goon/june)
gune, june / goon
gungle, jungle
gungul, jungle
guniur, junior
gunk, junk
gunker, junk(er)

gunkie, junkie
gunkshen, junction
gunksher, juncture
gunyer, junior
guppy,ppies, FISH
gurbel, gerbil
gurder, girder
gure, jury
gurer, juror
guresdiction, jurisdiction
gurgle,*,ed,ling, SOUNDS COMING FROM THE THROAT, BUBBLING SOUND
guri, jury
gurilla, guerilla / gorilla
gurk, jerk
gurl, girl
gurlfrend, girlfriend
gurm, germ
gurmenate, germinate
gurnelist, journal(ist)
gurney,*, A COT/STRETCHER TO CARRY BODIES (or see journey)
gurnol, journal
gurter, girder
gurth, girth
gus, goose / juice
gusd, gust / just
gusdefecation, justify(fication)
gusdefiable, justifiable
gusdes, justice
gusdify, justify
guse, goose / juice
gusee, juicy
gush,hes,hed,hing, SPEW FORTH IN SUDDEN BURST
gusle, guzzle
gust,*,ted,ting,ty,tier,tiest,tily,tiness, BIG BLOWS IN BURSTS, ERRATIC/HIGH WINDS (or see just)
gustefy, justify
gustes, justice
gustification, justify(fication)
gut,*,tted,tting, INSIDES OF LIVING THINGS, TO REMOVE INSIDES (or see good/jewt/jut)
gute, jute
gutir, gutter
guto, judo
gutter,*,red,ring,ral, ALONG ROOFS FOR RAIN COLLECTION
guttural,*,lly,lity,lism,lness,lizes,lized, lizing,lization, TYPE OF SOUND MADE IN THE THROAT

guverment, government
guviner, governor
guvinile, juvenile
guy,*, MALES, WIRE OR ROPE USED TO SUPPORT OR STEADY SOMETHING
guynacologist, gynecology(gist)
guzzle,*,ed,ling,er, RAPIDLY DRINK
gy, guy
gym,*,mnast,mnasium, A PLACE TO WORK-OUT (or see gem) "prefixes: multi"
gymnasium,*, A BUILDING WHERE PEOPLE DO PHYSICAL ACTIVITIES
gymnast,*,tics, ONE WHO PRACTICES THE ART OF MANIPULATING THEIR BODIES
gyn, PREFIX INDICATING "FEMALE" MOST OFTEN MODIFIES THE WORD
gyne, PREFIX INDICATING "FEMALE" MOST OFTEN MODIFIES THE WORD
gynecology,gical,gist, THE SCIENCE OF, ONE WHO STUDIES WOMEN'S ORGANS
gyno, PREFIX INDICATING "FEMALE" MOST OFTEN MODIFIES THE WORD
gyp,*,ped,ping, TO CHEAT/STEAL
gypsum, CHALKY ROCK
gypsy,sies, PEOPLE WHO CHOOSE TO BE ON THE FRINGE OF SOCIETY FOR WHATEVER REASON
gyrate,*,ed,ting,tion, TO SPIRAL "prefixes: multi"
ha, hay / hey
habachi, hibachi
habe, happy
haben, happen
habin, happen
habit,*,ted,ting,table,tability,tableness, tably,tant,tat,tation,tual, tuate, tuates,tuated,tuating,tuation,tude, tudinal,tus, DOING THE SAME THING OVER AND OVER
habitat,*,tation,tational,tor, NATURAL HOME FOR LIVING THINGS "prefixes: inter/non"
habitual,*,lly,lness,ate, SOMEONE WHO DEALS WITH MANY HABITS
habochi, hibachi
haby, happy
hach, hatch / hash / hack
hachet, hatchet
hachit, hatchet
hack,*,ked,king,kies,ker,ktivate,ktivism, ktivist, TO ILLEGALLY ACCESS

PRIVATE DATA ON COMPUTERS, CHOP AT
hactare, hectare
had, PAST TENSE FOR THE WORD "HAVE" (or see hat)
hade, hate
haden't, hadn't
hadint, hadn't
hadn't, CONTRACTION OF THE WORDS 'HAD NOT'
hadur, hot(tter)
hael, howl
haf, half / have / halve
hafen, haven / heaven
hafhasert, haphazard
hafhazard, haphazard
hafhazurdle, haphazard(ly)
hafint, haven't
hafnt, haven't
hafun, haven / heaven / have(ving)
hagerd, haggard
haggard,*,dly,dness, ROUGH, WORN
haggle,*,ed,ling,er, DEBATING OVER PRICE/CONTRACT
hagio, PREFIX INDICATING " HOLY " MOST OFTEN MODIFIES THE WORD
hagurd, haggard
haiku,*, FORM OF JAPANESE POETRY
hail,*,led,ling,ler, RAIN IN THE FORM OF ICE, LOUD VOCAL WELCOME (or see hale)
hainger, hanger
hainkerchef, handkerchief
hair,ry,rier,riest,riness, STRANDS OF WHICH GROW FROM THE SKIN (or see hare/heir/harry)
hak, hawk / hack
hakd, hack(ed)
haker, hack(er)
haktare, hectare'
hal, PREFIX INDICATING "SALT/ HALOGEN" MOST OFTEN MODIFIES THE WORD (or see hall/hale/hail/ haul/howl)
halagen, halogen
halagenic, halogen(ic)
halareus, hilarious
hale,*,ed,ling,er,est,eness, TO COMPLY, PULL/DRAG SOMEONE/ SOMETHING (or see hall/haul/hail/ holly)
halegram, hologram
halekopter, helicopter
haleluya, hallelujah

half,lve,lves, WHOLE MADE INTO TWO PARTS (or see have/halve)
halfhasard, haphazard
halfhasurdly, haphazard(ly)
halibut, A FISH
haligen, halogen
haligenic, halogen(ic)
hall,*, NARROW CORRIDOR WITH DOORS INSIDE A BUILDING (or see hale/haul/hail)
hallelujah,*, REJOICE
halloween,*, A HOLIDAY
halm, helm
halo,*,lation, REFLECTS LITE COMING FROM WITHIN SOMEONE, PREFIX INDICATING "SALT/HALOGEN" MOST OFTEN MODIFIES THE WORD (or see hollow/hello)
halogen,*,nate,nates,nating,nation,nic, NONMETALLIC/ REACTIVE CHEMICALS, TYPE OF LIGHT SOURCE
halokost, holocaust
halow, hollow / halo
halowen, halloween
halp, help
halpful, helpful
halt,*,ted,ting,ter, STOP NOW (or see haul(ed))
halter,*, GEAR FOR A HORSE, A SHIRT
halubet, halibut
halugram, hologram
halve,*,ed,ving, TO SEPARATE ONE INTO TWO PARTS (or see have)
haly, holly
ham,*,mmed,mming, PORK, TO BE GOOFY
hamak, hammock
hambergur, hamburger
hamburger,*, BEEF GROUND UP
hamer, hammer
hamileate, humiliate
hammer,*,red,ring,rer, FORCE SOMETHING IN, HANDTOOL
hammock,*, WOVEN FABRIC STRETCHED BETWEEN TWO POINTS TO SIT OR LIE IN
hamogenize, homogenize
hamper,*,red,ring, PUT CLOTHES INTO, GET IN THE WAY OF PROGRESS
hamster,*, A RODENT
hamuk, hammock
hamur, hammer

hand,*,ded,ding,dful,dy, AT THE END OF THE ARM WITH FINGERS ON IT "prefixes: over/un/under"
hande, handy
handeist, handy(diest)
handel, handle
handeur, handy(dier)
handicap,*,pped,pping,pper, UNABLE TO FUNCTION AT FULL CAPACITY, CHALLENGED "prefixes: multi"
handil, handle
handkerchief,*, SQUARE CLOTH
handle,*,ed,ling,er, FOR HANDS OR WITH HANDS "prefixes: mis"
handmade, MADE BY HAND NOT BY MACHINE
handout,*, GIVE SOMETHING TO SOMEONE IN NEED
handsome,ely,eness, GOOD LOOKING, SIZEABLE AMOUNT/BENEFITS
handul, handle
handy,dier,diest, SOMETHING EASILY AVAILABLE
hang,*,ged,ging,ger, SECURE SOMETHING ABOVE THE FLOOR ALLOWING FOR A VERTICAL POSITION "prefixes: over"
hangar,*, PLACE FOR LARGE TRANSPORTATION VESSELS (or see hanger)
hanger,*, FOR SUSPENSION OFF THE GROUND (or see hangar)
hank, hang
hankerchif, handkerchief
hansome, handsome
hant, hand
hantecap, handicap
hantel, handle
hantil, handle
hantmade, handmade
hantowt, handout
hantul, handle
hanty, handy
hapale, happy(pily)
hape, happy
hapeir, happy(pier)
hapeist, happy(piest)
hapele, happy(pily)
hapen, happen
hapenes, happy(piness)
hapeur, happy(pier)
haphazard,dly,dness, DO THINGS UNSAFELY, DISORGANIZED
hapie, happy

hapile, happy(pily)
hapin, happen
hapines, happy(piness)
happen,*,ned,ning, AN EVENT THAT HAS OCCURRED
happy,ppier,ppiest,ppily,ppiness, BEING JOYFUL IN LIFE "prefixes: un"
hapule, happy(pily)
hapun, happen
hapy, happy
hapyer, happy(pier)
hapyest, happy(piest)
hapynes, happy(piness)
har, hair / heir / hare
harass,sses,ssed,ssing,ssment, AGGRAVATE BEYOND NORMAL
haray, hurrah
harbor,*,red,ring,rer,rless,rage, WHERE BOATS DOCK, HOLD ONTO
hard,der,dest,den,dener,dy, CHALLENGING, DENSE, SOLID (or see heart) "prefixes: semi"
hardily, heart(ily)
hardin, hard(en)
hardles, heartless
hardly, BARELY, NOT QUITE
hardship,*, TOUGH TIMES
hardware,*, TOOLS, USE TO BUILD WITH, REPAIR MATERIAL
hardy,dier,diest,dily,diness, STRONG AND CAPABLE
hardyness, hardy(diness)
hare,*, A WILD RABBIT (or see hair(y)/harry/here)
haredetary, hereditary
haredity, heredity
harefy, horrify
harendus, horrendous
harer, horror
haretitary, hereditary
haretity, heredity
hareur, hair(ier)
hareust, hair(iest)
harfest, harvest
harifik, horrify(fic)
harindus, horrendous
harison, horizon
harm,*,med,ming,mful,mfully,mfulness, mless,mlessly,mlessness, TO INJURE "prefixes: un"
harmeny, harmony
harmfel, harm(ful)
harmlis, harm(less)
harmonica,*, MUSICAL INSTRUMENT

harmonize,*,ed,zing,er,zation, SYNCHRONIZE SOUNDS
harmony,nies,nic,nically,nious,niously, niousness,nist,nium,nize,nizes,nized, nizing,nizable,nization,nizer, VARIETY OF DIFFERENT SOUNDS VIBRATING AT A COMPATIBLE FREQUENCY "prefixes: dis/en/in/re/sub/un"
harmuny, harmony
harness,sses,ssed,ssing,sser, HOLD ONTO, GET HOLD OF "prefixes: un"
haroen, heroin / hero(ine)
haroik, hero(ic)
haroin, heroin / hero(ine)
haron, heron / heroin / hero(ine)
harp,*,ped,ping,per,pist, MUSICAL INSTRUMENT, TO NAG
harpoon,*,ned,ning,ner, TO STAB WITH A LONG METAL POLE WITH BARB ON THE END
harpsichord,*, A MUSICAL INSTRUMENT
harry,rries,rried,rrying, WAR PILLAGE/RAID, STRESS/DISTRESS (or see hair(y)/hare)
harsh,her,hest,hly,hness, STERN AND ROUGH
hart,*, MALE DEER (or see hard/heart)
harteist, heart(iest) / hard(iest)
harteur, heart(ier) / hard(ier)
harth, hearth
hartily, heart(ily)
hartiness, hardy(diness)
hartles, heartless
hartly, hardly
hartship, hardship
hartware, hardware
harty, heart(y) / hardy
haruble, horrible
harvest,*,ted,ting,ter, BRING IN RIPENED FOOD
hary, hair(y) / harry
has, ACQUIRED (or see have)
hasard, hazard
hase, haze / haze(y)
hasel, hassle / hazel
hasen, hasten
hash,hes,hed,hing,hish, A FOOD, TO TALK IT OVER
hasil, hassle
hasn't, CONTRACTION OF THE WORDS 'HAS NOT'
haspitality, hospitality

hassle,*,ed,ling, TO AGITATE
haste,*,ed,ting,en,ened,ening,ty,tier, tiest,tily,tiness, DO IT QUICKLY
hasten,ned,ning, TO SPEED UP
hasul, hassle / hazel
hat,*, COVERING FOR HEAD (or see had/hate)
hatch,hes,hed,hing,hling, COVER OF STORAGE AREA, LIVE THINGS COMING FROM EGGS
hatchet,*, SMALL AX
hate,*,ed,ting,eful,efully,efulness,eable, er,tred, MOST OPPOSITE FROM LOVE (or see haughty/hot)
haud, hod / hot / haul(ed)
haude, hod(ddie) / haughty / hood(y) / hot(ttie)
hauder, hot(tter)
hauefur, however
haughty,tier,tiest,tily,tiness, ACTING AS IF BETTER THAN OTHERS
hauk, hawk / hock
haul,*,led,ling,ler,lage, TRANSPORT A LOAD (or see hall) "prefixes: in/over"
hauleluea, hallelujah
haulo, hollow / wallow
haulter, halter / alter
haultur, halter
haunch,hes,hed,hless, REAR LEGS ON ANIMALS, ARCH
haund, hound
haunt,*,ted,ting,tingly,ter, TO SPOOK
haups, hops
haured, horrid
haurur, horror
haus, house
hausd, house(d)
hauspus, hospice
haustej, hostage
haustel, hostel / hostile
haustig, hostage
haut, hot / hod
haute, haughty / hod(ddie) / hood(y) / hot(ttie)
hauty, haughty / hod(ddie) / hood(y) / hot(ttie)
hauvel, hovel
hauztul, hostel / hostile
hav, halve / have / half
havd, halve(d)
have, TO POSSESS, ACQUIRE (or see half/halve)

haven,*, A SAFE PLACE (or see heaven/have(ving))
haven't, CONTRACTION OF THE WORDS 'HAVE NOT'
havin, haven / heaven
havint, haven't
havs, halve(s)
havun, haven / heaven
haw, how
hawever, however
hawk,*, A BIRD (or see hock)
hawl, howl / haul
hawle, holly
hawnd, hound
hawnt, hound
hawvul, hovel
hay,*,yed,ying, DRY GRASS, ALFALFA, WORKING WITH HAY (or see hey)
haz, has / haze
hazard,*,ded,ding,dous,dously, dousness, DANGEROUS "prefixes: bio"
haze,*,ed,zing,zy,zier,ziest,zily,ziness, SMOKE, MIST, DUST, BLURRY
hazel, A PLANT, A COLOR (or see hassle)
haznt, hasn't
hazurd, hazard
he, A MALE
he'd, CONTRACTION OF THE WORDS 'HE COULD, HE SHOULD, HE WOULD, HE HAD'
he'll, CONTRACTION OF THE WORDS 'HE WILL' (or see hell/heal/heel)
he's, CONTRACTION OF THE WORDS 'HE IS'
head,*,ded,ding,der,dy,dsier,diest,dily, diness, BODY PART ON TOP OF SHOULDERS, ON TOP OF, LEADING "prefixes: multi/over/sub"
heal,*,led,ling,ler,lable, TO CURE, SOMEONE WHO CURES, MEND (or see heel/he'll)
health,hy,hier,hiest,hily,hiness,hful, hfully,hfulness, OF SOUND BODY/MIND "prefixes: un"
heap,*,ped,ping, TO MOUND UP
hear,*,ring,rd, SOUND IN EARS (or see here) "prefixes: over"
heard, PAST TENSE FOR "HEAR "(or see herd) "prefixes: un"
hearsay, GOSSIP
hearse, A VEHICLE FOR MOVING CASKETS
hearst, hearse

heart,*,ty,tier,tiest,tily,tiness,tless, tlessly,tlessness, AN ORGAN IN A BODY (or see hard) "prefixes: dis"
hearth,*, SURROUNDING A FIREPLACE "prefixes: multi"
heartless,ssly,ssness, CRUEL
heat,*,ted,tedly,tedness,ting,er,tless, WARM, FOR MAKING WARM (or see heed/he'd) "prefixes: over/un"
heave,*,ed,ving, TO THRUST SOMETHING HEAVY USING FORCE
heaven,*,nly,nlier,nliest,nliness, A EUPHORIC STATE OF MIND, DIVINE
heavy,vier,viest,vily,viness, OF GREAT WEIGHT
hebachi, hibachi
hebapotamus, hippopotamus
hebnutize, hypnotize
heckle,*,ed,ling,er, ANNOYING NOISES/WORDS AIMED AT A SPEAKER
hecksugon, hexagon
heckup, hiccup
hectare,*, METRIC MEASUREMENT, 2.5 ACRES
hectic,cally, CONFUSING RUSH
hecto, PREFIX INDICATING "ONE HUNDRED" MOST OFTEN MODIFIES THE WORD
hed, head / hit / he'd / heat / heed
hedch, hitch / hedge
hedeus, hideous
hedge,*,ed,ging, BUSHES, TO TRIM BY CUTTING
hedid, heed(ed) / heat(ed) / head(ed)
hedud, heed(ed) / heat(ed) / head(ed)
heed,*,ded,ding, PAY ATTENTION, TAKE NOTICE OF (or see heat/he'd/heat) "prefixes: un"
heef, heave
heel,*,led,ling, PART OF THE FOOT (or see heal/he'll)
heep, heap
heet, heat
hefen, heaven
hefer, heifer
hefon, heaven
hefur, heifer
hefy, heavy
heg, hedge
heifer,*, IMMATURE COW
height,*,ten,tens,tened,tening,tener, MEASURE TOP TO BOTTOM, MAKE TALLER
heigth, height

heimlek, heimlich
heimlich, A MANEUVER WHICH CLEARS WINDPIPE FOR BREATHING
heir,*,rless,rship,ress, ONE WHO RECEIVES MONEY/PROPERTY BEQUEATHED TO THEM UPON SOMEONES DEATH (or see hair/air/err)
heirarchy, hierarch(y)
heirloom,*, SOMETHING PRECIOUS HANDED DOWN TO FOLLOWING GENERATIONS
heiroglyph, hieroglyph
heist,*,ted,ting,ter, THEFT, ROBBERY
heiten, height(en)
heith, height
heithen, height(en)
hej, hedge
heks, hex
heksigon, hexagon
heksugon, hexagon
hektare, hectare'
hektik, hectic
hekul, heckle
hekup, hiccup
hel, heel / hell / heal / he'll / hill
helakopter, helicopter
helareus, hilarious
held, PAST TENSE FOR THE WORD "HOLD"
heleom, helium
helicopter,*, FLYING MACHINE
helio, PREFIX INDICATING "SUN" MOST OFTEN MODIFIES THE WORD
helium, A GAS
hell,*,lled,lling,llish,llishly,llishness,llion, AN IMAGINARY PLACE OF GREAT DISCOMFORT (or see he'll/heal/heel)
hello,*, AMERICAN GREETING
helm,*, STEERING PART OF A BOAT
helmet,*,ted, A PROTECTIVE COVER FOR THE HEAD
helo, hello
help,*,ped,ping,pings,pful,per,pless, SOMEONE/SOMETHING BEING AIDED
helpd, help(ed)
helpful,lly,lness, THOSE WHO AID OTHERS "prefixes: un"
helpfulnes, helpful(ness)
helpless,ssly,ssness, UNABLE TO AID ONESELF
helpt, help(ed)

helt, held / hilt
helth, health
hem,*,mmed,mming, HAVING TO DO WITH BORDERS ON THINGS (or see him/hymn)
hema, PREFIX INDICATING "BLOOD" MOST OFTEN MODIFIES THE WORD
hemarag, hemorrhage
hemaroid, hemorrhoids
hemat, PREFIX INDICATING "BLOOD" MOST OFTEN MODIFIES THE WORD
hemato, PREFIX INDICATING "BLOOD" MOST OFTEN MODIFIES THE WORD
hemerag, hemorrhage
hemeroid, hemorrhoids
hemi, BRAND NAME, PREFIX INDICATING "HALF" MOST OFTEN MODIFIES THE WORD
hemirag, hemorrhage
hemisphere,*,ric,rical,rically, ONE HALF OF EARTH
hemmaroid, hemorrhoids
hemmoroid, hemorrhoids
hemo, PREFIX INDICATING "BLOOD" MOST OFTEN MODIFIES THE WORD
hemorag, hemorrhage
hemoroid, hemorrhoids
hemorrhage,*,ed,ging,gic, VALUABLE/ UNCONTROLLABLE LOSS
hemorrhoids,dal,dectomy, VARICOSE VEINS IN ANUS
hemosfere, hemisphere
hemp,*, A PLANT USEFUL FOR CLOTHING/MATERIAL/ROPE/PAPER
hemself, himself
hemurag, hemorrhage
hemuroid, hemorrhoids
hen,*, FEMALE CHICKEN
hena, henna
hence,*, THEREFORE, AND SO
hender, hinder
hendrance, hindrance
henge, hinge
henje, hinge
henna, PLANT FOR DYING HAIR/FABRIC, FOR TEMPORARY TATTOOS
hens, hen(s) / hence
hent, hint
hep, heap / hip
hepabotamus, hippopotamus
hepacrite, hypocrite
hepakrete, hypocrite
hepatitis, ILLNESS CAUSED BY VIRUS
hepnosis, hypnosis

hepnutize, hypnotize
hepobotamus, hippopotamus
hepokrite, hypocrite
hepopotamus, hippopotamus
hepothesis, hypothesis
hept, PREFIX INDICATING "SEVEN" MOST OFTEN MODIFIES THE WORD
hepta, PREFIX INDICATING "SEVEN" MOST OFTEN MODIFIES THE WORD
hepy, hip(py)
her,*, IN REFERRING TO A FEMALE (or see hear/here/hair/hare/heir)
heracane, hurricane
herass, harass
herb,*,bed,bal,balism,balist,baceous, baceously,bage,bivore, PLANTS FOR HEALING/COOKING WITH (THE "H" IS SILENT)
herbavor, herbivore
herbivore,*,rous, PLANT EATING ANIMAL (THE "H" IS SILENT)
herbulist, herb(alist)
herd,*,ded,ding,der, ANIMALS GATHERED INTO A GROUP FOR MOVING (or see heard/hurt)
herdle, hurdle / hurtle
herdul, hurdle / hurtle
here,*, IN THIS VICINITY, WHERE YOU ARE (or see hear/hair(y)/hare/ harry)
hered, hurry(ried)
hereditary,rily,riness, ABLE TO BE PASSED ON FROM ONE GENERATION TO ANOTHER
heredity,table,tability,tament,tarian, tarianism,tary,tarily,tariness, PASSED DOWN THROUGH GENERATIONS
hereist, hair(iest)
herendus, horrendous
heresay, hearsay
hereur, hair(ier)
hericane, hurricane
herison, horizon
herizun, horizon
herl, hurle
hermetic,cal,cally, PROTECTED/ AIRTIGHT ENVIRONMENT
hermit,*,tic,tical,tically, A RECLUSE, CRUSTACEAN
hernia,*,al, ABDOMINAL MUSCLE PROBLEM
hero,oes,oic,oics,oical,oically,oicalness, oine,oines,oism, BRAVE ACT TO SAVE SOMETHING FROM PERIL OR DEATH

heroek, hero(ic)
heroin, MANMADE DRUG TO EASE PAIN, ADDICTIVE (or see hero(ine))
heron,*, A BIRD (or see heroin/ hero(ine))
hers, hearse / her(s) / here(s) / hear(s)
herself, SHE ALONE, FEMALE SELF
herst, hearse
hert, hurt / heard / herd
hertful, hurt(ful)
herth, hearth
hertle, hurdle / hurtle
hertul, hurdle / hurtle
hery, hair(y) / hurry / harry
herz, hearse / her(s) / here(s) / hear(s)
hes, his / hiss / he's
hesatashen, hesitate(tion)
hesatation, hesitate(tion)
hesderical, hysterical
hesdorean, historian
hesdorik, historic
hesdory, history
hesdurekteme, hysterectomy
hesetashen, hesitate(tion)
hesetation, hesitate(tion)
hesitant,tly,nce,ncy,tate,tation, PAUSE TO CONSIDER BEFORE CONTINUING, CONSIDERING BEFORE STARTING
hesitashen, hesitate(tion)
hesitate,*,ted,ting,tingly,tant,tantly, tation,tive,er, TAKE A PAUSE BEFORE CONTINUING "prefixes: un"
hesterektomy, hysterectomy
hesterical, hysterical
hestorian, historian
hestorical, historic(al)
hestorik, historic
hestory, history
hesutashen, hesitate(tion)
hesutation, hesitate(tion)
het, head / hit / he'd / heat / heed
hetch, hitch
hetero, PREFIX INDICATING "OTHER/ DIFFERENT" MOST OFTEN MODIFIES THE WORD
heteus, hideous
hetid, heed(ed) / heat(ed) / head(ed)
hetud, heed(ed) / heat(ed) / head(ed)
heu, hue / who
heug, huge
heuj, huge
heumen, human

heve, heave / heavy
hevin, heaven
hevy, heavy
hew, hue / who
hewman, human / humane
hewmer, humor
hewmid, humid
hewmileate, humiliate
hex,xes,xed,xing,xer,xagon, CURSE, A COMPUTATION, PREFIX INDICATING "SIX" MOST OFTEN MODIFIES THE WORD
hexagon,*,nal, SIX-SIDED FIGURE/ SHAPE
hey, AN EXCLAMATION FOR GREETING/ FOR SURPRISE, WAY OF GREETING (or see hay)
hezetante, hesitant
hezitate, hesitate
hezutashen, hesitate(tion)
hi, A WELCOME GREETING (or see high)
hiarchy, hierarch(y)
hibachi,*, ROUND COOKING GRILL
hiberacteve, hyperactive
hibernate,*,ed,ting,tion,tor, SLEEP OVER THE WINTER
hibochi, hibachi
hibopotamus, hippopotamus
hibred, hybrid
hibrud, hybrid
hiccup,*,pped,pping, THROAT MUSCLE IN TEMPORARY SPASM
hid,dden, IN HIDING, PAST TENSE FOR THE WORD "HIDE", STORED FROM EYESIGHT (or see hide/height/hit)
hidch, hitch / hedge
hide,*,ding, STORE/PLACE OUT OF SIGHT, SKIN OFF OF ANIMAL (or see hid/height/hit)
hiden, hid(dden)
hideous,sly,sness, FRIGHTFULLY UGLY
hideout,*, WHERE SOMEONE GOES TO HIDE
hidout, hideout
hidrant, hydrant
hidrashen, hydrate(tion)
hidrat, hydrate
hidration, hydrate(tion)
hidrent, hydrant
hidroelectric, hydroelectric
hidrophonic, hydroponic
hidroponic, hydroponic
hidrugen, hydrogen

hierarch,*,hy,hies,hic,hical,hically,hize, hizes,hized,hizing,hization, OF FORMAL RANK
hieroglyph,*,hic, CARVED, PAINTED SYMBOLS FROM PAST PEOPLES
hiest, heist
hif, hive
hifen, hyphen
hifenate, hyphen(ate)
hifer, heifer
hifin, hyphen
higene, hygiene
higenist, hygiene(nist)
high,*,her,hest,hly,hness, ALTITUDE BETWEEN THE GROUND AND SPACE, A EUPHORIC SENSE UNDER THE INFLUENCE OF A HALLUCINOGEN (or see hi)
hight, height
hijack,*,ked,king,ker, TAKE VEHICLE/ VESSEL BY FORCE
hijene, hygiene
hike,*,ked,king,ker, TO WALK ON ROUGH/NATURAL TERRAIN
hikoo, haiku
hiku, haiku
hikup, hiccup
hilarious,sly,sness,ity, ABSOLUTELY FUNNY
hill,*,lled,lling,ller,lly, MOUNDS ON THE EARTH (or see he'll) "prefixes: up"
hilt,*, SWORD OR DAGGER HANDLE, COMPLETELY AND ABSOLUTELY
him, REFERENCE TO MALE OVER THERE, MALE/THIRD PERSON (or see hem/ hymn)
himarag, hemorrhage
himaroid, hemorrhoids
hime, hemi
himeroid, hemorrhoids
himesfere, hemisphere
himesphere, hemisphere
himiroid, hemorrhoids
himlek, heimlich
himluk, heimlich
himoroid, hemorrhoids
himp, hemp
himself, HIS OWN SELF
himuroid, hemorrhoids
hin, hen
hince, hence
hind, THE REAR PORTION OF AN ANIMAL

hinder,*,red,ring,rer,drance, IN THE WAY OF PROGRESS OR SUCCESS "prefixes: un"
hindrance,*, IN THE WAY OF PROGRESS/SUCCESS
hinge,*,ed,ging,eless, SWINGS BY WAY OF A PIN ENCASED IN A HINGE "prefixes: un"
hinje, hinge
hinse, hence
hint,*,ted,ting,tingly, TINY PORTION OF THE FULL FACT
hip,*,pper,ppest,pply,pness,ppy,ppier, ppiest, THE PELVIC AREA ON PEOPLE/ ANIMALS, TO BE COOL/ INDIFFERENT TO SOCIAL PRESSURE
hipadrete, hypocrite
hipapotamus, hippopotamus
hipatidus, hepatitis
hipauthusis, hypothesis
hipawthusis, hypothesis
hipe, hype / hip
hiperactive, hyperactive
hiperactuve, hyperactive
hipernate, hibernate
hipnosis, hypnosis
hipnosus, hypnosis
hipnutise, hypnotize
hipocrite, hypocrite
hipokrit, hypocrite
hipopotamus, hippopotamus
hipotenuse, hypotenuse
hipothurmeu, hypothermia
hipothusis, hypothesis
hippopotamus,*, LARGE/HEAVY HERBIVORE
hir, her / hire / here
hiracane, hurricane
hirarchy, hierarch(y)
hirass, harass
hird, heard / herd / hurt / hire(d)
hirdul, hurdle / hurtle
hire,*,ed,ring,rable,er, PAID TO WORK (or see high(er))
hirison, horizon
hirl, hurle
hirmet, hermit
hirmetic, hermetic
hiro, hero
hiroek, hero(ic)
hiroglif, hieroglyph
hiroin, hero(ine) / heroin
hirs, hearse / her(s) / hire(s)
hirself, herself

hirst, hearse
hirt, hurt / heard / herd
hirtul, hurdle / hurtle
hirz, her(s) / hearse / hire(s)
his, BELONGS TO HIM (or see hiss)
hisdarecal, hysterical
hisderektomy, hysterectomy
hisdorean, historian
hisdoric, historic
hisdurekteme, hysterectomy
hiself, himself
hiss,sses,ssed,ssing,ssy,sser, SOUND A SNAKE/STEAM MAKES (or see his)
hisself, himself
hist, PREFIX INDICATING "LIVING TISSUE" MOST OFTEN MODIFIES THE WORD
histare, history
histarical, hysterical
histere, history
histerical, hysterical
histo, PREFIX INDICATING "LIVING TISSUE" MOST OFTEN MODIFIES THE WORD
historian,*, PEOPLE WELL STUDIED IN HISTORY
historic,cal,calness,cally,city,cize,cizes, cized,cizing,ize,izes,ized,izing,izingly, ry,izedly,iographer,ization,iography, EVENT ABOUT THE PAST "prefixes: pre"
history,ries,ric,ricism,rize,ricization, riography, ABOUT THE PAST "prefixes: pre"
histrektomy, hysterectomy
histure, history
histurektemy, hysterectomy
hit,*,tting,ttable,tter, STRIKE A BLOW (or see height/hid/hide) "prefixes: over"
hitch,hes,hed,hing, JOIN TWO THINGS TOGETHER BY WAY OF (or see hedge) "prefixes: un"
hite, height / hide
hiten, height(en) / hid(dden)
hiteout, hideout
hiteus, hideous
hith, height
hithen, height(en)
hitout, hideout
hitrashen, hydrate(tion)
hitrate, hydrate
hitun, height(en)

hive,*, BUMPS ON A PERSON, HOME OF BEES OR WASPS
ho, hoe / who / hue
hoard,*,ded,ding,der, TO STOCKPILE MORE GOODS THAN NECESSARY (or see horde)
hoarse,er,est,ely,eness,en,ens,ened, ening, VOICE/THROAT IS RASPY/ ROUGH (or see horse)
hoax,xes, A TRICK IN DECEPTION
hobble,*,ed,ling, WALK WITH A LIMP
hobby,bies, A PASTTIME
hobe, hope / hobby
hobful, hope(ful)
hobil, hobble
hobless, hope(less)
hobt, hop(pped) / hope(d)
hobul, hobble
hoby, hobby
hock,*,ked,king, CUT OF MEAT/LEG, TO PAWN ITEMS (or see hawk/hog/ hokey)
hockey, A SKATING SPORT (or see hokey)
hocky, hokey / hockey
hod,*,ddie, HOLDER FOR MORTAR (or see hot/hold/hood)
hode, haughty / hod(ddie) / hood(y)
hodel, hotel
hoder, hot(tter)
hodir, hot(tter)
hody, haughty
hoe,*,ed,oing, A HAND TOOL (or see whole/whore)
hoest, hoist
hof, huff
hofel, hovel
hofer, hover
hoful, hovel
hofur, hover
hog,*,gged,gging, A PIG, SOMEONE WHO EATS LIKE A PIG
hoist,*,ted,ting, LIFT OR RAISE UP
hok, hawk / hock / hog
hokey,kier,kiest,yness,kily, CORNY, NOT REALISTIC (or see hockey)
hoks, hoax / hock(s)
hoky, hockey / hokey
hol, hole / whole / haul / hall
hold,*,ding,dings,held,der, KEEP FROM MOVING/FALLING, TO GRASP, KEEP STILL (or see haul(ed)) "prefixes: in/ up"

holder,*, SOMETHING THAT HOLDS THINGS
hole,*,ed,ling, AN OPENING/ SPACE/ ORIFICE/GAP (or see holy/holly/ whole(y)/wholly)
holegram, hologram
holeist, holy(liest)
holer, holler / haul(er) / hollow
holeur, holy(lier)
holey, wholly / whole(y) / holy
holi, holy / holly / whole(y) / wholly
holiday,*, A DAY OF REMEMBERANCE/ HONORING SOMEONE/EVENT
holigram, hologram
holl, hall / haul / whole / hole
holler,*,red,ring, YELLING/CALLING LOUDLY
hollow,*,wed,wing,wly,wness, TO DIG/ CARVE OUT SO INSIDE IS EMPTY (or see halo/haul(er))
holly,lies, PLANT (or see holy/hole/ whole/wholly)
holo, PREFIX INDICATING "WHOLE" MOST OFTEN MODIFIES THE WORD (or see hollow/hello)
holocaust,*, DEVASTATING DESTRUCTION OF PEOPLE/PLACES
hologram,*, A THREE DIMENSIONAL ILLUSION, VISUAL REFLECTED BY LASERS
holow, hollow
holoween, halloween
holsal, wholesale
holsel, wholesale
holsem, wholesome
holsome, wholesome
holster,*, HOLDER FOR A PISTOL
holsum, wholesome
holt, hold / halt / haul(ed)
holter, halter / hold(er)
holuday, holiday
holugram, hologram
holur, holler
holy,lier,liest,liness,lism,listic,listically, SACRED (or see hole/holly/wholly/ hole(y)/whole(y)) "prefixes: un"
hom, whom / home
homade, homemade
home,*,ey,ely,elier,eliest,eliness,eless, elessness, STRUCTURE WHERE SOMEONE LIVES
homeless,ssness, HAVING NO HOME
homely, PERSON WHO IS WITHDRAWN/ SHY

homemade, NOT MADE BY A MACHINE IN A FACTORY
homeny, hominy
homeo, PREFIX INDICATING "THE SAME" MOST OFTEN MODIFIES THE WORD
homer,*, HOME RUN IN BASEBALL
homevur, whomever
homey, HOME BOY
hominy, GROUND CORN
homir, homer
homless, homeless
homly, homely
homo, PREFIX INDICATING "THE SAME" MOST OFTEN MODIFIES THE WORD
homogenize,*,ed,zing,zation,er, CREAM/MILK MIXED TOGETHER
homogenous,sly,sness, SIMILAR/ UNIFORM TO, THE SAME AS
homur, homer
homy, homey
honch, haunch / hunch
hond, hone(d) / haunt / hound
hondred, hundred
hone,*,ed,ning,er, TO SHARPEN (or see honey)
honemoon, honeymoon
honemun, honeymoon
honer, honor
honerary, honorary
honest,ty,ties,tly,tness, TRUTHFUL ("H" IS SILENT) "prefixes: dis"
honey,*,yed,ying, A LIQUID FROM NECTAR MADE BY BEES
honeymoon,*,ned,ning,ners, WHAT A COUPLE HAS AFTER THEIR WEDDING
honimoon, honeymoon
honimun, honeymoon
honist, honest
honk,*,ked,king, A HORN SOUND, SOUND A GOOSE MAKES
honker, hunk(er) / honk
honor,*,red,ring,rer,rless,rable,rably, rableness,rarium,rary,ree, rific, RESPECT, STRONG MORAL INTEGRITY "prefixes: dis/re"
honorary, AWARD OF HONOR
hont, haunt / hone(d) / hunt
hontred, hundred
honur, honor
honymoon, honeymoon
hoo, hue / who

hood,*,ded,ding,dless,dy, JACKET/HAT COMBINATION, ENGINE COVER ON CAR, IN THE NEIGHBORHOOD (or see hoot/who'd)
hooever, whoever
hoof,*,fed,fing,fer,oves,oved, FEET OF SOME ANIMALS
hook,*,ked,king, A CURVED TOOL WITH SHARP TIP FOR GRABBING "prefixes: un"
hoomever, whomever
hoop,*,ped,ping, THINGS THAT ARE A CIRCLE USED AS A TOOL/TOY (or see hop)
hooray, hurrah
hoos, who's / whose / hue(s)
hoot,*,ted,ting,ter, SOUND OWL MAKES, FOND EXPRESSION TOWARDS SOMEONE (or see hood/who'd)
hoove,*,ed, MORE THAN ONE HOOF
hop,*,pped,pping,ppy, JUMP UP AND DOWN LIKE A RABBIT, A PLANT (or see hope)
hopd, hop(pped) / hope(d)
hope,*,ed,ping,er,eful,efully,efulness, eless,elessly,elessness, WISH FOR SOMETHING (or see hop/hops/hobby)
hopful, hope(ful)
hopless, hope(less)
hops, A PLANT (or see hope(s))
hopscotch, GAME
hopskoch, hopscotch
hor, hour / horror / whore
horable, horrible
horafid, horrify(fied)
horascope, horoscope
hord, hoard / hard / horde / horrid
horde,*,ed,ding, MANY THINGS/ PEOPLE ALL TOGETHER AT ONCE, SWARMS OF (or see hoard/hard/hardy/horrid)
hordervs, horsd'oevres
hordurves, horsd'oevres
horeble, horrible
hored, hoard / horrid / horde
horefik, horrify(fic)
horefy, horrify
horendous, horrendous
horer, horror
horescope, horoscope
horesontul, horizontal
horible, horrible

horify, horrify
horindus, horrendous
horir, horror
horiscope, horoscope
horizon,*,nal,ntal, WHERE THE SUN/ MOON RISES/SETS
horizontal,*,lly,lness,lity, POSITION SITUATED LINEAR WITH THE HORIZON
hormeny, harmony
hormful, harm(ful)
hormles, harm(less)
hormone,*,nal,nally, HEMICALS MANUFACTURED BY THE BODY (pineal gland) "prefixes: pro"
hormuny, harmony
horn,*,ned,ning,ny, INSTRUMENT PLAYED BY BLOWING, USED FOR SOUND ON VEHICLES AND VESSELS
horne, horny
hornet,*, LARGE VOLATILE WASP
horny, MADE OF HORN, SLANG FOR CERTAIN DESIRES
horoscope,*,pic, USING THE STARS TO GUESS THE FUTURE
horrendous,sness,sly, TERRIBLE, DREADFUL
horrible,ly,eness, AWFUL, UGLY, HORRENDOUS
horrid,dly,dness, HORROR, DREADFUL, OFFENSIVE
horrify,fies,fied,fying,fyingly,fication,fic, ror, VERY FRIGHTENING, BEYOND SCARY
horror,*, OVERPOWERING/ UNIMAGINABLE FEAR
horsd'oevres, TWO WORDS 'hors d'oevres', APPETIZERS
horse,*,ed,sing, ANIMAL(or see hoarse/horror) "prefixes: un"
hort, horde / hard
horte, horde / hardy
horuble, horrible
horufid, horrify(fied)
horufy, horrify
horur, horror
horuscope, horoscope
horusontel, horizontal
hos, hoe(s) / hose / who's / hue(s) / whose
hosbedul, hospital
hosbetality, hospitality
hosbidul, hospital
hosbitality, hospitality

hosbituble, hospitable
hosbitul, hospital
hosdege, hostage
hosdej, hostage
hosdel, hostel / hostile
hosdij, hostage
hosdul, hostel / hostile
hose,*,ed,sing, RUBBER TUBE(or see whose/who's)
hospetable, hospitable
hospetality, hospitality
hospetul, hospital
hospice,*, LODGING FOR TRAVELERS, PROGRAM FOR PATIENTS
hospitable,ly,leness, KIND/FRIENDLY TO GUESTS
hospital,*,lize,lized,lizing,lization, PLACE FOR SICK/INJURED PEOPLE "prefixes: multi/post"
hospitality,ties, KINDNESS TO GUESTS
host,*,ted,ting,tess, TO SPONSOR, ONE WHO ENTERTAINS/IS IN CHARGE
hostage,*, PERSON HELD AGAINST THEIR WILL
hostel,*,ler,ling,lry, SHELTERS AROUND THE WORLD WHERE TRAVELING PEOPLE MAY STAY CHEAPLY (or see hostile)
hoster, holster
hostes, host(ess)
hostige, hostage
hostile,lity,lities, ACTS AGGRESSIVE/ ANGRY (or see hostel)
hostis, host(ess)
hostle, hostile / hostel
hostul, hostel / hostile
hostus, host(ess)
hot,tter,ttest,ttie, CAN BURN, WARMER THAN WARM, IN REFERENCE TO SOMEONE VERY ATTRACTIVE (or see hod/hold/hood/hoot/who'd)
hote, haughty / hod(ddie) / hold / hood(y)
hotel,*, BUILDINGS WITH ROOMS FOR TRAVELERS TO STAY THE NIGHT
hoter, hot(tter)
hotur, hot(tter)
hoty, haughty / hod(ddie) / hood(y) / hot(ttie)
houefur, however
houl, howl / haul
hound,*,ded,ding, TO AGITATE SOMEONE, BE PERSISTENT LIKE A HOUND DOG ON A SCENT, A DOG

hour,*,rly, SECONDS (or see our)
house,*,ed,sing, STRUCTURE/ DWELLING TO LIVE IN
hovel,*, A TINY DWELLING, SMALL OPEN STRUCTURE
hover,*,red,ring, TO FLOAT ABOVE FOR A PERIOD OF TIME WITHOUT MOVING, TO FLOAT ABOVE
hovil, hovel
hovul, hovel
hovur, hover
how, EXPLAIN THE WAY SOMETHING IS SAID OR DONE, QUESTION THE WAY SOMETHING HAPPENS
however, IN ANY EVENT, ON THE OTHER HAND, STILL
howl,*,led,ling,lingly,ler, SOUND DOG MAKES, A LOUD SOUND
hownd, hound
hownt, hound
howse, house
hox, hoax / hock(s)
hoz, hose / hoe(s) / who's / whose
hozbetuble, hospitable
hozdul, hostel / hostile
hozpetality, hospitality
hozpitable, hospitable
hozt, host
hoztus, host(ess)
hu, hue / who
hub,*, THE CENTER OF SOMETHING WHICH HOLDS IT ALL TOGETHER, KEEPS IT MOVING
hubcap,*, COVER FOR WHEELS, COVERS THE HUB
huch, hutch / huge / hush
huckleberry,ries, AN EDIBLE BERRY
hud, hood / hoot / who'd / hut
huddle,*,ed,ling, FORM/HUNCH INTO A TIGHT GROUP
hude, hood / hoot / who'd
hudel, huddle
hue,*, SHADES, DEGREES OF THE SAME COLOR (or see who) "prefixes: multi/un"
huever, whoever
huf, hoof / huff / hoove
hufd, huff(ed) / hoove(d)
hufed, huff(ed) / hoove(d)
huff,*,ffed,ffing,ffy, DEEP GASPS FOR AIR, DEEP BREATH OUT
hug,*,gged,gging,ggable,ggably,gger, WRAP ARMS AROUND SOMEONE/ SOMETHING WITH GOOD INTENT (or see huge)
hugable, hug(ggable)
hugd, hug(gged)
huge,er,est,eness,ely, ENORMOUS IN BULK, TAKES UP ALOT OF SPACE (or see hutch)
hugible, hug(ggable)
hugt, hug(gged)
huguble, hug(ggable)
huj, huge / hutch
huk, hook / hug
hukd, hug(gged)
hukeble, hug(ggable)
huklbery, huckleberry
hukt, hook(ed) / hug(gged)
hul, hull / who'll
hulareus, hilarious
hull,*, MAINFRAME/COVER (or see who'll) "prefixes: multi"
hum,*,mmed,mming,mmer, A SOUND MADE WITH LIPS PURSED (or see whom)
human,*,ne,nness,nism,nist,nistic, nistically,nitarian,nitarianism, nity, nities,nize,nizes,nized,nizing, nization,nly, HOMO SAPIEN BEING (or see humane) "prefixes: in/neo/ sub"
humane,ely,eness, BE FAIR, CIVILIZED, REFINED (or see human) "prefixes: in"
humble,*,ed,ling,er,est,ly,eness, NOT SELF-RIGHTEOUS, ISN'T FLAGRANTLY PROUD OR OPINIONATED
humbul, humble
humdinger, OUTSTANDING
humed, humid
humeleate, humiliate
humen, human
humenbird, hummingbird
humengbird, hummingbird
humer, humor / hummer
humerus, humor(ous)
humes, hummus / humus
humever, whomever
humid,dity,dify,difies,dified,difier, difying,dification,dly, MOISTURE IN THE AIR
humiliate,*,ed,ting,tion,ity, BELITTLED, ATTACK ON SELF-ESTEEM, HARSH JUDGEMENT
humility, RESPECTFUL/MODEST

humin, human
huminbird, hummingbird
humis, hummus / humus
hummer,*, TYPE OF TRUCK
hummingbird,*, TINY BIRD
hummus, CHICKPEA, GARBONZO MIXTURE FOR AN EDIBLE SPREAD (or see humus)
humongous,sly, HUGE, ENORMOUS
humor,*,red,ring,rous,rously,rousness, rless,rlessly,rlessness,rist,resque, FUNNY (or see hummer)
hump,*,ped,ping, A BUMP, WHAT A MALE DOG DOES
humple, humble
humud, humid
humur, humor / hummer
humus, ORGANIC RICH SOIL (or see hummus)
hunch,hes,hed,hing, BENT OVER, HAVE AN IDEA
hundred,*,dth, A NUMBER USED IN THE U.S.
hunemoon, honeymoon
hung, PAST TENSE FOR THE WORD "HANG" "prefixes: over"
hunger,*,red,ring,gry,grily,griness, TO NEED/WANT SOMETHING DESPERATELY (or see hunker)
hungry,rier,riest,rily,riness, NEED FOOD
hunk,*,ker,ky, CHUNK OF SOMETHING (or see hung/honk)
hunker, hunk(er)
hunsh, hunch
hunt,*,ted,ting,ter, PURSUE TO LOCATE
huntch, hunch
huntret, hundred
huntrid, hundred
huntur, hunt(er)
huny, honey
hunymoon, honeymoon
hup, hoop / hub
hupcap, hubcap
hur, her
huracane, hurricane
hurass, harass
hurb, herb
hurbavore, herbivore
hurd, heard / herd / hurt
hurdid, herd(ed) / hurt(ed)
hurdle,*,ed,ling,er, JUMP OVER OBSTACLES (or see hurtle)
hure, hurry
huredetary, hereditary

hureditare, hereditary
huredity, heredity
huricane, hurricane
hurifek, horrify(fic)
hurisun, horizon
hurle,*,ed,ling,er, PITCH/SWING SOMETHING
hurmetic, hermetic
hurmit, hermit
huroik, hero(ic)
hurrah,*, YELL FOR JOY
hurricane,*, HIGH WINDS FROM THE SEAS
hurried, hurry(ried)
hurry,ries,ried,rying, TO GO FASTER THAN NORMAL "prefixes: un"
hurs, hearse / her(s)
hurself, herself
hurst, hearse
hurt,*,ting,tful,tfully,tfulness, PAIN, CAUSES PAIN (or see herd/heard) "prefixes: un"
hurtle,*,ed,ling, TO THROW/FLING VIOLENTLY WITH GREAT FORCE (or see hurdle)
hury, hurry
hurz, her(s) / hearse
hus, hue(s) / who's / whose
husband,*,dman,ubby, PARTNER OF A WIFE, MARRIED TERM
husbend, husband
husbind, husband
husderical, hysterical
hush,hes,hed,hing, BEING TOLD TO BE QUIET WITH A SOUND, GET SILENT
husk,*,ked,king,ker,ky, PROTECTIVE SHELLS ON THE FRUIT FROM PLANTS, TO REMOVE HUSKS
husky,kies,kier,kiest,kily,kiness, A DOG, SOMEONE WHO IS LARGER IN SIZE AND MUSCLE THAN PEERS
husle, hustle
husler, hustle(r)
huspend, husband
hustle,*,ed,ling,er, GET A MOVE ON IT, SOMEONE WHO GAMBLES AT POOL
hut,*, RAMSHACKLE STRUCTURE, WORD USED IN FOOTBALL (or see hoot)
hutch,hes, CAGE FOR ANIMALS, TO HOLD DISHES
hutel, huddle
hutul, huddle
huv, hoove

huz, who's / whose / hue(s)
huzbend, husband
huze, hue(s) / who's / whose
huzpend, husband
hybernate, hibernate
hybred, hybrid
hybrid,*,dism,dist,dity,dize,dizes,dized, dizing,dizable,dization, dizer, OFFSPRING FROM TWO ANIMALS OR PLANTS
hydr, PREFIX INDICATING "WATER/ LIQUID" MOST OFTEN MODIFIES THE WORD
hydrant,*, CAP FOR ACCESS TO STORED WATER
hydrate,*,ed,ting,tion,tor, ADD WATER "prefixes: de/re"
hydraulic,*, USE OF LIQUID UNDER PRESSURE TO MAKE PARTS MOVE
hydrint, hydrant
hydro, PREFIX INDICATING "WATER/ LIQUID" MOST OFTEN MODIFIES THE WORD
hydroelectric,cal,cally, USED TO RUN MACHINES VIA WATER PRESSURE THROUGH GENERATORS
hydrogen,nate,nates,nated,nating, nation,nator,nize,nizes,nized,nizing, nization,nous,eology,graphy, A COMMON/PLENTIFUL GAS
hydroponic,*,cally,cist,ist, USE OF WATER WITH ADDED VITAMINS/ MINERALS TO FEED ROOT PLANTS INSTEAD OF SOIL
hyfen, hyphen
hygene, hygiene
hygiene,nist,nics,nics,nically, CARE FOR THE EXTERIOR OF THE BODY "prefixes: un"
hygro, PREFIX INDICATING "MOISTURE" MOST OFTEN MODIFIES THE WORD
hyjack, hijack
hyke, hike
hymn,*,ned,ning,nal,nist, RELIGIOUS SONG (or see him/hem)
hymorag, hemorrhage
hypawthusis, hypothesis
hype, EXAGGERATING (or see hip)
hyper, PREFIX INDICATING "ABOVE/ OVER" MOST OFTEN MODIFIES THE WORD
hyperactive,vity, UNFOCUSED ENERGY
hypernate, hibernate
hypertherimia, hypothermia

hypethermia, hypothermia
hyphen,*,nate,nates,nated,nating, nation, A MARK WHICH SHOWS CONNECTION BETWEEN TWO WORDS
hyphenate, hyphen(ate)
hypnosis, SLIP TO A PLACE IN THE SUBCONSCIOUS MIND
hypnotic,cally,ize,ism, PUT INTO A SUBCONSCIOUS STATE OF MIND, MAGNETICALLY DRAWN TO SOMETHING
hypnotize,*,ed,zing,osis,ism, TALKED INTO A SUBCONSCIOUS STATE OF MIND
hypo, PREFIX INDICATING "BELOW/ UNDER" MOST OFTEN MODIFIES THE WORD
hypocrite,*,tical,tically,isy,isies, SOMEONE WHO SAYS ONE THING BUT DOES ANOTHER, LYING
hypotenuse, LONGEST SIDE OF TRIANGLE, USUALLY THE BASE
hypothermia, BODY BELOW NORMAL TEMPERATURE
hypothesis,ses, A THEORY FORMED DUE TO LACK OF INFORMATION OR TIME
hypothusis, hypothesis
hysdurekteme, hysterectomy
hysterectomy,mies, REMOVAL OF FEMALE ORGANS/UTERUS
hysterical,lly,lness, EXTREME EMOTION
hytrashen, hydrate(tion)
hytrat, hydrate
I, REFERS TO SELF (or see eye)
I'd, CONTRACTION OF THE WORDS 'I WOULD, I COULD, I SHOULD, I HAD'
I'll, CONTRACTION OF THE WORDS 'I WILL' (or see ill)
I'm, CONTRACTION OF THE WORDS 'I AM'
I've, CONTRACTION OF THE WORDS 'I HAVE'
ial, aisle
ibrau, eyebrow
ibreveate, abbreviate
ibreviate, abbreviate
ibrow, eyebrow
ice,*,ed,cing,cy,cily, FROZEN WATER
ich, itch / each
ichu, issue
ichuense, issue(uance)
ichuinse, issue(uance)

icicle,*, FROZEN ICE SHAPED LIKE DAGGERS
icing, TOPPING FOR BAKED GOODS
ickstensev, extensive
icon,*,nic,nical,nically,noclasm,noclast, noclastic,noclastically,nography, nographer,nographic,nographical, nolater,nology,nological,nologist, nomatic,nomaticism, SYMBOLS OR IMAGES THEY REPRESENT, PREFIX INDICATING "IMAGE" MOST OFTEN MODIFIES THE WORD
icono, PREFIX INDICATING "IMAGE" MOST OFTEN MODIFIES THE WORD
icselerate, accelerate
icy,cier,ciest,cily, FROZEN WATER
id, BASED ON FREUD'S EGO THEORY (or see eye(d)/I'd)
idalegy, ideology
idapt, adapt
idch, itch
idea,*,al,ally,alism,alist,alistic,alistically, ality,alize,alizes,alized,alizing,alizer, ally,ate,ates,ated,ating,ation,ational, ationally,ative, THE FORM/ THOUGHT OF SOMETHING
"prefixes: un"
idel, it'll / idle / idol
idelogical, ideological
idem, item
idemize, item(ize)
idenify, identify
idenity, identity
identical,lly,lness, EXACTLY THE SAME
identification,*, PICTURE/LEGAL DOCUMENT PROVING WHO A PERSON IS (I.D.)
identify,fies,fied,fying,fication,fier, fiable,fiably, fiability,ity, TO RECOGNIZE "prefixes: un"
identity,ties, A CHARACTERISTIC WHICH IDENTIFIES ONE FROM ANOTHER
idenufi, identify
ideo, PREFIX INDICATING "IDEA" MOST OFTEN MODIFIES THE WORD (or see idio)
ideology,gic,gical, OF IDEAS/THOUGHTS
"prefixes: un"
ideosy, idiocy
ideut, idiot
idilogical, ideological
idim, item
idimise, item(ize)
idinefy, identify

idinety, identity
idintekul, identical
idintufecation, identification
idio, PREFIX INDICATING "PRIVATE/ INDIVIDUAL/PROPER" MOST OFTEN MODIFIES THE WORD (or see ideo)
idiocy,cies, LACKS INTELLIGENCE
idiology, ideology
idiot,*,tic,tically,tness, ACTS LIKE A FOOL
idl, it'll / idle
idle,*,er,ling, RUN IN NEUTRAL, SITTING WITHOUT MOVING (or see idol/it'll)
idmire, admire
idmit, admit
idmyre, admire
idol,*,lator,latry,latrous,lize,lizes,lized, lizing,lization, ADMIRED, WORSHIPPED (or see idle)
idolegy, ideology
idological, ideological
idology, ideology
idolt, adult
idoo, adieu
idself, itself
idsetura, etcetera
idsulf, itself
idu, adieu
idul, idol / idle / it'll
idult, adult
idum, item
idvanse, advance
idvantige, advantage
idvize, advise / advice
ie, eye
iel, I'll / yell
ieng, eye(ying)
if, THEN THIS IF NOT THAT, IT COULD BE THIS OR THAT BASED ON WHETHER
ife, ivy / iffy
ifekt, effect / affect
iffy,fier,fiest,finess, PROBABILITY IT WILL/WILL NOT HAPPEN
ifre, ivory
ifree, every
ifry, ivory
ify, ivy / iffy
ig, PREFIX INDICATING "NOT" MOST OFTEN MODIFIES THE WORD
igalatarian, egalitarian
igalutarean, egalitarian
igloo,*, DOME DWELLING BUILT OF ICE BLOCKS
iglu, igloo

ignarent, ignorant
igneous, OLD ROCK FORMED BY HIGH HEAT
ignerants, ignorant(nce)
ignerent, ignorant
igneus, igneous
ignide, ignite
ignishin, ignition
ignite,*,ed,ting,tion,ter, SPARK TO MAKE IT START, START A FIRE "prefixes: pre"
ignition,*, ELECTRICAL SPARK TO START AN ENGINE "prefixes: pre"
ignor, ignore
ignorant,ntly,ance, LACKING INFORMATION
ignore,*,ed,ring,rant, PURPOSELY NOT PAY ATTENTION
ignurent, ignorant
igree, agree
igsajurate, exaggerate
igsakt, exact
igsample, example
igsberament, experiment
igsblanatory, explanatory
igsblod, explode
igsbozishen, expose(sition)
igsebshen, except(ion)
igsebt, except / accept
igsecutive, executive
igsempt, exempt
igsept, except / accept
igsert, exert
igsglude, exclude
igsilarate, exhilarate / accelerate
igsklute, exclude
igsotik, exotic
igspand, expand
igspans, expanse / expense
igspect, expect
igsperument, experiment
igspir, expire
igsplan, explain
igsplisit, explicit
igsplod, explode
igsplorashen, explore(ration)
igsploshen, explosion
igsplosive, explosive
igspoz, expose
igstend, extend
igstensev, extensive
igstenshen, extension
igstenuate, extenuate
igstereur, exterior

igstinkt, extinct
igstrakt, extract
igsturnel, external
igsurt, exert
igzajerate, exaggerate
igzakt, exact
igzample, example
igzasperate, exasperate
igzile, exile
igzist, exist
igzost, exhaust
igzurt, exert
ijusduble, adjust(able)
iknauleg, acknowledge
iknolege, acknowledge
iknor, ignore
iknurent, ignorant
ikon, icon
iksagerashen, exaggerate(tion)
iksajerashen, exaggerate(tion)
iksam, exam
iksamen, examine
iksamenashen, examine(nation)
iksampl, example
iksamunashen, examine(nation)
iksblan, explain
iksblod, explode
iksblor, explore
iksbloshen, explosion
iksblosive, explosive
iksboz, expose
ikschange, exchange
ikscuse, excuse
iksebt, except / accept
ikselirate, accelerate
ikseluratur, accelerate(tor)
iksepshen, except(ion)
iksept, except / accept
iksert, exert
iksglud, exclude
iksit, excite
iksitment, excite(ment)
ikskwisit, exquisite
iksost, exhaust
ikspans, expanse / expense
ikspant, expand
ikspektent, expect(ant)
ikspensef, expense(sive)
ikspereanse, experience
iksperement, experiment
ikspire, expire
iksplan, explain
iksplanatory, explanatory
iksplisitly, explicit(ly)

iksplod, explode
iksplor, explore
iksplorutory, explore(ratory)
iksploshen, explosion
iksplosive, explosive
ikspoz, expose
ikspreshen, express(ion)
ikspress, express
ikstend, extend
ikstengwish, extinguish
ikstensev, extensive
ikstenshen, extension
ikstenuate, extenuate
ikstereor, exterior
iksternul, external
ikstradite, extradite
ikstrem, extreme
ikstrordenair, extraordinaire
ikstrordinery, extraordinary
iksturmenate, exterminate
ikuate, equate
ikwalibreum, equilibrium
ikwalite, equality
ikwanimity, equanimity
ikwashun, equation
ikwate, equate
ikwater, equator
ikwaunimity, equanimity
ikwefalent, equivalent
ikwelbreum, equilibrium
ikwenox, equinox
ikwip, equip
ikwivalent, equivalent
ikwunimity, equanimity
ikzam, exam
ikzamen, examine
il, PREFIX INDICATING "NOT IN/INTO/ON" MOST OFTEN MODIFIES THE WORD (or see ill/aisle/i'll/eel)
iland, island
ilarm, alarm
ilash, eyelash
ilasteck, elastic
ilastick, elastic
ilastrate, illustrate
ilbow, elbow
ile, i'll
ilect, elect
ilectiv, elective
ilectrician, electrician
iledaret, illiterate
ilegal, illegal
ileganse, allegiance
ilegul, illegal

ilekul, illegal
ilend, island
ilent, island
ileptic, elliptic
ilesit, elicit / illicit
ilestrate, illustrate
ileterate, illiterate
iletest, elite(tist)
ileventh, eleven(th)
ileviate, alleviate
ilicit, elicit / illicit
iliderate, illiterate
iliderit, illiterate
iliiptical, elliptic(al)
iliktrishen, electrician
ilind, island
ilipsus, ellipsis
ilisit, elicit / illicit
iliterate, illiterate
ilive, alive
ill,lness, NOT WELL
illegal,lly,lity,lities,lize,lizes,lized,lizing, lization, AGAINST THE LAW, NOT LEGAL
illeterate, illiterate
illicit,tly,tness, PROHIBITED BY LAW, NOT ALLOWED (or see elicit)
illiptic, elliptic
illisit, elicit / illicit
illiterate, HARDLY ABLE TO READ AND WRITE, NOT EDUCATED
illogical,lly,lity,lities, NOT LOGICAL, NOT REALISTIC
illuminate,*,ed,ting,tingly,tion,ance,ant, OF BEING ENLIGHTENED/ INFORMED "prefixes: retro"
illumine,*,ed,ning,nance,nant,nate, nism, OF BEING ENLIGHTENED/ INFORMED
illusion,*,nal,nary,nist,nism, SENSE SOMETHING AS IF IT WERE PHYSICAL/REAL (or see allusion) "prefixes: dis"
illusive,ely,eness, SENSE SOMETHING AS IF IT WERE PHYSICAL/REAL (or see allusive)
illustrate,*,ed,ting,tive,tively,tion,tional, tor, DRAW A PICTURE, ONE WHO DRAWS
illustrious,sly,sness, FAMOUS FOR ACHIEVEMENT
ilness, ill(ness)
ilnus, ill(ness)
ilogikul, illogical

ilongate, elongate
ilop, elope
ilorm, alarm
ilostrious, illustrious
ilud, elude
ilujen, illusion / allusion
ilumenade, illuminate
iluminate, illuminate
ilund, island
ilur, allure
ilusdreus, illustrious
ilushen, illusion / allusion
ilusion, illusion / allusion
ilusive, illusive / allusive / elusive
ilustrate, illustrate
ilustrious, illustrious
ilute, elude
im, PREFIX INDICATING "NOT/IN/INTO/ ON" MOST OFTEN MODIFIES THE WORD (or see them/him)
imaculet, immaculate
image,*,ed,ery,er,ging,gine,gism, A PICTURE REAL OR IN THE MIND
imagenashen, imagine(nation)
imaginashen, imagine(nation)
imagine,*,ed,ning,nable,ary,native, nativeness,natively,nation, A PICTURE/THOUGHT IN THE MIND "prefixes: un"
imagrant, immigrant / emigrant
imagrate, immigrate / emigrate
imagrent, emigrant / immigrant
imagrints, emigrant(s) / immigrant(s)
imagrits, emigrant(s) / immigrant(s)
imagunashen, imagine(nation)
imaj, image
imajenashen, imagine(nation)
imanate, emanate
imanens, eminence / imminence/ immanence
imanint, eminent / imminent / immanent
imanserable, immensurable
imansopate, emancipate
imatashin, imitate(tion)
imatate, imitate
imaterial, immaterial
imature, immature
imbankment, embankment
imbargo, embargo
imbark, embark
imbasee, embassy
imbaudes, embody(dies)
imbeded, embed(dded)

imbelikul, umbilical
imberis, embarrass
imbet, embed
imbilakul, umbilical
imblim, emblem
imbodys, embody(dies)
imboss, emboss
imbotys, embody(dies)
imboudes, embody(dies)
imbrase, embrace
imbreo, embryo
imbrorder, embroider
imbrufment, improve(ment)
imbtee, empty
imbur, ember
imbuse, embassy
imediate, immediate
imeduetly, immediate(ly)
imenate, emanate
imenent, eminent / imminent / immanent
imense, immense
imensurable, immensurable
imerch, emerge
imerg, emerge
imergensi, emergency
imerj, emerge
imersable, immersible
imerse, immerse / emersed
imersion, immerse(sion)
imertality, immortal(ity)
imetashen, imitate(tion)
imeterial, immaterial
imeteut, immediate
imfasis, emphasis / emphasize
imfusis, emphasis / emphasize
imigrant, immigrant / emigrant
imigrashen, immigrate(tion) / emigrate(tion)
imigrate, immigrate / emigrate
imigration, immigrate(tion) / emigrate(tion)
imigrunt, immigrant / emigrant
iminate, emanate
iminens, eminence / imminence/ immanence
iminent, eminent / imminent / immanent
iminse, immense
iminsurable, immensurable
imirsable, immersible
imirsed, immerse(d) / emersed
imirshen, immerse(sion)
imirsion, immerse(sion)

imitate,*,ed,ting,tion,tional,tive,tively, tiveness, COPIES/REPRODUCTIONS OF THE REAL THING
imiterial, immaterial
imkombutent, incompetent
immaculate,ely,eness, NO SPOTS/STAINS/MARS/FLAWS
immagrate, immigrate/ emigrate
immanence,cy,nt, WITHIN, INTRINSIC (or see eminence/imminence)
immanent,tly, WITHIN, INTRINSIC (or see eminent/imminent)
immaterial,lly,lity,lism,lize,lizes,lized, lizing, NO IMPORTANT/ USEFUL FOR THE SITUATION
immature,ely,eness,rity, NOT OLD ENOUGH/MATURE/GROWN, FOOLISH
immeasurable,ly,bility, NOT ABLE TO MEASURE
immediate,ely,eness, RIGHT NOW
immense,ely,eness, GREAT IN SIZE, HUGE, VAST
immensurable,ely,bility,eness, IMPOSSIBLE TO MEASURE HOW VAST IT IS
immerchen, immerse(sion)
immerse,es,ed,sing,sion,sionist,sionism, sible, SINK INTO LIQUID/THOUGHT/ACTIVITY (or see emerse)
immershen, immerse(sion)
immersible, CAN BE SUBMERGED INTO LIQUID
immeterial, immaterial
immigrant,*, LEFT YOUR COUNTRY PERMANENTLY TO LIVE IN ANOTHER COUNTRY (or see emigrant) "prefixes: non"
immigrate,*,ed,ting,ant,tion,tioner, GOING TO ANOTHER COUNTRY (or see emigrate)
imminence,cy,nt,ntly, COULD POTENTIALLY HAPPEN (or see eminence/immanence)
imminent,tly,ncy, IT WILL HAPPEN NO MATTER HOW LONG IT TAKES, INEVITABLE (or see eminent/immanent)
immobile,lize,lizes,lized,lizing,lization, lizer,lity,lism, NOT ABLE TO MOVE/BE MOVED
immoral,lly,lity,lities,list, NOT PROPER/MORAL/ DECENT

immortal,lly,lity,lize,lizes,lized,lizing, lization, EXISTS FROM NOW ON, NEVER ENDING
immpresion, impression
immpresive, impressive
immune,nity,nities,nize, FREE FROM, EXEMPT, HEALTHY
immunize,*,ed,zing,er,zation, PHARMACEUTICALS INTRODUCED INTO THE BODY TO FIGHT MICRO ORGANISMS WHICH MAY/MAY NOT INVADE BODY
immurshen, immerse(sion)
immursion, immerse(sion)
imobile, immobile
imochen, emotion
imochun, emotion
imonate, emanate
imople, immobile
imoral, immoral
imorchen, immerse(sion)
imordle, immortal
imorshen, immerse(sion)
imortaledy, immortal(ity)
imortality, immortal(ity)
imorul, immoral
imoterial, immaterial
imownt, amount
impact,*,ted,ting,tion,tive, TWO BODIES OF MASS COLLIDING INTO ONE ANOTHER, SIZEABLE EFFECT
impair,*,red,ring,rer,rment, MAKE WORSE "prefixes: un"
impar, empower
imparer, emperor
imparical, empirical
imparment, empower(ment)
imparutev, imperative
impashent, impatient
impatient,tly,nce, NOT PATIENT, UNABLE TO RELAX
impaurment, empower(ment)
impeach,hes,hed,hing,her,hable,hment, CHARGE WITH CRIME/MISDEMEANOR "prefixes: un"
impeachuis, impetuous
impeccable,ly,bility, NO FLAWS/MISTAKES
impech, impeach
impechuous, impetuous
impede,*,ed,ding,er, DELAY/OBSTRUCT "prefixes: un"
impeed, impede
imper, impair

imperative,*,val,ely,eness, ABSOLUTELY ESSENTIAL, NECESSARY
imperfect,tly,tness,tion,tive,tiveness, NOT AS GOOD AS COULD BE
imperor, emperor
impersonal,lly,lity,lize,lizes,lized,lizing, ate, NOT ATTACHED IN A PERSONAL WAY, ABSENCE OF PERSONAL FEELINGS
impersonate,*,ed,ting,tion,tor,al, ACT/BEHAVE LIKE SOMEONE ELSE
impetuous,sly,sness,osity,osities, ACT/BEHAVE ON THE SPUR OF THE MOMENT
imphasis, emphasis / emphasize
impire, empire
impirical, empirical
implamint, implement
implant,*,ted,ting,tation, TO INSTILL IDEAS OR THOUGHTS, REPLACE BODY ORGAN WITH ANOTHER ONE
implecate, implicate
implement,*,ted,ting,tal,ter,tation, SOMETHING USED AS A TOOL, TO INCORPORATE INTO
implicate,*,ed,ting,tion,tional,tive,tively, BE TANGLED/INVOLVED IN, SUSPECTED PARTICIPATION
imploe, employee / employ
imploer, employer
imploy, employ / employee
imployer, employer
implucate, implicate
implucation, implicate(tion)
implument, implement
imply,lies,lied,ying,lication, SUGGEST SOMETHING/SOMEONE IS RESPONSIBLE
impolite,ely,eness, RUDE/FRANK/IMPERSONAL/HONEST
impols, impulse
impolsive, impulse(sive)
import,*,ted,ting,tation,table,tability, BRING INTO THE COUNTRY FROM ANOTHER COUNTRY
important,tly,nce, PRIORITY, MUST BE TENDED TO "prefixes: un"
impose,*,ed,sing,sition, TO INTERRUPT, SUGGESTED REFERENCE, UNWELCOME INCLUSION
imposebul, impossible
impossible,ly,bility, NOT POSSIBLE, COULD NEVER HAPPEN

imposter,*, UNWELCOME INCLUSION, BE WHERE ONE IS NOT WANTED, ILLEGITIMATE
impound,*,ded,ding, TAKE AWAY/ CONFISCATE/HOLD LAWFULLY
impour, empower
impourment, empower(ment)
impourtens, important(nce)
impourtent, important
impoverish,hed,her,hment, MARGINALIZED, UNABLE TO ADEQUATELY SUPPORT ONESELF
impovuresh, impoverish
impowerment, empower(ment)
impoze, impose
impractical,able,ability,ableness, NOT PRACTICAL/LOGICAL FOR SITUATION
impraktecle, impractical
imprasev, impressive
imprashen, impression
imprechen, impression
imprecise,ely,eness,sion, NOT PRECISE/FACTUAL
impregnable,bility,ly, NOT ABLE TO PENETRATE/GET INTO MOVE
impregnate,*,ed,ting,tion,tor,able, TO INTRODUCE/INJECT INTO, MAKE PREGNANT, INFUSE
impregnuble, impregnable
imprent, imprint
impresef, impressive
impreshen, impression
impresif, impressive
impresion, impression
impress,sses,ssed,ssing,ssion,ssive, ssivley,ssible,ssibly,ssibility, ssibilities,ssibleness,ssment, FAVORABLY AFFECTED "prefixes: over/re/un"
impression,*,nable,nability,nableness, nist,nistic,nism,ive, FAVORABLY AFFECTED, PRESSED/MOLDED/ EMBOSSED INTO "prefixes: re/un"
impressive,ely,eness, FAVORABLY AFFECTED "prefixes: re/un"
impretion, impression
imprint,*,ted,ting,ter, PRINT/STAMP INTO, TO LODGE/INSTILL INTO MEMORY
imprison,*,ned,ning,nment, PLACE INTO PRISON, CONFINE, INCARCERATE

improbable,ly,bility, HIGHLY UNLIKELY, NOT NORMALLY POSSIBLE, MOST LIKELY NOT
improbabol, improbable
improf, improve
impromptu, OFF THE TOP OF YOUR HEAD, SPUR OF THE MOMENT IDEA
impropar, improper
improper,rly,rness, NOT PROPER/ ACCEPTABLE
impropuble, improbable
improve,*,ed,ving,er,ement,vable, vability, MAKE BETTER THAN BEFORE, TOWARDS PERFECTION "prefixes: over/un"
improvise,*,ed,sing,er,sation,sational, sator,satorial, MAKE IT UP AS YOU GO, IMPROMPTU
improvusashen, improvise(sation)
impruf, improve
impte, empty
impulite, impolite
impulse,*,sion,sive,sively,siveness, SUDDEN ACT/MOVEMENT WITHOUT APPARENT THOUGHT
impurer, emperor
impurfekt, imperfect
impursenate, impersonate
impursonal, impersonal
impursonation, impersonate(tion)
impuseshen, impose(sition)
imput, input
imruld, emerald
imte, empty
imug, image
imugrant, immigrant / emigrant
imugrashen, immigrate(tion) / emigrate(tion)
imugrate, immigrate
imugrent, immigrant / emigrant
imuj, image
imun, immune
imunent, eminent / imminent / immanent
imunezashen, immunize(zation)
imunezation, immunize(zation)
imunise, immunize
imunity, immune(nity)
imunize, immunize
imurchen, immerse(sion)
imurgency, emergency
imursable, immersible
imurse, immerse / emersed
imurshen, immerse(sion)

imurtalety, immortal(ity)
imutashin, imitate(tion)
imutation, imitate(tion)
imuterial, immaterial
in, CONTAINED/BELONGS WITHIN, CONFINED,ENTER, PREFIX INDICATING "NOT" MOST OFTEN MODIFIES THE WORD (or see inn/en)
in-law,*, PEOPLE RELATED BY MARRIAGE
inabel, enable / unable
inability,ties, UNABLE, NOT ABLE TO, WITHOUT CAPACITY TO
inabishen, inhibit(ion)
inable, enable / unable
inabler, enable(r)
inabul, enable / unable
inaccessible,bility,eness,ly, CANNOT BE OBTAINED, UNREACHABLE, NO ACCESS
inaccurate,ely,eness,acy,acies, NOT CORRECT/FACTUAL/ACCURATE
inacsesable, inaccessible
inact, enact
inaction,*, NO ACTION, IDLE
inactive,ely,eness,vity,vate, NO ACTION, IDLE (or see enact(ive))
inaculation, inoculate(tion)
inacurate, inaccurate
inadequate,ely,eness,acy,acies, NOT ENOUGH, INADEQUATE, LACKING
inadmissible,bility,bly, NOT ALLOWED TO ENTER, NOT ADMISSABLE
inadvertent,tly,nce,ncy,ncies, NOT PAYING ATTENTION, NOT DIRECT/ STRAIGHTFORWARD
inadvisable,bility, ADVISE/ RECOMMEND AGAINST, BEST NOT TO DO/SAY SOMETHING
inakd, enact
inakshen, inaction
inaktif, enact(ive) / inactive
inakulation, inoculate(tion)
inaleable, inalienable
inaleuble, inalienable
inalienable,ly,bility, CANNOT TAKE AWAY
inalisis, analysis
inamel, enamel
inamet, intimate
inamul, enamel

inanimate,ely,eness, NOT ANIMATE, USUALLY AN OBJECT WHICH DOESN'T ACT/MOVE
inaple, enable / unable
inappreciative,able,ably, NOT APPRECIATED, ACTIONS NOT REGARDED AS USEFUL/NECESSARY (also unappreciative)
inapproachable, NOT ACCESSIBLE/ APPROACHABLE, UNREACHABLE
inappropriate,ely,eness, NOT PROPER/ APPROPRIATE/ACCEPTABLE AT THE MOMENT
inapul, enable / unable
inaqulate, inoculate
inaqurite, inaccurate
inarferins, interfere(nce)
inasinse, innocence
inate, innate
inatequit, inadequate
inatible, inaudible
inatly, innate(ly)
inatmisable, inadmissible
inatvertense, inadvertent
inatvizable, inadvisable
inatvurtent, inadvertent
inaudible,ly,bility, NOT ABLE TO HEAR, NOT AUDIBLE, CAN'T BE HEARD
inaugurate,*,ed,ting,tion,tor,al, FORMALLY INSTALL/BEGIN, ADDRESS TO THE PUBLIC
inaukulate, inoculate
inbankment, embankment
inbaris, embarrass
inbark, embark
inbasee, embassy
inbed, embed
inberis, embarrass
inbet, embed
inblem, emblem
inblum, emblem
inboard,*, BOAT WITH MOTOR/ENGINE INSIDE
inbord, inboard
inbosd, emboss(ed)
inboss, emboss
inbrase, embrace
inbreo, embryo
inbrorder, embroider
incadesent, incandescent
incamped, encamp(ed)
incampment, encamp(ment)

incandescent,tly,nce, A BULB TYPE WITH A FILAMENT THAT HEATS UP, BRIGHT/SHINING LITE
incantashen, incantation
incantation,*,nal,tory, SPELLS/CHANTS FOR MAGIC
incapable,ly,eness,bility, NOT CAPABLE/ ABLE TO, DON'T HAVE WHAT IT TAKES TO ACCOMPLISH
incapacitate,*,ed,ting,tion, OUT OF ORDER, UNABLE TO FUNCTION AS USUAL, LACKING POWER TO
incapacity,ties, NOT ABLE EITHER PHYSICALLY/MENTALLY TO PERFORM TASKS WELL
incarcerate,*,ed,ting,tion, SENTENCED TO CONFINEMENT
incarnate,*,ed,ting,tion, TAKE ON PHYSICAL FORM "prefixes: re"
incarserate, incarcerate
incase, encase
incast, encase(d)
incendiary,ries, ABLE TO CREATE FIRE, CIVIL UNREST
incense,ed,sing, AROMATIC PRESSED POWDER FOR BURNING
incentive,*,vize,vizes,vized,vizing, A MOTIVATION FOR PERFORMING A TASK "prefixes: dis"
incenurate, incinerate
incepshen, incept(ion)
incept,tor,tion,tive,tively, FROM THE BEGINNING, MOMENT OF CREATION
incercl, encircle
incerense, insure(rance)
incerkl, encircle
incesant, incessant
incessant,ncy,tly, CONTINUE WITHOUT STOPPING
incest,tuous,tuously,tuousness, SEX AMONGST THE FAMILY IF RELATED BY BLOOD
inch,hes,hed,hing, A U.S. MEASUREMENT
inchant, enchant
inchantmint, enchant(ment)
incher, ensure / insure / injure
inchoy, enjoy
inchur, ensure / insure / injure
incide, incite/ inside
incident,*,nce,ntal,ntally, HAPPENING ATTACHED TO A LARGER EVENT, DISTINCT BUT SEEMINGLY MINOR

incindiary, incendiary
incinerate,*,ed,ting,tor,tion, TO BURN, COOKS TO ASHES WITH FIRE
incircle, encircle
incise,*,ed,sing,sor,sion, CUT/CARVE INTO
incision,*,nal,ned, MAKE A CUT INTO
incist, insist
incite,*,ed,ting,tation,ement,er, TO ROUSE/SPUR/PROVOKE TO ACT/ REBEL (or see inside/insight)
incline,*,ed,ning,nation, A GRADUALLY ELEVATED PLANE, TO GO UP, MOST LIKELY TO "prefixes: dis"
inclood, include
inclose, enclose
incloser, enclose(sure)
inclosment, enclose(ment)
inclozur, enclose(sure)
include,*,ed,ding,usion,usive,usively, usiveness,dible,dable, ADD/ INVOLVE SOMETHING INTO GROUP OF OTHER THINGS
inclusef, inclusive
inclushen, include(usion)
inclusion,*,ive, ADD/INVOLVE SOMETHING INTO GROUP OF OTHER THINGS
inclusive,ely,eness, ADD/INVOLVE SOMETHING INTO GROUP OF OTHER THINGS
incognedo, incognito
incognito,*, DISGUISED TO BE UNRECOGNIZABLE
incoherent,tly,nce,ncy,ncies, UNABLE TO COMPREHEND UNDERSTAND, CANNOT COMMUNICATE LOGICALLY/ UNDERSTANDABLE
incokneto, incognito
incomber, encumber
incombutent, incompetent
income,*,ming, MONEY COMING IN
incommode,*,ed,ding,dious,diously, DISTURB SOMEONE BY HAVING THEM CATER TO YOUR NEEDS UNNECESSARILY
incomode, incommode
incomodious, incommode(dious)
incomparable,bility,bly, NOTHING TO COMPARE TO
incompas, encompass
incompatible,bility,eness,ly, NOT ABLE TO GET ALONG WITH, TOO MANY DIFFERENCES

incompetent,tly,nce,ncy, NOT ABLE TO COMPETE/KEEP UP, LACKS QUALIFICATIONS
incomplete,*,ely,eness,etion, NOT COMPLETE, NEEDS MORE TO FINISH
incompruble, incomparable
inconclusive,ely,eness, NO FINAL RESULTS, NO CERTAIN ANSWERS
inconsiderate,ely,eness,tion,ably, ableness, NOT CONCERNED WITH SOMEONE'S EMOTIONAL REACTION OR WELL BEING
inconsistent,tly,ncy,ncies, DOESN'T PERFORM STEADILY/PREDICTABLY
incontinent,nce,tly, NOT ABLE TO CONTAIN/CONTROL ONESELF
inconvenient,tly,nce,ncy,ncies, DOESN'T FIT INTO THE PLAN CAUSING DELAY OF FINISHING, NOT ON THE WAY THERE, UNPLANNED
incorect, incorrect
incoriguble, incorrigible
incorporate,*,ed,ting,tion,tive,tor,able, TO INCLUDE INTO THE WORKINGS OF, BROUGHT INTO A LARGER BODY, UNITE, COMBINE "prefixes: dis/un"
incorrect,tly,tness, NOT EXACT/FACTUAL/SUITABLE
incorrigible,ly,bility,eness, NOT ABLE TO BE CORRECTED/REFORMED TO MEET EXPECTED STANDARDS
incorugible, incorrigible
incounter, encounter
incownter, encounter
increase,*,ed,sing,singly,sable, TO MAKE MORE THAN THERE WAS, ADD MORE
incredible,ly,lity,eness, ASTONISHING, BEYOND EXPECTATION
incredulous,sly,sness, CROSS BETWEEN INCREDIBLE AND RIDICULOUS
incremenate, incriminate
increment,*,tal,tally, MOVE EXACT AMOUNT IN ONE DIRECTION, INCREASE
incriminate,*,ed,ting,tion, TO ACCUSE OR LEND SUSPICION, CHARGE WITH A CRIME
incroach, encroach
incrochment, encroach(ment)
incruments, increment(s)
incrust, encrust

incubate,*,ed,ting,tion,tional,tive,tor, TO PROTECT AN EGG IN PERFECT ENVIRONMENT FOR EMBRYO TO GROW INTO FULL FORM
incumbent,*,ntly,ncy,ncies, FILL A POST OR OFFICE
incumber, encumber
incumode, incommode
incumpatuble, incompatible
incunklusef, inconclusive
incunsideret, inconsiderate
incunsistent, inconsistent
incupasitate, incapacitate
incur,*,rred,rring,rrable, LIABLE FOR, ADDED DEBT IN ORIGINAL LOAN
incurable,ly,bility,eness, SEEMINGLY UNABLE TO CURE, EXTREMELY DIFFICULT TO HEAL
incureg, encourage / anchor(age)
incurekt, incorrect
incurig, encourage / anchor(age)
ind, and / end
indanger, endanger
indangurment, endanger(ment)
indanjer, endanger
indapendense, independent(nce)
indasishen, indecision
indau, endow
indaument, endow(ment)
indaveguel, individual
indavishual, individual
indebted,dness, OWE SOMETHING TO SOMEONE
indecent,ncy,ncies,ntly, NOT ACCEPTABLE BY SOCIETY'S STANDARDS
indecision, NOT ABLE TO BE FIRM IN MAKING A CHOICE
indecisive,eness,ely, NOT ABLE TO MAKE A FIRM CHOICE
inded, end(ed)
indeded, indebted
indedud, indebted
indeed, CERTAINLY, CONFIRMATION
indefer, endeavor
indeferent, indifferent
indefinite,ely,eness, WITH NO END OR FINAL GOAL, NOT DEFINED
indefur, endeavor
indefurent, indifferent
indego, indigo
indekat, indicate
indeks, index
indeleble, indelible

indelible,bility,ly, HARD TO REMOVE, NEARLY PERMANENT
indemafy, indemnify
indemic, endemic
indemnify,fies,fied,fying,fication,fier, COMPENSATE/REIMBURSE FOR LOSS
indent,*,ted,ting,tation, A DENT IN SOMETHING, DIFFERENT DEPTH FROM REST OF THE SURFACE
independent,*,tly,nce,ncy,ncies, ABLE TO STAND PRIMARILY ON ITS OWN, NOT DEPENDENT
inder, inter / enter
indermetant, intermittent
indesent, indecent
indeted, indebted
indever, endeavor
index,xes,dices,xed,xing,xical, TO CATEGORIZE, DIVIDE INTO GROUPS, PROVIDE A NAME FOR EASY RETRIEVAL "prefixes: sub"
indicate,*,ed,ting,tion,tive,tively,tor, tory, GIVE A SIGN TOWARDS A DIRECTION, PROVIDES INFORMATION, HELPS IN FIGURING ANSWER "prefixes: contra"
indicater, indicate(tor)
indict,*,ted,ting,table,ter,tor,tment, CHARGE WITH A CRIME ("C" IS SILENT)
indifferent,tly,nce, NOT PARTIAL OR CONCERNED WITH CHOICES/ACT/EVENT
indifrent, indifferent
indigenous, ORIGINAL TO THE LAND, NATIVE
indigo,*, DEEP BLUE COLOR, COLOR FROM A PLANT
indikate, indicate
indimec, endemic
indintashen, indent(ation)
indirmetant, intermittent
indite, indict
individual,*,lly,lism,lity,lize,lities,ization, ate, ON ITS OWN, DOESN'T BELONG TO A GROUP
indlis, endless
indoctrinate,*,ed,ting,tion,tor, FORCED TEACHING PRINCIPLES/IDEOLOGY TO ELIMINATE CREATIVE THINKING
indoer, endure
indoor,*, INSIDE A STRUCTURE/DWELLING

indoose, induce
indor, endure / indoor
indormetant, intermittent
indorse, endorse / indoor(s)
indorsment, endorse(ment)
indostry, industry
indou, endow
indoument, endow(ment)
indow, endow
indowment, endow(ment)
indrakit, intricate
indubitable,ly,bility, BEYOHND A DOUBT
inducate, indicate
induce,*,ed,cing,ement,er,cible, BRING ON, START/MAKE HAPPEN
induckshen, induct(ion)
inducktor, induct(or)
induct,*,ted,ting,tee,tance,tion,tional, tive,tively,tiveness,tor, ELECTRIC CURRENT CHANGE, BE ENLISTED, TERM IN PHYSICS/MILITARY/ EMBRYOLOGY/CHEMISTRY/ MATHEMATICS
indukshen, induct(ion)
induktor, induct(or)
indulge,*,ed,ging,gingly,ger,gence, gencies,gent,gently, TO AFFORD ONESELF A DESIRE, SATISFY AN IMPULSE "prefixes: over"
indur, inter / enter / endure
indurmitant, intermittent
induseshin, indecision
industrial,lly,list,lness,lism,lize,lized, lizing,lization, PRODUCTIVE, MANUFACTURES "prefixes: re"
industry,ries,rious,riously,rial, MACHINE/TECHNOLOGY/ MANUFACTURING "prefixes: re"
induvijual, individual
inebriate,*,ed,ting,tion,iety, DRUNK/ INTOXICATED
ineckwitable, inequitable
inecwity, inequity
inedible,ly, CANNOT OR SHOULD NOT EAT
inegma, enigma / enema
inekspensef, inexpensive
inekwality, inequality
inekwitable, inequitable
inekwity, inequity
inema, enema / anemia
inemut, intimate
inendashen, inundate(tion)

inendate, inundate
inengs, inning(s)
inept,tly,tness,titude, UNABLE, INCOMPETENT
inequality,ties, NOT EQUAL, DIFFERENCES EXIST
inequitable,ly,ty, NOT EQUAL, DIFFERENCES EXIST
inequity,ties, NOT FAIR/JUST/EQUAL
iner, inner / inter / enter
ineract, interact
inerchange, interchange
inercom, intercom
inerconnect, interconnect
inercors, intercourse
inerem, interim
inerferins, interfere(nce)
inerge, energy
inergetek, energetic
inerject, interject
inerjetek, energetic
inerkorse, intercourse
inerlock, interlock
inerlude, interlude
inermedeary, intermediary
inermingle, intermingle
inermishen, intermission
inermission, intermission
inermost, innermost
inernashenul, international
inernational, international
inernet, internet
inerrelate, interrelate
inersculastic, interscholastic
inersect, intersect
inersection, intersection
inerseksheh, intersection
inersperse, intersperse
inert,tly,tness, VISIBLY INACTIVE, NO APPARENT ACTION/MOVEMENT
inertwine, intertwine
inerupt, interrupt
inervene, intervene
inerview, interview
inervol, interval
inervue, interview
inervul, interval
inerwoven, interwoven
inescapable,ly,bility,bilities, CANNOT ESCAPE
inesent, innocence(nt)
inesheashen, initiate(tion)
ineshul, initial
inesince, innocence

inesthesia, anesthesia
inetiale, initial(lly)
inetuble, inedible
inetvizable, inadvisable
inevitable,bility,eness,ly, CANNOT AVOID
inexcesable, inaccessible
inexpensive,ely,eness, FAIR PRICE, NOT EXPENSIVE
inexperience,ed, DOESN'T HAVE SKILLS TO PERFORM
infachuashen, infatuate(tion)
infachuate, infatuate
infadek, emphatic
infallible,lity,eness,ly, FOR CERTAIN
infaluble, infallible
infant,*,ncy,ncies,thood,tlike, BABIES UP TO ONE YEAR OLD
infantry,ries,ymen, FOOT SOLDIERS
infasis, emphasis / emphasize
infatashen, invitation
infatik, emphatic
infatuate,ed,tion,edly, INSTANTLY ATTRACTED FOR BRIEF PERIOD OF TIME
infect,*,ted,ting,tion,tive,tor,tious, TO POLLUTE AN AREA "prefixes: dis/ retro"
infekshus, infect(ious)
infenatively, infinite(tively)
infent, infant
infentry, infantry
inferior,rity,rly,rity, LESSER THAN ANOTHER, NOT SUPERIOR
infermashen, inform(ation)
infermation, information
infermury, infirmary
infest,*,ed,ting,tation, THREATENINGLY OVERWHELM "prefixes: re"
infeureate, infuriate
infiltrate,*,ed,ting,tion,tive, PASS BEYOND BORDERS OF A SPACE WHERE UNINVITED
infinite,ely,eness,tude,tive,tival,tively,ty, ties, GOES ON AND ON PERHAPS FOREVER
infirmary,ries, SITE FOR MEDICAL CARE
infirmashen, information
infistructure, infrastructure
infite, invite
inflagingly, unflagging(ly)
inflame,*,ed,ming,er,mmable, mmability,mmation,mmatory, mmatorily, TO PROVOKE/INTENSIFY

ANGER/STRONG EMOTIONS, SWOLLEN TISSUE
inflammation,*, SWOLLEN TISSUE
inflapable, unflappable
inflashen, inflate(tion)
inflate,*,ed,ting,tion,tionism,tionist, table, TO AIR UP, RAISE, EXPAND/ INCREASE "prefixes: dis"
inflection,*,nal,nally,nless, CHANGE IN FORM/SOUND/SHAPE
inflekshen, inflection
infleksuble, inflexible
inflemashen, inflammation
inflewance, influence
inflexible,bility,eness,ly, WON'T BEND, STUBBORN, NOT FLEXIBLE
inflextion, inflection
inflict,*,ted,ting,tion,tor,tive, TO CAUSE PAIN, TO BRING ABOUT PUNISHMENT
inflimation, inflammation
influence,*,ed,cing,eable,er,ntial,ntially, TO IMPRESS/EXERT UPON, ONE WHO IMPRESSES OTHERS, AUTHORITY, POSITION OF POWER
inform,*,med,ming,mation,mer,mative, matively,mativeness, matory,mant, OFFER ADVICE/FACTS "prefixes: dis/un"
informal,lly,lity, NOT FORMAL, RELAXED/UNRESTRICTED
informant,*, SOMEONE WHO PROVIDES INFORMATION TO HIGHER AUTHORITY
information,nal, COLLECTION OF DATA "prefixes: dis/mis"
inforse, enforce
infotation, invitation
infra, PREFIX INDICATING "BENEATH" MOST OFTEN MODIFIES THE WORD
infraction,*, BREAK A RULE/LAW/ CONTRACT
infrared, A LASER TYPE, A LEVEL OF FREQUENCY NEAR THE COLOR RED
infrastructure, SKELETAL/FOUNDATION OF
infrenge, infringe
infrenj, infringe
infrequent,tly,ncy, OCCASIONALLY
infringe,*,ed,ging,er,ement, UNLAWFULLY OCCUPY/ DISREGARD SOMEONE'S BOUNDARIES
infugen, infuse(sion)
infultrate, infiltrate

infunently, infinite(ly)
infunit, infinite
infunsy, infant(ncy)
infunt, infant
infuntry, infantry
infuriate,*,ed,ting,tingly,tion,ely, ENRAGE, FURIOUSLY ANGRY
infurmation, inform(ation)
infurmery, infirmary
infuse,*,ed,sing,sibility,sible,sive,er, LIQUID INTRODUCED/INJECTED INTO ANOTHER LIQUID
infustashen, infest(ation)
infustrukture, infrastructure
infutashen, invitation
ingage, engage
ingaje, engage
ingalate, ungulate
inganuity, ingenuity
ingection, inject(ion)
ingekt, inject
ingen, engine
ingeneer, engineer
ingenious,sly,sness, ESPECIALLY CREATIVE IN PERSPECTIVE/IDEAS (or see ingenuous) "prefixes: dis"
ingenuity,ties, ABLE TO USE CREATIVE IMAGINATION "prefixes: dis"
ingenuous,sly,sness, GENUINELY HONEST/DIRECT/NAIVE/ TRUSTING (or see ingenious) "prefixes: dis"
inger, injure
ingery, injure(ry)
ingest,*,ted,ting,tive,tion, TO SWALLOW, SWALLOWED THROUGH THE MOUTH
inginuity, ingenuity
ingoeuble, enjoy(able)
ingolf, engulf
ingot,*, MASS OR CHUNK OF METAL
ingoy, enjoy
ingrafe, engrave
ingrain,*,ned,ning, ROUTED INTO, CARVED INTO, DEEPLY IMPRESSED WITHIN
ingrave, engrave
ingredient,*, VARIETY OF ELEMENTS COMBINED TO MAKE SOMETHING ELSE
ingulate, ungulate
ingulf, engulf
ingun, engine
inguneer, engineer
ingury, injure(ry)

ingustes, injustice
inhabetent, inhabit(ant)
inhabit,*,ted,ting,tation,table,tant, tancy,tancies, TO OCCUPY, LIVE IN "prefixes: un"
inhalant,*, A DEVICE FOR BREATHING IN MEDICINE
inhalashin, inhale(lation)
inhale,*,ed,ling,lation,lational,er,lator, BREATH IN
inhanse, enhance
inharent, inherent
inharet, inherit
inharitance, inherit(ance)
inharmonic,ious,iously,iousness,icity, icities,ny, TONES NOT PEAKING TOGETHER, FREQUENCY NOT SYNCHRONIZED or see enharmonic)
inherent,tly, BELONGS AS PART OF THE WHOLE, INSEPARABLE
inherit,*,ted,ting,tor,tress,table,tability, tableness,tance, GOODS AND MONEY RECEIVED WHEN SOMEONE DIES "prefixes: dis"
inhewmane, inhumane
inhibit,*,ted,ting,tor,tory,tive,ter,tion, KEEP BACK/RESTRAINED, TIMID/ SLOW TO ACT "prefixes: dis/un"
inhormonic, inharmonic / enharmonic
inhosbitable, inhospitable
inhospitable,eness,ly,ality,alities, NOT TREATED WARMLY/ FRIENDLY/ GENEROUSLY
inhubeshen, inhibit(ion)
inhulashen, inhale(lation)
inhumane,ely, CRUEL
inigma, enigma / enema
inima, enema / anemia
inime, enemy / enema
inimet, intimate
inimutle, intimate(ly)
ining, inning
iniquity,ties,tous,tously,tousness, COMPLETELY LACKS MORALITY/ JUSTICE/FAIRNESS
inisheation, initiate(tion)
inishul, initial
initial,*,led,ling,lly,lize,lizes,lized,lizing, lizer,lism, ORIGINALLY, THE BEGINNING, THE FIRST
initiate,*,ed,ting,tion,tive,tor,tory, BREAK INTO NEW KNOWLEDGE, BEGIN SOMETHING NEW "prefixes: un"

inje, inch
inject,*,ted,ting,tion,table,tive,tor, INSERT SOMETHING INTO SOMETHING ELSE
injekshen, inject(ion)
injelate, ungulate
injen, engine
injeneer, engineer
injeneus, ingenious
injenuidy, ingenuity
injenuous, ingenuous
injenyus, ingenuous
injest, ingest
injin, engine
injineer, engineer
injoy, enjoy
injoymint, enjoy(ment)
injoyuble, enjoy(able)
injulate, ungulate
injun, engine
injunction,*, COURT ORDER TO ACT
injure,*,ed,ring,ry,rious,riously, riousness,rer, DAMAGE, OFFEND, VIOLATE ANOTHER'S RIGHTS "prefixes: un"
injustice,*, NOT PLAYING FAIRLY, SOMEONE'S RIGHTS VIOLATED
ink,*,king,ky,kier,kiest, FLUID USED IN A PEN
inkabuble, incapable
inkadesent, incandescent
inkamped, encamp(ed)
inkampment, encamp(ment)
inkantashen, incantation
inkantation, incantation
inkarsurate, incarcerate
inkase, encase
inkast, encase(d)
inker, incur
inkerej, encourage / anchor(age)
inkewbate, incubate
inkline, incline
inkling, A FEELING/HINT/IDEA
inklood, include
inkloshur, enclose(sure)
inkloze, enclose
inklud, include
inklusev, inclusive
inkognito, incognito
inkomber, encumber
inkomodeus, incommode(dious)
inkompruble, incomparable
inkompus, encompass
inkonsistent, inconsistent

inkoreg, encourage / anchor(age)
inkoreguble, incorrigible
inkorpurate, incorporate
inkownter, encounter
inkreduble, incredible
inkredulus, incredulous
inkreese, increase
inkroach, encroach
inkrochment, encroach(ment)
inkrument, increment
inkrust, encrust
inkum, income
inkumbent, incumbent
inkumber, encumber
inkumblete, incomplete
inkumodeus, incommode(dious)
inkumpatuble, incompatible
inkumplete, incomplete
inkumpus, encompass
inkunsiduret, inconsiderate
inkunvenyunt, inconvenient
inkupacity, incapacity
inkurect, incorrect
inkwesishun, inquisition
inkwesutev, inquisitive
inkwire, inquire(ry)
inkwisative, inquisitive
inland,der, AWAY FROM THE SEA
inlarge, enlarge
inlargmint, enlarge(ment)
inlarje, enlarge
inles, unless
inlest, enlist
inlet,*,ting, RECESS BETWEEN LAND/ WATER, INSERTED
inlist, enlist
inliten, enlighten
inlund, inland
inmachure, immature
inmate,*, ONE CONFINED TO PRISON/ JAIL
inmature, immature
inmertaledy, immortal(ity)
inmortalidy, immortal(ity)
inn,*, A DWELLING TO SLEEP FOR THE NIGHT
innacurate, inaccurate
innate,ely,eness, BELONGS WITH THE BODY
inner,rly, TOWARDS THE CENTER (or see inter)
innerchange, interchange
innerlock, interlock
innerlude, interlude

innermingle, intermingle
innermission, intermission
innermost, DIRECTLY IN THE CENTER
innernational, international
innernet, internet
innerscolastic, interscholastic
innertwine, intertwine
innervene, intervene
inning,*, A SECTION OF PLAY IN A GAME OF SPORTS
innocence,cy,cies,nt, FREE FROM ULTERIOR MOTIVES
innocent,tly, FREE FROM ULTERIOR MOTIVES
innovate,tive,tion,tor,tory, IMPROVE SYSTEM WITH NEW CREATIVE IDEA INSTILLING CHANGE
innuendo,*, UNOBVIOUS/INDIRECT HINT OR MEANING
inoberable, inoperable
inoburatef, inoperable(ative)
inocent, innocence(nt)
inocreate, inaugurate
inoculate,*,ed,ting,able,ability,ation, ative,ator,lum,ant, TO INJECT A PATHOGEN
inoduble, inaudible
inof, enough
inogerashen, inaugurate(tion)
inogerate, inaugurate
inogeration, inaugurate(tion)
inogurate, inaugurate
inokewlate, inoculate
inokewlent, inoculate(ant)
inokulation, inoculate(tion)
inonemus, anonymous
inonseate, enunciate
inoperable,bly,bility,bleness,ative, ativeness, WILL NOT OPERATE
inopportune,ely,eness,nity, NOT THE BEST TIME TO ENSURE SUCCESS
inopurtune, inopportune
inoqulashen, inoculate(tion)
inoqulent, inoculate(ant)
inordinate,acy,ely,eness, EXCESSIVE WITHOUT RESTRAINT/CONTROL
inordunet, inordinate
inorge, energy
inorgetek, energetic
inormis, enormous
inormus, enormous
inorsect, intersect
inosense, innocence
inotable, inaudible

inougeration, inaugurate(tion)
inovadef, innovate(tive)
inovative, innovate(tive)
inownse, announce
inpar, impair
inpashent, impatient
inpatient,*, VISITS HOSPITAL FOR TREATEMENT (or see impatient)
inpech, impeach
inpecuble, impeccable
inpersonashen, impersonate(tion)
inpersonate, impersonate
inplie, imply
inpolite, impolite
inpolse, impulse
inport, import
inportant, important
inpose, impose
inposebul, impossible
inposition, impose(sition)
inpossible, impossible
inposter, imposter
inpound, impound
inpoverish, impoverish
inpownd, impound
inpractical, impractical
inpragnuble, impregnable
inprasise, imprecise
inpravize, improvise
inprecise, imprecise
inpregnable, impregnable
inpregnate, impregnate
inpregnuble, impregnable
inprent, imprint
inpres, impress / empress
inpresion, impression
inpresive, impressive
inpreson, imprison
inprint, imprint
inprison, imprison
inprobuble, improbable
inpromptu, impromptu
inpromtu, impromptu
inpropable, improbable
inproper, improper
inprove, improve
inprovement, improve(ment)
inprovisation, improvise(sation)
inprovise, improvise
inprufment, improve(ment)
inpruve, improve
inpruvize, improvise
inpulse, impulse
inpulsive, impulse(sive)

input,*,tted,tting, ADD TO EXISTING INFORMATION
inquazishen, inquisition
inqubate, incubate
inquire,*,ed,ring,ringly,ry,ries,er, TO ASK OF, SEEK FURTHER INFORMATION
inquisition,nal,nist,tor, TAKE PEOPLE IN AGAINST THEIR WILL TO INTERROGATE THEM
inquisitive,ely,eness,tor, TO SEEK ANSWERS/KNOWLEDGE
inquisitor,rial,rially, TO INTERROGATE
inquizadive, inquisitive
inquizeshen, inquisition
inrage, enrage
inraj, enrage
inrech, enrich
inrich, enrich
inrol, enroll
inrolmint, enroll(ment)
inroot, enroute
inroute, enroute
inrut, enroute
insabordinate, insubordinate
insacure, insecure
insadent, incident
insafishent, insufficient
insakuredy, insecure(rity)
insalate, insulate
insalin, insulin
insane,ely,eness,nity,nities, THINK IN UNPOPULAR MODALITY, MENTAL HEALTH IN DOUBT
insanetation, insanitary(ation)
insanifekent, insignificant
insanitary,ation, UNCLEAN/ UNACCEPTABLE
insarektion, insurrection
insatiable,ly,bility,eness,ate, APPETITE FOR SOMETHING THAT CANNOT BE SATIATED/SATISFIED
insatiate,ely,eness, APPETITE FOR SOMETHING THAT CANNOT BE SATIATED/SATISFIED
insawyuble, insoluble
insayuble, insoluble
insbarashen, inspire(ration)
insbekable, unspeakable
insboken, unspoken
insburashen, inspire(ration)
inscribe,*,ed,bing,bable,ber, LEAVE A MARK BY ANY METHOD

inscription,*,nal,nless,ive,ively, LEAVING A MARK BY MANY METHODS
inseam,*, SEAM ON THE INSIDE OF PANTLEGS
insebordinate, insubordinate
insect,*, BUGS (or see incest)
insecticide,*,dal, CHEMICALS TO KILL BUGS
insecure,ely,rity,rities,eness, ILL AT EASE, NOT SECURE/COMFORTABLE WITH ENVIRONMENT
insedent, incident
insedius, insidious
insefficient, insufficient
insegnea, insignia
insegnifakent, insignificant
insejen, incision
insekt, insect
insektaside, insecticide
insekurety, insecure(rity)
inselate, insulate
inselation, insulate(tion)
inseminate,*,ed,ting,tion, INJECT SEMEN INTO
insen, ensign
insenarade, incinerate
insendiary, incendiary
insenea, insignia
insense, incense
insenseer, insincere
insensible,ly,eness,bility,bilities, NOT MAKING SENSE TO PERCEIVER, MISUNDERSTOOD
insensitive,eness,vity,ely, DOESN'T EASILY REACT TO SENSORY INPUT
insentive, incentive
insentuf, incentive
insenuashen, insinuate(tion)
insenuate, insinuate
inseparable,bility,bly, WILL NOT BE DISJOINTED OR TAKEN APART
insepshen, incept(ion)
insept, incept
inseption, incept(ion)
inserekshen, insurrection
inserkle, encircle
insermountable, insurmountable
insert,*,ted,ting,ter,tion,tional, PLACE INTO ALREADY EXISTING FORM OR METHODOLOGY
inseshun, incision
insest, insist / incest / encyst
insestent, insist(ent)

insh, inch
insher, ensure / insure
insherance, insure(rance)
inshree, entry / entree
inshurans, insure(rance)
inshure, insure
insice, incise
insicor, incise(sor)
insicure, insecure
inside,*,er, INTERIOR OF A FORM (or see insight/incite)
insident, incident
insidious,sly,sness, ILL INTENT DETECTABLE, MANIPULATE TO HARM WITHOUT BEING PERCEIVED AS SO
insidnea, insignia
insificient, insufficient
insigen, incision
insight,*,tful,tfully,tfulness, ABILITY TO PERCEIVE FUTURE OUTCOMES OF CURRENT EVENT (or see inside/incite)
insightation, incite(tation)
insightment, incite(ment)
insignia,*, BADGES/MEDALS OF HONOR/AUTHORITY IN MILITARY
insignificant,tly,nce, NOT SIGNIFICANT/ WORTHY TO CALCULATE IN, NOT IMPORTANT
insiklopedea, encyclopedia
insimanation, inseminate(tion)
insime, enzyme
insin, ensign
insinarate, incinerate
insincere,ely,rity,rities, NOT SINCERE/ TRUTHFUL
insinsative, insensitive
insinseer, insincere
insinsuble, insensible
insintuf, incentive
insinuate,*,ed,ting,tion,tive,tingly,tor, LEADING TOWARDS ACCUSATION, INDIRECTLY IMPLYING
insishen, incision
insisor, incise(sor)
insist,*,ted,ting,tingly,tent,tently,tence, tency, MUST HAVE/BE, ABSOLUTE (or see encyst)
insitation, incite(tation)
insite, inside / insight / incite
insiteful, insight(ful)
insitement, incite(ment)
insiteus, insidious

insition, incision
insize, incise
inskribe, inscribe
inskripshen, inscription
insoluble,bility,eness,bly, WILL NOT DISSOLVE IN LIQUID
insolvable, NOT ABLE TO BE SOLVED, NO ANSWER
insolvent,*,ncy, NOT ENOUGH FLUID CAPITAL TO GET OUT OF DEBT, CANNOT BE LIQUIDATED
insomnia,ac, PROBLEM SLEEPING
insovable, insolvable
insparation, inspire(ration)
inspect,*,ted,ting,tion,tive,tor,torate, toral,torial,torship, EXAMINE FOR FLAWS
inspekable, unspeakable
insperation, inspire(ration)
inspire,*,ed,ring,ringly,er,ration, rational,rator, EMPOWER, INSTILL FAITH/HOPE "prefixes: un"
inspoken, unspoken
instagate, instigate
install,*,lled,lling,llation,ller,llment, PUT SOMETHING/SOMEONE INTO A PLACE TO PERFORM A FUNCTION, MAKE A PAYMENT (or see instill) "prefixes: un"
instance,*,ed,cing, AN EXAMPLE/ MOMENT
instant,tly,taneous, IN A WINK, RIGHT AWAY
instantaneous,sly,sness, HAPPENED SO QUICKLY THAT TIME COULDN'T BE MEASURED
instatushen, institute(tion)
instatute, institute
instaul, install
instaulment, install(ment)
instead, IN PLACE OF, A SUBSTITUTE
instegate, instigate
instenked, instinct
instense, instance
instentaneusly, instantaneous(ly)
instetution, institute(tion)
instigate,*,ed,ting,tion,tive,tor, PROVOKE, STIR UP, INITIATE AN ACTION
instill,*,lled,lling,llation, INTRODUCE GRADUALLY (or see install)
instinct,*,tual,tive,tively,tiveness, KNOWINGNESS WE'RE ALL BORN WITH

instinse, instance
instintaneusly, instantaneous(ly)
institute,*,ed,ting,er,tion,tive, ESTABLISH TO WORK AS A GROUP, FORMAL PLACE OF LEARNING
institution,*,nal,nalism,nalist,nally, nalize,nalizes,nalized,nalizing, nalization, FORMAL PLACE OF LEARNING
instol, install
instolashen, install(ation)
instolment, install(ment)
instrament, instrument
instriment, instrument
instruct,*,ted,ting,tor,tion,tional,tive, tively,tiveness, PROVIDE KNOWLEDGE TO/FOR OTHERS "prefixes: un"
instrument,*,tal,tally,talist,talism,tality, tation, AN ITEM WHICH MEASURES OR FUNCTIONS AS A DEVICE TO HELP WITH WORK, MUSICAL DEVICE "prefixes: bio"
instugate, instigate
instulation, install(ation) / instill(ation)
instunle, instant(ly)
instunlty, instant(ly)
instunt, instant
insubordinate,*,ely,tion, DOESN'T SUBMIT TO AUTHORITY
insucure, insecure
insue, ensue
insufficient,tly,ncy,ncies, NOT SUFFICIENT, NOT ENOUGH
insugnifakent, insignificant
insukurety, insecure(rity)
insulate,*,ed,ting,tion,tor, LAYER/COAT OF SOMETHING FOR PROTECTION/ BARRIER
insulin, SECRETED BY A HORMONE IN THE BODY, A MANMADE CHEMICAL TO TREAT DIABETES "prefixes: pro"
insult,*,ted,ting,tingly,ter, AN ATTEMPT TO LOWER ANOTHER'S SELF ESTEEM
insunseer, insincere
insurcle, encircle
insure,*,ed,ring,er,rable,rability,rance, PROTECT AGAINST MONETARY/ PROPERTY/JOB LOSS (or see ensure/assure) "prefixes: re/un/ under"
insurekshen, insurrection
insurens, insure(rance)

insurkle, encircle
insurmountable,ly, CANNOT BE ACHIEVED/OVERCOME
insurrection,nary,naries,nism,nal,nally, REVOLT AGAINST FIGURES OF AUTHORITY
insurshen, insert(ion)
insurt, insert
insyklopedia, encyclopedia
insyme, enzyme
intact,tness, NOT AFFECTED BY A POTENTIALLY DAMAGING EVENT
intaferance, interfere(rance)
intagral, integral
intagrate, integrate
intagration, integrate(tion)
intail, entail
intak, intact / intake
intake, A TUBE/DEVICE WHICH TAKES IN FLUID/AIR FOR MECHANICS (or see intact)
intale, entail
intalect, intellect
intalectual, intellect(ual)
intamit, intimate
intangible,*,bility,eness,ly, NOT REAL/ PHYSICAL
intarier, interior / anterior
intatee, entity
intecate, indicate
integer,*, TERM IN MUSIC AND MATH
integral,*,lly,lity, IMPORTANT PART OF THE WHOLE
integrate,*,ed,ting,ability,tion,tionist, tive,tor, INCLUDE INTO THE WHOLE, MAKE A PART OF A WHOLE "prefixes: dis"
integrity,ties, SOUND PRINCIPLES, HONORABLE
inteligible, intelligible
intellect,*,tion,tive,tual,tually,tuality, tualism,tualize, ABILITY FOR MENTAL COMPREHENSION
intelligent,tly,nce,er, LEVEL OF ABILITY TO PERFORM COMPLEX REASONING "prefixes: un"
intelligible,bility,ly, NOT UNDERSTANDABLE "prefixes: un"
intelugeble, intelligible
intenation, intonate(tion)
intend,*,ded,ding,der,dment, APPARENT GOAL (or see intent)
intense,ely,eness,sity,sities,sive,sively, sify,sifier,sification, FIRM/ FORWARD/ KEEN/VIGOROUS/ EXTREME
intenshin, intent(ion)
intent,*,tly,tness,tion,tional,tionally, tioned,tionality, THOUGHTFULLY PLAN COURSE OF ACTION "prefixes: un"
inter,*,rred,rring, TO BURY, PREFIX INDICATING "BETWEEN/AMONG" MOST OFTEN MODIFIES THE WORD (or see enter/intra)
interact,*,ted,ting,tion,tions,tional, tionism,tionist,tionists,tive,tively, tivity, EXCHANGE BETWEEN TWO/ MORE THINGS (or see enter)
interagate, interrogate
intercede,*,ed,ding,er, MEDIATE/ FACILITATE
intercept,*,ted,ting,ter,tion,tive, PASS BETWEEN/THROUGH A LINE/ OBSTRUCT A LINEAR ACTION
interchange,*,ed,ging,eability,eable, eableness,eably, EXCHANGE/ ALTERNATE BETWEEN/WITH
intercom, INTERCOMMUNICATION SYSTEM/COMMUNICATE BY MICROPHONE
interconnect,*,ted,ting,tion,tedness, tible, TO CONNECT BETWEEN TWO SOURCES
intercourse, INTERCHANGE OF FEELINGS/THOUGHTS, COPULATION
interdisciplinary,rity,rian, WHEN ALL FIELDS/SYSTEMS ARE INTERCONNECTED/ COMMUNICATING
interest,*,ted,tedly,ting,tingly, ATTENTIVENESS TO LEARN SOMETHING NEW, LENDERS COLLECT THIS "prefixes: dis/un"
interfere,*,ed,ring,ringly,er,ence,ential, TO INTERCEPT BETWEEN ONGOING EXCHANGE, PRESENCE OF SLOWS PROGRESS
interim, A TEMPORARY PAUSE IN AN ONGOING PROJECT
interior,*,rity,rly,rize,rizes,rized,rizing, rization, INSIDE A STRUCTURE (or see anterior)
interject,*,ted,ting,tion,tory,torily, INTERRUPT WITH INFORMATION
interlock,*,ked,king,ker, CHAINLIKE, ONE ENMESHED WITH ANOTHER, PART OF ONE MECHANISM EMBEDDED INTO THE OTHER
interlude,*,dial, PAUSE DURING A PERFORMANCE/ACTIVITY
intermediary,ries, FACILITATOR/ AMBASSADOR/AGENT WHO AIDS COMMUNICATION BETWEEN GROUPS
intermediate,*,ed,ting,tion,tor,ary, HELPS WITH COMMUNICATION BETWEEN PEOPLE/GROUPS "prefixes: dis"
intermetant, intermittent
intermingle,*,ed,ling,ement, MINGLE TOGETHER, INTERTWINED
intermission,*,ive, A BREAK BETWEEN EVENTS/ACTIVITY/PERFORMANCE
intermittent,nce,tly, STOPPING/ STARTING WITH PAUSES IN BETWEEN
intern,*,nship,nist,nment, A STUDENT PRACTICING UNDER SUPERVISION, SOMETHING CONFINED DURING WAR
internal,lly,lize,lization,lity, INSIDE A FORM/BODY
international,lity,lly,lism,list,lize,lization, OUTSIDE NATIONAL BOUNDARIES
internet, A COMPUTER WEB WHICH NETS BETWEEN COMPUTERS ALL OVER THE WORLD
interoj, entourage
interpherens, interfere(nce)
interpret,*,ted,ting,tability,table,ter, tive,tively,tation, REVIEW FACTS FOR FURTHER CLARIFICATION, BRING ABOUT THE MEANING OF
interpretation,nal, ACT OF REVIEWING FACTS FOR FURTHER CLARIFICATION
interprise, enterprise
interrelate,tion,tionship, TO RELATE THINGS TOGETHER, SECURE COMMON GROUND BETWEEN TWO THINGS
interrogate,*,ed,ting,tion,tional,tive, tively,tor,tory,tories, TRANSMIT A SIGNAL FOR SETTING OFF AN APPROPRIATE RESPONSE, INTENSE QUESTIONING BY AUTHORITIES
interrupt,*,ted,ting,tion,ter,tive, HINDER THE PROGRESS OF MOMENTARILY "prefixes: un"

interscholastic,*, ACTIVITIES BETWEEN SCHOOLS
intersect,*,ted,ting,tion,tive, POINT WHERE TWO LINE CRISSCROSS, PLACE WHERE OPPOSING LINES CROSS
intersection,*,nal, POINT WHERE TWO LINE CRISSCROSS, PLACE WHERE OPPOSING LINES CROSS
intersperse,*,ed,edly,sing,sion, TO SCATTER, BEING SCATTERED ABOUT
interstate,*, HIWAYS BETWEEN STATES, ROADS CONNECTING STATES
intertane, entertain
intertanment, entertain(ment)
intertwine,*,ed,ning,ningly,ement, WEAVE TOGETHER
interupt, interrupt
interval,*, A PAUSE OR GAP BETWEEN
intervene,*,ed,ning,ner,ntion,ntionist, ntionism, TO INTERFERE, GET BETWEEN
interview,*,wed,wing,wer,wee, QUESTIONING PERSON FOR QUALIFICATIONS OR ANSWERS
interwoven, INTERTWINED, BRAIDED TOGETHER
intestine,*,nal,nally, ORGAN INSIDE BODY WHERE FOOD IS PROCESSED
intety, entity
intever, endeavor
inthooseastik, enthuse(siastic)
inthooziazm, enthuse(siasm)
inthrall, enthrall
inthroll, enthrall
inthuseastek, enthuse(siastic)
inthusiasm, enthuse(siasm)
inticate, indicate
intication, indicate(tion)
intidle, entitle
intiger, integer
intigo, indigo
intil, until
intimadate, intimidate
intimate,ely,er,tion, CLOSE/BONDING, MAKE KNOWN
intimidate,*,ed,ting,tion,tor, ATTEMPT TO LOWER SOMEONE'S SELF ESTEEM/CONFIDENCE BY APPEARING GREATER THAN THEM
intinse, intense
intinshen, intent(ion)
intire, entire
intirle, entire(ly)

intirlee, entire(ly)
intirmediate, intermediate
intirmitant, intermittent
intirsept, intercept
intirty, entire(ty)
intise, entice
intite, entity
intitle, entitle
intlis, endless
into, ENTER TO THE INSIDE
intoishen, intuit(ion)
intolerable,eness,ly,bility,ance,ant,antly, WILL NOT TOLERATE, NOT ABLE TO DEAL WITH
intonate,*,ed,ting,tion,tional,er, ACCENT ON CERTAIN WORDS WHICH AFFECT MEANING
intormident, intermittent
intorse, endorse / indoor(s)
intortane, entertain
intourage, entourage
intoxicate,*,ed,edly,ting,tingly,ant,tion, DRUNK FROM ALCOHOL, INEBRIATED, HIGH WITH EXCITEMENT "prefixes: dis"
intra, PREFIX INDICATING "INSIDE/WITHIN" MOST OFTEN MODIFIES THE WORD (or see inter)
intradukshen, introduce(ction)
intraduse, introduce
intrakit, intricate
intramural,lly, EVENTS HAPPENING WITHIN, SCHOOL SPORTS
intrance, entrance
intranet,*, A WEB OF NETWORKING WITHIN A CLOSED/RESTRICTED COMPUTER SYSTEM
intraspect, introspect
intravenous,sly, INJECTING FLUID INTO VEINS
intrees, entry(ries) / entree
intrege, intrigue
intrense, entrance
intrensic, intrinsic
intres, entry(ries) / entree
intrest, interest / entrust
intricate,ely,eness,acy,acies, OF THE TINIEST DETAIL
intridukshen, introduce(ction)
intrigue,*,ed,uing,uingly,er, DEEPLY INTERESTED, CAPTIVATED
intrinsic,cal,cally,calness, ABSOLUTELY IMPORTANT, ESSENTIAL, CANNOT DO WITHOUT IT

intro, PREFIX INDICATING "INSIDE/WITHIN" MOST OFTEN MODIFIES THE WORD (or see inter)
introduce,*,ed,cing,er,ction,ctory,ctive, ctorily, ACQUAINTING PEOPLE TOGETHER, PRESENT SOMETHING
introduse, introduce
introspect,tion,tional,tive,tively, tiveness, TO GO WITHIN FOR KNOWLEDGE AND ANSWERS
introst, interest / entrust
introvert,*,ted,rsion, SOMEONE WHO SPENDS MOST OF THEIR TIME WITH THEMSELVES, DOESN'T SEEK THE OUTSIDE WORLD FOR ANSWERS
intrude,*,ed,ding,er,usion,usive, ENTER WITHOUT INVITATION, FISSURES FILLED WITH MOLTEN LAVA
intrukit, intricate
intrumural, intramural
intrunse, entrance
intrusion, ENTER WITHOUT INVITATION, ROCK FORM
intrusive,ely,eness, ENTER WITHOUT INVITATION
intrust, entrust / interest
intry, entry / entree
intuative, intuit(ive)
intueshen, intuit(ion)
intufer, interfere
intuger, integer
intugrate, integrate
intuishen, intuit(ion)
intuit,tion,tional,tionism,tionalism, tionist,tive,tively,tiveness, A KNOWINGNESS WE ARE ALL BORN WITH, CAN SEE OUR OWN FUTURE
intunate, intonate
intur, enter / inter
inturage, entourage
inturauj, entourage
inturmedeate, intermediate
inturmetant, intermittent
inturn, intern
inturnalize, internal(ize)
inturnil, internal
inturoj, entourage
inturpret, interpret
inturpretation, interpretation
inturprise, enterprise
intursede, intercede
intursept, intercept
inturtane, entertain
inturtaner, entertain(er)

inturtanment, entertain(ment)
intutes, entity(ties)
intwoet, intuit(ive)
intyre, entire
inubelidy, inability
inubishen, inhibit(tion)
inucent, innocence(nt)
inuendo, innuendo
inuf, enough
inuindo, innuendo
inume, enemy
inunciate, enunciate
inundate,*,ed,ting,tion, OVERWHELMED, OVERFLOWING, OVER ABUNDANCE
inunseade, enunciate
inupresheative, inappreciative
inuprochible, inapproachable
inupropreut, inappropriate
inur, inner
inuract, interact
inurcom, intercom
inurelate, interrelate
inurem, interim
inurge, energy
inurjetek, energetic
inurlock, interlock
inurlude, interlude
inurmediary, intermediary
inurmingle, intermingle
inurmission, intermission
inurmost, innermost
inurnashenul, international
inurnet, internet
inursculastic, interscholastic
inursection, intersection
inursperse, intersperse
inurt, inert
inurtwine, intertwine
inurupt, interrupt
inurval, interval
inurvene, intervene
inurvue, interview
inurwoven, interwoven
inuscapable, inescapable
inusense, innocence
inuvate, innovate
invade,*,ed,ding,er,asion,asive, OVERWHELM A TERRITORY OR PEOPLES BY UNWELCOME OCCUPATION, ENEMY WHO ENTERS TO OCCUPY A SYSTEM

invaginate,*,ed,ting,tion,tions, MEDICAL TERM INVOLVING FOLDING
invajenation, invaginate(tion)
invalid,dly,dity,date,dation,dator,dism, NOT VALID/LEGAL, VOIDED, A PERSON INCAPABLE OF FUNCTIONING NORMALLY
invalope, envelope
invaluable,ly,eness, WORTH MORE THAN CAN BE BOUGHT FOR, MOST VALUABLE
invariable,ly,bility,eness, CONSTANT, NEVER CHANGING
invashen, invasion
invashenate, invaginate
invasion,*,nary, ATTEMPT TO CONQUER IN A HOSTILE MANNER, HOSTILE OVERTHROW
invasive,ely,eness, HOSTILE TAKEOVER
invatation, invitation
invate, invade
inved, envy(vied)
invee, envy
invegorate, invigorate
invelop, envelope
invensable, invincible
invenshen, invent(ion)
invent,*,ted,ting,tion,tor,tible,tive, tively,tiveness, CREATION FROM THOUGHT "prefixes: dis/re"
inventory,ries,ried,rying, A CATALOG/ LIST OF GOODS
inverdebrate, invertebrate
inveriably, invariable(ly)
inverse,*,ely,sion,sive,rt, SWITCH AROUND, MAKE OPPOSITE, INSIDE OUT
inversion,*,ive, SWITCH AROUND, MAKE OPPOSITE, INSIDE OUT
invert,*,ed,tibility,tible,ter,rsion,rsive, SWITCH AROUND, MAKE OPPOSITE, INSIDE OUT
invertebrate,*, HAS NO SPINE/ BACKBONE
inves, envy(vies)
invesible, invisible
invest,*,ted,ting,tment, PUT TIME/ MONEY INTO SOMETHING/ PROJECT "prefixes: dis/re"
investigate,*,ed,ting,tion,tive,tor,tory, SEARCH FOR CLUES/ANSWERS/ SIGNS
investmunt, invest(ment)

invetation, invitation
inveuble, enviable
inveus, envious
invezible, invisible
invigorate,*,ed,ting,tingly,tion,tive, tively,ant,er, BRING EXCITEMENT TO, RENEW
invilope, envelope
invincible,eness,ly,bility, NOT ABLE TO CONQUER/PENETRATE
invintory, inventory
invious, envious
invirenment, environment
invirunmental, environment(al)
invisability, invisible(bility)
invisible,ly,eness,bility, NOT PERCEIVABLE, CANNOT SEE/FEEL
invitation,*,nal, ASKED TO COME TO AN EVENT, WELCOME TO VISIT
invite,*,ed,ting,tingly,tingness,ee,tor, tation,tatory, ASKED TO COME TO AN EVENT, WELCOME TO VISIT, OFFER PLEASURE "prefixes: dis/un"
invoice,*,ed,cing, A DETAILED BILL DUE AND OWING
involope, envelope
involuntary,rily,riness, DID NOT VOLUNTEER
involve,*,ed,ving,ement,er, BE CAUGHT UP IN, INTERACTING WITH, OBLIGATE TIME/THOUGHT "prefixes: un"
invotashen, invitation
invoyce, invoice
invulid, invalid
invurdabrae, invertebrate
invurt, invert
invy, envy
inward,*,dly,dness, FACING TOWARDS THE INSIDE, ON IN SIDE
inword, inward
inwrech, enrich
inwroll, enroll
inzyme, enzyme
iodine, A CHEMICAL ELEMENT
ion,*,nize,nizes,nized,nizing,nizer, nization,nizable, ATOM/PARTICLE WITH A CHARGE "prefixes: inter"
ionesfer, ionosphere
ionesphere, ionosphere
ionisfere, ionosphere
ionosphere,ric, A PROTECTIVE LAYER SURROUNDING THE EARTH ABOVE 43 MILES, HOLES MADE IN IT WITH

ROCKETS CREATE OZONE DEPLETION

iquevocate, equivocate
iquivocate, equivocate
iqwantense, acquaintance
ir, PREFIX INDICATING "NOT" MOST OFTEN MODIFIES THE WORD
irabrochuble, irreproachable
iradebul, irritable
iradek, erratic / erotic
iradekate, eradicate
iradesent, iridescent
iradiate, irradiate
iradic, erratic / erotic
iradubel, irritable
iradukashen, eradicate(tion)
iragardles, irregardless
iragashen, irrigate(tion)
iragate, irrigate
iraguardless, irregardless
iraknid, arachnid
iranment, arraign(ment)
irant, errant
iraplasible, irreplaceable
iraproachable, irreproachable
irasbonsuble, irresponsible
irase, erase
iraser, eraser
irashenul, irrational
irasistible, irresistible
iraspective, irrespective
iraspektif, irrespective
irasponsuble, irresponsible
iratable, irritable
iratant, irritant
iratashen, irritate(tion)
iratate, irritate
iratation, irritate(tion)
irate,ely,eness, ANGRY
iratent, irritant
iratic, erratic / erotic
irational, irrational
iratrevible, irretrievable
iratuble, irritable
iraudik, erratic / erotic
iravokuble, irrevocable
iraze, erase
irazer, eraser
irazistuble, irresistible
irchin, urchin
irebrochuble, irreproachable
iredescent, iridescent
iredesent, iridescent
iredubel, irritable

iregardless, irregardless
iregashen, irrigate(tion)
iregate, irrigate
iregation, irrigate(tion)
iregeuler, irregular
iregeuleredy, irregular(ity)
iregewler, irregular
ireglur, irregular
ireguardless, irregardless
iregular, irregular
ireguleredy, irregular(ity)
irekshen, erect(ion)
irekt, erect
irelavense, irrelevant(nce)
irelevant, irrelevant
irelevense, irrelevant(nce)
ireluvense, irrelevant(nce)
ireluvint, irrelevant
iren, iron
ireny, irony
ireperuble, irreparable
irepirable, irreparable
ireproachable, irreproachable
ireprochible, irreproachable
irepruble, irreparable
irepurable, irreparable
ires, iris
iresbonsuble, irresponsible
iresistible, irresistible
irespective, irrespective
irespektif, irrespective
iresponsuble, irresponsible
iretant, irritant
iretashen, irritate(tion)
iretate, irritate
iretibul, irritable
iretreavible, irretrievable
iretrievable, irretrievable
irevocable, irrevocable
irg, urge
irgint, urge(nt)
iribrochuble, irreproachable
irid, PREFIX INDICATING "IRIS/ RAINBOW" MOST OFTEN MODIFIES THE WORD
iridescent,tly,nce, A LIGHT REFLECTION WITH RAINBOW COLORS
irifd, arrive(d)
iriful, arrive(val)
irigardles, irregardless
irigashen, irrigate(tion)
irigate, irrigate
irigation, irrigate(tion)
iriplasible, irreplaceable

iris, PART OF THE EYE, A FLOWER
irisbonsuble, irresponsible
irisistible, irresistible
irispective, irrespective
irispektif, irrespective
irisponsuble, irresponsible
iritable, irritable
iritashen, irritate(tion)
iritate, irritate
iritation, irritate(tion)
iritrevible, irretrievable
irivokuble, irrevocable
irizisduble, irresistible
irj, urge
irk,*,ked,king, ANNOYING
irn, earn / urn / iron
irnd, earn(ed) / iron(ed)
irnest, earnest
irochun, erosion
irode, erode
irodinamic, aerodynamic
irodynamic, aerodynamic
irogate, irrigate
iron,*,ned,ning, A METAL, A TOOL FOR TAKING WRINKLES OUT OF CLOTHES/ TOOL FOR GOLF/ SMOOTH OUT WRINKLES
irone, irony
ironic,cal,cally,ny,calness, OPPOSITE TO WHAT YOU WOULD EXPECT
irony,nies, ODDLY COINCIDENTAL
irosbonsuble, irresponsible
irosef, erosive
iroshin, erosion
irosif, erosive
irosponsuble, irresponsible
irote, erode
irovokuble, irrevocable
irowze, arouse
irradescent, iridescent
irradiate,*,ed,ting,tion,tor,ant, ILLUMINATE, EXPOSE TO RADIATION
irragate, irrigate
irragation, irrigate(tion)
irrant, errant
irraplasible, irreplaceable
irraproachable, irreproachable
irratable, irritable
irratant, irritant
irratate, irritate
irrate, irate
irratic, erratic

irrational,lity,lness,lly,lism,list,listic, NOT RATIONAL, NOT ABLE TO PROVE RATIONALE
irredescent, iridescent
irregardless, NOT REGARDED, ASIDE FROM THAT
irregate, irrigate
irregation, irrigate(tion)
irregular,*,rly,rity, NOT REGULAR
irrelavent, irrelevant
irrelevant,ntly,nce,ncy, NOT RELEVANT, DOES NOT PERTAIN TO
irrepairable, irreparable
irreparable,ly,eness,bility, CANNOT BE REPAIRED
irreplaceable,ly,eness,bility, NOT ABLE TO BE REPLACED
irreproachable,ly,eness,bility, NOT ABLE TO BE APPROACHED, UNBLEMISHED
irresistible,ly,eness,bility, NOT ABLE TO RESIST
irrespective,ely, NOT TO BE CONSIDERED IN THE EQUATION/ CIRCUMSTANCE/EVENT
irresponsible,ly,eness,bility, NOT RESPONSIBLE
irretrievable,ly,eness,bility, NOT ABLE TO BE
irrevocable,ly,eness,bility, NOT REVERSIBLE, CANNOT BE UNDONE/ CHANGED
irridescent, iridescent
irrigate,*,ed,ting,tion,tional,tive,tor, METHOD OF PROVIDING WATER TO "prefixes: sub"
irriplasible, irreplaceable
irritable,ly,eness,bility, ANNOY/ AGGRAVATE/STIMULATE, INFLAMMED TISSUE
irritant,*,ncy,ncies, SOMETHING THAT IRRITATES
irritate,*,ed,ting,tion,tive,tingly,tor, ANNOY/AGGRAVATE/STIMULATE, INFLAMMED TISSUE
irrogate, irrigate
irrugation, irrigate(tion)
irruplacable, irreplaceable
irrupt,*,ted,ting,tion,tive,tively, SUDDENLY/FORCIBLY INVADE/ ENTER (or see erupt)
irth, earth
irrubshen, erupt(ion) / irrupt(ion)
irubt, erupt / irrupt
irubtif, erupt(ive) / irrupt(ive)
irudebul, irritable
irudibul, irritable
irugardles, irregardless
irugashen, irrigate(tion)
irugate, irrigate
irugation, irrigate(tion)
iruguardless, irregardless
irune, irony
iruplaseble, irreplaceable
iruprochuble, irreproachable
irupshen, erupt(ion) / irrupt(ion)
irupt, erupt / irrupt
iruptif, erupt(ive) / irrupt(ive)
iruption, erupt(ion) / irrupt(ion)
irus, iris
irusbonsuble, irresponsible
irusistible, irresistible
iruspective, irrespective
iruspektif, irrespective
irusponsuble, irresponsible
irutashen, irritate(tion)
irutate, irritate
irutation, irritate(tion)
irutrevible, irretrievable
irutrievable, irretrievable
irutuble, irritable
iruvokuble, irrevocable
iruzistuble, irresistible
is, THIRD PERSON SINGULAR, PRESENT IN TIME, PREFIX INDICATING "EQUAL" MOST OFTEN MODIFIES THE WORD (or see ease/eye(s))
isalashen, isolate(tion)
isalation, isolate(tion)
isay, essay
isbeshalee, especially
isbeshulee, especially
iscape, escape
isdeem, esteem
ise, ice / icy / eye(s)
iselate, isolate
iselation, isolate(tion)
isense, essence
isenshil, essential
isential, essential
ishew, issue
ishu, issue
ishuense, issue(uance)
isier, icy(cier)
isikle, icicle
isilate, isolate
isilation, isolate(tion)
ising, icing
isinshul, essential
iskape, escape
iskort, escort
island,*,der, BODY OF LAND SURROUNDED BY WATER, ONE WHO LIVES ON AN ISLAND "prefixes: inter"
ism,*, A SUFFIX WHICH MEANS A SYSTEM OF PRINCIPLES, A PRACTICE
isn't, CONTRACTION OF THE WORDS 'IS NOT'
iso, PREFIX INDICATING "EQUAL" MOST OFTEN MODIFIES THE WORD
isofigus, esophagus
isolashen, isolate(tion)
isolate,*,ed,ting,tion,tionism,tionist, TO PREVENT HAVING CONTACT WITH ANOTHER THING
isoteric, esoteric
ispeshalee, especially
ispeshulee, especially
issuanse, issue(uance)
issue,*,ed,uing,er,uance,uable, DISTRIBUTE/HAND OUT INFORMATION, POINT OF MATTER "prefixes: un"
issuence, issue(uance)
istablish, establish
istablush, establish
isteem, esteem
istrologe, astrology
isuance, issue(uance)
isue, issue
isuinse, issue(uance)
isulashen, isolate(tion)
isulate, isolate
isulation, isolate(tion)
it,*, PRONOUN REFERRING TO PERSON/ PLACE/THING/TIME/EVENT (or see eat/ate/eight)
it'll, CONTRACTION OF THE WORDS 'IT WILL'
it's, CONTRACTION OF THE WORDS 'IT IS'
itach, attach
itak, attack
italic,*,cize,cized,cizing,cization, SLANTED STYLE OF PRINT TO ATTRACT ATTENTION
italisize, italic(ize)
itch,hes,hed,hing,hy,hiness, DESIRE TO SCRATCH, A NEED TO SATISFY (or see etch)

item,*,mize,mizer,mization, ARTICLE/UNIT IN A COLLECTION, AN OBJECT
itenarary, itinerary
itenerate, itinerate
iteosy, idiocy
iternul, eternal
iteut, idiot
itinerary,ries,ate,ation, LIST OF DETAILS PERTAINING TO A TRIP
itinerate,*,ed,ting,ration,ary, LIST OF DETAILS PERTAINING TO A TRIP
itl, it'll / idle / idol
its, it's
itself, ONE ON ITS OWN
itsetera, etcetera
itul, idol / idle / it'll
itum, item
itumize, item(ize)
iturnal, eternal
iu, ewe / you / yew
iudine, iodine
iul, i'll
iun, ion
iunizur, ion(izer)
iurn, iron
ivacuate, evacuate
ivade, evade
ivakuashen, evacuate(tion)
ivakuate, evacuate
ivaluashen, evaluate(tion)
ivaluate, evaluate
ivant, event
ivaparate, evaporate
ivaporate, evaporate
ive, ivy
ivent, event
ivoke, evoke
ivolution, evolution
ivolve, evolve
ivory, A BONE OR HORN FROM MAMMALS
ivow, avow
ivry, ivory
ivy,vies,vied, A PLANT
ixagerate, exaggerate
ixajurate, exaggerate
ixamunashen, examine(nation)
ixblanatory, explanatory
ixempt, exempt
ixemshen, exempt(ion)
ixequtif, executive
ixitment, excite(ment)
ixkershen, excursion
ixklude, exclude

ixklute, exclude
ixkurjen, excursion
ixkus, excuse
ixost, exhaust
ixperiense, experience
ixpire, expire
ixplanatory, explanatory
ixplisitly, explicit(ly)
ixploet, exploit
ixseluratur, accelerate(tor)
izbeshulee, especially
izenshil, essential
izkape, escape
izkort, escort
izoteric, esoteric
iztablish, establish
izteem, esteem
jab,*,bbed,bbing, TO POKE, PUNCH (or see gab)
jabber,*,red,ring,ry, TALKS VERY FAST
jaber, jabber
jac, jack
jack,*,ked,king,ker, TO STEAL, TO RAISE/LIFT, A GAME, PREFIX INDICATING "MALE/LARGE/HEAVY" MOST OFTEN MODIFIES THE WORD
jackass,sses, MALE DONKEY
jacket,*,ted,tless, A COVERING, PROTECTIVE COAT
jacks,ses, TOOLS FOR HOLDING UP CARS, A GAME FOR KIDS
jacs, jacks
jad, jade
jade,*,ed,edly,edness, LACK OF ENTHUSIASM/INTEREST RESULTING FROM TOO MUCH OF SOMETHING, A PRECIOUS STONE
jag,*,gged,gging,gger,gless, UNEVEN CUTS, POKE/STAB/SPREE
jail,*, BUILDING WHERE PEOPLE WHO BREAK LAWS ARE CONFINED
jak, jack
jaket, jacket
jaks, jacks
jale, jail / jelly
jaly, july / jelly
jam,*, FRUIT SPREAD, BEING STUCK (or see jamb)
jamb,*, HOLDS A STABLE OPENING FOR A DOOR (or see jam)
janedic, genetic
janewery, january
janitor,*,tial, A CUSTODIAN, SOMEONE WHO SEES TO CLEANING/MAINTENANCE OF PUBLIC BUILDING

january, A MONTH OF THE YEAR (ENGLISH)
januery, january
janyuery, january
jar,*,rred,rring, STARTLE SOMEONE, GLASS CONTAINER WITH A LID
jargon,*, A DIALECT, THE WAY A LANGUAGE IS SPOKEN
jas, jazz
jasture, gesture
jau, jaw
jaundice,ed, AN UNHEALTHY BODY CONDITION
jauns, jounce
jaunt,*, SPONTANEOUS/BRIEF JOURNEY
jaus, joust / jaw(s)
jaust, joust
java, COMPUTER SOFTWARE, COFFEE BEVERAGE
jaw,*, PART OF THE MOUTH
jawalk, jaywalk
jawolk, jaywalk
jaywalk,*,ked,king,ker, CROSSING A STREET AT AN INAPPROPRIATE PLACE
jazz,zes,zed,zing,zy, TYPE OF MUSIC, TO MODERNIZE
jealous,sy,sness,sly,sies, EMOTION WHICH ERUPTS WHEN ONE IS INSECURE/FEARFUL
jean,*, THICK FABRIC USED FOR PANTS (or see gene)
jeaneul, genial
jeauluge, geology
jeb, gibe / jib / jibe
jebalashen, jubilant(ation)
jeburish, gibber(ish)
jech, jig / gig
jeens, jean(s) / gene(s)
jefe, jiffy
jegle, jiggle
jegsaw, jigsaw
jelatin, gelatin
jelatnus, gelatin(ous)
jele, jelly
jeli, july / jelly
jelis, jealous
jeliten, gelatin
jell,*,led,ling,ly,lify, CONSISTENCY BETWEEN LIQUID AND SOLID, A GELATIN (or see gel)

jello, A BRAND NAME FOR 'GEL', A GELATIN
jelly,llies,llied,llying,llify,llifying,llified, FRUIT SPREAD, SEMI SOLID SUBSTANCE
jeluten, gelatin
jely, july / jelly
jem, gem / gym
jemmy, jimmy
jemnaseum, gymnasium
jemnast, gymnast
jen, gene / jean
jenarashin, generation
jenarate, generate
jenarator, generator
jenarus, generous
jenaside, genocide
jendur, gender
jene, genie
jeneal, genial
jeneol, genial
jenerik, generic
jenerul, general
jenerus, generous
jenetic, genetics
jeneus, genius
jengle, jingle
jengur, ginger
jenicide, genocide
jenks, jinx
jenome, genome
jenrul, general
jens, jean(s) / gene(s)
jenter, gender
jentul, gentle
jentur, gender
jenuen, genuine
jenul, gentle
jenurulize, general(ize)
jenus, genus
jenyus, genius
jeografy, geography
jeological, geology(gical)
jeometry, geometry
jeopardy,dize,dizes,dized,dizing, GREAT RISK OF DANGER IF NOT SKILLFUL ENOUGH
jep, gyp
jepardy, jeopardy
jeperdize, jeopardy(dize)
jepsee, gypsy
jepsum, gypsum
jerbul, gerbil
jeresdikshen, jurisdiction

jerk,*,ked,king,kily,kiness,ky, QUICK MOTION/JOLT
jerky, DRIED MEAT
jermanate, germinate
jernal, journal
jernalist, journal(ist)
jerney, journey
jeror, juror
jery, jury
jest,ter,ting,tingly, IN FUN, TO MAKE LIGHT OF
jesture, gesture
jet,*,ted,ting,ty, A PLANE, A ROCK, TYPE OF STREAM ACTION (or see get)
jete, jetty
jeti, jetty
jetsam, WASTE/ITEMS ELIMINATED FROM A JET
jetty,ties, PIER/STRUCTURE AT AN OCEAN SHORE
jety, jetty
jeulogical, geology(gical)
jewbalee, jubilee
jewdeshul, judicial
jewdishes, judicious
jewel,*,lry,ler, DECORATIVE ORNAMENTS FOR THE BODY (or see joule)
jewly, july
jewn, june
jewse, juice
jewt, jute
jewvinile, juvenile
jib,*,bed,bing,ber, SAIL OF A BOAT, ARM OF A CRANE (or see jibe/gibe)
jibe,*,ed,bing, SAILING TERM, CONFORM, SHIFT (or see gibe)
jife, jiffy
jiffy, DONE FAST
jifi, jiffy
jig,*,ged,ging,ger, A DANCE, FISHING/ TOOLING DEVICE, TEMPLATE (or see gig) "prefixes: re"
jigantic, gigantic
jigger, A TOOL, THING THAT DOESN'T HAVE A NAME "A THING AMA JIGGER", MEASURING DEVICE
jiggle,*,ed,ling,ly, ACTION LIKE JELLO IN MOTION, DANCE MOVEMENT (or see giggle)
jigsaw,*,wed,wing, A CUTTING TOOL, A PUZZLE
jilatnus, gelatin(ous)

jilt,*,ted,ting,ter, REJECT SOMEONE'S AFFECTION
jily, july / jelly
jim, gem / gym / him
jimmy,mies,mied,ying, FORCE A LOCK TO OPEN
jimnaseum, gymnasium
jimnast, gymnast
jinarashin, generation
jinarate, generate
jinarator, generator
jinarulize, general(ize)
jinarus, generous
jinch, hinge
jind, hint / hind
jinder, gender / hinder
jindrens, hindrance
jindur, gender / hinder
jinerik, generic
jinetic, genetics
jinger, ginger
jingle,*,ed,ling,ly, BELL SOUNDS, BRIEF, CATCHY TUNE
jinks, jinx
jinocide, genocide
jinrul, general
jint, hint
jinter, gender
jintul, gentle
jinuen, genuine
jinurulize, general(ize)
jinus, genus
jinuside, genocide
jinusist, genesis
jinx,xes,xed, SOMETHING THAT CAUSES BAD LUCK
jiolugee, geology
jiometry, geometry
jip, gyp
jipse, gypsy
jipsum, gypsum
jirate, gyrate
jirble, gerbil
jirm, germ
jirmanate, germinate
jirney, journey
jirnul, journal
jirnulist, journal(ist)
jirur, juror
jiry, jury
jitter,*,red,ring,ry, BRIEF BURSTS OF SHAKING OR JIGGLING, A DANCE, FEARFUL REACTION

jive,*,ed,ving, A RHYTHM STYLE OF MUSIC AND ALL ASSOCIATED WITH IT, MISLEADING/PHONY
job,*,bless,blessness, WORKING CONSISTENTLY FOR INCOME
jock,*, SOMEONE WHO FOCUSES PRIMARILY ON SPORTS IN SCHOOL
jockey,*,yed,ying, RIDER IN HORSE RACING, METAPHOR FOR GETTING INTO POSITION TO WIN
joe, joy
joen, join
joent, joint / join(ed) / jaunt
joest, joist
jofeul, jovial
jog,*,ged,ging,ger, TYPE OF RUNNING
jogur, jog(gger)
join,*,ned,ning,nable,ner, BRING TWO OR MORE INDEPENDENT THINGS/ GROUPS TOGETHER IN UNION "prefixes: con/dis/en/re/sub/un"
joint,*,ted,ting, WHERE PARTS INTERSECT, JUNCTION "prefixes: con/dis/un"
joist,*, HORIZONTAL/PARALLEL BOARDS IN A STRUCTURE/ FOUNDATION
jok, jock / joke
joke,*,ed,king,kingly,er,ester, COMMENT/STORY INTENDED TO GENERATE LAUGHTER (or see jock)
joky, jockey
jol, joule / jewel
jole, jolly
jolly,lier,liest,lity, MERRY, LIVELY, GAY
jolt,*,ted,ting,ty, A SUDDEN HARSH ACTION
joly, jolly
jonc, junk
jonci, junkie
jondis, jaundice
jongal, jungle
jongul, jungle
jonk, junk
jonke, junkie
jonki, junkie
jont, jaunt / join(ed) / joint
jooly, july
joon, june
joot, jute
jop, job
jore, jury
jori, jury
jornul, journal

josel, jostle
josh,hing,her, TEASING WITH GOOD HUMOR
jostle,*,ed,ling,ement,er, TO PUSH/ JUMBLE/SHOVE/ BUMP/COLLIDE IN A CROWDED SITUATION
josul, jostle
jot,*,ted,ting, QUICKLY WRITE SOMETHING DOWN, WRITE A QUICK NOTE
jouel, jowl / joule
joule,*, A METHOD OF MEASURING (or see jewel)
jounce,*,ed,cing, TO BOUNCE AROUND
journal,*,lize,lizes,lized,lizing,lizer,lism, lization,list, AN ITEMIZED ACCOUNT OF AN EVENT OR SPAN OF TIME
journalist,*,tic,tically,ize,ism, ONE WHO DOCUMENTS/RECOUNTS AN EVENT OR SPAN OF TIME
journey,*,yed,ying, TO TRAVEL OR TAKE A TRIP
joust,*,ted,ting,ter, MEDIEVAL COMBAT
jovial,lity,lness,lly, JOLLY, GOOD CHEER/ HUMOR
jow, jaw
jowl,*,led, THE JAW, FISH HEAD (or see joule)
jownse, jounce
joy,yful,yfully,yfulness,yous,yously, yousness, A PLEASURABLE STATE OF BEING, HARMONIC "prefixes: en/over"
joyes, joy(ous)
joyesly, joy(ously)
joyfil, joy(ful)
joyis, joy(ous)
joyn, join
joynd, joint / join(ed)
joynt, joint / join(ed)
joyst, joist
joyusness, joy(ousness)
jubalashen, jubilant(ation)
jubilant,tly,lance,lancy,ation,ate,atory, EXHULTANT/TRIUMPHANT/FESTIVE
jubilee,*, A ROWDY/FESTIVE CELEBRATION NORMALLY HONORING A TIMESPAN
juce, juice / juicy
judeshal, judicial
judeshus, judicious
judge,*,ed,ging,gment,gmental, gmentally, MAKING A DECISION

BASED ON KNOWN INFORMATION "prefixes: mis/pre"
judicial,lly,ary, ACTS/ADMINISTRATION OF JUDGING
judicious,sly,sness, BEHAVING IN A JUDGEMENTAL FASHION
judo, SELF-DEFENSE SPORT
juel, joule / jewel
jug,*,gged,gging,gful, A LARGE CONTAINER FOR FLUIDS/LIQUID (or see judge)
juge, jug / judge
juggle,*,ed,ling,er, KEEP OBJECTS AFLOAT IN THE AIR SIMULTANEOUSLY
jugil, juggle
jugment, judge(ment)
juice,*,ed,er,cy,cier,ciest,eless, LIQUID FROM FRUIT
juicy,cier,ciest, EDIBLE FOOD LADEN WITH MOISTURE
juj, judge
jujment, judge(ment)
jul, joule / jewel
july, A MONTH OF THE YEAR (ENGLISH)
jumble,*,ed,ling, TO MIX TOGETHER WITHOUT ORDER
jump,*,ped,ping,py,piness,per, TO TAKE TO THE AIR FOR NANOSECONDS TO DEFY GRAVITY
junc, junk
juncer, junk(er)
junction,*,nal, PLACE WHERE THINGS MEET, TIME/PLACE INTERCHANGE "prefixes: dis/sub"
juncture,*, ONE POINT WHERE THINGS OR THOUGHTS MEET, PLACE FOR EXCHANGE
june, A MONTH OF THE YEAR (ENGLISH)
jungle,*,led,ly, PLACE WHERE PLANTS/ ANIMALS ARE ABUNDANT/FREE FROM HUMAN RESTRAINT
junior,*, A CLASS LEVEL IN SCHOOL, THE MALE OFFSPRING OF A FATHER
junk,ked,king,ky,ker,kie, OBJECTS CONSIDERED TO BE OF NO VALUE
junke, junkie
junkie,*, PERSON WITH HABITUAL DRUG PROBLEM
junkshen, junction
junksher, juncture
junky, junkie
junyer, junior
juol, jewel / joule

juometree, geometry
jurasdiction, jurisdiction
jurbel, gerbil
jure, jury
juresdiction, jurisdiction
jurisdiction,nal,nally, AN AREA/RANGE CONTROLLED BY PARTICULAR ENTITIES
jurk, jerk
jurky, jerky
jurm, germ
jurmenate, germinate
jurnal, journal
jurney, journey
jurni, journey
jurnil, journal
jurnilist, journal(ist)
jurnul, journal
juror,*, MEMBER OF A GROUP WHO SITS IN COURT AND JUDGES A DEFENDANT
jurusdikshen, jurisdiction
jury,ries,ried,ror,rist, A GROUP WHO SIT IN COURT AND JUDGES A DEFENDANT
jusd, just
jusdes, justice
jusdifiable, justifiable
jusdify, justify
jusdufecation, justify(fication)
juse, juice / juicy
juser, juice(r)
just,tly,tness, WHAT IS RIGHT BY SOCIAL NORMS "prefixes: un"
justefiable, justifiable
justefication, justify(fication)
justes, justice
justice,*,eless,elike,ciable,ciability, ONE WHO IS EMPLOYED BY THE GOVERNMNENT TO MAKE LAWFUL DECISIONS "prefixes: in"
justifiable,bility,bleness,ly, DEFENDS THAT THE ACTION REFLECTS THE CAUSE "prefixes: un"
justify,fies,fied,fying,fyingly,fier,fication,ficative,ficatory, DEFEND REACTIONS, ARGUE IN DEFENSE OF ACTION/ THOUGHT "prefixes: un"
jusy, juice(cy)
jut,*,tted,tting, STICKS OUT (or see jute)
jute, PLANT FIBER FOR WEAVING AND BRAIDING
juto, judo
juvenile,*,lism,lity, A YOUTH, IMMATURE
juxta, PREFIX INDICATING "NEAR/ CLOSE" MOST OFTEN MODIFIES THE WORD
kabduve, captive
kaben, cabin
kabenet, cabinet
kaberay, cabaret
kabich, cabbage
kabige, cabbage
kabin, cabin
kabinet, cabinet
kable, cable
kabnet, cabinet
kabnit, cabinet
kaboose, caboose
kabsher, capture
kabsul, capsule
kabten, captain
kabture, capture
kabul, cable
kabunet, cabinet
kabuse, caboose
kacdus, cactus
kach, catch / cache / cash
kacher, catcher / cashier
kackel, cackle
kacl, cackle
kactus, cactus
kadagore, category
kadagorize, categorize
kadagory, category
kadagurize, categorize
kadal, cattle
kadalize, catalyst(yze)
kadavir, cadaver
kade, caddy
kadecism, catechism
kadegore, category
kadegurize, categorize
kadekism, catechism
kadence, cadence
kadet, cadet
kadigore, category
kadigurize, categorize
kadikism, catechism
kadil, cattle
kadilist, catalyst
kadilog, catalog
kadinse, cadence
kadl, cattle
kadugore, category
kadugorize, categorize
kadugory, category
kadugurize, categorize
kadul, cattle
kadulist, catalyst
kadulize, catalyst(yze)
kadulog, catalog
kadur, cater
kaduract, cataract
kady, caddy
kaf, calf / cave
kafa, cafe
kafanated, caffeine(nated)
kafatirea, cafeteria
kafe, cafe / coffee
kafene, caffeine
kafetirea, cafeteria
kafi, coffee
kafinated, caffeine(nated)
kafine, caffeine
kafiterea, cafeteria
kafiteria, cafeteria
kafs, calves / cave(s)
kafunated, caffeine(nated)
kage, cage
kagol, cajole
kahoot, cahoot
kahute, cahoot
kail, kale
kainker, chancre / canker
kairful, careful
kaje, cage
kajole, cajole
kajuol, casual
kajwul, casual
kak, caulk / calk / cake / cock
kakd, cake(d)
kake, cake / khaki
kakil, cackle
kakoon, cocoon
kakt, cake(d)
kaktis, cactus
kakul, cackle
kakulashun, calculate(tion)
kakulation, calculate(tion)
kaky, khaki
kal, kale / call
kalamity, calamity
kalcefy, calcify
kalceum, calcium
kalculashun, calculate(tion)
kalculate, calculate
kalculus, calculus
kale, AN EDIBLE PLANT
kalebrate, calibrate

kaleidoscope,,pic,pical,pically, COLORFUL VIEWING OBJECT
kalek, colic
kalender, calendar / calender / colander
kalentur, calendar / calender / colander
kalepur, caliper / caliber
kaler, collar / call(er)
kales, callous / callus
kalesdenics, calisthenics
kalesterol, cholesterol
kalesthenics, calisthenics
kaliber, caliber
kalibrate, calibrate
kalide, collide
kalidoscope, kaleidoscope
kaliflower, cauliflower
kalindula, calendula
kalindur, calendar / calender / colander
kalintur, calendar
kalipur, caliper
kalir, collar / call(er)
kalire, calorie
kalis, callous / callus
kalisdenics, calisthenics
kalisthenics, calisthenics
kalk, calk / caulk
kalkewlashun, calculate(tion)
kalkewlate, calculate
kalkewlus, calculus
kalkilate, calculate
kalkulate, calculate
kalkulus, calculus
kalobrate, calibrate
kalokweul, colloquial
kalon, cologne / colon
kaloneil, colonial
kaloquial, colloquial
kalore, calorie
kalostemy, colostomy
kalqulus, calculus
kalsafy, calcify
kalseum, calcium
kalsufy, calcify
kaluber, caliber
kalubrate, calibrate
kaluper, caliper
kalury, calorie
kalus, callous / callus
kalusdenics, calisthenics
kalusthinics, calisthenics
kalvs, calves
kam, came
kamb, camp

kamend, commend
kamenduble, commendable
kamfer, camphor
kamil, camel
kaminduble, commendable
kamofloje, camouflage
kamp, camp
kampane, campaign
kampus, campus
kamru, camera
kamu, comma
kamul, camel
kamunecate, communicate
kamunety, community
kamute, commute
kancer, cancer / chancre / canker
kanded, candid
kandidat, candidate
kandil, candle
kandy, candy
kane, cane
kanebul, cannibal
kanebulize, cannibal(ize)
kaneon, canyon
kanepy, canopy
kanery, canary / cannery
kanesiology, kinesis(iology)
kanesis, kinesis
kangaroo,, LARGE MARSUPIAL ANIMAL
kangrues, congruous
kanibul, cannibal
kanibus, cannabis
kanikanik, kinnikinnick
kanin, cannon / canine
kaniry, cannery / canary
kanister, canister
kanker, chancre / canker
kanon, cannon
kanopy, canopy
kanselashin, cancellation
kanseld, cancel(lled)
kansilashun, cancellation
kansild, cancel(lled)
kansir, cancer
kansul, cancel
kansulashen, cancellation
kansult, cancel(lled)
kant, can't
kantalope, cantaloupe
kantankerus, cantankerous
kanted, candid
kanteen, canteen
kantelope, cantaloupe

kantiguis, contiguous
kantina, cantina
kantir, canter
kantrovert, controvert
kantulope, cantaloupe
kantur, canter
kanubelize, cannibal(ize)
kanubis, cannabis
kanuster, canister
kanves, canvas / canvass
kanvus, canvas / canvass
kanyun, canyon
kaos, chaos
kap, cap / cape
kapabul, capable
kapasety, capacity
kapdivate, captivate
kape, cap / cape
kapechulate, capitulate
kapedul, capital / capitol
kapedulism, capitalism
kapelary, capillary
kapetate, capitate
kapetul, capital / capitol
kapetulesm, capitalism
kapibilety, capability
kapibul, capable
kapilary, capillary
kapitulate, capitulate
kapoot, kaput
kapshun, caption
kapsil, capsule
kapsize, capsize
kapsul, capsule
kaptin, captain
kaption, caption
kaptuf, captive
kaptun, captain
kaptuvate, captivate
kapubilety, capability
kapubul, capable
kapulery, capillary
kaput, DIED, PASSED OUT, FELL OVER DEAD
kaputate, capitate
kapzize, capsize
kar, car
karacter, character
karaoke, GAME WHERE SONGS WITHOUT WORDS ARE SUNG TO
karat,, A MEASUREMENT FOR GEMS AND GOLD (or see karate/carrot/ carat/caret)

karate, MARTIAL ART FORM (or see karat)
karbin, carbon
karbinete, carbonate
karbon, carbon
karburator, carburetor
kard, card / care(d) / cart
kardboard, cardboard
kardeac, cardiac
kardenul, cardinal
kardilege, cartilage
kardnul, cardinal
kare, carry / care
karebu, caribou
karecatshure, caricature
karecter, character
kareer, career
karefree, carefree
karekteriz, character(ize)
kareless, careless
kareng, care(ring)
kareoke, karaoke
karer, career
kares, care(s) / caress
karet, carat /caret / carrot / karat
kareur, carrier
karevan, caravan
karf, carve
karfl, careful
karfre, carefree
karful, careful
kargo, cargo
karib, carob
kariboo, caribou
karisma, charisma
karit, carat / caret / carrot / karat
karkes, carcass
karkus, carcass
karlis, careless
karma, A BELIEF
karmil, caramel
karmu, karma
karmul, caramel
karnashun, carnation
karnevul, carnival
karnivore, carnivore
karob, carob
karoburate, corroborate
karode, corrode
karogen, corrode(osion)
karoke, karaoke
karosef, corrode(osive)
karosene, kerosene
karote, karate

karouse, carouse
karows, carouse
karpenter, carpenter
karpet, carpet
karpinder, carpenter
karpit, carpet
kars, care(s) / car(s)
karsenugen, carcinogen
karsinugin, carcinogen
kart, cart
kartoon, cartoon
kartreg, cartridge
kartrig, cartridge
kartuleg, cartilage
kartune, cartoon
karudge, carriage
karukter, character
karul, carol
karusen, kerosene
karv, carve
kary, carry
kasadilla, quesadilla
kascade, cascade
kase, case
kasedeya, quesadilla
kaseno, casino
kaset, cassette
kash, cash / cache
kashen, caution
kasher, cashier
kashes(ly), cautious(ly)
kashmer, cashmere
kashosly, cautious(ly)
kashu, cashew
kashual, casual
kasine, casino
kasing, casing
kasiroll, casserole
kask, cask
kaskera, cascara
kasket, casket
kast, cast / caste
kastrate, castrate
kasudilla, quesadilla
kasul, castle
kat, cat
kata, PREFIX INDICATING "APART/ DOWN" MOST OFTEN MODIFIES THE WORD
katagorize, categorize
katagory, category
katalize, catalyst(yze)
katch, cache / cash / catch
katecism, catechism

kategore, category
kategurize, categorize
katekisom, catechism
katel, cattle
katelog, catalog
katepiler, caterpillar
katepult, catapult
kater, cater
kateract, cataract
katigore, category
katigurize, categorize
katikism, catechism
katl, cattle
katugory, category
katukism, catechism
katul, cattle
katulist, catalyst
katulize, catalyst(yze)
katulog, catalog
katupiler, caterpillar
katupult, catapult
katurakt, cataract
kau, cow
kauchen, caution
kaudej, cottage
kaufe, coffee / cough
kaugorize, categorize
kauk, caulk / calk / cake / cock
kaul, call / cowl
kauleg, college
kaumu, comma
kaunasure, connoisseur
kauncekwently, consequent(ly)
kaunsaquently, consequent(ly)
kaunsuquenshul, consequent(ial)
kaunvex, convex
kausd, cause(d) / cost
kaushas, cautious
kaushen, caution
kaushon, caution
kaushos, cautious
kaut, caught / cot
kav, cave
kava, BEVERAGE FROM PLANT
kavety, cavity
kavilry, cavalry
kavirn, cavern
kavity, cavity
kavs, calves / cave(s)
kavude, cavity
kavulree, cavalry
kavurn, cavern
kawcus, caucus
kawshun, caution

kawshus, cautious
kawt, caught / cot
kayak,*,ker,king, CANOE-LIKE BOAT
kayen, cayenne
kaynine, canine
kayos, chaos
kaysadilla, quesadilla
kazadilla, quesadilla
kazual, casual
kazudilla, quesadilla
ke, key
kech, catch
kechen, kitchen
kechup, ketchup / catsup
ked, key(ed) / kid
kednapur, kidnap(pper)
kedny, kidney
kedul, kettle
kedy, kitty
keel,*,led,ling,less, FALL OVER, STRUCTURAL PART OF A BOAT
keen,nly,nness,ner, SHARP IN SENSES, VERY AWARE
keep,*,per,ping,pable, HOLD ONTO, WITHHOLD FROM SOMEONE, POSSESS "prefixes: up"
kek, kick
kel, kill / keel / kale
keld, kill(ed) / kelt
kell, kill
keln, kiln
kelo, kilo
kelokweul, colloquial
keloquial, colloquial
kelowatt, kilowatt
kelp, WATER PLANT
kelt, celt / kilt / kill(ed)
kelur, kill(er)
kemakol, chemical
kemecol, chemical
kemest, chemist
kemestri, chemistry
kemicol, chemical
kemist, chemist
kemistri, chemistry
kemokol, chemical
kemostry, chemistry
kemotherupy, chemotherapy
kemukol, chemical
kemustri, chemistry
ken, kin / keen / can
kendergarden, kindergarten
kendling, kindle(ling)
kendom, kingdom

kendred, kind(red)
kendul, kindle
kendurgarden, kindergarten
kenel, kennel
kenesiology, kinesis(iology)
kenesis, kinesis
keng, king / kink
kengdom, kingdom
kenikkanik, kinnikinnick
kenk, king / kink
kenly, keen(ly)
kennel,*,led,ling, FENCING/HOUSING FOR ANIMALS "prefixes: un"
kenol, kennel
kensum, consume
kentend, contend
kentenual, continue(ual)
kentling, kindle(ling)
kentred, kind(red)
kenturgarden, kindergarten
kenul, kennel
keosk, kiosk
keper, kipper
kepsize, capsize
kepur, kipper
ker, care
kerab, carob
keracter, character
keral, choral / coral / corral / chorale
keraoky, karaoke
kerat, carat / caret / carrot / karat
keravan, caravan
kerb, curb
kerd, curd
kerdeus, courteous
kerdul, curdle
kere, care / carry
kereb, carob
kerekt, correct
kerekturiz, character(ize)
kereoke, karaoke
keret, carat / caret / carrot / karat
kerf, curve
kerfle, careful / careful(lly)
kerfri, carefree
kerfue, curfew
kerful, careful
kerfule, careful(lly)
keri, carry
kerib, carob
kericuture, caricature
kerier, carrier
kerige, carriage / courage
kerikulum, curriculum

kerioke, karaoke
kerisel, carousel
kerisen, kerosene
kerit, carat / caret / carrot / karat
kerivan, caravan
kerl, curl
kerles, careless
kernal, colonel / kernel
kernel,*,ly, SMALL BITS/SECTIONS OF CORN COB/NUTS/SEEDS (or see colonel)
kernul, colonel / kernel
kerob, carob
keroberate, corroborate
kerol, carol
kerosell, carousel
kerosene, TYPE OF FUEL
kerot, carat / caret / carrot / karat
keroty, karate
kerp, curb
kersanthimum, chrysanthemum
kersash, corsage
kerse, curse / care(s)
kersive, cursive
kersoch, corsage
kersoje, corsage
kersuf, cursive
kertale, curtail
kertin, curtain
kertsy, curtsy
kertul, curdle
keruge, courage
kerunsy, currency
kerunt, currant / current
kerupt, corrupt
kerusel, carousel
kerusen, kerosene
kerut, caret / carrot / karat
keruvan, caravan
kerve, curve
kervicher, curvature
kervuchure, curvature
kery, curry / carry
kes, kiss
kesng, kiss(ing)
kest, kiss(ed) / cist
ket, kid / kit / kite
ketal, kettle
ketch, catch
ketchen, kitchen
ketcher, catcher
ketchup, TOMATO BASED CONDIMENT (also catsup)
keten, kitten

ketny, kidney
kets, kid(s) / kit(s) / kite(s)
kettle,*, LARGE IRON POT, METAL VESSEL WITH ROUNDED BOTTOM AND WIDE TOP
ketul, kettle
kety, kitty
keurader, curator
kew, cue
kewdos, kudos
kewe, kiwi
kewk, cook
kewth, couth
key,*,yed,ying, TOOL TO UNLOCK SOMETHING, IMPORTANT INFORMATION TO UNLOCK A MYSTERY
keylo, kilo
keyosk, kiosk
keysadilla, quesadilla
keysudeya, quesadilla
khaki,*, A TYPE OF COTTON PANT, A COLOR
ki, key
kiak, kayak
kian, cayenne
kibuse, caboose
kic, kick
kichen, kitchen
kick,*,ked,king,ker, STRIKE SOMETHING WITH FRONT OF FOOT
kid,*,ddy,dder,dding,ddingly,ddishness, dlike, YOUNG CHILD/ANIMAL, JOKING(or see kite/kit)
kiddy, kitty
kiden, kitten
kidnap,*,pped,pping,pper, ONE WHO STEALS AWAY WITH SOMEONE
kidnaper, kidnap(pper)
kidney,*, ORGANS IN THE BODY
kidny, kidney
kidur, kid(dder)
kidy, kid(ddy) / kitty
kigole, cajole
kijole, cajole
kik, kick
kil, kill / keel
kild, kill(ed) / kilt / keel(ed)
kiler, kill(er)
kill,*,led,ler,ling, TAKE LIFE AWAY FROM "prefixes: over"
kiln,*, A SPECIAL OVEN WHICH EXCEEDS 1,000°

kilo, PREFIX INDICATING "THOUSAND" MOST OFTEN MODIFIES THE WORD
kiloge, collage
kilokweul, colloquial
kiloneul, colonial
kiloquial, colloquial
kilor, kill(er)
kilosil, colossal
kilostomy, colostomy
kilowatt, ELECTRICAL MEASUREMENT
kilt,*, SKIRT OF SCOTTISH DESCENT (or see kill(ed))
kilur, kill(er)
kimast, chemist
kimecul, chemical
kimest, chemist
kimestry, chemistry
kimist, chemist
kimponent, component
kimustry, chemistry
kin,*,nsmen,nfolk, RELATIVES (or see can)
kinal, canal
kincdom, kingdom
kind,dred,dly,dest,dness,der, WHAT TYPE, BEING NICE WITHOUT ULTERIOR MOTIVES "prefixes: un"
kind of, SORT OF, SOMEWHAT
kinda, kind of
kindergarten,ner, A CLASS LEVEL IN SCHOOL
kindhearted,dly,dness, A GENTLE SPIRIT
kindle,*,ed,ling, MATERIAL USED AS A FIRE STARTER "prefixes: en/re"
kindolense, condolence
kindom, kingdom
kinducter, conductor
kinduf, kind of
kindukt, conduct
kindurgarden, kindergarten
kinery, canary / cannery
kinesis,iology, STUDY OF HEALTH/ MUSCLES OF THE BODY, HEALING USING KINERGETIC STUDY
kinet, PREFIX INDICATING "MOTION" MOST OFTEN MODIFIES THE WORD
kinfedy, confetti
kinfes, confess
kinfeshun, confession
kinfetion, confession
king,*,gdom, RULER IN A MONARCH
kingdom,*, AREA RULED BY MONARCHY "prefixes: sub"
kingradulashun, congratulation

kinikkanik, kinnikinnick
kink,*,ked,king,ky, SOMETHING THAT KNOT'S UP, A BEND/HOOK IN A LINEAR SYSTEM (or see king) "prefixes: un"
kinkdom, kingdom
kinnikinnick, A PLANT
kinol, kennel
kinsestincy, consistence(cy)
kinsistently, consistent(ly)
kinsole, console
kinspirusy, conspiracy
kinstrucshen, construction
kinstruct, construct
kinsult, consult
kinsumpshen, consumption
kint, kind / can't / couldn't
kinta, kind of
kintaminate, contaminate
kintergarden, kindergarten
kintred, kind(red)
kinul, kennel
kinverdable, convertible
kiosk,*, INFORMATION STATION
kiper, kipper
kipper,*, FISH AND RELATED
kiral, choral / coral / corral / chorale
kirnel, colonel / kernel
kiroberate, corroborate
kirogen, corrode(osion)
kiropraktor, chiropractor
kiroshen, corrode(osion)
kirote, karate
kirsanthemum, chrysanthemum
kirsoch, corsage
kirten, curtain
kirteus, courteous
kiruge, courage
kirupraktor, chiropractor
kirvucher, curvature
kis, kiss
kiset, cassette
kiss,sses,ssed,ssing,sser,ssable, TOUCH WITH THE LIPS
kist, cist / kiss(ed)
kit,*, ACCUMULATION OF ITEMS IN A CONTAINER TO USE FOR A SPECIFIC TASK (or see kite)
kitastrufy, catastrophe
kitchen,*, PLACE TO PREPARE FOOD
kite,*, FRAME WITH COVERING THAT SAILS IN THE WIND BY A STRING (or see kit)
kiten, kitten

kitny, kidney
kitten,*, IMMATURE CAT
kitty,tties,tten, IMMATURE CAT, GAMBLING TERM
kity, kitty
kiwi,*, FRUIT, BIRD
kiyak, kayak
kiyan, cayenne
kiyen, cayenne
klad, clad
klairvoyants, clairvoyance
klam, clam / claim
klamable, claim(able)
klament, claimant
klamp, clamp
klan, clan
klandistine, clandestine
klap, clap
klapse, collapse
klarecul, clerical
klaricul, clerical
klarity, clarity
klarvoyuns, clairvoyance
klaset, closet
klash, clash
klasha, cliche
klasic, classic
klasify, classify
klasp, clasp
klass, class
klasuc, classic
klasufy, classify
klauged, clog(gged) / cloak / clock(ed)
klaun, clown
klausterfobic, claustrophobic
klaw, claw
klawsit, closet
klawzet, closet
klay, clay
klebtomaniac, kleptomania(c)
klecter, collect(or)
kleerense, clearance
kleet, cleat
kleff, cliff
klen, clean
klench, clench / clinch
kleng, cling
klenik, clinic
klenikul, clinic(al)
klense, cleanse
klensh, clench / clinch
klenz, cleanse
klenzer, cleanser
klep, clip

kleptomania,ac,acs,acal, OBSESSION WITH STEALING
klepur, clipper
kler, clear
klerense, clearance
klerge, clergy
klerical, clerical
klerify, clarify
klerity, clarity
klerk, clerk
klervoyents, clairvoyance
klet, cleat
kletorus, clitoris
klevur, clever
klew, clue
kliant, client
klicha, cliche
klick, click / clique
kliff, cliff
klik, click / clique
klim, climb
klimax, climax
klimet, climate
klimut, climate
klinch, clench / clinch
kling, cling
klinik, clinic
klinsh, clench / clinch
klinzr, cleanser
klip, clip
klipur, clipper
klirk, clerk
klisha, cliche
klitorus, clitoris
kliunt, client
kloak, cloak
klober, clobber
kloester, cloister
klofe, clove
klofur, clover
kloger, closure
klojure, closure
klok, clock / cloak
klokd, clog(gged) / cloak / clock(ed)
klon, clown / clone / cologne
klorene, chlorine
klos, clothes / claw(s) / close / clause
kloser, close(r) / closure
klosher, closure
klosir, close(r) / closure
klosline, clothesline
klosterfobic, claustrophobic
klosturfobia, claustrophobia
klosur, close(r) / closure

klot, clot
kloth, cloth
kloud, cloud
kloun, clown
klout, clout
klove, clove
klovur, clover
klowd, cloud
klown, clown
klowsit, closet
klowt, clout
klowth, cloth / cloth(e)
klowz, clothes / claw(s) / close / clause
kloyster, cloister
kloz, clothes / claw(s) / close / clause
klozer, close(r) / closure
klozit, closet
klozline, clothesline
klu, clue
klub, club
kluch, clutch
kludch, clutch
kluder, clutter
klue, clue
klump, clump
klumze, clumsy
klurge, clergy
kluster, cluster
klutch, clutch
kluter, clutter
klutorus, clitoris
knack, HAVE A NATURAL SKILL/TALENT FOR
knap,*,pped,pping,pper,ppy, HAIR AFFECTATION
knead,*,ded,ding, PREPARING DOUGH FOR BAKING (or see knee(d)/need))
kned, knee(d) / knead
knee,*,ed,eing, BENDABLE JOINT HALFWAY DOWN LEG (or see need/ knead)
kneel,*,led,ling,ler, TO SIT ON YOUR KNEES
knel, kneel / knell
knell,*,led,ling, SOUND OF A BELL NORMALLY HEARD AT FUNERALS, A SOLEMN SOUND (or see kneel)
knes, knee(s) / niece
knew, PAST TENSE FOR THE WORD "KNOW" (or see new)
knewmerable, numerable
knick knack,*, SMALL COLLECTIBLES, TRINKETS (or see nick)

knife,ed,fing,ives, SHARP, METAL BLADE WITH HANDLE FOR CUTTING
knight,*,ted,ting,tly, MEDIEVAL SOLDIER
knit,*,tted,tting,tter, USING NEEDLES/ YARN "prefixes: inter/un"
knitch, niche
knob,*, HANDLES FOR DOORS AND DRAWERS
knock,*,ked,king,ker, SOUND MADE ON DOOR WITH FIST, USING THE FIST
knoll,*, SMALL ROUND HILL
knot,*,tted,tting,tty, ROPE/STRING TIED WITH LOOPING CONFIGURATION, SPOT WHERE LIMBS GREW FROM (or see not/naught)
know,*,wing,wn,wable,wer,wledge, HAVE IT IN YOUR MEMORY, ACCESS BY MEMORY (or see noun) "prefixes: un"
knowledge,gable,gableness,gably, HAVING A MEMORY BASE
known,*,PAST TENSE FOR THE WORD 'KNOW', INFORMED/AWARE OF
knuckle,*,ed,ling, FINGER JOINT BONE, TO FIST UP HAND TO DISPLAY BONE JOINTS
koagewlate, coagulate
koagulate, coagulate
koal, coal / cool
koalition, coalition
koap, co-op
koar, core / corp
koarse, course / coarse
koaster, coaster
koat, coat
kob, cob
kobalt, cobalt
kobolt, cobalt
kobra, cobra
kobweb, cobweb
kocane, cocaine
koch, coach
kochen, caution
kocher, kosher
koches, cautious
kock, cook / cock
kockroach, cockroach
kod, cod / code / could / cold / caught
kodage, cottage
kode, code
kodej, cottage
kodene, codeine
kodin, cotton

kodo, kudos
koduge, cottage
koed, coed
koel, coil
koen, coin
koenside, coincide
koensudent, coincident
koersment, coerce(ment)
kof, cough
kofe, cove / coffee / cough
kofen, coffin / cough(ing)
kofert, covert
kofin, coffin / cough(ing)
kofy, coffee
kognativ, cognitive
kognisant, cognizant
kognishun, cognition
kognition, cognition
kognutiv, cognitive
kohabutate, cohabitate
kohearent, coherent
koherent, coherent
kohersive, coerce(cive)
kohesuf, cohesive
kohesuve, cohesive
kohort, cohort
kohurse, coerce
koil, coil
koin, coin
koinside, coincide
koinsudent, coincident
kok, cock / cook
kokain, cocaine
kokane, cocaine
koke, kook(y)
koko, cocoa
kokonut, coconut
kokroch, cockroach
koks, coax
koktale, cocktail
kokunut, coconut
kol, call / cowl
koladerul, collateral
kolamedy, calamity
kolander, colander
kolaps, collapse
kolapsubl, collapse(sible)
kolasal, colossal
kolate, collate
kold, cold
koldsfoot, coltsfoot
kole, coal / call
koleage, colleague
koleague, colleague

kolecshin, collection
kolecter, collect(or)
koledg, college
koleg, college
kolegent, collegiate
kolekt, collect
kolem, column
kolen, colon
kolenary, culinary
kolendur, colander
koleng, call(ing) / cowl(ing)
kolenize, colonize
koleny, colony
koler, collar / call(er) / cooler
kolerd, collar(ed) / collard greens
kolesterol, cholesterol
kolic, colic
kolid, collide
koliflower, cauliflower
kolige, college
kolijin, collision
kolim, column
koliny, colony
kolishen, coalition
kolk, calk / caulk
kolm, calm
kolmenate, culminate
koloj, collage
kolostemy, colostomy
kolpret, culprit
kolsla, coleslaw
kolslow, coleslaw
kolt, cold / colt
koltivate, cultivate
koltsfoot, coltsfoot
koluge, college
kolum, column
kolun, colon
kolundir, colander
kolune, colony
kolunise, colonize
kolur, cooler / color / collar / call(er)
kolvurt, culvert
kom, calm / come / comb
koma, coma / comma
komand, command
komander, commander
kombat, combat
kombenation, combination
komber, cumber
kombinashun, combination
kombine, combine
kombinsashen, compensation
kombrahensiv, comprehensive

kombunashen, combination
kombustible, combustible
kombustion, combustion
komec, comic
komedian, comedian
komedy, comedy
komemerate, commemorate
komendable, commendable
komendation, commendation
komenduble, commendable
komense, commence
koment, comment
komentatur, commentator
koments, commence
komerse, commerce
komershul, commercial
komet, commit / comet
komfert, comfort
komfertible, comfortable
komfurter, comfort(er)
komic, comic
komidy, comedy
komimurate, commemorate
komin, common
komindation, commendation
kominduble, commendable
kominsurate, commensurate
komint, comment
komintator, commentator
komirse, commerce
komirshul, commercial
komisary, commissary
komishner, commissioner
komit, comet / commit
komitee, committee
komitment, commitment
komity, comedy
komodety, commodity
kompact, compact
kompar, compare
komparebul, comparable
kompartment, compartment
kompashun, compassion
kompashunet, compassionate
kompass, compass
kompatibility, compatible(bility)
kompeditor, competitor
kompel, compel
kompensashen, compensation
komper, compare
kompete, compete
kompetior, competitor
kompile, compile
kompinsate, compensate

kompitance, competent(nce)
kompizishen, composition
komplane, complain
komplasins, complacence / complaisance
komplecshun, complexion
kompleks, complex
kompleshun, completion
komplete, complete
komplians, compliant(nce)
kompliant, compliant
komplukashun, complication
komplukate, complicate
komplumint, complement / compliment
komply, comply
komponent, component
kompose, compose
komposier, composure
komposit, composite
kompost, compost
komposyer, composure
kompound, compound
kompownd, compound
komprahensive, comprehensive
kompramise, compromise
komprehend, comprehend
komprehenshun, comprehension
komprehinsef, comprehensive
kompreshun, compression
kompresor, compressor
kompress, compress
kompretion, compression
kompruble, comparable
komprumize, compromise
komptroler, comptroller
kompulsery, compulsory
kompulshun, compulsion
kompulsuve, compulsive
kompultion, compulsion
komputashun, computation
kompute, compute
komputer, computer
komputishen, competition
kompuzishen, composition
komrad, comrade
komtroler, comptroller
komudoor, commodore
komun, common / commune
komune, commune
komunest, communist
komunety, community
komunicate, communicate
komunism, communism

komunul, communal
komutable, commute(table)
kon, con / cone
konasur, connoisseur
koncaf, concave
koncafety, concave(vity)
koncakwently, consequent(ly)
koncavity, concave(vity)
koncavudy, concave(vity)
koncesion, concession
konch, conch
koncheinchus, conscientious
konchuse, conscious
konclewsef, conclusive
konclude, conclude
konclujen, conclusion
konclusef, conclusive
konclusion, conclusion
koncucrat, consecrate
koncution, concussion
kondem, condemn
kondensashen, condensation
kondense, condense
kondesend, condescend
kondewit, conduit
kondimeneum, condominium
kondiment, condiment
kondinsashun, condensation
kondisend, condescend
kondishen, condition
kondition, condition
kondolense, condolence
kondomeneum, condominium
kondone, condone
konduct, conduct
konducter, conductor
konduit, conduit
kondukt, conduct
kondum, condom
kondument, condiment
kone, cone
konekshen, connection
konekt, connect
konesur, connoisseur
konfederit, confederate
konfedont, confidant
konfeduret, confederate
konfedy, confetti
konfekshun, confection
konferanse, conference
konferm, confirm
konfermashun, confirmation
konfes, confess
konfeshun, confession

konfesion, confession
konfetty, confetti
konfide, confide
konfidense, confidence
konfidenshul, confidential
konfidential, confidential
konfidont, confidant
konfigurashun, configuration
konfine, confine
konfinment, confinement
konfirents, conference
konfirm, confirm
konfirmashun, confirmation
konfirmation, confirmation
konflict, conflict
konform, conform
konfrunt, confront
konfudense, confidence
konfudenshul, confidential
konfudont, confidant
konfujen, confusion
konfuranse, conference
konfuse, confuse
konfusion, confusion
konger, conjure
kongested, congest(ed)
konglomurete, conglomerate
kongradulashun, congratulation
kongratshulate, congratulate
kongregashun, congregation
kongres, congress
kongrewint, congruent
kongrewity, congruent(uity)
kongrigate, congregate
kongris, congress
kongruedy, congruent(uity)
kongrues, congruous
kongrugate, congregate
kongrugation, congregation
kongruint, congruent
kongunctivitis, conjunction(ivitis)
konifur, conifer
konisur, connoisseur
konjer, conjure
konjest, congest
konjestion, congest(ion)
konjewgul, conjugal
konjugul, conjugal
konjunction, conjunction
konjunctivitis, conjunction(ivitis)
konjunkshen, conjunction
konjure, conjure
konk, conch
konkaf, concave

konkavety, concave(vity)
konker, conquer
konklusive, conclusive
konkokt, concoct
konkrete, concrete
konkwest, conquest
konquest, conquest
konsacrat, consecrate
konsalidate, consolidate
konscientious, conscientious
konsecrashen, consecrate(tion)
konsecrat, consecrate
konsecutive, consecutive
konsedarashen, considerate(tion)
konseduration, considerate(tion)
konseed, concede
konseet, conceit
konseeve, conceive
konseevuble, conceivable
konsekwently, consequent(ly)
konsel, council / counsel / console
konsemate, consummate
konsent, consent
konsentrate, concentrate
konsentric, concentric
konsepshual, conceptual
konsepshun, conception
konsept, concept
konsequenshal, consequent(ial)
konserge, concierge
konsern, concern
konservation, conservation
konservator, conservator
konservatory, conservatory
konserve, conserve
konservutive, conservative
konseshun, concession
konsestenly, consistent(ly)
konsetion, concession
konseve, conceive
konshenshis, conscientious
konsider, consider
konsierge, concierge
konsikwense, consequence
konsimate, consummate
konsinet, consonant
konsinment, consignment
konsintrate, concentrate
konsiquence, consequence
konsirv, conserve
konsirvation, conservation
konsirvator, conservator
konsirvatory, conservatory
konsirvutive, conservative

konsise, concise
konsist, consist
konsistency, consistence(cy)
konsiter, consider
konsolashen, consolation
konsole, console
konsolidate, consolidate
konsoul, console
konspearusy, conspiracy
konspikuos, conspicuous
konspikyewus, conspicuous
konspirusy, conspiracy
konstancy, constancy
konstant, constant
konstatushen, constitution
konstilashen, constellation
konstinse, constancy
konstint, constant
konstipashen, constipation
konstitushen, constitution
konstrict, constrict
konstrucshen, construction
konstruct, construct
konstulashen, constellation
konstupashen, constipation
konstutushen, constitution
konsucrat, consecrate
konsucrating, consecrate(ing)
konsukration, consecrate(tion)
konsukwinse, consequence
konsulashun, consolation
konsult, consult
konsumate, consummate
konsume, consume
konsumshen, consumption
konsunet, consonant
konsurt, concert
konsurvation, conservation
konsurvator, conservator
konsurvatory, conservatory
konsurve, conserve
konsurvutive, conservative
kontagus, contagious
kontain, contain
kontakt, contact
kontamenate, contaminate
kontane, contain
konteguis, contiguous
kontekst, context
kontemporary, contemporary
kontemt, contempt
kontend, contend
kontent, content
kontenuel, continue(ual)

kontest, contest
kontiguis, contiguous
kontimplate, contemplate
kontimporary, contemporary
kontinet, continent
konting, content
kontinuance, continuance
kontorshenist, contortionist
kontradik, contradict
kontrak, contract
kontrasepshun, contraception
kontrast, contrast
kontraversy, controversy
kontravertible, controvert(ible)
kontrebute, contribute
kontrery, contrary
kontrishen, contrition
kontrol, control
kontrovert, controvert
kontrovertible, controvert(ible)
kontrudik, contradict
kontrusepshun, contraception
kontumplate, contemplate
kontunent, continent
konture, contour
konufir, conifer
konusur, connoisseur
konvay, convey
konvayor, convey(or)
konvene, convene
konvenyut, convenient
konversashen, conversation
konvershen, conversion
konvert, convert
konvex, convex
konvict, convict
konvinse, convince
konvinshen, convention
konvulesents, convalescence
konvulgin, convulsion
konvulshen, convulsion
konvursashen, conversation
konvursation, conversation
konvurtable, convertible
kood, could
koodos, kudos
kooger, cougar
kook,*,ky,kier,kiest,kily,kiness, NEW SNOWBOARDER, ODD/ECCENTRIC BEHAVIOR
kookoo, cuckoo
kooky, cookie
kool, cool
koop, coop / co-op

kooperate, cooperate
kooshin, cushion
kooth, couth
kope, cope / copy
kopeir, copy(pier)
koper, copper
kopier, copy(pier)
kopulate, copulate
kopur, copper
kopy, copy
kor, car
koral, choral / coral / corral / chorale
kord, cord / chord / court
kordaroy, corduroy
kordinate, coordinate
kords, cord(s) / chord(s) / court(s) / quart(s) / quartz
kordunate, coordinate
korduroy, corduroy
kore, core / corp
korekt, correct
kores, chorus / course / core(s) / caress
korespond, correspond
korgil, cordial
korgul, cordial
koridoor, corridor
korigate, corrugate
korilate, correlate
koriner, coroner
korinery, coronary
koris, chorus / course
korispond, correspond
korjil, cordial
kork, cork / quark
korn, corn
korner, corner / coroner
korneu, cornea
kornikopea, cornucopia
kornukopea, cornucopia
kornur, corner / coroner
korode, corrode
koroshen, corrode(osion)
korparul, corporal
korpirate, corporate
korps, corpse
korpural, corporal
korpurate, corporate
kors, course / coarse
korsd, coarse(d)
korsoge, corsage
kort, cord / court / quart
kort-marshul, court-martial
korteks, cortex
kortex, cortex

korts, quartz / court(s) / quart(s) / cord(s) /chord(s) / car(ts)
korudoor, corridor
korugate, corrugate
korul, choral / coral / corral / chorale
korulate, correlate
koruner, coroner
korunery, coronary
korupt, corrupt
korus, chorus / course
koruspond, correspond
korve, carve
kos, cause
kosd, cause(d) / cost / coast /
kosee, cozy
koshen, caution
kosher,*,red,ring, RESTRICTION IN FOOD PREPARATION, LEGITIMATE/ FIT FOR OCCASION
koshes, cautious
koshin, caution
koshus, cautious
kosmik, cosmic
kosmopolutin, cosmopolitan
kosmos, cosmos
kost, cost / cause(d) / coast
koster, coaster
kostic, caustic
kostum, costume
kostyume, costume
kosy, cozy
kot, caught / cot / coat
kotage, cottage
kotch, coach
koten, cotton
kotuge, cottage
kouch, couch
koulishun, coalition
kounsil, council / counsel / console
kount, count
koursif, coerce(cive)
koursment, coerce(ment)
kova, kava
kove, cove
kovenant, covenant
kover, cover
kovit, covet
kovu, kava
kovurt, covert
kow, cow
kowch, couch
kowculus, calculus
kowerd, coward
kowersev, coerce(cive)

kowkulate, calculate
kowl, call / cowl
kownder, counter
kownsul, council / counsel / console
kownt, count
kowntur, counter
kownty, county
kowurd, coward
kowursif, coerce(cive)
kowursment, coerce(ment)
koyel, coil
koyn, coin
koz, cause
kozd, cause(d) / cost
kozmik, cosmic
kozmopoletin, cosmopolitan
kozmos, cosmos
kozy, cozy
krab, crab
krader, crater / creator
kradul, cradle
kradur, crater / creator
krafe, crave
kraft, craft
krain, crane
kraink, crank
krak, crack
krakel, crackle
kraker, cracker
kral, crawl / corral
kram, cram
kramp, cramp
kranbery, cranberry
krane, crane
kraneum, cranium
krank, crank
krany, cranny
kraon, crayon
krap, crap / crepe
krape, crepe / crap(ppy)
krasee, crazy
krash, crash
krass, crass
krate, crate
krater, crater / creator
kraul, crawl
kraut, PICKLED CABBAGE
krave, crave
krawnik, chronic
krayon, crayon
krazy, crazy
kreader, creator
kreal, creel
kream, cream / creme

kreap, creep
kreapy, creep(y)
krease, crease
kreashun, creation
kreasul, creosol
kreate, create
kreatef, create(ive)
kreative, creative
kreator, creator
kreb, crib
krebd, crib(bbed)
krebeg, cribbage
krecher, creature
kredable, credible
kredeeder, creditor
kreder, critter
kredet, credit
kredible, credible
kredibul, credible
kredider, creditor
kredik, critic
kredisize, criticize
kredit, credit
kreditor, creditor
kreduble, credible
kreecher, creature
kreel, creel
kreen, careen
kreenkul, crinkle
kreep, creep
kreepy, creep(y)
kreer, career
kreisote, creosote
kreke, creak / creek
krekit, cricket
krel, creel
kremate, cremate
kreme, cream / creme
kremenul, criminal
kreminal, criminal
kremsun, crimson
kreng, cringe
krenj, cringe
krenkle, crinkle
krep, creep / crepe
kreple, cripple
kreptic, cryptic
krepy, creep(y)
krescross, crisscross
krese, crease
kresendo, crescendo
kresent, crescent
kresont, croissant
kresp, crisp

kress, caress
krest, crest
kretable, credible
kreteek, critique
kretik, critic
kretikul, critical
kreusol, creosol
kreusote, creosote
krevas, crevasse / crevice
krevus, crevasse / crevice
krew, crew
krewd, crude
krewshul, crucial
krewsufix, crucifix
krewton, crouton
kri, cry
krib, crib
kribage, cribbage
krid, cried
kridecal, critical
kridenshul, credential
krider, critter
kridesize, criticize
krien, cry(ing)
kriket, cricket
krime, crime
krimenal, criminal
krimson, crimson
kring, cringe
krinj, cringe
kriptic, cryptic
kripul, cripple
krisade, crusade
kriscross, crisscross
krisis, crisis
krismus, christmas
krisont, croissant
krisp, crisp
kristal, crystal
kristashen, crustacean
kritesize, criticize
kritik, critic
kritur, critter
kriz, cries
kroak, croak
kroan, crone
krok, crock / croak
krokedile, crocodile
kroket, croquet / croquette
krokudile, crocodile
krokus, crocus
krol, crawl
krom, chrome / crumb
kromizone, chromosome

kronac, chronic	kryptic, cryptic	kulid, collide
kronacle, chronicle	krystal, crystal	kulidescope, kaleidoscope
kronalogical, chronology(gical)	krysus, crisis	kulijin, collision
krone, crone / crony	ku, cue	kulishun, collision
krones, crony(s)	kuack, quack	kulition, collision
kronic, chronic	kuagmire, quagmire	kulmenate, culminate
kronicle, chronicle	kubby, cubby	kulminate, culminate
kronilogical, chronology(gical)	kube, cubby / cube	kuloge, collage
kronlogical, chronology(gical)	kubek, cubic	kuloje, collage
kronucle, chronicle	kubekle, cubicle	kulokweul, colloquial
kronulogikul, chronology(gical)	kuberd, cupboard	kulon, cologne / colon
krony, crony	kubic, cubic	kuloneal, colonial
krook, crook	kubicul, cubicle	kuloquial, colloquial
kroose, cruise / crew(s)	kuburd, cupboard	kulor, color / cooler
krop, crop	kubuse, caboose	kulosel, colossal
kroshay, crochet	kuchen, cushion	kulosil, colossal
kross, cross	kucky, cookie	kulown, cologne / colon
krotch, crotch	kucumber, cucumber	kulpret, culprit
krouch, crouch	kud, cud / could / cue(d)	kulsher, culture
krout, kraut	kudaver, cadaver	kult, cult
krow, crow	kudel, cuddle	kultavashen, cultivate(tion)
krowch, crouch	kudent, couldn't	kultivashen, cultivate(tion)
krowd, crowd	kudet, cadet	kultivate, cultivate
krown, crown	kudint, couldn't	kultsher, culture
krows, crow(s) / carouse	**kudos**, BONUS, CREDIT	kulture, culture
krowshay, crochet	kufer, cover	kultuvashen, cultivate(tion)
krowt, kraut	kuferege, coverage	kulvert, culvert
kru, crew	kuff, cuff	kum, come / cum
kruch, crutch	kufredge, coverage	kumand, command
krude, crude	kuger, cougar	kumander, commander
krudenshul, credential	kugole, cajole	kumbarsome, cumber(some)
krue, crew	kuhoot, cahoot	kumber, cumber
kruke, crook	kuhute, cahoot	kumberbun, cummerbund
kruks, crux	kuk, kook / cook	kumbine, combine
krum, crumb	kuke, cook / cookie / kook(y)	kumbirsome, cumber(some)
krumble, crumble / crumple	kukoon, cocoon	kumbur, cumber
krumple, crumble / crumple	kuku, cuckoo	kumbuschen, combustion
krunch, crunch	kukumber, cucumber	kumbustuble, combustible
krupt, corrupt	kukune, cocoon	kumedeun, comedian
krusade, crusade	kul, cool / cull	kumemerate, commemorate
kruse, cruise / crew(s)	kulamity, calamity	kumenduble, commendable
krusefix, crucifix	kulandur, colander	kumensirit, commensurate
krusendo, crescendo	kulaps, collapse	kuments, commence
krush, crush	kulapsebul, collapse(sible)	kumfert, comfort
krushul, crucial	kulcher, culture	kumferter, comfort(er)
krusont, croissant	kuldesac, cul-de-sac	kumfertible, comfortable
krust, crust	kuleckshun, collection	kuminduble, commendable
krustashen, crustacean	kulecter, collect(or)	kumit, commit
krutch, crutch	kulejet, collegiate	kumitment, commitment
kruteke, critique	kulekt, collect	kumity, committee
kruton, crouton	kulenary, culinary	kumodety, commodity
krux, crux	kulendula, calendula	kumpar, compare
kry, cry	kuler, color / cooler / collar	kumpareson, comparison
kryeng, cry(ing)	kulesterol, cholesterol	kumpartment, compartment

kumpashun, compassion
kumpashunate, compassionate
kumpeny, company
kumpile, compile
kumplane, complain
kumpleks, complex
kumplete, complete
kumplians, compliant(nce)
kumplient, compliant
kumply, comply
kumponint, component
kumposier, composure
kumposit, composite
kumpoze, compose
kumpozer, composure
kumpreshun, compression
kumpresor, compressor
kumpress, compress
kumpuder, computer
kumpulsery, compulsory
kumpulshun, compulsion
kumpuss, compass
kumpute, compute
kumputer, computer
kumulative, cumulative
kumunal, communal
kumuneon, communion
kumutable, commute(table)
kumutble, commute(table)
kumyewtable, commute(table)
kunal, canal
kuncideration, considerate(tion)
kunclusev, conclusive
kundem, condemn
kundinse, condense
kundishen, condition
kundition, condition
kundolense, condolence
kundone, condone
kundukt, conduct
kundukter, conductor
kunekshen, connection
kunekt, connect
kunfekshun, confection
kunferm, confirm
kunfermashun, confirmation
kunfes, confess
kunfeshun, confession
kunfety, confetti
kunfide, confide
kunfigerashun, configuration
kunfine, confine
kunfinment, confinement
kunflict, conflict

kunform, conform
kunfrunt, confront
kunfujen, confusion
kunfuze, confuse
kunglomurete, conglomerate
kungradulashun, congratulation
kungratshulate, congratulate
kungruedy, congruent(uity)
kungruint, congruent
kungruity, congruent(uity)
kungunctavitis, conjunction(ivitis)
kunikkunik, kinnikinnick
kuning, cunning
kunjest, congest
kunjested, congest(ed)
kunjunction, conjunction
kunklude, conclude
kunklujen, conclusion
kunklusef, conclusive
kunkokt, concoct
kunkushen, concussion
kunning, cunning
kunsecutive, consecutive
kunsedurashen, considerate(tion)
kunseed, concede
kunseel, conceal
kunseet, conceit
kunseevable, conceivable
kunseeve, conceive
kunsent, consent
kunsentric, concentric
kunsepshual, conceptual
kunsepshun, conception
kunsern, concern
kunservator, conservator
kunservatory, conservatory
kunserve, conserve
kunseshun, concession
kunsestently, consistent(ly)
kunsevable, conceivable
kunsider, consider
kunsinment, consignment
kunsirvator, conservator
kunsirvatory, conservatory
kunsirvutive, conservative
kunsise, concise
kunsist, consist
kunsistency, consistence(cy)
kunsiter, consider
kunsole, console
kunsoludate, consolidate
kunsoom, consume
kunsoul, console
kunspearucy, conspiracy

kunspikyus, conspicuous
kunstrict, constrict
kunstrucshen, construction
kunstruct, construct
kunsult, consult
kunsume, consume
kunsumshen, consumption
kunsurvatory, conservatory
kunsurve, conserve
kunsurvutive, conservative
kunsuvator, conservator
kuntagus, contagious
kuntain, contain
kuntamunate, contaminate
kuntane, contain
kunteguis, contiguous
kuntemporary, contemporary
kuntemt, contempt
kuntend, contend
kuntent, content
kuntenual, continue(ual)
kuntenuense, continuance
kuntenule, continue(ual)
kuntest, contest
kuntiguis, contiguous
kuntimporary, contemporary
kuntorshenist, contortionist
kuntrakshen, contraction
kuntree, country
kuntrery, contrary
kuntribute, contribute
kuntrishen, contrition
kuntrol, control
kunveenyut, convenient
kunvene, convene
kunvense, convince
kunvenshen, convention
kunvenyant, convenient
kunvergin, conversion
kunvershen, conversion
kunvert, convert
kunvertable, convertible
kunvict, convict
kunvulgin, convulsion
kunvulshen, convulsion
kup, cup / coop
kupasity, capacity
kupcake, cupcake
kupe, coop
kupil, couple
kupler, coupler
kupon, coupon
kupoot, kaput
kupul, couple

kuput, kaput	kurten, curtain	kwalefiur, qualify(fier)
kurable, curable	kurtesy, courtesy	kwaletatif, quality(tative)
kurader, curator	kurteus, courteous	kwalety, quality
kural, choral / coral / corral / chorale	kurtin, curtain	kwalifekashen, qualify(fication)
kurb, curb	kurtle, curdle	kwalify, qualify
kurd, curd	kurtse, curtsy	kwalitatif, quality(tative)
kurdesy, courtesy	kurupt, corrupt	kwalitee, quality
kurdeus, courteous	kurvachure, curvature	kwalm, qualm
kurdisy, courtesy	kurve, curve	kwandery, quandary
kurdle, curdle	kury, curry	kwandree, quandary
kure, cure	kus, cuss	kwant, quaint
kurect, correct	kusen, cousin	kwantefy, quantify
kureen, careen	kuset, cassette	kwantem, quanta(tum)
kureer, career	kushen, cushion	kwantetative, quantitative
kurege, courage	kusin, cousin	kwantety, quantity
kureje, courage	kusp, cusp	kwantify, quantify
kurekt, correct	kusped, cuspid	kwantifyer, quantify(fier)
kurekulum, curriculum	kuss, cuss	kwantim, quanta(tum)
kuren, careen / cure(ring)	kustedy, custody	kwantity, quantity
kurensy, currency	kustem, custom	kwantry, quandary
kurent, currant / current	kustemary, customary	kwantum, quanta(tum)
kureosety, curiosity	kustemize, customize	kward, quart
kureosudy, curiosity	kusterd, custard	kwarder, quarter
kures, care(s) / caress / cure(s)	kustimer, customer	kwarderly, quarter(ly)
kureur, courier	kustodeun, custodian	kwards, quartz / quart(s)
kureus, curious	kustomary, customary	kwardur, quarter
kureusol, creosol	kustomer, customer	kwardurly, quarter(ly)
kurf, curve	kustomize, customize	kwardz, quartz / quart(s)
kurfew, curfew	kut, cut / cat	kware, quarry
kurfue, curfew	kutastrufee, catastrophe	kwarel, quarrel
kuri, curry	kute, cute	kwarentene, quarantine
kurige, courage	kutecle, cuticle	kwaril, quarrel
kurin, curtain	kuth, couth	kwarintene, quarantine
kurinsy, currency	kutlury, cutlery	kwark, quark
kurint, current	kutukle, cuticle	kwarol, quarrel
kuriosity, curiosity	kuvenant, covenant	kwart, quart
kurisma, charisma	kuver, cover	kwarter, quarter
kurl, curl	kuvit, covet	kwarterly, quarter(ly)
kurnel, colonel / kernel	kuvridge, coverage	kwarts, quartz / quart(s)
kuroburate, corroborate	kuvunent, covenant	kwarul, quarrel
kurode, corrode	kuzn, cousin	kwary, quarry / query
kuroky, karaoke	kwack, quack / quake	kwasar, quasar
kurosef, corrode(osive)	kwad, quad	kwasy, quasi
kurote, karate	kwadrant, quadrant	kwaundre, quandary
kurotion, corrode(osion)	kwagmire, quagmire	kwaure, quarry
kuroty, karate	kwaik, quake	kwawrel, quarrel
kurowse, carouse	kwail, quail	kwawrul, quarrel
kursanthimum, chrysanthemum	kwaint, quaint	kwawry, quarry
kursathimum, chrysanthemum	kwak, quack / quake	kwaysar, quasar
kurse, curse	kwale, quail	kwazar, quasar
kursif, cursive	kwaledy, quality	kwazee, quasi
kursive, cursive	kwalefication, qualify(fication)	kwazene, cuisine
kursoge, corsage	kwalefikashen, qualify(fication)	kween, queen
kurtale, curtail	kwalefiuble, qualify(fiable)	kweer, queer, career

kwefir, quiver
kwefur, quiver
kwek, quick
kwekest, quick(est)
kwekly, quick(ly)
kweky, quick(ie)
kwel, quill
kwelt, quilt
kwench, quench
kwentuplet, quintuplet
kwer, queer, career
kwerk, quirk
kwerky, quirk(y)
kwery, query
kwes, quiz
kwesden, question
kwesekal, quiz(zzical)
kweshten, question
kwest, quest
kwestenair, question(nnaire)
kwesteun, question
kwestshunar, question(nnaire)
kwestun, question
kwet, quit / quite
kweter, quit(tter) / quiet(er)
kwever, quiver
kwez, quiz
kwezekal, quiz(zzical)
kwezene, cuisine
kwezt, quest
kwiet, quiet
kwietly, quiet(ly)
kwifir, quiver
kwifor, quiver
kwik, quick
kwikest, quick(est)
kwikly, quick(ly)
kwiky, quick(ie)
kwil, quill
kwilt, quilt
kwinch, quench
kwintuplet, quintuplet
kwire, choir
kwirk, quirk
kwiry, query
kwisekal, quiz(zzical)
kwisine, cuisine
kwit, quit / quite
kwiter, quit(tter) / quiet(er)
kwiut, quiet
kwiutly, quiet(ly)
kwiver, quiver
kwiyet, quiet
kwiz, quiz

kwizekal, quiz(zzical)
kwochent, quotient
kwod, quad
kwoda, quota
kwodabul, quote(table)
kwodashen, quote(tation)
kwode, quote
kwodrent, quadrant
kwodu, quota
kwoledy, quality
kwolefikashen, qualify(fication)
kwolefy, qualify
kwoletatif, quality(tative)
kwoletative, quality(tative)
kwolety, quality
kwolification, qualify(fication)
kwolifikashen, qualify(fication)
kwolifiuble, qualify(fiable)
kwolifiur, qualify(fier)
kwolitatif, quality(tative)
kwolitative, quality(tative)
kwolitee, quality
kwolm, qualm
kwolufy, qualify
kwondery, quandary
kwontefy, quantify
kwontefyer, quantify(fier)
kwontem, quanta(tum)
kwontetative, quantitative
kwontety, quantity
kwontify, quantify
kwontifyer, quantify(fier)
kwontim, quanta(tum)
kwontity, quantity
kwontre, quandary
kwontum, quanta(tum)
kworam, quorum
kword, quart
kworder, quarter
kworderly, quarter(ly)
kwords, quartz / quart(s)
kwordur, quarter
kwordurly, quarter(ly)
kwordz, quartz / quart(s)
kwore, quarry
kworel, quarrel
kworem, quorum
kworentene, quarantine
kworil, quarrel
kworim, quorum
kworintene, quarantine
kwork, quark
kworol, quarrel
kworom, quorum

kwort, quart
kworter, quarter
kworterly, quarter(ly)
kwortir, quarter
kworts, quartz / quart(s)
kwortur, quarter
kwortz, quartz / quart(s)
kworul, quarrel
kworum, quorum
kworuntene, quarantine
kwoshent, quotient
kwosy, quasi
kwota, quota
kwotabul, quote(table)
kwotashen, quote(tation)
kwotation, quote(tation)
kwote, quote
kwotu, quota
kwozy, quasi
kwurentene, quarantine
kwurintene, quarantine
kwurk, quirk
kwurky, quirk(y)
kwyit, quiet
kwyre, choir
kyak, kayak
la, law / lay
labarenth, labyrinth
labedo, libido
label,*,led,ling, A WAY TO REMEMBER/ SAVE/RETRIEVE/CATEGORIZE THINGS "prefixes: un"
laber, labor
laberatory, laboratory
labeul, labial
labi, PREFIX INDICATING "LIP" MOST OFTEN MODIFIES THE WORD
labial,lly,lize,lization, SOUND, OF THE LIPS, ORGAN PIPE "prefixes: bi"
labido, libido
labil, label
labio, PREFIX INDICATING "LIP" MOST OFTEN MODIFIES THE WORD
labl, label
lable, label
labor,*,red,ring,rious,riously,riousness, rism,rist,rer, PHYSICALLY WORKING "prefixes: un"
laboratory,ries, PLACE FOR STUDY/ EXPERIMENTS AND OBSERVATION
laborenth, labyrinth
labratory, laboratory
labrinth, labyrinth
labrutory, laboratory

labul, label
labur, labor
labyrinth,*, A MAZE, CHAOTIC CIRCUMSTANCES
lace,*,ed,cing,cy,cier,ciest,ciness, SECURE SHOES WITH, WOVEN STRING "prefixes: en/un"
lacerate,*,ed,ting,tion, GASH/RIP SOMETHING BY PENETRATION
lach, latch / lodge / lash
lack,*,ked,king, BELIEF THAT ONE DOES NOT HAVE ENOUGH OF SOMETHING (or see lake)
lackative, laxative
lacker, lacquer / lager
lacks, lax / lake(s) / lack(s)
lacktat, lactate
lacquer,*, VARNISH
lacrosse, ORIGINALLY A NATIVE AMERICAN SPORTS GAME
lacs, lax
lacsetive, laxative
lact, PREFIX INDICATING "MILK" MOST OFTEN MODIFIES THE WORD
lactate,*,ed,ting,tion, MILK BEING PRODUCED IN MAMMALS
lacti, PREFIX INDICATING "MILK" MOST OFTEN MODIFIES THE WORD
lacto, PREFIX INDICATING "MILK" MOST OFTEN MODIFIES THE WORD
lactose, SUGAR FROM COW MILK
lad,*, YOUNG MEN (or see laid/late)
ladder,*, TWO POLES WITH RUNGS FOR CLIMBING (or see later)
lade, laid / lady / late
ladel, ladle
laden, BURDENED DOWN, HEAVY LOAD
lader, ladder / later / latter
laderal, lateral
laderuly, lateral(ly)
ladery, lottery
lades, lattice / lady(dies) / lettuce
ladetude, latitude
ladir, latter / ladder / later
ladis, lattice / lady(dies) / lettuce
laditude, latitude
ladle,*,ed,ling, LONG HANDLE SPOON TO SERVE FOOD
ladul, ladle
ladur, later / ladder / latter
ladural, lateral
ladutude, latitude
lady,dies, A WOMAN
lae, lay

laed, laid / late
laeng, lay(ing)
laer, layer
laevo, PREFIX INDICATING "COUNTER-CLOCKWISE" MOST OFTEN MODIFIES THE WORD
laf, laugh
lafdur, laughter
lafender, lavender
laff, laugh
lafter, laughter
lag,*,gged,gging, BE SLOWER THAN THE OTHERS, SHAPE OR CASING, DELAY (or see log/lodge/lack/leg/lake)
lager, BEER (or see logger/lacquer)
lageslat, legislate
lagestics, logistic(s)
lagetamate, legitimate
lagicul, logic(al)
lagir, logger / lacquer
lagislat, legislate
lagistics, logistic(s)
lagitamate, legitimate
lagoon,*, ENCLOSED/NEARLY ENCLOSED SMALL BODY OF WATER NEAR LARGER BODY OF WATER
lagor, logger / lacquer
lagoslat, legislate
lagur, lacquer / lager / logger
laguslat, legislate
lai, lay
laid, PAST TENSE FOR THE WORD "LAY" (or see late)
lain, PAST TENSE FOR THE WORD "LAID" (or see lane/line)
laing, lay(ing) / lying
laingwege, language
lair,*,red,ring, ANIMALS DEN (or see lyre/layer)
laj, lodge
lajekul, logic(al)
lajeslat, legislate
lajislat, legislate
lajistics, logistic(s)
lajoslat, legislate
lajuslat, legislate
lake,*, LARGE BODY OF WATER FED BY SPRINGS (or see lack)
laker, lacquer / lager / logger
lakross, lacrosse
laks, lax / lake(s) / lack(s)
laksetif, laxative
laksutef, laxative
laktate, lactate

laktose, lactose
lam, RUNNING FROM TROUBLE (or see lamb/lame)
lama, llama
lamb,*, YOUNG SHEEP (or see lam/lame)
lame,ly,eness, PERMANENTLY INJURED LIMB/LIMBS THAT DON'T WORK (or see lam/lamb)
lamenate, laminate
lament,*,ted,ting,tingly,table,tably, tableness,tation,ter, MOURN THE LOSS OF SOMEONE, SPEND TIME IN THE PAST ON REGRETS
laminate,*,ed,ting,tion,tor,able, GLUE LAYERS TOGETHER "prefixes: inter/multi/non"
lamp,*, A LIGHT WITH A SHADE/COVER OVER THE BULB
lamunate, laminate
lance,*,ed,cing,er, MEDIEVAL WEAPON
lanch, launch
land,*,ded,ding,dless, EARTH, SETTLE ONTO, DIVIDING THE GROUND
landern, lantern
landers, launder(s)
landlord,*, OWNER WHO RENTS/LEASES PROPERTY
landscape,*,ed,ping,er, FOLIAGE/FAUNA/TERRAIN OF WHAT THE EYE SEES
landslide,*, WHEN LAND BREAKS AWAY FROM OTHER LAND DUE TO WATER
lane,*, PASSAGEWAYS/ROADS FOR VEHICLES, PATHS IN BOWLING (or see lain)
lanelin, lanolin
language,*, WORDS/MEANS OF COMMUNICATION IN DIFFERENT REGIONS "prefixes: inter"
langweg, language
lankwij, language
lanky,kily,kiness, TALL AND THIN
lanlord, landlord
lanolin, OIL FROM WOOL
lanqueg, language
lans, lance / lane(s) / land(s)
lanskap, landscape
lanskapur, landscape(r)
lant, land
lantern,*, FUELED FLAME WITHIN CONTAINER
lantlord, landlord
lantscape, landscape

lantslide, landslide
lanulin, lanolin
lap,*,pped,pping, TO GO AROUND, HOW ANIMALS DRINK, CREATED IN SITTING POSITION "prefixes: over"
lapadary, lapidary
lapel,*, COLLARS
lapidary,ries,rian, CUT/POLISH/ ENGRAVE STONES
laprutory, laboratory
laps, lapse / lap(s)
lapse,*,ed,sing, SLIPPING INTO, LOOSE A MOMENT IN TIME, PAUSE (or see lap(s)) "prefixes: pro"
lapudary, lapidary
lar, lair / layer
larch, large
lard, FAT FROM DEAD PIGS
larel, laurel
larengitis, laryngitis
lareut, laureate
large,er,est,ely,eness, BIG "prefixes: en"
larges, largess / large(st)
largess, GENEROUS GIFT/DONATION EXPECTING NOTHING IN RETURN
largist, large(st)
largly, large(ly)
lariet, laureate
lariette, laureate
larinex, larynx
larj, large
larjes, largess
lark,*, BIRD, PRANT, ON AN IMPULSE FOR FUN
larniks, larynx
larol, laurel
larva,al, BABY INSECT THAT RESEMBLES A WORM BEFORE IT BECOMES AN ADULT
larying, PREFIX INDICATING "LARYNX/ VOCAL ORGAN" MOST OFTEN MODIFIES THE WORD
laryngitis,ic, THROAT INFLAMMATION
larynx, THROAT
lasarate, lacerate
lasd, last / lace(d)
lase, lace / lace(y) / lazy
lasench, lozenge
laser,*, A LIGHT FREQUENCY
laserashen, lacerate(tion)
laserate, lacerate
laseration, lacerate(tion)
lash,hes,hed,hing,her, HAIRS ON THE EYE, USE SOMETHING SUCH AS ROPE TO STRIKE/TIE UP SOMETHING, THRUST OUT WITH ILL INTENT "prefixes: un"
lasinch, lozenge
lasirashen, lacerate(tion)
lasirate, lacerate
lasiration, lacerate(tion)
lass,ssie, GIRL
lasso,oes, SLIDING HOOP MADE OF ROPE
last,*,ted,ting,tly, NOT THE FIRST, WON'T GO AWAY FOR QUITE AWHILE (or see lace(d))
lasuit, lawsuit
lasurashen, lacerate(tion)
lasurat, lacerate
lasuration, lacerate(tion)
lasute, lawsuit
latch,hes,hed, CLOSURE FOR A DOOR/ LID
late,er,ely,eness,tish, NOT ON TIME, OF A PARTICULAR TIME (or see lady/ ladder/latter)
laten, laden
latent,tly,ncy, A TIME LAPSE BETWEEN WHEN IT HAPPENED AND THE REACTION
later, FURTHER ALONG IN TIME (or see late/ladder/latter)
lateral,lly, EXTENDS FROM THE SIDE, A MOVEMENT IN A SIDEWAYS DIRECTION "prefixes: bi/contra/ multi/uni"
latex,xes,tices, FORM OF MANMADE RUBBER/PLASTIC USED FOR GLOVES, PAINT, ETC.
lath,*, NARROW STRIPS OF WOOD USED TO BUILD WITH (or see lathe)
lathargic, lethargic
lathe,*,ed,hing, WOOD SHAPING MACHINE (or see lath)
lather,*,red,ring,ry,rer, SOAPY/FOAMY BUBBLES (or see leather)
latil, ladle
latincy, latent(ncy)
latise, lattice
latitude,*,dinal,dinally, LINES THAT RUN NORTH/ SOUTH
latle, ladle
latrine,*, MILITARY WORD FOR TOILET
latter,rly, MORE TOWARDS THE LAST (or see ladder)
lattice,ed, WOOD STRIPS CRISSCROSSED TOGETHER FOR DECORATION
latur, later / ladder / latter
latural, lateral
latury, lottery
laty, lady
lau, law
laud, loud
lauger, lager / logger
laugh,hes,hed,hing,hable,hably,hter, DISPLAY/EXPRESS GLEE/ ENJOYMENT IN VOCAL BURSTS
laughter, VOCAL EXPRESSION OF HAPPINESS/GLEE
lauk, lock / log
laukd, lock(ed)
laun, lawn
launch,hes,hed,hing,her, PROPEL/ SHOOT SOMETHING (or see lounge)
launder,*,rer,ry, WASH AND IRON CLOTHING
laundry, CLEANING/CARING OF CLOTHES
laung, lounge / long
laur, layer
laurch, large
laureate,eship, HONORED/ DISTINGUISHED POET
laurel, A TREE, REST ON PREVIOUS AWARDS
lausut, lawsuit
lauyer, lawyer
lava, MOLTEN ROCK
laven, leaven(ed)
lavender, A PLANT
lavesh, lavish
lavinder, lavender
lavish,hes,her,hly,hness,hment, TO BESTOW UPON SOMEONE GIFTS AND OTHER THINGS
lavun, leaven(ed)
lavunder, lavender
law,*,wful,wfully,wfulness,wless, wlessly, RULES SUPPORTED BY A GOVERNMENT "prefixes: un"
lawn,*, GRASSY AREAS
lawnch, launch
lawsuit,*, A CASE BROUGHT BEFORE A JUDGE CONCERNING THE LAW
lawyer,*, PAID PEOPLE TO HELP YOU WITH THE LAWS
lax,xly,xness,xity,xative, RELAXED, NO HURRY (or see lake(s)/lack(s))

laxative,*, PLANT/CHEMICALS FOR RELAXING THE BOWELS
laxsatif, laxative
laxsutif, laxative
laxutif, laxative
lay,*,aid,ying,yer, SET ASIDE/DOWN AN OBJECT, TO INSTALL, SOMEONE WHO IS TRAINING TO BE AN UPPER RANK, RECLINE (or see lie) "prefixes: in/inter/mis/over/re-/un/under"
layeng, lay(ing) / lying
layer,*,red,ring, THICKNESS OF SOMETHING OVER TOP OF ANOTHER, ONE LEVEL OVER ANOTHER "prefixes: bi/multi"
laytex, latex
layur, layer / lawyer
lazarashen, lacerate(tion)
laze, lazy
lazeng, lozenge
lazer, laser
lazeur, lazy(zier)
lazing, lozenge / laze(zing)
lazy,zier,ziest,zily,ziness, NO AMBITION TO DO ANYTHING (or see lace(y))
lbo, elbow
leach,hes,hed,hing, SEEPING/PERCOLATING LIQUID (or see leech)
lead,*,ded,dless,der,derless,ding,den, denly,denness, A HEAVY METAL, SOMEONE WHO TAKES CHARGE OF A SITUATION "prefixes: mis/un"
leader,*,rless,rship, ONE WHO TAKES CHARGE (or see letter/liter)
leaf,aves,fy,fier,fiest,finess, GROWS ON A TREE/BUSH "prefixes: inter"
league,*,er, GROUPS PARTICIPATING IN A SIMILAR ACTIVITY DIVIDED INTO REGIONS/ABILITIES "prefixes: pro"
leak,*,ked,king,kage,ky,kiness, WHEN LIQUID/INFORMATION SEEPS OUT (or see leek)
lean,*,nly,nness,ner,nest, VERY LITTLE FAT, VERTICAL POSITION LEANING TOWARDS A HORIZONTAL STATE (or see lien)
leap,*,ped,ping,pt, TO BOUND/JUMP
lear, leer
learn,*,ned,ning,nable,ner,nedly, nedness, TAKE IN INFORMATION AS KNOWLEDGE "prefixes: un"
leary, leery

lease,*,ed,sing,sable,ssee,er, BORROW/USE FOR AWHILE IN EXCHANGE FOR MONEY (or see lees) "prefixes: re-/sub"
leash,es,hed,hing, RESTRAINT FOR ANIMALS "prefixes: un"
leason, liaison
least,twise, SMALLEST AMOUNT, GREATER THAN "LESS" (or see lease(ed))
leasy, lessee
leather,*,red,ring, DRIED SKIN FROM ANIMALS
leave,*,ving,eft, TO GO AWAY, PAST TENSE FOR THE WORD "LEAF/LEAVE" (or see leaf/leaven) "prefixes: inter"
leaven,*,ned,ning, USED TO FERMENT DOUGH, TO RAISE MOODS/SPIRITS (or see leave(ving)) "prefixes: un"
leazon, liaison
lebarul, liberal
lebirate, liberate
lebrul, liberal
lebural, liberal
leburate, liberate
leburty, liberty
lecar, liquor / liqueur / lick(er)
lech, leech / leach / ledge
lechibol, legible
lecshur, lecture
lecture,*,ed,ring,er, TO SPEAK AT GREAT LENGTH ABOUT SOMETHING TO A GROUP OF PEOPLE
lecur, liquor / liqueur / lick(er)
led, PAST TENSE FOR THE WORD "LEAD" (or see lid/lead/let)
ledagation, litigate(tion)
ledal, little
ledaret, literate
leder, liter / litter / letter / leader
lederachure, literature
lederary, literary
lederul, literal
ledge,*,er, A FLAT LANDING ATOP A WALL/SECTION, A BOOK WHICH KEEPS ACCOUNTING RECORDS, AN OVERHANG
ledigation, litigate(tion)
ledir, leader / letter / liter / litter
ledis, lettuce
leds, let(s) / lead(s)
ledur, liter / litter / letter / leader

ledurasy, literacy
ledus, lettuce
leech,hes, BLOOD SUCKING BUG (or see leach)
leed, lead
leef, leaf / leave
leeg, league
leek, A VEGETABLE (or see leak)
leen, lean / lien
leenyency, leniency
leep, leap
leer,*,red,ring,ry, A LONG GLANCE WITH MALICIOUS INTENT
leery, SUSPICIOUS/WARY OF
lees, SEDIMENTS OF WINE/LIQUOR (or see lease)
leese, lease
leesh, leash
leest, least / lease(d)
leet, lead
leeward, AWAY FROM THE WIND
lef, leaf / live / leave / left
lefd, lift / left / leaf(ed) / live(d)
lefee, levee / levy / leaf(y)
lefol, level
left,*,ty, LEFT VS. RIGHT, PAST TENSE FOR THE WORD "LEAVE", APPEARS TO BE GONE (or see lift/live(d))
leful, level
leg,*,gged,gging,ggings, EXTREMITY ON THE LOWER END OF THE TORSO, SUPPORT FOR TABLE/CHAIRS, AN EXTENSION, COVER FOR LEGS (or see league/ledge)
legacy,cies, SOMETHING HANDED DOWN FROM PREDECESSORS
legal,ly,lity,lities,lize,lization,lism, RULES AS DECIDED BY THE SUPREME COURT "prefixes: il"
legament, ligament
leganse, allegiance / elegance
legasy, legacy
lege, ledge / league
legebul, legible
legecy, legacy
legend,*,dary,daries, A STORY HANDED DOWN THROUGH HISTORY
leger, leisure / ledge(r)
legeslat, legislate
legesy, legacy
legible,ly,bility, WRITING CAPABLE OF BEING READ "prefixes: il"
legibul, legible
legido, libido

legind, legend
legion,*,nary,naries, LARGE GROUP ASSOCIATED WITH THE MILITARY
legislat, legislate
legislate,*,ed,ting,tion,tive,tor,ture, RELATED TO LAWMAKING
legislation, PASSING AND CREATING LAWS
legislative,ely, RELATED TO LAWMAKING
legislature, LAWMAKING BRANCH
legistics, logistic(s)
legisy, legacy
legitimate,*,ed,ting,ely,eness,tize,acy, tion,mist,mize,mized,mizing,azation, mizer, LEGALLY RECOGNIZED "prefixes: il"
legium, legume
legoslat, legislate
leguble, legible
legue, league
legul, legal
legulize, legal(ize)
legume,*, SPECIES OF PLANT
legun, lesion / legion
leguse, legacy
leguslashen, legislation
leguslat, legislate
leguslative, legislative
leguslature, legislature
legusy, legacy
lei, lay
leier, layer
lein, lain / lane
leis, lace
leisure,ed,eless,ely,reliness,eness, RELAXED, UNHURRIED
lej, ledge / leech
lejable, legible
lejanse, allegiance
lejebul, legible
lejen, lesion / legion
lejend, legend
lejer, leisure / ledge(r)
lejeslat, legislate
lejibul, legible
lejin, legion / lesion
lejislashen, legislation
lejislat, legislate
lejislative, legislative
lejislature, legislature
lejitamet, legitimate
lejoslat, legislate
lejun, legion / lesion

lejuslat, legislate
lek, lick / leak / leek / league
leked, lick(ed) / leak(ed)
lekemia, leukemia
leker, liquor / liqueur / lick(er)
lekoresh, licorice
leksher, lecture
lekture, lecture
lekume, legume
lekur, liquor / liqueur / lick(er)
lekwefide, liquify(fied)
lekwid, liquid
lekwidate, liquid(ate)
lekwify, liquify
lem, limb
lemazene, limousine
lemb, limb
lember, limber
lembo, limbo
lemet, limit
lemfatic, lymph(atic)
lemintation, lament(tation)
lemit, limit
lemitation, limit(ation)
lemon,*,ny,nade, CITRUS FRUIT, JUICE
lemp, limp
lemphatic, lymph(atic)
lemune, lemon(y)
lemusine, limousine
lemutation, limit(ation)
lemuzene, limousine
len, lean / lien
lenament, liniment
lend,*,ding,nt,der, LET SOMEONE BORROW SOMETHING (or see lint/ lean(ed))
leneanse, leniency
lenear, linear
lenen, linen
leneuge, lineage
leneul, lineal
lenger, linger
lengo, lingo
length,*,hen,hener,hiness,hy, HOW LONG SOMETHING IS
lengual, lingual
lenguist, linguist
lenguistic, linguistic
lenguistics, linguistic(s)
lengwestic, linguistic
lengwist, linguist
lengwistics, linguistic(s)
lengwul, lingual
leniansy, leniency

leniency,cies,ce,nt,ntly, NOT RIGID OR TOO STRICT
lenin, linen / lean(ing)
leniuge, lineage
leniur, linear
lenk, link
lenkage, link(age)
lenker, linger
lenkth, length
lenkwol, lingual
lenoleum, linoleum
lenon, linen / lean(ing)
lens, PART OF THE EYE, USED IN GLASSES
lenseed, linseed
lent, PAST TENSE FOR THE WORD "LEND", LET SOMEONE BORROW, A RELIGIOUS EVENT (or see lint/lend/ lean(ed))
lenth, length
lentil,*, PLANT IN THE LEGUME FAMILY
lentul, lentil
lenument, liniment
lenyensy, leniency
leotard,*, HEAVYWEIGHT PANTYHOSE
lep, lip / leap
lepel, lapel
leqer, liquor / liqueur
lequid, liquid
lequidate, liquid(ate)
lequifide, liquify(fied)
lequify, liquify
leranex, larynx
lerch, lurch
lere, leery
lerengitis, laryngitis
leric, lyric
lerinex, larynx
leringitis, laryngitis
lerk, lurk
lern, learn
lernicks, larynx
lery, leery
les, less / lease
lesard, lizard
lesbian,*, WOMAN WHO PREFERS INTIMATE COMPANIONSHIP WITH ANOTHER WOMAN
lese, lessee
lesee, lessee
lesen, lessen / lesson / listen
leser, lesser / lessor
lesh, leash
leshun, lesion

lesi, lessee
lesin, lessen / lesson / listen
lesion,*, AN INJURED SPOT ON HUMAN TISSUE
lesir, lesser / lessor
lesless, listless
leson, lessen / lesson / listen
lesp, lisp
less,sser, NOT AS MUCH AS BEFORE OR AS EXPECTED
lessee,*, ONE WHO IS LEASING
lessen, TAKE SOME AWAY, REMOVE SOME (or see lesson)
lesser, NOT AS MUCH AS BEFORE, LESS THAN (or see lessor)
lesson,*, A TEACHING/LEARNING SECTION/SESSION (or see lessen)
lessor,*, ONE WHO LEASES OUT PROPERTY TO OTHERS (or see lesser)
lest, list / least
lesten, listen
lestless, listless
lesun, lessen / lesson / listen
lesur, lesser / lessor
let,*,tting, PERMIT, ALLOW (or see led/lead)
let's, CONTRACTION OF THE WORDS 'LET US'
leter, liter / litter / letter / leader
leteracy, literacy
leteral, literal
leterally, literal(ly)
leterary, literary
leterate, literate
leterature, literature
letes, lettuce
lethal,lly,lity, DEADLY "prefixes: non/semi"
lethargic,cally,gy, SLEEPY, NO ENERGY, SLUMPED
lethargy,gic, SLEEPY, HARD TO MOVE, NO ENERGY
lether, leather
lethergy, lethargy
lethul, lethal
letir, liter / litter / letter / leader
letiracher, literature
letis, lettuce
letmus, litmus
letrine, latrine
letter,*,red,ring, SYMBOLS OF THE ALPHABET, PAPER WITH WRITING TO SOMEONE, MAKE LETTER SHAPES (or see leader) "prefixes: un"
lettuce, AN EDIBLE PLANT
letur, liter / litter / letter / leader
leturacher, literature
letus, lettuce
leuc, PREFIX INDICATING 'WHITE/COLORLESS' MOST OFTEN MODIFIES THE WORD
leuco, PREFIX INDICATING 'WHITE/COLORLESS' MOST OFTEN MODIFIES THE WORD
leukemia,ic, A FATAL DISEASE
leuko, PREFIX INDICATING 'WHITE/COLORLESS' MOST OFTEN MODIFIES THE WORD
leutard, leotard
lev, PREFIX INDICATING 'COUNTERCLOCKWISE' MOST OFTEN MODIFIES THE WORD
levabul, live(vable)
leval, level
levatate, levitate
leve, leave / levy / levee
levee,*, TRENCH/EMBANKMENT FOR CONTROLLING WATER (or see levy)
level,*,led,ling,lly,lness,ler, STRAIGHT UP OR HORIZONTAL, TRUTHFUL WITH SOMEONE "prefixes: multi/un"
leven, leaven(ed)
lever,*,rage, APPLY PHYSICS/HARDWARE TO LIFT "prefixes: un"
levi, levee / levy
levid, livid
levil, level
levitate,*,ed,ting,tion,ty, DEFY GRAVITY
levo, PREFIX INDICATING "COUNTERCLOCKWISE" MOST OFTEN MODIFIES THE WORD
levol, level
levor, lever / liver
levs, leave(s)
levuble, live(vable)
levul, level
levun, leaven(ed)
levur, liver / lever
levury, livery
levutate, levitate
levy,vies,vied,vying,viable,vier, USED TO COLLECT MONEY, WAGE WAR (or see levee)
lew, lieu
lewb, lube
lewbrecashen, lubricate(tion)
lewbrecate, lubricate
lewbrikate, lubricate
lewcid, lucid
lewcratef, lucrative
lewd,dly,dness, OBSCENE, GIVEN TO LUST AND INDECENCY (or see loot)
lewdakris, ludicrous
lewducris, ludicrous
lewkrative, lucrative
lewkwarm, lukewarm
lewlu, lulu
lewmenary, luminary
lewmenesense, luminescence
lewmenosity, luminosity
lewmenus, luminous
lewmin, lumen
lewner, lunar
leword, leeward
lewpine, lupine
lewse, loose / lose
lewsid, lucid
lewsun, loose(n)
lewt, loot / lute / lewd
leyor, layer
lezard, lizard
lezbeun, lesbian
li, lie / lye / lay
liabelity, liable(bility)
liable,bility,bilities, SOMEONE TO BE BLAMED
liaison,*, FORMATION OF DEEP CONNECTION BETWEEN PEOPLE FOR MANEUVERING, BONDING
liar,*, SOMEONE WHO DOESN'T TELL THE TRUTH (or see lyre)
liatard, leotard
libary, library
libel,llant,lee,lous,lously, WRITE MALICIOUS WORDS ABOUT SOMEONE ELSE FOR PUBLIC VIEWING (or see liable)
liberal,*,lly,lness,lism,lity,lities,listic,list, MODERATE, TOLERANT, PROVIDE FREELY "prefixes: neo"
liberate,*,ed,ting,tion,tor, TO SET FREE
liberde, liberty
liberty,ties, THE ACT OF FREEDOM
libery, library
libido,dinal,dinally, THOUGHTS WHICH DRIVE THE SEXUAL IMPULSES
lible, libel / liable
libol, libel
liboral, liberal
liborashun, liberate(tion)

liborate, liberate
liboration, liberate(tion)
liborte, liberty
liborul, liberal
library,ries,rian, A PLACE WHICH COLLECTS AND DISSEMINATES WRITTEN HISTORY "prefixes: inter"
librul, liberal
libul, libel / liable
libural, liberal
licd, lick(ed) / like(d)
lice, PLURAL WORD FOR LOUSE, PARASITIC INSECT (or see like/lick/lie(s)/lay(s))
license,*,ed,sing,sable,see,er, A PERMIT TO OPERATE "prefixes: sub/un"
lich, leach / leech
lichen,*, MOSS, A FORM OF PLANT WITH HEALING QUALITIES (or see liken)
lichon, legion / lesion / lichen
licinse, license
lick,*,ked,king,ker, USING THE TONGUE (or see like) "prefixes: un"
licorice, A PLANT EXTRACT, A CANDY
lict, lick(ed) / like(d)
lid,*,dded,dless, TOP FOR A CONTAINER, A COVERING (or see lie(d)/light/lit)
lidagachon, litigate(tion)
lidagation, litigate(tion)
lidegashen, litigate(tion)
lidegate, litigate
lidel, little
lider, liter / litter / light(er) / leader
liderachure, literature
lideral, literal
liderally, literal(ly)
liderary, literary
liderasy, literacy
liderate, literate
liderature, literature
liderit, literate
lidigachen, litigate(tion)
lidigate, litigate
lidigation, litigate(tion)
lidirachure, literature
lidirary, literary
lidol, little
lidor, litter / leader / liter / letter
lidul, little
liduracher, literature
lidurally, literal(ly)
lidurare, literary

lie,*,ed,lying, TO NOT TELL THE TRUTH, BODY IN A RECLINED/FLAT POSITION, INACTIVE POSITION (or see lay/lye) "prefixes: under"
lien,*, SOMEONE WHO TAKES AWAY PROPERTY FOR MONEY DUE (or see lion)
lieng, lying
lier, liar / lyre
lieu, INSTEAD OF, IN PLACE OF
lieutenant,*, A MILITARY OFFICER
lif, life / live / leaf / leave
lifd, lift / live(d)
life,er,ive, ANIMATE MATTER/ ORGANISM "prefixes: pro-"
lifeble, live(vable)
lifle, live(ly)
liflehood, livelihood
liflehud, livelihood
lift,*,ted,ting,ter, PICK/HOIST UP (or see live(d)/left) "prefixes: up"
ligal, legal
ligale, legal(lly)
ligality, legal(ity)
ligament,*,tous,tal,tary, FIBROUS TISSUE IN THE BODY
ligan, legion / lesion / lichen
light,*,ted,ting,tly,it,ten,tens,tened, tening,tless,tness, VISIBLE WAVE/ PARTICLES, NOT HEAVY "prefixes: en"
lightening, ILLUMINATED ELECTRICAL BOLTS IN SKY
lightness, NOT HEAVY, FEATHER WEIGHT, DEGREE OF ILLUMINATION
ligol, legal
ligole, legal(lly)
ligoly, legal(lly)
ligon, legion / lesion / lichen
ligoon, lagoon
ligument, ligament
lik, lick / like / leak / leek
likd, lick(ed) / like(d)
like,*,ed,kable,eness,ely,elier,eliest, SIMILAR TO SOMETHING/ SOMEONE ELSE, ENJOY SOMETHING, ATTRACTED TO SOMETHING (or see lick) "prefixes: dis/un"
liken,*, SIMILAR TO, RESEMBLING (or see lichen/lick(ing))
likeness, SIMILAR TO, RESEMBLING
liker, liquor / liquer / lick(er)

likerish, licorice
likewise, SIMILARLY, ALSO
likness, likeness
likor, liquor / liqueur
likoresh, licorice
likt, like(d) / lick(ed)
likuble, like(kable)
likued, liquid
likuefi, liquify
likun, liken
likwed, liquid
likwid, liquid
likwidate, liquid(ate)
likwifide, liquify(fied)
likwify, liquify
likwise, likewise
lilac,*, AROMATIC PLANT
liluc, lilac
limasen, limousine
limazene, limousine
limb,*,bed,bing, BRANCHES OF TREES/ SHRUBS, TO REMOVE BRANCHES/ EXTRUSIONS FROM THE BODY TORSO
limber,*,red,ring,rly,rness, ABLE TO MOVE BODY SMOOTHLY, WITH DEXTERITY "prefixes: un"
limbo, PLACE BETWEEN HERE AND THERE, WITH UNCERTAINTY, A PHYSICAL GAME
lime,*, A CITRUS FRUIT, MINERAL FOR SETTING BRICKS/STONE
limelight,*, BEING IN THE SPOTLIGHT
limen, lemon
limesine, limousine
limet, limit
limetation, limit(ation)
limfatic, lymph(atic)
limit,*,ted,ting,tation,tless,tative,ter, tary, ONLY GO SO FAR, A FIXED VALUE "prefixes: il/sub/un"
limlite, limelight
limon, lemon
limosen, limousine
limousine,*, LONG AUTOMOBILE FOR TRANSPORTING PEOPLE
limozen, limousine
limp,*,ped,ping,ply,per, NOT STIFF/ RIGID, LOSS OF FUNCTION, LACK OF WILLFUL CONTROL OVER THE BODY
limphatic, lymph(atic)
limpt, limp(ed)
limusine, limousine
limuzene, limousine

lin, line / lean / lend
linament, liniment
lind, lend / lint / line(d)
line,*,ed,ning,er,eless,eable,eal,ear, eate, BETWEEN TWO POINTS, FOR FISHING "prefixes: inter/multi/un/under"
lineage,*, OUR ANCESTORS, FAMILY TREE, WHERE WE COME FROM
lineal,lly, HEREDITY FOLLOWING A DIRECT PATH "prefixes: bi/inter/multi/uni"
lineansi, leniency
linear,rly,rize,rizes,rized,rizing,rization, rity, PATH STRAIGHT AHEAD WITH NO DEVIATION "prefixes: bi/inter/multi/non/uni"
linen,*, TAN COTTON FABRIC (or see linin/lining) "prefixes: under"
lineng, lining
liner,*, COATING INSIDE A VESSEL FOR PROTECTION
lineur, linear
linger,*,red,ring,ringly,er, STAY AROUND LONGER, LOITER, WAITING
lingo,oes, WAY TO SAY SOMETHING, UNIQUE METHOD OF COMMUNICATION
lingual,lly, OF THE TONGUE/LANGUAGE "prefixes: bi/intra/multi/sub"
linguist,*,tic, ONE WHO SPECIALIZED IN LANGUAGES
linguistic,*,tical,tically, STUDY OF LANGUAGES AND SPEECH
lingwestic, linguistic
lingwist, linguist
lingwistics, linguistic(s)
lingwul, lingual
liniansi, leniency
liniment,*, HEALING OINTMENTS
linin, IN CELL NUCLEUS (or see linen/lining)
lining,*, LAYER INSIDE OF EXTERIOR LINING (or see linin/linen)
liniul, lineal
link,*,ked,king,kage,ker, TWO THINGS JOINED TOGETHER "prefixes: inter/up"
links, lynx / link(s)
linkth, length
linkuge, link(age)
linkwol, lingual
linoleum, FLOOR COVERING

lins, lens / line(s)
linseed, OIL
lint,*,ty,tless, FUZZ FROM MATERIAL (or see lent/line(d))
linth, length
lintul, lentil
linument, liniment
linur, liner
linx, lynx
linz, lens / line(s)
lion,*,ness, A WILD ANIMAL (or see lien)
lior, liar
liotard, leotard
lip,*,pped,pping,ppy,pless, PREFIX INDICATING "FATTY" MOST OFTEN MODIFIES THE WORD, FLESHY FOLDS WORKING TOGETHER, A RIM, PART OF THE MOUTH "prefixes: under"
lipo, PREFIX INDICATING "FATTY" MOST OFTEN MODIFIES THE WORD
liprul, liberal
liqer, liquor / liqueur
liqoresh, licorice
liqueur,*, A SWEETENED/FLAVORED ALCOHOLIC LIQUID (or see liquor)
liquid,*,date,dated,dating,dation,dize, dity,ify,uefy, FLUID
liquify,fiable,fier,fies,fied,fying,faction, factive,fier,uifiable,uifier,uifies, uified,uifying,uifaction,uifactive, uifier, ALSO SPELLED 'LIQUEFY', TURN TO LIQUID/FLUID
liquifying, liquify(ing)
liquor,*, FERMENTED ALCOHOLIC LIQUID (or see liqueur)
lir, leer / liar
lirch, lurch
lire, leery/ leer
lirec, lyric
liric, lyric
lirn, learn
lis, lie(s) / lease / list / lice
lisard, lizard
lisen, listen
lisense, license
liserd, lizard
lishan, legion / lesion
lisles, listless
lison, listen
lisp,*,pingly, PRONUNCIATION IS CHALLENGED BY SHAPE OF TEETH/JAW MUSCLE FORMATION

list,*,ted,ting, IDENTIFY OBJECTS BY ITEMIZING, ORGANIZING TECHNIQUE "prefixes: en/un"
listen,*,ned,ning, TO HEAR AND PAY ATTENTION
listless,ssly,ssness, NO ENERGY, LACKS INTEREST
lisun, listen
lisuns, license
lisurt, lizard
lit, PAST TENSE FOR THE WORD "LIGHT" (or see lite/lid/light/lie(d)) "prefixes: un"
lite, SHORT SPELLING OF "LIGHT", LOW IN SOMETHING (or see lid/lit/light/lie(d))
litegation, litigate(tion)
litel, little
litening, lightening
liter,*, METRIC MEASUREMENT (or see litter/light(er)) "prefixes: deca"
literacy, ABILITY TO WRITE AND READ "prefixes: il"
literal,lly,lity,lize,list,listic,lism, QUITE SO, PERFECT INTERPRETATION "prefixes: uni"
literale, literal(lly)
literary,rily,riness,ate, OF WRITTEN TEXT, LEARNED, EDUCATED "prefixes: sub"
literate,*,ely,acy,ture, EDUCATED, SKILLFUL "prefixes: il/pre/semi/sub"
literature, WRITINGS ABOUT EVERYTHING, TEXT "prefixes: sub"
lithal, lethal
lithargic, lethargic
lithargy, lethargy
lithol, lethal
litigate,*,ed,ting,tor,tion,gious, giousness, BRING DISPUTE INTO LAWFUL JUDGEMENT, TAKE TO COURT
litigation,*, A LAWSUIT
litle, little
litly, light(ly)
litmas, litmus
litmos, litmus
litmus, AN ACID TEST
litneng, lightening
litness, lightness
litning, lightening
litor, light(er) / litter / liter / leader
litr, light(er) / litter / liter / leader

litter,*,red,ring, TRASH/GARBAGE WHERE IT DOESN'T BELONG, GROUP OF INFANT ANIMALS IN A CERTAIN SPECIES (or see liter/light(er))
little, SMALL SIZE IN COMPARISON
litul, little
litur, litter / liter / light(er) / leader
liturally, literal(ly)
liu, lieu
liubility, liable(bility)
liur, liar / lyre
liv, live / life / alive
livad, livid
livapul, live(vable)
live,*,ed,ving,ely,vable,vability, PLACE WHERE YOU DWELL, NOT DEAD, ACTIVE/VITAL "prefixes: en/re/un"
liveable, live(vable)
livebul, live(vable)
livelihood,*, OCCUPATION
livelyhood, livelihood
liver,*, AN ORGAN IN THE BODY
livery,ries, UNIFORM, CARE OF HORSES
livid,dly,dness,dity, FURIOUS, BRUISED FLESH COLOR
livle, live(ly)
livlihood, livelihood
livly, live(ly)
livur, liver
livury, livery
lizard,*, A REPTILE
llama,*, A WOOLY MAMMAL
lo, low
load,*,ded,ding,der, BURDEN, WEIGHT, HEAP/PILE INTO A VESSEL, ADD AMMUNITION "prefixes: un/up"
loaf,*,fed,fing,fer,aves, OF BREAD, SOMEONE WHO LIES AROUND DOING NOTHING, A SHOE, FOOD SHAPE
loafer,*, SOMEONE WHO IS LAZY, A SHOE
loam,my, A RICH/ORGANIC SOIL
loan,*,ned,ning,lent, ALLOW SOMEONE TO BORROW SOMETHING (or see lone)
loathe,*,ed,hing,er,hsome,hsomely, hsomeness, DESPISES, STRONGLY DISLIKES
lob,*,bbed,bbing,bber, A HIGH, ROUNDED ARCH BY A BALL IN A SPORT (or see lobe/lop)

lobby,bbies,bbied,ying,yist,yism, WAITING/RESTING ROOM, TO COERCE POLITICAL LAWMAKERS FOR VOTES
lobd, lob(bbed)
lobe,*,ed,bule, BULBOUS PART OF THE EAR/A PLANT, ROUND SHAPE (or see lobby)
lobster,*, AN EDIBLE CRUSTACEAN
loby, lobby
loc, lock
locader, locate(tor)
local,*,lly,le,lism,lity,lities,lize, IN THE AREA, WITHIN DESIGNATED REGION
localety, local(ity)
localize,ed,zation, TO BE LOCATED IN A SPECIFIC REGION, IN THE AREA
locashen, locate(tion)
locate,*,ed,ting,tion,tive,tor, TO IDENTIFY A SPECIFIC PLACE "prefixes: dis/re"
locemoshen, locomotive
locer, locker
locest, locust
loch, lodge / lock
lock,*,ked,king,kage,kable,kless,ker, MECHANISM WHICH REQUIRES A KEY, SECURE, BE INEXCUSABLY INVOLVED, EXCLUDED "prefixes: inter/un"
locker,*, A CONTAINER WITH A LOCK
locksmith,*, ONE WHO WORKS WITH LOCKS
loco, CRAZY
locomotion, THE ACT OF MOVING, LOCATING FROM ONE PLACE TO ANOTHER
locomotive,*, THE BODILY OR PHYSICAL ACT OF MOVEMENT FROM ONE PLACE TO ANOTHER
locsmith, locksmith
locul, local
loculizashen, localize(zation)
loculize, localize
loculy, local(ly)
locumoshen, locomotion
locumotive, locomotive
locur, locker
locust,*, A BUG ("T" IS SILENT)
lod, load
lodery, lottery
lodge,*,ed,ging,gment, SOMETHING JAMMED INTO A TIGHT SPACE, HABITATION FOR VISITORS WHO OCCASIONALLY COME FOR THE NIGHT, BRING FORTH ACTION ("D" IS SILENT) "prefixes: dis"
lodis, lotus
lodury, lottery
lodus, lotus
loeder, loiter
loen, loin
loer, lower / lawyer
loest, low(est)
loeul, loyal
lof, loaf
lofa, lava
lofer, loafer
lofly, lovely
loft,*,ted,ting,ty,tily, SMALL LANDING ABOVE THE MAIN FLOOR, PROPEL SOMETHING INTO THE AIR
lofur, loafer
log,*,gged,gging,gger, MAKE A WRITTEN NOTE OF, REMOVED SECTION OF LIMB/TREE, TO REMOVE TIMBER, MEASURE VELOCITY (or see lodge)
logarithm,*,mic,mically, A MATH FUNCTION "prefixes: semi"
loge, lodge
logec, logic
logecul, logic(al)
loger, logger
logestics, logistic(s)
logger,*, SOMEONE WHO CUTS TREES (or see lager)
logic,*,cal,cally,cality,calness, TO MAKE SENSE OF, BE REASONABLE "prefixes: il"
logicul, logic(al)
logir, logger
logistic,*,cal,cally,cian, ARRANGING ACTIONS TO BENEFIT AN ADDITIONAL ACTION, CALCULATING
logo,*, A THEME OR SYMBOL WHICH IDENTIFIES
logrethm, logarithm
logrythm, logarithm
logur, logger
loider, loiter
loin,*, SECTION OF A BODY
loir, lower
loiter,*,red,ring, TO STAND AROUND, HANGING OUT
lojecul, logic(al)

lojek, logic
lojical, logic(al)
lojik, logic
lok, look / lock
lokality, local(ity)
lokashen, locate(tion)
lokate, locate
lokator, locate(tor)
lokel, local
lokelizashen, localize(zation)
lokelize, localize
lokely, local(ly)
lokemotive, locomotive
loker, locker / look(er) / logger
lokes, locust / look(s) / lock(s)
lokimoshen, locomotive
lokimotev, locomotive
lokir, locker / look(er) / logger
lokist, locust
loko, loco
loksmeth, locksmith
lokt, lock(ed) / look(ed)
lokul, local
lokule, local(ly)
lokulization, localize(zation)
lokulize, localize
lokumoshen, locomotion
lokumotef, locomotive
lokumotive, locomotive
lokur, locker / look(er) / logger
lokus, locust
lolegag, lollygag
lolepop, lollipop
loligag, lollygag
lollipop,*, CANDY
lollygag,*,gged,gging, TO LOITER/HANG AROUND DOING NOTHING
loly, low(ly)
lolypop, lollipop
lom, loam / loom
loma, llama
lomanesense, luminescence
lombur, lumber / lumbar
lome, loam
lomp, lump
lomunesense, luminescence
lomy, loam(y)
lon, lone / loan / lawn
lonch, launch / lunch
londer, launder
londry, laundry
londurer, launder(er)

lone,er,ely,eliness,esome,esomely, esomeness, BY ITSELF, SINGLED OUT, JUST ONE (or see loan)
long,ger,gest, THE LENGTH/DURATION OF SOMETHING, MEASURE OF TIME
longatude, longitude
longetudenul, longitude(dinal)
longir, long(er)
longist, long(est)
longitude,*,dinal,dinally, INVISIBLE LINE ON EARTH THAT RUNS EAST, WEST
lonir, lone(r)
lonjatude, longitude
lonjetudenul, longitude(dinal)
lonjitude, longitude
lonk, long
lonker, long(er)
lonkist, long(est)
lonly, lone(ly)
lons, lawn(s) / loan(s)
lonsem, lone(some)
lonsum, lone(some)
lonter, launder
lontre, laundry
lonur, lone(r)
loob, lube
loobrucate, lubricate
lood, lewd / load
loodekres, ludicrous
look,*,ked,king,ker, TO VIEW WITH THE EYES
lookwarm, lukewarm
looloo, lulu
loom,*,med,ming, INTO THE FUTURE, LATER IN TIME, A MACHINE FOR WEAVING YARN/THREAD (or see loam)
loomanocity, luminosity
loomenesent, luminescence(nt)
loomenocity, luminosity
loominesinse, luminescence
loominocity, luminosity
loominus, luminous
loomy, loam(y)
loon,*,ny, A BIRD, BEHAVING GOOFY (or see lune)
looner, lunar
loop,*,ped,ping,py, A SEMI-CIRCULAR SHAPE, WRAP/GO AROUND, BEHAVING ODDLY
loopen, lupine
loose,*,sing,en,ens,ened,ening, MISPLACE/FORGET SOMETHING, RELAX HOLD ON, UNTIGHTEN,

SLOPPY, GET RID OF (or see lose) "prefixes: un"
loosid, lucid
loot,*,ted,ting,ter, MONEY/GOODS, ONE WHO STEALS THINGS (or see lute/lewd)
looze, loose / lose
lop,*,pped,pping, ACT OF REMOVING, ROUGHLY (or see lobe/lope)
lope,*,er,ed,ping, EASY STRIDES WITH BOUNCE (or see lop)
lor, lore / low(er)
lorch, large
lord,*,ded,ding, MASTER, ONE WHO TAKES OWNERSHIP
lore,*, BELIEF IN THE FORM OF A STORY OF THE PAST
loreate, laureate
lorg, large
loriette, laureate
lorj, large
lort, lord
lorul, laurel
losd, lost
lose,*,er,sing,st, PAST TENSE FOR THE WORD "LOST", HAVING LOST (or see loose)
losenge, lozenge
losh, lush
loshen, lotion
loshin, lotion
losinge, lozenge
losinje, lozenge
losir, lose(r) / loose(r)
loss,ses, TAKEN AWAY, REMOVED
lost, PAST TENSE FOR THE WORD "LOOSE", CANNOT BE FOUND (or see lust)
loster, luster
losuit, lawsuit
losur, lose(r) / loose(r)
losute, lawsuit
lot,*,tted,tting, WHOLE BUNCH, A SPECIFIC SIZE OF SOMETHING, A SECTION AMONG MANY
lotery, lottery
lotes, lotus
lothe, loathe
lotion,*, CREAMY LIQUID TO APPLY TO THE BODY
lotis, lotus
lottery,ries, GAMBLING
lotury, lottery
lotus, A FLOWER, A POSITION, A PLANT

loud,dly,dness,der,dest, SOUND THAT IS BEYOND A COMFORTABLE HEARING RANGE
loul, loyal
lounch, lounge
lounge,*,ed,ging,er, TO LIE AROUND, RECLINED POSITION, ROOM WHERE PEOPLE REST/RELAX
lour, lower
louver,*, SHUTTERS
lova, lava
love,*,ed,ving,vable,vableness,vably, vability,er,eless, A SPECIAL/DEEP AFFECTION FOR
lovely,lier,liest,liness, PERFECTLY ATTRACTIVE "prefixes: un"
lovle, lovely
lovte, loft(y)
lovu, lava
low,wer,west,wly, CLOSE TO THE BOTTOM OR THE GROUND, LACK OF ENERGY
lowd, loud
lowder, loud(er)
lowdest, loud(est)
lowen, loin
lower,*,red,ring, ACT OF LETTING DOWN, CLOSE TO THE BOTTOM OR GROUND, LESSEN
lownch, lounge
lownge, lounge
lows, low(s) / loathe(s)
lowt, loud / load
lowtest, loud(est)
lowyer, lawyer
lowyul, loyal
loyal,list,lly,lty,lties, FAITHFUL "prefixes: dis"
loyer, lawyer
loyn, loin
loyulty, loyal(ty)
loyure, lawyer
lozenge,*, THROAT MEDICINE
lu, lieu
lub, lube
lube,*,ed,bing,bricate, GREASE
lubracashen, lubricate(tion)
lubracate, lubricate
lubricate,*,ed,ting,tion,ant, TO GREASE/ OIL UP
luc, look / luck
lucgireate, luxury(riate)
lucgiry, luxury
lucheus, luscious
luchious, luscious
luchness, lush(ness)
lucid,dity,dness,dly, A STATE OF BEING BETWEEN HERE AND THERE
lucjireate, luxury(riate)
lucjiry, luxury
luck,ky,kily,kier,kiest,kless, GOOD FORTUNE "prefixes: un"
lucke, luck(y)
luckgerious, luxurious
luckjiry, luxury
lucrative,ely,eness, COULD YIELD PROFIT OR GAIN
lucwarm, lukewarm
ludakris, ludicrous
lude, lewd / lute / loot
ludecris, ludicrous
luder, loot(er)
ludicrous,sly,sness, RIDICULOUS
luf, love
lufable, love(vable)
lufer, louver / love(r)
lufless, love(less)
lufly, lovely
lug,*,gged,gging, CARRY AROUND A HEAVY LOAD, ON A WHEEL, PULL (or see luck/look)
lugach, luggage
lugd, lug(gged)
lugege, luggage
luggage, TRAVELING BAGS
lugich, luggage
lugije, luggage
lugjureus, luxurious
lugshureant, luxuriant
lugshureous, luxurious
lugshury, luxury
lugt, lug(gged)
luk, look / luck / lug
lukchury, luxury
luke, luck / luck(y) / look
lukege, luggage
lukemea, leukemia
lukewarm, BETWEEN WARM AND HOT
lukgery, luxury
lukgureus, luxurious
lukiest, luck(iest)
lukige, luggage
lukjereus, luxurious
lukrative, lucrative
luks, look(s) / luck(s)
lukshereant, luxuriant
lukshury, luxury
luksuryant, luxuriant
lukwarm, lukewarm
luky, luck(y)
lull,*,led,ling, A PAUSE, GENTLY COAX, CAUSE TO RELAX
lulu,*, REAL WINNER
lum, loom
lumanesense, luminescence
lumbar,*, AREA IN LOWER BACK (or see lumber)
lumber,rer,rman,ring, BOARDS CUT FROM TIMBER (or see lumbar)
lumbir, lumber / lumbar
lumbur, lumber / lumbar
lume, loom
lumen,*,mina,minal,minous, OF LIGHT, GIVING OFF LIGHT, UNIT OF MEASURE "prefixes: il"
lumenary, luminary
lumenesense, luminescence
lumenesent, luminescence(nt)
lumenosidty, luminosity
lument, lament
lumentation, lament(ation)
lumenus, luminous
lumenusly, luminous(ly)
luminary,ria,ries, GIVING OFF LIGHT
luminescence,nt, GIVING OFF LIGHT "prefixes: bio"
luminosity,ties, INTENSITY OF LIGHT
luminous,sly,sness, AMOUNT OF LIGHT, OF LIGHT
luminus, lumen(ous)
lump,*,ped,ping,py, MASS OR AGGREGATE OF SOMETHING
lumunesense, luminescence
lun, loon / lune
lunar,ate,rian, OF THE MOON "prefixes: inter/semi/sub"
lunch,hes,hed,hing,heon, AFTERNOON MEAL (or see lunge)
lune,nula, MOON WHEN IT'S NOT FULL (or see loon)
luney, loon(y) / lune
lung,*, ORGAN OF THE BODY (or see lunge)
lunge,*,ed,ging, LEAP FORWARD TOWARDS SOMETHING, PULL QUICKLY/ HARD AGAINST RESTRAINTS
lunir, lunar
lunje, lunge
lunur, lunar
lup, loop
lupe, loop / loop(y)

lupel, lapel
lupen, lupine
lupine,*, A WOLF, A PLANT
lurch,hes,hed,hing,her, HANG ABOUT SUSPICIOUSLY, DRUNKEN STAGGER, LEAP INTO ACTION
lurk,*,ked,king,ker, STALK, SECRETLY WAIT TO AMBUSH
lus, loose / lose
luscious,sly,sness, GLORIOUS SENSORY EXPERIENCE OF SOMETHING USING TASTE/SMELL/SIGHT/TOUCH
lusd, lust
lusder, luster
lusdruss, lust(rous)
luse, loose / lose
lused, lucid
lusen, loose(n)
lush,hly,hness, ABUNDANT, OPULENT FLORAL AND FAUNA, RICH IN FOLIAGE, AN ALCOHOLIC
lusheous, luscious
lushus, luscious
lusid, lucid
lusin, loose(n)
lust,*,ted,ting,tful,tfully,tfulness,trous, TEMPORARY INTENSE DESIRE
luster,*,red,ring,rless, GLISTENING, WAY LIGHT REFLECTS, AS IF GLOWING, SHINY REFLECTION
lustious, luscious
lusty,tily,tiness, HEARTY AND JOVIAL, ROBUST
lut, lute / loot / lewd
lute,*, A MUSICAL INSTRUMENT (or see loot/lewd)
lutenant, lieutenant
luter, loot(er)
lutinant, lieutenant
lutrene, latrine
luv, love
luvabul, love(vable)
luver, louver / love(r)
luvle, lovely
luvless, love(less)
luxuriant,nce,ncy,tly, VERY HEALTHY, RICHLY ABUNDANT, PROFUSE
luxurious,sly,sness, EXPENSIVE COMFORT
luxury,ries,riate,riated,riating,rious, GREAT RICHNESS, OPULENT, OVERLY ABUNDANT
luz, loose / lose
ly, lye / lie

lye, WOOD ASH FOR SOAP (or see lie)
lying, NOT TELLING THE TRUTH, PAST TENSE FOR THE WORD "LIE" (or see lay(ing))
lymfatic, lymph(atic)
lymph,hatic, FLUID WITH WHITE BLOOD CELLS, OF THE BODY, PREFIX INDICATING "LYMPH/YELLOWISH" MOST OFTEN MODIFIES THE WORD
lympho, PREFIX INDICATING "LYMPH/ YELLOWISH" MOST OFTEN MODIFIES THE WORD
lynx,xes, A WILD ANIMAL
lyo, PREFIX INDICATING "DISSOLVED/ DISPERSED" MOST OFTEN MODIFIES THE WORD
lyre,*, AN INSTRUMENT (or see liar)
lyric,*,cal,cally,cism,cist, WORDS SANG IN A SONG
lys, PREFIX INDICATING "DISSOLVED/ DISPERSED"MOST OFTEN MODIFIES THE WORD
lyso, PREFIX INDICATING "DISSOLVED/ DISPERSED"MOST OFTEN MODIFIES THE WORD
m, am
ma, may
mab, mob
mabe, maybe
mabilety, mobile(lity)
mac, mach / make / mock / mace
macaroni,ies, CHEESY NOODLES
macaroon,*, A COOKIE
macasen, moccasin
macaw,*, A TROPICAL BIRD
mace,ed, SPICE, MEDIEVAL WEAPON, CHEMICAL SPRAY (or see make/ maize/ maze/mach)
mach, AMOUNT OF SPEED (or see make/match/mock/mash)
machenery, machine(ry)
macheng, match(ing) / mash(ing)
macherel, mackerel
macherly, mature(ly)
maches, match(es) / mash(es)
machestral, magistral
machestrate, magistrate
machete,*, A CHOPPING HAND TOOL
machine,*,nability,nable,nate,nation, nator,ery,eries,nist, DEVICE WITH MOVING PARTS THAT PERFORMS WORK
machis, match(es) / mash(es)
machistral, magistral

machistrate, magistrate
machurashen, mature(ration)
machure, mature
machuredy, mature(rity)
machuril, mackerel
machus, match(es) / mash(es)
mack, make / mach / mock
mackerel,*, EDIBLE FISH
macks, max / make(s)
macrame, LACED/WOVEN ROPE
macro, PREFIX INDICATING "DISSOLVED/DISPERSED" MOST OFTEN MODIFIES THE WORD
macrocosm,*,mic,mically, THE BIG PICTURE, INCORPORATES EVERYTHING BIG AND SMALL
macruma, macrame
macs, max / make(s)
macsimul, maximal
macuroni, macaroni
macuroon, macaroon
macusen, moccasin
mad,dder,ddest,dden,ddening, ddeningly,dness, NOT HAPPY, MORE THAN IRRITATED, ANGRY (or see made/maid/matte/mat/mate)
madch, match
made, PAST TENSE FOR THE WORD "MAKE", HAVING CREATED (or see maid/mate) "prefixes: re/un"
madekulus, meticulous
madel, modal /model / mottle
madena, matinee
mader, matter / mad(dder)
maderde, maitre d'
madereulise, materialize
madernize, modern(ize)
madernulistic, maternal(istic)
madesenul, medicine(nal)
madina, matinee
madir, mad(dder) / matter
madirde, maitre d'
madisenul, medicine(nal)
madist, mad(ddest)
madna, matinee
madnes, mad(dness)
mado, motto
madramony, matrimony
madreark, matriarch
madrearkul, matriarch(al)
madremony, matrimony
madren, matron
madress, mattress
madrexs, matrix

madricks, matrix
madrimony, matrimony
madris, mattress
madron, matron
madur, matter / mad(der)
madurde, maitre d'
mae, may
maer, mayor
maestro,*, MASTER OF ANY MEDIUM RELATED TO ART
mafe, mauve
maferick, maverick
mafrek, maverick
magacul, magic(al)
magazine,*, COMPILED PAGES OF WRITTEN ARTICLES, HAVING TO DO WITH WEAPONS
mager, major
magesine, magazine
magestral, magistral
magestrate, magistrate
magesty, majesty
maggot,*, LARVA OF AN INSECT
magic,cal,cally,cian, DIDN'T VISIBLY WITNESS THE CHANGE OF EVENTS WHICH LED TO AN EVENT
magir, major
magirete, major(ette)
magistral,lly,lity,ature,terial,terially, terialness,terium,ate, LOCAL OFFICIAL OFFICE
magistrate,*,acy,acies,ture,al, LOCAL OFFICIAL OFFICE
magisty, majesty
magit, maggot
magizene, magazine
magma,*,ata,atic, MOLTEN ROCK
magnate,*, PROMINENT INDUSTRIALIST (or see magnet))
magnatise, magnetize
magnatisum, magnet(ism)
magnatude, magnitude
magnedic, magnet(ic)
magnefacashen, magnify(fication)
magnefasent, magnificent
magnefesently, magnificent(ly)
magnefiable, magnify(iable)
magnefy, magnify
magnet,*,tic,tically,tism,tize, DRAWN TO, ORE FROM THE EARTH, TOWARD THE NORTH/SOUTH ENDS, PREFIX INDICATING "MAGNET" MOST OFTEN MODIFIES THE WORD (or see magnate) "prefixes: bio"

magnetize,*,ed,zing,zable,zation,zer, BE DRAWN TO, MAKE POLAR
magneto, PREFIX INDICATING "MAGNET" MOST OFTEN MODIFIES THE WORD
magnetude, magnitude
magnifesent, magnificent
magnificent,tly,nce, SPLENDID
magnify,fies,fied,ying,fiable,fier,fication, TO ENLARGE, GET CLOSER TO, MAKE BIGGER "prefixes: bio"
magnit, magnet / magnate
magnitise, magnetize
magnitude,*,dinous, THE SIZE OR EXTENT OF, THE DEGREE OF
magnufecashen, magnify(fication)
magnufy, magnify
magnutise, magnetize
magnutisum, magnet(ism)
magnutude, magnitude
magoredy, major(ity)
magorete, major(ette)
magority, major(ity)
magot, maggot
maguk, magic
magul, module
maguler, module(lar)
magur, major
magurete, major(ette)
magustrate, magistrate
maguzene, magazine
mai, may / my
maid,*,den, ONE WHO CLEANS BEHIND OTHERS FOR A LIVING (or see made/mate)
mail,*,led,ling,ler, SEND A PHYSICAL THING AWAY TO SOMEONE (or see male/mile)
maim,*,med,ming, TO MUTILATE/ DESTROY (or see mime)
main,*,nly, THE MOST IMPORTANT ONE, THE ONE THAT STANDS OUT (or see mane/mine)
maingy, mangy
maintain,*,ned,ning,nable,tenance, UPKEEP, KEEP IN GOOD REPAIR
maintenance, TO KEEP IN WORKING ORDER, TO FIX, SUPPORT, UPKEEP
maitre d',*, HEADWAITER/HOTEL MANAGER
maize,*, CORN (or see maze)
maj, image
majek, magic
majen, imagine

majer, major
majestral, magistral
majestrate, magistrate
majesty,tic,tically, OF AUTHORITY/ GRANDEUR, GREAT IMPRESSION
majewlate, modulate
majir, major
majistral, magistral
majistrate, magistrate
major,*,red,ring,rity,rities,rette, GREATEST NUMBER OF, A MILITARY RANK, FEMALE MARCHER, HIGHEST NUMBER OF
majoredy, major(ity)
majul, module
majulate, modulate
majur, major
majustrate, magistrate
mak, mach / make / mock
makanek, mechanic
makanekul, mechanic(al)
makanize, mechanize
makaril, mackerel
makarony, macaroni
makaroon, macaroon
makaw, macaw
make,*,ade,king,er, TO CREATE, BRING TO REALITY (or see mach/mock) "prefixes: re/un"
maked, made / mock(ed)
makerony, macaroni
makinate, machine(nate)
makir, make(r)
makirony, macaroni
makremay, macrame
makrocosim, macrocosm
makrumay, macrame
maks, max / make(s) / mock(s)
maksamis, maximize
maksemal, maximal
maksemize, maximize
maksimul, maximal
maksimum, maximum
maksumum, maximum
makuril, mackerel
makurone, macaroni
makusen, moccasin
makzemize, maximize
mal, PREFIX INDICATING "BAD" MOST OFTEN MODIFIES THE WORD (or see mall/maul/male/mail)
malable, malleable
maladek, melody(dic)

maladjusted,tment, NOT SITUATED AS SHOULD BE, IMPROPER ORIENTATION
malado, mulato
malady,dies, A DISORDER OR CONFLICT BETWEEN THE BODY AND MIND, ABNORMAL ARRANGEMENT
malajusted, maladjusted
malanosis, melanosis
malaria, DISEASE TRANSPORTED TO HUMANS BY SOME MOSQUITOES
malarkey, DOESN'T APPEAR TO BE THE TRUTH, CALLING A BLUFF
malas, malice
malases, molasses
mald, maul(ed) / mail(ed) / malt
male,*,eness, THE MASCULINE GENDER, THE INSERTION END (or see mail)
maleable, malleable
maleble, malleable
maledy, malady
malegnent, malignant
malegusted, maladjusted
malegustment, maladjusted(tment)
malejusted, maladjusted
malekule, molecule
malekuler, molecule(lar)
maleneum, millennium
malenoma, melanoma
malenosis, melanosis
malerd, mallard
malese, malice
malesha, militia
maleshes, malicious
malest, molest
malet, mallet
maleuble, malleable
malevolent,tly,nce, MALICIOUS, HATEFUL
malfunction,*,ned,ning, DOESN'T WORK AS IT WAS INTENDED
malfunkshen, malfunction
malible, malleable
malice,cious, DIRECT HATE TOWARDS ANOTHER, EMOTION OF FEAR/INSECURITY
malicious,ciously,ciousness, DIRECT HATE TOWARDS ANOTHER, EMOTION OF FEAR/INSECURITY
malignant,tly,ncy, ACT OF BEING MALICIOUS, DANGEROUS GROWTH "prefixes: pre"
maligusted, maladjusted
malineum, millennium

malinoma, melanoma
malinosis, melanosis
malisha, militia
malishes, malicious
malit, mallet
malitia, militia
mality, malady
maliuble, malleable
mall,*, LARGE BUILDING WITH SMALL STORES INSIDE (or see mail/male/maul)
mallard,*, WILD DUCK
malleable,billity,eness, SEEMINGLY STIFF MATERIAL/METAL THAT'S EASILY WORKED/MOLDED
mallet,*, HAMMER TYPE TOOL
malluble, malleable
malnerished, malnourished
malnewtrishen, malnutrition
malnourished, NOT ENOUGH NUTRITIONAL FOOD
malnureshed, malnourished
malnutrition, SUFFERING LACK OF NUTRITIOUS FOOD
malodic, melody(dic)
malos, malice
malpractice,*,cioner, DR. WHO PRODUCED A FATAL/SERIOUS INJURY WHILE PRACTICING MEDICINE
malpraktes, malpractice
malt,*,ted,ty, A FROTHY COLD DRINK (or see maul(ed)/molt)
maluble, malleable
maludy, malady
malugusted, maladjusted
malujustment, maladjusted(tment)
malunosis, melanosis
malurd, mallard
malus, malice
malut, mallet
mam, maim
mama, A MOTHER (or see mamma)
mamal, mammal
mamalean, mammal(ian)
mamary gland, mammary gland
mamel, mammal
mamento, memento
mamery gland, mammary gland
mameth, mammoth
mamil, mammal
maminto, memento
mamiry gland, mammary gland
mamith, mammoth

mamma, MILK SECRETING BREASTS/TEATS/ORGAN
mammal,*,lian, WARM BLOODED ANIMAL THAT GIVES BIRTH TO ITS YOUNG
mammary gland,*, GLANDS IN THE BREAST THAT SECRETES MILK
mammoth, ICE AGE ELEPHANT
mamory gland, mammary gland
mamoth, mammoth
mamt, maim(ed)
mamul, mammal
mamury gland, mammary gland
man, ADULT MALE (or see mane/main) "prefixes: un"
manacle,*, WRIST RESTRAINTS
manage,*,ed,ging,ement,eable,eably, eableness,er,erial, ABILITY TO DEAL WITH AND ORCHESTRATE AFFAIRS SMOOTHLY "prefixes: mis/un"
manakin,*, BIRD (or see mannikin/manikin/mannequin)
manakure, manicure
manark, monarch
manarkeul, monarch(ial)
manarky, monarch(y)
manase, mayonnaise
manchen, mansion
mandala,*, A SYMBOL OF SPIRITUAL SIGNIFICANCE
mandalin, mandolin
mandarin,*, FRUIT
mandate,*,ed,ting,tory, A COMMAND, RULE
mandatory,ries,rily, COMMANDE, ORDERED
mandel, mantel / mantle
mandelin, mandolin
manderin, mandarin
mandetory, mandatory
manditory, mandatory
mandle, mantel / mantle
mandola, mandala
mandolin,*, A STRINGED INSTRUMENT
mandrake, AN HERB
mandrel,*, A DEVICE TO AID IN CUTTING A SOLID MATERIAL
mandril, mandrel
mandrul, mandrel
mandul, mantel / mantle
manduren, mandarin
mandutory, mandatory
mane, HAIR ABOUT THE NECK OF AN ANIMAL (or see main/many)

manea, mania
maneac, maniac
manecure, manicure
manee, many
manefest, manifest
manefesto, manifest(o)
manefold, manifold
manege, manage
manegment, manage(ment)
maneje, manage
manekin, manikin / manakin / mannequin
manekul, manacle
manense, maintenance
maner, manner / manor / manure
manerism, manner(ism)
manerlee, manner(ly)
maneuver,*,red,ring,rable,rability,rer, SKILLFUL DISPLAY OF MOVEMENT
manevest, manifest
mang, mange
mange, A SKIN CONDITION
manger, TROUGH FOR ANIMALS
mangle,*,ed,ling,er, TO SHRED/TEAR UP, A LARGE IRON
mango,*, A FRUIT
mangul, mangle
mangy,gily,giness, SHABBY, ILL-KEPT
mania, NTENSE EMOTION
maniac,*,cal,cally, SOMEONE UNCONTROLLABLE ON A CONTINUOUS BASIS
manicle, manacle
manicure,*,ed,ring,rist, CARING OF FINGERNAILS
manifest,*,ted,ting,ter,tly,tation,tant, ter,to, DESIRED RESULT ACHIEVED WITH LITTLE EFFORT
manifold,*,ded,ding,der,dly,dness, ON A MOTOR, A COPY, TO MULTIPLY
manige, manage
manigment, manage(ment)
manikin, A MOLD OF A BODY FOR CLOTHING DISPLAY (or see manakin/mannequin)
manila, BUFF-COLORED HEMP PAPER
manipulate,*,ed,ting,tion,able,ability, table,tor,tory,tive,tively,tiveness, CONTROL ENVIRONMENT/EVENTS
manir, manner / manor / manure
manirism, manner(ism)
manirlee, manner(ly)
manj, mange
manjur, manger

manle, main(ly) / man(ly)
mannequin,*, LITTLE/DWARFED HUMAN, MODEL OF PART OF THE BODY OR ENTIRE TORSO, SOMEONE WHO MODELS CLOTHING, ALSO SPELLED 'MANNIKIN OR MANIKIN' (or see manakin/manikin)
manner,*,red,rless,rism,rist,ristic,rly, TO HANDLE ONESELF PROPERLY, BE POLITE (or see manor) "prefixes: un"
manofestation, manifest(ation)
manogumy, monogamy
manolith, monolith
manopuly, monopoly
manor,*, HOME OF MEDIEVAL TIMES (or see manure/manner)
manotny, monotony
manotone, monotone
manotunus, monotony(nous)
manshen, mansion
mansion,*, A VERY LARGE HOME
mantane, maintain
mantanuble, maintain(able)
mantel,*, FIREPLACE SHELF (or see mantle)
mantenanse, maintenance
mantil, mantel / mantle
mantle,*, A CLOAK, A CLOTH SLEEVE FOR A GAS LANTERN (or see mantel)
mantul, mantel / mantle
mantunense, maintenance
manual,*,lly, DIRECTIONS ON HOW TO USE SOMETHING, TO DO BY HAND
manucle, manacle
manuel, manual
manuely, manual(ly)
manufacture,*,ed,ring,rer,rable,ral, CREATE SOMETHING FROM RAW MATERIALS
manufaksher, manufacture
manufestation, manifest(ation)
manufold, manifold
manuge, manage
manugment, manage(ment)
manuil, manual
manukin, manakin
manul, mantel / mantle
manur, manner / manor / manure
manure,rial,er, WASTE FROM ANIMALS (or see manor/manner)
manurism, manner(ism)
manurly, manner(ly)

manuscript,*, STORY SOMEONE WRITES THAT MAY BECOME A BOOK/MOVIE
manuskrept, manuscript
manustery, monastery
manuver, maneuver
many, MORE THAN A FEW (or see mini)
manyewfaksher, manufacture
manyual, manual
manyuskrept, manuscript
maonase, mayonnaise
maor, mayor
map,*,pped,pping, DIRECTIONS/GUIDE TO A SPECIFIC AREA (or see mop)
mapal, maple
mapd, map(pped) / mop(pped)
mape, maybe
mapel, maple
maple,*, A TREE, SYRUP FROM TREE
mapul, maple
mar,*,rred,rring, TO RUIN/DETRACT FROM (or see mare/mayor)
maraje, mirage
marakulus, miracle(culous)
maranade, marinade / marinate
maranate, marinade / marinate
marange, meringue
marathon,*,ner, A LONG DISTANCE EVENT
marbel, marble
marble,*,ed,ling,ly,er, A LITTLE GLASS BALL, TYPE OF ROCK, A VISUAL EFFECT
marbul, marble
marc, mark
marcetable, market(able)
march,hes,hed,hing,her, BRISK FORM OF WALKING, MONTH OF THE YEAR
marchel, martial / marshal
marchel law, martial law
marchen, martian / march(ing) / margin(s)
marchenulize, marginalize
marchoram, marjoram
marchul, martial / marshal
marchul law, martial law
marden, martin
mardene, martini
mardengale, martingale
marder, martyr
mardin, martin
mardine, martini
mardingale, martingale
mardir, martyr

mardur, martyr
mare,*, FEMALE HORSE (or see marry/ mayor)
mared, married / mar(rred)
maredean, meridian
mareg, marriage
maregold, marigold
marej, marriage
marejuana, marijuana
marena, marina
marenad, marinade / marinate
marene, marine
mareonette, marionette
maret, merit
maretime, maritime
maretul, marital
mareunette, marionette
marewana, marijuana
marfilus, marvelous
margarine, A FAKE BUTTER
margen, margin
margenul, margin(al)
margenulize, marginalize
margerem, marjoram
margin,*,nal,nally,nality,nalize,nate, nates,nated,nating,nation, SPACE OUTSIDE OF THE TEXT/ BORDER AREA "prefixes: sub"
marginalize,*,ed,zing,zation,nate, BLOCK SOMEONE FROM SOMETHING THEY NEED/ WANT
margorem, marjoram
margurim, marjoram
mari, marry
marid, married
maridian, meridian
marig, marriage
marigold,*, A FLOWER
marij, marriage
marijuana, ALSO MARIHUANA, MEDICINAL PLANT (or see hemp)
marily, merry(rily)
marina,*, FOR BOAT MOORING
marinade,*,ate, SAUCE WITH SPICES THAT FISH/MEAT IS SOAKED IN (or see marinate)
marinate,*,ted,ting,tion,ade, THE ACT OF SOAKING FISH/MEAT IN A SAUCE (or see marinade)
marine,*,er, CONCERNED WITH THE OCEAN/ SEA
marionette,*, A PUPPET ON STRINGS
marit, merit

marital,lly, INVOLVES MARRIAGE "prefixes: pre"
marithon, marathon
maritime, OF THE OCEAN OR SEA
mariwana, marijuana
marjaren, margarine
marjen, margin
marjenalize, marginalize
marjenul, margin(al)
marjeren, margarine
marjin, margin
marjinul, margin(al)
marjinulize, marginalize
marjoram,*, HERBAL PLANT
mark,*,ked,king,ker,kedly, A GOUGE/ LINE/ SCRATCH/ IMPRESSION "prefixes: un"
markee, marquee / marquis
marker,*, A LINE OF MARKATION, A TOOL OR INSTRUMENT THAT MARKS
market,*,ted,ting,table,tability,ter, ABOUT SELLING GOODS "prefixes: sub"
marki, marquee / marquis
markit, market
markt, mark(ed)
markur, marker
marmalade, A FRUIT PRESERVE
marmulade, marmalade
marn, martin / marten
maroon,*,ned,ning, BE LEFT ABANDONED, STRANDED, A COLOR
marose, morose
marow, marrow
marquee, A BANNER, TENT, SIGN OVER ENTRANCEWAY (or see marquis)
marquis,ses,sate, BRITISH RANK (or see marquee)
marriage,*,eable,eability,eableness, TWO PEOPLE WHO LEGALLY BOND IN MATRIMONY "prefixes: inter"
married, PAST TENSE FOR THE WORD "MARRY"
marrow, INNER BONE, PARTNER, MATE
marry,ries,ried,ying,riage, TWO PEOPLE LEGALLY BONDING (or see merry) "prefixes: inter/un"
marsh,hes,hy, WETLAND
marshal,*,led,ling,lcy,lship, EUROPEAN OFFICER, SIMILAR TO A SHERIFF, TO LEAD, USHER (or see martial)
marshal law, martial law
marshen, martian / march(ing)

marshil, marshal / martial
marshin, martian / march(ing)
marshmallow, A SUGAR SWEET , AN HERBAL PLANT
marshmelow, marshmallow
marshul, marshal / martial
marsoopeal, marsupial
marsupeul, marsupial
marsupial, AN ANIMAL THAT SLEEPS DURING THE DAY
martch, march
marten, MEMBER OF THE WEASEL FAMILY (or see martin)
martengale, martingale
marteny, martini
marter, martyr
martial,lism,list,lly,lness, OF WAR (or see marshal)
martial law, PERMANENT MILITARY RULE IN THE U.S.
martian,*, PLANET MARS INHABITANTS
martin,*, A BIRD
martingale,*, A BIRD
martini,*, ALCOHOLIC DRINK
martir, martyr
martur, martyr
martyr,*,red,ring,rize,rdom, SOMEONE WHO RISKS THEIR LIVES FOR A CAUSE OF THEIR CHOOSING
marune, maroon
marut, merit
marutime, maritime
marvel,*,led,ling,lous,lously,lousness, GREATLY IMPRESSIVE, ATTENTION GETTER
marvelous,lously,lousness, VERY IMPRESSIVE
marvelus, marvelous
marvil, marvel
marvilus, marvelous
marvul, marvel
mary, marry / merry
maryonette, marionette
mas, mace / mass / moss / maize
masa, mesa
masach, massage
masacistic, masochism
masacur, massacre
masage, massage
masakistic, masochism(stic)
masakisum, masochism
masakur, massacre
masanine, mezzanine
masc, mask

mascara, A DYE PUT ON EYELASHES
mascarade, masquerade
mascot,*, A THING OF LUCK
masculine,ely,eness,nity,nize,nized, nizing, MALE
masd, mast
masdebashen, masturbate(tion)
masdek, mastic
masder, master
masderbade, masturbate
masdereus, mysterious
masdides, mastitis
masdik, mastic
masdir, master
masditis, mastitis
masdurful, master(full)
mase, mace / maize / maze
masectame, mastectomy
masectome, mastectomy
masecur, massacre
masef, massive
masekur, massacre
masen, mason
masenger, messenger
masenry, mason(ry)
maseurse, masseuse
maseve, massive
masgot, mascot
mash,hes,hed,hing,her, TO SHRED/PULVERIZE/SQUISH, TURN TO PASTE (or see match)
mashene, machine
mashenery, machine(ry)
mashenest, machine(nist)
mashes, mash(es) / match(es)
mashety, machete
mashin, machine / mash(ing)
mashinury, machine(ry)
mashis, mash(es) / match(es)
mashus, mash(es) / match(es)
masif, massive
masiker, massacre
masin, mason
masive, massive
mask,*,ked,king, COVER UP "prefixes: un"
maskalen, masculine
maskarade, masquerade
maskarate, masquerade
maskeet, mesquite
maskera, mascara
maskerate, masquerade
masketo, mosquito
maskewlen, masculine

maskot, mascot
maskulin, masculine
maskurade, masquerade
maskurate, masquerade
masochism,st, PATHOLOGICAL SELF-DESTRUCTION
masochist,tic,tically,sm, PATHOLOGICAL SELF-DESTRUCTION
masof, massive
masoge, massage
masoje, massage
masokism, masochism
masokistic, masochism(stic)
masokizum, masochism
mason,*,nry,nries,nic, WORKS WITH STONE
masoose, masseuse
masquerade,*,ed,ding,er, USE A MASK OR DISGUISE TO COVER IDENTITY
masquite, mesquite
mass,ses,sed,sing,sive, MEASURE OF VOLUME, WEIGHT, ACCUMULATION OF SIGNIFICANT AMOUNT "prefixes: bio"
massacre,*,ed,ring, KILLING OF SIGNIFICANT AMOUNT AT ONCE
massage,*,ed,ging, MANIPULATE/RUB SKIN TO AFFECT INTERNAL TISSUE (or see message)
masseur,*,use, MALE WHO GIVES MASSAGE
masseuse,*,ur, FEMALE WHO GIVES MASSAGE
massiuse, masseuse
massive,ely,eness, OF GREAT QUANTITY, SIZE
massuer, masseur
massuse, masseuse
mast, PART OF SAIL ON VESSEL, HOG FEED (or see mace(d))
mastectomy,mies, BREAST REMOVAL
mastek, mastic
master,*,red,ring,ry,rful,rfully,rfulness, rliness,rly,rhood, ONE WHO IS HIGHLY SKILLFUL/WISE "prefixes: over/re"
masterbashen, masturbate(tion)
masterbate, masturbate
mastereus, mysterious
mastic,*, RESIN OR SEALANT FOR PROTECTIVE COAT
mastidis, mastitis
mastique, mystique
mastir, master

mastirbashen, masturbate(tion)
mastirful, master(full)
mastitis,ic, INFLAMMED BREAST OR UDDER
masturbate,*,ed,ting,tion, TO STIMULATE ONE'S OWN SEXUAL ORGANS TO AROUSAL/ORGASM
masturly, master(ly)
mastytis, mastitis
masuese, masseuse
masukestik, masochism
masukistic, masochism(stic)
masure, masseur
masuse, masseuse
mat,*,tted,tting, FLAT ITEM FOR DOORSTEPS, FOR DISPLAYING VISUAL IMAGES, A FLAT MESH OF SOME MATERIAL (or see mad/made/mate/matte)
matabulism, metabolism
match,hes,hed,hing, PAIR UP, PUT SUITABLES TOGETHER, CHEMICALLY TREATED ITEM USED TO CREATE FLAME "prefixes: mis/over/re/un"
matcherashen, mature(ration)
matchure, mature
mate,*,ed,ting, TO JOIN TOGETHER, METHOD OF PROPOGATION, A CALL IN THE GAME OF CHESS (or see made/maid/matte) "prefixes: un"
matekulus, meticulous
matena, matinee
matenens, maintenance
mater, matter / mad(dder)
materde, maitre d'
materealise, materialize
matereul, material
material,*,lly,lism,list,listic,listically,lity, lities,lness,lize, NON-VIRTUAL, OF THE PHYSICAL PLANE, OF MASS, OF THE PHYSICAL "prefixes: bio/im/non"
materialize,*,ed,zing,zation,er, TO PHYSICALLY APPEAR "prefixes: im"
maternal,lly,listic,lism, MOTHERING, NURTURING
maternity,ties, A HUMAN STATE OF BEING PREGNANT
mateure, mature
math, LANGUAGE OF NUMBERS
mathematic,*,cal,cally,cian, SCIENCE AND LANGUAGE DEALING WITH NUMBERS "prefixes: bio"

mathology, mythology
matikulus, meticulous
matina, matinee
matinee,*, SPECIFIC AREA OF TIME WHEN A MOVIE IS SHOWN IN A THEATER
matir, mad(dder) / matter
matirde, maitre d'
matireal, material
matirnol, maternal
matirnulistic, maternal(istic)
matist, mad(ddest)
matna, matinee
matne, matinee
matness, mad(ness)
mato, motto
matramony, matrimony
matrearch, matriarch
matrearchal, matriarch(al)
matreark, matriarch
matreks, matrix
matremony, matrimony
matren, matron
matress, mattress
matrex, matrix
matriarch,*,hal,halism,hate,hy,hies, MOTHER IS LEADING ROLE
matricks, matrix
matriculate,*,ed,ting,tion, REGISTERED/ ENROLLED
matrimony,nies,nial,nially, OF MARRIAGE
matrin, matron
matris, mattress
matrix,xes,ices, MYSTERY/LABYRINTH/ RIDDLE
matron,*,nage,nly,nal,nage,nize, A FEMALE CHAPERONE/GUARDIAN/ ATTENDANT
matropolis, metropolis
matte, METAL STYLE, NON-GLOSSY SURFACE
matter,*,red, OF IMPORTANCE/ SUBSTANCE/PHYSICAL MATERIAL
mattress,ses, BED OF STUFFING FOR SLEEPING ON
matunens, maintenance
matur, matter / mad(der)
maturde, maitre d'
mature,*,ed,ring,rate,ration,rational, rative,ely,eness,rity, GROWN TO PHYSICAL PEAK "prefixes: im/pre"
maturnedy, maternity
maturnity, maternity

mauf, mauve
maugul, module
maujul, module
maul,*,led,ling, A TOOL, TO PHYSICALLY BATTER, REDUCE TO LESSER STATE (or see mall/mole)
mauld, maul(ed) / malt
maunaz, mayonnaise
maunten, mountain
mauntenus, mountain(ous)
mauroon, maroon
mausoleum, GRANDIOSE TOMB
mauve, A COLOR
mave, mauve
maverick,*, RADICALS, ONE'S WHO DON'T FOLLOW TRADITIONAL BELIEFS/ VALUES
mavrik, maverick
mavurek, maverick
mawntin, mountain
max,xes,xed,xing,ximal,ximize,ximum, SHORT FOR MAXIMUM
maximal,lly, THE MOST POSSIBLE
maximize,*,ed,zing,er,mum, THE MOST POSSIBLE
maximum,*, THE MOST POSSIBLE
may, ALLOWED TO, A MONTH IN THE YEAR (ENGLISH)
maybe, PERHAPS
maydreark, matriarch
mayenase, mayonnaise
mayer, mayor
mayonnaise, SPREAD OR SALAD DRESSING FOR FOOD
mayor,*,ral,ralty,ralties, POLITICAL POSITION
mazanine, mezzanine
mazdek, mastic
mazderful, master(full)
mazdik, mastic
mazdur, master
maze,*,ed,zing,zy, INABILITY TO MOVE/ THINK ALONG A CONTINUOUS PATH (or see mace/maize)
mazef, massive
mazeker, massacre
mazektomy, mastectomy
mazenine, mezzanine
mazif, massive
maziker, massacre
mazonry, mason(ry)
mazt, mast
mazturbate, masturbate
mazzanine, mezzanine

meadow,*, A FIELD GENERALLY WITHOUT TREES
meager,rly,rness, SMALL PORTION/ AMOUNT
meal,*,ly,lier,liest,liness, FOOD, FOOD EATEN AT CERTAIN TIME
mean,*,ning,ningful,ningfully, ningfulness,ningless,nt, ILL INTENT, EXPRESS THOUGHTS OF HARMFUL INTENT, METHOD OF ACHIEVING A GOAL, INTENT TO REFER/CONVEY SOMETHING "prefixes: un"
meant, PAST TENSE FOR THE WORD "MEAN", ATTEMPT TO EXPRESS THOUGHTS
mear, mere
measles, A VIRUS
measure,*,ed,ring,rable,rably,rability, rableness,ement, USE NUMBERS/ WORDS TO EXPLAIN SIZE/AMOUNT/ DISTANCE "prefixes: un"
meat,*,ty,tier,tiest,tiness, MUSCLE FIBER IN LIVING THINGS, EDIBLE PARTS (or see meet)
mecaneks, mechanic(s)
mechanic,*,cal,cally,calness,ist,istic, istically,ize,ism, WORKS WITH PARTS WHICH MAKES OBJECTS MOVE, SYSTEM OF APPROACH "prefixes: bio/un"
mechanize,*,ed,zing,zation,ist,istic, istically,er,ism, USE MACHINE TO PERFORM A TASK
mechen, mission
mechenary, mission(ary)
med, mid / meet
meda, meta
medabulism, metabolism
medacate, medicate
medafesic, metaphysic
medafisical, metaphysic(al)
medafore, metaphor
medagashen, mitigate(tion)
medagate, mitigate
medal,*,llic,llist,llion, A BADGE/OBJECT FOR AWARD (or see metal/mettle/ meddle/middle)
medamorfasis, metamorphosis
medaphore, metaphor
medaphysic, metaphysic
medaphysical, metaphysic(al)
medasen, medicine
medatashen, meditate(tion)

meddle,*,ed,ling,er,esome,esomeness, INTERFERE WITH OTHER'S THINGS/ AFFAIRS, (or see medal/metal/ mettle/middle) "prefixes: inter"
medea, media
medeader, mediate(tor)
medean, median
medeashen, mediate(tion)
medeat, mediate
medeator, mediate(tor)
medec, medic
medecal, medical
medefisic, metaphysic
medefl, medieval
medefol, medieval
medefore, metaphor
medek, medic
medekal, medical
medekulus, meticulous
medel, medal / metal / mettle / meddle / middle
medemorfasis, metamorphosis
medeokrity, mediocre(rity)
medeokur, mediocre
medeor, meteor
medeorite, meteorite
medeorology, meteorology
medephore, metaphor
meder, meter
medernedy, maternity
mederology, meteorology
medesin, medicine
medetashen, meditate(tion)
medeum, medium
medeur, meteor
medevul, medieval
medget, midget
media,*, AUDIO/VIDEO MEANS OF COMMUNICATION "prefixes: multi/ retro"
median,*,nly, OF THE MIDDLE, SEPARATION
mediate,*,ed,ting,tion,tive,tize,tor, tization, TO FACILITATE/DIFFUSE BETWEEN TWO OPPOSING PARTIES OR OBJECTS
medic,*, ONE'S WHO WORK WITH INJURIES, MEDICINE
medicable,ly, RESPONSIVE TO MEDICAL TREATMENT "prefixes: im/non/un"
medical,*,lly,cine,ate, OF MEDICINE, EXAMINATION "prefixes: bio/pre"
medicate,*,ed,ting,tion, GIVE MAN- MADE DRUGS TO "prefixes: pre"

medicine,*,nal,nally, MAN-MADE CHEMICALS TAKEN INTO THE BODY "prefixes: bio"
medieval,lism,list,lly, OF THE MIDDLE AGES
medifal, medieval
medifiseks, metaphysic(s)
medifl, medieval
medik, medic
medikulus, meticulous
medil, medal / metal / mettle / meddle / middle
mediocre,rity,rities, BETWEEN POOR AND GOOD QUALITY, IN-BETWEEN
mediocur, mediocre(rity)
medir, meter
medirology, meteorology
medisine, medicine
meditate,*,ed,ting,tion,tative,tatively, tor,tiveness, BE SILENT/STILL, ELIMINATE THOUGHT "prefixes: pre"
medium,*,mistic, COMMUNICATION USING THE VIRTUAL FIELD, TRANSLATE INFORMATION FROM ONE FORM OF MEDIA TO ANOTHER
medjet, midget
medl, medal / meddle / metal / mettle / middle
medle, medal / metal / mettle / meddle / middle
medo, meadow
medol, medal / metal / mettle / meddle / middle
medow, meadow
medrapolitan, metropolitan
medrek, metric
medric, metric
medropoletan, metropolitan
medst, midst
medtrik, metric
medufore, metaphor
medugation, mitigate(tion)
medukul, medical
medul, medal / metal / mettle / meddle / middle
medulsom, meddle(some)
medumorfasis, metamorphosis
medur, meter
medurology, meteorology
medusin, medicine
medutashen, meditate(tion)
medwife, midwife
meek,kly,kness, GENTLE/MILD TEMPERAMENT

meel, meal
meen, mean
meet,*,met,ting, COME TOGETHER, ARRIVE AT SAME DESTINATION AND TIME (or see meat)
mega, PREFIX INDICATING "MILLION/ VERY LARGE" MOST OFTEN MODIFIES THE WORD
megalo, PREFIX INDICATING "MILLION/ VERY LARGE" MOST OFTEN MODIFIES THE WORD
meger, meager / measure
megir, measure / major
megu, mega
megur, measure / meager
meiosis, CELLULAR PROCESS, UNDERSTATEMENT
mejer, measure / major
mejur, measure / major
mejut, midget
mek, meek
mekanek, mechanic
mekanekul, mechanic(al)
mekanise, mechanize
mekcher, mixture
mekenize, mechanize
meker, meager
mekschur, mixture
mekster, mixture
mekunize, mechanize
mekur, meager
mel, meal / mail / male
melado, mulato
meladramatic, melodrama(tic)
melady, melody
melameter, milli(meter)
melan, melon
melancholy,lies,lily,liness,lic, DESPONDENT, DEPRESSED, CONTEMPLATIVE
melancoli, melancholy
melanoma,*,ata,osis,nism, TUMOR, CELLS WITH DARK PIGMENT
melanosis,oma,nism, OVER PRODUCTION OF PIGMENT MELANIN IN SKIN/TISSUE
melasecond, millisecond
melatent, militant
melateristic, military(ristic)
melato, mulato
melaturize, military(rize)
meld,*,ded,ding, AS IF TO MELT TOGETHER, BLEND INTO ONE (or see melt/mill(ed))

meldoo, mildew
meldu, mildew
meledy, melody
melen, melon
melencholy, melancholy
melenium, millennium
melenkaly, melancholy
melenoma, melanoma
melenosis, melanosis
meleonaire, million(aire)
melet, millet
meletary, military
melin, melon
melincholy, melancholy
melinium, millennium
melinkoly, melancholy
melinoma, melanoma
melinosis, melanosis
melisha, militia
melit, millet
melitia, militia
melk, milk
mell, mill / meal
mellapede, millipede
mellinium, millennium
mellow,wly,wness, BECOME SOFTENED/RELAXED WITHOUT FEAR
melnutrishen, malnutrition
melo, mellow
melodrama,*,atic,atically,atist, EXAGERRATED ACT/EVENT, OVER EMPHASIS
melody,dies,dic,dically,dious,diousness, A SERIES OF SOUNDS/FREQUENCY, TUNES IN HARMONY
melogram, milli(gram)
melon,*, EDIBLE FRUIT
melonkoly, melancholy
melonosis, melanosis
melow, mellow
melt,*,ted,ting,table,tability,ter, TO CHANGE FROM SOLID TO LIQUID, CHANGE FORM (or see meld)
meltary, military
meludrumatek, melodrama(tic)
melugram, milli(gram)
meluleter, milli(liter)
melun, melon
meluncholy, melancholy
melunoma, melanoma
melunosis, melanosis
melupete, millipede
melusekund, millisecond

melutare, military
melutint, militant
melyonaire, million(aire)
melyun, million
memacree, mimic(ry)
memakry, mimic(ry)
member,*,rship, PART/PERSON WHICH BELONGS TO LARGER ORGANISM/ ORGANIZATION
membrane,*,nal,nous, LAYER OF THIN TISSUE "prefixes: non/semi"
memek, mimic
memento,*, ARTICLE/OBJECT REMINDER OF THE PAST
memerabelia, memorabilia
memerable, memorable
memerize, memorize
memic, mimic
memoir,*,rist, PRINTED REMINDER OF THE PAST
memok, mimic
memorabilia, REMINDERS OF THE PAST
memorable,ly,eness,bility,bilia, WORTHY OF REMEMBERING
memorais, memorize
memorial,*,list,lly,lize,lizes,lized,lizing, lization,lizer, AN OBJECT PLACED IN MEMORY OF THOSE WHO DIED "prefixes: im"
memorize,*,ed,zing,zable,er, STORE INTO MEMORY
memory,ries,rize, COLLECTION OF STORED INFORMATION
memrable, memorable
memrize, memorize
memruble, memorable
memry, memory
memuk, mimic
memurabilea, memorabilia
memurise, memorize
memwar, memoir
men,*, HUMAN ADULT MALE (or see mean)
menace,*,ced,cing, HARMFUL/ THREATENING, A NUISANCE
menacher, miniature
menamize, minimize
menamul, minimal
menamuly, minimal(y)
menamum, minimum
menapos, menopause
menarolization, mineral(ization)
menarul, mineral
menarulize, mineral(ize)

menas, menace
menasher, miniature
menaskewul, minuscule
menastrony, minestrone
menastry, minister(y)
mences, menses
menchen, mention
mend,*,ded,ding,dable, TO FIX/REPAIR (or see mint/meant)
mene, mean / mini / many
meneacher, miniature
menemize, minimize
menengidos, meningitis
menenjidus, meningitis
menerable, memorable
menerul, mineral
menes, menace
menestrony, minestrone
menestry, minister(y)
menet, minute
meneul, menial
mengul, mingle
meni, mini / many
menial,lly, REQUIRES LITTLE THOUGHT
meniature, miniature
menila, manila
meningitis,ic, VIRUS OF THE BODY
menipause, menopause
menipulate, manipulate
menis, menace
menk, mink
menmerable, memorable
mennow, minnow
meno, minnow
menogamy, monogamy
menokside, monoxide
menopause,sal, STOP HAVING MONTHLY ESTRUS CYCLES, ESTROGEN CHANGES IN FEMALES
menopuly, monopoly
menoscule, minuscule
menotnus, monotony(nous)
menotny, monotony
menoxide, monoxide
menruble, memorable
mens, men(s) / mean(s) / mince
menses, MENSTRUATION
menshen, mention
mensteration, menstruation
menstral, menstrual / minstrel
menstrashen, menstruation
menstration, menstruation

menstrual,uous,ate,uum,ation, MENSTRUATION (or see minstrel) "prefixes: pre"
menstruation, FEMALE MONTHLY UTERUS LINING DISCHARGE, A PERIOD
ment, mint / mend / meant
mental,lly,lity, THOUGHT, OF THE MIND
menthol, OIL
mention,*,ned,ning,nable,ner, CALLING BRIEF ATTENTION TO SOMETHING "prefixes: un/under"
mentle, mental
mentol, mental
mentor,*, A COACH, GUIDE
mentur, mentor
menu,*, LIST OF RESTAURANT MEALS
menuet, minuet
menumem, minimum
menumly, minimal(y)
menupause, menopause
menure, manure
menus, menace
menustrony, minestrone
menyew, menu
menyewet, minuet
menyon, mignon
meol, meal
mer, mere / mirror / mare
meracle, miracle
meraculus, miracle(culous)
merage, mirage
meragolt, marigold
meraje, mirage
merakle, miracle
merakulus, miracle(culous)
meral, morale / mural
meraly, merry(rily)
meranade, marinade / marinate
merange, meringue
merathon, marathon
mercantile,lism,list, COMMERCE, TRADE
mercenary,ries,rily,riness, HIRED TO KILL
merch, merge
merchandise,ed,sing,er,sable,sability, ize,izes,ized,izing,izer, GOODS FOR RETAIL SALE
merchant,*,table,ndise, ONE WHO DEALS IN GOODS FOR RETAIL
mercury,rial,rialism,rialize,rializes, rialized,rializing,rialization,ric, A PLANET, BEHAVIOR AS IF RULED BY THE PLANET, METALLIC ELEMENT USED IN THERMOMETERS
mercy,cies,ciful,cifully,ciless,cilessly, cilessness, PROVIDE COMPASSION/ BENEVOLENCE AT A CRUCIAL TIME "prefixes: un"
merder, murder
merdurer, murder(er)
mere,ely, SIMPLY FOR THE REASON OF, SMALL IN MATTER (or see marry/ merry/mirror)
merech, marriage
mered, married
meredian, meridian
mereg, marriage
meregold, marigold
mereinette, marionette
merej, marriage
merekul, miracle
meren, marine
merenate, marinade / marinate
mereod, myriad
mereonett, marionette
meret, merit
meretal, marital
merethon, marathon
meretime, maritime
meretul, marital
mereunett, marionette
merewana, marijuana
merg, merge
merge,*,ed,ging,er,ence, COME TOGETHER AS ONE "prefixes: sub/ un"
meri, marry / merry
meriad, myriad
merich, marriage
merid, married
meridg, marriage
meridian,*,nal,nally, INVISIBLE CIRCLE RUNNING AROUND EARTH THROUGH NORTH/SOUTH POLES
merigold, marigold
merijuana, marijuana
merily, merry(rily)
merin, marine
merina, marina
merinad, marinade / marinate
merinat, marinade / marinate
meringue, WHIPPED EGGS
merit,*,ted,tedly,tless,torious, WORTHY OF HONOR OR NOTE "prefixes: un"
merital, marital
merithon, marathon
meritime, maritime
meritol, marital
meriwana, marijuana
merje, merge
merk, murky
merkanteel, mercantile
merkury, mercury
merky, murky
merlen, merlin
merlin, BIRD
mermaid,*, ILLUSIONARY FISH WOMAN
mermer, murmur
mermur, murmur
mero, marrow
meroge, mirage
meroj, mirage
meror, mirror
merose, morose
merow, marrow
merry,rriment,rrily,rriness, CHEERY, HAPPY
mersenary, mercenary
mershandise, merchandise
mersinary, mercenary
mersy, mercy
merukul, miracle
merur, mirror
mery, marry / merry
mes, PREFIX INDICATING "MIDDLE" MOST OFTEN MODIFIES THE WORD
mesa,*, LAND PLATEAU
mesach, message / massage
mesage, message / massage
mesalaneus, miscellaneous
mesals, measles / missile(s)
mesanine, mezzanine
mesbahave, misbehave
mesbaleef, misbelief
mesbaleve, misbelieve
mesbok, misspoke
mesbokin, misspoke(n)
mescalculate, miscalculate
meschef, mischief
mesconstrue, misconstrue
mesdake, mistake
mesdamener, misdemeanor
mesderius, mysterious
mesdress, mistress
mesdriul, mistrial
mesdufy, mystify
mesdur, mister
mesdury, mystery
meseg, message
mesej, message

mesel, missile
meseness, mess(iness)
mesenger, messenger
mesenine, mezzanine
mesenturpet, misinterpret
meseur, mess(ier) / masseur
meseust, mess(iest)
mesfet, misfit
mesfire, misfire
mesforshen, misfortune
mesfortune, misfortune
mesgeving, misgiving
mesguge, misjudge
mesh,hes,hed,hing, INTERWOVEN METAL STRANDS TO CREATE A BLANKET/ NET "prefixes: en"
meshandle, mishandle
meshap, mishap
meshen, mission
meshenary, mission(ary)
meshur, measure
mesige, message
mesije, message
mesil, missile
mesils, measles / missile(s)
mesinene, mezzanine
mesinform, misinform
mesinger, messenger
mesinturpet, misinterpret
mesjef, mischief
mesjug, misjudge
meskalaneus, miscellaneous
meskarege, miscarriage
meskedo, mosquito
meskeet, mesquite
meskenstrew, misconstrue
meskownt, miscount
meskwote, misquote
mesled, misled
mesleed, mislead
mesmach, mismatch
mesmerize,*,ed,zing,ism,ic,ically,ist,er,zation, INTENSELY ATTENTIVE TO THE POINT OF EXCLUDING ALL OTHER THINGS
mesmurize, mesmerize
mesnomer, misnomer
meso, PREFIX INDICATING "MIDDLE" MOST OFTEN MODIFIES THE WORD
mesoje, massage
mesonderstand, misunderstand
mesonderstood, misunderstood
mesonine, mezzanine
mespell, misspell

mesplase, misplace
mespok, misspoke
mespokin, misspoke(n)
mesprent, misprint
mesprunounce, mispronounce
mesquite, LAND TYPE, A TREE, SHRUB
mesquote, misquote
mesred, misread
mesrepresent, misrepresent
mesruble, miserable
mess,ses,sed,sing,sy,sily,siness,sier,siest, SLOPPY, DISHEVELED, DISARRAY
message,*,ed,ging, SHORT NOTE OF VOICE/TEXT
messanine, mezzanine
messenger,*,red,ring, ONE WHO DELIVERS A NOTE
messusege, misuse(sage)
mest, mist / midst / miss(ed) / mess(ed)
mestake, mistake
mestakin, mistake(n)
mestamener, misdemeanor
meste, mist(y)
mesteek, mystique
mestefy, mystify
mesteik, mystic / mystique / mistake
mester, mister
mestereus, mysterious
mestic, mystic
mestides, mastitis
mestify, mystify
mestikul, mystic(al)
mestireus, mysterious
mestook, mistook
mestreat, mistreat
mestress, mistress
mestrete, mistreat
mestris, mistress
mestriul, mistrial
mestufy, mystify
mestuk, mistook
mestumener, misdemeanor
mestury, mystery
mesuge, message
mesuje, message
mesulaneus, miscellaneous
mesuls, measles / missile(s)
mesultoe, mistletoe
mesunderstand, misunderstand
mesunine, mezzanine
mesure, measure
mesurible, miserable
mesuse, masseuse / misuse
mesuseje, misuse(sage)

mesuze, misuse / masseuse
mesyews, misuse
met, PAST TENSE FOR THE WORD "MEET", (or see mitt/mite/meet/meat) "prefixes: un"
meta, PREFIX INDICATING "BEYOND/ CHANGE" MOST OFTEN MODIFIES THE WORD
metabolism,*,ize,ic,ically, THE CONVERSION OF ENERGY IN A LIVING ORGANISM, FUNCTION OF LIFE
metabolize,*,ed,zing,zable, CONCERNED WITH METABOLISM
metabulism, metabolism
metacate, medicate
metafisical, metaphysic(al)
metagate, mitigate
metal,*,led,ling,llic,llically,llurgy, CHEMICAL ELEMENTS FOUND IN THE EARTH (or see mettle/meddle/medal/middle) "prefixes: bi/non/semi/un"
metamorphosis, MAJOR TRANSFORMATION AS A CATERPILLAR TO A BUTTERFLY
metaphor,*,ric,rical,rically, EXPRESSING THOUGHT USING UNCONVENTIONAL COMPARISONS
metaphysic,*,cal,cally, STUDY OF THE SUPERNATURAL, INVISIBLE
metapolize, metabolize
metasen, medicine
metatashen, meditate(tion)
mete, meat(y)
metea, media
metean, median
meteashen, mediate(tion)
meteate, mediate
meteator, mediate(tor)
metefisical, metaphysic(al)
metek, medic
metekal, medical
metekulus, meticulous
metel, medal / metal / mettle / meddle / middle
metemorfusis, metamorphosis
meten, mitten
meteokrety, mediocre(rity)
meteokur, mediocre
meteor,*,ric,rite,rology, COMPACTED SAND AND ICE TRAVELING AT HIGH VELOCITY THROUGH SPACE

meteorite,*, METEOR THAT SURVIVES ENTRY THROUGH EARTH'S ATMOSPHERE
meteorology,gic,gical,gically,gist, STUDY OF THE ATMOSPHERE SUCH AS WEATHER/CLIMATE
metephysical, metaphysic(al)
meter,*,red,ring, FORM/INSTRUMENT OF MEASUREMENT "prefixes: deca/un"
metesen, medicine
metetashen, meditate(tion)
meteum, medium
meteurology, meteorology
metevul, medieval
meteyorite, meteorite
meth, SHORT FOR METHAMPHETAMINE
methad, method
methadology, methodolgy
methadone, MAN-MADE DRUG, DOWNER, HIGHLY ADDICTIVE
methakul, myth(ical)
methalogic, mythologic
methamphetamine,*, ABBREVIATION FOR METH, MANMADE CHEMICAL STIMULANT
methane, A GAS
methanfetamene, methamphetamine
methanol, TOXIC LIQUID
methanphetamine, methamphetamine
methasize, myth(icize)
methecul, myth(ical)
methed, method
methedology, methodology
methedone, methadone
methemfetamine, methamphetamine
methenphetamine, methamphetamine
methid, method
methidology, methodology
method,*,dize,dizes,dized,dizing,dizer, dical,dically,dicalness, dology, A SYSTEM/PROCEDURE/TECHNIQUE
methodology,gies,gical,gically,gist, A SYSTEM/ PROCEDURE/TECHNIQUE
metholugy, mythology
methonol, methanol
methud, method
methudology, methodology
methudone, methadone
methunol, methanol
metia, media
metic, medic
metical, medical

meticulous,sly,sness, EXCESSIVE ATTENTION TO DETAIL/ CLEANLINESS/ EXACTING
metil, medal / metal / mettle / meddle / middle
metin, mitten
meting, meet(ing)
metir, meter
metirology, meteorology
metisine, medicine
metitate, meditate
metle, medal / metal / mettle / meddle / middle
meto, meadow
metr, PREFIX INDICATING "WOMB/MOTHER" MOST OFTEN MODIFIES THE WORD
metrapolitan, metropolitan
metric,*,cal,cally,cate,cates,cated, cating,cation,cist,cize,cizes, cized, cizing, A MEASUREMENT SYSTEM "prefixes: bio"
metro, REFERRING TO TRANSIT SYSTEM IN CITY, SHORT FOR "METROPOLITAN"
metropolis,ses, CENTRAL CITY
metropolitan,nism, HUB OF CITY AND THOSE WHO DWELL THERE "prefixes: non"
metruk, metric
metst, midst
mettle,*,ed,esome, COURAGEOUS, SPIRITED (or see medal/metal/meddle/middle)
metukul, medical
metul, medal / metal / mettle / meddle / middle
metur, meter
meturnedy, maternity
meturnul, maternal
meturology, meteorology
metutashen, meditate(tion)
meuchuel, mutual
meudilate, mutilate
meukus, mucus
meul, meal / mule
meurol, mural
meus, muse
meusikul, music(al)
meut, mute
meutashen, mutate(tion)
meutat, mutate
meutene, mutiny
meutilate, mutilate

meutulashen, mutilate(tation)
meuzeim, museum
meuzek, music
meuzeshen, musician
mewfee, movie
mewfuble, move(vable)
mewkus, mucus
mewl, mule
mewn, moon
mewnisapaledy, municipal(ity)
mewnisepal, municipal
mewral, mural
mewse, muse/ moose/ mousse
mewseum, museum
mewsik, music
mewt, moot / mute
mewtashen, mutate(tion)
mewtelate, mutilate
mewteny, mutiny
mewtint, mutate(ant)
mewvee, movie
mewvuble, move(vable)
mewzishen, musician
mexcher, mixture
mexter, mixture
mez, mess
mezandul, mishandle
mezanine, mezzanine
mezdamener, misdemeanor
mezder, mister
mezdery, mystery
mezdumener, misdemeanor
mezenine, mezzanine
mezfet, misfit
mezfire, misfire
mezforchen, misfortune
mezhap, mishap
mezinform, misinform
mezinine, mezzanine
mezkwote, misquote
mezled, misled
mezleet, mislead
mezmach, mismatch
mezmurize, mesmerize
meznomer, misnomer
mezonine, mezzanine
mezpell, misspell
mezplase, misplace
mezprent, misprint
mezred, misread
mezreprezent, misrepresent
mezruble, miserable
meztake, mistake
meztamener, misdemeanor

meztek, mystic
mezter, mister
meztereus, mysterious
meztreat, mistreat
meztress, mistress
meztriul, mistrial
mezuls, measles
mezunine, mezzanine
mezury, misery
mezzanine,*, LOW UPPER FLOOR OR THEATER BALCONY
mfusiz, emphasize
mi, my
mibuleve, misbelieve
mic, meek
mica, ORGANIC, SILICATE
michanek, mechanic
michanekul, mechanic(al)
michen, mission
michenary, mission(ary)
micks, mix
micrawave, microwave
micro, VERY SMALL, PREFIX INDICATING "SMALL" MOST OFTEN MODIFIES THE WORD
microbe,*,bial,bian,bic, ORGANISMS SEEN ONLY UNDER A MICROSCOPE
micrometer, SYSTEM OF MEASUREMENT
micron,*,ra,nation, MICROMETER "prefixes: sub"
microphone,*, TRANSMITS SOUND
microscope,*,pic,pically,py,pist, INSTRUMENT WHICH ENLARGES OBJECTS FOR VIEWING WITH THE EYES "prefixes: sub"
microwave,*, ELECTROMAGNETIC WAVELENGTH, AN APPLIANCE
micu, mica
mid, PREFIX INDICATING "HALF/ MIDDLE" MOST OFTEN MODIFIES THE WORD (or see mitt)
midachondria, mitochondria
midagashen, mitigate(tion)
midagate, mitigate
middle, IN BETWEEN (or see medal/ metal/mettle/meddle)
midegate, mitigate
midegation, mitigate(tion)
mider, miter
midevil, medieval
midget,*, UNUSUALLY SMALL PERSON
midia, media
midian, median

midieit, mediate
midigashen, mitigate(tion)
midioker, mediocre
midium, medium
midival, medieval
midjet, midget
midle, middle
midochondria, mitochondria
midokondrea, mitochondria
midol, middle
midoses, mitosis
midst, LOCATED IN THE MIDDLE, AMONG
miduchondria, mitochondria
midul, medal / metal / mettle / meddle / middle
midur, miter
midwife,eves,ery, ASSISTS MOTHER THROUGH BIRTHING A CHILD
miff,*,fed,fing,fy, BE OFFENDED
miget, midget
might,ty,tier,tiest,tily,tiness, STRENGTH, POWER, PERHAPS, MAYBE (or see mite)
mignon,*, SMALL, DELICATE
migraine,*, A SERIOUS HEADACHE
migrant,*, ONE WHO IS CONTINUOUSLY MOVING
migrashen, migrate(tion)
migrate,*,ed,ting,tion,ant,tor,tory, TO MOVE LOCATION OF HOME BASED UPON THE SEASONS
migro, micro
migrunt, migrant
migrutory, migrate(tory)
mijet, midget
mika, mica
mikanek, mechanic
mikanekul, mechanic(al)
mikaw, macaw
mikcher, mixture
mikount, miscount
mikrafone, microphone
mikrascope, microscope
mikrawave, microwave
mikro, micro
mikrobe, microbe
mikrofone, microphone
mikrometer, micrometer
mikron, micron
mikrowave, microwave
mikshter, mixture
mikster, mixture
miku, mica

mil, mile / meal
milado, mulato
milage, mile(age)
milagram, milli(gram)
milaleter, milli(liter)
milameter, milli(meter)
milapede, millipede
milarea, malaria
milasecond, millisecond
milasus, molasses
milatent, militant
milato, mulato
milaturestic, military(ristic)
milaturise, military(rize)
mild,der,dest,dly,dness, PLEASANT (or see mill(ed))
mildew,*,wed,wing,wy, FUNGI
mildu, mildew
mile,*,eage, U.S. MEASUREMENT FOR DISTANCE
milegram, milli(gram)
milekuler, molecule(lar)
milemeder, milli(meter)
milenium, millennium
mileonaire, million(aire)
milepete, millipede
miler, mill(er)
milesekent, millisecond
milest, molest
milet, millet
miletary, military
mileturezation, military(rization)
miligram, milli(gram)
milileter, milli(liter)
milimeter, milli(meter)
milinium, millennium
milion, million
milionair, million(aire)
milipede, millipede
militant,tly,tness,ncy, ORDERLY, BY STRICT RULES
military,ries,rily,rism,rist,rize,rizes,rized, rizing,rization,ristic,ristically, GROUP OF PEOPLE BEING LED WITH STRICT RULES, AN ORDERLY GROUP
militia,*, GROUP ORGANIZED/TRAINED TO FIGHT
milk,ker,ky,kiness, WHITE LIFE-GIVING FLUID EXCRETED BY MOTHERS OF MAMMALS, ANY RESEMBLANCE TO MILK
mill,*,lled,lling,ller, GRINDS GRAIN/ REMOVAL OF HULL (or see mile)

millaliter, milli(liter)
millameter, milli(meter)
millenium, millennium
millennia,ial,ium, MEASUREMENT BY 1,000 "prefixes: pre"
millennium,*,ia, MEASUREMENT BY 1,000
millet, EDIBLE GRAIN, GRASS
milli,igram,iliter,imeter, LATIN THOUSAND/THOUSANDTH, PREFIX INDICATING "ONE THOUSANDTH" MOST OFTEN MODIFIES THE WORD
millinium, millennium
million,*,naire, U.S. NUMBER TO IDENTIFY QUANTITY "prefixes: multi"
millipede,*, INSECT
millisecond,*, METRIC NUMBER
miltary, military
miluge, mile(age)
milugram, milli(gram)
milumeter, milli(meter)
milupede, millipede
milutant, militant
milutare, military
milyen, million
milyonaire, million(aire)
mimakry, mimic(ry)
mimbrane, membrane
mimbur, member
mime,*,ed,ming, ACTOR WHO USES THE BODY TO ACT, COMMUNICATE WITHOUT USING WORDS
mimic,*,cking,cry,cries, TO COPY, IMITATE ANOTHER PERSON
mimorabilia, memorabilia
mimorabul, memorable
mimorealzation, memorial(ization)
mimoreul, memorial
mimorise, memorize
mimory, memory
mimuck, mimic
mimurabilia, memorabilia
mimwar, memoir
min, mine / mean
minacher, miniature
minamize, minimize
minamul, minimal
minamum, minimum
minapos, menopause
minaralize, mineral(ize)
minarul, mineral
minasher, miniature
minaskule, minuscule
minaster, minister

minastrony, minestrone
mince,*,ed,cing, CHOP SOMETHING INTO SMALL PIECES
minchen, mention
mind,*,ded,ding,dful,dfully,dfulness, dless,dlessly,dlessness, TO OBEY, PLACE WHERE THOUGHTS ARE GENERATED (or see mend/mint)
mine,*,ed,ning,er, PAST TENSE FOR THE WORD "MY", CLAIMING OWNERSHIP, A FORMED TUNNEL INTO THE GROUND WHICH BEARS PRECIOUS ROCKS/METALS, SUBSURFACE BOMB (or see mind/main)
mineature, miniature
minemal, minimal
minemize, minimize
minemum, minimum
minengidus, meningitis
mineon, mignon
miner, mine(r) / minor
mineral,*,lize,lizes,lized,lizing,lizable, lization,lizer,logy, ORGANIC SUBSTANCES "prefixes: bio"
mines, minus / mine(s) / mince / menace
mineskule, minuscule
minester, minister
minestrone, SOUP
minet, minute
mingle,*,ed,ling, TO BE AMONG, ASSOCIATE WITH "prefixes: inter"
mini, LATIN FOR SMALL, SHORT, BRIEF, PREFIX INDICATING "SMALL" MOST OFTEN MODIFIES THE WORD (or see many)
miniature,*,rist,rize,rizes,rized,rizing, rization, SMALL FORM OF ORIGINAL SIZE "prefixes: sub"
minimal,ly,lism, THE LEAST POSSIBLE
minimize,*,ed,zing, MAKE SMALLER, LESS
minimum,*, THE LEAST POSSIBLE "prefixes: sub"
miniscule, minuscule
minister,*,ry,ries,rial,rially, PREACHING ABOUT RELIGION
miniucher, miniature
mink,*, A RODENT
minnow,*,wed,wing, A VERY SMALL FISH
mino, minnow
minogumy, monogamy

minokside, monoxide
minon, mignon
minopos, menopause
minopuly, monopoly
minor,*, BELOW MAJOR, SMALLER THAN, MUSICAL CHORD (or see miner)
minority,ties, SMALLER NUMBER WHEN COMPARED TO PREDOMINANT GROUP
minos, minus / minnow(s)
minotnus, monotony(nous)
minotny, monotony
minow, minnow
minoxite, monoxide
minse, mince
minses, menses
minshen, mention
minsteration, menstruation
minstral, menstrual / minstrel
minstrel,*, ONE WHO ENTERTAINS WITH POETRY/SONG (or see menstrual)
mint,*,ted,ting, AN HERB, PLACE WHERE COINS ARE MADE (or see meant/mend)
mintalety, mental(ity)
mintel, mental
minter, mentor
minthol, menthol
mintle, mental
mintor, mentor
mintul, mental
minu, menu
minuet,*, SLOW RYTHM IN MUSIC, DANCE
minural, mineral
minure, manure
minus, MATH EXPRESSION, TAKE AWAY/SUBTRACT FROM (or see menace)
minuscule, OF LITTLE IMPORTANCE, TINY
minuskule, minuscule
minustrony, minestrone
minute,*,ely, MEASURE OF TIME, RECORD A MEETING, SLIGHT/SMALL
minuver, maneuver
minyew, menu
minyewet, minuet
minyon, mignon
miosis, meiosis
mir, mere / mire

miracle,*,culous,culously, EVENT PRECEDED BY MYSTERIOUS ACTIONS, SEEMINGLY IMPOSSIBLE OCCURRENCE
miraculus, miracle(culous)
mirage,*, AN OPTICAL ILLUSION
mirakle, miracle
miral, morale / mural
mirange, meringue
mircantile, mercantile
mirchandise, merchandise
mirchant, merchant
mire,*,ed,ing,ry, DIFFICULT, MUDDY
miread, myriad
mirekul, miracle
mireod, myriad
mirer, mirror
mirje, merge
mirkanteel, mercantile
mirky, murky
mirlin, merlin
mirmer, murmur
mirmur, murmur
miroge, mirage
miror, mirror
mirose, morose
mirquery, mercury
mirror,*,red,ring, REFLECTION
mirseful, mercy(ciful)
mirsy, mercy
mirukul, miracle
mirur, mirror
mirurd, mirror(ed)
mis, PREFIX INDICATING "BAD/WRONG/ WRONGLY" MOST OFTEN MODIFIES THE WORD (or see miss/mice)
misalaneus, miscellaneous
misandul, mishandle
misap, mishap
misapprehension,*, NOT CORRECT UNDERSTANDING/IMPRESSION
misbaleef, misbelief
misbaleve, misbelieve
misbehave,*,ed,ving,vior, TO NOT BEHAVE
misbehavior, NOT BEHAVE
misbelief, DO NOT BELIEVE
misbelieve,*,ed,ving, PAST TENSE FOR THE WORD "MISBELIEF"
misbok, misspoke
misbokin, misspoke(n)
misbuleef, misbelief
miscalculate,*,ed,ting,tion, NOT PROPER CALCULATION

miscarriage,*,ed,ging, LOSS IN CARRYING A FETUS TO FULL TERM
miscellaneous, VARIETY OF ELEMENTS/ THINGS WHICH HAVE NO RELEVANCE TO ONE ANOTHER
mischef, mischief
mischief,evous,evously,evousness, ACTION/BEHAVIOR THAT CREATES AGITATION FOR OTHERS
misconstrue,*,ed,uing, MISINTERPRET, INCORRECT UNDERSTANDING OF INFORMATION
miscount,*,ted,ting, COUNT DIDN'T COME OUT CORRECTLY
miscownt, miscount
misd, miss(ed) / mist
misdacism, mystic(icism)
misdaken, mistake(n)
misdamener, misdemeanor
misdemeanor,*, CITED FOR NOT OBEYING SET RULES
misdereus, mysterious
misdirection,*, WRONG DIRECTIONS/ INFORMATION
misdireus, mysterious
misdress, mistress
misdriul, mistrial
misdrus, mistress
misdufy, mystify
misdur, mister
misdury, mystery
mised, miss(ed) / mist
misel, missile
miself, my(self)
miseltoe, mistletoe
misenform, misinform
misenterpret, misinterpret
miser,rly,rliness, ONE WHO IS OVERLY FEARFUL ABOUT USING, SPENDING THEIR MONEY
miserable,ly,eness, EXTREMELY UNCOMFORTABLE, FEELING BEYOND CAPACITY
misery,ries, DREADFUL EMOTIONAL OR PHYSICAL STATE OF BEING
misfire,*,ed,ring, DIDN'T HIT THE TARGET
misfit,*, DOESN'T QUITE FIT IN WITH THE OTHERS
misfortune,*, UNPLANNED DISTURBING EVENT
misgef, mischief

misgiving,*, GIVEN TO DOUBT OR APPREHENSION IN MAKING A JUDGEMENT
misguge, misjudge
mishandle,*,ed,ling, TO NOT TREAT CAREFULLY
mishap,*, EVENT WHICH RENDERS UNCONTROLLABLE REACTIONS
mishen, mission
mishenary, mission(ary)
misinform,*,med,ming,mant,mer, mation, NOT CORRECT INFORMATION
misinterpret,*,ted,ting,tation, DOESN'T REPRESENT THE FACTS
mision, mission
misionary, mission(ary)
misjif, mischief
misjudge,*,ed,ging,ement, MAKE DECISION WITHOUT TAKING ALL FACTS INTO CONSIDERATION
misjuge, misjudge
miskalaneus, miscellaneous
miskalkulate, miscalculate
miskedo, mosquito
miskeet, mesquite
miskerage, miscarriage
miskeruge, miscarriage
miskonstrue, misconstrue
miskownt, miscount
miskunstrew, misconstrue
misle, missile
mislead,*,ed,ding, MANIPULATE INTO UNDESIRABLE DIRECTION
misled, PAST TENSE FOR THE WORD MISLEAD
misletoe, mistletoe
mismach, mismatch
mismatch,hes,hed,hing, DO NOT MATCH UP TOGETHER
misnomer,*, INCORRECT NAME FOR
misoge, massage
misoje, massage
misonderstand, misunderstand
misonderstood, misunderstood
mispell, misspell
misplace,*,ed,cing,ement, NOT PLACED WHERE IT NORMALLY BELONGS
mispoke, misspoke
mispokin, misspoke(n)
misprint,*,ted,ting, PRINTED INCORRECT INFORMATION
mispronounce,*,ed,cing,nunciation, WORD NOT SPOKEN CORRECTLY

misprunownse, mispronounce
misquote,*,ed,ting,tation, DIDN'T ACCURATELY REFLECT WHAT WAS ACTUALLY SAID
misread,*, TO NOT READ CORRECTLY
misred, misread
misrepresent,*,ted,ting,tation,tative,ter, DOESN'T ACCURATELY REPRESENT
misruble, miserable
miss,sses,ssed,ssing, NOT IN USUAL/PREFERRED PLACE, IN REFERENCE TO YOUNG UNMARRIED WOMAN
missile,*,ery, A THROWN OR SHOT PROJECTILE WITH INTENT TO INJURE
mission,*,nary,naries, SET OUT TO COMPLETE A TASK AS IF WITH AUTHORITY
misslede, mislead
misspell,*,lled,lling, TO SPELL INCORRECTLY
misspoke,en, DID NOT SAY WHAT WAS MEANT TO BE SAID, SPOKEN INCORRECTLY
missusage, misuse(sage)
missuse, misuse
mist,*,ted,ting,ty,tily,tiness, VERY LIGHT SPRAY OF WATER, A HAZE (or see midst/miss(ed))
mistacism, mystic(icism)
mistake,*,en,enly,enness,kable, THINK IT IS SOMETHING IT IS NOT, INCORRECT "prefixes: un"
mistakuble, mistake(kable)
mistamener, misdemeanor
misteek, mystique
mistefy, mystify
mistek, mystic / mystique / mistake
mistektamy, mastectomy
mister, MR.(ABBREVIATION), REFERENCE TO A MAN
mistereus, mysterious
mistic, mystic
misticul, mystic(cal)
mistique, mystique
mistireus, mysterious
mistletoe, PARASITIC PLANT ON A TREE
mistook, PAST TENSE FOR THE WORD 'MISTAKE'
mistreat,*,ted,ting,tment, TREAT SOMETHING/SOMEONE IMPROPERLY

mistress,sses, WOMAN IN POSITION OF COMMAND/RULE
mistret, mistreat
mistrial,*, UNABLE TO MAKE A JUDGEMENT IN A TRIAL DUE TO VARIOUS REASONS
mistro, maestro
mistufy, mystify
mistuk, mistook
misul, missile
misulaneus, miscellaneous
misulf, my(self)
misultoe, mistletoe
misunderstand,*,ding,tood, NOT ABLE TO COMPREHEND/UNDERSTAND
misunderstood, PAST TENSE FOR THE WORD "MISUNDERSTAND"
misur, miser
misuruble, miserable
misury, misery
misus, miss(es)
misuse,*,ed,sing,er,sage, NOT USING PROPERLY
misuze, misuse
mit, mitt / mite / might / meat / meet / met
mitabolize, metabolize
mitachondria, mitochondria
mitagashen, mitigate(tion)
mitagate, mitigate
mitapolize, metabolize
mite,*, TINY INSECT, ANIMAL, SOMETHING TINY (or see might/mitt/might(y))
miten, mitten
miter,*,red,ring, REFERENCE TO ANGLES (or see meter)
mitereul, material
miteur, might(ier)
mitevul, medieval
mith, myth
mithakul, myth(ical)
mithalogic, mythologic
mithasize, myth(icize)
mithecul, myth(ical)
mitholagize, mythologic(ize)
mithology, mythology
mitiest, might(iest)
mitigate,*,able,tion,tive,tor,tory, TO LESSEN A BURDEN OR SEVERITY "prefixes: un"
mitir, meter / miter

mitochondria,al,ion, ORGANELLES WITHIN A CELL WHICH ASSIST IN METABOLISM
mitoesis, mitosis
mitosis,ic, CELL DIVISION FROM ORIGINAL CELL "prefixes: endo"
mitropolis, metropolis
mitst, midst
mitt,*,ten, A COVERING FOR THE HAND (or see mite/might)
mitten,*, HAND COVERING TO PROTECT SKIN FROM GREAT TEMPERATURE DIFFERENCES
mitul, medal / metal / mettle / meddle / middle
mityest, might(iest)
mix,xes,xed,xing,xer, TO BLEND/STIR VARIOUS ELEMENTS/ARTICLES/INGREDIENTS TOGETHER ELIMINATING ORDER "prefixes: inter"
mixchur, mixture
mixture,*, COMBINE DIFFERENT THINGS TOGETHER TO CREATE SOMETHING ENTIRELY DIFFERENT "prefix: inter"
mizconstsrue, misconstrue
mizdakin, mistake(n)
mizdamener, misdemeanor
mizdereus, mysterious
mizdress, mistress
mizdrus, mistress
mizdur, mister
mizdury, mystery
mizenformation, misinform(ation)
mizenturpret, misinterpret
mizer, miser
mizeruble, miserable
mizfet, misfit
mizfire, misfire
mizforchen, misfortune
mizgeving, misgiving
mizhandul, mishandle
mizhap, mishap
mizinform, misinform
mizkunstrew, misconstrue
mizkwote, misquote
mizled, misled
mizleed, mislead
mizmach, mismatch
miznomer, misnomer
mizpell, misspell
mizplase, misplace
mizpronounce, mispronounce

mizread, misread
mizreprezent, misrepresent
miztake, mistake
miztakuble, mistake(kable)
miztamener, misdemeanor
mizteek, mystique
miztek, mystic
mizter, mister
miztereus, mysterious
miztress, mistress
miztret, mistreat
miztrial, mistrial
mizunderstand, misunderstand
mizur, miser
mizury, misery
mizuse, misuse
mo, mow
moan,*,ned,ning, A LOW, GUTTERAL SOUND COMING FROM THE THROAT
moat,*, DUG OUT TRENCH AROUND A STRUCTURE WHICH IS NORMALLY FILLED WITH WATER (or see mote)
mob,*,bbed,bbing, GATHERING OF LARGE GROUP OF PEOPLE
mobal, mobile
mobalezation, mobile(lization)
mobalize, mobile(lize)
mobelity, mobile(lity)
mobeluzation, mobile(lization)
mobile,lity,lize,lizes,lized,lizing,lization, ABILITY TO BE PHYSICALLY ON THE MOVE, TEMPORARY "prefixes: im"
moble, mobile
mobt, mop(ped) / mope(d)
mobul, mobile
mobulization, mobile(lization)
mobulize, mobile(lize)
moc, mach / make / mock
moca, mocha
mocasin, moccasin
moccasin,*, SOFT LEATHER SHOE/BOOT
mocha, COLOR, TYPE OF COFFEE
mochen, motion
mochenist, machine(nist)
mochure, mature
mock,*,ked,king,kery,keries,kingly,ker, DISRESPECTFULLY MIMIC/IMITATE SOMEONE (or see mach)
mocksy, moxie
mocusen, moccasin
mod, mode / mud / mood
modafekashen, modify(fication)
modafy, modify

modal,*,lly,lity,lities, OF MODE/ MANNER/FORM "prefixes: bi/inter"
modavashen, motive(vation)
modavate, motive(vate)
mode,*, POSITION/TYPE/USAGE/WAY/ FORM
modeef, motif
modef, motive
modefekashen, modify(fication)
modefy, modify
model,*,led,ling,ler, ABOUT SHAPE/ STYLE/FORM (or see modal/mottle/ motel/muddle)
moder, motor / mutter
moderate,*,ed,ting,tion,tor, BETWEEN EXTREMES OF HIGH/LOW, IN BETWEEN "prefixes: im"
moderet, moderate
modern,nism,nist,nistic,nize,nizes,nized, nizing,nizer,nization, CURRENT IN STYLE/FASHION, TRENDY
modest,tly,ty,ties, MODERATE IN DEMEANOR, NOT EXTREME "prefixes: im"
modevashen, motive(vation)
modevate, motive(vate)
modeve, motive
modewlashen, modulate(tion)
modgual, module
modgul, module
modi, mood(y) / muddy
modify,fies,fied,fying,fication,ficative, ficatory,fiable,fier, CHANGE/ALTER THE MODE/CONFIGURATION OR OPERATION OF
modil, modal / model / mottle
modir, motor
modirn, modern
modisly, modest(ly)
modist, modest
modisty, modest(y)
modivashen, motive(vation)
modivate, motive(vate)
modive, motive
modjual, module
modjulashen, modulate(tion)
modjule, module
modle, modal / model / mottle
modo, motto
moduf, motive
moduficashen, modify(fication)
modul, modal / model / module / mottle

modulate,*,ed,ting,tion,tor,tory, ABILITY TO ADJUST TO ACCEPTABLE FREQUENCY "prefixes: inter"
module,*,lar,larity,lus,li, A STANDARDIZED SIZE/SHAPE/ DIMENSION, PRE-MADE
modur, motor
modurashen, moderate(tion)
moduret, moderate
modurise, motor(ize)
modurn, modern
modurnasation, modern(ization)
moduvashen, motive(vation)
moduvate, motive(vate)
mody, mood(y)
moer, mow(er)
moest, moist
mof, mauve / move
mofment, move(ment)
mogma, magma
mogulate, modulate
mogule, module
moguler, module(lar)
mohair,*, HAIR OF ANGORA GOAT
mohare, mohair
moir, mow(er)
moist,ten,tens,tened,tening,ture,turize, turizes,turized,turizing, turizer,tness, BETWEEN DRY/ WET, MORE THAN DAMP
mojul, module
mojulate, modulate
mojulir, module(lar)
mok, mach / make / mock
moka, mocha
mokasen, moccasin
mokery, mock(ery)
mokesin, moccasin
moksy, moxie
moku, mocha
mol, mall / maul / mole
molakul, molecule
molakuler, molecule(lar)
molar,*,rity, A TOOTH, CHEMISTRY AMOUNT "prefixes: pre"
molarky, malarkey
molasis, molasses
molasses, RICH/DARK SYRUP
mold,*,ded,ding,dy,diness,dable, FUNGI, CONTAINER USED TO MAKE A FORM, USED FOR FRAMING/ FINISHING WORK (or see molt/ maul(ed)) "prefixes: un"
moldibul, mold(able)

molduble, mold(able)
mole,*, A CHEMISTRY MEASUREMENT OF WEIGHT, A RODENT, A BEAUTY MARK, GROWTH ON SKIN
molecule,*,lar,larly,larity, TINY PARTICLES SUSPECTED TO EXIST BUT CANNOT BE SEEN "prefixes: bi/bio/inter/intra"
molekuler, molecule(lar)
moler, molar
moleshes, malicious
molest,*,ted,ting,ter,tation, TO PHYSICALLY FORCE SOMEONE INTO AN UNACCEPTABLE SITUATION
molicious, malicious
molikule, molecule
moll, mall / maul / mole
mollusk,*, INVERTEBRAE GENERALLY WITH SHELLS AND NO SEGMENTS
molt,*,ted,ting,ter, TO SHED OUTER LAYER SUCH AS SKIN (or see mold/malt/maul(ed))
molur, molar
molusk, mollusk
mom,*,mma,mmy, PARENT WHO PERFORMED THE BIRTHING
moma, mamma
momendus, moment(ous)
moment,*,tary,tarily,tariness,tly,tous, tously,tousness,tum, VERY BRIEF MEASURE/AMOUNT OF TIME
momento, memento
momentus, moment(ous)
mominshus, moment(ious)
momint, moment
mominterily, moment(arily)
mominto, memento
momintum, moment(um)
momintus, moment(ous)
mon, PREFIX INDICATING "ALONG/ONLY/SINGLE" MOST OFTEN MODIFIES THE WORD (or see moan/moon)
monafilament, monofilament
monagram, monogram
monalith, monolith
monalithic, monolith(ic)
monalogue, monologue
monanukleosis, mononucleosis
monarale, monorail
monarch,*,hal,hial,hally,hical,hically, hism,hist,histic,hy,hies, LARGE BUTTERFLY, POWERFUL POSITION, SOLE RULER

monark, monarch
monarkial, monarch(ial)
monastery,ries,rial,tic,tical,ticism, PLACE OF ISOLATION
monater, monitor
monatone, monotone
mondane, mundane
monday,*, A DAY OF THE WEEK (ENGLISH)
mone, moan / money
monee, money
monegram, monogram
monelogue, monologue
monenukleosis, mononucleosis
monerale, monorail
monestasism, monastery(tacism)
monestery, monastery
monetary,rily,tize,tization,rist, OF MONEY
monetone, monotone
monetor, monitor
monewment, monument
money,nies, MINTED COIN AND PAPER USED FOR EXCHANGE OF ITEMS OR SERVICES
mongrel,*,ly,lism,lize,lizes,lized,lizing, lization, MIXED BREED OF DOG
mongril, mongrel
mongrul, mongrel
monie, money
monigram, monogram
monilogue, monologue
moninukleosis, mononucleosis
monirale, monorail
monistery, monastery
monitary, monetary
monitone, monotone
monitor,*,red,ring,ry,rship, ENFORCER OF RULES, A MACHINE THAT READS VITAL LIFE SIGNS "prefixes: bio"
monk,*,khood,kish,kishly,kishness,kery, keries, ONE WHO PRACTICES TO OVERCOME EGO
monkey,kies,ying, ANIMAL, MAMMAL, TO ACT LIKE A MONKEY
mono, SHORT FOR MONONUCLEOSIS, PREFIX INDICATING "ALONG/ONLY/SINGLE" MOST OFTEN MODIFIES THE WORD
monocular,*, ITEM WHERE ONE EYE CAN SEE MAGNIFICATION
monofilament,*, ONE FILAMENT IN A BULB

monogamy,mous,mic,mist,mistic, mously,mousness, ADULT WHO ACCEPTS ONLY ONE PARTNER
monogram,*,med,ming,matic, LETTER/CHARACTER REPRESENTING A NAME
monolith,hic,hically, SINGLE SKIN, STONE
monologue,*,gic,gist,gize, ONE PERSON WHO SPEAKS
mononucleosis, ONE-NUCLEUS BLOOD CELLS RESULTANT FROM A VIRUS
monopoly,lies, ONE COMPANY DOMINATES LEAVING NO CHOICE
monorail,*, A SINGLE RAIL FOR TRAVEL
monotary, monetary
monotone,*,nosity, ONE TONE
monotony,nous,nously,nousness, REPETITION, SAME THING OVER AND OVER AGAIN
monoxide, ONE OXYGEN ATOM IN A MOLECULE
monsoon,*, GREAT RUSH OF RAIN IN A CERTAIN SEASON WHICH LASTS FOR MONTHS
monster,*,red,ring,trance,trous,trosity, USED TO DESCRIBE SOMETHING UNUSUAL/FRIGHTENING, RELIGIOUS VESSEL, DRUNK
monstrasute, monstrosity
monstrausete, monstrosity
monstres, monstrous
monstrocity, monstrosity
monstrosete, monstrosity
monstrosity,sities,ous, USED TO DESCRIBE SOMETHING UNUSUAL/FRIGHTENING/ABNORMAL
monstrous,sly,sness,osity, USED TO DESCRIBE SOMETHING UNUSUAL/FRIGHTENING
monstrus, monstrous
monstur, monster
monsune, monsoon
monten, mountain
month,*,hly,hlies, A MEASURE OF TIME WHICH DIVIDES DAYS OF THE YEAR INTO SECTIONS "prefixes: bi/semi"
montin, mountain
monuer, manure
monugram, monogram
monulithic, monolith(ic)
monulogue, monologue

monument,*,tal,tally,talize, A MARKER/ STONE/ARTICLE/STRUCTURE IN HONOR OF SOMEONE/SOMETHING
monumint, monument
monurale, monorail
monure, manure
monustery, monastery
monutary, monetary
monutone, monotone
mony, money
monyument, monument
monzoon, monsoon
monzter, monster
mood,*,dy,dier,diest,dily,diness, AN EMOTIONAL STATE OF MIND (or see moot/mute)
moodyness, mood(iness)
moof, move
moofuble, move(vable)
moon,*,ned,ning,nish,nishly,ny, LARGEST PLANET SEEN AT NIGHT, A PRANK
moor,*,red,ring,rage, A BOG, A PLACE TO DOCK A BOAT, ACT OF DOCKING A SHIP (or see more) "prefixes: un"
moose, A LARGE MEMBER OF THE DEER FAMILY (or see mouse/mousse)
moot,tness, UP FOR DISCUSSION WITHOUT DECISION, ARGUABLE, DEBATABLE (or see mute/mood)
mootiness, mood(iness)
mooty, mood(y)
moove, move
mop,*,pped,pping, AN ITEM USED WET TO CLEAN FLOORS (or see mob/map)
mope,*,ed,ping,per,pey, TO BE DISINTERESTED DUE TO SADNESS/ BEING BORED, TO HAVE LOW SPIRITS (or see mop)
moped, mop(ped) / mope(d)
mopt, mop(ped) / mope(d)
mor, mar / more / moor / mow(er)
moral,*,lly,lism,list,listic,lize,lizes,lized, lizing,lization,lizer, ABILITY TO JUDGE/ BEHAVE RIGHT FROM WRONG (or see morale/morel) "prefixes: im/un"
morale,*,lity,lities, CONDITION/STATE OF ONE'S ABILITY TO JUDGE/ACT ON THOSE JUDGEMENTS (or see mural/moral/morel)
moralestic, moral(istic)
moraly, moral(ly)

moratorium,*,ry, A PURPOSELY IMPOSED DELAY FOR AN UNDETERMINED AMOUNT OF TIME
morbed, morbid
morbedly, morbid(ly)
morbel, marble
morbet, morbid
morbid,dly,dness,dity, AKIN TO DEATH/ DARKNESS
morbidety, morbid(ity)
morbil, marble
morbit, morbid
morbul, marble
morch, march
morchoery, mortuary
morchuery, mortuary
mordar, mortar
mordel, mortal
mordir, mortar
mordul, mortal
morduly, mortal(ly)
mordur, mortar
more, OF A GREATER NUMBER WHEN COMPARING, GREATER (or see moor/mow(er))
morege, moor(age)
morel,*, EDIBLE MUSHROOM (or see moral/morale)
morelise, moral(ize)
morelistic, moral(istic)
mores, SOCIAL ACCEPTANCE
moretoreum, moratorium
morgage, mortgage
morge, morgue
morgedge, mortgage
morgeje, mortgage
morgen, margin
morgenulize, marginalize
morgerin, margarine
morgije, mortgage
morgue,*, PLACE WHERE BODIES WITHOUT SPIRITS ARE TEMPORARILY HELD
morige, moor(age)
moril, moral / morel
morily, moral(ly)
moritoreum, moratorium
morjaren, margarine
morjenulize, marginalize
mork, morgue
morn, mourn / morning
mornen, morning / mourn(ing)
morneng, mourn(ing) / morning
mornful, mourn(ful)

mornin, morning / mourn(ing)
morning,*, MORN, FIRST PART OF THE DAY BEFORE 12 NOON (or see mourn(ing))
moroon, maroon
morose,ely,eness,sity, GLOOMY OR DARK THOUGHTS, IDEAS, BEHAVIOR
morotoreum, moratorium
morph, PREFIX INDICATING "SHAPE/ FORM/STRUCTURE" MOST OFTEN MODIFIES THE WORD
mors, mores
morshuery, mortuary
mortal,*,lly,lity,lities, RELATED TO DEATH/KILLING/DYING "prefixes: im"
mortaledy, mortal(ity)
mortalidy, mortal(ity)
mortar,*, MIXTURE USED FOR JOINTS TO HOLD BRICK, VESSEL SHAPE WITH A PESTLE
mortel, mortal
morter, mortar
mortgage,*,ed,ging,ger,gor, TITLE/ DEED OF PROPERTY HELD BY SOMEONE WHICH REQUIRES MONEY TO OWN/HAVE
mortil, mortal
mortir, mortar
mortuary,ries, A FUNERAL HOME
mortul, mortal
mortur, mortar
morul, moral
morulesm, moral(ism)
morulestic, moral(istic)
morulise, moral(ize)
moruly, moral(ly)
mos, moss / most
mosaic,*,cally,cist, MANY PIECES PLACED TOGETHER TO FORM A PICTURE
mosayic, mosaic
mosdereus, mysterious
mosdly, most(ly)
mose, moose / mousse
moseik, mosaic
mosektimy, mastectomy
moshen, motion
moshenist, machine(nist)
moshun, motion
mosk, mosque
moskeet, mesquite
mosketo, mosquito

moskewlur, muscle(cular)
mosly, most(ly)
mosoleum, mausoleum
mosoose, masseuse
mosque,*, A BUILDING WHERE MUSLIMS PRAY
mosquito,oes,oey, AN INSECT WHO SEEKS BLOOD
mosquler, muscle(cular)
moss,sses,ssy,ssier,ssiest,ssiness, A PLANT GROWTH
most,tly, PAST TENSE FOR THE WORD MORE, THE GREATEST AMOUNT IN COMPARISON TO ANOTHER AMOUNT (or see must) "prefixes: under/up/upper"
mostache, mustache / moustache
mostash, mustache / moustache
mostectemy, mastectomy
moster, monster / muster
mostereus, mysterious
mostique, mystique
mosuleum, mausoleum
mosuse, masseuse
mot, moat / mutt / mode / mote
motabolize, metabolize
motafikashen, modify(fication)
motapolize, metabolize
motavashen, motive(vation)
motchewlate, modulate
motchulashen, modulate(tion)
motchulate, modulate
mote, SPECK, PARTICLE (or see moat/ mode)
moteef, motif
motef, motif / motive
motel,*, LODGING WHERE YOU CAN PARK YOUR VEHICLE NEAR THE DOOR (or see mottle)
moter, motor / mutter
moterashen, moderate(tion)
moteret, moderate
motereul, material
moterise, motor(ize)
motern, modern
moternul, maternal
motevashen, motive(vation)
moth,*, A NOCTURNAL INSECT
mother,*,red,ring,rly,rless,rlessness, ONE WHO HAS GIVEN BIRTH, BACTERIAL COATING ON FERMENTING LIQUIDS, ORGINATOR OF LIFE

motif, RECURRING THEME IN VISUAL PRESENTATION (or see motive)
motil, modal / model / mottle
motion,*,nal,ned,ning,nless,nlessness, ACTIVITY, MOVEMENT
motir, motor
motirn, modern
motivashen, motive(vation)
motive,*,vate,vates,vated,vating,vation, vational,vative,vity, ENCOURAGE TO PERFORM ALONG IN A PLANNED DIRECTION (or see motif)
motle, mottle / modal / model
motled, mottle(d) / model(ed)
moto, motto
motor,*,red,ring,rist,rize,rized,rizing, rization, AN ENGINE/DEVICE USED TO CREATE MOTION
mottle,ed,er,ling, SPLOTCHY IN COLOR, PATCHES OF IRREGULAR SHAPES
motto,*, A CONCISE DESCRIPTION OF PRINCIPLE OR PURPOSE
motul, modal / model / mottle
motur, motor
moturashen, moderate(tion)
moturet, moderate
moturise, motor(ize)
moturn, modern
moturnize, modern(ize)
motuv, motive
motuvashen, motive(vation)
motuvate, motive(vate)
moucus, mucus
moud, mood / mode
mound,*,ded,ding, A SMALL HILL/PILE/ HEAP (or see mount)
mount,*,ted,ting, TO SIT ATOP OF, SHORT FOR MOUNTAIN, AFFIX SOMETHING, GET ON TOP OF "prefixes: dis/re/sur"
mountain,*,neer,nous,nously,nousness, GREAT HILLS OF ORGANIC MATTER, LARGE JUTTING EXTRUSIONS OF EARTH "prefixes: inter"
mounteneer, mountain(eer)
mountenus, mountain(ous)
mountin, mountain
mour, mow(er)
mourn,*,ned,ning,ningly,nful,nfully, nfulness,ner, EMOTIONALLY EXPERIENCE LOSS OF SOMETHING (or see morning)
mouse,er,sing,ey,mice, SMALL RODENT (or see moose/mousse)

mousse, DESSERT (or see mouse/ moose)
moustache, FACIAL HAIR GROWING ABOVE THE LIP (also spelled mustache)
moutenus, mountain(ous)
mouth,*,hed,hing,her,hful,hfuls,hy, ORIFICE ON THE FACE WHICH MAKES SOUNDS/INGESTS
mov, mauve / move
movd, move(d)
move,*,ed,ving,vingly,er,vable, vableness,vably,vability,eless, elessly,elessness,ement, CHANGE/ RELOCATE FROM ONE PLACE/ LOCATION TO ANOTHER, BE IN MOTION "prefixes: im/non/re/un"
movie,*, PICTURES IN MOTION
movment, move(ment)
mow,*,wed,wing,wer, CUT GRASS/ BRUSH WITH A TOOL/MACHINE, REMOVE/LOWER IN WIDE SWATHES
mowder, motor
mowenus, mountain(ous)
mownd, mound
mownden, mountain
mownt, mound / mount
mownten, mountain
mowse, mouse
mowten, mountain
mowteneer, mountain(eer)
mowtenus, mountain(ous)
mowth, mouth
mowtin, mountain
mowtinus, mountain(ous)
moxie, COURAGE, ASSERTIVE
moxy, moxie
moyeast, moist
moyster, moist(ure)
moysturize, moist(urize)
mozaek, mosaic
mozayic, mosaic
mozed, most
mozly, most(ly)
mozoleum, mausoleum
mozt, most
mozuleim, mausoleum
mperical, empirical
mpethy, empathy
mpithy, empathy
mportant, important
mportens, important(nce)
mportent, important

mpress, impress
mpurfikt, imperfect
mputhy, empathy
mr, mister
mrk, mark
mt, empty
mubiledy, mobile(lity)
mubility, mobile(lity)
mucaw, macaw
much, AMOUNT OF SOMETHING, SIZEABLE QUANTITY
muchanek, mechanic
muchanekul, mechanic(al))
muchene, machine
muchenist, machine(nist)
muchety, machete
muchual, mutual
muchure, mature
muchuredy, mature(rity)
muchurle, mature(ly)
muchyual, mutual
mucus,coid,citis,sity,cous, SLIPPERY SECRETED SUBSTANCE FOR PROTECTION OF SKIN
mud,*,dded,dding,ddy, DIRT MIXED WITH WATER (or see mood/mutt)
mudalate, mutilate
muddle,*,ed,ling, TO CONFUSE, MAKE UNCLEAR, MAKE A MESS, CREATE DISORDER
muddy,ddies,ddier,ddiest,ddying,ddily, ddiness, WATER MIXED WITH DIRT
mude, mood / mute / muddy
mudel, muddle
mudelate, mutilate
muden, mutton
mudeness, mood(iness)
muder, mutter
mudereul, material
mudereulise, materialize
mudernol, maternal
mudiest, muddy(diest)
mudil, muddle
mudilate, mutilate
mudir, mutter
mudle, muddle
mudon, mutton
mudul, muddle
mudur, mutter
mudy, muddy / mood(y)
mudyest, muddy(diest)
muer, moor
muerege, moor(age)
muf, move / muff

mufan, muffin / move(ving)
mufd, move(d) / muff(ed)
mufee, movie
mufen, muffin / move(ving)
muff,*,ffed,ffing, BE CLUMSY, BUNGLE SOMETHING, HAND WARMER, TUFT ON BIRDS /FOWL
muffen, muffin
muffin,*, BAKED DESSERT
muffler,*, KEEPS LOUD NOISES QUIET
mufin, muffin
mufler, muffler
mufment, move(ment)
muft, move(d)
mufuble, move(vable)
mug,*,gged,gging,gger,ggy, DRINKING VESSEL, SOMEONE WHO ASSAULTS WITH INTENT TO ROB, A FACE, WARM/DAMP/STILL AIR
mugd, mug(gged)
muge, muggy
mugeness, muggy(giness)
mugestekal, majesty(tical)
mugestik, majesty(tic)
muggie, muggy
muggy,ggily,gginess, WARM AND HUMID
mugi, muggy
mugishen, magic(ian)
mugority, major(ity)
mugy, muggy
mugynes, muggy(giness)
muir, moor
muj, much
mujestical, majesty(tical)
mujishen, magic(ian)
mukanek, mechanic
mukanekul, mechanic(al)
mukaw, macaw
mukus, mucus
mul, mull / mule / mole / mall
mulado, mulato
mularea, malaria
mularky, malarkey
mulasis, molasses
mulato,oes, MIXTURE OF RACES OR BREEDS
mulch,hes,hed,hing, TO TILL UP GROUND, ADD ORGANIC MATERIAL TO SOIL
muldaplekashen, multiplication
muldaplikation, multiplication
muldiply, multiply

mule,*,lish, HYBRID MAMMAL/PLANT, STUBBORN PERSON, SHOE WITHOUT A BACK (or see mull)
mulecious, malicious
mulekuler, molecule(lar)
muleneum, millennium
muleshes, malicious
mulest, molest
mulevolens, malevolent(nce)
mulevolent, malevolent
mulicious, malicious
mulignant, malignant
mulinium, millennium
mulk, milk
mull,*, A FABRIC, TO STUDY/THINK ABOUT, MUSLIN, HUMUS (or see mule)
mullenium, millennium
multaplekashen, multiplication
multaply, multiply
multch, mulch
multeply, multiply
multi, PREFIX INDICATING "MUCH/ MANY" MOST OFTEN MODIFIES THE WORD
multiple,*,ly,lies,lied,lying,lier,licity, lication, DUPLICATES, A NUMBER THAT CAN BE DIVIDED WITH NO REMAINDERS "prefixes: sub"
multiplekashen, multiplication
multiplication,tive,tively, THE ACT OF WORKING NUMBERS TIMES NUMBERS
multiply,lies,lied,lying,lier,licity, TO INCREASE NUMBERS BY REPRODUCTION, ADDING NUMBERS TIMES NUMBERS, MATH
mumble,*,ed,ling,er,lingly, TO SPEAK WITHOUT ANNUNCIATING OR BE UNINTELLIGIBLE,SPOKEN WORDS NOT UNDERSTANDABLE
mumbul, mumble
mume, mummy
mummy,mmies,mmify,mmification, A DRIED UP CORPSE, WORD FOR MOM IN ENGLAND
mumps, A VIRUS WHICH ATTACTS THE THROAT
mumy, mummy
mun, moon
munarkikul, monarch(ical)
munarky, monarch(y)
munda, monday
mundane,ely,eness, DULL ROUTINE

munday, monday
mune, moon / money
munepulate, manipulate
munesipality, municipal(ity)
munesipul, municipal
municipal,*,lity,lities,lly,lize,lization, TOWN/CITY GOVERNED BY/WITH ITS OWN LAWS
munie, money
munila, manila
munipulate, manipulate
munisepal, municipal
munisepality, municipal(ity)
munisipal, municipal
munk, monk
munkee, monkey
munky, monkey
munodnes, monotony(nous)
munogemy, monogamy
munogimy, monogamy
munokside, monoxide
munokuler, monocular
munopuly, monopoly
munorkeul, monarch(ial)
munotny, monotony
munotunus, monotony(nous)
munoxide, monoxide
munsoon, monsoon
munstrocity, monstrocity
munstrosedy, monstrocity
munsune, monsoon
munth, month
munthly, month(ly)
munure, manure
munuver, maneuver
muny, money
muraculus, miracle(culous)
muraje, mirage
murakulus, miracle(culous)
mural,*, LARGE PAINTING APPLIED ONTO A WALL
muraledy, morale(lity)
murality, morale(lity)
murange, meringue
murchandise, merchandise
murchant, merchant
murder,*,red,ring,rer,rous,rousness, KILL SOMEONE UNLAWFULLY
murdir, murder
murdur, murder
murege, moor(age)
murel, mural
murena, marina
murene, marine

murge, merge
murgur, merge(r)
muridean, meridian
muril, mural
murina, marina
murine, marine
murje, merge
murk, murky
murkanteel, mercantile
murkery, mercury
murky,kily,kiness, DARK, SILTY OR THICK LIQUID/AIR, GLOOMY
murlin, merlin
murmade, mermaid
murmer, murmur
murmir, murmur
murmur,*,rer,ring,ringly,rous,rously, A LOW STEADY STREAM OF SOUND, MUFFLED SOUND
muroge, mirage
muroje, mirage
murose, morose
mursenary, mercenary
mursinary, mercenary
mursy, mercy
mursyful, mercy(ciful)
murul, mural
murun, maroon
mus, mouse / mousse / moose
musal, mussel / muscle / muzzle
muscle,*,ed,ling,cular,cularity,cularly, THICK TISSUE WHICH MOVES BONES (or see mussel/muzzle) "prefixes: intra/non"
musdach, moustache
musdake, mistake
musdakin, mistake(n)
musderd, mustard
musdurd, mustard
muse,*,ed,sing,singly,er, WHAT INSPIRES AN ARTIST, A DEEP THINK/ CONTEMPLATION (or see moose/ mouse/mousse)
musec, music
musecal, music(al)
musecian, musician
musecul, music(al)
musek, music
musektome, mastectomy
musekul, music(al)
musel, mussel / muscle / muzzle
museshen, musician
museum,*, A STRUCTURE FOR EXHIBITS OF INTERESTING ITEMS

mushedy, machete
mushene, machine
mushenest, machine(nist)
mushete, machete
mushinary, machine(ry)
mushroom,*,med,ming, FUNGI WITH BELL SHAPED HEAD ON A STEM
mushrum, mushroom
mushual, mutual
music,cal,cally,cality,calness,cian, TONES, SOUNDS PLAYED IN HARMONY ON INSTRUMENTS, PLEASING SOUND TO EARS "prefixes: un"
musician,*,nly,nship, PROFESSIONALLY INVOLVED IN CREATING MUSIC
musik, music
musil, mussel / muscle / muzzle
musishen, musician
muskedo, mosquito
muskeet, mesquite
muskera, mascara
musketo, mosquito
muskuler, muscle(cular)
musle, mussel / muscle / muzzle
muslen, muslin
muslin,*, MEDIUM WEIGHT COTTON CLOTH
musoge, massage
musoje, massage
musol, muscle / mussel / muzzle
musoose, masseuse
musquedo, mosquito
musquler, muscle(cular)
mussel,*, EDIBLE MARINE MOLLUSK WITH SHELL (or see muscle/muzzle)
mussle, mussel / muscle / muzzle
must, HAS TO BE, IMPERATIVE
mustache,*, HAIR ON TOP OF THE UPPER LIP ON ADULT MALES (also spelled moustache)
mustake, mistake
mustakin, mistake(n)
mustang,*, WILD HORSES
mustard, AN HERB USED AS A CONDIMENT
muster,*,red,ring, TO GATHER/ COLLECT/ASSEMBLE
musterd, mustard
mustereus, mysterious
mustir, muster
mustird, mustard
mustireus, mysterious
musturd, mustard

musuese, masseuse
musul, muscle / mussel / muzzle
mususe, masseuse
mut, mutt / mute / mud / moot
mutabolize, metabolize
mutalate, mutilate
mutapolize, metabolize
mutashen, mutate(tion)
mutate,*,ed,ting,tive,tion,ant, ENDURED CHROMOSOME ALTERATION
mutch, much
mutchuel, mutual
mute,*,ed,ting,ely,eness,tism, NO SPEECH, UNABLE TO SPEAK (or see mutt/moot)
mutelate, mutilate
muten, mutton / mutate(ant)
mutent, mutate(ant)
muteny, mutiny
muter, mutter
mutereolise, materialize
mutereul, material
muternedy, maternity
muternol, maternal
muternulistek, maternal(istic)
muther, mother
muthor, mother
mutil, muddle
mutilashen, mutilate(tation)
mutilate,*,ed,ting,tion,tor, TO SHRED, RIP, TEAR BEYOND RECOGNITION
mutin, mutton
mutint, mutate(ant)
mutiny,nous, RESISTANCE TO AUTHORITY BY MORE THAN ONE ENTITY
mutir, mutter
mutireul, material
mutirnil, maternal
mutle, muddle
muton, mutton
mutony, mutiny
mutt,*, MIXED BREED (or see mute)
mutter,*,red,ring,ringly, TO MURMUR, SPEAK LOW AND UNINTELLIGIBLY, UNDECIPHERABLE SPEECH
mutton,*, SHEEP MEAT
mutual,*,lly,lism,list,listic,lity,lize, lization, CONSENT TO SHARE/ AGREE
mutul, muddle
mutulashen, mutilate(tation)
mutune, mutiny

mutur, mature / mutter
muty, muddy / mood(y)
muvd, move(d)
muve, move / movie
muvee, movie
muvi, movie
muvuble, move(vable)
muzdake, mistake
muzeim, museum
muzektame, mastectomy
muzekul, music(al)
muzel, muzzle
muzeshen, musician
muzeum, museum
muzik, music
muzikul, music(al)
muzishen, musician
muzlen, muslin
muzlin, muslin
muzt, must
muztake, mistake
muzter, muster
muztereus, mysterious
muzul, muzzle
muzzle,*,ed,ling,er, DEVICE TO RESTRAIN ANIMALS FROM BITING (or see muscle) "prefixes: un"
my, MYSELF, DENOTES OWNERSHIP, PREFIX INDICATING "MUSCLE" MOST OFTEN MODIFIES THE WORD
myc, PREFIX INDICATING "FUNGUS" MOST OFTEN MODIFIES THE WORD
mycrascope, microscope
mycrobeul, microbe(bial)
mycron, micron
mycrophone, microphone
myder, miter
mydokondrea, mitochondria
mydukondrea, mitochondria
mygrane, migraine
mygrashen, migrate(tion)
mygrate, migrate
mygratory, migrate(tory)
mykrafone, microphone
mykraskope, microscope
mykro, micro
mykrobe, microbe
mykrofone, microphone
mykrometer, micrometer
mykron, micron
mykrowave, microwave
myld, mild
myluge, mile(age)
myme, mime

myn, mine
mynd, mind / mend
myne, mine
myreod, myriad
myriad, MANY, MORE THAN TEN THOUSAND
mysdacism, mystic(icism)
mystecal, mystic(cal)
mysteek, mystique
mystek, mystique / mystic
mystereus, mysterious
mysterious,sly,sness, OF THE UNKNOWN, NOT ENOUGH FACTS TO UNDERSTAND
mystery,ries,rious, NOT ENOUGH FACTS TO UNDERSTAND, THE UNKNOWN
mystic,*,cal,cally,calness,cism,ify, A MYSTERY, THE UNSEEN/ UNEXPLAINED (or see mystique)
mystify,fies,fied,fying,fyingly,fication, PURPOSELY MISLEAD/BE VAGUE
mystique, BELIEF/AURA OF MYSTERIOUS POWER (or see mystic)
mystirious, mysterious
mystukul, mystic(cal)
mystury, mystery
mysulf, my(self)
myt, mitt / mite / might
myter, miter
myth,*,hic,hical,hically,hicize,hicizes, hicized,hicizing,hicization,hicizer, hography,hology, A STORY SURVIVING HISTORY THAT ISN'T SUPPORTED BY FACT
mythologic,cal,cally, OF MYTHS, LEGENDS, FOLKLORE
mythology,gies,gize,gizes,gized,gizing, gization,gize,gic, OF THE UNKNOWN, ATTEMPT TO EXPLAIN THE UNKNOWN
mytochondrea, mitochondria
mytokondrea, mitochondria
mytosis, mitosis
n, in / inn
nab,*,bbed,bbing,bber, TO GRAB/SEIZE/ CATCH UNEXPECTEDLY
naber, neighbor
naberhood, neighbor(hood)
nabir, neighbor
nabken, napkin
nabkin, napkin
nabor, neighbor
naborhud, neighbor(hood)

nabt, nab(bed) / nap(ped)
nabur, neighbor
naburhood, neighbor(hood)
nacessity, necessity
nach, notch
nacheirpath, naturopath
nachen, nation
nachenaluty, nation(ality)
nachenul, nation(al)
nacher, nature
nacheralist, natural(ist)
nacheropethy, naturopath(y)
nacherul, natural
nacheruly, natural(ly)
naches, nauseous
nachinal, nation(al)
nachir, nature
nachon, nation
nachral, natural
nachrul, natural
nachur, nature
nachuril, natural
nachurily, natural(ly)
nachuropath, naturopath
nachuropathy, naturopath(y)
nachus, nauseous
nadal, natal
nadef, native
nadefly, native(ly)
nadical, nautical
nadilus, nautilus
nadive, native
nadle, natal
nadol, natal
naduf, native
nady, naughty / knot(ty)
naefe, naive
naem, name
naevet, naive(te)
naevly, naive(ly)
nafee, navy
nafegashen, navigate(tion)
nafegubul, navigable
nafel, naval/ navel/ novel
nafigate, navigate
nafigubul, navigable
nafil, naval / navel / novel
nafol, naval / navel / novel
nafugate, navigate
nafuguble, navigable
naful, naval / navel / novel
nafulty, novelty
nafy, navy

nag,*,gged,gging,ggingly, AN ACT PERFORMED REPEATEDLY, IRRITATED BY REPETITION, YOUNG/ OLD HORSE
naglekt, neglect
nagosheate, negotiate
nagoshubul, negotiable
nagotiate, negotiate
nagutev, negative
naif, naive / knife
naighbor, neighbor
nail,*,led,ling,ler, SLENDER STEEL WITH POINT/HEAD FOR HAMMERING, PROTECTIVE GROWTH ON FINGERS/ TOES
naim, name
nait, night / knight
naive,ely,eness,ete,ety, LACKS INFORMATION, CLUELESS
nak, knack
naked,dly,dness, WITHOUT CLOTHES OR COVERING
nakit, naked
nale, nail
nalege, knowledge
namadik, pneumatic / nomad(ic)
name,*,ed,ming,ely,eless,elessly, elessness, LEGAL/PROPER TITLE, WHAT TO CALL SOMETHING/ SOMEONE "prefixes: mis/sur/un"
namles, name(less)
namly, name(ly)
nane, nanny
nanny,nies, SOMEONE WHO IS HIRED BY A FAMILY TO TAKE CARE OF THE CHILDREN, A FEMALE GOAT
nano, PREFIX INDICATING "ONE BILLIONTH/EXTREMELY SMALL" MOST OFTEN MODIFIES THE WORD
nany, nanny
nap,*,pped,pping,pper, SLEEP BRIEFLY, PILE/CLOTH/ SUBSTANCE/FUZZ (or see knap/nape)
nape, BACK OF NECK (or see nap/knap/ knap(ppy))
naped, nab(bed) / nap(pped)
napken, napkin
napkin,*, CLOTH/PAPER USED AT MEALTIME FOR FACE/HANDS
nappy, knap(ppy)
napt, nab(bed) / nap(ped)
narashen, narrate(tion)
narate, narrate
narative, narrate(tive)

narator, narrate(tor)
narcisim, narcissism
narcism, narcissism
narcissi,ssus,ssuses,ist,istic,istically,ism, EXCESSIVE SELF-LOVE
narcissism,st,stic,stically, EXCESSIVE SELF-LOVE
narcistic, narcissi(tic)
narcistik, narcissi(tic)
narco, PREFIX INDICATING "NARCOTIC/ STUPOR/SLEEP" MOST OFTEN MODIFIES THE WORD
narcotic,*,cally,ize,izes,ized,izing,ization, CHEMICAL WHICH ALTERS BODY METABOLISM
nare, nary
narely, narrow(ly)
nari, nary
narkotek, narcotic
naro, narrow
naroly, narrow(ly)
narou, narrow
narowd, narrow(ed)
narrate,*,ed,ting,tion,tional,tive,tively, tor, TO RECOUNT/TELL/RELATE A STORY
narrow,*,wed,wing,wer,west,wly, wness, NOT AS WIDE AS USUAL/ NORMAL, THIN STRIP, MAKE SMALLER
narsesm, narcissism
narsistic, narcissi(tic)
nary, NEVER, NOT
nasal,lity,lism,lly,lize,lization, INVOLVING THE NOSE AND ITS PASSAGEWAYS "prefixes: intra"
nasdeor, nasty(tier)
nasdursheum, nasturtium
nasdy, nasty
nasel, nasal
nasely, nasal(ly)
nasesidy, necessity
nasesitate, necessitate
nashen, nation
nashenaledy, nation(ality)
nashenul, nation(al)
nashinality, nation(ality)
nashonul, nation(al)
nashos, nauseous
nashunaludy, nation(ality)
nashuropathy, naturopath(y)
nasia, nausea
nasius, nauseous
nastee, nasty

nastershem, nasturtium
nastershum, nasturtium
nasti, nasty
nasturtium,*, A FLOWERING PLANT
nasty,tier,tiest,tily,tiness, UNDESIRABLE, OBJECTIONABLE, UNACCEPTABLE, NOT PROPER
nat, not / naught / knot / gnat
natal, OF/RELATING TO BIRTH "prefixes: neo"
natcheroputhy, naturopath(y)
natcherul, natural
natchural, natural
natchurely, natural(ly)
natecal, nautical
natef, native
nateuropath, naturopath
nateve, native
natical, nautical
natif, native
natilus, nautilus
nation,*,nal,nally,nalize,nalization, nhood,nless,nalism,nalist,nality, nalities, nalizer, DEVOTED/LOYAL TO A PEOPLE/COUNTRY "prefixes: bi/inter/intra/multi"
natiunality, nation(ality)
native,*,ely,eness,vism,vist,vistic,vity, vities, BORN/BELONG TO CERTAIN LAND/ AREA, RACE OF PEOPLES, NOT AN IMMIGRANT
natle, natal
natol, natal
natoreus, notorius
natorius, notorious
natsher, nature
natsheropethy, naturopath(y)
natshur, nature
natuf, native
natufly, native(ly)
natul, natal
natural,*,lly,lness,lism,list,listic,listically, lize,lization, NOT REFINED/ MODIFIED/ REARRANGED/ CHANGED/MOLDED OR MANIPULATED "prefixes: un"
naturapathy, naturopath(y)
nature,*,ral, BASIC ESSENCE OF THINGS, CHARACTER, COMBINATION OF QUALITIES
naturel, natural
naturilist, natural(ist)
naturopath,*,hy,hic, TREATS ILLNES/ INJURIES WITH NATURAL REMEDIES

natuv, native
nau, gnaw / know / now
naude, naughty / knot(ty)
naudical, nautical
nauev, naive
naught, NOTHING, NOT, DON'T NEED ANYTHING (or see not/knot)
naughty,tier,tiest,tily,tiness, IMPROPER BEHAVIOR, MISCHIEVOUS (or see knot(ty))
naumenol, nominal
nauminoly, nominal(lly)
naumune, nominee
naun, noun
nausdalgea, nostalgia
nausdalgik, nostalgic
nausdrel, nostril
nausea,ate,ating,atingly, FEELING ILL IN STOMACH
nauseous,sly,sness, STOMACH FEELING ILL
naushus, nauseous
nausious, nauseous
naustalgea, nostalgia
naustalgik, nostalgic
naustrel, nostril
naut, not / naught / knot
nautch, notch
nautical,ally, OCEAN NAVIGATION
nautilus,ses,li, SPIRAL OCEAN SHELL
nauves, novice
nauvulest, novel(ist)
nauvulte, novelty
navagate, navigate
navagation, navigate(tion)
naval, SHIPS, OF A NAVY (or see navel/ novel)
navee, navy
navegable, navigable
navegashen, navigate(tion)
navegate, navigate
navegation, navigate(tion)
navel,*, SPOT ON THE BELLY WHERE THE UMBILICAL CORD WAS SEVERED, MIDDLE/CENTRAL PLACE (or see naval/novel)
navember, november
navigable,bility,eness,ly, ABLE TO MANEUVER/GUIDE
navigate,*,ed,ting,tion,tional,tionally, tor, STEER OR MANEUVER, ONE WHO STEERS/MANEUVERS/GUIDES
navil, naval / navel / novel
navimber, november

navol, naval / navel / novel
navugashen, navigate(tion)
navugate, navigate
navugation, navigate(tion)
navuguble, navigable
navul, naval / navel / novel
navuldy, novelty
navy,vies,val, COLLECTION OF SHIPS BELONGING TO A NATION
naw, gnaw / now
nawleg, knowledge
nawstrel, nostril
nayber, neighbor
nazdeur, nasty(tier)
nazdursheum, nasturtium
nazdy, nasty
nazel, nasal
nazely, nasal(ly)
nazil, nasal
nazily, nasal(ly)
naztersheum, nasturtium
nazty, nasty
ne, knee
near,*,rer,rest,rly,rness, CLOSE TO
neat,ter,test,tly,tness, ORDERLY/ ORGANIZED, APPEALING (or see need/knead/ knee(d))
nebal, nibble
neber, neighbor
nebir, neighbor
neble, nibble
nebor, neighbor
nebul, nibble
nebur, neighbor
nec, niece / neck
necasery, necessary
necatene, nicotine
neccesary, necessary
neccesitate, necessitate
neccesity, necessity
neccessary, necessary
necdur, nectar
nece, niece
necesadi, necessity
necesary, necessary
necesitate, necessitate
necesite, necessity
necessary,rily,riness, MUST BE/HAVE, REQUIRED "prefixes: un"
necessatate, necessitate
necessitate,*,ed,ting,tion,tive, REQUIRED, ESSENTIAL
necessity,ties,tous,tously,tousness, REQUIRED, MUST HAVE

necesudi, necessity
neche, niche
nechel, nickel
necisary, necessary
neck,*,ked,king, PART OF THE BODY BETWEEN HEAD AND SHOULDERS, PART OF THE SPINE
necklace,*, ORNAMENT/ADORNMENT FOR THE NECK
necklajay, negligee
neckleshay, negligee
neclas, necklace
neclasha, negligee
neclos, necklace
neclus, necklace
necotine, nicotine
necramancer, necromancer
necrimancer, necromancer
necromancer,*,cy,ntic, PERSON OR OCCURRENCE WHICH REFLECTS OUR GREATEST FEAR, THE DARK/ UNAPPEALING SIDE OF OUR NATURE
nectar,*, SWEET JUICE OF A FLOWER
nectarine,*, CROSS BETWEEN PEACH/ PLUM
necterene, nectarine
nectir, nectar
nectirene, nectarine
nectur, nectar
necturene, nectarine
ned, need / neat / knead / knee(d)
nede, need(y)
neded, need(ed) / knead(ded)
nedel, needle / nettle
nedil, needle / nettle
nedle, needle / nettle
nedly, neat(ly)
nedul, needle / nettle
nedwurk, network
nedy, need(y)
nee, knee
need,*,ded,ding,diness,dy,dful,dfully, dfulness,dless,dlessly,dlessness, REQUIRED, ESSENTIAL, MANDATORY (or see knead/ knee(d)/neat)
needle,*,ed,ling, SLENDER METAL PIN WITH A SHARP POINT AT ONE END AND HOLE AT THE OTHER END, FOR SEWING (or see nettle)
needly, neat(ly)
neel, kneel
neer, near

neerer, near(er)
neerest, near(est)
neerly, near(ly)
nees, niece / knee(s)
nefew, nephew
nefir, never
nefiu, nephew
nefu, nephew
nefur, never
negative,*,ely,eness,vity,vism,vistic, MINUS, IN THE RED, OPPOSITE OF POSITIVE, FILM UNPROCESSED "prefixes: non"
negetiv, negative
neghbor, neighbor
neghborhood, neighbor(hood)
negitif, negative
negitive, negative
neglagay, negligee
neglagense, negligence
neglagent, negligence(nt)
neglagible, negligence(gible)
neglagint, negligence(nt)
neglaja, negligee
neglect,*,ted,ting,tful,tfully,tfulness,tor, NOT BE RESPONSIBLE/TAKE CARE OF
neglegable, negligence(gible)
neglegense, negligence
negligee,*, WOMEN'S UNDERGARMENTS
negligence,*,nt,ntly,gible,gibly,gibility, gibleness, NOT TAKE CARE OF OR BE RESPONSIBLE FOR
neglijay, negligee
neglijents, negligence
neglisha, negligee
neglugense, negligence
negodev, negative
negosheate, negotiate
negosheuble, negotiable
negoshubul, negotiable
negotef, negative
negotiable,bility, ABLE TO COME TO AGREEMENT
negotiate,*,ed,ting,tion,tor,able, COME TO AGREEMENT BY COMMUNICATING
negudev, negative
negutif, negative
negutive, negative
neibor, neighbor
neice, niece

neighbor,*,rly,rhood, PEOPLE WHO DWELL NEAR YOU, THOSE WHO LIVE CLOSE TO YOU
neither, NOT ONE OR THE OTHER, NOT THIS ONE OR THAT ONE
nek, neck / nick
nekatene, nicotine
nekdur, nectar
nekil, nickel
neklagent, negligence(nt)
neklajense, negligence
neklegent, negligence(nt)
nekles, necklace
neklesha, negligee
neklijent, negligence(nt)
neklis, necklace
neklisha, negligee
neklus, necklace
nekotene, nicotine
nekrumanser, necromancer
nekst, next
nektarine, nectarine
nekter, nectar
nekturene, nectarine
nekul, nickel
nekzd, next
nel, nil / kneel / nail
nemf, nymph
nemfomanea, nymphomania
nemonia, pneumonia
nemph, nymph
nemphomanea, nymphomania
neo, PREFIX INDICATING "NEW" MOST OFTEN MODIFIES THE WORD
neon, A NOBLE/INERT GAS, USED IN LAMPS
nep, nip
nepd, nip(pped)
nepe, nip(ppy)
nephew,*, FAMILY RELATION
nephu, nephew
nepil, nipple
nept, nip(pped)
nepul, nipple
nerador, narrrate(tor)
nerashen, narrate(tion)
nerate, narrate
neratek, neurotic
nerative, narrate(tive)
nerator, narrate(tor)
nercher, nurture
nere, near / nary
neresh, nourish
nereshen, narrate(tion)

nerf, nerve
nerfona, nirvana
nerfus, nervous
neri, nary
nerly, near(ly)
nero, narrow
nerodic, neurotic
neroly, narrow(ly)
neron, neuron
nerosis, neurosis
nerotic, neurotic
nerow, narrow
ners, nurse / near(s)
nerture, nurture
nerv, nerve
nervana, nirvana
nervas, nervous
nerve,*,ed,ving,eless,vous, SOFT TISSUE IN THE BODY WHICH RELATES BODY TO BRAIN BY ELECTRICAL IMPULSES, BODY'S FORM OF COMMUNICATION "prefixes: un"
nervous,sly,sness, UNGROUNDED, WORRIED, STRESSED, UNSURE, DOUBTFUL, FEARFUL
nervus, nervous
nery, nary
nes, knee(s) / niece
nesasary, necessary
nesd, nest
nesdalgik, nostalgic
nese, niece
nesesary, necessary
nesesitate, necessitate
nesesudy, necessity
nesil, nestle
nesisary, necessary
nesol, nestle
nesold, nestle(d)
nest,*,ted,ting,ter, A BIRD'S HOME
nestalgek, nostalgic
nestle,*,ed,ling,ler, COZY/SNUGGLE UP AGAINST
nestursheum, nasturtium
nesul, nestle
net,*,tted,tting,table,tlike, A WEB, WEAVING OF SOMETHING, COLLECTION OF (or see neat/knit) "prefixes: inter/intra"
netal, needle / nettle
nete, neat / need(y)
nethur, neither
netil, needle / nettle
netly, neat(ly)

netol, needle / nettle
netorius, notorius
netpiky, nitpick(y)
netrishu, nutricious
netrishun, nutrition
netsh, niche
nettle,*, AN HERB (or see needle)
netul, needle / nettle
network,*,ked,king,ker, JOIN/CONNECT TOGETHER "prefixes: inter"
netwurk, network
nety, need(y)
neuder, neuter
neur, PREFIX INDICATING "NERVE" MOST OFTEN MODIFIES THE WORD
neural,lly, OF THE NERVOUS SYSTEM
neuresh, nourish
neurish, nourish
neurodic, neurotic
neuron,*,nal,nally,osis,oses, OF THE NERVOUS SYSTEM "prefixes: inter"
neurosis, DISORDER OF NERVES/ EMOTIONS
neurotic,cally,cism,osis, DISORDER AFFECTING EMOTIONS AS IT RELATES TO THE NERVOUS SYSTEM
neuter,*,red,ring, A LIVING THING WITHOUT ABILITY TO REPRODUCE
neutral,lity,lly,lism,list,listic,lize,lizes, lized,lizing,lization,lizer, BETWEEN EXTREMES/OPPOSITES, IN THE MIDDLE
neutreshen, nutrition
neutreshus, nutritious
neutretive, nutritive
neutricious, nutritious
neutrino,*, TINY UNCHARGED PARTICLE
neutron,*,nic, UNCHARGED PARTICLE IN ATOM
nevember, november
never, NOT EVER
nevimber, november
nevor, never
new,*,wer,west,wish,wly,wness, JUST CAME INTO BEING, JUST CREATED (or see knew) "prefixes: re"
newborn,*, JUST BORN
newcleate, nuclear(ate)
newcleur, nuclear
newdul, noodle
newdur, neuter
newkleate, nuclear(ate)
newkleus, nucleus
newlewed, newlywed

newlywed,*, COUPLES IN FIRST YEAR OF MARRIAGE
newmadik, pneumatic / nomad(ic)
newmarible, numerable
newmaril, numeral
newmatek, pneumatic
newmerology, numerology
newmerus, numerous
newmirary, numerary
newmonia, pneumonia
newmresy, numeracy
newmurable, numerable
newmurader, numerate(tor)
newmurary, numerary
newmurecy, numeracy
newmurology, numerology
newmurus, numerous
newron, neuron
newsans, nuisance
newspaper,*, PAPER WITH PRINTED TEXT CIRCULATED AS NEWS
newsuns, nuisance
newter, neuter
newtral, neutral
newtrative, nutritive
newtreant, nutrient
newtreno, neutrino
newtril, neutral
newtrishen, nutrition
newtrishus, nutritious
newtrol, neutral
newtron, neutron
next, FOLLOWS AFTER, COMING UP
nezt, nest
ngoy, enjoy
ni, knee
nibble,*,ed,ling, TINY BITE/MORSEL TO EAT
nibul, nibble
nicatene, nicotine
nice,er,est,ely,ety, KIND, THOUGHTFUL, CONSIDERATE, APPEALING, PLEASANT
nicesity, necessity
niche,*, A CORNER OF, A LITTLE PLACE CARVED/ETCHED OUT OF SOMETHING
nichel, nickel
nicity, nice(ty)
nick,*,ked,king, SHALLOW MARK/CUT/ NOTCH, AT THE LAST MINUTE
nickel,*,led, U.S. COIN

nicotine,nic,nism, A CHEMICAL SUBSTANCE NATURALLY FOUND IN TOBACCO
nid, night / need / knead
nidal, needle
nider, neither
nidl, needle
nidol, needle
nidul, needle
niece,*, A RELATIVE BY BLOOD FAMILY
niese, niece
nif, knife
night,*,tly,tless, THE DARK PART OF A 24 HOUR PERIOD, WITHOUT THE SUN (or see knight) "prefixes: over"
niglekt, neglect
niglekted, neglect(ed)
nigosheate, negotiate
nigosheuble, negotiable
nigotiable, negotiable
nigotiate, negotiate
nik, nick
nikatene, nicotine
nikel, nickel
niknak, knick knack
nikotene, nicotine
nikul, nickel
nikutene, nicotine
nil, NOTHING, NONE (or see kneel)
nilon, nylon
nimf, nymph
nimfomanea, nymphomania
nimfomaneac, nymphomania(c)
nimonea, pneumonia
nimph, nymph
nimphomania, nymphomania
nindeith, nine(tieth)
nindes, nine(ties)
nindy, nine(ty)
nine,*,er,ety,eties,nth,neteenth,netieth, ENGLISH NUMBER BETWEEN EIGHT AND TEN
ninfomaneac, nymphomania(c)
ninphomania, nymphomania
nintenth, nine(teenth)
ninthe, nine(nth)
ninty, nine(ty)
nintys, nine(ties)
nio, neo
niol, kneel
nion, neon
nip,*,pped,pping,pper,ppy, TAKE A LITTLE BITE, TAKE IN JUST A LITTLE
niped, nip(pped)

niple, nipple
nipple,*, FORMED TIP EXTRUSIONS ON THE CHEST CAVITY, TIP WITH ORIFICE
nipul, nipple
nipy, nip(ppy)
nircher, nurture
nireshment, nourish(ment)
nirfona, nirvana
nirfus, nervous
niron, neuron
nirosis, neurosis
nirse, nurse
nirvana, A STATE OF BLISS WHERE ONE IS TRANSFORMED FROM THE MATERIAL PLANE
nirves, nervous / nerve(s)
nirvus, nervous
nis, nice / niece
nise, nice / niece
nisedy, nice(ty)
niser, nice(r)
nisesity, necessity
nisest, nice(st)
nistalgek, nostalgic
nit,*, PARASITIC LARVAE (or see night/ knit/net/knight)
nitch, niche
nite, night / knight / knit
nited, knit(tted) / knight(ed)
nither, neither
nitorius, notorious
nitpeky, nitpick(y)
nitpick,*,ky, BE OVERLY CONCERNED ABOUT MINISCULE DETAILS
nitpiky, nitpick(y)
nitr, PREFIX INDICATING "NITROGEN" MOST OFTEN MODIFIES THE WORD
nitragen, nitrogen
nitral, nitrile
nitregen, nitrogen
nitrel, nitrile
nitrigen, nitrogen
nitrile, CHEMICAL CLASSIFICATION
nitro, PREFIX INDICATING "NITROGEN" MOST OFTEN MODIFIES THE WORD
nitrogen,nous, A GAS
nitrul, nitrile
nitsh, niche
niu, new / knew
niw, new / knew
njoy, enjoy
no, NEGATORY (or see know)

nob,*,bby, BUMPS/EXTRUSIONS (or see knob)
nobel, noble
nobelity, nobility
nobil, noble
nobility,ties, SUPERIOR, REPUTABLE, OF QUALITY
noble,*,er,est,esse,eman,bility, OF RANK/REPUTATION, CHEMICALLY INERT "prefixes: en"
nobody, NO BODY, NO PERSON
noboty, nobody
nobul, noble
noc, nock / knock / nook
noch, notch / nudge
nochin, notion
nochus, nauseous
nock,*,ked,king, SETTING AN ARROW INTO PLACE ON BOW STRING, PART OF ARROW (or see knock)
nocol, knuckle
nocshos, noxious
noct, PREFIX INDICATING "NIGHT" MOST OFTEN MODIFIES THE WORD
nocturnal,lity,lly,ne, ACTIVE AT NIGHT
nod,*,dded,dding, UP AND DOWN HEAD MOVEMENT (or see not/ node)
nodafekashen, notify(fication)
nodariety, notorius(iety)
nodary, notary
nodch, notch
node,*,dal,dality, STUMP/BULGE (too many definitions please see standard dictionary) (or see note/ naughty/knot(tty)) "prefixes: inter"
nodefication, notify(fication)
nodefy, notify
nodekul, nautical
nodelus, nautilus
noderiety, notorius(iety)
noderize, notary(rize)
nodery, notary
nodes, notice / node(s)
nodical, nautical
nodier, naughty(tier)
nodiest, naughty(tiest)
nodify, notify
nodikal, nautical
nodiriety, notorius(iety)
nodirize, notary(rize)
nodiry, notary
nodis, notice
nodle, noodle

nodufikashen, notify(fication)
nodufy, notify
nodukul, nautical
nodure, notary
noduriety, notorius(iety)
nodurise, notary(rize)
nodus, notice
nody, naughty / knot(ty)
noefe, naive
noese, noise / noise(sy) / nosy
noeve, naive
noevet, naive(te)
nofa, nova
nofel, novel
nofelty, novelty
nofember, november
nofil, novel
nofilty, novelty
nofu, nova
noget, nugget
noglekted, neglect(ed)
nois, noise
noise,*,eless,elessly,elessness,sy,sily, siness, DISHARMONIC SOUND, AN ALARMING/OFFENSIVE SOUND
noisey, noise(y)
nok, nock / knock / nook
nokel, knuckle
nokshus, noxious
nokternul, nocturnal
nokturnal, nocturnal
nol, knoll / null
nole, knoll
nolech, knowledge
noleg, knowledge
nolige, knowledge
noll, knoll
nom, gnome / numb
nomad,*,dic,dically,dism, A WANDERER, WITHOUT A PERMANENT HOME (or see pneumatic) "prefixes: semi"
nomadek, pneumatic / nomad(ic)
nomanaded, nominate(d)
nomanate, nominate
nomanee, nominee
nomat, nomad
nomatic, nomad(ic) / pneumatic
nomenashen, nominate(tion)
nomenate, nominate
nomene, nominee
nomenoly, nominal(lly)
nominal,lly,lism,lize,lizes,lized,lizing, lization, LOW COST, OF A NAME, BANKING TERM, NOUN FORM "prefixes: pre/pro"
nominate,*,ted,ting,tion,tive,tor, SELECT PEOPLE WHO WILL BE IN AN ELECTION "prefixes: de"
nominee,*, SOMEONE SELECTED TO BE VOTED FOR, ONE WHOM IS SELECTED FOR ELECTION
nomunashin, nominate(tion)
nomunate, nominate
nomunee, nominee
non, PREFIX INDICATING "NOT" MOST OFTEN MODIFIES THE WORD (or see known/none/nun/noon)
noncense, nonsense
nonchalant,tly,nce, CASUAL, UNCONCERNED
nonchelot, nonchalant
nonchulot, nonchalant
none, WITHOUT ANY, ABSENT FROM (or see nun/noun/known)
nonfiction,nal, FACTUAL
nonsense,sical,sically,sicalness, ABSURB, GOOFY, NOT POSSIBLE, IRRATIONAL
nonsents, nonsense
nonshelont, nonchalant
nonshulot, nonchalant
nonsinse, nonsense
noo, new / knew
noocleate, nuclear(ate)
noodle,*, PASTA
noodul, noodle
nook,*, A CORNER/CREVICE/RECESSED AREA
noon, O'CLOCK P.M. (or see nun)
noos, noose / new(s)
noose, SLIPKNOT ROPE WITH A LOOPED END FOR HOLDING SOMETHING (or see new(s))
nooz, noose / new(s)
noozpaper, newspaper
nop, nob/ knob/ nope
nope, NO
nor, ANOTHER WORD FOR 'NEITHER'
norishment, nourish(ment)
norm,*,mal, SLANG FOR WHAT'S NORMAL
normal,lly,lity,lcy,lize,lizes,lized,lizing, lization, MIDDLE OF THE ROAD BEHAVIOR/THOUGHT/ACTION, IN BETWEEN, AVERAGE "prefixes: re/ sub/un"
normul, normal
normuly, normal(lly)
nors, nurse
norsism, narcissism
norsistik, narcissi(tic)
north,hen,hener,hern,hernmost,her, herly,herlies,herliness, ONE OF FOUR COMPASS/MAGNETIC DIRECTIONS
northirn, north(ern)
northurly, north(erly)
nos, nose / know(s)
nosdalgek, nostalgic
nosdalgia, nostalgia
nosdrul, nostril
nose,*,ed,sing,eless,sy, PROBOSCUS, FACIAL FEATURE REQUIRED FOR SMELLING AND BREATHING (or see know(s))
nosel, nozzle
noseus, nauseous
noshen, notion
noshes, nauseous
noshus, nauseous
nosil, nozzle
nosle, nozzle
nost, nose(d)
nostalgea, nostalgia
nostalgia,ic, REMINISCE/REFER TO THE PAST
nostalgic,cally, REMINISCE/REFER TO THE PAST
nostrel, nostril
nostril,*, ORIFICES ON NOSE WHICH EMPLOYS AIR MOVEMENT
nostrul, nostril
nosul, nozzle
nosy,sier,siest,sily,siness, FOLLOW THE NOSE, PRY/SNOOP AROUND IN ANOTHERS BUSINESS, ALSO SPELLED 'NOSEY'
not, THIS ONE/THAT ONE, NO (or see note/knot/naught)
notariety, notorius(iety)
notary,ries,rize,rizes,rized,rizing,rization, AN OFFICIAL WHO PREPARES LEGAL DOCUMENTS
notch,hes,hed,hing, TO CUT/KNOCK OUT A WEDGE IN SOMETHING, TO CARVE OUT OF
note,*,ed,ting,tice, WRITE TEXT ON PAPER, KEEP IN MIND, OBSERVE/ REMEMBER (or see node/knot/ naught)
notee, naughty / knot(ty)
notefication, notify(fication)

notefikashen, notify(fication)
notefy, notify
notekul, nautical
notelus, nautilus
noterize, notary(rize)
notery, notary
notes, notice / note(s)
notheng, nothing
nothing, NOT A THING
notice,*,ed,cing, TO TAKE NOTE OF, OBSERVE A DISCREPANCY "prefixes: un"
notiest, naughty(tiest)
notifacation, notify(fication)
notify,fies,fied,fying,fication, TO INFORM, COMMUNICATE TO SOMEONE BY VARIOUS MEANS
notikal, nautical
notilus, nautilus
notion,*, AN INKLING/VIEW/OPINION "prefixes: pre"
notiriety, notorius(iety)
notiry, notary
notis, notice
notorious,sly,sness,iety,ieties, WIDELY KNOWN BUT WITHOUT POSITIVE REGARD
notufikashen, notify(fication)
notufy, notify
notukul, nautical
noturiety, notorius(iety)
noturize, notary(rize)
notury, notary
notus, notice
noty, naughty / knot(ty)
noun,*, A WORD REFERRING TO PEOPLE PLACE/THING/TIME/PROPER NAME (or see known)
nourish,hes,hed,hing,her,hment, TO PROVIDE NECESSARY NUTRIENTS "prefixes: under"
nouse, noose
nova,*, STAR FLARE-UPS/BURSTS, NEW STAR
novel,*,list,listic,ette,lize,lization,lla,lty, FICTITIOUS WRITING, IMAGINED PLOT AND CHARACTERS, A CREATIVE IDEA OR DESIGN
novela, novel(lla)
novelty,ties, UNUSUAL AND CREATIVE
november, A MONTH OF THE YEAR (ENGLISH)
noves, novice
novice,*, A BEGINNER

novil, novel
novildy, novelty
novimber, november
novis, novice
novle, novel
novlety, novelty
novu, nova
novul, novel
novulest, novel(ist)
novulty, novelty
novus, novice
now, IN THE MOMENT/PRESENT
nowar, nowhere
noweesy, noise(sy)
nowere, nowhere
nowese, noise
nowhere, NO WHERE, NOT HERE NOW
nowleg, knowledge
nown, noun / known
noxious,sly,sness, HARMFUL TO HEALTH(or see nauseous)
noxus, noxious
noyse, noise
noze, nose / know(s)
nozeate, nausea(te)
nozel, nozzle
nozy, nosy
nozzle,*, AN APERTURE FOR SPRAYING
nu, new / knew
nuborn, newborn
nubshuel, nuptial
nuc, nook
nucle, PREFIX INDICATING "NUCLEUS/NUCLEAR" MOST OFTEN MODIFIES THE WORD
nuclear,ate,ates,ated,ating,ation, HAVING TO DO WITH A NUCLEUS "prefixes: bi/inter/intra/pro/sub"
nucleus,ei,eic,ein, CENTRAL HUB, PRIMARY CONTROL "prefixes: pro"
nud, nude
nuddy, nut(ty) / nude(ies)
nude,*,ely,eness,dism,dity,dities, WITHOUT COVERINGS "prefixes: semi"
nudel, noodle
nuder, neuter
nudesm, nude(dism)
nudety, nude(dity)
nudge,*,ed,ging, GENTLY POKE/PUSH
nudil, noodle
nudl, noodle
nudmeg, nutmeg
nudol, noodle

nudril, neutral
nudul, noodle
nudy, nut(ty)
nue, new / knew
nuendo, innuendo
nuer, new(er)
nufember, november
nuge, nudge
nuget, nugget
nugget,*, A SMALL CHUNK OF SOMETHING
nugit, nugget
nuglekt, neglect
nuglere, nuclear
nugleus, nucleus
nugosheate, negotiate
nugoshiable, negotiable
nugotiable, negotiable
nugotiate, negotiate
nuindo, innuendo
nuisance, ANNOYING, OBNOXIOUS, CONTINUOUS IRRITATION
nuist, new(est)
nujt, nudge(d)
nuk, nook
nukle, knuckle
nukleate, nuclear(ate)
nukleir, nuclear
nukleus, nucleus
nukul, knuckle
nul, null
nulefy, nullify
nulewed, newlywed
nulify, nullify
null,llity,llities,llify, OF NO VALUE
nullify,fies,fied,fying,fier,fication,ity, RENDER NOT VALUABLE/NECESSARY
nuly, new(l)
nulywed, newlywed
num, numb
numadik, pneumatic / nomad(ic)
numarader, numerate(tor)
numarery, numerary
numaril, numeral
numatic, pneumatic / nomad(ic)
numb,*,bed,bing,bness, VOID OF FEELING, INABILITY TO FEEL ANYTHING
number,*,red,ring,ral, A UNIT/SYMBOL WHICH REPRESENTS AN AMOUNT "prefixes: un"
numberible, numerable
numbroble, numerable

numerable, CAN BE COUNTED, COUNTABLE "prefixes: in"
numeracy, COMMON MATH "prefixes: in"
numeral,*,lly,ate,ary,ric,ator, ONE NUMBER/DIGIT, OF A DIGIT, ADD/SUBTRACT
numerary, ABOUT NUMBERS
numerate,*,ed,ting,tion,tor,tors, BASIC MATH "prefixes: en/in"
numeric,*,rical,rically,rous, USE OF NUMBERS
numerology, SCIENCE OF NUMBERS/FREQUENCY
numeros, numerous
numerous,sly,sness, MANY IN NUMBER "prefixes: in"
numirator, numerate(tor)
numirology, numerology
numirus, numerous
numonia, pneumonia
numorator, numerate(tor)
numper, number
numpir, number
numral, numeral
numrecy, numeracy
numrisy, numeracy
numrul, numeral
numurery, numerary
numurologe, numerology
numurus, numerous
nun,*, RELIGIOUS WOMAN WHO VOWS TO OBEY RULES AS A NUN (or see non/none/known/noun/noon)
nundo, innuendo
nune, noon
nupshuel, nuptial
nuptial,lly, CONCERNS WEDDING/RITUAL
nuradic, neurotic
nurcher, nurture
nuresh, nourish
nurfus, nervous
nurish, nourish
nurishment, nourish(ment)
nurodic, neurotic
nuron, neuron
nurosis, neurosis
nurotic, neurotic
nurs, nurse
nurse,*,ed,sing,er,ery,eries, TO NURTURE AND/OR PROTECT VULNERABLE THINGS/PEOPLE

nurture,*, PROVIDE NECESSARY NOURISHMENT TO
nurve, nerve
nurvis, nervous
nurvus, nervous
nus, new(s) / noose
nusans, nuisance
nusdalgik, nostalgic
nuse, noose / new(s)
nusel, nuzzle
nusense, nuisance
nusesidy, necessity
nusesitate, necessitate
nusil, nuzzle
nusinse, nuisance
nusle, nuzzle
nuspaper, newspaper
nustalgek, nostalgic
nusul, nuzzle
nut,*,tty, HIGH PROTEIN WOODY FRUIT, SOMEONE WHO DOESN'T BEHAVE LOGICALLY
nute, nude
nutedy, nude(dity)
nutel, noodle
nuter, neuter
nutesm, nude(dism)
nuthen, nothing
nuthing, nothing
nutil, noodle
nutle, noodle
nutmeg, A SPICE
nutoreus, notorius
nutral, neutral
nutrality, neutral(ity)
nutralize, neutral(ize)
nutreant, nutrient
nutreno, neutrino
nutreshen, nutrition
nutreshus, nutritious
nutrichas, nutritious
nutrient, FOOD THAT NOURISHES LIVING THINGS
nutril, neutral
nutrino, neutrino
nutrishen, nutrition
nutrishenal, nutrition(al)
nutrition,nal,nally,nist,ous,ive, GIVES/PROVIDES NOURISHMENT
nutritious,sly,sness, PROVIDES NOURISHMENT
nutritive,ely,eness, PROVIDES NOURISHMENT
nutron, neutron

nuty, nut(ty)
nuvember, november
nuvimber, november
nuwkleus, nucleus
nuwlewed, newlywed
nuz, new(s)
nuzle, nuzzle
nuzpaper, newspaper
nuzzle,*,ed,ling, TO SNUGGLE/DIG IN/THRUST GENTLY INTO
nve, envy
nylon, A MANMADE CHEMICAL FIBER
nymph,*, ENTITIES, DEITIES, A STAGE IN THE DEVELOPMENT OF AN INSECT
nymphomania,ac, CONTINUAL/INTENSE FOCUS ON SEXUAL ACTIVITY
nyn, nine
nyte, night / knight / knit
nzime, enzyme
o, oh
o'clock, SHORT FOR "ON THE CLOCK"
oak,*, A DECIDUOUS TREE WITH ACORNS
oar,*,red, USED TO ROW A BOAT (or see or)
oarthodox, orthodox
oases, oasis
oasis, SPOT OF TREES/WATER IN THE DESERT, COMFORT AMIDST AN UNCOMFORTABLE ENVIRONMENT
oat,*, A GRAIN (or see ode)
oath,*, PLEDGE/OBLIGATE TO CERTAIN RULES/LAWS
oatmeal, EDIBLE OAT GRAIN
ob, PREFIX INDICATING "AGAINST/TOWARDS/IN THE WAY OF" MOST OFTEN MODIFIES THE WORD
obay, obey
obazit, opposite
obecity, obese(sity)
obedeinse, obedience
obedeint, obedient
obedience,*,nt, TO COMPLY/OBEY "prefixes: dis"
obedient,ly,nce, TO COMPLY/OBEY "prefixes: dis"
obees, obese
obese,ely,seness,sity, OVERLY HEAVY, EXCESSIVELY OVERWEIGHT
obetchuery, obituary
obeteinse, obedience

obey,*,yed,ying,edient, COMPLY, FOLLOW RULES AND LAWS "prefixes: dis"
obfeus, obvious
obgectif, object(ive)
obgectivity, object(ivity)
obgekshen, object(ion)
obgektif, object(ive)
obichuery, obituary
obideinse, obedience
obituary,ries, LIST OF PEOPLE WHO HAVE TRANSPIRED FROM THIS PHYSICAL PLANE
object,*,ted,ting,tion,tive,tively,tivism, tion,tionable,tionably,tionability, PHYSICAL/TANGIBLE THINGS, ARGUE IN DEFENSE OF, NEUTRAL POSITION
oblagation, obligate(tion)
oblederate, obliterate
oblefeus, oblivious
oblegate, obligate
obleterate, obliterate
obleveus, oblivious
oblevion, oblivion
oblifeus, oblivious
oblig, oblige(d)
obligate,*,ed,ting,tion,tory,torily, toriness, ACCEPT TERMS/ RESPONSIBILITY TO PERFORM
oblige,*,ed,ging,gingly, WILLING TO HELP "prefixes: dis"
oblij, oblige(d)
obliterate,*,ed,ting,tion,tive,tor, TO DESTROY COMPLETELY
oblivion,ous, COMPLETELY FORGET
oblivious,ously,ousness,on, COMPLETELY FORGET
oblong, LONGER LENGTH THAN SIDES, LONG/ROUND
oblugashen, obligate(tion)
oblugate, obligate
obnoksheus, obnoxious
obnoxious,sly,sness, OFFENSIVE, ROUGH FREQUENCY, DISHARMONIC IN NATURE
obozit, opposite
obreble, operable
obruble, operable
obsalesens, obsolescent(nce)
obsalesent, obsolescent
obscene,ely,eness,nity,nities, VERY UNDESIRABLE, INDECENT

obscure,*,ed,ring,ely,eness,ration,er, est,rity,rities, VAGUE, UNFOCUSED, DIFFICULT TO EXPLAIN/ UNDERSTAND
obselesens, obsolescent(nce)
obselesent, obsolescent
obselete, obsolete
obsene, obscene
observe,*,ed,ving,vingly,vance,vant, vantly, TO WATCH/SEE AND STUDY "prefixes: in"
obseshen, obsess(ion)
obsesive, obsess(ive)
obsess,sses,ssed,ssive,ssively,ssion, ssional,ssionally, TO BECOME OVERWHELMED WITH THOUGHT ABOUT ONE THING, COMPULSIVE
obshen, option
obsilesens, obsolescent(nce)
obsilete, obsolete
obsinety, obscene(nity)
obsolescent,nce,tly, NOT MODERN, OUT OF DATE
obsolesens, obsolescent(nce)
obsolete,ely,eness, NO LONGER MODERN
obsquire, obscure
obssesed, obsess(ed)
obssesion, obsess(ion)
obstacle,*, OBSTRUCTION, SOMETHING IN THE PATH
obstatrician, obstetrician
obstatrishen, obstetrician
obstetric,*,cal,cally,cian, SCIENCE INVOLVING WOMEN IN CHILDBEARING PROCESS (or see obstetrician)
obstetrician,*, PERSON PRACTICING MEDICINE ON WOMEN IN THE CHILDBEARING PROCESS
obstikul, obstacle
obstinate,ely,eness,acy,acies, RESOLVED IN PURPOSE/OPINION, UNABLE TO ARGUE WITH, STUBBORN
obstruct,*,ted,ting,tion,tionist,tive, tively,tiveness,tor, GET INTO THE PATH OF, PREVENT FROM TRAVELING FURTHER
obstukel, obstacle
obstunint, obstinate
obsulesens, obsolescent(nce)
obsulesense, obsolescent
obsulete, obsolete

obsurvashen, observe(vation)
obt, opt
obtain,*,ned,ning,nment,nable, ACQUIRE, COME INTO POSSESSION OF
obtametry, optometry
obtamist, optimist
obtamize, optimize
obtane, obtain
obtek, optic
obtekul, optic(al)
obtemal, optimal
obtemist, optimist
obtemize, optimize
obtemum, optimum
obteshen, optician
obtience, obedience
obtik, optic
obtikul, optic(al)
obtimesum, optimism
obtimum, optimum
obtishen, optician
obtometrist, optometry(rist)
obtometry, optometry
obtomitrist, optometry(rist)
obtreshen, optician
obtroosive, obtrusive
obtrude,*,ed,ding,usion,usive,er, STICKS OUT, FORCED PRESENCE IN UNWELCOME WAY
obtrusive,ely,eness,ion, INTRUDES ON OTHERS, NOT WELCOME, THRUSTS OUT "prefixes: un"
obtumal, optimal
obtumem, optimum
obtumist, optimist
obtumistek, optimist(ic)
obtumize, optimize
obtumizum, optimism
obulent, opulent
obulint, opulent
obusev, abuse(sive)
obusif, abuse(sive)
obuzit, opposite
obveus, obvious
obvious,sly,sness, MOST APPARENT, PLAIN TO SEE/INTERPRET
obzurvashen, observe(vation)
oc, PREFIX INDICATING "AGAINST/ TOWARDS/IN THE WAY OF" MOST OFTEN MODIFIES THE WORD
ocashen, occasion
ocasional, occasion(al)

occasion,*,ned,nal,nally,nalism, NOT FREQUENT/OFTEN
occularist, ocular(ist)
occult,*,tism, A SCHOOL OF THOUGHT OUTSIDE OF SOCIETAL NORMS, KNOWLEDGE CONCERNING THE ESOTERIC SCIENCES
occupancy,cies, SPECIFIC NUMBER OF SPACES SET ASIDE FOR PEOPLE TO OCCUPY
occupation,*,nal, JOB/ACTIVITY, BE IN A CERTAIN SPACE IN TIME "prefixe: non/pre"
occupy,pies,pied,pying,pation,piable, pier, TO FILL A SPACE "prefixes: pre/un"
occur,*,rred,rring,rrence,rrences,rrent, TO TAKE PLACE/HAPPEN
occurinse, occur(rrence)
ocean,*,nic, LARGEST BODIES OF WATER "prefixes: inter/sub"
ocen, ocean
ocerents, occur(rrence)
ocra, A COLOR (or see okra)
oct, PREFIX INDICATING "EIGHT" MOST OFTEN MODIFIES THE WORD
octa, PREFIX INDICATING "EIGHT" MOST OFTEN MODIFIES THE WORD
octagon, SIDED SHAPE WITH ANGLES
octahedron,*,ra,ral, FACED SOLID
octane,*, METHANE HYDROCARBON
octave,*, SECTION OF 8 TONES
octif, octave
octihedron, octahedron
octo, PREFIX INDICATING "EIGHT" MOST OFTEN MODIFIES THE WORD
october, A MONTH OF THE YEAR (ENGLISH)
octopus,pi, SEA CREATURE WITH 8 ARMS
octuf, octave
octugon, octagon
octuhedron, octahedron
octupus, octopus
ocular,rist,rly,ulist, OF THE EYE AND EYESIGHT "prefixes: intra"
ocult, occult
ocupancy, occupancy
ocupashen, occupation
ocupation, occupation
ocupied, occupy(pied)
ocupy, occupy
ocurence, occur(rrence)
ocurinse, occur(rrence)

od, odd / ode / ought
odamin, ottoman
odamotive, automotive
odd,*,ddly,ddish,ddness,ddity, NOT EVEN/NORMAL (or see ode/ought)
oddesy, odyssey
ode, POEM (or see odd/ought)
odeanse, audience
odeble, audible
odeinse, audience
odem, autumn
odeo, audio
oder, odor / otter / outer / utter / udder / other / odd(er)
odeshen, audition
odesy, odyssey
odet, audit
odete, odd(ity)
odetion, audition
odetoreum, auditorium
odety, odd(ity)
odible, audible
odim, autumn
odio, audio
odir, odor / otter / outer / utter / udder / other / odd(er)
odishun, audition
odissy, odyssey
odisy, odyssey
odit, audit
odite, odd(ity)
odition, audition
oditorium, auditorium
odity, odd(ity)
odle, odd(ly)
odly, odd(ly)
odmeal, oatmeal
odnes, odd(ness)
odobiaugrufe, autobiography
odograf, autograph
odomashen, automatic(ion)
odomatik, automatic
odomen, ottoman
odometer,*, INSTRUMENT THAT MEASURES NUMBER OF REVOLUTIONS OF A WHEEL AND DISTANCE
odomobeel, automobile
odomotive, automotive
odor,*,rous,rless, SMELL (or see otter/udder) "prefixes: in"
oduble, audible
odum, autumn
odumin, ottoman

odur, odor / otter / outer / utter / udder / other / odd(er)
odyssey,*, A JOURNEY
oel, oil
oeng, owe(wing)
oer, or / oar / over
oestur, oyster
oeul, oil
oeuly, oil(y)
of, A WORD WHICH HELPS TO PULL SENTENCE STRUCTURE TOGETHER (or see off)
ofarall, overall
ofary, ovary
ofashen, ovation
ofation, ovation
ofecial, official
ofel, awful / oval
ofem, ovum
ofen, oven / often
ofend, offend
ofense, offense
ofensive, offense(sive)
ofer, offer / over
oferbering, overbearing
ofercast, overcast
ofercot, overcoat
ofercum, overcome
oferien, ovary(rian)
oferkame, overcame
oferkast, overcast
oferkot, overcoat
oferkum, overcome
oferlay, overlay
oferly, over(ly) / overly
oferot, overwrought
ofert, overt / avert
oferture, overture
oferwelming, overwhelm(ing)
ofery, ovary
ofes, office
ofeser, office(r)
ofeshul, official
ofewlate, ovulate
off, NOT OPERATING, NOT ON (or see of)
offend,*,ded,ding,nse, TO IRRITATE/ANNOY, BREAK RULES
offense,*,eless,sive,sively,siveness, INITIATE, MAKE THE FIRST MOVE "prefixes: in"
offer,*,red,ring, TO GRANT/GIVE
offes, office

office,*,er, A PLACE/PERSON CONDUCTING BUSINESS "prefixes: inter"
official,*,lly,lism, ASSIGNED BY DUTY, CONFIRMED BY AUTHORITY "prefixes: semi/un"
offurt, overt/ avert
ofice, office
oficer, office(r)
oficial, official
ofil, awful / oval
ofim, ovum
ofin, oven / often
ofind, offend
ofinse, offense
ofinsuf, offense(sive)
ofir, offer / over
ofirbering, overbearing
ofircame, overcame
ofircast, overcast
ofircot, overcoat
ofircum, overcome
ofirkame, overcame
ofirkast, overcast
ofirkot, overcoat
ofirkum, overcome
ofirly, over(ly)
ofirot, overwrought
ofirwelming, overwhelm(ing)
ofiry, ovary
ofis, office
ofiser, office(r)
ofishul, official
ofishuly, official(lly)
ofol, oval
often, FREQUENTLY, DO SOMETHING MORE THAN NOT
oftin, often
oful, awful / oval
ofulashen, ovulate(tion)
ofulate, ovulate
ofulation, ovulate(tion)
ofum, ovum
ofur, offer / over
ofurall, overall
ofurbering, overbearing
ofurcame, overcame
ofurcast, overcast
ofurla, overlay
ofurly, over(ly) / overly
ofurot, overwrought
ofurt, overt / avert
ofurture, overture
ofurwelming, overwhelm(ing)

ofury, ovary
ofus, office
ofuser, office(r)
ofvir, over
ofvur, over
ogast, august
oger, auger / ogre
ogern, adjourn
ogest, august
ogir, ogre / auger
ogirn, adjourn
ogist, august
ogli, ugly
ogly, ugly
ogment, augment
ogmint, augment
ogorn, adjourn
ogre,*, UGLY AND MEAN (or see auger)
ogua, aqua
ogur, ogre / auger
ogust, august
ogwa, aqua
ogwu, aqua
ogzelery, auxiliary
ogzilery, auxiliary
oh, AN EXCLAMATION OF SURPRISE OR SUDDENNESS
oil,*,led,ler,ling,ly,lier,liest, SLIPPERY/ LUBRICATING SUBSTANCE
oing, owe(wing)
ointment,*, A SALVE/LOTION APPLIED TO THE SKIN FOR HEALING
oister, oyster
ojern, adjourn
ojorn, adjourn
ok, okay / oak
okashenul, occasion(al)
okashiun, occasion
okay, O.K./YES/FINE
okerinse, occur(rrence)
okest, august
okewpansy, occupancy
okewpie, occupy
okist, august
oklok, o'clock
okra, A VEGETABLE (or see ocra)
oks, ox
oksadashen, oxide(dation)
oksadate, oxidant
oksagen, oxygen
oksedation, oxide(dation)
oksejin, oxygen
oksen, ox(en)
okshin, auction

oksid, oxide
oksidashen, oxide(dation)
oksidation, oxide(dation)
oksigen, oxygen
oksijen, oxygen
oksilery, auxiliary
oksin, ox(en)
oksudashen, oxide(dation)
oksudation, oxide(dation)
oksugen, oxygen
oktahedron, octahedron
oktane, octane
oktegon, octagon
oktehedron, octahedron
oktev, octave
oktif, octave
oktihedron, octahedron
oktober, october
oktopus, octopus
oktuf, octave
oktugon, octagon
okularest, ocular(ist)
okult, occult
okupashen, occupation
okupensy, occupancy
okupit, occupy(pied)
okupy, occupy
okur, occur
okurinse, occur(rrence)
okust, august
okwa, aqua
okwadukt, aqueduct
okwafer, aquifer
okward, awkward
okwefer, aquifer
okword, awkward
okwu, aqua
okwurd, awkward
okzilery, auxiliary
ol, owl / all / awl / old
olastick, elastic
olau, allow
olaw, allow
olcer, ulcer
old,der,dest, PAST ITS PRIME, OF THE PAST
ole, old / all / awl
olef, olive
olempek, olympic
olempic, olympic
olesit, elicit / illicit
oleve, olive
olfebet, alphabet
olif, olive

olimpic, olympic
olisit, elicit / illicit
olive,*, A FRUIT FROM A TREE
oll, all
olmenak, almanac
olmost, almost
olone, alone
olser, ulcer
olso, also
olt, old
oltegether, altogether
olter, altar / alder / alter
olternativ, alternative
olternutev, alternative
oltigether, altogether
oltirnutev, alternative
oltugethur, altogether
oltur, altar / alder / alter
olturnativ, alternative
olturnutev, alternative
oluf, aloof / olive
oluv, olive
olwaz, always
olympic,*, RELATING TO GAMES/ COUNTRY/MOUNTAIN
om, home / them
omaga, omega
omed, omit / emit
omeded, omit(tted) / emit(tted)
omega, LAST, AT THE END
omeka, omega
omenus, ominous
omesable, omit(issible)
omeshin, omission / emission
omet, omit / emit
ometion, omission / emission
ominous,sly,sness, A SIGN, THREATENING DUE TO LACK OF UNDERSTANDING, FOREBODING
ominus, ominous
omishen, omission / emission
omissible, LEAVE SOMETHING OUT
omission,*,ible, THE ACT OF LEAVING SOMETHING OUT (or see emission)
omit,*,tted,tting,issible,ission, LEAVE SOMETHING OUT (or see emit))
omition, omission / emission
omne, omni
omnefurus, omnivore(ous)
omnevore, omnivore
omnevorus, omnivore(ous)
omni, ALL AS ONE, HAVING IT ALL, ALL OF IT, PREFIX INDICATING "ALL" MOST OFTEN MODIFIES THE WORD

omniferus, omnivore(ous)
omniverus, omnivore(ous)
omnivore,*,rous,rously, EATS ANYTHING DIGESTIBLE
omnuvore, omnivore
on, OPERATING, FUNCTIONING, PERFORMING (or see own/one)
onarary, honorary
once, ONLY ONE TIME, FORMER (or see want(s)/ounce)
oncore, encore
ond, own(ed)
one,*,eness, SINGLE, NUMERAL MEANING LESS THAN TWO BUT MORE THAN ZERO (or see won/ own)
onebreated, inebriate(d)
oneng, awning / own(ing)
oner, honor / owner
onerable, honor(able)
onest, honest
onibreated, inebriate(d)
oning, awning / own(ing)
onion,*, A VEGETABLE
onir, honor / owner
onirable, honor(able)
onist, honest
onkore, encore
onle, only
only, NO EXCEPTIONS, EXCLUSIVELY, MERELY
onomaly, anomaly
onor, honor / owner
onoruble, honor(able)
onry, ornery / honorary
ons, own(s) / ounce
onsbekable, unspeakable
onsboken, unspoken
onse, once / one(s) / own(s) / ounce
ont, own(ed)
onto, ON/TO, ABOUT/TOWARDS (or see unto)
ontra, entree
ontrapreneur, entrepreneur
ontre, entree
ontrupreneur, entrepreneur
ontu, onto
onurary, honorary
onvasef, invasive
onward,*, FORWARD
onwry, ornery / honorary
onwurd, onward
onyen, onion
onyun, onion

oos, ooze
ooserp, usurp
oosurp, usurp
ooze,*,ed,zing, GENTLE FLOW, GENERAL OVERALL APPEARANCE OF EXCESSIVE, HEAVY MOISTURE
op, PREFIX INDICATING "AGAINST/ TOWARDS/IN THE WAY OF" MOST OFTEN MODIFIES THE WORD
opake, opaque
opal,*, AN IRRIDESCENT STONE
opalescence,nt, HAVING A COATING/ APPEARANCE OF RAINBOW COLORED/ IRREDESCENT LIGHT, FILMY/COLORFUL
opaque,*,ely, NON-TRANSPARENT, DULL, DENSE
oparade, operate
oparate, operate
opaset, opposite
opasit, opposite
opazeshen, oppose(sition)
opazit, opposite
opeate, opiate
open,*,ned,ning,nness,ner, INVITING, ALLOWING, PENETRABLE, ACCEPTING "prefixes: re"
openeun, opinion
openyun, opinion
opera,*,retta, PLAY/DRAMA WITH MUSIC/SINGING
operable,bility,ly, CAN BE OPERATED ON "prefixes: in/inter"
operade, operate
operader, operate(tor)
operashen, operate(tion)
operate,*,ed,ting,tion,tional,tive,tivity, tively,tor, MAKE FUNCTIONAL, PUT INTO EFFECT, MAKE ACTIVE, REMEDY WITH ACTION "prefixes: in/post/pre"
operater, operate(tor)
opertune, opportune
opertunedy, opportune(nity)
opertunest, opportune(st)
opertunity, opportune(nity)
opesishen, oppose(sition)
opesit, opposite
opeum, opium
opeute, opiate
opewlent, opulent
opezit, opposite
opfeis, obvious
opfeus, obvious

ophil, awful
ophul, awful
opiate,*, DRUG/NARCOTIC USED TO DULL PAIN AND INDUCE SLEEP
opilesent, opalescence(nt)
opilesinse, opalescence
opilessence, opalescence
opin, open
opinion,*,ned,nated, A JUDGEMENT/ THOUGHT
opirashen, operate(tion)
opirate, operate
opirtune, opportune
opirtunedy, opportune(nity)
opirtunist, opportune(st)
opirtunity, opportune(nity)
opiruble, operable
opisit, opposite
opium, JUICE FROM FLOWERING POPPY FRUIT
opizit, opposite
oplagashen, obligate(tion)
opleveus, oblivious
opligate, obligate
oplige, oblige(d)
oplij, oblige(d)
opliveus, oblivious
oplivion, oblivion
oplong, oblong
oplugashen, obligate(tion)
oplugate, obligate
opnokshes, obnoxious
oponent, opponent
oponit, opponent
oporashin, operate(tion)
oporate, operate
oportune, opportune
opose, oppose
oposet, opposite
opossum, A MARSUPIAL ANIMAL
opostrufe, apostrophe
opozishen, oppose(sition)
oppasite, opposite
oppazit, opposite
oppezit, opposite
opponent,*, THE OTHER SIDE IN COMPETITION, ONE OF TWO SIDES COMPETING
opportune,ely,eness,nism,nist,nistic, nistically,nity,nities, FAVORABLE MOMENT TO ACT/MAKE A CHANGE "prefixes: in"

oppose,*,ed,sing,site,sitely,siteness, sition, ADVERSE/ CONTRARY/ CONTRASTING "prefixes: un"
opposishen, oppose(sition)
opposite,*,ely,eness,tion, ADVERSE/ CONTRARY/CONTRASTING
opposum, opossum
oppreshen, oppress(ion)
oppress,sses,ssed,ssing,ssion,ssive, ssively,ssiveness,ssor, CONTROL OTHER'S FREEWILL BEYOND REASONABLE EXTENT, TYRANNIZE, CRUEL/UNUSUAL PUNISHMENT
opptimism, optimism
opptomistic, optimist(ic)
oppusite, opposite
opra, opera
oprasef, opress(ive) / abrasive
oprasuf, opress(ive) / abrasive
oprater, operate(tor)
opres, oppress
opreshen, oppress(ion)
opror, uproar
opru, opera
oprut, uproot
opsalesens, obsolescent(nce)
opsalesent, obsolescent
opscure, obscure
opseen, obscene
opselesens, obsolescent(nce)
opselete, obsolete
opsenity, obscene(nity)
opserve, observe
opshin, option
opsilesens, obsolescent(nce)
opsilesent, obsolescent
opsilete, obsolete
opsirvashen, observe(vation)
opskure, obscure
opsolesens, obsolescent(nce)
opsolete, obsolete
opstatrishen, obstetrician
opstekul, obstacle
opstenit, obstinate
opstikul, obstacle
opstinesy, obstinate(acy)
opstitrishen, obstetrician
opstrukshen, obstruct(ion)
opstrukt, obstruct
opstukel, obstacle
opstunint, obstinate
opstutrishen, obstetrician
opsulesens, obsolescent(nce)
opsulesense, obsolescent

opsulete, obsolete
opsurvashen, observe(vation)
opt,ted,ting,tion, THE ACT OF MAKING A CHOICE, PREFIX INDICATING "EYE/ VISION" MOST OFTEN MODIFIES THE WORD
optametry, optometry
optamism, optimism
optamist, optimist
optamistek, optimist(ic)
optamisum, optimism
optamize, optimize
optane, obtain
optek, optic
optemal, optimal
optemistic, optimist(ic)
optemisum, optimism
optemum, optimum
opteshen, optician
optic,*,cal,cally, CONCERNING THE EYE
optician,*, DOCTOR WHO WORKS WITH EYES
optico, PREFIX INDICATING "EYE/ VISION" MOST OFTEN MODIFIES THE WORD
optimal,lly,lity, BEST THAT CAN BE ACHIEVED
optimesm, optimism
optimism,stic, BELIEF BASED ON HOPE/ FAITH, LOOKS ON THE BRIGHT SIDE
optimist,tic,tically,sm,ize,ization, BASED ON HOPE/FAITH, HOPE FOR A BRIGHTER FUTURE
optimize,*,ed,zing,zation,mum, TO MAXIMIZE, REAP GREATEST BENEFIT FROM
optimum,*, OPTIMAL, HOPE FOR THE BEST
option,*,ned,nal,nally, A CHOICE
optishen, optician
opto, PREFIX INDICATING "EYE/VISION" MOST OFTEN MODIFIES THE WORD
optometry,rist,ric,rical, DOCTOR OF THE EYES
optrood, obtrude
optrude, obtrude
optrusive, obtrusive
optumem, optimum
optumist, optimist
optumistek, optimist(ic)
optumle, optimal
opul, opal
opulent,tly,nce, OVER ACCUMULATION OF WEALTH AND/OR POWER

opulesense, opalescence
opulesent, opalescence(nt)
opulessence, opalescence
opulint, opulent
opun, open
opura, opera
opurader, operate(tor)
opurashen, operate(tion)
opurate, operate
opurtune, opportune
opurtunedy, opportune(nity)
opurtunest, opportune(st)
opurtunity, opportune(nity)
opusishen, oppose(sition)
opusit, opposite
opuzet, opposite
opuzishen, oppose(sition)
opuzit, opposite
opveus, obvious
opzerve, observe
oqua, aqua
oquelarist, ocular(ist)
oquepy, occupy
oqupensy, occupancy
oqupied, occupy(pied)
oqupy, occupy
oqwa, aqua
or, WORD USED AS A CONJUNCTION, OTHERWISE (or see oar/ore/over/are)
oracle,*,lar,larity,larly, PERSON/THING WHO HOLDS GREAT/SECRET WISDOM (or see auricle)
orador, orator
orafes, orifice
orafus, orifice
oragen, origin
orageno, oregano
oragin, origin
orajin, origin
orajinate, originate
orakul, oracle / auricle
oral,lly, OF/FROM THE MOUTH
orange,*, COLOR, FRUIT
orashen, orator(tion)
orator,tion,tor,torical,torically,ry,ries, SPOKEN FROM THE MOUTH, PUBLIC SPEAKING
orb,*,bit,bited,biting,bital,biter,bitary, bicular,bicularly,bicularity,biculate, biculately,biteer,biteering, SPHERE, GLOBE, CIRCULAR "prefixes: sub"
orbut, orb(it)
orbutrate, arbitrate

orcanek, organic
orcanekly, organic(ally)
orcasem, orgasm
orced, orchid
orcestra, orchestra
orchard,*, FIELD OF FRUIT TREES
orchart, orchard
orchastra, orchestra
orchen, organ
orcherd, orchard
orchestra,*,al,ally,ate,ated,ating,ator, ation, GROUPS OF PEOPLE WITH INSTRUMENTS PERFORMING MUSIC TOGETHER IN SYNCHRONICITY
orchid,*, A FLOWER
orchird, orchard
orchistra, orchestra
orchurt, orchard
orcid, orchid
ordain,*,ned,ning,ner,nment, APPOINT "prefixes: pre"
ordane, ordain
ordanery, ordinary
ordaninse, ordinance
ordeal,*, MORE DRAMA THAN NECESSARY
ordel, ordeal
ordenary, ordinary
ordenate, ordinate
ordenense, ordinance
order,*,red,ring,rly,rliness, ORGANIZED, PROPER PLACEMENT, FOLLOWING SET OF RULES/LAWS "prefixes: dis/sub"
ordervs, horsd'oevres
ordinance,*, A LAW
ordinary,*, COMMON, EVERYDAY, AVERAGE "prefixes: sub"
ordinate,*, VERTICAL PLACEMENT/POSITION "prefixes: sub"
ordinence, ordinance
ordinery, ordinary
ordir, order
ordirves, horsd'oevres
ordninse, ordinance
ordunery, ordinary
ordur, order
ordurvs, horsd'oevres
ore,*, ROCK CONTAINING METAL (or see oar)
orefis, orifice
orefus, orifice
oregano, AN HERB/SPICE

oregen, origin
oregenate, originate
oregeno, oregano
oregin, origin
oreginate, originate
oregino, oregano
oreint, orient
oreintul, orient(al)
orejen, origin
orejenal, origin(al)
orejenashen, originate(tion)
orejenat, origin(ate)
orejin, origin
orejinul, origin(al)
orel, oral
orenge, orange
orenj, orange
oretor, orator
oreundashen, orient(ation)
oreunt, orient
oreuntashen, orient(ation)
orfan, orphan
orfun, orphan
organ,*,nist, MUSICAL INSTRUMENT, A MAJOR INTERNAL BODY PART
organek, organic
organic,*,cally,city,cism, ALL NATURAL SUBSTANCE, FROM THE EARTH "prefixes: bio/in"
organism,*,mic,mically, A LIFE FORM
organization,*,nal,nally, SYSTEM/METHOD OF OPERATION WHICH KEEPS A BODY/HOST ALIVE, COLLECTION OF WORKING PARTS WHICH MAKE UP THE WHOLE "prefixes: dis"
organize,*,ed,zing,zable,er,zation, TO CREATE/USE A METHOD/SYSTEM WHICH CREATES ORDER/FUNCTION BETWEEN MOVING PARTS "prefixes: dis/re/un"
orgasm,*,mic,mically, THE ELEVATED POINT/HEIGHT OF AN EMOTIONAL/PHYSICAL EXPERIENCE/EVENT
orgazem, orgasm
orge, orgy
orgen, organ
orgenise, organize
orgenism, organism
orgenuzashen, organization
orgin, organ / origin
orginazation, organization
orginesm, organism
orginise, organize

orginuzashen, organization
orgon, organ
orgunise, organize
orgunism, organism
orgy,gies, COMBINING NUMBERS OF BODIES WHO EXCESSIVELY INDULGE THEMSELVES
oriendul, orient(al)
orient,*,ted,ting,tates,tation,tational, tive, DEFINITE POSITION/BEARING IN REFERENCE TO SPECIFIC POINTS, OF THE EAST "prefixes: dis"
oriental,*,lly,lism,list,lize, EASTERN PLACE IN RELATION TO THE REST OF THE WORLD
orifice,*, OPENINGS
origen, origin
origin,*,nal,nally,nality,nalities,nate, BEGINNING OF CREATION, FIRST THOUGHT, THE BEGINNING
originate,*,ed,ting,tion,tor,tive,tively, tion, FROM WHERE IT BEGAN, FIRST THOUGHT
orijenal, origin(al)
orijenate, originate
orijinal, origin(al)
orikul, oracle / auricle
oril, oral
oringe, orange
orinj, orange
orivul, arrive(val)
orjy, orgy
orkan, organ
orkanek, organic
orkanekly, organic(ally)
orkanik, organic
orkanism, organism
orkanize, organize
orkanusashen, organization
orkastra, orchestra
orkasum, orgasm
orked, orchid
orken, organ
orkenasashen, organization
orkenism, organism
orkenize, organize
orkenuzashen, organization
orkestra, orchestra
orkestrete, orchestra(ate)
orket, orchid
orkid, orchid
orkin, organ
orkinasation, organization
orkinazashen, organization

orkinism, organism
orkinize, organize
orkistra, orchestra
orkit, orchid
orkunise, organize
orkunism, organism
orkustra, orchestra
ormer, armor
ormur, armor
ornade, ornate
ornament,*,tal,tally,tation, DECORATIONS, ACCESSORIZE, BEAUTIFY
ornamintal, ornament(al)
ornate,ely,eness, ARTISTICALLY DETAILED, EMBELLISHED
ornement, ornament
ornemintal, ornament(al)
ornery,riness, STUBBORN/ADVERSE DISPOSITION OR ATTITUDE
ornge, orange
ornry, ornery
ornument, ornament
ornumentul, ornament(al)
orocle, oracle
orofes, orifice
orp, orb
orpet, orb(it)
orphan,*,nage,nhood, ONE LEFT WITHOUT PARENTS, PLACE FOR THOSE WITHOUT PARENTS
orphen, orphan
orpit, orb(it)
orput, orb(it)
orsherd, orchard
orshurd, orchard
ortanery, ordinary
ortenanse, ordinance
ortenary, ordinary
orter, order
orth, PREFIX INDICATING "MAKE NORMAL/CORRECTION" MOST OFTEN MODIFIES THE WORD
orthodontic,*,ia,ist, TEETH/DENTISTRY
orthodox,xes,xly,xy,xies, OF SOCIAL CUSTOM/PRACTICE "prefixes: un"
orthopedic,*,cally,ist, TEETH/ DENTISTRY
orthridus, arthritis
orthudox, orthodox
ortinanse, ordinance
ortinary, ordinary
ortir, order
ortnense, ordinance

ortunense, ordinance
ortur, order
orufis, orifice
orugin, origin
orujin, origin
orukle, oracle / auricle
orukul, oracle / auricle
orul, oral
orunj, orange
orupt, erupt / irrupt
oryent, orient
oryentashen, orient(ation)
oryentul, orient(al)
oryindashen, orient(ation)
os, us / owe(s)
osalate, osculate / oscillate
osanefurus, ozone(niferous)
oscillate,*,ed,ting,tion,tor,tory, VOLUME OF MOVEMENT/ VIBRATION IN BETWEEN, MOVE TO/ FRO (or see osculate)
osculate,*,ed,ting,tion,tor,tory, KISS, COME IN CONTACT, TWO OR MORE COINCIDENT POINTS (or see oscillate) "prefixes: inter"
osdrege, ostrich
osdrich, ostrich
osdrije, ostrich
ose, owe(s)
oselate, osculate / oscillate
osheanic, ocean(ic)
osher, usher
oshin, ocean
osilate, osculate / oscillate
osmose,ed,sing,sis,otic,otically, PENETRATION OF A BARRIER WHERE TWO SHARE THE SAME AS ONE, SHARING OF INFORMATION BETWEEN TWO "prefixes: end"
osmoses, osmose(sis)
osone, ozone
osonic, ozone(nic)
osonusfere, ozone(nosphere)
ost, PREFIX INDICATING "BONE" MOST OFTEN MODIFIES THE WORD
ostracize,*,ed,zing,ism, TO EXPEL OR EXCLUDE FROM A GROUP
ostrech, ostrich
ostreje, ostrich
ostresize, ostracize
ostrich,hes, A LARGE BIRD
ostrisize, ostracize
ostrusize, ostracize
osulashen, oscillate(tion)

osulate, osculate / oscillate
osum, awesome / assume
osuniferus, ozone(niferous)
ot, PREFIX INDICATING "EAR" MOST OFTEN MODIFIES THE WORD (or see oat/ odd/ought/ode)
otamate, automate
otamotive, automotive
otej, outage
otem, autumn
otemin, ottoman
oteo, audio
oter, odor / otter / outer / utter / udder
otesm, autism
otest, attest
otesy, odyssey
otezum, autism
oth, oath
othentik, authentic
other,*, THAT ONE NOT THIS ONE, THE FURTHER ONE, THE ALTERNATIVE (or see author)
othintik, authentic
othir, author
othoretarean, authoritarian
othorety, authority
othoritarean, authoritarian
othority, authority
othoruterein, authoritarian
otim, autumn
otiman, ottoman
otimobil, automobile
otimotive, automotive
otir, odor / otter / outer / utter / udder
otism, autism
otisum, autism
otisy, odyssey
otitoreum, auditorium
otizum, autism
otle, odd(ly)
otluk, outlook
otmel, oatmeal
otmost, utmost
oto, PREFIX INDICATING "EAR" MOST OFTEN MODIFIES THE WORD
otobiografe, autobiography
otograf, autograph
otomadik, automatic
otoman, ottoman
otomashen, automatic(ion)
otomate, automate
otomobel, automobile
otomotive, automotive
otoneme, autonomy

otonume, autonomy
otopse, autopsy
otor, odor / otter / outer / utter / udder
otter,*, WATER MAMMAL
ottoman,*, FOOTSTOOL/COUCH WITHOUT BACK/ARMS
otur, odor / otter / outer / utter / udder
ou, oh / owe
ouch, SOUND ASSOCIATED WITH PAIN/ GETTING HURT
oud, out / ode
oudacity, audacity
oudasedy, audacity
ouder, outer / odor
ouding, outing
oudsmart, outsmart
oudstand, outstand
oudwerd, outward
oudwet, outwit
oughn, own
ought, SHOULD/WOULD/COULD TAKE ACTION/DO SOMETHING
ounce,*, MEASUREMENT FOR DRY PRODUCTS (or see once)
ouns, ounce / own(s)
our,*, BELONGS IN THE GROUP, OWNERSHIP (or see hour/oar)
ourle, hour(ly)
out,tting,tage,ter, NOT IN, EXIT, NOT THERE ANYLONGER, BEYOND THE MAIN/ OBJECT, DOESN'T EXIST AS IT ONCE DID (or see ought)
outage,*, QUIT WORKING, LACKING WITHOUT
outer, BEYOND THE MAIN AREA OR BODY, NOT PART OF THE WHOLE ANY LONGER, EXTERIOR
outfit,*,tted,tting,tter, EXTERNAL GEAR/ CLOTHING
outgo,oes,oing, AWAY FROM THE CENTER, LEAVING THE AREA, REMOVED FROM THE PREVIOUS PLACE
outij, outage
outing,*, TAKE A SMALL EXCURSION AWAY, GO AWAY BRIEFLY
outlaw,*, PEOPLE WHO PERFORM ACTS OUTSIDE OF THE LAW
outlet,*, A WAY TO GET OUT
outline,*,ed,ning, BOUNDARIES OF, DEFINING PRINCIPLES, SKETCH OR WORDS DESCRIBING THE INSIDE
outlook, PERSPECTIVE OF THE OBSERVER, WAY OF PERCEPTION

outluk, outlook
outlying, ON THE OUTSKIRTS, OUTSIDE OF, BEYOND
outpost,*, A STATION OR POST OUTSIDE OF THE MAIN CONFINES, A REMOTE SETTLEMENT
output, THE RESULT OF MANUFACTURING, WHAT IS PRODUCED
outrage,*,ed,ging,eous,eously,eousness, EXCESSIVE EMOTIONAL REACTION, SUDDEN OUTBURST
outright, WITHOUT CONCEALMENT OR RESTRAINT, OPEN, STRAIGHT OUT
outset, AT THE BEGINNING
outside,er, NOT IN THE MAIN PORTION, REMOTE FROM THE CENTER
outskirt,*, AT THE EDGES OF TOWN, BORDER DISTRICTS
outskurt, outskirt
outsmart,*,ted,ting, OUTWIT
outstand,ding, STANDS OUT, PROTRUDES, APART FROM THE REST, LEAVE PORT
outward,*,dly,dness, AWAY FROM CENTER, TOWARDS THE EXTERIOR, ON THE OUTSIDE
outwit,*,tted,tting, OUTSMART, THINK FASTER THAN
oval,*,lly,lness, ELONGATED CIRCLE, SHAPE OF EGG
ovalable, available
ovart, overt / avert
ovarwelming, overwhelm(ing)
ovary,ries,rian,rial,ritis,riotomy, riectomy, REPRODUCTIVE GLANDS
ovashen, ovation
ovashin, ovation
ovation,*, ENTHUSIASTIC APPLAUSE
ovau, avow
ovekt, evict
ovel, oval
ovem, ovum
oven,*,nable, CONTAINER BUILT FOR HIGH HEAT TO COOK/BAKE THINGS
ovent, event
oventful, eventful
over,rly, ABOVE AND BEYOND, MORE THAN NORMAL, PREFIX INDICATING "EXCESSIVELY/COMPLETELY/ UPPER/ABOVE/OUTER" MOST OFTEN MODIFIES THE WORD
overall, SUMMARY, WITH ALL THINGS TAKEN INTO ACCOUNT

overbearing,gly, DOMINATING, OPPRESSING, TYRANNICAL, FORCEFUL
overbering, overbearing
overcame, PAST TENSE FOR THE WORD "OVERCOME"
overcast,ting, SHADOWING, GLOOMS OVER, SEWING ROUGH EDGES
overcoat,*, TO APPLY A COAT OVER ANOTHER
overcome,ming,came, TO RISE ABOVE AN OBSTACLE, TO MANAGE THROUGH A PROBLEM, RISE ABOVE OPPOSITION
overcum, overcome
overhang,*,ging, LEDGE/OUTCROP WHICH JUTS OUT/OVER, OVER AN UDERCUT, HANGS UNDER
overien, ovary(rian)
overkame, overcame
overkast, overcast
overkot, overcoat
overkum, overcome
overlap,*,pped,pping, LAYER THAT PARTIALLY COVERS/LAPS THE EDGE OF ANOTHER LAYER
overlay,*,aid,ain,ying, A COAT/COVER AS TOP FOR PROTECTION
overly, TOO MUCH, TOO EXTREME
overot, overwrought
overt,tly,tness, NO ATTEMPT TO CONCEAL/HIDE (or see avert)
overter, overture
overture,*, INTRODUCTION/ BEGINNING TO
overwelming, overwhelm(ing)
overwhelm,*,med,ming,mingly, OVERLOAD, OVERPOWERING, RESISTANCE IS FUTILE
overwrot, overwrought
overwrought, EMOTIONAL DISTRESS, TOO MUCH TO HANDLE GRACEFULLY
overy, ovary
oveulate, ovulate
ovewlate, ovulate
ovil, oval
ovim, ovum
ovin, oven
ovint, event
ovintful, eventful
ovios, obvious
ovir, over
ovirall, overall
ovirbering, overbearing
ovircast, overcast
ovircot, overcoat
ovircum, overcome
ovirkast, overcast
ovirkot, overcoat
ovirkum, overcome
ovirla, overlay
ovirle, overly
ovirly, over(ly)
ovirot, overwrought
ovirshur, overture
ovirture, overture
ovirwelming, overwhelm(ing)
oviry, ovary
ovow, avow
ovul, oval
ovulashen, ovulate(tion)
ovulate,*,ed,ting,tion, TO RELEASE AN EGG (OVUM) FROM THE OVARY "prefixes: pre"
ovum,*, AN EGG
ovur, over
ovurall, overall
ovurbering, overbearing
ovurcast, overcast
ovurcoat, overcoat
ovurcum, overcome
ovure, ovary
ovurkame, overcame
ovurkast, overcast
ovurkot, overcoat
ovurkum, overcome
ovurla, overlay
ovurly, over(ly)
ovurot, overwrought
ovurt, overt / avert
ovurwelming, overwhelm(ing)
ovury, ovary
ow, owe
owch, ouch
owd, out / ought / owe(d)
owdacity, audacity
owdamotive, automotive
owdasedyy, audacity
owdege, outage
owdemotive, automotive
owdeng, outing
owdfit, outfit
owdimotive, automotive
owdir, outer
owdishun, audition
owdition, audition
owdline, outline
owdpost, outpost
owdrage, outrage
owdrit, outright
owdskirt, outskirt
owdsmart, outsmart
owdstand, outstand
owe,*,ed,wing, TO BE INDEBTED FOR
owl,*, NOCTURNAL BIRD (or see oil)
own,*,ned,ning,ner, HAVE FULL RIGHTS TO TITLE/PROPERTY (or see one/ on) "prefixes: dis"
owner,*, ONE WHO HOLDS RIGHTS/ TITLE TO PROPERTY
owns, ounce/ own(s)
owperable, operable
owr, are / hour / our
owra, aura
owrie, awry
owrit, outright
owrle, hour(ly)
owry, awry
owsh, ouch
owson, ozone
owt, out / ought
owtege, outage
owtej, outage
owtfit, outfit
owtige, outage
owting, outing
owtir, outer
owtlaw, outlaw
owtlet, outlet
owtlieng, outlying
owtline, outline
owtlook, outlook
owtluk, outlook
owtpost, outpost
owtput, output
owtragus, outrage(ous)
owtraj, outrage
owtrite, outright
owtset, outset
owtside, outside
owtskirt, outskirt
owtsmart, outsmart
owtstand, outstand
owtwet, outwit
owtwit, outwit
owtwurd, outward
owur, hour / our
ox,xen,xes, TYPE OF BOVINE (CATTLE)
oxa, PREFIX INDICATING "OXYGEN/ ADDITIONAL OXYGEN" MOST OFTEN MODIFIES THE WORD

oxajen, oxygen
oxedate, oxidant
oxedation, oxide(dation)
oxejen, oxygen
oxejin, oxygen
oxidant,*,ation,ative, OXYGEN ACTIVELY PARTICIPATING WITH OTHER ELEMENTS
oxidashen, oxide(dation)
oxidate, oxidant
oxide,*,dic,dize,dizes,dized,dizing,dizer, dizable,dation,dant, INTERACTION BETWEEN OXYGEN AND OTHER ELEMENTS "prefixes: sub"
oxijen, oxygen
oxilery, auxiliary
oxin, ox(en)
oxo, PREFIX INDICATING "OXYGEN/ ADDITIONAL OXYGEN" MOST OFTEN MODIFIES THE WORD
oxsadashen, oxide(dation)
oxsagen, oxygen
oxsigen, oxygen
oxsudashen, oxide(dation)
oxudiz, oxide(dize)
oxugen, oxygen
oxujin, oxygen
oxy, PREFIX INDICATING "OXYGEN/ ADDITIONAL OXYGEN" MOST OFTEN MODIFIES THE WORD
oxydate, oxidant
oxygen,nic,nicity,nate,nation, A GAS, GAS USED FOR RESPIRATION OF ALL LIVING THINGS
oyle, oil / oil(y)
oyntment, ointment
oyster,*, MARINE SHELLFISH, MOLLUSK
oystur, oyster
ozmosis, osmose(sis)
ozone,*,nic,niferous,nous,nide,nize, nized,nizing,nizer,nosphere, PURE AIR, FORM OF OXYGEN, LAYER AROUND THE EARTH
p, pea
pa, paw / pay
paber, paper / papier mache'
pabreka, paprika
pabur, paper / papier mache'
pace,*,ed,cing,er, RATE OF PROGRESS/ MOVEMENT, A GAIT/STEP
pach, patch
pachen, passion
pachendly, patient(ly)
pachense, patience / patient(s)

pachin, passion
pachindly, patient(ly)
pachints, patience / patient(s)
pacht, patch(ed)
pacific, PEACEFUL, THE PACIFIC OCEAN
pacify,fies,fied,fying,fication,ficatory, fier,fism, TO CODDLE/APPEASE/ SETTLE/ SOOTHE
pack,*,ked,king,kage,kaged,kaging,ker, ket, PREPARE FOR TRANSPORT "prefixes: pre/retro/un"
packet,*, SMALL COLLECTION OF DATA/ MATERIAL PROVIDING INFORMATION
packit, packet
pact,*, AN AGREEMENT (or see pack(ed))
pacterul, pectoral
pad,*,dded,dding,ddy, LAYER OF MATERIAL OF VARYING THICKNESS FOR PROTECTION, A RESIDENCE, BOTTOM OF PAW (or see pat/paid)
pada, pate'
paddle,*,ed,ling,er, TO USE OARS/FEET FOR MOBILIZATION, ITEM USED FOR ROWING, A SPANKING
paddock,*, SMALL AREA TO CONFINE ANIMALS/VEHICLES TEMPORARILY
paddy,dies, HAVING TO DO WITH RICE (or see patty)
pade, paid / paddy / patty / pate'
paded, pad(dded) / pat(tted)
padel, paddle
paden, patent
padeo, patio
padern, pattern
padestrein, pedestrian
padid, pad(dded) / pat(tted)
padik, paddock
padil, paddle
padin, patent
padio, patio
padirn, pattern
padled, paddle(d)
padlock,*, LOCK WITH KEY OR COMBINATION DIAL
padok, paddock
padreark, patriarch
padrearkul, patriarch(al)
padreit, patriot / patriate
padren, patron
padrenize, patron(ize)
padreodic, patriot(ic)
padreut, patriot / patriate

padriarch, patriarch
padrin, patron
padrinize, patron(ize)
padrun, patron
padrunize, patron(ize)
padryet, patriot / patriate
padsee, patsy
padthulogical, pathology(gical)
padtult, paddle(d)
paduk, paddock
paduled, paddle(d)
padurn, pattern
pady, paddy / patty
pae, pay / pay(ee)
pael, pail / pale
paer, pay(er)
paet, paid
paf, pave
pafd, pave(d)
pafeleon, pavilion
paferty, poverty
pafileon, pavilion
pafmint, pave(ment)
paft, pave(d)
pafurted, pervert(ed)
pagamus, pajamas
pagan,*,nish,nism,nize,nizes,nized, nizing,nizer, PEOPLE WHO SUPPORT NATURE AS THEIR DEITY
page,*,ed,ging,ginate,gination,er, SHEET IN A BOOK, TO CALL FOR "prefixes: un"
pageant,*,try,tries, A SHOWY DISPLAY
pagen, pagan
pagenashen, page(gination)
pagenate, page(ginate)
pagense, patience / patient(s)
pagent, pageant
pagentre, pageant(ry)
pagin, pagan
paginashen, page(gination)
pagint, pageant
pagonism, pagan(ism)
pagun, pagan
pai, pay / pie / pi
paibul, pay(yable)
paid, PAST TENSE FOR THE WORD "PAY" (or see pad) "prefixes: pre/ re/un"
pail,*, BUCKET TYPE VESSEL (or see pal/ pale/pall)
pain,*,ned,nful,nfully,nfulness,nless, nlessly,nlessness, INTERPRETATION BY THE BRAIN FROM NERVE

ENDINGS SENSING HARM/THREAT (or see pane/pine)
paint,*,ted,ting,table,ter, MANMADE OR NATURAL BASED COLORANT, VIVID DESCRIPTION "prefixes: re/under"
pair,*,red,ring, TWO IDENTICAL/SIMILAR ITEMS TOGETHER (or see par/parr/pare/pear) "prefixes: un"
pairadox, paradox
pairalise, paralyze
pairudox, paradox
pait, paid
paj, page
pajamas, SLEEPING GARMENTS
pajenashen, page(gination)
pajenate, page(ginate)
pajense, patience / patient(s)
pajent, pageant
pajinashen, page(gination)
pajint, pageant
pakd, pact / pack(ed)
pakeg, pack(age)
paket, packet
pakij, pack(age)
pakt, pact / pack(ed)
pakut, packet
pal,*,lled,lling, A FRIEND, SOMEONE YOU ENJOY HANGING OUT WITH (or see pail/pale/pall)
palace,*, DWELLING OF ROYALTY
palas, palace
palate,table,tableness,tability,tably,tal, tally,tize, ROOF OF THE MOUTH AS A SENSOR (or see pallet/palette/pallid) "prefixes: un"
pale,*,ed,ling,lish,ely,eness,llid,llidly, llidity, DIM/WAN, STAKE WITH SHARP END, SPACE WITHIN A FIXED BOUNDARY (or see pail/pal/pall)
paled, pale(d) / palate / palette / pallet / pallid
paleduble, palate(table)
paleintology, paleontology
palenate, pollinate
paleo, PREFIX INDICATING "EARLY/ANCIENT/PREHISTORIC" MOST OFTEN MODIFIES THE WORD
paleontology,gies, SCIENCE CONCERNED WITH ALL LIFE IN THE PAST
paleredy, polar(ity)
palerity, polar(ity)
pales, palace / police / pale(s)

palesh, polish
palesy, policy
palet, palate / palette / pallet / pallid
paletical, politic(al)
palette,*, PAINTER'S BOARD, VARIETY OF COLORS/TECHNIQUES (or see pallet/palate)
paleuntology, paleontology
palid, pallid / palate / palette / pallet
paliduble, palate(table)
paligamus, polygamy(mous)
paligemy, polygamy
paligine, polygyny
palin, pollen
palinize, pollen(ize)
palip, polyp
palise, palace
palish, polish
palisy, policy
palit, palate / palette / pallet / polite / pallid
palitasize, politic(ize)
palite, palate / palette / pallet / polite / pallid
palitecal, politic(al)
palituble, palate(table)
pall,*, EVOKES A DULL/OPPRESSIVE ATMOSPHERE, COVERING FOR A COFFIN (or see palor pale/pail)
pallet,*,tize,tized,tizing, PLATFORM TO HOLD GOODS, A TOOL, IN A CLOCK/WATCH, POTTER'S TOOL (or see palette/palate/pallid)
pallid,dly,dness, LACKS COLOR (or see palette/palate/pallet)
palm,*, THE HAND, A PLANT
palpitate,*,ed,ting,tion, PULSATE, TREMBLE
palt, pale(d)
palud, pallid
paluduble, palate(table)
paluse, palace
palushen, pollute(tion)
palut, palate / palette / pallet / pollute
palutent, pollute(tant)
palutics, politic(s)
palution, pollute(tion)
palygamus, polygamy(mous)
palyginy, polygyny
palyintology, paleontology
pam, palm
pamendo, pimento
pament, pay(ment)
pamento, pimento

pamflet, pamphlet
pamint, pay(ment)
pamphlet,*, PUBLICATION CONSISTING OF FOLDED PIECES OF PAPER WITH TEXT
pamplet, pamphlet
pamunt, pay(ment)
pan,*,nned,nning, FLAT METAL ITEM WITH SIDES, A COOKING UTENSIL, PREFIX INDICATING 'ALL' MOST OFTEN MODIFIES THE WORD (or see pane/pain)
pancho, poncho
pancreas,atic,atin, PART OF THE STOMACH
pancreus, pancreas
pand, pond / pant
panda,*, A BLACK/WHITE BEAR
pandees, pant(ies)
pander, ponder
pandilunes, pantaloon(s)
pandre, pantry
pandulunes, pantaloon(s)
pane,*, FRAME TO PLACE GLASS/PHOTOGRAPHS, DIAMOND FACE (or see pain)
panek, panic
panel,*,led,ling,list, FLAT SHEET USED FOR COVER/DECORATION, PEOPLE WORKING AS A GROUP TO MAKE A DECISION
panemine, pantomime
panensula, peninsula
paneramic, panorama(mic)
panic,*,cked,cking,cky, SUDDEN OVERWHELMING FEAR WHICH CAUSES REACTION
panik, panic
panil, panel
panimine, pantomime
paninsula, peninsula
paniramic, panorama(mic)
pankreus, pancreas
panol, panel
panomine, pantomime
panorama,*,mic,mically, ABILITY TO VIEW/OBSERVE ENTIRE EVENT/SCENE WITHOUT OBSTRUCTION
panoramic, panorama(mic)
pant,*,ted,ting,ties, BREATH/GASP HEAVILY, ARTICLE OF CLOTHING FOR LEGS/ LOWER TORSO, UNDERWEAR (or see paint/pan(nned)) "prefixes: under"

pantaloon,*, LOOSE FITTING PANTS
pantees, pant(ies)
panteloons, pantaloon(s)
pantemime, pantomime
panther,*, LARGE WILD CAT
panthur, panther
pantilunes, pantaloon(s)
pantimime, pantomime
pantomime,*,ed,ming,mist,mic, COMMUNICATE WITH GESTURES, NON SPEAKING PERFORMANCE
pantre, pantry
pantry,ries, A FOOD STORAGE CLOSET/ROOM
pantu, panda
pantulunes, pantaloon(s)
pantumime, pantomime
pantys, pant(ies)
panul, panel
panulist, panel(ist)
panumine, pantomime
paode, peyote
paodur, powder
paond, pound
paonse, pounce
paont, pound
paote, peyote
papaya,*, A FRUIT
papcorn, popcorn
paper,*,red,ring,rer,riness,ry,rless, USABLE SHEET OF MATERIAL FOR INK/PAINT, MADE OF WOOD/HEMP PULP, TO APPLY PAPER
papier mache', DIFFERENT TYPES OF PAPER PUT TOGETHER, COLLAGE OF PAPER (or see paper)
papir, paper / papier mache'
papreka, paprika
paprika, *, A SPICE
papur, paper / papier mache'
papyu, papaya
par,rred,rring,rity, AN AVERAGE OR NORMAL, BALANCE EQUALLY, A PREFIX, SPORTS TERM (or see parr/pear/pair/pare) "prefixes: sub"
para, PREFIX INDICATING "BESIDE/BEYOND" MOST OFTEN MODIFIES THE WORD
parable,*,list, SHORT STORY/SENTENCES WHICH REFLECTS HUMAN EMOTIONAL WISDOMS (or see parabola)
parabola,*,lic, BOWL SHAPE (or see parable)

parachute,*,ed,ting,tist, DEVICE FOR DROPPING FROM GREAT HEIGHT/PLANES
parade,*,ed,ding, AN ORGANIZED CEREMONIAL MARCH DOWN STREETS OF A CITY
paradigm,*,matic, MAKING RELATIVE COMPARISONS, CATEGORIZING INTO A DEFINED SET
paradox,xes,xical,xically, A CONTRADICTION OF TERMS, WORDS/ACTIONS WHICH CANCEL EACH OTHER OUT
paraffin,nic, MELTABLE/WAXY SUBSTANCE
paragraph,*, SEVERAL SENTENCES TOGETHER SUPPORTING A THEME
parakeet,*, A TROPICAL BIRD
paralasis, paralysis
paralel, parallel
parallel,*,led,ling, EACH GOING THE SAME DIRECTION, SIDE BY SIDE, BELONG TOGETHER "prefixes: un"
parallyzed, paralyze(d)
paralusis, paralysis
paralysis,ytic,yze, LOOSE ABILITY TO MOVE VOLUNTARILY
paralyze,*,ed,zing,ysis,ytic,ytically, LOOSE ABILITY TO MOVE VOLUNTARILY
paramater, parameter / perimeter
paramedic,*,cal, MEDICAL PROFESSIONAL WHO TRAVELS TO GATHER INJURED/SICK PEOPLE
parameter,*,tric,trical, A DEFINED BOUNDARY WHICH BELONGS AS A UNIT, A MATH EXPRESSION
parametic, paramedic
paramiter, parameter / perimeter
paramount,tly,tcy, UPMOST IN IMPORTANCE, AT THE TOP, SUPERIOR TO ANYTHING ELSE
paranoia,id,ic, FEAR WITHOUT APPARENT REASON
paranoyd, paranoia(id)
paraplegia,ic, PARALYSIS OF LOWER TORSO, LOWER HALF OF BODY CANNOT BE MOVED VOLUNTARILY
parasite,*,tic,tical,tically,ticide,ticidal, tism,tize,tology,tosis, TAKES NOURISHMENT FROM ANOTHER WITHOUT PERMISSION/WILLINGNESS FROM HOST "prefixes: endo"

parate, parade
paratrooper,*, ONE WHO JUMPS FROM PLANE WITH A PARACHUTE
parcel,*,led,ling, A SMALL PACKAGE, BOXED ITEMS, SMALL SECTION OF LAND, TO SECTION OFF
parch,hed,hment, DRY, NEEDS MOISTURE
parcht, parch(ed)
parcle, parcel
pard, part / pair(ed) / pare(d)
pardake, partake
parde, party
pardekul, particle
pardes, party(ties)
pardesapate, participate
pardesubate, participate
pardezan, partisan
pardikul, particle
pardisubant, participate(ant)
pardisupate, participate
pardizan, partisan
pardner, partner
pardnur, partner
pardon,*,ned,ning,nable,nably, FORGIVE "prefixes: un"
pardukle, particle
pardun, pardon
parduzen, partisan
pardy, party
pare,*,ed,ring, TRIM, CUT-OFF (or see par/parr/pair/pear)
parebolic, parabola(lic) / parable(lic)
paredime, paradigm
paredoks, paradox
parefen, paraffin
pareferul, peripheral
paregraf, paragraph
paregraph, paragraph
pareid, parade
parekeet, parakeet
parel, peril
parelel, parallel
parelize, paralyze
paremedic, paramedic
paremeter, perimeter / parameter
paremider, perimeter / parameter
paremount, paramount
parend, parent
parendul, parent(al)
pareneul, perennial
parenial, perennial
parenoid, paranoia(id)
parense, parent(s)

parent,*,ted,ting,tal,tage, PROVIDER OF DNA TO BIRTHED OFFSPRING "prefixes: bi"
parenthesis,es,etic,tical,tically,ize,izes, ized,izing, TWO MARKS (SHAPED LIKE CRESCENT MOONS) ON EITHER SIDE OF WORDS INSERTED INTO A SENTENCE
parepheral, peripheral
pareplegic, paraplegia(ic)
parescope, periscope
paresh, parish / perish
paretruper, paratrooper
parews, peruse
parfa, parfait
parfae, parfait
parfait, DESSERT
pari, PREFIX INDICATING "EQUAL" MOST OFTEN MODIFIES THE WORD
paribolic, parabola(lic) / parable(lic)
paride, parity / parody / parrot(y)
paridime, paradigm
paridokical, paradox(ical)
paridoks, paradox
parifen, paraffin
parifuril, peripheral
parigraf, paragraph
parikeet, parakeet
parilel, parallel
parilize, paralyze
parimiter, perimeter / parameter
parimount, paramount
parind, parent
parinoid, paranoia(id)
parinse, parent(s)
parint, parent
parintal, parent(al)
parinthases, parenthesis
paripheral, peripheral
pariplegic, paraplegia(ic)
pariscope, periscope
parish,hes,hioner, CHURCH CONGREGATION (or see perish)
parishute, parachute
parisite, parasite
paritrooper, paratrooper
parituper, paratrooper
parity, THE ACT OF CUTTING/DIVIDING (or see parody/parrot(y))
park,*,ked,king,ker, LAND FOR PUBLIC REST/RECREATION, SITUATE A VEHICLE WHERE IT WILL BE IMMOBILE FOR A PERIOD OF TIME
parka,*, HEAVY COAT WITH FUR

parkay, parquet
parkeet, parakeet
parket, parquet
parkt, park(ed)
parku, parka
parodoks, paradox
parody,dies,died,dying,dic,dical,dically, dist, A STORY MAKING LIGHT OF A SERIOUS DRAMA/SITUATION (or see parity/parrot(y))
parogative, prerogative
parokside, peroxide
parole,ed,ling, UNDER COURT SUPERVISION
parona, piranha
paroose, peruse
parot, parrot
paroxside, peroxide
parportional, proportion(al)
parquet,*,try, TYPE OF WOOD FLOORING
parr, YOUNG FISH (or see par/pare/ pear/pair)
parrot,*,ted,ting,ter,ty, A TROPICAL BIRD, TO REPEAT LIKE THE BIRD (or see parody)
parsel, parcel
parsen, parson
parshal, partial
parshul, partial
parsil, parcel
parsin, parson
parsle, parcel
parsley, AN EDIBLE HERB
parsly, parsley
parsnip,*, VEGETABLE
parson,*,nage,nic,nical, IN CHARGE OF CHURCH PARISH
parsul, parcel
parsun, parson
part,*,ted,ting,tition,titioned,titioning, SELECT PART OF THE WHOLE, LET GO OF "prefixes: under"
partake,*,king,took, TAKE PART, BE INVOLVED IN AN ASPECT OF
partekul, particle
partekularly, particular(ly)
parten, pardon
partequler, particular
partequlurly, particular(ly)
partesan, partisan
partesapate, participate
parteshen, partition

partial,*,led,lling,lly,lity,lities,lness, PORTION/SECTION FROM THE WHOLE, FOCUS ON ONE
participate,*,ed,ting,tion,ant,tive,tor, tory, WORK/PLAY WITH A GROUP, BE A PART OF
particle,*, OF SMALL PIECE/FRAGMENT IN SCIENTIFIC TERMS, PERTAINS TO ENGLISH GRAMMAR
particular,rate,rity,rities,rism,rist,ristic, rize,rization,rly,ate, REFERRING SPECIFICALLY TO A SMALL PIECE/ FRAGMENT/ PART
partiel, partial
partikquler, particular
partikul, particle
partikularly, particular(ly)
partin, pardon
partiquler, particular
partisan,*, SUPPORTS A SPECIFIC POLITICAL DOGMA
partisapate, participate
partisapunt, participate(ant)
partishen, partition
partisupent, participate(ant)
partition,*,ned,ning,ner,nment, SEGMENT OFF, DIVIDE UP INTO PARTS "prefixes: re"
partner,*,red,ring, ASSOCIATE, RELATIONS BETWEEN TWO PEOPLE/ GROUPS, ONE OF TWO PEOPLE
partook, PAST TENSE FOR THE WORD "PARTAKE", BE INVOLVED IN
partreg, partridge
partridge,*, A GAME BIRD
partrij, partridge
partucle, particle
partuk, partook
partukle, particle
partun, pardon
partusen, partisan
party,ties,tied,tying,yer, PEOPLE GATHERING FOR FUN/SPORT/ LAUGHTER/SPECIFIC REASON "prefixes: intra"
paruchute, parachute
parudime, paradigm
parudoks, paradox
parugraf, paragraph
parukeet, parakeet
parul, peril
parulel, parallel
parulize, paralyze
parumont, paramount

parunt, parent
paruplegic, paraplegia(ic)
paruse, peruse
parushute, parachute
parusite, parasite
paruskope, periscope
parutruper, paratrooper
paruze, peruse
parzly, parsley
parznip, parsnip
pas, pass / pause / pase
pasable, pass(able)
pasage, passage
pascripshen, prescript(ion)
pasd, past / paste / pass(ed)
pasdasheo, pistachio
pasdel, pastel
pasder, pastor / pasture
pasderize, pasteurize
pasdirize, pasteurize
pasdor, pastor / pasture
pasdrame, pastrami
pasdre, pastry
pasdree, pastry
pasdrome, pastrami
pasdur, pastor / pasture
pasduresashen, pasteurize(zation)
pasdurize, pasteurize
pase, pace
paseble, pass(able)
pasedge, passage
pasef, passive
pasefikashen, pacify(fication)
pasefy, pacify
paseg, passage
pasej, passage
pasenger, passenger
pases, possess / pass(es) / pause(s)
paseshen, position / possess(ion)
pasesuf, possess(ive)
pasev, passive
pashen, passion
pashendly, patient(ly)
pashenit, passion(ate)
pashens, patience / patient(s)
pashin, passion
pashindly, patient(ly)
pashins, patience / patient(s)
pashinute, passion(ate)
pashun, passion
pashunit, passion(ate)
pasif, passive
pasific, pacific
pasification, pacify(fication)

pasify, pacify
pasig, passage
pasij, passage
pasinger, passenger
pasinjur, passenger
pasion, passion
pasionate, passion(ate)
pasishen, position
pasition, position
pasive, passive
paskrepshen, prescript(ion)
paskripshen, prescript(ion)
paskription, prescript(ion)
pass,sses,ssed,ssing,ssable,ssably, SKIP FROM ONE TO THE NEXT, MOVE ALONG WITHOUT STOPPING, TO GO AROUND WITHOUT STOPPING "prefixes: over/sur"
passage,*,ged,ging,eway, A NARROW WAY THROUGH, INTERCHANGE, CORRIDOR
passenger,*, PEOPLE RIDING ON/IN A VEHICLE/VESSEL TO SOME DESTINATION
passion,*,nate,nately,nal,nality,nless, DEEPLY DEVOTED DESIRE FOR SOMETHING "prefixes: dis"
passive,ely,eness,vity, HAS NO REACTION TO ACTION, DOESN'T GENERATE ACTION
past, PAST TENSE FOR THE WORD "PASS", YESTERDAY AND BEYOND, BACK THERE (or see pass(ed)/paste)
pasta, PASTE USED TO MAKE NOODLES
pastachio, pistachio
pastasheo, pistachio
paste,*,ed,ting,ty, A THICK/VISCOUS LIQUID TEXTURE MADE OF A VARIETY OF MATERIAL (or see past)
pastel,*,list, PALE IN COLOR, TYPE OF PAINTING
paster, pastor / pasture
pasteurize,*,ed,zing,zation,zer, HIGH TEMPERATURE OVER PERIOD OF TIME TO KILL BACTERIA
pastirize, pasteurize
pastor,*,rship, ONE IN CHARGE OF A CHURCH CONGREGATION (or see pasture)
pastrami, PICKLED BEEF
pastrome, pastrami
pastry,ries, DESSERT, BAKED GOODS

pasture,*,ed,ring,rage,rer, GRASS FIELD USED FOR GRAZING ANIMALS (or see pastor)
pasturesashen, pasteurize(zation)
pasturize, pasteurize
pasuble, pass(able)
pasuf, passive
pasufi, pacify
pasuges, passage(s)
pasuj, passage
pasuve, passive
pat,*,tted,tting, TO LIGHTLY/GENTLY SLAP/STROKE USING THE HANDS/ FEET (or see paid/pate')
pata, pate'
patado, potato
pataseum, potassium
patato, potato
patch,hes,hed,hing,hy, COVER A HOLE WITH SOMETHING, PROTECTION FOR OPENING
pate',*, A PASTE (or see paid/pat(tty))
pateet, petite
patel, paddle
paten, patent
patenchul, potential
patenshil, potential
patent,*,ted,ting,ncy,tly,tability,table, tor, LEGAL OWNERSHIP OF A PROPERTY/IDEA/INVENTION
patential, potential
pateo, patio
paterbed, perturb(ed)
patern, pattern
paternal,lly,lism,list,listic,nity, MALE PARENT
pateshen, petition
patet, petite
path,*,hway, A DEFINED TRAIL
pathalogical, pathology(gical)
pathetic,cally, MISERY, INHUMANE QUALITY, UNAGREEABLE CONDITION
patho, PREFIX INDICATING "DISEASE" MOST OFTEN MODIFIES THE WORD
pathology,gies,gic,gical,gically, SCIENCE FIELD WHICH STUDIES DISEASE
patience, RELAX AND ALLOW A NATURAL COURSE (or see patient(s))
patient,*,tly, PAST TENSE FOR THE WORD "PATIENCE", PERSON UNDERGOING MEDICAL CARE (or see patience) "prefixes: im/in"

patil, paddle
patina,*, CHEMICAL APPLICATION FOR METAL
patinchul, potential
patint, patent
patintial, potential
patio,*, OUTSIDE AREA NEAR DOOR INTO DWELLING
patirn, pattern
patirnal, paternal
patishen, petition
patite, petite
patition, petition
patle, paddle
patlok, padlock
patluc, potluck
patreark, patriarch
patrearkul, patriarch(al)
patreit, patriot / patriate
patren, patron
patrenize, patron(ize)
patreotic, patriot(ic)
patreut, patriot / patriate
patriarch,hal,hy,hies, MALE WHO IS HEAD OF HOUSEHOLD, DOMINANT MALE
patriate,*,ed,ting, TAKE CONTROL OF COUNTRY UNDER FORMER COLONIAL POWER (or see patriot)
patrinize, patron(ize)
patriot,*,tic,tically,tism, SOMEONE WITH STRONG EMOTIONAL TIES TO THEIR COUNTRY (or see patriate)
patrol,*,lled,lling, ONE WHO COVERS PRESCRIBED/DESIGNATED AREA FOR SECURITY, TO PATROL
patroleum, petrol(eum)
patron,*,nal,nage,nize,nized,nizing, nizingly, SOMEONE WHO PROVIDES SUPPORT FOR GROUPS OF PEOPLE IN NEED, CLIENT
patronise, patron(ize)
patrude, protrude
patrun, patron
patrunize, patron(ize)
patrushen, protrude(usion)
patryarkle, patriarch(al)
patse, patsy
patsy,sies, THE SCAPEGOAT, TAKES THE BLAME
pattern,*,ned,ning, A SHAPE MADE TO REPRESENT AN ORIGINAL TO BE REPRODUCED, ORIGINAL TO BE REPRODUCED

patty,tties, FLAT/ROUND SHAPE (or see paddy)
patunia, petunia
patunya, petunia
paturbed, perturb(ed)
paturn, pattern
paturnal, paternal
paty, patty / paddy
pauble, pay(yable)
pauch, pouch
pauder, powder
pauer, power
paulanize, pollen(ize)
paulen, pollen
paulenize, pollen(ize)
pauletics, politic(s)
paulip, polyp
paum, palm
paun, pawn
paund, pound / pawn(ed) / pond
paunder, pound(er) / ponder
pauns, pounce / pound(s) / pawn(s)
paur, pay(er) / power
paus, pause / paw(s)
pauschur, posture
pausder, posture
pausdur, posture
pause,*,ed,sing,sal, A BRIEF MOMENT OF SILENCE BETWEEN, BRIEF HESITATION (or see paw(s))
paustr, posture
pausture, posture
paut, pout
pauvurde, poverty
pauwer, power
pauwr, power
pauzder, posture
pave,*,ed,ving,ement, TO LAY/PREPARE A TRAIL/ROAD/PATH FOR SMOOTHER TRAVEL, APPLY A COMPOSITE ON TOP OF THE GROUND
paverdy, poverty
pavershen, pervert(rsion)
pavilion,*, SMALL ADDITION TO A LARGER BUILDING WHICH IS NORMALLY EXPOSED TO THE ELEMENTS
pavillion, pavilion
pavmint, pave(ment)
pavt, pave(d)
pavurted, pervert(ed)
paw,*,wed,wing, ANIMAL FOOT
pawer, power

pawir, power
pawlen, pollen
pawn,*,ned,ning, BORROW MONEY AGAINST AN ARTICLE FOR LATER RETRIEVAL, TO PLEDGE
pawur, power
paxs, pack(s)
pay,es,aid,ying,yment,yable,yee,yer, TO GIVE MONEY IN EXCHANGE FOR GOODS/SERVICES (or see pad/paid/ pie) "prefixes: pre/re"
payd, paid
payleontology, paleontology
payn, pain / pane / pine
paynt, paint / pane(d) / pain(ed)
payode, peyote
payote, peyote
payst, paste
payt, paid
pazd, past / paste / pass(ed)
pazdel, pastel
pazdry, pastry
pazefy, pacify
pazenjer, passenger
pazinger, passenger
pazishen, position
pazt, past / paste / pass(ed)
pe, pee / pay
pea,*, LEGUME/FOOD (or see pee/ peace/piece)
peace,eful,efully,efulness,eable, eableness,eably, ATTITUDE/AIRE OF CALM/ QUIET (or see piece)
peach,hes,hy, A FRUIT
peacock,*, A COLORFUL BIRD
peak,*,ked,king,kedness, THE CLIMAX/ HIGHEST POINT OF A WAVE/ OBJECT, MAXIMUM POINT (or see peek/pique)
peakok, peacock
peal, SOUNDS/RINGS (or see peel)
peano, piano
peanut,*, A LEGUME, SMALL NUT
pear,*, A FRUIT (or see pare/pair)
pearl,*,ly,lized, PRODUCED BY OYSTER, HAVING THE QUALITIES OF A PEARL
peasant,*,try, SIMPLE PERSON WHO LIVES OFF THE LAND (or see pheasant)
peasful, peace(ful)
peat,ty, DRIED PLANTS PARTIALLY DECAYED (or see pit)
peave, peeve
pebble,*, TINY ROCKS/STONES

pebel, pebble
peber, pepper
pebil, pebble
pebir, pepper
pebl, pebble
pebol, pebble
pebul, pebble
pebur, pepper
pec, peck / pick / pig / pique / peak / peek
pecalo, piccolo
pecan,*, AN EDIBLE NUT
pecd, pick(ed) / peck(ed) / peak(ed)
pecdorul, pectoral / pictorial
pech, peach / pitch
peched, pitch(ed)
pecher, pitcher / picture
pechr, pitcher / picture
peck,*,ked,king,ker, BIRDS USING THEIR BILLS TO STAB/JAB, A MEASUREMENT OF WEIGHT (or see pick/pig/pique/peak/peek)
pecnic, picnic
pecok, peacock
pecon, pecan
pecs, SHORT FOR PECTORAL MUSCLES(or see peck(s))
pecsher, picture / pitcher
pect, pick(ed) / peck(ed) / peak(ed)
pecten,*, A SCIENTIFIC PROCESS (or see pectin)
pectin, WAXY SUBSTANCE COLLECTED FROM WALLS OF PLANTS, USED TO STIFFEN (or see pecten)
pecton, pectin / pecten
pectoral,*, OF THE CHEST/BREAST, FINS ON FISH
pectorial, pectoral / pictorial
pectun, pectin / pecten
pecturul, pectoral
peculiar,rly,rity,rities, STRANGE, UNUSUAL
ped, PREFIX INDICATING "FOOT/CHILD" MOST OFTEN MODIFIES THE WORD
pedagogy,gies,gogue,gic,gical,gically, gics, ART/SCIENCE OF TEACHING, AN EDUCATOR
pedagree, pedigree
pedakure, pedicure
pedal,*,led,ling, USE FOOT/LEVER TO CREATE MOVEMENT/ACTION (or see petal/peddle)

peddle,*,ed,ling,er, MOVING/GOING ABOUT SELLING WARES/GOODS (or see petal/pedal)
pede, petty / pity
pedeatrician, pediatrician
pedeatrics, pediatrics
pedeatrishen, pediatrician
pedecoat, petticoat
pedegogy, pedagogy
pedegree, pedigree
pedekote, petticoat
pedekure, pedicure
pedel, pedal / petal / peddle
pedestal,*,led,ling, A BASE/STAND/PODIUM
pedestle, pedestal
pedestrian,*, ONE WHO TRAVELS BY FOOT/ON THEIR FEET, SOMEONE WHO IS WALKING
pedeutrishen, pediatrician
pedi, PREFIX INDICATING "FOOT/CHILD" MOST OFTEN MODIFIES THE WORD
pediatrician,*, DOCTOR FOR CHILDREN
pediatrics, SCIENCE THAT WORKS WITH CHILDREN
pediatrishen, pediatrician
pedicoat, petticoat
pedicure,*,rist, WORKING WITH THE FEET
pedid, pet(tted)
pedigogy, pedagogy
pedigree,*,eed, HAS LEGAL PAPERS SHOWING ANCESTRY
pedikote, petticoat
pedil, pedal / petal / peddle
pedir, peter
pedistal, pedestal
pedle, pedal / petal / peddle
pedo, PREFIX INDICATING "FOOT/CHILD" MOST OFTEN MODIFIES THE WORD
pedol, pedal / petal / peddle
pedrafication, petrify(fication)
pedrify, petrify
pedrol, petrol
pedroleim, petrol(eum)
pedrufy, petrify
peds, pet(s)
pedugogy, pedagogy
pedugree, pedigree
pedul, pedal / petal / peddle
pedur, peter

pedustal, pedestal
pedy, petty / pity
pee,*,eed,eeing, TO URINATE (or see pea)
peech, peach
peed, peat / pee(d)
peek,*,ked,king,ker, TO GET A QUICK GLIMPSE OF, TO LOOK QUICKLY (or see peak)
peekt, peek(ed)
peel,*,led,ling,ler, TO REMOVE OUTER LAYER/SKIN
peenk, pink
peep,*,ped,ping,per, LOOK/GLIMPSE INTO
peeple, people
peer,*,rless,rlessly,rlessness, OF THE SAME AGE/RANK/STATUS, TO FOCUS YOUR GAZE FARAWAY, LOOK INTO (or see pyre/pierce/pier(s))
peeroet, pirouette
peers, pier(s) / peer(s) / pierce
pees, pea(s) / peace / piece / pee(s)
peeve,*,vish,vishly,vishness, IRRITATE/AGGRAVATE
pef, peeve
pefs, peeve(s)
peg,*,gged,gging, A SPIKE OF ANY MATERIAL USED TO HOLD UP/DOWN SOMETHING "prefixes: un"
pegamus, pajamas
pegated, picket(ed)
pegen, pigeon
peget, picket
pegul, pickle
pegy, pig(ggy) / pick(y)
pein, pain / pane
peiny, peony
peiper, paper
peiper mache, paper mache
peir, pier / peer / pyre
peirce, pierce
peirse, pierce / pier(s) / peer(s)
pejamus, pajamas
pejen, pigeon
pek, peck / pick / pig / pique / peak / peek
pekalo, piccolo
pekan, pecan
pekel, pickle
peker, pick(er) / peck(er)
pekewler, peculiar
pekit, picket

peknik, picnic
pekok, peacock
pekol, pickle
pekon, pecan
peksher, picture / pitcher
pektin, pectin / pecten
pektoral, pectoral / pictorial
pektun, pectin / pecten
pekture, picture / pitcher
pekul, pickle
pekuler, peculiar
pekuleur, peculiar
pekur, pick(er) / peck(er)
peky, pick(y)
pel, peel / peal / pill / pale
pelacan, pelican
pelaf, pilaf
pelage, pillage
pelakan, pelican
pelar, pillar
pelaredy, polar(ity)
pelej, pillage
pelekan, pelican
peler, pillar
pelese, police
pelet, pellet
peletical, politic(al)
pelgrem, pilgrim
pelgremege, pilgrim(age)
pelgrim, pilgrim
pelican,*, A LARGE BIRD WHO EATS FISH
peligamus, polygamy(mous)
peligamy, polygamy
pelit, pellet / polite
pelitecal, politic(al)
pellet,*, ANYTHING SMALL/ROUND/ HARD
pellow, pillow
pelminary, pulmonary
pelof, pilaf
pelot, pellet
pelow, pillow
pelt,*,ted,ting, ANYTHING SMALL/ ROUND/HARD HITTING SOMETHING, THE HIDE/HAIR FROM SMALL ANIMAL
peluch, pillage
peludge, pillage
peluge, pillage
pelukin, pelican
pelushen, pollute(tion)
pelut, pellet / pollute
pelutent, pollute(tant)

pelution, pollute(tion)
pelvek, pelvic
pelves, pelvis
pelvic, LARGE BONE ON LOWER TORSO WHERE LEGS ARE ATTACHED
pelvis,es,ic, LARGE BONE ON LOWER TORSO WHERE LEGS ARE ATTACHED
pelygamus, polygamy(mous)
pelygamy, polygamy
peminto, pimento
pemp, pimp
pempul, pimple
pemt, pimp(ed)
pen,*,nned,nning, INSTRUMENT WITH INK FOR WRITING, HAVING BEEN WRITTEN/COMPOSED, FEMALE SWAN, CAGE FOR PIGS (or see pin/ pent)
penacle, pentacle / pinnacle
penada, pinata
penagon, pentagon
penagram, pentagram
penakle, pinnacle / pentacle
penal,lize,lizes,lized,lizing,lization,lly,lty, lties, PUNISHMENT
penasilen, penicillin
penatentiary, penitentiary
penatinchory, penitentiary
penatrable, penetrable
penatrashen, penetrate(tion)
penatrate, penetrate
penc, pink
pench, pinch
penchant, DESIRE MOSTLY, STRONG LIKING FOR, BIAS
penchers, pinch(ers) / pincers
pencil,*,led,ling, WOODEN/GRAPHITE WRITING INSTRUMENT, TO USE TO WRITE
pendalum, pendulum
pendant,dent,*, ITEM HANGING FROM SOMETHING, SUSPENDED ITEM
pendelum, pendulum
pending, ACTION IN PROCESS AIMED FOR COMPLETION
pendlum, pendulum
pendo, pinto
pendulum,*,lar, SUSPENDED FROM A FIXED POINT, ENDS FREE TO SEEK BALANCE/EQUILIBRIUM
peneal gland, pineal gland
penecilin, penicillin
penecle, pinnacle / pentacle

penegram, pentagram
penensula, peninsula
peneol gland, pineal gland
penes, penis
penesilin, penicillin
penetrable,bility,eness,ly, EXPOSED, ACCEPT/EXPERIENCE INCOMING PENETRATION, BOUNDARIES ALLOWING FOR INFILTRATION
penetrate,*,ed,ting,tion,ant,tive,tively, tiveness, ENTER/PIERCE/AFFECT "prefixes: inter"
pengalum, pendulum
pengilum, pendulum
penguin,*, BIRD OF THE ANTARCTIC
pengwen, penguin
peni, penny
penial gland, pineal gland
penicillin,ium,ia, ANTIBIOTIC DERIVED FROM A MOLD, USED FOR KILLING BACTERIA
penikul, pentacle / pinnacle
peninsula,*,ar, FINGER/PORTION OF LAND JUTTING FROM THE MAINLAND, SURROUNDED BY WATER
penis, MALE ORGAN USED FOR COPULATION/URINATION (or see penny(nies))
penitenchery, penitentiary
penitentiary,ries, PRISON, ROMAN CATHOLIC TERM
penitintiary, penitentiary
penjalum, pendulum
penjulem, pendulum
penk, pink
penkwen, penguin
penky, pink(y)
pennicilin, penicillin
penny,nnies, A U.S. COIN
pennyul gland, pineal gland
pensel, pencil
pensers, pincers / pinch(ers)
penshen, pension
penshent, penchant
pensil, pencil
pension,*,nable,nary,naries,ner, A REGULARLY ALLOTTED ALOWANCE
pensul, pencil
pent, CLOSED OFF, SHUT IN (or see pen(ned)/pint)
pentacle,*, A FIVE POINT STAR
pentagon,nal,nally, U.S. OFFICE OF DEFENSE

pentagram,*, A PENTACLE, FIVE POINT STAR
pentalum, pendulum
pentegram, pentagram
pentigon, pentagon
pentilum, pendulum
penting, pending
pento, pinto
pentucle, pentacle / pinnacle
pentugon, pentagon
pentulem, pendulum
penud, peanut
penugon, pentagon
penugram, pentagram
penukel, pentacle / pinnacle
penulize, penal(ize)
penulty, penal(ty)
penus, penis
penusilen, penicillin
penut, peanut
penutrashen, penetrate(tion)
penutruble, penetrable
peny, penny
penyada, pinata
penyoda, pinata
peode, peyote
peol, pail / pale / peel
peony,nies, A FLOWER
people,*, HUMANS
peote, peyote
pep,*,pped,pping,ppy, VIGOR/ENERGY, ENERGETIC (or see peep)
pepal, people
pepe, pep(ppy)
peper, pepper
pepil, people
pepir, pepper
pepiu, papaya
pepl, pebble / people
peple, people
peporshenal, proportion(al)
pepper,*,red,ring,ry, A SPICE/ VEGETABLE, TO BE SPRINKLED/ PELTED BY
pepul, people
pepur, pepper
pepy, pep(ppy)
pequleur, peculiar
per, BY/THROUGH/EACH, PREFIX INDICATING "COMPLETELY/ THOROUGHLY" MOST OFTEN MODIFIES THE WORD (or see peer/ purr/pear/pier/pair/pare)
perabolic, parabola(lic) / parable(lic)

perabul, parable
perade, parade
peradime, paradigm
peradox, paradox
perafen, paraffin
peragative, prerogative
peragraf, paragraph
perakeet, parakeet
peralasis, paralysis
peralel, parallel
peralises, paralysis
peralusis, paralysis
peramaunt, paramount
peramedur, parameter / perimeter
perametic, paramedic
perametur, parameter / perimeter
peramid, pyramid
peramitur, parameter / perimeter
peramount, paramount
peranoid, paranoia(id)
peranoyd, paranoia(id)
perant, parent
peraplegic, paraplegia(ic)
perascope, periscope
perashute, parachute
perasite, parasite
perate, parade
peratruper, paratrooper
peraty, parody / parity / parrot(y)
perbendikuler, perpendicular
perceive,*,ed,ving,er, SEE/ UNDERSTAND/KNOW
percent,*,tage,tages,tile,tum, PORTION OF THE WHOLE AMOUNT
percept,tion,tional,tive,tively,tiveness, tivity,tual,tually, TO KNOW/ PERCEIVE WITH THE SENSES
perceptible,bility,bly, KNOW/PERCEIVE WITH SENSES
perceve, perceive
perch,hes,hed,hing, A FISH, WHERE BIRDS ROOST, TINY BUILDING OUTCROP (or see purge)
perchus, purchase / perch(es)
percieve, perceive
percintage, percent(age)
percipatation, precipitate(tion)
percivere, persevere
percrastination, procrastinate
percushen, percussion
percussion,*,nist,ive,ively,iveness, IMPACT BETWEEN TWO BODIES OF MATTER, MUSICAL INSTRUMENT GROUP

pereadontek, periodontic
pereadontist, periodontist
pereatic, periodic
pereaudic, periodic
perebolic, parabola(lic) / parable(lic)
perebul, parable
perechute, parachute
peredime, paradigm
peredox, paradox
peredy, parody / parity / parrot(y)
pereferul, peripheral
perefin, paraffin
peregraf, paragraph
perekeet, parakeet
perel, peril
perelel, parallel
perelize, paralyze
peremedic, paramedic
peremont, paramount
peremownt, paramount
perend, parent
perenial, perennial
perennial,*,lly, EXISTS/GROWS ALL YEAR LONG
perenoya, paranoia
perens, parent(s)
perent, parent
pereod, period
pereodic, periodic / periotic
pereot, period
pereotecul, periodic(al)
pereotic, periodic / periotic
pereotical, periodic(al)
perepheral, peripheral
pereple, parable
pereplegic, paraplegia(ic)
perescope, periscope
peresh, parish / perish
pereshute, parachute
peresite, parasite
peret, parrot
peretruper, paratrooper
pereud, period
pereudonteks, periodontic(s)
pereudontest, periodontist
perfect,*,ted,ting,tion,tness,tible, tionism,tionist,tive,tiveness, tivity, tly,to, GREAT AT THE MOMENT, SYNCHRONOUS, HARMONIC
perfekshen, perfect(ion)
perferted, pervert(ed)
perfeum, perfume
perfikt, perfect
perfium, perfume

perform,*,med,ming,mance,mances, mable,mer, ACT/PLAY OUT/ MOTION/ FUNCTIONABLE "prefixes: over/under"
performence, perform(ance)
perfume,*,ed,ming,ery,eries, SCENT/ SMELL WHICH COMES NATURALLY OR IS APPLIED
pergatory, purgatory
perge, purge
perger, perjure
pergery, perjure(ry)
pergitory, purgatory
pergury, perjure(ry)
pergutory, purgatory
perhaps, COULD BE, LIKELY, POSSIBLE
peri, PREFIX INDICATING "AROUND/ ABOUT" MOST OFTEN MODIFIES THE WORD
periadontist, periodontist
peribolic, parabola(lic) / parable(lic)
peribul, parable
perichute, parachute
peridime, paradigm
peridox, paradox
peridy, parody / parity / parrot(y)
perifen, paraffin
perifuril, peripheral
perigraf, paragraph
perikeet, parakeet
peril,*,led,ling,lous,lously,lousness, CAUTION, GREAT DANGER, HAZARDOUS (or see pearl)
perilel, parallel
perilize, paralyze
perimed, pyramid
perimedic, paramedic
perimeter,*,tric,trical,trically,try, AROUND A PARTICULAR AREA, CIRCUMFERENCE, BOUNDARY/ SIDES (or see parameter)
perimetic, paramedic
perimider, perimeter / parameter
perimiter, perimeter / parameter
perimount, paramount
perind, parent
perinoid, paranoia(id)
perinoya, paranoia
perinse, parent(s)
perint, parent
period,*, A PUNCTUATION MARK, SPAN OF TIME, MENSTRUATION

periodic,cal,cally,city, RECURRING, PREDICTABLE PATTERN (or see periotic)
periodontic,*,tal,ia,ium, SCIENCE/ STUDY OF TEETH/GUMS
periodontist, DENTIST/DOCTOR, OF TEETH
periotic, OF THE EAR (or see periodic)
peripheral,ric,rally,ry,ries, GENERAL EXTERIOR AREA AROUND A NUCLEUS/ CENTER/TOWN, CIRCUMFERENCE
periple, parable
periplegic, paraplegia(ic)
periscope,*,pic,pical, USED IN SUBMARINES/TANKS FOR VIEWING ABOVE THE VESSEL/WATER
perish,hes,hed,hing,hable,hably,hability, hableness, STOP BEING ALIVE, END OF GROWING/BREATHING, BEGIN TO ROT (or see parish)
perisite, parasite
perit, parrot
peritruper, paratrooper
perity, parody / parity / parrot(y)
perje, purge
perjure,*,ed,ring,er,ry,ries,rious,riously, KNOWINGLY MAKE A FALSE STATEMENT UNDER OATH
perkeet, parakeet
perkrastination, procrastinate
perkushen, percussion
perkusion, percussion
perl, pearl
permanence,cy,cies,nt, THE STATE OF BEING PERMANENT/FIXED
permanent,tly,tness,nce, CHEMICAL TREATMENT TO HAIR, FIXED POSITION, NONMOVING "prefixes: semi"
permanins, permanence
permeable,ly,bility, FILTERS/SPREADS/ ABSORBS, FILLS SPACE IN BETWEEN "prefixes: semi"
permeate,*,ed,ting,tion,tive,ance,able, ableness,ably,ability, FILTERS/ SPREADS/ ABSORBS, FILLS SPACE IN BETWEEN
permenant, permanent
permenence, permanence
permeuble, permeable
permiable, permeable
permiate, permeate
permichen, permission

perminet, permanent
permisable, permissible
permisen, permission
permishen, permission
permisive, permissive
permissible,ly,bility, HAVE APPROVAL FOR/OF, ALLOWABLE "prefixes: non"
permission,ible,ive, HAVE APPROVAL FOR/OF
permissive,ely,eness,ion,ible, MORE ALLOWABLE THAN THE NORM
permisuble, permissible
permisuf, permissive
permit,*,tted,tting,tter, RECEIPT/ LICENSE/ALLOWING APPROVAL (or see pyramid)
permited, permit(tted)
permition, permission
permunins, permanence
permunint, permanent
perodox, paradox
perody, parody / parity / parrot(y)
peroet, pirouette
perogative, prerogative
perograf, paragraph
perokside, peroxide
perole, parole
perona, piranha
peront, parent
peroose, peruse
perosity, porosity
peroty, parody / parity / parrot(y)
peroxide,ed,ding, A CHEMICAL
perpel, purple
perpendicular,rity,rly, RIGHT ANGLE TO A PLANE
perpes, purpose
perpesly, purpose(ly)
perpetrate,*,ed,ting,tion,tor, EXECUTE, COMMIT
perpetshuate, perpetual(ate)
perpetual,lly,ate,able,ation,ator,uity, ONGOING, FOREVER, CONTINUOUS
perpetuity,uties, FOREVER, ONGOING, CONTINUOUS
perpil, purple
perpindicular, perpendicular
perpis, purpose
perpisly, purpose(ly)
perpitrate, perpetrate
perpituity, perpetuity
perple, purple
perplex,xes,xed,xing,xingly,xity,xities, NOT UNDERSTANDING, CONFUSED

perpol, purple
perporshenal, proportion(al)
perportional, proportion(al)
perpos, purpose
perposly, purpose(ly)
perposterus, preposterous
perpul, purple
perpus, purpose
perpusle, purpose(ly)
perputrate, perpetrate
perrenial, perennial
pers, pierce / purse / pier(s) / peer(s)
persacute, persecute
persafere, persevere
persanu, person(a)
persarverance, persevere(rance)
persavere, persevere
persbektif, perspective
persbiration, perspiration
persbire, perspire
perscripshen, prescript(ion)
perse, pierce / purse / pier(s) / peer(s)
persebduble, perceptible
persebtf, percept(ive)
persecute,*,ed,ting,tion,tive,tor, AGGRAVATE/HARASS/PUNISH (or see prosecute)
persede, precede / proceed
persenality, personality
persenaly, personal(lly)
persenel, personnel
persent, percent
persentige, percent(age)
persentil, percent(ile)
persenuble, person(able)
persenulize, personal(ize)
persepatashen, precipitate(tion)
persepshen, percept(ion)
perseptable, perceptible
perseptef, percept(ive)
perseption, percept(ion)
perseptive, percept(ive)
perserverance, persevere(rance)
perservere, persevere
perseshen, precision / procession / precession
persest, persist
persestince, persist(ence)
persev, perceive
perseve, perceive
persevere,*,ed,ring,ringly,rance, TO PERSIST, CONTINUE ON DESPITE ODDS/ OBSTACLES
persh, perch / purge

pershis, purchase / perch(es)
persikute, persecute
persin, person
persinaledy, personality
persinel, personnel
persint, percent
persinuble, person(able)
persinul, personal
persinulize, personal(ize)
persinuly, personal(lly)
persipetashen, precipitate(tion)
persipitation, precipitate(tion)
persirverance, persevere(rance)
persishen, precision
persist,*,ted,ting,tence,tency,tent, tently, CONSISTENT IN FOCUS, TENACIOUS
persition, precision
persiv, perceive
persivere, persevere
persiverense, persevere(rance)
perskripshen, prescript(ion)
persokut, persecute
person,*,na,nable,nably,nability, nableness,nage,nal,nate,nality, nation,nator, nify,nnel,nhood, ONE HUMAN BEING "prefixes: un"
personal,*,ly,lism,lity,lize, AURA/ ESSENCE/ATTITUDE/BEHAVIOR OF A PERSON, CAN RELATE TO OTHERS "prefixes: im/inter/intra/un/uni"
personality,ties, A PERSON'S ATTITUDE/ BEHAVIOR
personefication, person(ification)
personel, personnel / personal
personify,fies,fied,fying,fication,fier, TO REPRESENT AS HUMAN, ACT LIKE, ACT AS IF
personnel, GROUP/BODY OF PEOPLE, DEPARTMENT WHICH HANDLES EMPLOY OF PEOPLE
persoo, pursue
perspective,*,ely, FROM A CERTAIN POINT OF VIEW
persperashen, perspiration
perspiration, TO SWEAT, RELEASE WATER FROM THE PORES TO COOL OFF
perspire,*,ed,ring,ration,ratory, TO SWEAT, RELEASE WATER FROM THE PORES TO COOL OFF
persu, pursue
persuade,*,ed,ding,asion,dable,asive, asively,asiveness,asion, COERCE/ SWAY/ IMPRESS SOMEONE/ SOMETHING TO COMMIT TO YOUR IDEALS "prefixes: over"
persuasion,ive, COERCE/SWAY/ IMPRESS SOMEONE
persude, pursue(d)
persun, person
persunal, personal
persunality, personality
persunaly, personal(lly)
persunel, personnel
persute, pursue(uit)
persuvere, persevere
perswade, persuade
perswaseve, persuade(asive)
perswashen, persuade(asion)
perswasif, persuade(asive)
pert,tly,tness, BRIGHT, LIVELY
pertain,*,ned,ning, ASSOCIATED WITH, BELONGS TO
pertane, pertain
pertishen, partition
pertrayal, portray(al)
pertrude, protrude
perturb,*,bed,bing,bable,bation, bational, BOTHERED BY, DISTURBED "prefixes: un"
peruble, parable
perudime, paradigm
perudox, paradox
perufin, paraffin
perugraf, paragraph
perukeet, parakeet
perul, peril
perulel, parallel
perulised, paralyze(d)
perulize, paralyze
perumedic, paramedic
perumid, pyramid
perumount, paramount
perund, parent
perunoid, paranoia(id)
perunoya, paranoia
perunt, parent
peruphen, paraffin
peruplegic, paraplegia(ic)
perupul, parable
peruse,*,ed,sing,sal, TO READ/ EXAMINE CAREFULLY
perushute, parachute
perusite, parasite
peruskope, periscope
perut, parrot
perutruper, paratrooper

pervade,*,ed,ding,er,asion,asive,asively, asiveness, PERMEATE, SPREAD THROUGHOUT
pervashen, pervade(asion)
pervasif, pervade(asion)
perversef, pervert(rsive)
pervert,*,ted,tedly,tedness,ter,tible,rse, rsely,rseness,rsion,rsity, rsities,rsive, rsively,rsiveness, DEVIANT BY SOCIETAL NORMS
pervirsive, pervert(rsive)
perzakute, persecute
perzaverinse, persevere(rance)
pes, peace / piece / pee(s) / pea(s)
pesa, pizza
pesamist, pessimism(st)
pesamistic, pessimism(stic)
pesamisum, pessimism
pesant, peasant
pesd, pest
pesdalense, pestilence
pesdasheo, pistachio
pesdaside, pesticide
pesdrome, pastrami
pesdulinse, pestilence
pesebly, peace(ably)
pesel, pestle
pesemisum, pessimism
pesent, peasant
peses, possess
pesesuf, possess(ive)
pesful, peace(ful)
pesher, pitcher / picture
pesibly, peace(ably)
pesific, pacific
pesil, pestle
pesimesum, pessimism
pesimist, pessimism(st)
pesimistic, pessimism(stic)
pesint, peasant
pesishen, position
pesition, position
peskripshen, prescript(ion)
pesol, pestle
pesont, peasant
pessimism,st,stic, CONTRARY TO, THE DOWNSIDE
pessimistic,cally, CONTRARY TO, THE DOWNSIDE
pest,*,ty, ANNOYANCE, BOTHERSOME
pestachio, pistachio
pestal, pestle / pistol / pistil
pestalinse, pestilence
pestasheo, pistachio

pestaside, pesticide
pestel, pistil / pistol / pestle
pestelinse, pestilence
pesten, piston
pesticide,*,dal, HARMFUL/POISONOUS CHEMICALS USED TO KILL INSECTS/ ANIMALS/PLANTS
pestil, pistil / pistol / pestle
pestilence, DISEASE WHICH SPREADS THROUGHOUT
pestin, piston
pestle,*,ed,ling, GRIND/PULVERIZE/ CRUSH/SMASH AGAINST A SURFACE WITH THIS AS A TOOL, NORMALLY ASSOCIATED WITH MORTAR/PESTLE
pestrome, pastrami
pestul, pistil / pistol / pestle
pestuled, pestle(d)
pestun, piston
pestuside, pesticide
pesuble, peace(able)
pesubly, peace(ably)
pesul, pestle
pesumisem, pessimism
pesumistic, pessimism(stic)
pesunt, peasant
pet,*,tted,tting, AN ANIMAL KEPT CONFINED AND FED BY HUMANS, TO STROKE (or see peat)
peta, PREFIX INDICATING "FIVE" MOST OFTEN MODIFIES THE WORD
petado, potato
petagogy, pedagogy
petagojik, pedagogy(gic)
petagree, pedigree
petakure, pedicure
petal,*,led, PART OF FLOWER(or see pedal/peddle)
petaseum, potassium
petasium, potassium
petato, potato
petch, pitch
petcher, pitcher / picture
petchir, pitcher/ picture
pete, petty / pity
peteatriks, pediatrics
peteatrishen, pediatrician
petecoat, petticoat
peted, pet(tted)
petegree, pedigree
petekote, petticoat
petekure, pedicure
petel, pedal / petal / peddle

petena, patina
peteness, petty(ttiness)
peter,*,red,ring, TO GET TIRED, RUN OUT OF ENERGY
petestul, pedestal
peteutrishen, pediatrician
pethetic, pathetic
peti, petty
petiatrics, pediatrics
peticoat, petticoat
peticure, pedicure
petier, petty(ttier)
petiest, petty(ttiest)
petigree, pedigree
petikote, petticoat
petikure, pedicure
petil, pedal / petal / peddle
petina, patina
petinchul, potential
petiness, petty(ttiness)
petinshul, potential
petir, peter
petistul, pedestal
petite,eness, SMALL WITH NORMAL PROPORTIONS
petition,*,ned,ning, SOLICIT/ APPROACH/REQUEST SOMETHING
petle, pedal / petal / peddle
petnik, picnic
petr, PREFIX INDICATING "STONE/ PETROLEUM" MOST OFTEN MODIFIES THE WORD
petrafikashen, petrify(fication)
petrafy, petrify
petrefication, petrify(fication)
petrefy, petrify
petrewd, protrude
petrify,fies,fied,fying,fication,factive, faction, FROZEN WITH HORROR, TURNED TO STONE
petro, PREFIX INDICATING "STONE/ PETROLEUM" MOST OFTEN MODIFIES THE WORD
petrol,*,leum, HYDROCARBON/OIL/ FUEL
petrolium, petrol(eum)
petrude, protrude
petrushen, protrude(usion)
petsa, pizza
petticoat,*, UNDERGARMENT, LAYERED SLIP
petty,ttier,ttiest,ttily,ttiness, SMALL/ RESTRICTIVE/HABITUAL OUTLOOK LOOK FOR FLAWS

petugogy, pedagogy
petugree, pedigree
petul, pedal / petal / peddle
petunia,*, A FLOWER
petur, peter
peturbed, perturb(ed)
peturnol, paternal
petustel, pedestal
pety, petty / pity
peu, pew
peub, pube
peuberdy, puberty
peubesent, pubescent
peubik, pube(bic)
peuburdy, puberty
peuk, puke
peunatef, punitive
peune, peony / puny
peunutive, punitive
peuny, peony / puny
peupul, pupil
peur, pier / peer / pyre / pure
peuraficashen, purify(fication)
peure, puree'
peurefide, purify(fied)
peurefy, purify
peurly, pure(ly)
peury, puree'
peutrid, putrid
pev, peeve
pevurted, pervert(ed)
pew,*, BENCH SEATS IN CHURCH
pewbesent, pubescent
pewder, pewter
pewding, pudding / putt(ing)
pewdur, pewter
pewne, puny
pewpul, pupil
pewt, put
pewter,rer, MOLDABLE METAL MADE WITH LEAD, USED AS DISHES/ VESSELS
pewtrid, putrid
pex, pick(s) / peck(s)
peyer, pure
peyeree, puree'
peyerify, purify
peyerly, pure(ly)
peyir, pure
peyote,*,tle, CACTUS, PRODUCES MESCALINE
peyur, pure
peyuree, puree'
peyurefide, purify(fied)

peyurify, purify
peyurly, pure(ly)
pez, pea(s) / peace / piece
peza, pizza
pezamistic, pessimism(stic)
pezd, pest
pezdalense, pestilence
pezdaside, pesticide
pezent, peasant
pezes, possess
pezful, peace(ful)
pezt, pest
pezubly, peace(ably)
pezunt, peasant
phalanthropy, philanthropy
phalek, philli(c)
phalicity, felicity
phalli,ic,icism,ism,icist,lluses, OF THE PENIS
phalosify, philosophy
phanetik, phonetic / fanatic
phanik, phonic
phanomena, phenomena
phanomenal, phenomenal
phantem, phantom
phantom,*, AN ILLUSIVE/SURREAL APPARITION, NOT PHYSICAL
pharaoh,*,onic,onical, EGYPTIAN KINGS
pharmac, PREFIX INDICATING "DRUGS/ MEDICINES" MOST OFTEN MODIFIES THE WORD
pharmaceutic,*,cal,cally, DISPENSING OF MANMADE CHEMICALS/DRUGS "prefixes: bio"
pharmacist,*, ONE WHO DISPENSES MANMADE CHEMICALS/DRUGS/ MEDICINE
pharmasutical, pharmaceutic(al)
pharmicist, pharmacist
pharmusutical, pharmaceutic(al)
pharoh, pharaoh
phase,*,ed,sing, AN ASPECT/PORTION OF AN OVERALL PROJECT/DESIGN, CHANGES/MOVEMENT (or see faze) "prefixes: in/inter/multi"
phasek, physique
phaselity, facility
phasic, physique
phasility, facility
phasishen, physician
phasphate, phosphate
phausfate, phosphate
phaze, phase / faze
pheasant,*, GAME BIRD

pheladendron, philodendron
phelanthrapist, philanthropy(pist)
phelanthropek, philanthropy(pic)
phelarmonic, philharmonic
phelicity, felicity
phelodendron, philodendron
phelosofy, philosophy
pheludindron, philodendron
phenaminan, phenomenon
phenomena,al, OF THE INCREDIBLE, EXTRAORDINARY
phenomenal,ly,lism,list,listic,listically, INCREDIBLE, EXTRAORDINARy
phenomenon,*, STRANGE/ UNCHARACTERISTIC BEHAVIOR/ EVENT, GIVEN TO THE INVISIBLE
phenominon, phenomenon
pheroh, pharaoh
phesant, pheasant
phesasist, physicist
phesek, physique / physic
pheselity, facility
phesent, pheasant
pheseology, physiology
phesesist, physicist
phesic, physic / physique
phesility, facility
phesint, pheasant
phesod, facade
phesunt, pheasant
phil, PREFIX INDICATING "LOVE" MOST OFTEN MODIFIES THE WORD
philadendron, philodendron
philanthrapist, philanthropy(pist)
philanthropek, philanthropy(pic)
philanthropy,pies,pic,pical,pically,pist, GIVE TO MANKIND VIA A KIND ACT/ MONEY, A BENEFACTOR
philarmonic, philharmonic
philasofical, philosophy(hical)
philasophical, philosophy(hical)
philermonic, philharmonic
philharmonic,*, LOVE OF HARMONICS, ENJOYMENT OF HARMONIC MUSICAL INSTRUMENTS
philodendron,*, A TROPICAL PLANT
philosofy, philosophy
philosophy,hies,her,hic,hical,hically, hize,hizer, ACQUISITION/ ACCUMULATION OF WISDOM WHETHER PHYSICAL OR METAPHYSICAL
philudindron, philodendron
philurmonic, philharmonic

phinaminan, phenomenon
phinaumena, phenomena
phinetik, phonetic / fanatic
phinite, finite
phinomenal, phenomenal
phinominan, phenomenon
phisasist, physicist
phisecal, physical
phisek, physique / physic
phiseks, physics
phiseologikul, physiology(gical)
phiseology, physiology
phisesist, physicist
phishen, fission
phisic, physic / physique
phisical, physical
phisiks, physics
phisiology, physiology
phisisist, physicist
phisyological, physiology(gical)
phisyologist, physiology(gist)
phlabadumist, phlebotomy(mist)
phlabitis, phlebitis
phlabodumist, phlebotomy(mist)
phlabotomy, phlebotomy
phlebitis,ic, VEIN INFLAMMATION/
    SWELLING
phlebodomist, phlebotomy(mist)
phlebotomy,mic,mist,mize, OPENING
    VEINS TO RELIEVE PRESSURE
phlegm,my, MUCUS
phlem, phlegm
phlibites, phlebitis
phlibodumist, phlebotomy(mist)
phlibotomy, phlebotomy
phlim, phlegm
phlubotomy, phlebotomy
phnegraf, phonograph
phobea, phobia
phobia,*,bic, UNFOUNDED FEAR, NO
    APPARENT REASON FOR FEAR/
    DREAD
phodagraf, photo(graph)
phodasinthesis, photosynthesis
phodegraf, photo(graph)
phodesinthesis, photosynthesis
phodo, photo
phodograf, photo(graph)
phodon, photon
phodosynthesis, photosynthesis
phodugraf, photo(graph)
phon, PREFIX INDICATING "SOUND"
    MOST OFTEN MODIFIES THE WORD
    (or see phone/fawn)

phone,*,ed,ning, SPEAKING/HEARING
    COMMUNICATION DEVICE
    "prefixes: inter"
phonegraph, phonograph
phoneme,*,mic,mics, DISTINCT
    SOUNDS OF LETTERS
phonetic,*,cal,cally, HOW WORDS ARE
    HEARD/SPOKEN/TRANSMITTED,
    THE SOUND/AUDIO CONCERNING
    WORDS "prefixes: un"
phonic,*, IDENTIFYING/SPELLING
    WORDS ACCORDING TO THEIR
    SOUNDS
phonigraf, phonograph
phonimic, phoneme(mic)
phonograph,*,hic,hical,hically, RECORD
    PLAYER
phony,ney,nies,nier,niest,nily,niness,
    FAKE, NOT REAL (also spelled
    phoney)
phosfade, phosphate
phosfate, phosphate
phosphate,*, A CHEMICAL/SALT
phot, PREFIX INDICATING "LIGHT"
    MOST OFTEN MODIFIES THE WORD
photagraf, photo(graph)
photasinthesis, photosynthesis
photigraf, photo(graph)
photo,*,ograph,ographable,ographer,
    ography,ographic,ogenic, ogenically,
    PICTURE CREATED IN A PROCESS
    USING LIGHT "prefixes: un"
photograf, photo(graph)
photon,*,nic, A QUANTUM PARTICLE
    WITH NO MASS/CHARGE
photosinthesis, photosynthesis
photosynthesis,ize,etic,etically,
    PROCESS WHERE PLANTS TURN
    LIGHT INTO ENERGY
photugraf, photo(graph)
phsycist, physicist
phulanthrapy, philanthropy
phulicity, felicity
phulosefy, philosophy
phunamina, phenomenon
phunomenal, phenomenal
phusility, facility
phuzek, physique
phycisian, physician
phycisist, physicist
physasist, physicist
physecal, physical
physek, physique / physic
physeks, physics

physekul, physical
physeological, physiology(gical)
physeology, physiology
physeshan, physician
physesist, physicist
physi, PREFIX INDICATING "PHYSICAL/
    NATURAL" MOST OFTEN MODIFIES
    THE WORD
physic,*,cist, OF NATURE (or see
    physique/physics)
physical,*,lly,lity,lities, CAN BE SEEN/
    SENSED WITH THE EYE, AN EXAM
physician,*, LICENSED TO PRACTICE
    MEDICINE
physicist,*, ONE WHO STUDIES PHYSICS
physico, PREFIX INDICATING
    "PHYSICAL/NATURAL" MOST OFTEN
    MODIFIES THE WORD
physics,cist, THE STUDY OF SUBATOMIC
    PARTICLES, A SCIENCE (or see
    physic/physique) "prefixes: bio"
physik, physique / physic
physiology,gist,gical,gically,gist,
    CONCERNING PLANTS/ANIMALS,
    SCIENCE OF NATURE
physique, PHYSICAL BODY/STRUCTURE
physisist, physicist
phyt, PREFIX INDICATING "PLANT"
    MOST OFTEN MODIFIES THE WORD
pi, GREEK LETTER WHICH STANDS FOR
    MATHEMATICAL RATIO 3.141592
    (or see pie/pea/pee)
pial, pile
pianeer, pioneer
piano,*, USING KEYS TO STRIKE
    STRINGS OF THIS INSTRUMENT
    HOUSED IN A LARGE WOODEN BOX
pibe, pipe
pic,*, SMALL/TRIANGULAR/FLAT/RIGID
    ITEM USED TO STRUM STRINGS OF
    A MUSICAL INSTRUMENT (or see
    pick/pig/pique/peak/peek/pike)
picalo, piccolo
piccolo,*,list, INSTRUMENT/FLUTE
picdorul, pectoral / pictorial
pich, pitch / peach
pichen, pigeon
picher, pitcher / picture
pichon, pigeon
pichur, pitcher / picture
pichy, pitch(y)
pick,*,ked,king,kier,kiest,ky,ker,
    CHOOSE/SELECT FROM AMONGST
    OTHERS, ACQUIRE (or see pic/pig/

pique/peak/ peek/pike) "prefixes: un"
pickalo, piccolo
picket,*,ter,ted,ting, WOODEN POST WITH SHARPENED END, BARRIER/ FENCE AS IN A UNION STRIKE, POST GUARD
pickle,*,ed,ling, TO SOAK/MARINATE FOOD IN A BRINE/SALT SOLUTION
picknic, picnic
pickul, pickle
picnic,*, A LUNCH OUTDOORS
picol, pickle
picon, pecan
picsher, picture / pitcher
pict, pick(ed) / pig(gged)
picter, picture / pitcher
pictorial,*,lly,lism,lness, VISION/ ENVISIONED AS A PICTURE
picture,*,ed,ring, A VISUAL REPRESENTATION OF A SCENE
piculear, peculiar
pid, pit
pide, pity
pidestreun, pedestrian
pidi, pity
pidiatrics, pediatrics
pidiatrishan, pediatrician
pidy, pity
pie,*, FOOD ITEM INCORPORATING A CRUST AND FILLING (or see pi)
piece,*,ed,cing,er, ONE PART OF THE WHOLE, ONE AMONGST MANY (or see peace)
piel, pile
pieneer, pioneer
pieni, peony
pieno, piano
pier,*, MANMADE OUTCROP ON THE WATER FOR DOCKING BOATS/ FISHING (or see peer/pierce/pyre)
pierce,*,ed,cing,cingly, TO PENETRATE/ PUNCTURE (or see peer(s)/pier(s))
pies, pious
piethon, python
pif, peeve
pig,*,gged,gging,ggish,ggy, DOMESTICATED SWINE/BOAR (or see peg/pick/pic)
pigal, pickle
pigamus, pajamas
pigated, picket(ed)
pigen, pigeon

pigeon,*, A CITY BIRD, OF THE DOVE FAMILY
piget, picket
pigeted, picket(ed)
pigil, pickle
pigin, pigeon
pigit, picket
pigle, pickle
pigme, pygmy
pigmi, pygmy
pigul, pickle
pigy, pig(ggy)
pijamus, pajamas
pijen, pigeon
pik, pic / pick / pike / pig
pikal, pickle
pikalo, piccolo
pikcher, picture / pitcher
pikchir, picture / pitcher
pikchor, picture / pitcher
pikchr, picture / pitcher
pikchur, picture / pitcher
pikd, pick(ed) / pique(d)
pike,*,ed,king, A FISH, STAFF WITH POINTED TIP USED AS WEAPON/ TOOL, A POINT, TURNPIKE (or see pick/pig/ pique/peak/peek)
pikel, pickle
piker, pick(er)
piket, picket
pikeust, pick(iest)
piki, pick(y)
pikiest, pick(kiest)
pikir, pick(er)
pikit, picket
pikl, pickle
pikle, pickle
piknik, picnic
pikol, pickle
pikon, pecan
piksher, picture / pitcher
pikshor, picture / pitcher
pikshr, picture / pitcher
pikt, pick(ed) / pique(d)
piktorul, pectoral / pictorial
pikture, picture / pitcher
pikul, pickle
pikuleur, peculiar
pikur, pick(er)
piky, pig(ggy) / pick(y)
pil, pill / pile / peel
pilach, pillage
pilaf, ASIAN STYLE OF RICE
pilage, pillage

pilar, pillar
pilaredy, polar(ity)
pile,*,ed,ling,lings, MOUND/ ACCUMULATION OF SOMETHING, A POST/ TIMBER/PILLAR WITH POINTED END, NAP OF FABRIC, HEMORRHOIDS (or see peel/pill)
pilech, pillage
pileg, pillage
pilej, pillage
pilengs, pile(lings)
piler, pillar
pilerity, polar(ity)
pilese, police
pilet, pilot
pilgrim,*,mage, ORIGINAL SETTLERS IN AMERICA FROM EUROPE, THOSE WHO TRAVEL TO UNSEEN PLACES
pilich, pillage
pilig, pillage
pilij, pillage
pilite, polite / pilot
pill,*, TABLET/CAPSULES
pillach, pillage
pillage,*,ed,ging, TO GO THROUGH OTHER PEOPLES STUFF, TO PLUNDER/ TAKE AWAY/STEAL
pillar,*, A POST/MONUMENT/SUPPORT
pillow,*, A CUSHION, HEAD SUPPORT WHEN LYING DOWN, CUSHION TO PROTECT FROM HARM
pilo, pillow
pilot,*,ted,ting,tage,tless, ONE WHO NAVIGATES/OPERATES A VESSEL, ONE THAT STEERS, FLAME ON A GAS APPLIANCE
pilow, pillow
pils, pill(s) / pile(s) / peel(s)
piluch, pillage
piludge, pillage
piluge, pillage
pilur, pillar
pilushen, pollute(tion)
pilut, pilot / pollute
pilutent, pollute(tant)
pilution, pollute(tion)
pimento,*, A SWEET PEPPER
pimp,*,ped,ping, VIOLENT/ABUSIVE PERSON WHO CAPITALIZES OFF OF WOMEN, INSIGNIFICANT, PETTY, COOL
pimpel, pimple
pimple,*, INFLAMED SKIN PORES
pimpul, pimple

pin,*,nned,nning,nner, TO FASTEN, SHARP TIPPED THIN OBJECT (or see pen/pent/pine) "prefixes: un"
pinacle, pentacle / pinnacle
pinada, pinata
pinagon, pentagon
pinagram, pentagram
pinakle, pinnacle / pentacle
pinalty, penal(ty)
pinaple, pineapple
pinapple, pineapple
pinasilun, penicillin
pinata,*, A PAPIER MACHE PARTY DECORATION FILLED WITH GOODIES FOR CHILDREN
pinatentiary, penitentiary
pinatrate, penetrate
pinatruble, penetrable
pinc, pink
pincers, USED FOR GRIPPING, CLAWLIKE (or see pinch(ers))
pinch,hes,hed,hing,her, SQUEEZE TOGETHER FOR HOLDING SOMETHING, TWO SIDES COMING TOGETHER (or see pincers)
pinchent, penchant
pinchers, pinch(ers) / pincers
pind, pine(d) / pin(nned)
pindalem, pendulum
pindent, pendant / pendent
pinding, pending
pindlum, pendulum
pindo, pinto
pindulum, pendulum
pine,*,ed,ning, EVERGREEN TREE, PAINFULLY LONG FOR SOMEONE/ SOMETHING (or see pain/pane)
pineal gland, PINE CONE SHAPED ORGAN IN THE BODY WHICH SECRETES MELATONIN
pineapple,*, A TROPICAL FRUIT
pinecillin, penicillin
pinecle, pinnacle / pentacle
pineer, pioneer
pinegon, pentagon
pineng, pine(ning) / pin(nning)
pines, pine(s) / penis
pinetentiary, penitentiary
pinetrate, penetrate
pingalum, pendulum
pinguin, penguin
pingwen, penguin
pinial gland, pineal gland
piniselin, penicillin

pinitenchery, penitentiary
pinjalum, pendulum
pinjulim, pendulum
pink,*,ky, A COLOR, THE LITTLE FINGER ON THE HAND
pinkwen, penguin
pinnacle,*, PEAK/POINT/CREST/CONE (or see pentacle)
pinol, penal
pinos, penis
pinot, peanut
pinotrashen, penetrate(tion)
pinotrate, penetrate
pinsel, pencil
pinsers, pincers / pinch(ers)
pinshen, pension
pinshent, penchant
pinsil, pencil
pinsion, pension
pinsul, pencil
pint,*, A U.S. FORM OF MEASUREMENT FOR LIQUIDS (or see paint/pine(d)/ pent/pin(nned))
pintacle, pentacle / pinnacle
pintagon, pentagon
pintagram, pentagram
pintalum, pendulum
pintegon, pentagon
pinting, pending
pinto,*, SPOTTED HORSE/BEAN
pintucle, pentacle / pinnacle
pintulem, pendulum
pinugram, pentagram
pinukle, pinnacle / pentacle
pinulize, penal(ize)
pinulty, penal(ty)
pinusilun, penicillin
pinut, peanut
pinutentiary, penitentiary
pinutrashen, penetrate(tion)
pinutrate, penetrate
pinutruble, penetrable
piny, penny / pine(y)
pinyada, pinata
pioneer,*,red,ring, ONE WHO DISCOVERS NEW TERRITORY/THE UNKNOWN
pious,sly,sness, HOLIER THAN THOU, INTENSELY MOTIVATED ABOUT THEIR GOD, REVERENCE FOR
pipe,*,ed,ping, TUBULAR/HOLLOW FORM
piporshenal, proportion(al)

pique,*,ed,uing, HEIGHTEN/STIMULATE, RIBBED/RAISED EFFECT (or see peak/peek)
piqueur, peculiar
pir, per / purr / peer / pier
pirade, parade / pirate
piraet, pirouette
piralusis, paralysis
piramid, pyramid
pirana, piranha
piranha,*, FLESH EATING FRESH WATER FISH (or see prana)
pirat, parade / pirate
pirate,*,ed,ting,acy, ONE WHO TRAVERSES THE SEAS STEALING FROM OTHERS, TAKE FROM OTHERS WITHOUT PERMISSION "prefixes: bio"
pirbendikuler, perpendicular
pirceive, perceive
pircent, percent
pirceptible, perceptible
pirch, perch / purge
pirchus, purchase / perch(es)
pircushen, percussion
pircusion, percussion
pirdly, pert(ly)
piremid, pyramid
pireneal, perennial
pireod, period
pireodic, periodic / periotic
pireodontic, periodontic
pireodontist, periodontist
pireot, period
pireoticul, periodic(al)
piret, pirate
pireud, period
pireut, period
pirews, peruse
pirfect, perfect
pirfekd, perfect
pirferted, pervert(ed)
pirfeum, perfume
pirfikt, perfect
pirfium, perfume
pirform, perform
pirformence, perform(ance)
pirfume, perfume
pirgatory, purgatory
pirge, purge
pirger, perjure
pirgery, perjure(ry)
pirgetory, purgatory
pirgury, perjure(ry)

pirgutory, purgatory
pirhaps, perhaps
piright, pyrite
piriodontic, periodontic
piriodontist, periodontist
pirit, pirate / pyrite
pirje, purge
pirjury, perjure(ry)
pirkrastination, procrastinate
pirkushen, percussion
pirmanence, permanence
pirmanent, permanent
pirmeate, permeate
pirmenant, permanent
pirmesabul, permissible
pirmet, permit
pirmeuble, permeable
pirmishen, permission
pirmisive, permissive
pirmisuf, permissive
pirmit, permit
pirmition, permission
pirmnent, permanent
piro, pyro
piroet, pirouette
pirogative, prerogative
pirokside, peroxide
pirole, parole
pirona, piranha
pirosedy, porosity
pirosity, porosity
pirot, pirate
pirouette,*, TO TWIRL ABOUT ON THE TIPS OF TOES
piroxside, peroxide
pirpechuel, perpetual
pirpendicular, perpendicular
pirpes, purpose
pirpeshual, perpetual
pirpesly, purpose(ly)
pirpetrate, perpetrate
pirpetshuate, perpetual(ate)
pirpetual, perpetual
pirpetuate, perpetual(ate)
pirpetuity, perpetuity
pirpis, purpose
pirpisly, purpose(ly)
pirple, purple
pirpleksity, perplex(ity)
pirplexity, perplex(ity)
pirporshenal, proportion(al)
pirportional, proportion(al)
pirpos, purpose
pirposful, purpose(ful)

pirposly, purpose(ly)
pirpus, purpose
pirpusly, purpose(ly)
pirputrate, perpetrate
pirs, purse / pierce / peer(s) / pier(s)
pirsacute, persecute
pirsavere, persevere
pirsbektif, perspective
pirsbiration, perspiration
pirsbire, perspire
pirscripshen, prescript(ion)
pirscription, prescript(ion)
pirsebtef, percept(ive)
pirsecute, persecute
pirsen, person
pirsenal, personal
pirsenaledy, personality
pirsenality, personality
pirsenaly, personal(lly)
pirsenel, personnel
pirsent, percent
pirsentage, percent(age)
pirsenuble, person(able)
pirsenulize, personal(ize)
pirseptable, perceptible
pirseptive, percept(ive)
pirseshen, precision
pirsest, persist
pirsestans, persist(ence)
pirseve, perceive
pirseverense, persevere(rance)
pirsh, perch / purge
pirshes, purchase / perch(es)
pirsikute, persecute
pirsinuble, person(able)
pirsinulize, personal(ize)
pirsistence, persist(ence)
pirskripshen, prescript(ion)
pirson, person
pirsona, person(a)
pirsonality, personality
pirsonefication, person(ification)
pirsonel, personnel / personal
pirsonification, person(ification)
pirsonifikashen, person(ification)
pirsonify, personify
pirsonuble, person(able)
pirsoo, pursue
pirspective, perspective
pirspektif, perspective
pirspiration, perspiration
pirspire, perspire
pirsu, pursue
pirsuade, persuade

pirsuasion, persuade(asion)
pirsuasive, persuade(asive)
pirsude, pursue(d)
pirsunal, personal / personnel
pirsunel, personnel / personal
pirsute, pursue(uit)
pirsuvere, persevere
pirswade, persuade
pirswashen, persuade(asion)
pirswasif, persuade(asive)
pirt, pert
pirtain, pertain
pirtane, pertain
pirtly, pert(ly)
pirtray, portray
pirtrayal, portray(al)
pirturb, perturb
pirumid, pyramid
piruse, peruse
pirut, pirate
pirvade, pervade
pirvashen, pervade(asion) / provision
pirvasif, pervade(asion)
pirvershen, pervert(rsion)
pirversive, pervert(rsive)
pirvert, pervert
pirvirsev, pervert(rsive)
piryte, pyrite
pirzukewt, persecute
pis, peace / piece / pie(s) / pea(s)
pisa, pizza
pisdachio, pistachio
pisdasheo, pistachio
pisdrome, pastrami
pises, possess
piseshen, position
pisesif, possess(ive)
pisher, pitcher / picture
piskrepshin, prescript(ion)
pistachio,*, AN EDIBLE NUT
pistasheo, pistachio
pisten, piston
pistil,*,llate, PART OF A FLOWER (or see pistol)
pistol,*,led,ling, HANDGUN/FIREARM (or see pistil)
piston,*, PART OF AN ENGINE
pistrome, pastrami
pistul, pistil / pistol / pestle
pistun, piston
pit,*,tted,tting, THE SEED OF A FRUIT, A HOLLOWED DEPRESSION (or see pet/peat)
pitado, potato

pitaseum, potassium
pitasium, potassium
pitato, potato
pitch,hes,hed,hing,hy, TAR, BASEBALL MANEUVER "prefixes: over/un"
pitcher,*, POSITION IN THE GAME OF BASEBALL, A VESSEL FOR HOLDING LIQUIDS (or see picture)
pite, pity
pitena, patina
pitenchul, potential
pitenshil, potential
pithon, python
piti, pity
pitifol, pity(tiful)
pitina, patina
pitinshil, potential
pitnik, picnic
pitrol, patrol
pitroleum, petrol(eum)
pitrood, protrude
pitrude, protrude
pitrushen, protrude(usion)
pitsa, pizza
pituitary,ries, PERTAINING TO A GLAND PRODUCING HORMONES
pitunia, petunia
piturbed, perturb(ed)
pity,ties,tied,tying,tier,tiful,tifully, tifulness,tiless,tilessly,tilessness, ying,tiable, tiably,tiableness, FEEL SYMPATHY/GRIEF/COMPASSION FOR SOMEONE
piu, pew
piuder, pewter
piul, pile
piuneer, pioneer
piuny, puny
pius, pious
piuter, pewter
piutrid, putrid
piv, peeve
pivurted, pervert(ed)
piwrite, pyrite
piwro, pyro
pix, pick(s) / pic(s)
piyuree, puree'
pizdromy, pastrami
pizes, possess
piztacheo, pistachio
pizza,*, A FLAT BREAD WITH OTHER FOODS COOKED ON TOP OF IT
pla, play

placard,*, FLAT CARD DISPLAYING INFORMATION
placate,*,ed,ting,er,tion,tive,tory, TO PACIFY/APPEASE/LET THEM HAVE THEIR WAY
place,*,ed,cing,ement, POSITION/AREA "prefixes: dis/mis/re/un"
placebo,*, AN IMITATION/FAKE, PRETENDING TO BE THE REAL THING
placed, placid / place(d)
placenta,*,al,ary,ation, LINING OF A MAMMALS WOMB/UTERUS WHICH HOLDS THE FETUS
placerd, placard
placid,dity,dness,dly, CALM/GENTLE/QUIET
plack, plaque
placment, place(ment)
placurd, placard
plad, plaid / plait / play(ed) / plate
pladenum, platinum
plader, platter
pladform, platform
pladinum, platinum
pladir, platter
pladnum, platinum
pladur, platter
plaeng, play(ing)
plag, plague
plagarism, plagiarism
plager, please(sure)
plagerism, plagiarism
plagiarism,st,stic,ize,izes,ized,izing,izer, COPY SOMEONE ELSES WORK WITHOUT PERMISSION
plagiresm, plagiarism
plague,*,ed,uing, A SPREADING DISEASE WHICH CAUSES HARM, A NUISANCE (or see plaque)
plagur, please(sure)
plagurism, plagiarism
plai, play / ply
plaid,*,ded, A CROSS WEAVING PATTERN (or see plait/play(ed))
plaigerism, plagiarism
plain,*,nly,nness, WITHOUT ACCENTS/ ORNAMENTS, NO OUTSTANDING FEATURES (or see plane)
plait,*,ted,ting,ter, BRAID/ FOLD OVER/ INTERWOVEN (or see plate/plaid)
plajer, please(sure)
plajerism, plagiarism
plajir, please(sure)

plajur, please(sure)
plajurism, plagiarism
plak, plaque
plakard, placard
plakate, placate
plakurd, placard
plan,*,nned,nning,nner, TO CONTRIVE/ DREAM/CONJURE/DESIGN (or see plane/plain) "prefixes: un"
planaterium, planetary(rium)
plancton, plankton
plane,*,ed,ning,er,nar,narity, FLAT/ LEVEL SURFACE, FLYING VESSEL (or see plan/plain) "prefixes: bi/de/en/uni"
planet,*, A SPHERICAL BODY IN SPACE
planetary,rium,riums, OF/CONCERNING BODIES OF MATTER IN SPACE
planit, planet
planitareum, planetary(rium)
plank,*,ked,king, FLAT/WIDE BOARD
plankton,nic, TINY WATER ORGANISMS
plant,*,ted,ting,ter, ORGANISM WHICH TRANSFORMS LIGHT ENERGY AND HAS NO NERVOUS SYSTEM, TO TAKE A STAND, TAKE ROOT "prefixes: re"
plantain,*, ANTI-BACTERIAL/ INFLAMMATORY/VIRAL/HEALING PLANT
plantane, plantain
plantashen, plantation
plantation,*, ESTATE WHICH GROWS LARGE FIELDS OF CROPS
planter,*, VESSEL/CONTAINER WHICH HOLDS PLANTS/DIRT
planut, planet
plaque,*, A COATING OF SOMETHING, A FLAT BOARD WITH TEXT COMMEMORATING SOMEONE
plasa, plaza
plasdur, plaster
plasebo, placebo
plased, placid
plashur, please(sure)
plasible, plausible
plasinta, placenta
plasit, placid
plasma,mic, CONCERNS THE BLOOD "prefixes: endo"
plasment, place(ment)
plastek, plastic

plaster,*,red,ring,ry, A GYSUM OR OTHER PASTE MATERIAL THAT SPREADS, TO COAT WITH
plastic,*, MOLDABLE/VERSATILE SUBSTANCE
plasu, plaza
plasuble, plausible
plat,*,tted,tting, MAP/CHART/PLOT, A BRAID (or see plate/plait/play(ed))
platau, plateau
plate,*,ed,ting, FLAT/ROUND VESSEL (or see plat/plait/play(ed)) "prefixes: retro"
plateau,*, ELEVATED AREA OF LAND WITH A FLAT TOP
platepus, platypus
plater, platter
platform,*, ELEVATED FORM WITH A FLAT TOP/AREA
platibus, platypus
platinum,*, A METAL
platipus, platypus
platir, platter
platnem, platinum
platnum, platinum
plato, plateau
platonic,ism,ist,istic,ize, LOVE/ FRIENDSHIP WITHOUT SEX, SPIRITUAL, OF PLATO
platoon,*, A GROUP/UNIT IN MILITARY
platter,*, A FLAT PLATE/VESSEL
platur, platter
platypus,ses,pi, UNDERWATER MAMMAL WITH BIRD-LIKE QUALITIES
plauding, plod(dding) / plot(tting)
plausible,bility,eness,ly,ive, POSSIBLE/ CONVINCING
plauteng, plod(dding) / plot(tting)
plaw, plow
play,*,yed,ying,yer,yful,yfully,yfulness, BEHAVE CHEERFULLY/JOYFULLY/ HAPPY "prefixes: inter/over/re/ under"
playkate, placate
plaza, A SQUARE CITY CENTER/TOWN
plazma, plasma
plaztek, plastic
plea,*,ad, BEG/DECLARE/ARGUE FOR (or see pleat)
plead,*,ded,ding,dable,der, BEG/ DECLARE/ARGUE FOR (or see pleat) "prefixes: inter/mis"

pleasant,try,tly,tness,try,tries, AMIABLE/ENJOYABLE/ UNDRAMATIC EXPERIENCE "prefixes: un"
please,*,ed,sing,singly,singness,surable, surableness,surably,sure,sures, sured, SATISFY/QUENCH/APPEASE/ PROVIDE COMFORT "prefixes: dis"
pleat,*,ted,ter, FOLDS/CREASES (or see plead)
plecebo, placebo
plecenta, placenta
plech, pledge
plecher, please(sure)
plecht, pledge(d)
plechur, please(sure)
plecksiglass, plexiglass
plecseglas, plexiglass
plecsiglas, plexiglass
pleded, plea(ded)
pledge,*,ed,ging,ger, OFFER A PROMISE/GUARANTEE
pledonic, platonic
pleduble, plea(dble)
pleed, plead
plees, please / plea(s)
pleet, pleat / plead
plege, pledge
pleger, please(sure)
plegeurism, plagiarism
plegir, please(sure)
plegt, pledge(d)
plegur, please(sure)
pleig, plague
plein, plain / plane
pleit, plait / plate
pleje, pledge
plejer, please(sure)
plejir, please(sure)
plejor, please(sure)
plejur, please(sure)
pleksaglass, plexiglass
pleksiglass, plexiglass
plendiful, plenty(tiful)
plendy, plenty
plentaful, plenty(tiful)
plenty,tiful,tifully,tifulness,teous, teously,teousness, ENOUGH/ AMPLE AMOUNT
pleral, plural
pleril, plural
ples, please / plea(s)
plesant, pleasant
plesebo, placebo

plesent, pleasant
pleser, pleas(sure) / please(r)
plesher, please(sure)
pleshur, please(sure)
plesinta, placenta
plesunt, pleasant
plesure, please(r)
plet, pleat / plead
pleted, plea(ded)
pleto, plateau
pletonic, platonic
pletoon, platoon
pletune, platoon
plewm, plume
plewrel, plural
plewtonium, plutonium
plexaglass, plexiglass
plexiglass, CLEAR SHEET OF PLASTIC
plez, please / plea(s)
plezent, pleasant
plezint, pleasant
pli, ply / plea
pliable,bility,eness,ly, BENDABLE/ FLEXIBLE
plicebo, placebo
plieble, pliable
plight,*, SITUATION/CONDITION (or see polite)
plintaful, plenty(tiful)
plinty, plenty
plirul, plural
plis, please / ply(lies)
plisebo, placebo
plisenta, placenta
plit, plight / polite / pleat
plito, plateau
plitonic, platonic
plitune, platoon
pliuble, pliable
pliwood, plywood
pliwute, plywood
plod,*,dded,dding,ddingly,dder, MOVE ABOUT WITHOUT ENTHUSIASM, IN THE DOLDRUMS, HEAVY/SLOW WALKING (or see plot)
ploded, plod(dded) / plot(tted)
plodeng, plod(dding)/ plot(tting)
ploding, plod(dding) / plot(tting)
ploe, ploy
plog, plug
ploi, ploy
plom, plum / plumb / plume / plump
plomber, plumb(er)

plomer, plumb(er)
plomet, plummet
plomp, plump
plomr, plumb(er)
ploom, plume
plop,*,pped,pping, SOUND/ MOVEMENT RESEMBLING DROPPING SOMETHING HEAVY/ FLAT
ploped, plop(pped)
plopt, plop(pped)
plos, plus
ploseble, plausible
plosh, plush
plosible, plausible
plot,*,tted,tting,tter,ttage, MAP/PLAN/ CHART OUT (or see plod) "prefixes: sub/under"
ploted, plot(tted)
ploteng, plod(dding) / plot(tting)
ploter, plot(tter)
plotoon, platoon
plotune, platoon
plow,*,wed,wing,wable,wer, PHYSICALLY CAUSE TO TURN OVER/ ROLL/REARRANGE "prefixes: un"
plowee, ploy
ploy,*, A TRICK
plozible, plausible
pluc, pluck
plucenta, placenta
pluck,*,ked,ker,king,ky,kily,kiness, PULL STRINGS ON INSTRUMENT, REMOVE FEATHERS
pludonic, Platonic
plug,*,gged,gging, AN OBJECT WHICH FILLS/FITS INTO HOLES, SHOOT, BULLET (or see pluck) "prefixes: un"
pluk, pluck / plug
plum,*, A FRUIT (or see plumb/plume)
plumb,*,bed,ber,bing, USE PIPES TO TRANSPORT LIQUIDS/GAS, TO SQUARE/ MAKE LEVEL (or see plum) "prefixes: un"
plume,*,ed,ming,my, BILLOWY CLOUD OF MATTER FROM VOLCANO, BIRD'S FEATHERS (or see plum/ plumb)
plumer, plumb(er)
plumit, plummet
plummet,*,ted,ting, FALL STRAIGHT DOWN, USED TO TEST FOR PERPENDICULAR LEVEL

plump,ply,pish, ROUND/FULL/CHUBBY, HEAVY FALLING SOUND (or see plumb)
plunch, plunge
plunder,*,red,ring,rer,rable,rous,rage, TO FORCIBLY ROB
plunge,*,ed,ging,er, DIVE/DELVE/ THRUST INTO
plunje, plunge
plunter, plunder
plural,lly,lism,list,listic,lity,lities,lize, lized,lizing,lization, MORE THAN ONE
plus,ses, TO ADD/GAIN/POSITIVE "prefixes: non"
plusebo, placebo
plusenta, placenta
plush,hier,hiest,hy,hly, THICK/SOFT/ LUXURIOUS
plusinta, placenta
pluto, plateau
plutonic, platonic
plutonium, A CHEMICAL ELEMENT
plutoon, platoon
plutune, platoon
pluwrel, plural
ply,lies,lied,ying,liable, TO DO/ FURNISH/WORK AT, OF LAYERS
plyible, pliable
plys, ply(lies) / please
plyt, plight / polite
plyuble, pliable
plywood, FORMED SHEET CONSISTING OF LAYERS OF WOOD/COMPOSITE
plywude, plywood
plywute, plywood
pneumatic,*,cally, USING COMPRESSION TO OPERATE TOOLS, AIR/GAS SCIENCE
pneumonia,ic, LUNG INFLAMMATION
pnewmatic, pneumatic
pnumatic, pneumatic
pnumonia, pneumonia
poach,hes,hed,hing,her, WAY TO COOK EGGS, UNLAWFULLY TAKE/KILL ANIMALS/FISH (or see pouch)
poatry, poetry
pob, pub
poblec, public
poblecher, publish(er)
poblecis, publicize
poblecist, publicist
poblek, public
poblesh, publish

poblesist, publicist
poblesiz, publicize
poblic, public
poblicis, publicize
poblicist, publicist
poblisest, publicist
poblisher, publish(er)
poblisist, publicist
poblisiz, publicize
poc, poke / pock
pocediv, positive
poces, possess
poceshen, possess(ion)
pocetion, possess(ion)
pocetiv, positive
poch, poach
pocht, poach(ed)
pock, SCAR/PIT/ERUPTION ON THE SKIN (or see poke)
pocker, poker
pocket,*,ted,ting,tful, A FOLD IN CLOTHING WHICH HOLDS THINGS, STORAGE PLACE IN CLOTHING
pocks, pox
pocreate, procreate
pod,*,dded,dding, THAT WHICH ENVELOPES SOME OF MANY (or see pot) "prefixes: uni"
podable, potable
podary, potter(y)
pode, potty
podebul, potable
poded, pot(tted) / pod(dded)
podel, puddle / poodle
podend, potent
podeng, pudding
podensy, potent(ncy)
podent, potent
poder, potter
podery, potter(y)
podestrein, pedestrian
podeum, podium
podibul, potable
podid, pot(tted) / pod(dded)
podind, potent
poding, pudding
podinsy, potent(ncy)
podir, potter
podiry, potter(y)
podium,*, A PLATFORM FOR SPEAKERS, PEDESTAL
podl, puddle
podlach, potlatch
podlage, potlatch

podluk, potluck
podol, puddle
podpory, potpourri
poduble, potable
podunsy, potent(ncy)
podur, potter
podury, potter(y)
pody, potty
poed, poet
poedik, poet(ic)
poem,*, TEXT/WRITINGS WHICH DEPICT A STORY/THOUGHT/ EMOTION
poenseda, poinsettia
poenseta, poinsettia
poent, point
poenyent, poignant
poenzeda, poinsettia
poes, poise / pose
poesin, poison
poet,*,tic,tical,tically,ticize,ticized, ticizing, SOMEONE WHO WRITES/IS GIVEN TO POETRY
poetry, LITERARY VERSE PROJECTING EMOTIONS/EVENT/IDEA
poez, poise
poezun, poison
pof, puff
poferdy, poverty
pofirty, poverty
pofurdee, poverty
poger, poker
poid, poet
poignant,tly,ncy, TO THE POINT, PRECISE, EXACT
poim, poem
poinant, poignant
poinseda, poinsettia
poinsettia,*, A SEASONAL FLOWERING PLANT
point,*,ted,ter,ting,ty,tless,tlessly, tlessness, THE TIP, DIRECT, AIM, SHOW, PRIMARY THEME/ISSUE
poinyent, poignant
poinzeta, poinsettia
poise,ed, IN POSITION TO, SUSPENDED ACTION, IN EQUILIBRIUM
poison,*,ned,ning,nous,nously, TOO HIGH A DOSE OF THIS WILL KILL, ABILITY TO HARM
poit, poet
poitry, poetry
poizen, poison
pok, poke / pock

pokd, poke(d)
poke,*,ed,king,ey, USE SOMETHING TO PRY/PUSH/MOVE, TO BE SLOW (or see pock)
poker, A CARD GAME, A TOOL
poket, pocket
pokit, pocket
pokreate, procreate
poks, pox
pokut, pocket
poky, poke(y)
pol, pole / poll / pool / pall
polar,rity,rities,rize,rization, OPPOSITE ELECTRICAL IMPULSE/ STREAM "prefixes: bi/de/re/sub/uni"
polaredy, polar(ity)
polarization, OF CELL ELECTRICAL SIGNALS "prefixes: re"
polarize,*,ed,zing,zation,zable,er, OPPOSITE FREQUENCY/PULSE/ POLES
polatics, politic(s)
pold, poll(ed)
poldes, poultice
poldis, poultice
poldre, poultry
poldus, poultice
pole,*, ROD, STAFF, (too many definitions please see standard dictionary) (or see poll)
polegimy, polygamy
polegon, polygon
polegraf, polygraph
polegraph, polygraph
polehedron, polyhedron
polemur, polymer
polen, pollen
polenade, pollinate
polenate, pollinate
polenation, pollinate(tion)
polenize, pollen(ize)
poleo, polio
polep, polyp
poler, polar
polerize, polarize
polese, police
polesh, polish
polester, polyester
polesy, policy
polet, pullet
poletics, politic(s)
poleticul, politic(al)
poletishen, politic(ian)
poley, pulley

poli, pulley
police,*,ed,cing, KEEP WATCH OVER A DESIGNATED AREA, ONE WHO KEEPS WATCH
policy,cies, RULES ESTABLISHED BY PRINCIPLES WHICH GUIDE BUSINESS AFFAIRS
polie, pulley
poliester, polyester
poligamus, polygamy(mous)
poligamy, polygamy
poligine, polygyny
poligon, polygon
poligraf, polygraph
poligraph, polygraph
polihedren, polyhedron
polimer, polymer
polin, pollen
polinate, pollinate
polination, pollinate(tion)
polinize, pollen(ize)
polio, POLIOMYELITIS, A CRIPPLING DISEASE
polip, polyp
polir, polar
polirize, polarize
polis, police
polish,hes,hed,hing,her, USE CHEMICAL/FRICTION TO REMOVE OXYDATION, A NATIONALITY
polit, pullet
polite,ely,eness, CONSIDERATE, RESPECTFUL
politecal, politic(al)
politecize, politic(ize)
politeshen, politic(ian)
politic,*,cal,cally,cian,cize,cized,cizing, CONCERNING GOVERNMENT "prefixes: de"
politicize,*,ed,zing,zation, MAKE AWARE OF/ABOUT POLITICS "prefixes: de"
poll,*,lled,lling,ller, USED TO TAX/ SURVEY/VOTE, PART OF HEAD WITH HAIR (or see pole) "prefixes: un"
pollen,*,nize,nizes,nized,nizer,nizing, nate,nia,nium, MICROSCOPIC SPORES PRODUCED BY PLANTS
pollenate, pollinate
pollinate,*,ed,ting,tion,tor,niferous, nize,nizes,nizer,nizing, POLLEN TRANSMITTED FROM ONE PLANT TO ANOTHER

pollute,*,ed,er,tant,ting,tion, HARMFUL (BYPRODUCTS) RELEASED INTO THE ENVIRONMENT "prefixes: de"
polm, palm
polomer, polymer
polre, polar
pols, poll(s) / pole(s) / pulse
polt, poll(ed)
poltes, poultice
poltice, poultice
poltis, poultice
poltree, poultry
poltry, poultry
poltus, poultice
polun, pollen
polunize, pollen(ize)
polup, polyp
polur, polar
polurize, polarize
polusee, policy
polushen, pollute(tion)
polusy, policy
polut, pullet / pollute
polutent, pollute(tant)
poluteshen, politic(ian)
polutics, politic(s)
polution, pollute(tion)
poly, PREFIX INDICATING "MANY" MOST OFTEN MODIFIES THE WORD
polyester,rification, CHEMICAL CHAIN WHICH IS USED TO MAKE PRODUCTS
polygamus, polygamy(mous)
polygamy,mist,mous, MAN/WOMAN HAVING MORE THAN ONE LEGAL PARTNER/SPOUSE AT A TIME (or see polygyny)
polyginy, polygyny
polygon,*,nal,nally, THREE OR MORE STRAIGHT SIDES
polygraph,*,hic, VERSATILE INSTRUMENT FOR REPLICATING/ RECORDING
polygyny,nous, HAVING MORE THAN ONE WIFE AT A TIME (or see polygamy)
polyhedren, polyhedron
polyhedron,*,ra,ral, A SOLID SURROUNDED BY MANY PLANED SURFACES
polymer,*,ric,rism,rization,rize, COMPOUNDS OF TWO OR MORE WITH A SIMILAR RELATIONSHIP
polymir, polymer

polyp,*,pous,pary, MANY GROWTHS/ TUMORS
pom, palm / poem
pomagranate, pomegranate
pombus, pompous
pomegranate,*, A FRUIT
pomel, pummel
pomigranate, pomegranate
pomil, pummel
pomkin, pumpkin
pomp, pump
pompis, pompous
pompkin, pumpkin
pompous,sly,sness, EXAGGERATED EXPRESSION TO SHOW SELFIMPORTANCE
pompus, pompous
pomugranate, pomegranate
pomul, pummel
pon, pawn
ponc, punk
ponchent, pungent
poncho,*, BLANKET/COAT
poncsher, puncture
poncshual, punctual
poncshuate, punctuate
ponctshur, puncture
pond,*, SMALL BODY OF WATER (or see pawn(ed))
ponder,*,rance,red,ring,rable,rer,rous, rously,rousness, TAKE TIME TO CONTEMPLATE SOMETHING "prefixes: pre"
pondificate, pontificate
pondir, ponder
pondoon, pontoon
pondune, pontoon
pondur, ponder
pone, pony
ponk, punk
ponsho, poncho
pont, pond / pawn(ed) / punt
pontcho, poncho
ponteficate, pontificate
ponter, ponder
pontificate,*,ed,ting,tion,tor, HAVE DOGMATIC CHARACTERISTICS, RELIGIOUS EXPRESSION
pontoon,*, FLOATS ON A PLANE IN PLACE OF WHEELS, A TYPE OF BOAT
pontune, pontoon
pontur, ponder
pony,nies, YOUNG/SMALL HORSE
pooch,hes, DOG

pood, put
pooding, pudding / putt(ing)
poodle,*, A BREED OF DOG (or see puddle)
pool,*,led,ling, PLACE TO SWIM, GAME USING BALLS/STICKS, COLLECTION/ ACCUMULATION OF LIQUID
poold, pull(ed) / pool(ed)
poolt, pull(ed) / pool(ed)
poor,rish,rly,rness, LACKING BASIC NECESSITIES (or see pore/pour)
poos, puss
poosh, push
pooshis, push(es)
pooshy, push(y)
poosy, puss(y)
poot, put
pootal, poodle
pooting, pudding / putt(ing)
pootle, poodle
pop,*,pped,pping,pper, A SOUND, A SOFT DRINK, SOMETHING BURSTING (or see pup)
popalashen, populate(tion)
popaler, popular
popcorn,*, COOKED CORN KERNEL
pope, pup(ppy) / poppy
popelashen, populate(tion)
popelur, popular
popery, potpourri
popet, puppet
popewlashen, populate(tion)
popewler, popular
popi, pup(ppy) / poppy
popilashen, populate(tion)
popiler, popular
poping, pop(pping)
popiry, potpourri
popit, puppet
popiuleit, populate
popkorn, popcorn
poplar,*, A TREE (or see popular)
poplashen, populate(tion)
poplur, poplar / popular
poporshenal, proportion(al)
poppy,ppies, A FLOWER
popree, potpourri
popt, pop(pped)
populachen, populate(tion)
popular,ly,rity,rize,rization,rizer, DESIRABLE BY MANY (or see poplar) "prefixes: un"
populashen, populate(tion)

populate,*,ed,ting,tion,list,lous,lously, lousness, TWO OR MORE THINGS THRIVING TOGETHER "prefixes: de/over/sub"
populus, populate(lous)
popury, potpourri
popy, poppy
popya, papaya
por, poor / pour / pore
porc, pork / park
porcalin, porcelain
porcelain, FINE/TRANSLUCENT CERAMIC "prefixes: semi"
porcepine, porcupine
porch,hes, A PLATFORM/STOOP/LANDING ADDED TO THE OUTSIDE OF A STRUCTURE
porchen, portion
porchun, portion
porcipine, porcupine
porcupine,*, LARGE RODENT WITH EXTERIOR QUILLS
pord, port / pour(ed)
pordable, portable
pordal, portal
pordeble, portable
pordel, portal
porder, porter
pordfolio, portfolio
pordible, portable
pordol, portal
porduble, portable
pordul, portal
pordur, porter
pore,*,ed,ring,rous, ONE OF MANY LOCATION ON THE SKIN/SURFACE FOR RESPIRATION, LOOK/EXAMINE WITH PERSERVERANCE (or see poor/pour)
pores, porous / pore(s)
porform, perform
poris, porous
pork,ky,ker, MEAT/OF PIGS/BOAR
porkepine, porcupine
porkewpine, porcupine
porkipine, porcupine
porkupine, porcupine
porogative, prerogative
porole, parole
porosity,sities, NUMBER/AMOUNT OF OPENINGS/PORES
porous,sly,sness, MANY OPENINGS/PORES
porpis, porpoise

porpoise,*, LARGE FISH THAT LOOKS LIKE A DOLPHIN, A CETACEAN
porpus, porpoise
porqupine, porcupine
porsalin, porcelain
porselan, porcelain
porsh, porch
porshin, portion
porsilan, porcelain
porsion, portion
porslin, porcelain
port,*,ted,ting,tly,table, A PLACE ON LAND WHERE VESSELS DOCK, TYPE OF WINE
portable,*,bility,bly, ABLE TO BE MOVED ABOUT EASILY
portal,*, OPENING ALLOWING ABILITY TO MOVE FROM ONE PLACE TO ANOTHER, PART OF THE LIVER
portch, porch
porteble, portable
porteon, portion
porter,*, AN ATTENDANT ON RAILCARS
portfolio,*, A DELIBERATE COLLECTION OF SPECIFIC PAPERS FOR PRESENTATION
portible, portable
portil, portal
portion,*,ned,ning, PART OF THE WHOLE "prefixes: pro"
portir, porter
portle, portal
portrait,*,tist, PAINTING/PHOTO OF A PERSON
portrat, portrait
portray,*,yed,ying,yal,yer, ATTEMPT TO PERSONIFY/DESCRIBE
portret, portrait
portuble, portable
portul, portal
portur, porter
porus, porous / peruse
porusness, porous(ness)
pos, pause / paw(s) / pose
posabiledy, possible(bility)
posability, possible(bility)
posative, positive
posatron, positron
posbone, postpone
poscher, posture
posd, post / pose(d)
posda, pasta
posdal, postal
posdchur, posture

posdel, postal
posder, poster / posture
posderety, posterior(ity)
posderior, posterior
posderity, posterior(ity)
posdil, postal
posdir, poster / posture
posdireor, posterior
posdle, postal
posdmark, postmark
posdpardum, postpartum
posdr, posture / poster
posdu, pasta
posdul, postal
posdulate, postulate
posdur, poster / posture
pose,*,ed,sing,er, STRIKE/HOLD AN ATTITUDE/POSTURE (or see posse/posy)
posebiledy, possible(bility)
posebly, possible(ly)
posebul, possible
posechon, position
posee, posy / posse
posem, opossum
poses, possess / pose(s) / posy / posse
poseshon, position
posesuf, possess(ive)
posetef, positive
posetive, positive
posetron, positron
posey, posse / posy
poshin, potion
poshon, potion
posibiledy, possible(bility)
posibly, possible(ly)
posibul, possible
posichen, position
posichon, position
posie, posse / posy
posim, opossum
posishen, position
positef, positive
position,*,ned,ning,nal,ner, POSTURE/ATTITUDE/STANCE/PLACEMENT "prefixes: contra/dis/inter/pre/pro"
positive,*,ely,eness,vism,vist,vistic, TYPE OF CHARGE, ON THE UP SIDE, OPTIMISTIC "prefixes: contra/dis/pre"
positron,*, PARTICLE OF POSITIVE CHARGE
posl, puzzle
posmordum, postmortem

posmortem, postmortem
posol, puzzle
posom, opossum
posotive, positive
pospartum, postpartum
pospone, postpone
posse, A GROUP OUT TO COLLECT JUSTICE
possess,sses,ssed,ssing,ssion,ssive, ssively,ssiveness, OWN/HAVE "prefixes: dis/pre"
possesuf, possess(ive)
possible,bility,bilities,ly, MOST LIKELY COULD BE DONE/PERFORMED "prefixes: im"
possum, opossum
post,*,ted,ting,ter,terize, MAKE INFORMATION PUBLIC, VERTICAL SUPPORT TO ATTACH SOMETHING TO (or see pose(d))
posta, pasta
postage,al, PRICE TO SHIP/FREIGHT SOMETHING TO A MAILBOX/ LOCATION
postaj, postage
postal,age, MAIL BY POST, PAY TO MAIL "prefixes: semi"
postasheo, pistachio
postcher, posture
postege, postage
postej, postage
postel, postal
poster,*, LARGE/BLOWN-UP PICTURE/ DIGITAL IMAGE (or see posture)
posterety, posterior(ity)
posterior,rly, THE REAR, FOLLOWS
posterity, CONCERNING THE FUTURE
postige, postage
postij, postage
postil, postal
postir, poster / posture
postireor, posterior
postle, postal
postmark,*,ked,king, AN INKED STAMP SHOWING DATE SOMETHING WAS MAILED
postmordem, postmortem
postmortem, A BODY ONCE THE SPIRIT IS REMOVED, AFTER DEATH
postpartum, AFTER GIVING BIRTH
postpone,*,ed,ning,nable,ement,er, PUT OFF UNTIL ANOTHER TIME
postr, posture / poster
postu, pasta

postuge, postage
postulate,*,ed,ting,tion,tor, TO CLAIM/ PETITION, ASSUME WITHOUT TRUTH
postur, poster / posture
posture,*,ed,ring, STANCE/PHYSICAL ATTITUDE
posubel, possible
posubility, possible(bility)
posubly, possible(ly)
posum, opossum
posutron, positron
posy,sies, A FLOWER (or see posse)
pot,*,tted,tting,table,tability,tableness, FLAT BOTTOM CONTAINER FOR COOKING/PLANTS (or see pod)
potable,bility,eness, WATER YOU CAN DRINK
potary, potter(y)
potaseum, potassium
potassium,ic, METALLIC CHEMICAL ELEMENT
potato,oes, A STARCHY VEGETABLE
pote, putty / potty
poteble, potable
poted, pot(tted) / pod(dded)
potee, potty
poten, potent
potenchul, potential
potend, potent
potenshul, potential
potensy, potent(ncy)
potent,ncy,ncies,tly, AMOUNT/DEGREE OF STRENGTH "prefixes: pre/sub/ uni"
potential,*,lly,lity,lities, STRONG POSSIBILITY "prefixes: bi"
poter, potter
potery, potter(y)
poteum, podium
poti, putty / potty
potible, potable
potid, pot(tted) / pod(dded)
potin, potent
potinchul, potential
potind, potent
potinshul, potential
potinsy, potent(ncy)
potint, potent
potintial, potential
potintiale, potential(lly)
potintialy, potential(lly)
potion,*, LIQUID WITH SPIRITUAL POWERS

potir, potter
potiry, potter(y)
potium, podium
potlach, potlatch
potlatch,hes, FESTIVAL/PARTY EXCHANGING GIFTS/GOODS
potlege, potlatch
potluck,*, A GATHERING OF PEOPLE WHERE EACH BRINGS A DISH OF FOOD TO SHARE
potluk, potluck
potpery, potpourri
potpourri,*, DRIED PLANTS COMBINED FOR THEIR AROMATHERAPY
potrude, protrude
potrushen, protrude(usion)
potter,*, ONE WHO WORKS WITH CLAY
pottery,ries, THINGS MADE OF CLAY THEN FIRED IN A KILN
potty,tties, A TOILET
potuble, potable
potun, potent
potunsy, potent(ncy)
potury, potter(y)
poty, potty
pouch,hes,hed, BAG/SACK/CAVITY FOR HOLDING THINGS (or see poach)
poud, pout
pouder, powder
poudir, powder
pouer, power
poultes, poultice
poultice,*,ed,cing, CRUSHED PLANTS/ HERBS MIXED WITH A BASE FOR APPLICATION
poultry,ries, EDIBLE BIRDS/FOWL
poum, poem
pounce,*,ed,cing, JUMP/LEAP TOWARDS AS IF TO GRAB/ATTACK, A POWDER
pound,*,ded,ding, U.S. MEASUREMENT FOR SOLIDS, TO HAMMER/STRIKE, BRITISH MONEY, AN AREA OF CONFINEMENT/HOLDING
pounse, pounce
pount, pound
pouperi, potpourri
pour,*,red,ring, WHEN TRANSFERRING LIQUID, A STREAMING FROM ONE PLACE TO ANOTHER (or see pore/ poor/power) "prefixes: in"
pourus, porous
pous, pose

pout,*,ted,ting,ter, TO SULK, BE SULLEN, A FISH (or see poet)
pouwir, power
pouwur, power
poverdy, poverty
poverty, WITHOUT BASIC NEEDS BEING FULFILLED
povileon, pavilion
povirty, poverty
povurty, poverty
powar, power
powch, pouch
powd, pout
powder,*,red,ring,rer,ry, FINELY CRUSHED MINERAL/PLANT, PULVERIZED
powdir, powder
powdur, powder
power,*,red,ring,rful,rfully,rfulness, rless,rlessly,rlessness, A CHARGE, RAISING FREQUENCY, EUPHORIC SENSE OF SUPREMACY/MASTERY (or see poor/pour) "prefixes: over"
powir, power
powlar, polar
powlur, polar
pownd, pound
pownse, pounce
pownt, pound
powr, power
powt, pout
powtch, pouch
powtur, powder
powur, power
pox, INDICATION THAT ONE IS DISTURBED BY A VIRUS IN THE BODY
poynt, point
poynyent, poignant
poyse, poise
poysin, poison
poz, pause / paw(s) / pose
pozd, pose(d) / pause(d)
pozda, pasta
pozderedy, posterior(ity)
pozdmark, postmark
pozdmordum, postmortem
pozdr, posture
pozdu, pasta
pozdul, postal
poze, pose / pause / posy / paw(s)
pozeble, possible
pozebly, possible(ly)
pozee, posy

pozetron, positron
pozible, possible
pozishen, position
pozitef, positive
pozol, puzzle
pozpardum, postpartum
pozpone, postpone
pozt, post / pose(d) / pause(d)
pozta, pasta
poztaj, postage
poztal, postal
pozteg, postage
poztej, postage
poztel, postal
pozter, poster / posture
poztereur, posterior
pozterior, posterior
poztij, postage
poztil, postal
poztir, poster / posture
poztmordum, postmortem
poztpardim, postpartum
poztu, pasta
poztul, postal
poztur, poster / posture
pozuble, possible
pozubly, possible(ly)
pozutif, positive
pozy, posy
pra, pray / prey
prababelity, probable(bility)
prabable, probable / probable(ly)
prabared, prepare(d)
prabebly, probably
praberty, property
prabibly, probably
prabirty, property
prablem, problem
prablum, problem
prabobelity, probable(bility)
prabozkus, proboscis
prabubilety, probable(bility)
prabubly, probably
prabugate, propagate
prabur, proper
praburly, proper(ly)
praburty, property
pracareus, precarious
pracaushen, precaution
pracawshen, precaution
pracedure, procedure
praceedure, procedure
pracepitous, precipitous
pracess, process

pracipitashen, precipitate(tion)
pracipitous, precipitous
pracise, precise
pracisly, precise(ly)
pracktus, practice
praclame, proclaim
praclemashen, proclamation
praclevity, proclivity
praclimation, proclamation
praclivedy, proclivity
praclivity, proclivity
praclution, preclusion
pracoshus, precocious
pracrastination, procrastinate(tion)
pracrastunate, procrastinate
practekul, practical
practes, practice
practeshener, practitioner
practical,lly,lity,lness, BEING LOGICAL, EASE OF USE/ OPERATION/ FUNCTION "prefixes: im/un"
practice,*,ed,cing,cal, PERFORM REPEATEDLY TO ACHIEVE MASTERY "prefixes: un"
practishener, practitioner
practitioner,*, ONE WHO PRACTICES
practus, practice
prad, parade / prod / pray(ed) / prey(ed)
pradasheus, predacious
pradatious, predacious
pradecament, predicament
pradector, predict(or)
pradegul, prodigal
pradegy, prodigy
pradekament, predicament
pradekshen, predict(ion)
pradekt, predict
pradektability, predict(ability)
pradektable, predict(able)
pradicament, predicament
pradict, predict
pradiction, predict(ion)
pradictor, predict(or)
pradigul, prodigal
pradigy, prodigy
pradikament, predicament
pradikshen, predict(ion)
pradiktability, predict(ability)
pradiktable, predict(able)
pradomenate, predominate
pradomenatly, predominate(ly)
pradominate, predominate
pradukshen, product(ion)

praduktion, product(ion)
prae, pray / prey
praer, pray(er)
prafale, prevail
prafanedy, profane(nity)
prafanity, profane(nity)
prafedik, prophet(ic)
prafes, profess
prafeser, professor
prafeshenul, profession(al)
prafeshinul, profession(al)
prafesy, prophecy / prophesy
prafet, profit / prophet
prafetable, profit(able)
prafetek, prophet(ic)
prafetible, profit(able)
prafetik, prophet(ic)
prafide, provide
prafiduble, provide(dable)
prafishent, proficient
prafit, profit / prophet
prafiteer, profit(eer)
prafoundly, profound(ly)
prafusy, prophecy / prophesy
prageks, project(s)
pragekshin, project(ion)
pragektile, project(ile)
pragektor, project(or)
pragesterone, progesterone
pragmadik, pragmatic
pragmatic,*,cal,cally,ism,ist,istic, BUSINESSLIKE, OFFICIAL ACTIVITY, OF PRACTICALITY/TRUTH
pragmatism, pragmatic(ism)
pragmitist, pragmatic(ist)
pragmutism, pragmatic(ism)
pragmutist, pragmatic(ist)
pragreshen, progress(ion)
pragresive, progress(ive)
pragress, progress
pragretion, progress(ion)
prahebatif, prohibit(ive)
prahebit, prohibit
prahibative, prohibit(ive)
prahibetory, prohibit(ory)
prahibit, prohibit
praid, parade / pride
praink, prank
prair, pray(er)
prairie,*, LARGE AREA OF LAND MOSTLY VOID OF TREES
praise,*,ed,sing, TO CONDONE/ COMPLIMENT SOMEONE/ SOMETHING (or see price) "prefixes: dis"
prajection, project(ion)
prajeks, project(s)
prajekshun, project(ion)
prajektile, project(ile)
prajektor, project(or)
prajesterone, progesterone
prakawshen, precaution
praklaim, proclaim
praklemashen, proclamation
praklemation, proclamation
praklevity, proclivity
praklimation, proclamation
praklivity, proclivity
praklude, preclude
praklumation, proclamation
praklusion, preclusion
praklusive, preclusive
prakoshen, precaution
prakoshious, precocious
prakotius, precocious
prakrastenate, procrastinate
prakrastination, procrastinate(tion)
praktekul, practical
praktes, practice
prakteshener, practitioner
praktetioner, practitioner
praktical, practical
praktikul, practical
praktis, practice
praktishener, practitioner
praktitioner, practitioner
praktus, practice
praleminary, preliminary
pralene, praline
pralimenary, preliminary
praline,*, CANDY
pralong, prolong
pralongate, prolong(ate)
pralood, prelude
pralude, prelude
pramenant, prominent
pramenit, prominent
pramere, premier
prames, promise
prameskuis, promiscuity(uous)
pramesuble, permissible
praminade, prom(enade)
praminent, prominent
pramis, promise
pramisable, permissible
pramiskuis, promiscuity(uous)
pramisquety, promiscuity
pramisquos, promiscuity(uous)
pramoder, promote(r)
pramonishen, premonition
pramoshen, promote(tion)
pramoter, promote(r)
pramotion, promote(tion)
prana, LIFE/ENERGY OF THE BREATH (or see piranha)
pranaunse, pronounce
prance,*,ed,cing,er, TO LIGHTLY DANCE ABOUT, TO WALK A GAIT WITH A PROUD/BOLD POSTURE
prank,*,kish,kster, TO PULL A TRICK ON SOMEONE, A SHOWFUL TRICK
pranounce, pronounce
pranownse, pronounce
pranse, prance / prawn(s)
pranunseashen, pronunciate(tion)
pranunsiate, pronunciate
pranunsiation, pronunciate(tion)
prapablee, probably
prapare, prepare
praparidness, prepare(dness)
prapegate, propagate
prapel, propel
prapeler, propel(ller)
prapelint, propel(llant)
praper, proper / prepare
praperedness, prepare(ness)
praperly, proper(ly)
praperty, property
praphat, prophet / profit
praphisy, prophecy / prophesy
praphut, prophet / profit
prapigate, propagate
prapir, proper
prapirty, property
praplum, problem
prapogate, propagate
praponint, proponent
praporshen, proportion
praportion, proportion
praposal, propose(sal)
prapose, propose
praposition, proposition
praposterus, preposterous
prapostureis, preposterous
prapoze, propose
prapozishen, proposition
praprietor, proprietor
prapubly, probably
prapuganda, propaganda
prapugashen, propagate(tion)
prapugate, propagate

prapur, proper
prapurty, property
prare, prairie
prarogative, prerogative
prary, prairie
prascribe, prescribe / proscribe
prascription, prescript(ion)
prascriptive, prescript(ive)
prasdeje, prestige
prasdrate, prostrate / prostate
prase, praise
prasechen, precision / procession / precession
prasecute, prosecute
prasede, precede / proceed
prasedger, procedure
praseet, precede
prasejur, procedure
prasekushen, prosecute(tion)
prasekute, prosecute
prasentuble, present(able)
praserve, preserve
prases, process / precess
praseshen, precision / procession / precession
prasetchur, procedure
prasetion, precision / procession / precession
prasetyur, procedure
prasicute, prosecute
praside, preside
prasidger, procedure
prasijer, procedure
prasikushen, prosecute(tion)
prasintable, present(able)
prasipatate, precipitate
prasise, precise
prasishen, precision / procession / precession
prasisly, precise(ly)
prasited, preside(d)
praskrepshen, prescript(ion)
praskribe, prescribe / proscribe
praskribshen, prescript(ion)
praskript, prescript / prescribe(d)
prasomtif, presume(mptive)
praspect, prospect
praspective, prospect(ive)
praspekt, prospect
praspektif, prospect(ive)
prasperus, prosper(ous)
praspur, prosper
prastate, prostate / prostrate
prastegis, prestige(gious)

prasteje, prestige
prastejus, prestige(gious)
prastetute, prostitute
prasthesis, prosthesis
prasthesus, prosthesis
prastrate, prostrate / prostate
prasukushen, prosecute(tion)
prasum, presume
prasumptive, presume(mptive)
prasumshen, presume(mption)
prasumtif, presume(mptive)
prasumtion, presume(mption)
prasumtuis, presume(mptuous)
prasurve, preserve
pratect, protect
pratection, protect(ion)
pratekshen, protect(ion)
pratekt, protect
pratektuf, protect(ive)
pratend, pretend
pratended, pretend(ed)
pratind, pretend
pratrude, protrude
pratrugin, protrude(usion)
pratrusef, protrude(usive)
pratrusion, protrude(usion)
praublem, problem
praud, proud
praudly, proud(ly)
praufet, prophet / profit
praufut, prophet / profit
praukse, proxy
praul, prowl
praun, prawn
prauphet, prophet / profit
prauses, process
praustat, prostate / prostrate
praut, proud
prautly, proud(ly)
pravale, prevail
pravalent, prevalent
pravelent, prevalent
pravense, province
pravenshen, prevent(ion)
pravent, prevent
praventable, prevent(able)
praventive, prevent(ive)
praverb, proverb
praverbeul, proverb(ial)
pravide, provide
praviduble, provide(dable)
pravilent, prevalent
pravinse, province
pravinshen, prevent(ion)

pravinshul, province(cial)
pravint, prevent
pravintable, prevent(able)
pravirb, proverb
pravirbeal, proverb(ial)
pravocative, provocative
pravock, provoke
pravokative, provocative
pravoke, provoke
pravulent, prevalent
pravurb, proverb
pravurbeul, proverb(ial)
prawdly, proud(ly)
prawess, prowess
prawl, prowl
prawn,*, LARGE SHRIMP
prawt, proud
prawtly, proud(ly)
pray,*,yed,ying,yer, TO FOCUS ON A THOUGHT OR A DESIRE YOU WISH TO PHYSICALLY MANIFEST IN THE MOMENT OR THE FUTURE (or see praise/prey)
praylene, praline
prayr, pray(er)
prayree, prairie
praze, praise / pray(s)
prazens, presence / present(s)
prazent, present
prazentuble, present(able)
prazerve, preserve
prazint, present
prazumtues, presume(mptuous)
prazurve, preserve
pre, PREFIX INDICATING "BEFORE" MOST OFTEN MODIFIES THE WORD
preach,hes,hed,hing,hingly,her,hify, hified,hifying,hy, VOCALLY TEACH A LESSON
preamble, BRIEF INTRODUCTION, PREFACE
preample, preamble
preampt, preempt
prebozkus, proboscis
precadent, precedent / president
precarious,sly,sness, UNCERTAIN ABOUT STABILITY OR FIRM POSITION, NOT SECURE
precastinate, procrastinate
precaushen, precaution
precaution,*,nary,nal,ous, TAKE STEPS TO PREPARE TO AVERT DANGER/ HARM

precede,*,ed,ding,ence,ency,ent, GOING/BEING BEFORE, SETS GUIDELINES FOR ALL THAT FOLLOWS (or see proceed)
precedent,*,tly,tial,tially, GOING/BEING BEFORE, SETS GUIDELINES FOR ALL THAT FOLLOWS (or see proceed) "prefixes: un"
precens, presence / present(s)
precent, present
precentashen, presentation
precepitate, precipitate
precepitous, precipitous
precersory, precursor(y)
precess,ssion, FIRST IN ORDER/RANK/TIME, BEHAVIOR OF PLANETS/AXIS/MOTION
precession,ssional, FIRST IN ORDER/RANK/TIME, BEHAVIOR OF PLANETS/ AXIS/MOTION (or see procession/precision)
prech, preach
precher, preach(er)
precidense, precede(nce) / president(s)
precident, precede(nt) / president / precedent
precinct,*, AREAS DIVIDED FOR VOTING/CONTROL
precious,ly,ness, HIGHLY CHERISHED, VALUABLE "prefixes: semi"
precipitate,*,ed,ting,able,ely,eness,tive, tor,tion,ant,ancy,antly, FALLING MOISTURE, BRING ABOUT
precipitous,sly,sness, BRING ABOUT QUICKLY WITHOUT MUCH THOUGHT, STEEP HEIGHT
precise,ely,eness,sion, EXACT/CLOSE TO PERFECT, CAREFUL ATTENTION TO DETAIL
precishen, precision / procession / precession
precision,nist, EXACT/CLOSE TO PERFECT, CAREFUL ATTENTION TO DETAIL (or see procession/precession)
precius, precious
preclame, proclaim
preclude,*,ed,ding,usion,usive, PREVENT OR EXCLUDE SOMEONE/SOMETHING
preclushen, preclusion
preclusion, PREVENT/EXCLUDE SOMEONE/SOMETHING

preclusive,ely,ion, PREVENT/EXCLUDE SOMEONE/SOMETHING
preclution, preclusion
precochusly, precocious(ly)
precocious,sly,sness,sity, MATURING EARLY/QUICKLY
precognative, precognitive
precognishen, precognition
precognition,ive, ABLE TO SENSE/KNOW THE FUTURE
precognitive, ABILITY TO SENSE/KNOW THE FUTURE
precoshen, precaution
precoshus, precocious
precotion, precaution
precotious, precocious
precrastination, procrastinate
precugnishen, precognition
precursor,ry,sive, COMES BEFORE
predacious,sness,sity,ation, PREDATORY/PREYS, ATTACKING/KILLING/HUNTING
predacity, predacious(ity)
predasesor, predecessor
predasheus, predacious
predater, predator
predatious, predacious
predator,*,rial,rily,ry, ATTACKING/KILLING/HUNTING
predatoreul, predator(ial)
prede, pretty
predecesor, predecessor
predecessor,*, WHO LIVED/CAME BEFORE, ANCESTOR
predekshen, predict(ion)
predekt, predict
predesesor, predecessor
predespasition, predispose(sition)
predespazishen, predispose(sition)
predespose, predispose
predetor, predator
predetorial, predator(ial)
predeur, pretty(ttier)
prediar, pretty(ttier)
predicament,*,tal, TO BE IN AN AWKWARD/CHALLENGING/DIFFICULT POSITION
predicesor, predecessor
predict,*,ted,ting,table,tably,tability, tion,tive,tively,tiveness,tor, TO FORETELL THE FUTURE "prefixes: un"
predier, pretty(ttier)
prediest, pretty(ttiest)

predikament, predicament
prediktable, predict(able)
predisesor, predecessor
predispazishen, predispose(sition)
predispose,*,ed,sing,sition, TENDENCY TOWARDS BEFOREHAND
preditor, predator
preditorial, predator(ial)
predomenashen, predominate(tion)
predominate,ely,tion,nant,nantly,ance, ancy, DOMINATE/AUTHORITY/CONTROL OVER
predsul, pretzel
preduction, product(ion)
predukshen, product(ion)
predusesor, predecessor
predutor, predator
predutoreul, predator(ial)
predutory, predator(y)
predy, pretty
predyest, pretty(ttiest)
preech, preach
preechy, preach(y)
preempt,tor,ption,ptive,ptively, TO OCCUPY/SEIZE/ACQUIRE BEFORE ANYONE ELSE CAN ACQUIRE OWNERSHIP
preemshen, preempt(ion)
preemt, preempt
preface,ed,cing, REMARKS/INTRODUCTION BEFORE A BOOK/LITERARY WORK
prefale, prevail
prefanedy, profane(nity)
prefanity, profane(nity)
prefeks, prefix
prefer,*,rred,rring,rence,rences,rable, rableness,rability,rably,rential, rentialist, rentialism,rentiality, rentially,rment, CHOOSE OVER OTHERS, MOST DESIRABLE
preferinse, prefer(ence)
preferuble, prefer(able)
prefese, preface
prefeshenul, profession(al)
prefesur, professor
prefex, prefix
preficks, prefix
prefide, provide
prefiduble, provide(dable)
prefiks, prefix
prefir, prefer
prefirability, prefer(ability)
prefirable, prefer(able)

prefirense, prefer(ence)
prefirenshul, prefer(ential)
prefirential, prefer(ential)
prefis, preface
prefix,xes,xal,xally,xation,xion, LETTERS BEFORE A BASE WORD THAT MODIFIES IT'S MEANING, EXISTS PRIOR TO
preforenshul, prefer(ential)
prefound, profound
prefoundly, profound(ly)
prefur, prefer
prefurabiledy, prefer(ability)
prefurable, prefer(able)
prefurenshul, prefer(ential)
prefurential, prefer(ential)
prefurinse, prefer(ence)
prefuse, preface
prefy, privy
pregadis, prejudice
pregedis, prejudice
pregekshin, project(ion)
pregesterone, progesterone
pregidis, prejudice
pregnant,tly,ncy,ncies,able,ability, BODY CARRYING AN EMBRYO
pregnensy, pregnant(ncy)
pregnet, pregnant
pregnint, pregnant
pregnonsy, pregnant(ncy)
pregnunt, pregnant
pregnut, pregnant
pregodis, prejudice
pregreshen, progress(ion)
pregretion, progress(ion)
pregudis, prejudice
prei, prey / pray
preimshen, preempt(ion)
preimt, preempt
preimtif, preempt(ive)
preimtive, preempt(ive)
preis, prey(s) / pray(s) / praise
prejadis, prejudice
prejekshin, project(ion)
prejidis, prejudice
prejodis, prejudice
prejudice,*,ed,cing,cial,cially, AN OPINION/ATTITUDE ABOUT SOMETHING/ SOMEONE WITHOUT BASIS OF FULL KNOWLEDGE
prek, prick
prekareus, precarious
prekarius, precarious
prekastinate, procrastinate

prekaution, precaution
prekawshen, precaution
preked, prick(ed)
prekersery, precursor(y)
prekirsor, precursor
prekirsory, precursor(y)
preklame, proclaim
preklewd, preclude
preklude, preclude
preklushen, preclusion
preklusive, preclusive
preklution, preclusion
preknet, pregnant
preknit, pregnant
preknut, pregnant
prekognative, precognitive
prekognishen, precognition
prekognition, precognition
prekoshen, precaution
prekoshious, precocious
prekoshus, precocious
prekotius, precocious
prekrastination, procrastinate
prekursor, precursor
prekursory, precursor(y)
preleminary, preliminary
prelene, praline
prelewt, prelude
preliminary,ries,rily, INTRODUCTION TO THE MAIN
prelong, prolong
prelongate, prolong(ate)
prelood, prelude
prelude,*,ded,ding,er,usive,usively, usorily,usory, LEADING UP/ INTRODUCTORY TO
prelute, prelude
prem, prim
premachure, premature
premanishen, premonition
premanition, premonition
prematif, primitive
prematively, primitive(ly)
premature,ely,eness,rity, BEFORE RIPE/ MATURE/FULLY FORMED
premear, premier
premechure, premature
premedatate, premeditate
premeditate,*,ed,ting,tion,tive, PLAN OUT BEFORE THE ACT OF "prefixes: un"
premeim, premium
premeneshen, premonition
premenishen, premonition

premenstrual,lly, PRIOR TO/BEFORE MENSTRUATION
premenzdrul, premenstrual
premere, premier
premese, premise
premetetate, premeditate
premetitate, premeditate
premeum, premium
premichure, premature
premier,*, PLAY/OPERA/MOVIE FIRST PUBLIC EXPOSURE
preminishen, premonition
preminstral, premenstrual
preminstrul, premenstrual
premiom, premium
premir, premier
premisabul, permissible
premise,*, ASSUMPTION, BEFOREHAND, LAND WITH TENANTS, BEGINNING OF, PROPOSITION
premiskues, promiscuity(uous)
premitive, primitive
premiture, premature
premium,*, BONUS, ADDITIONALLY
premoder, promote(r)
premoneshen, premonition
premonition,*, SENSE/FEELING BEFORE AN EVENT
premose, premise
premoshen, promote(tion)
premote, promote
premotion, promote(tion)
premoture, premature
premp, primp
prempt, primp(ed)
premuchure, premature
premunishen, premonition
premunition, premonition
premuse, premise
premutif, primitive
premuture, premature
prence, prince / print(s)
prenceses, princess(es)
prencess, princess
prenciple, principle / principal
prend, print
prendable, print(able)
prender, print(er)
prendible, print(able)
prenduble, print(able)
prenoense, pronounce
prenounce, pronounce
prensabul, principle / principal
prensaple, principle / principal

prense, prince / print(s)
prenses, princess / prince(s)
prensibul, principle / principal
prensipul, principle / principal
prensis, princess / prince(s)
prensuple, principle / principal
prent, print
prentabul, print(able)
prenter, print(er)
prentible, print(able)
prentr, print(er)
prentur, print(er)
prenunseate, pronunciate
prenunsiation, pronunciate(tion)
prenus, apprentice
prep,*,pped,pping,pper,ppy, PREPARE/ MAKE READY FOR
prepare,*,ed,edness,ring,ration,rative, ratively,rator,ratory,rer, EQUIP/ COMPOSE/ASSEMBLE/ MANUFACTURE/CONDITION SOMETHING/ SOMEONE FOR ACTIVITY/EVENT "prefixes: un"
prepaseshen, preposition / proposition / prepossess(ion)
prepazishen, preposition / proposition / prepossess(ion)
preperashen, prepare(ration)
preperatory, prepare(ratory)
preperidness, prepare(ness)
prepiration, prepare(ration)
prepiratory, prepare(ratory)
prepiseshen, preposition / proposition / prepossess(ion)
preponent, proponent
preporashen, prepare(ration)
preporshen, proportion
preportion, proportion
preposal, propose(sal)
prepose, propose
preposeshun, prepossess
preposesing, prepossessing
preposishen, preposition / proposition / prepossess(ion)
preposition,*,ned,ning,nal,nally, ENGLISH LANGUAGE TERM (or see proposition)
prepossess,ssing,ssion, POSSESS BEFORE SOMEONE ELSE DOES, TO IMPRESS
prepossessing,gly,gness,ion, TO IMPRESS/CHARM FAVORABLY "prefixes: un"

preposterous,sly,sness, BEYOND RATIONAL, GOES AGAINST COMMON SENSE
preposturis, preposterous
prepoze, propose
prepozes, prepossess
prepozishen, preposition / proposition / prepossess(ion)
prepozle, propose(sal)
prepriator, proprietor
prepurashen, prepare(ration)
prepuration, prepare(ration)
prepusition, proposition
prepuzishen, preposition / proposition / prepossess(ion)
prer, pray(er)
prere, prairie
prerogative,*, PRIVILEGED
prery, prairie
pres, press
presadense, precede(nce) / president(s)
presadenshul, president(ial)
presadent, precedent/ president
presadinse, precede(nce) / president(s)
presadint, precede(nt) / president
prescrebshin, prescript(ion)
prescribe,*,ed,bing,er, RULE/COURSE/ ACTION TO BE FOLLOWED (or see prescript/proscribe)
prescripshen, prescript(ion)
prescript,tible,tion,tive,tively,tiveness, tivism, CLAIM/CUSTOM/RULE/ RIGHT/ TITLE TO (or see prescribe)
prescrishen, prescript(ion)
presd, press(ed)
presdeje, prestige
presdo, presto
presede, precede / proceed
presedent, precede(nt) / president
presedential, president(ial)
presedger, procedure
presedintial, president(ial)
presedyur, procedure
presee, prissy
preseet, precede
preseger, procedure
presejur, procedure
presence, OF BEING PRESENT, IN IMMEDIATE VICINITY OF (or see present)
presenked, precinct
presenkt, precinct
presens, presence / present(s)

present,*,ted,ter,ting,tly,tness,table, tableness,tability,tably,tment,tation, nce, GIVEN FREELY, ACCEPTABLE, TO OFFER SOMETHING, IN IMMEDIATE VICINITY OF, MAKE VISIBLE (or see presence) "prefixes: re,-re"
presentation,*,nal,ive, PRESENT/ OFFER/EXHIBIT SOMETHING "prefixes: re,-re"
presepitous, precipitous
preser, pressure / press(er)
preservashen, preserve(vation)
preserve,*,ed,er,vable,vation,ving, PROTECT FROM, PREVENT CONDITION FROM BEING ALTERED/ EXPLOITED/CHANGED
preses, precess
preseshen, precision / procession / precession
presetgur, procedure
presetion, precision / procession / precession
presh, preach
presher, pressure
presherize, pressure(rize)
preshes, precious
preshir, pressure
preshis, precious
preshorize, pressure(rize)
preshur, pressure
preshurize, pressure(rize)
preshus, precious
preside,*,ed,ding,er, ONE IN A HIERARCHAL POSITION OVER, THE AUTHORITY OF THE GROUP, OVERSEEING
presidense, precede(nce) / president(s)
presidenshul, president(ial)
president,*,ncy,ncies,tial, LEADERSHIP POSITION (or see precedent)
presiger, procedure
presijur, procedure
presim, prism
presin, prison
presinct, precinct
presiner, prison(er)
presinked, precinct
presinkt, precinct
presinse, presence
presint, present
presintable, present(able)
presintashen, presentation
presintation, presentation

presintly, present(ly)
presints, present(s) / presence
presipatate, precipitate
presipatation, precipitate(tion)
presipitate, precipitate
presipitous, precipitous
presiputashen, precipitate(tion)
presir, pressure / press(er)
presirvation, preserve(vation)
presis, precise / press(es)
presishen, precision / procession / precession
presisly, precise(ly)
presited, preside(d)
presition, precision/procession
preskrepshen, prescript(ion)
preskribe, prescribe / proscribe
preskribshen, prescript(ion)
presm, prism
presmadik, prism(atic)
presodent, precede(nt) / president
presomtif, presume(mptive)
preson, prison
press,sses,ssed,ssing,sser, APPLY/EXERT FORCE, SQUEEZE, COMPACT "prefixes: re,-re"
pressure,*,ed,ring,rize,rizer,rizing, rization, THE APPLICATION/ EXERTION OF FORCE, SQUEEZE, COMPACT, REMOVE AIR "prefixes: over"
prest, priest / press(ed)
prestege, prestige
prestegus, prestige(gious)
prestej, prestige
prestene, pristine
prestess, priest(ess)
presthesus, prosthesis
presthood, priest(hood)
prestige,gious,giousness,giously, OF DISTINCTION RANK/QUALITY
prestigous, prestige(gious)
prestine, pristine
prestly, priest(ly)
presto, INSTANT/AUTOMATIC/ SUDDEN/QUICK
presudent, precede(nt) / president / precedent
presum, prism / presume
presume,*,ed,ming,er,mption,mptive, mptively,tuous,tuously, tuousness, MOST PROBABLE WITHOUT PROOF, CONCLUSION/SUPPOSING WITHOUT FACTS

presumshen, presume(mption)
presumtif, presume(mptive)
presumtion, presume(mption)
presumtuis, presume(mptuous)
presumtuous, presume(mptuous)
presun, prison
presur, pressure / press(er)
presurf, preserve
presurvashen, preserve(vation)
presurve, preserve
presus, press(es)
presy, prissy
prete, pretty
pretekt, protect
pretektif, protect(ive)
pretektive, protect(ive)
pretend,*,ded,ding,der,nse, ACT AS IF REAL, MAKE BELIEVE, DECEPTIVE "prefixes: un"
pretense,*,sion,sionless,sive,ntious, ACT AS IF REAL, MAKE BELIEVE, DECEPTIVE
pretenshen, pretense(sion)
pretentious,sly,sness, FIRMLY CONFIDENT, OVERSTEPS OTHERS' BOUNDARIES "prefixes: un"
preteur, pretty(ttier)
pretiest, pretty(ttiest)
pretind, pretend
pretinse, pretense
pretinshen, pretense(sion)
pretrude, protrude
pretrusion, protrude(usion)
pretsul, pretzel
pretty,ttier,ttiest,tties,ttiness,ttily,ttyish, ttify,ttifier,ttifying,ttification, ATTRACTIVE/VISUALLY PLEASING
prety, pretty
pretzel,*,led, DOUGHY FOOD TWISTED INTO A KNOT
prevade, pervade
prevail,*,led,ling, WILL ENDURE, ONGOING, WILL NOT BE OVERCOME
prevale, prevail
prevaleg, privilege
prevalense, prevalent(nce)
prevalent,tly,nce, WILL PREVAIL, MOST COMMON/POPULAR
prevalige, privilege
prevalijes, privilege(s)
prevalinse, prevalent(nce)
prevalint, prevalent
prevalt, prevail(ed)

preveis, previous
preveisly, previous(ly)
prevelent, prevalent
prevelinse, prevalent(nce)
prevelint, prevalent
prevenshen, prevent(ion)
prevent,*,ted,ting,tion,tability,table,ter, tive,tively,tiveness,tative, STOP/ PREPARE/KEEP FROM HAPPENING
preveos, previous
preveosly, previous(ly)
preveus, previous
preveusly, previous(ly)
previde, provide
previduble, provide(dable)
previlege, privilege
previlense, prevalent(nce)
previlent, prevalent
previnshun, prevent(ion)
previntion, prevent(ion)
previntive, prevent(ive)
previous,sly, HAPPENED/OCCURRED BEFORE
previus, previous
previusly, previous(ly)
prevlej, privilege
prevlig, privilege
prevocative, provocative
prevok, provoke
prevokative, provocative
prevokt, provoke
prevulense, prevalent(nce)
prevulent, prevalent
prevulinse, prevalent(nce)
prevy, privy
prey,*,yed,ying,yer, STALK/HUNT DOWN SOMEONE/SOMETHING FOR SATISFACTION/NOURISHMENT (or see pray)
prezadinshul, president(ial)
prezadint, precede(nt) / president
prezedinshul, president(ial)
prezedint, precede(nt) / president
prezent, present
prezentashen, presentation
prezents, presence / present(s)
prezervashen, preserve(vation)
prezerve, preserve
prezident, precede(nt) / president
preziner, prison(er)
prezint, present
prezintly, present(ly)
prezints, presence / present(s)
prezodent, precede(nt) / president

prezomtuis, presume(mptuous)
prezt, priest
prezudenshul, president(ial)
prezudent, precede(nt) / president
prezum, prism
prezumtues, presume(mptuous)
prezunt, present
prhaps, perhaps
pri, pry / pre
priboskus, proboscis
pric, prick / price
pricarius, precarious
pricashen, precaution
pricastinate, procrastinate
pricaushen, precaution
pricaution, precaution
price,*,ed,cing,ey,eless, COST OF/FOR SOMETHING (or see prick) "prefixes: under"
pricechen, precession / procession / precision
pricede, precede / proceed
pricersor, precursor
prices, price(s) / precess
priceshen, precession / procession / precision
pricise, precise
pricisely, precise(ly)
pricishen, precession / procession / precision
pricision, precession / procession / precision
prick,*,ked,king,kley,klier,kliest,kliness, PIERCE/PUNCTURE WITH SHARP POINT, SLANG FOR MALE ORGAN
priclame, proclaim
priclude, preclude
priclushen, preclusion
priclution, preclusion
pricochen, precaution
pricognative, precognitive
pricogneshen, precognition
pricognition, precognition
pricoshus, precocious
pricotion, precaution
pricotious, precocious
pricursor, precursor
pricy, price(y)
pridachus, predacious
pridacity, predacious(ity)
pridashius, predacious
pridatious, predacious

pride,*,ded,ding,eful,efully,efulness, roud, EGO PROTECTING ITS SELF-ESTEEM, BOASTFUL, ARROGANT
pridear, pretty(ttier)
pridecament, predicament
pridect, predict
pridekter, predict(or)
pridespose, predispose
prideur, pretty(ttier)
pridful, pride(ful)
pridfulness, pride(fulness)
pridfuly, pride(fully)
pridi, pretty
pridicament, predicament
pridictable, predict(able)
pridiction, predict(ion)
pridiest, pretty(ttiest)
pridikament, predicament
pridikshen, predict(ion)
pridikt, predict
pridispose, predispose
pridominate, predominate
pridukshen, product(ion)
priduktion, product(ion)
pridy, pretty
pridyest, pretty(ttiest)
priempt, preempt
priemt, preempt
prieng, pry(ing)
prier, prior
prieredy, prior(ity)
priest,*,tly,tliness,thood,tess, ASSIGNED PERSON TO REPRESENT A RELIGIOUS BELIEF
prifale, prevail
prifasee, private(acy)
prifatize, private(tize)
prifatlee, private(ly)
prifee, privy
prifer, prefer
prifes, profess
prifeshen, profession
prifeshinol, profession(al)
prifesor, professor
prifesy, private(acy)
prifet, private
prifetize, private(tize)
prifetlee, private(ly)
prifex, prefix
prifide, provide
prifir, prefer
prifisee, private(acy)
prifit, private
prifitize, private(tize)

prifitlee, private(ly)
prifix, prefix
prifot, private
prifotize, private(tize)
prifound, profound
prifur, prefer
prifusy, private(acy)
prifut, private
prifutize, private(tize)
prifutlee, private(ly)
prify, privy
prigekshen, project(ion)
prignostik, prognostic
prigreshen, progress(ion)
prijekshen, project(ion)
prijektile, project(ile)
prijidus, prejudice
prik, prick
prikareus, precarious
prikashen, precaution
prikastinate, procrastinate
prikaushen, precaution
prikd, prick(ed)
priked, prick(ed)
prikereous, precarious
priklame, proclaim
prikle, prick(ly)
priklusion, preclusion
priklusive, preclusive
prikognishen, precognition
prikoshen, precaution
prikoshus, precocious
prikotion, precaution
prikotius, precocious
prikrastination, procrastinate
prikt, prick(ed)
prilemenary, preliminary
prilimenary, preliminary
prilong, prolong
prilongate, prolong(ate)
prim,mmer,mmest,mly,mness, FORMAL/PROPER (or see prime)
primachur, premature
primade, primate
primal, PRIMITIVE, BASE, FUNDAMENTAL
primary,ries,rily, MAIN ONE, CENTRAL, MOST IMPORTANT, FUNDAMENTAL
primate,*,eship,tial, MAMMALS, MAN/ MONKEYS/APES
primatif, primitive
primative, primitive
primativly, primitive(ly)

prime,ed,ming,eness,er, AT ITS PEAK, READY, PREPARED FOR AN EVENT, TYPE OF NUMBER "prefixes: un"
primechur, premature
primeditate, premeditate
primel, primal
primenstral, premenstrual
primer, premier / prime(r)
primerily, primary(rily)
primery, primary
primir, prime(r) / premier
primise, premise
primitive,*,ely,eness,vism,vist,vistic, SIMPLE, EARLIEST EXPRESSION, CRUDE, GEOMETRIC EXPRESSION
primle, primal
primly, prim(mmly) / prime(ly)
primoder, promote(r)
primol, primal
primoshen, promote(tion)
primote, promote
primoter, promote(r)
primotion, promote(tion)
primp,*,ped,ping, TO ADORN/GROOM/ DRESS UP
primul, primal
primur, prime(r) / prim(mmer)
primutif, primitive
prinaunse, pronounce
princabol, principal/ principle
prince,*,edom, MALE POSITION OF ROYALTY
princepol, principal/ principle
princess,sses, FEMALE POSITION OF ROYALTY
principal,*,lly,lship,lity,lities,lly, PRIMARY/FIRST IN POSITION/ IMPORTANCE, TERM HAVING TO DO WITH MONEY/LAW (or see principle) "prefixes: sub"
principle,*,ed, MAIN POINT, GENERAL TRUTH, ADOPTED METHOD/RULE/ LAW (or see principal) "prefixes: un"
principol, principal / principle
prind, print
prinounce, pronounce
prinownse, pronounce
prins, prince / print(s)
prinsabul, principle / principal
prinse, prince / print(s)
prinsepul, principle / principal
prinses, princess / prince(s)
prinseses, princess(es)

prinsipul, principle / principal
prinsuple, principle / principal
print,*,ted,ting,table,tability,ter,tery, tless, USE OF TEXT TO COMMUNICATE "prefixes: mis/ over/pre/un"
printuble, print(able)
printur, print(er)
prinunseashen, pronunciate(tion)
prinunseate, pronunciate
prinunsiation, pronunciate(tion)
prior,rly,rship,rate,rity,rities, FIRST, BEFORE, EARLIER, RELIGIOUS RANK
priorety, prior(ity)
prioridy, prior(ity)
pripare, prepare
pripeler, propel(ller)
priper, prepare
priponent, proponent
priporshen, proportion
priportion, proportion
priposal, propose(sal)
pripose, propose
priposteros, preposterous
pripozle, propose(sal)
pripriator, proprietor
pririogative, prerogative
pris, price / prize
priscraib, prescribe
priscribe, prescribe / proscribe
priscript, prescript
prisdeje, prestige
prise, price / price(y) / prize
prisechen, precision / procession / precession
prised, precede / proceed / price(d)
prisedger, procedure
prisee, prissy / price(y)
priseet, precede / proceed
prisejur, procedure
prisem, prism
prisen, prison
prisener, prison(er)
prisentable, present(able)
prisentashin, presentation
prisentation, presentation
priserv, preserve
priservation, preservation
priserve, preserve
prises, price(s)/ precess
priseshen, precision / procession / precession
prisetgur, procedure

prisetion, precision / procession / precession
priside, preside / precede
prisigur, procedure
prisim, prism
prisin, prison
prisipatate, precipitate
prisipatation, precipitate(tion)
prisise, precise
prisisly, precise(ly)
priskrepshen, prescript(ion)
priskribe, prescribe / proscribe
prisless, price(less)
prislis, price(less)
prism,*,matic,matically, GEOMETRICAL SHAPE, OPTICAL/CRYSTAL/ RAINBOW EFFECT
prismadik, prism(atic)
prisom, prism
prisomtif, presume(mptive)
prison,*,ner, BUILDING USED TO CONFINE/HOLD, A FEELING OF INVOLUNTARY RESTRAINT
prisontation, presentation
prissy,ssily,ssiness, ARROGANTLY PRIM, GIRLY GIRL
prist, priest / price(d)
pristege, prestige
pristegus, prestige(gious)
pristeje, prestige
pristene, pristine
pristine,ely, UNCONTAMINATED, PURE
prisum, prism / presume
prisumptive, presume(mptive)
prisumtion, presume(mption)
prisumtuis, presume(mptuous)
prisun, prison
prisuner, prison(er)
prisurf, preserve
prisurve, preserve
prisy, prissy / price(y)
prit, pride
pritear, pretty(ttier)
pritect, protect
pritection, protect(ion)
prited, pride(d)
pritekshen, protect(ion)
pritekt, protect
pritektif, protect(ive)
pritenchus, pretentious
pritend, pretend
pritenshen, pretense(sion)
pritenshus, pretentious
pritentious, pretentious

priteur, pretty(ttier)
pritful, pride(ful)
priti, pretty
pritiest, pretty(ttiest)
pritinchos, pretentious
pritinshus, pretentious
pritintious, pretentious
pritrude, protrude
pritrushen, protrude(usion)
pritrusion, protrude(usion)
prity, pretty
priur, prior
prival, prevail
privaledged, privilege(d)
privalent, prevalent
privalije, privilege
privalt, prevail(ed)
privasee, private(acy)
private,*,ely,acy,tness,tize,tized,tizing, tization,tion,tist,tism, MUST GAIN PERMISSION TO ACCESS, SECLUDED, U.S.MILITARY RANK, NON-GOVERNMENTAL "prefixes: semi"
privatisation, private(tization)
privatly, private(ly)
privecy, private(acy)
privee, privy
priveisly, previous(ly)
priveledged, privilege(d)
privelent, prevalent
privelige, privilege
privenshen, prevent(ion)
privent, prevent
priventable, prevent(able)
priventive, prevent(ive)
priverbeul, proverb(ial)
privese, private(acy)
privet, private
privetisation, private(tization)
privetly, private(ly)
priveus, previous
priveusly, previous(ly)
privicy, private(acy)
prividuble, provide(dable)
privilege,*,ed,ging, SPECIAL, HONORARY, FAVORED, CHOSEN "prefixes: under"
privilent, prevalent
privilige, privilege
privios, previous
privit, private
privitly, private(ly)
priviusly, previous(ly)
privocative, provocative

privock, provoke
privokative, provocative
privoke, provoke
privokt, provoke(d)
privolent, prevalent
privulej, privilege
privusee, private(acy)
privut, private
privutization, private(tization)
privutly, private(ly)
privvy, privy
privy,vies,vier,viest, OUTDOOR TOILET, IN ON A PRIVATE MATTER/SECRET
privyed, privy(vied)
prize,*,ed,zing, GIFT/REWARD/AWARD FOR ACCOMPLISHMENT/WINNING (or see price/pry(s))
prizen, prison
prizener, prison(er)
prizent, present
prizerve, preserve
prizin, prison
prizis, prize(s) / price(s)
prizm, prism
prizmadik, prism(atic)
prizmatic, prism(atic)
prizomtuis, presume(mptuous)
prizoner, prison(er)
prizum, prism
prizumshen, presume(mption)
prizumtues, presume(mptuous)
prizun, prison
prizuner, prison(er)
prizus, prize(s) / price(s)
pro,*, SHORT FOR PROFESSIONAL (or see prose) "prefixes: semi"
prob, prop / probe
probabil, probable
probable,ly,bilism,bilist,bilistic,bility, bilities, MOST LIKELY, CHANCE TO OCCUR/HAPPEN "prefixes: im"
probably, MOST LIKELY TO OCCUR/ HAPPEN
probade, probate
probaganda, propaganda
probagashen, propagate(tion)
probagate, propagate
probane, propane
probashen, probate(tion)
probashinul, probate(tional)
probate,*,ed,ting,tion,tional,tionary, tionally,tioner,tive,tory, EXAMINATION/ INVESTIGATE THE TRUTH/VALIDITY/GENUINENESS/ AUTHENTICITY "prefixes: re"
probatid, probate(d)
probe,*,ed,bing,er, DEEPLY INVESTIGATE/OBSERVE, INSTRUMENT/ACT FOR RELAYING FACTUAL INFORMATION (or see prop)
probebly, probably
probebul, probable
probeganda, propaganda
probegashen, propagate(tion)
probegate, propagate
prober, proper
proberte, property
probibly, probably
probibul, probable
probiganda, propaganda
probigashen, propagate(tion)
probigate, propagate
probirty, property
problem,*,matic,matical,matically, CHALLENGING SITUATION/ INFORMATION WHICH REQUIRES RESOLUTION/ANSWERS/RESULTS
problum, problem
probobul, probable
proboganda, propaganda
probogation, propagate(tion)
proboscis,ses,ides, SNOUT/NOSE/ TRUNK
probs, probe(s) / prop(s)
probubilety, probable(bility)
probuble, probable
probuganda, propaganda
probugashen, propagate(tion)
probugate, propagate
probur, proper
proburty, property
procede, proceed
procedure,*,ral,rally, NORMAL/PROPER ACTION/METHOD/PROCESS
proceed,*,ded,ding, GO AHEAD/ VENTURE FORTH, PROFIT/REVENUE FROM EVENT (or see precede)
proceedure, procedure
proces, process
proceshen, precision / procession / precession
procesion, precision / procession / precession
process,sses,ssed,ssing,ssor,ssion, ssional,ssionally, STEPS TO ACHIEVE

A GOAL, INCREMENTAL/GRADUAL CHANGES "prefixes: bio"
procession,nal,nally, MOVING ALONG AS A GROUP (or see precession/precision)
procetion, precision / procession / precession
prockreashen, procreate(tion)
proclaim,*,med,ming,mer, MAKE VERBAL ANNOUNCEMENT WITH AUTHORITY
proclamashen, proclamation
proclamation,*, ANNOUNCE/DECLARE TO THE PUBLIC
proclimashen, proclamation
proclimation, proclamation
proclivity,ties, A TENDENCY TOWARDS
proclumashen, proclamation
proclumation, proclamation
procram, program
procrastinate,*,ed,ting,tion,tor, REPEATEDLY PUT OFF UNTIL LATER
procreashen, procreate(tion)
procreate,*,ed,ting,tion,tive,tor, TO REPRODUCE/PRODUCE
prod,*,dded,dding,dder, POKE/JAB, POLE/STICK WITH POINTED END
prodakol, protocol
prodatipe, prototype
prodegul, prodigal
prodegy, prodigy
prodekol, protocol
prodest, protest
prodetipe, prototype
prodews, produce
prodicol, protocol
prodigal,lity,lly, ONE WHO SPENDS/ WASTES TOO MUCH MONEY
prodigul, prodigal
prodigy,gies, YOUTH WITH REMARKABLE TALENTS/SKILLS/ APTITUDE
prodikol, protocol
prodikt, predict
proditipe, prototype
prodon, proton
prodotype, prototype
produce,*,ed,cing,cible,er, CREATE/ MANUFACTURE/BRING FORTH, FRUIT/ VEGETABLE "prefixes: re"
producol, protocol
producshen, product(ion)

product,*,tion,tive, SOMETHING PRODUCED/MANUFACTURED/ DEVELOPED AS SALEABLE GOOD, ACT OF CREATING GOODS "prefixes: pre/re"
productive,ely,eness,vity,ion, SOMETHING PRODUCED/ DEVELOPED/ MANUFACTURED AS SALEABLE GOOD, ACT OF CREATING GOODS "prefixes: re/un"
produgee, prodigy
produgil, prodigal
produkol, protocol
produkshen, product(ion)
produktion, product(ion)
produse, produce
produtipe, prototype
prof, proof / prove
profable, prove(vable)
profail, prevail / profile
profalaktik, prophylactic
profale, prevail
profane,ely,eness,er,nity,nities, TO MISUSE WORDS, VULGAR LANGUAGE
profanedy, profane(nity)
profat, profit / prophet
profedik, prophet(ic)
profelaktik, prophylactic
profeser, professor
profeshen, profession
profeshenul, profession(al)
profesional, profession(al)
profesor, professor
profess,sses,ssed,ssedly,ssing, TO VOW, CLAIM ALLEGIANCE/ACCEPTANCE
profession,*,nal,nally,nalism,nalize, LOYAL TO A VOCATION, ADEPT IN THEIR FIELD "prefixes: semi/sub/un"
professor,*,rial,rially,rate,riate,rship, TEACHER ON COLLEGE/UNIVERSITY STAFF
profesy, prophecy / prophesy
profet, profit / prophet
profetable, profit(able)
profeteer, profit(eer)
profetible, profit(able)
profetik, prophet(ic)
proficient,tly,ncy, SKILLED/ KNOWLEDGEABLE
profide, provide
profiduble, provide(dable)
profilaktik, prophylactic

profile,*,ed,ling, SIDE VIEW OF FACE, OUTLINE/CONTOUR, BIOGRAPHICAL OUTLINE
profishent, proficient
profisy, prophecy / prophesy
profit,*,ted,ting,tless,table,tably,tability, tableness,teer, GAIN ON THE SALE OF SOMETHING (or see prophet) "prefixes: un"
profituble, profit(able)
profolaktik, prophylactic
profound,dly,dness, DEEP/SIGNIFICANT IN KNOWLEDGE/INSIGHT
profownd, profound
profowndly, profound(ly)
profownt, profound
profulaktik, prophylactic
profusy, prophecy / prophesy
progeks, project(s)
progekshin, project(ion)
progekt, project
progektile, project(ile)
progesterone, CHEMICAL PRODUCED BY FEMALES HUMANS/MAMMALS
prognastic, prognostic
prognosis,ses, A MEDICAL OPINION
prognostic,*,cate,cative,cator,cation, PREDICT A MEDICAL CONDITION'S OUTCOME
program,*,mmed,mming,mmer,mmatic, mmatically, OUTLINE OF EVENTS/ ACTIONS/SCHEDULES "prefixes: de/ pre/sub"
programt, program(mmed)
progreshen, progress(ion)
progresive, progress(ive)
progress,sses,ssed,ssing,ssion,ssional, ssionist,ssive, FORWARD MOVEMENT, ADVANCEMENT, EVOLUTION
progressive,ely,eness, ADVANCEMENT/ EVOLUTION/FORWARD MOVEMENT
progretion, progress(ion)
progris, progress
prohabeshin, prohibit(ion)
prohebatory, prohibit(ory)
prohebit, prohibit
prohebition, prohibit(ion)
prohibatif, prohibit(ive)
prohibetory, prohibit(ory)
prohibit,*,ted,ting,tive,tively,tion, tionist,tory, NOT ALLOWED TO DO, FORBID, PREVENT

project,*,ted,ting,table,tile,tion,tional, tionist,tive,tively,tivity,tor, PLAN/OBJECTIVE/UNDERTAKING TO BE CARRIED OUT, JUT OUT, PROTRUDE, PRESENT
projekshin, project(ion)
projeksion, project(ion)
projektile, project(ile)
projesterone, progesterone
projestirone, progesterone
prokastinate, procrastinate
proklaim, proclaim
proklame, proclaim
proklemashen, proclamation
proklevidy, proclivity
proklimation, proclamation
proklumation, proclamation
proklusion, preclusion
proklusive, preclusive
proknosis, prognosis
prokram, program
prokrastinate, procrastinate
prokrastination, procrastinate(tion)
prokreashen, procreate(tion)
prokreate, procreate
prokreation, procreate(tion)
prokriate, procreate
prokse, proxy
proksemate, proximate
proksimety, proximate(mity)
proksumit, proximate
proleminary, preliminary
prolimenary, preliminary
prolog, prologue
prologue,*,ed,uing,uize,uized,uizing, INTRO/PREFACE/SPEECH BEFORE A BOOK/PLAY/POEM/NOVEL
prolok, prologue
prolong,*,ged,ging,gate,gates,gated, gating,gation, EXTEND/LENGTHEN/ELONGATE TIME
prolongade, prolong(ate)
prolonk, prolong
prom,*,menade,menaded,menading, menader, FORMAL DANCE
promanent, prominent
promanintly, prominent(ly)
promanitly, prominent(ly)
promd, prompt
promded, prompt(ed)
promdly, prompt(ly)
promenant, prominent
promenintly, prominent(ly)
promes, promise

promeskuis, promiscuity(uous)
promesquis, promiscuity(uous)
promesquity, promiscuity
prominade, prom(enade) / prominent
prominate, prom(enade) / prominent
prominent,tly,ncy, PRONOUNCED/DISTINCT/JUTS OUT/STANDS OUT/NOTICEABLE
prominet, prominent
promiscuity,uous,uously,uousness, GIVEN TO CONDUCTING SEXUAL/RANDOM/INDISCRIMINATE ACTIVITY WITH MANY
promise,*,ed,sing,ser,see,sor,sory, PLEDGE, AGREE, LOYAL TO FOLLOW THROUGH AS STATED "prefixes: un"
promiskuis, promiscuity(uous)
promisquis, promiscuity(uous)
promisquity, promiscuity
promist, promise(d)
promote,*,ed,ting,tion,tional,tive, tiveness,er, ADVERTISE/PRESENT/ENGAGE TO FURTHER A PROJECT/EVENT/SALE
prompnes, prompt(ness)
prompt,*,ted,ting,tly,tness,ter,titude, TIMELY/EXACT/TO REMIND/PUNCTUAL "prefixes: un"
promt, prompt
promted, prompt(ed)
promtlee, prompt(ly)
promunetly, prominent(ly)
promus, promise
prona, prana / piranha
pronaun, pronoun
pronaunse, pronounce
prondo, pronto
prone,eness, GIVEN/INCLINED TO, HAVE AN AFFILIATION FOR
prones, prone(ness) / prawn(s)
pronnis, prone(ness)
pronoun, CLASS OF WORDS IN ENGLISH GRAMMAR
pronounce,*,ed,edly,cing,eable,er, ement, ARTICULATE/ANNUNCIATE SPEAKING, DEFINE, SPEAK WITH CONFIDENCE/AUTHORITY "prefixes: mis/un"
pronown, pronoun
pronto, QUICKLY/IMMEDIATELY
pronu, prana / piranha
pronunciate,*,ed,ting,tion, ARTICULATE, BE SPECIFIC IN SPEECH/SPEAKING
pronunseashen, pronunciate(tion)

pronunseate, pronunciate
pronunsiation, pronunciate(tion)
prood, prude
proodish, prude(dish)
proof,*,fed,fing,fer, FACTUAL EVIDENCE, SUPPORT THE TRUTH, TESTED (or see prove) "prefixes: dis/over/re"
proon, prune
proot, prude
proove, prove
prop,*,pped,pping, THEATER STAGE SET TERM, A SUPPORT, AIRPLANE PROPELLER (or see probe) "prefixes: under"
propabel, probable
propabelity, probable(bility)
propable, probable / probably
propabul, probable
propagade, propagate
propaganda,dist,distic,distically,dism, dize, MISINFORMATION, PURPOSEFUL HALF-TRUTHS
propagashen, propagate(tion)
propagate,*,ed,ting,tion,tional,tive,tor, BREED/REPRODUCE/MAKE MORE OF
propain, propane
propane, A GAS
propasishen, preposition / proposition / prepossess(ion)
propasterus, preposterous
propazishen, preposition / proposition / prepossess(ion)
propd, prop(pped) / robe(d)
propebly, probably
proped, prop(pped) / probe(d)
propeganda, propaganda
propegashen, propagate(tion)
propegate, propagate
propegation, propagate(tion)
propel,*,lled,lling,llant,ller, EXERT/GIVE MOMENTUM/START INTO ACTION, MOVING PART ON A PLANE, ELEMENT USED TO CREATE MOVEMENT "prefixes: bi"
propeler, propel(ller)
propelint, propel(llant)
proper,rly,rness, CORRECT/ACCURATE
properedness, prepare(dness)
properidness, prepare(dness)
property,ties,tied,tyless, SOMETHING TANGIBLE/PHYSICAL TO BE OWNED BY SOMEONE
prophalaktik, prophylactic

prophecy,cies, PREDICTION OF A DIRE/ UNDESIRABLE FUTURE (or see prophesy)
prophelaktik, prophylactic
prophesy,sies,sied,sying,siable,sier, PREDICTION OF THE FUTURE (or see prophecy)
prophet,*,tic,ecy,esy, ONE WHO IS BELIEVED TO HAVE CONNECTION TO THE UNKNOWN SOURCE FOR PREDICTIONS/ANSWERS (or see profit)
prophilaktik, prophylactic
prophile, profile
prophisy, prophecy / prophesy
prophit, prophet / profit
propholaktik, prophylactic
prophylactic,*,cally, ITEM USED FOR CONTRACEPTION
propibly, probably
propigade, propagate
propiganda, propaganda
propigashen, propagate(tion)
propigate, propagate
propigation, propagate(tion)
propiseshen, preposition / proposition / prepossess(ion)
proplem, problem
proplum, problem
propogate, propagate
proponent,*, ONE WHO MAKES A PROPOSAL
proporshen, proportion
proportion,*,ned,ning,nal,nally,nable, nality,nate,nately,nateness, PARTS EQUAL/RELATIVE IN PERSPECTIVE/ SIZE "prefixes: dis/over"
propose,*,ed,er,sing,sal,sition, OFFER/ PRESENT AN IDEA (or see preposition)
proposishen, preposition / proposition / prepossess(ion)
proposition,nal,nally, OFFER/PRESENT AN IDEA/SUGGESTION
proposterus, preposterous
propozishen, preposition / proposition / prepossess(ion)
propriater, proprietor
proprietor,rship,ty,ties,tary, LEGAL OWNER/TITLE HOLDER
propriuter, proprietor
propseshen, preposition / proposition / prepossess(ion)
propt, prop(pped) / probe(d)

propubil, probable
propubiledy, probable(bility)
propubly, probably
propuganda, propaganda
propugashen, propagate(tion)
propugate, propagate
propugation, propagate(tion)
propur, proper
propurle, proper(ly)
propuzishen, preposition / proposition / prepossess(ion)
pros, prose / pro(s)
prosberity, prosper(ity)
proscribe,*,ed,bing,er, OUTLAW/ PROHIBIT (or see prescribe)
prosdatoot, prostitute
prosdetushen, prostitute(tion)
prosditute, prostitute
prosdition, prostitute(tion)
prosdrate, prostrate / prostate
prose, MORE LIKE NORMAL WRITTEN LANGUAGE THAN POETRY (or see pro(s))
prosechin, precision / procession / precession
prosecute,*,ed,ting,tion,tor, FOLLOW THROUGH, FINAL DETERMINATION, ENFORCE THE LAW, INITIATE A LAWSUIT (or see persecute)
prosed, proceed
proseds, proceed(s)
proseets, proceed(s)
proseetsher, procedure
proseger, procedure
prosejur, procedure
prosekewt, prosecute
prosekushen, prosecute(tion)
prosekution, prosecute(tion)
proses, process
proseshen, precision / procession / precession
prosetion, precision / procession / precession
prosicute, prosecute
prosidger, procedure
prosijur, procedure
prosikushen, prosecute(tion)
prosikute, prosecute
prosis, process
prosparidy, prosper(ity)
prospect,*,ted,ting,tor,tive,tively,tus, EXPECTING/FUTURE/POSSIBLE EVENT/ SITUATION, MINING FOR SOMETHING "prefixes: bio"

prospectif, prospect(ive)
prospekt, prospect
prospektif, prospect(ive)
prosper,*,red,ring,rity,rities,rous,rously, rousness, BENEFIT GREATLY, BE SUCCESSFUL
prosperidy, prosper(ity)
prospir, prosper
prospirus, prosper(ous)
prospures, prosper(s) / prosper(ous)
prostate,ectomy,ectomies,tism, PERTAINS TO A GLAND AROUND THE MALE URETHRA (or see prostrate)
prostatution, prostitute(tion)
prostetute, prostitute
prostetution, prostitute(tion)
prosthesis,etic,etically, ARTIFICIAL REPLACEMENT OF A BODY PART
prosthesus, prosthesis
prostitute,*,tion,tor, PERSON WHO TRADES SEXUAL FAVORS FOR MONEY/GOODS
prostrade, prostrate / prostate
prostrate,*,ed,ting,tion,tor, TO PLACE ONE'S BODY INTO A SUBMISSIVE POSITION/POSTURE, ASSUME A HUMILIATED/HELPLESS/ POWERLESS POSITION (or see prostate)
prosukushen, prosecute(tion)
prot, prod
protacol, protocol
protaga, protege'
protagenist, protagonist
protaginest, protagonist
protagonist,*, LEADING/PRINCIPAL CHARACTER
protajay, protege'
protakol, protocol
protatype, prototype
protean, protein
protecol, protocol
protect,*,ted,ting,tion,tionism,tionist, tive,tor, GUARD/SHIELD/PREVENT FROM DANGER/HARM/ DESTRUCTION "prefixes: un"
protectif, protect(ive)
protega, protege'
protege',*, YOUNG PERSON UNDER CARE/PROTECTION OF AN ELDER/ MASTER (or see prodigy)
protein,*, CHEMICAL COMPOUNDS
protejay, protege'

protekol, protocol
protekshen, protect(ion)
protekt, protect
protektuf, protect(ive)
protene, protein
protes, protest
protest,*,ted,ting,ter, TAKE ACTION AGAINST A PERCEIVED INJUSTICE TO AFFECT CHANGE
protestur, protest(er)
protetipe, prototype
protetype, prototype
proticol, protocol
protiga, protege'
protijay, protege'
protikol, protocol
protitype, prototype
protocol,*,led,ling, GENERAL RULE WHETHER FORMALIZED OR NOT
proton,*,nic, A MOLECULAR PARTICLE OF POSITIVE CHARGE
protonek, proton(ic)
prototipe, prototype
prototype,*,pal,pic, A MODEL/ REPLICATE OF ORIGINAL, FIRST MODEL
protract,tion,tive,ted,tor, DRAW OUT/ LENGTHEN TIME/SPACE/DISTANCE, A TOOL FOR DRAWING
protrakt, protract
protrakter, protract(or)
protrude,*,ed,ding,ent,usible,usion, usile,usive,usively,usiveness, EXTENDS/PROJECTS OUT
protrugin, protrude(usion)
protrushen, protrude(usion)
protrusuf, protrude(usive)
protukol, protocol
prototipe, prototype
proud,dly,dness, PAST TENSE FOR THE WORD" PRIDE", HAPPY ABOUT AN ACCOMPLISHMENT
proues, prowess
prouis, prowess
proul, prowl
provacation, provocative(ion)
provakashen, provocative(ion)
prove,*,ed,ving,vable,vably, BRING FORTH FACTS, MAKE TRUTH KNOWN (or see proof) "prefixes: dis/re"
proveable, prove(vable)
proveble, prove(vable)
provecation, provocative(ion)

provekation, provocative(ion)
provence, province
provencial, province(cial)
provensial, province(cial)
provent, prevent
provents, province / prevent(s)
proverb,*,bial,bially, POPULAR/WISE SAYING
proverbeil, proverb(ial)
proverbeul, proverb(ial)
proveshen, provision
provible, prove(vable)
provication, provocative(ion)
provide,*,ed,ding,er,dable, MAKE AVAILABLE/GIVE/EXPOSE "prefixes: un"
provikation, provocative(ion)
province,*,cial,cially,ciality,cialize, cialities,cialist,cialize,cialism, DESIGNATED AREA OUTSIDE OF MAINSTREAM GIVEN TO A SPECIFIC ORDER/RULE
provinshul, province(cial)
provint, prevent
provints, province
provirb, proverb
provirbeul, proverb(ial)
provision,*,ned,ning,ner, SUPPLIES, ALLOWANCES, PROVIDE FOR
provocative,ely,eness,ion, STIMULATE/ ENTICE TO REACT
provokative, provocative
provoke,*,ed,king,kingly,ocation, ENTICE/LURE/MANIPULATE TO REACT
provost,tship, CHURCH/EDUCATIONAL SUPERIOR
provuble, prove(vable)
provukashen, provocative(ion)
provukation, provocative(ion)
provurb, proverb
provurbeul, proverb(ial)
provurbial, proverb(ial)
prowd, proud
prowdly, proud(ly)
prowess, EXCEPTIONAL BRAVERY/SKILL
prowis, prowess
prowl,*,led,ling,ler, SOMEONE SNEAKING AROUND IN SEARCH OF SOMETHING/SOMEONE
prowt, proud
prowtly, proud(ly)
proxamit, proximate
proxemidy, proximate(mity)

proximate,ely,eness,mity,al, NEXT/ NEAR IN TIME/SPACE, CLOSE TO (or see approximate)
proxsemity, proximate(mity)
proxumit, proximate
proxy,xies, AUTHORIZED/LEGAL TO SUBSTITUTE FOR
prozdatute, prostitute
prozdetushen, prostitute(tion)
prozditushin, prostitute(tion)
prozdrate, prostrate / prostate
proztate, prostate / prostrate
prubaskis, proboscis
prubozkis, proboscis
prucede, precede / proceed
prucedure, procedure
prucepitous, precipitous
pruclivity, proclivity
pruclusion, preclusion
pruclusive, preclusive
prude,ery,eries,dish,dishness, SOMEONE UNCOMFORTABLE WITH SEX RELATED ISSUES
prudence,nt,ntly,ntial,ntially, PRACTICING CAUTION/GOOD JUDGEMENT
prudense, prudence
prudesh, prude(dish)
prudikament, predicament
prudinse, prudence
prudunt, prudence(nt)
pruf, proof / prove
prufanedy, profane(nity)
prufanity, profane(nity)
prufedik, prophet(ic)
prufeshen, profession
prufeshinul, profession(al)
prufesional, profession
prufible, prove(vable)
prufide, provide
prufiduble, provide(dable)
prufuble, prove(vable)
prugektile, project(ile)
prugnostik, prognostic
prugnoztek, prognostic
prugreshen, progress(ion)
prugresif, progress(ive)
prugresive, progress(ive)
prugretion, progress(ion)
pruhebit, prohibit
pruhibatif, prohibit(ive)
pruhibet, prohibit
prujektile, project(ile)
pruklivedy, proclivity

pruklivity, proclivity
pruklusion, preclusion
pruklusive, preclusive
pruleminary, preliminary
prulimenary, preliminary
prumere, premier
prumiskues, promiscuity(uous)
prumoder, promote(r)
prumoshen, promote(tion)
prumote, promote
prumoter, promote(r)
prumotion, promote(tion)
prune,*,ed,ning, DRIED PLUM, TRIM A SHRUB/TREE
prunownse, pronounce
prupare, prepare
prupel, propel
prupeler, propel(ller)
prupelint, propel(llant)
prupelir, propel(ller)
prupelt, propel(lled)
pruponent, proponent
pruporshen, proportion
pruporshenate, proportion(al)
pruportion, proportion
prupose, propose
pruposition, proposition
pruposle, propose(sal)
prupoze, propose
prupozel, propose(sal)
prupozishen, proposition
prupriater, proprietor
pruprietor, proprietor
prusdej, prestige
prusdejus, prestige(gious)
prusechen, precision / procession / precession
prusede, precede / proceed
prusejur, procedure
prusepitous, precipitous
pruseshin, precision / procession / precession
prusetgur, procedure
prusetion, precision / procession / precession
prusipitous, precipitous
prusiputashen, precipitate(tion)
prusishen, precision
prusisly, precise(ly)
prusition, precision / procession / precession
pruskribe, prescribe / proscribe
prusteg, prestige
prustegis, prestige(gious)

prustejus, prestige(gious)
prute, prude
prutective, protect(ive)
prutekshen, protect(ion)
prutektuf, protect(ive)
prutish, prude(dish)
prutrude, protrude
prutrushen, protrude(usion)
prutrusion, protrude(usion)
pruv, prove
pruvale, prevail
pruvencial, province(cial)
pruvenshen, prevent(ion)
pruvenshul, province(cial)
pruvent, prevent
pruventable, prevent(able)
pruventive, prevent(ive)
pruverbeul, proverb(ial)
pruvide, provide
pruviduble, provide(dable)
pruvinshul, province(cial)
pruvint, prevent
pruvintable, prevent(able)
pruvokative, provocative
pruzentuble, present(able)
pruzumshen, presume(mption)
pry,ries,ried,ying,yingly,rier, PEEP IN, METHOD OF OPENING SOMETHING THAT'S TIGHTLY CLOSED
pryer, prior
prymate, primate
psalm,*, BIBLICAL SONG
psariasis, psoriasis
pseudo, PREFIX INDICATING 'FALSE/ PRETEND/IMITATION' MOST OFTEN MODIFIES THE WORD
pseudonym,*, USING ANOTHER NAME
psicheatric, psychiatric
psichopathologist, psychopath(ologist)
psikeatric, psychiatric
psikik, psychic
psikilegekul, psychology(gical)
psikilegy, psychology
psikologekul, psychology(gical)
psikologest, psychology(gist)
psikology, psychology
psikopath, psychopath
psikopathic, psychopath(ic)
psikopatholagist, psychopath(ologist)
psikosis, psychosis
psikotic, psychotic
psoriasis,atic, SKIN PROBLEM
psudo, pseudo
psuriesis, psoriasis

psych, PREFIX INDICATING "MIND/ MENTAL" MOST OFTEN MODIFIES THE WORD
psychadelic, psychedelic
psyche,edelic, OVERALL ESSENCE OF THE HUMAN BEING, SOUL/BODY/ MIND/ SPIRIT (or see sic/sick)
psycheatric, psychiatric
psychedelic,*, HALLUCINATION/ DELUSION/MIND ALTERING
psychiatric,*,cally, FIELD OF SCIENCE WHICH STUDIES THE MIND/ EMOTIONS
psychiatry,rist, PHYSICIAN WHO STUDIES THE MIND, STUDY OF THE MIND/ EMOTIONS
psychic,*,cal,cally, USE OF THE MORPHOGENIC FIELD TO SEE PAST/ PRESENT/ FUTURE EVENTS, EXTRA- SENSORY PERCEPTION "prefixes: intra"
psychidelic, psychedelic
psychietrist, psychiatry(rist)
psychietry, psychiatry
psychiotrist, psychiatry(rist)
psycho,*, SLANG FOR SOMEONE WHO IS BEING LUDICROUS/CRAZY
psychodelic, psychedelic
psycholagy, psychology
psycholgekul, psychology(gical)
psychology,gies,gical,gically,gism,gist, gize, FIELD OF SCIENCE RELATED TO STUDYING THE MIND/MENTAL "prefixes: bio"
psychopath,*,hic,hically,hy,hology, hylogical,hologist, SOMEONE WHO HAS OR WORKS WITH A PERSONALITY DISORDER
psychopathic, psychopath(ic)
psychopatholagist, psychopath(ologist)
psychosis, A MENTAL DISORDER WHICH RENDERS A PERSON DISATTACHED FROM NORMAL REALITY
psychotic,cally, MENTAL DISORDER THAT RENDERS A PERSON DISATTACHED FROM NORMAL REALITY "prefixes: non"
psychudelic, psychedelic
psycik, psychic
psykadelic, psychedelic
psykapathic, psychopath(ic)
psykeatric, psychiatric
psykedelic, psychedelic
psykek, psychic

psykepathic, psychopath(ic)
psykiatric, psychiatric
psykiatrist, psychiatry(rist)
psykiatry, psychiatry
psykidelic, psychedelic
psykik, psychic
psykipathic, psychopath(ic)
psykiutry, psychiatry
psyko, psycho
psykolegy, psychology
psykoligekul, psychology(gical)
psykoligy, psychology
psykologekul, psychology(gical)
psykologest, psychology(gist)
psykology, psychology
psykopath, psychopath
psykopathic, psychopath(ic)
psykopathologist, psychopath(ologist)
psykosis, psychosis
psykotic, psychotic
psykudelic, psychedelic
psykyatric, psychiatric
pu, pew
pub,*, A TAVERN (or see pube)
pube,*,bic,escent,escence,escency, HAIR ON GENITALS WHICH APPEAR DURING PUBERTY, THE DOWN ON PLANTS
pubek, pube(bic)
puberdy, puberty
puberty, BECOMING OF AGE FOR REPRODUCTION
pubescent,nce,ncy, GOING THROUGH PUBERTY "prefixes: pre"
pubirty, puberty
publacation, publication
publacist, publicist
publakashen, publication
publakation, publication
publash, publish
publasher, publish(er)
publasist, publicist
publasize, publicity(ize)
publecation, publication
publecist, publicist
publecity, publicity(ity)
publek, public
publekashin, publication
publekation, publication
publesher, publish(er)
publeshuble, publish(able)
publesist, publicist
publesity, publicity(ity)
publesize, publicity(ize)

public,cly,cness, NOT PRIVATE
publicashen, publication
publication,*, ISSUE PRINTED MATERIAL FOR PUBLIC
publicist,ity,ize,cation, INVOLVED IN THE PRODUCTION/DISSEMINATION OF WRITTEN TEXT
publicity, USING MEDIA TO GAIN PUBLIC ATTENTION
publicize,*,ed,zing, ADVERTISE, MAKE PUBLICLY KNOWN
publikashen, publication
publikation, publication
publisaty, publicist(ity)
publisety, publicity(ity)
publish,hes,hed,hing,hable,her, INVOLVED IN PRODUCTION/ DISSEMINATION OF WRITTEN TEXT/ INFORMATION "prefixes: un"
publishuble, publish(able)
publisist, publicist
publisity, publicist(ity)
publisize, publicity(ize)
publokashen, publication
publosher, publish(er)
publosist, publicist
publosize, publicity(ize)
publucation, publication
publucist, publicist
publukation, publication
publush, publish
publushable, publish(able)
publusher, publish(er)
publusist, publicist
publusize, publicity(ize)
puburdy, puberty
puc, puck / puke
puch, pooch / push
puck,*, A DISC USED IN HOCKEY (or see puke)
pud, put
pudado, potato
pudal, puddle / poodle
puddil, puddle / poodle
pudding, A CREAMY DESSERT (or see putt(ing))
puddle,*,ed,ling, SMALL POOL OF LIQUID (or see poodle)
puddul, puddle / poodle
pude, put / putty
pudel, puddle / poodle
pudeng, pudding / putt(ing)
puder, pewter / putt(er)
pudestrein, pedestrian

pudgie, pudgy
pudgy, A BIT OVERWEIGHT
pudil, puddle / poodle
puding, pudding / putt(ing)
pudir, pewter / putt(er)
pudje, pudgy
pudl, puddle / poodle
pudul, puddle / poodle
pudur, pewter / putt(er)
pudy, putty
puer, poor / pour / pore
puf, puff
pufeleon, pavilion
pufer, puff(er)
puff,*,ffed,ffing,ffer, SHORT/SUDDEN BURST OF AIR/SMOKE, TO INHALE/ EXHALE SMOKE
pufileon, pavilion
pufs, puff(s)
puft, puff(ed)
pugamus, pajamas
puge, pudgy
puir, poor / pour / pore
puit, put
pujamus, pajamas
puje, pudgy
pujomus, pajamas
puk, puck / puke
puke,*,ed,king, TO VOMIT/THROW-UP (or see puck)
pukon, pecan
pukuleur, peculiar
pul, pull / pool
pularity, polar(ity)
puld, pull(ed) / pool(ed)
pule, pool / pulley
puled, pull(ed) / pool(ed)
pulegimy, polygamy
puleridy, polar(ity)
pules, police / pulley(s)
pulet, pullet
pulewshen, pollute(tion)
puley, pulley
pulferise, pulverize
pulfurise, pulverize
puli, pulley
pulies, pulley(s)
puligamus, polygamy(mous)
puligemy, polygamy
puligine, polygyny
puling, pull(ing) / pool(ing)
pulit, pullet / polite
pull,*,lled,lling,ller,lley, TO DRAW/ BRING TOWARDS, TUG

SOMETHING/SOMEONE (or see pool)
pullet,*, YOUNG DOMESTICATED HEN
pulley,*, TOOL USED WITH ROPE FOR LIFTING/PULLING
pullit, pullet
pulmanery, pulmonary
pulmonary, PERTAINING TO THE LUNGS
pulmunery, pulmonary
pulp,piness,py, FIBROUS/THICK SUBSTANCE LEFT BEHIND WHEN VEGETABLE/ FRUIT/PLANTS ARE COOKED/ SMASHED
pulpet, pulpit
pulpit, CHURCH PLATFORM
pulsashen, pulsate(tion)
pulsate,*,ed,ting,tile,tion,tor,tory, PULSE/THROB
pulse,*,ed,sing, THROB/BEAT RYTHMICALLY
pult, pull(ed) / pool(ed)
pulushen, pollute(tion)
pulut, pollute / pullet
pulutent, pollute(tant)
pulution, pollute(tion)
pulverize,*,ed,zing,er, REDUCE TO POWDER/PULP
pulvirise, pulverize
pulvorise, pulverize
puly, pulley
pulygamus, polygamy(mous)
pulygamy, polygamy
pulyginy, polygyny
pulzate, pulsate
pumal, pummel
pumas, pumice
pumb, pump
pumbt, pump(ed)
pumcan, pumpkin
pumel, pummel
pumes, pumice
pumice,eous, VOLCANIC STONE USED FOR SANDING
pumil, pummel
pumis, pumice
pumkan, pumpkin
pumkun, pumpkin
pumle, pummel
pummel,*,led,ling, POMMEL/HIT REPEATEDLY CAUSING DAMAGE
pumol, pummel
pumos, pumice

pump,*,ped,ping,per, FORCE LIQUID/ OBJECT TO MOVE INTO A DESIGNATED DIRECTION
pumpken, pumpkin
pumpkin,*, A LARGE SQUASH
pumpt, pump(ed)
pumul, pummel
pumus, pumice
pun,*,nned,nning, TO USE WORDS SIMILAR BUT DIFFERENT FOR HUMOROUS INTENT
punatef, punitive
punative, punitive
punch,hes,hed,hing,her, STRIKE AGAINST SOMETHING WITH FORCE, TO PIERCE, DRINK MIXTURE
puncherd, puncture(d)
puncht, punch(ed)
punchuate, punctuate
puncsher, puncture
puncshuate, punctuate
puncshuel, punctual
punctewashen, punctuate(tion)
punctual,lity,lly, ARRIVE ON TIME
punctuashen, punctuate(tion)
punctuate,*,ed,ting,tion,tor, USE MARKS/SYMBOLS IN TEXT FOR CLARIFICATION
puncture,*,ed,ring,rable, PIERCE/ PERFORATE/PRICK THROUGH SOMETHING
pund, punt / pun(nned)
punech, punish
puneched, punish(ed)
punechmint, punish(ment)
punensula, peninsula
punesh, punish
puneshmint, punish(ment)
punesht, punish(ed)
punetive, punitive
pungensy, pungent(ncy)
pungent,tly,ncy, STRONG/SHARP SMELL OR TASTE
punginsy, pungent(ncy)
pungunt, pungent
punich, punish
punichment, punish(ment)
puninsula, peninsula
punish,hes,hed,hing,her,hable,hment, APPLY MEASURES TO CORRECT INTOLERABLE ACT
punishmint, punish(ment)
punisht, punish(ed)

punitive,ely,eness, INFLICT/IMPOSE PUNISHMENT
punjensy, pungent(ncy)
punjinsy, pungent(ncy)
punjunt, pungent
punk,*,ker, STICK USED FOR STARTING FIREWORKS, DERAGATORY WORD FOR BAD BEHAVIOR
punkchashen, punctuate(tion)
punkcher, puncture
punkchewashen, punctuate(tion)
punkchewate, punctuate
punkchir, puncture
punkchuate, punctuate
punkchuation, punctuate(tion)
punkchur, puncture
punkir, punk(er)
punksher, puncture
punkshewal, punctual
punkshewashen, punctuate(tion)
punkshewate, punctuate
punkshewul, punctual
punkshir, puncture
punkshooate, punctuate
punkshooation, punctuate(tion)
punkshooel, punctual
punkshor, puncture
punkshual, punctual
punkshuashen, punctuate(tion)
punkshuate, punctuate
punkshuation, punctuate(tion)
punkshuol, punctual
punkshur, puncture
punktual, punctual
punktuate, punctuate
punotif, punitive
punsh, punch
punshur, puncture / punch(er)
punt,*,ted,ting,ter, DROP/KICK A BALL, PROPEL, OF A POINTED NATURE, GAMBLE (or see pun(ed))
punuched, punish(ed)
punuchment, punish(ment)
punudeve, punitive
punudive, punitive
punushed, punish(ed)
punushment, punish(ment)
punutive, punitive
puny,nier,niest, INSIGNIFICANT, SMALL, WEAK IN SIZE/STRENGTH
pup,*,ppy,ppies, A NEWBORN DOG/ SEAL (or see pop)
pupal, pupil
pupater, puppet(eer)

pupatree, puppet(ry)
pupe, pup(ppy)
pupel, pupil
pupet, puppet
pupeteer, puppet(eer)
pupetry, puppet(ry)
pupil,*,llary, PART OF THE EYE, STUDENT UNDER TUTELAGE OF INSTRUCTOR/GUARDIAN "prefixes: inter"
pupit, puppet
pupiteer, puppet(eer)
pupitry, puppet(ry)
pupiya, papaya
puplasher, publish(er)
puplasist, publicist
puplasize, publicity(ize)
puple, pupil
puplek, public
puplekashin, publication
puplesh, publish
puplesist, publicist
puplik, public
puplikashen, publication
puplish, publish
puplisher, publish(er)
puplisist, publicist
puplisize, publicity(ize)
puplosher, publish(er)
puplosist, publicist
puplukashin, publication
puplusher, publish(er)
puplusize, publicity(ize)
pupol, pupil
puporshenal, proportion(al)
puportion, proportion
puppateer, puppet(eer)
puppet,*,try,teer, A DOLL/FIGURE/ MARIONETTE RESEMBLING ANIMAL/HUMAN
puppiteer, puppet(eer)
pupput, puppet
pupputeer, puppet(eer)
pupul, pupil
puput, puppet
puputer, puppet(eer)
puputry, puppet(ry)
pupy, pup(ppy)
pupyu, papaya
pur, purr / per / pure / pour / poor
purabula, parabola
purade, parade
purafecashen, purify(fication)
purafication, purify(fication)

puragative, prerogative
puralasis, paralysis
puralises, paralysis
puramedur, parameter / perimeter
puramiter, parameter / perimeter
purapula, parable
purate, parade
purbendikuler, perpendicular
purceptible, perceptible
purch, perch / purge
purchase,*,ed,sing,er,sable, ACQUIRE/ SECURE OWNERSHIP OF
purchis, purchase / perch(es)
purcivere, persevere
purdly, pert(ly)
pure,ely,er,est,eness, NOT MIXED, FREE OF IMPURITIES/CONTAMINANTS
puree', FOOD BOILED INTO A PULP AND RUN THROUGH A STRAINER/SIEVE
purefacation, purify(fication)
pureferul, peripheral
pureficashen, purify(fication)
purefide, purify(fied)
purendal, parent(al)
pureneul, perennial
purental, parent(al)
purenthases, parenthesis
purfect, perfect
purfekshen, perfect(ion)
purfektion, perfect(ion)
purfert, pervert
purferted, pervert(ed)
purfikt, perfect
purform, perform
purformence, perform(ance)
purfume, perfume
purgatory,ries,tive, THEORETICAL PLACE WHERE A PERSON MAY SPEND TIME AFTER DEATH
purge,*,ed,ging,ger, PURIFY/CLEANSE/ GET RID OF/FREE/REMOVE
purger, perjure
purgery, perjure(ry)
purgetory, purgatory
purgury, perjure(ry)
purgutory, purgatory
purhaps, perhaps
purifecation, purify(fication)
puriferul, peripheral
purificashen, purify(fication)
purifide, purify(fied)
purify,fies,fied,ying,ficator,fication, ACT OF CLEANSING/RIDDING/FREEING/ REMOVING

purineal, perennial
purintal, parent(al)
purinthusees, parenthesis
purje, purge
purjury, perjure(ry)
purkushen, percussion
purl, pearl
purly, pure(ly)
purmanence, permanence
purmanent, permanent
purmanins, permanence
purmeate, permeate
purmenint, permanent
purmeuble, permeable
purmishen, permission
purmisive, permissive
purmit, permit
purmited, permit(tted)
purmition, permission
purmnent, permanent
purogative, prerogative
purokside, peroxide
purole, parole
purona, piranha
purooze, peruse
purosedy, porosity
purosity, porosity
puroxside, peroxide
purpel, purple
purpendicular, perpendicular
purpes, purpose
purpeshual, perpetual
purpesly, purpose(ly)
purpetrate, perpetrate
purpetshual, perpetual
purpetshuate, perpetual(ate)
purpetual, perpetual
purpetuate, perpetual(ate)
purpetuity, perpetuity
purpil, purple
purpindicular, perpendicular
purpis, purpose
purpisly, purpose(ly)
purpitrate, perpetrate
purple,lish, A COLOR
purpleksity, perplex(ity)
purplex, perplex
purplexity, perplex(ity)
purporshenal, proportion(al)
purportional, proportion(al)
purpose,*,ed,sing,eful,efully,efulness, eless,ely,sive,sively,siveness, elessness, REASON FOR/MISSION/ GOAL, DESIGN FOR "prefixes: multi"

purposly, purpose(ly)
purpul, purple
purpus, purpose
purpusly, purpose(ly)
purr,*,rred,rring, GUTTURAL SOUND COMING FROM A CATS THROAT WHEN PLEASED
pursacute, persecute
pursavere, persevere
pursbektif, perspective
pursbiration, perspiration
pursbire, perspire
purscription, prescript(ion)
purse,*,ed,sing, HAND BAG, PRIZE MONEY, SQUEEZE TIGHTLY TOGETHER
pursebduble, perceptible
pursebtef, percept(ive)
pursecute, persecute
pursen, person
pursenality, personality
pursenaly, personal(lly)
pursenel, personnel
pursent, percent
pursentige, percent(age)
pursentil, percent(ile)
pursenuble, person(able)
pursenul, personal
pursenulize, personal(ize)
pursepdable, perceptible
pursepshen, percept(ion)
purseptef, percept(ive)
purseption, percept(ion)
purseptive, percept(ive)
purseshen, precision
pursest, persist
purseve, perceive
purseverense, persevere(rance)
purshis, purchase / perch(es)
pursikute, persecute
pursin, person
pursinaledy, personality
pursinel, personnel
pursint, percent
pursinuble, person(able)
pursinulize, personal(ize)
pursinuly, personal(lly)
pursipatation, precipitate(tion)
pursishen, precision
pursist, persist
pursistence, persist(ence)
purskripshen, prescript(ion)
purson, person
pursona, person(a)

pursonality, personality
pursonefication, person(ification)
pursonifekashen, person(ification)
pursonify, personify
pursoo, pursue
pursparashen, perspiration
purspective, perspective
pursperashen, perspiration
purspiration, perspiration
purspire, perspire
pursuade, persuade
pursuasion, persuade(asion)
pursuasive, persuade(asive)
pursude, pursue(d)
pursue,*,ed,uing,er,uant,uit, SEEKING/ STRIVING TO OVERCOME/ OVERTAKE
pursute, pursue(uit)
pursuvere, persevere
purswade, persuade
purswashen, persuade(asion)
purswasif, persuade(asive)
purt, pert
purtain, pertain
purtane, pertain
purterb, perturb
purterbt, perturb(ed)
purteshen, partition
purtishen, partition
purtrayal, portray(al)
purtrayed, portray(ed)
puruficashun, purify(fication)
purufied, purify(fied)
puruse, peruse
purvade, pervade
purvashen, pervade(asion)/provision
purvasif, pervade(asion)
purversev, pervert(rsive)
purvert, pervert
purvirsev, pervert(rsive)
purvurshen, pervert(rsion)
pury, puree'
purzakute, persecute
pus, FLUID/INFLAMMATION PRESENT AS THE RESULT OF AN INFECTION (or see puss)
pusdasheo, pistachio
pusdromy, pastrami
pusefic, pacific
pusel, puzzle
puseld, puzzle(d)
puses, possess
push,hes,hed,hing,hier,hiest,her,hy,hily, hiness, FORCE/EXERT MOVEMENT

pushenis, push(iness)
pushir, push(er)
pusie, puss(y)
pusific, pacific
pusil, puzzle
pusiled, puzzle(d)
pusishen, position
puskrepshen, prescript(ion)
pusl, puzzle
puss,ssy,ssies, A CAT, THE FACE WHERE THE MOUTH IS, SLANDER FOR A WHIMP (or see pus)
pustasheo, pistachio
pustrome, pastrami
pusul, puzzle
pusy, puss(y)
put,*,tted,tting,tter, TO PLACE (or see putt)
putado, potato
putal, puddle / poodle
putato, potato
pute, putty / putt
putees, putty(tties)
putel, puddle / poodle
putena, patina
putenchul, potential
puteng, pudding / putt(ing) / put(tting)
putenshul, potential
putential, potential
puter, pewter / putt(er)
puterbd, perturb(ed)
puternol, paternal
putestrein, pedestrian
puthetic, pathetic
putil, puddle / poodle
putina, patina
putinchul, potential
puting, pudding / putt(ing) / put(tting)
putintial, potential
putir, pewter / putt(er)
putishen, petition / beautician
putition, petition
putle, puddle / poodle
putol, puddle / poodle
putoto, potato
putrid,dity,dness,dly, ROTTEN, CORRUPT, VILE
putrol, patrol
putrood, protrude
putrude, protrude
putt,*,tting,tter, A GOLF STROKE (or see put)
puttle, puddle / poodle

putty,tties,ttied,ttying, TACKY/PASTY SUBSTANCE
putul, puddle / poodle
puty, putty
puveleon, pavilion
puvileon, pavilion
puvirted, pervert(ed)
puwding, pudding / putt(ing) / put(tting)
puzel, puzzle
puzeld, puzzle(d)
puzes, possess
puzil, puzzle
puzl, puzzle
puzled, puzzle(d)
puzzle,*,ed,ling,er,ement, PROBLEM WITH ONLY ONE SOLUTION, MANY PARTS MAKE UP THE BIG PICTURE
pygme, pygmy
pygmy,mies, VERY SMALL/DWARFED IN COMPARISON TO OTHERS IN ITS SPECIES
pyis, pious
pyke, pike
pyle, pile
pype, pipe
pyramid,*, FOUR-SIDED/TRIANGULAR STRUCTURE
pyrana, piranha
pyranna, piranha
pyre,*, MOUND OF COMBUSTIBLE MATERIAL WHERE AN EXPIRED BODY IS PLACED FOR CEREMONIAL CREMATION (or see pier/peer/pierce)
pyrite,*,tic, YELLOW COLORED METAL
pyro,*, SLANG FOR SOMEONE WHO PLAYS WITH FIRE, PREFIX INDICATING "FIRE/HEAT" MOST OFTEN MODIFIES THE WORD
pyrona, piranha
python,*, A VENOMOUS SNAKE
q, cue
qkumber, cucumber
qkwant, quaint
qords, quartz / quart(s)
qork, quark / cork
qorts, quartz / quart(s)
qu, cue
quack,*,ked,king, SOUND A DUCK MAKES, SLANG FOR A 'NO GOOD DOCTOR' (or see quake)
quad,*, SHORT FOR QUADRANT, FOUR, QUADRANGLE, QUADRUPLET

quadrant,*,tal, ONE QUARTER OF A CIRCLE
quadrint, quadrant
quael, quail
quaent, quaint
quagmire,*, BOG, SOFT EARTH HEAVY WITH MOISTURE
quail,*, A GAME BIRD
quaint,tly,tness, PLEASING/COMFORTABLE/PICTURESQUE
quak, quack
quake,*,ed,king, A TREMBLING/SHAKING (or see quack)
quakmire, quagmire
qual, quail
qualedy, quality
qualefy, qualify
qualefyable, qualify(fiable)
qualetatif, quality(tative)
qualetative, quality(tative)
qualety, quality
qualidy, quality
qualify,fies,fied,fying,fiedly,fier,fiable,fying,fication, IS ELIGIBLE/CAPABLE/SKILLFUL ENOUGH "prefixes: dis/over/un"
qualifyable, qualify(fiable)
qualifyer, qualify(fier)
qualitatif, quality(tative)
quality,ties,tative,tatively, A MEASURE/GUAGE OF RESULTS IN THE OUTCOME OF AN EFFORT, A SCALE WHICH RATES THE BEST/WORST
qualm,*,mish,mishly,mishness, FEELING OF DOUBT/TWINGE/UNEASINESS
qualufecashen, qualify(fication)
qualufi, qualify
quandary,ries, DIFFICULTY/HESITANCY/PERPLEXING
quandery, quandary
quandre, quandary
quanetative, quantitative
quanitative, quantitative
quanotative, quantitative
quant, quaint
quanta,tum, SMALLEST AMOUNT OF ENERGY CAPABLE OF EXISTING ON ITS OWN, QUALITY/EXTENT
quantefy, quantify
quantefyer, quantify(fier)
quantem, quanta(tum)
quantery, quandary
quantetative, quantitative
quantety, quantity

quantify,fies,fied,fying,fiable,fication,fier, MEASURE/DETERMINE THE AMOUNT OF
quantim, quanta(tum)
quantitative,ely, MEASURE BY QUALITY RATHER THAN QUANTITY
quantity,ties, MEASURE OF THE AMOUNT/FREQUENCY OF OCCURENCE
quantom, quanta(tum)
quantry, quandary
quarantine,*,ed,ning,nable, SECTION OFF/ISOLATE FROM EVERYTHING ELSE
quarder, quarter
quarderly, quarter(ly)
quardur, quarter
quardurly, quarter(ly)
quare, quarry / query
quarel, quarrel
quarentene, quarantine
quari, query
quaril, quarrel
quarinteen, quarantine
quark,*, BASIC/ELEMENTARY PARTICLE (or see cork)
quarol, quarrel
quarontene, quarantine
quarrel,*,led,ling,lsome,lsomely, lsomeness, BICKER, ARGUE, BE AT ODDS WITH, ENHARMONIC, SQUARE SHAPED HEAD, A TOOL
quarry,rries,rried,ying,rrier, DIG A PIT INTO THE EARTH FOR STONE/DIRT, PURSUED GAME
quart,*, U.S. MEASUREMENT OF LIQUID (or see quartz)
quarter,*,red,ring,rage,rly,rlies, ONE-FOURTH OF THE WHOLE, U.S. COIN
quartirly, quarter(ly)
quartur, quarter
quarturly, quarter(ly)
quartz,zite,zose,zous, MINERAL/ROCK (or see quart(s))
quarunteen, quarantine
quasadilla, quesadilla
quasar,*, ASTRONOMICAL OBJECT WITH HIGH ENERGY OUTPUT
quasi, SORT OF, SIMILAR, NOT CERTAIN
quawry, quarry
quazar, quasar
qucumber, cucumber
quean, queen
queck, quick

queckest, quick(est)
queen,*,ned,nliness,nly, A FEMALE OF ROYALTY
queer,*,rly,rness, STRANGE/ODD, HOMOSEXUAL
quefer, quiver
queint, quaint
quek, quick
queke, quick(ie)
quekest, quick(est)
quekly, quick(ly)
quel, quill / quail / kale
quelt, quilt
quemulutive, cumulative
quench,hes,hed,hing,hable,her,hless, TO SATISFY, PUT AWAY, EXTINGUISH
quentuplet, quintuplet
querable, curable
queri, query
querk, quirk
querky, quirk(y)
query,ries,ried,rying,rist, ASK OF, QUESTION, INQUIRE
quesadilla,*, FLOUR TORTILLAS WITH FILLING
quesdun, question
quest,*,ted,ting,ter, ON A JOURNEY/ ADVENTURE SEEKING SOMETHING "prefixes: in"
questen, question
question,*,ned,ning,nable,nably, nability,nary,naries,nnaire, ASK/ INQUIRE, HAVE DOUBT, NEED INFORMATION ON MATTER/ SUBJECT "prefixes: un"
questshunar, question(nnaire)
questun, question
quet, quit / quite
queter, quit(tter) / quiet(er)
quevor, quiver
quevur, quiver
quez, quiz
quezene, cuisine
quezt, quest
quick,kly,ker,kest,kness,ken,kie,kener, FAST, WITHOUT DELAY, BRIEF, SKIN UNDER NAILS
quiet,ter,test,tly,tness,tism,tude, SILENT, CALM, STILL, TRANQUIL (or see quit/quite) "prefixes: dis/un"
quifur, quiver
quik, quick
quikest, quick(est)

quikly, quick(ly)
quiky, quick(ie)
quil, quill / kill / keel
quill,*, WING/TAIL FEATHER OF LARGE BIRD
quilt,*,ted,ting,ter, HANDMADE/ STITCHED BLANKET, THICKLY BLANKETED (or see kilt)
quin, keen / kin / queen
quinch, quench
quinsh, quench
quintuplet,*, FIVE OF ANYTHING
quirk,*,ky,kily,kiness, GIVEN TO ERRATIC MOVEMENT, JERKING, SUDDEN CHANGES
quiry, query
quisadilla, quesadilla
quisen, cuisine
quisine, cuisine
quit,*,tted,tting,tter, STOP (or see quite)
quite, COMPLETELY CERTAIN/CLEAR (or see quit/quiet)
quiut, quiet
quiutly, quiet(ly)
quiver,*,red,ring, CASE TO CARRY ARROWS, TREMBLE/SHAKE/ TREMOR
quivor, quiver
quiz,zzes,zzed,zzing,zzical,zzically, zzicality,zzer, TO TEST/WONDER, BE CONFUSED
qukumber, cucumber
qumulotive, cumulative
quochent, quotient
quochiunt, quotient
quoda, quota
quode, quote
quodrant, quadrant
quodrunt, quadrant
quodu, quota
quoledy, quality
quolm, qualm
quondery, quandary
quondry, quandary
quontefy, quantify
quontefyer, quantify(fier)
quontem, quanta(tum)
quontery, quandary
quontety, quantity
quontify, quantify
quontim, quanta(tum)
quontity, quantity
quontre, quandary

quontum, quanta(tum)
quord, quart
quorderly, quarter(ly)
quordir, quarter
quordorly, quarter(ly)
quords, quartz / quart(s)
quordurly, quarter(ly)
quordz, quartz / quart(s)
quore, quarry
quorel, quarrel
quorem, quorum
quorentene, quarantine
quoril, quarrel
quorim, quorum
quorintene, quarantine
quork, quark
quorol, quarrel
quorom, quorum
quort, quart
quorter, quarter
quorterly, quarter(ly)
quortir, quarter
quortirly, quarter(ly)
quorts, quartz / quart(s)
quorturly, quarter(ly)
quortz, quartz / quart(s)
quorum, THE MAJORITY OF A SELECTED GROUP
quoruntene, quarantine
quory, quarry
quoshent, quotient
quoshunt, quotient
quota,*, A PERMITTED NUMBER/ QUANTITY
quotashen, quote(tation)
quote,*,ted,ting,tation,table,tability,ta, tient, IDENTIFY/CITE/REPEAT EXACTLY WHAT WAS HEARD, STATE FACTS, USE MARKS AROUND WORDS SPOKEN "prefixes: un/ under"
quotient,*, A MATHEMATICAL RESULT
quowry, quarry
qurader, curator
qureus, curious
qutikle, cuticle
qwack, quack
qwad, quad
qwadrent, quadrant
qwagmire, quagmire
qwaint, quaint
qwak, quack / quake
qwakmire, quagmire
qwale, quail

qwaledy, quality
qwalefieur, qualify(fier)
qwalefiuble, qualify(fiable)
qwaletatif, quality(tative)
qwalety, quality
qwalidy, quality
qwalifecation, qualify(fication)
qwalifikashen, qualify(fication)
qwalitative, quality(tative)
qwalitee, quality
qwalm, qualm
qwant, quaint
qwantefy, quantify
qwantefyer, quantify(fier)
qwantem, quanta(tum)
qwantety, quantity
qwantify, quantify
qwantifyer, quantify(fier)
qwantim, quanta(tum)
qwantity, quantity
qwantum, quanta(tum)
qwarder, quarter
qwards, quartz / quart(s)
qwardur, quarter
qwarel, quarrel
qwarentene, quarantine
qwaril, quarrel
qwarintene, quarantine
qwark, quark
qwarol, quarrel
qwarter, quarter
qwarts, quartz / quart(s)
qwartur, quarter
qwarul, quarrel
qwary, query
qwasar, quasar
qwasy, quasi
qwazar, quasar
qwazy, quasi
qwear, queer
qween, queen
qweer, queer
qwek, quick
qwekest, quick(est)
qwekly, quick(ly)
qweky, quick(ie)
qwel, quill
qwelt, quilt
qwench, quench
qwensh, quench
qwentuplet, quintuplet
qwerk, quirk
qwerky, quirk(y)
qwery, query

qwes, quiz
qwesden, question
qwesekal, quiz(zzical)
qweshten, question
qwest, quest
qwestchenair, question(nnaire)
qwestshun, question
qwestunair, question(nnaire)
qwet, quit / quite
qweter, quit(tter) / quiet(er)
qwevir, quiver
qwevur, quiver
qwez, quiz
qwezekal, quiz(zzical)
qwik, quick
qwikest, quick(est)
qwikly, quick(ly)
qwiky, quick(ie)
qwil, quill
qwilt, quilt
qwinch, quench
qwinsh, quench
qwintuplet, quintuplet
qwirk, quirk
qwirky, quirk(y)
qwiry, query
qwis, quiz
qwit, quit / quite
qwiter, quit(tter) / quiet(er)
qwivur, quiver
qwiz, quiz
qwizekal, quiz(zzical)
qwochent, quotient
qwod, quad
qwoda, quota
qwodashen, quote(tation)
qwodation, quote(tation)
qwode, quote
qwodrent, quadrant
qwodrunt, quadrant
qwodu, quota
qwoduble, quote(table)
qwoledy, quality
qwolefikashen, qualify(fication)
qwolefiuble, qualify(fiable)
qwolefiur, qualify(fier)
qwoletatif, quality(tative)
qwolety, quality
qwolifekation, qualify(fication)
qwolm, qualm
qwomtum, quanta(tum)
qwondry, quandary
qwontefy, quantify
qwontefyer, quantify(fier)

qwontem, quanta(tum)
qwontery, quandary
qwontety, quantity
qwontify, quantify
qwontifyer, quantify(fier)
qwontim, quanta(tum)
qwontity, quantity
qworam, quorum
qworder, quarter
qwords, quartz / quart(s)
qwordur, quarter
qworel, quarrel
qworem, quorum
qworentene, quarantine
qworil, quarrel
qworim, quorum
qworintene, quarantine
qwork, quark
qworol, quarrel
qworom, quorum
qworter, quarter
qworts, quartz / quart(s)
qwortur, quarter
qworul, quarrel
qworum, quorum
qwoshent, quotient
qwosy, quasi
qwota, quota
qwotashen, quote(tation)
qwotation, quote(tation)
qwote, quote
qwotuble, quote(table)
qwozy, quasi
qwurentene, quarantine
qwurintene, quarantine
qwurk, quirk
qwurky, quirk(y)
r, are
ra, ray / raw
rabbi,*, JEWISH RELIGIOUS TITLE
rabbit,*, LONG-EARED RODENT
rabcity, rhapsody
rabed, rabbit / rabid / rapid
rabees, rabid(ies)
rabel, rebel
rabeleon, rebel(llion)
rabeleus, rebel(llious)
rabelius, rebel(llious)
rabet, rabbit/rabid/rapid
rabi, rabbi
rabid,dity,dly,dness,ies, MADNESS/
    FURIOUSNESS/UNREASONABLE,
    DISEASE (or see rapid)
rabit, rabbit / rabid / rapid

rablie, reply
rabodek, robot(ic)
rabot, rabbit / rabid / rapid
rabotik, robot(ic)
rabsady, rhapsody
rabsudy, rhapsody
rabt, rape(d) / wrap(pped) / rap(pped)
rabud, rabbit / rabid / rapid
rabut, rabbit / rabid / rapid / rebut
rabutal, rebut(ttal)
rac, rack / rake / wrack / rock
racat, racket / racquet
racateer, racketeer
raccoon,*, PLANTIGRADE CARNIVOROUS MAMMAL
raccune, raccoon
race,*,ed,cing,er,cy, COMPETITION WITH MORE THAN ONE, GAME WITH A BEGINNING/END, CATEGORY FOR HUMAN TYPES (or see raise) "prefixes: de"
racede, recede
raceptecle, receptacle
racepter, receptor
racepticle, receptacle
raception, reception
raceptucle, receptacle
racet, racket / racquet
raceteer, racketeer
rach, rash
rachal, racial
rachen, ration
racheo, ratio
rachet, ratchet
rachil, racial
rachin, ration
rachio, ratio
rachit, ratchet
rachon, ration
rachul, racial
rachun, ration
rachunil, rational
rachut, ratchet
racial,lly,lism,list,listic,ism,ist, CHARACTERISTICS/DIFFERENCES IN RACES/PEOPLE "prefixes: bi/inter"
racipeint, recipient
raciprocation, reciprocate(tion)
racism,*, HUMAN FEAR/IGNORANCE TOWARDS PEOPLE OF A DIFFERENT COLOR/RACE
racist,*, HUMAN FEAR/IGNORANCE TOWARDS PEOPLE OF A DIFFERENT COLOR/RACE

racit, racket / racquet / recite
raciteer, racketeer
rack,*,ked,king,ker,ket, APPARATUS USED FOR HANGING/STRETCHING THINGS (or see rake/wrack/rock)
racket,*,teer, NOISY SOUND, USED IN SPORTS TO HIT A BALL (or see racquet)
racketeer,*,ring, SLANG FOR SOMEONE ENGAGED IN ILLEGAL ACTIVITY
rackit, racket / racquet
rackiteer, racketeer
rackoteer, racketeer
rackut, racket / racquet
rackuteer, racketeer
raconasinse, reconnaissance
raconstitushen, reconstitute(tion)
raconstitute, reconstitute
racoon, raccoon
racquet,*, STRINGED TOOL FOR SPORT (or see racket)
racrute, recruit
racruter, recruit(er)
racumbent, recumbent
racut, racket / racquet
racuteer, racketeer
rad, raid / rate
radar,*, A RADIO WAVE FREQUENCY
raddle, rattle
rade, raid
radeal, radial
radeans, radiance
radeant, radiant
radeashen, radiate(tion)
radeate, radiate
radeater, radiate(tor)
radeation, radiate(tion)
radecal, radical
radech, radish
radechulus, ridiculous
radeemible, redeem(able)
radefy, ratify
radeil, radial
radeim, radium
radeinse, radiance
radeint, radiant
radeints, radiance
radekly, radical(lly)
radekul, radical
radel, rattle
rademe, redeem
rademption, redemption
rademshin, redemption
rademtif, redemption(ive)

rademtion, redemption
rademtive, redemption(ive)
rademuble, redeem(able)
radeo, radio
radeol, radial
radeom, radium
radeos, radius / radio(es)
radequelus, ridiculous
radesh, radish
radeul, radial
radeum, radium
radeunse, radiance
radeunt, radiant
radeus, radius
radial,*,lly, CENTER WITH SPOKES/RAYS GOING OUT FROM THE CENTER, TYPE OF TIRE "prefixes: bi/inter"
radiance,cy,cies,nt,ntly, BRIGHT/ SHINING LIKE A STAR, GLOWING BRIGHT
radians, radiance
radiant,ntly,nce, TYPE OF HEAT/WAVE/ LIGHT, TO GLOW "prefixes: ir"
radiashen, radiate(tion)
radiate,*,ed,ting,tion,tional,tive,tor, EMIT/GIVE FORTH/EXUDE "prefixes: ir/re"
radiater, radiate(tor)
radical,*,lly,lness,lism, FAR-SWEEPING CHANGE/ACT/ATTITUDE FROM THE EXISTING IDEALISM
radicaly, radical(lly)
radich, radish
radicle, radical
radicly, radical(lly)
radiel, radial
radiem, radium
radient, radiant
radify, ratify
radikle, radical
radikly, radical(lly)
radikul, radical
radil, rattle
radio,*,oed,oing, WIRELESS AUDIO TRANSMITTING/RECEIVING DEVICE, PREFIX INDICATING "RADIO/ RADIATION" MOST OFTEN MODIFIES THE WORD, FROM ANCIENT WORD "RADIUS" (RAY)
radiol, radial
radiquelus, ridiculous
radish,hes, A VEGETABLE
radiul, radial

radium, A METALLIC ELEMENT WHICH IS RADIOACTIVE
radiunse, radiance
radius,ii,ses, AREA WITHIN A CIRCLE, RAY EXTENDING FROM CENTER OF CIRCLE, BONE DESCRIPTIONS
radol, rattle
radon, A CHEMICAL ELEMENT
rador, radar
raduction, reduce(ction)
radufy, ratify
radukle, radical
radukly, radical(lly)
radukshen, reduce(ction)
radul, rattle
radundense, redundant(ncy)
radundent, redundant
radundunse, redundant(ncy)
radusable, reduce(cible)
raduse, reduce
radush, radish
raelm, realm
raelrod, railroad
raen, rain / reign / rein
raenbo, rainbow
raenj, range
raer, rare
raesesem, racism
raf, rave
rafal, raffle / ravel
rafalee, reveille
rafan, raven
rafash, ravish
rafd, raft / waft
rafded, raft(ed)
rafdur, raft(er)
rafe, rave
rafel, raffle / ravel / reveal
rafelashen, revelation
rafen, raven / ravine
rafenge, revenge
rafenje, revenge
rafenus, raven(ous)
rafeole, ravioli
rafer, revere / refer
rafers, reverse / refer(s)
rafesh, ravish
rafeusil, refuse(sal)
rafewsel, refuse(sal)
raffle,*,ed,ling, A GAME
rafiew, review / revue
rafif, revive
rafiful, revival
rafil, raffle / ravel

rafilee, reveille
rafin, raven / refine
rafinable, refine(nable)
rafinery, refine(ry)
rafinje, revenge
rafinment, refine(ment)
rafinuble, refine(nable)
rafinury, refine(ry)
rafinus, raven(ous)
rafioly, ravioli
rafirse, reverse
rafish, ravish
raflashen, revelation
rafle, raffle / ravel
raflect, reflect
raflection, reflect(ion)
raflective, reflect(ive)
raflekshen, reflect(ion)
raflektor, reflect(or)
rafol, raffle
rafolee, reveille
raformutory, reform(atory)
rafractory, refract(ory)
rafrain, refrain
rafraktory, refract(ory)
rafrane, refrain
rafregirant, refrigerate(ant)
rafregirator, refrigerate(tor)
rafresh, refresh
rafreshment, refresh(ment)
rafrigerant, refrigerate(ant)
rafrigerator, refrigerate(tor)
raft,*,ted,ting,ter, A SMALL BOAT MADE WITH A MATERIAL FILLED WITH AIR (or see rave(d))
raftur, raft(er) / waft(er)
rafue, review / revue
raful, raffle / ravel
rafulashen, revelation
rafulation, revelation
rafulee, reveille
rafun, raven
rafunus, raven(ous)
rafurbish, refurbish
rafurse, reverse
rafusel, refuse(sal)
rafute, refute
rag,*,gged,ggedness,ggedly,ggedy, TATTERED/TORN/WORN OUT MATERIAL/CLOTH (or see rack/rage)
ragalia, regal(ia)
ragardless, regard(less)
ragd, rage(d) / rag(gged)

rage,*,ed,ging,gingly, INTENSE/VIOLENT ANGER, OF INTENSE/GREAT FORCE "prefixes: en"
raged, rag(gged) / racket
ragedy, rag(ggedy)
ragektion, reject(ion)
rager, roger
raget, rag(gged) / racket
ragid, rag(gged) / racket
ragidy, rag(ggedy)
ragir, roger
ragit, rag(gged) / racket
ragity, rag(ggedy)
ragret, regret
ragreted, regret(tted)
ragretful, regret(ful)
ragretfuly, regret(fully)
ragt, rage(d) / rake(d) / rack(ed) / wrack(ed)
ragud, rag(gged) / racket
ragudy, rag(ggedy)
ragut, rag(gged) / racket
raid,*,ded,ding,der, A SUDDEN ENTRY/ATTACK/SALE (or see rate/ride)
rail,*,led,ling,ler, METAL/WOOD BARS/POSTS, TO PUNISH/SCOLD, A BIRD (or see rale) "prefixes: de"
railroad,*,ded,ding,der, ROAD MADE OF RAILS, BRING A FALSE CHARGE AGAINST SOMEONE, OF LOCOMOTIVES
rain,*,ned,ning,ny, WATER RELEASED FROM CLOUDS (or see reign/rein)
rainbow,*, AN ARC/BOW OF COLORS NORMALLY CAUSED BY RAIN
rainder, reindeer
raing, range
rair, rare
rairly, rare(ly)
rais, rise / raise / ray(s)
raise,es,ed,sing,er, TO LIFT/BRING/TAKE UP (or see ray(s)/razor) "prefixes: un/up"
raisin,*, A DRIED PLUM
rait, rate / right / rite / write / wright
raive, rave
raj, rage
rajd, rage(d)
rajekshen, reject(ion)
rajekt, reject
rajektion, reject(ion)
rajer, roger
rajur, roger
rak, rack / rake / wrack / rag

rakat, racket / racquet
rakateer, racketeer
rake,*,ed,king, TOOL/IMPLEMENT TO MOVE ORGANIC MATERIAL AROUND (or see rack/wrack)
raket, racket / racquet
raketeer, racketeer
rakit, racket / racquet
rakiteer, racketeer
rakonesinse, reconnaissance
rakonstitute, reconstitute
rakonusents, reconnaissance
rakoon, raccoon
rakord, record
rakorder, record(er)
rakot, racket / racquet
rakoteer, racketeer
rakrute, recruit
rakruter, recruit(er)
rakt, rake(d) / rack(ed) / wrack(ed)
rakumbent, recumbent
rakune, raccoon
rakut, racket / racquet
rakuteer, racketeer
rakwest, request
rakwire, require
rakwirment, require(ment)
rakwit, requite
rakwitable, requite(table)
rakwrute, recruit
ralaks, relax
ralax, relax
rale, A BREATHING SOUND (or see rail/rally)
raleenkwish, relinquish
ralef, relief
ralejis, religion(ous)
ralek, rollick
ralenkwish, relinquish
ralenqwish, relinquish
ralent, relent
ralentless, relentless
ralerode, railroad
ralese, release
raleve, relieve
ralevens, relevance
ralevent, relevant
ralevir, relieve(r)
rali, rely / rally
raliable, reliable
raliant, reliance(nt)
ralick, rollick
ralie, rally
raliense, reliance

raligeon, religion
raligis, religion(ous)
ralijus, religion(ous)
ralik, rollick
ralinkwish, relinquish
ralinquish, relinquish
ralintless, relentless
ralish, relish
raliubility, reliable(bility)
raliuble, reliable
raliunts, reliance
ralivens, relevance
ralivent, relevant
rally,llies,llied,ying,llier, BRING/CALL SUMMON FORTH SPIRIT/ACTION/ENTHUSIASM
ralm, realm
ralrod, railroad
ralrot, railroad
ralrus, walrus
raluctant, reluctant
raluctinse, reluctant(nce)
raluktint, reluctant
raluvence, relevance
raluvent, relevant
ralwrod, railroad
raly, rally / rely
ram,*,mmed,mming,mmer, MALE SHEEP, DEVICE USED TO STRIKE/FORCE/ CRUSH/POUND
ramadik, rheumatic
ramafication, ramification
ramafikashen, ramification
ramain, remain / romaine
ramander, remain(der)
ramane, remain / romaine
ramantek, romantic
ramantic, romantic
ramantisize, romantic(ize)
ramarkible, remark(able)
ramatik, rheumatic
rambal, ramble
rambant, rampant
rambint, rampant
ramble,*,ed,ling,er, WANDER/MEANDER, STYLE OF HOME
rambul, ramble
rambunctious,sly,sness, NOISY/BOISTEROUS/LOUD
rambunktious, rambunctious
rambunt, rampant
ramd, ram(mmed)
ramedeul, remedy(dial)
ramediashen, remedy(diation)

ramediation, remedy(diation)
ramefekashen, ramification
ramefekation, ramification
ramember, remember
ramembranxe, remember(ance)
ramesable, remissible
rameshen, remission
ramet, remit
rameteul, remedy(dial)
ramidal, remit(ttal)
ramifekashen, ramification
ramification,*, THE RESULT/RESPONSE OF AN ACTION
ramifikation, ramification
ramindur, remind(er)
ramint, remind
ramintur, remind(er)
ramishen, remission
ramisible, remissible
ramision, remission
ramit, remit
ramital, remit(ttal)
ramition, remission
ramituble, remit(ttable)
ramofer, remove(r)
ramorse, remorse
ramorsless, remorse(less)
ramote, remote
ramotly, remote(ly)
ramover, remove(r)
ramp,*,ped,ping,part, DEVICE TO CREATE INCLINE/SLOPE FOR MOVING/RAISING FROM ONE LEVEL TO ANOTHER
rampage,*,ed,ging,eous,eously, BOISTEROUS/VIOLENT/PASSIONATE BEHAVIOR
rampaje, rampage
rampant,tly,ncy, RUN AMUCK/WILD/UNPREDICTABLY
rampel, ramble
rampent, rampant
rampint, rampant
rample, ramble
rampt, ramp(ed)
rampunkshes, rambunctious
rampunt, rampant
ramsum, ransom
ramt, ram(mmed)
ramuf, remove
ramufecation, ramification
ramufekashen, ramification
ramufel, remove(val)
ramufible, remove(vable)

ramufication, ramification
ramufikashen, ramification
ramufil, remove(val)
ramufucation, ramification
ramuneration, remunerate(tion)
ramuvable, remove(vable)
ramuval, remove(val)
ran, PAST TENSE FOR THE WORD "RUN" (or see rain/rein/reign) "prefixes: re"
ranbo, rainbow
ranbow, rainbow
ranced, rancid
ranch,hes,hed,hing,her, WHERE HORSES/CATTLE ARE RAISED/ BOARDED, A TYPE OF DRESSING
ranchi, raunch(y)
ranchur, ranch(er)
rancid,dity,dness, SMELL/TASTE OF FOOD THAT IS SPOILED/ROTTEN
rancud, rancid
rand, rant / rain(ed)
randam, random
rander, reindeer
randim, random
random,mly,mness, WITHOUT AN APPARENT/RECOGNIZABLE ORDER "prefixes: non/un"
rane, rain / reign / rein
ranege, renege
range,*,ed,ging,er, DEFINED/SPECIFIC AREA WHICH HOLDS DATA/ INFORMATION/ANIMALS (or see ranch) "prefixes: de"
rangel, wrangle
ranglur, wrangle(r)
rangt, range(d)
rangul, wrangle
rangur, range(r)
ranige, renege
ranik, renege
ranj, range / ranch
rank,*,ked,king,ker,kest,kly,kness, CHRONOLOGICAL/LINEAR ORDER, A BAD/ OFFENSIVE SMELL/ODOR
ranone, renown
ranoserus, rhinoceros
ranosirus, rhinoceros
ranouncement, renounce(ment)
ranounse, renounce
ranown, renown
ranownsment, renounce(ment)

ransack,*,ked,king,ker, PLUNDER/ SEARCH THROUGH PEOPLE'S BELONGINGS
ransak, ransack
ransam, ransom
ransed, rancid
ransem, ransom
ransh, ranch
ransher, ranch(er)
ransid, rancid
ransim, ransom
ransit, rancid
ransom,*,mer, FORCE SOMEONE TO PAY FOR THE RETURN OF GOODS/ PEOPLE
ransud, rancid
ransum, ransom
ransut, rancid
rant,*,ted,ting,tingly,ter, TALK/UTTER LOUD AGITATED OR AGGRESSIVE WORDS
rantsum, ransom
rantum, random
ranumerate, remunerate
ranzak, ransack
ranzum, ransom
raon, rayon
rap,*,pped,pping,pper, TYPE OF MUSIC AND THAT ASSOCIATED WITH IT, TYPE OF SOUND, BLAME/ PUNISHMENT/FOR AN ILLEGAL ACT NOT RESPONSIBLE FOR (or see wrap/rape)
rapad, rapid
rapar, repair
rapcher, rapture
rapcherus, rapture(rous)
rapchur, rapture
rapcity, rhapsody
rape,*,ed,ping,pist, VIOLENTLY/ FORCEFULLY/PHYSICALLY PENETRATE A PERSON AGAINST THEIR WILL (or see rap/wrap)
rapeal, repeal
rapeat, repeat
raped, rape(d) / rapid / rabid
rapededly, repeat(edly)
rapedly, rapid(ly)
rapedutif, repetitive
rapeel, repeal
rapel, rappel / repeal / repel
rapelein, rebel(llion)
rapelent, repellent
rapeleon, rebel(llion)

rapelinsy, repellent(ncy)
rapelint, repellent
rapenins, repent(ance)
rapent, repent
rapentinse, repent(ance)
raper, rap(pper) / rape(r) / wrap(pper)
rapest, rape(pist)
rapete, repeat
rapetedly, repeat(edly)
rapid,*,dly,dness,dity, QUICK (or see rabid)
rapinens, repent(ance)
rapint, repent
rapintense, repent(ance)
rapir, rap(pper) / rape(r) / wrap(pper)
raplacment, replace(ment)
raplase, replace
raplasmint, replace(ment)
raplenish, replenish
raplenishment, replenish(ment)
raplid, reply(lied)
raplinesh, replenish
rapor, rapport
raporder, report(er)
raport, rapport / report
raporter, report(er)
rapository, repository
rapour, rapport
rapozitory, repository
rappel,*,lled,lling, DESCEND FROM A HEIGHT WITH A ROPE (or see repel)
rapport, HARMONY/AFFILIATION WITH
rapreshen, repress(ion)
rapresion, repress(ion)
rapress, repress
rapresuve, repress(ive)
raproch, reproach
raprochuble, reproach(able)
rapsety, rhapsody
rapshur, rapture
rapsuty, rhapsody
rapt, rape(d) / wrap(pped) / rap(pped)
raptcher, rapture
raptor,*, BIRD OF PREY (or see rapture)
raptur, raptor / rapture
rapture,*,ed,ring,rous,rously,rousness, EXTREME DELIGHT/JOY/PLEASURE (or see raptor) "prefixes: en"
rapublek, republic
rapublekan, republic(an)
rapublikan, republic(an)
rapud, rapid
rapugnense, repugnant(nce)
rapugnent, repugnant

rapulshen, repulse(ion)
rapulsif, repulse(sive)
rapulsion, repulse(ion)
rapuplekan, republic(an)
rapur, rap(pper) / rap(er) / wrap(pper)
rapust, rape(pist)
rapute, repute
raqet, racket / racquet
raqeteer, racketeer
raqrute, recruit
raquire, require
raquirment, require(ment)
raquitable, requite(table)
raquite, requite
raqut, racket / racquet
raquteer, racketeer
raqwest, request
raqwire, require
raqwirment, require(ment)
rar, rare
rare,ely,er,est,eness,rity,rities,efy,efies, efied,efying,efiable, MOST UNCOMMON, UNUSUAL, SCARCE, MEAT BARELY COOKED
rarety, rare(rity)
rarist, rare(rist)
rarity, rare(rity)
rarly, rare(ly)
rarudy, rare(rity)
raruty, rare(rity)
ras, race / raise / ray(s)
rasbery, raspberry
rascal,*,lly,lity,lities, MISCHIEVOUS/ PLAYFUL/ROQUISH BEHAVIOR
rascul, rascal
rasd, race(d) / raise(d)
raseat, receipt
rasebshenist, receptionist
rasebshin, reception
rasebter, receptor
rasebtif, receptive
rasebtive, receptive
raseed, recede
rasefe, receive
rasefible, receive(vable)
rasemblinse, resemble(lance)
rasembul, resemble
rasen, raisin / race(cing) / raise(sing)
rasentful, resent(ful)
rasentment, resent(ment)
rasepdekle, receptacle
rasepe, recipe
rasepeunt, recipient
raseprikul, reciprocal

raseprocation, reciprocate(tion)
raseprokashen, reciprocate(tion)
raseprokate, reciprocate
rasepshenist, receptionist
rasepshun, reception
raseptacle, receptacle
raseptef, receptive
raseptikle, receptacle
raseptionest, receptionist
raseptive, receptive
raseptor, receptor
raseptukle, receptacle
raser, razor / raise(r) / race(r)
raserekshen, resurrect(ion)
raservation, reservation
raservist, reserve(vist)
rasesem, racism
raseshun, recess(ion)
rasesif, recess(ive)
rasesion, recess(ion)
rasesive, recess(ive)
rasession, recess(ion)
rasest, racist
rasestef, resist(ive)
rasestif, resist(ive)
rasestinse, resist(ance)
rasestint, resist(ant)
rasestive, resist(ive)
rasesum, racism
rasete, receipt
rasetion, recess(ion)
raseve, receive
rasevuble, receive(vable)
rash,hes, A SKIN FORMATION
rashal, racial
rashel, racial
rashen, ration
rashenaledy, rational(ity)
rashenality, rational(ity)
rashenalization, rational(ization)
rashent, ration(ed)
rashenul, rational
rasheo, ratio
rasheonalization, rational(ization)
rasheunolezashen, rational(ization)
rashil, racial
rashin, ration
rashinal, rational
rashinaledy, rational(ity)
rashinality, rational(ity)
rashint, ration(ed)
rashinul, rational
rashinulization, rational(ization)
rashio, ratio

rashon, ration
rashonality, rational(ity)
rashonalization, rational(ization)
rashonel, rational
rashs, rash(es)
rashul, racial
rashun, ration
rashunal, ration(al)
rashunaledy, rational(ity)
rashunality, rational(ity)
rashunalization, rational(ization)
rashund, ration(ed)
rashunil, rational
raside, reside
rasiduel, residue(ual)
rasign, resign
rasiliency, resilient(ncy)
rasilient, resilient
rasimblanse, resemble(lance)
rasimble, resemble
rasin, raisin / race(cing) / raise(sing)
rasintful, resent(ful)
rasipeant, recipient
rasipeint, recipient
rasiprikul, reciprocal
rasiprocation, reciprocate(tion)
rasiprokashen, reciprocate(tion)
rasiprokate, reciprocate
rasiprokle, reciprocal
rasiprokul, reciprocal
rasir, razor / raise(r) / race(r)
rasirekshen, resurrect(ion)
rasirvation, reservation
rasirvist, reserve(vist)
rasis, race(s) / raise(s) / racist
rasisem, racism
rasism, racism
rasist, racist / resist
rasistef, resist(ive)
rasistense, resist(ance)
rasistent, resist(ant)
rasister, resist(or)
rasistive, resist(ive)
rasisum, racism
rasite, recite
rasitle, recite(tal)
rasitul, recite(tal)
rasizm, racism
rasizum, racism
raskel, rascal
raskle, rascal
rasn, raisin / raise(sing) / race(cing)
rasodo, risotto
rasolve, resolve

rasolvuble, resolve(vable)
rasor, razor / raise(r) / race(r)
rasort, resort
rasoto, risotto
rasotto, risotto
rasp,*,per,pingly,py, A TOOL WHICH ROUGHS/SCRAPES/SANDS, A ROUGH SOUND
raspberry,rries, AN EDIBLE BERRY
raspect, respect
raspectful, respect(ful)
raspective, respect(ive)
raspectuble, respect(able)
raspekt, respect
raspektful, respect(ful)
raspektif, respect(ive)
raspektuble, respect(able)
raspite, respite
raspond, respond
rasponder, respond(er)
rasponse, response
rasponsef, response(sive)
rasponsive, response(sive)
rasponsuble, response(sible)
rast, race(d) / raise(d)
rastore, restore
rastrant, restrain(t)
rastrektif, restrict(ive)
rastrektion, restrict(ion)
rastrikshen, restrict(ion)
rastrikt, restrict
rastriktive, restrict(ive)
rasume, resume
rasun, raisin / raise(sing) / race(cing)
rasur, razor / raise(r) / race(r)
rasurekshen, resurrect(ion)
rasus, racist / race(s)
rasusatate, resuscitate
rasuscitate, resuscitate
rasusitashen, resuscitate(tion)
rasusitate, resuscitate
rasusitator, resuscitate(tor)
rasust, racist
rasy, race(y)
rat,*,tted,tting,tty, RODENT, SOMEONE WHO REVEALS OTHERS PRIVATE INFORMATION WITHOUT PERMISSION, TANGLED HAIR (or see rate/raid)
ratainer, retain(er)
rataleashen, retaliate(tion)
rataleate, retaliate
rataleation, retaliate(tion)
ratane, retain

rataner, retain(er)
ratar, radar
ratash, radish
ratchat, ratchet
ratchet,*,ted,ting, A DEVICE/TOOL
ratchut, ratchet
rate,*,ed,ting,table, RANK, QUALIFY, QUANTIFY, PROVIDE A VALUE FOR (or see raid) "prefixes: de/over/pro/under"
rateal, radial
rateant, radiant
rateashen, radiate(tion)
rateate, radiate
rateater, radiate(tor)
rateation, radiate(tion)
ratecal, radical
ratech, radish
rated, rate(d) / rat(tted) / rot(tted)
ratefy, ratify
rateil, radial
rateim, radium
rateinse, radiance
rateint, radiant
rateints, radiance
rateis, radius
ratekly, radical(lly)
ratekul, radical
ratel, rattle
ratenshun, retention
ratentif, retentive
ratention, retention
ratentive, retentive
rateo, ratio / radio
rateod, radio(ed)
rateol, radial
rateom, radium
ratesh, radish
rateul, radial
rateum, radium
rateunse, radiance
rateunt, radiant
rateus, radius
rath, wrath
rather, THIS OVER THAT, PREFERENCE
rathful, wrath(ful)
rathur, rather
ratiate, radiate
ratiater, radiate(tor)
ratical, radical
ratich, radish
raticly, radical(lly)
ratid, rat(tted) / rate(d)
ratiel, radial

ratiem, radium
ratient, radiant
ratify,fies,fied,fying,fication,fier, APPROVE/CONFIRM/MAKE FORMAL
ratikly, radical(lly)
ratikul, radical
ratikuly, radical(lly)
ratil, rattle
ratinshun, retention
ratintion, retention
ratio,*, COMPARISON OF AMOUNTS
ratiol, radial
ration,*,ned,ning, A SPECIFIC/LIMITED AMOUNT
rational,le,lly,lness,lism,list,listic, listically,lity,lities,lize,lizer,lization, FACTUAL/ LEVEL-HEADED/NON EMOTIONAL THOUGHT "prefixes: ir"
rationalezation, rational(ization)
rationulization, rational(ization)
ratire, retire
ratirment, retire(ment)
ratisery, rotisserie
ratish, radish
ratisury, rotisserie
ratiul, radial
ratium, radium
ratiunse, radiance
ratius, radius
ratl, rattle
ratol, rattle
raton, radon
ratorical, rhetoric(al)
ratrakshen, retract(ion)
ratrakted, retract(ed)
ratrefe, retrieve
ratrefer, retrieve(r)
ratreful, retrieve(val)
ratreve, retrieve
ratrevul, retrieve(val)
ratrevur, retrieve(r)
rattle,*,ed,ling,er,ly,lier,liest, INSTRUMENT/TOY WITH BEADS INSIDE TO CREATE SOUND
ratufy, ratify
ratukle, radical
ratukly, radical(lly)
ratul, rattle
ratush, radish
raty, rat(tty)
raudy, rowdy
rauk, rock

raunch,hy,hier,hiest, INDECENT/FOUL
raund, round
raunyin, reunion
raunyun, reunion
raust, roust
raut, wrought / route
rauty, rowdy
rav, rave
ravage,*,ed,ging, TO VIOLENTLY DAMAGE/DESTROY/DEVASTATE
ravaje, ravage
raval, ravel
ravalashen, revelation
ravalee, reveille
ravalve, revolve
ravan, raven
ravash, ravish / ravage
rave,*,ed,ving,er, DELIRIOUS/WILD/ EXCESSIVE, CARRYING ON, INCESSANT ABOUT
ravech, ravish / ravage
raveel, reveal
raveer, revere
ravege, ravage
ravegen, revise(sion)
raveje, ravage
ravejen, revise(sion)
ravel,*,led,ling,ler,lment, BECOME FRAYED/ENTANGLED (or see reveal) "prefixes: un"
ravelation, revelation
ravelee, reveille
ravelt, reveal(ed)
raven,*,ner,ning,ningly,nous,nously, nousness,ner, BIRD, PLUNDER/ DEVOUR GREEDILY, VORACIOUS APPETITE (or see ravine/rave(ving))
ravench, revenge
ravene, ravine
ravenge, revenge
ravengful, revenge(ful)
ravenje, revenge
ravenjful, revenge(ful)
ravenus, raven(ous)
raveoly, ravioli
raverberate, reverberate
raverbirate, reverberate
ravere, revere
raversuble, reverse(sible)
ravert, revert
ravesh, ravish / ravage
raveshen, revise(sion)
ravesion, revise(sion)
raview, review / revue

ravige, ravage
ravigen, revise(sion)
ravije, ravage
ravijen, revise(sion)
ravil, ravel
ravilashen, revelation
ravilation, revelation
ravilee, reveille / ravel
ravin, raven / ravine
ravinch, revenge
ravine,*, A DEEP GORGE/DRIED RIVER BED WORN AWAY BY WATER (or see raven)
ravinge, revenge
ravingful, revenge(ful)
ravinje, revenge
ravinjful, revenge(ful)
ravinous, raven(ous)
ravinus, raven(ous)
ravioli,*, STUFFED PASTA/NOODLE
ravirberate, reverberate
ravirse, reverse
ravirsuble, reverse(sible)
ravirt, revert
ravise, revise
ravish,hes,hed,hing,her,hment, CARRY AWAY/TRANSPORT/TAKE BY FORCE, OVERWHELM EMOTIONALLY
ravishen, revise(sion)
ravision, revise(sion)
ravival, revival
ravive, revive
ravivle, revival
ravivuble, revive(vable)
ravize, revise
ravl, ravel
ravocable, revocable
ravokable, revocable
ravoke, revoke
ravokt, revoke(d)
ravol, ravel
ravolashen, revelation
ravolation, revelation
ravolee, reveille
ravolfe, revolve
ravolfer, revolve(r)
ravolt, revolt
ravolushen, revolution
ravolutioniz, revolution(ize)
ravolve, revolve
ravolver, revolve(r)
ravon, raven / rave(ving)
ravonous, raven(ous)
ravu, review / revue

ravuge, ravage
ravuje, ravage
ravul, ravel
ravulashen, revelation
ravulation, revelation
ravulee, reveille
ravurbarate, reverberate
ravurse, reverse
ravurt, revert
raw,wly,wness,wish, UNFINISHED, UNCOOKED, UNADULTERATED, IN ITS NATURAL STATE
raward, reward
rawdy, rowdy
rawlik, rollick
rawnd, round
rawnt, round
raword, reward
rawst, roust
rawty, rowdy
ray,*, STREAM OF LIGHT/HOPE/ ENERGY (or see rye)
raybees, rabid(ies)
raydar, radar
raydeans, radiance
raydon, radon
rayl, rail / rale
rayn, rain / reign / rein
raynbo, rainbow
rayon, SYNTHETIC FIBER
raysd, raise(d) / race(d)
rayunyon, reunion
razberee, raspberry
razd, race(d) / raise(d)
raze, raise / ray(s) / race
razeleant, resilient
razemble, resemble
razemblinse, resemble(lance)
razen, raisin / raise(sing) / race(cing)
razent, resent
razentment, resent(ment)
razer, razor
razervation, reservation
razervist, reserve(vist)
razesd, racist
razesm, racism
razest, racist / resist
razide, reside
raziduel, residue(ual)
razilyent, resilient
razimble, resemble
razimbul, resemble
razin, raisin / raise(sing) / race(cing) / resign

razir, razor
razirvation, reservation
razisd, racist
razism, racism
razist, racist / resist
razistef, resist(ive)
razistense, resist(ance)
razistent, resist(ant)
razistur, resist(or)
razite, recite
razizum, racism
razkel, rascal
razkul, rascal
razodo, risotto
razolve, resolve
razon, raisin / raise(sing) / race(cing)
razoom, resume
razor,*, SHARP BLADE INSTRUMENT FOR CUTTING HAIR
razort, resort
razoto, risotto
razt, raise(d) / race(d)
razume, resume
razun, raisin / raise(sing) / race(cing)
razur, razor
razust, racist
re, PREFIX INDICATING "BACK/AGAIN/IN RESPONSE" MOST OFTEN MODIFIES THE WORD
reach,hes,hed,hing, STRETCH FURTHER THAN NORMAL TO ACHIEVE/GRASP/ACQUIRE "prefixes: over"
reacshen, react(ion)
react,*,ted,ting,tion,tional,tionary, tionaries,tionist,tive,tance,tor, RESPOND/ ACT/MOVE IN RESPONSE TO STIMULUS "prefixes: bio/over/un"
reacter, react(or)
reactur, react(or)
read,*,ding,dable,dability,dableness, dably,der, ABLE TO VIEW/SEE/DECIPHER TEXT/LETTERS/NUMBERS/SYMBOLS (or see red) "prefixes: mis/un"
ready,died,dying,dily,diness, PREPARED TO ACT/PERFORM/RESPOND (or see read) "prefixes: un"
reaf, reef
reak, wreak / reek / wreck
reaked, wreck(ed) / wreak(ed) / reek(ed)
reaks, react(s) / reek(s) / wreak(s)
reakshen, react(ion)

reakshun, react(ion)
reakt, react
reakted, react(ed)
reaktef, react(ive)
reakter, react(or)
reaktif, react(ive)
reaktion, react(ion)
reaktir, react(or)
reaktive, react(ive)
reaktor, react(or)
reaktuf, react(ive)
reaktur, react(or)
real,lness,lism,list,listic,listically,lly,lize, lizes,lized,lizing,lity, PHYSICAL/TRUTHFUL/FACTUAL (or see reel/realty) "prefixes: ir/neo/sur"
realdy, realty
realedy, reality
realestic, real(istic)
realety, reality
realidy, reality
reality,ties, PHYSICAL, TRUTHFUL, FACTUAL (or see reel/realty) "prefixes: un"
really, TRULY, ACTUALLY, INDEED
realm,*, AREA OF SCOPE/INTEREST
realty,ties,tor, OF REAL ESTATE/PROPERTY
ream,*,med,ming,mer, BUNDLED PAPER, ENLARGE/BORE/BEVEL/ENLARGE/ SQUEEZE WITH A TOOL
reanlistment, reenlist(ment)
reap,*,ped,ping,per, ACCEPT, RECEIVE, HARVEST FOR YOUR EFFORTS
rear,*,red,ring, THE END/LAST/BOTTOM OF SOMETHING, TO RISE UP ON HINDQUARTERS "prefixes: up"
reary, weary
reason,*,ned,ning,nable,nably, nableness, WEIGH LOGIC AGAINST EMOTIONS IN MAKING DECISIONS, USE MODERATE JUDGEMENT "prefixes: un"
reastat, rheostat
reath, wreath / wreathe
reatret, retreat
reaultee, realty
reax, react(s)
reb, rib
rebade, rebate
rebaflavin, riboflavin
rebal, rebel
reban, ribbon

rebate,*,er, TO RETURN BACK
rebatishen, repetition
rebeit, rebate
rebel,*,lled,lling,llion,llious,lliously, lliousness, RISE UP/GO AGAINST THE MAINSTREAM OF RULE/THOUGHT
rebelion, rebel(llion)
rebelyus, rebel(llious)
reben, ribbon
reberkushen, repercussion
reberkution, repercussion
rebertwa, repertoire
rebertwor, repertoire
rebetishen, repetition
rebeut, rebut / reboot
rebeutashen, repute(tation)
rebeutel, rebut(ttal)
rebewk, rebuke
rebewt, rebut / reboot
rebewtel, rebut(ttal)
rebil, rebel
rebin, ribbon
rebirkushen, repercussion
rebirkution, repercussion
rebirtwa, repertoire
rebirtwor, repertoire
reble, rebel
rebled, rebel(lled)
rebleka, replica
reblekashen, replica(tion)
reblika, replica
reblikate, replica(te)
reblikation, replica(tion)
rebluka, replica
reblukashen, replica(tion)
reblukate, replica(te)
reblukation, replica(tion)
rebof, rebuff
reboflavin, riboflavin
rebol, rebel
rebon, ribbon
reboot,*,ted,ting, RESTART A COMPUTER/MEMORY/ACTION (or see rebut)
reborkushen, repercussion
rebotek, robot(ic)
rebound,ded,ding, REPERCUSSION/REACTION TO A COLLISION WITH EMOTIONS/ATTITUDES/SOMETHING PHYSICAL
rebownd, rebound
rebownt, rebound
rebrahensible, reprehensible

rebrkushen, repercussion
rebt, rib(bbed) / rip(pped)
rebtile, reptile
rebtileun, reptile(lian)
rebudal, rebut(ttal)
rebudle, rebut(ttal)
rebuf, rebuff
rebuff,*,ffed,ffing, REFUSE/REJECT
rebuflavin, riboflavin
rebuke,*,ed,king,er, SEVERE/SHARP REJECT/REFUSE
rebul, rebel
rebuled, rebel(lled)
rebun, ribbon
reburkushen, repercussion
reburkution, repercussion
reburtwa, repertoire
reburtwor, repertoire
rebut,*,tted,tting,ttable,ttal, ARGUE/REFUTE/OPPOSE/THRUST BACK (or see reboot) "prefixes: sur"
rebutal, rebut(ttal)
rebutashen, repute(tation)
rebute, reboot
rebutishen, repetition
rebutle, rebut(ttal)
rec, wreck
recal, recall
recall,*,lled,lling,llable, CALL/SOLICIT SOMETHING BACK TO THE SOURCE/CREATOR
recamend, recommend
recansile, reconcile
recant,*,ted,ting, CONTRADICT/RETRACT WHAT WAS JUST SAID
recap,*,pped,pping, SUMMARIZE/RECOAT/RESURFACE
recaul, recall
reccomend, recommend
reccomendable, recommend(able)
reccomendation, recommend(ation)
reccomended, recommend(ed)
reccomenduble, recommend(able)
recd, wreck(ed) / wreak(ed) / reek(ed)
recede,*,ed,ding, RETREAT/WITHDRAW/YIELD TO PREVIOUS/PRIOR
receipt,*, ACKNOWLEDGEMENT/INVOICE FOR HAVING RECEIVED SERVICES/ GOODS
receive,*,ed,ving,vable,vables,er,ership, ACCEPT/ACQUIRE/ACCUMULATE
recensile, reconcile

recent,tly,tness,ncy, HAVING OCCURED NEAR/CLOSE TO THE PRESENT TIME (or see resent)
recepe, recipe
receprocate, reciprocate
receprokul, reciprocal
recepshen, reception
recepshenist, receptionist
recepshin, reception
receptacle,*, A PLACE TO DELIVER, A RECEIVING PLACE, ELECTRICAL SOURCE
recepticle, receptacle
reception,*, AN EVENT/CEREMONY/DEVICE WHICH RECEIVES/ACKNOWLEDGE/ACCEPTS INCOMING
receptionist,*, SOMEONE WHO ACCEPTS INCOMING CALLS/VISITORS/CUSTOMERS
receptive,ely,eness,vity,tor, ABLE TO TAKE IN/RECEIVE
receptor,*, THAT WHICH RECEIVES
receptucle, receptacle
recer, recur
reces, recess
recess,sses,ssed,ssing,ssion,ssional, ssionary,sive,sively,siveness, TO TAKE A BREAK, RECEDE
receve, receive
rech, wreck / wreak / reek / reach / wretch / rich
rechd, wreck(ed) / wreak(ed) / reek(ed) / reach(ed)
reched, reach(ed) / wreck(ed) / wreak(ed) / reek(ed)
rechem, regime
rechim, regime
rechis, reach(es) / rich(es)
rechister, register
rechistrashen, registration
rechly, rich(ly)
recht, wreck(ed) / wreak(ed) / reek(ed) / reach(ed)
rechual, ritual
rechuol, ritual
recicle, recycle
recieve, receive
recipe,*, DIRECTIONS FOR COOKING
recipient,*, THOSE WHO RECEIVE/IN RECEIPT OF
recipracate, reciprocate
reciprocal,lity,lly, GIVE AND TAKE, BACK AND FORTH, MUTUALLY RESPONSIVE

reciprocate,*,ted,ting,tion,tive,tor, MOVES BACK AND FORTH, MUTUALLY RESPONSIVE
reciproqueit, reciprocate
recir, recur
recite,*,ed,ting,tal,tation,tative, REPEAT/RELATE GIVE ACCOUNT FROM MEMOR
reck, wreck / wreak / reek
reckamendation, recommend(ation)
recken, wreck(ing) / reek(ing)
reckensile, reconcile
reckety, rickety
reckin, wreck(ing) / reek(ing)
reckinsile, reconcile
reckits, rickets
recklaim, reclaim / reclame
recklamashen, reclamation
recklame, reclaim / reclame
reckless,ssly,ssness, BE UNAWARE/CARELESS OF SURROUNDING ENVIRONMENT POSING POTENTIAL DANGER/PAIN
reckline, recline
recklus, recluse / reckless
reckognition, recognition
reckomend, recommend
reckon,*,ned,ning, SUPPOSE, TO BE CONSIDERED "prefixes: un"
reckonsile, reconcile
reckumend, recommend
reckumendation, recommend(ation)
reckun, reckon
reckunsile, reconcile
reclaim,*,med,ming,mer,mable,mant, mation, TAKE BACK, MAKE PURE/USABLE AGAIN (or see reclame) "prefixes: ir"
reclaimable,*,bility, TAKE BACK, MAKE PURE/USABLE AGAIN "prefixes: ir"
reclamashen, reclamation
reclamation,*, TAKE BACK, MAKE PURE/USABLE
reclame,*, ADVERTISE ONESELF, PUBLIC ATTENTION/NOTORIETY (or see reclaim)
reclamer, reclaim(er)
recles, reckless
recline,*,ed,ning,er, RECUMBENT POSITION/LIE BACK
reclumashen, reclamation
reclumation, reclamation

recluse,*,sion,sive,sively,siveness, SHUT ONESELF OFF/AWAY FROM SOCIETY/ SOCIAL ENVIRONMENT
reclushen, recluse(sion)
recochet, ricochet
recogneshen, recognition
recognetion, recognition
recognition,ive,tory, TO FIND FAMILIAR, FRIENDLY ATTENTION "prefixes: non"
recognize,*,ed,zing,zable,zability,zance, FIND FAMILIAR, KNOW, ACKNOWLEDGE "prefixes: de"
recognizuble, recognize(zable)
recoil,*,led,ling,lless, SUDDEN JERK/ DRAW BACK/SHRINKING FROM
recol, recoil / recall
recold, recall(ed)
recolt, recall(ed)
recomendable, recommend(able)
recomendashen, recommend(ation)
recomindation, recommend(ation)
recommend,*,ded,ding,dation,dable, datory, ADVISE/SUGGEST FAVORABLY
recommendashen, recommend(ation)
reconaisanse, reconnaissance
reconasinse, reconnaissance
reconcile,*,ed,ling,lable,lability, lableness,lably,ement,liation, liatory, REBUILD FRIENDSHIP, RESTORE UNION, ADJUST TO DIFFERENCES "prefixes: ir"
reconnaissance, EXAMINE PARAMETER/ TERRITORY
reconsile, reconcile
reconsileashen, reconcile(liation)
reconsileation, reconcile(liation)
reconstatute, reconstitute
reconstetushen, reconstitute(tion)
reconstetute, reconstitute
reconstitute,*,ed,ting,tion, RECONSTRUCT FROM A CONDENSED/DRIED STATE
reconstruct,*,ted,ting,tion,tive,tible,tor, TO CONSTRUCT AGAIN, RESTORE "prefixes: un"
recoop, recoup
recooped, recoup(ed)
recooperashen, recuperate(tion)
recooperate, recuperate
record,*,ded,ding,dable,der, DOCUMENT/TAPE/WRITE/DEFINE AN EVENT FOR POSTERITY, PRESERVE EVIDENCE "prefixes: pre"
recorse, recourse
recoup,*,ped,ping,pable,pment, TO REGAIN, BE COMPENSATED
recourse, RETURN FOR BACK-UP HELP, ONLY OPTION
recover,*,red,ring,rable,ry, TO GET BACK TO NORMAL/HEALTHY, BECOME OPERABLE AGAIN "prefixes: ir"
recreashen, recreation
recreate,*,ed,ting,tion,tive,tor, AMUSEMENT/DIVERSION/PLAY
recreation,nal,ive, AMUSEMENT/ DIVERSION/PLAY
recreminate, recriminate
recriminate,*,ed,ting,tion,tive,tor,tory, TO ACCUSE THE ONE WHO ACCUSED ORIGINALLY
recruit,*,ted,ting,ter,tment, ORGANIZE/ ENLIST/ENTICE PEOPLE TO JOIN
recrut, recruit
recruter, recruit(er)
rect, wreck(ed) / wreak(ed) / reek(ed)
rectafy, rectify
rectal,lly,tum,ta, INVOLVES/ PERTAINING TO THE RECTUM
rectatude, rectitude
rectem, rectum
rectifie, rectify
rectify,fies,fied,fying,fiable,fication, itude, AMEND/CORRECT/MAKE RIGHT
rectil, rectal
rectim, rectum
rectitude,dinous, RIGHTEOUS IN FORM/ INTEGRITY
rectol, rectal
rectom, rectum
rectul, rectal
rectum,*,ta, THE LOWER LARGE INTESTINE
rectutude, rectitude
recufer, recover
recufry, recover(y)
recuisit, requisite
recumbent,tly,ncy, RECLINING/LYING POSITION
recumendashen, recommend(ation)
recunsdrucdev, reconstruct(ive)
recunsile, reconcile
recunstruct, reconstruct
recupe, recoup

recuped, recoup(ed)
recuperashen, recuperate(tion)
recuperate,*,ed,ting,tion,tive,tory, RECOVER/REGAIN FROM ILLNESS/ FINANCIAL STRESS
recur,*,rred,rring,rrent,rrently,rrence, REPEATEDLY HAPPENING
recurd, record
recuver, recover
recuvry, recover(y)
recwuzit, requisite
recycle,*,ed,ling,er,lable,lables,lability, REUSE, USE AGAIN
red,*,dder,ddest,dding,dness,dden, A COLOR, PERTAINING TO THE COLOR (or see read)
redabel, read(able)
redabul, read(able)
redal, riddle
redard, retard
redasent, reticent
redasint, reticent
rede, ready
redeam, redeem
redeble, read(able)
reded, ready(died) / read
redeem,*,med,ming,mer,mable, CLEAR PAYMENT, RECOVER, FULFILL PLEDGE "prefixes: ir"
redeemible, redeem(able)
redempshun, redemption
redemption,*,nal,ner,ive,tory, TO BE/ ACT OF BEING REDEEMED
redemshen, redemption
redemtion, redemption
redemtive, redemption(ive)
redemuble, redeem(able)
redents, rid(ddance)
reder, red(dder) / read(er)
redern, return
redge, ridge
redi, ready
redible, read(able)
redicint, reticent
redicule, ridicule
rediculus, ridiculous
redimtive, redemption(ive)
redin, red(dden)
redio, radio
redir, red(dder) / read(er)
redisent, reticent
redium, radium
redle, riddle
redna, retina

redniss, red(ness)
redo,oes,did,oing,one, DO AGAIN/OVER
redoo, redo
redoose, reduce
redor, read(er) / red(dder)
redroactive, retroactive
redroaktif, retroactive
redrograte, retrograde
redrospection, retrospect(ion)
redrospekshin, retrospect(ion)
redubel, read(able)
redubol, read(able)
reduce,*,ed,cing,er,cible,cibly,cibility, ction,ctional,ctive, TO LOWER/ DIMUTION/DIVIDE "prefixes: ir"
reducshen, reduce(ction)
reduing, redo(ing)
redukshen, reduce(ction)
reduktion, reduce(ction)
redul, riddle
redun, red(dden)
redundant,tly,ncy,ncies, OVER AND OVER, REPEATEDLY/REPETITION/ UNNECESSARY
redundensy, redundant(ncy)
redur, red(dder) / read(er)
redurn, return
redusable, reduce(cible)
reduse, reduce
redusent, reticent
redusint, reticent
redy, ready
reech, reach
reed,*,ding,dy, A PLANT, CONVEX MOLDING, RIDGES (or see read)
reederate, reiterate
reef,*,fer, OCEAN LEDGE, PART OF A SAIL, SLANG FOR ROLLED MARIJUANA, REFRIGERATOR
reek,*,ked,king,ker,kingly,ky, OFFENSIVE/STRONG/AWFUL ODOR (or see wreak/wreck)
reel,*,led,ling,ler,lable, TO WIND/PULL IN, A DANCE, WOUND UP, REVOLVING TOOL (or see real) "prefixes: un"
reem, ream
reemberse, reimburse
reembersment, reimburse(ment)
reemburse, reimburse
reembursment, reimburse(ment)
reenact,*,ted,ting,tment, REPLICATE A PERFORMANCE/EVENT
reenaktment, reenact(ment)

reenforse, reinforce
reenforsment, reinforce(ment)
reenlestment, reenlist(ment)
reenlist,*,ted,ting,tment, TO ENLIST AGAIN
reep, reap
reept, reap(ed)
reer, rear
reeth, wreath / wreathe
reeturate, reiterate
ref, reef / referee
refal, revel
refalashen, revelation
refalation, revelation
refald, revel(lled)
refalee, reveille
refar, river
refarmashen, reform(ation)
refarmation, reform(ation)
refeel, reveal
refel, revel / refill
refelable, refill(able)
refelashen, revelation
refelation, revelation
refeld, revel(lled) / refill(ed)
refelee, reveille
refeloble, refill(able)
refer,*,rred,rring,rable,rral, RECOMMEND/HAND OVER/ REQUEST/ASSIGN SOMEONE ELSE, SLANG FOR REFRIGERATOR (or see reef(er)/river)
referal, refer(rral)
referbash, refurbish
referbish, refurbish
referbishment, refurbish(ment)
referd, refer(rred)
refere, referee
referee,*,eed,eeing, ASSIGNED TO SETTLE DISPUTES/MAKE JUDGEMENT CALLS
reference,*,ed,cing, DIRECTION, ALLUSION, GUIDE
referendum,*,da, MEASURE PUT BEFORE PUBLIC FOR VOTE
referil, refer(rral)
referindum, referendum
referinse, reference
refermashen, reform(ation)
refermation, reform(ation)
referse, reverse
refeuge, refuge
refeugy, refugee
refeuje, refuge

refeuse, refuse
refeusil, refuse(sal)
refeuze, refuse
refewge, refuge / refugee
refewje, refuge
refews, refuse
refewsel, refuse(sal)
refiew, review / revue
refiful, revival
refil, refill
refilable, refill(able)
refilashen, revelation
refilation, revelation
refild, revel(lled)
refilee, reveille
refill,*,lled,lling,llable, FILL AGAIN
refine,*,ed,ning,ery,nable,ement, REMOVE IMPURITIES/ALLOYS, MAKE FINE "prefixes: un"
refinment, refine(ment)
refinury, refine(ry)
refir, refer / reef(er) / river
refiral, refer(rral)
refirans, reference
refirbash, refurbish
refirbish, refurbish
refird, refer(rred)
refired, refer(rred)
refiree, referee
refirence, reference
refirendum, referendum
refirense, reference
refirmashen, reform(ation)
refirmation, reform(ation)
refirse, reverse
reflashen, revelation
reflecks, reflex / reflect(s)
reflecksef, reflex(ive)
reflect,*,ted,ting,tion,tive,tively, tiveness,tor,torize, MIRROR/CAST BACK/ REPRODUCE AN IMAGE (or see reflex) "prefixes: retro/un"
reflectif, reflect(ive)
refleks, reflex / reflect(s)
reflekshen, reflect(ion)
refleksif, reflex(ive)
reflekt, reflect / reflex(ed)
reflektif, reflect(ive)
reflektion, reflect(ion)
reflektor, reflect(or)
reflex,xes,xed,xing,xly,xive,xively, xiveness,xivity, REACTION/ RESPONSE (or see reflect) "prefixes: ir"

reflexsif, reflex(ive)
reflext, reflex(ed)
refol, revel
refolashen, revelation
refolation, revelation
refold, revel(lled)
refolee, reveille
refor, river / refer / reef(er)
reform,*,med,ming,mer,mation,mable, matory,matories,mative, CHANGE/MODIFY/RETRAIN/REARRANGE/RESTORE "prefixes: ir"
reformashen, reform(ation)
reformd, reform(ed)
reformitory, reform(atory)
reformutory, reform(atory)
refract,*,ted,ting,tion,tive,tory, DEFLECT/REFLECT INTO A DIFFERENT DIRECTION/DENSITY
refrain,*,ned,ning,nment, REPETITIVE BREAK/INTERRUPTION, TO REPRESS/ ABSTAIN
refrakt, refract
refraktory, refract(ory)
refrane, refrain
refrans, reference / refrain(s)
refred, referee(d)
refree, referee
refregirant, refrigerate(ant)
refregirator, refrigerate(tor)
refrendum, referendum
refrense, reference
refresh,hes,hed,hing,her,hment, TO MAKE FRESH AGAIN/ INVIGORATE
refrigerate,*,ed,ting,tion,ant, USED TO KEEP THINGS COOL/ COLD
refrigerator, refrigerate(tor)
refrigerent, refrigerate(ant)
refrindum, referendum
refrinse, reference
refry, referee
reft, rift
refuch, refuge
refuchi, refugee
refue, review / revue
refuge,*, SANCTUARY/SHELTER, SAFE PROTECTION
refugee,*, ONE ESCAPING PERSECUTION FROM A FOREIGN COUNTRY
refugy, refugee
refuje, refuge
reful, revel
refulashen, revelation

refulation, revelation
refulee, reveille
refund,*,ded,ding,dable, RETURN/COMPENSATE/GIVE BACK
refundible, refund(able)
refunduble, refund(able)
refunt, refund
refur, refer / reef(er) / river
refurbeshment, refurbish(ment)
refurbish,hes,hed,hing,hment, RENOVATE/MAKE FRESH AGAIN
refurd, refer(rred)
refured, refer(rred)
refuree, referee
refurendum, referendum
refurense, reference
refuril, refer(rral)
refurindum, referendum
refurmashen, reform(ation)
refurse, reverse
refus, raffle / refuse
refuse,*,ed,sing,sal,er, NOT ACCEPT, DENY/REJECT, TO DISCARD UNUSABLES/ TRASH
refusel, refuse(sal)
refute,*,ed,ting,tability,table,tably, tation, CHANGE/MODIFY/RETRAIN/REARRANGE/RESTORE "prefixes: ir"
refuze, refuse
reg, rig / ridge
regal,lly,lia,le,led,ling,lity,lities, PERTAINING TO LAVISH FEASTS/ROYALTY
regalea, regal(ia)
regaledy, regal(ity)
regamen, regime(n)
regamentashen, regime(ntation)
regamentation, regime(ntation)
regamin, regime(n)
regamint, regime(nt)
regan, region
regard,*,ded,ding,dful,dfully,dfullness, dless,dlessly,dlessness, TO CONSIDER, SHOW CONCERN/ATTENTION/RESPECT "prefixes: dis/ir"
regart, regard
regaster, register
regastrashen, registration
regastration, registration
regect, reject
regekshen, reject(ion)
regekt, reject
regektion, reject(ion)

regel, regal
regementation, regime(ntation)
regemin, regime(n)
regemint, regime(nt)
regemintation, regime(ntation)
regen, region
regenal, region(al)
regenerate,*,ed,ting,able,acy,tely,tion, tive,tively,tor, RENEW, RESTORE, REPLACE, REVITALIZE "prefixes: un"
regenuradive, regenerate(tive)
reger, rigor
regergetate, regurgitate
regerjutate, regurgitate
regestir, register
regestrashen, registration
regestration, registration
reget, rigid
regeuler, regular
regeulerly, regular(ly)
regewlashen, regulate(tion)
regewlate, regulate
regewlation, regulate(tion)
regewlerly, regular(ly)
regewvinate, rejuvenate
regid, rigid
regil, regal
regime,*,en,ent,ental,entally,entation, MODE/SYSTEM OF RULE/MANAGEMENT
regimentashen, regime(ntation)
regimin, regime(min)
regimint, regime(nt)
regimintation, regime(ntation)
regin, region
reginal, region(al)
reginuradive, regenerate(tive)
reginurate, regenerate
reginurative, regenerate(tive)
region,*,nal,nally,nalism,nalist,nalistic, AN AREA/PART/SECTION OF "prefixes: inter/sub"
regirus, rigor(ous)
register,*,red,ring,tration, SIGN UP/ENROLL TO PARTICIPATE "prefixes: de"
registrashen, registration
registration,*, SIGN UP/ENROLL TO PARTICIPATE
regit, rigid
regiular, regular
reglar, regular
reglate, regulate
regle, regal

reglerly, regular(ly)
reglir, regular
reglurly, regular(ly)
regoise, rejoice
regon, region
regonal, region(al)
regoyse, rejoice
regres, regress
regresif, regress(ive)
regresive, regress(ive)
regress,sses,ssed,ssing,ssion,ssive,
    ssively,ssiveness,ssor, GOING BACK/
    REVERSION
regresuf, regress(ive)
regret,*,tted,tting,tful,tfully,tfulness,
    ttable,ttably,tter, SENSE OF LOSS/
    SORROW, SORRY
regreted, regret(tted)
regretfuly, regret(fully)
reguard, regard
reguardless, regard(less)
regul, regal
regular,*,rly,rity,rize, NORMAL/
    AVERAGE/TYPICAL "prefixes: ir"
regulashen, regulate(tion)
regulate,*,ed,ting,tion,tive,tor,tory,
    NORMALIZE, KEEP WITHIN LIMITS/
    STANDARDS "prefixes: de"
reguler, regular
regulerly, regular(ly)
regulur, regular
regument, regime(nt)
regumentashen, regime(ntation)
regumentation, regime(ntation)
regumin, regime(n)
regumint, regime(nt)
regunal, region(al)
regurgitate,*,ed,ting,tion, RUSH/SURGE
    BACK AND FORTH
regurjitate, regurgitate
regurs, rigor(s)
regurus, rigor(ous)
regustir, register
regustrashen, registration
regustration, registration
reguvanashen, rejuvenate(tion)
reguvanate, rejuvenate
reguvanation, rejuvenate(tion)
reguvinate, rejuvenate
reguvination, rejuvenate(tion)
reguvunate, rejuvenate
regwasit, requisite
regwazit, requisite

rehab,*,bber,bilitate, SLANG FOR
    REHABILITATION
rehabeletashen, rehabilitate(tion)
rehabeletate, rehabilitate
rehabilitate,*,ed,ting,tion,tive,
    RESTORE/REINSTATE/REESTABLISH
rehap, rehab
rehearse,*,ed,sing,sal, TO PRACTICE
    REPEATEDLY FOR A PERFORMANCE
rehebilatation, rehabilitate(tion)
rehersal, rehearse(sal)
reherse, rehearse
rehersul, rehearse(sal)
rehirsul, rehearse(sal)
rehubelatashen, rehabilitate(tion)
rehubilatate, rehabilitate
rehubiletation, rehabilitate(tion)
rehurse, rehearse
rehursil, rehearse(sal)
reiderate, reiterate
reidurate, reiterate
reign,*,ned,ning, HAVE RULE/POWER/
    SOVEREIGNITY (or see rain/rein)
reil, real / reel / rale / rail
reilistec, real(istic)
reiltee, realty
reilty, realty
reimberse, reimburse
reimbirsment, reimburse(ment)
reimburse,*,ed,sing,sable,ement,er,
    PAY BACK/REFUND/COMPENSATE
rein,*,ned,ning,nless, RESTRAINT/
    CURB/CONTROL (or see rain/reign)
reinacment, reenact(ment)
reinacted, reenact(ed)
reinakt, reenact
reinaktment, reenact(ment)
reindeer,*, IN THE DEER FAMILY
reinforce,*,ed,cing,ement, INCREASE/
    STRENGTHEN
reinforse, reinforce
reinforsment, reinforce(ment)
reinlest, reenlist
reinlisment, reenlist(ment)
reinlist, reenlist
reinlistment, reenlist(ment)
reip, rape / ripe / reap
reis, race / rise / raise
reiterate,*,ed,ting,tion,tive,tively, TO
    REPEAT/SAY AGAIN
reiturate, reiterate
rej, ridge / reach
rejament, regime(nt)
rejamin, regime(n)

rejamintashen, regime(ntation)
rejamintation, regime(ntation)
rejan, region
rejaster, register
reject,*,ted,ting,tion,ter,tive, REFUSE
    TO RECEIVE/RECOGNIZE/
    ACKNOWLEDGE/ACCEPT
rejekshen, reject(ion)
rejekt, reject
rejektion, reject(ion)
rejen, region
rejenaradive, regenerate(tive)
rejenarative, regenerate(tive)
rejenul, region(al)
rejenurate, regenerate
rejestir, register
rejestrashen, registration
rejestration, registration
rejet, rigid
rejewvinate, rejuvenate
rejid, rigid
rejimen, regime(n)
rejiment, regime(nt)
rejin, region
rejinarate, regenerate
rejinul, region(al)
rejinuradive, regenerate(tive)
rejister, register
rejistrashen, registration
rejistration, registration
rejit, rigid
rejoese, rejoice
rejoice,*,ed,cing,er,cingly, TO DISPLAY
    JOY/GLADNESS
rejon, region
rejonal, region(al)
rejoyse, rejoice
rejumen, regime(n)
rejument, regime(nt)
rejumentashen, regime(ntation)
rejumentation, regime(ntation)
rejumin, regime(n)
rejumint, regime(nt)
rejumintashen, regime(ntation)
rejumintation, regime(ntation)
rejun, region
rejunal, region(al)
rejustir, register
rejustrashen, registration
rejustration, registration
rejuvanashen, rejuvenate(tion)
rejuvenate,*,ed,ting,tion,tor,nize,
    nescence, MAKE YOUTHFUL AGAIN
rejuvinashen, rejuvenate(tion)

rejuvinate, rejuvenate
rejuvination, rejuvenate(tion)
rek, wreck / wreak / reek
rekal, recall
rekamend, recommend
rekamendation, recommend(ation)
rekamenduble, recommend(able)
rekamented, recommend(ed)
rekanize, recognize
rekansile, reconcile
rekansileashun, reconcile(liation)
rekant, recant
rekap, recap
rekapt, recap(pped)
rekashay, ricochet
rekd, reek(ed) / wreck(ed) / wreak(ed)
rekedy, rickety
rekegnise, recognize
reken, reckon
rekendil, rekindle
rekendul, rekindle
rekenize, recognize
rekensile, reconcile
rekensileashun, reconcile(liation)
reker, recur / wrecker
rekerd, record
rekety, rickety
rekeulir, regular
rekewlashen, regulate(tion)
rekewpt, recoup(ed)
rekewpurate, recuperate
rekidy, rickety
rekimented, recommend(ed)
rekin, reckon
rekindle,*,ed,ling, RENEW
rekindul, rekindle
rekinise, recognize
rekinsile, reconcile
rekir, recur / wrecker
rekird, record
rekits, rickets
rekity, rickety
reklaimuble, reclaimable
reklamashen, reclamation
reklamation, reclamation
reklame, reclaim / reclame
reklamshen, reclamation
reklamuble, reclaimable
reklas, reckless
reklemashen, reclamation
rekless, reckless
reklimashen, reclamation
reklimation, reclamation
rekline, recline

reklinur, recline(r)
reklir, regular
reklis, reckless
rekloos, recluse
reklumation, reclamation
reklus, reckless
rekluse, recluse
rekochet, ricochet
rekofry, recover(y)
rekogneshen, recognition
rekognise, recognize
rekognition, recognition
rekognize, recognize
rekognizuble, recognize(zable)
rekoil, recoil
rekol, recall
rekold, recall(ed)
rekole, recoil / recall
rekolt, recall(ed)
rekomend, recommend
rekomendashen, recommend(ation)
rekomented, recommend(ed)
rekon, reckon
rekonasents, reconnaissance
rekonisense, reconnaissance
rekonize, recognize
rekonsdructive, reconstruct(ive)
rekonsile, reconcile
rekonsileat, reconcile(ate)
rekonsileation, reconcile(liation)
rekonstatute, reconstitute
rekonstetushen, reconstitute(tion)
rekonstetute, reconstitute
rekonstitution, reconstitute(tion)
rekonstruct, reconstruct
rekonusinse, reconnaissance
rekoop, recoup
rekooperate, recuperate
rekor, wrecker
rekord, record
rekorder, record(er)
rekorse, recourse
rekover, recover
rekoyl, recoil
rekreashen, recreation
rekreate, recreate
rekreation, recreation
rekreative, recreate(tive)
rekreminate, recriminate
rekrimenate, recriminate
rekroot, recruit
rekrute, recruit
rekruter, recruit(er)
reks, reek(s) / wreck(s) / wreak(s)

rekt, reek(ed) / wreck(ed) / wreak(ed)
rektafy, rectify
rektal, rectal
rektatude, rectitude
rektel, rectal
rektem, rectum
rektify, rectify
rektitude, rectitude
rektol, rectal
rektom, rectum
rektufy, rectify
rektul, rectal
rektum, rectum
rekuasit, requisite
rekufer, recover
rekufry, recover(y)
rekugnise, recognize
rekugnishen, recognition
rekugnize, recognize
rekugnizuble, recognize(zable)
rekulade, regulate
rekular, regular
rekulashen, regulate(tion)
rekulate, regulate
rekulation, regulate(tion)
rekumbent, recumbent
rekumend, recommend
rekumendashen, recommend(ation)
rekumenduble, recommend(able)
rekumented, recommend(ed)
rekumind, recommend
rekun, reckon
rekunize, recognize
rekunsile, reconcile
rekunsileashen, reconcile(liation)
rekunsileation, reconcile(liation)
rekunstruct, reconstruct
rekunstrukdive, reconstruct(ive)
rekupe, recoup
rekuperate, recuperate
rekuperation, recuperate(tion)
rekupirate, recuperate
rekupt, recoup(ed)
rekupurashen, recuperate(tion)
rekur, recur / wrecker
rekurd, record
rekushet, ricochet
rekuver, recover
rekuvry, recover(y)
rekwasit, requisite
rekwest, request
rekwire, require
rekwirment, require(ment)
rekwrute, recruit

rekwuzit, requisite
rel, real / reel / rill / rail / rale
rela, relay
relabs, relapse
relagashen, relegate(tion)
relagate, relegate
relagation, relegate(tion)
relaks, relax
relantless, relent(less)
relaps, relapse
relapse,*,ed,sing,er, TO BACKSLIDE/ FALL BACK
relashen, relate(tion)
relashunship, relate(tionship)
relate,*,ed,ting,tion,tional,table, tionship,edness, BE ALLIED/ ASSOCIATED/CONNECTED WITH, TO TELL/NARRATE "prefixes: inter"
relatevity, relativity
relatif, relative
relative,*,ely,eness,vism,vist,vistic,vity, ASSOCIATED/SIMILAR/CLOSE/ CONNECTION "prefixes: ir"
relativity,vities, THAT WHICH IS RELATIVE
relativly, relative(ly)
relavance, relevant(nce)
relavant, relevant
relavence, relevance
relavent, relevant
relax,xes,xed,xing,xation,xedly,xedness, xer,xant, BECOME CALM/LOOSE/ SLACK "prefixes: un"
relay,*,yed,ying, USE OF MACHINERY/ ELECTRICITY/PEOPLE/ TECHNOLOGY/ANIMALS TO SEND/ TRANSMIT/RETRIEVE
rele, really / reel / real
release,*,ed,sing,er,sable, TO FREE
relef, relief
relegate,*,ed,ting,tion, SEND AWAY
releive, relieve
relek, relic
relent,*,ted,ting,tless, INTENSELY PERSISTENT/DEMANDING/ PUNISHING "prefixes: un"
relentless,ssly,ssness, MERCILESS/ HARSH
relese, release
relesh, relish
reletif, relative
reletivity, relativity
reletivly, relative(ly)
relevance, relevant(nce)

relevant,tly,nce,ncy, PERTAINS/ APPLICABLE TO, IMPORTANT/ SUPPORTIVE "prefixes: ir"
releve, relieve
relevence, relevance
relevent, relevant
relever, relieve(r)
relevur, relieve(r)
reli, really / rely
reliable,bility,leness,ly, CONFIDENCE/ TRUST IN, DEPEND ON "prefixes: un"
reliance,cy,nt,ntly, CONFIDENCE/ TRUST/DEPENDENT
reliaple, reliable
relic,*, MEMENTOS/PRESERVED/KEEP SAKES
relichon, religion
relidy, reality
relief,eve, EASE/REMOVAL/ ALLEVIATION FROM PAIN
relieve,*,ed,ving,er,vable, EASED/ REMOVED/ALLEVIATED FROM PAIN (or see relief)
religashen, relegate(tion)
religate, relegate
religation, relegate(tion)
religeon, religion
religion,*,ous,ously,ousness, BELIEF IN A GOD IN A SPECIFIC/PARTICULAR WAY "prefixes: inter/ir"
religon, religion
religus, religion(ous)
relik, relic
relinkwish, relinquish
relinquish,hes,hed,hing,hment,her, GIVE UP POSSESSION OF
relintless, relent(less) / relentless
relish,hes,hed,hing,hable, APPETIZER, PICKLED CONDIMENT, BE GRATIFIED/ PLEASED/LIKE/SAVOR SOMETHING
relity, reality
reliubility, reliable(bility)
reliuble, reliable
reliunse, reliance
reliunt, reliance(nt)
relivance, relevant(nce)
relivant, relevant
relivence, relevance
relivent, relevant
reliver, relieve(r)
relm, realm
reloctant, reluctant

relogate, relegate
relogation, relegate(tion)
reltifly, relative(ly)
relty, realty
reluctant,tly,nce, APPREHENSIVE/ RESISTANT/UNWILLING
reluctinse, reluctant(nce)
reluctint, reluctant
relugashen, relegate(tion)
relugate, relegate
relugation, relegate(tion)
reluktant, reluctant
reluktense, reluctant(nce)
reluktint, reluctant
relur, regular
relush, relish
relutif, relative
relutivly, relative(ly)
reluvence, relevance
reluvent, relevant
rely,lies,lied,lying,liable,liability, liableness,liably, TRUSTWORTHY/ SUPPORTIVE/DEPENDABLE (or see really)
rem, ream / realm / rim
remade, remedy
remadik, rheumatic
remain,*,ned,ning,nder, STAY BEHIND/ LEFT OVER (or see romaine)
reman, remain / romaine
remanis, reminisce
remanisent, reminisce(nt)
remantisize, romantic(ize)
remar, ream(er)
remark,*,ked,king,kable,kably, kableness, WORTHY OF COMMENT/ OBSERVATION/NOTICE "prefixes: un"
remarkuble, remark(able)
rematik, rheumatic
rematy, remedy
rembunctious, rambunctious
rembunkshes, rambunctious
reme, ream
remede, remedy
remediashen, remedy(diation)
remedy,dies,died,dying,diable, diableness,diably,diless,dial, diation, FIX/IMPROVE DAMAGE, RELIEVE DISORDER "prefixes: ir"
remember,*,red,ring,brance,brancer, ACKNOWLEDGE/THINK OF/ RECOLLECT THE PAST "prefixes: dis"
remembrinse, remember(ance)

remembur, remember
remenis, reminisce
remenisent, reminisce(nt)
remer, ream(er)
remeshen, remission
remet, remit
remety, remedy
remidal, remit(ttal)
remidy, remedy
remind,*,ded,ding,der,dful, CAUSE TO RECOLLECT/REMEMBER
remindur, remind(er)
reminis, reminisce
reminisce,*,ed,cing,ent,ently, LONGINGLY REMEMBER/THINK OF THE PAST
reminisent, reminisce(nt)
remintur, remind(er)
remir, ream(er)
remishen, remission
remision, remission
remissible,bility, CAN BE FORGIVEN "prefixes: ir"
remission, ABATEMENT, TEMPORARY REDUCTION/DISAPPEARANCE
remit,*,tted,tting,tment,ttable,tter, ttance,ttent,ttently,ttal, TRANSMIT/ SEND/GIVE BACK "prefixes: un"
remital, remit(ttal)
remited, remit(tted)
remition, remission
remituble, remit(ttable)
remity, remedy
remnant,*, LEFT OVERS/REMAINS/ SCRAPS
remnet, remnant
remnint, remnant
remofer, remove(r)
remonis, reminisce
remoof, remove
remooval, remove(val)
remoovil, remove(val)
remorse,eful,efully,efulness,eless, elessly,elessness, PAIN/GUILT WHEN LOOKING TO SOMETHING IN THE PAST
remorsful, remorse(ful)
remorsless, remorse(ful)
remote,*,ely,eness, REMOVED FROM SOCIAL CENTERS, FAR OFF IN DISTANCE/TIME
remotly, remote(ly)

remove,*,ed,ving,vable,vability, vableness,vably,val,ver, TAKE AWAY/ERASE "prefixes: ir"
remudy, remedy
remufe, remove
remufer, remove(r)
remufible, remove(vable)
remufil, remove(val)
remunerashen, remunerate(tion)
remunerate,*,ed,ting,able,ability,tion, tive,tively, PAY FOR LOSS/REPAY/ COMPENSATE/REWARD
remuneration, remunerate(tion)
remunirate, remunerate
remuniration, remunerate(tion)
remunis, reminisce
remur, ream(er)
remutoed, rheumatic(toid)
remuty, remedy
remuvable, remove(vable)
remuve, remove
remuvel, remove(val)
remuvul, remove(val)
ren, wren
renagade, renegade
renaisance, renaissance
renaissance, PERIOD OF TIME IN EUROPE
renasance, renaissance
renasons, renaissance
renauserus, rhinoceros
renavashen, renovate(tion)
renavate, renovate
renavation, renovate(tion)
renawserus, rhinoceros
rench, wrench
rendal, rent(al)
render,*,red,ring,rable,rer, RETURN/ GIVE IN/SUBMIT/FURNISH/ SURRENDER/CAUSE (or see rent(er))
rendezvous, ARRANGE TO MEET, MEET UP WITH
rendur, render
renegade,*,do, ONE WHO DESERTS, A TRAITOR
renege,*,ed,ging,er, TO FAIL/GO BACK ON WORD, VIOLATE CARD GAME RULE
renevashen, renovate(tion)
renevate, renovate
renevation, renovate(tion)

renew,*,wed,wing,wable,wably, wability,wal,wer, REFRESH/MAKE LIKE NEW/REFURBISH/UPDATE
reng, ring / rink / wring
renger, ring(er) / ranger
renig, renege
renigade, renegade
renik, renege
renisance, renaissance
renissance, renaissance
renk, ring / rink / wring
renkle, wrinkle
renkul, wrinkle
renlistment, reenlist(ment)
renone, renown
renoserus, rhinoceros
renosirus, rhinoceros
renosonse, renaissance
renounce,*,ed,cing,eable,ement,er, DISOWN/REJECT/CAST OFF
renounse, renounce
renounsment, renounce(ment)
renovaded, renovate(d)
renovashen, renovate(tion)
renovate,*,ed,ting,tion,tor, REPAIR TO LIKE NEW CONDITION
renown,ned, ACHIEVEMENTS/ REPUTATION KNOWN FAR AND WIDE
renownse, renounce
renownsment, renounce(ment)
rens, rinse / wren(s) / rent(s)
rensd, rinse(d)
rensur, rinse(r)
rent,*,tal,ted,ting,table,ter,tor, PAY SOMEONE TO BORROW THE USE OF PROPERTY
rentel, rent(al)
renter, render / rent(er)
rentible, rent(able)
rentil, rent(al)
rentuble, rent(able)
rentul, rent(al)
renu, renew
renuable, renew(able)
renuel, renew(al)
renugade, renegade
renuil, renew(al)
renumerate, remunerate
renumeration, remunerate(tion)
renusans, renaissance
renusons, renaissance
renussance, renaissance
renuvadid, renovate(d)

renuvashen, renovate(tion)
renuvate, renovate
renuvation, renovate(tion)
renuzons, renaissance
reol, real / reel / rail / rale
reolistic, real(istic)
reoltee, realty
reolty, realty
reostat, rheostat
rep, rip / ripe / reep
repair,*,red,ring,rer,arable,aration, TO FIX/RESTORE TO A USABLE CONDITION "prefixes: dis"
repal, rebel / ripple
reparable,ly,bility,ative,ation, ABLE TO BE REPAIRED "prefixes: ir"
reparashen, reparation
reparation,*, ABLE TO BE REPAIRED
reparcushen, repercussion
repare, repair
reparkushen, repercussion
repateshen, repetition
repatishus, repetition(ous)
repatition, repetition
repatitious, repetition(ous)
repd, rip(pped) / reep(ed)
repeal,*,led,ling,lable, TO END/ABOLISH A LAW (or see repel/rappel) "prefixes: ir"
repeat,*,ted,ting,ter,tedly,table,tability, TO SAY/DO/HAPPEN AGAIN, MORE THAN ONCE "prefixes: un"
reped, rip(pped) / reep(ed)
repedatif, repetitive
repededly, repeat(edly)
repedutif, repetitive
repeel, repeal
repeet, repeat
repel,*,lled,lling,ller,llency,llent, KEEP SOMETHING AWAY/OFF OF, REJECTS/RESISTS (or see rappel/repeal/ripple)
repelent, repellent
repelinsy, repellent(ncy)
repellent,*,tly,ncy, REJECT/RESIST, KEEP OFF OF
repellinsy, repellent(ncy)
repense, repent(s)
repent,*,ted,ting,tance,tant,ter, REALIZE/REMEDY WRONGDOING
repentinse, repent(ance)
reperable, reparable
reperashen, reparation
reperation, reparation

repercushen, repercussion
repercussion,*,ive, THE EFFECTS/DEVELOPMENT ACHIEVED/RESULTING FROM AN ACTION
reperkushen, repercussion
reperkution, repercussion
repertoire,*, LIST OF DRAMAS/PERFORMANCES/TALENTS/AVAILABLE RESOURCES
repertor, repertoire
repertwa, repertoire
repertwor, repertoire
repete, repeat
repetedly, repeat(edly)
repetishen, repetition
repetishus, repetition(ous)
repetition,*,ous,ously,ousness,ive, REPEAT/SAY/DO SOMETHING OVER AND OVER, ROUTINE
repetitive,ely,eness,ion, REPEAT OVER AND OVER
repetitous, repetition(ous)
repeutashen, repute(tation)
repeutation, repute(tation)
repeutuble, repute(table)
rephund, refund
repil, rebel / ripple
repint, repent
repintense, repent(ance)
repirable, reparable
repirashen, reparation
repiration, reparation
repircushen, repercussion
repirkution, repercussion
repirtoire, repertoire
repirtwor, repertoire
repitishen, repetition
repitishus, repetition(ous)
repitition, repetition
repititious, repetition(ous)
repl, repel / ripple / rebel
replacation, replica(tion)
replace,*,ed,cing,ement,eable,er, PUT SOMETHING IN PLACE OF SOMETHING ELSE "prefixes: ir"
replacment, replace(ment)
replakation, replica(tion)
replasmint, replace(ment)
reple, rebel / ripple
repleca, replica
replecation, replica(tion)
repleka, replica
replekate, replica(te)
replekation, replica(tion)

repleneshment, replenish(ment)
replenish,hes,hed,hing,her,hment, TO RESTOCK/REFILL
replica,*,ate,ated,ating,ation, MAKE AN EXACT COPY OF
replika, replica
replikate, replica(te)
replucation, replica(tion)
repluka, replica
replukate, replica(te)
replukation, replica(tion)
reply,lies,lied,lying,lier, TO ANSWER BACK/RESPOND
repoflavin, riboflavin
repoire, rapport
repol, rebel / ripple
repor, rapport
reporashen, reparation
reporation, reparation
reporder, report(er)
reporkushen, repercussion
report,*,ted,tedly,ting,ter,table,tage,torial,torially, GIVE ACCOUNT OF AN EVENT/OCCURRENCE "prefixes: mis/under"
repository,ries, A PLACE/SHELTER/DWELLING WHICH STORES/PRESERVES/ SAFEKEEPS
reposutory, repository
repoteshen, repetition
repour, rapport
repozitory, repository
reprable, reparable
repraduction, reproduce(ction)
repradukshen, reproduce(ction)
repraduse, reproduce
reprahensible, reprehensible
repramand, reprimand
reprasent, represent
reprazintation, represent(ation)
repreble, reparable
repreduction, reproduce(ction)
reprehensible,bility,bly, UNACCEPTABLE/TO BE CENSURED, SUPPORTIVE/IMPORTANT "prefixes: ir"
reprehinsible, reprehensible
repremand, reprimand
represent,*,ted,ting,table,ter,tation, tational,tative,tatively, tativeness, TO ACT ON BEHALF OF SOMEONE/SOMETHING ELSE "prefixes: mis/under"
represhin, repress(ion)

represif, repress(ive)
represion, repress(ion)
represive, repress(ive)
repress,sses,ssed,ssing,ssion,sser, PREVENT/SUPPRESS/BLOCK NATURAL EXPRESSION (or see oppress) "prefixes: de/ir"
represuve, repress(ive)
reprible, reparable
reprimand,*,ded,ding, TO BE REPRESSED/REPROVED/FORMALLY REBUKED
reprisent, represent
reprkushen, repercussion
reproach,hes,hed,hing,hingly,hable, hableness,hably,her, BLAMED/ CRITICIZED FOR WRONGDOING "prefixes: ir"
reproch, reproach
reprochuble, reproach(able)
reproduce,*,ed,cing,cible,cibility,er, ction,ctive,ctively,ctiveness, PRODUCE ANEW, DUPLICATE/ REPEAT/REMEMBER "prefixes: ir"
reprodukshen, reproduce(ction)
reproduse, reproduce
repruble, reparable
repruduction, reproduce(ction)
reprudukshen, reproduce(ction)
reprumand, reprimand
reprusent, represent
repruzentation, represent(ation)
rept, reap(ed) / rip(pped) / reep(ed)
repteleun, reptile(lian)
reptile,*,lian, COLD BLOODED VERTEBRATE
reptilein, reptile(lian)
reptishus, repetition(ous)
republek, republic
republekin, republic(an)
republic,*,can, A TYPE OF POLITICAL SYSTEM "prefixes: pre"
republikan, republic(an)
repugnant,tly,nce,ncy, STRONG OPPOSITION/DISLIKE/AVERSION
repugnense, repugnant(nce)
repugnent, repugnant
repul, ripple / rebel
repuld, ripple(d)
repulse,*,ed,sing,sion,sive,sively, siveness, REPEL/AVERT/REBUFF/ FORBID
repulshen, repulse(ion)
repulsif, repulse(sive)

repult, ripple(d)
repurable, reparable
repurashen, reparation
repuration, reparation
repurcushen, repercussion
repurkution, repercussion
repurtoire, repertoire
repurtwa, repertoire
repurtwor, repertoire
reputashen, repute(tation)
repute,ed,edly,table,tably,tability, tation, TYPE OF CHARACTER "prefixes: dis"
reputeshen, repetition
reputishus, repetition(ous)
reputition, repetition
reputitious, repetition(ous)
reqrute, recruit
request,*,ted,ting, ASK/PETITION/ SOLICIT FOR
require,*,ed,ring,ement, ESSENTIAL/ NECESSARY
requisite,*,ely,eness, REQUIRED/ NECESSARY "prefixes: de/pre"
requisition,*,ned,ning,nary, REQUEST TO OBTAIN, FORMAL DEMAND "prefixes: de"
requite,*,ed,ting,table,tably,tal,ement, er, ASK/PETITION/SOLICIT FOR "prefixes: un"
requpe, recoup
reqwasit, requisite
reqwest, request
reqwire, require
reqwirement, require(ment)
rer, rear / rare
rerd, rear(ed)
rere, weary
reridy, rare(rity)
rerity, rare(rity)
resadenshul, reside(ntial)
resadensy, reside(ncy)
resadential, reside(ntial)
resadinshul, reside(ntial)
resadinsy, reside(ncy)
resadue, residue
resal, wrestle
resalushen, resolute(tion)
resan, reason / resin / rise(n)
resanate, resonate / resinate
resandly, recent(ly)
resanense, resonance
resanent, resonance(nt)
resaninse, resonance

resanuble, reason(able)
resape, recipe
resarektion, resurrect(ion)
resatashen, recite(tion)
resauluble, resoluble
rescue,*,ed,uing,er, SAVE/SPARE FROM DANGER/HARM
resdrane, restrain
research,hes,hed,hing,her, TO STUDY/ OBSERVE/DERIVE FROM FACTS
resebshen, reception
resebshinist, receptionist
resebter, receptor
resebtif, receptive
resebtive, receptive
resede, recede
reseded, recede(d)
resedenshul, reside(ntial)
resedential, reside(ntial)
resedinse, reside(ncy)
resedue, residue
reseed, recede
reseef, receive
reseet, receipt
reseeve, receive
resefe, receive
resefuble, receive(vable)
resegnation, resign(ation)
reselute, resolute
resemble,*,ed,ling,lance, SIMILAR/ LIKENESS
resemblinse, resemble(lance)
resen, reason / resin / rise(n)
resenate, resonate / resinate
resenation, resonate(tion)
resenator, resonate(tor)
resendly, recent(ly)
reseninse, resonance
resent,*,ted,ting,tful,tfully,tfulness, tment, FEEL SORRY FOR ONESELF, DOESN'T FEEL APPRECIATED FOR A DEED DONE (or see recent)
resenuble, reason(able)
resepdkle, receptacle
resepe, recipe
resepeunt, recipient
reseprocal, reciprocal
reseprocation, reciprocate(tion)
reseprokashen, reciprocate(tion)
resepshen, reception
resepshenist, receptionist
resepshun, reception
reseptacle, receptacle
resepticle, receptacle

reseptif, receptive
reseption, reception
reseptionest, receptionist
reseptive, receptive
reseptor, receptor
reseptukle, receptacle
reserch, research
reserect, resurrect
reserection, resurrect(ion)
reserf, reserve
reserfd, reserve(d)
reserginse, resurge(nce)
resergint, resurgent
reservation,*,nist, RESERVE/KEEP BACK/WITHHOLD SOMETHING, TERRITORY MANAGED BY NATIVE TRIBES
reserve,*,ed,ving,edly,edness,vist, vation, HAVE EXTRA/SPARE/ STORED UP "prefixes: un"
reservoir,*, WHERE WATER IS COLLECTED/STORED
reservor, reservoir
reses, recess
reseshun, recess(ion)
resesif, recess(ive)
resesion, recess(ion)
resesive, recess(ive)
resession, recess(ion)
reset, receipt
resetion, recess(ion)
reseve, receive
resevuble, receive(vable)
reside,*,ed,ding,er,ence,ency,encies, ent,ential,entially,entiary,entiaries, PLACE/AREA WHERE PEOPLE DWELL/LIVE/OCCUPY "prefixes: non"
residenshul, reside(ntial)
residensy, reside(ncy)
residinsy, reside(ncy)
residue,*,ual,ually,uary, WHAT'S LEFT OVER/REMAINING AFTER A SEPARATION PROCESS
residuel, residue(ual)
resign,*,ned,ning,nation,nedness,ner, GIVE UP/RELINQUISH A POSITION/ AUTHORITY
resignashin, resign(ation)
resikle, recycle
resil, wrestle
resiliensy, resilient(ncy)
resilient,tly,nce,ncy, ABILITY TO SPRING BACK/BE FLEXIBLE/ELASTIC

resilute, resolute
resimblanse, resemble(lance)
resimble, resemble
resin,*,nous,nate, ORGANIC/ INORGANIC CHEMICAL USED FOR VARNISH/ PLASTIC/MANY USES (or see reason/rise(n))
resinate,*,ed,ting, TO IMMERSE IN RESIN (or see resonate)
resination, resonate(tion)
resinator, resonate(tor)
resindly, recent(ly)
resinense, resonance
resinent, resonance(nt)
resint, recent
resintly, recent(ly)
resinuble, reason(able)
resipe, recipe
resipeant, recipient
resipeint, recipient
resipient, recipient
resiprekul, reciprocal
resiprocal, reciprocal
resiprocation, reciprocate(tion)
resiprokashen, reciprocate(tion)
resiprokate, reciprocate
resirch, research
resirect, resurrect
resirection, resurrect(ion)
resirf, reserve
resirgense, resurge(nce)
resirgent, resurgent
resirgint, resurgent
resirvation, reservation
resirvd, reserve(d)
resirve, reserve
resirvist, reserve(vist)
resirvor, reservoir
resist,*,ted,ting,tance,tant,ter,tible, tibility,tibly,tive,tively,tivity, tless, tor, DEFEND/PROTECT AGAINST "prefixes: ir"
resitashen, recite(tion)
resitation, recite(tion)
resite, recite
resitle, recite(tal)
resitul, recite(tal)
resk, risk
resked, risk(ed)
reskeu, rescue
reskiu, rescue
reskt, risk(ed)
resku, rescue
reskud, rescue(d)

resl, wrestle
resnibul, reason(able)
resnuble, reason(able)
resodo, risotto
resol, wrestle
resoluble,bility,eness, CAN BE SOLVED/ RESOLVED, DISSOLVED TWICE "prefixes: ir"
resolushin, resolute(tion)
resolute,*,ely,eness,tion, HAVE FIRM DETERMINATION/RESOLVE, FIXED PURPOSE/DECISION "prefixes: ir"
resolve,*,ed,ving,vable,er,ent, FINAL DETERMINATION/SETTLEMENT "prefixes: ir/un"
resolvuble, resolve(vable)
reson, reason / resin / rise(n)
resonance,nt,ntly, A SYMPATHETIC VIBRATION/SYNCHRONIZED WAVES
resonate,*,ed,ting,tion,tor, RESOUND/ ECHO/EXTENDED EFFECT/BE FAMILIAR (or see resinate)
resondly, recent(ly)
resonense, resonance
resonent, resonance(nt)
resoninse, resonance
resontly, recent(ly)
resope, recipe
resorse, resource
resorsful, resource(ful)
resort,*,ted,ting,ter, RECOURSE/ REVERBERATE, PLACE TO RELAX, FALL BACK ON
resorvor, reservoir
resoto, risotto
resotto, risotto
resource,*,eful,efully,efulness, AVAILABLE MEANS/MEASURE/ PROPERTY/ SOURCES
resparater, respiration(tor)
respect,*,ted,ting,tful,tfully,tfulness,ter, table,tably,tableness,tability, tabilities, tive,tively,tiveness, TO HONOR/PAY TRIBUTE/RELATE/ REGARD/HOLD IN HIGH ESTEEM "prefixes: dis/ir"
respectif, respect(ive)
respektful, respect(ful)
respektif, respect(ive)
resperashen, respiration
resperater, respiration(tor)
resperation, respiration
respirashen, respiration
respirater, respiration(tor)

respiration,nal,tor,tory, INHALE/ EXHALE OF THE BREATH IN PLANTS/ ANIMALS
respite, REST/RELIEF FROM LABOR/ SUFFERING/FEAR
respond,*,ded,ding,dent,der, ANSWER/ REPLY/CORRESPOND
respondint, respond(ent)
response,*,sible,sibility,sibilities, sibleness,sibly,sive,sively, siveness, ANSWER/ REPLY/CORRESPOND "prefixes: ir/non/un"
responsef, response(sive)
responsive, response(sive)
responsuble, response(sible)
respont, respond
respurashen, respiration
respurater, respiration(tor)
respuration, respiration
resque, rescue
resqwu, rescue
resrektion, resurrect(ion)
rest,*,ted,ting,tful,tfully,tfulness, TIME/ TRANQUILITY/PEACE BETWEEN MOMENTS OF MENTAL/PHYSICAL EXERTION (or see wrest/wrist) "prefixes: un"
restaraunt, restaurant
restaront, restaurant
restatushen, restitution
restatution, restitution
restatutive, restitution(ive)
restaurant,*, A PUBLIC EATERY
restauront, restaurant
resterashen, restore(ration)
resteration, restore(ration)
restetushen, restitution
restetution, restitutions
restfuly, rest(fully)
restid, rest(ed) / wrest(ed)
restirashen, restore(ration)
restiration, restore(ration)
restitushen, restitution
restitution,*,tive,itory, COMPENSATING/GIVING BACK FOR A LOSS
restorant, restaurant
restorashen, restore(ration)
restoraunt, restaurant
restore,*,ed,ring,er,ration,rative, REFURBISH/REFINISH BACK TO NEAR ORIGINAL
restrain,*,ned,ning,nt,nable, STOP/ CONTROL SOMETHING/SOMEONE FROM DOING SOMETHING "prefixes: un"
restrane, restrain
restrant, restaurant / restrain(t)
restrektif, restrict(ive)
restrict,*,ted,ting,tion,tive,tively, tiveness, CONTROL/LIMIT THE FLOW OF "prefixes: de/un"
restrikshen, restrict(ion)
restrikt, restrict
restriktion, restrict(ion)
restriktive, restrict(ive)
restront, restaurant
resturashen, restore(ration)
resturation, restore(ration)
restutushen, restitution
restutution, restitution
resucitate, resuscitate
resudenshul, reside(ntial)
resudensy, reside(ncy)
resudent, reside(nt)
resudential, reside(ntial)
resudinshul, reside(ntial)
resudinsy, reside(ncy)
resudue, residue
resugnashin, resign(ation)
resugnation, resign(ation)
resul, wrestle
result,*,ted,ting,tant, THE OUTCOME/ REACTION/CONDITION OF AN ACTION
resulushin, resolute(tion)
resulute, resolute
resuma, resume
resume,*,ed,ming,mable, CONTINUE/ CARRY ON, SUMMARY OF SOMEONE'S WORK HISTORY
resun, reason / resin / rise(n)
resunate, resonate / resinate
resunation, resonate(tion)
resunator, resonate(tor)
resundly, recent(ly)
resunense, resonance
resunent, resonance(nt)
resuninse, resonance
resuntly, recent(ly)
resunuble, reason(able)
resupe, recipe
resurch, research
resurect, resurrect
resurection, resurrect(ion)
resurfs, reserve(s)
resurge,*,ed,ging,ent,ence, RISE UP/ STRENGTHEN AGAIN
resurgense, resurge(nce)
resurgent,*,nce, RISE UP/STRENGTHEN AGAIN
resurginse, resurge(nce)
resurgint, resurgent
resurrect,*,ted,ting,tion,tional,tionist, tionism, RAISE FROM THE DEAD, TO REINSTATE/RESTORE
resurvd, reserve(d)
resurve, reserve
resurvor, reservoir
resusatashen, resuscitate(tion)
resusatator, resuscitate(tor)
resuscitate,*,ed,ting,tion,tive,tor, RESTORE LIFE TO BREATHING AGAIN
resusitate, resuscitate
resusitator, resuscitate(tor)
resycle, recycle
ret, red / read
retabul, read(able)
retail,*,led,ling,ler, SALE OF GOODS IN SMALL QUANTITIES TO CONSUMERS
retain,*,ned,ning,ner,nable,nability, nment, TO CONTINUE/HOLD/KEEP IN POSSESSION
retal, retail
retaleashen, retaliate(tion)
retaleate, retaliate
retaleation, retaliate(tion)
retaler, retail(er)
retaliate,*,ed,ting,tion, TO RETURN A PUNISHMENT, DELIBERATE HARM IN REVENGE
retan, retain
retaner, retain(er)
retanse, rid(ddance)
retard,*,ded,ding,dant,dation,dative, date,der, DEVELOPMENT/GROWTH IS SLOWED DOWN/CURBED/ DELAYED
retardashen, retard(ation)
retardat, retard(ate)
retardint, retard(ant)
retardir, retard(er)
retardunt, retard(ant)
retaric, rhetoric
retasense, reticent(nce)
retasent, reticent
retashin, rotate(tion)
retasint, reticent
retch, rich / wretch
reted, ready(died) / read

retee, ready
retenshun, retention
retentif, retentive
retention,ive,ivity, ABLE TO HOLD/ MAINTAIN/REMEMBER
retentive,vity,vities, ABLE TO HOLD/ MAINTAIN/REMEMBER
reter, red(dder) / read(er)
retern, return
reternd, return(ed)
reth, wreath / wreathe
rethem, rhythm
rethum, rhythm
reti, ready
reticent,tly,nce, RESERVED/ APPREHENSIVE IN SPEAKING FREELY
reticint, reticent
retina,*,al,nitis, ASSOCIATED WITH THE EYE
retinse, rid(ddance)
retinshun, retention
retintion, retention
retir, read(er) / retire
retire,*,ed,ring,ringly,ringness,rement, REMOVE/RETREAT/WITHDRAW FROM SOME FORM OF ACTIVITY/ CIRCULATION/WORK "prefixes: semi"
retirec, rhetoric
retirment, retire(ment)
retirn, return
retirndt, return(ed)
retisense, reticent(nce)
retisent, reticent
retisint, reticent
retna, retina
retnu, retina
retor, read(er)
retorec, rhetoric
retoric, rhetoric
retorical, rhetoric(al)
retract,*,ted,ting,tion,tability,table, tation,tile,tive, WITHDRAW/ REMOVE/TAKE BACK "prefixes: un"
retraction, retract(ion)
retrad, retread
retrakshen, retract(ion)
retrakted, retract(ed)
retread,*,ded,ding, RESURFACE/RECAP/ GO OVER AGAIN
retreat,*,ted,ting,ter,tal,tive,tful,tant, tism,tist, WITHDRAW/FALL BACK/ REFUGE/ASYLUM/DO AGAIN

retred, retread
retreded, retreat(ed)
retredid, retread(ed)
retrefe, retrieve
retrefer, retrieve(r)
retreful, retrieve(val)
retret, retreat
retreted, retreat(ed)
retrevul, retrieve(val)
retrevur, retrieve(r)
retrieve,*,ed,ving,val,er, RESTORE/ REMEDY/SAVE/GET SOMETHING BACK, A TYPE OF DOG "prefixes: ir"
retrive, retrieve
retro, PREFIX INDICATING "BACKWARDS" MOST OFTEN MODIFIES THE WORD
retroactif, retroactive
retroactive,ely, BACK TO SOME POINT IN THE PAST
retroaktif, retroactive
retroaktive, retroactive
retrograde,*,ed,ding,dation,ely, MOVING CONTRARY/BACKWARDS/ REVERSE/INVERSE
retrogratashen, retrograde(dation)
retrogreat, retrograde
retrosbekt, retrospect
retrospect,tion,tive,tives,tively, RECOLLECTION/REVIEW OF THE PAST
retrospekt, retrospect
retrospektion, retrospect(ion)
retsee, ritzy
retsy, ritzy
retual, ritual
retubil, read(able)
retuble, read(able)
retul, riddle
retur, red(dder) / read(er)
returec, rhetoric
returic, rhetoric
return,*,ned,ning,ner,nable, GO BACK TO THE PLACE OF THE ORIGINATION/BEGINNING/ MOMENT
returndt, return(ed)
retusense, reticent(nce)
retusent, reticent
retusint, reticent
rety, ready
retzy, ritzy
reul, real / reel
reuldee, realty

reuldy, realty
reulestic, real(istic)
reulistic, real(istic)
reulty, realty
reum, realm
reunacment, reenact(ment)
reunactment, reenact(ment)
reunakt, reenact
reunaktment, reenact(ment)
reunforse, reinforce
reunforsment, reinforce(ment)
reunion,*, GATHERING, COMING TOGETHER
reunyun, reunion
reustat, rheostat
reval, revel
revalation, revelation
revalee, reveille
revaler, revel(er)
revalushen, revolution
revalution, revolution
revalutioniz, revolution(ize)
revalve, revolve
revaly, reveille
revar, river
revarent, reverent
reveal,*,led,ling,ler,lingly, EXPOSE/ MAKE KNOWN/UNCOVER, BE FRANK (or see revel)
reveelt, reveal(ed)
reveer, revere
reveille,*, MILITARY WAKE-UP CALL/ SIGNAL
revejen, revise(sion)
revel,*,led,ling,ler, PLEASURE/ ENJOYMENT IN SOMETHING (or see reveal/reveille)
revelashen, revelation
revelation,*,nal,tory, SUDDEN REALIZATION/UNDERSTANDING OF VALUABLE/ SURPRISING INFORMATION
reveld, revel(lled) / reveal(ed)
revelee, reveille
revelir, revel(er)
revelushen, revolution
revelutioniz, revolution(ize)
revely, reveille
revench, revenge
revene, ravine / raven
revenge,eful,efully,er, BE RETALIATORY/ HARMFUL WITH INTENT
revengful, revenge(ful)
rever, revere / river

reverberate,*,ed,ting,ant,tion,tive,tor, AN ECHO, REFLECTION OF WAVES OFF A SURFACE
reverbirate, reverberate
revere,*,ed,ring, DEEPLY ADMIRE/ RESPECT SOMEONE
reverent,tly,nce,tial,tially, EXPRESS AWE/RESPECT "prefixes: ir"
reverse,*,ed,sing,sal,sely,er,sible,sibly, sibility, CHANGE TO OPPOSITE, INSIDE OUT/BACKWARD "prefixes: ir"
reversuble, reverse(sible)
revert,*,ted,ting,ter,tible, GO BACK TO PREVIOUS/FORMER/ORIGINAL
reveshen, revise(sion)
revesion, revise(sion)
revew, review / revue
review,*,wed,wing,wable,wer, EXAMINE/INSPECT/CRITIQUE/ SURVEY/ASSESS (or see revue)
revigen, revise(sion)
revil, revel / reveal
revilashen, revelation
revilation, revelation
revild, revel(lled)
revilee, reveille
reviler, revel(er)
revilushen, revolution
revilutioniz, revolution(ize)
revily, reveille
revinch, revenge
revine, ravine
revingful, revenge(ful)
revir, river
revirberate, reverberate
revirent, reverent
revirse, reverse
revirsuble, reverse(sible)
revirt, revert
revise,*,ed,sing,sion,sable,er,sory, ADJUST/UPDATE/ALTER/IMPROVE UPON
revishen, revise(sion)
revision, revise(sion)
revival,*, RENEWAL/RECOVERY/ REESTABLISHMENT OF
revive,*,ed,ving,vable,er,val, BECOME CONSCIOUS/FLOURISH/VIGOROUS AGAIN
revivle, revival
revivuble, revive(vable)
revlashen, revelation

revocable,ly,bility, ABILITY TO BE CANCELLED/CALLED BACK IN "prefixes: ir"
revokability, revocable(bility)
revokable, revocable
revoke,*,ed,king,er,ocable, MAKE NULL AND VOID, CANCEL, SUMMON SOMEONE/SOMETHING BACK
revol, revel
revolashen, revelation
revolation, revelation
revold, revolt / revel(lled)
revolee, reveille
revolfe, revolve
revolt,*,ted,ting, REBEL/DEFY AUTHORITY, REPULSED
revoltid, revolt(ed)
revolution,*,nary,naries,nize,nizes, nized,nizing,nism,nist,nists, REBEL/ DEFY POWERS THAT BE, OF CIRCULAR SHAPE/ MOTION
revolve,*,ed,ving,er,vable, RECURRING CIRCULAR MOVEMENT, A TYPE OF GUN
revorent, reverent
revue,*, MUSICAL EVENT (or see review)
revul, revel
revulashen, revelation
revulation, revelation
revuled, revel(lled)
revulee, reveille
revuler, revel(er)
revulushen, revolution
revulutioniz, revolution(ize)
revuly, reveille
revur, river
revurbarate, reverberate
revurent, reverent
revurse, reverse
revursuble, reverse(sible)
revurt, revert
rew, rue / roux
reward,*,ded,ding, SOMETHING RECEIVED FOR HAVING DONE SOMETHING COMMENDABLE
rewbe, ruby
rewd, rude
rewdest, rude(st)
rewf, roof
rewge, rouge
rewje, rouge
rewl, rule
rewlet, roulette

rewm, room
rewmer, rumor
rewmur, rumor
reword, reward
rewral, rural
rewralee, rural(lly)
rewrul, rural
rewrulee, rural(lly)
rewsdir, rooster
rewsdur, rooster
rewse, ruse
rewstur, rooster
rewt, route / root / rude
rewteen, routine
rewthles, ruthless
rewtlee, rude(ly)
rey, ray
reyewnyin, reunion
reyunyon, reunion
rezadenshul, reside(ntial)
rezadensy, reside(ncy)
rezadinsy, reside(ncy)
rezadue, residue
rezalushen, resolute(tion)
rezalute, resolute
rezalution, resolute(tion)
rezan, reason / resin / rise(n)
rezand, recent
rezandly, recent(ly)
rezanense, resonance
rezanent, resonance(nt)
rezant, recent
rezanuble, reason(able)
rezarection, resurrect(ion)
rezarektion, resurrect(ion)
rezedue, residue
rezegnation, resign(ation)
rezelute, resolute
rezen, reason / resin / rise(n)
rezenate, resinate / resonate
rezenator, resonate(tor)
rezend, recent
rezendly, recent(ly)
rezent, recent / resent
rezenuble, reason(able)
rezerect, resurrect
rezerf, reserve
rezervation, reservation
rezervor, reservoir
rezide, reside
rezidensy, reside(ncy)
rezidinsy, reside(ncy)
rezidual, residue(ual)
rezidue, residue

rezignashin, resign(ation)
rezilute, resolute
rezin, reason / resin / rise(n)
rezinate, resonate / resinate
rezinator, resonate(tor)
rezind, recent
rezindly, recent(ly)
rezine, resign
rezinent, resonance(nt)
rezint, recent / resent
rezinuble, reason(able)
rezirect, resurrect
rezirvation, reservation
rezirvor, reservoir
rezist, resist
rezistense, resist(ance)
rezistent, resist(ant)
rezistif, resist(ive)
rezistor, resist(or)
reznuble, reason(able)
rezodo, risotto
rezolushin, resolute(tion)
rezolute, resolute
rezolve, resolve
rezom, resume
rezon, reason / resin / rise(n)
rezonate, resonate / resinate
rezondly, recent(ly)
rezonense, resonance
rezontle, recent(ly)
rezoom, resume
rezort, resort
rezorvor, reservoir
rezoto, risotto
rezrekshen, resurrect(ion)
rezt, rest / wrist / wrest
rezudensy, reside(ncy)
rezudinsy, reside(ncy)
rezudue, residue
rezult, result
rezultent, result(ant)
rezultunt, result(ant)
rezulushen, resolute(tion)
rezulute, resolute
rezulution, resolute(tion)
rezume, resume
rezun, reason / resin / rise(n)
rezunate, resonate / resinate
rezunation, resonate(tion)
rezund, recent
rezundly, recent(ly)
rezunense, resonance
rezunent, resonance(nt)
rezunt, recent

rezunuble, reason(able)
rezurect, resurrect
rezurection, resurrect(ion)
rezurekshen, resurrect(ion)
rezurf, reserve
rezurve, reserve
rezurvor, reservoir
rezuvor, reservoir
rhain, rain / reign / rein
rhanoceros, rhinoceros
rhanosirus, rhinoceros
rhapsady, rhapsody
rhapsedy, rhapsody
rhapsody,dies, IRREGULAR/INTENSE IMPROVISATION IN REGARD TO MUSIC/EXPRESSION/LITERATURE
rhapsuty, rhapsody
rhatorecal, rhetoric(al)
rhatorical, rhetoric(al)
rhedaric, rhetoric
rheduric, rhetoric
rhein, rain / reign / rein
rheindeer, reindeer
rhen, rain / reign / rein
rhenoceros, rhinoceros
rhenosirus, rhinoceros
rheostat,*,tic, ELECTRONIC DEVICE
rhetarec, rhetoric
rheteric, rhetoric
rhethm, rhythm
rhethym, rhythm
rhetoric,*,cal,cally, THE ART OF SPEAKING/WRITING EFFECTIVELY/ PERSUASIVELY
rheturec, rhetoric
rheumatic,*,ism,toid,toidal, ASSOCIATED WITH STIFF JOINTS/ MUSCLES IN THE BODY
rhime, rhyme
rhinasurus, rhinoceros
rhinauserus, rhinoceros
rhinestone,*, FAKE GEMS
rhino,*, SHORT FOR RHINOCEROS
rhinoceros,ses, A MAMMAL/ANIMAL
rhinosurus, rhinoceros
rhinstone, rhinestone
rhisome, rhizome
rhithm, rhythm
rhithum, rhythm
rhitorecal, rhetoric(al)
rhitorical, rhetoric(al)
rhiz, PREFIX INDICATING "ROOT" MOST OFTEN MODIFIES THE WORD
rhizome,*, TYPE OF PLANT ROOT

rhod, PREFIX INDICATING "RED" MOST OFTEN MODIFIES THE WORD
rhodadendron, rhododendron
rhodidendron, rhododendron
rhodo, PREFIX INDICATING "RED" MOST OFTEN MODIFIES THE WORD
rhododendron,*,rum, CAN BE SPELLED EITHER WAY, FLOWERING PLANT/ BUSH
rhodudindron, rhododendron
rhotorical, rhetoric(al)
rhubarb, AN EDIBLE PLANT
rhunoceros, rhinoceros
rhunosirus, rhinoceros
rhutorecal, rhetoric(al)
rhutorical, rhetoric(al)
rhyme,*,ed,ming,er, PUT WORDS TOGETHER IN SPEECH WHICH SOUND LIKE EACH OTHER
rhysome, rhizome
rhythm,*,mic,mical,mically, REPETITIOUS BEAT/FREQUENCY/ PATTERN "prefixes: bio"
rhyzome, rhizome
ri, rye / wry
riact, react
rial, real / rile
rib,*,bbed,bbing, BONES IN TORSO
ribaflavin, riboflavin
riban, ribbon
ribaund, rebound
ribbin, ribbon
ribbon,*,ny, THIN STRIP OF SOMETHING, A DECORATION USED AS AN AWARD
ribbun, ribbon
ribeled, rebel(lled)
ribeleon, rebel(llion)
ribeleus, rebel(llious)
riben, ribbon
ribin, ribbon
riblase, replace
riblie, reply
ribodek, robot(ic)
ribof, rebuff
riboflavin,*, A CHEMICAL COMPOUND/ VITAMIN
ribon, ribbon / rib(bbing)
ribt, rib(bbed) / rip(pped)
ribuf, rebuff
ribulican, republic(an)
ribun, ribbon / rib(bbing)
ribut, rebut / reboot
ributle, rebut(ttal)

ric, reek / rice
ricachet, ricochet
ricant, recant
ricap, recap
ricashay, ricochet
rice, A GRAIN (or see rise)
ricebder, receptor
ricebdif, receptive
riced, recede
ricent, recent
ricepter, receptor
ricerch, research
rices, recess
rich,hes,her,hest,hly,hness, ABUNDANT/PLENTIFUL/FERTILE/PRODUCTIVE (or see reach/ridge/wretch) "prefixes: en"
richas, right(eous) / rich(es)
richecshen, reject(ion)
richect, reject
riched, rigid
richem, regime
riches, right(eous) / rich(es)
richewul, ritual
richid, rigid
richoal, ritual
richon, region
richos, right(eous) / rich(es)
richuol, ritual
richus, right(eous) / rich(es)
ricid, reside / recede
ricipient, recipient
ricis, recess
ricit, receipt / recite
riciv, receive
rickets, VITAMIN DEFICIENCY DISEASE
rickety, UNSTABLE CONDITION
rickidy, rickety
rickits, rickets
rickity, rickety
rickliner, recline(r)
rickonusinse, reconnaissance
riclusion, recluse(sion)
ricochet,*,ted,ting, THE ACTION OF REBOUNDING/BOUNCING OFF AN OBJECT
ricoil, recoil
ricomben, recumbent
riconisans, reconnaissance
riconsile, reconcile
riconstitushen, reconstitute(tion)
riconstitute, reconstitute
ricord, record
ricors, recourse

ricoshay, ricochet
ricover, recover
ricrut, recruit
ricuest, request
ricumbent, recumbent
ricup, recoop
ricuperate, recuperate
ricushay, ricochet
rid,*,dded,dding,ddance, BE DISPOSED OF/DONE AWAY WITH (or see ride/red/read/reed/right)
ridakeul, ridicule
ridakule, ridicule
ridal, riddle
ridanse, rid(ddance)
ridar, ride(r) / write(r)
ridch, ridge
riddle,*,ed,ling,er, PUZZLE OF WORDS "prefixes: un"
ride,*,ding,rode,er, BE CARRIED/MOVED ALONG IN/ON SOMETHING (or see write/right) "prefixes: over"
ridecule, ridicule
rideculus, ridiculous
rideemible, redeem(able)
ridekule, ridicule
ridekulus, ridiculous
ridem, redeem
ridempshun, redemption
ridemtion, redemption
ridemuble, redeem(able)
ridense, rid(ddance)
ridents, rid(ddance)
ridge,*,ed, RAISED AREA
ridicule,*,ed,ling,er,lous, TO MAKE FUN OF
ridiculous,sly,sness, NOT POSSIBLE/ACCEPTABLE
ridikule, ridicule
ridikulus, ridiculous
ridim, redeem
ridinse, rid(ddance)
ridle, riddle
ridol, riddle
ridondent, redundant
ridoose, reduce
ridu, redo
riduction, reduce(ction)
ridukeul, ridicule
ridukshen, reduce(ction)
riduktion, reduce(ction)
ridul, riddle
ridundensy, redundant(ncy)
ridundent, redundant

ridundinsy, redundant(ncy)
ridundint, redundant
ridus, reduce
ridusable, reduce(cible)
rie, rye / wry
riel, rile
riemburs, reimburse
rienact, reenact
rienlist, reenlist
riestat, rheostat
riet, riot
rieterate, reiterate
rif, reef / rift
rifal, rifle
rifar, river / refer
rifeel, reveal
rifeelt, reveal(ed)
rifel, rival / rifle
rifenge, revenge
rifenje, revenge
rifer, river / refer
riferbishment, refurbish(ment)
riferse, reverse
rifeusil, refuse(sal)
rifewsel, refuse(sal)
rififul, revival
rifil, rival / rifle
rifin, refine
rifinable, refine(nable)
rifine, refine
rifinery, refine(ry)
rifinje, revenge
rifinment, refine(ment)
rifinury, refine(ry)
rifle,*,ed,ling, A GUN, SWIFTLY GO THROUGH, LOOK THROUGH STUFF TO STEAL "prefixes: un"
riflecs, reflect(s) / reflex
riflect, reflect
riflection, reflect(ion)
riflective, reflect(ive)
riflector, reflect(or)
riflekshen, reflect(ion)
riflekt, reflect
riflektif, reflect(ive)
riflektor, reflect(or)
rifletive, reflect(ive)
rifol, rifle
rifond, refund
rifor, river / refer
riformitory, reform(atory)
rifract, refract
rifractory, refract(ory)
rifrain, refrain

rifrakt, refract
rifraktory, refract(ory)
rifrane, refrain
rifresh, refresh
rifresher, refresh(er)
rifreshment, refresh(ment)
rifrigerator, refrigerate(tor)
rift,*,ted,ting, SLOWLY SPREAD APART, GROWING CHASM
riful, rival / rifle
rifur, river / refer
rifural, refer(rral)
rifurbishment, refurbish(ment)
rifurse, reverse
rifusel, refuse(sal)
rig,*,gged,gging,gger, ASSEMBLE DEVICES TOGETHER (or see ridge)
rigal, wriggle / regal
rigaledy, regal(ity)
rigalia, regal(ia)
rigality, regal(ity)
rigard, regard
rigardless, regard(less)
rige, ridge
rigect, reject
riged, rigid
rigekshen, reject(ion)
rigekt, reject
rigektion, reject(ion)
riger, rigor
riget, rigid
right,*,ted,ting,table,ter,tness,teous, teously,teousness,tful,tfully,tfulness, tism,tist,tly,ty, BE CORRECT, SPECIFIC DIRECTION/ORIENTATION, OTHER SIDE OF LEFT (or see rite/ write/ wright/writ) "prefixes: un/ up"
rigid,dly,dness,dity,dizer,dify,ification, STIFF/UNYIELDING "prefixes: semi"
rigirs, rigor(s)
rigit, rigid
rigle, wriggle
rigol, wriggle
rigor,*,rous,rously,rousness, CONDITIONS INVOLVING HARDSHIP/SEVERITY/TOUGH DEMANDS
rigres, rigor(ous) / regress
rigreshen, regress(ssion)
rigresif, regress(ive)
rigresive, regress(ive)
rigress, regress
rigret, regret

rigreted, regret(tted)
rigretful, regret(ful)
rigretfuly, regret(fully)
rigrus, rigor(ous)
rigul, wriggle
rigurs, rigor(s)
rigurus, rigor(ous)
rij, ridge
rijed, rigid
rijekshen, reject(ion)
rijekt, reject
rijektion, reject(ion)
rijet, rigid
rijid, rigid
rijit, rigid
rikachet, ricochet
rikashay, ricochet
rikedy, rickety
rikendal, rekindle
rikerus, rigor(ous)
rikeshay, ricochet
rikete, rickety
rikets, rickets
rikidy, rickety
rikishay, ricochet
rikity, rickety
rikliner, recline(r)
rikochet, ricochet
rikonasinse, reconnaissance
rikonstitute, reconstitute
rikonusins, reconnaissance
rikord, record
rikorder, record(er)
rikrute, recruit
rikruter, recruit(er)
rikumbent, recumbent
rikurus, rigor(ous)
rikwest, request
rikwire, require
rikwirment, require(ment)
ril, real / reel / rile / rill
rilacs, relax
rilaps, relapse
rilat, relate
rilax, relax
rile,*,ed,ling, PROVOKE INTO ACTION (or see rill/really)
rilef, relief
rilegeon, religion
rilegon, religion
rilegous, religion(ous)
rilenquish, relinquish
rilentles, relentless
rilese, release

rilevar, relieve(r)
rileve, relieve
rilevir, relieve(r)
rili, rely / really
rilians, reliance
riliaple, reliable
rilichon, religion
rilients, reliance
rilif, relief
riligen, religion
rilis, release
riliubility, reliable(bility)
riliuble, reliable
riliunse, reliance
riliunt, reliance(nt)
riliv, relieve
rill,*, NARROW VALLEY/CHANNEL (or see real/reel/rile)
rilly, really
rilm, realm
rilte, realty
riluctanse, reluctant(nce)
riluctant, reluctant
riluktense, reluctant(nce)
riluktint, reluctant
rily, really / rely
rim,*,mmed,mming, CURVED/ CIRCULAR OUTER EDGE (or see ream/rhyme)
rimadik, rheumatic
rimander, remain(der)
rimane, remain / romaine
rimanis, reminisce
rimanisent, reminisce(nt)
rimantek, romantic
rimantisize, romantic(ize)
rimark, remark
rimarkible, remark(able)
rimarkt, remark(ed)
rimarkuble, remark(able)
rimatik, rheumatic
rimaty, remedy
rimbunctious, rambunctious
rimbunkshes, rambunctious
rime, rhyme
rimedeul, remedy(dial)
rimedial, remedy(dial)
rimediashen, remedy(diation)
rimediation, remedy(diation)
rimembranse, remember(ance)
rimembur, remember
rimeng, rhyme(ming)
rimenis, reminisce
rimenisent, reminisce(nt)

rimet, remit
rimeted, remit(tted)
rimetuble, remit(ttable)
rimety, remedy
rimidy, remedy
rimind, remind
rimindur, remind(er)
riming, rhyme(ming)
rimintur, remind(er)
rimishen, remission
rimission, remission
rimit, remit
rimital, remit(ttal)
rimition, remission
rimity, remedy
rimnent, remnant
rimnet, remnant
rimnint, remnant
rimofer, remove(r)
rimonis, reminisce
rimonisent, reminisce(nt)
rimors, remorse
rimorsful, remorse(ful)
rimorsless, remorse(less)
rimot, remote
rimotly, remote(ly)
rimover, remove(r)
rimudy, remedy
rimufel, remove(val)
rimufer, remove(r)
rimufible, remove(vable)
rimunerashen, remunerate(tion)
rimunerate, remunerate
rimunirate, remunerate
rimuniration, remunerate(tion)
rimunis, reminisce
rimunisent, reminisce(nt)
rimuty, remedy
rimuv, remove
rimuvable, remove(vable)
rin, wren
rinagade, renegade
rinasonse, renaissance
rinasonts, renaissance
rinasurus, rhinoceros
rinaun, renown
rinauns, renounce
rinauserus, rhinoceros
rinavashen, renovate(tion)
rinavate, renovate
rinavation, renovate(tion)
rinawserus, rhinoceros
rinch, wrench

rind,*, THE EXTERIOR COVERING/SKIN OF SOME FRUIT/TREES/CHEESE
rinder, render
rindur, render
rineg, renege
rinegade, renegade
rinesonse, renaissance
rinestone, rhinestone
rinevashen, renovate(tion)
rinevate, renovate
rinevation, renovate(tion)
ring,*,ged,ging,ger,rung, A SOUND, ARTICLE OF JEWELRY, CIRCULAR SHAPE (or see wring/rink)
ringur, ring(er) / ranger
rinige, renege
rink,*, PLACE FOR SKATING (or see ring)
rinkle, wrinkle
rinkul, wrinkle
rino, rhino
rinone, renown
rinoserus, rhinoceros
rinosonse, renaissance
rinosurus, rhinoceros
rinounce, renounce
rinouncement, renounce(ment)
rinovadid, renovate(d)
rinovashen, renovate(tion)
rinovate, renovate
rinovation, renovate(tion)
rinown, renown
rinownse, renounce
rinownsment, renounce(ment)
rinoz, rhino(s)
rins, rinse / rind(s) / wren(s)
rinsd, rinse(d)
rinse,*,ed,sing,er, TO WASH/CLEAN WITH A LIQUID
rinstone, rhinestone
rinsur, rinse(r)
rint, rind / rent
rinter, render / rent(er)
rintible, rent(able)
rintuble, rent(able)
rinu, renew
rinuable, renew(able)
rinual, renew(al)
rinuel, renew(al)
rinugade, renegade
rinumerate, remunerate
rinusonts, renaissance
rinuvadid, renovate(d)
rinuvashen, renovate(tion)
rinuvat, renovate

rinztone, rhinestone
riol, rile / real / reel
riole, really
riostat, rheostat
riot,*,ted,ting,ter, ANGRY CROWD/ MOB OF PEOPLE WHO MAY OR MAY NOT BE VIOLENT
rip,*,pped,pping,pper, TO TEAR/SLICE SOMETHING OPEN/APART (or see ripe/reap) "prefixes: un"
ripaflavin, riboflavin
ripair, repair
ripal, ripple
ripar, repair
ripd, rip(pped)
ripe,en,ened,er,est,ening,eness, FULLY MATURE/PRIME IN DEVELOPMENT (or see rip) "prefixes: over/un"
ripeal, repeal
ripeat, repeat
riped, rip(pped)
ripededly, repeat(edly)
ripeel, repeal
ripeet, repeat
ripel, rappel / repeal / repel
ripelent, repellent
ripeleon, rebel(llion)
ripelinsy, repellent(ncy)
ripelint, repellent
ripellinsy, repellent(ncy)
ripend, ripe(ned)
ripenins, repent(ance)
ripense, repent(s)
ripent, repent
riper, repair / rip(pper)
ripercoshon, repercussion
ripetative, repetitive
ripete, repeat
ripetedly, repeat(edly)
ripil, repeal
ripin, ripe(n) / rip(pping)
ripit, repeat
riplace, replace
riplacement, replace(ment)
riplase, replace
riplasmint, replace(ment)
riple, ripple
riplenesh, replenish
riplenish, replenish
riplenishment, replenish(ment)
riplid, reply(lied)
riplied, reply(lied)
riply, reply
ripnes, ripe(ness)

ripoblic, republic
ripoflavin, riboflavin
ripognant, repugnant
ripoire, rapport
ripol, ripple
ripold, ripple(d)
ripols, repulse
ripolsev, repulse(sive)
ripon, ribbon / ripe(n)
ripor, rapport / rip(pper)
riporder, report(er)
riport, report
riporter, report(er)
ripository, repository
riposutory, repository
ripozitory, repository
ripple,*,ed,ling, A SMALL WAVE
ripreshen, repress(ion)
ripresif, repress(ive)
ripresion, repress(ion)
ripresive, repress(ive)
ripress, repress
ripresuve, repress(ive)
riproch, reproach
riprochuble, reproach(able)
riproductive, reproduce(ctive)
riprodus, reproduce
riprouch, reproach
ripublek, republic
ripublekan, republic(an)
ripublic, republic
ripublican, republic(an)
ripugnense, repugnant(nce)
ripugnent, repugnant
ripul, ripple / rebel
ripuld, ripple(d)
ripuls, repulse
ripulshen, repulse(ion)
ripulsif, repulse(sive)
ripulsion, repulse(ion)
ripult, ripple(d)
ripun, ripe(n)
ripund, ripe(ned)
ripunt, ripe(ned)
ripuplecan, republic(an)
ripuplican, republic(an)
ripur, ripe(r)
ripust, ripe(st)
riqrute, recruit
riquest, request
riqueti, rickety
riquire, require
riquirment, require(ment)
riquite, requite

riqwire, require
riqwirment, require(ment)
rir, rear / we're / were / whirr
risbond, respond
risbons, response
risdrane, restrain
rise,*,sing,en,er,rose, ASSOCIATED WITH UPWARDS/MOVING UP/ UPWARD BOUND (or see rice) "prefixes: up"
riseat, receipt
risebdef, receptive
risebtif, receptive
risebtive, receptive
riseed, recede
riseef, receive
riseet, receipt
risefe, receive
riseleant, resilient
risemblanse, resemble(lance)
risent, recent / resent
risentful, resent(ful)
risentment, resent(ment)
risepdekle, receptacle
risepdikul, receptacle
risepeant, recipient
risepeunt, recipient
risepshun, reception
riseptacle, receptacle
riseptef, receptive
riseptekle, receptacle
risepter, receptor
riseption, reception
riseptive, receptive
riseptukle, receptacle
riserch, research
riserv, reserve
riservist, reserve(vist)
riseshun, recess(ion)
risesif, recess(ive)
risesion, recess(ion)
risesive, recess(ive)
risession, recess(ion)
risestanse, resist(ance)
risestor, resist(or)
risete, receipt
risetion, recess(ion)
risevuble, receive(vable)
rishis, right(eous) / rich(es)
rishuel, ritual
rishus, right(eous) / rich(es)
riside, reside / recede
risign, resign
risileant, resilient

risilyent, resilient
risipeunt, recipient
risir, rise(r)
risit, receipt / recite
risitle, recite(tal)
risitul, recite(tal)
risiv, receive
risk,*,ked,king,ky, TAKE A CHANCE/ GAMBLE
riskt, risk(ed)
risodo, risotto
risolt, result
risoltant, result(ant)
risolv, resolve
risolvuble, resolve(vable)
risome, rhizome
rison, reason / rise(n) / rhizome
risor, rise(r)
risors, resource
risort, resort
risoto, risotto
risotto, TYPE OF EDIBLE DISH/FOOD
rispect, respect
rispectful, respect(ful)
rispective, respect(ive)
rispectuble, respect(able)
rispekt, respect
rispektful, respect(ful)
rispektif, respect(ive)
rispektuble, respect(able)
rispite, respite
rispond, respond
rispondent, respond(ent)
risponder, respond(er)
risponse, response
risponsive, response(sive)
risponsuble, response(sible)
rispont, respond
rist, wrist
ristor, restore
ristrain, restrain
ristraint, restrain(t)
ristrane, restrain
ristrant, restrain(t)
ristrect, restrict
ristrikt, restrict
ristriktive, restrict(ive)
risuma, resume
risume, resume
risurgent, resurgent
risurs, rise(rs)
risusatator, resuscitate(tor)
risusetate, resuscitate
risusitashen, resuscitate(tion)

rit, rite / write / wright / writ / right / rid
ritacule, ridicule
ritainer, retain(er)
ritakule, ridicule
rital, riddle
ritaleashen, retaliate(tion)
ritaleate, retaliate
ritaleation, retaliate(tion)
ritaliation, retaliate(tion)
ritane, retain
ritaner, retain(er)
ritanse, rid(ddance)
ritard, retard
ritashen, rotate(tion)
ritch, rich / wretch
ritches, right(eous) / rich(es)
ritchly, rich(ly)
ritchuil, ritual
ritchus, right(eous) / rich(es)
rite,*, A CEREMONY/OBSERVANCE (or see right/write/white/writ/wright)
ritein, retain
ritel, retail
ritense, rid(ddance)
ritenshun, retention
ritentif, retentive
rith, writhe
rithem, rhythm
rithm, rhythm
rithum, rhythm
ritinshun, retention
ritire, retire
ritirment, retire(ment)
ritle, riddle
ritorical, rhetoric(al)
ritous, right(eous) / rich(es)
ritracted, retract(ed)
ritraction, retract(ion)
ritrakshen, retract(ion)
ritrakted, retract(ed)
ritrefe, retrieve
ritrefer, retrieve(r)
ritreful, retrieve(val)
ritreve, retrieve
ritrevul, retrieve(val)
ritrevur, retrieve(r)
ritsee, ritzy
ritsy, ritzy
ritual,*,lly,lism,list,listic,listically,lize, lization, CEREMONY
rituil, ritual
ritukeul, ridicule
ritul, riddle

riturn, return
ritzy,zier,ziest, SWANKY/ELEGANT
riul, rile
riunyen, reunion
riunyun, reunion
riuse, ruse
riut, riot
riuted, riot(ed)
riuter, riot(er)
rivais, revise
rival,*,led,ling,lry,lries, COMPETITOR
    "prefixes: un"
rivalfe, revolve
rivalree, rival(ry)
rivalve, revolve
riveel, reveal
riveelt, reveal(ed)
riveer, revere
rivegen, revise(sion)
rivejen, revise(sion)
rivel, rival / arrival
rivench, revenge
rivenge, revenge
rivengful, revenge(ful)
rivenje, revenge
river,*, TRIBUTARY/CHANNEL OF WATER, SOMETHING FLOWING
    "prefixes: up"
riverberate, reverberate
rivere, revere
rivers, river(s) / reverse
riversuble, reverse(sible)
rivert, revert
riview, review / revue
rivigen, revise(sion)
rivijen, revise(sion)
rivil, revel
riving, revenge
rivingful, revenge(ful)
rivinje, revenge
rivir, revere
rivirbarate, reverberate
rivirs, reverse
rivirt, revert
rivise, revise
rivishen, revise(sion)
rivision, revise(sion)
riviu, review
rivival, revival
rivive, revive
rivivuble, revive(vable)
rivivul, revive(val)
rivize, revise
rivlree, rival(ry)

rivocability, revocable(bility)
rivocable, revocable
rivokability, revocable(bility)
rivokable, revocable
rivoke, revoke
rivokt, revoke(d)
rivol, rival / arrival
rivolfe, revolve
rivolfer, revolve(r)
rivolree, rival(ry)
rivolt, revolt
rivolv, revolve
rivolver, revolve(r)
rivul, rival / arrival
rivulree, rival(ry)
rivurbarate, reverberate
rivurse, reverse
rivurt, revert
riward, reward
riword, reward
riyewnyen, reunion
riyunyun, reunion
rizalfe, resolve
rize, rise / rice
rizelyent, resilient
rizemblanse, resemble(lance)
rizemble, resemble
rizent, resent
rizentful, resent(ful)
rizentment, resent(ment)
rizer, rise(r)
rizid, reside
rizilyent, resilient
rizine, resign
rizist, resist
rizite, recite
rizodo, risotto
rizolve, resolve
rizolvuble, resolve(vable)
rizom, resume
rizome, rhizome
rizoom, resume
rizort, resort
rizoto, risotto
rizultent, result(ant)
rizultunt, result(ant)
rizum, resume
rizuma, esume / resume'
rizume, resume / resume'
rizur, rise(r)
ro, row / raw
roach,hes, AN INSECT, BUTT END OF HERB CIGARETTE

road,*,dy, A PATH/PASSAGE/WIDE TRAIL TO TRAVEL ON (or see rode/wrote) "prefixes: in"
roam,*,med,ming,mer, TO WANDER/MOVE ABOUT AIMLESSLY (or see room)
roar,*,red,ring, LOUD/DEEP SOUND/EXPRESSION COMING FROM THE THROAT (or see row(er)) "prefixes: up"
roast,*,ted,ting,ter, SLOWLY COOK IN AN OVEN, BAKE WITHOUT A FLAME
rob,*,bbed,bbing,bber, STEAL/TAKE AWAY FROM WITHOUT PERMISSION (or see robe/rope)
robd, robe(d) / rob(bbed) / rope(d)
robe,*,ed,bing, LONG/LOOSE SLEEVED GARMENT (or see rob/rope) "prefixes: dis/en"
robed, robe(d) / rob(bbed) / rope(d)
robeled, rebel(lled)
robeleus, rebel(llious)
roben, robin / rob(bbing)
rober, rob(bber)
robin,*, A TYPE OF BIRD (or see rob(bbing))
robodezashen, robot(ization)
robodik, robot(ic)
robost, robust
robot,*,tic,tism,tize,tization, A MACHINE WHICH WORKS FOR PEOPLE
robotisashen, robot(ization)
robotizashen, robot(ization)
robt, rob(bbed) / rope(d) / robe(d)
robudezashin, robot(ization)
robun, robin / rob(bbing)
robushus, robust(ious)
robust,tly,tness,tious,tiously,tiousness, FULL/HEALTHY/STRONG
robustus, robust(ious)
robutesation, robot(ization)
robuzd, robust
roch, roach
rocher, roger
roches, roach(es)
rochir, roger
rochur, roger
rock,*,ked,king,ker,ky, HARD MINERAL, BACK AND FORTH MOTION
rockateer, rocket(eer)
rocket,*,try,teer, A FUELED CYLINDER WITH POINTED TIP

rod,*,dded,dding,dless, THIN ROUND/CYLINDRICAL STAFF/POLE/STICK SHAPE (or see rotor/road/rode/wrote)
rodadendron, rhododendron
rodadindron, rhododendron
rodant, rodent
rodar, rotor
rodaree, rotary
rodary, rotary
rodatelir, rototiller
rodatilur, rototiller
rode, PAST TENSE FOR THE WORD "RIDE" (or see road/wrote) "prefixes: over"
rodedendron, rhododendron
rodedindron, rhododendron
rodent,*, A SMALL MAMMAL
rodeo,*,oed,oing, GAME IN ARENA USING HORSES/COWS/ROPES
roder, rotor
rodery, rotary
rodetilur, rototiller
rodidendron, rhododendron
rodidindron, rhododendron
rodint, rodent
rodio, rodeo
rodiquelus, ridiculous
rodir, rotor
roditelur, rototiller
rododendrem, rhododendron
rodotiler, rototiller
rodudindron, rhododendron
rodunt, rodent
rodur, rotor
roduree, rotary
rodury, rotary
rodutiler, rototiller
roeal, royal
roeul, royal
roeyul, royal
rof, rove / rough
rofeelt, reveal(ed)
rofer, revere / refer / rove(r)
roferse, reverse
rofeusil, refuse(sal)
rofiew, review / revue
rofiful, revival
rofir, rove(r) / rough(er)
rofirst, reverse
rofol, ruffle
rofue, review / revue
rofur, rove(r) / rough(er)
rofurse, reverse

rofute, refute
rog, rogue / rouge
roged, rugged
roger, RADIO COMMUNICATION WHICH MEANS "OKAY", SOMEONE'S NAME
rogir, roger
rogue,*,uish,uishly,uishness,ery,eries, SWINDLER/TRICKY/DEVIANT BEHAVIOR (or see rouge)
rogur, roger
roiel, royal
roiul, royal
rojer, roger
rojur, roger
rok, rock / rogue
rokateer, rocket(eer)
roket, rocket
roketeer, rocket(eer)
rokut, rocket
rokuteer, rocket(eer)
rokwit, requite
rokwitable, requite(table)
rol, roll / role
rolar, roll(er)
role,*, A PART/CHARACTER IN A PLAY (or see roll)
rolec, rollick
roled, roll(ed)
rolek, rollick
rolent, relent
roler, roll(er)
rolic, rollick
rolik, rollick
rolir, roll(er)
roll,*,lled,lling,ller, A BREAD SHAPE, MOVES/GOES AROUND IN CIRCULAR FASHION (or see role) "prefixes: un"
rollick,*,ked,king, TO PLAYFULLY ROLL/TUMBLE/JUMP/SKIP AROUND
rolor, roll(er)
rolres, walrus
rolrus, walrus
rolur, roll(er)
rom, roam / room / rum
romach, rummage
romadik, rheumatic
romaine, TYPE OF LETTUCE (or see remain)
romance,*,ed,cing,er,ntic, FANCIFUL/WHIMSICAL/EXTRAVAGANT EXPERIENCE WITH INFATUATION/LOVE BETWEEN TWO PEOPLE

romane, romaine / remain
romanek, romantic
romanse, romance
romantic,cally,cism,cist,cize,cization, INVOLVES ROMANCE
romantisize, romantic(ize)
romark, remark
romatik, rheumatic
romatoyd, rheumatic(toid)
romb, romp
rombed, romp(ed) / roam(ed)
rombl, rumble / rumple
rombol, rumble / rumple
romediashen, remedy(diation)
romediation, remedy(diation)
romeshen, remission
rometeul, remedy(dial)
romidal, remit(ttal)
romind, remind
romindur, remind(er)
romintur, remind(er)
romishen, remission
romision, remission
romission, remission
romital, remit(ttal)
romited, remit(tted)
romition, remission
romituble, remit(ttable)
romp,*,ped,ping,per, PLAYFULLY FROLIC/JUMP/BOUNCE AROUND (or see rump)
rompt, romp(ed)
roms, room(s) / roam(s)
romufel, remove(val)
romufible, remove(vable)
romufil, remove(val)
romunerate, remunerate
romunirashen, remunerate(tion)
romunirate, remunerate
romuvable, remove(vable)
romuver, remove(r)
romy, room(y)
ron, run
ronchee, raunch(y)
ronchy, raunch(y)
rondavous, rendezvous
rondavu, rendezvous
ronduvu, rendezvous
ronege, renege
rong, wrong / rung / wrung
rongle, wrong(ly)
ronige, renege
ronk, wrong
ronouncement, renounce(ment)

ronounse, renounce
ronownse, renounce
ronownsment, renounce(ment)
ronshy, raunch(y)
ront, runt
rontavu, rendezvous
rontchy, raunch(y)
rontivu, rendezvous
roobarb, rhubarb
rood, rude / root
roodly, rude(ly)
rooen, ruin
rooenus, ruin(ous)
roof,*,fed,fing,fer, TOP/COVER OF A DWELLING/STRUCTURE
rooin, ruin
rooinus, ruin(ous)
rook,*, A BIRD, CHEAT MONEY OUT OF SOMEONE, GAME PIECE IN CHESS
roold, rule(d)
rooler, rule(r)
roolet, roulette
roolir, rule(r)
roolt, rule(d)
roolur, rule(r)
room,*,med,ming,mer,mful,my,miness, mily, CUBICLE/SPACE/PLACE WITH WALLS WITHIN A LARGER DWELLING/STRUCTURE (or see roam)
rooman, rumen
roomanu, rumina
roomatoyd, rheumatic(toid)
roomen, rumen
roomena, rumina
roomenate, rumina(te)
roomenator, rumina(tor)
roomin, rumen
roominate, rumina(te)
roominator, rumina(tor)
roomon, rumen
roon, rune
roonashen, ruin(ation)
roonation, ruin(ation)
roose, ruse
roost,*,ted,ting,ter, SIT ATOP SOMETHING TO REST/SLEEP, NORMALLY HOW BIRDS SLEEP (or see roast/rust/roust)
rooster,*, A MALE CHICKEN
root,*,ted,ting,ter,tage,tless,ty, PART OF PLANT THAT'S UNDERGROUND "prefixes: up"
rop, rope / rob

ropair, repair
ropare, repair
ropcher, rupture
rope,*,ed,ping,er, MANY STRANDS WOVEN TOGETHER INTO ONE (or see robe)
ropeel, repeal
ropeet, repeat
ropel, rappel / repeal / repel
ropelinsy, repellent(ncy)
ropent, repent
ropete, repeat
roplenish, replenish
roposutory, repository
roquitable, requite(table)
roquite, requite
ror, roar / row(er)
ros, rose / row(s)
rosaree, rosary
rosary,ries, STRAND OF BEADS WITH A CROSS ON IT
rosdrane, restrain
rose,*,eate,eately,ette,etta, A FLOWER, COLOR, PAST TENSE FOR "RISE" (or see row(s))
rosebshin, reception
rosebshinist, receptionist
rosebtif, receptive
rosefe, receive
rosefible, receive(vable)
rosen, rosin
rosepdekle, receptacle
rosepdikul, receptacle
rosepeunt, recipient
roseprikul, reciprocal
rosepshen, reception
rosepshenist, receptionist
roseptekle, receptacle
roseptif, receptive
roseptionest, receptionist
roseptive, receptive
roseree, rosary
roseshun, recess(ion)
rosesive, recess(ive)
rosetion, recess(ion)
roseve, receive
rosevuble, receive(vable)
rosh, rush
rosin,*,ned,ny, OIL FROM TURPENTINE
rosipeant, recipient
rosipeint, recipient
rosiprekul, reciprocal
rosiree, rosary
rosodo, risotto

rosoto, risotto
rospective, respect(ive)
rospektif, respect(ive)
rost, roast / rust
rostar, roster / roast(er) / rooster
roster,*, LIST OF NAMES/EVENTS (or see roast(er)/rooster)
rostic, rustic
rostir, roster / roast(er) / rooster
rostore, restore
rostrain, restrain
rostrane, restrain
rostrektif, restrict(ive)
rostrikshen, restrict(ion)
rostrikt, restrict
rostriktion, restrict(ion)
rostriktive, restrict(ive)
rostur, roster / roast(er) / rooster
rosun, rosin
rosuree, rosary
rot,*,tted,tting, DETERIORATE, DISINTEGRATE (or see rod/rode/ wrote/rote/ wrought)
rotade, rotate
rotaleation, retaliate(tion)
rotaliation, retaliate(tion)
rotan, rotten
rotaree, rotary
rotary,ries, A SPINNING/ROTATION ON AN AXIS/HUB
rotashen, rotate(tion)
rotashenul, rotate(tional)
rotashun, rotate(tion)
rotate,*,ed,ting,table,tion,tional,tive, tor,tory, TAKE TURNS, REVOLVE/ ALTERNATE
rotatelur, rototiller
rotatiller, rototiller
rote, REPETITION, OVER AND OVER (or see wrote/rotor/road/rode)
roten, rotten
roteo, rodeo
roter, rotor
rotery, rotary
rotesaree, rotisserie
rotesuree, rotisserie
rotetiller, rototiller
rotin, rotten
rotio, rodeo
rotir, rotor / retire
rotiry, rotary
rotisaree, rotisserie
rotisserie,*, A FOOD COOKER
rotisuree, rotisserie

rotitelir, rototiller
rotor,*, TO DO WITH ROTATION/HUB
rototiler, rototiller
rototiller,*, MACHINE TO TILL GROUND
rotten, PAST TENSE FOR "ROT"
rotun, rotten
rotur, rotor
rotury, rotary
rou, row
roub, robe
roudy, rowdy
rouf, rough / roof
roug, rogue / rouge
rouge, RED MAKE-UP FOR FACE (or see rogue)
rough,*,hed,hing,hen,her,hest,hly, hness,hage,hen,hish, ABRASIVE/ FIBROUS/ UNREFINED/UNEVEN
roulette, GAME WITH SPINNING DISK/ BALL
rounation, ruin(ation)
round,*,ded,ding,der,dest,dish,dly, dness, CIRCULAR SHAPE, AROUND, MAKE MORE EVEN/SMOOTH TO SHAPE "prefixes: un"
rount, round
roust,*,ted,ting, WAKEN/AROUSE, FORCE TO ACTION (or see roost)
rout, route / rote / wrote
route,*,ed,ting,er, SPECIFIC/ PARTICULAR PATH/NETWORK/ LINES (or see root)
routeen, routine
routine,*,ely,nize,nized,nizing, PERFORM SPECIFIC FUNCTION ON CONTINUOUS BASIS "prefixes: sub"
routy, rowdy
roux, A PASTE FOR SAUCE/GRAVY (or see rue)
rovalfe, revolve
rove,*,ed,ving,er, TO WANDER/MOVE AIMLESSLY SEEKING FOR SOMETHING "prefixes: un"
roveel, reveal
roveelt, reveal(ed)
rovegen, revise(sion)
rovejen, revise(sion)
rovench, revenge
rovene, ravine
rovenge, revenge
rovengful, revenge(ful)
rovenjful, revenge(ful)
roverberate, reverberate
roverbirate, reverberate

rovere, revere
roverse, reverse
rovert, revert
roveshen, revise(sion)
rovesion, revise(sion)
roview, review / revue
rovigen, revise(sion)
rovijen, revise(sion)
rovinch, revenge
rovinjful, revenge(ful)
rovir, rove(r)
rovirbarate, reverberate
rovirberate, reverberate
rovirse, reverse
rovirsuble, reverse(sible)
rovirt, revert
rovise, revise
rovishen, revise(sion)
rovision, revise(sion)
rovival, revival
rovive, revive
rovivle, revival
rovivuble, revive(vable)
rovize, revise
rovocability, revocable(bility)
rovolfe, revolve
rovolfer, revolve(r)
rovolve, revolve
rovue, review / revue
rovur, rove(r)
rovurse, reverse
rovurt, revert
row,wed,wer,wing, USE OF OARS/ PADDLES TO NAVIGATE THROUGH WATER
roward, reward
rowbot, robot
rowch, roach
rowdy,dier,diest, TALK LOUD, BE ROUGH/RAMBUNCTIOUS
rowmane, romaine
rowmanse, romance
rownd, round
rownt, round
roword, reward
rowp, rope
rowr, row(er) / roar
rowst, roust
rowtee, rowdy
rowty, rowdy
royal,lty,lties,lly,lism,list, OF KINGS/ QUEENS, A SOVEREIGN POWER/ RIGHT, PERCENTAGE AS GAIN
royel, royal

royul, royal
roz, rose / row(s)
rozaree, rosary
roze, rose / row(s)
rozen, rosin
rozeree, rosary
rozin, rosin
roziree, rosary
rozodo, risotto
rozt, roast
rozter, roster
roztur, roster
rozun, rosin
rozuree, rosary
rub,*,bbed,bbing,bber, USE MOTION/ MASSAGE TO WORK AN AREA
rubal, rubble
rubar, rubber
rubarb, rhubarb
rubash, rubbish
rubber,*,rize,rizes,rized,rizing,ry, MATERIAL DERIVED FROM PETROLEUM/TREES
rubbish, GARBAGE/TRASH, WORTH REJECTING/ELIMINATING
rubble, ROCKS/DEBRIS LAYING AROUND
rube, ruby
rubed, rub(bbed)
rubee, ruby
rubel, rubble
rubeled, rebel(lled)
rubelein, rebel(llion)
rubeleus, rebel(llious)
rubelyon, rebel(llion)
ruber, rubber
ruberize, rubber(ize)
rubesh, rubbish
rubil, rubble
rubir, rubber
rubirize, rubber(ize)
rubish, rubbish
rublase, replace
ruble, rubble
rublie, reply
rubodek, robot(ic)
rubodizashen, robot(ization)
ruborb, rhubarb
rubotek, robot(ic)
rubotiks, robot(ics)
rubt, rub(bbed)
rubul, rubble
rubur, rubber
ruby,bies, A GEMSTONE

rucede, recede
rucepter, receptor
ruch, rush
ruciprocation, reciprocate(tion)
ruck, rug
ruclaimuble, reclaimable
rucumbent, recumbent
rudder,*,rless, A BLADE ON A BOAT WHICH STEERS
rude,er,est,dly,eness, TO OFFEND SOMEONE WITH BEHAVIOR/ WORDS, UNREFINED/RAW
rudeculus, ridiculous
rudeemible, redeem(able)
rudeme, redeem
rudemption, redemption
rudemshen, redemption
ruder, rudder
rudikulus, ridiculous
rudir, rudder
rudist, rude(st)
rudur, rudder
ruduse, reduce
rudusible, reduce(cible)
rue,*, AN HERB (or see roux)
ruebarb, rhubarb
ruel, rule
ruelur, rule(r)
ruen, ruin
ruenashen, ruin(ation)
ruenation, ruin(ation)
ruenus, ruin(ous)
ruf, roof / rough / ruff
rufag, rough(age)
rufal, ruffle
rufeel, reveal
rufeelt, reveal(ed)
rufeer, revere
rufeg, rough(age)
rufej, rough(age)
rufel, ruffle
rufen, ravine / rough(en)
rufenge, revenge
rufenje, revenge
rufer, roof(er) / rough(er) / refer
rufere, revere / refer
ruferse, reverse / refer(s)
rufest, rough(est)
ruff,*,ffed, ELABORATE COLLAR, CARD GAME TERM (or see rough/roof)
ruffle,*,ed,ling, TO MESS UP/DISTURB "prefixes: un"
rufiew, review revue
rufiful, revival

rufig, rough(age)
rufij, rough(age)
rufil, ruffle
rufinable, refine(nable)
rufine, refine
rufinery, refine(ry)
rufinje, revenge
rufinment, refine(ment)
rufinuble, refine(nable)
rufinury, refine(ry)
rufir, rough(er) / roof(er) / refer
rufirse, reverse
rufist, rough(est)
rufle, ruffle
ruflection, reflect(ion)
ruflee, rough(ly)
ruflekshen, reflect(ion)
ruflekt, reflect
ruflektion, reflect(ion)
ruflektor, reflect(or)
rufly, rough(ly)
rufol, ruffle
rufor, rough(er) / roof(er) / refer
rufractory, refract(ory)
rufrain, refrain
rufraktory, refract(ory)
rufrane, refrain
rufregirant, refrigerate(ant)
rufregirator, refrigerate(tor)
rufresher, refresh(er)
rufreshment, refresh(ment)
rufrigerant, refrigerate(ant)
rufrigerator, refrigerate(tor)
rufs, roof(s) / ruff(s)
ruft, roof(ed) / rough(ed)
rufue, review / revue
ruful, ruffle
rufur, rough(er) / roof(er) / refer
rufurse, reverse
rufursuble, reverse(sible)
rufust, rough(est)
rufute, refute
rug,*, REMOVABLE FLOOR COVERING
rugard, regard
ruge, rouge
ruged, rugged
rugged,dly,dness, ROUGH/COARSE/ UNREFINED/IRREGULAR "prefixes: semi"
rugit, rugged
rugresif, regress(ive)
rugresive, regress(ive)
rugret, regret
rugreted, regret(tted)

rugretful, regret(ful)
rugretfuly, regret(fully)
rugud, rugged
rugut, rugged
ruil, rule
ruin,*,ned,ning,nation,nous, BREAK/ DESTROY, COMPLETE FAILURE/ DECAY
ruj, rouge
ruk, rug / rook
ruklamuble, reclaimable
rukliner, recline(r)
rukord, record
rukorder, record(er)
rukumbent, recumbent
rukwest, request
rukwire, require
rukwirment, require(ment)
rukwit, requite
rul, rule
rulaks, relax
rular, rule(r)
rulax, relax
ruld, rule(d)
rule,*,ed,ling,er, LAW/COMMAND/ METHOD, PERIOD OF GOVERNING, DEVICE TO MEASURE "prefixes: mis/ over"
rulegis, religion(ous)
rulejis, religion(ous)
rulenquish, relinquish
rulent, relent
rulentless, relentless
rulese, release
rulet, roulette
rulette, roulette
ruleve, relieve
rulever, relieve(r)
ruli, rely
ruliability, reliable(bility)
rulianse, reliance
ruliense, reliance
ruligeon, religion
ruligous, religion(ous)
rulijes, religion(ous)
rulinkwish, relinquish
rulinqish, relinquish
rulintless, relentless
rulir, rule(r)
rult, rule(d)
ruluktense, reluctant(nce)
ruluktint, reluctant
rulur, rule(r)
ruly, rely

rum,*,mmer,mmy, LIQUOR, UNUSUAL
rumach, rummage
rumadik, rheumatic
rumadoed, rheumatic(toid)
rumage, rummage
rumain, remain / romaine
rumaje, rummage
rumanater, rumina(tor)
rumander, remain(der)
rumane, remain / romaine
rumanek, romantic
rumantek, romantic
rumanticize, romantic(ize)
rumantisize, romantic(ize)
rumanu, rumina
rumar, rumor
rumared, rumor(ed)
rumark, remark
rumarkt, remark(ed)
rumarkuble, remark(able)
rumatezum, rheumatic(ism)
rumatik, rheumatic
rumatism, rheumatic(ism)
rumatizum, rheumatic(ism)
rumatoed, rheumatic(toid)
rumb, rump
rumbal, rumble / rumple
rumble,*,ed,ling,er,ly, DEEP/ROLLING SOUND, A FIGHT (or see rumple)
rumbul, rumble / rumple
rume, room
rumech, rummage
rumedeal, remedy(dial)
rumedge, rummage
rumedial, remedy(dial)
rumediashen, remedy(diation)
rumediation, remedy(diation)
rumedoed, rheumatic(toid)
rumege, rummage
rumeje, rummage
rumember, remember
rumen,*,mina, STOMACH IN RUMINANT ANIMALS (many stomachs)
rumena, rumina
rumenate, rumina(te)
rumenator, rumina(tor)
rumer, rumor / room(er)
rumered, rumor(ed)
rumert, rumor(ed)
rumes, room(s)
rumeshen, remission
rumet, remit
rumetisem, rheumatic(ism)

rumetism, rheumatic(ism)
rumetoid, rheumatic(toid)
rumich, rummage
rumidal, remit(ttal)
rumidoed, rheumatic(toid)
rumige, rummage
rumije, rummage
rumina,al,ant,antly,ate,ation,ative, atively,ator, PERTAINING TO CHEWING OF CUD, FIRST STOMACH
rumind, remind
rumindur, remind(er)
rumintur, remind(er)
rumir, rumor / room(er)
rumired, rumor(ed)
rumishen, remission
rumission, remission
rumit, remit
rumitable, remit(ttable)
rumited, remit(tted)
rumitezum, rheumatic(ism)
rumition, remission
rumitizum, rheumatic(ism)
rumitoed, rheumatic(toid)
rumitoid, rheumatic(toid)
rummage,*,ed,ging, GO THROUGH/ SEARCH/RANSACK
rummige, rummage
rumofer, remove(r)
rumor,*,red, GOSSIP/HEARSAY/ GENERAL TALK
rumorse, remorse
rumorsful, remorse(ful)
rumorsless, remorse(ful)
rumote, remote
rumotisem, rheumatic(ism)
rumotism, rheumatic(ism)
rumotly, remote(ly)
rumovable, remove(vable)
rumover, remove(r)
rump,*, REAR/TAIL END, BUTTOCKS
rumple,*,ed,ling, CREASE/FOLD/ WRINKLE (or see rumble)
rums, room(s)
rumuch, rummage
rumufer, remove(r)
rumufible, remove(vable)
rumuge, rummage
rumun, rumen
rumunerashen, remunerate(tion)
rumunerate, remunerate
rumuneration, remunerate(tion)
rumunirashen, remunerate(tion)
rumunirate, remunerate

rumur, rumor
rumurt, rumor(ed)
rumutezim, rheumatic(ism)
rumutizem, rheumatic(ism)
rumy, room(y)
run,*,nning,nner,nny,ran, MOVE QUICKLY USING LEGS, MOVING LIQUID (or see rune) "prefixes: over/re/under"
runar, run(nner)
rund, runt
rune,*,nic, SYMBOLS/ALPHABET (or see run/ruin/run(nny))
runege, renege
runer, run(nner)
rung,*, PAST TENSE FOR THE WORD "RING", STEPS/LEVELS OF A LADDER, STEERING FOR SHIP (or see wrung)
runige, renege
runik, renege
runir, run(nner)
runone, renown
runoserus, rhinoceros
runosirus, rhinoceros
runounsment, renounce(ment)
runown, renown
runownse, renounce
runownsment, renounce(ment)
runre, run(nner)
runt,*,tier,tiest,tiness,ty, SMALLEST OF A GROUP/LITTER/ SPECIES
runumerate, remunerate
runur, run(nner)
rup, rip / ripe / rub
rupair, repair
rupal, rubble
rupare, repair
rupcher, rupture
rupchur, rupture
rupeal, repeal
rupeat, repeat
rupedidly, repeat(edly)
rupedutif, repetitive
rupee, ruby
rupeel, repeal
rupeet, repeat
rupel, rappel / repeal / repel / rubble
rupelein, rebel(llion)
rupelent, repellent
rupelinsy, repellent(ncy)
rupelint, repellent
rupense, repent(s)
rupent, repent
rupentinse, repent(ance)

ruper, rubber
rupesh, rubbish
rupete, repeat
rupetedly, repeat(edly)
rupil, rubble
rupinens, repent(ance)
rupint, repent
rupintense, repent(ance)
rupir, rubber
rupish, rubbish
ruplace, replace
ruplasmint, replace(ment)
ruple, rubble
ruplenesh, replenish
ruplenish, replenish
ruplid, reply(lied)
ruplied, reply(lied)
ruply, reply
rupor, rapport
ruporder, report(er)
ruport, report
ruporter, report(er)
rupository, repository
rupozitory, repository
rupreshen, repress(ion)
rupresif, repress(ive)
rupress, repress
rupresuve, repress(ive)
ruproch, reproach
ruprochuble, reproach(able)
rupshar, rupture
rupsheruble, rupture(rable)
rupshir, rupture
rupshiruble, rupture(rable)
rupshur, rupture
rupshuruble, rupture(rable)
rupt, rub(bbed)
rupture,*,ed,ring,rable, BURST/BREACH CONTAINER
rupublekan, republic(an)
rupublican, republic(an)
rupugnenst, repugnant(nce)
rupugnint, repugnant
rupul, rubble
rupulshin, repulse(ion)
rupulsion, repulse(ion)
rupur, rubber
ruquire, require
ruquirment, require(ment)
ruquitable, requite(table)
ruquite, requite
ruqwest, request
ruqwire, require
ruqwirment, require(ment)

rur, roar
rural,lly,lity,lism,list,lize,lization, CITY OUTSKIRTS "prefixes: semi"
ruril, rural
rurilee, rural(lly)
rurul, rural
rurulee, rural(lly)
rus, ruse
rusde, rust(y)
rusder, rooster
rusdrane, restrain
rusdur, rooster
ruse, A TRICK
ruseat, receipt
rusebshin, reception
rusebshinist, receptionist
rusebtif, receptive
rusebtive, receptive
ruseed, recede
ruseef, receive
ruseet, receipt
rusefible, receive(vable)
ruseliensy, resilient(ncy)
rusemblinse, resemble(lance)
rusentful, resent(ful)
rusentment, resent(ment)
rusepdekle, receptacle
rusepdikul, receptacle
rusepeunt, recipient
ruseprocation, reciprocate(tion)
ruseprocul, reciprocal
rusepshen, reception
rusepshenist, receptionist
ruseptef, receptive
ruseptekle, receptacle
rusepter, receptor
ruseptickle, receptacle
ruseption, reception
ruseptionest, receptionist
ruseptive, receptive
ruserved, reserve(d)
ruseshun, recess(ion)
rusesif, recess(ive)
rusesion, recess(ion)
rusesive, recess(ive)
rusession, recess(ion)
rusestinse, resist(ance)
rusestive, resist(ive)
rusete, receipt
rusetion, recess(ion)
ruseve, receive
rusevuble, receive(vable)

rush,hes,hed,hing,hy, UNEXPECTEDLY/ FORCEFULLY MOVE FORWARD, HURRY ALONG "prefixes: in"
rushd, rush(ed)
ruside, reside
rusiduil, residue(ual)
rusileant, resilient
rusilient, resilient
rusimblense, resemble(lance)
rusimbul, resemble
rusine, resign
rusintment, resent(ment)
rusipeint, recipient
rusiprocation, reciprocate(tion)
rusiprocul, reciprocal
rusiprokate, reciprocate
rusiprokle, reciprocal
rusirfed, reserve(d)
rusist, resist
rusistanse, resist(ance)
rusistense, resist(ance)
rusistent, resist(ant)
rusister, resist(or)
rusistive, resist(ive)
rusitil, recite(tal)
rusitle, recite(tal)
rusodo, risotto
rusolve, resolve
rusort, resort
rusoto, risotto
rusotto, risotto
ruspect, respect
ruspectful, respect(ful)
ruspective, respect(ive)
ruspectuble, respect(able)
ruspekt, respect
ruspektful, respect(ful)
ruspektif, respect(ive)
ruspektuble, respect(able)
ruspite, respite
ruspond, respond
ruspondent, respond(ent)
rusponder, respond(er)
rusponse, response
rusponsef, response(sive)
rusponsive, response(sive)
rusponsuble, response(sible)
ruspont, respond
rust,*,ted,ting,ty,tier,tiest, OXIDATION OF METAL (or see roost)
rustek, rustic
ruster, rooster

rustic,*,cally,cate,cates,cated,cating, cation,cator,city,cities, COUNTRY STYLE, SIMPLE
rustid, roost(ed)
rustik, rustic
rustir, rooster
rustore, restore
rustrain, restrain
rustraint, restrain(t)
rustrane, restrain
rustrant, restrain(t)
rustrekt, restrict
rustrektif, restrict(ive)
rustrikshen, restrict(ion)
rustrikt, restrict
rustriktion, restrict(ion)
rustriktive, restrict(ive)
rustuk, rustic
rustur, rooster
rusurfed, reserve(d)
rususcitate, resuscitate
rususetate, resuscitate
rususitashen, resuscitate(tion)
rususitate, resuscitate
rususitator, resuscitate(tor)
rut,*,tted,tting, NOISE DEER MAKES, A TRENCH/GROOVE/FURROW (or see route/root/rude/wrought)
rutainer, retain(er)
rutaleashen, retaliate(tion)
rutaleate, retaliate
rutaleation, retaliate(tion)
rutaliation, retaliate(tion)
rutane, retain
rutaner, retain(er)
rutashen, rotate(tion)
rute, rude / root / route
ruted, rut(tted)
ruteen, routine
rutenshun, retention
rutentif, retentive
rutention, retention
rutentive, retentive
ruter, rudder
rutesary, rotisserie
rutest, rude(st)
ruthlesnes, ruthless(ness)
ruthless,ssly,ssness, SPEAKING/ACTING WITHOUT MERCY
ruthlis, ruthless
rutine, routine
rutinshun, retention
rutintion, retention
rutir, rudder

rutire, retire
rutirment, retire(ment)
rutisary, rotisserie
rutisury, rotisserie
rutlee, rude(ly)
rutorekle, rhetoric(al)
rutorikle, rhetoric(al)
rutracted, retract(ed)
rutraction, retract(ion)
rutrakshen, retract(ion)
rutrakted, retract(ed)
rutre, rudder
rutref, retrieve
rutrefer, retrieve(r)
rutreful, retrieve(val)
rutreve, retrieve
rutrevur, retrieve(r)
rutur, rudder
ruvalfe, revolve
ruvalve, revolve
ruveel, reveal
ruveelingly, reveal(ingly)
ruveelt, reveal(ed)
ruveer, revere
ruvegen, revise(sion)
ruvejen, revise(sion)
ruvench, revenge
ruvene, ravine
ruvenge, revenge
ruvengful, revenge(ful)
ruvenje, revenge
ruvenjful, revenge(ful)
ruverbarate, reverberate
ruverbirate, reverberate
ruvere, revere
ruversuble, reverse(sible)
ruvert, revert
ruveshen, revise(sion)
ruvesion, revise(sion)
ruview, review / revue
ruvigen, revise(sion)
ruvijen, revise(sion)
ruvinch, revenge
ruvine, ravine
ruving, revenge
ruvingful, revenge(ful)
ruvinje, revenge
ruvinjful, revenge(ful)
ruvirberate, reverberate
ruvirse, reverse
ruvirsuble, reverse(sible)
ruvirt, revert
ruvise, revise
ruvishen, revise(sion)

ruvision, revise(sion)
ruvival, revival
ruvive, revive
ruvivle, revival
ruvivuble, revive(vable)
ruvize, revise
ruvocability, revocable(bility)
ruvocable, revocable
ruvokability, revocable(bility)
ruvokable, revocable
ruvoke, revoke
ruvokt, revoke(d)
ruvolfe, revolve
ruvolfer, revolve(r)
ruvolt, revolt
ruvoltid, revolt(ed)
ruvolve, revolve
ruvolver, revolve(r)
ruvue, review / revue
ruvurse, reverse
ruvurt, revert
ruward, reward
ruwidable, requite(table)
ruword, reward
ruwul, rural
ruzemblinse, resemble(lance)
ruzentful, resent(ful)
ruzentment, resent(ment)
ruzerved, reserve(d)
ruzestif, resist(ive)
ruzestir, resist(or)
ruzide, reside
ruziduil, residue(ual)
ruzileant, resilient
ruzilient, resilient
ruzimble, resemble
ruzimblense, resemble(lance)
ruzine, resign
ruzintful, resent(ful)
ruzintment, resent(ment)
ruzist, resist
ruzistanse, resist(ance)
ruzistant, resist(ant)
ruzistef, resist(ive)
ruzistense, resist(ance)
ruzistent, resist(ant)
ruzister, resist(or)
ruzodo, risotto
ruzolfe, resolve
ruzolve, resolve
ruzort, resort
ruzoto, risotto
ruzt, rust / roost
ruztek, rustic

ruztid, rust(ed)
ruztuk, rustic
ruzty, rust(y)
ruzurfs, reserve(s)
ry, rye / wry
rye, A GRAIN (or see wry)
ryle, rile
ryme, rhyme
ryno, rhino
rynstone, rhinestone
rysome, rhizome
ryth, writhe
rythem, rhythm
rythom, rhythm
ryut, riot
ryzome, rhizome
sa, saw / say
sabal, sable
sabateur, saboteur
sabatoj, sabotage
sabature, saboteur
saber,*,red,ring, BROADSWORD, LIGHTWEIGHT SWORD WITH BLUNT TIP
sabereoredy, superior(ity)
sabereority, superior(ity)
sabereur, superior
sabetaje, sabotage
sabetoge, sabotage
sabeture, saboteur
sabil, sable
sabir, saber
sabitaje, sabotage
sabiteur, saboteur
sabitoge, sabotage
sabitoj, sabotage
sabiture, saboteur
sable,*, CARNIVOROUS ANIMAL
sableng, sapling
sabling, sapling
sabol, sable
sabor, saber
sabotage,*,ed,ging,teur, HINDER/ DAMAGE SOMEONE'S ATTEMPTS/ POSSESSIONS/EFFORTS
sabotaje, sabotage
saboteur,*, ONE WHO COMMITS SABOTAGE
saboture, saboteur
sabre, saber
sabul, sable
sabur, saber
sabutaje, sabotage
sabuteur, saboteur

sabutoge, sabotage
sabutoj, sabotage
saccaren, saccharin
saccerin, saccharin
saccharin,ne,nely,nity, MANMADE SUGAR
saccuren, saccharin
sacede, secede
sacha, sachet
sachal, satchel
sacharate, saturate
sacharation, saturate(tion)
sachatory, statutory
sachay, sashay / sachet
sache, sachet
sacheable, sate(tiable)
sacheatid, sate(tiated)
sachel, satchel
sacherashen, saturate(tion)
sacherate, saturate
sacheration, saturate(tion)
sacherin, saccharin
sachet,*, SMALL/AROMATIC BAG (or see sashay)
sachetory, statutory
sacheuble, sate(tiable)
sachil, satchel
sachirashen, saturate(tion)
sachirate, saturate
sachiration, saturate(tion)
sachiren, saccharin
sachol, satchel
sachul, satchel
sachurate, saturate
sachuration, saturate(tion)
sachutory, statutory
sack,*,ked,king,ker,kful, BAG MADE OF VARIOUS MATERIALS USED TO CONTAIN/HOLD SOMETHING, TO BAG/TACKLE (or see sax)
sackarin, saccharin
sackralegus, sacrilege(gious)
sackralijes, sacrilege(gious)
sackrament, sacrament
sackrul, sacral
sackrument, sacrament
sackuren, saccharin
saclusion, seclusion
saclusive, seclusive
sacrafise, sacrifice
sacral, ASSOCIATED WITH RITES
  "prefixes: de"
sacraleje, sacrilege
sacraligous, sacrilege(gious)

sacrament,*,tal,tally,tality,talism,talist, tarian,tarianism, THAT WHICH IS SACRED
sacrasankt, sacrosanct
sacred,dly,dness, OF REVERENCE/ WORSHIPPED
sacrefise, sacrifice
sacrel, sacrum(ral)
sacreleje, sacrilege
sacreligus, sacrilege(gious)
sacrem, sacrum
sacremint, sacrament
sacresanct, sacrosanct
sacreshen, secrete(tion)
sacresion, secrete(tion)
sacrete, secrete / sacred
sacretion, secrete(tion)
sacrid, sacred
sacrifice,*,ed,cing,er,cial,cially, GIVE UP WITHOUT PROFIT/RETURN, DENY ONESELF
sacril, sacrum(ral)
sacrilege,gious,giously,giousness, VIOLATION OF SACRED
sacrim, sacrum
sacrosanct,tity,tness, TOO HOLY TO BE CRITICIZED/SLANDERED
sacrud, sacred
sacrufise, sacrifice
sacrul, sacrum(ral)
sacruleje, sacrilege
sacruligus, sacrilege(gious)
sacrum,ral, LUMBAR VERTEBRAE ON THE SPINE
sacrument, sacrament
sacumb, succumb
sacure, secure
sad,dly,dness,dden,dder,ddest, SORROWFUL/MOURNFUL, UNHAPPY WITH RESULTS (or see sat)
sadalight, satellite
sadalite, satellite
sadarday, saturday
sadasfaction, satisfy(faction)
sadasfakshen, satisfy(faction)
sadasfy, satisfy
sadashen, sedate(tion)
sadasion, sedate(tion)
sadate, sedate
sadation, sedate(tion)
saddle,*,ed,ling,er, DEVICE/SEAT USED TO RIDE ON A FOUR LEGGED ANIMAL "prefixes: un"

sadel, saddle
sadelite, satellite
sademize, sodomy(mize)
saden, sad(dden) / satin
sadentary, sedentary
sadeny, satin(y)
saderday, saturday
sadesfaction, satisfy(faction)
sadesfakshen, satisfy(faction)
sadesfy, satisfy
sadesum, sadism
sadews, seduce
sadil, saddle
sadilight, satellite
sadilite, satellite
sadimize, sodomy(mize)
sadin, sad(dden) / satin
sadintary, sedentary
sadiny, satin(y)
sadirday, saturday
sadisfaction, satisfy(faction)
sadisfakshen, satisfy(faction)
sadisfy, satisfy
sadism,stic,st,stically, SEXUALLY AROUSED BY PAIN/TORTURE
sadisum, sadism
sadle, saddle
sadnes, sad(ness)
sadnis, sad(ness)
sadolite, satellite
sadomasakisum, sadomasochism
sadomasochism,st,stic, ASSOCIATED WITH SADISM
sadomasukezim, sadomasochism
sadoose, seduce
sadosfaction, satisfy(faction)
sadosfakshen, satisfy(faction)
saducshen, seduce(ction)
saductive, seduce(ctive)
saduktion, seduce(ction)
saduktive, seduce(ctive)
sadul, saddle
saduld, saddle(d)
sadulite, satellite
sadun, sad(dden) / satin
sadurday, saturday
saduse, seduce
sadusfakshen, satisfy(faction)
sadusfy, satisfy
sae, say
saed, said / set
saen, sane / sain
saend, sound
saent, saint

safari,*, HUNTING EXPEDITION
safd, save(d)
safe,ely,er,est,eness,ety, PROTECT FROM HARM (or see salve)
safekate, suffocate
safekation, suffocate(tion)
safeks, suffix
safestikashen, sophisticate(tion)
safestikated, sophisticate(d)
safestikation, sophisticate(tion)
safex, suffix
safflower, FLOWERS WHICH PRODUCED OIL
saffron, A FLOWER/COLOR
saficashen, suffocate(tion)
saficate, suffocate
safication, suffocate(tion)
safichent, sufficient
saficient, sufficient
safikashen, suffocate(tion)
safikate, suffocate
safikation, suffocate(tion)
safiks, suffix
safinth, seventh
safir, safe(r) / savor / sapphire
safire, sapphire
safise, suffice
safishent, sufficient
safishently, sufficient(ly)
safishunt, sufficient
safist, safe(st)
safistakashen, sophisticate(tion)
safistakated, sophisticate(d)
safistakation, sophisticate(tion)
safix, suffix
saflawur, safflower
saflee, safe(ly)
saflour, safflower
saflower, safflower
safly, safe(ly)
safmore, sophomore
safocashen, suffocate(tion)
safocate, suffocate
safocation, suffocate(tion)
safron, saffron
safrun, saffron / sovereign
saftee, safe(ty)
safucashen, suffocate(tion)
safucate, suffocate
safucation, suffocate(tion)
safukashen, suffocate(tion)
safukate, suffocate
safur, safe(r) / savor
safy, savvy

safyur, savior
sag,*,gged,gging,ggy, TO BOW/BEND IN A CERTAIN AREA (or see sack/sage)
sagd, sag(ged) / sage(d)
sage,*,ed,ging,ely,eness, AN HERB/ PLANT, SOMEONE WISE
saged, sag(gged) / sage(d)
sagee, sag(ggy)
sagis, sage(s)
saguaro,*, A CACTUS
sagus, sage(s)
sagy, sag(ggy)
said, PAST TENSE FOR THE WORD "SAY" (or see set) "prefixes: un"
sail,*,led,ling,lor, OF/GIVEN TO A BOAT WITH SAILS, USE OF WIND TO NAVIGATE BOAT/VESSEL (or see sale/sailor))
sailor,*, PEOPLE WHO OPERATE SEAGOING VESSELS (or see sail(er))
saim, same
sain, MAKE THE SIGN OF THE CROSS (or see sane/say(ing))
sainkshuary, sanctuary
saint,*,ted,ting,tly,tdom,thood, OFFICALLY RECOGNIZED IN DYING FOR A HOLY CAUSE, A VERY KIND PERSON
saje, sage
sajed, sage(d)
sak, sack / sake / sag / sax
sakaren, saccharin
sakarin, saccharin
sakd, sack(ed)
sake, PURPOSE/BENEFIT OF, JAPANESE ALCOHOL BEVERAGE (or see sack)
saker, soccer / sack(er)
sakeren, saccharin
sakerin, saccharin
sakeuridy, secure(rity)
sakewr, secure
sakewrity, secure(rity)
sakful, sack(ful)
sakir, soccer / sack(er)
sakiuredy, secure(rity)
sakiutrest, psychiatry(rist)
saklooded, seclude(d)
saklude, seclude
sakluded, seclude(d)
saklusive, seclusive
saklution, seclusion
sakrafise, sacrifice
sakraleje, sacrilege
sakralige, sacrilege

sakraligus, sacrilege(gious)
sakrament, sacrament
sakramintal, sacrament(al)
sakrasinkt, sacrosanct
sakred, sacred
sakrefise, sacrifice
sakrel, sacral
sakrem, sacrum
sakrement, sacrament
sakren, saccharin
sakreshen, secrete(tion)
sakresion, secrete(tion)
sakret, sacred
sakrete, secrete
sakrid, sacred
sakrifice, sacrifice
sakril, sacral
sakrilege, sacrilege
sakrim, sacrum
sakriment, sacrament
sakrimental, sacrament(al)
sakrin, saccharin
sakrit, sacred
sakrom, sacrum
sakrosankt, sacrosanct
sakrud, sacred
sakrufise, sacrifice
sakrufishul, sacrifice(cial)
sakrul, sacral
sakruleje, sacrilege
sakruligus, sacrilege(gious)
sakrum, sacrum
sakrument, sacrament
sakrun, saccharin
sakrusankt, sacrosanct
sakrut, sacred
saks, sack(s) / sag(s) / sax
saksafone, saxophone
saksaphone, saxophone
saksufone, saxophone
saksuphone, saxophone
sakt, sack(ed)
sakum, succumb
sakur, soccer / sack(er)
sakure, secure
sakuren, saccharin
sakurin, saccharin
sakurity, secure(rity)
sakwenshul, sequence(ntial)
sakwential, sequence(ntial)
sakwoia, sequoia
sal, sale / sail / saw
salad,*, COLD MIXED FOOD DISH, TOSSED GREENS

saladerity, solidarity
salal, plant
salamander,*, AMPHIBIOUS LIZARD
salami, A SAUSAGE
salar, sail(er) / sailor
salaree, salary / celery
salary,ries,ried, STEADY PAY IN COMPENSATION FOR WORK PERFORMED
salatood, solitude
salatude, solitude
sald, salt / sail(ed)
salder, solder(ed)
saldered, solder(ed)
sale,*,eable,sell, SELL GOODS/SERVICES (or see sail) "prefixes: pre/re"
salebrity, celebrity
salective, select(ive)
saled, sail(ed) / salad
saledarity, solidarity
saledify, solid(ify)
saleen, saline
saleks, select(s)
salekshen, select(ion)
salekt, select
salektif, select(ive)
salektion, select(ion)
salektive, select(ive)
salelaquy, soliloquy
salem, solemn
salemandur, salamander
salemantur, salamander
salemly, solemn(ly)
salen, saline
salenity, saline(nity)
salenium, selenium
salenoid, solenoid
saler, sail(er) / sailor
saleree, salary celery
salesteal, celestial
salet, salad
saleutation, salute(tation)
salevate, saliva(te)
salewtashen, salute(tation)
salfent, solvent
salfint, solvent
salicit, solicit
salicitation, solicit(ation)
saliciter, solicit(er)
salid, salad / solid
salidarity, solidarity
salidefy, solid(ify)
salidness, solid(ness)
salilakwy, soliloquy

salilaqwy, soliloquy
salim, solemn
salimandur, salamander
salimly, solemn(ly)
saline,na,nity,nization, PERTAINS TO SALT "prefixes: de"
salinidy, saline(nity)
salinoid, solenoid
salir, sail(er) / sailor
saliry, salary / celery
salis, solace
saliset, solicit
saliseter, solicit(er)
salisit, solicit
salisitation, solicit(ation)
salisiter, solicit(er)
salit, salad
salitefy, solid(ify)
saliva,ary,ate,ation, FLUID SECRETED BY GLANDS IN THE MOUTH "prefixes: in"
salm, psalm
salmin, salmon
salmon, a fish
salmonela, salmonella
salmonella, BACTERIA WHICH POISONS FOOD
salmun, salmon
salod, salad
salomander, salamander
salomantur, salamander
salomee, salami
salon,*, CUTS/STYLES HAIR
saloon,*, TYPE OF DRINKING ESTABLISHMENT
saloot, salute
salt,*,ted,ting,ty,tier,tiest,ter, SODIUM/ CHEMICAL COMPOUND (or see sail(ed)) "prefixes: de"
salud, salad
saludid, salute(d)
saludness, solid(ness)
salum, solemn
salumandur, salamander
salumly, solemn(ly)
salune, saloon
salunization, saline(nization)
salunoid, solenoid
salur, sail(er) / sailor
saluree, salary / celery
salus, solace
salushen, solution
salut, salad
salutashen, salute(tation)

salute,*,ed,ting,tary,tarily,tariness, tation,tational,tatorian,tor,tories, ter, METHOD OF GREETING
salutid, salute(d)
salution, solution
saluvate, saliva(te)
salvage,*,ed,ging,eable,er, THOUGH DAMAGED, IS STILL WORTHY OF SAVING
salvashen, salvation
salvation,nal,nism, PRESERVE/PROTECT FROM DANGER/HARM
salve,*,ed,ving, AN OINTMENT/BALM USED FOR HEALING SORES (or see solve)
salvech, salvage
salved, solve(d)
salvige, salvage
salvije, salvage
salvuble, solve(vable)
salvug, salvage
salyewble, soluble(ize)
salyutashen, salute(tation)
saman, salmon
samanela, salmonella
samantics, semantics
same,eness, ALIKE/SIMILAR
samen, salmon
samenela, salmonella
samesdur, semester
samester, semester
sametrek, symmetry(ric)
sametric, symmetry(ric)
samin, salmon
saminela, salmonella
samonela, salmonella
sampal, sample
sample,*,ed,ling,er, A SMALL AMOUNT/ TASTE OF SOMETHING "prefixes: re/ sub"
samplir, sample(r)
sampul, sample
samun, salmon
samunela, salmonella
san, sane / sain / sand
sanada, sonata
sanareo, scenario
sanatarium, sanitorium
sanatate, sanitate
sanatesation, sanitize(zation)
sanatezashen, sanitize(zation)
sanatization, sanitize(zation)
sanatize, sanitize
sanatoreum, sanitorium

sanatu, sonata
sancshen, sanction
sancshin, sanction
sancshuary, sanctuary
sancshun, sanction
sanctafie, sanctify
sanctify,fies,fied,fying,fication,fier, MAKE HOLY
sanction,*,ned,ning,ner,nable, FORMAL/BINDING PERMISSION
sanctofie, sanctify
sanctuary,ries, REPRIEVE FROM PROBLEMS, PLACE OF IMMUNITY
sanctuery, sanctuary
sanctufy, sanctify
sand,*,ded,ding,dy,der, TINY ROCKS, SMOOTH A SURFACE BY SANDING
sandal,*, TYPE OF SHOE
sandee, sand(y)
sandel, sandal
sandul, sandal
sandur, sand(er)
sandwech, sandwich
sandwich,hes,hed,hing, MEAT/ VEGETABLES BETWEEN TWO PIECES OF BREAD, PHYSICALLY BE BETWEEN TWO THINGS
sandwitch, sandwich
sane,ely,eness,nity,nities, OF SOUND MIND/JUDGEMENT (or see sain/ sand)
sanedy, sanity
sanek, sonic
sanelity, senile(lity)
sanereo, scenario
sanerist, scenario(ist)
sanetareum, sanitorium
sanetary, sanitary
sanetate, sanitate
sanetery, sanitary
sanetize, sanitize
sanetoreum, sanitorium
sanetorium, sanitorium
sanety, sanity
sanidy, sanity
sanility, senile(lity)
sanitareum, sanitorium
sanitarium, sanitorium
sanitary,rian,rily,riness, CLEAN/FREE OF MOST HARMFUL BACTERIA "prefixes: in"
sanitate,*,ed,ting,tion, CLEAN/RID OF HARMFUL BACTERIA
sanitery, sanitary

sanitezation, sanitize(zation)
sanitised, sanitize(d)
sanitize,*,ed,zing,zation,er, CLEAN/RID OF HARMFUL BACTERIA
sanitizer, sanitize(r)
sanitorium,*, RESORT/FACILITY FOR LONG-TERM CARE OF ILLNESS/HEALTH
sanity,ties, RELATED TO A SOUND MIND/JUDGEMENT
sankchuery, sanctuary
sankdefide, sanctify(fied)
sankdefy, sanctify
sankdify, sanctify
sankdufide, sanctify(fied)
sankdufy, sanctify
sankshen, sanction
sankshin, sanction
sankshuery, sanctuary
sankshun, sanction
sanktafi, sanctify
sanktify, sanctify
sanktion, sanction
sanktofie, sanctify
sanktuary, sanctuary
sanktuery, sanctuary
sanktufie, sanctify
sanoda, sonata
sanografee, scenography
sanopsis, synopsis
sanota, sonata
sant, saint
sante, sand(y)
santels, sandal(s)
santly, saint(ly)
santuls, sandal(s)
santur, sand(er)
santwech, sandwich
santwitch, sandwich
sanuc, sonic
sanudy, sanity
sanuk, sonic
sanut, sonnet
sanutareum, sanitorium
sanutary, sanitary
sanutate, sanitate
sanutery, sanitary
sanutezashen, sanitize(zation)
sanutisation, sanitize(zation)
sanutised, sanitize(d)
sanutize, sanitize
sanutizer, sanitize(r)
sanuty, sanity
sanwech, sandwich

saons, se'ance
sap,*,pped,pping,ppy, THE LIFEBLOOD OF PLANTS
saped, sap(pped)
sapena, subpoena
sapenid, subpoena(ed)
sapenud, subpoena(ed)
saperb, superb
saperblee, superb(ly)
sapereor, superior
sapereoredy, superior(ity)
sapereority, superior(ity)
saperlative, superlative
saperlutif, superlative
saphire, sapphire
saphmore, sophomore
sapinud, subpoena(ed)
sapirb, superb
sapirblee, superb(ly)
sapireor, superior
sapireority, superior(ity)
sapirlutif, superlative
sapleminul, subliminal
sapleng, sapling
sapli, supply
saplier, supply(lier)
sapling,*, YOUNG TREES
sapliur, supply(lier)
saply, supply
saport, support
saportef, support(ive)
saportive, support(ive)
sapose, suppose
sapository, suppository
saposubly, suppose(dly)
sapoze, suppose
sapozetory, suppository
sapozitory, suppository
sapozubly, suppose(dly)
sapphire,*, A GEM STONE
sappresion, suppress(ion)
saprechen, suppress(ion)
sapreem, supreme
sapremacy, supremacy
sapreme, supreme
sapremusist, supremacy(cist)
sapremusy, supremacy
sapreno, soprano
sapres, suppress
sapreshen, suppress(ion)
sapretion, suppress(ion)
saprimosy, supremacy
saprino, soprano
sapt, sap(pped)

sapurb, superb
sapurblee, superb(ly)
sapurlative, superlative
sapurlitef, superlative
sapurlutif, superlative
sapy, sap(ppy)
saquential, sequence(ntial)
saquer, secure
saquir, secure
saquoia, sequoia
sar, czar
saran, A THIN PLASTIC
sarandipity, serendipity
sarape, serape
sarcafagus, sarcophagus
sarcasm,*,stic, REMARKS MEANT TO BE DEMEANING/MOCKERY TO ANOTHER
sarcastecly, sarcastic(ally)
sarcastek, sarcastic
sarcastekly, sarcastic(ally)
sarcastic,cally, REMARKS MEANT TO BE DEMEANING/MOCKERY TO ANOTHER
sarcastikly, sarcastic(ally)
sarcastuk, sarcastic
sarcazum, sarcasm
sarcophagus,ses,gi, STONE COFFIN
sardeen, sardine
sardene, sardine
sardine,*, TINY EDIBLE FISH
sardo, sourdough
sarebrul, cerebral
sarel, sorrel / surreal
sarench, syringe
sarender, surrender
sarendipity, serendipity
sarene, serene
sarenge, syringe
sarenity, serene(nity)
sarenje, syringe
sarenk, saw(ing)
sargeant, sergeant / surgent
sargent, sergeant / surgent
sargint, sergeant / surgent
sari, saury / sorry
saribrol, cerebral
sarinch, syringe
sarinder, surrender
sarindipity, serendipity
saring, saw(ing)
saringe, syringe
sarinje, syringe
sarink, saw(ing)

sariosis, psoriasis
sariusis, psoriasis
sarjent, sergeant
sarjint, sergeant
sarkafigus, sarcophagus
sarkasem, sarcasm
sarkasim, sarcasm
sarkastek, sarcastic
sarkastiklee, sarcastic(ally)
sarkastuk, sarcastic
sarkawfegus, sarcophagus
sarkazum, sarcasm
sarkofigus, sarcophagus
sarkofugus, sarcophagus
sarkophagus, sarcophagus
sarkrowt, sauerkraut
saro, sorrow
saroful, sorrow(ful)
sarong,*, MATERIAL/CLOTH USED TO WRAP AROUND THE LOWER TORSO
sarope, serape
saroredy, sorority
sarority, sorority
saround, surround
sarow, sorrow
sarowful, sorrow(ful)
sarownd, surround
sarrated, serrate(d)
sarration, serrate(tion)
sarro, sorrow
sarundipity, serendipity
sarundipudy, serendipity
sary, saury / sorry
sas, sass / say(s)
sasafras, sassafras
sascha, sashay / sachet
sased, sass(ed) / secede
sasede, secede
sasefras, sassafras
saseg, sausage
sasej, sausage
sasenked, succinct
sasenkt, succinct
sasenktly, succinct(ly)
saseptible, susceptible
saseptif, susceptive
saseptive, susceptive
saseptuble, susceptible
saseptuf, susceptive
saser, saucer
saseshen, secession
sasesion, secession
saset, secede
sasetion, secession

sasha, sachet
sashay,*, WISPILY WALK AS IF DANCING (or see sachet)
sasheable, sate(iable)
sasheated, sate(tiated)
sashet, sashay / sachet
sasheuble, sate(iable)
sasifras, sassafras
sasig, sausage
sasij, sausage
sasinked, succinct
sasinkt, succinct
sasinktly, succinct(ly)
sasir, saucer
sasofras, sassafras
sasor, saucer
saspekt, suspect
saspend, suspend
saspender, suspender
saspeshus, suspicious
saspishus, suspicious
sass,sses,ssing,ssy, SPEAK IMPUDENTLY, SMART BACK AT
sassafras, USEFUL TREE ROOTBARK
sasufras, sassafras
sasur, saucer
sasy, saucy / sass(y)
sat, PAST TENSE WORD FOR 'SIT' (or see sate/sad)
sata, saute / sate
satalite, satellite
satanek, satanic
satanic,cal,cally,ism,ist, MOCKERY OF CHRISTIAN RITUAL
satanuk, satanic
satanukel, satanic(al)
satarate, saturate
satarday, saturday
satasfaction, satisfy(faction)
satasfakshen, satisfy(faction)
satasfy, satisfy
satay, saute / sate
satchal, satchel
satcharashen, saturate(tion)
satcharate, saturate
satchatory, statutory
satchel,*, BAG/CARRYING CASE
satcherashen, saturate(tion)
satcherate, saturate
satchetory, statutory
satchil, satchel
satchirashen, saturate(tion)
satchirate, saturate
satchitory, statutory

satchul, satchel
satchurashen, saturate(tion)
satchurate, saturate
satchutory, statutory
sate,ed,ting,tiable,tiably,tiability,tiate, tiates,tiated,tiating,tiation,tiety, TO BE COMPLETELY SATISFIED (or see saute) "prefixes: in"
sateable, sate(tiable)
satel, saddle
satelite, satellite
satellite,*, A PLANET OR MANMADE DEVICE WHICH ORBITS THE EARTH "prefixes: bio"
satemize, sodomy(mize)
saten, sad(dden) / satin
satentary, sedentary
sateny, satin(y)
saterate, saturate
saterday, saturday
saterikul, satire(rical)
satesfaction, satisfy(faction)
satesfakshen, satisfy(faction)
satesfy, satisfy
satesm, sadism
satiaty, sate(tiety)
satilite, satellite
satimize, sodomy(mize)
satin,ny, A SOFT FABRIC
satintary, sedentary
satirate, saturate
satirday, saturday
satire,*,ric,rical,rically,rist,rize,rizes, rized,rizing,rization,rizer, EMPLOY IRONY/WIT/SARCASM (or see satyr)
satirest, satire(rist)
satisfakshen, satisfy(faction)
satisfy,fies,fied,fying,fiable,fier,fyingly, faction,factory,factorily, NEEDS/ DEMANDS/EXPECTATIONS FULFILLED "prefixes: dis/un"
satisum, sadism
satle, saddle
satlee, sad(ly)
satnis, sad(ness)
satolite, satellite
satomasakisum, sadomasochism
satomasochism, sadomasochism
satosfaction, satisfy(faction)
satosfakshen, satisfy(faction)
satshetory, statutory
satul, saddle
satulite, satellite

saturate,*,ed,ting,tion,tor, UNABLE TO ABSORB ANYMORE LIQUID "prefixes: de/un/under"
saturday,*, A DAY OF THE WEEK (ENGLISH)
satusfakshen, satisfy(faction)
satusfy, satisfy
satutory, statutory
satyerashen, saturate(tion)
satyirate, saturate
satyr,*,ric,rical, MYTHOLOGICAL CREATURE (or see satire)
satyurate, saturate
satyuration, saturate(tion)
sau, saw
sauble, say(able)
sauce,*,ed,cing,cy, A THICK LIQUID WITH SPICES/HERBS/FLAVORINGS ADDED
saucer,*, A SMALL PLATE, SHAPE OF A PLATE
sauciur, saucy(cier)
saucy,cier,ciest,cily,ciness, BEING IMPUDENT/FLIPPANT TOWARD SUPERIORS
saud, sod / sold / saw
sauder, solder
sauderd, solder(ed)
saudumize, sodomy(mize)
saudumy, sodomy
sauer, sour
sauerdo, sourdough
sauerkraut, FERMENTED CABBAGE
saufari, safari
saufen, soft(en)
saufet, soffit
saufiner, soft(ener)
saufit, soffit
saufmore, sophomore
saufunir, soft(ener)
saugee, soggy
saught, saute / sought
sauir, sour
sauirdo, sourdough
sauirkrowt, sauerkraut
saulanoid, solenoid
saulder, solder
saulesmint, solace(ment)
saulid, solid
saulis, solace
saulisment, solace(ment)
saulitare, solitaire / solitary
sauluderity, solidarity
saulus, solace

saulutare, solitaire / solitary
saulutude, solitude
saulyewble, soluble(ize)
sauna,*, ROOM WITH MOIST HEAT/ STEAM
saund, sound
saunek, sonic
saunet, sonnet
saunik, sonic
saunit, sonnet
saunt, sound
saunter,*,red,ring, A LEISURLY WALK/ STROLL
saunu, sauna
saunut, sonnet
saur, sour
saurdo, sourdough
sauree, sorry / saury
sauro, sorrow
saury,ries, A FISH (or see sorry)
saus, sauce
sausage,*, MINCED MEAT WITH FLAVORINGS
sauseur, saucy(cier)
sausier, saucy(cier)
saut, sought
saute,*,eed,eing, QUICKLY FRY IN A PAN/WOK (or see sate)
sauter, solder
sautered, solder(ed)
sauvren, sovereign
sauvter, soft(er)
sauvuble, solve(vable)
sauyubil, soluble
sav, save / salve / solve
savach, savage
savage,*,ely,eness,ery,eries, BEASTLY/ RUDE/BARBARIAN
savagly, savage(ly)
savana, savanna
savanna, MEADOW/PLAIN WITH SHRUBS/TREES
savant,*, A WISE/LEARNED PERSON
savar, savor / save(r)
savaren, sovereign
savd, save(d)
save,*,ed,ving,er, RESCUE FROM DANGER/HARM/ALTERCATION (or see safe/savvy/salve)
savech, savage
savechry, savage(ry)
savee, savvy
savege, savage
savegly, savage(ly)

savegry, savage(ry)
saveje, savage
saver, save(r) / savor
saveridy, severe(rity)
saverin, sovereign
saverity, severe(rity)
savich, savage
savichry, savage(ry)
savier, savvy(vvier) / savior
savigly, savage(ly)
savigry, savage(ry)
savije, savage
savinth, seventh
savior,*, ONE CHOSEN BY PEOPLE TO LEAD THEM FROM IGNORANCE INTO ENLIGHTENMENT
savir, savor / save(r) / savior
savird, savor(ed)
saviren, sovereign
savlawur, safflower
savlee, safe(ly)
savont, savant
savor,*,red,ring,rer,ry, FOOD WITH MOST PALATABLE FLAVOR/SMELL/ TASTE (or see savior) "prefixes: un"
savree, savor(y)
savren, sovereign
savron, saffron / sovereign
savrun, sovereign
savry, savor(y)
savtee, safe(ty)
savuch, savage
savugly, savage(ly)
savugry, savage(ry)
savuje, savage
savur, savor / save(r) / savior
savurd, savor(ed)
savuren, sovereign
savurin, sovereign
savvy,vvies,vvied,vvying,vviest, INTELLIGENT/SHREWD UNDERSTANDING
savy, savvy
savyer, savior
savyur, savior
saw,*,wed,wing,wer, PAST TENSE FOR THE WORD "SEE", BLADE WITH TEETH THAT CUTS (or see sauce) "prefixes: over"
sawardo, sourdough
sawarkrowt, sauerkraut
sawaro, saguaro
sawdemise, sodomy(mize)
sawdemy, sodomy

sawder, solder
sawdered, solder(ed)
sawdimy, sodomy
sawdumize, sodomy(mize)
sawdur, solder
sawer, sour
sawerdo, sourdough
sawerkraut, sauerkraut
sawfenir, soft(ener)
sawfet, soffit
sawfin, soft(en)
sawfinur, soft(ener)
sawfit, soffit
sawfmore, sophomore
sawfun, soft(en)
sawfuner, soft(ener)
sawgee, soggy
sawir, sour
sawirdo, sourdough
sawirkraut, sauerkraut
sawirkrowt, sauerkraut
sawker, soccer
sawled, solid
sawlesmint, solace(ment)
sawletare, solitaire / solitary
sawlf, solve
sawlid, solid
sawlidness, solid(ness)
sawlis, solace
sawlisment, solace(ment)
sawlitness, solid(ness)
sawlud, solid
sawludness, solid(ness)
sawlutare, solitaire / solitary
sawlutude, solitude
sawnd, sound
sawnek, sonic
sawnet, sonnet
sawnik, sonic
sawnut, sonnet
sawor, sour
saworo, saguaro
sawp, sop / sob
sawpee, sop(ppy)
sawree, saury / sorry
sawrely, sorry(rily)
sawrench, syringe
sawri, sorry / saury
sawro, saguaro / sorrow
sawrong, sarong
sawry, sorry / saury
saws, saw(s) / sauce / souse
sawsege, sausage
sawseje, sausage

sawser, saucer
sawsige, sausage
sawsor, saucer
sawst, souse(d)
sawsuge, sausage
sawsuje, sausage
sawsur, saucer
sawsy, saucy
sawt, saw(ed)
sawtay, saute / sate
sawte, saute / sate
sawtemy, sodomy
sawtered, solder(ed)
sawtimise, sodomy(mize)
sawtumy, sodomy
sawuble, soluble(ize)
sawur, sour
sawurdo, sourdough
sawurkraut, sauerkraut
sawurkrowt, sauerkraut
sawvuble, solve(vable)
sawyebul, soluble
sawyubil, soluble
sawzy, saucy
sax, SLANG FOR SAXOPHONE (or see sack(s))
saxophone,*,nic,nist, HORN INSTRUMENT
saxsifone, saxophone
saxsuphone, saxophone
say,*,yer,ying,aid, WHAT HAS BEEN SPOKEN, TO SPEAK VERBALLY "prefixes: un"
sayabil, soluble
sayans, se'ance
sayn, sain / sane / say(ing)
sayons, se'ance
sayulose, cellulose
sbase, space / space(y)
sbaser, space(r)
sbast, space(d)
sbasur, space(r)
sbasy, space(y)
sbegut, spigot
sbekit, spigot
sbekot, spigot
sbidel, spittle
sbidul, spittle
sbiget, spigot
sbikit, spigot
sbikot, spigot
sbital, spittle
sbitul, spittle
sblash, splash

sblat, splat
sblendur, splinter / splendor
sblent, splint
sblerge, splurge
sblerje, splurge
sblet, split
sbletur, split(tter)
sblices, splice(s)
sblin, spline / spleen
sblindur, splinter / splendor
sblint, splint
sblirge, splurge
sblirje, splurge
sblis, splice
sbliser, splice(r)
sblist, splice(d)
sblisur, splice(r)
sblit, split
sbliter, split(tter)
sblitur, split(tter)
sbloch, splotch
sblochy, splotch(y)
sblotch, splotch
sblotchee, splotch(y)
sblurje, splurge
sboel, spoil
sboeld, spoil(ed) / spoilt
sboeleg, spoil(age)
sboil, spoil
sboild, spoil(ed) / spoilt
sboiled, spoil(ed) / spoilt
sboileg, spoil(age)
sboke, spoke
sbon, spoon
sboon, spoon
sbore, spore
sboyl, spoil
sbra, spray
sbraket, sprocket
sbran, sprain
sbrauket, sprocket
sbraul, sprawl
sbre, spree
sbreg, sprig
sbrews, spruce
sbrig, sprig
sbrocket, sprocket
sbroket, sprocket
sbroose, spruce
sbruse, spruce
sbun, spun / spoon
sburd, spur(rred)
sburt, spur(rred)

scab,*,bbed,bbing,bby, CRUST FORMED ON SKIN OVER OPEN WOUND, TERM FOR STRIKE WORKERS
scabard, scabbard
scabbard,*, SWORD SHEATH/ SHEATHE
scabburd, scabbard
scabed, scab(bbed)
scabees, scabies
scaberd, scabbard
scabies,etic,ious, SKIN DISEASE
scaburd, scabbard
scaby, scab(bby)
scad,*, EDIBLE FISH, LARGE NUMBER/ QUANTITY
scader, skate(r) / scatter
scadered, scatter(ed)
scadir, skate(r) / scatter
scadured, scatter(ed)
scaffold,*,ding, TEMPORARY FRAMEWORK WITH PLANKS USED TO BUILD
scafold, scaffold
scair, scare
scairslee, scarce(ly)
scairsness, scarce(ness)
scalar, A PHYSICS EXPRESSION, OF MASS AND TIME
scald,*,ded,ding, SURFACE BURN
scale,*,ed,ling,eless,eliness,lable,ly, INSTRUMENT FOR MEASURING WEIGHT, MUSICAL LADDER, TO CLIMB (or see scaly) "prefixes: de/over/re/up"
scaleness, scaly(liness)
scaleon, scallion
scalep, scallop
scaleun, scallion
scaley, scaly
scalion, scallion
scalip, scallop
scallion,*, TYPE OF ONION
scallop,*,per, SHELLFISH, TYPE OF DISH/ SHAPE
scalop, scallop
scalor, scalar
scalp,*,ped,ping, SKIN ON HUMAN SKULL, WAY OF SELLING TICKETS (or see scallop)
scalpal, scalpel
scalpel,*, A SURGICAL KNIFE
scalpul, scalpel
scalup, scallop
scaly,liness,leless, SIMILAR/SAME AS SCALES ON A FISH

scalyin, scallion
scalyun, scallion
scamatic, scheme(matic)
scan,*,nned,nning,nner, A MACHINE WHICH COPIES/TAKES DIGITAL IMAGES "prefixes: over"
scandal,*,lize,lous,lously,lousness, EVENT WHICH DEGRADES/ OFFENDS A SOCIAL VALUE/IDEA
scandel, scandal
scandelus, scandal(ous)
scandil, scandal
scandolus, scandal(ous)
scandul, scandal
scandulus, scandal(ous)
scaner, scan(nner)
scanerio, scenario
scanir, scan(nner)
scanography, scenography
scant,tily,tness, LIMITED RESOURCE
scantuly, scant(ily)
scanur, scan(nner)
scapala, scapula
scapel, scalpel
scapeula, scapula
scapewla, scapula
scapil, scalpel
scapila, scapula
scapul, scalpel
scapula,*, SHOULDER BLADE
scar,*,rred,rring, A PHYSICAL MARK LEFT AFTER A BODILY INJURY HAS HEALED (or see scare)
scarce,ely,city,eness, IN DEMAND, RARE
scarcedy, scarce(city)
scare,*,ed,ring,ry, FRIGHTEN/ALARM
scared, scare(d) / scar(rred)
scarf,fes,fed,fing,rves, A LIGHTWEIGHT MATERIAL WORN ON THE HEAD, TO WOLF DOWN FOOD/DRINK
scarfd, scarf(ed)
scarfs, scarf(rves)
scarft, scarf(ed)
scarlet, A COLOR
scarlut, scarlet
scarse, scarce
scarsedy, scarce(city)
scarsity, scarce(city)
scarsly, scarce(ly)
scarsness, scarce(ness)
scarsudy, scarce(city)
scart, scar(rred) / scare(d)
scary, scare(y)

scat,*,tted,tting, SINGING IMPROVISATION, TO HURRY AWAY, FISH, ANIMAL FECAL (or see skat/ skate)
scater, scatter
scathe,*,ed,hing,hingly, TO INJURE/ HARM "prefixes: un"
scatir, scatter
scatter,*,red,ring,rable, DISPERSED ABOUT IRREGULARLY (or see skate(r))
scatur, scatter
scauler, scholar
scaulerly, scholar(ly)
scavage, scavenge
scavager, scavenge(r)
scavenge,*,ed,ging,er, SEARCH/SEEK FOR USABLE ITEMS
scavuge, scavenge
scavunjer, scavenge(r)
scawler, scholar
scawlerly, scholar(ly)
scem, scheme / skim
scenac, scene(nic)
scenario,*,ist, TO OUTLINE SCENES/ CHARACTERS FOR PLAY/MOVIE
scenary, scene(ry)
scene,*,ery,eries,nic,nerio,nography, VISUAL PRESENTATION OF A PLACE/ EVENT
scenic, scene(nic)
sceniry, scene(ry)
scenography,hic,her, RULES IN CREATING PERSPECTIVE
scent,*,ted,tless,tlessness, ODOR/ FRAGRANCE
scenur, skinner
sceptacism, skeptic(ism)
sceptasisum, skeptic(ism)
scepter,*,red,ring, ROD OF AUTHORITY/ ROYALTY
scepticism, skeptic(ism)
sceptik, skeptic
sceptir, scepter
sceptisitum, skeptic(ism)
sceptor, scepter
sceptuk, skeptic
sceptur, scepter
sceptusisum, skeptic(ism)
scer, scare
scerfy, scurvy
sceris, scirrhus / cirrus
scersity, scarce(city)
scersly, scarce(ly)

scersudy, scarce(city)
scerus, scirrhus / cirrus
scery, scurry
scesurs, scissor(s)
scewbu, scuba
scewp, scoop
scewper, scoop(er)
schalastic, scholastic
schaler, scholar
schalerly, scholar(ly)
schamatic, scheme(matic)
schaulerly, scholar(ly)
schedewl, schedule
schedule,*,ed,ling, AN ITEMIZED LIST CONCERNING TIME AND APPOINTMENTS "prefixes: re"
scheem, scheme
schelastic, scholastic
scheme,*,ed,ming,er,ma,mata,matic, matically,matism,matist,matize, matization,matizer, PLAN/PLOT/ PROJECT
schemir, skim(mmer) / scheme(r)
schemur, skim(mmer) / scheme(r)
schilastic, scholastic
schimatic, scheme(matic)
schist,tose,tous, ROCK TYPE DETERMINED BY THE WAY IT EXFOLIATES
schitzophrenia, schizophrenia
schizofrenia, schizophrenia
schizoid, PERTAINING TO SCHIZOPHRENIA
schizophrenia,ic, MENTAL PROBLEM
schizoyd, schizoid
scholar,*,rly,rliness, ONE WHO HAS STUDIED/LEARNED A GREAT DEAL
scholastic,*,cal,cally,cate,cism, RELATED/CONCERNING SCHOOL "prefixes: inter"
scholer, scholar
scholerly, scholar(ly)
school,*,led,ling,ler, A PLACE TO LEARN "prefixes: pre/un"
schooner,*, TYPE OF SAILING VESSEL
schuel, school
schulastic, scholastic
schule, school
schumatic, scheme(matic)
schuner, schooner
sciadeca, sciatic(a)
sciadica, sciatic(a)
scianse, science
sciantifek, scientific

sciantifekaly, scientific(ally)
sciantificly, scientific(ally)
sciatek, sciatic
sciatic,ca,cally MAJOR NERVES IN THE BODY NEAR THE HIPS
sciatik, sciatic
science,*,ntific,ntist, FIELDS OF GENERAL LAWS CONCERNING EVERYTHING IN OUR REALITY "prefixes: bio"
scientest, scientist
scientifek, scientific
scientific,cally, OF FIELDS OF SCIENCE "prefixes: un"
scientifik, scientific
scientifikaly, scientific(ally)
scientist,*,sm, MAJORS IN THE FIELD OF SCIENCE "prefixes: bio"
scif, skiff
scikyatrus, psychiatry(rist)
scimatic, scheme(matic)
scinario, scenario
scinerio, scenario
scinography, scenography
scint, scent
scinur, skinner
scirfy, scurvy
scirhus, scirrhus / cirrus
scirrhus,hoid,hous, CONCERNING TUMORS IN THE BODY (or see cirrus)
scirus, scirrhus / cirrus
sciry, scurry
scisers, scissor(s)
scissor,*, TOOL TO CUT/SEVER
scisurs, scissor(s)
scith, scythe
sciuntefikaly, scientific(ally)
sciuntist, scientist
scizurs, scissor(s)
scof, scoff
scofed, scoff(ed)
scoff,*,ffed,ffing,ffingly,ffer, SHOW MOCKERY/DISTASTE, RIDUCULE
scold,*,ded,ding, TO FIND FAULT/ REPRIMAND SOMEONE FOR THEIR BEHAVIOR (or see scald)
scoleosis, scoliosis
scoliosis,ic, CURVATURE OF THE SPINE
scolt, scold / scald
sconce,*,ed,cing, LIGHTS ON THE WALL, FORT, SKULL
scone,*, A BREAD CAKE
scons, scone(s) / sconce

sconts, sconce
scooba, scuba
scooder, scoot(er)
scoop,*,ped,ping,per,pful, GATHER UP QUANTITY OF SOMETHING ALL AT ONCE
scoopir, scoop(er)
scoot,*,ted,ting,ter, GO/SEND HASTILY ALONG, SLIDE OVER (or see scute)
scorch,hes,hed,hing,her, LIGHTLY BURN
score,*,ed,ring,er,eless, MARK BY GOUGING/SCRATCHING, POINTS IN COMPETITION "prefixes: over/re/ under"
scorlis, score(less)
scorn,*,ned,ning,ningly,nful,nfully, nfulness, EXPRESS DISTATE/ CONTEMPT
scornfuly, scorn(fully)
scorpeon, scorpion
scorpion,*, AN ARACHNOID
scoul, scowl
scouled, scowl(ed)
scoundrel,*,lly, MEAN PERSON WHO HAS NO HONOR FOR OTHERS
scoundril, scoundrel
scoundrle, scoundrel
scour,*,red,ring,rer, SCRUB CLEAN, GO OVER, PURGE
scourd, scour(ed)
scourge,*,ed,ging,er, TORMENT/ TORTURE/SEVERLY PUNISH
scout,*,ted,ting,ter, TO HUNT/SEARCH FOR
scouwl, scowl
scower, scour
scowl,*,led,ling, WEARING A LOOK OF ANGER
scowndrel, scoundrel
scowr, scour
scowt, scout
scowurd, scour(ed)
scrach, scratch
scrag,*,gged,gging,ggy,gily,gginess,ggly, JAGGED/SKINNY/DISHEVELED/ BONEY/SCRAWNY/LEAN
scraggly,lies,lier,liest,ggily,gginess, UNEVEN/IRREGULAR/DISHEVELED/ MESSY
scragleur, scraggly(lier)
scragliest, scraggly(liest)
scragly, scrag(ily) / scraggly
scrakly, scrag(ily) / scraggly

scram,*,mmed,mming, GO AWAY QUICKLY
scrambal, scramble
scrambil, scramble
scramble,*,ed,ling,er, MIX UP TOGETHER, CLUMSILY TAKE ACTION "prefixes: de/un"
scrambul, scramble
scrap,*,pped,pping,pper,ppage, SMALL PARTICLE/PIECE/FRAGMENT, LEFTOVERS, PICK A FIGHT (or see scrape)
scrape,*,ed,ping,er,pable, RASP/GRATE/ DAMAGE, NOISE BY DRAGGING SOMETHING/MARKS (or see scrap)
scrapt, scrap(pped) / scrape(d)
scrapuble, scrap(able)
scratch,hes,hed,hing,her,hy, MARK/ CUT/CROSS OUT
scrawl,*,led,ling,ly,ler, AWKWARD/ IRREGULAR MARKS AS IF DONE HASTILY
screach, screech
scream,*,med,ming,mer,mingly, A LOUD/SHRILL OUTCRY FROM THE THROAT
screan, screen
screanable, screen(able)
screbul, scribble
screch, screech
scred, screed
screech,hes,hed,hing, SHARP/SHRILL/ LOUD SOUND
screed,*,ded,ding, SEPARATE PARTICLES FROM ONE ANOTHER, PLASTER/ MORTAR TECHNIQUE
screem, scream
screen,*,ned,ning,ner,nable, MATERIAL FOR WINDOWS, TO SORT/SIFT THROUGH
scremp, scrimp
scremshaw, scrimshaw
scren, screen
screped, script
screpsher, scripture
scrept, script
screpture, scripture
screw,*,wed,wing,wer,wy, SMALL CYLINDRICAL OBJECT WITH POINTED TIP/SLOTTED HEAD "prefixes: un"
screwdnee, scrutiny
screwge, scrooge
screwje, scrooge

screwpul, scruple
screwpulus, scrupulous
screwtney, scrutiny
scribble,*,ed,ling,er, SCRAWL, UNDECIPHERABLE MARKS
scribd, scribe(d) / script
scribe,*,ed,bing,er,bal, A WRITER
scrible, scribble
scribul, scribble
scrimage, scrimmage
scrimmage,*,ed,ging, PHYSICAL ROUGH ABOUT WITH OTHERS IN A GAME
scrimp,*,ped,ping,py, TIGHT BUDGET/ SPENDING HABIT
scrimshaw, IVORY CARVING
scrimuge, scrimmage
scrimuje, scrimmage
scripshur, scripture
script,*,ted,ting, THE CHARACTERS/ TEXT OF A PLAY/MOVIE/ BROADCAST/ PROGRAM "prefixes: re/un"
scripture,*,ral,rally,ralness, RELIGIOUS WRITING "prefixes: un"
scroge, scrooge
scroje, scrooge
scrol, scrawl / scroll
scroll,*,lled,lling, PARCHMENT/PAPER ROLLED UP
scrooge, A MISER, TIGHTWAD
scrooje, scrooge
scrooteny, scrutiny
scrounge,*,ed,ging,gy,gier,giest, FORAGE AROUND, A DISHEVELED/ UNKEPT LOOK
scroungy, scrounge(y)
scrowl, scrawl
scrowngy, scrounge(y)
scrownje, scrounge / scrounge(y)
scru, screw
scrub,*,bbed,bbing,bber,bby, RUB/ SCOURGE BRISKLY, LOW GROWTH TREE/SHRUBS
scrudnee, scrutiny
scruf, scruff
scruff,ffy, BACK/NAPE OF NECK
scrufy, scruff(y)
scruge, scrooge
scruje, scrooge
scruny, scrutiny
scrup, scrub
scrupel, scruple
scrupewlus, scrupulous

scruple,*,ed,ling, REMAIN CONSCIOUSLY AWARE/ALERT
scrupol, scruple
scrupulous,osity,sness,sly, BEING CAREFUL CONCERNING WHAT IS RIGHT/PROPER "prefixes: un"
scrut, screw(ed)
scruteny, scrutiny
scrutiny,nize,nizes,nized,nizing,nization, nizer, CLOSELY EXAMINE/EVALUATE
scruwy, screw(y)
scruy, screw(y)
scuba,*, UNDERWATER DEVICE FOR BREATHING
scuder, scoot(er)
scuf, scuff
scufel, scuffle
scuff,*,ffed,ffing, LEAVE MARKS BY WEARING/USAGE/WALKING
scuffle,*,ed,ling, DISORDERLY PHYSICAL STRUGGLE/FIGHT
scufil, scuffle
scuful, scuffle
scul, school / skull
sculbed, sculpt
sculbshir, sculpt(ure)
sculpshir, sculpt(ure)
sculpt,*,ted,ting,tor,ture,tural,turally, FORM BY HUMAN/NATURAL PROCESS TO CREATE 3D IMAGES
sculpter, sculpt(ure)
scum,*,mmed,mming,mmy, NASTY/ VILE/WORTHLESS, RESIDUE LEFT BEHIND
scumatic, scheme(matic)
scumy, scum(mmy)
scunario, scenario
scuner, schooner
scup, scoop
scupd, scoop(ed)
scupt, scoop(ed)
scurfy, scurvy
scurry,rries,rried,rrying, TO SCAMPER/ HURRY
scurvy,vies,vier,viest,vily,viness, A DISEASE
scury, scurry
scute,*, BONY PLATE/SHIELD (or see scoot)
scuter, scoot(er)
scwaled, squalid
scwolid, squalid

scythe,*,ed,hing, A TOOL WITH LONG BLADE USED IN SWEEPING MOTIONS TO CUT GRASS/GRAIN
sdabul, stable
sdaroyd, steroid
sdash, stash
sdemulashen, stimulate(tion)
sdemulate, stimulate
sdemulation, stimulate(tion)
sderdy, sturdy
sdergen, sturgeon
sderjon, sturgeon
sderoed, steroid
sderoet, steroid
sderoyd, steroid
sderty, sturdy
sdewdeo, studio
sdewdeus, studious
sdewpendus, stupendous
sdewper, stupor
sdewpid, stupid
sdewpir, stupor
sdewpur, stupor
sdifel, stifle
sdiful, stifle
sdil, style / still
sdilesh, style(lish)
sdilest, style(list)
sdilist, style(list)
sdilush, style(lish)
sdime, stymie
sdimulashen, stimulate(tion)
sdimulate, stimulate
sdimulation, stimulate(tion)
sdirafom, styrofoam
sdirdy, sturdy
sdirefom, styrofoam
sdirty, sturdy
sdirufom, styrofoam
sdo, stow / store
sdoe, stow
sdoek, stoic
sdogee, stogy
sdogy, stogy
sdoik, stoic
sdok, stuck
sdol, stole
sdolen, stole(n)
sdolun, stole(n)
sdon, stun
sdools, stool(s)
sdooped, stupid
sdoopid, stupid
sdoopidudy, stupid(ity)

sdoopiduty, stupid(ity)
sdoopir, stupor
sdoopufid, stupefy(fied)
sdoopur, stupor
sdopid, stupid
sdored, story(ried)
sdoree, story
sdoreg, storage
sdorej, storage
sdores, story(ries)
sdorig, storage
sdorij, storage
sdorm, storm
sdormee, storm(y)
sdow, stow
sdowek, stoic
sdowik, stoic
sdra, straw / stray
sdradagee, strategy
sdradajist, strategy(gist)
sdrade, stray(ed) / straight
sdrades, stratus
sdradis, stratus
sdradugee, strategy
sdradugist, strategy(gist)
sdradus, stratus
sdrae, stray
sdrain, strain
sdrand, strain(ed) / strand
sdrane, strain
sdrap, strap
sdras, stress
sdratagee, strategy
sdrategek, strategic
sdrategekly, strategic(ally)
sdrategist, strategy(gist)
sdrategy, strategy
sdratejik, strategic
sdratejikly, strategic(ally)
sdratejist, strategy(gist)
sdrates, stratus
sdratesfere, stratosphere
sdratesphere, stratosphere
sdratigek, strategic
sdratigekly, strategic(ally)
sdratis, stratus
sdratosfere, stratosphere
sdratosphere, stratosphere
sdratugee, strategy
sdratugist, strategy(gist)
sdratus, stratus
sdratusfere, stratosphere
sdratusphere, stratosphere
sdraw, straw

sdrayd, stray(ed) / straight
sdreakee, streak(y)
sdrech, stretch
sdrecher, stretch(er)
sdrechr, stretch(er)
sdrechur, stretch(er)
sdreek, streak
sdreem, stream
sdreet, street
sdrek, streak
sdrekd, strict / streak(ed)
sdreke, streak(y)
sdreknine, strychnine
sdrekun, stricken
sdreky, streak(y)
sdrem, stream
sdremer, stream(er)
sdremur, stream(er)
sdreneus, strenuous
sdrenewus, strenuous
sdreng, string
sdrengee, string(y)
sdrengint, stringent
sdrenjint, stringent
sdrenkth, strength
sdrenth, strength
sdrenues, strenuous
sdrep, strep/ strip /stripe
sdrepd, stripe(d) / strip(pped)
sdreped, stripe(d) / strip(pped)
sdreper, stripe(r) / strip(pper)
sdrepur, stripe(r) / strip(pper)
sdres, stress
sdresh, stretch
sdret, street
sdreun, strewn
sdrew, strew
sdriashen, striate(tion)
sdriate, striate
sdriation, striate(tion)
sdrife, strife / strive
sdrik, strike
sdrikd, strict
sdriked, strict
sdriken, stricken
sdriknin, strychnine
sdrikun, stricken
sdrinewus, strenuous
sdring, string
sdringee, string(y)
sdrinjint, stringent
sdrinkth, strength
sdrinth, strength
sdrinues, strenuous

sdrip, strep/ strip /stripe
sdriped, stripe(d) / strip(pped)
sdripur, stripe(r) / strip(pper)
sdrivd, strive(d)
sdrive, strive / strife
sdro, straw
sdrobe, strobe
sdroganoff, stroganoff
sdroginof, stroganoff
sdroke, stroke
sdrol, stroll
sdroler, stroll(er)
sdrolur, stroll(er)
sdrong, strong
sdrongist, strong(est)
sdrongur, strong(er)
sdroodel, strudel
sdroodul, strudel
sdroon, strewn
sdrope, strobe
sdru, strew
sdruc, struck
sdud, stood / stud
sdrudel, strudel
sdrudid, strut(tted)
sdrudil, strudel
sdrudul, strudel
sdrueng, strew(ing)
sdrugel, struggle
sdrugul, struggle
sdruk, struck
sdrukchur, structure
sdrukshur, structure
sdrukul, struggle
sdrum, strum
sdrumer, strum(mmer)
sdrun, strewn
sdrung, strung
sdrut, strut
sdrutegek, strategic
sdrutegekly, strategic(ally)
sdrutejik, strategic
sdrutigekly, strategic(ally)
sdruz, strew(s)
sdryate, striate
sdubee, stub(bby)
sdubel, stubble
sdubern, stubborn
sduble, stubble
sduborn, stubborn
sdubul, stubble
sduburn, stubborn
sduby, stub(bby)
sduded, study(died) / stud(dded)

sdudee, study
sdudeo, studio
sduder, stutter
sdudes, study(dies)
sdudeus, studious
sdudio, studio
sdudir, stutter
sdudius, studious
sdudur, stutter
sdudy, study
sduel, stool
sdufee, stuff(y)
sduil, stool
sduk, stuck
sduko, stucco
sdule, stool
sdump, stump
sdumpee, stump(y)
sdun, stun
sdunk, stunk
sdunt, stunt / stun(nned)
sduol, stool
sdupafid, stupefy(fied)
sduped, stub(bbed) / stupid
sdupedudy, stupid(ity)
sdupeduty, stupid(ity)
sdupefy, stupefy
sdupel, stubble
sdupendus, stupendous
sduper, stupor
sdupidudy, stupid(ity)
sdupiduty, stupid(ity)
sdupify, stupefy
sdupil, stubble
sdupindus, stupendous
sdupir, stupor
sduple, stubble
sdupt, stub(bbed)
sdupud, stupid
sdupufie, stupefy
sdupul, stubble
sdupur, stupor
sdurdy, sturdy
sdurgen, sturgeon
sdurjon, sturgeon
sduter, stutter
sduty, study
sdwaple, squabble
sdylesh, style(lish)
sdyme, stymie
sdyrafom, styrofoam
se'ance, A COMMUNICATION WITH SPIRITS BEYOND THE PHYSICAL PLANE

sea,*, LARGE SALTWATER BODY/OCEAN (or see see) "prefixes: over/under"
seable, see(able)
seabul, see(able)
sead, seed / said
seaesta, siesta
seafood,*, EDIBLE SHELLFISH/AQUATIC ANIMALS
seal,*,led,ling,ler,lery,leries, AQUATIC MAMMAL, CLOSE SOMETHING TIGHTLY "prefixes: un/under"
sealeng, seal(ing) / ceiling
seam,*,med,ming,mer,mless,mlessly, mlessness,my, A LINE/ PLACE WHERE TWO PIECES OF MATERIAL ARE JOINED (or see seem) "prefixes: in/un"
seamen, semen
seamin, semen
seamly, seem(ly)
seamstress,ter, ONE WHO SEWS
sean, scene / seen
sear,*,red,ring, SCORCH/BURN/GRAZE A SURFACE (or see seer)
seara, sierra
search,hes,hed,hing,her,hable,hingly, hingness, TO LOOK/SEEK FOR SOMETHING "prefixes: un"
searchuble, search(able)
searus, scirrhus / cirrus
seas, cease / sea(s) / see(s) / seize
seasan, season
seashell,*, SHELL OF A MOLLUSK
seasin, season
season,*,ned,ning,nal,nally,ner,nable, nably,nableness, TIME OF THE YEAR, MIXTURE OF HERBS/SPICES FOR FOOD, EXPERIENCED/SKILLED "prefixes: un"
seasun, season
seat,*,ted,ting,ter, A PLACE/CHAIR/ BENCH TO SIT, SOMETHING FIRMLY FIT INTO PLACE, VACANCY FOR A PERSON "prefixes: re/un"
seath, seethe
seaz, seize
sebconchus, subconscious
sebkonshes, subconscious
sebkontrakt, subcontract
sebling, sibling
sebtek, septic
sebtember, september
sebtik, septic
sebtimbur, september

seburat, separate
sec, sic / sick
secandery, second(ary)
secandly, second(ly)
secant,*, MATHEMATICAL EXPRESSION, DIVIDE INTO TWO PARTS (or see second/secund)
secede,*,ed,ding,er, POLITICAL WITHDRAWAL
secendly, second(ly)
secesion, secession
secession,nal,nism,nist, TO SECEDE/WITHDRAW
secewler, secular
sech, sedge
sechewashen, situate(tion)
sechewation, situate(tion)
sechuate, situate
sechuation, situate(tion)
secindery, second(ary)
seckal, sickle
secks, sex
seckstee, sixty
seclude,ed,ding,usion,usive, BECOME PRIVATE/ISOLATED/SHELTERED FROM
seclushen, seclusion
seclusion,ive, BECOME SECLUDED
seclusive,ely,eness, BECOME SECLUDED
seclution, seclusion
second,*,ded,dly,dary,darily,der, AFTER THE FIRST, NOT PRIMARY, MEASURE OF TIME (or see secant/secund)
secondery, second(ary)
secoority, secure(rity)
secragate, segregate
secrat, secret
secratary, secretary
secratereul, secretary(rial)
secratery, secretary
secrative, secret(ive)
secreshen, secrete(tion)
secret,*,tly,tness,ecy,tive,tively,tiveness, PRIVATE KNOWLEDGE ONLY FEW SHARE, HIDE FROM OTHERS (or see secrete) "prefixes: post/semi"
secretareul, secretary(rial)
secretary,ries,rial, ONE WHO MAINTAINS PRIMARY OPERATIONS OF AN OFFICE "prefixes: under"
secrete,*,ed,ting,tion,tionary,tor,tory, FLUIDS THAT EXCRETE/DISCHARGE FROM ANIMALS/PLANTS/HUMANS

secretion, secrete(tion)
secrit, secret
secritary, secretary
secritereul, secretary(rial)
secritery, secretary
secritive, secret(ive)
secritly, secret(ly)
secrut, secret
secrutary, secretary
secrutereul, secretary(rial)
secrutery, secretary
secrutive, secret(ive)
secrutly, secret(ly)
secshen, section
secshenul, section(al)
secshun, section
secshunal, section(al)
sect,*,tarian,tarianism,tarianize, tarianizes,tarianized,tarianizing,tary, tile,tility, tion, SEGMENT/SECTION OF SOMETHING "prefixes: bi"
secter, sector
section,*,ned,ning,nal,nally,nalize, nalizes,nalized,nalizing,nalization, nalism, ONE PART OF THE WHOLE "prefixes: inter/re/sub"
sectir, sector
sector,*,rial, A PART/DIVISION OF THE WHOLE "prefixes: bi"
sectur, sector
secular,rly,rism,rist,ristic,rity,rities,rize, rizer, UNBIND FROM RELIGIOUS BELIEF
seculir, secular
secumb, succumb
secund,dly, BOTANICAL TERM (or see second/secant)
secundery, second(ary)
secundly, second(ly)
secure,*,ed,ring,rable,ely,eness,ement, er,rity,rities, PROTECT FROM CERTAIN ELEMENTS, KEEP FIRMLY IN PLACE "prefixes: bio/in/un"
securety, secure(rity)
securidy, secure(rity)
sed, said / set / seed
sedalment, settle(ment)
sedam, sedum
sedamentary, sediment(ary)
sedamint, sediment
sedan,*, TYPE OF VEHICLE
sedantary, sedentary
sedashen, sedate(tion)
sedasion, sedate(tion)

sedate,*,ed,ting,ely,eness,tion,tive, APPEASE/SUBSIDE/CALM
sedelment, settle(ment)
sedem, sedum
sedemint, sediment
sedentary,riness, NOT MUCH MOVEMENT/STILL
sedews, seduce
sedge,*,gy, A SWAMP GRASS WITH EDGES
sedil, settle
sedilment, settle(ment)
sedim, sedum
sediment,*,tary,tal,tation,tology,tologic, tologist, ACCUMULATION OF MATTER CARRIED BY LIQUID
sedle, settle
sedlers, settle(rs)
sedling, seedling / settle(ling)
sedlment, settle(ment)
sedol, settle
sedom, sedum
sedoose, seduce
seduce,*,ed,cing,er,cible,ction,ctive, ement,ctively,ctiveness, COERCED/ENTICED AWAY FROM NORMAL PATTERN OF BEHAVIOR
seducshen, seduce(ction)
seductif, seduce(ctive)
seduktion, seduce(ction)
seduktive, seduce(ctive)
sedul, settle
sedulers, settle(rs)
sedulment, settle(ment)
sedum,*, A PLANT
sedumentary, sediment(ary)
sedumint, sediment
seduntary, sedentary
seduse, seduce
sedy, seed(y)
see,*,eeable,eeing,een,eeing,eer,saw, USE OF THE EYES, VISUAL IMAGING (or see sea/seize) "prefixes: over"
seed,*,ded,ding,dless,dful,der,dy,dling, PLANT POD THAT HOLDS THE FUTURE, DNA BLUEPRINTS "prefixes: re/un"
seedling,*, GROWTH BURSTING FROM A SEED
seefood, seafood
seefud, seafood
seeg, siege
seej, siege
seek,*,ked,king,ker, TO SEARCH FOR

seekratif, secret(ive)
seekrutif, secret(ive)
seel, seal
seeld, seal(ed)
seem,*,med,ming,mingly,mingness,mly, mliness, APPEARS TO BE FACTUAL/ TRUTHFUL/REAL, COULD BE (or see seam) "prefixes: un"
seemstras, seamstress
seemstrus, seamstress
seen, PAST TENSE FOR THE WORD "SEE" (or see scene/seine) "prefixes: un"
seena, sienna
seengle, single
seengul, single
seengulerety, singular(ity)
seep,*,ped,ping,py,page, THE OOZING OF LIQUID THROUGH A BARRIER (or see sipe/ sip)
seepige, seep(age)
seepuge, seep(age)
seer,*, ONE WHO SEES/HAS SPIRITUAL INSIGHT/PREDICTOR OF THE FUTURE (or see sear)
seera, sierra
sees, see(s) / sea(s) / seize / cease / say(s)
seesan, season
seeshell, seashell
seesin, season
seesta, siesta
seesun, season
seethe,*,ed,hing,hingly, STATE OF AGITATION/EMOTION THAT IS BARELY CONTAINED
seety, seed(y)
seez, seize / cease / sea(s) / see(s)
sef, sieve
sefal, civil
sefalezation, civil(ization)
sefalis, syphilis
seful, civil
sefulization, civil(ization)
sefan, seven
sefanteen, seventeen
sefanth, seventh
sefaree, safari
sefenteith, seventieth
sefestikashen, sophisticate(tion)
sefestikation, sophisticate(tion)
sefichent, sufficient
sefichunt, sufficient
sefin, seven
sefinteen, seventeen
sefinteith, seventieth
sefinth, seventh
sefise, suffice
sefishent, sufficient
sefishunt, sufficient
sefistukashen, sophisticate(tion)
sefistukation, sophisticate(tion)
seflus, syphilis
sefon, seven
sefonteen, seventeen
sefood, seafood
sefral, several
sefrense, severance
sefril, several
sefrinse, severance
sefrul, several
sefrunse, severance
sefud, seafood
seful, civil
sefules, syphilis
sefulezation, civil(ization)
sefulization, civil(ization)
sefun, seven
sefunteen, seventeen
sefunteith, seventieth
sefunth, seventh
seg, siege / sedge
segar, cigar
segaret, cigarette
sege, sedge / siege
seged, siege(d)
seger, seize(zure)
seges, sedge(s) / siege(s)
segir, seize(zure)
segis, sedge(s)
segjest, suggest
segjestion, suggest(ion)
segjestshen, suggest(ion)
segma, sigma
segment,*,ted,ting,tary,tal,tally,tation, ONE PORTION/SECTION OF THE WHOLE
segmentul, segment(al)
segmintul, segment(al)
segmu, sigma
segnafiable, signify(fiable)
segnafier, signify(fier)
segnature, signature
segnifukent, significant
segnucher, signature
segnul, signal
segnushure, signature
segragashen, segregate(tion)
segragate, segregate
segregate,*,ed,ting,tion,tionist,tive,tor, able,ant, SET APART, SEPARATE/ DIVIDE FROM THE WHOLE
segrigate, segregate
segrugashen, segregate(tion)
segrugate, segregate
segur, seize(zure)
seguret, cigarette
segus, sedge(s)
seible, see(able)
seige, siege / sage
seine, A NET (or see seen/scene)
seing, see(ing)
seir, sear / seer
seira, sierra
seism,mic,mical,mically,micity,micities, mism,mogram,mograph,mology, mologist, FREQUENCY/WAVES OF THE EARTH, EARTHQUAKE
seista, siesta
seize,*,ed,zing,zure,zer, TO GRAB/ CONFISCATE QUICKLY/ FORECEFULLY (or see cease) "prefixes: dis"
sej, sedge / siege
sejd, siege(d)
sejer, seize(zure)
sejes, sedge(s)
sejt, siege(d)
sejur, seize(zure)
sejus, sedge(s)
sek, sic / sick / seek
sekal, sickle
sekamore, sycamore
sekand, secant / second / secund
sekandery, second(ary)
sekandly, second(ly)
sekendly, second(ly)
sekent, secant / second / secund
sekently, second(ly)
sekeuridy, secure(rity)
sekewlir, secular
sekewlur, secular
sekewr, secure
sekewrity, secure(rity)
sekiatrist, psychiatry(rist)
sekiatry, psychiatry
sekil, sickle
sekind, secant / second / secund
sekindery, second(ary)
sekindly, second(ly)
sekintly, second(ly)
sekir, seek(er)

sekle, sickle
seklushen, seclusion
seklusion, seclusion
seklusive, seclusive
sekma, sigma
sekment, segment
sekmentul, segment(al)
sekmint, segment
seknafiur, signify(fier)
seknafy, signify
seknashure, signature
seknifukent, significant
seknishure, signature
seknol, signal
seknucher, signature
seknul, signal
sekol, sickle
sekondery, second(ary)
sekragashen, segregate(tion)
sekragate, segregate
sekragation, segregate(tion)
sekrat, secret
sekratary, secretary
sekratereul, secretary(rial)
sekratery, secretary
sekratif, secret(ive)
sekrative, secret(ive)
sekregation, segregate(tion)
sekreshen, secrete(tion)
sekresion, secrete(tion)
sekret, secret / secrete
sekretive, secret(ive)
sekretly, secret(ly)
sekrigashen, segregate(tion)
sekrigate, segregate
sekrigation, segregate(tion)
sekrit, secret
sekritary, secretary
sekritereul, secretary(rial)
sekritery, secretary
sekritive, secret(ive)
sekritly, secret(ly)
sekrogate, segregate
sekrtly, secret(ly)
sekrugashen, segregate(tion)
sekrugate, segregate
sekrugation, segregate(tion)
sekrut, secret
sekrutary, secretary
sekrutef, secret(ive)
sekrutereul, secretary(rial)
sekrutery, secretary
sekrutive, secret(ive)
sekrutly, secret(ly)

seks, seek(s) / sex
sekshen, section
sekshenul, section(al)
sekshin, section
sekshinul, section(al)
sekshuel, sexual
sekshuil, sexual
sekshun, section
sekshunal, section(al)
sekshwal, sexual
seksion, section
seksis, sex(es)
seksless, sex(less)
sekst, sex(ed)
sekstant, sextant
sekste, sixty
seksteen, sixteen
seksteenth, sixteen(th)
sekstent, sextant
sekstet, sextet
seksteuth, sixtieth
seksth, sixth
sekstile, sextile
sekstileon, sextillion
sekstillion, sextillion
sekstiuth, sixtieth
sekstuple, sextuple
sekstuplet, sextuplet
sekstupul, sextuple
seksty, sixty
seksualedy, sexual(ity)
seksuality, sexual(ity)
seksus, sex(es)
seksy, sex(y)
sekt, sect / seek(ed)
sekter, sector
sekth, sixth
sektion, section
sektional, section(al)
sektir, sector
sektur, sector
sekul, sickle
sekular, secular
sekulir, secular
sekum, succumb
sekund, secant / second / secund
sekundery, second(ary)
sekundly, second(ly)
sekuntly, second(ly)
sekure, secure
sekuredy, secure(rity)
sekurity, secure(rity)
sekurly, secure(ly)
sekwal, sequel

sekwel, sequel
sekwen, sequin
sekwense, sequence
sekwenshul, sequence(ntial)
sekwential, sequence(ntial)
sekwents, sequence
sekwil, sequel
sekwin, sequin
sekwinse, sequence
sekwoia, sequoia
sekwoya, sequoia
sekwul, sequel
sekwunts, sequence
sel, seal / sell / sale / cell / sail
selabet, celibate
selabil, syllable
selable, syllable
selabrate, celebrate
selabus, syllabus
selafane, cellophane
selakit, silica(te)
selal, salal
selami, salami
selanoid, solenoid
selaphane, cellophane
selar, cellar / sell(er) / seal(er)
selareum, solarium
selary, celery
selawet, silhouette
seld, seal(ed) / sold
seldem, seldom
seldemly, seldom(ly)
seldom,mly,mness, RARELY/
    INFREQUENTLY
seldumly, seldom(ly)
selebrety, celebrity
selebusy, celibate(acy)
select,*,ted,ting,tion,tionist,tness,tor,
    tee,tive,tively,tiveness, tivity,
    CHOOSE ONE AMONG MANY
    "prefixes: de"
selee, silly
selekshen, select(ion)
selekt, select
selektif, select(ive)
selektion, select(ion)
selektive, select(ive)
seleng, ceiling / seal(ing)
selenic,ide,iferous,ious,ite,ium,
    CHEMICAL ELEMENT
selenium,iferous, NONMETALLIC
    ELEMENT
selenoid, solenoid
seler, cellar / seal(er) / sell(er)

selery, celery
self,lves,flessly,flessness,fish, FIRST PERSON
selfer, silver
selferware, silverware
selfesh, selfish
selfeshly, selfish(ly)
selfir, silver
selfish,hly,hness, LESS THOUGHT FOR OTHERS THAN FOR SELF "prefixes: un"
selfishlis, selfish(less)
selflis, self(less)
selflisness, self(lessness)
selfs, self(lves)
selfurware, silverware
selfury, silver(y)
selfush, selfish
seli, silly
selibet, celibate
selibrate, celebrate
selibuse, celibate(acy)
selicon, silicon / silicone
selifane, cellophane
selilaquy, soliloquy
selines, silly(lliness)
seling, ceiling / sell(ing) / seal(ing)
selinoid, solenoid
selir, cellar / seal(er) / sell(er)
seliset, solicit
selisetation, solicit(ation)
seliseter, solicit(er)
selivu, saliva
selk, silk
selkun, silk(en)
selky, silk(y)
sell,*,lling,ller,sale,sold, TRADE GOODS/ SERVICES FOR MONEY (or see sail/ sale/sill/seal) "prefixes: over/un/ under"
seller, cellar / sell(er)
sellfish, selfish
selluler, cellular
sellur, cellar / sell(er) / seal(er)
seloet, silhouette
selofane, cellophane
selomee, salami
selon, salon
selonoid, solenoid
seloon, saloon
seloot, salute
selor, cellar / seal(er) / sell(er)
sels, sell(s) / seal(s) / sail(s)
selseus, celsius

selt, seal(ed) / sold / silt / sail(ed)
seltashen, silt(ation)
seltation, silt(ation)
seltem, seldom
seltum, seldom
selty, silt(y)
selubasy, celibate(acy)
selubel, syllable
selubet, celibate
selubrate, celebrate
selubus, syllabus
selufane, cellophane
selukon, silicon / silicone
selular, cellular
selulite, cellulite
selulose, cellulose
selune, saloon
selunoid, solenoid
selur, cellar / sell(er) / seal(er)
selure, celery
selushen, solution
selute, salute
selution, solution
selverware, silverware
selvir, silver
selvurware, silverware
selvury, silver(y)
sely, silly
semalarity, similar(ity)
semaler, similar
semalerly, similar(ly)
semanar, seminar
semantics,cal,cally,cist, STUDY OF LANGUAGE/WORDS
semar, simmer
semashen, sum(mation)
semation, sum(mation)
sematry, symmetry
sembal, symbol
sembalism, symbol(ism)
sembathetik, sympathetic
sembathy, sympathy
sembeodik, symbiotic
sembeosis, symbiosis
sembeotek, symbiotic
sembilism, symbol(ism)
sembiosis, symbiosis
semblance,*, SIMILARITY/ RESEMBLANCE
semble, symbol
semblents, semblance
semblinse, semblance
sembolek, symbol(ic)
sembolik, symbol(ic)

sembul, cymbal / symbol
sembulism, symbol(ism)
sembuthetik, sympathetic
sembuthy, sympathy
semdum, symptom
semecolon, semicolon
semekolun, semicolon
semelur, similar
semelurly, similar(ly)
semen,miniferous,minal, SUBSTANCE CONTAINING MALE SPERM
semenal, seminal
semenar, seminar
sement, cement
semenul, seminal
semesder, semester
semester,*,tral,trial, SIX MONTH PERIOD OF TIME
semetary, cemetery
semetric, symmetry(ric)
semetry, symmetry
semeulate, simulate
semewlation, simulate(tion)
semfeny, symphony
semfonic, symphony(nic)
semfune, symphony
semi, PREFIX INDICATING "HALF/ PARTLY" MOST OFTEN MODIFIES THE WORD
semicolon,*, A PUNCTUATION MARK
semikolin, semicolon
semilarity, similar(ity)
semiler, similar
semilerly, similar(ly)
semin, semen
seminal,lly,niferous, CAPABLE OF CREATING LIFE/FUTURE DEVELOPMENT
seminar,*,rian,ries,ry, A GROUP OF PEOPLE CONVERGING TOGETHER TO LEARN ONE THING IN PARTICULAR
semingly, seem(ingly)
semir, simmer
semitary, cemetery
semliness, seem(liness)
semly, seem(ly)
semon, semen
semonal, seminal
semonar, seminar
semoolader, simulate(tor)
sempal, simple
sempalest, simple(st)
sempaly, simple(ly)

sempathee, sympathy
sempathetic, sympathetic
sempathize, sympathy(hize)
sempathy, sympathy
sempdum, symptom
sempel, simple
sempelist, simple(st)
sempethy, sympathy
semphonek, symphony(nic)
semphonic, symphony(nic)
semphuny, symphony
sempithize, sympathy(hize)
sempithy, sympathy
semple, simple
sempler, simple(r)
semplest, simple(st)
semplisity, simple(licity)
semplistec, simple(listic)
semply, simple(ly)
sempol, simple
sempoler, simple(r)
sempolest, simple(st)
semposeum, symposium
sempozeum, symposium
semptem, symptom
semptum, symptom
sempul, simple
sempuler, simple(r)
sempulest, simple(st)
sempuly, simple(ly)
semputhee, sympathy
semputhetic, sympathetic
semputhize, sympathy(hize)
semstras, seamstress
semstrus, seamstress
semtem, symptom
semtum, symptom
semulader, simulate(tor)
semularly, similar(ly)
semulashen, simulate(tion)
semulate, simulate
semulation, simulate(tion)
semulator, simulate(tor)
semuler, similar
semulerly, similar(ly)
semullarety, similar(ity)
semun, semen
semunal, seminal
semunar, seminar
semur, simmer
semutare, cemetery
semutree, symmetry
semwat, somewhat
semwere, somewhere

semwhat, somewhat
semwhere, somewhere
semwot, somewhat
sen, seen / scene / seine / sin
senada, sonata
senak, scene(nic)
senamon, cinnamon
senanem, synonym
senapse, synapse
senapsis, synapsis
senaptek, synaptic
senaptic, synaptic
senareo, scenario
senary, scene(ry)
senaster, sinister
senate,tor, A BODY/HOUSE OF U.S. GOVERNMENT
senator,*,rial,rially,rship, ELECTED MEMBER OF THE U.S. GOVERNMENT
senatoriel, senator(ial)
senatu, sonata
senc, sync / sink / since
sench, cinch
senched, singe(d) / cinch(ed)
senchro, synchro
senchronus, synchrony(nous)
sencht, singe(d) / cinch(ed)
senchual, sensual
sencro, synchro
sencronize, synchrony(nize)
sencrony, synchrony
send,*,ding,der,nt, PUSH/ENCOURAGE SOMETHING TO LEAVE YOUR VICINITY, HAVE DELIVERED
sendamental, sentiment(al)
sendamintal, sentiment(al)
sender, cinder / send(er)
sendicate, syndicate
sendication, syndicate(tion)
sendikation, syndicate(tion)
sendiket, syndicate
sendral, central
sendrem, syndrome
sendrum, syndrome
sendukit, syndicate
sendumentil, sentiment(al)
sendumeter, centimeter
sene, scene / seen
sened, sin(nned)
senek, scene(nic)
senema, cinema
seneority, senior(ity)
sener, sin(nner)

senerist, scenario(ist)
senery, scene(ry)
senete, senate
senetor, senator
senew, sinew
senful, sin(ful)
senfuly, sin(fully)
seng, sing / sink / singe / cinch
sengal, single
senge, singe / cinch
senged, singe(d) / cinch(ed)
sengel, single
senger, sing(er)
sengewler, singular
sengle, single
sengs, sing(s) / sink(s)
sengt, singe(d) / cinch(ed)
sengul, single
sengularedy, singular(ity)
sengularly, singular(ly)
senguled, single(d)
senguler, singular
senguleridy, singular(ity)
senguly, single(ly)
senical, cynical
senik, cynic / scene(nic)
senile,lity, WHEN THE MIND CEASES TO STAY SHARP/ALERT DUE TO AGING
senilidy, senile(lity)
senior,*,rity, UPPER RANK, OLDER THAN MOST, HIGHER IN CLASS
senir, sin(nner)
senirgy, synergy
seniry, scene(ry)
senistur, sinister
senite, senate
senitor, senator
senitoreul, senator(ial)
senj, singe / cinch
senjt, singe(d) / cinch(ed)
senk, sync / sink
senker, sink(er) / sing(er)
senkewler, singular
senkil, single
senkir, sink(er) / sing(er)
senkle, single(ly)
senkranes, synchrony(nous)
senkro, synchro
senkrone, synchrony
senkronize, synchrony(nize)
senkrunus, synchrony(nous)
senkt, sink(ed)
senkul, single
senkularedy, singular(ity)

senkularly, singular(ly)
senkuler, singular
senkur, sink(er) / sing(er)
senles, sin(less)
senoda, sonata
senodu, sonata
senografee, scenography
senography, scenography
senonemus, synonym(ous)
senonim, synonym
senonimus, synonym(ous)
senonym, synonym
senopsis, synopsis
senota, sonata
senotor, senator
sens, sense / since / cent(s) / sin(s) / scene(s)
sensability, sensible(bility)
sensable, sensible
sensaridy, sincere(rity)
sensarity, sincere(rity)
sensashen, sensation
sensation,*,nal,nally,nalism,nalist, nalistic, A FEELING/SENSE/ KNOWINGNESS OF AN AFFECT
sensative, sensitive
sensatize, sensitize
sensd, sense(d)
sense,*,ed,sing,eless,sor,sors,sorial, sorially,sorium,sory, FEEL/KNOW THE SIX SENSES; SOUND/SIGHT/ SMELL/TASTE/ TOUCH/FEEL (or see sent/cent(s)/scene(s)) "prefixes: non"
sensebility, sensible(bility)
senseble, sensible
senser, sincere / censor
sensere, sincere / censor
senseredy, sincere(rity)
senserity, sincere(rity)
senserly, sincere(ly)
sensetize, sensitize
senshewality, sensual(ity)
senshewus, sensuous
senshual, sensual
senshuality, sensual(ity)
senshues, sensuous
senshuil, sensual
senshury, century
sensible,eness,ly,bility,bilities, BE NORMAL/PREDICTABLE TO OTHERS "prefixes: in"
sensir, sensor / censor / censure

sensitive,ely,eness,vity,vities,ize,ization, izer, READILY RESPONDS TO STIMULUS "prefixes: de/in/pre"
sensitivity, sensitive(vity)
sensitize,*,ed,zing,zation,er, BECOME VERY SENSITIVE TO STIMULUS "prefixes: de"
sensless, sense(less)
sensor,*,red,ring,rial,rially,rium,ry, ABLE TO RESPOND TO A PARTICULAR STIMULUS/IMPULSE (or see censor/censure) "prefixes: bio"
sensoreal, sensor(ial)
sensual,lity,lly,lism,list,listic,lize,lization, uous, OPEN TO THE BODY'S EXPRESSION/DESIRE/FEELINGS, UNINHIBITED
sensuble, sensible
sensuous,sly,sness, OF BEING SENSUAL
sensur, sensor / censor / censure
sensus, census / sense(s)
sensutive, sensitive
sensutivity, sensitive(vity)
sensutize, sensitize
sent, PAST TENSE FOR THE WORD 'SEND' (or see scent/sin(nned))
sentaks, syntax
sentamental, sentiment(al)
sentax, syntax
sentchuous, sensuous
sented, scent(ed)
senteince, sentient(ncy)
senteint, sentient
sentekit, syndicate
sentement, sentiment
sentemental, sentiment(al)
sentence,*,ed,cing,ntial,ntially, COMPLETE THOUGHT GRAMMATICALLY, FORMAL JUDGEMENT/DECISION
senteneul, centennial
sentennial, centennial
sentense, sentence
senter, center
senthasis, synthesis
senthasize, synthesize
senthedik, synthetic
senthesis, synthesis
senthetic, synthetic
senthusis, synthesis
sentient,tly,nce,ncy, ABILITY/FACULTY TO PERCEIVE CONSCIOUSLY "prefixes: in/pre"

sentigrade, centigrade
sentiment,*,tal,tally,tality,talities,talism, talist,talize,talizes,talized,talizing, talization, EMOTIONALLY SWAYED BY THE PAST
sentimeter, centimeter
sentineol, centennial
sentinse, sentence
sentipede, centipede
sentless, scent(less)
sentrul, central
sentrulize, centralize
sentry,ries, A GUARD FOR GATE/ENTRY
sents, since / sense / cent(s) / scent(s)
senttance, sentence
sentument, sentiment
sentumental, sentiment(al)
sentury, century
senu, sinew
senuee, sinew(y)
senuk, scene(nic)
senunem, synonym
senupeded, centipede
senur, sin(nner)
senurgy, synergy
senury, scene(ry)
senuster, sinister
senute, senate
senutor, senator
senutoreul, senator(ial)
senutorial, senator(ial)
senuw, sinew
senuy, sinew(y)
senyer, senior
senyority, senior(ity)
senyuee, sinew(y)
senyur, senior
seonse, se'ance
sep, seep / sip / sipe
sepage, seep(age)
sepal,*,led,lous,loid, PART OF A FLOWER
separable,bility,eness,bly, ABLE TO BE SEPARATED "prefixes: in"
separador, separator
separashen, separate(tion)
separate,*,ed,ting,tion,ely,eness,tist, tism,tistic,tive,tor, DIVIDE/BREAK APART FROM THE WHOLE "prefixes: bio"
separator,*, THAT WHICH ENCOURAGES SEPARATION
separet, separate
separite, separate

sepausatory, suppository
sepd, sip(pped) / seep(ed)
sepea, sepia
sepege, seep(age)
sepej, seep(age)
sepena, subpoena
seperabul, separable
seperader, separator
seperashen, separate(tion)
seperate, separate
seperately, separate(tly)
seperation, separate(tion)
seperatly, separate(tly)
seperator, separator
seperible, separable
seperubil, separable
sepeu, sepia
sephelis, syphilis
sephules, syphilis
sepia, A COLOR/PIGMENT, A FISH
sepige, seep(age)
sepij, seep(age)
sepil, sepal
sepirable, separable
sepirador, separator
sepirashen, separate(tion)
sepirate, separate
sepiration, separate(tion)
sepirator, separator
sepirlative, superlative
sepiruble, separable
sepkonshes, subconscious
sepkontrakt, subcontract
seplant, supplant
seple, sepal
sepli, supply
seplier, supply(lier)
sepling, sibling
sepliur, supply(lier)
seply, supply
sepol, sepal
seport, support
seportive, support(ive)
sepose, suppose
seposetory, suppository
seposubly, suppose(dly)
sepozatory, suppository
sepoze, suppose
sepozubly, suppose(dly)
seprabul, separable
seprashen, separate(tion)
seprat, separate
sepratisem, separate(tism)
seprative, separate(tive)

sepratly, separate(tly)
seprator, separator
seprechen, suppress(ion)
sepreem, supreme
sepreme, supreme
sepres, suppress
sepreshen, suppress(ion)
sepret, separate
sepretion, suppress(ion)
sepretism, separate(tism)
sepretive, separate(tive)
sepretly, separate(tly)
sepribul, separable
seprino, soprano
seprit, separate
sepritesm, separate(tism)
sepritly, separate(tly)
sepruble, separable
seprut, separate
seprutly, separate(tly)
septar, scepter
septek, septic / styptic
september, A MONTH OF THE YEAR (ENGLISH)
septer, scepter
septic,*,cally,city, THAT WHICH CAUSES PUTREFACTION OR SEPSIS, OF BEING ROTTEN
septik, styptic
septimber, september
septir, scepter
septisity, septic(ity)
septor, scepter
septupil, septuple
septuple,*,ed,ling, SEVEN TIMES/FOLD
septur, scepter
sepuge, seep(age)
sepuj, seep(age)
sepul, sepal
sepurabul, separable
sepurador, separator
sepurashen, separate(tion)
sepurate, separate
sepurately, separate(tly)
sepurater, separator
sepuration, separate(tion)
sepurb, superb
sepurblee, superb(ly)
sepurible, separable
sepurlative, superlative
sequel,*,litis, CONTINUATION ON THE STORY

sequence,*,ed,cing,cy,er,ntial,ntially, SERIES/PARTS ALIGNED IN ORDER/PATTERN
sequenshil, sequence(ntial)
sequer, secure
sequerity, secure(rity)
sequerly, secure(ly)
sequill, sequel
sequin,*,ned, SMALL REFLECTIVE DECORATIONS USED ON CLOTHING
sequir, secure
sequoia,*, TYPE OF TREE, A TRIBE
seqwen, sequin
ser, seer / sir / sear
seraget, surrogate
seran, saran
seranade, serenade
serandipity, serendipity
serandipudy, serendipity
serap, syrup
serape,*, OUTER GARMENT/BLANKET/SHAWL
serashen, serrate(tion)
serated, serrate(d)
seration, serrate(tion)
serbent, serpent
sercafigus, sarcophagus
sercamscribe, circumscribe
sercas, circus
sercemscribe, circumscribe
serch, search
sercharj, surcharge
serchuble, search(able)
sercit, circuit
sercle, circle
sercomscribe, circumscribe
sercophagus, sarcophagus
sercot, circuit
sercumfurens, circumference
sercumscribe, circumscribe
sercumsize, circumcise
sercumstans, circumstance
sercus, circus
sercut, circuit
serdafication, certificate(tion)
serdanly, certain(ly)
serdatude, certitude
serdenly, certain(ly)
serdufication, certificate(tion)
serdufy, certify
serdunly, certain(ly)
serdutude, certitude
sereal, serial / cereal / surreal
serealism, surrealism

serebral, cerebral
serebrul, cerebral
serees, series
serel, sorrel / surreal
serelism, surrealism
serenade,*,ed,ding,er, SOLITARY PERFORMANCE BY SOMEONE FOR SOMEONE IN PARTICULAR
serender, surrender
serendipity,tous, UNEXPECTED/ ACCIDENTAL HAPPY ENDING
serene,nly,eness,nity,nities, TRANQUIL/ PEACEFUL
sereol, serial / cereal
serep, syrup
sereul, serial / cereal
sereulizum, surrealism
sereus, serious
sereusly, serious(ly)
serf,*,fage,fdom,fhood,fish, WORKER WHO BELONGED WITH THE LAND (or see surf/serve)
serface, surface
serfdum, serf(dom)
serfee, surf(y)
serfej, serf(age)
serfes, surface
serfis, surface / service
serfuge, serf(age)
serfunt, servant
serfur, surf(er)
serfus, surface / service
sergd, surge(d)
serge, A TWILLED FABRIC (or see surge)
sergeant,*,ncy, A RANK/POSITION WITHIN THE U.S. MILITARY/POLICE
sergen, surgeon
sergent, sergeant / surgent
sergeon, surgeon
sergery, surgery
sergikul, surgical
sergin, surgeon
sergiry, surgery
sergon, surgeon
sergree, surgery
sergukle, surgical
serguree, surgery
serial,lly,list,lize,lization, SUCCESSIVE NUMBER/SERIES (or see cereal) "prefixes: uni"
seriasis, psoriasis
series, CORRESPONDING/SUCCESSIVE EVENTS/ITEMS
serim, serum

serimony, ceremony
serinade, serenade
serinder, surrender
serindipity, serendipity
serindipudy, serendipity
serious,sly,sness, EARNEST/SOLEMN/ GRAVE
serip, syrup
seris, scirrhus / cirrus
seriulesm, surrealism
serius, serious
seriusis, psoriasis
serjakle, surgical
serjaree, surgery
serje, surge / serge
serjen, surgeon
serjent, sergeant / surgent
serjikul, surgical
serjint, sergeant / surgent
serjon, surgeon
serjree, surgery
serjukle, surgical
serkemscribe, circumscribe
serkemsize, circumcise
serkes, circus
serket, circuit
serkimscribe, circumscribe
serkimsize, circumcise
serkimstans, circumstance
serkis, circus
serkit, circuit
serkle, circle
serkofegus, sarcophagus
serkofigus, sarcophagus
serkomscribe, circumscribe
serkulate, circulate
serkuler, circular
serkumfurense, circumference
serkumsize, circumcise
serkumstans, circumstance
serkus, circus
serkut, circuit
serlee, surly
serloin, sirloin
serly, surly
serman, sermon
sermize, surmise
sermon,*,nic,nize,nizer, A RELIGIOUS DISCOURSE
sermun, sermon
serogate, surrogate
serondipity, serendipity
serong, sarong
serope, serape

seroredy, sorority
serority, sorority
seros, scirrhus / cirrus
seround, surround
serownd, surround
serpas, surpass
serpent,*, A SNAKE
serpentene, serpentine
serpentine, SHAPED/MOVEMENT OF A SNAKE
serpint, serpent
serpintene, serpentine
serplus, surplus
serprize, surprise
serrate,*,ed,ting,tion, JAGGED/ TOOTHED OUTLINE LIKE A SAW
serrender, surrender
sersharge, surcharge
sertafy, certify
sertanle, certain(ly)
sertatude, certitude
sertefication, certificate(tion)
sertenly, certain(ly)
sertification, certificate(tion)
sertificut, certificate
sertifikashen, certificate(tion)
sertifucate, certificate
sertin, certain
sertinle, certain(ly)
sertinly, certain(ly)
sertufie, certify
sertunly, certain(ly)
seruget, surrogate
serum,*, A FLUID OF INOCULATION
serumony, ceremony
serunade, serenade
serundipety, serendipity
serundipudy, serendipity
serup, syrup
serus, cirrus / scirrhus
serva, survey
servaer, survey(or)
servailense, surveillance
servalinse, surveillance
servant,*, ONE EMPLOYED/OWNED TO PERFORM DOMESTIC CHORES/ WORK
servatood, servitude
servatude, servitude
servaur, survey(or)
servayer, survey(or)
serve,*,ed,ving,er,vant,vice,vitude, ONE WHO PUTS A BALL INTO PLAY,

PERFORM DUTIES FOR OTHERS "prefixes: sub"
serveilinse, surveillance
servent, servant
serveor, survey(or)
serves, service
serveyor, survey(or)
service,*,ed,cing,eable,eability, eableness,eably, PROVIDE OR ACCOMMODATE SOMEONE/ SOMETHING "prefixes: dis/inter"
servife, survive
serviks, cervix
servint, servant
servisuble, service(cable)
servitude, TO BE IN THE SERVICE OF OTHERS
servive, survive
serviver, survive(vor)
servivul, survive(val)
servunt, servant
servusable, service(cable)
servutude, servitude
ses, see(s) / sea(s) / seize / cease
sesal, sizzle
sesame,*, AN EDIBLE SEED
sesan, season
sesdamadik, system(atic)
sesdamatic, system(atic)
sesdan, sustain
sesdum, system
sesdumadik, system(atic)
sesdumatic, system(atic)
sesede, secede
sesee, sissy
sesel, sizzle
sesen, season
seseptability, susceptible(bility)
seseptif, susceptive
seseptive, susceptive
sesers, scissor(s)
seset, secede
sesetion, secession
seshell, seashell
seshon, session
sesil, sizzle
sesime, sesame
sesin, season
sesion, session
sesirs, scissor(s)
sesle, sizzle
sesmek, seism(ic)
sesmic, seism(ic)
sesmical, seism(ical)

sesmik, seism(ic)
sesome, sesame
seson, season
sesors, scissor(s)
sespend, suspend
sespishus, suspicious
session,*,nal, A PERIOD/COURSE/ SPECIFIC OF TIME "prefixes: inter"
sest, cyst / zest
sestain, sustain
sestane, sustain
sestanuble, sustain(able)
sester, sister
sestim, system
sestir, sister
sestum, system
sestumatic, system(atic)
sestur, sister
sesturly, sister(ly)
sesturn, cistern
sesul, sizzle
sesume, sesame
sesun, season
sesurs, scissor(s)
sesy, sissy
set,*,tting,ttee,tter,sat, COLLECTION OF SIMILAR ITEMS, PUT INTO PLACE (or see sit/seat/said) "prefixes: in/over/pre/re/sub/un/under"
setal, settle
setalment, settle(ment)
setament, sediment
setamentary, sediment(ary)
setamint, sediment
setanic, satanic
setanikul, satanic(al)
setantary, sedentary
setchuashen, situate(tion)
setee, set(ttee)
setel, settle
setelment, settle(ment)
setemint, sediment
setemintary, sediment(ary)
setentary, sedentary
seter, set(tter)
seterical, satire(rical)
seth, seethe / scythe
setil, settle
setilment, settle(ment)
setintary, sedentary
setion, session
setir, set(tter)
setle, settle
setling, seedling / settle(ling)

setlment, settle(ment)
settle,*,ed,ling,ement,er, FINAL AGREEMENT, BECOME STATIONARY "prefixes: re/un"
setuashen, situate(tion)
setuation, situate(tion)
setul, settle
setulers, settle(rs)
setulment, settle(ment)
setumentary, sediment(ary)
setuntary, sedentary
setur, set(tter) / seat(er) / seed(er)
sety, city
seubil, see(able)
seuble, see(able)
seuler, cellular
seur, sear / seer
sev, sieve
sevan, seven
sevandy, seventy
sevant, savant
sevanteen, seventeen
sevanteith, seventieth
sevanth, seventh
sevanty, seventy
sevanu, savanna
sevarul, several
seven,*,nteen,nth,ntieth,nty, A NUMBER
sevendeith, seventieth
sevendy, seventy
seventeen, A DOUBLE DIGIT NUMBER
seventh, PLACE IN THE NUMBER SEQUENCE WHICH COMES AFTER THE 6TH
seventieth, COMES AFTER THE 69TH IN NUMBER SEQUENCE
seventy,ties, COMES AFTER 69 IN NUMBER SEQUENCE
sever,*,red,ring,rable,ralty,rance, TO CUT OFF/ SEPARATE FROM THE HOST (or see severe)
several,lly, MORE THAN TWO
severance, SEPARATION/SPLIT/ PARTING, FROM THE WORD "SEVER"
severe,ely,eness,rity,rities, EXTREME/ HARSH/PUNISHING (or see sever)
severedy, severe(rity)
severinse, severance
severly, severe(ly)
severt, sever(ed)
severul, several
severunse, severance

sevik, civic
sevil, civil
sevilean, civilian
sevin, seven
sevindeith, seventieth
sevindy, seventy
sevinteen, seventeen
sevinteith, seventieth
sevinth, seventh
sevinty, seventy
seviral, several
seviranse, severance
sevird, severe(d)
sevire, severe / sever
sevirly, severe(ly)
sevirt, sever(ed)
sevirunse, severance
sevlazation, civil(ization)
sevlization, civil(ization)
sevlozation, civil(ization)
sevluzation, civil(ization)
sevol, civil
sevolazation, civil(ization)
sevon, seven
sevondeith, seventieth
sevondy, seventy
sevont, savant
sevonteen, seventeen
sevonteith, seventieth
sevor, sever
sevr, sever
sevral, several
sevrense, severance
sevrul, several
sevrunse, severance
sevt, sift / sieve(d)
sevun, seven
sevundeith, seventieth
sevundy, seventy
sevunteen, seventeen
sevunteith, seventieth
sevunth, seventh
sevunty, seventy
sevur, sever
sevural, several
sevuranse, severance
sevurd, sever(ed)
sew,*,wed,wing,wer,wn, TO JOIN/ UNITE PIECES WITH STITCHES (or see so/sow) "prefixes: over"
sewage, WASTE MATTER
sewaro, saguaro
sewd, sue(d) / sew(ed)
sewdanim, pseudonym

sewdo, pseudo
sewdonim, pseudonym
sewer,*,wage,rage, A CHANNEL FOR WASTE/WATER, SOMEONE WHO SEWS (or see sew(er))
sewfaner, souvenir
sewfineer, souvenir
sewflay, souffle'
sewfuner, souvenir
sewkrose, sucrose
sewn, PAST TENSE FOR THE WORD "SEW" (or see son/sown)
seworo, saguaro
sewpee, soup(y)
sewperb, superb
sewpurb, superb
sewpy, soup(y)
sewt, soot / suit
sewtanim, pseudonym
sewto, pseudo
sewtonim, pseudonym
sewture, suture
sex,xes,xed,xing,xless,xy,xier,xiest,xily, xiness,xual, CONCERNING THE REPRODUCTIVE AREAS "prefixes: de/inter/over/ under/uni"
sexest, sexist
sexis, sex(es)
sexist,*, A MAN WHO EXPLOITS/ DISCRIMINATES AGAINST WOMEN "prefixes: non"
sexshen, section
sexshin, section
sexshinul, section(al)
sexshualedy, sexual(ity)
sexshuality, sexual(ity)
sexshunol, section(al)
sexshwal, sexual
sextant,*, SIXTH PART OF A CIRCLE, AN INSTRUMENT
sexteen, sixteen
sextenth, sixteen(th)
sextet,*, SIX IN A GROUP
sexth, sixth
sextile,llion, ASTRONOMICAL/ STATISTICAL EXPRESSION, 1/6TH OF ANYTHING
sextileon, sextillion
sextilion, sextillion
sextillion,*,nth, A NUMBER FOLLOWED BY 21 OR 36 ZEROS
sextint, sextant
sextion, section
sextional, section(al)

sextuple,*,ed,ling,et, SIX FOLDS/PARTS/ TIMES
sextuplet,*, SIX EQUAL
sexual,lly,lity,lize,lizes,lized,lizing, PERTAINING TO THE FIRST SEAL/ CHAKRA, FEATURE OF REPRODUCTION "prefixes: bi/de/ inter/intra/non/uni"
sexuol, sexual
sexuoly, sexual(lly)
sexus, sex(es)
sexyewality, sexual(ity)
sexyewul, sexual
sexyuality, sexual(ity)
sexyuol, sexual
seyer, sear / seer
seyons, se'ance
seyur, sear / seer
sez, seize / cease / sea(s) / see(s)
sezal, sizzle
sezen, season
sezil, sizzle
sezin, season
sezle, sizzle
sezmek, seism(ic)
sezmic, seism(ic)
sezmical, seism(ical)
sezors, scissor(s)
sezul, sizzle
sezun, season
sezurs, scissor(s)
sfarekil, sphere(rical)
sfeer, sphere
sfencks, sphinx
sfencter, sphincter
sfenktur, sphincter
sfenx, sphinx
sfer, sphere
sferakil, sphere(rical)
sfere, sphere
sferekul, sphere(rical)
sferical, sphere(rical)
sferukle, sphere(rical)
sfincter, sphincter
sfinks, sphinx
sfinktur, sphincter
sfinx, sphinx
sgoundrel, scoundrel
sgowndrul, scoundrel
sgragliest, scraggly(liest)
sgrakleur, scraggly(lier)
shabby,bbier,bbiest,bbily,bbiness, WORN, THREADBARE
shabely, shabby(bbily)

shabiness, shabby(bbiness)
shaby, shabby
shack,*,ked,king, SHANTY, PRIMITIVE HUT, CABIN (or see shag/shake)
shackle,*,ed,ling,er, A FASTENER, CUFFS "prefixes: un"
shade,*,ed,ding,dy,eless, OVERHEAD PROTECTION FROM THE SUN
shader, shatter
shadey, shade(dy)
shadir, shatter
shado, shadow
shadow,*,wed,wing,wer,wy, AREA WHERE THE LIGHT DOESN'T PENETRATE, SCREEN/PROTECT "prefixes: over"
shadur, shatter
shaem, shame
shaemful, shame(ful)
shaenk, shank
shafd, shaft / shave(d) / chafe(d)
shafe, shave / chafe
shafed, shaft / shave(d)
shaft,*,ted,ting, NARROW COLUMN/ CYLINDER (or see chafe(d)/ shave(d))
shag,gged,gging,ggy,ggier,ggiest, CARPET, TO RETRIEVE, LOOSE THREADS (or see shack)
shagier, shag(ggier)
shagiest, shag(ggiest) / shake(kiest)
shagy, shag(ggy)
shaim, shame
shaimless, shame(less)
shaink, shank
shak, shack / shake
shake,*,ed,king,er,ky,kier,kiest,hook, JUMBLE, JOSTLE, VIBRATE, MOVE UP/DOWN, BUILDING MATERIAL (or see shack) "prefixes: un"
shaked, shack(ed) / shake(d)
shakel, shackle
shakul, shackle
shakult, shackle(d)
shakyest, shake(kiest)
shal, shall / shale / shawl
shale,*, TYPE OF CLAY/ROCK (or see shell)
shalet, shallot
shalit, shallot
shall, COULD, ALLOWED/ABLE TO (or see shawl)
shallot,*, PLANT BULBS USED IN COOKING

shallow,*,wly,wness, OF LITTLE DEPTH, SUPERFICIAL
shalo, shallow
shaloness, shallow(ness)
shalons, chalant(nce)
shalont, chalant
shalot, shallot
shalow, shallow
shalowness, shallow(ness)
shalut, shallot
sham,mmed,mming,mmer, COVER-UP FOR THE TRUTH (or see shame)
shaman,*,nic,nism,nist,nistic, WISE ONE WITH SPIRITUAL POWERS
shambal, shamble
shamble,*,ed,ling, UNSTEADY, DISORDER
shambul, shamble
shame,*,ed,ming,eful,efully,efulness, eless, DISGRACED, DISHONORED (or see sham)
shamed, shame(d) / sham(mmed)
shamen, shaman
shamer, sham(mmer)
shamful, shame(ful)
shamin, shaman
shaminesm, shaman(ism)
shamless, shame(less)
shamonek, shaman(ic)
shamonism, shaman(ism)
shample, shamble
shampoo,*,ooed,ooing,ooer, USE SOAP TO CLEAN HAIR/CARPET/ UPHOLSTERY
shampoor, shampoo(er)
shampu, shampoo
shampuer, shampoo(er)
shampuir, shampoo(er)
shampul, shamble
shamrock,*, PLANT
shamrok, shamrock
shanal, channel
shanalize, channelize
shananigen, shenanigan
shananugin, shenanigan
shandalere, chandelier
shandulere, chandelier
shange, change
shanil, channel
shanilize, channelize
shank,*, PART OF THE BODY
shanty,ties, ROUGH/FRONTIER STRUCTURE
shantys, shanty(ties)

shape,*,ed,ping,pable,eless,elessness, elessly,eliness,ely,er, OF FORM/ FIGURE "prefixes: re/un"
shapeable, shape(pable)
shaperd, shepherd
shaplis, shape(less)
shaply, shape(ly)
shapuble, shape(pable)
shar, share / chair / char
sharade, charade
sharck, shark
shard,*, FRAGMENT
share,*,ed,ring, TO DIVIDE INTO PORTIONS "prefixes: over"
sharee, sherry
sharef, sheriff
shari, sherry
sharif, sheriff
shark,*, MARINE FISH, LIKE A SHARK
sharp,ply,pness,pen,pens,pened,pening, pener,per,pest,pie, DISTINCT POINT/TIP
sharpin, sharp(en)
sharpind, sharp(ened)
sharpinur, sharp(ener)
sharpnis, sharp(ness)
sharpuner, sharp(ener)
sharpy, sharp(ie)
sharry, sherry
sharuf, sheriff
shate, shade
shater, shatter
shatir, shatter
shato, shadow
shatord, shatter(ed)
shatoy, shadow(y)
shatter,*,red,ring, REDUCE TO PIECES/ FRAGMENTS
shaturd, shatter(ed)
shauk, chalk / choke / shock / chock
shavar, shave(r)
shave,*,ed,ving,er, TO REDUCE THE SURFACE/OUTCROP, SCRATCH/ GRAZE THE SURFACE
shavir, shave(r)
shavur, shave(r)
shawer, shower
shawir, shower
shawl,*, EXTERIOR GARMENT FOR SHOULDERS
shawmen, shaman
shawmonism, shaman(ism)
shawur, shower
she,*, THAT FEMALE

she'd, CONTRACTION OF THE WORDS 'SHE HAD/WOULD' (or see shed)
she'll, CONTRACTION OF THE WORDS 'SHE WILL' (or see shell)
sheaf,aves, BOUND STALKS, QUIVER OF ARROWS
shear,*,red,ring,rer,horn, CUT WITH CLIPPERS (or see sheer)
sheath,hes,hed,hing, CLOSE FITTING CASE/COVERING, ALSO SPELLED 'SHEATHE'
sheberd, shepherd
sheburd, shepherd
shechul, special
shed,*,dded,dding, SMALL STRUCTURE (or see she'd/sheet)
sheef, sheaf
sheek, chic
sheeld, shield
sheen,*,ned,ning,nier,niest,ny, RADIANT/BRIGHT/LIGHT (or see shin)
sheengul, shingle
sheep,pish,pishly,pishness, A RUMINANT ANIMAL
sheer,*,red,ring,rer,rly,rness, NAUTICAL TERM, OF LITTLE BODY/SUBSTANCE, NEAR TRANSPARENT (or see shear)
sheet,*,ted,ting, THIN/FLAT SUBSTANCE/MATERIAL
sheeth, sheath
shef, chef / chief / sheaf
shefor, shiver
sheft, shift
shefur, shiver
sheild, shield
sheilt, shield
shel, she'll / shell / shale
shelak, shellac
sheld, shield / shell(ed)
sheldur, shelter
sheldurless, shelter(less)
shelf,lves, HORIZONTAL LEDGE TO PLACE THINGS ON (or see shelve)
shelfs, shelve(s)
shell,*,lled,lling,ller, HOUSING/ PROTECTION FOR CREATURES, LAYERS OF ATOM, HAND OVER (or see she'll) "prefixes: sub"
shellac,*,ced,cing, A CHEMICAL SOLUTION, USED IN VARNISH
shelont, chalant
shelt, shell(ed)

shelter,*,red,ring,rless, COVER/ PROTECTION/REFUGE
sheltired, shelter(ed)
sheltur, shelter
shelturd, shelter(ed)
shelturless, shelter(less)
shelve,*,ed,ving,er, PLURAL FOR SHELF, LEDGE TO PLACE ITEMS
shem, shim
shemed, shim(mmed) / shimmy(mmied)
shemee, shimmy
shemir, shimmer
shemmiry, shimmer(y)
shemonic, shaman(ic)
shemur, shimmer
shemury, shimmer(y)
shemy, shimmy
shen, sheen / shin / chin
shenanigan,*, NONSENSE TRICKERY
shengle, shingle
shengul, shingle
shep, sheep / ship / chip
shepard, shepherd
sheper, ship(pper) / chip(pper)
sheperd, shepherd
shepherd,*, THAT WHICH GUARDS/ PROTECTS
shepird, shepherd
shepish, sheep(ish)
sheprek, shipwreck
shept, ship(pped) / chip(pped)
shepur, ship(pper) / chip(pper)
shepurd, shepherd
shepwreck, shipwreck
sher, sure / share / chair / cheer
sherba, sherbet
sherbert, sherbet
sherbet,*, FRUIT FLAVORED ICE DESSERT
sherbirt, sherbet
sherburt, sherbet
sherd, shear(ed) / sheer(ed) / share(d)
shered, shear(ed) / sheer(ed) / share(d)
sheredy, surety
sheri, sherry
sheridy, surety
sherif, sheriff
sheriff,*, LAW ENFORCEMENT OFFICIAL
sherir, shear(er)
sherity, surety
sherly, sure(ly)
sheror, shear(er)
sherrif, sheriff

sherry,ries, TYPE OF WINE
shert, shear(ed) / sheer(ed) / shirt
sheruf, sheriff
sherur, shear(er)
shery, sherry
shet, shed / sheet / she'd
shethd, sheath(ed)
sheult, shield
shevir, shiver
shevt, shift
shevtur, shift(er)
shevulry, chivalry
shevur, shiver
shew, shoe / chew
shewr, sure
shews, shoe(s)
shewt, chute / shoot / chew(ed)
shi, shy / she
shid, shy(hied) / she'd
shield,*,ded,ding, USED FOR DEFENSE/ PROTECTION
shier, shy(er)
shift,*,ted,ting,tingly,tingness,ter,tless, tlessly,tlessness,ty,tily,tiness, LEAVE ONE GEAR/FOCUS/PLACE/POINT TO GO TO ANOTHER "prefixes: un/up"
shiftur, shift(er)
shifur, shiver
shil, she'll / shell
shilak, shellac
shild, shield
shilee, shy(ly)
shilons, chalant(nce)
shilont, chalant
shily, shy(ly)
shim,*,mmed,mming, A THIN STRIP OF SOME MATERIAL USED TO FILL GAPS
shimanik, shaman(ic)
shimee, shimmy
shimer, shimmer
shimery, shimmer(y)
shimes, shimmy(mmies) / shim(s)
shimmer,*,ry, LIGHT/GLEAMING
shimmy,mmies,mmied,mmying, VIBRATION/WOBBLING
shimonic, shaman(ic)
shimur, shimmer
shimury, shimmer(y)
shimy, shimmy
shimyd, shimmy(mmied)
shimys, shimmy(mmies)

shin,*,nned,nning, PART OF THE LEG, SPLINT OF WOOD (or see shine/chin)
shinanigan, shenanigan
shinanugan, shenanigan
shind, shine(d) / shin(nned)
shine,*,ed,ning,er,ny,nier,niest,niness, RADIANT/REFLECTIVE (or see chin/shin/shiny)
shineist, shiny(niest)
shiness, shy(ness)
shineur, shiny(nier)
shingle,*,ed,ling, ROOF COVERING, PAINFUL VIRAL INFECTION
shingul, shingle
shinguled, shingle(d)
shinie, shiny
shiny, nier,niest,niness, RADIANT/REFLECTIVE
shinyest, shiny(niest)
shinyness, shiny(niness)
ship,*,pped,pping,pper, WATER/NAUTICAL VESSEL, SEND ITEM BY ROAD/SEA/AIR (or see chip) "prefixes: un"
shipd, ship(pped) / chip(pped)
shiper, ship(pper) / chip(pper)
shiprek, shipwreck
shipur, ship(pper) / chip(pper)
shipwreck,*,ked, BOAT WHICH WRECKS IN THE SEA
shipwrek, shipwreck
shir, sure / shy(er) / shear
shirbert, sherbet
shirbet, sherbet
shirburt, sherbet
shiredy, surety
shirety, surety
shirly, sure(ly)
shirt,*, UPPER TORSO GARMENT "prefixes: over/under"
shister, shyster
shiur, shy(er)
shivalry, chivalry
shiver,*,red,ring, SHAKE/TREMBLE FROM COLD/FEAR
shivt, shift
shivulry, chivalry
shivur, shiver
sho, show
shoal,*, SHALLOW AREA ASSOCIATED WITH A BODY OF WATER, SCHOOL OF FISH
shoar, shore / chore

shock,*,ked,king,ker,kingly, SUDDEN/ABRUPT/UNPREDICTABLE EVENT, JOLT OF ELECTRICITY, SUDDEN IMPACT
shod,*,ddy, TO SHOE A HORSE (or see show(ed)/shoot/shoe(d)/should) "prefixes: un"
shoddy,ddier,ddiest,ddily,ddiness, INFERIOR PRODUCT/SERVICE PRODUCED TO MOCK FINE QUALITY
shode, shoddy
shody, shoddy
shoe,*,ed,eing,er, FOOT/HOOF COVERING
shofel, shovel
shofer, chauffeur
shok, chalk / choke / shock / chock
shoked, shock(ed) / choke(d) / chock(ed)
shol, shawl / shoal
sholak, shellac
sholder, shoulder
sholdur, shoulder
shole, shoal / shawl
sholont, chalant
sholtur, shoulder
shoman, shaman
shomenism, shaman(ism)
shomin, shaman
shoo, shoe
shood, should / shoe(d)
shook, PAST TENSE FOR THE WORD "SHAKE", A SET OF PREFABRICATED PARTS (or see shuck)
shoot,*,ting,ter,hot, AIM AT SOMETHING TO DISCHARGE INTO/PIERCE/ CAPTURE AN IMAGE (or see shut/should) "prefixes: over/under"
shop,*,pped,pping,pper, SEEK TO PURCHASE GOODS ITEMS, PLACE TO MANUFACTURE/PERFORM RETAIL ACTIVITIES (or see chop)
shoper, shop(pper)
shopur, shop(pper)
shor, shore / chore / sure
shord, shore(d) / short
shordist, short(est)
shore,*,ed,ring, PLACE WHERE BODY OF WATER MEETS LAND (or see chore) "prefixes: in"
shork, shark
shorn, PAST TENSE FOR THE WORD "SHEAR"

shorp, sharp
shors, shore(s) / chore(s)
short,*,ted,ter,test, BRIEF/ABRUPT, SMALLER/LESS THAN NORMAL (or see shore(d)/shorts)
shortir, short(er)
shortist, short(est)
shorts,*, MEDIA LENGTH, PANTS TO THE KNEES (or see shore(d)) "prefixes: under"
shortur, short(er)
shos, shoe(s)
shot, PAST TENSE FOR THE WORD 'SHOOT', TAKE A HIT OF/FROM SOMETHING, TO FILM (or see shod)"prefixes: up"
shoty, shoddy
shoud, shout
shoul, shawl
should, PAST TENSE FOR THE WORD 'SHALL'
should've, CONTRACTION OF THE WORDS 'SHOULD HAVE'
shoulder,*,red,ring, BODY PART HOLDING THE ARM, TO USE THE SHOULDER
shouldn't, CONTRACTION OF THE WORDS 'SHOULD NOT'
shout,*,ted,ting, TO SPEAK/VOICE WORDS LOUDLY
shove,*,ed,ving, TO PUSH/RAM AGAINST
shovel,*,led,ling, AN IMPLEMENT/TOOL FOR DIGGING/MOVING/SCRAPING ORGANIC MATERIAL (or see shuffle)
show,*,wed,wing,wn,wy, TO DISPLAY FOR SOMEONE
shower,*,red,ring,ry, RAIN OR THE IMITATION OF
showfer, chauffeur
showir, shower
showl, shawl
showmin, shaman
showt, shout / show(ed)
showur, shower
shoy, show(y)
shrapnel, SHELL FRAGMENTS
shrapnul, shrapnel
shreak, shriek
shred,*,dded,dding,dder, TO TEAR/CUT INTO SLIVERS/THIN STRIPS/PIECES
shredur, shred(dder)
shreek, shriek
shreful, shrivel

shrel, shrill
shrelness, shrill(ness)
shremp, shrimp
shrempy, shrimp(y)
shrenk, shrink
shrenkable, shrink(able)
shrevle, shrivel
shrevul, shrivel
shrew,*,wish,wishly,wishness, SMALL MAMMAL, TO BE ILL TEMPERED
shrewd,dly,dness, TO BE DISCERNING/ PRACTICAL
shrewtly, shrewd(ly)
shriek,*,ked,king, A SHRILL/SHARP YELL OR SHOUT SOUNDED WHEN FRIGHTENED/ANGRY
shrifle, shrivel
shril, shrill
shrill,lly,llness, PIERCING/HIGH PITCHED SOUND
shrilness, shrill(ness)
shrimp,*,py, EDIBLE CRUSTACEANS, SMALL/TINY
shrine,*, A STRUCTURE WITH RELIGIOUS IMPLICATIONS "prefixes: en"
shrink,*,runk,king,kable, BECOME SMALLER THAN ORIGINAL SIZE, SLANG FOR MENTAL DOCTOR
shrivel,*,led,ling, TO WRINKLE/SHRINK
shrivle, shrivel
shronk, shrunk
shroo, shrew
shrood, shrewd
shroodly, shrewd(ly)
shrooish, shrew(ish)
shroot, shrewd
shroud,*,ded,ding, HIDE/COVER/ CONCEAL "prefixes: en"
shrowd, shroud
shru, shrew
shrub,*,bbery,bby, LOW GROWING TREES/BUSHES "prefixes: sub/ under"
shrubery, shrub(bbery)
shrubry, shrub(bbery)
shrud, shrewd
shrudly, shrewd(ly)
shrue, shrew
shrug,*,gged,gging, USE THE SHOULDERS FOR EMOTIONAL EXPRESSION
shrunk, PAST TENSE FOR 'SHRINK' "prefixe: pre"

shrupree, shrub(bbery)
shrut, shrewd
shrutly, shrewd(ly)
shryn, shrine
shu, shoe
shuch, shush
shuck,*,ked,king,ker, REMOVE HULLS/ SHELLS/OUTER HOUSING (or see shook)
shuckir, shuck(er)
shud, should / shut
shudal, shuttle
shudder,*,red,ring,ry, PHYSICAL/ EMOTIONAL RESPONSE TO SOMETHING GROTESQUE/ REPULSIVE (or see shutter)
shudel, shuttle
shuder, shutter / shudder / shoot(er)
shuderd, shudder(ed) / shutter
shudery, shudder(y)
shudil, shuttle
shudir, shutter / shudder / shoot(er)
shudol, shuttle
shudur, shutter / shudder / shoot(er)
shuf, shove
shufal, shuffle / shovel
shuffle,*,ed,ling,ler, MOVE AROUND BY DRAGGING, AN ACT IN A CARD GAME, MOVE AS A CHESS PIECE ON GAMEBOARD (or see shovel) "prefixes: re"
shufil, shuffle / shovel
shuful, shovel / shuffle
shugar, sugar
shugur, sugar
shuk, shook / shuck
shukd, shuck(ed) / shook
shuker, sugar / shuck(er)
shukur, sugar / shuck(er)
shulak, shellac
shuld, should
shulont, chalant
shun,*,nned,nning, TO AVOID
shunanegin, shenanigan
shunanigen, shenanigan
shund, shun(nned) / shunt
shuner, shun(nner)
shunir, shun(nner)
shunt,*ted,ter, SHIFT, RID OF, MOVE ASIDE (or see shun(nned))
shuntur, shunt(er)
shur, sure / shoe(r)
shurade, charade
shurba, sherbet

shurbert, sherbet
shurbet, sherbet
shurburt, sherbet
shuredy, surety
shurity, surety
shurly, sure(ly)
shurt, shirt
shus, shoe(s)
shush, TO ENCOURAGE TO BE QUIET
shut,*,tter,tting, TO CLOSE/STOP (or see should/shoot/chute)
shutal, shuttle
shute, chute / shoot
shuter, shutter / shudder / shoot(er)
shutir, shutter / shudder / shoot(er)
shutled, shuttle(d)
shutol, shuttle
shutter,*, A HINGED FLAP/COVER OVER AN OPENING (or see shudder)
shuttle,*,ed,ling, CARRY/TRANSPORT TO ANOTHER PLACE
shutur, shutter / shudder / shoot(er)
shuve, shove
shuvel, shovel
shuvul, shovel
shuw, shoe
shuz, shoe(s)
shy,hies,hied,ying,hier,hiest,yly,yness, yster, LESS THAN WILLING TO ACCEPT/FACE HEAD-ON/ CONFRONT
shyster,*, ONE WHO IS UNETHICAL
shystur, shyster
si, sigh / see / sea
siadeka, sciatic(a)
siadika, sciatic(a)
sianide, cyanide
sianse, science
siantifek, scientific
siantist, scientist
siants, science
siatek, sciatic
siateka, sciatic(a)
siatic, sciatic
siatika, sciatic(a)
sibkonchus, subconscious
sibkontrakt, subcontract
siblengs, sibling(s)
sibling,*, LEGAL BROTHERS/SISTERS
siborg, cyborg
siburnetiks, cybernetics
sic, WORD USED FOR REPLACEMENT IN TEXT, TO ENCOURAGE SOMETHING TO ATTACK (or see sick/psyche)

sicede, secede
sicheatric, psychiatric
sichek, psychic
sichewashen, situate(tion)
sichewation, situate(tion)
sichiatric, psychiatric
sichic, psychic
sicholegist, psychology(gist)
sichologekul, psychology(gical)
sichologest, psychology(gist)
sichology, psychology
sichopath, psychopath
sichopatholagist, psychopath(ologist)
sichosis, psychosis
sichuaded, situate(d)
sichuashen, situate(tion)
sichuate, situate
sichuation, situate(tion)
sichudelic, psychedelic
sick,kish,kishness,kly,kliness,kness, PHYSICALLY/MENTALLY ILL (or see psyche)
sickal, sickle / cycle
sickle,*,ed,ling, TOOL USED FOR CUTTING GRASS/GRAIN, CRESCENT MOON SHAPE (or see cycle)
sicks, six
sickstee, sixty
sickteith, sixtieth
sickth, sixth
siclone, cyclone
sico, psycho
sicodek, psychotic
sicological, psychology(gical)
sicology, psychology
sicreshen, secrete(tion)
sicrete, secrete
sicretion, secrete(tion)
sicuer, secure
sicuerity, secure(rity)
sicuerly, secure(ly)
sicumb, succumb
sid, sigh(ed) / side / sight / seed
sidan, sedan
sidar, sit(tter) / cider / side(r)
sidashen, sedate(tion)
sidasion, sedate(tion)
sidate, sedate
sidation, sedate(tion)
side,*,ed,ding,er, BE NEAR OR BESIDE BUT NOT ON, POSITION OFF FROM CENTER (or see site/sight) "prefixes: under/up/sub"
sideng, side(ding) / site(ting) / sight(ing)

sider, sit(tter) / cider / side(r)
sidewse, seduce
sidir, sit(tter) / cider / side(r)
sidokshen, seduce(ction)
sidoose, seduce
sidor, sit(tter) / cider / side(r)
sids, sit(s) / set(s) / side(s)
siducshen, seduce(ction)
sidukshen, seduce(ction)
siduktion, seduce(ction)
siduktive, seduce(ctive)
sidur, sit(tter) / cider / side(r)
siduse, seduce
siduzen, citizen
siege,*,ed,ging, TAKE/STEAL CONTROL OF FUNCTIONS
siegur, seize(zure)
siejur, seize(zure)
sienna, A COLOR/PIGMENT
siense, science
sienses, science(s)
sientifekly, scientific(ally)
sientific, scientific
sientifikly, scientific(ally)
sientist, scientist
sier, sigh(er)
siera, sierra
sierra, SECTION OF HILLS/RANGE, A FISH
siesta,*, AFTERNOON NAP
sieve,*,ed,ving, STRAINER/NET FOR SOLIDS/LIQUIDS
sieze, seize
sif, sieve
sifal, civil
sifalis, syphilis
sifaree, safari
sifd, sieve(d) / sift
sifen, siphon
sifenul, siphon(al)
sifinal, siphon(al)
sifise, suffice
siflazation, civil(ization)
siflus, syphilis
sifol, civil
sifolization, civil(ization)
sifon, siphon
sift,*,ted,ting,ter, SEPARATION OF VARIOUS GRAIN SIZES, SORT FOR A SPECIFIC THING (or see sieve(d))
siftur, sift(er)
sifules, syphilis
sifunil, siphon(al)
sigar, cigar

sigaret, cigarette
siger, seize(zure)
sigeret, cigarette
siggesdeve, suggest(ive)
siggestion, suggest(ion)
sigh,*,hed,hing, A DEEP/RELEASING BREATH
sight,*,ted,ting,table,ter,tless,tlessly, tlessness,tly,tliness, VISUAL, ABLE TO SEE (or see site) "prefixes: in/ over/un"
sigjesdeve, suggest(ive)
sigjestion, suggest(ion)
sigjestive, suggest(ive)
sigjestshen, suggest(ion)
sigma, GREEK ALPHABET LETTER
sigmu, sigma
sign,*,ned,ning,ner, WRITTEN TEXT, SYMBOL WITH MEANING, A PLACARD/ BOARD WITH WORDS/ SYMBOLS, A SIGNATURE (or see sine) "prefixes: con/-re/un/under"
signacher, signature
signafiable, signify(fiable)
signafier, signify(fier)
signafy, signify
signal,*,led,ling,ler,lly,lize,lized,lizing, IMAGE/GESTURE USED TO COMMUNICATE
signature,*,tory,tories, A PERSON'S NAME/MARK, TO SIGN SOMETHING "prefixes: bio"
signefiable, signify(fiable)
signefukent, significant
signeture, signature
signifacantly, significant(ly)
significant,tly,nce,ation,ative,atively, OF IMPORTANCE, OUTSTANDING "prefixes: in"
signify,fied,fying,fiable,fier, INDICATE, POINT OUT
signuchur, signature
signufy, signify
signul, signal
signushure, signature
sigur, seize(zure)
siguret, cigarette
sijur, seize(zure)
sik, sick / psyche / seek
sikadelic, psychedelic
sikal, sickle / cycle
sikamore, sycamore
sike, psyche / sick / sic
sikeatree, psychiatry

sikeatric, psychiatric
sikedelic, psychedelic
sikek, psychic
sikel, sickle / cycle
sikepath, psychopath
sikeur, secure
sikeurety, secure(rity)
sikeurly, secure(ly)
sikewr, secure
sikgest, suggest
sikgestion, suggest(ion)
sikiatree, psychiatry
sikiatrist, psychiatry(rist)
sikik, psychic
sikil, sickle / cycle
sikiotrist, psychiatry(rist)
sikiutrest, psychiatry(rist)
sikiutry, psychiatry
sikjest, suggest
sikjestion, suggest(ion)
sikjestshen, suggest(ion)
sikle, sickle
siklude, seclude
siklushen, seclusion
siklusive, seclusive
siklution, seclusion
sikma, sigma
siknacher, signature
siknafier, signify(fier)
siknashure, signature
siknature, signature
siknefakent, significant
siknefy, signify
sikneture, signature
siknifakent, significant
siknify, signify
siknishure, signature
siknol, signal
siknufy, signify
siknul, signal
siknuture, signature
siko, psycho
sikodelic, psychedelic
sikodik, psychotic
sikolegy, psychology
sikologekul, psychology(gical)
sikologest, psychology(gist)
sikology, psychology
sikopath, psychopath
sikopathic, psychopath(ic)
sikopatholagist, psychopath(ologist)
sikosis, psychosis
sikotic, psychotic
sikreshen, secrete(tion)

sikresion, secrete(tion)
sikrete, secrete
siks, six
sikstee, sixty
siksteen, sixteen
siksteenth, sixteen(th)
siksteith, sixtieth
sikstiuth, sixtieth
siksty, sixty
sikteith, sixtieth
sikth, sixth
sikudelic, psychedelic
sikul, sickle / cycle
sikulest, cyclist
sikum, succumb
sikumore, sycamore
sikure, secure
sikurity, secure(rity)
sikwenshul, sequence(ntial)
sikwential, sequence(ntial)
sikwoia, sequoia
sikwoya, sequoia
siky, psyche / sick
silabes, syllabus
silabil, syllable
silacon, silicon / silicone
silakit, silica(te)
silakon, silicon / silicone
silal, salal
silami, salami
silanoid, solenoid
silanse, silence
silant, silent
silantly, silent(ly)
silantness, silent(ness)
silareum, solarium
silawet, silhouette
sild, silt
sildashen, silt(ation)
silebus, syllabus
sileca, silica
silecate, silica(te)
silective, select(ive)
silee, silly
sileka, silica
silekshen, select(ion)
silekt, select
silektif, select(ive)
silektion, select(ion)
silektive, select(ive)
silence,*,ed,cing,er, QUIET, NO SOUND
silendur, cylinder
sileness, silly(lliness)
sileng, ceiling / seal(ing)

silenium, selenium
silenoid, solenoid
silense, silence
silensur, silence(r)
silent,tly,tness, BEING QUIET, NO SOUND
silerium, solarium
silesit, solicit
silesitation, solicit(ation)
silesiter, solicit(er)
silesteul, celestial
sileur, silly(llier)
silewet, silhouette
silfer, silver
silferware, silverware
silfur, silver
silfurware, silverware
silfury, silver(y)
silhouete, silhouette
silhouette,*,ed,ting, THE SHAPE/ OUTLINE OF SOMETHING
silica,ate, A NATURAL CHEMICAL COMPOUND
silicon, A NATURALLY OCCURING ELEMENT (or see silicone)
silicone,*, A SILICON SUBSTITUTE, MANMADE CHEMICAL (or see silicon)
siliest, silly(lliest)
silinder, cylinder
siliness, silly(lliness)
siling, ceiling / seal(ing)
silinoid, solenoid
silins, silence
silinser, silence(r)
silivu, saliva
silk,*,ken,ky,kily,kiness, THREAD/ FABRIC MADE FROM SILKWORMS
silkee, silk(y)
silkeness, silk(iness)
silkun, silk(en)
sill,*, A HORIZONTAL SHELF (or see sell)
silly,llier,lliest,llies,lliness, GOOFY/ FUNNY, NOT SERIOUS
silo,*,oed,oing, A STRUCTURE/ HOUSING FOR GRAIN/MISSILES/ ROCKETS
siloet, silhouette
silomee, salami
silon, salon
siloon, saloon
siloot, salute
silow, silo

silt,tation,ty, A VERY FINE DIRT/
    SEDIMENT
siltashen, silt(ation)
silubel, syllable
silubes, syllabus
silubil, syllable
siluca, silica
silucone, silicon / silicone
siludid, salute(d)
siluet, silhouette
siluka, silica
siluket, silica(te)
silukon, silicon / silicone
silune, saloon
silunoid, solenoid
siluns, silence
silunsed, silence(d)
silunser, silence(r)
silunt, silent
siluntly, silent(ly)
siluntness, silent(ness)
silute, salute
silver,red,ry,riness, A TYPE OF SOFT
    METAL, THE COLOR OF SHINY GRAY
silverware, UTENSILS COATED IN
    SILVER
silvir, silver
silvur, silver
silvurware, silverware
silvury, silver(y)
sily, silly
sim, seem / seam
simalarly, similar(ly)
simaler, similar
simalerety, similar(ity)
simalerly, similar(ly)
simaltaneus, simultaneous
simaltaneusly, simultaneous(ly)
siman, semen
simantics, semantics
simar, simmer
simashen, sum(mmation)
simation, sum(mmation)
simatry, symmetry
simbal, symbol
simbalism, symbol(ism)
simbathetik, sympathetic
simbathy, sympathy
simbeodek, symbiotic
simbeosis, symbiosis
simbeotek, symbiotic
simbethe, sympathy
simbethetic, sympathetic
simbiosis, symbiosis

simblanse, semblance
simblants, semblance
simble, symbol
simblense, semblance
simbol, cymbal / symbol
simbolek, symbol(ic)
simbolik, symbol(ic)
simbul, symbol
simbulism, symbol(ism)
simbuthe, sympathy
simbuthetic, sympathetic
simdum, symptom
simelarity, similar(ity)
simeltaneus, simultaneous
simeltaneusly, simultaneous(ly)
simelur, similar
simelurly, similar(ly)
simen, semen
siment, cement
simer, simmer
simesder, semester
simester, semester
simetrek, symmetry(ric)
simetric, symmetry(ric)
simetry, symmetry
simewlate, simulate
simfeny, symphony
simfonic, symphony(nic)
simfune, symphony
similar,rly,rity,rities, RESEMBLES
    SOMETHING ALMOST LIKE IT, NOT
    THE SAME BUT CLOSE (also spelled
    "simular") "prefixes: dis"
similur, similar
similurly, similar(ly)
simin, semen
simmer,*,red,ring, COOK GENTLY WITH
    LOW HEAT, TO CALM DOWN
simoltaneous, simultaneous
simoltaneus, simultaneous
simoltaneusly, simultaneous(ly)
simoolader, simulate(tor)
simpal, simple
simpalest, simple(st)
simpaly, simple(ly)
simpathee, sympathy
simpathetic, sympathetic
simpathize, sympathy(hize)
simpathy, sympathy
simpdum, symptom
simpel, simple
simpelest, simple(st)
simpely, simple(ly)
simpethize, sympathy(hize)

simpethy, sympathy
simphonek, symphony(nic)
simphonic, symphony(nic)
simphuny, symphony
simpithy, sympathy
simple,er,est,leness,ly,licity,licities,lify,
    lification,lifier,lism,listic,listically,
    NOT COMPLICATED, BASIC,
    UNDERSTANDABLE "prefixes: over"
simplisity, simple(licity)
simplistec, simple(listic)
simplur, simple(r)
simposeum, symposium
simpozeum, symposium
simptom, symptom
simptum, symptom
simpul, simple
simpuler, simple(r)
simpulest, simple(st)
simpuly, simple(ly)
simputhee, sympathy
simputhetic, sympathetic
simputhize, sympathy(hize)
simtem, symptom
simtum, symptom
simualtaneus, simultaneous
simuladur, simulate(tor)
simularity, similar(ity)
simularly, similar(ly)
simulashen, simulate(tion)
simulate,*,tive,tion,tor,
    REPRODUCTION OF ORIGINAL
    "prefixes: dis"
simuler, similar
simulerity, similar(ity)
simulerly, similar(ly)
simultaneous,sly,eity, HAPPENING AT
    SAME TIME
simultaneusly, simultaneous(ly)
simur, simmer
simurd, simmer(ed)
simurt, simmer(ed)
simutary, cemetery
simutree, symmetry
sin,*,nned,nning,nner,nful,nfully,
    nfulness, KNOWINGLY COMMIT AN
    IMMORAL ACT (or see sine/sign/
    seine/seen)
sinada, sonata
sinanem, synonym
sinapse, synapse
sinapsis, synapsis
sinaptek, synaptic
sinaptic, synaptic

sinareo, scenario
sinas, sinus
sinaster, sinister
sinata, sonata
sinatorial, senator(ial)
sinatur, senator
sinc, sync / sink
since, REFERRING TO THE PAST, FROM THEN UP UNTIL NOW, BECAUSE OF (or see sense/cent(s)/sin(s)/scent(s))
sincere,ely,rity,eness, HONEST/GENUINE "prefixes: in"
sincerly, sincere(ly)
sinch, cinch
sinched, singe(d) / cinch(ed)
sinchro, synchro
sinchronus, synchrony(nous)
sincht, singe(d) / cinch(ed)
sincronize, synchrony(nize)
sincrony, synchrony
sind, send / sign(ed) / sin(nned)
sinder, cinder / send(er)
sindicate, syndicate
sindication, syndicate(tion)
sindikation, syndicate(tion)
sindiket, syndicate
sindrem, syndrome
sindrulize, centralize
sindrum, syndrome
sindukit, syndicate
sindur, send(er)
sine, MATHEMATICAL FUNCTION (or see sign/sin)
sined, sign(ed) / sin(nned)
sinegrade, centigrade
sinek, cynic
sinekal, cynical
sinema, cinema
sinemin, cinnamon
sineority, senior(ity)
sinepede, centipede
siner, sin(nner)
sinereo, scenario
sinergy, synergy
sinerist, scenario(ist)
sines, sign(s) / sin(s) / sinus
sinester, sinister
sinetor, senator
sinetorial, senator(ial)
sinew,wy, TENDONS, TO STRENGTHEN
sinfuly, sin(fully)

sing,*,ging,ger, CREATE MELODIC NOTES/SONGS WITH THE VOICE/THROAT (or see singe/sink)
singal, single
singar, sing(er)
singe,*,ed,ging, SCORCH/SLIGHTLY BURN SOMETHING (or see sing/cinch)
singel, single
singewlerety, singular(ity)
singil, single
singir, sing(er)
single,*,ed,ling,lism,ly, ONLY ONE, NOT WITH OTHERS
singul, single
singular,rly,rness,rize,rity,rities, OF BEING ONE/ONCE, INDIVIDUAL "prefixes: non"
singuler, singular
singulerety, singular(ity)
singuleridy, singular(ity)
singulerly, singular(ly)
singuly, single(ly)
singur, sing(er)
singus, singe(s) / cinch(es)
sinic, cynic
sinical, cynical
sinima, cinema
sinior, senior
sinir, sin(nner)
sinister,rous,rously,rly,rness, SOMETHING EVIL/FOREBODING
sinj, singe / cinch
sinjd, singe(d) / cinch(ed)
sinjt, singe(d) / cinch(ed)
sink,*,sunk,king,ker,kage,kable, TO DESCEND/LOWER/RECLINE/SUBMERGE, A BASIN (or see sync)
sinkd, sink(ed)
sinkewler, singular
sinkil, single
sinkir, sink(er) / sing(er)
sinkle, single
sinkly, single(ly)
sinkranes, synchrony(nous)
sinkrenus, synchrony(nous)
sinkro, synchro
sinkronee, synchrony
sinkronize, synchrony(nize)
sinkronus, synchrony(nous)
sinkrony, synchrony
sinkt, sink(ed)
sinkul, single
sinkularedy, singular(ity)

sinkularly, singular(ly)
sinkuler, singular
sinkur, sink(er) / sing(er)
sinles, sin(less)
sinnless, sin(less)
sinoda, sonata
sinodu, sonata
sinografee, scenography
sinography, scenography
sinome, tsunami
sinonemus, synonym(ous)
sinonim, synonym
sinonimus, synonym(ous)
sinonym, synonym
sinopsis, synopsis
sinota, sonata
sinoter, senator
sins, sign(s) / sin(s) / since / sense / cent(s)
sinsable, sensible
sinsaredy, sincere(rity)
sinsaridy, sincere(rity)
sinsashen, sensation
sinsation, sensation
sinsative, sensitive
sinsativity, sensitive(vity)
sinsatize, sensitize
sinse, since / sense / cent(s) / scent(s)
sinseer, sincere
sinseerly, sincere(ly)
sinsere, sincere
sinseredy, sincere(rity)
sinserity, sincere(rity)
sinserly, sincere(ly)
sinsery, sensor(y)
sinsetive, sensitive
sinseur, sincere / censor / censure / sensor
sinshere, century
sinshewality, sensual(ity)
sinshewus, sensuous
sinshual, sensual
sinshuality, sensual(ity)
sinshuos, sensuous
sinshure, century
sinsiry, sensor(y)
sinsless, sense(less)
sinsor, censor / censure
sinsoreal, sensor(ial)
sinsory, sensor(y)
sinst, sense(d)
sinsual, sensual
sinsuble, sensible
sinsus, census / sense

sinsutive, sensitive
sinsutivity, sensitive(vity)
sinsutize, sensitize
sint, sent / cent / scent / sin(nned) / sign(ed)
sintaks, syntax
sintament, sentiment
sintamental, sentiment(al)
sintax, syntax
sintchuis, sensuous
sintekit, syndicate
sintement, sentiment
sinteneul, centennial
sintense, sentence
sinter, center
sinthasis, synthesis
sinthasize, synthesize
sinthedik, synthetic
sinthesis, synthesis
sinthetek, synthetic
sinthusis, synthesis
sinthusize, synthesize
sintimental, sentiment(al)
sintineul, centennial
sintinse, sentence
sintrie, sentry / centri
sintrul, central
sintrulize, centralize
sintry, sentry / centri
sintrys, sentry(ries)
sintugrade, centigrade
sintumental, sentiment(al)
sintury, century
sinu, sinew
sinuee, sinew(y)
sinugrade, centigrade
sinumeter, centimeter
sinumon, cinnamon
sinunem, synonym
sinupede, centipede
sinur, sin(nner)
sinurgy, synergy
sinus,ses,sitis, RESPIRATORY CAVITIES/ PASSAGES IN THE FACE, BOTANICAL TERM
sinuster, sinister
sinutor, senator
sinutorial, senator(ial)
sinuy, sinew(y)
sinyor, senior
sinyority, senior(ity)
sinyuee, sinew(y)
siontefikly, scientific(ally)
siontest, scientist
siontifek, scientific
siontist, scientist
sip,*,pped,pping,pper,ppingly, TO PURSE THE LIPS TO DRINK, SMALL DRINKS (or see sipe/seep)
sipasetory, suppository
sipausatory, suppository
sipe,*,ed,ping, SOAK/DRIP THROUGH (or see sip/seep)
sipereor, superior
sipereority, superior(ity)
sipereur, superior
siperlitef, superlative
siphelis, syphilis
siphen, siphon
siphenul, siphon(al)
siphilis, syphilis
siphon,*,ned,ning,nal,nic,nless, USE PRESSURE/SUCTION TO RELOCATE FLUIDS (also spelled syphon)
siphules, syphilis
sipkonchus, subconscious
siplant, supplant
sipli, supply
siplier, supply(lier)
sipling, sibling
sipliur, supply(lier)
siply, supply
siport, support
siportef, support(ive)
siportive, support(ive)
siposatory, suppository
sipose, suppose
siposubly, suppose(dly)
sipoze, suppose
sipozubly, suppose(dly)
sipreem, supreme
sipreno, soprano
sipres, suppress
sipreshun, suppress(ion)
siptek, styptic
siptik, styptic
sipur, sip(pper)
sipurb, superb
sipurblee, superb(ly)
sipurlitef, superlative
siquential, sequence(ntial)
siquerly, secure(ly)
siquir, secure
siquirety, secure(rity)
siquoia, sequoia
sir,*, TITLE OF A MAN (or see sire)
siraded, serrate(d)
siraget, surrogate
siragit, surrogate
siramik, ceramic
siran, saran / siren
sirape, syrup / serape
sirashen, serrate(tion)
sirated, serrate(d)
siration, serrate(tion)
sircal, circle
sircas, circus
sircemscribe, circumscribe
sircharge, surcharge
sirchuble, search(able)
sircimscribe, circumscribe
sircit, circuit
sircle, circle
sircol, circle
sircomfurinse, circumference
sircomscribe, circumscribe
sircophagus, sarcophagus
sircot, circuit
sircul, circle
sircumferenc, circumference
sircumpherence, circumference
sircumsize, circumcise
sircumstans, circumstance
sircus, circus
sircut, circuit
sirdify, certify
sire,*,ed,ring, MALE PARENT OF A MAMMAL (or see sir)
sireal, serial / cereal / surreal
sirealism, surrealism
sireilisum, surrealism
sirel, sorrel / surreal
sirelism, surrealism
sirem, serum
siren,*, LOUD/PIERCING SOUNDS FROM A DEVICE, SEA NYMPHS
sirench, syringe
sirendur, surrender
sirene, serene
sireng, syringe
sirenidy, serene(nity)
sirenity, serene(nity)
sirenj, syringe
sireol, serial / cereal
sireous, serious
sirep, syrup
sires, series / sire(s) / cirrus / scirrhus
sireul, cereal / serial
sireulizum, surrealism
sireus, serious
sireusly, serious(ly)
sirf, surf / serf / serve

sirface, surface
sirfdum, serf(dom)
sirfege, serf(age)
sirfeje, serf(age)
sirfes, surface / service
sirfibul, surf(able)
sirfis, surface
sirfunt, servant
sirfur, surf(er)
sirg, surge / serge
sirgakle, surgical
sirgekul, surgical
sirgen, surgeon
sirgent, sergeant / surgent
sirgeon, surgeon
sirgon, surgeon
sirgree, surgery
sirgukle, surgical
sirguree, surgery
siriasis, psoriasis
sirim, serum
sirin, siren
sirios, serious
siriosly, serious(ly)
siris, series
sirius, serious
sirjakle, surgical
sirje, surge / serge
sirjekul, surgical
sirjen, surgeon
sirjon, surgeon
sirjree, surgery
sirjukle, surgical
sirjuree, surgery
sirkawfigus, sarcophagus
sirkemscribe, circumscribe
sirkes, circus
sirkewler, circular
sirkis, circus
sirklar, circular
sirkofegus, sarcophagus
sirkomscribe, circumscribe
sirkulate, circulate
sirkumferinse, circumference
sirkumscribe, circumscribe
sirkumsize, circumcise
sirlee, surly
sirloin,*, A CUT OF BEEF
sirly, surly
sirman, sermon
sirmize, surmise
sirmon, sermon
sirogate, surrogate
sirom, serum

siron, siren
sirong, sarong
sirope, serape / syrup
siroredy, sorority
sirority, sorority
siros, scirrhus / cirrus
siround, surround
sirownd, surround
sirpas, surpass
sirpent, serpent
sirpentene, serpentine
sirpint, serpent
sirpintent, serpentine
sirplus, surplus
sirprize, surprise
sirrated, serrate(d)
sirrus, cirrus / scirrhus
sirtenly, certain(ly)
sirtin, certain
sirtunly, certain(ly)
sirum, serum
sirun, siren
sirup, syrup
sirus, cirrus / scirrhus
sirv, serve
sirva, survey
sirvailense, surveillance
sirvalense, surveillance
sirvatood, servitude
sirvatude, servitude
sirvaur, survey(or)
sirvayer, survey(or)
sirve, serve / survey
sirveilinse, surveillance
sirveor, survey(or)
sirves, service / survey(s) / serve(s)
sirvesable, service(cable)
sirveyor, survey(or)
sirvife, survive
sirvint, servant
sirvis, service
sirvitude, servitude
sirvive, survive
sirvivul, survive(val)
sirvont, servant
sirvunt, servant
sirvusable, service(cable)
sirvutude, servitude
sirys, series
sis, size /cease / seize
sisabul, size(zable)
sisal, sizzle
sisd, size(d) / cyst
sisdamadik, system(atic)

sisdamatic, system(atic)
sisdan, sustain
sisdem, system
sisdum, system
sisdumadik, system(atic)
sisdumatic, system(atic)
sise, size / sissy
siseble, size(zable)
sisede, secede
siseded, secede(d)
sisee, sissy
sisel, sizzle
siseptible, susceptible
siseptif, susceptive
siseptive, susceptive
siseptuble, susceptible
siseptuf, susceptive
sisers, scissor(s)
siseshen, secession
sisesion, secession
siset, secede
sisetion, secession
sisle, sizzle
sismec, seism(ic)
sismic, seism(ic)
sismical, seism(ical)
sismik, seism(ic)
sisors, scissor(s)
sispend, suspend
sissy,ssies,ssified,ssiness,yness,yish, BEHAVE LIKE A COWARD, UNMASCULINE
sist, cist / cyst
sistain, sustain
sistane, sustain
sistanuble, sustain(able)
sistem, system
sister,*,rly,hood, FEMALES WHO HAVE A STRONG AFFINITY/RELATIONSHIP, FEMALE SIBLING BY LAW/BLOOD
sistre, sister
sistum, system
sistumatic, system(atic)
sistur, sister
sisturly, sister(ly)
sisturn, cistern
sisubil, size(zable)
sisuble, size(zable)
sisul, sizzle
sisurs, scissor(s)
sisus, size(s)
sisy, sissy
sit,*,tting,tter,sat, POSITION RESTING ON THE BUTTOCKS, WHAT

SOMETHING OCCUPYING SPACE/
POSITION DOES (or see set/site/
side)
sitanic, satanic
sitanikul, satanic(al)
sitashun, citation
sitation, citation
sitchuashen, situate(tion)
sitchuate, situate
site,*, AREA OF SIGNIFICANCE (or see
sight/side)
siter, sit(tter)/ cider/ side(r)
siterical, satire(rical)
sitesin, citizen
sith, scythe
sitir, sit(tter) / cider / side(r)
sitor, sit(tter) / cider / side(r)
sitrek, citric
sitrik, citric
sitrus, citrus
situashen, situate(tion)
situate,*,ed,ting,tion,tional,tionally,
LOCATION/POSITION OF OBJECTS/
EVENTS
situatid, situate(d)
situr, sit(tter) / cider
situzin, citizen
sity, city
siunide, cyanide
siunse, science
siuntest, scientist
siuntifek, scientific
siuntifekaly, scientific(ally)
siuntist, scientist
siur, sigh(er)
siv, sieve
sival, civil
sivalization, civil(ization)
sivana, savanna
sivant, savant
sivd, sieve(d) / sift
sivear, severe
sived, sieve(d) / sift
sivere, severe
siverity, severe(rity)
siverly, severe(ly)
sivic, civic
sivil, civil
sivilean, civilian
sivlazation, civil(ization)
sivluzation, civil(ization)
sivol, civil
sivolazation, civil(ization)
sivont, savant

sivt, sift / sieve(d)
sivted, sift(ed)
sivter, sift(er)
sivul, civil
sivulization, civil(ization)
siworo, saguaro
six,xes, AN ENGLISH NUMBER AFTER
FIVE
sixis, six(es)
sixstenth, sixteen(th)
sixtee, sixty
sixteen,nth, AN ENGLISH NUMBER
AFTER FIFTEEN, 16 PARTS OF A
WHOLE
sixteith, sixtieth
sixten, sixteen
sixth,*, AN ENGLISH NUMBER AFTER
THE FIFTH, OF SIX EQUAL PARTS
sixtieth, ENGLISH NUMBER AFTER 59,
OF 60 EQUAL PARTS
sixty,ties, AN ENGLISH NUMBER AFTER
59
sixtyn, sixteen
sixus, six(es)
siz, size /seize / sight(s) / see(s) / sea(s)
sizabil, size(zable)
sizal, sizzle
sizars, scissor(s)
sizd, size(d) / seize(d)
size,*,ed,zing,zable,zably,zableness,
AREA/DIMENSION OF SOMETHING
"prefixes: over/under"
sizebul, size(zable)
sizel, sizzle
sizers, scissor(s)
sizible, size(zable)
sizis, size(s)
sizle, sizzle
sizmek, seism(ic)
sizmekul, seism(ical)
sizmik, seism(ic)
sizmikul, seism(ical)
sizold, sizzle(d)
sizors, scissor(s)
siztur, sister
sizuble, size(zable)
sizul, sizzle
sizurs, scissor(s)
sizus, size(s)
sizzle,*,ed,ling,er, A COOKING/FRYING/
SIZZLING SOUND
skab, scab
skabard, scabbard
skabbard, scabbard

skabed, scab(bbed)
skabees, scabies
skaburd, scabbard
skaby, scab(bby)
skabys, scabies
skad, scat / skate / skat / scad
skader, skate(r) / scatter
skaffold, scaffold
skafolding, scaffold(ing)
skair, scare
skairslee, scarce(ly)
skalar, scalar
skalastic, scholastic
skalb, scalp
skalber, scalp(er)
skald, scald / scale(d)
skale, scale
skalee, scaly
skaleness, scaly(liness)
skaleon, scallion
skalep, scallop
skaleun, scallion
skaley, scaly
skalip, scallop
skaliun, scallion
skallion, scallion
skallop, scallop
skalor, scalar
skalp, scalp
skalpel, scalpel
skalper, scalp(er)
skalpul, scalpel
skalt, scald / scale(d)
skalup, scallop
skaly, scaly
skalyin, scallion
skalyun, scallion
skamatek, scheme(matic)
skan, scan
skand, scan(nned)
skandal, scandal
skandelus, scandal(ous)
skandul, scandal
skandulus, scandal(ous)
skaner, scan(nner)
skanir, scan(nner)
skant, scant / scan(nned)
skantily, scant(ily)
skantuly, scant(ily)
skanur, scan(nner)
skapal, scalpel
skapala, scapula
skapel, scalpel
skapela, scapula

skapeula, scapula
skapil, scalpel
skapila, scapula
skapul, scalpel
skapula, scapula
skar, scar / scare
skarcedy, scarce(city)
skarcity, scarce(city)
skare, scare / scare(y)
skarf, scarf
skarlut, scarlet
skarse, scarce / scare(s)
skarsedy, scarce(city)
skarsly, scarce(ly)
skarsness, scarce(ness)
skarves, scarf(rves)
skat, A CARD GAME (or see scat/skate)
skatar, skate(r) / scatter
skate,*,ed,ting,er, MOVE ABOUT WITH ROLLERS/BLADES ATTACHED TO SHOES, TO MOVE IN GLIDING MOTION (or see skat/scat)
skater, scatter / skate(r)
skathe, scathe
skator, skate(r) / scatter
skattur, scatter / skate(r)
skatur, skate(r) / scatter
skauler, scholar
skaulerly, scholar(ly)
skavage, scavenge
skavege, scavenge
skaveger, scavenge(r)
skavenger, scavenge(r)
skavinger, scavenge(r)
skavuge, scavenge
skavunger, scavenge(r)
skawler, scholar
skawlerly, scholar(ly)
skeam, scheme
skeat, skeet
skech, sketch
skechily, sketch(ily)
skechis, sketch(es)
skecht, sketch(ed)
skechuly, sketch(ily)
skechus, sketch(es)
skechwal, schedule
skechwul, schedule
sked, ski(ed) / scare(d) / skid
skedchule, schedule
skedule, schedule
skeed, ski(ed) / skid
skeem, scheme
skeemer, skim(mmer) / scheme(r)

skeen, skein / ski(iing)
skeet, TYPE OF TRAPSHOOTING
skef, skiff
skein, FLOCK OF WILD BIRDS, BUNDLE OF THREAD/YARN (or see ski(iing)/ skin)
skeing, ski(iing)
skeir, skier
skel, skill / skull / school
skelastic, scholastic
skelaten, skeleton
skelatul, skeletal
skelatun, skeleton
skeld, skill(ed)
skeled, skill(ed)
skeletal,tally, BONES OF A BODY, BASIC FRAMEWORK "prefixes: exo/endo"
skeletin, skeleton
skeleton,*,tal,nize,nizer, BONES OF A BODY, BASIC FRAMEWORK "prefixes: endo/exo"
skeletun, skeleton
skelful, skill(ful)
skelit, skillet
skeliton, skeleton
skelitul, skeletal
skelitun, skeleton
skelut, skillet
skelutin, skeleton
skem, scheme / skim
skematik, scheme(matic)
skemd, skim(mmed) / scheme(d)
skeme, scheme
skemer, skim(mmer) / scheme(r)
skemur, skim(mmer) / scheme(r)
sken, skein / skin
skenee, skinny
skenir, skinner
skeniur, skinny(nier)
skeniust, skinny(niest)
skenlus, skin(less)
skenur, skinner
skeny, skinny
skeor, skier
skep, skip
skepir, skipper
skeps, skip(s)
skept, skip(pped)
skeptacism, skeptic(ism)
skeptak, skeptic
skeptic,*,cal,cally,calness,cism, ONE WHO CHALLENGES/DOUBTS DOCTRINATED BELIEFS (also spelled "sceptic")

skeptucism, skeptic(ism)
skeptuk, skeptic
skeptusisum, skeptic(ism)
sker, scare / skier
skerd, skirt / scare(d)
skere, scare(y)
skerfy, scurvy
skerge, scourge
skerje, scourge
skers, skier(s) / scare(s) / scarce
skersedy, scarce(city)
skersity, scarce(city)
skersly, scarce(ly)
skersness, scarce(ness)
skersudy, scarce(city)
skert, skirt / scare(d)
skervy, scurvy
skery, scurry
skeryd, scurry(ried)
skes, ski(s) / sky(kies)
skeshily, sketch(ily)
sket, skeet / skit
sketch,hes,hed,hing,her,hy,hily,hiness, BRIEF/ROUGH OUTLINE/DRAWING/ IDEA
sketchewl, schedule
sketsh, sketch
skeu, skew
skeuer, skewer
skeuner, schooner
skeur, skier / skewer
skew,*,wed,wing,wness, SLANTED/ SLOPED/DISTORTED/OBLIQUE POSITION
skewbu, scuba
skewdur, scoot(er)
skewer,*, THIN/LONG INSTRUMENT FOR HOLDING MEAT/VEGETABLES FOR GRILLING
skewir, skewer
skewp, scoop
skewpur, scoop(er)
skewtur, scoot(er)
skewur, skewer
skezafrinea, schizophrenia
ski,*,ied,iing,ier, LONG DEVICES ATTACHED TO FEET TO ACHIEVE SPEED/ GLIDING ON VARIOUS SURFACES (or see sky)
skid,*,dded,dding, FRAMEWORK TO HELP SOMETHING SLIDE ALONG, SLIDE WHEN COMING TO A STOP (or see ski(ed)/skit)
skidesh, skittish

skidush, skittish
skier,*, SOMEONE WHO SKIS
skif, skiff
skiff,*, SMALL BOAT
skiier, skier
skiir, skier
skiis, ski(s)
skil, skill
skilastic, scholastic
skilet, skillet
skilful, skill(ful)
skilfuly, skill(fully)
skill,*,led,lful,lfully,lfulness,less, GAIN APTITUDE/EXPERIENCE PERFORMING A CRAFT/TRADE/ACT "prefixes: re/semi/un"
skillet,*, LONG HANDLED FRYING PAN
skilut, skillet
skim,*,mmed,mming,mmer, BE ON/ GLANCE OVER A SURFACE, REMOVE THE SURFACE (or see scheme)
skimatik, scheme(matic)
skimer, skim(mmer) / scheme(r)
skin,*,nned,nning,nner,nless, SURFACE ORGANISM THAT PROTECTS BODILY FLUIDS/CONTENTS, REMOVE COVER/ LAYER OF PROTECTION FROM SOMETHING (or see skein)
skinee, skinny
skiner, skinner
skineust, skinny(niest)
sking, ski(iing)
skinles, skin(less)
skinner,*,ry, ONE WHO REMOVES SKIN
skinny,nnier,nniest, BONEY, NOT MUCH MUSCLE/FAT ON THE BODY
skinur, skinner
skiny, skinny
skip,*,pped,pping, PASS OVER/MISS A BEAT/LEVEL
skiper, skipper
skipir, skipper
skipper,*, CAPTAIN OF A SHIP/BOAT, AN INSECT, ONE WHO SKIPS
skipur, skipper
skir, skier
skireed, scurry(ried)
skirfy, scurvy
skirt,*,ted,ting,ter, A GARMENT WORN TO COVER/PROTECT THE LOWER TORSO, TO EVADE/PASS AROUND AND ISSUE/EVENT "prefixes: under"
skirvy, scurvy
skiry, scurry

skisoed, schizoid
skisophrenea, schizophrenia
skit,*, A BRIEF/SHORT PLAY
skitesh, skittish
skitish, skittish
skitsafrenea, schizophrenia
skitsophrenia, schizophrenia
skittish,hly, EASILY FRIGHTENED
skitush, skittish
skitzafrenea, schizophrenia
skiur, skewer
skizoed, schizoid
skizofrenea, schizophrenia
skizoid, schizoid
skizophrenia, schizophrenia
skof, scoff
skolar, scholar
skolarly, scholar(ly)
skolastic, scholastic
skold, scold / scald
skoleosis, scoliosis
skoler, scholar
skolerly, scholar(ly)
skoliosis, scoliosis
skolir, scholar
skolirly, scholar(ly)
skolt, scold / scald
skolur, scholar
skolurly, scholar(ly)
skomatik, scheme(matic)
skone, scone
skons, scone(s) / sconce
skonts, sconce
skoobu, scuba
skooder, scoot(er)
skool, school
skooner, schooner
skoop, scoop
skooper, scoop(er)
skoot, scoot / scute
skooter, scoot(er)
skor, scar
skorch, scorch
skore, score
skorles, score(less)
skorn, scorn
skornfuly, scorn(fully)
skorpeon, scorpion
skorpeun, scorpion
skorsh, scorch
skorur, score(r)
skoul, scowl
skour, scour
skout, scout

skouter, scout(er)
skower, scour
skowir, scour
skowl, scowl
skowndrel, scoundrel
skowr, scour
skowt, scout
skowter, scout(er)
skowurd, scour(ed)
skquer, skewer
skquir, skewer
skrabs, scrap(s) / scrape(s)
skrach, scratch
skrag, scrag
skragliest, scraggly(liest)
skragly, scrag(ily) / scraggly
skrakleur, scraggly(lier)
skrakly, scrag(ily) / scraggly
skram, scram
skrambul, scramble
skrampul, scramble
skrap, scrap / scrape
skraper, scrape(r) / scrap(pper)
skrapuble, scrap(able)
skratch, scratch
skreach, screech
skream, scream
skrean, screen
skreblur, scribble(r)
skrebul, scribble
skrech, screech
skred, screed
skreech, screech
skreed, screed
skreem, scream
skreen, screen
skreenuble, screen(able)
skremage, scrimmage
skremije, scrimmage
skremp, scrimp
skremshaw, scrimshaw
skremuge, scrimmage
skremuje, scrimmage
skren, screen
skrenuble, screen(able)
skreped, script
skrepshur, scripture
skrept, script
skrepture, scripture
skrew, screw
skrewge, scrooge
skrewje, scrooge
skrewpal, scruple
skrewpel, scruple

skrewpewlis, scrupulous	skuar, skewer	skwabil, squabble
skrewpils, scruple(s)	skuba, scuba	skwabul, squabble
skrewpul, scruple	skuder, scoot(er)	skwad, squad / squat
skrewpules, scrupulous	skued, squid	skwader, squat(ttor)
skrewpulisle, scrupulous(ly)	skueel, squeal	skwadir, squat(ttor)
skrewteny, scrutiny	skuegul, squiggle	skwadrin, squadron
skrewtiney, scrutiny	skuel, school	skwadron, squadron
skrewy, screw(y)	skuelched, squelch(ed)	skwadur, squat(ttor)
skribe, scribe	skuelsh, squelch	skwair, square
skrible, scribble	skuer, skewer	skwairly, square(ly)
skribler, scribble(r)	skuesh, squish	skwal, squall
skribul, scribble	skueshy, squish(y)	skwaled, squalid
skrimage, scrimmage	skuf, scuff	skwalid, squalid
skrimije, scrimmage	skufel, scuffle	skwalor, squalor
skrimp, scrimp	skuful, scuffle	skwander, squander
skrimshaw, scrimshaw	skuid, squid	skwantur, squander
skrimuge, scrimmage	skuigul, squiggle	skwapel, squabble
skrimuje, scrimmage	skuir, skewer	skwapul, squabble
skriped, script	skuish, squish	skward, square(d)
skripshur, scripture	skuishy, squish(y)	skware, square
skript, script	skul, school / skull	skwarlee, square(ly)
skripture, scripture	skulastic, scholastic	skwart, square(d) / squirt
skripuld, scribble(d)	skulbd, sculpt	skwash, squash
skrol, scrawl / scroll	skulbsher, sculpt(ure)	skwat, squad / squat
skroo, screw	skulbshir, sculpt(ure)	skwater, squat(ttor)
skrooge, scrooge	skulbt, sculpt	skwatir, squat(ttor)
skrooje, scrooge	**skull**,*, BONE IN THE HEAD (or see school)	skwatrin, squadron
skrooy, screw(y)		skwaudren, squadron
skroul, scrawl	skulpsher, sculpt(ure)	skwauled, squalid
skrounge, scrounge	skulpshur, sculpt(ure)	skwaulid, squalid
skrowl, scrawl	skulpt, sculpt	skwaulir, squalor
skrownge, scrounge / scrounge(y)	skum, scum	skwaulur, squalor
skrowngy, scrounge(y)	skumatek, scheme(matic)	skwaut, squad / squat
skrownje, scrounge / scrounge(y)	skumy, scum(mmy)	skwautrin, squadron
skru, screw	skuner, schooner	skwautron, squadron
skrub, scrub	**skunk**,*, OMNIVOROUS BLACK/WHITE MAMMAL WITH STRONG SCENT GLANDS	skweak, squeak
skrud, screw(ed)		skwed, squid
skrudnee, scrutiny		skweegee, squeegee
skruf, scruff	skupe, scoop	skweeje, squeegee
skrufy, scruff(y)	skuper, scoop(er)	skweek, squeak
skruge, scrooge	skurage, scourge	skweel, squeal
skruje, scrooge	skuraje, scourge	skweemish, squeamish
skrup, scrub	skured, scurry(ried) / skewer(ed)	skwees, squeeze
skrupel, scruple	skureed, scurry(ried)	skweesir, squeeze(r)
skrupeulus, scrupulous	skurfy, scurvy	skweeze, squeeze
skrupul, scruple	skurge, scourge	skwegal, squiggle
skrupules, scrupulous	skurige, scourge	skwegee, squeegee
skrupulous, scrupulous	skurje, scourge	skwegul, squiggle
skruteny, scrutiny	skurt, skirt	skwegy, squeegee
skrutiny, scrutiny	skurvy, scurvy	skwejee, squeegee
skruwe, screw(y)	skury, scurry	skwel, squeal
skruy, screw(y)	skuryd, scurry(ried)	skwelch, squelch
sku, skew	skut, skew(ed) / scoot / scute	skweler, squeal(er)
skual, squall	skuter, scoot(er)	skwelir, squeal(er)

skwelsh, squelch
skweltch, squelch
skwelur, squeal(er)
skwemesh, squeamish
skwemish, squeamish
skwent, squint
skweral, squirrel
skwerl, squirrel
skwerly, squirrel(y)
skwerm, squirm
skwermy, squirm(y)
skwerol, squirrel
skwert, squirt
skwerul, squirrel
skwes, squeeze
skweser, squeeze(r)
skwesh, squish
skweshy, squish(y)
skwesir, squeeze(r)
skwesur, squeeze(r)
skwet, squid
skweze, squeeze
skwezur, squeeze(r)
skwiarly, square(ly)
skwid, squid
skwigal, squiggle
skwigul, squiggle
skwint, squint
skwire, squire
skwirl, squirrel
skwirm, squirm
skwirmy, squirm(y)
skwirt, squirt
skwirul, squirrel
skwish, squish
skwishy, squish(y)
skwobil, squabble
skwobul, squabble
skwod, squad / squat
skwodir, squat(ttor)
skwodrin, squadron
skwodron, squadron
skwodur, squat(ttor)
skwol, squall
skwoled, squalid
skwolid, squalid
skwolor, squalor
skwondur, squander
skwontur, squander
skwopel, squabble
skwopil, squabble
skwosh, squash
skwot, squad / squat
skwoter, squat(ttor)

skwotir, squat(ttor)
skwotrin, squadron
skwotron, squadron
skwotur, squat(ttor)
skwural, squirrel
skwurl, squirrel
skwurly, squirrel(y)
skwurm, squirm
skwurmt, squirm(ed)
skwurmy, squirm(y)
skwurt, squirt
sky,kies, FIRMAMENT/FIELD ABOVE A PLANET (or see ski)
sla, slay / sleigh
slab,*,bbed,bbing, LARGE/FLAT/SOLID MATERIAL (or see slap)
slabt, slept / slap(pped)
slack,*,ked,king,ker,ken, NOT TAUT/TIGHT, PAIR OF DRESS PANTS, NOT SHARP/ALERT (or see slag)
slade, slay(ed) / slate
slader, slaughter
slae, slay / sleigh
slafe, slave
slafree, slave(ry)
slafry, slave(ry)
slag, WASTE REMNANTS FROM METALS (or see slack)
slag hamer, sledge hammer
slai, slay / sleigh
slain, PAST TENSE FOR THE WORD "SLAY", KILL VIOLENTLY
slak, slack
slaker, slack(er)
slakur, slack(er)
slam,*,mmed,mming,mmer, SHUT/CLOSE/STRIKE
slamur, slam(mmer)
slan, slain
slander,*,red,ring,rer,rous,rously, rousness, FALSE/UNTRUE REMARKS/WORDS
slanderus, slander(ous)
slandured, slander(ed)
slanduris, slander(ous)
slang,*,gily,giness,gy, NON-STANDARD USAGE OF WORDS, SHORT-LIVED WORDS
slank, slang
slant,*,ted,ting, SLOPING/OBLIQUE STANCE, NOT LEVEL, BIASED
slantur, slander

slap,*,pped,pping,pper, TO STRIKE WITH AN OPEN HAND, A CRISP/SHORT BLOW
slapir, slap(pper)
slapt, slap(pped) / slept
slas, sleigh(s) / slay(s) / slaw(s)
slash,hes,hed,hing,her, TO DRIVE A SWEEPING STROKE/BLOW, TO CUT/OPEN WITH A BLADE
slashur, slash(er)
slat,*,ted,ting,ty, THIN STRIPS OF WOOD/METAL (or see slate/slay(ed))
slate,*,ed,ting,ty, CLAY/SHALE/COAL TYPES OF ROCK, AN APPOINTMENT (or see slat/slay(ed))
slath, sloth
slau, slaw
slaudir, slaughter
slaudur, slaughter
slaughter,*,red,ring,rer,rous,rously, VIOLENTLY KILL/DESTROY
slauterus, slaughter(ous)
slave,*,ed,ving,ery, ONE WHO IS FORCED TO WORK FOR SOMEONE WITHOUT PAY, WORK HARDER THAN REASONABLE "prefixes: en"
slaven, sloven
slavenly, sloven(ly)
slavry, slave(ry)
slaw,*, COLD CABBAGE/VEGETABLE DISH
slawb, slob
slawderus, slaughter(ous)
slawdur, slaughter
slawter, slaughter
slawterus, slaughter(ous)
slay,*,yed,ying,yer,slew,slain, KILL VIOLENTLY (or see sleigh)
sleak, sleek
sleaken, sleek(en)
sleaknes, sleek(ness)
sleat, sleet
sleave, sleeve
sleazy,zier,ziest,zily,ziness, OF CHEAP/POOR CHARACTER/QUALITY
sleber, sleep(er)
slebir, sleep(er)
slebry, slip(ppery)
slebt, slept
slebur, sleep(er)
sleck, slick
slecker, slick(er)
sleckly, sleek(ly)

sled,*,dded,dding,dder, TO SLIDE/GLIDE SMOOTHLY ALONG THE GROUND (or see sleigh/slid)
sledge hammer, LARGE/HEAVY HAMMER
sledir, sled(dder)
sledur, sled(dder)
sleef, sleeve
sleek,ken,kens,kened,kening,ker,kly, kness, SHINY/SMOOTH/SOOTHING
sleeknis, sleek(ness)
sleep,*,ping,slept,per,pless,py,piness, pily, SLOW DOWN BASIC FUNCTIONS TO REST, BECOME UNCONSCIOUS, PLACE TO SLEEP "prefixes: over"
sleepee, sleep(y)
sleeseist, sleazy(ziest)
sleesy, sleazy
sleet,*,ted,ting, ICY SNOW, FROZEN PRECIPITATION
sleeve,*,ed,ving,eless, COVER FOR MANY THINGS
sleezee, sleazy
sleezyest, sleazy(ziest)
slefs, sleeve(s)
slefur, sliver
sleg, slick
slege hamer, sledge hammer
sleigh,*,hed,hing, A CONTRAPTION DESIGNED TO GLIDE/SLIDE ALONG THE GROUND (or see sled)
sleight,*,ted,ting, ADROIT/NIMBLE OF BODY/MIND, 'SLEIGHT OF HAND' (or see slight)
sleit, slight / sleight / slate
sleje hamer, sledge hammer
slek, slick / sleek
sleker, slick(er) / sleek(er)
slekly, sleek(ly) / slick(ly)
sleknis, slick(ness) / sleek(ness)
slekur, slick(er) / sleek(er)
slem, slim
slemd, slim(mmed) / slime(d)
slemest, slim(mmest)
slemir, slim(mmer)
slemt, slim(mmed) / slime(d)
slemur, slim(mmer)
slemust, slim(mmest)
slender,rly,rness,rize, SLIM
slendir, slender
slendirness, slender(ness)
slendur, slender
slendurness, slender(ness)

sleng, sling
slenger, sling(er)
slengur, sling(er)
slenk, sling / slink
slenky, slink(y)
slenter, slender
slentur, slender
slep, sleep / slip / slept
slepd, slept / slip(pped)
sleper, sleep(er)
slepir, sleep(er)
slepless, sleep(less)
slepry, slip(ppery)
sleps, sleep(s) / slip(s)
slept, PAST TENSE FOR THE WORD 'SLEEP', TO TAKE A DEEP REST WITH EYES CLOSED
slepur, sleep(er)
slepy, sleep(y)
sler, slur
sleried, slurry(ried)
slerp, slurp
slerpt, slurp(ed)
slert, slur(rred)
slery, slurry
sleryed, slurry(ried)
slesee, sleazy
sleseer, sleazy(zier)
sleseist, sleazy(ziest)
sleseur, sleazy(zier)
slesy, sleazy
slet, sled / slid
sleter, sled(dder)
sletir, sled(dder)
slets, sleet(s)
sletur, sled(dder)
sleuth,*, TRACK/TRAIL/DETECTIVE
sleve, sleeve
sleved, sleeve(d)
slever, sliver
slevir, sliver
slevs, sleeve(s)
slevur, sliver
slew, PAST TENSE FOR THE WORD "SLAY", LARGE AMOUNT/NUMBER OF SOMETHING, TO PIVOT, ALSO "SLUE" (or see slue/slough)
slewth, sleuth
sley, slay / sleigh
slezee, sleazy
slezeist, sleazy(ziest)
slezeur, sleazy(zier)
slezy, sleazy
sli, sly

slibree, slip(ppery)
slibry, slip(ppery)
sliburee, slip(ppery)
slice,*,ed,cing,er, TO CUT
slick,kly,kness,ker,kest, SLIPPERY/ SMOOTH
slid, PAST TENSE FOR THE WORD "SLIDE", GLIDE/MOVE ALONG SMOOTHLY WITHOUT RESISTANCE (or see sled/slide/slit/sleight/slight)
slide,*,ding,er,slid, GLIDE/MOVE ALONG SMOOTHLY WITHOUT RESISTANCE (or see slid/slit/slight/ sleight)
slided, slide(d) / slight(ed)
slidlee, slight(ly)
slifur, sliver
slig, slick
slight,*,ted,ted,test,ting,tingly,tly,tness, NEGLIGENT, PETTY, SLENDER, FRAIL, DISRESPECTFUL (or see sleight)
slightist, slight(est)
slik, slick / sleek
sliker, slick(er) / sleek(er)
slikness, slick(ness)
sliknis, slick(ness)
slikur, slick(er)
slily, sly(ly)
slim,*,mmer,mmest,mmed,mming,mly, UNDER PROPORTION, SMALL, UNSUBSTANTIAL (or see slime)
slimd, slim(mmed) / slime(d)
slime,*,ed,ming,my,mier,miest,mily, miness, VISCOUS/MUCOUS/OOZEY SECRETION (or see slim)
slimed, slim(mmed) / slime(d)
slimee, slime(y)
slimely, slim(ly)
slimeness, slime(miness)
slimeur, slime(mier)
slimiest, slime(miest)
slimiur, slime(mier)
slimt, slim(mmed) / slime(d)
slimur, slim(mmer) / slim(er)
slimy, slime(y)
slimyest, slime(miest)
slinder, slender
slindurness, slender(ness)
sliness, sly(ness)
sling,*,slung,ging,ger, DEVICE DESIGNED TO STRADLE/HOLD, TO FLING (or see slink) "prefixes: un/ under"
slingt, sling(ed) / slink(ed)

slingur, sling(er)
slink,*,ked,lunk,king,ky, MOVE/CREEP/ WALK QUIETLY/SECRETIVELY, BORN PREMATURELY
slinkd, slink(ed) / sling(ed)
slinkey, slink(y)
slinkt, slink(ed) / sling(ed)
slinter, slender
slip,*,pped,pping,ppery, SLIDE/GLIDE/ FALL AWAY, LOSS OF TRACTION/ FOOTING, AN UNDERGARMENT (or see sleep)
sliparee, slip(ppery)
slipry, slip(ppery)
slipt, slip(pped)
slipuree, slip(ppery)
slirp, slurp
sliry, slurry
slise, slice
sliser, slice(r)
slit,*,tting,tter, CUT SLOTS/OPENINGS INTO (or see slid/slide/slight/ sleight/sleet)
slited, sleight(ed)/ slight(ed)/ slide(d)
slither,*,red,ring,ry, TO SNAKE/SLIDE ALONG
slithry, slither(y)
slithur, slither
slitly, slight(ly)
sliver,*,red,ring, SMALL/THIN PIECE OF MATTER WHICH SPLINTERS/ SEPARATES FROM LARGER OBJECT
slivir, sliver
slivur, sliver
slo, slaw / slow
slob,*,bbed,bbing, SOMEONE WHO IS UNKEPT/UNCLEAN/UNHEALTHY (or see slab/slop)
slobber,*,red,ring,ry, DROOL/WET SECRETION FROM THE MOUTH
slober, slobber
slobery, slobber(y)
slobur, slobber
slobury, slobber(y)
slod, slot / slow(ed)
slodder, slaughter
slode, slot / slow(ed)
sloder, slaughter
slods, slot(s)
slodur, slaughter
slodurus, slaughter(ous)
sloe, slough / slow
sloer, slow(er)
sloest, slow(est)

slof, slough
slofenly, sloven(ly)
slofun, sloven
slofunly, sloven(ly)
slogan,*, A CATCHWORD/PHRASE/ MOTTO/BATTLE CRY
slogun, slogan
sloir, slow(er)
sloist, slow(est)
sloken, slogan
slokun, slogan
slole, slow(ly)
sloly, slow(ly)
slonis, slow(ness)
sloo, slew / slue / slough
sloose, sluice
slooth, sleuth
slop,*,pped,pping,ppy,ppier,ppiest, ppily,ppiness, CARELESS, SPILLED LIQUID, NASTY FOOD, SLUSHY/ MUDDY (or see slob/slope)
slopd, slope(d) / slop(pped)
slope,*,ed,ping,er,pingly,pingness, AN INCREASE/DECREASE IN ANGLE ALONG A HORIZONTAL/VERTICAL PLANE (or see slop) "prefixes: up"
slopee, slop(ppy)
slopeir, slop(ppier)
slopely, slop(ppily)
slopery, slobber(y)
slopeur, slop(ppier)
slopily, slop(ppily)
slopiness, slop(ppiness)
slopry, slobber(y)
slopt, slope(d) / slop(pped)
slopule, slop(ppily)
slopury, slobber(y)
slopy, slop(ppy)
slopyer, slop(ppier)
slopyest, slop(ppiest)
slopyness, slop(ppiness)
slos, sloth(es)
slosh,hes,hed,hing,hy, LIQUID SPLASHING AROUND
sloshee, slosh(y)
slot,*,tted,tting, NARROW OPENING/ CUT CREATED TO ALLOW INSERTION OF SOMETHING (or see slow(ed))
sloted, slot(tted)
sloter, slaughter
sloth,*, SLOW TREE-DWELLING MAMMAL (or see slough)

slouch,hes,hed,hing,her,hily,hiness,hier, hiest, DROOPS INTO A NON-ERECT POSITION
slough,hy,hiness, SHED/CAST OFF, MARSHY/SWAMPY AREA, CONDITION OF DEGRADATION (or see slew/slue)
slour, slow(er)
sloutsh, slouch
sloutshed, slouch(ed)
sloven,nly,nliness,nlier,nliest, UNTIDY/ CARELESSLY CLAD
slovin, sloven
slovinly, sloven(ly)
slovun, sloven
slovunliness, sloven(liness)
slovunly, sloven(ly)
slow,*,wed,wing,wer,west,wly,wish, wness, PERFORM AT LESS THAN NORMAL/ AVERAGE SPEED (or see slough)
slowb, slob
slowch, slouch
slowcheur, slouch(ier)
slowchily, slouch(ily)
slowist, slow(est)
slowur, slow(er)
slu, slew / slue / slough
sluce, sluice
slud, slue(d) / slough(ed) / slew(ed) / sleuth
sludch, sludge
sludchy, sludge(gy)
sludge,*,gier,giest,gy, A THICK/VISCOUS LIQUID WITH HEAVY SEDIMENT
sludgeur, sludge(gier)
sludje, sludge
slue,*,ed,uing, TO PIVOT/SWING AROUND, HAVING TO DO WITH SLEW (or see slew/slough)
sluee, slough(y)
slueness, slough(iness)
sluf, slough
slug,*,gged,gging,ggish,ggishly, ggishness,gger, REMNANT OF BULLET THAT'S BEEN SHOT, HIT/ LUG SOMETHING, GASTROPOD THAT EATS PLANTS
slugar, slugger
sluge, sludge
sluger, slugger
slugesh, slug(ggish)
slugeshness, slug(ggishness)
slugeur, sludge(gier)

slugger,*, ONE WHO HITS HARD/HEAVY
slugir, slugger
slugish, slug(ggish)
slugishnes, slug(ggishenss)
slugt, slug(gged)
slugur, slugger
slugush, slug(ggish)
slugy, sludge(gy)
sluice,*,ed,cing, A CHANNEL/CANAL OF WATER, ITEM USED TO PAN FOR GOLD
sluje, sludge
slujeir, sludge(gier)
slujy, sludge(gy)
sluk, slug
sluker, slugger
slukesh, slug(ggish)
slukir, slugger
slukishnes, slug(ggishness)
slukur, slugger
slum,*,mmed,mming,mmer, POOR/HIGHLY POPULATED/DIRTY AREA
slumber,*,red,ring,rer,rless,rous,ry, rously,rousness, TO SLEEP, BE QUITE INACTIVE, LIGHT SLEEP/DOZE
slumbir, slumber
slumbrus, slumber(ous)
slumbrusly, slumber(ously)
slumbrusness, slumber(ousness)
slumbry, slumber(y)
slumbur, slumber
slumd, slum(mmed)
slump,*,ped,ping, DIP IN PRODUCTION, A SURFACE/VALUE
slumper, slumber
slumpur, slumber
slumur, slum(mmer)
slung, PAST TENSE FOR "SLING"
slunk, slung
slur,*,rred,rring, TO SMEAR/SMUDGE WORDS/SPEECH, INARTICULATE, CARELESS
slureng, slurry(ing) / slur(rring)
slurp,*,ped,ping, LOUD SIPPING SOUNDS WITH MOUTH
slurry,ried,ying, SOFT/ORGANIC MATERIAL CHOPPED UP IN LIQUID
slury, slurry
sluryed, slurry(ried)
slurz, slur(s)
slus, sluice
sluse, sluice

slush,hy,hiness, BETWEEN LIQUID AND SOLID
slushyness, slush(iness)
slutch, sludge
slutge, sludge
sluth, sleuth
slutje, sludge
sluy, slough(y)
sly,yly,yness, SMOOTH/DISCREET/QUIET
slym, slim / slime
slynis, sly(ness)
slynke, slink(y)
slyse, slice
slyt, slight / slide / slid
smack,*,ked,king,ker, TO DO WITH THE MOUTH, A SHARP BLOW, DIRECT, STRAIGHT, SAILING VESSEL
smak, smack
smaker, smack(er)
smal, small
smaler, small(er)
smalest, small(est)
smalist, small(est)
small,ller,llest,llness, NOT AS LARGE COMPARED TO NORMAL/AVERAGE
smarden, smart(en)
smardest, smart(est)
smardin, smart(en)
smart,*,ted,ten,ter,test,ting,tly,tness,ty, SHARP/QUICK/ALERT/PRACTICAL
smartie, smart(y)
smartist, smart(est)
smash,hes,hed,hing,her, BLAST/CRUSH/DEMOLISH TO PIECES, DESTROY BY VIOLENT BLOWS
smashur, smash(er)
smear,*,red,ring,ry, TO SPREAD/WIPE INTO, CAUSE TO RUN TOGETHER, SLANDER
smedin, smite(tten)
smeer, smear
smeery, smeer(y)
smel, smell
smeld, smell(ed) / smelt
smelder, smelter
smeldur, smelter
smelee, smell(y)
smell,*,led,ling,ly,lt, PERCEIVE WITH THE NOSE/OLFACTORY
smelt, FISH (or see smell(ed))
smelter,*, METAL MELTING PROCESS
smely, smell(y)
smer, smear

smerk, smirk
smerker, smirk(er)
smethureens, smithereens
smetin, smite(tten)
smiden, smite(tten)
smil, smile
smile,*,ed,ling,er,ey,lier,liest, FACIAL EXPRESSION STATING THAT ALL IS WELL, FRIENDLY EXPRESSION
"prefixes: un"
smily, smile(y)
smirk,*,ked,king,ker,kingly, SMUG SMILE EXPRESSING SUPERIORITY/CONCEIT
smirkd, smirk(ed)
smit, smite
smite,*,ting,mote,tten, SERIOUSLY/DEEPLY STRUCK/AFFECTED, EXACT
smiten, smite(tten)
smithereens, BLOW/SMASH TO PIECES/BITS
smithureens, smithereens
smitin, smite(tten)
smiwree, smeer(y)
smock,*, OUTER GARMENT LOOSELY COVERING MAIN TORSO (or see smoke)
smog,ggy,ggier,ggiest,ggless,gginess, HEAVY AIRBORNE POLLUTION (or see smock/smoke)
smogy, smog(ggy)
smok, smock / smog / smoke
smokd, smoke(d) / smog(gged)
smoke,*,ed,king,kier,kiest,kily,kiness,er, eless,ey, CLOUD OF GAS RESULTING FROM BURNED MATERIAL (or see smock)
smokir, smoke(r)
smokless, smoke(less)
smoklus, smoke(less)
smokt, smoke(d) / smog(ed)
smokur, smoke(r)
smoky, smoke(y) / smog(ggy)
smol, small
smold, smolt
smolder,*,red,ring, SLOWLY COOK IN SMOKE WITHOUT FLAME
smoler, small(er)
smolir, small(er)
smolt, A STAGE IN SALMON/FISH GROWTH
smolter, smolder
smoltur, smolder
smolur, small(er)

smooch,hes,hed,hing, TO HUG/KISS
smooth,hes,hed,hing,her,hest,hly,hness, hen,hie, NOT ROUGH, PLEASANT TO THE SENSES
smoothie,*, A FRUIT SLUSH/DRINK
smoothin, smooth(en)
smoothnis, smooth(ness)
smoothy, smoothie
smorgasboard,*, BUFFET WITH CONGLOMERATION/SELECTION OF FOODS
smorgusboard, smorgasboard
smort, smart
smoth, smooth
smother,*,red,ring, COVER, PUT OUT, STIFLE, SUPPRESS, SUFFOCATE (or see smooth(er))
smuch, smooch / smudge
smuched, smooch(ed) / smudge(d)
smuches, smooch(es) / smudge(s)
smudeist, smut(ttiest)
smudeness, smut(ttiness)
smudeur, smut(ttier)
smudge,*,ed,ging,er, SMEAR/STAIN, A SMOLDERING FIRE/SMOKE FOR PROTECTION
smudy, smut(tty)
smug,gly,gness, SELF-SATISFIED/ CONCEITED (or see smooch)
smugal, smuggle
smugaler, smuggle(r)
smuge, smudge
smuggle,*,ed,ling,er, TRANSPORT SOMETHING ACROSS A LAWFUL BORDER WITHOUT PERMISSION
smuglir, smuggle(r)
smugul, smuggle
smuj, smudge
smuk, smug
smukil, smuggle
smuklee, smug(ly)
smukler, smuggle(r)
smukly, smug(ly)
smuknes, smug(ness)
smukul, smuggle
smukuler, smuggle(r)
smurk, smirk
smut,tted,tting,tty,ttier,ttiest,ttily, ttiness, SOOTY/SMUDGED, INDECENT LANGUAGE, PLANT AFFECTED BY FUNGUS SPORES
smuteir, smut(ttier)
smuteist, smut(ttiest)
smuteness, smut(ttiness)

smuth, smooth
smuthen, smooth(en)
smuther, smooth(er) / smother
smuthie, smoothie
smuthir, smooth(er) / smother
smuthist, smooth(est)
smuthly, smooth(ly)
smuthness, smooth(ness)
smuthy, smoothie
smuty, smut(tty)
snabur, snap(pper)
snach, snatch
snachir, snatch(er)
snack,*,ked,king, BITS OF FOOD BETWEEN MEALS (or see snake/ snag)
snael, snail
snafoo, snafu
snafu,ued,uing, UNEXPECTED/CHAOTIC TURN OF EVENTS
snag,*,gged,gging,ggy,ggier,ggiest, BE CAUGHT UP/ENTANGLED (or see snack) "prefixes: un"
snageist, snag(ggiest)
snaggier, snag(ggier)
snail,*, GASTROPOD MOLLUSK WITH SHELL
snair, snare
snak, snack / snake / snag
snakd, snack(ed) / snake(d) / snag(gged)
snake,*,ed,king,ky,kily, REPTILE WITHOUT ARMS/LEGS (or see snack)
snakey, snake(ky)
snaks, snack(s) / snake(s) / snag(s)
snakt, snack(ed) / snake(d) / snag(gged)
snale, snail
snap,*,pped,pping,pper, A QUICK/ BITING MOTION, CRISP BREAK, BRITTLE/TENSE "prefixes: un"
snaper, snap(pper)
snapper,*, A FISH
snapur, snap(pper)
snard, snare(d)
snare,*,ed,ring,er, A TRAP/NOOSE FOR CATCHING THINGS, USED FOR INSTRUMENT "prefixes: en"
snarl,*,led,ling,ler,ly,lingly, TO ENTANGLE/COMPLICATE, A THREATENING SOUND "prefixes: en/un"
snarlee, snarl(y)
snart, snare(d)

snasee, snazzy
snaseur, snazzy(zier)
snasiest, snazzy(ziest)
snasy, snazzy
snatch,hes,hed,hing,her, SUDDEN/ SWIFT MOVE TO GRASP/SEIZE SOMETHING
snaul, snail
snawt, snout
snazeir, snazzy(zier)
snazeist, snazzy(ziest)
snazeur, snazzy(zier)
snazy, snazzy
snazzy,zzier,zziest, FANCY
sneak,*,ked,king,kingly,kily,kiness,ky, ker, ENGAGE IN ACTIVITY IN A SECRETIVE MANNER
sneaker,*, TENNIS SHOES, SOMEONE WHO SNEAKS AROUND
sneakey, sneak(y)
sneakuly, sneak(ily)
snear, sneer
sneaze, sneeze
sneazy, sneeze(zy)
snech, snitch
snechur, snitch(er)
sneek, sneak
sneeker, sneaker
sneeky, sneak(y)
sneer,*,red,ring,rer,ringly, FACIAL EXPRESSION OF CONTEMPT/SCORN
sneesy, sneeze(zy)
sneeze,*,ed,zing,zy, AN INVOLUNTARY GUST OF AIR FORCED THROUGH THE NASAL PASSAGES TO RELIEVE THEM OF AN IRRITANT
snef, sniff
snefdur, snifter
snefel, sniffle
snefer, sniff(er)
sneftur, snifter
sneful, sniffle
snefur, sniff(er)
snek, sneak
sneker, sneaker
snekily, sneak(ily)
snekir, sneaker
snekuly, sneak(ily)
snekur, sneaker / snicker
sneky, sneak(y)
snep, snip
snepee, snip(ppy)
snepit, snippet
snept, snip(pped)

sner, snare / sneer
snert, snare(d) / sneer(ed)
snesy, sneeze(zy)
snetch, snitch
sneveler, snivel(ller)
snevil, snivel
snevlur, snivel(ller)
snevul, snivel
snevult, snivel(lled)
snewdy, snooty
snewp, snoop
snews, snooze
sneze, sneeze
snezy, sneeze(zy)
snibt, snip(pped) / snipe(d)
snich, snitch
snicher, snitch(er)
snicker,*,red,ring, EMOTE A NEGATIVE SNEERING LAUGH OUT OF DISRESPECT
snide,er,est,ely, INSINUATING/ SARCASTIC
snidly, snide(ly)
snif, sniff
snifal, sniffle
snifd, sniff(ed)
snifdur, snifter
snifer, sniff(er)
sniff,*,ffed,ffing,ffer, TO SMELL FOR, USE NOSE FOR DETECTION
sniffle,*,ed,ling,er, A NASAL SOUND
snifter,*, STYLE OF GLASS DRINKING VESSEL
sniftur, snifter
sniful, sniffle
snifur, sniff(er)
sniker, snicker
snikur, snicker
snip,*,pped,pping,ppy, CUT OFF A SMALL PORTION OF SOMETHING (or see snipe)
snipe,*,ed,ping,er, TYPE OF BIRD, TO SHOOT FROM A CAMOUFLAGED POSITION (or see snip)
sniped, snip(pped) / snipe(d)
snipee, snip(ppy)
snipet, snippet
snippet,*, SMALL BITS/FRAGMENTS/ PARTS
snipur, snipe(r)
sniput, snippet
snitch,hes,hed,hing,her, FINK/RAT ON SOMEONE, BE AN INFORMANT
snite, snide

snitly, snide(ly)
snivel,*,lled,lling,ller, WHINE/CRY WHILE EXCREMENTING SNOT/ MUCOUS FROM NOSE
snivlur, snivel(ller)
snivul, snivel
sno, snow
snob,*,bby,bbery,bberies,bbish,bbishly, bbishness, SOMEONE APPEARING TO DISPLAY SUPERIORITY/ SMUGNESS/SELF-RIGHTEOUSNESS
snobeshnis, snob(bbishness)
snobish, snob(bbish)
snoby, snob(bby)
snod, snow(ed) / snot
snody, snot(tty)
snoker, snooker
snoodeist, snooty(tiest)
snoody, snooty
snooker,*, GAME OF BILLIARDS
snoop,*,ped,ping,per,pier,piest,py, SOMEONE WHO IS NOSY/PRYING/ PROWLING
snoose, snooze
snooty,tier,tiest,tily,tiness, SNOBBISH, BELIEVE THEY'RE EXCLUSIVE
snooze,*,ed,zing,er, SLEEP/NAP
snop, snob
snopee, snob(bby)
snopy, snob(bby)
snore,*,ed,ring,er, EMIT LOUD BREATHING SOUND DURING SLEEP, TO SLEEP WITH THE MOUTH OPEN
snorkel,*,led,ling, UNDERWATER BREATHING APPARATUS
snorkul, snorkel
snorl, snarl
snorlingly, snarl(lingly)
snort,*,ted,ting,ty, LOUD/QUICK BURST OF AIR FORCED FROM THE NOSE
snot,tty, MUCOUS EXCREMENTED IN THE SINUS CAVITIES, SOMEONE WHO HAS AN AIR OF SUPERIORITY/ CALLOUSNESS
snotee, snot(tty)
snoud, snout
snout,*,ted, THE NOSE/MUZZLE OF ANIMALS
snow,*,wed,wing,wy, WHITE/LIGHT PRECIPITATION FALLING FROM CLOUDS, BURY/COVER/FOOL SOMEONE LIKE SNOW AS A BLANKET
snowd, snow(ed) / snout

snowee, snow(y)
snowt, snout / snow(ed)
snub,*,bbed,bbing,bness,bby,bbiness, TURNED UP NOSE WITH ATTITUDE, REBUKE/REBUFF/NEGLECT (or see snoop)
snube, snub(bby) / snoop(y)
snubed, snoop(ed) / snub(bbed)
snubiness, snub(bbiness)
snubt, snoop(ed)
snuby, snub(bby)
snudy, snooty
snuf, snuff
snuff,*,ffer,ffy,ffier,ffiest, PAST TENSE FOR THE WORD "SNIFF", PUT OUT/ EXTINGUISH/END, POWDERED TOBACCO
snuffely, snuffle(ly)
snuffle,*,ed,ling,ly, SNIFFLE/NASAL CONGESTION
snufil, snuffle
snufir, snuff(er)
snufuly, snuffle(ly)
snufur, snuff(er)
snug,gger,ggest,gged,gging,gness,ggery, FIRMLY/COMFORTABLY IN PLACE
snugelt, snuggle(d)
snuger, snug(gger)
snuggle,*,ed,ling,ly, COZY/NESTLE UP COMFORTABLY AGAINST SOMETHING/ SOMEONE
snugle, snuggle
snugly, snuggle(ly)
snugnis, snug(ness)
snugul, snuggle
snuker, snooker
snukle, snuggle
snuklee, snuggle(ly)
snupe, snoop
snuper, snoop(er)
snupy, snoop(y)
snuse, snooze
snuteir, snooty(tier)
snuteist, snooty(tiest)
snuty, snooty
snuze, snooze
snyd, snide
so, THAT WHICH IS APPROXIMATE (or see sew/sow)
soak,*,ked,king,ker, EXPOSE TO MOISTURE UNTIL SATURATED
soap,*,ped,ping,py,piness, MANMADE COMPOUND USED FOR CLEANING (or see sop)

soar,*,red,ring,rer, RISE TO GREAT HEIGHTS EITHER LITERALLY/ FIGURATIVELY (or see sore)
soaside, suicide
sob,*,bbed,bbing, CRY WITH DEEP GASPS/EMOTION (or see sop/soap/sub)
sobcity, subsidy
sobconshos, subconscious
sobcontract, subcontract
sobdue, subdue
sobed, sob(bbed) / soap(ed) / sop(pped)
sober,*,red,ring,ringly,rness, NOT INTOXICATED/DRUNK, INFORMATION WHICH IS SERIOUS/ GRAVE IN NATURE
soberb, suburb
sobgekt, subject
sobir, sober
sobirnes, sober(ness)
sobject, subject
sobkonshus, subconscious
sobleminal, subliminal
soblime, sublime
soblimenal, subliminal
sobmarine, submarine
sobmerge, submerge
sobmesev, submissive
sobmeshin, submission
sobmesiv, submissive
sobmet, submit
sobmirge, submerge
sobmisev, submissive
sobmishon, submission
sobmit, submit
sobmuren, submarine
sobordenate, subordinate
sobordenation, subordinate(tion)
sobort, support
sobpena, subpoena
sobpina, subpoena
sobragate, subrogate
sobregate, subrogate
sobriaty, sobriety
sobriety, BEING SOBER, FREE FROM EXCESS/EXTRAVAGANCE, SERIOUS/ GRAVE "prefixes: in"
sobriudy, sobriety
sobrogate, subrogate
sobrugate, subrogate
sobsedy, subsidy
sobsequent, subsequent
sobsikwent, subsequent

sobstans, substance
sobstanshal, substantial
sobstins, substance
sobt, sop(pped) / sob(bbed)
sobtract, subtract
sobur, sober
soburnes, sober(ness)
sobvergin, subversion
sobvershen, subversion
sobversive, subversive
sobvert, subvert
sobvirgin, subversion
sobvirsev, subversive
sobvirshen, subversion
sobvirt, subvert
sobvurgin, subversion
sobvurshen, subversion
sobvursive, subversive
sobvurt, subvert
soccer, A TYPE OF FOOTBALL GAME
socebdubility, susceptible(bility)
socer, soccer
sochably, sociable(ly)
sochalist, social(ist)
sochaly, social(lly)
sochealugist, sociology(gist)
sochebul, sociable
sochel, social
sochelize, social(ize)
sochely, social(lly)
socheolegy, sociology
socheolugist, sociology(gist)
socher, soldier
sochibly, sociable(ly)
sochibul, sociable
sochil, social
sochilest, social(ist)
sochilize, social(ize)
sochily, social(lly)
sochioligy, sociology
sochuble, sociable
sochubly, sociable(ly)
sochul, social
sochulee, social(lly)
sochulist, social(ist)
sochulize, social(ize)
sochur, soldier
sociable,bility,eness,ly, ABILITY TO INTERACT WITH OTHERS "prefixes: un"
social,*,lism,list,listic,listically,lite,lity, lize,lized,lizing,lization,lizer,lly, INTERACTION WITH OTHERS "prefixes: sub/un"

socialest, social(ist)
socialigest, sociology(gist)
socialise, social(ize)
socialy, social(lly)
society,ties,tal, GROUPS OF PEOPLE WITH COMMONALITIES "prefixes: non"
socioligest, sociology(gist)
sociology,gical,gically,gist, SCIENCE OF STUDYING HOW SOCIAL INTERACTION IS CONDUCTED
socir, soccer
sociubly, sociable(ly)
sock,*,ked,king, A CLOTH FOOT COVERING, BE PUNCHED BY SOMEONE, WINDSOCK FOR WIND DIRECTION (or see soak)
socket,*, SOMETHING WITH THE SHAPE OF A HOLLOWED OUT/SHORT CYLINDER WITH A BASE
sockit, socket
sockut, socket
socom, succumb
socseshan, succession
socsesion, succession
socshen, suction
socshun, suction
socur, soccer / secure
socurity, secure(rity)
socurly, secure(ly)
sod,dded,dding,ddy, TURF, GRASS WITH ROOTS (or see sold/saw(ed)/ sought/ sew(ed))
soda,*, CARBONATED DRINK, COMPOUNDS OF SODIUM
sodame, sodomy
sodan, sedan
sodden,nly,nness, HEAVY WITH MOISTURE, SOGGY
soded, sod(dded) / sold
sodeim, sodium
sodemize, sodomy(mize)
sodemy, sodomy
soden, sodden
sodeum, sodium
sodimise, sodomy(mize)
sodimy, sodomy
sodin, sodden
sodinly, sodden(ly)
sodium, METALLIC/NATURAL/ACTIVE ELEMENT
sodn, sudden
sodomy,mize,mized,mizing, HATEFUL, SELF-CENTERED ACT OF ANAL

PENETRATION FORCED ONTO ANOTHER
sodu, soda
sodumee, sodomy
sodumize, sodomy(mize)
sodun, sodden
sodunly, sodden(ly)
sody, sod(ddy)
soe, soy
soeal, soil
soebean, soybean
soee, soy
soeil, soil
soeled, soil(ed)
soem, psalm
soerdo, sourdough
soeul, soil
sofaree, safari
sofaren, sovereign
sofari, safari
sofecate, suffocate
sofekate, suffocate
sofeks, suffix
sofen, soft(en)
sofenir, soft(ener)
sofer, suffer
soferin, sovereign
sofeshent, sufficient
sofet, soffit
sofex, suffix
soffit,*, NECESSARY GEOMETRIC COMPONENT OF A STRUCTURE
soficate, suffocate
sofics, suffix
sofin, soft(en)
sofineer, souvenir
sofinur, soft(ener)
sofiren, sovereign
sofise, suffice
sofishent, sufficient
sofit, soffit
sofmore, sophomore
sofomore, sophomore
sofr, suffer
sofrech, suffrage
sofren, sovereign
sofrenity, sovereign(ity)
sofrenudy, sovereign(ity)
sofrin, sovereign
sofrinedy, sovereign(ity)
sofrun, sovereign
soft,tly,tness,ten,tener,ty, SMOOTH/GENTLE/COMFORTABLE "prefixes: semi"

softenur, soft(ener)
softur, soft(er)
sofun, soft(en)
sofuner, souvenir / soft(ener)
sofunir, soft(ener) / souvenir
sofuren, sovereign
sofut, soffit
sogee, soggy
sogenis, soggy(gginess)
soger, soldier
soggy,ggier,ggiest,ggily,gginess, THOROUGHLY SOAKED
sogir, soldier
sogjesgen, suggest(ion)
sogjest, suggest
sogur, soldier
sogy, soggy
sogyness, soggy(gginess)
soht, sought/ sew(ed)
soi, soy
soibeen, soybean
soil,*,led,ling,lless,lage, DIRT, ORGANIC DECAYED MATTER "prefixes: sub"
soing, sew(ing) / sow(ing)
soirdow, sourdough
sok, sock / soak
sokd, sock(ed) / soak(ed)
soked, sock(ed) / soak(ed)
sokee, soggy
sokenis, soggy(gginess)
soker, soccer / soak(er)
soket, socket
sokeulent, succulent
sokgeschen, suggest(ion)
sokir, soccer
sokit, socket
sokl, suckle
sokshen, suction
sokt, sock(ed) / soak(ed)
sokulent, succulent
sokur, soccer
sokut, socket
soky, soggy
sokynis, soggy(gginess)
sol, sole / soul / saw
solace,*,ed,cing, PROVIDE COMFORT, ALLEVIATION FROM WORRY/ SORROW/GRIEF
solad, solid / salad
soladerity, solidarity
solami, salami
solanoyd, solenoid

solar,rize,rizes,rized,rizing,rization,rium, HEAT/LIGHT PRODUCED BY SUN "prefixes: sub"
solarium,*, ENCLOSURE WHICH ALLOWS MAXIMUM PENETRATION OF THE SUNS RAYS
solas, solace / soul(ess) / sole(eless)
solatare, solitaire / solitary
solatarily, solitary(rily)
solatary, solitary
solatood, solitude
solatude, solitude
solcher, soldier
solchur, soldier
sold, PAST TENSE FOR THE WORD 'SELL' "prefixes: over/un/under"
solder,*,red,ring,rer, USE OF FLUX/ SOFT METAL TO MELD SEVERAL PIECES OF METAL TOGETHER
soldier,*,rly,rship,ry,ries, PEOPLE TRAINED TO PARTICIPATE IN WAR/ BATTLE
soldir, solder / soldier
soldired, solder(ed)
sole,*,ely,eness,eless, ONE AND ONLY, THE BOTTOM OF FEET/SHOES (or see soul) "prefixes: in"
solective, select(ive)
soled, solid
soledarity, solidarity
soledify, solid(ify)
soledness, solid(ness)
solee, sole(ly)
solelukwy, soliloquy
solem, solemn
solemly, solemn(ly)
solemn,nly,nness,nity,nities,nize, nization, OBSERVANCE OF CELEBRATIONS/RITES, OF A GRAVE/ SERIOUS ACTIVITY OR DISPOSITION
solen, sullen
solenium, selenium
solenoid,*,dal,dally, MAGNETICALLY CONTROLLED
soler, solar
solereum, solarium
solerize, solar(ize)
soles, solace / soul(ess) / sole(eless)
solesit, solicit
solesitation, solicit(ation)
solesiter, solicit(er)
solesment, solace(ment)
solet, solid
soletare, solitaire / solitary

soletarily, solitary(rily)
soletary, solitary
soletness, solid(ness)
soletood, solitude
soletude, solitude
solf, solve
solfely, soul(fully)
solfint, solvent
solfite, sulfite / sulfide
solfor, sulfur
solfuly, soul(fully)
solfunt, solvent
solger, soldier
solgur, soldier
solicit,*,ted,ting,tor,tation,tous,tously, tousness, REQUEST/SEEK/APPLY/INFLUENCE/PETITION FOR AN ACTION/OPPORTUNITY/FUNDING "prefixes: un"
solid,*,dly,dify,difiable,dification,dness, dity,dities,darity, GIVE THE IMPRESSION OF BEING HARD/FIRM/COMPACT/THICK "prefixes: semi"
solidarity,ties, PEOPLE WHO FORM SOLID RELATIONSHIPS BASED ON COMMONALITIES
solidefy, solid(ify)
soliderity, solidarity
solilaquy, soliloquy
soliloquy,uies,uist,uizer, TALK TO ONESELF, SHARE THOUGHTS OUTLOUD IN FRONT OF AN AUDIENCE
solim, solemn
solimly, solemn(ly)
solin, sullen
solinoid, solenoid
solir, solar
solirise, solar(ize)
solis, solace / soul(ess) / sole(eless)
soliset, solicit
solisetation, solicit(ation)
soliseter, solicit(er)
solisment, solace(ment)
solit, solid
solitaire,ry, CARD GAME PLAYED ALONE
solitary,ries,rily,riness, OF BEING COMPLETELY ALONE, SECLUDED
solitness, solid(ness)
solitude, ALONE/REMOTE/LONELY
solivu, saliva
soljer, soldier
soljur, soldier

solking, sulk(ing)
solm, psalm
solo,*,oed,oing,oist, TO PERFORM ALONE
solomi, salami
solon, salon
solonoid, solenoid
soloon, saloon
soloot, salute
solstice,*,itial,itially, TIME OF THE YEAR BASED UPON SUN'S POSITION
solstis, solstice
solt, sold / soil(ed) / salt
soluble,eness,ly,bility,bilities,bilize, bilizes,bilized,bilizing,bilization, ABLE TO DISSOLVE IN WATER "prefixes: dis/in/re"
solud, solid
solum, solemn
solumly, solemn(ly)
solun, sullen
solune, saloon
solunoid, solenoid
solur, solar
solurize, solar(ize)
soluse, solace / soul(ess) / sole(eless)
solutare, solitaire / solitary
solutarily, solitary(rily)
solutary, solitary
solute, salute
solution,*, A COMBINATION OF CHEMICAL FORMS, THE ANSWER TO A PROBLEM, SETTLEMENT
solutood, solitude
solutude, solitude
solvant, solvent
solvashin, salvation
solve,*,ed,ving,vable,vability,vableness, er, REMEDY/FIX/UNDERSTAND (or see salve) "prefixes: in"
solvent,ency,ently, ABLE TO BE DISSOLVED
solvuble, solve(vable)
solvunt, solvent
soly, sole(ly)
solyewble, soluble(ize)
solyubel, soluble
som, psalm / sum / some
somber,rly,rness, MELANCHOLY/GRAVE/DEPRESSING IN MOOD/ATTITUDE
sombir, somber
sombirly, somber(ly)

sombreo, sombrero
sombrero,*, A WIDE BRIM HAT
sombur, somber
somburly, somber(ly)
somchuos, sumptuous
some, PARTIAL, AN INDEFINITE AMOUNT/DISTANCE (or see sum)
somersault,*,ted,ting, AN ENTIRE BODY MANEUVER WITH HEELS GOING OVER HEAD
somester, semester
somet, summit
something, WANT FOR, INDETERMINABLE AMOUNT/TYPE/OBJECT OF, OPPOSITE OF NOTHING
sometime,*, UNSPECIFIED TIME
somewar, somewhere
somewat, somewhat
somewere, somewhere
somewhat, INDETERMINATE MEASURE
somewhere, UNSPECIFIED PLACE
somewot, somewhat
somewut, somewhat
somirsalt, somersault
somirsolt, somersault
somit, summit
somon, summon
somp, sump
sompchuos, sumptuous
somper, somber
somptuous, sumptuous
sompur, somber
somtheng, something
somthing, something
somtime, sometime
somting, something
somwar, somewhere
somwat, somewhat
somwer, somewhere
somwhare, somewhere
somwhere, somewhere
somwot, somewhat
somwut, somewhat
son,*,nless,nny, PARENT'S MALE OFFSPRING (or see sun/sown/sewn/sunn)
sona, sauna
sonar, ACRONYM FOR SOUND NAVIGATION AND RANGING (or see soon(er))
sonareo, scenario
sonata, A FORM FOR INSTRUMENTS IN MUSIC
sonda, sunday

sondree, sundry
sondrys, sundry(ries)
sonec, sonic
sonek, sonic
sonereo, scenario
sonet, sonnet
song,*,gful,gless, COLLECTION/ ARRANGEMENT OF MUSICAL NOTES AND/OR ACCOMPANYING WORDS
sonic,cally, SOUNDWAVE/FREQUENCY "prefixes: sub/super"
sonik, sonic
sonit, sonnet
sonk, song
sonkles, song(less)
sonks, song(s)
sonnet,*,teer,tize,tization, A COMPLETE IDEA WRITTEN POETICALLY IN 14 LINES
sonor, sonar
sonseer, sincere
sonter, saunter
sontir, saunter
sontre, saunter
sontree, sundry
sontres, sundry(ries)
sontur, saunter
sonu, sauna
sonuk, sonic
sonut, sonnet
sooaside, suicide
soodar, suitor
soodir, suitor
soodo, pseudo
soodor, suitor
soody, soot(y)
sooet, suet
soofaneer, souvenir
soofineer, souvenir
soofla, souffle'
sooflay, souffle'
soofuneer, souvenir
sooit, suet
sookrose, sucrose
soon,ner,nest, BEFORE IT'S TOO LATE, CLOSE TO NOW, READILY PREFER (or see sun/son)
soopereur, superior
sooperfishul, superficial
sooperioredy, superior(ity)
soopireur, superior
soopirfishul, superficial
soopurb, superb

soopurfishul, superficial
soot,ty, BLACK CARBON RESULTANT OF BURNED MATERIAL (or see suit)
sooter, suitor
soothe,*,ed,hing,hingly,hingness, TO CALM, RELIEVE AGITATION
sootir, suitor
sootor, suitor
soour, sewer
soovaneer, souvenir
soovuneer, souvenir
sop,*,pped,pping,ppy, ABSORB/ SATURATE SOMETHING WITH LIQUID (or see soap/soup/sob/sap)
sopausetori, suppository
sopazeshan, supposition
sopd, sop(pped) / sob(bbed) / soap(ed)
sope, soap / sop / soap(y) / sop(ppy)
soped, sop(pped) / sob(bbed) / soap(ed)
sopee, soap(y)
soper, sober / sob(bber) / supper
soperioredy, superior(ity)
soperiority, superior(ity)
sophisticate,*,ed,edly,tion, IMPROVED QUALITY OF "prefixes: un"
sophmore, sophomore
sophomore,*,ric,rical,rically, STUDENT IN THE SECOND YEAR OF A FOUR-YEAR COURSE
soplant, supplant
soport, support
sopos, suppose
soposetori, suppository
soposishon, supposition
soprano,*, HIGHEST OCTAVE ABLE TO BE OBTAINED BY VOICE OR INSTRUMENT
soprechen, suppress(ion)
sopremosy, supremacy
sopreno, soprano
sopres, suppress
sopreshen, suppress(ion)
sopretion, suppress(ion)
soprietee, sobriety
soprim, supreme
soprino, soprano
sopscrepshon, subscription
sopsekwent, subsequent
sopsequent, subsequent
sopsid, subside
sopsikwent, subsequent
sopstans, substance
sopstanshal, substantial

sopt, sop(pped) / sob(bbed) / soap(ed)
sopy, soap(y) / sop(ppy)
soquer, secure
soquerity, secure(rity)
soquerly, secure(ly)
sor, sore / soar
soran, saran
sorape, serape
sorce, source
sorcerur, sorcery(rer)
sorcery,rer,rous, USING THE "SOURCE"/ INVISIBLE FIELD TO CREATE PHYSICAL THINGS/ACTIONS
sord, soar(ed) / sword / sort
sorded, sordid / sort(ed)
sordedly, sordid(ly)
sordeen, sardine
sordene, sardine
sorder, sort(er)
sordid,dly,dness, OF BEING DIRTY/ MEAN (or see sort(ed))
sordir, sort(er)
sordud, sordid / sort(ed)
sordudly, sordid(ly)
sordur, sort(er)
sore,*,er,est,ely,eness, PAIN, INFLAMMATION, PERTURBED (or see soar/sorry)
sored, soar(ed) / sword
soree, sorry / saury
sorel, sorrel / surreal
soren, serene
sorender, surrender
sorenidy, serene(nity)
sorenity, serene(nity)
soresury, sorcery
sorf, surf
sorfas, surface
sorfis, surface
sorgem, sorghum
sorgent, sergeant / surgent
sorghum, GRAIN USED FOR MANY PURPOSES
sorgint, sergeant / surgent
sorgum, sorghum
sori, sorry / saury
sorial, surreal
sorialism, surreal(ism)
soriasis, psoriasis
sorily, sorry(rily)
sorinder, surrender
soriol, surreal
soriolism, surreal(ism)
sorir, sore(r)

sorist, sore(st)
soriusis, psoriasis
sorkazem, sarcasm
sorkem, sorghum
sorkum, sorghum
sorly, sore(ly)
sorness, sore(ness)
sornis, sore(ness)
soro, sorrow
soroful, sorrow(ful)
sorority,ties, FEMALE COLLEGE ORGANIZATIONS
sorow, sorrow
sorowful, sorrow(ful)
sorples, surplus
sorplus, surplus
sorpris, surprise
sorrel, AN EDIBLE PLANT (or see surreal)
sorro, sorrow
sorrow,*,wful,wfully,wfulness, GRIEF, SADNESS, REGRET
sorry,rrier,rriest,rrily,rriness, APOLOGETIC, REGRETFUL, RESENTFUL (or see saury)
sors, source / sore(s) / czar(s)
sorseree, sorcery
sorserer, sorcery(rer)
sorsuree, sorcery
sorsurer, sorcery(rer)
sort,*,ted,ting,ter,table, CATEGORIZE/ COMPARTMENTALIZE/ARRANGE BY ASSOCIATION (or see sword/sordid) "prefixes: re-"
sortar, sort(er)
sorted, sordid / sort(ed)
sortedly, sordid(ly)
sortidly, sordid(ly)
sortir, sort(er)
sortud, sordid / sort(ed)
sortudly, sordid(ly)
sortur, sort(er)
sorur, sore(r)
sorva, survey
sory, saury / sorry
sorz, source / sore(s)
sos, sauce / saw(s) / sew(s)
sosbect, suspect
sosbenchen, suspension
sosbended, suspend(ed)
sosbenders, suspender(s)
sosbens, suspense
sose, saucy
sosege, sausage

soseje, sausage
soseptef, susceptive
soseptif, susceptive
soseptubility, susceptible(bility)
soser, saucer
soseshen, secession
sosetion, secession
soseur, saucy(cier)
soshable, sociable
soshaly, social(lly)
soshealegy, sociology
soshebul, sociable
soshel, social
soshelize, social(ize)
sosheolugest, sociology(gist)
sosheolugy, sociology
soshible, sociable
soshibly, sociable(ly)
soshibul, sociable
soshil, social
soshilist, social(ist)
soshilize, social(ize)
soshily, social(lly)
soshubil, sociable
soshubly, sociable(ly)
soshul, social
soshulist, social(ist)
soshulize, social(ize)
soshuly, social(lly)
sosiatal, society(tal)
sosiaty, society
sosiedle, society(tal)
sosier, saucy(cier)
sosietal, society(tal)
sosiety, society
sosige, sausage
sosije, sausage
sosiology, sociology
sosir, saucer
sosiudil, society(tal)
sosiudy, society
sosiutul, society(tal)
sosoge, sausage
sosoje, sausage
sospact, suspect
sospect, suspect
sospenchen, suspension
sospens, suspense
sospeshen, suspicion
sospeshes, suspicious
sospinchen, suspension
sospinded, suspend(ed)
sospins, suspense
sospishon, suspicion

sospishus, suspicious
sosuge, sausage
sosuje, sausage
sosur, saucer
sosy, saucy
sot, sought / suite / soot
sota, soda
sotame, sodomy
sotanic, satanic
sotay, saute / sate
sote, saute / sate
soted, saute(d)
soteim, sodium
sotemy, sodomy
soteum, sodium
sotiably, sociable(ly)
sotiabul, sociable
sotialy, social(lly)
sotu, soda
sotume, sodomy
souerdow, sourdough
souffle',*,ed, A BAKED FLUFFY DISH
soufle', souffle'
sought, PAST TENSE FOR THE WORD "SEEK" "prefixes: un"
souirdow, sourdough
soul,*,lful,lfully,lfulness,lless,llessly, llessness, INVISIBLE FIELD/DESTINY/ SPIRIT THOUGHT TO EXIST WITHIN THE BODY (or see sole/sol) "prefixes: en/in/over"
soulenoid, solenoid
sound,*,ded,ding,der,dest,dly,dness, dless,dlessly,dlessness, AUDIBLE/ HEAR WITH EARS, RELIABLE, A FREQUENCY, LAND NEAR WATER "prefixes: un"
sounly, sound(ly)
soup,*,py,pier,piest, EDIBLE LIQUID BASE WITH BROTH AND/OR VEGETABLES/MEAT
sour,*,red,ring,rish,rly,rness, GONE BAD/RANCID, TYPE OF TASTE REGISTERED ON A CERTAIN PLACE ON THE TONGUE
source,*,ed,cing, POINT OF ORIGINATION OF SOMETHING, BEGINNING/PRIMARY "prefixes: in/ out"
sourcrowt, sauerkraut
sourdough,*, TYPE OF BREAD, NICKNAME FOR CANADIAN/ ALASKAN NATIVES
sourkraut, sauerkraut

sourkrowt, sauerkraut
souse,*,ed,sing, BE IMMERSED/ DRENCHED/SATURATED IN, INTOXICATED
soust, souse(d)
sout, sought
souted, saute(d)
south,hern,herner,hernly,herly,herlies, NAVIGATIONAL DIRECTION
souvaneer, souvenir
souvenir,*, A TOKEN WHICH REMINDS/ SHOWS WHAT YOU HAVE DONE OR WHERE YOU HAVE BEEN
souvuneer, souvenir
sovana, savanna
sovant, savant
sovaren, sovereign
sovereign,nly,nty,nties, SELF-SUFFICIENT, FREE OF OUTSIDE CONTROL
soverin, sovereign
soverity, severe(rity)
soviren, sovereign
sovont, savant
sovren, sovereign
sovrenedy, sovereign(ity)
sovrin, sovereign
sovrinedy, sovereign(ity)
sovrun, sovereign
sovt, soft
sovtur, soft(er)
sovurin, sovereign
sow,*,wed,wing,wer,wn, TO PLANT/ IMPLANT/PROPAGATE, FEMALE PIG (or see so/sewn/son/sun/souse)
sowarkraut, sauerkraut
sowd, sew(ed) / sow(ed)
sowded, sound(ded)
sower, sour
sowerdrow, sourdough
sowerkrowt, sauerkraut
sowir, sour
sowirdo, sourdough
sowirkraut, sauerkraut
sowlitare, solitaire / solitary
sown, PAST TENSE FOR THE WORD "SOW" (or see sewn)
sownd, sound
sownded, sound(ded)
sowndlis, sound(less)
sowndly, sound(ly)
sownly, sound(ly)
sownt, sound
sownted, sound(ded)

sowpee, sop(ppy)
sowr, sour / sow(er)
sowree, saury / sorry
sows, sauce / sow(s) / souse / saw(s)
sowsd, souse(d) / sauce(d)
sowt, sew(ed) / sow(ed) / sought
sowth, south
sowuble, soluble(ize)
sowur, sour
sowurdo, sourdough
sowurkraut, sauerkraut
sowurkrowt, sauerkraut
soy, A SOYBEAN SAUCE/CONDIMENT
soybean,*, A PLANT/LEGUME
soybeen, soybean
soyible, soluble
soyl, soil
soyld, sold / soil(ed)
soyuble, soluble(ize)
soyul, soil
soz, sauce / saw(s)
sozy, saucy
spa,*, RETREAT/RESORT/HOT TUB/ MINERAL SPRINGS FACILITY (or see spay)
space,*,ed,cing,er,eless,ey,cious, PLACE WHERE NO APPARENT MATTER EXISTS, NOT OF THIS EARTH "prefixes: inter/sub"
spachela, spatula
spachula, spatula
spacious,sly,sness, OPEN/VAST/BROAD AREA
spackel, spackle
spackle,*,ed,ling,er, PASTE FOR REPAIRING DAMAGE
spacy, space(y)
spad, spade / spay(ed)
spadchewla, spatula
spadchula, spatula
spade,*,ed,ding, A SHOVEL/SYMBOL/ SHAPE
spadshewlu, spatula
spadshula, spatula
spaenk, spank
spagedi, spaghetti
spagem, sphagnum
spageti, spaghetti
spaghetti, LONG/SLENDER PASTA MADE OF FLOUR
spagnem, sphagnum
spagnum, sphagnum
spagum, sphagnum
spaink, spank

spaircity, sparse(sity)
spairs, sparse / spare(s)
spairsly, sparse(ly)
spakel, spackle
spakil, spackle
spakul, spackle
span,*,nned,nning,nner, TOOL, MATCHED PAIR, SPACE/DISTANCE BETWEEN
spangle,*,ed,ling, SPARKLING/GLITTERY ORNAMENTS ON SOMETHING
spank,*,ked,king, OPEN HANDED SWATS ON BUTTOCKS, SPRITELY, LIVELY, NEW
spar,*,rred,rring,rry, PHYSICAL DISPUTE WITH, CRYSTAL-LINED MINERAL (or see spare)
sparadik, sporadic
sparadikly, sporadic(ally)
sparcity, sparse(sity)
sparckul, sparkle
spare,*,ed,ring,eable,ely,eness,ringly, LEFT OVER, EXTRA, TO SAVE, REFRAIN FROM, BOWLING EXPRESSION (or see spar) "prefixes: un"
sparengly, spare(ringly)
spark,*,ked,king,ky, RESULT BETWEEN TWO ELECTRICAL CHARGES COLLIDING, PARTICLES OF GLOWING MATTER
sparkal, sparkle
sparkil, sparkle
sparkle,*,ed,ling,er, GLITTERY/ FLASHING LIGHT
sparkul, sparkle
sparo, sparrow
sparrow,*, A BIRD
sparse,er,est,ely,eness,sity, RARE, NOT MANY OF, MEAGER (or see spare(s)/spar(s))
sparsedy, sparse(sity)
sparsidy, sparse(sity)
sparsly, sparse(ly)
sparsudy, sparse(sity)
spart, spare(d) / spar(rred)
spas, spa(s) / space / spay(s)
spasam, spasm
spasdek, spastic
spasdik, spastic
spase, space
spasee, space(y)
spasefik, specific
spasefikly, specific(ally)

spasem, spasm
spaser, space(r)
spashel, spatial
spashely, spatial
spashes, spacious
spashesness, spacious(ness)
spasheus, spacious
spashewla, spatula
spashil, spatial
spashily, spatial(lly)
spashis, spacious
spashisnes, spacious(ness)
spashius, spacious
spashle, spatial
spashul, spatial
spashula, spatula
spashuly, spatial(lly)
spashus, spacious
spashusnes, spacious(ness)
spasifek, specific
spasifekly, specific(ally)
spasific, specific
spasim, spasm
spasiousness, spacious(ness)
spasir, space(r)
spasm,*,modic,modical,modically, MUSCLE CONTRACTION
spasom, spasm
spastek, spastic
spastic,cally, OCCURENCE OF MUSCLE SPASMS
spastuk, spastic
spasum, spasm
spasur, space(r)
spasy, space(y)
spat, PAST TENSE FOR THE WORD "SPIT" (or see spay(ed)/spade)
spatchela, spatula
spatchula, spatula
spate, spade / spat / spay(ed)
spatial,lly,lity, SPACE WITH NO PHYSICAL MATTER APPARENT (or see special)
spatialy, spatial(lly)
spatious, spacious
spatiuly, spatial(lly)
spatshewla, spatula
spatshula, spatula
spatula,*, FLAT/BROAD BLADE HAND IMPLEMENT/TOOL
spatulu, spatula
spause, spouse
spaut, spout
spautles, spot(less)

spaw, spa
spawn,*,ned,ning, INCUBATE, GIVE BIRTH TO, PRODUCE OFFSPRING
spaws, spouse
spawt, spout
spawtles, spot(less)
spay,*,yed,ying, NEUTER TO PREVENT FROM CREATING OFFSPRING
spazam, spasm
spazdek, spastic
spazduk, spastic
spazem, spasm
spazim, spasm
spaztek, spastic
spaztuk, spastic
spazum, spasm
speach, speech
speachless, speech(less)
spead, speed
speady, speed(y)
speak,*,poke,ker,king, COMMUNICATE WITH VERBAL SOUNDS (or see speck) "prefixes: mis/un"
speakible, speak(able)
speakuble, speak(able)
speal, spiel
spear,*,red,ring, LONG SHAFT WITH SHARP POINTED/PIERCING INSTRUMENT ON ONE END
spec, speech / speak / speck
specafy, specify
specamen, specimen
specemin, specimen
specewlate, speculate
specewlum, speculum
spech, speech
spechal, special
spechalist, special(ist)
spechalize, special(ize)
spechelty, special(ity)
speches, speech(es)
spechil, special
spechilist, special(ist)
spechilize, special(ize)
spechis, speech(es)
spechle, special
spechles, speech(less)
spechlist, special(ist)
spechlize, special(ize)
spechlus, speech(less)
spechol, special / speck(le)
specholist, special(ist)
specholize, special(ize)
specholty, special(ity)

spechulist, special(ist)
spechulize, special(ize)
spechulty, special(ity)
special,*,lly,list,lty,lties,lism,list,listic, lization,lize,lizes,lized,lizing,lity, UNLIKE OTHERS, RARE, UNUSUAL, SPECIFIC CATEGORY "prefixes: sub/un"
species, ORGANISMS GROUPED BY ABILITY TO BREED TOGETHER "prefixes: intra/sub"
specific,*,cally,city,cation, CLEARLY AND DISTINCTLY STATE/DEFINE/MAKE KNOWN "prefixes: con/inter/intra/non"
specifide, specify(fied)
specify,fies,fied,fying,fier,fiable, CLEARLY AND DISTINCTLY STATE/DEFINE/MAKE KNOWN/REVEAL "prefixes: un"
specimen,*, SAMPLE/EXAMPLE OF SOMETHING
speck,*,kle,kles,kled,kling, TINY FLECKS/SPOTS (or see specs/speak)
specktrum, spectrum
speckulashen, speculate(tion)
speckulation, speculate(tion)
specs, SHORT FOR SPECTACLES/GLASSES/DRAWINGS (or see speck)
spectacle,*,ed, GLASSES FOR THE EYES, FOR PUBLIC EXHIBITION/VIEW "prefixes: be"
spectacul, spectacle
spectacular,rly,rity,rization,rism,rized, MOST IMPRESSIVE EVENT/ACTIVITY/ OCCURENCE "prefixes: un"
spectader, spectator
spectadur, spectator
spectakewler, spectacular
spectator,*,rial,rship, SOMEONE WATCHING AN EVENT WITHOUT PARTICIPATING
spectecul, spectacle
specter,*, SPIRIT, GHOST APPEARANCE, APPARITION
specticle, spectacle
specticul, spectacle
spectir, specter
spector, specter
spectral,lity,lness,lly, GIVEN TO BE LIKE A SPIRIT/GHOST
spectrim, spectrum
spectrol, spectral

spectrom, spectrum
spectrul, spectral
spectrum,*, RANGE OF SOMETHING BETWEEN TWO GIVEN POINTS
spectucle, spectacle
spectur, specter
specufy, specify
speculashen, speculate(tion)
speculate,*,ed,ting,tor,tion,tive, tiveness,tory, THEORIZE BASED UPON FACTS/KNOWINGNESS
speculim, speculum
speculum,*, MEDICAL INSTRUMENT USED TO EXAMINE MORE CLOSELY
sped, PAST TENSE FOR THE WORD "SPEED"
spede, speed(y)
spedeness, speed(iness)
speder, speed(er)
spedeur, speed(ier)
spedily, speed(ily)
spedir, speed(er)
spedul, spittle
speduly, speed(ily)
spedur, speed(er)
spedy, speed(y)
speech,hes,hless,hlessness, VOCALLY EMPHASIZE SOUNDS/WORDS
speed,*,ded,ding,dier,diest,der,dy,dily, diness, RATE/VELOCITY OF MOVEMENT, TRAVEL FASTER THAN NORMAL
speedeness, speed(iness)
speeker, speak(er)
speekt, speak
speel, spiel
speer, sphere / spear
speget, spigot
spegit, spigot
spegot, spigot
spekabul, speak(able)
spekal, speck(le)
speker, speak(er)
spekeulate, speculate
spekeulatif, speculate(tive)
spekewlashen, speculate(tion)
spekewlate, speculate
spekewlation, speculate(tion)
spekewlative, speculate(tive)
spekewlem, speculum
spekible, speak(able)
spekil, speck(le)
spekir, speak(er)
spekol, speck(le)

spekor, speak(er)
speks, specs / speak(s) / speck(s)
spekt, spoke
spektadur, spectator
spektakewler, spectacular
spektakle, spectacle
spektakul, spectacle
spektakuler, spectacular
spektar, specter
spektator, spectator
spektekul, spectacle
spekter, specter
spektikul, spectacle
spektir, specter
spektor, specter
spektrality, spectral(ity)
spektram, spectrum
spektrel, spectral
spektrem, spectrum
spektrul, spectral
spektrum, spectrum
spektukul, spectacle
spektur, specter
spekuble, speak(able)
spekul, speck(le)
spekulashen, speculate(tion)
spekulate, speculate
spekulation, speculate(tion)
spekulative, speculate(tive)
spekulem, speculum
spekulotif, speculate(tive)
spekulum, speculum
spekulutive, speculate(tive)
spekur, speak(er)
spekyewlem, speculum
spekyulate, speculate
spekyulatif, speculate(tive)
spel, spiel / spell / spill
spelar, spell(er)
speld, spill(ed) / spelt / spell(ed)
speler, spell(er)
spell,*,led,ling,ler, FORMULATE LETTERS INTO ACCEPTABLE FORMAT, BE SUBCONSCIOUSLY CONTROLLED "prefixes: mis"
spellur, spell(er)
spelor, spell(er)
spelt, PAST TENSE FOR THE WORD "SPELL", A TYPE OF WHEAT (or see spell(ed)/spill(ed)/ spiel(ed))
spelur, spell(er)
spen, spin / spend
spenatch, spinach

spend,*,nt,ding,der,dy, TRADE OUTGOING FOR INCOMING (or see spent/spin(nned)) "prefixes: mis/over/under"
spendal, spindle
spended, spent
spendir, spend(er)
spendle, spindle
spendly, spindle(y)
spendul, spindle
spenech, spinach
spenich, spinach
spent, PAST TENSE FOR THE WORD "SPEND" (or see spend)
spentle, spindle
spentul, spindle
spenuch, spinach
spenur, spin(nner)
spenutch, spinach
speol, spiel
sper, spare / spear / spur
speradik, sporadic
spercity, sparse(sity)
sperd, spear(ed) / spur(rred)
sperds, spurt(s)
sperichual, spiritual
sperichualidy, spiritual(ity)
speringly, spare(ringly)
sperit, spirit
speritshuality, spiritual(ity)
sperm,*, A METHOD OF CARRYING MALE DNA FOR PROCREATION, SEMEN "prefixes: endo"
spero, sparrow
sperow, sparrow
spers, sparse / spare(s) / spear(s) / spur(s)
spersity, sparse(sity)
sperslee, sparse(ly)
spersly, sparse(ly)
spersudy, sparse(sity)
spert, spurt / spare(d) / spear(ed)
spesaficashen, specify(fication)
spesafide, specify(fied)
spesafikation, specify(fication)
spesafy, specify
spesamen, specimen
spesamin, specimen
spesefakation, specify(fication)
spesefide, specify(fied)
spesefukation, specify(fication)
spesefy, specify
spesemin, specimen
speshal, special

speshalist, special(ist)
speshalize, special(ize)
speshelty, special(ity)
speshez, species
speshil, special
speshilest, special(ist)
speshilty, special(ity)
speshis, species
speshle, special
speshlist, special(ist)
speshlize, special(ize)
speshol, special
spesholty, special(ity)
speshul, special
speshulist, special(ist)
speshulize, special(ize)
speshulty, special(ity)
spesial, special
spesies, species
spesifakation, specify(fication)
spesifek, specific
spesificashen, specify(fication)
spesification, specify(fication)
spesifide, specify(fied)
spesifik, specific
spesifucashen, specify(fication)
spesifukation, specify(fication)
spesify, specify
spesimen, specimen
spesofecashen, specify(fication)
spesofecation, specify(fication)
spesofide, specify(fied)
spesufication, specify(fication)
spesufide, specify(fied)
spesufy, specify
spesumen, specimen
spesumin, specimen
spet, sped
spetil, spittle
spetle, spittle
spetoon, spittoon
spetul, spittle
spetune, spittoon
spetur, spit(tter)
speu, spew
speul, spiel / spill
spew,*,wed,wing,wn, RUN/FLOW FORTH, EJECT FROM WITHIN, VOMIT
sphagnum,nous, VARIETY OF MOSS
spharikul, sphere(rical)
spharukil, sphere(rical)
sphenctur, sphincter
sphenktur, sphincter

spherakil, sphere(rical)
sphere,*,ed,ring,ral,rical,rics,ry,ricity, CIRCLE/AREA EXTENDED AROUND THE CENTER WHERE DISTANCE IS EQUAL FROM THE CENTER "prefixes: bio/en/non"
spherekil, sphere(rical)
spherikul, sphere(rical)
sphincter,ral,rial,rate,ric, MUSCLE WHICH CONTRACTS THE ORIFICE ON THE LOWER TORSO
sphinkter, sphincter
sphinx,xes,xian, A FIGURE WITH THE HEAD OF ONE THING AND BODY OF SOMETHING DIFFERENT
sphire, sphere
spic, speak / spike / spice
spice,*,ed,cing,ery,cy, OF OR GIVEN TO SPICES, CULINARY PLANTS
spictacular, spectacular
spictakuler, spectacular
spid, spy(pied) / spite / speed / spit
spider,*,ry, EIGHT LEGGED ARACHNID
spidful, spite(ful)
spidul, spittle
spidur, spider
spidury, spider(y)
spiel,*, TALK/EXPLAIN AT LENGTH WITH PERSUASION
spiget, spigot
spigot,*, DEVICE/FAUCET FOR ALLOWING/STOPPING FLOW OF LIQUIDS
spigut, spigot
spike,*,ed,king,ker,ky, STIFF/SHARP, USED TO IMPALE/PIERCE, SHAPED LIKE A NAIL
spikt, spike(d)
spiktakewler, spectacular
spiktakuler, spectacular
spiky, spike(ky)
spil, spill
spill,*,lled,lling,llage, SOMETHING LOOSE/LIQUID TO FLOW FROM CONTAINER/SOURCE, TO DIVULGE (or see spiel/spell) "prefixes: over"
spin,*,pun,nning,nner, TO WEAVE/ TWIST/WRAP AROUND, TELL A STORY, PERFORM CIRCULAR MOTION (or see spine/spend) "prefixes: under"
spinach, VEGETABLE/PLANT
spinal,lly, ASSOCIATED WITH THE SPINE
spinatch, spinach

spind, spend / spin(nned)
spinded, spent
spinder, spend(er)
spindil, spindle
spindle,*,ed,ling,ly, A ROD/PIN, TO WIND/SPIN/TWIST SOMETHING AROUND
spindly, spindle(y)
spindul, spindle
spindur, spend(er)
spine,*,eless,elessly,elessness,ny, escent,escence, BACKBONE/ VERTEBRATE OF BODIES, A LONG CREST/SET OF PEAKS
spinech, spinach
spinel, spinal
spiner, spin(nner)
spinlesness, spine(lessness)
spinless, spine(less)
spinol, spinal
spinor, spin(nner)
spint, spent
spinter, spend(er)
spintil, spindle
spintir, spend(er)
spintul, spindle
spintur, spend(er)
spinuch, spinach
spinul, spinal
spinur, spin(nner)
spinutch, spinach
spiny, spine(y)
spir, spur / spire / spear
spiradek, sporadic
spiradik, sporadic
spiradikly, sporadic(ally)
spiral,*,led,ling,lly, REPEATED CIRCULAR CURVE WHOSE EVOLUTION AROUND CONSISTENTLY ASCENDS OR DESCENDS, CONTINUOUS CIRCULAR MOTION IN ONE DIRECTION OR ANOTHER
spiraly, spiral(lly)
spird, spire(d) / spur(rred) / spurt / spear(ed)
spire,ed,ring,ry, COMING TO A POINT, PYRAMID SHAPE
spirechualedy, spiritual(ity)
spirechuil, spiritual
spirel, spiral
spireshuil, spiritual
spiret, spirit
spiretshualety, spiritual(ity)

spirichual, spiritual
spirichualidy, spiritual(ity)
spirichuel, spiritual
spiril, spiral
spirit,*,ted,tism,tist,tistic,tual, CHARACTER/DISPOSITION AND ESSENCE OF ENERGY, THAT WHICH ANIMATES/MAKES THINGS LIFELIKE OR ALIVE, TYPE OF ALCOHOL "prefixes: di"
spiritchuel, spiritual
spiritual,lly,lness,lism,list,listic,lity,lities, lize,lized,lizing, IMMATERIAL ESSENCE/SPIRIT/LIFE, OF THE UNKNOWN, NOT PHYSICAL
spirm, sperm
spirt, spurt / spire(d)
spirul, spiral
spiruly, spiral(lly)
spisd, spice(d)
spise, spice / spice(y) / spy(pies)
spised, spice(d)
spisury, spice(ry)
spisy, spice(y)
spit,*,tted,tting,pat,tter, PROJECT/FORCE SALIVA FROM THE MOUTH, ROD/PIN FOR HOLDING MEAT WHILE COOKING, NARROW SLENDER EXTENSION OF LAND SURROUNDED BY WATER
spital, spittle
spite,ed,ting,eful,efully,efulness, OF MALICIOUS INTENT/DISPOSITION
spitel, spittle
spiter, spider / spit(tter)
spitful, spite(ful)
spitle, spittle
spitoon, spittoon
spittle, SECRETION BY INSECTS
spittoon,*, VESSEL FOR SPIT
spittune, spittoon
spitul, spittle
spitune, spittoon
spitur, spider / spit(tter)
spiz, spy(pies) / spice
spize, spice / spy(pies) / spice(y)
spla, splay
splach, splotch / splash
splachy, splotch(y)
splad, splat / splay(ed)
splader, splatter
spladur, splatter
splaer, splay(er)

splash,hes,hed,hing,her,hy,hily,hiness, PARTICLES OF LIQUID SCATTERED INTO THE AIR
splat, BACK OF A CHAIR, A TYPE OF SOUND
splater, splatter
splator, splatter
splatter,*,red,ring, TO SPLASH A LIQUID
splatur, splatter
splaur, splay(er)
splay,*,yed,yer, SPREAD OUT/FLARE/FAN, CREATE CURVE
splean, spleen
spledur, split(tter)
spleen,*,nful,ny, AN ORGAN IN THE BODY, ILL HUMOR/ IRRITABLE
splen, spleen
splendant, splendent
splendedly, splendid(ly)
splendent, BRILLIANT/RADIANT IN APPEARANCE
splender, splendor / splinter
splendid,dly,dness, GRAND/MAGNIFICENT
splendint, splendent
splendir, splendor / splinter
splendit, splendid
splendor,*,rous, BRILLIANCE, LUSTER (or see splinter)
splendrus, splendor(ous)
splendunt, splendent
splendur, splendor / splinter
splene, spleen / spleen(y)
splent, splint
splented, splendid
splentor, splendor / splinter
splentrus, splendor(ous)
splentur, splendor / splinter
spleny, spleen(y)
splerge, splurge
splerje, splurge
splet, split
spletor, split(tter)
splice,*,ed,cing,er, GRAFT/PIECE TOGETHER PERFECTLY, CUT TO JOIN
splider, split(tter)
splin, spline / spleen
splindant, splendent
splinded, splendid
splindedly, splendid(ly)
splindint, splendent
splindir, splendor / splinter
splindit, splendid
splindrus, splendor(ous)

splindud, splendid
splindunt, splendent
splindur, splendor / splinter
spline,*,ed,ning, INTERNAL PART OF A WHEEL, A SLAT, WAY TO SECURE A PART, MATHEMATICAL EXPRESSION (or see spleen)
splint,*,ter, USED TO REPAIR FRACTURES
splinted, splendid
splinter,*,red,ring,ry, A SMALL SLICE/PIECE BROKEN/CUT OFF LENGHTWISE, A SLIVER
splintird, splinter(ed)
splintor, splendor / splinter
splintrus, splendor(ous)
splintur, splendor / splinter
splirge, splurge
splirje, splurge
splisur, splice(r)
split,*,tting,tter, BROKEN/TORN APART/SEPARATED
splitor, split(tter)
sploch, splotch
sploche, splotch(y)
splotch,hes,hed,hing,hy,hier,hiest, AN IRREGULAR SPOT/SPLASH OF LIQUID/ COLOR/STAIN
splurch, splurge
splurgd, splurge(d)
splurge,*,ed,ging, TO OVER SPEND
spo, spa
spock, spoke
spod, spot
spodable, spot(able)
spoded, spot(tted)
spodee, spot(tty)
spodible, spot(able)
spodid, spot(tted)
spodlis, spot(less)
spoduble, spot(able)
spoel, spoil
spoeld, spoil(ed) / spoilt
spoeleg, spoil(age)
spoelij, spoil(age)
spoelt, spoil(ed) / spoilt
spoeluj, spoil(age)
spogedi, spaghetti
spogeti, spaghetti
spoil,*,led,ling,lage,ler,lable,lt, TO GO BAD, DAMAGE, RENDER UNFIT "prefixes: un"
spoild, spoil(ed) / spoilt
spoileg, spoil(age)

spoilej, spoil(age)
spoilt, PAST TENSE FOR THE WORD "SPOIL " (or see spoil(ed))
spoiluje, spoil(age)
spoke,*,en, PAST TENSE FOR THE WORD "SPEAK", RODS/WIRES RADIATING FROM THE HUB OF A WHEEL "prefixes: mis/un"
spokun, spoke(n)
spon, spawn / spoon
sponch, sponge
sponge,*,ed,ging,gy,gier,giest,giness,er, SEA ANIMAL, SKELETON OF SEA ANIMALS USED TO CLEAN/ABSORB LIQUIDS
sponser, sponsor
sponsor,*,red,ring,rial,rship, SOMEONE WHO PAYS/SUPPORTS SOMEONE ELSE
sponsur, sponsor
spont, spawn(ed) / spoon(ed)
spontaineus, spontaneous
spontaneity,eities,eous, ABLE TO ACT QUICKLY ON IMPULSE WITHOUT CONSTRAINT
spontaneous,sly,sness, ACT QUICKLY ON IMPULSE WITHOUT CONSTRAINT
spontaneus, spontaneous
spontenaity, spontaneity
spontinaedy, spontaneity
spontunaity, spontaneity
sponzur, sponsor
spoof,*, TO TEASE/DECEIVE WITH GOOD INTENT
spook,*,ked,king,ky,kish, GHOST, SPECTER, APPARITION
spool,*,led,ling,ler, ROUND/CYLINDER SHAPE HOLDING LENGTHS OF SOMETHING WOUND AROUND IT
spoon,*,ned,ning,nful, UTENSIL WITH HANDLE AT ONE END AND A BOWL SHAPE ON THE OTHER
spor, spar / spore
sporadic,cal,cally, ERRATIC/ UNPREDICTABLE OCCURENCES
sporadikly, sporadic(ally)
sporded, sport(ed)
spordee, sport(y)
spordid, sport(ed)
spordy, sport(y)
spore,*,red,ring,ral,roid,riferous,rulate, REPRODUCTIVE SEEDS OF BACTERIA AND SOME PLANTS

sporol, spore(ral)
sport,*,ted,ting,tive,tively,tiveness,ty, ATHLETIC/OUTDOOR GAMES, TO CARRY, GOOD ATTITUDE
sportee, sport(y)
sportef, sport(ive)
sportif, sport(ive)
sportud, sport(ed)
sporul, spore(ral)
spos, suppose
spot,*,tted,tting,tty,ttier,ttiest,tter, table,tless,tlessly,tlessness, FLAW/ MARK/ BLEMISH, A PARTICULAR/ SPECIFIC PLACE, TO SEE "prefixes: un"
spoted, spot(tted)
spotee, spot(tty)
spotible, spot(able)
spotid, spot(tted)
spotuble, spot(able)
spoty, spot(tty)
spouse,*,sal, ONE WHO IS ENGAGED/ VOWED/MARRIED TO ANOTHER
spout,*,ted,ting,ter, PIPE/NOZZLE PROJECTING FROM VESSEL FOR LIQUID
spown, spawn
spowse, spouse
spowsul, spouse(sal)
spowt, spout
spoyl, spoil
spoyleg, spoil(age)
spoylej, spoil(age)
spra, spray
spraer, spray(er)
spraget, sprocket
spragit, sprocket
sprain,*,ned,ning, TWIST/WRENCH/ OVER STRETCH A MUSCLE IN THE BODY
spraket, sprocket
spral, sprawl
spran, sprain
spraor, spray(er)
sprat, spray(ed)
spraukit, sprocket
spraul, sprawl
spraur, spray(er)
spraut, sprout
sprawl,*,led,ling, TO EXTEND/SPREAD OUT IN IRREGULAR POSITION/ MANNER
sprawt, sprout

spray,*,yed,ying,yer, PARTICLES OF LIQUID RELEASED/FORCED INTO THE AIR
spre, spree
spread,*,ding,der, FORCE/EXTEND INTO A THIN LAYER OVER SUBSTANTIAL DISTANCE/TIME/SPACE
spred, spread
spredur, spread(er)
spree,*, TO FROLICK, HAVE A MERRY TIME
spreg, sprig
sprein, sprain / spray(ing)
sprencol, sprinkle
spreng, spring
sprengee, spring(y)
sprengy, spring(y)
sprenk, spring
sprenkal, sprinkle
sprenkil, sprinkle
sprenkler, sprinkle(r)
sprenklor, sprinkle(r)
sprenkul, sprinkle
sprenkuler, sprinkle(r)
sprent, sprint
sprentur, sprint(er)
spret, spread
spreter, spread(er)
spretur, spread(er)
sprews, spruce
spri, spry / spree
sprig,*, SMALL BRANCH FROM PLANT
sprilee, spry(ly)
sprily, spry(ly)
sprincol, sprinkle
spring,*,ging,rang,gy,gier,giest,gily, giness, A RIVULET OF WATER, COILED DEVICE "prefixes: up"
springey, spring(y)
sprinis, spry(ness)
sprink, spring
sprinkel, sprinkle
sprinkle,*,ed,ling,er, SHOOT/RELEASE/ SPRAY HEAVY DROPS OF LIQUID
sprinklor, sprinkle(r)
sprinkul, sprinkle
sprinkuler, sprinkle(r)
sprint,*,ted,ting,ter, RACE/SPEED A SHORT DISTANCE
sprintor, sprint(er)
sprintur, sprint(er)
sprocket,*, PART OF A WHEEL/CHAIN
sprogit, sprocket
sprokut, sprocket

sprol, sprawl
sproose, spruce
sprout,*,ted,ting,ter, TO GERMINATE, GROW INTO THE DAYLIGHT, SHOW GROWTH
sprowt, sprout
spruce,*,ed,cing,ely,eness,er,est, TYPE OF TREE, GET DRESSED UP, GET FANCY
sprung, PAST TENSE FOR THE WORD SPRING "prefixes: un"
spruse, spruce
spry,yly,yness, LIVELY/NIMBLE
sprynis, spry(ness)
spuc, spook
spud,*,dded,dding, POTATOE, TOOL, TO WEED OUT
spuder, sputter
spudor, sputter
spue, spew
spufe, spoof
spugedi, spaghetti
spugeti, spaghetti
spuk, spook
spuky, spook(y)
spule, spool
spun, PAST TENSE FOR THE WORD "SPIN" (or see spoon) "prefixes: over"
spunch, sponge
spune, spoon / spun
spunful, spoon(ful)
spung, sponge / spunk
spungee, sponge(gy)
spungenis, spunk(iness)
spungy, sponge(gy)
spunj, sponge
spunjy, sponge(gy)
spunk,ky,kily,kiness,kier,kiest, SPIRITED/COURAGEOUS, TINDER FROM FUNGUS
spunkenis, spunk(iness)
spur,*,rred,rring,rious,riously,riousness, STIMULATE/ENCOURAGE TO GO ON, DEVICE FOR BOOTS/RIDING (too many definitions, please see standard dictionary) (or see spurt)
spuradek, sporadic
spuradikly, sporadic(ally)
spurm, sperm
spurt,*,ted,ting, SUDDEN JOLT/GROWTH/MOVEMENT, SHORT PERIOD OF TIME
spusefikly, specific(ally)

spusifikly, specific(ally)
sput, spud
sputer, sputter
sputter,*,red,ring,rer, TO RAPIDLY/INCOHERENTLY SPEAK, ERRATIC/HALTING MOTION/SOUND
sputur, sputter
spy,pies,pied,pying, SECRET SURVEILLANCE/MONITORING
spyd, spy(pied)
spyder, spider
spydful, spite(ful)
spydur, spider
spyeng, spy(ing)
spyke, spike
spyse, spy(pies) / spice
spytur, spider
sqeek, squeak
squabble,*,ed,ling,er, MINOR SCUFFLE/DISPUTE
squad,*,dron, SMALL GROUP OF SPECIFIC PEOPLE (or see squat)
squadir, squat(tter)
squadron,*, SMALL MILITARY/POLICE GROUP
squadur, squat(tter)
squaemish, squeamish
squaled, squalid
squalid,dly,dness,dity, NEGLECTED/FOUL/FILTHY
squall,*,lled,lling,llier,lliest,lly, SUDDEN/STRONG GUSTS OF WIND/RAIN/SLEET
squalor, NEGLECTED/FOUL/FILTHY
squander,*,red,ring, RECKLESSLY LET GO OF/USE/WASTE
square,*,ed,ring,ely,eness,rish,rishly, OF BEING FOUR EQUAL SIDES, TO BE PROPORTIONAL, SOMEONE DULL, A MATH OPERATION
squarly, square(ly)
squash,hes,hed,hing, A VEGETABLE, A GAME, TO SMASH/CRUSH SOMETHING
squat,*,tted,tting,tter, REST ON HAUNCHES, LOWER THE UPPER TORSO, TO SIT (or see squad)
squator, squat(tter)
squeak,*,ked,king,kingly,ker,ky, A SHORT/SHRILL SOUND
squeal,*,led,ling,ler, LOUD/SHRILL SOUND PRODUCED BY GLEE/HAPPINESS, TELL A TRUTH ABOUT

SOMEONE WITHOUT THEIR PERMISSION
squeamish,hly,hness, UNEASY/UNSETTLING, DISGUSTED ABOUT SOMETHING
squed, squid
squeegee,*,eed,eeing, AN INSTRUMENT/IMPLEMENT FOR REMOVING WATER/LIQUID
squeejy, squeegee
squeek, squeak
squeel, squeal
squeelur, squeal(er)
squeemish, squeamish
squeese, squeeze
squeeze,*,ed,zing,er,zingly,zable,zably, TO FORCE BY TIGHTENING GRIP
squegy, squeegee
squejy, squeegee
squel, squeal
squelch,hed,hing,her, SILENCE/CRUSH/SUPPRESS, A SOUND
squelur, squeal(er)
squemish, squeamish
squent, squint
squerl, squirrel
squerm, squirm
squermy, squirm(y)
squert, squirt
squesh, squish
squeshy, squish(y)
squesur, squeeze(r)
squeze, squeeze
squid,*, A CEPHALOPOD FOUND IN SALT WATER
squiggle,*,ed,ling, SQUIRM/TWIST
squigy, squeegee
squint,*,ted,ting, TO CLOSE EYES TO A NARROW OPENING FOR PROTECTION
squire,*,ed,ring, MAN OF ARISTOCRATIC BIRTH, MAN WHO ESCORTS
squirel, squirrel
squirl, squirrel
squirm,*,med,ming,mer,my,mier,miest, WRITHE/WRIGGLE LIKE A WORM
squirrel,*,lly, A RODENT, TO BEHAVE LIKE A SQUIRREL
squirt,*,ted,ting, NARROW STREAM OF LIQUID EMITTED FROM AN ORIFICE
squish,hes,hed,hing,hy,hier,hiest, SQUASH/SMASH
squrt, squirt

sqwal, squall
sqwalid, squalid
srgekul, surgical
sta, stay
stab,*,bbed,bbing,bber, TO POKE/ THRUST A BLADE WITH SHARP TIP INTO SOMETHING/SOMEONE
stabalize, stabilize
stabelity, stability
stabilise, stabilize
stability,ties,ize, OF FIRM GROUND/ FORM/FOUNDATION "prefixes: in"
stabilize,*,ed,zing,er,zation, TO PROVIDE/ENSURE FIRM GROUND/ FORM "prefixes: de"
stabiludy, stability
stable,*,ed,ling,ly,eness,bilize, OF FIRM GROUND/FORM, SHELTER FOR ANIMAL "prefixes: un"
stablize, stabilize
stabulize, stabilize
stac, stack / stake / steak / stalk / stock
stacado, staccato / stoccado
staccato,*, SHARP/BRIEF MUSICAL NOTE (or see stoccado)
stachatory, statutory
stachur, stature
stachutory, statutory
stack,*,ked,king,ker, ORGANIZE/PILE/ SET UP ITEMS ONE ON TOP OF ANOTHER (or see stake/steak/stalk)
stad, staid / stay(ed) / state
stadeim, stadium
stadek, static
stades, status
stadeum, stadium
stadiem, stadium
stadik, static
stadis, status
stadium,*, A LARGE ARENA FOR PEOPLE TO GATHER
stadus, status
staf, staff / staph / stave
stafed, staff(ed)
staff,*,ffed,ffing, GROUP OF HIRED PEOPLE, LONG POLE/STICK TO BE CARRIED/ USED BY HAND (or see staph) "prefixes: over"
staft, staff(ed) / stave(d)
stag,*,gged,gging,gger, MALE IN THE DEER FAMILY, MALE UNACCOMPANIED AT A GATHERING (or see stage/stack)
stagd, stag(gged) / stage(d)

stage,*,ed,ging,er,ey, PLATFORM DESIGNED FOR PLAYS/THEATER, TO PERFORM (or see stag) "prefixes: sub"
staged, stag(gged) / stage(d)
stagee, stodgy
stager, stagger
stagger,*,red,ring,rer,ringly, TO SWAY/ WAVER/WALK UNSTEADILY, SHOCKED, HORSE/COW HIT BY A DISEASE
stagir, stagger
stagnade, stagnate
stagnant,tly,ncy, NO MOVEMENT/ MOTION
stagnashen, stagnate(tion)
stagnate,*,ed,ting,tion, QUIT MOVING, BECOME DULL/QUIET
stagnatid, stagnate(d)
stagnit, stagnant
stagnunt, stagnant
stagnut, stagnant
stagred, stagger(ed)
stagt, stag(gged) / stage(d)
stagur, stagger
stagy, stodgy
staid,dly,dness, IN PLACE OF, FIXED/ STEADY (or see stead/stay(ed))
stain,*,ned,ning,nable,ner,nless,nlessly, UNDESIRABLE MARK, PERMANENTLY PLACE/AFFIX COLOR
stair,*, STEPS MAKING A RISE IN ELEVATION (or see stare)
stak, stack / stake / steak / stalk / stock
stakabul, stack(able)
stakado, staccato / stoccado
stakato, staccato / stoccado
stakd, stack(ed) / stake(d) / stalk(ed) / stock(ed)
stake,*,ed,king, LEVERAGE/PLEDGE/ WAGER/SUPPORT FOR SOMETHING, HAVE A VESTED INTEREST IN, BROAD POINTED POST FOR STRIKING/DRIVING INTO GROUND (or see steak/stack/stalk/stock)
staked, stack(ed) / stake(d) / stalk(ed) / stock(ed)
staker, stagger / stack(er) / stalk(er) / stock(er)
stakibel, stack(able)
stakibul, stack(able)
stakir, stagger / stack(er) / stalk(er) / stock(er)
staknade, stagnate

staknashen, stagnate(tion)
staknate, stagnate
staknation, stagnate(tion)
staknunt, stagnant
stakodo, staccato / stoccado
stakoto, staccato / stoccado
stakt, stack(ed) / stake(d) / stalk(ed) / stock(ed)
stakubil, stack(able)
stakuble, stack(able)
stakur, stagger / stack(er) / stalk(er) / stock(er)
stal, stall / stale
stale,*,ed,ling,er,est,ely,eness, LOSS OF ACTION/TASTE/FLAVOR (or see stall)
staleon, stallion
staliun, stallion
stalk,*,ked,king,ker, FOLLOW SOMEONE/SOMETHING WITH INTENT WITHOUT THEIR KNOWING, MAIN PORTION OF A POLE SHAPED PLANT
stall,*,lled,lling, A DWELLING FOR HORSES, TO HESITATE/QUIT/PAUSE (or see stale)
stallion,*, MALE HORSE CAPABLE OF BREEDING
stalwart,tly,tness, UNCOMPROMISING/ STRONG IN RESOLUTION
stalwort, stalwart
stalyun, stallion
stamen,*,nal, PLANT ORGAN
stamenu, stamina
stamer, stammer
stamin, stamen
stamina, LONGEVITY IN STRENGTH
stamir, stammer
stammer,*,red,ring,ringly, PAUSE/ HESITATE IN SPEECH
stamp,*,ped,ping,per, AFFIXED TO A POSTAL LETTER, A MARK LEFT BY PRESSING
stampede,*,ed,ding, A MAD/SUDDEN RUSH IN ONE DIRECTION BY MANY
stampet, stampede
stampir, stamp(er)
stampur, stamp(er)
stamun, stamen
stamur, stammer
stan, stain
stance, A STAND/ATTITUDE/POSITION
stanchen, stanchion
stancheon, stanchion

stanchion,*, BEAM/POST FOR SUPPORT
stand,*,ding,der,tood, PARTICULAR POSITION, BE UPRIGHT IN FOOTING "prefixes: up"
standard,*,dize,dized,dizing,dization, GENERAL CONSENSUS ON METHODOLOGY/DIMENSIONS/ DEGREE OF MEASURMENT "prefixes: non/sub"
standerd, standard
standerdazation, standard(ization)
standurd, standard
standurdize, standard(ize)
stane, stain
staneble, stain(able)
stanible, stain(able)
stank, PAST TENSE FOR THE WORD "STINK"
stans, stance / stain(s) / stand(s)
stansa, stanza
stanshen, stanchion
stanshon, stanchion
stansu, stanza
stant, stand
stanuble, stain(able)
stanza,*, FOUR OR MORE IN A VERSE/ POEM
stap, stab
stapel, staple
staph, SHORT FOR STAPHYLOCOCCUS (or see staff)
staple,*,ed,ling,er, FASTENER MADE OF METAL, BASIC REQUIREMENTS FOR SURVIVAL
stapul, staple
star,*,rred,rring,rless,rry, CELESTIAL/ SHINING BODY IN SPACE, PERSON WHO ACHIEVES THE LIMELIGHT, GEOMETRIC SHAPE (or see stare/ stair/store)
staralize, sterile(lize)
starc, stark
starch,hes,hed,hing,hiness,hy, NATURALLY OCCURING CHEMICAL USED TO MAKE THINGS STIFF
starchenes, starch(iness)
stard, start / stare(d) / star(rred)
starder, starter
stardil, startle
stardul, startle
stardur, starter
stare,*,ed,ring, AFFIX EYES ONTO A SINGLE POINT WITHOUT MOVING (or see star/stair/star/rry))

stared, stare(d) / star(rred)
stareledy, sterile(lity)
starelidy, sterile(lity)
stareo, stereo
starf, starve
staril, sterile
starilety, sterile(lity)
starilize, sterile(lize)
stark,kly,kness, GRIM/DESOLATE SCENE WITH LITTLE TO ENTERTAIN THE EYE
starling,*, A BIRD
staroed, steroid
staroid, steroid
stars, stair(s) / stare(s) / star(s)
start,*,ted,ting,ter, BEGIN, INITIAL ACTION (or see stare(d)) "prefixes: up"
starter,*, ELECTRIC MOTOR, BEGIN/ INITIATE ACTION
startil, startle
startir, starter
startle,*,ed,ling, BE ALARMED/ SURPRISED BY SUDDEN ACTION/ EVENT
startul, startle
startur, starter
starul, sterile
starulize, sterile(lize)
starvashen, starvation
starvation, SERIOUSLY LACK NOURISHMENT/BASIC ESSENTIALS
starve,*,ed,ving,vation, SERIOUSLY LACK NOURISHMENT/BASIC ESSENTIALS
stas, stay(s)
stases, stasis
stash,hes,hed,hing, TO HIDE/PUT SOMETHING AWAY
stashatory, statutory
stashen, station
stashenary, stationary / stationery
stasher, stature
stashetory, statutory
stashewesk, statue(sque)
stashewtory, statutory
stashin, station / stash(ing)
stashinary, stationary / stationery
stashir, stature
stashitory, statutory
stashonery, stationary / stationery
stashoot, statute
stashu, statue
stashuary, statuary

stashuery, statuary
stashuesk, statue(sque)
stashun, station
stashunery, stationary / stationery
stashur, stature
stashute, statute
stashutory, statutory
stasis, EQUILIBRIUM, FROZEN IN TIME/ MOVEMENT, INACTIVITY
stasus, stasis
stat,*, HOSPITAL EMERGENCY EXPRESSION, SHORT FOR STATISTICS (or see state/stay(ed))
statchuesk, statue(sque)
state,*,ed,ting,ely,elier,eliest,eliness, LAND WITH SPECIFIC/DIVISIVE BORDER, CURRENT CONDITION "prefixes: inter/intra/over/re/up"
statek, static
statement,*, SUMMARY/REVIEW OF CONDITION/STATUS
states, status / state(s)
stateur, stature
stateutory, statutory
static,*,cal,cally, NO MOVEMENT/ ACTION, AT REST
statik, static
station,*, PLACE TO MOMENTARILY REST/RECEIVE SERVICES "prefixes: inter/sub"
stationary, REST, STOP, BE STILL (or see stationery) "prefixes: non"
stationery, ENVELOPE/PAPER FOR WRITING (or see stationary)
statis, status
statistic,*,cal,cally, A MATHEMATICAL ACCOUNT OF CURRENT SITUATION/ CONDITION
statiur, stature
statment, statement
statmunt, statement
stats, state(s) / stat(s)
statshu, statue
statshuery, statuary
statuary,ries, COLLECTION OF STATUES
statue,*,esque,ette, SOLID/ STATIONARY FORM CARVED/ MOLDED TO RESEMBLE SOMETHING/SOMEONE
statuery, statuary
statuesk, statue(sque)
stature, PHYSICAL DIMENSIONS OF A LIVING THING
status, CURRENT POSITION/STANDING

statute,*,tory, A FIXED PERMANENT LAW
statutory,rily, IMPOSED BY A STATUTE
stauk, stock
staunch,hly,hness, RIGID/FIRM STRUCTURE/FORM, LIQUID RESILIENT
staut, stout
stave,*,ed,ving, FIGHT OFF AN ATTACK, A ROD/POLE/STICK
stawgines, stodgy(giness)
stawk, stock / stalk
stawked, stock(ed) / stoke(d)
stawt, stout
stay,*,yed,ying, TO REMAIN BEHIND/IN ONE PLACE, DON'T FOLLOW/MOVE "prefixes: over"
stead, TO BE IN SOMEONE'S PLACE/POSITION WHILE THEY'RE AWAY (or see steed/staid)
steadeness, steady(diness)
steadfast,tly,tness, HOLDING FIXED/FIRM/UNWAVERING (alternate spelling for 'stedfast')
steady,dies,died,dying,dier,diest,dily, diness, FIXED/FIRM/CONSTANT "prefixes: un"
steak,*, A CUT OF BEEF (or see stake)
steal,*,ling,tole, TAKE SOMETHING FROM SOMEONE WITHOUT THEIR PERMISSION (or see steel/stile/still)
stealth,hy,hily,hiness, SECRECY
steam,*,med,ming,mer,mily,miness,my, HOT WATER TURNED TO GASEOUS STATE
stear, steer
stebel, steeple / stipple
stebul, steeple / stipple
stebulashen, stipulate(tion)
stebulation, stipulate(tion)
stebulatory, stipulate(tory)
stec, stick
stecado, staccato / stoccado
stech, stitch
sted, SHORT FOR "INSTEAD" (or see stead/steed)
stede, steady
stedeness, steady(diness)
stedes, steady(dies)
stedfast,tly,tness, HOLDING FIXED/FIRM/UNWAVERING (alternate spelling for 'stedfast')
stedfastnes, steadfast(ness)
stedily, steady(dily)

stediness, steady(diness)
stedness, staid(ness) / stead(ness)
steduly, steady(dily)
stedy, steady
steed,*, HORSE WITH SPIRIT, STALLION (or see stead)
steel,ly,lier,liest,liness, TYPE OF METAL (or see steal/stile/still)
steenkur, stink(er)
steenky, stink(y)
steep,*,ped,ping,ply,pness,per,pen, SHARP SLOPE, SOAK/IMMERSE (or see step/steppe)
steeple,*, TALL ROOF COMING TO A POINT AT THE TOP
steer,*,red,ring,rable,rer,rage, MANIPULATE/CONTROL INTO PARTICULAR DIRECTION, CASTRATED BOVINE "prefixes: over/under"
steerible, steer(able)
steeruble, steer(able)
stef, stiff
stefin, stiff(en)
stefnis, stiff(ness)
stegma, stigma
stegmadik, stigma(tic)
stegmatist, stigma(tist)
stein,*, BEER MUGS (or see stain/stay(ing))
stek, stick / steak / stake
stekado, staccato / stoccado
stekato, staccato / stoccado
stekir, stick(er)
stekler, stickler
steklur, stickler
stekmu, stigma
stekodo, staccato / stoccado
stekor, stick(er)
stekoto, staccato / stoccado
stekur, stick(er)
steky, stick(y)
stel, steel / steal / still / stile / stale
stelar, stellar
stelir, stellar
stellar, OF THE STARS "prefixes: inter/sub"
stelnis, still(ness)
stelnus, still(ness)
stelre, stellar
stels, still(s) / steal(s)
stelt, stilt / steal(ed) / still(ed)
stelth, stealth
stelur, stellar

stem,*,mmed,mming, BRANCH OF A WOODY PLANT, SUGGESTING OF A BRANCH, THE BASE/BASIS OF SOMETHING
stemely, steam(ily)
stemer, steam(er)
stemewlasheon, stimulate(tion)
stemily, steam(ily)
stemir, steam(er)
stemulashen, stimulate(tion)
stemulate, stimulate
stemulation, stimulate(tion)
stemuly, steam(ily)
stemur, steam(er)
stenaugrafer, stenograph(er)
stench, POWERFUL STINK
stenchee, stingy
stencil,*,led,ling,ler, A FORM/OUTLINE/TEMPLATE FOR REPRODUCING
steng, sting
stengd, sting(ed) / stink
stengee, stingy
stenger, sting(er) / stink(er)
stengles, sting(less)
stengt, sting(ed) / stink
stengur, sting(er) / stink(er)
stengyness, stingy(giness)
stenjee, stingy
stenjenes, stingy(giness)
stenk, stink
stenkee, stink(y)
stenkenes, stink(iness)
stenkur, stink(er)
steno, SHORT FOR STENOGRAPHER
stenografir, stenograph(er)
stenograph,her,hers,hy,hic,hical,hically, USE OF SHORTHAND, A TYPE OF TYPEWRITER
stensh, stench
stenshee, stingy
stensil, stencil
stensul, stencil
stent, stint
step,*,pped,pping, RISE/MOVE UP, RISER, UP IN INCREMENTS (or see steep/steppe) "prefixes: mis/over"
stepel, steeple / stipple
stepend, stipend
stepeulashen, stipulate(tion)
stepewlation, stipulate(tion)
stepil, steeple / stipple
stepind, stipend
steple, steeple / stipple

steppe,*, A PLAIN WITHOUT TREES (or see step)
stepul, steeple / stipple
stepulashen, stipulate(tion)
stepulation, stipulate(tion)
ster, stare / steer / stir
steral, sterile
steralize, sterile(lize)
sterchen, sturgeon
sterd, stare(d) / steer(ed) / stir(rred)
sterdy, sturdy
stered, stare(d) / steer(ed) / stir(rred)
stereledy, sterile(lity)
stereo,*, SOUND SYSTEM, PREFIX INDICATING "THREE DIMENSIONAL OR SOLID" MOST OFTEN MODIFIES THE WORD
stergen, sturgeon
stergon, sturgeon
sterib, stirrup
sterible, steer(able)
sterile,lity,lize,lizes,lized,lizing,lization, lizer, FREE FROM BACTERIA/ CONTAMINATION, UNPRODUCTIVE "prefixes: inter/un"
sterilety, sterile(lity)
sterip, stirrup
sterjen, sturgeon
sterjon, sturgeon
sterleng, sterling
sterling, A STANDARD/DEGREE OF SILVER
stern,ner,nest,nly,nness, HIND/BACK END, BE HARSH/RIGID
sternem, sternum
sternness, stern(ess)
sternum,*, PART OF THE SKELETON
steroed, steroid
steroet, steroid
steroid,*,dal, CHEMICAL COMPOUND
sterol, sterile
steror, stir(rrer)
steroyd, steroid
stert, steer(ed) / stir(rred)
sterty, sturdy
sterub, stirrup
steruble, steer(able)
sterul, sterile
sterulize, sterile(lize)
sterup, stirrup
stesh, stitch
stetch, stitch
stethaskope, stethoscope
stethiskopek, stethoscope(pic)

stethoscope,*,pic,pical,pically,py, INSTRUMENT A MEDICAL EXAMINER USES
stethuskope, stethoscope
stethuskopik, stethoscope(pic)
stetistiks, statistic(s)
steudeo, studio
steudint, student
steul, stool
steve, stiff
stew,*,wed,wing, A THICK SOUP
steward,*,dess,desses, ONE WHO MANAGES THE AFFAIRS OF OTHERS
stewardes, steward(ess)
stewbud, stupid
stewdeis, studious
stewdent, student
stewdeo, studio
stewdeus, studious
stewdio, studio
stewg, stooge
stewj, stooge
stewlee, stool(ie)
stewp, stoop
stewpendus, stupendous
stewper, stupor
stewpid, stupid
stewpidety, stupid(ity)
stewpir, stupor
stewpud, stupid
stewpur, stupor
stewul, stool
stewurd, steward
stey, stay
sti, sty
stibe, stipe
stible, stipple
stibul, stipple
stibulashen, stipulate(tion)
stibulation, stipulate(tion)
stibulatory, stipulate(tory)
sticado, staccato / stoccado
stich, stitch
stick,*,king,ky,ker,kier,kiest,kiness,kily, tuck, A BRANCH, SOMETHING TACKY, BE AFFIXED/ADHERED TO "prefixes: un"
stickler,*, TO BE PARTICULAR, MYSTERIOUS/PUZZLING
stif, stiff
stifal, stifle
stifel, stifle
stifen, stiff(en)
stifenur, stiff(ener)

stiff,*,ffed,ffing,ffer,ffest,ffish,ffly,ffness, ffen,ffener, RIGID/TENSE/ UNBENDING/SEVERE
stifle,*,ed,ling,er,lingly, DIFFICULT TO MOVE/BREATH, OPPRESSIVE, MAMMAL'S JOINT
stifnes, stiff(ness)
stiful, stifle
stifun, stiff(en)
stifuner, stiff(ener)
stigma,*,ata,atist,atic,atically,atism, atize,atizes,atized,atizing,atization, atizer, BLEMISH/MARK, TO BRAND
stigmadik, stigma(tic)
stigmutist, stigma(tist)
stik, stick
stikado, staccato / stoccado
stiker, stick(er)
stikir, stick(er)
stikler, stickler
stiklur, stickler
stikmu, stigma
stikodo, staccato / stoccado
stikor, stick(er)
stikoto, staccato / stoccado
stikur, stick(er)
stiky, stick(y)
stil, still / stile / style
stild, still(ed) / stilt / style(d)
stile,*, FOR ASCENDING/MOUNTING, A SHAPE (or see style/still/steal/steel)
stiled, still(ed) / steal(ed) / style(d)
stiles, stylus / style(s)
stilesh, style(lish)
stilest, style(list)
stilis, stylus
stilish, style(lish)
stilishly, style(lishly)
stilize, style(lize)
still,*,lled,lling,llness, MOTIONLESS, DEVICE FOR DISTILLATION (or see stile/style/steal/steel)
stilness, still(ness)
stilnus, still(ness)
stils, still(s) / steal(s) / style(s)
stilt,*, PAIR OF LONG MANMADE LEGS (or see still(ed)/style(d))
stilus, stylus
stilush, style(lish)
stim, stem / steam
stime, stymie
stimed, stem(mmed) / stymie(d) / steam(ed)
stimee, stymie / steam(y)

stimulashen, stimulate(tion)
stimulate,*,ed,ting,tion,ant,ants,tive,tor,lus, ENCOURAGE/MOTIVATE TO MOVE/PERFORM "prefixes: bio"
stinaugrafur, stenograph(er)
stinch, stench
stinchee, stingy
stine, stein
sting,*,tung,ging,ger,gingly,gless, PAINFUL FEELING SENSATION, A COVERT OPERATION
stingd, sting(ed) / stink
stingee, stingy
stinglus, sting(less)
stingt, sting(ed) / stink
stingur, sting(er) / stink(er)
stingy,gier,giest,gily,giness, LACK GENEROSITY, TIGHT WITH RESOURCES, UNSHARING (or see sting)
stingyness, stingy(giness)
stinjee, stingy
stinjenes, stingy(giness)
stink,*,king,ky,kiness,kingly,ker,tank,tunk, FOUL/OFFENSIVE SMELL
stinkee, stink(y)
stinkur, stink(er)
stino, steno
stinografur, stenograph(er)
stinsel, stencil
stinsul, stencil
stint,*,ted,ter,tunt, LIMITED TIME/AMOUNT, BRIEF ACTIVITY "prefixes: un"
stintud, stint(ed)
stipe, RESEMBLES A STEM
stipend,*,diary,diaries, CONSISTENT/STEADY PAYMENT/COMPENSATION
stipeulate, stipulate
stipeulutory, stipulate(tory)
stipewlate, stipulate
stiplur, stipple(r)
stipple,ed,ling,er, MANY DOTS TO CREATE A SCENE/PICTURE
stiptek, styptic
stiptik, styptic
stipulashen, stipulate(tion)
stipulate,*,ed,ting,tion,tive,tory, AGREEMENT WITH GUIDELINES
stir,*,rred,rring,rrer,rringly, CREATE MOTION/MOVEMENT
stirafom, styrofoam
stird, stir(rred)
stirdy, sturdy

stirefom, styrofoam
stirgen, sturgeon
stirgeon, sturgeon
stirjun, sturgeon
stirleng, sterling
stirn, stern
stirnem, sternum
stirnly, stern(ly)
stirnness, stern(ess)
stirnum, sternum
stirrup,*, PART ON A HORSE SADDLE
stirt, stir(rred)
stirty, sturdy
stirufom, styrofoam
stirup, stirrup
stish, stitch
stitch,hes,hed,hing,her, SEW TOGETHER, USE OF A NEEDLE
stiulize, style(lize)
stive, stiff
sto, stow / store
stoakul, stoic(al)
stob, stop
stobur, stop(pper)
stoc, stalk / stock / stoke
stocado, staccato / stoccado
stocato, staccato / stoccado
stoccado, TO STAB/THRUST WITH A WEAPON (or se stocatta)
stoccato, staccato / stoccado
stock,*,ked,king,ker,ky, TO COLLECT/AMASS/ACCUMULATE SOMETHING, HOLDING INTEREST IN A COMPANY (or see stalk/stoke/stocking) "prefixes: over"
stocking,*, MATERIAL FOR COVERING LEGS/FEET
stodgeness, stodgy(giness)
stodgy,gily,giness,gier,giest, DULL/NOT INTERESTING, HEAVY/THICK (or see stogy)
stodgyest, stodgy(giest)
stoec, stoic
stoecul, stoic(al)
stoeg, stow(age)
stoej, stow(age)
stoek, stoic
stoekul, stoic(al)
stof, stove / stuff
stofs, stove(s) / stuff(s)
stoge, stogy / stodgy / stooge
stogeist, stodgy(giest)
stogenis, stodgy(giness)
stogey, stogy

stogiest, stodgy(giest)
stogines, stodgy(giness)
stogy, CIGAR, BOOT (or see stodgy)
stogyest, stodgy(giest)
stogyness, stodgy(giness)
stoic,*,cal,cally,cism, SECT WHO BELIEVES FREEDOM FROM PASSION/GRIEF/ JOY IS A VIRTUE
stoicul, stoic(al)
stoig, stow(age)
stoij, stow(age)
stoikal, stoic(al)
stok, stock / stoke / stalk / stuck
stokada, staccato / stoccado
stokato, staccato / stoccado
stokd, stock(ed) / stoke(d)
stoke,*,ed,king,er, TO STIR/FEED/POKE (or see stock(y)/stalk)
stoked, stoke(d) / stack(ed) / stake(d) / stalk(ed) / stock(ed)
stokee, stock(y) / stogy
stoker, stagger / stack(er) / stalk(er) / stock(er)
stokur, stagger / stack(er) / stalk(er) / stock(er)
stoky, stock(y) / stogy
stol, stall
stold, stall(ed)
stole,en, PAST TENSE FOR THE WORD "STEAL", FUR ACCESSORY FOR THE SHOULDERS
stolin, stole(n)
stolk, stalk / stock
stolker, stalk(er)
stolun, stole(n)
stolwart, stalwart
stolwort, stalwart
stomach,*,hic,hy, POUCH IN THE BODY WHICH HOLDS FOOD FOR DIGESTION
stomek, stomach
stomik, stomach
stomp,*,ped,ping,per, USING THE FOOT FOR FORCEFUL/HEAVY STEPS (or see stump)
stompur, stomp(er)
stomuk, stomach
ston, stun / stone
stonch, staunch
stone,*,ed,ning,er,ny,nier,niest,nily,niness, ROCK UNDER HEAVY INFLUENCE OF SOMETHING
stoney, stone(ny)
stonsh, staunch

stonshly, staunch(ly)
stooart, steward
stoobid, stupid
stood, PAST TENSE FOR THE WORD 'STAND', UPRIGHT
stooerd, steward
stooge,*, TO BE TRICKED/FOILED, A COMEDIAN
stool,*,lie, SMALL SEAT WITH NO BACK/ARMS, FECES, AN INFORMER
stoole, stool(ie)
stoop,*,ped,ping, BEND OVER, LOWER IN STATUS, SMALL PORCH
stooped, stoop(ed) / stupid
stoopedity, stupid(ity)
stooper, stupor
stoopir, stupor
stoopud, stupid
stoopufid, stupefy(fied)
stoopur, stupor
stop,*,pped,pping,ppage,pper, PUT AN END TO, HALT PROGRESS OF, BLOCK "prefixes: non/un"
stopud, stupid
stopur, stop(pper)
stor, store / star
storach, storage
storage,*, KEEP/STOCKPILE THINGS/INFORMATION
storck, stork
stord, store(d) / star(rred)
store,*,ed,ring,er,eable,rage, PUT AWAY FOR SAFE KEEPING, RETAIL ESTABLISHMENT (or see story) "prefixes: over/under"
storech, storage
storeg, storage
storij, storage
stork,*, A BIRD
storm,*,med,ming,my, CLASHING/MEETING OF TWO DIFFERENT ENERGY FRONTS AND THE REPURCUSSIONS AS A RESULT
stormee, storm(y)
stort, store(d) / star(rred)
storuch, storage
storug, storage
storuj, storage
story,ries,ried, A TALE/EXPLANATION OF AN EVENT/OCCURRENCE, VARIOUS FLOOR LEVELS WITHIN A BUILDING/ HOME
storyd, story(ried)
storys, story(ries)

stot, stow(ed) / stood
stoug, stow(age)
stouj, stow(age)
stout,*, SOLID/HARDY/ROBUST/STRONG/RESISTANT
stove,*, AN APPLIANCE/APPARATUS FOR COOKING/HEATING
stovs, stove(s) / stuff(s)
stow,*,wed,wing,wage,waway, PUT/PLACE SOMETHING/CARGO AWAY
stoweg, stow(age)
stowej, stow(age)
stowek, stoic
stowgee, stogy
stowic, stoic
stowig, stow(age)
stowij, stow(age)
stowik, stoic
stowt, stout / stow(ed)
stra, straw / stray
stradagee, strategy
stradajist, strategy(gist)
straddle,*,ed,ling,er, SIT ATOP OF SOMETHING, BE IN BETWEEN/THE MIDDLE OF, BE ON BOTH SIDES OF SOMETHING AT THE SAME TIME
strade, stray(ed) / straight / strait
stradegist, strategy(gist)
stradejist, strategy(gist)
stradel, straddle
straden, straight(ened)
strades, stratus
stradigest, strategy(gist)
stradil, straddle
stradin, straight(ened)
stradis, stratus
stradle, straddle
strados, stratus
straduge, strategy
stradugist, strategy(gist)
stradujist, strategy(gist)
stradul, straddle
stradun, straight(ened)
stradus, stratus
strae, stray
stragel, straggle
strageler, straggle(r)
stragely, straggle(ly)
straggle,er,ly,lier,liest, WANDER OFF COURSE IN IRREGULAR PATTERN, DISORGANIZED/DISHEVELED/UNTIDY
straght, straight / strait
stragil, straggle

stragiler, straggle(r)
stragily, straggle(ly)
stragle, straggle
straglee, straggle(ly)
stragleist, straggle(st)
straglur, straggle(r)
stragul, straggle
straguly, straggle(ly)
straight,ten,tens,tened,tening,tener, BE LINEAR/LEVEL/TRUE, WITHOUT DEVIATION BETWEEN POINT A AND B (or see strait)
strain,*,ned,ning,ner, STRETCH/PUSH/PULL TO MAXIMUM CAPACITY, SIFT/SIEVE OUT LARGER PARTICLES, REMOVE PARTICULATE MATTER "prefixes: un"
straingly, strange(ly)
strainj, strange
strait,*,ten,tly,tness, NARROW PASSAGEWAY BETWEEN TWO BODIES OF WATER, DIFFICULT/DESPERATE POSITION, CLOSE, STRICT, TIGHT (or see straight)
strakly, straggle(ly)
stran, strain
stranch, strange
strand,*,ded,ding, ONE ALL ALONE, BE SINGLED OUT AWAY FROM OTHERS
straner, strain(er)
strangal, strangle
strange,ely,er,est,eness, UNFAMILIAR/ODD/WEIRD
strangel, strangle
strangeulat, strangulate(tion)
strangir, strange(r)
strangist, strange(st)
strangle,*,ed,ling,er,gulate, CHOKE/HINDER/STOP/CLOSE OFF
strangor, strange(r)
strangul, strangle
strangulashen, strangulate(tion)
strangulate,*,ed,ting,tion, CHOKE/HINDER/STOP/CLOSE OFF
strangur, strange(r)
stranir, strain(er)
stranj, strange
stranjer, strange(r)
stranjest, strange(st)
stranjly, strange(ly)
stranjur, strange(r)
strankel, strangle
strankler, strangle(r)
strankul, strangle

strankulate, strangulate
stranor, strain(er)
stransh, strange
strant, strand
stranur, strain(er)
strap,*,pped,pping, NARROW/THIN STRIP OF SOMETHING, TIE DOWN/ FASTEN/SECURE WITH
strapeng, strap(pping)
stras, stray(s) / stress
strat, straight / strait / stray(ed)
stratagee, strategy
stratagist, strategy(gist)
strategek, strategic
strategekly, strategic(ally)
strategic,*,cal,cally, PERFORM ALONG A GUIDELINE/METHODOLOGY, HAVE A PLAN "prefixes: un"
strategy,gies,gist, HAVE A METHOD/ PLAN TO PERFORM AN ACTION/ EVENT/ PLAY
stratejik, strategic
stratejikly, strategic(ally)
stratel, straddle
straten, straight(en)
stratend, straight(ened)
strates, stratus
stratesfere, stratosphere
stratesphere, stratosphere
stratigek, strategic
stratigekly, strategic(ally)
stratigest, strategy(gist)
stratil, straddle
stratin, straight(en)
stratis, stratus
stratle, straddle
stratnur, straight(ener)
straton, straight(en)
stratoned, straight(ened)
stratos, stratus
stratosfere, stratosphere
stratosphere,ric, LAYER SEVEN MILES ABOVE EARTH "prefixes: sub"
stratugee, strategy
stratugist, strategy(gist)
stratugy, strategy
stratul, straddle
stratum,*,ta,tal,us, LAYER, LEVEL OF A SYSTEM/ FORMATION "prefixes: sub"
stratun, straight(ened)
stratuned, straight(ened)
stratus, UNIFORM/WEAK LAYER OF CLOUDS

stratusfere, stratosphere
stratusphere, stratosphere
straw,*, STALK OF GRAIN, A TUBE TO SIP LIQUIDS
stray,*,yed,ying,yer, WANDER FROM THE GROUP/CENTER
strayd, stray(ed) / straight
streak,*,ked,king,ky,kily,kiness, SMEARED AS IF WIPED, A BLURRED IMAGE
stream,*,med,ming,mer, GENTLE/ FLOWING/CONSISTENT MOVEMENT "prefixes: un/up"
strech, stretch
strecher, stretch(er)
strechnine, strychnine
strechur, stretch(er)
streekee, streak(y)
streem, stream
streemer, stream(er)
streengy, string(y)
street,*, A ROADWAY/PATH WIDE ENOUGH FOR ALL TYPES OF TRAVEL
strek, streak
strekd, strict / streak(ed)
streke, streak(y)
strekin, stricken
strekly, strict(ly)
streknine, strychnine
strekt, strict / streak(ed)
strekun, stricken
streky, streak(y)
strem, stream
stremer, stream(er)
stremur, stream(er)
streneus, strenuous
strenewus, strenuous
streng, string
strengee, string(y)
strengensees, stringent(ncies)
strengently, stringent(ly)
strengint, stringent
strength,*,hen,hened,hening,hener, STRONG ENOUGH, ENDURANCE "prefixes: under"
strenjint, stringent
strenkth, strength
strenth, strength
strenthin, strength(en)
strenues, strenuous
strenuous,sity,sness, STRAINING POINT/ CHALLENGE
strep,ptococcal,ptococcus, SHORT FOR STREPTOCOCCAL, BACTERIA AFFECTING THE THROAT (or see strip/stripe)
strepdokokus, streptococcus
strepir, stripe(r) / strip(pper)
streptococcus,cal, BACTERIA AFFECTING THE THROAT
streptokokus, streptococcus
strepur, stripe(r) / strip(pper)
stres, stress
stresh, stretch
stress,sses,ssed,ssing,ssful,ssfully,ssless, sslessness, STRETCHED BEYOND NORMAL LIMIT OF ACCEPTANCE, CHALLENGE TO DEAL WITH "prefixes: pre/un"
stret, street
stretch,hes,hed,hing,her,hability,hable, PULL AGAINST, EXTEND OUT/ BEYOND "prefixes: over/up"
streu, strew
strew,*,wed,wing,wn, SCATTER/ SPREAD ABOUT
strewn, PAST TENSE FOR THE WORD "STREW", SCATTER/THROW
striashen, striate(tion)
striate,*,ed,ting,tion, PARALLEL STREAKS/SMEARS/FURROWS "prefixes: un"
strichnine, strychnine
stricken, PAST TENSE FOR THE WORD "STRIKE", AFFLICTED WITH/ CHALLENGED, DEALT A BLOW (or see strike)
strict,ter,test,tly,tness, EXTREMELY FIRM/GUARDED/DISCIPLINED
stride,*,ed,rode,dden,ding,er, LARGE/ LONG STEPS, A TYPE OF GAIT WHEN WALKING "prefixes: over"
strife,eless,eful, OPPOSITION/ QUARREL/CONFLICT (or see strive)
strikd, strict
strike,*,king,kingly,ruck,er, DEALT A SHARP/FORCEFUL BLOW,TERM IN SPORTS, TO IGNITE (or see stricken) "prefixes: re"
striken, stricken
strikly, strict(ly)
striknine, strychnine
strikon, stricken
strikt, strict
strikun, stricken
strinewus, strenuous

string,*,ged,ging,ger,gy, THIN ROPE, LONG/THIN/TWISTED SUBSTANCE "prefixes: un"
stringensees, stringent(ncies)
stringent,tly,ncy,ncies, TO BE NARROW/THIN/BOUND/TIGHT/STRICT/SEVERE
stringth, strength
strinjint, stringent
strinkth, strength
strinth, strength
strinues, strenuous
strip,*,pped,pping,pper, TO REMOVE EXCESS/EXTERNAL LAYER, REMOVE CLOTHES (or see stripe)
stripd, stripe(d) / strip(pped)
stripdokokus, streptococcus
stripe,*,ped,ping,per,py,pier,piest, THIN/NARROW/LONG UNIFORM SHAPE (or see strip)
stript, stripe(d) / strip(pped)
striptokokus, streptococcus
stripur, stripe(r) / strip(pper)
strite, stride
strive,*,ed,ving, WORK/EXERT TO ACCOMPLISH A GOAL/END RESULT (or see strife)
strivt, strive(d)
stro, straw
strobe,*, STROBOSCOPE, TYPE OF LIGHT
stroganoff, TYPE OF COOKED DISH WITH PASTA
stroginof, stroganoff
stroke,*,ed,king,er, FORCE/BLOW TO MOVE SOMETHING, SWEEPING MOVEMENT, MEDICAL TERM "prefixes: up"
strol, stroll
stroler, stroll(er)
stroll,*,lled,lling,ller, A CASUAL GAIT IN WALKING, MOVE ABOUT WITH WHEELS
strolur, stroll(er)
strong,ger,gest,gly,gish, GREAT IN STRENGTH FORCE/MASS/POSITION/MOVEMENT
strongist, strong(est)
strongur, strong(er)
stronkist, strong(est)
stronkur, strong(er)
stroodel, strudel
stroon, strewn
strope, strobe

strow, straw
stru, strew
struck, PAST TENSE FOR THE WORD "STRIKE", A SHARP/FORCEFUL BLOW, TERM IN SPORTS, TO IGNITE
structure,*,ed,ring,reless,relessness,ral,rally, PLANNED/SPECIFIC/FORM/SHAPE/ARRANGEMENT, A DWELLING "prefixes: sub/re/un"
strudel, TYPE OF PASTRY
strudul, strudel
struen, strewn
strugel, struggle
struggle,*,ed,ling,er, TO RESIST/FIGHT/CONTEND WITH
strugle, struggle
strugul, struggle
struk, struck
strukcher, structure
strukel, struggle
strukle, struggle
struksher, structure
strukture, structure
strukul, struggle
strum,*,mmed,mming,mmer, USE FINGERS TO LIGHTLY TRAVEL OVER SEVERAL STRINGS OF AN INSTRUMENT
strumer, strum(mmer)
strun, strewn
strung, PAST TENSE FOR THE WORD STRING "prefixes: over/un"
strut,*,tted,tting, A DEVICE USED TO BRACE/SUPPORT, TO WALK WITH A PROUD GAIT
strutegek, strategic
strutejik, strategic
strutejikly, strategic(ally)
strutigekly, strategic(ally)
struz, strew(s)
stryate, striate
strychnine, POISON ORIGINATING FROM A PLANT
stryknine, strychnine
stu, stew
stualee, stool(ie)
stuardes, steward(ess)
stuart, steward
stuartes, steward(ess)
stub,*,bbed,bbing,bby, A KNOB/STUMP, OF A THEATER TICKET, RECEIVE A STRIKING BLOW

stubble,*,ed,ly, SHORT STALKS THAT REMAIN AFTER CUTTING OFF TIP/TOPS
stubborn,ner,nest,nly,ness, FIRMLY UNREASONABLE
stubed, stupid / stub(bbed)
stubee, stub(bby)
stubel, stubble
stubelidy, stability
stubelity, stability
stubern, stubborn
stubid, stupid
stubil, stubble
stubiledy, stability
stubility, stability
stubirn, stubborn
stuble, stubble
stuborn, stubborn
stubud, stupid
stubul, stubble
stuburn, stubborn
stucado, staccato / stoccado
stucato, staccato / stoccado
stucco,*,oed,oing, CEMENT/PLASTER USED FOR WALL COVERING
stuch, stooge / stuck
stuck, PAST TENSE FOR THE WORD STICK "prefixes: un"
stuco, stucco
stucodo, staccato / stoccado
stucoto, staccato / stoccado
stud,*,dded,dding, STALLION, BREEDING MALE, BEAM/POST/BOARD IN WALLS/ROOF OF A STRUCTURE (or see stew(ed)/stood)
studar, stutter
stude, study
studed, study(died) / stud(dded)
studeis, studious
studens, student(s)
student,*, PERSON WHO IS LEARNING/FORMING KNOWLEDGE ABOUT SOMETHING
studeo, studio
studer, stutter
studes, study(dies)
studeus, studious
studid, study(died) / stud(dded)
studint, student
studio,*, SPACE/ROOM FOR CREATING ARTWORK OF ANY MEDIUM
studious,sly,sness, DEVOTED TO GAINING KNOWLEDGE ABOUT SOMETHING "prefixes: un"

studir, stutter
studunt, student
studur, stutter
study,dies,died,ying, TAKE MENTAL NOTE OF, LEARN, READ UP ON, A ROOM TO READ/WRITE "prefixes: un/under"
stue, stew
stuel, stool
stuelee, stool(ie)
stuepiduty, stupid(ity)
stuerd, steward
stuerdes, steward(ess)
stuerdis, steward(ess)
stuf, stuff
stufee, stuff(y)
stuff,*,ffed,ffing,ffy,ffier,ffiest, CRAM/FORCE/PACK SOMETHING INTO CONTAINMENT, REFERENCE TO A BUNCH OF THINGS, TIGHTLY CONFINED
stufy, stuff(y)
stuge, stooge
stuil, stool
stuird, steward
stuirdes, steward(ess)
stuje, stooge
stuk, stuck
stukado, staccato / stoccado
stuko, stucco
stul, stool
stulie, stool(ie)
stumach, stomach
stumb, stump
stumbel, stumble
stumble,*,ed,ling,er,lingly, FAULTER/TRIP/BUMBLE/FALL INTO
stumbul, stumble
stumek, stomach
stump,*,ped,ping,per,py,pier,piest, END OF SOMETHING WITH MAIN PART CUT OFF/ELIMINATED/REMOVED, TO BE AT A LOSS (or see stomp)
stumpee, stump(y)
stumpul, stumble
stumuk, stomach
stun,*,nned,nning,nner,nningly, BE SURPRISED/IMMOBILIZED EITHER PHYSICALLY/MENTALLY/PSYCHOLOGICALLY OR EMOTIONALLY
stund, stun(nned) / stunt
stunk, PAST TENSE FOR THE WORD "STINK", TO SMELL FOUL

stunt,*,ted,ting,tedness, A SHORT/UNDEVELOPED/QUICK ACT/MOVEMENT, A STINT (or see stun(nned))
stuol, stool
stup, stoop
stupafid, stupefy(fied)
stupafie, stupefy
stuped, stupid / stub(bbed) / stoop(ed)
stupedity, stupid(ity)
stupee, stub(bby)
stupefy,fied,fying,fiedness,fyingly, faction, SHOCK/OVERWHELM/MAKE STUPID
stupendous,sly,sness, GREAT/GRAND/ASTONISHING
stupendus, stupendous
stuper, stupor
stupid,der,dest,dly,dness,dity,dities, BEHAVIOR GIVEN TO BE DULL/BORING
stupify, stupefy
stupindus, stupendous
stupir, stupor
stupor,rous, MENTAL LACK OF STABILITY/SENSIBILITY
stupt, stoop(ed) / stub(bbed)
stupufie, stupefy
stupy, stub(bby)
stur, stir
sturchan, sturgeon
sturdes, steward(ess) / steward(s)
sturdy,dier,diest,dily,diness, OF FIRM/STABLE/STRONG STATURE/FORM
sturep, stirrup
sturgen, sturgeon
sturgeon, A FISH
sturgon, sturgeon
sturip, stirrup
sturjen, sturgeon
sturjun, sturgeon
sturling, sterling
sturn, stern
sturnem, sternum
sturnim, sternum
sturnly, stern(ly)
sturnness, stern(ess)
sturnum, sternum
sturor, stir(rrer)
sturty, sturdy
stuter, stutter
stutestiks, statistic(s)
stutir, stutter
stutistiks, statistic(s)

stutor, stutter
stutter,*,red,ring,rer,ringly, STAMMER/REPEAT SECTIONS OF WORDS IN SPEAKING
stuwardes, steward(ess)
sty,ties, SWINE ENCLOSURE, EYE INFLAMMATION
style,*,ed,ling,er,eless,elessness,lish, lishly,lishness,list,listic,listical, listically,lize,lization,lizer, MANNER OF FORM/EXPRESSION OF THE ERA "prefixes: re"
styles, style(s) / stylus
stylest, style(list)
stylis, stylus
stylus,ses, POINTED INSTRUMENT FOR THE HAND TO USE FOR WRITING/ENGRAVING/DRAWING (or see style(list))
stymed, stymie(d)
stymie,*,ed,mying, A DIFFICULT SITUATION/POSITION, BALL POSITION IN SPORTS
styn, stein
stype, stipe
styptic,cal,city, STOPS BLEEDING
styrafom, styrofoam
styrofoam, MANMADE SPONGEY MATERIAL WITH VARIOUS USES
styrufoam, styrofoam
su, sue / zoo
suad, suede / sway(ed) / swat
suade, suede / sway(ed)
suaf, suave
suafly, suave(ly)
suage, sewage
suaje, sewage
suar, sewer
suareje, sewer(age)
suaside, suicide
suasidul, suicide(dal)
suasite, suicide
suate, suede / sway(ed) / swat
suave,er,est,ely,eness,vity, SMOOTH, PLEASANT, SOPHISTICATED
suavidy, suave(vity)
suavly, suave(ly)
sub,*, SHORT FOR SUBSTITUTE/SUBMARINE, TYPE OF SANDWICH, PREFIX INDICATING "BELOW/UNDER/NEAR/IN PLACE OF SECONDARY " MOST OFTEN MODIFIES THE WORD
subcity, subsidy

subconchisly, subconscious(ly)
subconchus, subconscious
subconscious,sly,sness, NOT CONSCIOUS/FULLY AWARE OF, UNDERLYING CONSCIOUSNESS
subconshes, subconscious
subconshus, subconscious
subcontract,*,ted,ting,tor, PERFORM UNDER ANOTHER PERSON'S CONTRACT
subdavejen, subdivision
subdevide, subdivide
subdevishen, subdivision
subdew, subdue
subdivide,*,ed,ding,dable,er,ision, TO DIVIDE UP INTO PARTS UNDER A CATEGORY
subdivision,*, HOUSING DEVELOPMENT
subdo, subdue
subdue,*,ed,uing,uer,ual, OVERCOME, OVERPOWER, INFLUENCE
subduvide, subdivide
subduvigun, subdivision
subduvishen, subdivision
subee, soup(y)
suber, sup(pper) / super
suberb, suburb / superb
suberbea, suburb(ia)
suberben, suburb(an)
suberentendent, superintendent
subereur, superior
suberfishul, superficial
suberintendint, superintendent
subfert, subvert
subgegate, subjugate
subgekdif, subject(ive)
subgekt, subject
subgektive, subject(ive)
subgektivedy, subject(ivity)
subgigate, subjugate
subgugate, subjugate
subir, super / supper
subirb, suburb / superb
subirbea, suburb(ia)
subirben, suburb(an)
subirentendent, superintendent
subjagashen, subjugate(tion)
subjagate, subjugate
subjagation, subjugate(tion)
subject,*,ted,ting,tion,tive,tively, tiveness,tivity,tivism,tivist,tivistic, UNDER RULE/AUTHORITY/ SCRUTINY, OPEN TO CRITERIA

subjegate, subjugate
subjekt, subject
subjektef, subject(ive)
subjektivety, subject(ivity)
subjugate,*,ed,ting,tion,tor,tive, CONQUER/DOMINATE/ENSLAVE
subjugation, subjugate(tion)
subkonshus, subconscious
subkonshusly, subconscious(ly)
subkontrakt, subcontract
sublamashen, sublime(mation)
sublamate, sublime(mate)
subleminaly, subliminal(lly)
subleminul, subliminal
sublimashen, sublime(mation)
sublime,er,est,ed,ming,ely,eness,er, mate,mation,mity,mities,minal, LOFTY/ ELEVATED/SUPERIOR/ EXALTED/HIGHER STATE OF BEING
sublimenaly, subliminal(lly)
sublimenul, subliminal
subliminal,lly, UNDERLYING, NOT FULLY AWARE OF
sublumashen, sublime(mation)
sublyme, sublime
submareen, submarine
submaren, submarine
submarine,*, BULLET SHAPED OCEAN GOING VESSEL WHICH CAN SUBMERGE/ GO UNDER WATER
submechen, submission
submerge,*,ed,ging,gible,gence,rse, BE UNDER LIQUID
submerj, submerge
submerjebul, submerge(gable)
submerse,*,ed,sing,sible,sion, SURROUND WITH LIQUID "prefixes: semi"
submershen, submerse(sion)
submersible, submerse(sible)
submertion, submerse(sion)
submeshen, submission
submesif, submissive
submesive, submissive
submet, submit
submetid, submit(tted)
submetion, submission
submichen, submission
submirj, submerge
submirse, submerse
submirshen, submerse(sion)
submirtion, submerse(sion)
submisefly, submissive(ly)
submisevly, submissive(ly)

submishen, submission
submisive, submissive
submisivly, submissive(ly)
submission,*, RELINQUISH/AGREE TO, ABIDE BY, UNDER THE AUTHORITY OF
submissive,ely,eness,ion, CAPABLE OF/ GIVEN TO SUBMIT/COMPLY/ SURRENDER
submisuf, submissive
submit,*,tted,tting,ttal,ission,issive, TO COMPLY/SURRENDER/COMMIT/ YIELD
submitid, submit(tted)
submition, submission
submoren, submarine
submuren, submarine
submurg, submerge
submurj, submerge
submurjebul, submerge(gable)
submurs, submerse
submurshen, submerse(sion)
submurtion, submerse(sion)
subordenation, subordinate(tion)
subordenit, subordinate
subordinashen, subordinate(tion)
subordinate,*,ed,ting,ely,eness,tion, LESSER IN RANK/ORDER/ SECONDARY/ DEPENDANT, BANKING TERM "prefixes: in"
subordnet, subordinate
subpenu, subpoena
subpoena,*,aed,aing, A LAWFUL PROCESS/MANDATE TO CALL SOMEONE FORTH FOR INFORMATION
subregation, subrogate(tion)
subriedy, sobriety
subriety, sobriety
subrigate, subrogate
subrigation, subrogate(tion)
subriode, sobriety
subrogashen, subrogate(tion)
subrogate,*,ed,ting,tion, REPLACE/ SUBSTITUTE SOMEONE/ SOMETHING
subsadize, subsidy(dize)
subsaqwently, subsequent(ly)
subscrebshen, subscription
subscreption, subscription
subscribe,*,ed,bing,er,iption, COMMIT PAYMENT TO RECEIVE SOMETHING, SIGNED STATEMENT "prefixes: over/un"

subscribshen, subscription
subscription,*, AGREE TO COMMIT MONEY IN EXCHANGE FOR GOODS, SIGNATURE OF COMMITMENT
subsdanshul, substantial
subsdatushen, substitute(tion)
subsdents, substance
subsdratem, substrate(tum)
subsdutoot, substitute
subsdutushin, substitute(tion)
subsdutut, substitute
subsede, subsidy
subsedens, subsidy(dence)
subsediary, subsidiary
subsedize, subsidy(dize)
subsedy, subsidy
subsekwint, subsequent
subsekwintly, subsequent(ly)
subsequent,tly,nce, AFTER/FOLLOWING IN A CERTAIN SEQUENCE/ORDER
subseqwint, subsequent
subserveint, subservient
subserveintly, subservient(ly)
subserveints, subservient(nce)
subservient,tly,nce, FACILITATES PROMOTION OF/ACT TO CREATE, TO SERVE
subsestense, subsistence
subsestinse, subsistence
subside,*,ed,ding,ence, TO SETTLE/ SINK/FALL TO A LOWER LEVEL
subsidens, subsidy(dence)
subsidiary,ries,rily, AID/ASSIST WITH A CONTRIBUTION
subsidy,dies,dize,dizes,dized,dizing, dization,dizer, ORGANIZATION/ GOVERNMENT WHO HELPS OTHERS BY PROVIDING MONEY/SERVICES TOWARD OVERALL NEEDS OF SPECIFIC PEOPLE
subsikwent, subsequent
subsikwently, subsequent(ly)
subsirveins, subservient(nce)
subsirveint, subservient
subsistence,nt, BASIC FOUNDATION WHICH SUPPORTS LIFE
subsite, subside
subsitearee, subsidiary
subsitinse, subside(nce)
subsity, subsidy
subskrebshin, subscription
subskreption, subscription
subskrib, subscribe
subskripshen, subscription

subskription, subscription
substance,*, MATTER, FIRMNESS, REAL
substancheate, substantiate
substanchel, substantial
substanchely, substantial(lly)
substanchiative, substantiate(tive)
substanchil, substantial
substanchuly, substantial(lly)
substansheate, substantiate
substansheative, substantiate(tive)
substanshul, substantial
substantial,lly,lity,lness, OF ENOUGH, MORE THAN A LITTLE, REWARDING AMOUNT "prefixes: in/un"
substantiate,*,ed,ting,tion,tive, OF SUBSTANCE, FACTUAL/REAL "prefixes: un"
substashial, substantial
substatushen, substitute(tion)
substatute, substitute
substatution, substitute(tion)
substechuent, substituent
substense, substance
substetuent, substituent
substetute, substitute
substetution, substitute(tion)
substichuent, substituent
substinse, substance
substishuent, substituent
substitoot, substitute
substituent,*, REPLACE ONE PERSON FOR ANOTHER
substitushen, substitute(tion)
substitute,*,ed,ting,tion,table,tional, tionally,tionary,tive,tively, REPLACE ONE FOR ANOTHER
substrade, substrate
substradem, substrate(tum)
substrate,*,tum,tums, LAYER BELOW
substutushen, substitute(tion)
subsukwently, subsequent(ly)
subsuquently, subsequent(ly)
subsurveanse, subservient(nce)
subsurveint, subservient
subsurviently, subservient(ly)
subtavigen, subdivision
subtle,er,eness,ety,eties,ly, NOT OBVIOUS, SLIGHT HINT OF, SUGGESTIVE WITHOUT SPECIFICS
subtract,*,ted,ting,tion,ter,tive, TAKE AWAY FROM THE WHOLE/ ORIGINAL PART
subtrakshin, subtract(ion)
subtrakshun, subtract(ion)

subtrakt, subtract
subtraktion, subtract(ion)
subur, super / supper
suburb,*,bia,ban,banite,banize, DISTRICT OUTSIDE OF MAJOR POPULATED AREA
suburbea, suburb(ia)
suburben, suburb(an)
suburintendent, superintendent
subversef, subversive
subvershen, subversion
subversion,sary, REMOVE THE BASIS/ FOUNDATION OF ANYTHING IN ORDER TO DESTROY IT
subversive,rsively,rsiveness, REMOVE THE BASIS/FOUNDATION OF ANYTHING TO DESTROY IT
subvert,*,ted,ting,ter,rsive, REMOVE BASIS/FOUNDATION OF ANYTHING IN ORDER TO DESTROY IT
subvertion, subversion
subvirsef, subversive
subvirshen, subversion
subvirsion, subversion
subvirt, subvert
subvursef, subversive
subvurshen, subversion
subvursive, subversive
subvurt, subvert
subvurtion, subversion
subwa, subway
subway,*, UNDERGROUND ELECTRIC TRAIN, A SANDWICH
succeed,*,ded,ding, IMPROVE/GAIN/ OVERCOME
succeses, success(es)
succesful, success(ful)
succesion, succession
success,es,ssful,ssfully,ssfulness, IMPROVING/GAINING/ OVERCOMING/ ADVANCING "prefixes: un"
succession,nal,nally, SEQUENCE/SERIES/ ONE AFTER THE OTHER OF SOMETHING/SOMEONE
successive,ely,eness, FOLLOW IN ORDER WITHOUT INTERRUPTION
succinct,tly,tness, BRIEF/SHORT/ SUMMARY
succor,rer, OFFER RELIEF/SUPPORT/AID IN TIME OF NEED (or see suck(er))
succsed, succeed

succulent,*,tly,nce,ncy, JUICY/ DELICIOUS TO THE PHYSICAL SENSES
succumb,*,bed, SURRENDER/RETIRE TO, FALL FOR, YIELD/GIVE WAY TO
sucdhen, suction
sucebdubility, susceptible(bility)
sucede, secede
sucenct, succinct
suceptability, susceptible(bility)
suceptable, susceptible
sucer, succor / suck(er)
sucession, succession
such, USED TO MAKE A COMPARISON WITH SOMETHING IMPLIED BY CONTEXT
sucher, suture / suck(er)
suchur, suture / suck(er)
sucinct, succinct
sucjestion, suggest(ion)
suck,*,ked,king,ker, FORCEFULLY PULL/ DRAW SOMETHING AWAY FROM ITS SOURCE, A FISH, LOLLIPOP (or see succor)
suckle,*,ed,ling, THE ACT OF BREAST FEEDING
suckshun, suction
sucol, suckle
sucom, succumb
sucor, succor / suck(er)
sucour, succor / suck(er)
sucreshen, secrete(tion)
sucrete, secrete
sucretion, secrete(tion)
sucrose, SUGAR OBTAINED FROM PLANTS
sucsashen, succession
sucseed, succeed
sucses, success
sucsesful, success(ful)
sucseshon, succession
sucsesif, successive
sucsesiflee, successive(ly)
sucsetion, succession
sucsinkt, succinct
suction, FORCEFULLY DRAW SOMETHING FROM ITS SOURCE, CREATE A VACUUM/ADHERENCE
suculent, succulent
suculint, succulent
sucumb, succumb
sucure, secure
sucurity, secure(rity)
sucurly, secure(ly)

sud, sue(d) / suds / suit
sudan, sedan
sudanem, pseudonym
sudanim, pseudonym
sudar, suitor
sudashen, sedate(tion)
sudasion, sedate(tion)
sudate, sedate
sudation, sedate(tion)
sudden,nly,nness, IMMEDIATELY, NO TIME LAPSE
sude, sue(d) / soot(y)
suden, sudden
sudenim, pseudonym
sudenly, sudden(ly)
suder, suitor
sudews, seduce
sudin, sudden
sudinem, pseudonym
sudinly, sudden(ly)
sudir, suitor
sudn, sudden
sudo, pseudo
sudon, sudden
sudonem, pseudonym
sudonim, pseudonym
sudonly, sudden(ly)
sudoose, seduce
sudor, suitor
suds,sy, BUBBLES, FOAMY, LATHER, FROTH
suducshen, seduce(ction)
suductive, seduce(ctive)
suduktion, seduce(ction)
suduktive, seduce(ctive)
sudun, sudden
sudunly, sudden(ly)
suduse, seduce
sudy, soot(y)
sue,*,ed,uing, LEGALLY ATTEMPT TO FORCE SOMEONE TO PAY MONEY FOR A WRONGDOING
suecher, suture
suede, LEATHER (or see sway(ed))
suege, sewage
sueje, sewage
suenome, tsunami
suer, sewer
suereje, sewer(age)
sueside, suicide
suesidul, suicide(dal)
suesite, suicide
suet, PART OF ANIMALS WHICH YIELDS TALLOW (or see suit/sweet)

sufaneer, souvenir
sufaree, safari
sufary, safari
sufecashen, suffocate(tion)
sufecate, suffocate
sufecation, suffocate(tion)
sufeer, severe
sufeerly, severe(ly)
sufekashen, suffocate(tion)
sufekate, suffocate
sufeks, suffix
sufeneer, souvenir
sufer, suffer / severe
suferd, suffer(ed)
sufere, severe
suferly, severe(ly)
sufestikashen, sophisticate(tion)
sufestikated, sophisticate(d)
sufestikation, sophisticate(tion)
sufex, suffix
suffer,*,red,ring,rable,rableness,rably, rer,rance, REACTION TO PAIN/ INFLICTION "prefixes: in"
suffice,ed,cing,cient, SUFFICIENT, ADEQUATE, SATISFIED
suffichent, sufficient
sufficient,tly,ncy, ENOUGH, ADEQUATE, SATISFIED "prefixes: in"
suffishent, sufficient
suffix,xes,xed,xal,xally,xion,xation, END ATTACHED TO A WORD/ SOMETHING
suffocate,*,ed,ting,tion,tive,tingly, SMOTHER, CHOKE OFF, REMOVE OXYGEN
suffrage,ette,gist, VOTING AND RIGHTS TO VOTE
suficashen, suffocate(tion)
suficate, suffocate
sufication, suffocate(tion)
sufice, suffice
suficent, sufficient
sufichent, sufficient
suficient, sufficient
suficiently, sufficient(ly)
sufikashen, suffocate(tion)
sufikate, suffocate
sufikation, suffocate(tion)
sufiks, suffix
sufiksis, suffix(es)
sufir, suffer / severe
sufird, suffer(ed)
sufirly, severe(ly)
sufise, suffice

sufishent, sufficient
sufishintly, sufficient(ly)
sufishunt, sufficient
sufistakashen, sophisticate(tion)
sufistakation, sophisticate(tion)
sufix, suffix
sufixes, suffix(es)
sufla, souffle'
suflay, souffle'
sufocashen, suffocate(tion)
sufocate, suffocate
sufocation, suffocate(tion)
sufor, suffer
suford, suffer(ed)
suforeg, suffrage
sufr, suffer
sufrage, suffrage
sufragist, suffrage(gist)
sufraje, suffrage
sufranse, suffer(ance)
sufrech, suffrage
sufreje, suffrage
sufrige, suffrage
sufrigest, suffrage(gist)
sufrije, suffrage
sufrinse, suffer(ance)
sufrugist, suffrage(gist)
sufucashen, suffocate(tion)
sufukate, suffocate
sufukation, suffocate(tion)
sufuner, souvenir
sufur, suffer
sufurd, suffer(ed)
sugar,*,rless,red,ry,rless, SUCROSE, SUBSTANCE OBTAINED FROM PLANTS "prefixes: non"
sugchestshen, suggest(ion)
suger, sugar
sugest, suggest
suggesdiv, suggest(ive)
suggest,*,ted,ting,ter,tion,tive,tively, tiveness,tible, OFFER A FACT/ THEORY TO BE CONSIDERED
suggestshen, suggest(ion)
sugjesdiv, suggest(ive)
sugjesgen, suggest(ion)
sugjest, suggest
sugjestion, suggest(ion)
sugjestive, suggest(ive)
sugnefakent, significant
sugnifukent, significant
sugwaro, suguaro
suicide,*,dal,dally, TAKE ONE'S OWN LIFE

suicidul, suicide(dal)
suige, sewage
suir, sewer
suireje, sewer(age)
suiside, suicide
suisidul, suicide(dal)
suisite, suicide
suit,*,ted,ting,table,tability,tableness, tably, PANTS/JACKET SET, IN A CARD GAME, PROPER/AGREEABLE/ FITTING (or see suite/sweet) "prefixes: un"
suite,*, TYPE OF ROOM (too many definitions, please consult standard dictionary) (or see suit/sweet)
suitor,*, ONE WHO SUES, MAN COURTING A WOMAN
sujest, suggest
suk, suck
sukal, suckle
sukchen, suction
sukchest, suggest
sukchun, suction
sukel, suckle
suker, succor / suck(er)
sukeurly, secure(ly)
sukewlent, succulent
sukewlunt, succulent
sukewr, secure
sukewrity, secure(rity)
sukgeshin, suggest(ion)
sukgest, suggest
sukgestion, suggest(ion)
sukgestshen, suggest(ion)
sukiatrist, psychiatry(rist)
sukiatry, psychiatry
sukil, suckle
sukini, zuchinni
sukir, succor / suck(er)
sukiulent, succulent
sukiutrest, psychiatry(rist)
sukjesdev, suggest(ive)
sukjest, suggest
sukjestion, suggest(ion)
sukjestshen, suggest(ion)
sukle, suckle
sukluded, seclude(d)
suklusion, seclusion
suklusive, seclusive
sukol, suckle
sukor, succor / suck(er)
sukour, succor / secure / suck(er)
sukqulent, succulent
sukreshen, secrete(tion)

sukresion, secrete(tion)
sukrete, secrete
sukrose, sucrose
suksed, succeed
sukses, success
suksesful, success(ful)
sukseshen, succession
suksesif, successive
suksesiflee, successive(ly)
sukshen, suction
sukshun, suction
sukul, suckle
sukulent, succulent
sukum, succumb
sukur, suck(er) / succor / secure
sukurity, secure(rity)
sukwenshul, sequence(ntial)
sukwential, sequence(ntial)
sukwoya, sequoia
sulal, salal
sulami, salami
sulareum, solarium
suldree, sultry
sulebrity, celebrity
sulective, select(ive)
suledify, solid(ify)
suleks, select(s)
sulekshen, select(ion)
sulekt, select
sulektion, select(ion)
sulektive, select(ive)
sulektof, select(ive)
suleluquy, soliloquy
sulen, sullen
sulenity, saline(nity)
sulenium, selenium
sulerium, solarium
sulesit, solicit
sulesitation, solicit(ation)
sulesiter, solicit(er)
sulesteul, celestial
sulewshen, solution
sulewtion, solution
sulfade, sulfate
sulfate,*,ed,ting, ALSO SULPHATE, A SULFURIC ACID SALT "prefixes: bi"
sulfats, sulfate(s)
sulfer, sulfur
sulferik, sulfur(ic)
sulfide,*, A SULFUR CHEMICAL COMPOUND "prefixes: bi"
sulfir, sulfur
sulfirek, sulfur(ic)

sulfite,*,tic, A SULFUR CHEMICAL
COMPOUND "prefixes: bi"
sulfur,ric,rize,rous,rously, ALSO
SULPHUR, NONMETALLIC ELEMENT
"prefixes: de"
sulfurik, sulfur(ic)
sulicit, solicit
sulicitation, solicit(ation)
suliciter, solicit(er)
sulidefy, solid(ify)
sulilakwee, soliloquy
sulin, sullen
sulinidy, saline(nity)
sulisetation, solicit(ation)
sulisit, solicit
sulisiter, solicit(er)
sulitefy, solid(ify)
sulivu, saliva
sulk,*,ked,king,ky,kier,kiest,kily,kiness,
UPSET AT NOT GETTING ENOUGH
ATTENTION, REACTION TO BEING
OFFENDED
sulkey, sulk(y)
sullen,nly,nness, ALONE/GLOOMY/
DISMAL
sulomee, salami
sulon, salon
suloon, saloon
suloot, salute
sulowl, salal
sulphade, sulfate
sulphate, sulfate
sulpher, sulfur
sulpherik, sulfur(ic)
sulphide, sulfide
sulphir, sulfur
sulphurek, sulfur(ic)
sultan,*,nic, DOMESTICATED FOWL,
DESPOT/TYRANT
sultin, sultan
sultree, sultry
sultry,rily,riness, SWEATY/HEAVY/HOT,
OVERPOWERING COMBINATION
sultun, sultan
sulun, sullen / saloon
sulushen, solution
sulute, salute
sulution, solution
sum,*,mmed,mming,mmation,
mmational,mmary, TOTAL OF,
ALTOGETHER (or see some/zoom)
sumachin, sum(mmation)
suman, summon
sumantics, semantics

sumarely, summary(rily)
sumarize, summary(rize)
sumaruly, summary(rily)
sumary, summary / summer(y)
sumashen, sum(mmation)
sumation, sum(mmation)
sumb, sump
sumbreo, sombrero
sumbrero, sombrero
sumchewus, sumptuous
sumchuis, sumptuous
sumd, sum(mmed)
sumding, something
sumedul, summit(ttal)
sumen, summon
sumener, summon(er)
sument, cement
sumer, summer
sumerily, summary(rily)
sumerise, summary(rize)
sumersolt, somersault
sumeruly, summary(rily)
sumery, summary / summer(y)
sumesder, semester
sumester, semester
sumet, summit / submit
sumetal, summit(ttal)
sumetrek, symmetry(ric)
sumetric, symmetry(ric)
sumfing, something
sumidul, summit(ttal)
sumin, summon
sumint, cement
sumir, summer
sumiry, summary / summer(y)
sumit, summit / submit
sumitul, summit(ttal)
summary,ries,rize,rizes,rized,rizing,rizer,
rist,rily,riness, CONCISE/SIMPLIFIED
SHORT VERSION
summen, summon
summer,*,red,ring,rly,ry, SEASON
FROM JUNE THROUGH SEPTEMBER
summin, summon
summit,*, THE HIGHEST PART/PEAK/
POINT/RANK OF (or see submit)
summon,*,ned,ning,ner, TO PETITION/
CALL/SEND/ORDER FOR
ATTENDANCE
sumon, summon
sumoner, summon(er)
sump, DEPRESSION WHERE POOL OF
LIQUID CAN COLLECT
sumpchewus, sumptuous

sumpshues, sumptuous
sumptues, sumptuous
sumptuous,sly,sness, IMPRESSIVE,
LUXURIOUS, MAGNIFICENT
sumshuis, sumptuous
sumt, sum(mmed)
sumteng, something
sumthing, something
sumtime, sometime
sumting, something
sumur, summer
sumuree, summary / summer(y)
sumurees, summary(ries)
sumurize, summary(rize)
sumursolt, somersault
sumury, summary / summer(y)
sumut, summit / submit
sumware, somewhere
sumwat, somewhat
sumwer, somewhere
sumwhat, somewhat
sumwhere, somewhere
sumwot, somewhat
sumwut, somewhat
sun,*,nned,nning,nny, SOLAR PLANET
THAT ALL PLANETS IN THE SYSTEM
REVOLVE AROUND (or see son/
sunn/soon)
sunada, sonata
suname, tsunami
sunapsis, synapsis
sunaptek, synaptic
sunaptic, synaptic
sunareo, scenario
sunatu, sonata
sunc, sung / sunk
sunda, sunday
sunday,*, A DAY OF THE WEEK
(ENGLISH)
sundiket, syndicate
sundree, sundry
sundres, sundry(ries)
sundry,ries, MANY SMALL THINGS
sundukit, syndicate
sune, sun(nny) / son(y)
sunelity, senile(lity)
sunereo, scenario
sunerist, scenario(ist)
sung, PAST TENSE FOR THE WORD
'SING' "prefixes: un"
sunility, senile(lity)
sunk, PAST TENSE FOR THE WORD
'SINK'
sunn, A SHRUB (or see sun/son)

sunoda, sonata
sunografee, scenography
sunome, tsunami
sunonimus, synonym(ous)
sunopsis, synopsis
sunota, sonata
sunseer, sincere
sunseerly, sincere(ly)
suntree, sundry
suny, sun(nny) / son(y)
suoge, sewage
suor, sewer
suosidel, suicide(dal)
suove, suave
sup,*,pped,pping,pper, SHORT FOR HAVING SUPPER/DINNER, TO SIP (or see sub/soup)
supal, supple
suparlatif, superlative
suparstishus, superstitious
supasetory, suppository
supasition, supposition
supasitory, suppository
supausatory, suppository
supazeshen, supposition
supazishen, supposition
supcity, subsidy
supconchesly, subconscious(ly)
supconshus, subconscious
supcontrakt, subcontract
supdavide, subdivide
supdavijin, subdivision
supdevid, subdivide
supdevide, subdivide
supdew, subdue
supdo, subdue
supdu, subdue
supduvide, subdivide
supe, soup(y)
supel, supple
supenu, subpoena
super,rable,rably,rableness, GREAT/ EXCESSIVE/HIGH UP/ STRONG, PREFIX INDICATING "OVER/ABOVE/ TO A VERY HIGH DEGREE" MOST OFTEN MODIFIES THE WORD (or see supper)
superb,bly,bness, GRAND/SPLENDID (or see suburb)
superbea, suburb(ia)
superentendent, superintendent
supereoredy, superior(ity)
supereority, superior(ity)
supereur, superior

superfichul, superficial
superficial,lity,lities,lly,lness, UNREAL/ ILLUSION/FAUX/FALSE LAYER
superfishul, superficial
superflewus, superfluous
superflues, superfluous
superfluous,sly,sness, EXCESS
superintendent,*, ONE WHO OVERSEES/MANAGES
superior,*,rity,rly, RANK/AUTHORITY OVER ANOTHER, ELEVATED, BETTER QUALITY/GRADE
superioridy, superior(ity)
superlatif, superlative
superlative,*,ely,eness, SURPASSES ALL DEGREES/ RANK BY COMPARISON
superlutif, superlative
supersdishen, superstition
supersteshus, superstitious
superstition,*,ous, ALLOW SOMETHING SEEMINGLY IRRATIONAL TO FORETELL FUTURE EVENTS
superstitious,sly,sness, ALLOW SOMETHING SEEMINGLY IRRATIONAL TO FORETELL FUTURE EVENTS
supervise,*,ed,sing,sor,sory,sion, PROVIDE OVERSIGHT/DIRECTION TO OTHERS
supervishen, supervise(sion)
supervizury, supervise(sory)
supesition, supposition
supgekt, subject
supgektif, subject(ive)
supil, supple
supina, subpoena
supir, sup(pper) / super
supirb, suburb / superb
supirblee, superb(ly)
supirentendent, superintendent
supireority, superior(ity)
supireur, superior
supirfichul, superficial
supirfishul, superficial
supirflewus, superfluous
supirfluis, superfluous
supirlatif, superlative
supirlative, superlative
supirlutif, superlative
supirsdishen, superstition
supirsteshus, superstitious
supirstition, superstition
supirveshin, supervise(sion)
supirvise, supervise

supirvisery, supervise(ry)
supirvishen, supervise(sion)
supirvision, supervise(sion)
supizeshen, supposition
supjekt, subject
supjektid, subject(ed)
supjektif, subject(ive)
supkonchisly, subconscious(ly)
supkonchus, subconscious
supkonshesly, subconscious(ly)
supkonshus, subconscious
supkontrakt, subcontract
suplamashen, sublime(mation)
suplament, supplement
suplamentul, supplement(al)
suplamint, supplement
suplant, supplant
suple, supple
suplement, supplement
suplementul, supplement(al)
suplemint, supplement
supleminul, subliminal
supli, supply
suplier, supply(lier)
suplime, sublime
supliment, supplement
suplimentul, supplement(al)
suplimenul, subliminal
suplument, supplement
suplumentul, supplement(al)
suply, supply
suplyer, supply(lier)
supmareen, submarine
supmaren, submarine
supmerg, submerge
supmerjebul, submerge(gable)
supmerse, submerse
supmersible, submerse(sible)
supmet, submit
supmeted, submit(tted)
supmichen, submission
supmirj, submerge
supmit, submit
supmited, submit(tted)
supmureen, submarine
supmurg, submerge
supmurjebul, submerge(gable)
supmurs, submerse
supmursabul, submerse(sible)
supmurshen, submerse(sion)
supol, supple
supor, super / supper
supordenate, subordinate
supordinet, subordinate

supordunet, subordinate
suport, support
suportef, support(ive)
suportive, support(ive)
suporvise, supervise
supose, suppose
suposetory, suppository
suposidly, suppose(dly)
suposition, supposition
supository, suppository
suposubly, suppose(dly)
supozatory, suppository
supoze, suppose
supozeshin, supposition
supozetory, suppository
supozitory, suppository
supozubly, suppose(dly)
supper, DINNER, MEAL IN EVENING (or see super)
supplament, supplement
supplamentul, supplement(al)
supplant,*,ted,ting,tation,ter, FORCEFUL/UNDERHANDED REMOVAL OF SOMETHING/ SOMEONE
supple,ely,ly,eness, FLEXIBLE/ GRACEFULLY CONFORMING (or see supply)
supplement,*,ted,ting,tal,tary,tation, IN ADDITION TO THE BASIC
supplimentul, supplement(al)
supplument, supplement
supplumentul, supplement(al)
supply,lies,lied,lying,lier, SUPPORT/ PROVIDE GOODS/SERVICES
support,*,ted,ting,tive,tively,tiveness, ter,table,tably, TO ENABLE/ EMPOWER/ SUSTAIN/ASSIST/ STRUCTURE SOMETHING OR SOMEONE "prefixes: in/un"
suppose,*,ed,sing,edly,sable,sably, PROPOSE/SUGGEST/IMPLY AS TO THE WAY SOMETHING COULD BE "prefixes: pre"
supposition,*,nal,nally,ous,ously,ive, HYPOTHESIS/ASSUMPTION
suppository,ries, PREPARATION FOR INSERTION INTO ORIFICE ON THE LOWER HALF OF THE BODY
suppreshun, suppress(ion)
suppresion, suppress(ion)
suppress,sses,ssed,ssing,ssible,ssor, ssion,ssive,ssant, PREVENT/ RESTRAIN

suprechen, suppress(ion)
supreem, supreme
supremacy,macist, BELIEVES THEY ARE SUPERIOR OVER OTHERS
supremasist, supremacy(cist)
supreme,ely,eness, HIGHEST OF QUALITY/DEGREE
supremusee, supremacy
supremusist, supremacy(cist)
supremusy, supremacy
supreno, soprano
supres, suppress
supreshen, suppress(ion)
supress, suppress
supression, suppress(ion)
supretion, suppress(ion)
suprino, soprano
suprogate, subrogate
suprveshin, supervise(sion)
suprvishen, supervise(sion)
supsakwently, subsequent(ly)
supscrepshon, subscription
supsdents, substance
supsditushen, substitute(tion)
supsedy, subsidy
supsekwent, subsequent
supsekwint, subsequent
supsekwintly, subsequent(ly)
supseqwint, subsequent
supserveint, subservient
supsestinse, subsistence
supside, subside
supsideary, subsidiary
supsidinse, subside(nce)
supsikwent, subsequent
supsikwently, subsequent(ly)
supsirveint, subservient
supsistense, subsistence
supsite, subside
supskrepshen, subscription
supskrib, subscribe
supskription, subscription
supstanchily, substantial(lly)
supstans, substance
supstansheate, substantiate
supstanshol, substantial
supstanshul, substantial
supstanshulee, substantial(lly)
supstantiate, substantiate
supstatoot, substitute
supstatushen, substitute(tion)
supstense, substance
supstetoot, substitute
supstichuent, substituent

supstinse, substance
supstishuent, substituent
supstitoot, substitute
supstitushen, substitute(tion)
supstitute, substitute
supstradem, substrate(tum)
supstrate, substrate
supstratem, substrate(tum)
supsurveint, subservient
suptract, subtract
suptrakchin, subtract(ion)
suptrakshun, subtract(ion)
suptrakt, subtract
supul, supple
supur, super / supper
supurb, suburb / superb
supurblee, superb(ly)
supurfichul, superficial
supurfishul, superficial
supurintendent, superintendent
supurlative, superlative
supurlutif, superlative
supurstishus, superstitious
supurstition, superstition
supurveshin, supervise(sion)
supurvise, supervise
supurvision, supervise(sion)
supusition, supposition
supuzishen, supposition
supvert, subvert
supvurt, subvert
supwa, subway
supy, soup(y)
suquential, sequence(ntial)
suquir, secure
suquirity, secure(ly)
suquirly, secure(ly)
suqulent, succulent
sur, PREFIX INDICATING "OVER/ABOVE/ TO A VERY HIGH DEGREE," MOST OFTEN MODIFIES THE WORD (or see sir/sure)
suraget, surrogate
suragit, surrogate
suramik, ceramic
suran, saran
surape, serape
suratid, serrate(d)
surbent, serpent
surcal, circle
surcas, circus
surcel, circle
surces, circus
surch, serge /surge /search

surchacol, surgical
surchan, surgeon
surcharge,*,ed,ging, AN EXCESS CHARGE/TAX OVER AND ABOVE THE NORM
surchari, surgery
surcharj, surcharge
surches, search(es) / surge(s)
surchon, surgeon
surchuble, search(able)
surcle, circle
surcol, circle
surcumcise, circumcise
surcumfirense, circumference
surcut, circuit
sure,er,est,ely,eness, MOST CERTAINLY, OF COURSE, INEVITABLE, CONFIDENTLY (or see surly) "prefixes: en/un"
sureal, surreal
surealism, surrealism
suree, surrey
sureilisum, surrealism
surel, sorrel / surreal
surelism, surrealism
surender, surrender
surene, serene
surenge, syringe
surenidy, serene(nity)
surenity, serene(nity)
surenje, syringe
sureolesum, surrealism
surety,ties, ONE WHO IS BOUND/ LIABLE/RESPONSIBLE
sureulist, surrealism(st)
sureulizum, surrealism
surf,*,fed,fing,fable,fer,fy, WHERE OCEANS WAVES BREAK, CRUISE THE INTERNET/TV (or see serf/ serve)
surface,*,ed,cing,eless,er,ficial, TOP/ EXTERNAL/OUTSIDE PORTION OF (or see service) "prefixes: bio/re/ sub/under"
surfase, surface
surfd, surf(ed)
surfeje, serf(age)
surfent, servant
surfes, surface
surfibul, surf(able)
surfis, surface / service
surft, serve(d) / surf(ed)
surfunt, servant
surfur, surf(er)

surg, surge
surgakle, surgical
surgaree, surgery
surgarge, surcharge
surgd, surge(d)
surge,*,ed,ging, ENERGETIC SWELLING/ BURST/FLUCTUATION OF SOMETHING (or see search(ed)) "prefixes: re/up"
surgen, surgeon
surgent, UPRISING, SWELLING, STRONG FLUCTUATION (or see sergeant)
surgeon,*,ncy,ncies, DOCTOR WHO PERFORMS SURGICAL PROCEDURES
surgery,ries, PERFORM A MEDICAL OPERATION "prefixes: bio"
surgical,lly, ASSOCIATED WITH MEDICAL OPERATIONS
surgikul, surgical
surgin, surgeon
surgint, surgent / sergeant
surgis, surge(s)
surgon, surgeon
surgree, surgery
surgukle, surgical
suriasis, psoriasis
suringe, syringe
surinje, syringe
surjakle, surgical
surjaree, surgery
surje, surge
surjen, surgeon
surjent, surgent / sergeant
surjikul, surgical
surjon, surgeon
surjree, surgery
surjukle, surgical
surkawfigus, sarcophagus
surkewlate, circulate
surkofegus, sarcophagus
surkulir, circular
surkumfurens, circumference
surkumstans, circumstance
surkus, circus
surlee, surly
surloen, sirloin
surloin, sirloin
surly,lier,liest,liness, ROUGH/RUDE (or see sure(ly))
surmin, sermon
surmise,*,ed,sing, ASSUME/GUESS
surmize, surmise
surmon, sermon
surogate, surrogate

surong, sarong
surope, serape
suroredy, sorority
surority, sorority
suround, surround
surownd, surround
surpass,sses,ssed,ssing,ssable,ssingly, GO BEYOND EXPECTATIONS
surpent, serpent
surpentene, serpentine
surpint, serpent
surpintene, serpentine
surplus,ses,sage, MORE THAN NEEDED/ NECESSARY, OVERABUNDANCE
surprise,*,ed,sing,sal,ser,singly, UNEXPECTEDLY SHOWING UP/ APPEARING/ OCCURING "prefixes: un"
surprize, surprise
surrated, serrate(d)
surreal,lism,list,listic,listically,lism, NOT OF THIS PLANE/ WORLD, UNREAL, TIME PERIOD IN ART
surrealism, NOT OF THIS PLANE/ WORLD, UNREAL,TIME PERIOD IN ART
surrender,*,red,ring, GIVE UP, RELINQUISH POWER
surrey, SMALL HORSE DRAWN CARRIAGE
surrogate,*,ed,ting, TO SUBSTITUTE SOMEONE AND THEIR DUTIES
surround,*,ded,ding, ENCOMPASS/ ENCIRCLE/ENCLOSE AROUND
surry, surrey
surtatude, certitude
surten, certain
surthener, south(erner)
surtifecate, certificate
surtify, certify
surva, survey
survalinse, surveillance
survas, survey(s) / service
survatood, servitude
survatude, servitude
survaur, survey(or)
survayer, survey(or)
survd, serve(d)
surveilance, surveillance
surveillance,nt, OBSERVE/WATCH OVER SOMEONE/SOMETHING, SPYING
survent, servant
surveor, survey(or)
surves, service

survesable, service(cable)
survey,*,yed,ying,yor, TO CAPTURE FACTS/VIEW/DOCUMENT AN AREA/ SITUATION
survife, survive
surviks, cervix
survint, servant
survis, service
survisable, service(cable)
survive,*,ed,ving,val,vor, REMAIN ALIVE AFTER A TRAGIC/SOLEMN EVENT
survivul, survive(val)
survont, servant
survunt, servant
survus, service
sury, surrey
susaptible, susceptible
susbect, suspect
susbend, suspend
susbenders, suspender(s)
susbind, suspend
susbinded, suspend(ed)
susbinders, suspender(s)
susceptible,eness,ly,bility, PRONE/ LIKELY/GIVEN TO BE AFFECTED "prefixes: in"
susceptive,eness,vity,ible, ABLE/LIKELY TO BE AFFECTED "prefixes: non/un"
suscinkt, succinct
susdan, sustain
susdanuble, sustain(able)
susdeninse, sustenance
susdinense, sustenance
susede, secede
susenked, succinct
susenktly, succinct(ly)
suseptibility, susceptible(bility)
suseptible, susceptible
suseptif, susceptive
suseptive, susceptive
suseptuble, susceptible
suseptuf, susceptive
suseshen, secession
susesion, secession
susete, secede
sush, such
susiadul, society(tal)
susiete, society
susietul, society(tal)
susiety, society
susinkt, succinct
susinktly, succinct(ly)
susiudil, society(tal)
susiuty, society

suspect,*,ted,ting, LIKELY TO BE INVOLVED IN AN EVENT "prefixes: un"
suspekt, suspect
suspenchen, suspension
suspend,*,ded,ding,der,nsion, TEMPORARILY BAR/RELIEVE/ REMOVE FROM DUTY, HANG IN THE AIR
suspender,*, SHOULDER HOLDERS FOR PANTS, ONE WHO SUSPENDS
suspense,eful,sive,sively,siveness, TO WAIT WITH UNCERTAINTY
suspensful, suspense(ful)
suspenshen, suspension
suspension, HANGING/FLOATING IN LIQUID
suspent, suspend
suspention, suspension
suspeshen, suspicion
suspeshesly, suspicious(ly)
suspeshus, suspicious
suspicion,*,ous, SUSPECT TO/OF, TO SUPPOSE WITHOUT CLEAR EVIDENCE
suspicious,sly,sness, SUSPECT, TO SUPPOSE WITHOUT CLEAR EVIDENCE
suspind, suspend
suspinder, suspender
suspinse, suspense
suspinsful, suspense(ful)
suspinshen, suspension
suspintion, suspension
suspishes, suspicious
suspishesly, suspicious(ly)
suspishun, suspicion
suspitious, suspicious
sustain,*,ned,ning,nable,ner,nment, tenance, ENDURE/CONFIRM
sustane, sustain
sustanense, sustenance
sustanible, sustain(able)
sustanuble, sustain(able)
sustenance, BASIC PROVISIONS FOR SURVIVAL
susteninse, sustenance
sustunense, sustenance
sut, soot / suit / suite
sutal, subtle
sutaltee, subtle(ty)
sutanic, satanic
sutanikul, satanic(al)
sutar, suitor

sutcher, suture
sutchur, suture
sutel, subtle
suteltee, subtle(ty)
suten, sudden
sutenly, sudden(ly)
suter, suitor
suterical, satire(rical)
suth, soothe
sutherly, south(erly)
suthern, south(ern)
suthirnur, south(erner)
suthurn, south(ern)
sutil, subtle
sutiltee, subtle(ty)
sutin, sudden
sutinly, sudden(ly)
sutir, suitor
sutle, subtle
sutly, subtle(ly)
suto, pseudo
sutol, subtle
sutoltee, subtle(ty)
suton, sudden
sutonem, pseudonym
sutonim, pseudonym
sutor, suitor
suts, suds
sutultee, subtle(ty)
sutun, sudden
sutunly, sudden(ly)
suture,*,ed,ring,rally, USED TO STITCH A WOUND CLOSED
suty, soot(y)
suvana, savanna
suvaner, souvenir
suvant, savant
suvear, severe
suvearly, severe(ly)
suveleun, civilian
suveneer, souvenir
suvere, severe
suverity, severe(rity)
suverly, severe(ly)
suviner, souvenir
suvire, severe
suvont, savant
suvuneer, souvenir
suvunir, souvenir
suwar, sewer
suwaro, saguaro
suwer, sewer
suwerige, sewer(age)
suwero, saguaro

suwir, sewer
suworo, saguaro
suwrench, syringe
suwurege, sewer(age)
svenks, sphinx
svenkter, sphincter
svenx, sphinx
svinks, sphinx
svinktur, sphincter
svinx, sphinx
swa, sway
swab,*,bbed,bbing, ABSORBENT MATERIAL TO DAB/ MOP/CLEAN (or see swap)
swabed, swap(pped) / swab(bbed)
swabt, swap(pped) / swab(bbed)
swach, swatch
swad, suede / sway(ed)
swaddle,ed,ling, TO WRAP WITH STRIPS OF CLOTH
swade, suede / sway(ed)
swadul, swaddle
swae, sway
swaf, suave
swafly, suave(ly)
swag,*,gged,gging, HANG LOOSE (or see swage)
swage,ed,ging, BLACKSMITHS TOOL (or see swag)
swager, swagger
swagger,*,red,ring,rer,ringly, STRUT LIKE A BULLY/DRUNK
swagur, swagger
swair, swear
swak, swag
swaker, swagger
swallow,*,wed,wing, TO TAKE DOWN THE THROAT, A BIRD
swalo, swallow
swalow, swallow
swam, PAST TENSE FOR THE WORD "SWIM"
swamp,*,ped,ping,py,pier,piest,piness,per, MARSHY/WATERY LAND
swan,*, A LONG-NECKED BIRD
swang, PAST TENSE FOR THE WORD "SWING" (or see swank)
swank,ker,kily,kiness,ky, SOMEONE WHO MOVES WITH AN AIR OF DASHING SMARTNESS (or see swang)
swankee, swank(y)
swap,*,pped,pping, TRADE/BARTER (or see swab)

swaped, swap(pped) / swab(bbed)
swapt, swap(pped) / swab(bbed)
swar, swear
swarm,*,med,ming,mer, GROUP OF MANY BEES/ZOOSPHERES/PEOPLE
swarn, sworn
swasteka, swastika
swastika,*, A SYMBOLIC SHAPE
swat,*,tted,tting,tter, A STRIKING BLOW (or see sway(ed)/suede)
swatch,hes, PIECE/SAMPLE OF MATERIAL
swate, suede / sway(ed) / swat
swath,hes, TRAVEL IN LONG STRIPS GOING BACK AND FORTH IN SEQUENTIAL PARALLEL MOVEMENTS
swatul, swaddle
swave, suave
swavedy, suave(vity)
swavity, suave(vity)
swavly, suave(ly)
sway,*,yed,ying,yable,yer, SWING BACK AND FORTH, SAG
swayd, suede / sway(ed)
sweap, sweep
swear,*,ring,wore,worn,rer, TO USE PROFANITY, PLEDGE, PROMISE
sweat,*,ted,ting,ty,ter, MOISTURE COMING THROUGH PORES OF SKIN TO COOL BODY DOWN, BE ANXIOUS, HEAT TO MELTING (or see sweet)
sweater,*, A KNITTED ARTICLE OF CLOTHING
swebt, swept
swech, switch
sweder, sweater / sweet(er)
swedur, sweater / sweet(er)
swedy, sweat(y) / sweet(ie)
sweep,*,ped,ping,per,wept, REMOVE LOOSE DIRT FROM FLOOR/GROUND, A GESTURE/STROKE/MOTION "prefixes: up"
sweet,*,ter,test,tly,tness,ten,tie,tish, PALATABLE/PLEASANT TASTE,WITH SUGAR (or see sweat/suit/suite) "prefixes: semi"
sweft, swift
sweg, swig
swek, swig
swel, swell
sweld, swell(ed)
swelder, swelter

sweldur, swelter
swell,*,lled,lling,wollen, TEMPORARILY BECOME
swelt, swell(ed)
swelter,*,red,ring,ringly, AFFECTED BY OPPRESSIVE HEAT
sweltir, swelter
sweltur, swelter
swem, swim
swemur, swim(mmer)
swendul, swindle
sweng, swing
swengur, swing(er)
swep, sweep / swept
sweper, sweep(er)
swept, PAST TENSE FOR THE WORD "SWEEP"
swepur, sweep(er)
swerf, swerve
swerl, swirl
swerve,*,ed,ving, SUDDENLY SWAY/ VEER DIRECTION "prefixes: un"
swesh, swish
swet, sweet / sweat
swetch, switch
swete, sweet(ie) / sweat(y)
sweten, sweet(en)
sweter, sweater / sweet(er)
swetin, sweet(en) / sweat(ing)
swetir, sweater / sweet(er)
swetle, sweet(ly)
swetur, sweater / sweet(er)
swevel, swivel
swevul, swivel
swich, switch
swifd, swift
swifdly, swift(ly)
swifdnes, swift(ness)
swift,tly,tness, RAPID MOVEMENT
swig,*,gged,gging,gger, TAKE LARGE DRINKS OF ALCOHOLIC LIQUID
swik, swig
swill,ller, FOOD FOR SWINE, TO GUZZLE
swim,*,wam,mming,mmer, USE APPENDAGES OF BODY TO MOVE THROUGH WATER
swimd, swim(mmed)
swimt, swim(mmed)
swimur, swim(mmer)
swin, swine
swindal, swindle
swindle,*,ed,ling,er, ONE WHO CHEATS/SCHEME'S/MANIPULATES MONEY FRAUDULENTLY

swindul, swindle
swine,*,nish,nishly,nishness, DOMESTICATED PIG/BOAR
swing,*,ging,ger,wang,wung, GLIDE/MOVE/SWAY BACK AND FORTH, TYPE OF DANCE/RELATIONSHIP "prefixes: in/up"
swip, swipe
swipe,*,ed,ping, TAKE/STRIKE/HIT, MOVE ACROSS A SCANNER
swirf, swerve
swirl,*,led,ling,lly,lier,liest, MOVE IN CIRCULAR MOTION, TWIST/CURL
swirve, swerve
swish,her,hy,hingly, A SOUND, A WISPY/QUICK/SWEEPING MOVEMENT
switch,hes,hed,hing,her, CHANGE/FLIP/DIVERT FROM ONE WAY/SOURCE TO ANOTHER, STICK
swivel,*,led,ling,ler, MOVEMENT CONSTRAINED TO A SINGLE PIVOT POINT
swivle, swivel
swivul, swivel
swob, swap / swab
swobed, swap(pped) / swab(bbed)
swobt, swap(pped) / swab(bbed)
swoch, swatch
swodel, swaddle
swodul, swaddle
swof, suave
swofly, suave(ly)
swolen, swollen
swollen, PAST TENSE FOR THE WORD "SWELL"
swolo, swallow
swolun, swollen
swomp, swamp
swompe, swamp(y)
swomper, swamp(er)
swompy, swamp(y)
swon, swan / swoon
swond, swoon(ed)
swoon,*,ned,ning,ner,ningly, FAINT/DIZZY FROM LACK OF OXYGEN OR FROM FEELINGS OF ELATION
swoop,*,ped,ping, DESCEND TO CAPTURE THEN ASCEND, BIRD'S MOVEMENT
swoosh,hed,hing, FAST/RUSHING SOUND/MOVEMENT
swop, swap / swab
swopt, swap(pped) / swab(bbed)
swor, swore
sword,*, A POINTED/LONG/SHARP DOUBLE-EDGED WEAPON
swore, PAST TENSE FOR THE WORD "SWEAR"
sworm, swarm
swormer, swarm(er)
sworn, PAST TENSE FOR THE WORD "SWEAR"
swosteku, swastika
swostiku, swastika
swot, swat
swotch, swatch
swoth, swath
swov, suave
swovity, suave(vity)
swovly, suave(ly)
swoztiku, swastika
swune, swoon
swung, PAST TENSE FOR THE WORD "SWING"
swup, swoop
swurf, swerve
swurl, swirl
swurve, swerve
swush, swoosh
sy, sigh
syanide, cyanide
sybernetics, cybernetics
syborg, cyborg
sycadelic, psychedelic
sycamore,*, A TREE/FRUIT
sycek, psychic
sychadelic, psychedelic
syche, psyche / sick / sic
sychic, psychic
sycho, psycho
sychologekul, psychology(gical)
sychology, psychology
sychopath, psychopath
sychosis, psychosis
sychotic, psychotic
syclone, cyclone
sycological, psychology(gical)
syfalis, syphilis
syfen, siphon
syflus, syphilis
syfules, syphilis
syfun, siphon
sykadelic, psychedelic
sykamore, sycamore
syke, psyche / sick / sic
sykeatric, psychiatric
sykek, psychic
sykiatrist, psychiatry(rist)
sykik, psychic
sykilogekul, psychology(gical)
sykle, cycle
syklist, cyclist
syko, psycho
sykodik, psychotic
sykologee, psychology
sykologest, psychology(gist)
sykopath, psychopath
sykopathic, psychopath(ic)
sykopathalagist, psychopath(ologist)
sykosis, psychosis
sykotic, psychotic
syksteen, sixteen
syl, PREFIX INDICATING "TOGETHER/UNITED/ALIKE" MOST OFTEN MODIFIES THE WORD
sylable, syllable
sylabus, syllabus
syllable,*,ed,ling, WORD THAT CAN BE DIVIDED INTO PARTS BASED UPON PHONETIC SOUNDS "prefixes: deca/dis"
syllabus,ses, AN OUTLINE/SUMMARY OF LECTURES/TEACHINGS
sym, PREFIX INDICATING "TOGETHER/UNITED/ALIKE" MOST OFTEN MODIFIES THE WORD
symatry, symmetry
symbal, symbol
symbalism, symbol(ism)
symbathe, sympathy
symbathetic, sympathetic
symbeotic, symbiotic
symbethe, sympathy
symbethetic, sympathetic
symbiosis,otic, TWO LIVE BODIES COEXISTING WITH MUTUAL BENEFITS "prefixes: endo"
symbiotic,cally, TWO LIVE BODIES COEXISTING WITH MUTUAL BENEFITS "prefixes: endo"
symbol,*,lic,lical,lically,lism,list,lize,lizes, lized,lizing,lization,lizer,logy, LETTER/ SHAPE WHICH HAS MEANING (or see cymbal)
symbolek, symbol(ic)
symbulism, symbol(ism)
symbuthe, sympathy
symbuthetic, sympathetic
symdum, symptom
symetrik, symmetry(ric)
symetry, symmetry
symfeny, symphony

symfonic, symphony(nic)
symfuny, symphony
symmetry,ries,ric,rical,rically,ricalness, rize,rization, MATHEMATICAL EXPRESSION, WHERE LINES ARE CONSISTENT WITHIN GUIDELINES "prefixes: dis"
sympathetic,cally, ABILITY TO RELATE/ REVERBERATE IN FREQUENCY/ FEELINGS
sympathy,hies,hetic,hize,hizes,hized, hizing,hizer, ABILITY TO RELATE/ REVERBERATE IN FREQUENCY/ FEELINGS
sympethy, sympathy
symphonek, symphony(nic)
symphony,nies,nic,nically,nious, HARMONIC WAVES/FREQENCY, ORCHESTRA
symphuny, symphony
sympl, simple / symbol
symposeum, symposium
symposium,*, CONFERENCE/MEETING WHERE VIEWS ARE DISCUSSED
sympozeum, symposium
symptom,*,matic,matically, REACTION TO SOME UNSEEN AFFECTATION
symptum, symptom
symputhee, sympathy
symputhize, sympathy(hize)
symtem, symptom
symtum, symptom
symutree, symmetry
syn, PREFIX INDICATING "TOGETHER/ UNITED/ALIKE" MOST OFTEN MODIFIES THE WORD
synanem, synonym
synapse,*,ed,sing,ptic, WHERE TWO NERVE ENDINGS COMMUNICATE
synapsis, MEIOSIS PHASE WITH CHROMOSOMES (or see synapse)
synapsus, synapsis
synaptek, synaptic
synaptic, MEIOSIS PHASE WITH CHROMOSOMES (or see synapse)
sync, SHORT FOR SYNCHRONIZE (or see sink)
synchro, SHORT FOR SYNCHRONIZE
synchronus, synchrony(nous)
synchrony,nal,nic,nical,nically,nism, nistic,nistically,nize,nizes,nized, nizing, nous,nously,nousness, WHEN HARMONY BETWEEN THINGS/PEOPLE/ WAVES/ FREQUENCY HAPPENS SIMULTANEOUSLY "prefixes: de/ un"
syncronize, synchrony(nize)
syncrony, synchrony
syndecate, syndicate
syndicashen, syndicate(tion)
syndicate,*,ed,tion,tor, COMPANIES/ CORPORATIONS BOUND FOR A FINANCIAL VENTURE
syndikation, syndicate(tion)
syndiket, syndicate
syndrem, syndrome
syndrome,*,mic, COMBINATION OF CIRCUMSTANCES/SYMPTOMS HAPPENING AT THE SAME TIME
syndrum, syndrome
synducate, syndicate
syndukit, syndicate
synergy,gies,getic,gism,gist,gistic, gistically, PARTS WORKING TOGETHER COOPERATIVELY
synik, cynic
synikal, cynical
synirgy, synergy
synkrenus, synchrony(nous)
synkronee, synchrony
synkronize, synchrony(nize)
synkrunus, synchrony(nous)
synonemus, synonym(ous)
synonim, synonym
synonimus, synonym(ous)
synonym,*,mic,mical,mity,mize,mized, mizing,mizer,mous,mously, ABOUT THE SAME/SIMILAR CHARACTERISTICS
synopses, synopsis
synopsis, CONCENTRATED VERSION OF SOMETHING WRITTEN, SUMMARY
syntaks, syntax
syntax,xes, A GRAMMAR RULE
syntekit, syndicate
synthasis, synthesis
synthasize, synthesize
synthedik, synthetic
synthesis,sist, HUMAN MODIFICATION/ COMBINATION OF FREQUENCY/ ELEMENTS PRODUCING SOMETHING DIFFERENT "prefixes: bio"
synthesize,*,ed,zing,zation, HUMAN MODIFICATION/ COMBINATION OF FREQUENCY/ELEMENTS PRODUCING SOMETHING DIFFERENT
synthetek, synthetic
synthetic,*,cal,cally, HUMAN MADE CHEMICAL COMPOUNDS "prefixes: retro"
synthusis, synthesis
synumen, cinnamon
synunem, synonym
syphelis, syphilis
syphen, siphon
syphilis,itic, A VENEREAL DISEASE
syphin, siphon
syphon, siphon
syphules, syphilis
syrenge, syringe
syrinch, syringe
syringe,*, TUBE WITH A PISTON FOR PULLING/EXPELLING LIQUIDS
syrinje, syringe
syrip, syrup
syrup,*,py, A VISCOUS/THICK SUGAR BASED LIQUID
sysdamadik, system(atic)
sysdamatic, system(atic)
sysdem, system
sysdum, system
sysdumadik, system(atic)
sysdumatic, system(atic)
syst, cist / cyst
system,*,mless,matic,matical,matically, maticness,matism,matist,matize, matization,matizer,mic,mically,mize, mization,mizer, OF/PERTAINING TO A PLAN/METHODOLOGY WITH PARTICULAR ORDER/ ARRANGEMENT, A CLASSIFICATION "prefixes: bio/sub"
systumatic, system(atic)
syterical, satire(rical)
syth, scythe
t, tea / tee
t-shirt,*, SHORT SLEEVE/COLLARLESS SHIRT
tab,*,bbed,bbing,bby, BILL FOR SERVICE PERFORMED, A SPACER (or see tap/ tape)
tabaco, tobacco
tabako, tobacco
tabal, table
tabby,bbies,bbied,ying, STYLE OF FUR ON A CAT
tabd, tab(bbed) / tap(pped)
tabe, tabby

tabel, table
tabernacle,*,ed,ling,cular, A NICHE/ DWELLING FOR SYMBOLIC STATUE, PART OF A BOAT
taberqulosis, tuberculosis
tabeulate, tabulate
tabew, taboo
tabewlashen, tabulate(tion)
tabewlate, tabulate
tabewlation, tabulate(tion)
tabewler, tabular
tabil, table
tabirnakle, tabernacle
tablau, tableau
table,*,ed,ling, GET RID OF, USUABLE SURFACE TO SET ITEMS, PLATFORM OF INFORMATION "prefixes: re"
tableau,*, PRESENTATION/ ARRANGEMENT WITH PICTURES
tablet,*, BOUND COMPILATION OF PAPERS, PILL SHAPE, FLAT WRITING SURFACE
tablit, tablet
tablo, tableau
tabloed, tabloid
tabloid,*, GOSSIP NEWSPAPER WITH PICTURES
tabloyd, tabloid
tablut, tablet
tabogin, toboggan
taboo,*,ooed,ooing, PROHIBITED/ BANNED/DISCRIMINATED AGAINST
tabt, tape(d) / tab(bbed) / tap(pped)
tabu, taboo
tabul, table
tabular,rly, RESEMBLING/CAN BE USED AS A TABLE
tabulashen, tabulate(tion)
tabulate,*,ed,ting,tion,tor, ENTER/LIST/ FORMULATE ONTO/INTO A TABLE
tabuld, table(d)
tabuler, tabular
tabulir, tabular
taburnakle, tabernacle
taby, tabby
tacd, tact / tack(ed)
tacdil, tactile
tacdul, tactile
tacet, MUSICAL TERM/ACTION (or see tacit)
tachometer,rically,ry, A DEVICE TO MEASURE LIQUID VELOCITY/ MOVEMENT
tachomitur, tachometer

tachy, PREFIX INDICATING "RAPID" MOST OFTEN MODIFIES THE WORD
tacit,tly,tness, IMPLIED WITHOUT SPEAKING IN WORDS (or see tacet)
tack,*,ked,king,ky,ker, ATTACH/AFFIX TO, SAILING TERM, POINTED OBJECT WITH A BROAD HEAD FOR AFFIXING THINGS (or see take/tact)
tackle,*,ed,ling,er, PURSUE/ OVERCOME/ACCOMPLISH
tacksonamy, taxonomy
tacky,kiness, STICKY, DISORDERLY/ SHABBY (or see tachy)
taco,*, SHAPED CORN TORTILLA FILLED WITH FOODS
tacs, take(s) / tax / tack(s)
tacshoal, tactual
tacshuel, tactual
tact,*,tful,tfully,tfulness,tless,tlessly, tlessness, DIPLOMATIC/ APPROPRIATE IN PRESENTATION (or see tack/take)
tactakul, tactic(al)
tactek, tactic
tactekil, tactic(al)
tactic,*,cal,cally,cian, STRATEGY/PLAN TO PERFORM A MANEUVER/ EXPERIMENT/ACTION
tactick, tactic
tactikel, tactic(al)
tactile,lity, PERTAINING TO THE SENSE OF TOUCH
taction, ACT OF TOUCHING
tactual,lly, PERTAINING/GIVEN TO SENSE OF TOUCH
tactukil, tactic(al)
tada, today
tader, tater / tatter / potato
tador, tater / tatter / potato
tadpole,*, YOUNG FROG LARVAE
tadpowl, tadpole
tadur, tater / tatter / potato
tael, tail / tale / towel
taelur, tailor
taent, taint
tafe, taffy
tafedu, taffeta
tafee, taffy
tafeta, taffeta
taffeta, TYPE OF WOVEN FABRIC
taffy, A CANDY
tafy, taffy

tag,*,gged,gging, TO LABEL/IDENTIFY SOMETHING, A GAME OF CHASE (or see tack/take)
tagethur, together
tagle, toggle
tail,*,led,ling,lless, APPENDAGE ON THE REAR OF SOMETHING, TO FOLLOW SOMEONE CLOSELY (or see tale/ tell/tall/towel)
tailor,*,red,ring, CUSTOM MAKES CLOTHING
taim, thyme / time / tame
taingo, tango
taint,*,ted,ting,tless, DISTRACTING IMPREFECTION, CORRUPT/ POLLUTED
tak, tack / take / tact
takal, tackle
takamidur, tachometer
takchen, taction
takchun, taction
takd, tact / talk(ed) / tack(ed)
takdel, tactile
take,*,took,king,en, ACQUIRE FOR ONE'S SELF, REMOVE FROM SOMETHING/ SOMEONE (too many definitions, please consult standard dictionary) (or see tack/tag) "prefixes: over/re/under/up"
taked, tact / tack(ed) / took
takee, tacky / take
takel, toggle
takela, tequila
taken, PAST TENSE FOR THE WORD "TAKE"
takil, tackle / toggle
takila, tequila
takin, taken / tack(ing)
takle, tackle / toggle
tako, taco
takol, tackle
takomeder, tachometer
takomitur, tachometer
taks, take(s) / tack(s)
taksachen, tax(ation)
taksation, tax(ation)
taksebul, tax(able)
taksed, taxi(ed)
taksedermy, taxidermy
taksee, taxi
takseng, taxi(iing) / tax(ing)
takshen, taction
takshuil, tactual
takshun, taction

taksibul, tax(able)
taksidermy, taxidermy
taksieng, taxi(iing)
taksobel, tax(able)
taksonimy, taxonomy
taksuble, tax(able)
taksudirmy, taxidermy
taksy, taxi
takt, tact / tack(ed)
taktakil, tactic(al)
taktek, tactic
taktekul, tactic(al)
taktik, tactic
taktikul, tactic(al)
taktil, tactile
taktion, taction
taktuk, tactic
taktukel, tactic(al)
taktul, tactile
takul, tackle / toggle
takun, taken / tack(ing)
taky, tacky / tachy
tal, tall / towel / tale / tail
talasman, talesman / talisman
talaspore, teliospore
talc, A CHEMICAL COMPOUND (or see talk)
tale,*, A STORY (or see tail/tall/towel)
talee, tally
talen, talon
talent,*,ted, HAVE NATURAL ABILITY FOR SOMETHING
taleology, teleology
talepathee, telepathy
taleputhee, telepathy
taler, tailor / tall(er)
talerible, tolerable
tales, tail(less)
talesman, SOMEONE PICKED FROM A COURTROOM TO SERVE ON A JURY (or see talisman)
talin, talon
talint, talent
talir, tailor / tall(er)
talirate, tolerate
talirense, tolerance
talisman, A CHARM/FIGURINE FOR GOOD LUCK (or see talesman)
talk,*,ked,king,ker,kative,kativeness,kie, ky, USE THE MOUTH/VOICE TO EXPRESS THOUGHT/FEELING "prefixes: up"
talkatif, talk(ative)

tall,ller,llest,llish,llness, MORE THAN AVERAGE HEIGHT (or see tale/tail/towel)
tallow,wy, ANIMAL FAT
tally,llies,llied,llying, REGISTER/RECORD/LABEL, KEEP SCORE/COUNT
talness, tall(ness)
talo, tallow
talon,*,ned, CLAWS OF A BIRD OF PREY
talor, tailor
talosman, talesman / talisman
talow, tallow
talr, tailor
talun, talon
talunt, talent
talur, tailor / tall(er)
talurashen, tolerate(tion)
talurate, tolerate
talurense, tolerance
talurent, tolerant
talurible, tolerable
talurint, tolerant
talusman, talesman / talisman
taly, tally
tambaren, tambourine
tambourine,*, A MUSICAL INSTRUMENT
tamburen, tambourine
tame,*,ed,ming,er,est,mable,mability, mableness,ely,eness,eless, TO DOMESTICATE/CONTROL, CALM DOWN, MODIFY, ALTER
tamoro, tomorrow
tamp,*,ped,ping,per,pered,pering,perer, HAMMER/ STRIKE LIGHT BLOWS, DISRUPT/CORRUPT
tampan, tampon
tampon,*, FEMININE HYGIENE PRODUCT
tampurd, tamp(ered)
tamulchuous, tumult(uous)
tamult, tumult
tan,*,nned,nning,nnish,nner, TO CHANGE/MODIFY SKIN, PREFIX INDICATING "EXTEND/EXPAND/SPREAD/CONTINUE/SPIN OUT/WEAVE/PUT FORTH/SHOW/MANIFEST" MOST OFTEN MODIFIES THE WORD
tanage, tannage
tand, tan(nned)
tandem, ONE BEFORE THE OTHER
tandim, tandem

tandrem, tantrum
tandrum, tantrum
tandum, tandem
tanej, tannage
tanel, tunnel
taner, tan(nner)
tang,ged,gy,gier,giest, A SHARP SOUND/TASTE, CHISEL STYLE TOOL
tangabul, tangible
tangarene, tangerine
tangebul, tangible
tangee, tang(y)
tangel, tangle
tangent,*,ncy,tial,tially,tally, STRAIGHT LINE RADIATING/DIVERGING AWAY FROM A COMMON POINT "prefixes: sub"
tanger, tanker
tangerine,*, A CITRUS FRUIT
tangeur, tang(ier)
tangible,*,bility,eness,ly, ABLE TO BE FELT/ACQUIRED/ACCOMPLISHED PHYSICALLY "prefixes: in"
tangibul, tangible
tangil, tangle
tangint, tangent
tangirene, tangerine
tangle,*,ed,ling,er,ly,ement, TWISTED UP, PERPLEXING, CONFUSING "prefixes: en/un"
tanglee, tangle(ly)
tanglmint, tangle(ment)
tango,*,oed,oing, A DANCE
tangol, tangle
tangubul, tangible
tangul, tangle
tangur, tanker
tangurene, tangerine
tanige, tannage
tanil, tunnel
tanir, tan(nner)
tanjable, tangible
tanjarene, tangerine
tanjebul, tangible
tanjent, tangent
tanjerine, tangerine
tanjibul, tangible
tanjint, tangent
tanjubul, tangible
tanjurene, tangerine
tank,*,ker, CONTAINER FOR LIQUIDS, A CONTAINER

tanker, CONTAINER WHICH TRANSPORTS LIQUIDS OVER A DISTANCE
tanko, tango
tankur, tanker
tannage, ACT/RESULT OF TANNING HIDES
tanol, tunnel
tanpon, tampon
tansy,sies, A BITTER HERB
tant, taunt / taint / tan(nned)
tantalize,*,ed,zing,er,zingly, ENCOURAGE/TEASE/TORMENT WITHOUT HOPES OF RECEIVING AN END RESULT
tantamount, EQUIVALENT/SIMILAR TO
tantelize, tantalize
tantem, tandem
tantilize, tantalize
tantim, tandem
tantimount, tantamount
tantra,rism,rist, RITUAL INVOLVING MOVEMENT OF FIRST LEVEL ENERGY
tantrem, tantrum
tantrest, tantra(rist)
tantrim, tantrum
tantru, tantra
tantrum,*, ANGRY/EMOTIONAL OUTBURST
tantulise, tantalize
tantum, tandem
tantumownt, tantamount
tanuj, tannage
tanul, tunnel
tanur, tan(nner)
tap,*,pped,pping,pper, LIGHT BLOWS, A FAUCET/VALVE USED TO ACCESS LIQUIDS FROM A CONTAINER (or see tape) "prefixes: un"
tapastre, tapestry
tape,*,ed,ping,er, STICKY PLASTIC USED TO SECURE/WRAP/MEND, LONG FLAT FLEXIBLE DEVICE/MATERIAL (or see tap)
tapek, topic
tapekul, topical
tapeoka, tapioca
taper,*,red,ring, DESCRIPTION FOR SOMETHING LONG THAT DECREASES IN WIDTH AS IT REACHES THE END/TIP/POINT

tapestry,ries, LARGE WOVEN FABRIC/ THREADS ILLUSTRATING A DESIGN/ PICTURE
tapik, topic
tapioca, PUDDING DERIVED FROM STARCHY PLANT
tapir, tater / tatter / potato
tapistre, tapestry
taploed, tabloid
taploid, tabloid
taployd, tabloid
taps, A MUSICAL SIGNAL USED FOR LIGHTS OUT IN MILITARY (or see tap(s)/tape(s))
tapt, tape(d) / tap(pped)
tapuk, topic
tapur, taper / tap(pper)
tapustree, tapestry
taquela, tequila
taquila, tequila
tar,*,rred,rring, A WOOD/COAL COMBINATION BY-PRODUCT (or see tare/tear)
tara, terra
tarafy, terrify
taragen, tarragon
taragon, tarragon
tarain, terrain / terrane
taranchula, tarantula
tarane, terrain / terrane
taranshula, tarantula
tarantula,*, A LARGE SPIDER
tararium, terrarium
taraso, terrazzo
tarazo, terrazzo
tard, tar(rred) / tart / tare(d) / tear(ed)
tardee, tardy
tardenes, tardy(diness)
tardur, tartar
tardy,dier,diest,dily,diness, LATE
tare,*,ed,ring, METHOD OF WEIGHING GOODS (or see tar/tear/tarry)
tarebly, terrible(ly)
tarebul, terrible
tared, tare(d) / tar(rred) / tear(ed) / tarry(ried)
taref, tariff
tarefic, terrific
tarefy, terrify
tarereim, terrarium
taresdreul, terrestrial
tarestreal, terrestrial
tarestrial, terrestrial
tareur, terrier

target,*,ted,ting, A POINT/AREA TO AIM AT/FOR
targit, target
targut, target
taribul, terrible
tarier, terrier
tarif, tariff
tarifek, terrific
tariff,*, A TAX
tarific, terrific
tarify, terrify
tarit, terret
tariur, terrier
tarlatan,*, LOOSELY WOVEN MATERIAL
tarletin, tarlatan
tarluten, tarlatan
tarmac,*, MATERIAL USED FOR ROADS/ LANDING PADS/PARKING
tarmak, tarmac
tarnesh, tarnish
tarnish,hes,hed,hing,hable, OXYDATION WHICH DISCOLORS, CAUSE TO LOOSE LUSTER/SHINE/STATE OF BEING
tarnush, tarnish
tarp,*,ped,ping, A LARGE/WOVEN MATERIAL FOR COVERING/ OVERHEAD PROTECTION
tarpalene, tarpaulin
tarpaulin,*, A WEATHERPROOF MATERIAL USED FOR A COVERING
tarpeline, tarpaulin
tarpin, tarpon
tarpon,*, LARGE OCEAN FISH
tarpulene, tarpaulin
tarpun, tarpon
tarragon, AN HERB/PLANT
tarrazzo, terrazzo
tarrestrial, terrestrial
tarrif, tariff
tarry,rries,rried,ying,rrier, LOITERING/ LINGERING, NOT MOVING ALONG, COVERED IN TAR
tars, PREFIX INDICATING "EYELID/ ANKLE/ BONES" MOST OFTEN MODIFIES THE WORD
tart,*,tish,tishly,tly,tness, SOUR TASTE, PASTRY (or see tar(rred)/tear(ed)/ tare(d)/tort/torte)
tartar, CALCIUM PHOSPHATE DEPOSIT, DEPOSIT FROM WINEMAKING, A SAUCE
tartir, tartar
tartoof, tartuffe

tartuffe,ery, COMIC DEPICTING A HYPOCRITE, ALSO SPELLED TARTUFE
tartur, tartar
taru, terra
taruf, tariff
tarufy, terrify
tarutoree, territory
tary, tarry
taryd, tarry(ried)
tasc, task
tasd, taste
tasde, taste(ty)
tasel, tassel
taset, tacet / tacit
tasil, tassel
tasit, tacet / tacit
task,*,ked,king, CHORE/WORK TO BE DONE, CHALLENGE INVOLVING HARDSHIP
tasles, taste(less)
tasol, tassel
tassel,*, HANGING THREADED ORNAMENT
taste,*,ed,ting,er,eful,efully,efulness, eless,elessly,elessness,ty,tier,tiest, tily,tiness, SENSE/FEELING WITHIN THE MOUTH "prefixes: dis"
tastee, taste(ty)
tasteir, taste(tier)
tastenes, taste(tiness)
tasteur, taste(tier)
tastful, taste(ful)
tastfule, taste(fully)
tastfuly, taste(fully)
tastur, taste(r)
tasul, tassel
tat, taught / taut
tatel, tattle
tater,*, SHORT FOR POTATOE (or see tatter)
tatewist, tattoo(ist)
tatil, tattle
tatir, tater / tatter
tatle, tattle
tatlur, tattle(r)
tatoist, tattoo(ist)
tatol, tattle
tatoo, tattoo
tator, tater / tatter
tatter,*,red,ring, WORN/SHREDDED MATERIAL (or see tater)

tattle,*,ed,ling,er, TO RAT/FINK/TELL/ EXPOSE SOMEONE'S WORDS/ BEHAVIOR/ ACT
tattoo,*,ooed,ooing,ooer,ooist, TO APPLY PERMANENT INK INTO THE SKIN WITH A NEEDLE
tatuist, tattoo(ist)
tatul, tattle
tatur, tater / tatter
taturd, tatter(ed)
tauer, tower
taught, PAST TENSE FOR THE WORD "TEACH" (or see taut/tout) "prefixes: un"
taugt, taught / taut / tout
tauko, taco
tauksik, toxic
tauksufy, toxify(fication)
taul, towel / tall
tauler, tall(er)
taulir, tall(er)
taulk, talk / talc
taulky, talk(y)
taulur, tall(er)
taulurinse, tolerance
taun, town
taunt,*,ted,ting, TEASE/PROVOKE/ MANIPULATE SOMEONE TO REACT (or see tout)
taupe, A COLOR (or see toupee)
taupikul, topical
taut,ten,tly,tness, HOLD/STRETCH TIGHT (or see taught/taunt/tout)
tavern,*,ner, PLACE WHICH SELLS SPIRITS/ALCOHOLIC BEVERAGES
tavurn, tavern
tawer, tower
tawir, tower
tawn, town
tawnt, taunt
tawp, taupe / top
tawt, taught / taut / tout
tax,xes,xed,xing,xable,xability,xation, CHARGE ADDED ONTO GOODS/ RESOURCES/SERVICE COLLECTED BY THE CITY/STATE/FEDERAL GOVERNMENTS, A CHALLENGE (or see taxi) "prefixes: over/sur"
taxadermy, taxidermy
taxashen, tax(ation)
taxe, taxi
taxed, taxi(ed) / tax(ed)
taxedirmy, taxidermy

taxi,*,ied,iing, VEHICLE HIRED FOR TRANSPORTATION, NAVIGATE A PLANE/ BOAT AT SLOW SPEED, MEDICAL TERM (or see tax)
taxidermy,mies,mist, ONE WHO EMBALMS/STUFFS ANIMALS
taxieng, taxi(iing)
taxonimy, taxonomy
taxonomy,mic,mical,mically,mist, METHOD TO CLASSIFY/CATEGORIZE ANIMALS/PLANTS
taxs, tax(es)
taxsachen, tax(ation)
taxsashen, tax(ation)
taxse, taxi
taxsedermy, taxidermy
taxsible, tax(able)
taxsuble, tax(able)
taxsudermy, taxidermy
taxudermy, taxidermy
taxus, tax(es)
tayler, tailor
taylur, tailor
taynt, taint
te, tea / tee
tea,*, DRIED PLANTS STEEPED IN WATER (or see tee)
teach,hes,taught,hing,her,hable,hability, hableness,hably, TRAIN/COACH/ INSTRUCT, INFORMATION/ KNOWLEDGE BEING PASSED ON TO OTHERS "prefixes: un"
teachs, teach(es)
teachuble, teach(able)
teachur, teach(er)
teak, A TREE
teal, A COLOR (or see teil)
team,*,med,ming, GROUP ATTEMPT TO WORK/PLAY/PERFORM TOGETHER (or see teem)
teanager, teenager
tear,*,red,ring,ry,rful,rfully,rfulness, rless, TO RIP, LIQUID COMING FROM THE EYES RELATED TO AN EMOTIONAL THOUGHT/EVENT (or see tier)
tearu, tiara
tease,*,ed,sing,er,sable,singly, TAUNT/ PROVOKE/ANNOY AS A DISTRACTION
teat,*, TIT/NIPPLE/UDDER
tebaco, tobacco
tebagen, toboggan
tebako, tobacco

tebea, tibia
tebogin, toboggan
tebse, tip(sy)
tech,*, SHORT FOR TECHNICAL (or see teach)
techable, teach(able)
techer, teach(er)
teches, teach(es)
techi,*, SHORT FOR TECHNICIAN
techible, teach(able)
techir, teach(er)
techis, teach(es)
technalogical, technology(gical)
technawlugee, technology
technecal, technical
technek, technique
techneque, technique
technical,lly,lness,lity,lities, DETAILED/ SPECIFIC, SPECIFIC TO THE LANGUAGE/ SCHOOL/TRADE "prefixes: bio"
technikality, technical(ity)
technilogikul, technology(gical)
technique,*, METHOD OF PERFORMING SOMETHING FOR SPECIFIC END RESULTS
technology,gies,gist,gic,gical,gically, INDUSTRIAL SCIENCE/ART "prefixes: bio"
technolugee, technology
technukality, technical(ity)
techuble, teach(able)
techur, teach(er)
techus, teach(es)
tecnec, technique
tecnic, technique
tecst, text
tectonic,*,cally, SCIENCE/ART OF CONSTRUCTING/STUDYING FORMS/ SHAPES
teda, today
tedbet, tidbit
tedbit, tidbit
teder, teeter
tedeus, tedious
tedeusly, tedious(ly)
tedious,sly,sness, DETAILED/SLOW/ MONOTONOUS
tedir, teeter
tedius, tedious
tedur, teeter
tee,*,ed,eing, A TERM IN THE GAME OF GOLF, TO BE IRRITATED, SHAPE/ LETTER, ALL COMES TOGETHER SUITABLY/PERFECTLY (or see tea)
teecher, teach(er)
teechuble, teach(able)
teechur, teach(er)
teek, teak
teel, teal / teil
teem,*,med,ming, OVERFLOWING/ ABUNDANT/COMING FORTH (or see team)
teen,*,ny,nier,niest,nager, SHORT FOR TEENAGER, SOMETHING VERY SMALL
teenager,*, PRE-ADULT AGE (13-19 YEARS)
teeneur, teen(ier)
teenksher, tincture
teenkur, tinker
teenyer, teen(ier)
teepee,*, A CONICAL SHAPED DWELLING COMMON TO NATIVE AMERICANS
teers, tear(s) / tier(s)
teery, tear(y)
tees, tease / tea(s) / tee(s)
teet, teat / tit
teeter,*,red,ring, SHIFT WEIGHT BACK AND FORTH AS IN A ROCKING MOTION, HORIZONTAL BALANCING MOVEMENT/MANEUVER
teeter-totter,*, SEESAW/TOY, LONG BOARD ON A FULCRUM WHICH MOVES UP/DOWN WITH SHIFTING OF WEIGHT
teeth,hing,her,tooth, MORE THAN ONE TOOTH, ACT OF GROWING FIRST SET OF TEETH
teetur, teeter
tef, tiff
teil, A LIME TREE (or see teal)
teir, tier / tear
teird, tier(ed) / tear(ed)
tek, teak / tech
tekal, tickle
tekdile, textile
teke, tiki
tekel, tickle
tekela, tequila
teket, ticket
teki, techi / tiki
tekil, tickle
tekit, ticket
tekle, tickle
teklech, tickle(lish)
teklish, tickle(lish)
teknakaledy, technical(ity)
teknalogical, technology(gical)
teknalugee, technology
teknek, technique
teknekality, technical(ity)
teknekul, technical
tekneque, technique
teknikul, technical
teknilogikul, technology(gical)
teknolugee, technology
teknukalety, technical(ity)
teknukil, technical
teknulogical, technology(gical)
tekol, tickle
tekot, ticket
teksd, text
teksdeur, texture
teksdile, textile
tekst, text
tekster, texture
tekstile, textile
teksture, texture
tekt, text / tick(ed)
tektonek, tectonic
tektonic, tectonic
tekul, tickle
tekut, ticket
teky, tiki
tel, PREFIX INDICATING "END/FAR" MOST OFTEN MODIFIES THE WORD (or see teil/teal)
telacast, telecast
telafase, telophase
telafone, telephone
telafoto, telephoto
telagraf, telegraph
telagram, telegram
telagraph, telegraph
telakanesis, telekinesis
telakast, telecast
telakinetic, telekinetic
telakunesis, telekinesis
telaphase, telophase
telaphone, telephone
telaphoto, telephoto
telapromptur, teleprompter
telar, teller
telaskope, telescope
telaskopic, telescope(pic)
telathon, telethon
telatipe, teletype
telavichen, television
telavision, television

telavize, televise
teld, tell / told / till(ed)
tele, PREFIX INDICATING "DISTANCE" MOST OFTEN MODIFIES THE WORD
telealogy, teleology
teleaspore, teliospore
telecast,*,ted,ting,ter, BROADCAST BY TELEVISION
telefone, telephone
telefoto, telephoto
telegraf, telegraph
telegram,*, SEND MESSAGE/MONEY BY WIRE
telegraph,her,hist,hic,hically, MESSAGE/TRANSMISSION SENT BY USING AN INSTRUMENT, WIRE TRANSFER
telekinesis, OBJECTS MOVING WHICH HAVE NO VISIBLE EXPLANATION AS TO CAUSE
telekinetic,*, OBJECTS MOVING WHICH HAVE NO VISIBLE EXPLANATION AS TO CAUSE
telekunesis, telekinesis
telekunetic, telekinetic
teleology,gism,gist, SCIENCE WHICH STUDIES ETHICS/CAUSES/ACTS IN NATURE
telepathee, telepathy
telepathy,hic,hically,hist, COMMUNICATE BY WAVELENGTH, MIND COMMUNICATION
telephone,*,nic,nically, INSTRUMENT FOR VERBAL COMMUNICATION
telephoto,ography,ographic, TAKING PHOTOS AT LONG DISTANCE
teleprompter,*, A DEVICE WHICH ENLARGES TEXT FOR THOSE ON CAMERA TO READ FROM
teleputhee, telepathy
teler, teller
telescope,*,ed,ping,pic,pically, INSTRUMENT THAT SEEMINGLY REDUCES DISTANCE BY USE OF LENSES (or see microscope)
telethon,*, A TELEVISION BROADCAST WHICH LASTS A LONG TIME
teletipe, teletype
teletype, DEVICE USED TO TRANSMIT MESSAGES
teleupromtur, teleprompter
teleuspore, teliospore
televigen, television
televijan, television

televise,*,ed,sing,sion, USING TELEVISION TO TRANSMIT/BROADCAST
television,*,nary, VISUAL IMAGES SENT BY WAVES THROUGH DEVICE WHICH INTERPRETS THEM
teli, telly
telialegy, teleology
teliaulugy, teleology
telicast, telecast
telifone, telephone
telifoto, telephoto
teligraf, telegraph
teligram, telegram
teligraph, telegraph
telikanesis, telekinesis
telikast, telecast
telikunesis, telekinesis
teliology, teleology
teliospore,*,ric, METHOD OF FUNGI GERMINATION
teliphone, telephone
teliphoto, telephoto
telipromptur, teleprompter
telipromtur, teleprompter
telir, teller
teliskope, telescope
teliskopic, telescope(pic)
telithon, telethon
telitipe, teletype
teliuspore, teliospore
telivishen, television
telivision, television
telivize, televise
tell,*,ling,told, TO COMMUNICATE INFORMATION ALONG (or see teal/teil) "prefixes: re"
teller,*, ONE WHO DEALS DIRECTLY WITH CUSTOMERS AT A BANK, NARRATOR, ONE WHO FACILITATES COMMUNICATION BETWEEN OTHERS
telltale,er, TATTLER, ONE WHO PASSES ALONG GOSSIP/HERESAY, A TOOL FOR NAVIGATION
telly, SHORT FOR TELEVISION
telo, PREFIX INDICATING "END/FAR" MOST OFTEN MODIFIES THE WORD
telofase, telophase
telokanesis, telekinesis
telokunesis, telekinesis
telophase,sic, BIOLOGICAL TERM
telor, teller
teloskope, telescope

teloskopic, telescope(pic)
telothon, telethon
telovishen, television
telt, till(ed) / told / tilt
teltail, telltale
teltale, telltale
telufase, telophase
telufone, telephone
telufoto, telephoto
telugraf, telegraph
telugram, telegram
telugraph, telegraph
telukanesis, telekinesis
telukast, telecast
telukenetick, telekinetic
telukinetik, telekinetic
telukunesis, telekinesis
teluphase, telophase
teluphone, telephone
teluphoto, telephoto
telupromtur, teleprompter
telur, teller
teluskope, telescope
teluskopic, telescope(pic)
teluthon, telethon
telutipe, teletype
teluvegun, television
teluvision, television
teluvize, televise
tem, team / teem
temaro, tomorrow
tembir, timber
tembrachure, temperature
tembrament, temperament
tembramentul, temper(mental)
tembrushure, temperature
tembur, timber
temd, team(ed) / teem(ed)
temed, timid
temidly, timid(ly)
temod, timid
temoro, tomorrow
tempal, temple
temparamint, temperament
tempararely, temporary(rily)
temparary, temporary
temparize, temporize
temper,*,red,ring,rament,ramental, ramentally,rance,rate,rability,rable, rer,rature, EMOTIONS WORKED INTO AN ANGRY STATE, HEATING UP CARBON MATERIAL TO FORCE MOLECULAR REALIGNMENT
tempera, tempura

temperament,*,tal,tally, OVERALL EMOTION/PHYSICAL/MENTAL TRAITS OF A PERSON/LIVING THING "prefixes: non/un"
temperarily, temporary(rily)
temperary, temporary
temperate,ely,eness, HEATING UP CARBON MATERIAL TO FORCE MOLECULAR REALIGNMENT, STABLE "prefixes: in/sub"
temperature,*, MEASUREMENT OF HOT/COLD VARIANCES
temperize, temporize
tempermint, temper(ment)
tempeshues, tempest(uous)
tempest,tuous,tuously,tuousness, BEING STORMY/WINDY/TURBULENT
tempil, temple
tempir, temper
tempirament, temperament
tempirashure, temperature
tempirment, temper(ment)
templat, template
template,*, SOMETHING TO SUPPORT/ALLOW THE FORM OF SOMETHING, FOR MAKING REPLICAS
temple,*,ed, RELIGIOUS STRUCTURE FOR WORSHIP, SPOT ON THE HEAD OF THE BODY
templut, template
tempo,*, THE RHYTHM OF A WAVE, RATE/SPEED/PACE OF MOVEMENT
tempol, temple
tempor, PREFIX INDICATING "TIME/TEMPLES" MOST OFTEN MODIFIES THE WORD
temporal,lly,lness,lity,lities, OF OR GIVEN TO THIS TIME/SPACE/DISTANCE
temporarely, temporary(rily)
temporary,rarily,riness, SHORT DURATION IN TIME
temporely, temporal(lly)
temporize,*,ed,zing,zer,zation,zingly, GAIN/DELAY/YIELD/MANIPULATE TIME
temporment, temper(ment)
temporo, PREFIX INDICATING "TIME/TEMPLES" MOST OFTEN MODIFIES THE WORD
temporul, temporal
tempra, tempura
temprachure, temperature

tempral, temporal
tempramentul, temper(mental)
temprary, temporary
temprashure, temperature
temprature, temperature
tempremintul, temper(mental)
tempreruly, temporary(rily)
temprery, temporary
temprment, temperament
tempru, tempura
temprumintul, temper(mental)
tempt,*,ted,ting,tingly,table,ter, tingness,tress,tation, TO ENTICE/ALLURE/SEDUCE/INVITE
temptashen, temptation
temptation,*, APPREHENSION IN RESPONDING TO INVITATION/ENTICEMENT/SEDUCTION
tempul, temple
tempur, temper
tempura, BATTER DIPPED VEGETABLES/FISH
tempurarily, temporary(rily)
tempurary, temporary
tempurely, temporal(lly)
tempureruly, temporary(rily)
tempurery, temporary
tempurize, temporize
tempurment, temper(ment)
tempust, tempest
temt, tempt / team(ed) / teem(ed)
temtashen, temptation
temtation, temptation
temted, tempt(ed)
temtres, tempt(ress)
temulchuis, tumult(uous)
temulchuous, tumult(uous)
temult, tumult
temut, timid
ten,*,nth, ENGLISH NUMBER AFTER NINE/BEFORE ELEVEN (or see tin/teen)
tenabel, tenable
tenable,bility,eness,ly, CAN SURVIVE ATTEMPT AT BEING TAKEN/CARRIED AWAY "prefixes: un"
tenachus, tenacious
tenacious,sly,sness,ity, PERSISTENT/CONSISTENT, WITHOUT FAULTER
tenacity, OF BEING TENACIOUS
tenacle, tentacle
tenager, teenager
tenakle, tentacle
tenament, tenement

tenansy, tenant(ncy)
tenant,*,tncy,tcies,try, BORROWER OF LAND/STRUCTURE/PROPERTY HELD/OWNED BY ANOTHER "prefixes: sub"
tenasedy, tenacity
tenashus, tenacious
tenasity, tenacity
tenasuty, tenacity
tenat, tenet / tenant
tenatef, tentative
tenatious, tenacious
tenative, tentative
tencity, tense(sity)
tend,*,ded,ding,der,dency, HAVE LEANING AFFINITY/TENDENCY TOWARDS, TAKE CARE OF (or see tin(nned)/tent/tint)
tendatev, tentative
tendency,cies,ntious,ntiously, ntiousness, HAVE A LEANING/INCLINATION TOWARDS, DISPOSITION/CAPABILITY OF
tendenus, tendon(dinous)
tender,*,rly,rness,rer,rize,rizes,rized, rizing,rization,rizer, SOFTENED FIBERS, SOFT/GENTLE IN NATURE/TEMPERAMENT, OFFER TOWARDS DEBT (or see tinder)
tenderloin,*, CUT OF BEEF
tendid, tend(ed) / tint(ed)
tendin, tendon
tendinsy, tendency
tendir, tender / tinder
tendirloin, tenderloin
tendon,*,dinous,nitis, PART OF A MUSCLE
tendorize, tender(ize)
tendril,*, CURLING OF A PLANT/HAIR
tendrul, tendril
tendun, tendon
tendunitus, tendon(itis)
tendunus, tendon(dinous)
tendur, tender / tinder
tendurize, tender(ize)
tendurloin, tenderloin
tendurly, tender(ly)
tendutif, tentative
tene, teen(y) / tin(nny)
tenekle, tentacle
tenement,*,tary, DWELLING WHERE PEOPLE LIVE AS TENANTS, PERMANENT PROPERTY
tenen, tenon

tenensy, tenant(ncy)
tener, tenor
tenet,*, DOCTRINE/BELIEF/DOGMA HELD TO BE TRUE (or see tenant)
tenetif, tentative
tenetive, tentative
teneur, tenure / teen(ier)
teneust, teen(iest)
tenewus, tenuous
tenfold, TEN TIMES OVER/GREATER
teng, ting / tinge
tenible, tenable
teniest, teen(iest)
tenikle, tentacle
teniment, tenement
tenin, tenon
tenir, tenor
tenis, tennis
tenit, tenet / tenant
tenite, tonight
tenj, tinge
tenkchur, tincture
tenker, tinker
tenkil, tinkle
tenkir, tinker
tenkol, tinkle
tenkshir, tincture
tenkture, tincture
tenkul, tinkle
tenkur, tinker
tennis, A RACQUET GAME
tenon, A CARPENTRY TOOL
tenor,*, A PITCH/LEVEL OF SOUND
tenos, tennis
tenparery, temporary
tenpermint, temperament
tenpest, tempest
tenpirery, temporary
tenpist, tempest
tenplit, template
tenpo, tempo
tenpol, temple
tenporal, temporal
tenporary, temporary
tenporat, temper(ate)
tenprachur, temperature
tenpral, temporal
tenprament, temperament
tenpret, temper(ate)
tenpriment, temperament
tenprit, temper(ate)
tenprochur, temperature
tenprot, temper(ate)

tens, ten(s) / tent(s) / tense / tint(s) / tend(s)
tense,*,ed,sing,ely,eness,sity,eless,sion, sional,sionless,sive, STRETCHED/PUSHED/STRAINED BEYOND A COMFORTABLE POSITION, TIGHT, IN RELATION TO TIME (or see tent(s))
tensul, tinsel
tent,*,ted,ting, SHARP PEAK WITH TWO EQUAL SLOPES, TEMPORARY/PORTABLE SHELTER, SURGICAL PROCEDURE (or see tint/tend/tin(nned))
tentacle,*,ed,cular, LONG/FLEXIBLE APPENDAGES ON A LIVING THING
tentakle, tentacle
tentative,ely,eness, TEMPORARY PLAN/TIME, NOT CERTAIN AS OF YET
tented, tint(ed) / tent(ed) / tend(ed)
tentekle, tentacle
tentetive, tentative
tenth,*, ONE PART OUT OF TEN
tentikle, tentacle
tentukle, tentacle
tentutive, tentative
tenuble, tenable
tenues, tenuous
tenukle, tentacle
tenument, tenement
tenunsy, tenant(ncy)
tenunt, tenant
tenuous,sly,sness, DELICATE/WEAK/FINE/DILUTED
tenur, tenor
tenure,ed,rial,rially, HOLDING/POSSESSING PROPERTY OR POSITION
tenus, tennis
tenutef, tentative
tenutive, tentative
teny, teen(y) / tin(nny)
tenyewr, tenure
tenyewus, tenuous
tenyir, tenure
tenyur, tenure
tenzul, tinsel
tep, tip
tepakle, typical
tepd, tip(pped)
tepe, teepee
teped, tepid
tepekul, typical
teper, tip(pper)

tepid,dity,dness,dly, LUKEWARM, WARM TO TOUCH
tepikul, typical
tepod, tepid
tepor, tip(pper)
tepse, tip(sy)
tepud, tepid
tepufy, typify
tepukle, typical
tepur, tip(pper)
tequila, A LIQUOR/ALCOHOL
ter, PREFIX INDICATING "THREE" MOST OFTEN MODIFIES THE WORD
tera, PREFIX INDICATING "ONE TRILLION/MONSTER" MOST OFTEN MODIFIES THE WORD
terable, terrible
terace, terrace
terafy, terrify
teragen, tarragon
teragin, tarragon
terain, terrain / terrane
teranchula, tarantula
terane, terrain / terrane / tyranny
teranshulu, tarantula
terantula, tarantula
terareim, terrarium
terarium, terrarium
teras, terrace
terastrial, terrestrial
terat, terret
teratoreul, territory(rial)
teratory, territory
terazo, terrazzo
terazzo, terrazzo
terben, turban / turbine
terbin, turban / turbine
terbo, turbo
terbulens, turbulent(nce)
terbulent, turbulent
terbun, turban / turbine
terd, tier(ed) / tear(ed) / tour(ed)
terdle, turtle
tere, tear(y)
tereble, terrible
terefic, terrific
terefy, terrify
terene, tyranny
terer, terror
terereim, terrarium
teres, terrace
teresdreul, terrestrial
teresm, tour(ism)
terest, tour(ist)

terestrial, terrestrial
teret, turret / terret
tereur, tarry(rier) / terrier
terf, turf
terfil, tear(ful)
terful, tear(ful)
terible, terrible
teribly, terrible(ly)
terif, tariff
terifek, terrific
terify, terrify
teriny, tyranny
terir, terror
teris, terrace
terism, tour(ism)
terist, tour(ist)
terit, turret / terret
teritoree, territory
teritoreul, territory(rial)
teriur, terrier
terkoes, turquois
terkois, turquois
term,*,med,mless, INVOLVING A SPECIFIC PERIOD OF TIME, FIXED/ SPECIFIC QUANTITY/VALUE
termarek, turmeric
termd, term(ed)
termenal, terminal
termenashen, terminate(tion)
termenate, terminate
termenation, terminate(tion)
termenator, terminate(tor)
termenolegy, terminology
termenul, terminal
termerik, turmeric
terminal,*,lly,able,ableness,ably, STATION/CONDUIT/CIRCUIT, TERMINATE, COME TO AN END "prefixes: sub"
terminashen, terminate(tion)
terminate,*,ed,ting,tive,tively,tor,tion, tional, TO END
terminology,gies,gical,gically, SPECIFIC WORDS/LANGUAGE WITHIN A SCIENCE/ART TO EXPLAIN PROCESSES
terminul, terminal
termite,*, WOOD EATING INSECT
termoel, turmoil
termonel, terminal
termunate, terminate
termunolegy, terminology
tern,*, A BIRD (or see turn)
ternament, tournament

ternd, turn(ed)
ternep, turnip
terniment, tournament
ternip, turnip
ternument, tournament
teror, terror
terpentin, turpentine
terpewlent, turbulent
terpulent, turbulent
terpuntine, turpentine
terra, PLANETS MOUNTAINOUS AREA
terrace,*,ed,cing, VARIOUS LEVEL AREAS CUT INTO A SLOPE
terrain, NATURALLY SHAPED LANDSCAPE (or see terrane)
terrane, GROUP OF NATURAL FORMATIONS PARTICULARLY ROCK (or see terrain) "prefixes: sub"
terrarium,*, CONTAINER FOR PLANTS/ ANIMALS TO LIVE/BE VIEWED
terrazzo, MOSAIC PIECES OF STONE/ TILE
terrestrial,*,lly,lness, BY/OF LAND/ EARTH "prefixes: semi/sub"
terret,*, ON A SADDLE/HARNESS (or see turret)
terreur, terrier
terrible,eness,ly, HORRIBLE/AWFUL/ UNCOMFORTABLE/STRESSFUL
terrier,*, BREED OF DOG
terrif, tariff
terrific,cally, EXCELLENT/EXCITING/ WONDERFUL
terrify,fies,fied,ying,yingly, STRICKEN WITH TERROR, HORRIFY/FRIGHTEN
terrir, terror
territory,ries,rial,rially,rialism,rialist, riality,lize,lized,lization, A SPECIFIC REGION/AREA OF TURF/LAND
terror,*,rism,rist,ristic,rless,rize,rizes, rized,rizing,rization,rizer, EXTREME FEAR/ HORROR "prefixes: bio"
terrur, terror
ters, tear(s) / tier(s)
terse,er,est,ely,eness, FREE OF FRIVOLTIES/SUPERFICIALITY
tersheary, tertiary
tershury, tertiary
tert, tier(ed) / tear(ed)
tertiary,ries, THREE/THIRD/THIRDS OF SOMETHING
tertil, turtle
tertul, turtle
teru, terra

terubil, terrible
terubly, terrible(ly)
teruf, tariff
terufy, terrify
terugen, tarragon
terugin, tarragon
terur, terror
terus, terrace
terut, turret
terutoree, territory
terutoreul, territory(rial)
terutory, territory
tery, tear(y) / tarry
terz, tear(s) / tier(s)
tes, tease / test
tesabel, tease(sable)
tesdamoneul, testimony(nial)
tesdee, testy
tesdekle, testicle
tesdi, testy
tesdukle, testicle
tesdumoneul, testimony(nial)
teseble, tease(sable)
tesh, teach
teshu, tissue
tesible, tease(sable)
test,*,ted,ting,ter,ty, TO CHALLENGE, EXPERIMENT FOR REACTION, A SHELL "prefixes: pre"
testafide, testify(fied)
testafy, testify
testament,*,tary,tal, WITNESS, CREATE A WILL "prefixes: inter"
testamint, testament
testamoneul, testimony(nial)
teste, testy
testefide, testify(fied)
testefy, testify
testekle, testicle
testemint, testament
testemony, testimony
testicle,*,cular,culate, MALE REPRODUCTIVE GLANDS
testify,fies,fied,fying,fier, TO DECLARE UNDER OATH/AS A WITNESS
testikle, testicle
testikuler, testicle(cular)
testiment, testament
testimony,nies,ial, PROVIDE WRITTEN/ VERBAL ACCOUNT AS A WITNESS
testir, test(er)
testufid, testify(fied)
testufy, testify
testukle, testicle

testument, testament
testumoneul, testimony(nial)
testumony, testimony
testur, test(er)
testy,tily,tiness, TOUCHY/IRRITABLE
tesu, tissue
tesubil, tease(sable)
tesuble, tease(sable)
tesy, tizzy
tetanus, A BACTERIA WHICH ENTERS OPEN WOUNDS
tetbit, tidbit
teter, teeter
teth, teeth
tether,*,red,ring, CORD/ROPE/ STRANDS TO SECURE SOMETHING FROM MOVING AWAY (or see teeth(er))"prefixes: un"
tethur, tether
tetir, teeter
tetnus, tetanus
tetra,*, FRESH WATER TROPICAL FISH, PREFIX INDICATING "FOUR" MOST OFTEN MODIFIES THE WORD
tetru, tetra
tetur, teeter
teuburkwulosis, tuberculosis
teul, teal / tell / teil
teurd, tier(ed) / tear(ed)
teurism, tour(ism)
teusday, tuesday
tewb, tube
tewbles, tube(less)
tewbuler, tube(bular)
tewl, tool
tewm, tomb
tewnik, tunic
tewt, toot
tewth, tooth
tewthles, tooth(less)
texder, texture
texdile, textile
texsdure, texture
text,*,ted,ting,tual,tually,tualism,tualist, PRINTED/WRITTEN LETTERS TO FORM WORDS "prefixes: inter/sub"
textile,*, ANY MATERIAL THAT CAN BE WOVEN
texture,*,ed,ring,ral,rally, ANY RAISED/ VARIANT PORTION OF A FLAT/ SMOOTH SURFACE "prefixes: inter"
tez, tease
tezzy, tizzy
tha, thaw / they

thad, they'd
thael, they'll
thair, there / their / they're
thal, they'll
thalamus,mi,mic,mically, PART OF A BRAIN/FLOWER
thalas, thallus
thalimus, thalamus
thallus, NEW BUD OF A PLANT WITHOUT LEAVES, ETC.
thalumus, thalamus
thalus, thallus
thamadik, theme(matic)
than, WORD USED TO COMPARE/ CONTRAST
thanck, thank
thang, thong / thing
thank,*,ked,king,kful,kfully,kfulness, kless,klessly,klessness, APPRECIATION/ GRATITUDE
thanklis, thank(less)
thar, there / their / they're
tharbi, thereby
thare, there / their / they're
tharepist, therapy(pist)
tharepudik, therapy(peutic)
tharepy, therapy
tharfor, therefor / therefore
tharfour, therefor / therefore
tharipist, therapy(pist)
tharipudik, therapy(peutic)
tharipy, therapy
tharof, thereof
tharupist, therapy(pist)
tharupudik, therapy(peutic)
tharupy, therapy
thasoris, thesaurus
that,*, SOMEONE/SOMETHING NOT IN THE IMMEDIATE AREA/TIME FRAME, PREVIOUSLY MENTIONED, A PRONOUN (or see thought)
thatch,hes,hed,hing,her, MATTED/ LAYERED ORGANIC MATERIAL, SURFACE COVERING
thau, thaw / thou
thaud, thaw(ed) / thought
thaung, thong
thausend, thousand
thaut, thaw(ed) / thought
thaw,*,wed,wing, TEMPERATURE WARMING AWAY FROM FREEZING, UNFREEZING (or see thou)
thawt, thaw(ed) / thought
thayd, they'd

thayl, they'll
the, AN IDENTIFYING/SPECIFYING WORD PRIOR TO A NOUN (or see thee)
theader, theater
theadir, theater
theadrekul, theatric(al)
theadrikal, theatric(al)
theadur, theater
thealegy, theology
theam, theme
theater,*,tre, A STRUCTURE FOR PERFORMING THE ARTS
theatir, theater
theatrek, theatric
theatrekul, theatric(al)
theatric,*,cal,calism,cality,calize,cally, THE ART OF PERFORMING, DRAMATIC "prefixes: non"
theatur, theater
thed, they'd
thee, REFERS TO A PERSON (or see the)
theef, thief / thieves
theem, theme
theesm, theism
thef, thief / they've
thefd, theft
theft,*, STEALING
theid, they'd
theif, thief / they've
theifs, thief(s)
theil, they'll
their,*, REFERS TO PEOPLE, POSSESSIVE PLURAL PRONOUN (or see there/ they're)
theism,st,stic,stical,stically, BELIEF IN ONE DEITY
theive, thief / thieves
thek, thick
thekin, thick(en)
thekinur, thick(ener)
thekist, thick(est)
thekit, thicket
theknur, thick(ener)
thekun, thick(en)
thekuner, thick(ener)
thekust, thick(est)
thekut, thicket
thel, they'll
them,mselves, PRONOUN REFERRING TO MORE THAN ONE (or see theme)
themadik, theme(matic)
themble, thimble

thembul, thimble
theme,*,matic,matically, A SPECIFIC TOPIC/SUBJECT
themselves, PLURAL PRONOUN POSSESSIVE
then, SIGNIFIES TIME/PLACE (or see thin/than)
thener, thin(nner)
theng, thing
thenir, thin(nner)
thenk, think
thenkar, think(er)
thenkur, think(er)
thenly, thin(ly)
thenur, thin(nner)
theo, PREFIX INDICATING "GOD" MOST OFTEN MODIFIES THE WORD (or see thio)
theology,gies,gian,gic,gical,gically,gize,gizer, PHILOSOPHY CONCERNING RELIGION
theolugy, theology
theory,ries,rize,rizes,rized,rizing,rem, rematic,rematically,retic,retical, retically, PRINCIPLES/TECHNIQUES/ BELIEF IN AN ATTEMPT TO EXPLAIN/ UNDERSTAND EVENTS
ther, there / their / they're
therapudik, therapy(peutic)
therapy,pies,pist,peutic,peutics, peutically,peutist, TREATMENT TO REMEDY A MALADY "prefixes: bio/ sub"
therasik, thoracic
therbi, thereby
therd, third
therdly, third(ly)
there,*, FOLLOWS NOUN/PRONOUN TO DESCRIBE PLACE/TIME/ EMPHASIS (or see their/they're)
thereby, IN WHICH CASE/INSTANCE
therefor, FOR IT/THIS/THAT (or see therefore)
therefore, IN REFERENCE TO THE BEFORE MENTIONED (or see therefor)
thereof, BECAUSE OF THAT
therepeudik, therapy(peutic)
therfor, therefor / therefore
therfour, therefor / therefore
therm,mic,mical,mal, CALORIES, PREFIX INDICATING "HEAT" MOST OFTEN MODIFIES THE WORD "prefixes: endo/exo"

thermal,*,lly, RELATED TO HEAT
thermamedur, thermometer
thermometer,*,tric,trical,trically,try, INSTRUMENT WHICH MEASURES HOT/COLD VARIANCES
thermomuder, thermometer
thermul, thermal
thero, thorough
therof, thereof
therough, thorough
therow, thorough
thers, there(s) / their(s)
thersd, thirst
thersde, thursday / thirst(y)
thersdy, thursday / thirst(y)
therst, thirst
thersty, thursday / thirst(y)
thert, third
theru, through / threw
theruf, thereof
therupist, therapy(pist)
therupudik, therapy(peutic)
therupy, therapy
thery, theory
thes, this / these
thesal, thistle
thesares, thesaurus
thesaurus,ses, BOOK OF SYNONYMS
thesbein, thespian
these, PLURAL TENSE OF "THIS" (or see this)
thesis,ses, SET/PUT DOWN/ DOCUMENT/PROVE
thesle, thistle
thesores, thesaurus
thespein, thespian
thespian,*, ACTOR/ACTRESS
thesul, thistle
thesus, thesis
theury, theory
thev, thief / thieves
thevaree, thieves(ry)
thevury, thieves(ry)
thewre, theory
they, PLURAL OF "PERSONS IN GENERAL"
they'd, CONTRACTION OF OF THE WORDS 'THEY HAD/ WOULD'
they'll, CONTRACTION OF OF THE WORDS 'THEY SHALL/ WILL'
they're, CONTRACTION OF OF THE WORDS 'THEY ARE' (or see there/ their)

they've, CONTRACTION OF THE WORDS 'THEY HAVE'
theyl, they'll
thez, this
thi, PREFIX INDICATING "SULFUR" MOST OFTEN MODIFIES THE WORD (or see the/thigh/thy/thee)
thiadur, theater
thiamen, thiamine
thiamine, VITAMIN COMPOUND
thiazine, CHEMICAL COMPOUND
thick,ken,kens,kened,kening,kener,ker, kest,kness,kly,kish,ket, HAVING NOTICEABLE DEPTH/VISCOSITY/ DENSITY, EXCESSIVE
thicket,*,ted,ty, DENSE/THICK SHRUBS
thief,*,eves, ONE WHO STEALS
thiemin, thiamine
thieves,ed,ving,ery,eries,vish,vishly, vishness, THOSE WHO STEAL
thiezene, thiazine
thigh,*, PORTION OF LEG ABOVE THE KNEE
thik, thick
thiken, thick(en)
thiket, thicket
thikist, thick(est)
thikit, thicket
thiknur, thick(ener)
thikuner, thick(ener)
thikust, thick(est)
thikut, thicket
thim, theme / them
thimadek, theme(matic)
thimadik, theme(matic)
thimas, thymus
thimatik, theme(matic)
thimble,*, DEVICE FOR PROTECTION OF FINGERTIPS
thimbul, thimble
thimes, thymus
thimomedur, thermometer
thimple, thimble
thimpul, thimble
thimselfs, themselves
thimselvs, themselves
thimus, thymus
thin,*,nned,nning,nner,nly,nness,nnish, LESS VISCOSITY/ WEIGHT/ THICKNESS/ DEPTH THAN PREFERRED/ NORMAL (or see then/ than/thine)
thind, thin(nned)

thine,hou,hy, THIRD PERSON PRONOUN MEANING YOU/ YOURS (or see thin)
thiner, thin(nner)
thing,*, GENERIC TITLE FOR THAT WHICH IS NOT KNOWN/ UNDERSTOOD, WITHOUT A NAME (or see think)
think,*,king,ker,thought,kable,kingly, TO ENGAGE THE MIND, TO SUPPOSE/ CONTEMPLATE/ CONSIDER (or see thing) "prefixes: un"
thinkur, think(er)
thinur, thin(nner)
thio, PREFIX INDICATING "SULFUR" MOST OFTEN MODIFIES THE WORD (or see theo)
thirasik, thoracic
third,*,dly, NUMBER/ONE MORE AFTER THE SECOND, 33.3% OF THE WHOLE
thirdlee, third(ly)
thirm, therm
thirmal, thermal
thirmamedur, thermometer
thirmamiter, thermometer
thirmek, therm(ic)
thirmel, thermal
thirmometur, thermometer
thirmul, thermal
thiro, thorough
thiroed, thyroid
thirogh, thorough
thiroid, thyroid
thirow, thorough
thiroyd, thyroid
thirsd, thirst
thirsde, thursday / thirst(y)
thirst,*,ty,tier,tiest,tily,tiness, STRONG DESIRE FOR LIQUIDS, CRAVE SENSORY/MENTAL INPUT
thirsty, thursday / thirst(y)
thirt, third
thirty,ties, NUMBER AFTER 29
thiry, theory
this, PRONOUN/POSSESSIVE PRESENT TIME (or see these)
thisal, thistle
thisares, thesaurus
thises, thesis
thisle, thistle
thisoris, thesaurus
thistle,*, A PLANT
thisul, thistle

thisus, thesis
thiumen, thiamine
thiuzene, thiazine
thiwroed, thyroid
thiz, this
tho, though / thou / thaw
thogh, though
thoght, thought
thoghtles, thought(less)
thong,*, SHOES, UNDER GARMENT, LEATHER STRAP
thonk, thong
thoracic,cally, THE CHEST AREA
thoraks, thorax
thorasik, thoracic
thorax,xes, THE CHEST AREA
thorn,*,ny,nless, A SHARP/PRICKLY POINT ON A PLANT/TREE
thornee, thorn(y)
thornlis, thorn(less)
thoro, thorough
thorough,hly,hness, COMPLETE/ DETAILED/ACCURATE
thorow, thorough
thos, those / thus
those, PRONOUN FOR REMOTE
thosend, thousand
thosund, thousand
thot, thaw(ed) / thought
thotful, thought(ful)
thotles, thought(less)
thou,hy,hine, THIRD PERSON PRONOUN MEANING YOU/YOURS (or see though)
though, PLURAL ADJECTIVE MEANING THAT/BUT/HOWEVER
thought,*,tful,tfully,tfulness,tless, tlessly,tlessness, PAST TENSE FOR THE WORD "THINK/CONTEMPLATE" "prefixes: un"
thousand,*,dth, ENGLISH NUMBER AFTER 999
thousend, thousand
thousind, thousand
thousund, thousand
thow, thou / thaw / though
thowsand, thousand
thowsund, thousand
thowsunth, thousand(th)
thoz, those
thrab, throb
thrach, thrash
thral, thrall
thrall, ENSLAVED/SLAVE/BONDAGE

thrash,hes,hed,hing,her, FLAIL ABOUT VIOLENTLY, TO BEAT/KICK/TALK OVER AGAIN
thraul, thrall
thre, three
thread,*,ded,ding,der,dless,dy,diness, A THIN STRAND/FILAMENT/CORD "prefixes: un"
threat,*,ten,tens,tened,tening,teningly, CHALLENGE AGAINST SOMEONE/ SOMETHINGS IDEALS/ EXPECTATIONS
threch, thresh
threchhold, threshold
threchold, threshold
thred, thread / threat
threden, threat(en)
thredined, threat(ened)
thredun, threat(en)
thredund, threat(ened)
three,*,rice, ENGLISH NUMBER AFTER TWO
threft, thrift
threfty, thrift(y)
threl, thrill
threlur, thrill(er)
thresh,hes,hed,hing,her, BEAT GRAIN
threshhold, threshold
threshold,*, A DOOR WAY/SILL, ENTRANCE "prefixes: sub"
thret, thread / threat
thretind, threat(ened)
thretund, threat(ened)
threw, PAST TENSE FOR THE WORD "THROW" (or see thru through)
thrice, THREE TIMES
thrif, thrive
thrifd, thrift / thrive(d)
thrifde, thrift(y)
thrifs, thrive(s)
thrift,ty,tily,tiness, MINDS/WATCHES/ CONTROLS SPENDING/USE OF RESOURCES (or see thrive(d))
thril, thrill
thriler, thrill(er)
thrill,*,lled,lling,ller, EMOTION EXAGERRATED IN A POSITIVE FASHION, DELIGHT
thrilur, thrill(er)
thrise, thrice
thrive,*,ed,ving,vingly,er, TO EXIST SUCCESSFULLY
thro, throe / throw / through

throat,*,ted,ty,tily,tiness, CONICAL/ HOLLOW ENTRANCE/ PASSAGEWAY, FRONT PART OF NECK
throb,*,bbed,bbing,bber, PULSATE/ VIBRATE
throd, throat / throw(n)
throdul, throttle
throe,*, AMIDST STRONG PAIN/ AGONY/EMOTIONAL TURMOIL (or see throw)
throl, thrall
throne,*,ed,ning,eless, SOVEREIGN/ AUTHORITATIVE PLACEMENT, A CHAIR (or see thrown) "prefixes: en"
throng,*, IN A CROWD/MULTITUDE OF PEOPLE/THINGS (or see thong)
thronk, throng
throsd, thrust
throst, thrust
throt, throat / throw(n)
throtal, throttle
throtil, throttle
throttle,*,ed,ling,er, CONTROL OF FLOW THROUGH AN ORIFICE/ OPENING/ THROAT
throtul, throttle
through, TO PENETRATE/PASS/MAKE IT TO THE END (or see threw)
throughout, PENETRATES/EXISTS COMPLETELY
throw,*,wing,wn, TO TOSS/ELIMINATE/ GET RID OF (or see throe/throne) "prefixes: mis/over/up"
thrown, PAST TENSE FOR THE WORD "THROW" (or see throne)
throwt, throw(n) / throat
thru, TO PENETRATE/PASS/MAKE IT TO THE END (or see threw)
thruch, thrush
thrusd, thrust
thrush, A BIRD, A CHILDRENS DISEASE
thrust,*,ted,ting,ter, TO PLUNGE/ DRIVE/FORCE FORWARD "prefixes: under/up"
thruzd, thrust
thud,*,dded,dding, A SOLID/HEAVY/ DROPPING/FALLING SOUND
thug,*, ROBBERS/IMMORAL PEOPLE
thuk, thug
thum, thumb
thumadik, theme(matic)
thumatik, theme(matic)

thumb,*,bed,bing, OPPOSABLE DIGIT ON THE HAND, USE OF THE THUMB (or see thump)
thumbt, thumb(ed) / thump(pped)
thump,*,ped,ping, FALLING/HEAVY SOUND, SOUND OF HEARTBEAT (or see thumb)
thumpt, thumb(ed) / thump(pped)
thumselfs, themselves
thunder,*,red,ring,ringly, RUMBLING SOUND IN A RAIN STORM, SOUND MADE WHEN WEATHER FRONTS CONVERGE
thuntur, thunder
thurasik, thoracic
thurd, third
thurdly, third(ly)
thurm, therm
thurmal, thermal
thurmamiter, thermometer
thurmic, therm(ic)
thurmil, thermal
thurmometer, thermometer
thurmomuder, thermometer
thuro, thorough
thurow, thorough
thursd, thirst
thursday,*, A DAY OF THE WEEK (ENGLISH)
thursde, thursday / thirst(y)
thursdy, thursday / thirst(y)
thurst, thirst
thurste, thursday / thirst(y)
thursty, thursday / thirst(y)
thurt, third
thurtly, third(ly)
thus, IN EFFECT, THEREFORE, AS A RESULT
thusares, thesaurus
thusores, thesaurus
thwart,*,ted,tedly,ting, TO INTERVENE/ WARD OFF/DISTRACT A MISSION/ EVENT OR ACTION FROM IT'S GOAL/ACCOMPLISHMENT
thwort, thwart
thy,hine,hou, THIRD PERSON PRONOUN MEANING YOU/YOURS (or see thigh)
thymas, thymus
thyme, AN HERBAL PLANT (or see time)
thymis, thymus
thymus,ses,mi, A GLAND IN THE BODY
thyroid,*,dless, GLAND/CARTILAGE IN THE THROAT OF A BODY

thyuzene, thiazine
ti, tie / tea / tee
tiara,*, SMALL CROWN/CORONET FOR HEAD
tibaco, tobacco
tibagen, toboggan
tibako, tobacco
tibea, tibia
tiberqulosis, tuberculosis
tibia,al, SHIN BONE IN LEG
tibogin, toboggan
tibse, tip(sy)
tic, A TWITCHING IN THE BODY/FACE (or see tick)
tick,*,ked,king,ker, SMALL BLOOD SUCKING INSECT, RYTHMIC CLOCK SOUND, A MARK ETCHED INTO SOMETHING, MATTRESS/PILLOW COVERING, TELEGRAPH INSTRUMENT (or see tic)
ticket,*,ted,ting, PIECE OF PAPER ISSUED WHICH BEARS INFORMATION SOLICITING YOUR PERSONAL APPEARANCE/ VISIT
tickle,*,ed,ling,er,lish,lishness, SENSATION TO SKIN/ EMOTIONS WHICH GENERATES SMILE/ LAUGHTER/ RESPONSE
ticol, tickle
tid, tide / tied / tight
tida, today
tidal,lly, CONCERNING THE EBB AND FLOW OF THE SEA/OCEAN (or see title) "prefixes: inter/sub"
tiday, today
tidbet, tidbit
tidbit,*, A SNIPPET/SMALL PORTION OF SOMETHING GREATER/LARGER
tide,*,ed,ding,eful,eless,elessness,dings, dal, CONCERNING THE RISE/FALL OF OCEAN/SEA/ECONOMICS (or see tight/tied/tidy)
tided, tidy / tide(d) / tied
tidel, tidal / title
tiden, tight(en)
tideness, tidy(diness)
tidil, tidal / title
tidin, tight(en)
tidings, INFORMATION/KNOWLEDGE SHARING
tidle, tidal / title
tidon, tight(en)
tidond, tight(ened)
tidul, tidal / title

tidun, tight(en)
tidy,dies,died,dying,dily,diness, GET/KEEP THINGS ORGANIZED/IN ORDER "prefixes: un"
tie,*,ed,tying,ed, TO HOLD/BUNDLE/TIGHTEN THINGS TOGETHER USING TWINE/STRING/ROPE "prefixes: re/un/under"
tied, PAST TENSE FOR THE WORD "TIE" (or see tight/tide)
tieng, tying
tier,*,red,ring, ELEVATE IN INCREMENTAL STEPS, RISERS, A LAYERED ARRANGEMENT OF ROWS (or see tear/tire)
tiera, tiara
tif, tiff
tifes, typhus
tiff, small argument
tifis, typhus
tifoid, typhoid
tifoon, typhoon
tifun, typhoon
tifus, typhus
tigar, tiger
tiger,*,rish, LARGE WILD FELINE
tigethur, together
tight,*,tly,tness,ten,tened,tening, APPLY PRESSURE/RESTRAINT/SUPPRESSION "prefixes: up"
tights, SNUG FITTING OUTER WEAR
tigor, tiger
tigress, FEMALE WILD FELINE
tigur, tiger
tikal, tickle
tike,*, SMALL/YOUNG CHILD (or see tiki)
tikel, tickle
tiker, tiger / tick(er)
tiket, ticket
tiki, A CARVED MYTHOLOGICAL FIGURE, OF POLYNESIAN CULTURE
tikil, tickle
tikir, tiger
tikit, ticket
tikle, tickle
tiklech, tickle(lish)
tiklush, tickle(lish)
tikol, tickle
tikor, tiger
tikot, ticket
tikres, tigress
tikt, tick(ed)
tikul, tickle

tikur, tiger
tikut, ticket
tiky, tiki
til, tile / till / teach / teal
tild, tile(d) / till(ed) / tilt
tile,*,ed,ling,er, FLAT/THIN SLAB OF VARIOUS MATERIAL, TO STACK (or see till)
tilepathee, telepathy
tileputhee, telepathy
till,*,lled,lling,ller,llage, PERFORM LABOR, PLACE FOR MONEY IN A BANK, ROTATING SOIL (too many definitions, please see standard dictionary) (or see tile/teach)
tilt,*,ted,ting,ter, TO ROTATE OFF-CENTER, LEAN ONE WAY/ANOTHER (or see till(ed)/tile(d))
tim, team / time
timado, tomato
timados, tomato(es)
timaro, tomorrow
timato, tomato
timber,*,rly, TREES VIEWED AS LUMBER (or see timbre)
timbrachure, temperature
timbre, A TONAL QUALITY (or see timber)
timbrushure, temperature
timbur, timber
timd, time(d)
time,*,ed,ming,er,ely,elier,eliest,eliness, eless,elessness, HUMAN CONSTRUCT TO DIFFERENTIATE BETWEEN PLACE/SPACE, TO GUAGE HOW MANY SECONDS/ MINUTES/HOURS/DAYS/MONTHS/YEARS (or see thyme) "prefixes: over/un/under"
timed, timid / time(d)
timedly, timid(ly)
timet, timid
timid,dly,dity,dness, HESITANT/CAUTIOUS
timly, time(ly)
timod, timid
timpal, temple
timparary, temporary
timparize, temporize
timparment, temperament
timper, temper
timperal, temporal
timperary, temporary
timperashure, temperature

timperize, temporize
timperol, temporal
timperushure, temperature
timpeshues, tempest(uous)
timpest, tempest
timpestuous, tempest(uous)
timpil, temple
timplat, template
timplut, template
timpo, tempo
timpol, temple
timporarely, temporary(rily)
timporul, temporal
timprachure, temperature
timpral, temporal
timpramentul, temper(mental)
timprary, temporary
timprashure, temperature
timprature, temperature
timprery, temporary
timpromintal, temper(mental)
timprumental, temper(mental)
timptashen, temptation
timptation, temptation
timptres, tempt(ress)
timpul, temple
timpur, temper
timpura, tempura
timpurarely, temporary(rily)
timpurary, temporary
timpurize, temporize
timpurment, temperament
timpust, tempest
timt, tempt
timtashen, temptation
timtation, temptation
timted, tempt(ed)
timtres, tempt(ress)
timud, timid
timulchuis, tumult(uous)
timulchuous, tumult(uous)
timult, tumult
timur, time(r)
timut, timid
tin,*,nned,nning,nnier,nniest,nny,nnilly, nniness, TYPE OF METAL, USE OF METAL, TINSMITH (or see tenor tine/tint/tiny/tend/teen)
tinable, tenable
tinachus, tenacious
tinacity, tenacity
tinakle, tentacle
tinament, tenement
tinamint, tenement

tinansy, tenant(ncy)
tinant, tenant
tinasedy, tenacity
tinashus, tenacious
tinasity, tenacity
tinatef, tentative
tinatif, tentative
tinatious, tenacious
tinative, tentative
tinchd, tinge(d)
tincity, tense(sity)
tincture,*, PLANTS SUBMERGED IN ALCOHOL FOR MEDICINAL USE
tind, tin(nned) / tend
tindatev, tentative
tinded, tend(ed) / tint(ed)
tinden, tendon
tindensy, tendency
tindenus, tendon(dinous)
tinder,ry, USED FOR KINDLING (or see tender)
tinderize, tender(ize)
tinderloin, tenderloin
tinderly, tender(ly)
tindernes, tender(ness)
tindinsy, tendency
tindirloin, tenderloin
tindon, tendon
tindor, tinder / tender
tindorize, tender(ize)
tindrel, tendril
tindrul, tendril
tindun, tendon
tindur, tender / tinder
tindurize, tender(ize)
tindurloin, tenderloin
tindurly, tender(ly)
tindutif, tentative
tine,*, A POINT ON A TOOL/INSTRUMENT/HORN/FORK (or see tin/tiny)
tinekle, tentacle
tinemint, tenement
tinen, tenon
tinensy, tenant(ncy)
tinent, tenant
tiner, tenor
tines, tennis / tine(s) / time(s)
tinet, tenet / tenant
tineur, tenure
tinewus, tenuous
tinfold, tenfold
ting, A SOUND (or see tinge)

tinge,*,ed,ging, A HINT/TRACE/SMALL BIT OF CHANGE IN COLOR/QUALITY (or see ting)
tinible, tenable
tinikle, tentacle
tinir, tenor
tinit, tenet / tenant / tonight
tinj, tinge
tink, ting
tinkal, tinkle
tinkchur, tincture
tinker,*,red,ring,rer, TOY/FONDLE/MEND/HANDLE SOMETHING
tinkle,*,ed,ling,ly,er, A FAINT LITTLE SOUND
tinkol, tinkle
tinksher, tincture
tinkture, tincture
tinkul, tinkle
tinkur, tinker
tinon, tenon
tinor, tenor
tinpal, temple
tinparery, temporary
tinpermint, temperament
tinpest, tempest
tinpirery, temporary
tinpist, tempest
tinplit, template
tinpo, tempo
tinpol, temple
tinporal, temporal
tinporary, temporary
tinporat, temper(ate)
tinprachur, temperature
tinpral, temporal
tinprament, temperament
tinpret, temper(ate)
tinpriment, temperament
tinprit, temper(ate)
tinprochur, temperature
tinprot, temper(ate)
tins, tin(s) / tent(s) / tense / tint(s) / tend
tinse, tense / tent(s)
tinsel,*,led,ling, SHINY/METALLIC STRIPS FOR DECORATION
tinsil, tinsel
tinsity, tense(sity)
tinsle, tinsel
tinsness, tense(ness)
tinsul, tinsel
tint,*,ted,ting,tless, CHANGE/APPLY SHADE OF COLOR (or see tent/

tense/tin(nned)/tend) "prefixes: under"
tintakle, tentacle
tintative, tentative
tinted, tint(ed) / tent(ed) / tend(ed)
tintetive, tentative
tinth, tenth
tintid, tint(ed) / tent(ed) / tend(ed)
tintikle, tentacle
tintuckle, tentacle
tintud, tint(ed) / tent(ed) / tend(ed)
tintukle, tentacle
tintutive, tentative
tinuble, tenable
tinuis, tenuous
tinukle, tentacle
tinument, tenement
tinunsy, tenant(ncy)
tinunt, tenant
tinur, tenor
tinus, tennis
tinutef, tentative
tinutive, tentative
tiny,nier,niest,niness, LITTLE, VERY SMALL IN SCALE (or see tin(nny))
tinyewr, tenure
tinyewus, tenuous
tinyir, tenure
tinyur, tenure
tinzul, tinsel
tip,*,pped,pping,pper,ppy,ppable,pless,psy, TO LEAN SOMETHING OFF-CENTER FROM ITS POINT OF GRAVITY (or see type)
tipakle, typical
tipd, tip(pped) / type(d)
tipe, type / tip(ppy)
tipekul, typical
tiper, tip(pper) / type(r)
tiphoon, typhoon
tiphune, typhoon
tipi, teepee / tip(ppy)
tipikul, typical
tipist, type(pist)
tipo, typo
tipography, topography
tipogrufe, topography
tipse, tip(sy)
tipt, tip(pped) / type(d)
tipufy, typify
tipukle, typical
tipur, tip(pper) / type(r)
tiquila, tequila
tir, tire / tear

tirade,*, VERBAL/VIOLENT OUTBURST
tiranchula, tarantula
tirane, terrain / terrane / tyranny
tiranekul, tyrannical
tiranikul, tyrannical
tiranshulu, tarantula
tirant, tyrant
tirantula, tarantula
tirate, tirade
tirazo, terrazzo
tirben, turban / turbine
tirbo, turbo
tirbulens, turbulent(nce)
tirbulent, turbulent
tirbun, turban / turbine
tird, tire(d)
tirdle, turtle
tire,*,ed,ring,eless,elessly,elessness, edly,edness,esome,esomely, esomeness, RUN OUT OF ENERGY, USED ON WHEELS "prefixes: un"
tirene, tyranny
tirent, tyrant
tireny, tyranny
tiresdreul, terrestrial
tirestrial, terrestrial
tirf, turf
tirit, turret
tirkoes, turquois
tirkoys, turquois
tirles, tire(less)
tirlis, tire(less)
tirm, term
tirmenashen, terminate(tion)
tirmenate, terminate
tirmenation, terminate(tion)
tirmenator, terminate(tor)
tirmenology, terminology
tirmenul, terminal
tirminate, terminate
tirmination, terminate(tion)
tirminator, terminate(tor)
tirminolegy, terminology
tirminul, terminal
tirmite, termite
tirmoel, turmoil
tirmonel, terminal
tirmunolegy, terminology
tirn, tern / turn
tirnament, tournament
tirnep, turnip
tirnument, tournament
tirpentine, turpentine
tirpewlent, turbulent

tirpulent, turbulent
tirpuntine, turpentine
tirrazo, terrazzo
tirse, terse
tirsheary, tertiary
tirsnes, terse(ness)
tirsum, tire(some)
tirtil, turtle
tirtul, turtle
tirunt, tyrant
tirut, turret
tise, tizzy
tishew, tissue
tissue,*, A SMALL/LIGHTWEIGHT PIECE OF PAPER
tisue, tissue
tisy, tizzy
tit,*,tty,tties, NIPPLE ON FEMALE OF SPECIES, TEAT (or see tied/tight/ tights)
tital, title / tidal
titan, tight(en)
titbet, tidbit
titbit, tidbit
tite, tidy / tight / tied
titel, title / tidal
titen, tight(en)
titend, tight(ened)
titenes, tidy(diness)
tithe,*,ed,hing,hable, A PERCENTAGE TO BE GIVEN AWAY TO SOMEONE/ SOMETHING
titil, title / tidal
titind, tight(ened)
title,*,ed,ling,list, A NAME (or see tidal/ tight(ly)) "prefixes: inter/re/sub/ sur/un"
titly, tight(ly)
titond, tight(ened)
titul, title / tidal
titun, tight(en)
titund, tight(ened)
tity, tidy
tiung, tying
tizzy, A FRENZIED STATE, A DITHER
to, PREPOSITION IN THE ENGLISH LANGUAGE TO SHOW RELATIONSHIP BETWEEN PERSON/ PLACE/THING (or see toe/too/tow)
toad,*, AN AMPHIBIAN MOSTLY FOUND IN DRY TERRAIN (or see told/toe(d)/ toady)

toady,dies,died,dying,dyish,dism,diness, TO GROVEL/FLATTER OTHERS FOR SELF-SERVING REASONS
toagrife, topography
toast,*,ted,ting,ter, TO BROWN FOOD WITH A HEAT SOURCE, HONORING SOMETHING/SOMEONE BEFORE HAVING A DRINK
tobacco, PLANT WHOSE LEAVES CONTAIN NICOTINE
tobaco, tobacco
tobagen, toboggan
tobako, tobacco
toberkulosis, tuberculosis
tobogan, toboggan
toboggan,*,ner,nist, TYPE OF SLED
tobogin, toboggan
toch, touch
tocsufy, toxify(fication)
tod, toad / toe(d) / tow(ed)
toda, today
todal, total
today, THE DAY WHICH IS PRESENT NOW
toddler,*, SMALL CHILD LEARNING TO WALK
toddy,ddies, ALCOHOLIC MIXED DRINK (or see toady)
tode, toad / toddy / toe(d) / toady
todee, toddy / toady
todel, total
todem, totem
todil, total
todim, totem
todler, toddler
todlur, toddler
todom, totem
todul, total
todum, totem
tody, toddy / toady
toe,*,ed,eless,eing, INDEX ON A FOOT (or see to/tow/toy)
toel, toil
toeld, toil(ed) / told
toelet, toilet
toeng, toe(ing) / toy(ing) / tow(ing)
tofu, A SOYBEAN BASED FOOD
toga,*, A WRAP AS WORN BY ROMANS
togal, toggle
togel, toggle
together,rness, BROUGHT/COLLECTED/ ROUNDED UP INTO ONE PLACE
toggle,*,ed,ling,er, LEVER/SWITCH FOR ALTERING ELECTRICAL CURRENT, A

SYSTEM DEVISED TO FACILITATE MOVEMENT
toght, taught / taut / tout
togle, toggle
togu, toga
togul, toggle
toi, toy
toid, toy(ed)
toil,*,led,ling,ler, TO LABOR/WORK VERY HARD
toild, toil(ed)
toilet,*, A FIXTURE FOR CAPTURING URING/FECES
tok, tuck / took
toka, toga
tokel, toggle
tokela, tequila
token,*, A SMALL DISK/COIN/PAPER RESEMBLING SOMETHING OF VALUE
tokik, toxic
tokil, toggle
tokila, tequila
tokin, token
tokle, toggle
toko, taco
toksakolegy, toxicology
toksek, toxic
toksen, toxin
toksikolegy, toxicology
toksufy, toxify(fication)
toksukolegy, toxicology
toksun, toxin
toku, toga
tokul, toggle
tokun, token
tol, tall / toll
tolarense, tolerance
tolarent, tolerant
tolarible, tolerable
tolarinse, tolerance
told, PAST TENSE FOR THE WORD "TELL" (or see toll(ed)) "prefixes: re/un"
tole, toll
toler, tall(er)
tolerable,eness,bility,ly, BE PATIENT WITH DESPITE THE IRRITATION "prefixes: in"
tolerance, BE PATIENT WITH DESPITE THE IRRITATION "prefixes: in"
tolerant,ntly, BE PATIENT WITH DESPITE IRRITATION "prefixes: in"
tolerashen, tolerate(tion)

tolerate,*,ed,ting,able,ance,ant,ative,ation, BE PATIENT WITH DESPITE THE IRRITATION
tolerinse, tolerance
tolerint, tolerant
tolir, tall(er)
tolirashen, tolerate(tion)
tolirate, tolerate
tolirense, tolerance
toliruble, tolerable
tolk, talk / talc
toll,*,lled,lling, BELL RINGING, A REQUIRED FEE (or see tall)
tolness, tall(ness)
tolorinse, tolerance
tolur, tall(er)
tolurashen, tolerate(tion)
tolurate, tolerate
toluration, tolerate(tion)
tolurense, tolerance
tolurent, tolerant
tolurible, tolerable
tolurinse, tolerance
tolurint, tolerant
tomado, tomato
tomaro, tomorrow
tomato,oes, A FRUIT/VEGETABLE
tomb,*, STONE ENCLOSURE FOR A LIFELESS BODY "prefixes: en"
tomoro, tomorrow
tomorrow, THE DAY AFTER TODAY
ton,*,nnage, POUNDS (or see tone/toon)
tonaledy, tone(nality)
tone,*,ed,ning,nal,nality,nally,eless, elessly,elessness, SOUND FREQUENCY, MAKE FIRM/STRONG "prefixes: over/semi/under"
tonej, ton(nnage)
tonek, tonic
tong,*, TOOL USED FOR GRASPING/PICKING THINGS UP (or see tongue)
tongue,*,ed,uing, MOVABLE ORGAN IN THE MOUTH, PART OF A HITCH, POINT ON LAND (or see tong)
tonic,*,cally, A MIXTURE, RELATED TO TONE "prefixes: sub"
tonight, THE NIGHT OF PRESENT TENSE
tonij, ton(nnage)
tonik, tonic
tonite, tonight
tonk, tong / tongue
tonles, tone(less)
tons, taunt(s) / ton(s) / tone(s)

tonsalodemy, tonsillotomy
tonsel, tonsil
tonselodemy, tonsillotomy
tonsil,*,llotomy, TISSUE HANGING IN THE THROAT
tonsillotomy, ACT OF REMOVING THE TONSILS
tonsilotomy, tonsillotomy
tonsul, tonsil
tonsulodemy, tonsillotomy
tont, taunt
tonul, tone(nal)
too, PREPOSITION MEANING ALSO/MORE THAN ENOUGH (or see to/toe/tow/ two)
toob, tube
tooba, tuba
tooch, tush
toocha, touche'
took, PAST TENSE FOR THE WORD "TAKE", TO TAKE SOMETHING "prefixes: over/re/under"
tool,*,led,ling,lless, DEVICE DESIGNED TO HELP WITH WORK "prefixes: re"
toolip, tulip
toom, tomb
toomer, tumor
toomur, tumor
toon,*, SHORT FOR CARTOON (or see tune)
toona, tuna
toonek, tunic
toonik, tunic
toonu, tuna
toopa, toupee
toopay, toupee
toosday, tuesday
toosh, tush
toot,*,ted,ting, A SOUND FROM A HORN
tooth,hless,hlessly,hy,hily,hiness,teeth, ENAMELED BONE PROJECTILES IN THE MOUTH, AN OUTCROP ON GEARS
tootoo, tutu
top,*,pped,pping,pper,pless, HEAD/TIP/UPPERMOST PART OF SOMETHING, A SPINNING TOY (or see taupe/toupee)
topa, toupee
topagrafik, topography(hic)
topagraphical, topography(hical)
topagraphy, topography
topal, topple

topalegy, topology
tope, toupee / taupe
topeary, topiary
topek, topic
topekul, topical
toper, top(pper)
tophu, tofu
topiary,ries, THE SCIENCE OF TRIMMING PLANTS
topic,*, SUBJECT/TITLE/THEME "prefixes: sub"
topical,lly,lity,lities, THE SURFACE, SHALLOW (or see tropical)
topiery, topiary
topigrafik, topography(hic)
topigrafikul, topography(hical)
topigraphic, topography(hic)
topigraphical, topography(hical)
topil, topple
tople, topple
toples, top(pless)
topo, PREFIX INDICATING "PLACE" MOST OFTEN MODIFIES THE WORD
topography,hies,hic,hical,hically,her, A SCIENCE WHICH IDENTIFIES ELEVATIONS/DEPRESSION ON THE EARTH
topol, topple
topolegy, topology
topology,gic,gical,gically,gist, SCIENCE THAT CAN IDENTIFY ELEVATION/ DEPRESSION ON THE EARTH
topple,*,ed,ling, OVERTHROWN, COME DOWN, FALL OVER
topugrafik, topography(hic)
topugrafikul, topography(hical)
topugraphical, topography(hical)
topuk, topic
topukil, topical
topul, topple
tor, tar / tore
torc, torque
torch,hes,hed,hing, STAFF/BRANCH WITH FIRE ON THE END
torcher, torture
torcherus, torture(rous)
torchur, torture
tord, toward / tour(ed) / tar(rred) / tore
tordis, tortoise
tordus, tortoise
tore, PAST TENSE FOR THE WORD "TEAR"
torenshul, torrent(ial)
torent, torrent

torential, torrent(ial)
tores, torus
torget, target
torgut, target
torifek, terrific
torinshul, torrent(ial)
torint, torrent
toris, torus
tork, torque
torment,*,ted,ting,ter, TO EXTEND/ APPLY CRUELTY/PAIN TO SOMETHING/ SOMEONE
tormint, torment
tornado,oes,dic, A HIGH/SWIRLING WIND WHICH BEGINS IN THE SKY THEN TOUCHES THE GROUND
tornados, tornado(es)
tornato, tornado
tornesh, tarnish
tornushd, tarnish(ed)
toros, torus
torp, tarp
torpedo,oes,oed,oing, A CONICAL/ BULLET-SHAPED MISSILE THAT PROPELS ITSELF THROUGH WATER
torpedod, torpedo(ed)
torque, AN EXERTED FORCE, AN ORNAMENT
torrent,*,tial,tially, A VIOLENT/SUDDEN GUSH/RUSH OF GREAT VOLUME
torsh, torch
torshen, torsion
torsher, torture
torshun, torsion
torshur, torture
torsion,nal,nally, TO TWIST SOMETHING OPPOSINGLY
torso,*,si, THE MAIN PORTION/TRUNK OF A BODY
tort,*, WRONG/IMPROPER (or see torte/tart)
torte,*, A HEAVILY MADE CAKE (or see tort/tart)
tortelu, tortilla
tortes, tortoise
torteu, tortilla
torteus, tortuous
tortila, tortilla
tortilla,*, CORN BASED ROUND/FLAT CAKE
tortis, tortoise
tortoise, A TURTLE LIVING ON LAND
tortuous,sly,sness, OF BEING TWISTED/ CROOKED/BENT BY NATURE

torture,*,ed,ring,rable,edly,er,esome, ringly,rous,rously, PURPOSEFUL INFLICTION OF PAIN
tortus, tortoise
torus, RING SHAPED/BULGE/RIDGE
tos, toss / toe(s) / two(s) / tow(s)
tosd, toast / toss(ed)
tosday, tuesday
tosder, toast(er)
tosdur, toast(er)
toss,sses,ssed,ssing, GENTLY THROW WITH UPWARD MOTION (or see toe(s)) "prefixes: re"
tost, toast / toss(ed)
tostur, toast(er)
tot,*,tted,tting, A SMALL AMOUNT, WORD FOR YOUNG CHILD/ TODDLER, SHORT WORD FOR 'TOTAL' (or see taught/taut/tout/ tote)
total,*,led,ling,lly,lity,lize,lizer, SUM OF ALL PARTS, COMPLETELY "prefixes: re/sub"
totalitarian,*,nism, CENTRALIZED/ DICTATORIAL GOVERNMENT
tote,*,ed,ting, TO CARRY (or see tot/ taught/taut/tout)
totel, total
totem,*,mic,mism,mist,mistic, CARVED/ SYMBOLIC REPRESENTATION
toten, taut(en)
totil, total
totile, total(lly)
totim, totem
totin, taut(en)
totler, toddler
totlur, toddler
totnes, taut(ness)
totoletarian, totalitarian
totom, totem
totule, total(lly)
totum, totem
toty, toddy / toady
touch,hes,hed,hing,hable,her,hy,hily, hiness, CONTACT/PRESSURE/ EFFECT/SENSATION AFFECTING SOME PART OF THE BODY (or see touche'/tush) "prefixes: re/un"
touche', FENCING/SPORT EXPRESSION (or see touch/tush)
tough,her,hest,hen,hener,hly,hness,hy, CHALLENGING/DIFFICULT TO PENETRATE/AFFECT/CONVINCE/ ASSUME

tought, tuft
toul, towel / tool
toun, town
toupee, FALSE HAIR PIECE (or see taupe)
tour,*,red,ring,rism,rist, PERUSE/VISIT/ TRAVEL TO SITES WITHIN A SPECIFIC TIME FRAME
tournament,*, COMPETITION IN SPORTS
tousil, tousle
tousle,*,ed,ling, RUFFLE/MESS UP
tout,*,ted,ting, TO SOLICIT FOR VOTES/ SALES/INFORMATION (or see taut/ taught)
tow,*,wed,wing,wer, TO HAUL/PULL BEHIND (or see toe/two/too/to/ toe(d)) "prefixes: under"
toward,*,dly,dliness, IN THE DIRECTION OF, EXPRESSING DIRECTION "prefixes: un"
towd, tow(ed) / toe(d) / toad
towel,*,led,ling, CLOTH/MATERIAL FOR USE IN DEALING WITH LIQUID
tower,*,red,ring, VERTICAL RISE, STRUCTURE WITH GREAT HEIGHT
towir, tower
town,*,nie, DESIGNATED AREA WHERE PEOPLE LIVE/ COHABITATE/ CONDUCT BUSINESS "prefixes: up"
towsil, tousle
towst, toast
towt, tout / taut / taught
towur, tower
tox, PREFIX INDICATING "POISON" MOST OFTEN MODIFIES THE WORD
toxakology, toxicology
toxek, toxic
toxen, toxin
toxi, PREFIX INDICATING "POISON" MOST OFTEN MODIFIES THE WORD
toxic,*,cally,cant,cation,city,cities, POISONOUS "prefixes: de/endo"
toxico, PREFIX INDICATING "POISON" MOST OFTEN MODIFIES THE WORD
toxicology,gic,gical,gically,gist,cosis, SCIENCE/STUDY OF POISONS
toxify,fies,fied,fying,fication, POISONED "prefixes: de"
toxik, toxic
toxikology, toxicology
toxin,*, POISON "prefixes: endo/exo"
toxun, toxin
toy,*,yed,ying, PLAYTHING

toyl, toil
toylet, toilet
tozdur, toast(er)
tozt, toast
tra, PREFIX INDICATING "ACROSS/ OVER/BEYOND" MOST OFTEN MODIFIES THE WORD (or see tray)
trac, track / trace
trace,*,ed,cing,er,eable,eableness,eably, eless, PATH/LINE/SCENT/CLUES LEADING TO ORIGINATION/ BEGINNING POINT (or see tray(s)/ track) "prefixes: re"
trach, trash
trachea,al,ate,eitis, TUBE PLACED IN THE THROAT FOR AIR/FOOD
trachoma,atous, EYELID INFLAMMATION/INFECTION
track,*,ked,king,ker,kable,kless, klessness, PATH/RAILS TO TRANSPORT/ NAVIGATE ALONG (or see tract)
trackshen, traction
tract,*,table,tion, A STRETCH/AREA OF SPACE/TIME/ DISTANCE (or see track(ed))
tractable,tability,tableness,tably, EASILY MANIPULATED/ FORMED (or see track(able))
tracter, tractor
traction,nal,ive, FIRM GRIP FOR MOMENTUM, METHOD TO RELIEVE STRESS ON THE BODY "prefixes: re"
tractor,*, EQUIPMENT USED FOR WORK
tractur, tractor
tracuble, trace(able)
tracur, trace(r)
trade,*,ed,ding,er,dable, EXCHANGE ONE THING FOR ANOTHER (or see trait) "prefixes: over"
traden, trod(dden) / trot(tting)
tradeshenul, tradition(al)
tradeshin, tradition
tradetion, tradition
tradin, trod(dden) / trot(tting)
tradir, trade(r) / traitor
tradishenul, tradition(al)
tradition,*,nal,nally,nalism,nalist, nalistic, PRACTICED REPEATEDLY THROUGHOUT TIME
tradur, trade(r) / traitor
trae, tray
trael, trail
traf, trough

trafek, traffic
trafel, travel
traffic,cked,cking, MANY PEOPLE USING SAME ROADWAY/PATH/AVENUE/ METHOD ROUTINELY
trafik, traffic
trafil, travel
trafler, travel(er)
trafuk, traffic
traful, travel
tragedy,dies,gic, A GREAT CATASTROPHIC/DISASTROUS EVENT
tragek, tragic
tragekle, tragic(ally)
tragekt, traject
tragektery, traject(ory)
tragety, tragedy
tragic,cally, A TRAGEDY
tragide, tragedy
tragik, tragic
tragude, tragedy
trail,*,led,ling,ler, A PATH/ROUTE "prefixes: en"
trailer,*, CONTAINER ON WHEELS WITH HITCH, MOVIE PREVIEW (or see trail(er)) "prefixes: semi"
trailor, trawl(er) / trail(er) / trailer
train,*,ned,ning,ner,nable, LOCOMOTIVE/RAILWAY CARS, DISCIPLINE TO FOLLOW DIRECTIONS AS COMMANDED/ INSTRUCTED "prefixes: de/en/re"
trainkwol, tranquil
trainqwil, tranquil
trainuble, train(able)
traipse,*,ed,sing, TO WALK AROUND WITHOUT PURPOSE
trait,*, SPECIFIC QUALITIES/FEATURES (or see trade)
traitor,*,rous,rously, ONE WHO BETRAYS ANOTHER
traject,*,ted,ting,tion,tory,tories, THE CURVE/ARC OF DIRECTION WHEN AIMING/CASTING/SHOOTING
trajectery, traject(ory)
trajek, tragic
trajekle, tragic(ally)
trajekt, traject
trajektery, traject(ory)
trajide, tragedy
trajik, tragic
trajude, tragedy
trak, track / tract

trakd, track(ed) / tract
trakea, trachea
traker, track(er)
trakia, trachea
trakible, track(able) / tract(able)
trakiu, trachea
traklis, track(less)
trakomu, trachoma
trakshen, traction
trakshun, traction
trakt, track(ed) / tract
traktor, tractor
trakuble, track(able) / tract(able)
trakur, track(er)
tral, trawl / troll / trowel
trale, trail / trolley
traler, trawl(er) / trail(er) / trailer
traley, trolley
tralur, trawl(er) / trail(er) / trailer
tram,*,mmed,mming, MECHANICALLY ADJUST, TRANSPORTER ON RAILS, WOVEN SILK TECHNIQUE
trama, trauma
tramadik, trauma(tic)
tramatis, trauma(tize)
tramb, tramp
trambalen, trampoline
trambon, trombone
trambulen, trampoline
tramel, trommel
tramendus, tremendous
tramindusle, tremendous(ly)
tramol, trommel
tramp,*, STEP HEAVILY, TRAVEL ON FOOT FROM PLACE TO PLACE FOR SUBSTINENCE WITHOUT A HOME
trampalen, trampoline
trampil, trample
trample,*,ed,ling, STEP/STOMP HEAVILY CAUSING HARM/INJURY
tramplen, trampoline
trampol, trample
trampoline,*,er,nist, MATERIAL STRETCHED ACROSS A FRAME SUPPORTED BY SPRINGS TO JUMP ON
trampul, trample
trampulen, trampoline
tramu, trauma
tramul, trommel
tramutize, trauma(tize)
tran, PREFIX INDICATING "ACROSS/OVER/BEYOND" MOST OFTEN MODIFIES THE WORD (or see train)

trance,*,ed,cing, A SUBCONSCIOUS STATE OF MIND "prefixes: en"
trancefigurashen, transfigure(ration)
trancefushen, transfuse(sion)
trane, train
traneble, train(able)
tranes, train(s) / tran(s) / trance
trangretion, transgress(ion)
tranible, train(able)
tranir, train(er)
trankwel, tranquil
tranquil,lly,lness,lize,lizes,lized,lizer, lizing,lity, PEACEFUL/CALM/RELAXING
tranqwul, tranquil
trans, trance / train(s) / tran(s)
transacshun, transact(ion)
transact,ted,ting,tion,tional, CARRY OUT/MAKE EXCHANGE IN BUSINESS
transaktion, transact(ion)
transatif, transit(ive)
transbertashen, transport(ation)
transbir, transpire
transbirtashen, transport(ation)
transblant, transplant
transbonder, transponder
transbort, transport
transburtachen, transport(ation)
transcend,*,ded,ding,dent,dence,dency, dently,dental,dentally,dentalism, dentalist, NOT OF THE MATERIAL/PHYSICAL PLANE/FREQUENCY
transcrepshen, transcription
transcribe,*,ed,bing,er,iption, PHYSICALLY/LITERALLY MAKE NOTATION/COPY, AVAILABLE FOR VIEWING
transcripshen, transcription
transcription,*,tional,tive, PHYSICALLY/LITERALLY MAKE NOTATION/COPY, AVAILABLE FOR VIEWING
transdews, transduce
transdewsur, transduce(r)
transduce,*,er,ction, CHANGE ONE TYPE OF FREQUENCY/ENERGY INTO ANOTHER
transduction,*,nal, CHANGE TYPE OF FREQUENCY/ENERGY INTO ANOTHER BIOLOGICALLY
transduse, transduce
transduxshin, transduction
transeant, transient
transechen, transit(ion)

transect,*,ted,ting,tion, DIVIDE/SEVER/CUT ACROSS
transekt, transect
transem, transom
transend, transcend
transendense, transcend(ence)
transendent, transcend(ent)
transendentul, transcend(ental)
transendul, transcend(ental)
transent, transcend
transeshenul, transit(ional)
transestur, transistor
transet, transit
transetif, transit(ive)
transetional, transit(ional)
transetory, transit(ory)
transeunt, transient
transexshen, transect(ion)
transfeks, transfix
transfer,*,rred,rring,rrer,rral,rrals,rable, rability,ree,rence,rential, MOVE/SHIFT FROM ONE PLACE TO ANOTHER "prefixes: re"
transfermashen, transform(ation)
transfeugin, transfuse(sion)
transfews, transfuse
transfex, transfix
transfigure,*,ed,ring,rement,ration, CHANGE APPEARANCE OF
transfirens, transfer(ence)
transfirmation, transform(ation)
transfiruble, transfer(able)
transfix,xes,xed,xing,xion, HOLD/FROZEN IN PLACE
transfor, transfer
transform,*,med,ming,mer,mation, mational,mationally,mative,mable, CHANGE FROM ONE TO ANOTHER, AN EVOLUTION "prefixes: inter/re"
transformur, transform(er)
transfujen, transfuse(sion)
transfurd, transfer(rred)
transfurens, transfer(ence)
transfurmashen, transform(ation)
transfuruble, transfer(able)
transfuse,ed,sing,sable,sion, TRANSMISSION/MOVEMENT OF LIQUID/BLOOD
transgreshen, transgress(ion)
transgresif, transgress(ive)
transgress,sses,ssed,ssing,ssive,ssor, ssively,ssion, VIOLATING A LAW
transgretion, transgress(ion)
transichenul, transit(ional)

transient,*,tly,nce,ncy, PHYSICAL TEMPORARY/PASSING
transim, transom
transind, transcend
transindense, transcend(ence)
transindentul, transcend(ental)
transishen, transit(ion)
transistor,*,rize, ELECTRONIC DEVICE
transit,*,ted,ting,tion,tional,tionally, tive,tively,tiveness,tivity,tory,torily, toriness, PASSING OVER/THROUGH/ACROSS
transkribe, transcribe
translachen, translate(tion)
translade, translate
transladuble, translate(table)
transladur, translate(tor)
translate,*,ed,ting,tability,table,tor,tion, tional,tive, MOVE/CONVEY INFORMATION/ITEMS/EFFECT, REPRODUCE WHILE RETAINING THE ORIGINAL
translatir, translate(tor)
translatuble, translate(table)
translewsed, translucid
translewsins, translucent(nce)
translewsint, translucent
transloused, translucid
translucent,nce,ncy,ntly,cid, LIGHT CAN PENETRATE
translucid, LIGHT CAN PENETRATE
translusent, translucent
translusinse, translucent(nce)
translusit, translucid
transmechen, transmission
transmedable, transmit(ttable)
transmedal, transmit(ttal)
transmedur, transmit(tter)
transmesable, transmissible
transmeshen, transmission
transmetuble, transmit(ttable)
transmewt, transmute
transmewtuble, transmute(table)
transmichen, transmission
transmiduble, transmit(ttable)
transmidul, transmit(ttal)
transmidur, transmit(tter)
transmisability, transmissible(bility)
transmision, transmission
transmissible,bility, PASSED ALONG, MOVEABLE, ABLE TO TRANSMIT
transmission,*, GEARS WHICH ENCOURAGE MOVEMENT, EFFECTIVE COMMUNICATION
transmisuble, transmissible
transmit,*,tted,tting,ttable,ttal,ttance, ttancy,tter,ission,issible, PASS FROM ONE TO ANOTHER
transmitable, transmit(ttable)
transmiter, transmit(tter)
transmition, transmission
transmitle, transmit(ttal)
transmituble, transmit(ttable)
transmutachen, transmute(tation)
transmute,*,ted,ting,ter,table, tableness,tability,tably,tation,tative, TRANSFORM/CHANGE FROM ONE FORM TO ANOTHER
transmutible, transmute(table)
transmutuble, transmute(table)
transom,*,med, BEAM/CROSSBOAR, VENTILATION WINDOW
transparensy, transparent(ncy)
transparent,*,tly,tness,ncy,ncies, CLEAR, ALLOWS VISUAL PENETRATION
transparint, transparent
transperinsy, transparent(ncy)
transperint, transparent
transpertashen, transport(ation)
transpire,*,ed,ring,rable,ratory, SWEAT/PERSPIRE, TO HAPPEN, COME ABOUT
transpirtachen, transport(ation)
transpirtasion, transport(ation)
transplant,*,ted,ting,table,tation,ter, MOVE/TRANSFER FROM ONE LOCATION TO ANOTHER
transplantuble, transplant(able)
transponder,*, A RADIO
transporduble, transport(able)
transport,*,ted,ting,tability,table,ter, tation,tive, CARRY/RELOCATE
transportashen, transport(ation)
transportuble, transport(able)
transpose,*,ed,sing,sable,sition,sitional, MOVE
transpoz, transpose
transpurtachen, transport(ation)
transpuzishen, transpose(sition)
transum, transom
transutif, transit(ive)
transutory, transit(ory)
transverse,*,ely,sal,sally, LYING ACROSS THE SAME LINE TWICE, CROSSING
transvurs, transverse
tranuble, train(able)
tranur, train(er)
tranzacktion, transact(ion)
tranzakt, transact
tranzatef, transit(ive)
tranzbirtashen, transport(ation)
tranzblant, transplant
tranzbonder, transponder
tranzbort, transport
tranzbortuble, transport(able)
tranzdukshen, transduction
tranzdusir, transduce(r)
tranzeant, transient
tranzechen, transit(ion)
tranzekt, transect
tranzendentul, transcend(ental)
tranzeshenul, transit(ional)
tranzeshin, transit(ion)
tranzestur, transistor
tranzet, transit
tranzetory, transit(ory)
tranzfeks, transfix
tranzfermashen, transform(ation)
tranzfeugen, transfuse(sion)
tranzfewshen, transfuse(sion)
tranzfewz, transfuse
tranzfex, transfix
tranzfikyerashen, transfigure(ration)
tranzfir, transfer
tranzfix, transfix
tranzform, transform
tranzformashen, transform(ation)
tranzformur, transform(er)
tranzfujin, transfuse(sion)
tranzfur, transfer
tranzfuruble, transfer(able)
tranzgres, transgress
tranzgreshen, transgress(ion)
tranzgresif, transgress(ive)
tranzichen, transit(ion)
tranzishenul, transit(ional)
tranzit, transit
tranzitional, transit(ional)
tranzitory, transit(ory)
tranzkribe, transcribe
tranzlachen, translate(tion)
tranzlade, translate
tranzladuble, translate(table)
tranzladur, translate(tor)
tranzlate, translate
tranzlater, translate(tor)
tranzlatible, translate(table)
tranzlation, translate(tion)
tranzlewsed, translucid
tranzlewsense, translucent(nce)
tranzlewsint, translucent
tranzlousent, translucent

tranzlousid, translucid
tranzlused, translucid
tranzlusense, translucent(nce)
tranzlusent, translucent
tranzmedable, transmit(ttable)
tranzmedur, transmit(tter)
tranzmeshin, transmission
tranzmesuble, transmissible
tranzmet, transmit
tranzmetuble, transmit(ttable)
tranzmetur, transmit(tter)
tranzmeut, transmute
tranzmewtashen, transmute(tation)
tranzmichen, transmission
tranzmidul, transmit(ttal)
tranzmidur, transmit(tter)
tranzmishen, transmission
tranzmision, transmission
tranzmisuble, transmissible
tranzmit, transmit
tranzmition, transmission
tranzmitur, transmit(tter)
tranzmutachen, transmute(tation)
tranzmutasion, transmute(tation)
tranzmute, transmute
tranzmutuble, transmute(table)
tranzpazichen, transpose(sition)
tranzperint, transparent
tranzplant, transplant
tranzplantuble, transplant(able)
tranzponder, transponder
tranzporduble, transport(able)
tranzport, transport
tranzportashen, transport(ation)
tranzpoz, transpose
tranzutif, transit(ive)
tranzvurs, transverse
trap,*,pped,pping,pper, CATCH/HOLD/ PREVENT SOMETHING FROM ITS NORMAL MOVEMENT/ACTION MUSICAL INSTRUMENT, DEVICE FOR TRAPPING "prefixes: en"
trapazoed, trapezoid
trapekul, tropic(al)
traper, trap(pper)
trapes, trapeze
trapeze,zist, A TYPE OF SWING
trapezoid,dal, A GEOMETRIC SHAPE
traphek, traffic
trapickul, tropic(al)
trapik, tropic
trapikul, tropic(al)
trapir, trap(pper)
trapizoed, trapezoid

trapse, traipse
trapur, trap(pper)
trapuzoed, trapezoid
tras, tray(s) / trace
trasabul, trace(able)
trase, trace / tray(s)
trash,hes,hed,hing,hily,hiness,hy, GARBAGE, DISPOSABLE/DISCARDED ITEMS
trashd, trash(ed)
trashe, trash(y)
trasible, trace(able)
trasuble, trace(able)
trat, trade / trait
trater, trade(r) / traitor
trats, trait(s) / trade(s)
tratur, trade(r) / traitor
trau, trough / trowel
traudishen, tradition
traudition, tradition
trauf, trough
traul, trawl/ troll/ trowel
traule, trolley
trauma,*,tic,tically,tism,tize,tizes,tized, tizing, SUDDEN/VIOLENT SHOCK TO THE SYSTEM
trausers, trousers
travail,*, ENDURE A HARDSHIP
travel,*,led,ling,ler, PHYSICALLY MOVE ABOUT/AWAY (or see travail) "prefixes: un"
traverse,*,ed,sing,sable,sal,ser, TO CROSS/ACCOMPLISH A BARRIER/ BOUNDARY
travesty,ties,tied,tying, RIDICULE BY DISTORTING/DEBASING/MOCKING AN ACTUAL EXPERIENCE
travil, travel
travirs, traverse
travisty, travesty
travler, travel(er)
travoste, travesty
travul, travel
travusde, travesty
trawl,*,led,ling,ler, BAITED HOOKS IN A LONG LINE/NET FOR CATCHING FISH (or see troll/trowel)
trawmu, trauma
trawpek, tropic
trawpekul, tropic(al)
trawpik, tropic
trawsers, trousers
trawt, trot / trout

tray,*, SHALLOW PAN WITH SIDES FOR CARRYING/HOLDING ITEMS "prefixes: under"
traykoma, trachoma
tre, tree / tray
treacherous,sly,sness, DANGEROUS FOR VARIETY OF REASONS
treachery,ries,rous, RISKY, OF TREASON/BETRAYAL/TRICKERY
tread,*,ded,ding,der,trod,trodden, HEAVY/SLOW WALK, SWIM IN PLACE, TIRE IMPRINT (or see tree(d)) "prefixes: re"
tready, treaty
treason,nable,nous,nably, BEFRIEND THE ENEMY
treasure,*,ed,ring,rable,er,ry, SOMETHING WORTHY/VALUABLE
treasury,ries, MANAGES MONEY "prefixes: sub"
treat,*,ted,ting,ter,table,tability,ty, tment, TASTY MORSEL TO EAT, PAY THE CHARGE/BILL FOR SOMEONE, TAKE FINANCIAL RESPONSIBILITY AS AN ACT OF KINDNESS "prefixes: en/ in/mis/pre/re"
treaty,ties,tise, WRITTEN SETTLEMENT OF AGREEMENT BETWEEN TWO POWERS/FACTIONS
treazen, treason
trebel, treble
trebeulashen, tribulation
trebeun, tribune
trebeut, tribute
trebeutery, tributary
trebewlashen, tribulation
trebewn, tribune
trebil, treble
treble,ed,ling, TREBLE CLEF, MUSICAL PITCH/NOTES, OF TRIPLE/THREE, SYMBOL
trebul, treble
trebulashen, tribulation
trebun, tribune
trebute, tribute
trebutery, tributary
trechirus, treacherous
trechury, treachery
treck, trek
tred, tread / tree(d) / treat
trede, treaty
tredid, tread(ed) / treat(ed) / trade(d)
tredment, treat(ment)
treduble, treat(able)

tree,*,eed,eeing,eeless,eelessness, LARGE WOODY PLANT (or see tread)
treety, treaty
treezin, treason
trefea, trivia
treger, treasure / trigger
tregery, treasury
tregunometry, trigonometry
tregur, treasure / trigger
trejere, treasury
trejur, treasure
trek,*,kked,kking,kker,kkie, TO JOURNEY/TRAVEL/MIGRATE SLOWLY
trekal, trickle
treked, trek(kked) / trick(ed)
trekil, trickle
trekinoses, trichinosis
trekir, trigger
trekol, trickle
trekoma, trachoma
trekt, trek(kked) / trick(ed)
trekul, trickle
trekur, trigger
trel, trill / trail
trelege, trilogy
treleim, trillium
treleon, trillion
treles, trellis
treleum, trillium
trelion, trillion
trelis, trellis
trellis,sed, DECORATIVE LATTICE
treluge, trilogy
trelus, trellis
trelyen, trillion
trem, trim
tremadik, trauma(tic)
tremar, tremor
trematik, trauma(tic)
trembil, tremble
tremble,*,ed,ling,er,lingly, VIBRATE/ SHAKE INVOLUNTARILY
trembul, tremble
tremd, trim(mmed)
tremendous,sly,sness, SUBSTANTIAL IN SIZE/AMOUNT
tremendus, tremendous
tremer, trim(mmer) / tremor
tremindus, tremendous
tremor,*,rous, INVOLUNTARY VIBRATION/SHAKING, RESULT OF EARTH CRUST MOVEMENT (or see trim(mmer))
trempul, tremble
tremur, trim(mmer) / tremor
trench,hes,hed,hing,her,hable,hment, hable,hment, DITCH/FURROW DUG INTO A FLAT SURFACE "prefixes: en/re/un"
trend,*,dy, A TEMPORARY MOVEMENT IN DESIGN/ CLOTHING/STYLE "prefixes: up"
trende, trend(y)
trenedy, trinity
trenity, trinity
trenket, trinket
trenkit, trinket
trensh, trench
trent, trend
trente, trend(y)
trenute, trinity
treo, trio
trep, trip
trepul, triple / treble
tresal, trestle
tresen, treason
treser, treasure
tresere, treasury
treshery, treachery / treasury
treshure, treachery / treasure
treshures, treacherous
tresil, trestle
tresin, treason
tresir, treasure
tresle, trestle
treson, treason
trespas, trespass
trespass,sses,ssed,ssing,sser, ENTER ONTO PROPERTY WITHOUT INVITATION/ PERMISSION
tresspas, trespass
trestle,*, SUPPORT FRAME/BEAM
tresul, trestle
tresun, treason
tresure, treasure / treasury
tret, treat
trete, treaty
tretid, tread(ed) / treat(ed) / trade(d)
tretment, treat(ment)
tretuble, treat(able)
treuth, truth
trevail, travail
trevet, trivet
treveul, trivia(l)
trevia, trivia
trevit, trivet
treviul, trivia(l)
trew, drew / true
trewant, truant
trewbador, troubadour
trewent, truant
trewezm, true(uism)
trewint, truant
trewly, true(uly)
trewp, troop / troupe
trewpur, troop(er)
trews, truce
trewth, truth
trezen, treason
trezer, treasure
trezery, treasury
trezpas, trespass
trezun, treason
trezure, treasure / treasury
tri, PREFIX INDICATING "THREE" MOST OFTEN MODIFIES THE WORD (or see try)
triad,*,dic,dically, CONSISTING OF THREE PARTS/ELEMENTS
trial,*, A MOMENT/PERIOD/PLACE OF CONSIDERATION/ REVIEW/ JUDGEMENT "prefixes: mis/re/under"
triamverite, triumvirate
triangewlate, triangular(ate)
triangewlur, triangular
triangle,*, THREE SIDED GEOMETRIC SHAPE
triangul, triangle
triangular,rity,rly,ate,ates,ated,ating,ation, MAKE INTO THREE SIDES/ PARTS/ AREAS
triankl, triangle
triankulate, triangular(ate)
triankuler, triangular
triat, triad
trib, tribe
tribe,*,bal,bally,balism,balistic, PEOPLE OF A SOCIETY WHO SHARE COMMON BELIEFS/VALUES/ MORALS "prefixes: de/sub"
tribel, tribe(bal)
tribeun, tribune
tribeunul, tribune(nal)
tribeut, tribute
tribeutary, tributary
tribewlashen, tribulation
tribewn, tribune
tribewnul, tribune(nal)

tribewtery, tributary
tribul, tribe(bal)
tribulation, TRIAL/STRESS/TROUBLE
tribune,*,nal,eship,nate, THAT WHICH CHAMPIONS PEOPLES RIGHTS, COURT OF LAW, A PLATFORM
tribunel, tribune(nal)
tribunul, tribune(nal)
tributary,ries,rily, FLOWING/ STREAMING OF LIQUID/ WATER/ RESOURCES/MONEY WHICH FEEDS/ MOVES INTO A LARGER BODY
tribute,*,ulation, TO OFFER/SUPPLY GRATITUDE/MONEY
triceps, ARM MUSCLES
trichanosis, trichinosis
trichinosis, DISEASE IN INTESTINES CAUSED BY WORMS
trichunosis, trichinosis
trick,*,ked,king,ker,kery,keries,ky, kiness, PRANK/HOAX (or see trek)
trickle,*,ed,ling, TINY FLOWING STREAM
trickunosis, trichinosis
tricycle,*,ed,ling, THREE WHEELED BIKE
trid, tried / trite
trident,*,tate,tal, THREE PRONGED FORK/BARB, BALLISTIC MISSILE SYSTEM
tridint, trident
tried, PAST TENSE FOR THE WORD "TRY", INSIGHTED FOR A CRIME, TESTED (or see trite) "prefixes: un"
triel, trial
triemverat, triumvirate
triemverint, triumvirate
trieng, try(ing)
trifea, trivia
trifil, trifle
trifle,*,ed,ling,er,lingly,lingness, SMALL/ MINIMAL AMOUNT, NOT TAKE SERIOUSLY, IDLE TIME
triful, trifle
trigar, trigger
trigenometry, trigonometry
trigger,*,red,ring,rless, PART OF GUN WHICH RELEASES BULLET
trigonometry, MATH WITH SYMBOLS/ DESIGNS
trigur, trigger
trihedras,al,ron, OF THREE INTERSECTING LINES
trihedril, trihedron(ral)

trihedron,*,ras,ral, THREE INTERSECTING LINES
trihedrul, trihedron(ral)
trik, trick
trikal, trickle
trikanosis, trichinosis
trikel, trickle
trikenoses, trichinosis
trikery, trick(ery)
trikul, trickle
trikure, trick(ery)
triky, trick(y)
tril, trial / trill
trilabit, trilobite
triladerul, trilateral
trilateral,lity,lly, THREE SIDED
trilaturil, trilateral
trilebit, trilobite
trilege, trilogy
trilengwul, trilingual
trileon, trillion
trileum, trillium
trilingual,lly, THREE LANGUAGES
trilingwul, trilingual
trilion, trillion
trilium, trillium
trill, TYPE OF SOUND
trillion,*,nth, ONE MILLION TIMES ONE MILLION
trillium, A LAWFULLY PROTECTED PLANT
trilobite,*,tic, EXTINCT ARTHROPOD, THREE LOBES
trilogy,gies, THREE PARTS TOGETHER IN A MUSICAL/LITERARY/FILMED/ DRAMATIC WORK
trilubit, trilobite
triluge, trilogy
trilyun, trillion
trim,*,mmed,mming,mmer, TO REMOVE EXCESS, CREATE A CLEAN/ TIDY/ FINISHED APPEARANCE
trimer, trim(mmer) / tremor
trimur, trim(mmer) / tremor
trin, trine
trinch, trench
trind, trend
trine,*,nal,nity, OF THREE PARTS
trinedy, trinity
tring, try(ing)
trinity,ties, OF THREE PARTS
trinket,*, SMALL KNICK KNACK/ ORNAMENT
trinsh, trench

trint, trend
trio,*, THREE PARTS
trip,*,pped,pping,pper,ppingly, JOURNEY AWAY FROM, STUMBLE (too many definitions, please see standard dictionary) (or see tripe)
tripal, triple
tripd, trip(pped)
tripe, COW/SHEEP STOMACH, POOR IN QUALITY
tripel, triple
tripewlashen, tribulation
triple,*,ed,ling,ly,let,licate,lication, THREE OF, THREE TIMES/FOLD
tripod,*, THREE LEGGED
tripol, triple
tripot, tripod
tripul, triple
tripulashen, tribulation
tripuld, triple(d)
trisebs, triceps
trisekel, tricycle
triseps, triceps
trisycle, tricycle
trit, tried / trite / treat
trite,ely,eness, OF LITTLE INTEREST IN (or see tried)
tritle, trite(ly)
tritly, trite(ly)
tritnes, trite(ness)
triul, trial
triumf, triumph
triumfent, triumph(ant)
triumph,*,hal,hant,hantly, A GAIN/ VICTORY/SUCCESS
triumphent, triumph(ant)
triumvaret, triumvirate
triumvirate, GROUP OF THREE
triveal, trivia(l)
trivet,*, STAND WITH THREE LEGS
triveu, trivia
triveul, trivia(l)
trivia,al,alness,ality,alities,alization,alize, ally, INSIGNIFICANT/UNIMPORTANT
trivit, trivet
troc, truck
trod,*,dden, PAST TENSE FOR THE WORD "TREAD", WALK HEAVILY/ SLOWLY WITH NO AMBITION (or see trot)
troden, trod(dden) / trot(tting)
trodeshinul, tradition(al)
trodin, trod(dden) / trot(tting)
trodition, tradition

troditional, tradition(al)
troe, troy
trof, trough / trove
trofe, trophy
trofl, truffle
trofy, trophy
trogectery, traject(ory)
troi, troy
trojektery, traject(ory)
trok, truck
trol, trawl / troll / trowel
trole, trolley / troll
troll,*,ller, TYPE OF SINGING, DRAGGING A HOOK, IMAGINARY CREATURE (or see trawl)
trolley,*, A CART/VEHICLE WITH WHEELS ON RAILS
troly, trolley
troma, trauma
tromatizd, trauma(tized)
trombone,*, A MUSICAL INSTRUMENT
tromel, trommel
trommel, ROUND SCREEN FOR SEPARATING VARIOUS SIZES OF ORGANIC MATERIAL
tromp,*,ped,ping, BIG/HEAVY FOOT STEPS, BEAT SOMEONE EXCESSIVELY (or see trump)
trompet, trumpet
tromu, trauma
tromul, trommel
tromutize, trauma(tize)
troobudor, troubadour
troop,*,ped,ping,per, AN ASSEMBLY/ GROUP/FLOCK (or see troupe)
troos, truce
tropeckul, tropic(al)
tropek, tropic
tropekul, tropic(al)
tropes, trapeze
trophe, trophy
trophy,hies,hic, MOUNTED HEAD OF ANIMAL, A COIN/ FIGURINE DESIGNED FOR AWARD/ ACHIEVEMENT
tropic,*,cal,cally, CONTINUOUS WARM WEATHER CLIMATE "prefixes: inter/ semi/sub"
tropickul, tropic(al)
tropik, tropic
tropikul, tropic(al)
trost, trust

trot,*,tted,tting,tter, STYLE OF WALKING/RUNNING (or see trout/ trod)
trotin, trod(dden) / trot(tting)
troubadour, POETS OF ANTIQUITY
trouble,*,ed,ling,esome,esomely, esomeness,lous, DIFFICULT/ CHALLENGING "prefixes: un"
trouf, trough / trove
trough,*, VESSEL FOR ANIMALS TO FEED/DRINK, RECTANGULAR/ SHALLOW CHANNEL/SHAPE
troul, trowel / troll
troupe,*,ped,ping, THEATER GROUP/ PERFORMERS (or see troop)
trousers, PANTS
trout, TYPE OF FISH
trouwl, trowel
trove,*, A FIND / DISCOVERY
trovers, traverse
trowel,*,led,ling,ler, HAND TOOL TO WORK PLASTER/MUD/MORTAR
trowsers, trousers
trowt, trout
trowzurs, trousers
troy, MEASUREMENT FOR WEIGHT OF PRECIOUS METALS
tru, true / through / thru / drew
truant,*,tly,ncy, NOT AT SCHOOL WITHOUT GOOD REASON
trubador, troubadour
trubel, trouble
trubidor, troubadour
trubudor, troubadour
trubul, trouble
truc, truck / truce
truce, COME TO AGREEMENT AFTER FIGHT/ARGUMENT (or see truss)
truch, trudge
truck,*,ked,king,ker, VEHICLE FOR HAULING/MOVING
trudeshin, tradition
trudeshinul, tradition(al)
trudge,*,ed,ging, WALK SLOWLY WITH HEAVY FEET
trudishenul, tradition(al)
trudition, tradition
truditional, tradition(al)
true,uly,uism,eness,uth, ACCURATE/ FACTUAL/REAL/STRAIGHT UP/ON THE LEVEL "prefixes: un"
truent, truant
truews, truce
truezm, true(uism)

trufal, truffle
truffle,*,ed, AN EDIBLE FUNGI, A CANDY
truful, truffle
trug, trudge
trugekt, traject
trugektery, traject(ory)
truint, truant
truizm, true(uism)
truj, trudge
trujd, trudge(d)
trujectery, traject(ory)
trujekt, traject
trujektery, traject(ory)
truk, truck
truker, truck(er)
trule, true(uly)
trumadik, trauma(tic)
trumendus, tremendous
trumindus, tremendous
trump,*,ped,ping,per,pery, OVERRANK/ SURPASS/DECEIVE (or see tromp)
trumpd, trump(ed) / tromp(ed)
trumpet,*,ter, BRASS HORNED INSTRUMENT
trumput, trumpet
trunc, trunk
truncate,*,ed,ting,tion, CUT OFF TIP/ END/PART OF, CUT SHORT
trundel, trundle
trundle,er, CIRCLE/WHEEL FOR ROTATION
trundul, trundle
trunk,*, MAIN BODY/PART FROM WHICH ALL THINGS EXTEND BEYOND, CONTAINER FOR ITEMS, ELEPHANT NOSE
trunkate, truncate
trupe, troop / troupe
trupel, trouble
truper, troop(er)
trupes, trapeze
trupir, troop(er)
trupl, trouble
trups, troop(s) / troupe(s)
trupul, trouble
trupur, troop(er)
trus, truce / truss
truse, truce / truss
truss,sses,sser, TO BOLSTER/SECURE/ SUPPORT WITH BEAMS/TIES/ROPE (or see truce)
trust,*,ted,ting,tee,tful,tfully,tfulness,ty, tiness, PLACE HOPE/ FAITH/BELIEF/

CONFIDENCE IN "prefixes: dis/en/mis"
truste, trust(y)
truth,*,hless,hful,hfully,hfulness, ACCEPTED AS FACT/CONSTANCY/ACTUAL "prefixes: un"
truvale, travail
truvers, traverse
truwent, truant
truz, truce / truss
try,ries,ried,ying,yingly, PUT TO THE TEST, ATTEMPT, DIFFICULT/CHALLENGE TO ACCOMPLISH "prefixes: re"
tryd, tried / trite
trydent, trident
tryeng, try(ing)
tryn, trine
tsunami,ic, GIGANTIC TIDAL WAVE
tsunome, tsunami
tu, two / to / too
tub,*,bbable,bby,bbier,bbiest,bbiness, LARGE VESSEL/CONTAINER FOR LIQUID, ROUND LIKE A TUB (or see tube)
tuba,*, HORNED INSTRUMENT
tubaco, tobacco
tubagen, toboggan
tubako, tobacco
tube,*,ed,bing,er,eless,erous,bular, bularity,bule,bulous, CYLINDER/ROUND SHAPE (or see tub)
tubequlosis, tuberculosis
tuberculosis,ous,ously, DISEASE OF THE LUNGS
tuberquelosis, tuberculosis
tubeulur, tube(bular)
tubir, tube(ber)
tubirquelosis, tuberculosis
tubles, tube(less)
tubogin, toboggan
tubu, tuba
tubur, tube(ber)
tuby, tub(bby)
tuc, took / tuck
tuch, touch / tush
tucha, touche'
tuche, touch(y) / touche'
tuchible, touch(able)
tuck,*,ked,king,ker,kered, TO PULL/SECURE EDGES, PLACE AWAY SAFELY, WEARY/TIRED FROM WORKING
tuda, today

tuder, tutor
tudur, tutor
tuel, tool
tuesday,*, A DAY OF THE WEEK (ENGLISH)
tuf, tough
tufen, tough(en)
tufer, tough(er)
tufest, tough(est)
tuff, tough
tufin, tough(en)
tufir, tough(er)
tufist, tough(est)
tuft,*,ty,tier,tiest, CLUMP/CLUSTER/BUNCH OF THREADS/ HAIR/MATERIAL/ FUR
tufun, tough(en)
tufur, tough(er)
tug,*,gged,gging, TO PULL/DRAG/HAUL
tugethur, together
tugt, tug(gged)
tuil, tool
tuk, tuck / tug / took
tukd, tuck(ed) / tug(gged)
tuke, took
tukela, tequila
tukila, tequila
tuksedo, tuxedo
tuksido, tuxedo
tukt, tuck(ed) / tug
tukurd, tuck(ered)
tul, tool
tule, tool
tulep, tulip
tuleputhee, telepathy
tulip,*, A FLOWER
tum, tomb
tumaro, tomorrow
tumato, tomato
tumauro, tomorrow
tumbel, tumble
tumble,*,ed,ling,er, BE TOSSED ABOUT, A DRINKING VESSEL/CAM/LOCKING PART, BOLT ACTION, ACROBATICS
tumblir, tumble(r)
tumbul, tumble
tumer, tumor
tumerus, tumor(ous)
tumor,*,rous, A CLUMP/MASS OF TISSUE
tumoro, tomorrow
tumulchewus, tumult(uous)
tumulchuis, tumult(uous)

tumult,tuary,tuous,tuously,tuousness, DISTURBANCE/AGITATED/DISORDER
tumures, tumor(ous)
tun, tune / toon / ton
tuna,*, SALT WATER FISH
tunacity, tenacity
tunaledy, tone(nality)
tunasedy, tenacity
tunasity, tenacity
tundra, ARCTIC PLAINS AROUND NORTH/SOUTH POLES
tundru, tundra
tune,*,ed,ning,er,eful,efully,efulness, eless, SET/ADJUST HARMONY/FREQUENCY (or see toon) "prefixes: de"
tuneg, ton(nnage)
tunej, ton(nnage)
tunek, tunic
tunel, tunnel
tungsten,nic, METAL ELEMENT, TYPE OF FILAMENT IN LIGHT BULBS
tungstin, tungsten
tunic,*, LONG GARMENT, A COVERING
tunig, ton(nnage)
tunij, ton(nnage)
tunil, tunnel
tunir, tune(r)
tunite, tonight
tunl, tunnel
tunnel,*,led,ling,ler, TUBULAR SHAPED OPENING GOING INTO A SURFACE
tunor, tune(r)
tuns, tune(s) / ton(s) / toon(s)
tunsten, tungsten
tunstun, tungsten
tunt, tune(d)
tuntru, tundra
tunu, tuna
tunuk, tunic
tunul, tunnel
tunur, tune(r)
tup, tub
tupa, toupee
tupagrufe, topography
tupay, toupee
tupe, tube / tub(bby)
tupht, tuft
tupography, topography
tupogrufe, topography
tupuler, tube(bular)
tuquela, tequila
tuquila, tequila

tur, tour
turain, terrain / terrane
turanchula, tarantula
turane, terrain / terrane
turanshulu, tarantula
turantula, tarantula
turareum, terrarium
turazo, terrazzo
turban,*, LONG SCARF WRAPPED AS A HEADDRESS (or see turbine)
turben, turban / turbine
turbeulent, turbulent
turbin, turban / turbine
turbine,*, MOTOR WITH ROTORS SUPPLIED BY A CONSTANT FLOW (or see turban)
turbo,*, POWERED BY/AS IF BY A TURBINE MOTOR
turbon, turban / turbine
turbulens, turbulent(nce)
turbulent,tly,nce, ROUGH/ERRATIC/ RANDOM FLOW
turcoys, turquois
turd, tour(ed)
turdul, turtle
ture, tour
turefic, terrific
turenshul, torrent(ial)
turereum, terrarium
turesdreul, terrestrial
turestrial, terrestrial
turet, turret
turf,*,fy,fier,fiest, GRASS/ORGANIC MATERIAL FORMING A SURFACE BLANKET
turifek, terrific
turific, terrific
turist, tour(ist)
turisum, tour(ism)
turit, turret
turkes, turkey(s)
turkey,*, EDIBLE BIRD
turkie, turkey
turkois, turquois
turky, turkey
turm, term
turmaric, turmeric
turmenashen, terminate(tion)
turmenate, terminate
turmenator, terminate(tor)
turmenolegy, terminology
turmenul, terminal
turmeric, SPICE FROM A PLANT
turmeruk, turmeric

turminashen, terminate(tion)
turminate, terminate
turmination, terminate(tion)
turminator, terminate(tor)
turminolegy, terminology
turminul, terminal
turmoel, turmoil
turmoil, STATE OF STRESS/CONFUSION
turmonel, terminal
turn,*,ned,ning, CHANGE DIRECTION, ROTATE/CURVE/BEND IN COURSE "prefixes: over/up"
turnado, tornado
turnament, tournament
turnato, tornado
turnep, turnip
turniment, tournament
turnip,*, A VEGETABLE
turnument, tournament
turpentine, MINERAL SPIRIT WITH VOLATILE OIL
turpewlent, turbulent
turpulent, turbulent
turpuntine, turpentine
turquois, BLUE/GREEN GEMSTONE
turrestrial, terrestrial
turret,*, CYLINDRICAL OUTCROP AS SEEN ON CASTLES
turse, terse
tursheare, tertiary
turshury, tertiary
tursnes, terse(ness)
turtle,*, REPTILE WITH A SHELL
turut, turret
tusday, tuesday
tush,hes, REAR END, BUTTOCK (or see touch)
tusha, touche'
tusk,*,ked, LARGE EXTERIOR TOOTH
tusled, tousle(d)
tute, toot
tuter, tutor
tuth, tooth
tuthee, tooth(y)
tuthles, tooth(less)
tutir, tutor
tutolatarian, totalitarian
tutor,*,red,ring,rage,rial,elage, TO MENTOR/TEACH OR BE A GUARDIAN OF SOMEONE "prefixes: un"
tutu,*, OUTER GARMENT DANCERS WEAR
tutur, tutor

tuxedo, FORMAL ATTIRE FOR MEN
twain, RIVERBOAT TERM
twalth, twelfth
twan, twain
twang,gy, A VIBRATIONAL TONE
twank, twang
twead, tweed
tweak,*,ked,king,ker,ky, TO ADJUST
tweat, tweet
tweazer, tweezer
twed, tweed
twede, tweed(y)
tweder, tweeter
twedul, twiddle
twedur, tweeter
tweed,*,dy,dier,diest,diness, TYPE OF WOOL/WEAVE
tweek, tweak
tweenkul, twinkle
tweet,*, SOUND OF A BIRD
tweeter, TYPE OF SPEAKER FOR SOUND EQUIPMENT
tweezer,*, TOOL FOR PLUCKING/ PINCHING
tweg, twig
twek, tweak / twig
tweke, tweak(y)
twelf, twelve
twelfth,*, ONE OUT OF TWELVE
twelth, twelfth
twelve,*, ENGLISH NUMBER AFTER ELEVEN
twelvth, twelfth
twen, twin
twench, twinge
twende, twenty
twenge, twinge
twenj, twinge
twenkul, twinkle
twenteith, twentieth
twentes, twenty(ties)
twentie, twenty
twentieth, ONE PART OF TWENTY PARTS
twenty,ties,tieth, ENGLISH NUMBER AFTER NINETEEN
twentys, twenty(ties)
twerl, twirl
twerp, A DEROGATORY SLANG
tweser, tweezer
twest, twist
twesur, tweezer
twet, tweet
twetur, tweeter

twezer, tweezer
twhirl, twirl
twice, TWO TIMES
twidal, twiddle
twiddle,*,ed,ding,er, TO ROTATE ONE AROUND ANOTHER, IDLY TOY WITH SOMETHING
twidul, twiddle
twig,*,ggy, PART OF A WOODY BRANCH
twik, twig
twilid, twilight
twilight, SUNSET/SUNRISE
twilite, twilight
twin,*, TWO IDENTICAL/SIMILAR (or see twine)
twinch, twinge
twindy, twenty
twine,*,ed,ning, BRAIDED/TWISTED ROPE/THREAD (or see twin) "prefixes: en/inter"
twinge,*,ed,ging, SHARP/SUDDEN JERK RELATED TO PAINFUL SCENE/ EXPERIENCE
twinj, twinge
twinkal, twinkle
twinkle,*,ed,ling,er, SPARKLE/GLEAM OF LIGHT
twintieth, twentieth
twinty, twenty
twirl,*,led,ling,ler,ly, SPIN/WHIRL AROUND
twirp,*, DEROGATORY SLANG
twis, twice
twist,*,ted,ting,ter,ty, COILED ROTATION IN ACTION "prefixes: en/ in/inter/re"
two,*, ENGLISH NUMBER AFTER ONE (or see too/to)
twoberkeuloses, tuberculosis
twobu, tuba
twobuler, tube(bular)
twocha, touche'
twonik, tunic
twonu, tuna
twopa, toupee
tworl, twirl
twotwo, tutu
twurl, twirl
twurp, twerp / twirp
ty, tie
tydengs, tidings
tyeng, tying
tyfoed, typhoid
tyfus, typhus

tying, PRESENT PARTICIPLE FOR THE WORD 'TIE', TO FASTEN/LOOP/ ATTACH STRING/CORD, TO AFFIX "prefixes: re/un/under"
tyk, tike / tick
tynkshur, tincture
type,*,ed,ping,er,eable,eability,pist, USE OF A MACHINE TO CREATE TEXT (or see tip) "prefixes: mis/pre/ re/sub/un"
typecul, typical
typefy, typify
typhis, typhus
typhoid, DISEASE OF THE INTESTINES
typhoon,*, HURRICANE
typhus,hous, A DISEASE CAUSED BY FLEAS
typical,lly,lness,lity, PREDICTABLE/ CHARACTERISTIC
typicul, typical
typify,fies,fied,fying,fication, SYMBOLIZES
typikul, typical
typo,*, TEXT ERROR
typukle, typical
tyrane, tyranny
tyranekal, tyrannical
tyranikul, tyrannical
tyrannical,lly,lness, OF BEING CRUEL/ PREDATORY
tyranny,nnies,nnous,nnously, nnousness,nnize,nnizes,nnized, nnizing,nnizer, nnic,nnical,nnically, nnicalness,nnicide, EVENT INVOLVING CRUEL/VICIOUS PREDATOR WHO EXPLOITS VICTIMS
tyrant,*,nny, CRUEL VICIOUS PREDATOR, ONE WHO EXPLOITS VICTIMS
tyreny, tyranny
u, you / yew / ewe
ubart, apart
ubat, abate
ubatment, abate(ment)
ubedeins, obedience
ubedeint, obedient
ubeding, abet(tting)
ubedy, uppity
ubel, appeal
ubelaty, ability
ubelte, ability
ubet, abet
ubeting, abet(tting)
ubikwety, ubiquity

ubilde, ability
ubiledy, ability
ubilte, ability
ubiquity,tous,tary,tously,tousness, OMNIPRESENT, EXISTS EVERYWHERE
ubity, uppity
ubleveus, oblivious
ubli, apply
ublid, apply(lied)
ublig, oblige(d)
ublij, oblige(d)
ubliveus, oblivious
ubliz, apply(lies)
ubolesh, abolish
ubord, aboard / abort
uborded, abort(ed)
ubort, abort / aboard
ubprnetis, apprentice
ubpropreat, appropriate
ubrenis, apprentice
ubresheate, appreciate
ubreshen, oppress(ion)
ubretiate, appreciate
ubreveashen, abbreviate(tion)
ubreveat, abbreviate
ubriged, abridged
ubroch, approach
ubrod, abroad
ubroof, approve
ubropreat, appropriate
ubrosh, approach
ubruf, approve
ubruv, approve
ubsakwently, subsequent(ly)
ubserd, absurd
ubsesd, obsess(ed)
ubseshen, obsess(ion)
ubset, upset
ubsolv, absolve
ubstane, abstain
ubstrakshen, obstruct(ion) / abstract(ion)
ubstrukt, obstruct
ubtane, obtain
ubtrude, obtrude
ubtrusive, obtrusive
ubzerd, absurd
ubzerve, observe
ubzolv, absolve
ubzorb, absorb
ubzurv, observe
ucemble, assemble
ucend, ascend

ucenshen, ascension
uchamed, ashamed
ucher, assure
ucide, aside
ucimbul, assemble
ucinshen, ascension
ucompany, accompany
ucumpany, accompany
ucumulate, accumulate
udalize, utilize
udapt, adapt
udder,*, TEATS ON A MILKING ANIMALS (or see utter)
udendum, addendum
uder, odor / otter / outer / utter / udder
uderus, uterus
udeshen, edition / add(ition)
udindum, addendum
udir, odor / otter / outer / utter / udder
udirens, utter(ance)
udirus, uterus
udishen, edition / add(ition)
udopt, adopt
udor, udder / utter / adore / odor/ otter
udrausety, atrocity
udroit, adroit
udrosity, atrocity
udulize, utilize
udur, odor / otter / outer / utter / udder
ufael, avail
ufermutif, affirm(ative)
ufeshent, efficient
ufileashen, affiliate(tion)
ufileate, affiliate
ufishent, efficient
ugilede, agile(ty)
ugilety, agile(ty)
ugle, ugly
ugleist, ugly(liest)
ugleur, ugly(lier)
ugly,lies,lier,liest, UNATTRACTIVE
ugre, agree
ugresev, aggressive
ugreshen, aggression
ugresuv, aggressive
ugretion, aggression
uhbart, apart
uhbli, apply
uhblid, apply(lied)
uhbliz, apply(lies)
uhbprnetis, apprentice

uhbpropreat, appropriate
uhbrenis, apprentice
uhbresheate, appreciate
uhbreshete, appreciate
uhbretiate, appreciate
uhbroch, approach
uhbroof, approve
uhbropreat, appropriate
uhbrosh, approach
uhbruhf, approve
uhcemble, assemble
uhcend, ascend
uhcenshen, ascension
uhchamed, ashamed
uhcher, assure
uhcide, aside
uhcimbul, assemble
uhcinshen, ascension
uhdrausety, atrocity
uhdrosity, atrocity
uhod, ahold
uhold, ahold
uhpairent, apparent
uhpairul, apparel
uhpalugize, apology(gize)
uhpalugy, apology(gize)
uhparent, apparent
uhpart, apart
uhpartment, apartment
uhparul, apparel
uhpastrufe, apostrophe
uhpauluge, apology
uhpaulugize, apology(gize)
uhpaurtment, apartment
uhpaustrufe, apostrophe
uhpealing, appeal(ing)
uhpearanc, appearance
uhpearinse, appearance
uhpeel, appeal
uhpel, appeal
uhperense, appearance
uhperent, apparent
uhperinse, appearance
uhperul, apparel
uhpil, appeal
uhplaud, applaud
uhplaus, applause
uhpli, apply
uhplod, applaud
uhplos, applause
uhpoent, appoint
uhpoentment, appointment
uhpoint, appoint
uhpointment, appointment

uhpoluge, apology
uhpolugize, apology(gize)
uhport, apart
uhportment, apartment
uhpostrufe, apostrophe
uhpotment, appointment
uhpoynt, appoint
uhppearanc, appearance
uhpperinse, appearance
uhpperul, apparel
uhpplaud, applaud
uhpplause, applause
uhpplod, applaud
uhpply, apply
uhpprentis, apprentice
uhppreshiate, appreciate
uhppropriate, appropriate
uhpprove, approve
uhpproximate, approximate
uhpproximately, approximate(ly)
uhpraisul, appraisal
uhprased, appraise(d)
uhpraz, appraise
uhprazul, appraisal
uhpreceashun, appreciate(tion)
uhprecheat, appreciate
uhpreciate, appreciate
uhprenis, apprentice
uhprentis, apprentice
uhpresheate, appreciate
uhpresheation, appreciate(tion)
uhpreshete, appreciate
uhpreshetion, appreciate(tion)
uhpretiate, appreciate
uhprintes, apprentice
uhprisheate, appreciate
uhproach, approach
uhprobreat, appropriate
uhproch, approach
uhproksamit, approximate
uhproksamitly, approximate(ly)
uhproksumit, approximate
uhproksumitly, approximate(ly)
uhproof, approve
uhproovul, approve(val)
uhpropreit, appropriate
uhprosh, approach
uhproximate, approximate
uhproximatly, approximate(ly)
uhpruhf, approve
uhpruhval, approve(val)
uhrain, arraign
uhraingment, arrange(ment)
uhrainment, arraign(ment)

uhrane, arraign
uhrangment, arrange(ment)
uhranjment, arrange(ment)
uhranment, arraign(ment)
uhrear, arrear
uhreighnment, arraign(ment)
uhreinment, arraign(ment)
uhrena, arena
uhrer, arrear
uhrest, arrest
uhriful, arrival
uhrina, arena
uhrivul, arrival
uhroma, aroma
uhround, around
uhrouz, arouse
uhrownd, around
uhrows, arouse
uhrrear, arrear
uhrrest, arrest
uhrrivol, arrival
uhsacin, assassin
uhsail, assail
uhsal, assail
uhsalant, assail(ant)
uhsalt, assault
uhsasen, assassin
uhsault, assault
uhsberugus, asparagus
uhscend, ascend
uhscention, ascension
uhsdonesh, astonish
uhsdrawnumy, astronomy
uhsdronumy, astronomy
uhsemble, assemble
uhsemelate, assimilate
uhsemilate, assimilate
uhsemlate, assimilate
uhsend, ascend
uhsenshen, ascension
uhsent, assent
uhsention, ascension
uhsershen, assert(ion)
uhsert, assert
uhsertion, assert(ion)
uhses, assess / use(s)
uhsesment, assessment
uhsest, assist
uhsestens, assist(ance)
uhsestins, assist(ance)
uhseum, assume
uhsfekseate, asphyxiate
uhshamed, ashamed
uhside, aside

uhsign, assign
uhsilem, asylum
uhsimbul, assemble
uhsimelate, assimilate
uhsin, assign
uhsind, ascend
uhsinment, assignment
uhsinshen, ascension
uhsint, assent
uhsirshen, assert(ion)
uhsirt, assert
uhsirtion, assert(ion)
uhsist, assist
uhsistens, assist(ance)
uhsleep, asleep
uhslep, asleep
uhsocheat, associate
uhsocheation, associate(tion)
uhsociate, associate
uhsociation, associate(tion)
uhsolt, assault
uhsosheashun, associate(tion)
uhsosheut, associate
uhsoshiat, associate
uhsoshiation, associate(tion)
uhsparugus, asparagus
uhsperugus, asparagus
uhsphikseate, asphyxiate
uhspire, aspire
uhssal, assail
uhssasin, assassin
uhssenble, assemble
uhstonish, astonish
uhstraunume, astronomy
uhstronumy, astronomy
uhstrownumy, astronomy
uhsum, assume
uhsumpshen, assumption
uhsur, assure
uhsurt, assert
uhsylim, asylum
uhtach, attach
uhtachment, attach(ment)
uhtack, attack
uhtain, attain
uhtainable, attain(able) / obtain(able)
uhtak, attack
uhtanable, attain(able) / obtain(able)
uhtane, attain
uhtanmint, attain(ment)
uhtash, attach
uhtempt, attempt
uhtemt, attempt
uhtend, attend

uhtendens, attend(ance)
uhtending, attend(ing)
uhtenshen, attention
uhtentef, attentive
uhtentefness, attentive(ness)
uhtention, attention
uhtentive, attentive
uhtimt, attempt
uhtind, attend
uhtindens, attend(ance)
uhtinding, attend(ing)
uhtinshen, attention
uhtintef, attentive
uhtintion, attention
uhtintive, attentive
uhtintiveness, attentive(ness)
uhtire, attire
uhtrausety, atrocity
uhtrochus, atrocious
uhtroshes, atrocious
uhtrosity, atrocity
uhwrest, arrest
uhwround, around
uhwrous, arouse
ujar, ajar
ujaur, ajar
ujiledy, agile(lity)
ujilety, agile(lity)
ujor, ajar
ukalale, ukulele
ukaumplish, accomplish
ukews, accuse
ukilale, ukulele
ukle, ugly
ukomplesh, accomplish
ukomplis, accomplice
ukomplish, accomplish
ukomudate, accommodate
ukord, accord
ukordant, accord(ant)
ukount, account
ukresif, aggressive
ukulale, ukulele
ukulayle, ukulele
ukulele,*, SMALL FOUR STRING GUITAR
ukumpany, accompany
ukumplish, accomplish
ukumulate, accumulate
ukumulation, accumulate(tion)
ukustemed, accustom(ed)
ukuz, accuse
ukwire, acquire
ularm, alarm

ulcer,*,red,rate,rated,rating,ration, rative,rous,rousness, FESTERED SORES IN THE LINING OF THE STOMACH
ulceradid, ulcer(ated)
ulcir, ulcer
ulcirashen, ulcer(ation)
ulcur, ulcer
uldamatum, ultimatum
uldamitle, ultimate(ly)
uldimatum, ultimatum
uldimetle, ultimate(ly)
uldrusonek, ultrasonic
uldumatum, ultimatum
uldumetle, ultimate(ly)
ule, you'll / yule
ulecit, elicit / illicit
uliens, alliance
ulif, alive
ulike, alike
ulin, align
ulinment, align(ment)
ulions, alliance
uliptic, elliptic
uliset, elicit / illicit
uliv, alive
uloof, aloof
ulope, elope
ulostrious, illustrious
ulow, allow
ulowanse, allowance
ulser, ulcer
ulseradid, ulcer(ated)
ulserashen, ulcer(ation)
ulsirashen, ulcer(ation)
ulsur, ulcer
ulsurashen, ulcer(ation)
ulsurated, ulcer(ated)
ultamatem, ultimatum
ultament, ultimate
ultametle, ultimate(ly)
ultemit, ultimate
ultereur, ulterior
ulterior,rly, UNDERLYING, SECRETIVE, NOT UP FRONT (or see alterior)
ultimate,ely,eness, THE GREATEST OF ALL
ultimatum,ta, FINAL, DO THIS OR A PENALTY RESULTS
ultimetly, ultimate(ly)
ultireor, ulterior
ultra, THE GREATEST/MOST/BEST/ EXTREME

ultrasonic,*, ABOVE 20,000 VIBRATIONS PER SECOND
ultru, ultra
ultrusonek, ultrasonic
ultumetle, ultimate(ly)
ultumint, ultimate
ultumit, ultimate
uluf, aloof
ulustrious, illustrious
um, them
umaunt, amount
umbelikul, umbilical
umbilical,ate,ated,ation, RELATING TO THE NAVEL
umbrella,*, DOME-SHAPED COVER FOR PROTECTION "prefixes: sub"
umeba, amoeba
umend, amend
umindment, amend(ment)
umonea, ammonia
umount, amount
umpede, impede
un, PREFIX INDICATING THAT "NOT/ REVERSAL" MOST OFTEN MODIFIES THE WORD (or see prefix in/en)
unable, NOT ABLE/CAPABLE(or see enable/inability)
unabridged, IN ITS FULL LENGTH
unabriged, unabridged
unacceptable, WILL NOT BE ALLOWED, NOT ACCEPTABLE
unacdev, enact(ive) / inactive
unacebtible, unacceptable
unacorn, unicorn
unacseptible, unacceptable
unactive, enact(ive) / inactive
unacurate, innacurate
unacycle, unicycle
unadime, anatomy
unafekachen, unification
unafi, unify
unafid, unify(fied)
unafiuble, unify(fiable)
unaform, uniform
unaformety, uniform(ity)
unaformly, uniform(ly)
unakdev, enact(ive)/ inactive
unakorn, unicorn
unakseptible, unacceptable
unaktef, inactive / enact(ive)
unaktive, enact(ive) / inactive
unakuret, inaccurate
unamoly, anomaly
unanamus, unanimous

unanimous,sly,mity, AGREED TO BY TWO OR MORE PEOPLE
unanomus, unanimous
unapel, unable
unapl, unable
unappreciative, inappreciative
unapresheative, inappreciative
unapropreat, inappropriate
unasen, unison
unasikle, unicycle
unasycle, unicycle
unat, innate
unate, unity
unaterein, unitary(rian)
unatery, unitary
unathekol, (un)ethic(al)
unathical, (un)ethic(al)
unatize, unite(tize)
unaty, unity
unaumily, anomaly
unavers, universe
unaversal, universal
unaversity, university
unaversule, universal(lly)
unavirs, universe
unavirsity, university
unavirsul, universal
unavurs, universe
unavursal, universal
unavursity, university
unaxseptible, unacceptable
unbanone, unbeknown
unbanonst, unbeknown(st)
unbeknown,nst, NOT KNOWN
unbenon, unbeknown
unbenonst, unbeknown(st)
unbenownst, unbeknown(st)
unbinone, unbeknown
unbinonst, unbeknown(st)
unbunownst, unbeknown(st)
uncal, uncle
uncane, uncanny
uncanily, uncanny(nnily)
uncanines, uncanny(niness)
uncanny,nnier,nniest,nily,nniness, NOT FORESEEN/ORDINARY
uncanuly, uncanny(nily)
uncany, uncanny
uncase, encase
uncased, encase(d)
uncel, uncle
unchues, unction(tuous)
uncil, uncle

uncle,*, THE BROTHER OF A FATHER/ MOTHER
uncoherent, incoherent
unconscionable,eness,ly, COMPLETELY UNACCEPTABLE
uncroach, encroach
uncrust, encrust
uncshen, unction
uncshuosity, unction(tuosity)
unction,*,tuous,tuosity,tuously, tousness, INSINCERE FLATTERY/ CHARM, VERY SOFT/RICH, OILY/ SOOTHING SUBSTANCE
undemic, endemic
under, PREFIX INDICATING THAT "BELOW/INCOMPLETE" MOST OFTEN MODIFIES THE WORD
undergerd, undergird
undergird,*,ded,ding,rt, SUPPORT/ SECURE FROM BELOW
underhand,ded,dedly,dedness, DISHONEST
undermine,*,ed,ning,er, REMOVE CREDIBILITY OF SOMEONE, ETCH AWAY AT THE FOUNDATION/ BASE/ FOOTING OF SOMETHING/ SOMEONE
underneath, BELOW/UNDERSIDE/ LOWER, NOT VISIBLE
underneeth, underneath
underneth, underneath
underpass,sses, ROAD UNDER A BRIDGE
underpin,*,nned,nning,nnings, SUPPORT/FOUNDATION FOR SOMETHING
understand,*,tood,ding,dability,dable, dably,dingly, KNOW/ COMPREHEND/ PERCEIVE "prefixes: mis"
understate,*,ed,ting,ement,ements, NOT FULLY RELEASING THE FACTS/ IMPORTANCE
understood, PAST TENSE FOR THE WORD "UNDERSTAND"
underway, ACTIVELY MOVING ALONG, IN THE PROCESS TOWARDS COMPLETION
underwear, UNDER CLOTHING
undes, undies
undeulate, undulate
undewlashen, undulate(tion)
undewlate, undulate
undewlated, undulate(d)

undewly, unduly
undies, SHORT FOR UNDERWEAR
undirhand, underhand
undirhandedly, underhand(edly)
undirhandid, underhand(ed)
undirmind, undermine(d)
undirmine, undermine
undirneth, underneath
undirstand, understand
undirstood, understood
undirstude, understood
undirwa, underway
undirwar, underwear
undole, unduly
undoly, unduly
undoole, unduly
undulashen, undulate(tion)
undulate,*,ed,ting,tion,tory,ant, WAVE MOTION
unduly, BEYOND MODERATION, UNLAWFUL
undurhand, underhand
undurhandidly, underhand(edly)
undurmind, undermine(d)
undurmine, undermine
undurneth, underneath
undurstand, understand
undurstood, understood
undurstude, understood
undurwa, underway
uneak, unique
unearth,*,hed,hing,hly,hliness, REMOVE FROM THE EARTH/DIRT, SOLVE A MYSTERY, NOT OF THIS PLANE/REALITY
unebreated, inebriate(d)
unebriated, inebriate(d)
unebriged, unabridged
unecorn, unicorn
unecycle, unicycle
uneek, unique
uneekle, unique(ly)
uneeknes, unique(ness)
unefi, unify
unefid, unify(fied)
unefikashen, unification
uneform, uniform
uneformedy, uniform(ity)
uneformety, uniform(ity)
uneformly, uniform(ly)
unefy, unify
unegma, enigma / enema
unek, unique
unekle, unique(ly)

uneknes, unique(ness)
unekorn, unicorn
unekwitable, inequitable
unekwity, inequity
unekwul, inequal
uneladeral, unilateral
unelateral, unilateral
unema, enema / anemia
unemea, anemia / enema
unemek, anemic
uneonize, union(ize)
uneque, unique
unequitable, inequitable
unequity, inequity
unerth, unearth
unerthd, unearth(ed)
unesikul, unicycle
uneson, unison
unesunus, unison(ous)
unesycle, unicycle
unet, unit
unetarean, unitary(rian)
unetary, unitary
unete, unity
unethecal, (un)ethic(al)
unethical, (un)ethic(al)
unety, unity
uneversal, universal
unevursal, universal
unferl, unfurl
unflagging,gingly, TIRELESS, UNCHANGING
unflagingly, unflagging(ly)
unflapable, unflappable
unflappable,bility,ly, ABLE TO MAINTAIN CONSISTENT COMPOSURE NO MATTER WHAT
unfleched, unfledged
unfledged, INMATURE, LACKS ADULT FEATHERS
unflegd, unfledged
unflejd, unfledged
unfortunate,*,ely,eness, WILL/DID NOT TURN OUT AS PLANNED
unfurl,*,led,ling, TO UNROLL OR SPREAD OUT
ungainly,liness, AWKWARD IN MOVEMENT/APPEARANCE
unganly, ungainly
ungulate,*,ed, MAMMAL WITH HOOVES
uni, PREFIX INDICATING THAT "ONE/ SINGLE" MOST OFTEN MODIFIES THE WORD

unibreated, inebriate(d)
unicorn,*, A MYTHICAL HORSE WITH A HORN COMING FROM IT'S FOREHEAD
unicycle,*,ling, ONE-WHEELED CYCLE (or monocycle)
unifekachen, unification
unifi, unify
unification, BROUGHT TOGETHER AS ONE/UNIFIED PART
unifid, unify(fied)
unifikachen, unification
uniform,*,med,mly,mity,mness, mitarian,mitarianism, NEAR EXACT IN FORM/ SHAPE/APPEARANCE/ CHARACTER
uniformedy, uniform(ity)
uniformety, uniform(ity)
unify,fies,fied,fier,fying,fiable,fication, ABILITY TO BE BROUGHT TOGETHER AS ONE/UNIFIED PART "prefixes: non/re/un"
unifyable, unify(fiable)
unigma, enigma / enema
unikle, unique(ly)
unilateral,*,lly,lism,list, ONE UNIFIED/ LATERAL SIDE OF AN AXIS/LINEAGE/ ORGANISM/PART
unimea, anemia / enema
union,*,nism,nist,nize,nized,nizing, nization,nism, BRING/FORM TOGETHER AS ONE, ALL PARTS COMING TOGETHER WORKING AS ONE (or see onion) "prefixes: dis/re"
unique,ely,eness, UNMATCHED, ONE OF A KIND
unirth, unearth
unirthd, unearth(ed)
unisen, unison
unisikul, unicycle
unison,nal,nous, ONE IN SOUND
unisycle, unicycle
unit,*,tage,ty, ONE PART/COMPONENT OF THE WHOLE "prefixes: sub"
unitarein, unitary(rian)
unitary,rian,rianism, CHARACTER WITHIN A UNIT, AS A UNIT
unite,*,ed,ting,table,er,edly,tive,tize, tizes,tized,tizing,tization,ty, ALL PARTS/ SECTIONS/FACTIONS COMING TOGETHER/ FUNCTIONING AS ONE/WHOLE (or see unity) "prefixes: dis/re"

uniterein, unitary(rian)
unituble, unite(table)
unity, ALL AS ONE, A JOINING (or see unite) "prefixes: dis"
universal,*,lly,lness,lism,list,lity,lities, lize,lization, APPLIES/ACCEPTED/ RELATING TO EVERYWHERE/ EVERYONE/EVERYTHING
universe,*, OF ONE, ALL TOGETHER
university,ties, A PLACE OF HIGHER EDUCATION
univurs, universe
univursal, universal
univursity, university
univursuly, universal(lly)
unjulate, ungulate
unkal, uncle
unkanely, uncanny(nily)
unkanenes, uncanny(niness)
unkany, uncanny
unkapacitated, incapacitate(d)
unkarnate, incarnate
unkase, encase
unkel, uncle
unkoherent, incoherent
unkonsheonable, unconscionable
unkroch, encroach
unkrust, encrust
unkshen, unction
unkshues, unction(tuous)
unkshuosedy, unction(tuosity)
unkshuosity, unction(tuosity)
unktion, unction
unkul, uncle
unles, unless
unless, OR, IN PLACE OF, AN EXCEPTION
unoculate, inoculate
unogeration, inaugurate(tion)
unoint, anoint
unokulate, inoculate
unomaly, anomaly
unovers, universe
unoversity, university
unowgeration, inaugurate(tion)
unoy, annoy
unroole, unruly
unruly,lier,liest,liness, NOT OBEDIENT/ CONFORMING
unsanitere, insanitary
unsbekable, unspeakable
unsboken, unspoken
unshuous, unction(tuous)

unspeakable,eness,ly,poken, NOT MAKE VERBAL SOUNDS, NOT MEANT TO BE SAID/SPOKEN
unspoken, NOT MAKE VERBAL SOUNDS, NOT TO BE SAID/SPOKEN
untel, until
until, TIME BETWEEN NOW AND THE FUTURE/NEXT TIME
unto, SAME AS THE WORD 'UNTIL', SOMETHING ACCOMPLISHED (or see onto)
untoward,*,dly,dness, NOT APPROPRIATE/PROPER, ADVERSE
untuord, untoward
untuosity, unction(tuosity)
untuword, untoward
untwo, unto / onto
untwoward, untoward
unubriged, unabridged
unucorn, unicorn
unufikachen, unification
unufikashen, unification
unuformady, uniform(ity)
unukorn, unicorn
unupropreat, inappropriate
unurth, unearth
unurthd, unearth(ed)
unusin, unison
unut, unit
unuvers, universe
unuversity, university
unuversule, universal(lly)
unuvirs, universe
unvasef, invasive
unvashen, invasion
unweting, unwitting
unwetingly, unwitting(ly)
unwitting,gly, NOT KNOWING/AWARE
unwrule, unruly
unyen, union / onion
unyon, union / onion
unyunize, union(ize)
up, DIRECTION TOWARDS THE SKY, PREFIX INDICATING THAT "MOST RECENTLY/HIGHER" MOST OFTEN MODIFIES THE WORD "prefixes: re"
upairent, apparent
upairul, apparel
upald, appall(lled)
upalugize, apology(gize)
upalugy, apology(gize)
upar, upper
uparent, apparent
upart, apart

upartment, apartment
uparul, apparel
upastrufe, apostrophe
upauld, appall(lled)
upauluge, apology
upaulugize, apology(gize)
upaurtment, apartment
upaustrufe, apostrophe
upbeat, HIGHER NOTE/FREQUENCY/ ATTITUDE
upbet, upbeat
upealing, appeal(ing)
upearanc, appearance
upearinse, appearance
upedy, uppity
upeel, appeal
upel, appeal
uper, upper
uperense, appearance
uperent, apparent
uperinse, appearance
uperul, apparel
upety, uppity
upheave,*,ed,ving,val, A LIFTING/ RISING OF
upheeve, upheave
uphev, upheave
uphevel, upheave(val)
uphevul, upheave(val)
uphold,*,held,ding, SUPPORT/ MAINTAIN
upholestury, upholstery
upholsdure, upholstery
upholster,*,red,ring,rer,ry, OF COVERING FURNITURE "prefixes: re"
upholstery,ries,rer, FABRICS FOR COVERING "prefixes: re"
upholsture, upholstery
upil, appeal
upir, upper
upity, uppity
upland, HIGHER REGION/GROUND
uplaud, applaud
uplaus, applause
uplefeus, oblivious
uplend, upland
upleveus, oblivious
upli, apply
uplifeus, oblivious
uplige, oblige(d)
upliveus, oblivious
uplod, applaud
uplos, applause

upoent, appoint
upoentment, appointment
upoint, appoint
upointment, appointment
upold, appall(lled) / uphold
upolstri, upholstery
upoluge, apology
upolugize, apology(gize)
upon, VERY CLOSE TO, UP ON
upord, aboard
uport, apart
uportment, apartment
upostrufe, apostrophe
upotment, appointment
upov, above
upoynt, appoint
uppearanc, appearance
upper, THE HIGHER LEVEL
upperinse, appearance
upperul, apparel
uppity,yness, SOMEONE BEHAVING STUCK-UP
upplaud, applaud
upplause, applause
upplod, applaud
upply, apply
upprentis, apprentice
uppreshiate, appreciate
uppropriate, appropriate
upprove, approve
upproximate, approximate
upproximately, approximate(ly)
upraisul, appraisal
uprased, appraise(d)
uprasef, abrasive
uprasul, appraisal
upraz, appraise
uprazel, appraisal
uprazif, abrasive
upreceashun, appreciate(tion)
uprecheat, appreciate
upreciate, appreciate
uprenis, apprentice
uprentis, apprentice
upresheat, appreciate
upresheate, appreciate
upresheation, appreciate(tion)
upreshen, oppress(ion)
upreshetion, appreciate(tion)
upress, oppress
upression, oppress(ion)
upretiate, appreciate
upreveate, abbreviate

upright,tly,tness, BE VERTICAL, BE IN THE RIGHT
uprintes, apprentice
uprise,*,rose,sing, STAND UP FOR/ AGAINST/WITH, RISE UP
uprisheate, appreciate
uprite, upright
uproach, approach
uproar,rious,riously,riousness, COMMOTION/DISTURBANCE, ELEVATED EMOTIONAL STATE
uprobreat, appropriate
uproch, approach
uproksamit, approximate
uproksumit, approximate
uproksumitly, approximate(ly)
uproof, approve
uproot,*,ted,ting,ter, REMOVE ROOTS FROM THE GROUND
uproovul, approve(val)
upropreit, appropriate
upror, uproar
uprose, PAST TENSE FOR THE WORD UPRISE
uprosh, approach
uproximate, approximate
uproximatly, approximate(ly)
upruf, approve
uprut, uproot
uprutid, uproot(ed)
upruv, approve
upruval, approve(val)
upserd, absurd
upsesed, obsess(ed)
upseshion, obsess(ion)
upset,*,tting, A DISTURBANCE/ IMBALANCE
upsolv, absolve
upstag, upstage
upstage,*,ed,ging, TO DISTRACT THE AUDIENCE FROM SOMEONE ELSE, BACK OF THE STAGE
upstairs, GO TO UPPER LEVEL BY MEANS OF STAIRS
upstaj, upstage
upstajd, upstage(d)
upstars, upstairs
upsters, upstairs
upsurd, absurd
uptane, obtain
uptrood, obtrude
uptroosiv, obtrusive
uptrude, obtrude
upur, upper

upward,*, MOVE UP
upwerd, upward
upwholstery, upholstery
upwird, upward
upwort, upward
upwright, upright
upwrite, upright
upwror, uproar
upwruted, uproot(ed)
upwurd, upward
upzolv, absolve
uracer, eraser
uradiate, irradiate
uradik, erotic / erratic
urain, arraign
uraingment, arrange(ment)
urainment, arraign(ment)
uralogy, urology
uran, urine / arraign
uraneum, uranium
urangment, arrange(ment)
uranium, A METAL CHEMICAL
uranjment, arrange(ment)
uranment, arraign(ment)
uranology,gies,gical, STUDY OF ASTRONOMY/THE HEAVENS
urase, erase
uraser, eraser
urater, ureter
urathane, urethane
uraudik, erotic
urban,nism,nist,nistic,nistically,nite,nity, nities,nize,nizes,nized,nizing, nization, LIFE ON THE OUTSKIRSTS OF CITY "prefixes: sub"
urben, urban
urbenite, urban(ite)
urbon, urban
urbonite, urban(ite)
urchen, urchin
urchin,*, A SEA CREATURE
urea,al,eic, CHEMICAL IN URINE
urear, arrear
uregenal, origin(al)
uregenate, originate
ureighnment, arraign(ment)
ureik, urea(eic)
ureinment, arraign(ment)
urejenate, originate
urejinal, origin(al)
urek, uric
uren, urine
urena, arena
urenaded, urinate(d)

urenary, urinary
urenate, urinate
urenology, uranology
urenul, urinal
urer, arrear
urest, arrest
ureter,ral,ric, CANAL FROM KIDNEY TO BLADDER CONTAINED WITHIN THE BODY
uretha, urethra
urethane, A MANMADE CHEMICAL
urethra,*,al, TUBE IN THE BODY WHICH FUNNELS URINE FOR DISCHARGE
urgd, urge(d)
urge,*,ed,ging,er,gingly,ency,ent,ently, OVERWHELMING DESIRE TO ACCOMPLISH/FULFILL
urgint, urge(nt)
urgis, urge(s)
uri, awry
uria, urea
uric, OF THE URINE
urif, arrive
uriful, arrival
uriginal, origin(al)
uriginate, originate
urijenal, origin(al)
urik, uric
urin, urine
urina, arena
urinal, A DEVICE/VESSEL FOR MALE'S TO URINATE INTO
urinary, OF THE URINE
urinate,*,ed,ting,tion, ACT OF RELEASING/DISCHARGING URINE
urine, LIQUID WASTE SECRETION
urinery, urinary
urinology, uranology
urinul, urinal
uriter, ureter
urithane, urethane
urithra, urethra
uriv, arrive
urivul, arrival
urj, urge
urjd, urge(d)
urjent, urge(nt)
urjinse, urge(ncy)
urli, early
urn,*, VESSEL USED TO MAKE BUTTER, HOLD CONTENTS (or see earn/ yearn/urine)
urodik, erotic
urolegy, urology

urology,gic,gical,gist, FIELD OF SCIENCE STUDYING THE URINARY TRACT
urolugy, urology
uroma, aroma
uron, urine
uround, around
urouz, arouse
urownd, around
urows, arouse
urrear, arrear
urrest, arrest
urrivol, arrival
urs, your(s)
urunal, urinal
urunate, urinate
urunery, urinary
urunology, uranology
us, PEOPLE INCLUDING SELF (or see ooze/use/yew(s))
usabil, usable
usable,*,bility,ly,eness, ABLE TO BE USED "prefixes: re/un"
usacin, assassin
usage,*, ABILITY TO BE USED/UTILIZED "prefixes: mis"
usail, assail
usal, assail
usalant, assail(ant)
usalt, assault
usary, usury
usasen, assassin
usault, assault
usberugus, asparagus
uscend, ascend
uscention, ascension
usd, use(d)
usdonesh, astonish
usdrawnumy, astronomy
usdronumy, astronomy
use,*,ed,sing,sable,sability,sage,sance, eful,efully,efulness,eless,elessly, elessness,er,sable, EMPLOY/ EXPLOIT/UTILIZE TO ACCOMPLISH/ ACHIEVE SUCCESS, EXPLOIT RESOURCES (or see yew(s)) "prefixes: dis/mis/multi/non/over/ re/un/under"
useage, usage
usebil, usable
useble, usable
usech, usage
usedik, acetic / acidic / ascetic
useful,lly,lness, ABLE TO BE UTILIZED EASILY

useg, usage
usej, usage
useless,sly,sness, NOT ABLE TO BE UTILIZED EASILY
uselis, useless
usemble, assemble
usemelate, assimilate
usemilate, assimilate
usemlate, assimilate
usend, ascend
usenshen, ascension
usent, assent
usention, ascension
user,*, ONE WHO EXPLOITS OTHERS/ RESOURCES, THOSE WHO USE DRUGS (or see usury)
usere, usury
userp, usurp
userped, usurp(ed)
usershen, assert(ion)
usert, assert
usertev, assert(ive)
usertion, assert(ion)
usery, usury
uses, assess / use(s)
useshun, accession
usesment, assessment
usest, assist
usestens, assist(ance)
usestins, assist(ance)
useum, assume
usfekseat, asphyxiate
usfikseat, asphyxiate
usfixeat, asphyxiate
usful, useful
ushamed, ashamed
usher,*,red,ring, TENDS TO GUESTS AT PUBLIC GATHERING, INDUCE/ ESCORT/ BRING ABOUT(or see assure)
ushir, usher / assure
ushwaly, usual(lly)
ushwule, usual(lly)
usibil, usable
usible, usable
usich, usage
uside, aside
usig, usage
usign, assign
usij, usage
usilem, asylum
usimbul, assemble
usimelate, assimilate
usin, assign

usind, ascend
usinment, assignment
usinshen, ascension
usint, assent
usir, user
usirshen, assert(ion)
usirt, assert
usirtif, assert(ive)
usirtion, assert(ion)
usiry, usury
usist, assist
usistens, assist(ance)
usitic, acetic / acidic / ascetic
usleep, asleep
uslep, asleep
uslis, useless
uslus, useless
usocheat, associate
usocheation, associate(tion)
usociate, associate
usociation, associate(tion)
usofegus, esophagus
usog, usage
usolt, assault
usordid, assorted
usortment, assortment
usosheashun, associate(tion)
usosheut, associate
usoshiat, associate
usoshiation, associate(tion)
usparugus, asparagus
usperugus, asparagus
usphikseate, asphyxiate
uspire, aspire
usry, usury
ussal, assail
ussasin, assassin
ussemble, assemble
ust, use(d)
ustonish, astonish
ustraunume, astronomy
ustronumy, astronomy
ustrownumy, astronomy
usual,lly,lness, MOST COMMON/ PREDICTABLE "prefixes: un"
usuch, usage
usug, usage
usuj, usage
usum, assume
usumpshen, assumption
usumshen, assumption
usur, user / assure
usure, usury

usurp,*,ped,ping,pation,per, TO UNLAWFULLY ASSUME POSSESSION OF
usurt, assert
usury,ries,rer,rious,riously,riousness, CHARGE EXORBITANT/UNLAWFUL AMOUNT OF INTEREST FOR A LOAN
usylim, asylum
utachment, attach(ment)
utack, attack
utain, attain
utainable, attain(able) / obtain(able)
utak, attack
utanable, attain(able) / obtain(able)
utane, attain
utanmint, attain(ment)
utash, attach
uteludy, utility
utempt, attempt
utemt, attempt
utend, attend
utendens, attend(ance)
utending, attend(ing)
utenshen, attention
utensil,*, DEVICE/INSTRUMENT/TOOL FOR WORK
utensul, utensil
utentef, attentive
utentefness, attentive(ness)
utention, attention
utentive, attentive
uter, odor / otter / outer / utter / udder
uterus,ri, HOME FOR EMBRYO IN FEMALE MAMMALS "prefixes: intra"
utest, attest
uther, other
utilatarian, utilitarian
utilety, utility
utilitarian,*,nism, FOCUS ON USEFUL/ PRACTICALITY
utility,ties,ize, A USEFUL SERVICE FOR THE COMMON GOOD OF THE PEOPLE "prefixes: dis"
utilize,*,ed,zing,zable,zation,zer, MAKE USE OF "prefixes: mis/re"
utilude, utility
utiluty, utility
utimt, attempt
utind, attend
utindens, attend(ance)
utinding, attend(ing)
utinsel, utensil
utinshen, attention

utinsul, utensil
utintef, attentive
utintion, attention
utintive, attentive
utintiveness, attentive(ness)
utir, odor / otter / outer / utter / udder / attire
utmost, BEST / HIGHEST IN ORDER OF IMPORTANCE
utopia,an, IDEAL SITUATION
utor, odor / otter / outer / utter / udder
utrausety, atrocity
utrochus, atrocious
utroshes, atrocious
utrosity, atrocity
utter,*,red,ring,rance,rable,rer, TO SPEAK (or see udder) "prefixes: un"
utur, odor / otter / outer / utter / udder
uturd, utter(ed)
uvale, avail
uvert, avert / advert / overt
uvou, avow
uvow, avow
uwa, away
uwil, awhile
uwrest, arrest
uwround, around
uwrous, arouse
uzd, use(d)
uzing, use(sing) / ooze(zing)
uzre, usury / use(r)
vacabeulery, vocabulary
vacalate, vacillate
vacancy,ncies, UNOCCUPIED DWELLING
vacant,tly,tness,ncy, DWELLING NEEDING/WITHOUT OCCUPANCY
vacashend, vacation(ed)
vacashun, vacation
vacate,*,ed,ting, TO LEAVE PERMANENTLY
vacation,*,ned,ning,nless,ner,nist, GO AWAY FOR A BRIEF VISIT/ EXCURSION WITH THE INTENT OF ENJOYMENT/RELAXATION
vaccen, vaccine
vaccenate, vaccinate
vaccilate, vacillate
vaccinate,*,ned,tion, INOCULATE WITH A CHEMICAL/MEDICINE TO AFFECT THE BODY
vaccine,*,nal, USED TO STIMULATE THE BODY TO PRODUCE ANTIBODIES, USED TO PROTECT AGAINST A VIRUS

vacculate, vacillate
vaccum, vacuum
vacelate, vacillate
vacenity, vicinity
vacensy, vacancy
vacent, vacant
vachaina, vagina
vacilate, vacillate
vacillate,*,ed,ting,tingly,tion,tor,tory, MOVE BACK AND FORTH, TO AND FRO, FLUCTUATE BETWEEN TWO POINTS
vacinate, vaccinate
vacine, vaccine
vacinity, vicinity
vacsenate, vaccinate
vacsinate, vaccinate
vacsination, vaccinate(tion)
vacum, vacuum
vacuole,*,lar,late,lates,lated,lating,lization, LACKING SUBSTANCE/ INTELLIGENCE/AWARENESS
vacuous,sly,sness, LACKS SUBSTANCE/ INTELLIGENCE/AWARENESS
vacuum,*,med,ming, MACHINE USED TO PULL/SUCK/PICK UP, SPACE CREATED BY REMOVING PARTICLES
vacuus, vacuous
vad, vat
vag, vague
vagabond,*,dish,dism, ONE WHO ROAMS WITHOUT A PERMANENT HOME/ SUSTENANCE
vagary,ried,rious,riously, WHIMSICAL, UNPREDICTABLE IN MOVEMENT/ BEHAVIOR
vage, vague
vagebond, vagabond
vagenul, vagina(l)
vagery, vagary
vagina,*,al,ally, TUBULAR SHAPED CANAL FOUND IN PLANTS/FEMALE BODIES
vaginul, vagina(l)
vagiry, vagary
vagist, vague(st)
vagle, vague(ly)
vagly, vague(ly)
vagobond, vagabond
vagrant,*,tly,ncy,ncies, HOMELESS WHO WANDER/ROAM
vagre, vagary
vagrense, vagrant(ncy)
vagrent, vagrant

vagrunse, vagrant(ncy)
vagry, vagary
vagubond, vagabond
vague,er,est,ely,eness, HAZY, UNCLEAR
vagury, vagary
vagust, vague(st)
vahement, vehemence(nt)
vahemins, vehemence
vail,*, TO LOWER/REMOVE (or see vale/ veil/vile)
vain,nly,nness, TO ATTEMPT WITHOUT SUCCESS, BE SELF-ABSORBED WITH ONE'S OWN SHALLOW VALUES (or see vane/vein)
vajenul, vagina(l)
vajina, vagina
vajinul, vagina(l)
vajunal, vagina(l)
vak, vague
vakabeulery, vocabulary
vakabulery, vocabulary
vakachend, vacation(ed)
vakachun, vacation
vakadid, vacate(d)
vakashen, vacation
vakashend, vacation(ed)
vakashun, vacation
vakat, vacate
vakatid, vacate(d)
vakchenashin, vaccinate(tion)
vakchunashen, vaccinate(tion)
vake, vague
vakense, vacant(ncy)
vakent, vacant
vakently, vacant(ly)
vakeum, vacuum
vakeuol, vacuole
vakinse, vacant(ncy)
vakint, vacant
vakium, vaccum
vakle, vague(ly)
vakly, vague(ly)
vakoum, vacuum
vakrent, vagrant
vakrint, vagrant
vakseen, vaccine
vaksen, vaccine
vaksenate, vaccinate
vakshenashin, vaccinate(tion)
vaksinate, vaccinate
vaksination, vaccinate(tion)
vaksine, vaccine
vaksunashen, vaccinate(tion)
vakual, vacuole

vakum, vacuum
vakumd, vacuum(ed)
vakunse, vacant(ncy)
vakunt, vacant
vakuol, vacuole
vakuous, vacuous
vakuus, vacuous
vakyewm, vacuum
vakyewol, vacuole
vakyual, vacuole
vakyum, vacuum
val, vail / vale / veil
vala, valet
valacity, velocity
valadectory, valedictory
valadiction, valediction
valadiktorean, valedictorian
valance,es,ed, SHORT CURTAIN (or see valence) "prefixes: uni"
valans, valance / valence
valantine, valentine
valatil, volatile
vale, A VALLEY (or see vail/veil/valley/valet)
valeant, valiant
valed, valid / veil(ed)
valediction, A VALEDICTORY
valedictorian, ONE WHO SPEAKS AT A SCHOOL COMMENCEMENT
valedictory,ries, SCHOOL FINAL/ FAREWELL CEREMONY
valediktorian, valedictorian
valediktory, valedictory
valedity, valid(ity)
valei, valley
valeint, valiant
valence,cy,nt, A WAY TO MEASURE THE STRENGTH OF AN ATOM (or see valance) "prefixes: bi"
valens, valance / valence
valent, valence(nt) / valiant
valentine,*, TO HONOR ONE WHOM YOU ARE ATTRACTED TO IN A ROMANTIC WAY
valer, valor
valerean, valerian
valerian, AN HERB
valerus, valor(ous)
valet, ONE WHO PARKS CARS FOR GUESTS AT AN EVENT/PUBLIC PLACE
valeubul, value(uable)
valeunt, valiant
valeuntly, valiant(ly)

valey, valley
valf, valve
valiant,tly,tness, OF COURAGE/ STRONG/BRAVE
valid,dly,dness,date,dates,dating,dation, dity,dities,dness, REAL, FACTUAL, ACTUAL, TO ACKNOWLEDGE AUTHENTICITY "prefixes: in/un"
validectory, valedictory
validete, valid(ity)
validety, valid(ity)
validiction, valediction
validictorian, valedictorian
validiktory, valedictory
valie, valley
valins, valance / valence
valint, valence(nt) / valiant
valintine, valentine
valir, valor
valirus, valor(ous)
valit, valid
valitel, volatile
valkano, volcano
valley,*, AREA BETWEEN THE MOUNTAINS AT THE LOWEST POINTS
valoor, velour / velure / valor
valor,rous,rously,rousness, QUALITY ATTRIBUTED TO MALE WHO DISPLAYS BRAVERY/FIRM RESOLVE (or see velour/velure)
valosedy, velocity
valosety, velocity
valotel, volatile
valu, value
valubel, value(uable)
valubul, value(uable)
valud, valid / value(d)
valudectory, valedictory
valudikshen, valediction
valudiktory, valedictory
value,*,ed,uing,eless,elessness,uable, uableness,uably,uate,uator,uation, uational,uationally, WHAT SOMETHING IS WORTH "prefixes: de/dis/in/un/ under"
valules, value(less)
valum, volume
valuns, valance
valuntery, voluntary
valuntine, valentine
valupshuis, voluptuous
valuptuous, voluptuous
valur, velour / velure / valor

valut, valid
valutel, volatile
valv, valve
valve,*,eless, AN APETURE/OPENING TO REGULATE FLOW OF AIR/ LIQUID/ MOLECULES "prefixes: bi/ un/uni"
valy, valley
valyant, valiant
valyently, valiant(ly)
valyew, value
valyewbul, value(uable)
valyint, valiant
valyu, value
valyubil, value(uable)
valyuble, value(uable)
valyum, volume
valyunt, valiant
valyuntle, valiant(ly)
vamb, vamp
vambir, vampire
vamp,*,ped,ping, MOVE BITS/PIECES AROUND TO CHANGE FLOW/ DIRECTION OF SOMETHING, IMPROVISE
vampire,*,ric,rism, ONE THAT DWELLS IN THE NIGHT AND USES BLOOD FOR SUSTENANCE
van,*,nned,nning, TYPE OF VEHICLE (or see vane/vain/vein/feign) "prefixes: de"
vandal,*,lic,lism,listic,lize,lizes,lized, lizing, BREAK IN AND DESTROY ANOTHERS PROPERTY
vandel, vandal
vandelism, vandal(ism)
vandelize, vandal(ize)
vandiktif, vindictive
vandil, vandal
vandilize, vandal(ize)
vandulism, vandal(ism)
vandulize, vandal(ize)
vane,*,ed,eless, DEVICE MOUNTED TO DISPLAY WIND DIRECTION, FEATHER ON AN ARROW (or see van/vain/vein/feign)
vanech, vanish
vanedy, vanity
vaneer, veneer
vanela, vanilla
vaner, veneer
vanesh, vanish
vaneshd, vanish(ed)
vanesht, vanish(ed)

vanety, vanity
vangard, vanguard
vangart, vanguard
vanguard, THE FEW WHO ARE AHEAD OF THE GROUP
vanich, vanish
vanide, vanity
vanila, vanilla
vanilla, TYPE OF FRUIT/BEAN
vanish,hes,hed,hing, TO DISAPPEAR
vanishd, vanish(ed)
vanity,ties, OF BEING VAIN, SELF-ABSORBED WITH SHALLOW VALUES
vankuesh, vanquish
vankwesh, vanquish
vankwish, vanquish
vankwishd, vanquish(ed)
vanquesh, vanquish
vanqueshd, vanquish(ed)
vanquish,hes,hed,hing,hable, OVERCOME/SUBDUE/DEFEAT
vanqwesh, vanquish
vanqweshd, vanquish(ed)
vanqwish, vanquish
vantage,*, A SUPERIOR POSITION/LOCATION
vantech, vantage
vantej, vantage
vantich, vantage
vantig, vantage
vantuj, vantage
vanude, vanity
vanush, vanish
vanushd, vanish(ed)
vanute, vanity
vaper, vapor
vaperize, vapor(ize)
vapir, vapor
vapirize, vapor(ize)
vapor,*,rer,rish,rishness,rific,ring,rize, rizes,rized,rizing,rizable,rization, rizer, rous,rously,rousness,rosity,ry, FUMES/CLOUD EMITTED/GIVEN OFF BY SOMETHING WHEN EXPOSED TO THE AIR
vapur, vapor
vapurize, vapor(ize)
vaqium, vacuum
vaqum, vacuum
varashis, veracious / voracious
varcity, varsity
vare, vary / very
vareagashen, variegate(tion)
vareashen, variate(tion)

vareation, variate(tion)
vared, vary(ried)
varefication, verify(fication)
varefy, verify
vareins, variant(nce)
vareint, variant
vares, vary(ries)
vareuble, variable
vareuns, variant(nce)
vareunt, variant
vareus, vary(rious)
vari, vary / very
variable,*,bility,eness,ly, CHANGE IN VALUE OF SOMETHING, THE GIVENS IN AN EQUATION, RATE OF SPEED/FLOW/FREQUENCY "prefixes: in"
variant,*,nce, RANGE OF SPEED/FLOW/FREQUENCY
variate,tion,tional,tionally,tive,tively, RATE OF CHANGE/ FLOW/SPEED/ DIRECTION/FREQUENCY "prefixes: bi"
variedy, variety
variegate,*,ed,ting,tion, OF A VARIETY
variety,ties,tal,tally, A RANGE OF CHOICES
varificashen, verify(fication)
varify, verify
varis, vary(ries)
variuble, variable
variugashen, variegate(tion)
variuns, variant(nce)
varius, vary(rious)
variuty, variety
varment, A TROUBLESOME ANIMAL
varmint, varment
varmun, varment
varnesh, varnish
varneshd, varnish(ed)
varnish,hes,hed,hing,her,hy, TRANSPARENT CHEMICAL COATING FOR PROTECTION "prefixes: un"
varnush, varnish
varsedy, varsity
varsety, varsity
varsity,ties, TYPE OF SCHOOL SPORTS TEAM
varsudes, varsity(ties)
varsuty, varsity
varufi, verify
vary,ries,ried,ying,yingly,rious,riously, riousness, MOVEABLE RANGE/RATE OF CHANGE/SELECTION (or see very)
varyd, vary(ried)
varys, vary(ries)
vas, vase
vasalashen, vacillate(tion)
vasalate, vacillate
vasalation, vacillate(tion)
vascular,rity,rly, FLOW WITHIN A SYSTEM "prefixes: intra/non"
vasd, vast
vase,*, A CONTAINER
vasectomy,mies, SURGICAL PROCEDURE FOR MALES
vasektumy, vasectomy
vaselashen, vacillate(tion)
vaselate, vacillate
vaselation, vacillate(tion)
vasenedy, vicinity
vasenety, vicinity
vasilashen, vacillate(tion)
vasilate, vacillate
vasilation, vacillate(tion)
vasinedy, vicinity
vasinety, vicinity
vaskeuler, vascular
vaskewler, vascular
vaskiular, vascular
vaskuler, vascular
vasnes, vast(ness)
vasqueler, vascular
vasquler, vascular
vast,tly,tness,ty,tier,tiest,titude,tity, GREAT AMOUNT IN RANGE/ DEGREES/ FREQUENCY/AREA
vasul, vessel
vasulashen, vacillate(tion)
vasulate, vacillate
vasulation, vacillate(tion)
vat,*,tted,tting, A VESSEL FOR LIQUIDS
vau, vow
vauch, vouch
vaucher, vouch(er)
vaud, vow(ed)
vaudku, vodka
vaul, vowel
vaulatil, volatile
vaulcano, volcano
vaule, volley
vaulenteer, volunteer
vauli, volley
vaulinter, volunteer
vaulkano, volcano

vault,*,ted,ting,ter, HOLDING/CONTAINER TO PROTECT VALUABLES, ARCHED HEIGHT WITHIN A DWELLING/SPACE/CONTAINER, LEAP HIGH (or see volt)
vaulum, volume
vauluntery, voluntary
vaulutil, volatile
vauly, volley
vaumet, vomit
vaumit, vomit
vaush, vouch
vausher, vouch(er)
vautku, vodka
vauz, vase
vaw, vow
vawch, vouch
vawcher, vouch(er)
vawd, vow(ed)
vawl, vowel
vawle, volley
vaygari, vagary
vea, via
veakul, vehicle
veal, MEAT FROM THE CALF OF A BOVINE
vecenity, vicinity
vechen, vision
vechenary, vision(ary)
veches, vicious
vechetal, vegetal
vechetarian, vegetarian
vechetate, vegetate
vechitarian, vegetarian
vechtable, vegetable
vechualize, visual(ize)
vechulante, vigil(ante)
vechun, vision
vechunary, vision(ary)
vechus, vicious
vechutarian, vegetarian
vecinity, vicinity
vecks, vex
vectomize, victim(ize)
vectumizashen, victim(ization)
vectumize, victim(ize)
vedeo, video
vederan, veteran
vedio, video
vedo, veto
vedod, veto(ed)
vedran, veteran
vedrify, vitrify

vedurin, veteran
veer,*,red,ring,ringly, SWERVE IN MOVEMENT, MOVE TOWARDS PARTICULAR DIRECTION
vegatashen, vegetate(tion)
vegatate, vegetate
vegatuble, vegetable
vegduble, vegetable
vegel, vigil
vegelante, vigil(ante)
veger, vigor
vegerus, vigor(ous)
vegetable,*, CATEGORY OF EDIBLE PLANTS
vegetal, OF BEING A VEGETABLE
vegetarian,*,nism, EATS PRIMARILY VEGETABLES "prefixes: non"
vegetate,*,ed,ting,tion,tional,tionless,tive,tively,tivness, SIT/AGE/RIPEN AS A VEGETABLE WITHOUT MOVEMENT "prefixes: re"
vegetuble, vegetable
vegetul, vegetal
vegil, vigil
vegilante, vigil(ante)
vegilent, vigil(ant)
veginu, vagina
vegir, vigor
vegirus, vigor(ous)
vegitashen, vegetate(tion)
vegitate, vegetate
vegiterean, vegetarian
vegituble, vegetable
vegitul, vegetal
vegolante, vigil(ante)
vegorus, vigor(ous)
vegtable, vegetable
vegtuble, vegetable
vegual, visual
vegulante, vigil(ante)
veguol, visual
veguolize, visual(ize)
vegur, vigor
vegurus, vigor(ous)
vegutarean, vegetarian
vegutashen, vegetate(tion)
vegutate, vegetate
vehecle, vehicle
vehekul, vehicle
vehemence,cy,nt,ntly, STRONG/FORCEFUL FEELINGS BROUGHT ON BY AN EMOTIONAL STATE/PASSION, STRONG/FORCEFUL EVENT
vehemint, vehemence(nt)

vehicle,*,cular, MOVING/POWERED VESSELS
vehicul, vehicle
vehikul, vehicle
veic, vague
veig, vague
veigary, vagary
veikle, vehicle
veil,*,led,ling, THIN/TRANSPARENT/REMOVABLE COVER (or see vail/vale) "prefixes: un"
vein,*,ned,ning,nal,ny,nlet, TUBE/CHANNEL THAT ALLOWS FLOW OF LIQUID (or see vane/vain) "prefixes: de"
veis, vase
veiwed, view(ed)
vejalante, vigil(ante)
vejalent, vigil(ant)
vejatashen, vegetate(tion)
vejatate, vegetate
vejaterean, vegetarian
vejdible, vegetable
vejduble, vegetable
vejetarean, vegetarian
vejetashen, vegetate(tion)
vejetul, vegetal
vejewelize, visual(ize)
vejinu, vagina
vejitarean, vegetarian
vejitashen, vegetate(tion)
vejitate, vegetate
vejitul, vegetal
vejolent, vigil(ant)
vejtuble, vegetable
vejual, visual
vejulante, vigil(ante)
vejulent, vigil(ant)
vejuolize, visual(ize)
vejutarean, vegetarian
vejutashen, vegetate(tion)
vejutate, vegetate
vekabeulery, vocabulary
vekabulery, vocabulary
veker, vigor
vekir, vigor
vekor, vigor
veks, vex
veksashen, vex(ation)
veksation, vex(ation)
vektem, victim
vektemize, victim(ize)
vektumize, victim(ize)
vekur, vigor

vel, vale / vail / veil
vela, villa
velafy, vilify
velage, villa(ge)
velanus, villain(ous)
velarean, valerian
velcom, welcome
veledictore, valedictory
veledictorean, valedictorian
veledictori, valedictory
velefy, vilify
velege, villa(ge)
velej, villa(ge)
velen, villain
velenus, villain(ous)
velidety, valid(ity)
velin, villain
velocity,ties,tize,tizes,tized,tizing, tization, RATE/AMOUNT OF MOVEMENT/ SPEED
velon, villain
velour,*,red,ring, TYPE OF FABRIC/ VELVET (or see velure)
velu, villa
veluch, villa(ge)
velufy, vilify
velug, villa(ge)
veluj, villa(ge)
velun, villain
velunus, villain(ous)
velure,*,ed,ring, TYPE OF FABRIC (or see velour)
velutch, villa(ge)
velvet,*,ted,ting,teen,ty, THICK/SILKY/ SOFT FABRIC
velvity, velvet(y)
velvude, velvet(y)
velvut, velvet
vem, vim
vemens, vehemence
venager, vinegar
venagrey, vinaigrette
venaker, vinegar
venam, venom
venamus, venom(ous)
venasin, venison
vench, venge
vencher, venture
venchful, venge(ful)
venchurd, venture(d)
vend,*,ded,ding,der,dition, TO SELL (or see vent)
vendacation, vindicate(tion)
vendalashen, ventilate(tion)

vendalate, ventilate
vendalation, ventilate(tion)
vendecate, vindicate
vendecation, vindicate(tion)
vendeda, vendetta
vendekduf, vindictive
vendektif, vindictive
vendetta,*, HAS A STRONG/DEEP GRUDGE/DISPUTE/DISAGREEMENT WITH
vendicashen, vindicate(tion)
vendicate, vindicate
vendiktif, vindictive
venducation, vindicate(tion)
vendulashen, ventilate(tion)
veneer,*,red,ring,rer,rable,rability, rableness, THIN OVERLAYMENT USED FOR SURFACING
venegrey, vinaigrette
venela, vanilla
venem, venom
venemus, venom(ous)
venerate,*,ed,ting,tor,tion,able,ability, ableness,ably, CANONIZE/ WORSHIP/ PUT IN HIGH ESTEEM OVER ONESELF
venew, venue
venge,*,ed,ging,eance,eful,efully, efulness, SEEK AVENGE FOR A WRONG, BE VINDICTIVE/ RELENTLESS IN PURSUIT OF SATISFACTION
vengens, venge(ance)
vengful, venge(ful)
venguns, venge(ance)
veniger, vinegar
venigra, vinaigrette
venila, vanilla
venim, venom
venimus, venom(ous)
venir, veneer
venirate, venerate
venison, TERM FOR THE MEAT OF THE DEER FAMILY
venj, venge
venjens, venge(ance)
venjful, venge(ful)
venjuns, venge(ance)
veno, vino
venom,*,mous,mously,mousness, POISON
venomus, venom(ous)
venorate, venerate
venosen, venison

vensable, vincible
vensher, venture
vensubul, vincible
vent,*,ted,ting, ALLOWS THE RELEASE OF AIR/STEAM/HEAT/EMOTIONS (or see vend) "prefixes: bio"
ventag, vintage
ventalashen, ventilate(tion)
ventalate, ventilate
ventalation, ventilate(tion)
venteg, vintage
ventej, vintage
ventilashen, ventilate(tion)
ventilate,*,ed,ting,tion,tive,tor,tory, ENCOURAGE THE FLOW OF AIR
ventricle,*,cular,culus,culi, TUBES/ ARTERIES "prefixes: inter/intra"
ventrikul, ventricle
ventriloquist,tic,sm,uy,ial,ially,ize, TO THROW/PROJECT THE VOICE WITHOUT MOVING THE LIPS
ventrilukwist, ventriloquist
ventrukle, ventricle
ventuge, vintage
ventuj, vintage
venture,*,ed,ring, GO ON BRAVE/ DARING ADVENTURE, MOVE TOWARDS UNKNOWN TERRITORY
venu, venue
venue,*, WAYS/PATHS, A LEGAL TERM
venuger, vinegar
venugray, vinaigrette
venuker, vinegar
venumus, venom(ous)
venurate, venerate
venusin, venison
venyou, venue
veol, vail / vale / veil / veal
ver, veer
veracious,sly,sness, TRUTHFUL/ UNERRING (or see voracious)
veracity,ties, EAGERNESS/SUPPORT FOR THE TRUTH
verafecation, verify(fication)
verafikashen, verify(fication)
verafy, verify
verasedy, veracity / voracity
verashes, voracious / veracious
verasious, voracious / veracious
verasity, veracity / voracity
verb,*,bal, WORD WHICH DENOTES ACTION
verbadum, verbatim

verbal,lly,lism,list,listic,lize,lizes,lized, lizing,lization,lizer, VOICE/SPEAK FROM THE MOUTH, MAKE THOUGHTS HEARD "prefixes: non"
verbatim, EXACT WORDS
verbatum, verbatim
verble, verbal / verbal(lly)
verblize, verbal(ize)
verboly, verbal(lly)
verbose,ely,eness,sity, TOO WORDY, USES TOO MANY WORDS TO DESCRIBE/COMMUNICATE
verbosity, verbose(sity)
verbosudy, verbose(sity)
verbule, verbal / verbal(lly)
verbulize, verbal(ize)
verch, verge
verchen, version / virgin
verchew, virtue
verchewul, virtual
verchoo, virtue
verchualedy, virtual(ity)
verchuality, virtual(ity)
verchuol, virtual
verd, veer(ed)
verdabra, vertebra
verdacal, vertical
verdago, vertigo
verdekly, vertical(lly)
verdekt, verdict
verdekul, vertical
verdibra, vertebra
verdical, vertical
verdict,*, FINAL DECISION/JUDGEMENT
verdigo, vertigo
verdikly, vertical(lly)
verdikul, vertical
verdubra, vertebra
verdukol, vertical
vere, vary / very
vereability, variable(lity)
vereabl, variable
vereant, variant
vereas, vary(rious)
vereashen, variate(tion)
vereate, variate
vereation, variate(tion)
vered, vary(ried)
verefikashen, verify(fication)
verefukashen, verify(fication)
verefy, verify
veregate, variegate
veres, vary(ries)
vereuble, variable

vereugate, variegate
vereuns, variant(nce)
vereunt, variant
vereus, vary(rious)
verge,*,ed,ging, EDGE/RIM/PIVOT/ PEAK PRIOR TO
vergen, version / virgin
vergun, version / virgin
veri, vary / very
veriabol, variable
veriagashen, variegate(tion)
veriagate, variegate
veriant, variant
veriants, variant(nce)
veriate, variate
verient, variant
verietal, variety(tal)
veriety, variety
verifikashen, verify(fication)
verifucation, verify(fication)
verify,fies,fied,fying,fication,ficative, ficatory,fiability,fiable,fiableness, fier, AUTHENTICATE/ ACKNOWLEDGE/RECOGNIZE FOR TRUTH
verigate, variegate
veriubility, variable(lity)
veriuble, variable
veriugate, variegate
veriuns, variant(nce)
verius, vary(rious)
verj, verge
verjen, version / virgin
vermakulite, vermiculite
vermekulite, vermiculite
vermen, vermin
vermiculite, TYPE OF ROCK
vermikewlite, vermiculite
vermin,nous,nously, ANNOYING/PESTY LIVING THING IN GREAT QUANTITIES
vermiqulite, vermiculite
vermooth, vermouth
vermouth, ALCOHOLIC APERITIF
vermuth, vermouth
vernacular,rly,rism, WORD USED AS IT ORIGINATED, NATIVE USE OF WORD
vernakular, vernacular
verp, verb
verply, verbal(lly)
verpul, verbal
vers, verse / veer(s)

versatile,ely,eness,lity, ABLE TO CONFORM TO MANY GIVEN SITUATIONS
versatilety, versatile(lity)
verse,*,ed,sing,sify,sifies,sified,sifying, sifier,sification, ONE PART/STANZA OF A GREATER PIECE/STORY, TO MAKE VERSE (or see versus)
versetul, versatile
vershin, version
vershu, virtue
vershuality, virtual(ity)
vershun, version
version,*, ONE PART/VIEW/ PERSPECTIVE OF A STORY/EVENT
versis, verse(s) / versus
versital, versatile
versitilety, versatile(lity)
versus, AGAINST, TWO PERSPECTIVES IN OPPOSITION (or see verse(s))
versutil, versatile
versutilety, versatile(lity)
vert, veer(ed)
vertabra, vertebra
vertebra,*,al,ally,ate,ation, A BONE IN THE SPINE "prefixes: inter"
vertego, vertigo
vertekul, vertical
vertibra, vertebra
vertical,lity,lness,lly, OPPOSED TO THE HORIZONTAL, AN UPRIGHT POSITION
verticly, vertical(lly)
vertigo,oes, DIZZY
vertikul, vertical
vertucly, vertical(lly)
vertue, virtue
vertugo, vertigo
verufecation, verify(fication)
verufikashen, verify(fication)
verufy, verify
verul, virile
very, MUCH/LOTS, GREAT AMOUNT (or see vary)
veryus, vary(rious)
vesa, visa
vesabul, visible
vesatashen, visit(ation)
vesater, visit(or)
vesatir, visit(or)
vesatude, vicissitude
vescosedy, viscous(ity)
vescosity, viscous(ity)
vescosudy, viscous(ity)

vesdabule, vestibule
vesdubule, vestibule
vesectomy, vasectomy
vesel, vessel
vesenedy, vicinity
vesenety, vicinity
vesetashen, visit(ation)
veseter, visit(or)
veshen, vision
veshenary, vision(ary)
veshes, vicious
veshuel, visual
veshun, vision
veshunary, vision(ary)
veshus, vicious
vesil, vessel
vesinedy, vicinity
vesinety, vicinity
vesit, visit
vesitashen, visit(ation)
vesiter, visit(or)
vesitude, vicissitude
veskes, viscous
veskosedy, viscous(ity)
veskosity, viscous(ity)
veskus, viscous
vesle, vessel
vessel,*, A CONTAINER
vest,*,ted,ting, SLEEVELESS OUTER GARMENT, POSSESS POWER/ POSITION
vestabule, vestibule
vestibule,*,ed,ling,lar,late, A CHAMBER/ CAVITY
vestubule, vestibule
vesu, visa
vesubel, visible
vesubiledy, visibility
vesuble, visible / visible(ly)
vesul, vessel
vesut, visit
vesutashen, visit(ation)
vesuter, visit(or)
vesutude, vicissitude
vet,*, SHORT FOR VETERINARIAN AND VETERAN
vetaren, veteran
veteran,*, ONES WHO SURVIVED A WAR/BATTLE OR GAINED WISDOM THOROUGH STUDY/ SERVICE
vetiren, veteran
veto,oes,oed,oing,oer, TO REJECT/ FORBID
vetod, veto(ed)

vetos, veto(es)
vetran, veteran
vetrefy, vitrify
vetrify, vitrify
veturen, veteran
veu, via / view
veud, view(ed)
veukle, vehicle
veva, viva
veved, vivid
vevidly, vivid(ly)
vevu, viva
vew, view
vex,xes,xed,xing,xingly,xation,xatious, xatiously, xatiousness,xedly,xedness, TO PLAGUE/IRRITATE/CAUSE COMMOTION
vexashen, vex(ation)
veygari, vagary
veyude, view(ed)
vezabel, visible
vezabelity, visibility
vezabiledy, visibility
vezatashen, visit(ation)
vezibiledy, visibility
vezit, visit
vezitashen, visit(ation)
vezubelity, visibility
vezubiledy, visibility
vezutashen, visit(ation)
via, BY WAY/MEANS OF
viable,bility,ly, POSSIBLE/CAPABLE "prefixes: non"
viabul, viable
viaduct,*, CHANNELS WHICH ALLOW FLOW/TRANSPORT
viaduk, viaduct
vial,*,led,ling, SMALL BOTTLE (or see vile)
vialashen, violate(tion)
vialate, violate
vialation, violate(tion)
vialen, violin
vialens, violent(nce)
vialet, violet
vialin, violin
vialint, violent
vialunt, violent
vibd, vibe(d)
vibe,*,bing, SHORT FOR VIBRATION, A RYTHMIC SYNCHRONICITY, RESOUNDS WELL TOGETHER
vibrachun, vibrate(tion)
vibraded, vibrate(d)

vibrant,ncy,tly, PULSING WITH ENERGY/ LIFE
vibrashen, vibrate(tion)
vibrate,*,ed,ting,tion,tor,ant, PULSATING RYTHM/WAVES
vibratid, vibrate(d)
vibrator,*,ry, MACHINE PRODUCING PULSES OF WAVES/FREQUENCY
vibrensy, vibrant(ncy)
vibrent, vibrant
vibrently, vibrant(ly)
vibrinsy, vibrant(ncy)
vibrutory, vibrator(y)
vicabulary, vocabulary
vice,*, REPLACING ONE INFERIOR WITH ANOTHER, INSTEAD OF (or see vise)
vicenity, vicinity
vichen, vision
vichenary, vision(ary)
viches, vicious
vichol, vigil
vichos, vicious
vichualize, visual(ize)
vichulante, vigil(ante)
vichun, vision
vichunary, vision(ary)
vichus, vicious
vichwal, visual
vichwulize, visual(ize)
vicinity,ties, WITHIN THE AREA
vicious,sly,sness, HATEFUL DISPOSITION, LASHING OUT WITH DARK/ NEGATIVE EMOTION
vicisitude, vicissitude
vicissitude,dinary,dinous, TO MOVE FROM ONE FREQUENCY TO ANOTHER, A MUTATION
victamize, victim(ize)
victem, victim
victim,*,mize,mizes,mized,mizing, mization,mizer, RECEIVER OF ILL WILL, HELPLESS, INABILITY TO GAIN POWER IN A SITUATION
victomizashen, victim(ization)
victomize, victim(ize)
victum, victim
victumizashen, victim(ization)
victumize, victim(ize)
vidal, vital
vidamen, vitamin
videl, vital
videmen, vitamin

video,*,oed,oing, MOVING/VISUAL FILM WITH MANY FRAMES/PICTURES
vidio, video
vidl, vital
vidrefy, vitrify
vidul, vital
vidumen, vitamin
vidumin, vitamin
vieble, viable
viebul, viable
viecol, vehicle
vieduk, viaduct
vielashen, violate(tion)
vielate, violate
view,*,wed,wing,wer, TO SEE WITH THE EYES "prefixes: over/pre"
vigalanty, vigil(ante)
vigalent, vigil(ant)
vigel, vigil
vigelent, vigil(ant)
vigeng, viking
viger, vigor
vigerus, vigor(ous)
vigil,la,lance,lant,lantly,lante,lantism, TO WATCH OVER, PAY CAREFUL ATTENTION TO "prefixes: in"
viging, viking
viginu, vagina
vigir, vigor
vigirus, vigor(ous)
vigolante, vigil(ante)
vigor,*,rous,roso,rously,rousness, OF VITALITY/STRENGTH "prefixes: in"
vigorus, vigor(ous)
vigual, visual
vigulante, vigil(ante)
vigulent, vigil(ant)
viguol, visual
vigur, vigor
vigurus, vigor(ous)
vijalante, vigil(ante)
vijalent, vigil(ant)
vijewelize, visual(ize)
vijinu, vagina
vijolent, vigil(ant)
vijual, visual
vijulante, vigil(ante)
vijulent, vigil(ant)
vijwel, visual
vijwul, visual
vijwulize, visual(ize)
vikabeulery, vocabulary
vikabulery, vocabulary

vikeng, viking
viker, vigor
viking,*, SCANDINAVIAN WARRIOR
vikir, vigor
vikor, vigor
viktem, victim
viktemizashen, victim(ization)
viktemize, victim(ize)
viktim, victim
viktumizashen, victim(ization)
viktumize, victim(ize)
vikur, vigor
vila, valet / villa
vilafy, vilify
vilage, villa(ge)
vilan, villain
vilanus, villain(ous)
vilarean, valerian
vile,*,ely,eness, DISGUSTING (or see vial/villa/valet)
vilefy, vilify
vilege, villa(ge)
vilej, villa(ge)
vilen, villain / violin
vilenus, villain(ous)
vilerean, valerian
vilet, valet
vilify,fies,fied,fier,vying,fication, TO DEFACE/SLANDER/DEGRADE
vilij, villa(ge)
vilin, villain / violin
vilinus, villain(ous)
villa,*,age,ager,agery, A RURAL/COUNTRY TOWN (or see valet)
villain,*,nous,nously,nousness,ny,nies, THE BAD GUY/ANTAGONIST, OF EVIL CHARACTER
villian, villain
vilofi, vilify
vilon, villain
vilosedy, velocity
vilosety, velocity
vilu, villa
viluch, villa(ge)
vilufy, vilify
vilug, villa(ge)
viluj, villa(ge)
vilun, villain
vilunus, villain(ous)
vilur, velure / velour
vilutch, villa(ge)
vim, OF STRENGTH/ENTHUSIASM
vin, vine
vinager, vinegar

vinagra, vinaigrette
vinagrette, vinaigrette
vinaigrette, SALAD DRESSING WITH MOSTLY VINEGAR
vinaker, vinegar
vinal, vinyl
vinamus, venom(ous)
vinasin, venison
vinch, venge
vincher, venture
vinchful, venge(ful)
vinchurd, venture(d)
vincible,lity,eness, CAN BE OVERCOME/CONQUERED
vind, vend / vent
vindalashen, ventilate(tion)
vindalate, ventilate
vindecate, vindicate
vindedu, vendetta
vindekdef, vindictive
vindektif, vindictive
vindeta, vendetta
vindetta, vendetta
vindicashen, vindicate(tion)
vindicate,*,ed,ting,able,ation,ative,ator,atory,ctive, TO BE LIBERATED BY AVENGING
vindictef, vindictive
vindictive,ely,eness, HAS A REVENGE
vindikduv, vindictive
vindiktif, vindictive
vinducation, vindicate(tion)
vindulashen, ventilate(tion)
vindulate, ventilate
vine,*,ey, A TRAILING PLANT SUCH AS IVY/GRAPE
vineer, veneer
vinegar,*,ry,rish, RESULT OF FERMENTATION
vinegre, vinaigrette
vinegrette, vinaigrette
vinel, vinyl
vinemus, venom(ous)
viner, veneer
vinerate, venerate
vinew, venue
ving, venge
vingents, venge(ance)
vingful, venge(ful)
viniger, vinegar
vinigre, vinaigrette
vinigrette, vinaigrette
vinil, vinyl
vinila, vanilla

vinj, venge
vinjents, venge(ance)
vinjful, venge(ful)
vino, WINE
vinol, vinyl
vinosen, venison
vinsable, vincible
vinsher, venture
vinsuble, vincible
vint, vint / vend
vintage, RESULT OF A SUPERIOR CROP SEASON
vintalashen, ventilate(tion)
vintalate, ventilate
vintalation, ventilate(tion)
vinteg, vintage
vintelate, ventilate
vintilate, ventilate
vintrecal, ventricle
vintrecular, ventricle(cular)
vintrelukwist, ventriloquist
vintrical, ventricle
vintrikul, ventricle
vintrikuler, ventricle(cular)
vintrilukwist, ventriloquist
vintrukle, ventricle
vintuge, vintage
vintuj, vintage
vintulate, ventilate
vintur, venture
vintured, venture(d)
vinu, venue
vinuger, vinegar
vinugrey, vinaigrette
vinuker, vinegar
vinul, vinyl
vinumus, venom(ous)
vinurate, venerate
vinusen, venison
viny, vine(y)
vinyl, TYPE OF PLASTIC
vinyou, venue
viola, STRINGED INSTRUMENT
violadid, violate(d)
violashen, violate(tion)
violate,*,ed,ting,tive,tor,tion, TO BASH BOUNDARIES/LAWS SET FORTH BY PEOPLE/NATURE "prefixes: in"
violen, violin
violens, violent(nce)
violent,tly,nce, USE OF AGGRESSIVE FORCE "prefixes: non"
violet, DARK COLOR OF RED/BLUE
violin,*, STRINGED INSTRUMENT

violint, violent
violunt, violent
vipe, vibe
viper,*,rish,rous,rously, POISONOUS SNAKE
vipir, viper
viporus, viper(ous)
viprus, viper(ous)
vipur, viper
vir, veer
viracedy, veracity / voracity
viracious, voracious / veracious
viracity, veracity / voracity
viral,lly, OF A VIRUS (or see virile) "prefixes: non/retro"
viralent, virulent
viralint, virulent
virasedy, veracity / voracity
virashes, voracious / veracious
virasious, voracious / veracious
virasity, veracity
virb, verb
virbadum, verbatim
virbatum, verbatim
virble, verbal
virblize, verbal(ize)
virbly, verbal(lly)
virboly, verbal(lly)
virbos, verbose
virbosity, verbose(sity)
virbosudy, verbose(sity)
virbul, verbal
virbule, verbal(lly)
virbulize, verbal(ize)
virch, verge
virchen, version
virchew, virtue
virchewul, virtual
virchoo, virtue
virchual, virtual
virchualedy, virtual(ity)
virchuality, virtual(ity)
virchuil, virtual
virchuol, virtual
virdabra, vertebra
virdago, vertigo
virdego, vertigo
virdek, verdict
virdekly, vertical(lly)
virdekul, vertical
virdibra, vertebra
virdict, verdict
virdigo, vertigo
virdikly, vertical(lly)

virdikt, verdict
virdikul, vertical
virdubra, vertebra
virdugo, vertigo
virdukil, vertical
virdukly, vertical(lly)
virel, viral / virile
vires, virus
virge, verge
virgen, version / virgin
virgin,*,nal, PRISTINE/NATURAL, HASN'T BEEN EXPLOITED/ ALTERED (or see version)
virgun, version / virgin
virile,lity,lism, HEALTHY MASCULINE QUALITIES (or see viral)
viris, virus
viriudy, variety
viriuty, variety
virje, verge
virjen, virgin
virjin, version / virgin
virmeculite, vermiculite
virmen, vermin
virmikewlite, vermiculite
virmikulite, vermiculite
virmin, vermin
virmiqulite, vermiculite
virmooth, vermouth
virmuth, vermouth
virnakuler, vernacular
virol, viral / virile
virolent, virulent
viros, virus
virp, verb
virply, verbal(lly)
virpul, verbal
virs, verse
virsatil, versatile
virsatilety, versatile(lity)
virsetal, versatile
virshen, version
virshuality, virtual(ity)
virsutil, versatile
virsutilety, versatile(lity)
virtebra, vertebra
virtego, vertigo
virtekul, vertical
virtibra, vertebra
virtigo, vertigo
virtikul, vertical
virtual,lity,lly, NOT PHYSICAL TO THE TOUCH

virtue,uosity,uosities,uoso,uous,uously, uousness, KNOWS OF EXCELLENCE, ONE WITH SUPRA KNOWLEDGE
virtugo, vertigo
virtukle, vertical(lly)
virul, viral / virile
virulent, VERY BITTER/POISONOUS/ DANGEROUS
virulint, virulent
virus,ses, LIVING ORGANISM "prefixes: pro/retro/sub"
visa,aed,aing, A PASS/PASSPORT
visabelity, visibility
visabil, visible
visabiledy, visibility
visabilety, visibility
visably, visible(ly)
visatashen, visit(ation)
visater, visit(or)
visatude, vicissitude
viscos, viscous
viscosedy, viscous(ity)
viscosity, viscous(ity)
viscous,sly,sness,osity, TEXTURE/ CONSISTENCY OF SYRUP "prefixes: non"
viscus, viscous
vise,*,ed,sing, A TOOL/PRESS FOR GRIPING/HOLDING ITEMS IN PLACE (or see vice)
visectomy, vasectomy
visekteme, vasectomy
visenedy, vicinity
visenety, vicinity
viser, visor
viset, visit
visetashen, visit(ation)
visetation, visit(ation)
viseter, visit(or)
visetude, vicissitude
vishen, vision
vishenary, vision(ary)
vishes, vicious
vishon, vision
vishos, vicious
vishuel, visual
vishun, vision
vishunary, vision(ary)
vishus, vicious
visibility,ties, THE DEGREE OF ABILITY TO SEE WITH THE NAKED EYE
visible,eness,ly, ABLE TO BE SEEN WITH THE EYE
visinedy, vicinity

visinety, vicinity
vision,*,nal,nally,nary,naries,nariness, nless, TO CONCEIVE/VIEW THAT BEYOND OUR EYE'S ABILITY, ABILITY TO SEE "prefixes: en/pre"
visir, visor
visit,*,ted,ting,table,tant,tation,tational, tatorial,tor, GO SEE SOMEONE/ SOMETHING BRIEFLY, RECEIVE GUESTS, BE A GUEST
visitashen, visit(ation)
visiter, visit(or)
visitude, vicissitude
viskes, viscous
viskosedy, viscous(ity)
viskosity, viscous(ity)
viskus, viscous
visor,*, GUARD/SHIELD TO PROTECT SUN'S GLARES
vista,*, A LONG/STRETCHING VIEW
visu, visa
visual,*,lly,lize,lization,lizer, USE OF EYES TO SEE, TO SEE AS IF WITH THE EYES "prefixes: non"
visubel, visible
visubelity, visibility
visubiledy, visibility
visuble, visible / visible(ly)
visur, visor
visut, visit
visutashen, visit(ation)
visutation, visit(ation)
visuter, visit(or)
visutude, vicissitude
vital,*,lly,lness,lism,listic,lity,lities,lize, lizes,lized,lizing,lization, LIFE ENERGY/ PROPERTIES, ESSENTIAL PROCESSES FOR CONTINUATION OF LIFE "prefixes: de/intra"
vitaledy, vital(ity)
vitalidy, vital(ity)
vitamen, vitamin
vitamin,*, ORGANIC NUTRIENTS/ MINERALS
vitel, vital
vitemen, vitamin
vitl, vital
vito, veto
vitrify,fies,fied,fying,fiability,fiable, BECOME/CHANGE INTO GLASS "prefixes: de"
vitul, vital
vitumen, vitamin
vitumin, vitamin

viu, view
viubil, viable
viuble, viable
viud, view(ed)
viuduk, viaduct
viuladid, violate(d)
viulashen, violate(tion)
viulation, violate(tion)
viulens, violent(nce)
viulet, violet
viva,acity,acities, LIFE
vivaches, vivacious
vivachusnes, vivacious(ness)
vivacious,sly,sness,ity,ities, BOUNDING WITH LIFE/ENERGY/ SPIRIT
vivashes, vivacious
vivashous, vivacious
vivashusnes, vivacious(ness)
vived, vivid
vivedly, vivid(ly)
vivid,dly,dness, BRIGHT/DRAMATIC/ CLEAR
vivu, viva
viyudukt, viaduct
vizabelity, visibility
vizabil, visible
vizabiledy, visibility
vizably, visible(ly)
vizatashen, visit(ation)
vizater, visit(or)
vizer, visor
vizet, visit
vizetashen, visit(ation)
vizetur, visit(or)
vizibelity, visibility
vizibiledy, visibility
vizibul, visible
vizir, visor
vizit, visit
vizitashen, visit(ation)
viziter, visit(or)
vizivelity, visibility
vizor, visor
vizubel, visible
vizubelity, visibility
vizubiledy, visibility
vizuble, visible
vizubly, visible(ly)
vizur, visor
vizutashen, visit(ation)
vizuter, visit(or)
vocabeulery, vocabulary

vocabulary,ries, WORDS IN A PARTICULAR LANGUAGE USED FOR COMMUNICATION
vocal,*,lly,lness,lize,lizes,lized,lizing, lization,list,lism,lizer, USING THE VOICE "prefixes: de/inter/sub/uni"
vocalise, vocal(ize)
vocashen, vocation
vocashenul, vocation(al)
vocation,*,nal,nally, AN ACQUIRED/ NATURAL SKILL/ PROFESSION USED TO EARN MONEY "prefixes: in"
vocel, vocal
vocul, vocal
voculize, vocal(ize)
voded, vote(d)
vodef, votive
voder, vote(r)
vodev, votive
vodid, vote(d)
vodif, votive
vodir, vote(r)
vodiv, votive
vodka, ALCOHOLIC SPIRITS
vodur, vote(r)
voed, void
voeg, voyage
voej, voyage
voes, voice
voezd, voice(d)
vog, vogue
vogue, IN FASHION
voice,*,ed,cing,eful,efulness,eless, elessly,elessness, SOUND COMING FROM THE MOUTH "prefixes: de/un"
void,*,ded,ding,dable,dableness,der, dness,dance, ONE VAST NOTHING MATERIALLY ALL THINGS POTENTIALLY, RETURN TO NOTHING
voig, voyage
voij, voyage
vois, voice
voist, voice(d)
vok, vogue
vokabeulery, vocabulary
vokabulery, vocabulary
vokalize, vocal(ize)
vokashen, vocation
vokashenul, vocation(al)
vokation, vocation
vokationul, vocation(al)
vokeishon, vocation

vokel, vocal
vokelize, vocal(ize)
vokil, vocal
vokilize, vocal(ize)
vokul, vocal
vokulize, vocal(ize)
volanteer, volunteer
volanterd, volunteer(ed)
volatel, volatile
volatile,eness,lity,lize,lization, ABLE TO CHANGE SUDDENLY IN COMPOSITION, EXPLOSIVE "prefixes: de"
volcano,oes,nic,nically,nism,nicity,nist, nize,nizes,nized,nizing,nization, MOUNTAIN ERUPTION FROM ITS CORE
volcher, vulture
vold, vault / volt
vole, volley
volee, volley
volenter, volunteer
volenterd, volunteer(ed)
volentery, voluntary
voleum, volume
volgar, vulgar
voli, volley
volinter, volunteer
volisity, velocity
volitel, volatile
volkano, volcano
volley,*,yed,ying,yer, TO GO BACK AND FORTH, DISCHARGE OF MANY THINGS AT ONCE
volly, volley
volnerable, vulnerable
volnirable, vulnerable
volnrable, vulnerable
volopchuis, voluptuous
volosedy, velocity
volshur, vulture
volt,*,tage,taic, ELECTRICAL MEASUREMENT OF POWER (or see vault)
voltaec, voltaic
voltage,*, TYPE OF ELECTRICAL ACTION "prefixes: over"
voltaic,*, TYPE OF ELECTRICAL ACTION
voltauk, voltaic
voltshur, vulture
volume,*,ed,ming,minous,minously, minosity, LEVEL OF SOUND/ FREQUENCY, MANY THINGS

BROUGHT TOGETHER, FORM OF MEASUREMENT
voluntary,rism,rist,ristic,ries,rily,riness, teer, FREELY OFFER SERVICE WITHOUT EXPECTING PAY/MONEY/ EXCHANGE "prefixes: in"
volunteer,*,red,ring, FREELY OFFER SERVICE WITHOUT EXPECTING PAY/ MONEY/EXCHANGE
volunter, volunteer
volunterd, volunteer(ed)
voluntery, voluntary
voluptuous,sly,sness, OF SENSUALITY
volutel, volatile
volutil, volatile
volva,ate, FUNGI MEMBRANE (or see vulva)
voly, volley
volyewm, volume
vomet, vomit
vomit,*,ted,ting,tous,tory,tories, turition,tus, THE ENERGETIC DISCHARGE OF CONTENTS OF THE STOMACH THROUGH THE MOUTH
vomut, vomit
voner, veneer
voodoo, FICTITIOUS PRACTICE OF SORCERY
voracious,sly,sness, DEVOUR WITH EXTREME GREED/ENTHUSIASM (or see veracious)
voracity,ious, VORACIOUS/EAGER/ RAVENOUS CONSUMPTION, GREAT APPETITE FOR (or see veracity)
vorashus, voracious / veracious
vorasity, veracity
vordes, vortice
vordex, vortex
vorteks, vortex
vortes, vortice
vortesis, vortex(es) / vortice(s)
vortex,xes,tices,tical,tically,ticose, A SWIRLING/SPIRAL MOVEMENT
vortice,*,cal,cally,cose, SWIRLING/ SPIRAL MOVEMENT AS IN A VORTEX
vortisus, vortex(es)
vos, vase
vosektumy, vasectomy
vot, vote
vote,*,ed,ting,er,eless, TO MAKE A CHOICE/DECISION BETWEEN TWO OR MORE THINGS
votef, votive

voteve, votive
votid, vote(d)
votif, votive
votive, DEDICATED WITH A VOW
votka, vodka
votku, vodka
votuve, votive
vouch,hes,hed,hing,her,hee, CONFIRM/ATTEST/UPHOLD THE LEGITIMACY/VALIDITY OF SOMEONE/SOMETHING
vouchd, vouch(ed)
voug, voyage
vouj, voyage
voul, vowel
vow,*,wed,wing, TAKE AN OATH, SWEAR TO UPHOLD
vowch, vouch
vowchur, vouch(er)
vowel,*, ONE OF SIX LETTERS OF THE ENGLISH ALPHABET WITH CERTAIN CHARACTERISTICS "prefixes: semi"
vowl, vowel
voyage,*,ed,ging,er, A JOURNEY/TRIP BY SEA
voyd, void
voyg, voyage
voyj, voyage
voys, voice
voyst, voice(d)
voz, vase
vucabeulery, vocabulary
vucinity, vicinity
vud, view(ed)
vudu, voodoo
vue, view
vugina, vagina
vuhemint, vehemence(nt)
vujina, vagina
vukabulery, vocabulary
vula, valet
vularean, valerian
vulchur, vulture
vuledity, valid(ity)
vulerean, valerian
vulerian, valerian
vulet, valet
vulfa, vulva / volva
vulgar,rly,rness,rian,rism,rity,rities,rize,rization,rizer, OFF COLOR IN BEHAVIOR/LANGUAGE/MANNERISM
vulgaredy, vulgar(ity)
vulger, vulgar

vulgeredy, vulgar(ity)
vulgurly, vulgar(ly)
vulidete, valid(ity)
vulnerable,bility,eness,bly, NOT WELL PROTECTED "prefixes: in"
vulnuruble, vulnerable
vulopchues, voluptuous
vulosedy, velocity
vulosety, velocity
vulsher, vulture
vulture,*, A LARGE SCAVENGER BIRD
vulupchuis, voluptuous
vuluptuis, voluptuous
vuluptuous, voluptuous
vulur, velour / velure
vulva, EXTERNAL FEMALE GENITALIA (or see volva)
vuneer, veneer
vunela, vanilla
vuner, veneer
vunila, vanilla
vuracious, voracious / veracious
vurashes, voracious / veracious
vurasity, veracity
vurb, verb
vurbadum, verbatim
vurbatum, verbatim
vurbelize, verbal(ize)
vurblize, verbal(ize)
vurbose, verbose
vurbuliz, verbal(ize)
vurchen, version / virgin
vurchew, virtue
vurchewul, virtual
vurchoo, virtue
vurchual, virtual
vurchuol, virtual
vurdabra, vertebra
vurdago, vertigo
vurdekly, vertical(lly)
vurdekt, verdict
vurdekul, vertical
vurdibra, vertebra
vurdigo, vertigo
vurdikly, vertical(lly)
vurdikt, verdict
vurdikul, vertical
vurdubra, vertebra
vurdukil, vertical
vurge, verge
vurgen, version / virgin
vurgun, version / virgin
vuriedy, variety
vurietal, variety(tal)

vuriety, variety
vurje, verge
vurjen, version / virgin
vurjun, version / virgin
vurmeculite, vermiculite
vurmikulite, vermiculite
vurmouth, vermouth
vurmuth, vermouth
vurnaculer, vernacular
vurnakuler, vernacular
vurp, verb
vurple, verbal / verbal(lly)
vurs, verse
vursatilety, versatile(lity)
vursitelity, versatile(lity)
vurtabra, vertebra
vurtego, vertigo
vurtekul, vertical
vurtibra, vertebra
vurtigo, vertigo
vurtikul, vertical
vurtue, virtue
vurtugo, vertigo
vusectemy, vasectomy
vusekteme, vasectomy
vusenedy, vicinity
vusinity, vicinity
vyle, vial / vile
wa, way / weigh / whey
wabel, wobble
wabul, wobble
wac, wake / walk / wok / whack
wach, wage / wash / watch / wake / wok / walk
wacher, washer / wage(r)
waches, wage(s) / watch(es)
wachir, washer / wage(r)
wachis, wage(s) / watch(es)
wachul, waggle
wachus, wage(s) / wash(es)
wack, wake / walk / wok / whack
wacks, wax / whack(s) / walk(s)
wacky,kily,kiness, SILLY, ERRATIC, CRAZY
wackyness, wacky(kiness)
wacs, wax / whack(s) / walk(s) / wake(s) / wok(s)
wad,*,dded,dding, CRUMPLE/CRINKLE/ROLL SOMETHING UP INTO A BALL SHAPE (or see wade/what/watt/wait/weight)
waddle,*,ed,ling,er,ly, MOVE BACK AND FORTH IN MOVEMENT SUCH AS A PENGUIN WALKING

wade,*,ed,ding,er,ers, WALK/ NAVIGATE THROUGH SHALLOW WATER/ LIQUID/RESISTANT MATERIAL (or see wait/wad/ weight)
wadel, waddle / what'll
wader, wader / water / waiter
wadercres, watercress
waderfol, waterfall
waderproof, waterproof
waderpruf, waterproof
waders, LONG RUBBER BOOTS FOR FEET TO PROTECT AGAINST DEEP WATER (or see waiter(s))
wadertite, watertight
wadevr, whatever
wadid, wad(dded) / wait(ed) / wed(ed)
wadil, waddle / what'll
wadir, wader / water / waiter
wadirproof, waterproof
wadirpruf, waterproof
wadirs, waders / waiter(s) / water(s)
wadirtite, watertight
wadle, waddle / what'll
wadol, waddle / what'll
wador, wader / water / waiter
wadres, waitress
wadrus, waitress
wadud, wad(dded) / wait(ed) / wade(d)
wadul, waddle / what'll
wadur, wader / water / waiter
wadurd, water(ed)
wadurfol, waterfall
wadurproof, waterproof
wadurpruf, waterproof
wadurs, waders / waiter(s) / water(s)
wae, way / weigh / whey
wael, whale / wail / wale
waen, wain / wane
waest, waist / waste
waet, wait / weight
waf, wave
wafd, waft / raft / wave(d) / waive(d)
wafe, wave / wave(vy)
wafel, waffle
wafer,*, THIN SLICE OF SOMETHING (or see waiver)
waffle,*,ed,ling, BATTER COOKED IN A WAFFLE MAKER
wafil, waffle
wafir, wafer / waiver
wafle, waffle
waflis, wave(less)
wafor, wafer / waiver

waft,*,ted,ting,ty,tage, SMALL PENNANT SHAPED FLAG, BE CARRIED ALONG ,FLOAT (or see raft/wave(d)/waive(d))
waful, waffle
wafur, wafer / waiver
wag,*,gged,gging,gger,ggle,ggles,ggled, ggling, QUICKLY MOVE BACK AND FORTH SUCH AS A DOGS TAIL (or see wage)
wagd, wag(gged) / wage(d)
wage,*,ed,ging,eless,er,erer, MONEY EARNED BY WORKING,MAKE A BET, CREATE CONFLICT/WAR (or see wag) "prefixes: un"
wagel, waggle
wagen, wagon
waggle,*,ed,ling,ly,ggingly, QUICKLY MOVE BACK AND FORTH SUCH AS A DOGS TAIL
wagil, waggle
wagin, wagon
wagir, wage(r)
wagle, waggle / waggle(ly)
wagly, waggle(ly)
wagon,*,ner, VESSEL WITH BOX SHAPED BASE AND FOUR WHEELS FOR CARRYING THINGS
wagul, waggle
wagun, wake(n) / wagon
wagur, wage(r)
wail,*,led,ling,ler,lingly,lful,lfully, VERY HEAVY/LOUD/ PAINFUL CRY (or see wale/whale)
wain, TYPE OF WAGON (or see wane)
wainscot,ted,ting, WOOD/SUBSTANCE ONLY COVERING LOWER HALF OF A WALL
wainskot, wainscot
waist, MIDDLE SECTION/MIDRIFF OF A BODY BETWEEN RIBCAGE AND HIPS (or see waste)
wait,*,ted,ting,ter, TEMPORARILY PAUSE/STOP MOMENTUM TO SERVICE ANOTHER'S NEEDS (or see wade/weight)
waiter,*, ONE WHO SERVES PATRONS FOOD AT A RESTAURANT/CAFE/ DINER (or see waders)
waitress,ses, FEMALES WHO SERVE PATRONS FOOD AT A RESTAURANT/ CAFE/ DINER

waive,*,ed,ving,er, RELINQUISH/LET GO OF YOUR RIGHTS TO SOMETHING (or see wave)
waiver,*, A TEMPORARY PASS, TO GIVE UP RIGHTS
wajd, wage(d)
wajer, wage(r)
wajur, wage(r)
wak, walk / whack / wake / wok
wake,*,en,woke,eful,efully,efulness, eless,king, BE AWARE OF PHYSICAL REALITY AFTER BEING ASLEEP, WAVE CAUSED BY MOVEMENT, RITUAL PERFORMED FOR DECEASED (or see whack/wok/ wacky)
waken, wake(n) / wagon
wakenes, wacky(kiness)
waker, walker / wake(n) / whack(er)
wakin, wake(n) / wagon
wakle, waggle
wakon, wake(n) / wagon
waks, wax / whack(s) / walk(s) / wake(s) / wok(s)
wakse, wax(y)
wakser, wax(er)
waksy, wax(y)
wakul, waggle
wakun, wake(n) / wagon
waky, wacky
wakynes, wacky(kiness)
wal, wall / wail / whale
wald, wail(ed) / wale(d) / wall(ed)
wale,*,ed,ling, A WELT CAUSED BY A WHIPPING, SUPPORT FOR OUTSIDE PLANKING OF A BOAT (or see wail/ whale/wall)
walep, wallop
walet, wallet
walip, wallop
walit, wallet
walk,*,ked,king,ker, MOVING/ TRAVELING ON FOOT
walker,*, A DEVICE TO HELP PEOPLE WALK (or see walk(er))
walkor, walk(er) / walker
wall,*,lled,lling, VERTICAL SECTION OF A DWELLING/STRUCTURE (or see wail/wale)
wallet,*, HOLDER FOR MONEY AND I.D.
wallit, wallet
wallop,*,ped,ping, THRASH/STRIKE A BLOW TO

wallow,*,wed,wing,wer, LIKE A PIG SQUIRMING IN THE MUD, TO LIE/BE DEEP INTO SOMETHING
wallut, wallet
walnut,*, A NUT
walo, wallow
walod, wallow(ed)
walop, wallop
waloped, wallop(ed)
walow, wallow
walowed, wallow(ed)
walres, walrus
walrus,ses, A CARNIVOROUS/MARINE MAMMAL
wals, waltz / wall(s) / wale(s) / wail(s)
walts, waltz
waltsd, waltz(ed)
waltz,zes,zed,zing,zer, DANCE TO 3/4 TIME MUSIC
walup, wallop
waluped, wallop(ed)
walupt, wallop(ed)
walut, wallet
walz, waltz
walzed, waltz(ed)
wamp, whomp
wan,*, WASHED OUT/WEAK IN COLOR/ ENERGY/MOTION (or see wain/ wane/ won/one)
wand,*, SLENDER STICK USED FOR MANY PURPOSES (or see want/ won't)
wander,*,red,ring,ringly,rer, TO MOVE/ TRAVEL AIMLESSLY ABOUT (or see wonder)
wanderful, wonderful
wandurer, wander(er)
wane,*,ed,ning,ey,nier,niest, ON THE DOWNSIDE OF A PEAK/WAVE, TO DIMINISH (or see wan/wain)
wans, once
wanscoat, wainscot
wanskot, wainscot
want,*,ted,ting, DESIRE SOMETHING (or see won't/wand)
wanten, wanton
wanton,nly,nness, WANT FOR NOTHING, FREE/UNBOUND/ UNRESTRAINED
wantun, wanton
wantunes, wanton(nness)
wantunle, wanton(ly)
wapen, weapon
wapun, weapon

war,*,rred,rring,rless, DISPLAY OF HOSTILITY/OPPOSITION BETWEEN FORCES (or see wore/wear/where/ ware/we're/weir) "prefixes: pre"
warale, weary(rily)
warant, warrant
warante, warrant(y)
waras, whereas
warbil, warble
warble,*,ed,ling,er, TYPE OF VIBRATION/SOUND, A TUMOR/ SWELLING
warbler,*, A BIRD
warbul, warble
ward,*,ded,ding,den, TERRITORY/AREA, FEND OFF, DEFEND AGAINST (or see word/wart/war(rred)/where'd)
warden,*, A PAID OVERSEER IN A PRISON SYSTEM
wardon, warden
wardrobe,*, COLLECTION OF CLOTHING, PLACE WHERE CLOTHING IS KEPT
wardun, warden
ware,*, BE WATCHFUL OF, SPECIAL ITEMS OF USE/VALUE (or see war/ wear/ where/weary)
warefur, wherever
wareir, warrior
warele, weary(rily)
waren, warren
warent, warrant
warente, warrant(y)
warenty, warrant(y)
wareur, warrior
warevur, wherever
warf, wharf
warier, warrior
warily, weary(rily)
warin, warren
warint, warrant
warinte, warrant(y)
warinted, warrant(ed)
warinty, warrant(y)
warl, where'll
warm,*,med,ming,mer,mest,mth,mly, mish,mness, TEMPERATURE BETWEEN HOT/COLD, BECOME COMFORTABLE WITH (or see worm)
warmist, warm(est)
warn,*,ned,ning,ningly, TO CAUTION SOMEONE AGAINST HARM/ PUNISHMENT (or see worn/warren)
warp,*,ped,ping, BECOME TWISTED/ BENT/BOWED IN SHAPE

warrant,*,ted,ting,ty,ties,ter, GUARANTEE/CONTRACT/ AUTHORIZATION "prefixes: un"
warren,*, ENCLOSURE FOR BREEDING GAME
warrior,*, BRAVE FIGHTER IN WARFARE
warrun, warren
wars, war(s) / where(s) / wear(s) / was / worse / worst
warsh, wash
warshd, wash(ed)
wart,*,ted,ty, A BUMPY SKIN GROWTH FROM A VIRUS
wartrobe, wardrobe
warule, weary(rily)
warun, warren
warunt, warrant
warunte, warrant(y)
warunted, warrant(ed)
warunty, warrant(y)
warwithal, wherewithal
wary,rier,riest,rily,riness, BE CAUTIOUS/ CAREFUL OF (or see weary) "prefixes: un"
was, PAST TENSE FOR THE WORD "IS" (or see weigh(s)/way(s))
wasd, waist / waste
wash,hes,hed,hing,her,hable,hy, TO CLEANSE WITH WATER/LIQUID "prefixes: pre/un"
washe, wash(y)
washeble, wash(able)
washepl, wash(able)
washer,*, APPLIANCE TO WASH CLOTHES/PARTS, SOMEONE WHO WASHES
washible, wash(able)
washipl, wash(able)
washir, washer
washt, wash(ed)
washuble, wash(able)
washur, washer
wasn't, CONTRACTION OF THE WORDS "WAS NOT", PAST TENSE FOR THE WORD "IS NOT"
wasp,*, A STINGING/FLYING INSECT
wast, waist / waste
waste,*,ed,ting,er,tage,eness,tingly, MORE THAN NECESSARY, LEFTOVERS, REMAINS OF SOMETHING (or see waist)
wastid, waste(d)
wat, wait / weight / what / watt / wade / wad

watal, waddle / what'll
watch,hes,hed,hing,hful,hfully,hfulness, MONITOR/LOOK AFTER, A DEVICE WORN ON THE WRIST "prefixes: un"
wated, wade(d) / wait(ed) / wad(dded)
watel, waddle / what'll
water,*,red,ring,ry,rless, CLEAR/ NATURAL SOLUTION THAT CONFORMS TO ICE/LIQUID/GAS "prefixes: un/under"
watercress, AN EDIBLE PLANT
waterd, water(ed)
waterfall, A DOWNFLOWING OF WATER
waterfaul, waterfall
waterfol, waterfall
waterkres, watercress
waterproof,*,fed,fing,fer, WATER CANNOT PENETRATE
waterpruf, waterproof
waters, waders / waiter(s) / water(s)
watertight,tness, SEALS AGAINST WATER ENTERING
watertite, watertight
watever, whatever
watevur, whatever
watid, wade(d) / wait(ed) / wad(dded)
watil, waddle / what'll
watir, wader / water / waiter
watird, water(ed)
watirfal, waterfall
watirfol, waterfall
watirkres, watercress
watirproof, waterproof
watirpruf, waterproof
watirs, waders / waiter(s) / water(s)
watl, waddle / what'll
watle, waddle / what'll
wator, wader / water / waiter
watres, waitress
watrus, waitress
watt,*,ttage, MEASURE OF ELECTRICITY (or see what/wad)
watud, wade(d) / wait(ed) / wad(dded)
watul, waddle / what'll
watur, wader / water / waiter
waturcres, watercress
waturfal, waterfall
waturfol, waterfall
waturproof, waterproof
waturpruf, waterproof
waturs, waders / waiter(s) / water(s)
waubel, wobble

waubil, wobble
wauch, watch
wauchful, watch(ful)
wauded, wade(d) / wait(ed) / wad(dded)
waudel, waddle / what'll
wauder, water
waudertight, watertight
waudid, wade(d) / wait(ed) / wad(dded)
waudil, waddle / what'll
waudul, waddle / what'll
waufel, waffle
wauful, waffle
wauk, wok / walk
waul, whale / wail / wale / wall
waulep, wallop
waulet, wallet
waulk, walk
waulker, walk(er) / walker
waulkur, walk(er) / walker
waulnut, walnut
waulo, wallow
waulop, wallop
waulow, wallow
waults, waltz
waulup, wallop
waulut, wallet
waun, won / one
waund, wound
waunder, wander / wonder
waunt, want
wauper, whopper
waupur, whopper
waur, war(s) / where(s) / wear(s) / was / worse / worst
waurl, where'll
waurp, warp
waurs, war(s) / where(s) / wear(s) / was / worse / worst
waut, watt / what / wad
wautercres, watercress
wautertite, watertight
wavd, wave(d) / waive(d)
wave,*,ed,ving,eless,vy,vily,viness,er, SERPENTINE ACTION DISPLAYING UP/DOWN/BACK/FORTH MOVEMENTS
wavenes, wave(viness)
waver,*, FLUCTUATE UP/DOWN/BACK/ FORTH (or see waiver/wafer) "prefixes: un"
wavir, waiver / wafer
wavles, wave(less)

wavur, waiver / wafer
wavynes, wave(viness)
wax,xes,xed,xing,xer,xen,xy,xier,xiest, xiness, INCREASE IN INTENSITY/ SIZE/ STRENGTH, MATTER PRODUCED BY BEE/PETROLEUM (or see whack(s)/ wake(s))
waxin, wax(en)
waxse, wax(y)
way,*,yless, METHOD, FASHION, STYLE, DIRECTION (or see weigh/whey)
wayv, wave
waz, way(s) / weigh(s) / was
wazp, wasp
we, MORE THAN ONE WITH SELF INCLUDED (or see wee/whee/ whey)
we'd, CONTRACTION OF THE WORDS "WE WOULD/HAD" (or see wed/ weed/ wheat/whet)
we'll, CONTRACTION OF THE WORDS "WE WILL" (or see well/wheel)
we're, CONTRACTION OF THE WORDS "WE ARE" (or see were/where/ weir/ whirr)
we've, CONTRACTION OF THE WORDS "WE HAVE" (or see weave)
weak,ker,kest,ken,kened,kening,kish, kishly,kishness,kener,kling,kly, kliness, kness, LACKING IN SKILL/ STRENGTH/KNOWLEDGE (or see week)
weald,*, PRISTINE/UNCULTIVATED FIELD AMIDST A FOREST (or see wield/ wheel(ed))
wealth,hy,hier,hiest,hily,hiness, AN OVER ABUNDANCE, MORE THAN ONE NEEDS
wean,*,ned,ning,ner,nling, SLOWLY REDUCE NEED FOR NOURISHMENT FROM THE MOTHER/PRIMARY FOOD SOURCE (or see ween)
weane, weeny
weapan, weapon
weape, weep(y)
weaped, weep(ed) / wept / reap(ed)
weapen, weapon
weapon,*,nry,nless, TOOL/ INSTRUMENT FOR PROTECTION OR TO HURT/KILL "prefixes: bio"
weapun, weapon
weapy, weep(y)
wear,*,ring,wore,worn,rable, USE SOMETHING UNTIL NO LONGER

NEW, COVERING, CLOTHING (or see ware/where/we're/weir)
weard, weird
weary,rier,riest,ried,rying,rily,riness, riful,rifully,rifulness,riless,risome, risomely,risomeness, TIRED/EXHAUSTED/FATIGUED (or see wary) "prefixes: un"
weasel,*,led,ling, CARNIVOROUS/SLINKY/RODENT/MAMMAL
weather,*,red,ring,rability,rly,rliness, ELEMENTS/ATMOSPHERE AROUND THE EARTH (or see whether/wether/wither)
weathur, weather / wether / wither / whether
weave,*,woven,ving,er, CRISS-CROSS PERPENDICULAR FIBERS ONE INTO/THROUGH/ACROSS THE OTHER (or see we've) "prefixes: in/inter"
web,*,bbed,bbing,bby, INTERCONNECTING STRANDS CRISSCROSSING ONE ANOTHER, A NET, STRETCHED SKIN ON DUCK FEET (or see wept)
webd, web(bbed) / wept / weep(ed)
webt, web(bbed) / wept / weep(ed)
wech, which / witch / wedge
wechd, wedge(d)
wecht, wedge(d)
wed,*,dded,dding, GET MARRIED (or see wet/we'd/weed/whet/wheat)
weded, wed(dded) / weed(ed) / wet(tted)
wedeir, weed(er) / wet(tter)
wedel, whittle
weder, weed(er) / wet(tter) / weather
wedge,*,ed,ging,gie,gier,giest, A TRIANGULAR SHAPE, METHOD FOR RAISING/LEVELING
wedible, wet(able)
wedid, wed(dded) / weed(ed) / wet(tted)
wediest, weed(iest)
wedil, wheedle / whittle
wedir, weed(er) / wet(tter) / weather
wedle, wheedle / whittle
wedlock, MARRIAGE
wedlok, wedlock
wednesday,*, A DAY OF THE WEEK (ENGLISH)
wedo, widow
wedol, wheedle / whittle
wedr, weed(er) / wet(tter) / weather

wedth, width
wedud, wed(dded) / weed(ed) / wet(tted)
wedul, wheedle / whittle
wedur, weed(er) / wet(tter) / weather
wee, TINY/SMALL (or see we/whee)
weed,*,ded,ding,dy,dier,diest,dless,der, dily,diness, PLANTS MISUNDERSTOOD/UNDERAPPRECIATED FOR THEIR MEDICINAL QUALITIES (or see we'd)
week,*,kly, SEVEN DAYS IN A ROW (or see weak) "prefixes: bi/semi"
weekle, week(ly)
weels, wheel(s) / wield(s)
ween,*,ned,ning, DESIRE/EXPECT SOMETHING (or see wean)
weeny,nies,nier,niest,nsy, TINY/SMALL, A TYPE OF HOTDOG/WEINER
weep,*,ped,ping,py,pier,piest, PASSIONATE/SAD/INTENSE CRYING, AN OOZING/LEAKING/DRIPPING OF FLUIDS (or see wept/reap)
weery, weary
weevil,*,led,ly, AN INSECT/BEETLE WHICH BORES INTO PLANTS
wef, weave / we've
weful, weevil
weg, wedge / wig
wegal, wiggle
wegd, wedge(d)
wege, wedge / wedge(gy)
weged, wedge(d) / wig(gged)
wegis, wedge(s)
wegle, wiggle
wegul, wiggle
wegus, wedge(s)
weigh,*,hed,hing,hable,her,ht, THE ACT OF MEASURING THE WEIGHT OF SOMETHING, TO FEEL WEIGHT (or see way/whey)
weight,*,ted,ting,ty,tier,tiest,tless, tlessly,tlessness,ty,tier,tiest,tily, tiness, MEASUREMENT OF VOLUME/DENSITY/MASS (or see wait/whet) "prefixes: over/under"
weild, wield / weald / weld
weiner,*, A HOTDOG/SMOKED SAUSAGE, ALSO SPELLED 'WIENER', SHORT FOR WIENER WURST VIENNESE SAUSAGE (or see wean(er))

weir,*, WALL/DAM BUILT TO SLOW DOWN THE FLOW OF WATER (or see were/ we're/wear/where)
weird,der,dest,dly,dness, STRANGE/UNCOMMON/UNKNOWN/UNLIKELY
wej, wedge
wejt, wedge(d)
wek, weak / week / wick
weked, wicked / wick(ed)
weker, wicker
wekle, week(ly)
wekur, wicker / weak(er)
wel, well / we'll / wheel
welcome,*,ed,ming,ely,eness,er, INVITE/HONOR/ENCOURAGE/ACKNOWLEDGE THE ARRIVAL OF SOMETHING/SOMEONE
welcomnes, welcome(ness)
welcum, welcome
weld,*,ded,ding,der,dability,dable, dment, FUSE TWO PIECES OF SUBSTANCE TOGETHER USING A FILLER, HERB (or see wheel(ed)/wield/weald)
weldid, weld(ed) / wield(ed)
weldir, weld(er) / wield(er)
weldmint, weld(ment)
welduble, weld(able) / wield(able)
weldur, weld(er) / wield(er)
weldurnes, wilderness
weler, wheel(er)
welfare,rism, ABLE TO FARE WELL AND FUNCTION NORMALLY/PROPERLY
welfer, welfare
welkem, welcome
welkumd, welcome(d)
welkumt, welcome(d)
well,*,lled,lling, FIT, HEALTHY, STRUCTURE THAT HOLDS WATER SEEPING UP FROM A SPRING, WORD POSED AS A QUESTION, ALSO, IN ADDITION TO (or see will/we'll/ wheel) "prefixes: un/up"
wellth, wealth
welo, willow
wels, wheel(s) / wield(s)
welt,*, DISCOLORED/RAISED AREA ON THE SKIN WHERE DAMAGE OCCURED (or see weld/weild/wheel(ed)/weald/wilt)
welter, weld(er) / wield(er)
welth, wealth
welthe, wealth(y)

weltheist, wealth(iest)
welthenes, wealth(iness)
weltheur, wealth(ier)
welur, wheel(er)
wem, whim
weman, women
wemin, women
wempe, wimp(y)
wemped, wimp(ed)
wemper, whimper
wempur, whimper
wemsekul, whimsical
wemsukil, whimsical
wen, wean / ween / win / when
wenar, win(nner) / whine(r) / weiner
wence, wince
wench,hes,hing, DEROGATORY WORD FOR A WOMAN WHO IS FROM THE COUNTRY/PROMISCUOUS (or see winch/wrench)
wenchis, wench(es) / winch(es) / wrench(es)
wencht, wench(ed) / winch(ed) / wrench(ed)
wend,*,ded,ding, TRAVELING ALONG A PATH/ROUTE (or see wean(ed)/ ween(ed)/wind)
wende, wind(y)
wendeur, wind(ier)
wendy, wind(y)
wene, weeny / whinny / weiner
wenefer, whenever
wenefur, whenever
wener, win(nner) / whine(r) / weiner / wean(er)
weng, wing / wink
wenging, wing(ing)
wenie, weeny / weiner / whinny
wenir, win(nner) / weiner
wenk, wing / wink
wenking, wing(ing)
wenor, win(nner) / whine(r) / weiner
wens, whence / win(s) / wince
wensda, wednesday
wensh, wench / winch / wrench
wenshd, wench(ed) / winch(ed) / wrench(ed)
went, PAST TENSE FOR THE WORD "GO" (or see wind) "prefixes: under"
wenter, winter
wentre, wintery
wentur, winter
wenur, win(nner) / whine(r) / weiner

weny, weeny / whinny / weiner
wenzda, wednesday
wep, web / weep / whip
wepd, web(bbed) / wept / weep(ed)
wepe, weep(y)
weped, weep(ed) / wept / reap(ed)
wepen, whip(pping) / weapon
wepenre, weapon(ry)
weperwil, whippoorwill
wepeur, weep(ier)
wepin, whip(pping) / weapon
wepinre, weapon(ry)
wept, PAST TENSE FOR THE WORD 'WEEP', CRY (or see web(bbed)) "prefixes: un"
wepun, whip(pping) / weapon
wepunre, weapon(ry)
wepurwil, whippoorwill
wepy, weep(y)
wepyer, weep(ier)
wer, wear / ware / where / we're / were / weir
werable, wear(able)
werafir, wherever
weras, whereas
werd, word / weird / where'd
werder, weird(er)
werdest, weird(est)
werdist, weird(est)
werdly, weird(ly)
werdnes, weird(ness)
were, PAST TENSE FOR THE WORD "WAS/IS" (or see where/we're/ whirr/weary/wire/weir/ worry)
wereble, wear(able)
werefur, wherever
weren't, CONTRACTION OF THE WORDS "WERE NOT"
werever, wherever
weri, wary / weary / worry
werible, wear(able)
werkd, work(ed)
werkt, work(ed)
werkuble, work(able)
werl, whirl / whorl / where'll
werld, whirl(ed) / world / whorl(ed)
werlpool, whirlpool
werlpul, whirlpool
werlwend, whirlwind
werlwind, whirlwind
werm, worm
wernd, weren't / warn(ed)
wernt, weren't

wers, where's / wear(s) / ware(s) / worse / worst
wershep, worship
wership, worship
wert, weird / word / where'd
werth, worth
werubel, wear(able)
weruble, wear(able)
werwithal, wherewithal
wery, weary / wary / worry
wes, wheeze
wesal, weasel
wesd, whiz(zzed)
wesdim, wisdom
wesdum, wisdom
wesdwurd, west(ward)
wesel, whistle
weseld, weasel(ed)
wesenes, wheeze(ziness)
weserd, wizard
weses, whiz(zzes)
wesh, wish
weshd, wish(ed)
wesil, weasel
wesk, whisk
weskd, whisk(ed)
weske, whiskey
wesker, whisker
weskur, whisker
wesky, whiskey
wesol, weasel / whistle
wesp, wisp
wespe, wisp(y)
wesper, whisper
wesperd, whisper(ed)
wespur, whisper
wespurd, whisper(ed)
wespy, wisp(y)
west,terly,tern,ternize,ternized,ting, tward, ONE OF THE FOUR DIRECTIONS ON THE EARTH
westirea, wisteria
westirly, west(erly)
westirn, west(ern)
westirnise, west(ernize)
westle, whistle
westorn, west(ern)
westornize, west(ernize)
westurle, west(erly)
westurly, west(erly)
westurn, west(ern)
westurnise, west(ernize)
westwerd, west(ward)
westwurd, west(ward)

wesul, weasel / whistle
wesuld, weasel(ed) / whistle(d)
wesuls, weasel(s) / whistle(s)
wesurd, wizard
wesus, whiz(zzes)
wet,*,tted,tting,tter,ttest,tly,tness, ttable,ttish, BATHED/COATED/ AFFECTED BY A LIQUID (or see wheat/wed/whet/we'd/weed/wit)
wetch, which / witch
wetel, whittle
weter, wet(tter) / whet(tter)
wetesh, wet(ish)
weth, with
wethar, weather / wether / wither / whether
wethaut, without
wethdrau, withdraw
wethdro, withdraw
wethdron, withdraw(n)
wethdroul, withdraw(al)
wetheld, withheld
wethen, within
wether, A RAM/BUCK THAT HAS BEEN CASTRATED (or see weather/ wither/whether)
wethhold, withhold
wethin, within
wethir, weather / wether / wither / whether
wethold, withhold
wethout, without
wethrdraul, withdraw(al)
wethstand, withstand
wethstood, withstood
wethstud, withstood
wethur, weather / wether / wither / whether
wethurle, weather(ly)
wetir, wet(tter) / whet(tter)
wetl, whittle
wetlok, wedlock
wetnes, witness / wet(ness)
wetnus, witness / wet(ness)
wetnusd, witness(ed)
weto, widow
wetuble, wet(able)
wetul, whittle
wetur, wet(tter) / whet(tter)
wety, wit(tty)
weuld, wield / weald / weld
weurd, weird
weurdest, weird(est)
weurl, where'll / whirl

wev, weave / we've
wevd, weave(d)
wevel, weevil
wevor, weave(r)
wevul, weevil
wevur, weave(r)
wewre, weary
wey, way / weigh / whey
wez, wheeze / whiz
wezard, wizard
wezd, whiz(zzed)
weze, wheeze(zy)
wezel, weasel
wezeld, weasel(ed)
wezil, weasel
wezines, wheeze(ziness)
wezt, west
wezul, weasel
wezuld, weasel(ed)
wezurd, wizard
whack,*,ked,king,ky, A SOUND, A SLAPPING ACTION
whad, wad / what / wade / wait
whaddle, waddle / what'll
whadul, waddle / what'll
whake, wacky / wake
whakiness, wacky(kiness)
whaky, wacky
whale,*,ed,ling,er, LARGE AQUATIC MAMMAL, CETACEAN, TO BEAT/ THRASH/WHIP (or see wale/wail)
whalep, wallop
whalup, wallop
whar, wear / ware / where / we're
wharas, whereas
whard, where'd
whare, where / ware / wear / were
wharevur, wherever
wharf,es, PLACE FOR BOATS TO DOCK AND UNLOAD/LOAD ALONG A BODY OF WATER
whars, where's / ware(s) / wear(s)
wharwithal, wherewithal
what,*, A GENERAL WORD USED TO ASK A QUESTION OR LEARN MORE ABOUT SOMETHING (or see watt)
what'll, CONTRACTION OF THE WORDS "WHAT WILL/ SHALL" (or see waddle)
whatel, what'll / waddle
whatever, EITHER WAY, NOT THAT IMPORTANT
whatul, what'll / waddle

wheat,*, A GRAIN (or see weight/weed/ we'd)
wheb, web
whech, which / witch
whed, wed / we'd / weed / wheat
whedil, wheedle / whittle
whedlok, wedlock
whedul, wheedle / whittle
whee, EXPRESSION OF JOY, SUDDEN EXCITEMENT (or see we/wee)
wheedle,*,ed,ling,er,lingly, USE WORDS TO COAX/ENTICE SOMEONE TO GIVE YOU SOMETHING (or see whittle)
wheel,*,led,ling,ler, ROUND SHAPED DEVICE USED TO ROLL/TRANSPORT (or see we'll/well/weld/weald)
wheeze,*,ed,zing,zily,ziness,zy,ziness, RASPY BREATHING SOUND DUE TO LUNG IRRITATION
wheld, wheel(ed) / weld / wield / weald
whelm,*,med,ming, OVERTAKE, OVERPOWER, SUBMERGE "prefixes: over/under"
whem, whim
when, REFERENCE TO TIME (or see win/ wean/ween)
whence, REFERS TO "FROM/ORIGIN/ WHEN" (or see wince)
whenever, NO SPECIFIC TIME
whenevur, whenever
whens, whence / wean(s) / wince
whent, went
whep, whip
whepurwil, whippoorwill
wher, where / were / we're / ware / weir
wheras, whereas
wherd, where'd / weird
where,*, IN REFERENCE TO PLACE (or see ware/were/we're/whirr)
where'd, CONTRACTION OF THE WORDS "WHERE DID" (or see weird)
where'll, CONTRACTION OF THE WORDS "WHERE WILL", SLANG WORD (or see whirl)
where's, CONTRACTION OF THE WORDS "WHERE IS" (or see ware(s)/wear(s))
whereas, ALTHOUGH, EXCEPT THAT, OTHER THAN
wherever, NO SPECIFIC PLACE

wherewithal, TO HAVE THE RESOURCES/TIME
wherl, whirl / whorl / where'll
wherlpool, whirlpool
wherlwind, whirlwind
whers, where's / wear(s) / ware(s)
whert, where'd / weird
wherwithal, wherewithal
whesk, whisk
whesky, whiskey
whet,*,tted,tting, SMALL AMOUNT REMOVED/ADDED/CARVED OUT (or see wet/wheat/wit/wed)
whether, WHEN ONE OF SEVERAL CHOICES HASN'T BEEN DECIDED, REFERRING TO CHOICE (or see weather/wether/wither)
whetle, whittle
whetlok, wedlock
whetul, whittle
whew, DEEP SIGH OF RELIEF AFTER A STRESSFUL MOMENT (or see woo/hue/who)
whey, INGREDIENT IN SOME ANIMALS MILK (or see way/weigh)
whez, whiz / wheeze
wheze, wheeze(zy)
whezines, wheeze(ziness)
which, CHOICE BETWEEN, CHOOSE ONE (or see witch)
whid, wide / white
while, REFERENCE TO TIME, IN THE MEANTIME, DURING THE SAME TIME (or see will/wile)
whim,msy,msies,msical, SPONTANEOUS, WITHOUT MUCH FORETHOUGHT
whimper,*,red,ring,rer, SOFT CRYING/WHINING SOUND
whimsical,lly,lity,lness, WITH A FRIVOLOUS NATURE, ADVENTUROUS/FANTASY
whine,*,ed,ning,ey,er, A NASAL/NEEDY/PLEADING/WANTING SOUND (or see wine/whinny)
whinefur, whenever
whinevur, whenever
whinny,nnies,nnied,nnying, SOUND A HORSE MAKES (or see whine(y))
whint, went
whiny, whine(y) / whinny
whip,*,pped,pping,pper, BEAT/WORK INTO A LATHER, LONG DEVICE MADE OF WOVEN LEATHER STRIPS (or see wipe)
whiperwil, whippoorwill
whippoorwill, A BIRD
whipurwil, whippoorwill
whirl,*,led,ling,ler,ly, SPIN AROUND (or see whorl)
whirlpool,*, A CIRCULAR/SPIRAL MOTION IN THE WATER
whirlwind,*, CIRCULAR/SPIRAL MOTION IN THE WIND
whirr,*,rred,rring, TYPE OF SOUND LIKE A MOTOR/SPIRAL (or see were/we're/where/whirl)
whisel, whistle
whisk,*,ked,king, BRUSH AWAY AS IF BY THE WIND
whisker,*,red,ry, LONG SENSITIVE/SENSORY HAIRS AROUND ANIMALS NOSE/ SNOUT, FACIAL HAIR
whiskey, ALCOHOL FERMENTATION
whisky, whiskey
whisol, whistle
whisper,*,red,ring,rer,ry, SPEAK QUIETLY/FAINTLY
whistle,*,ed,ling,er, FORCED AIR FROM BETWEEN PURSED LIPS PRODUCING SOUND
whisul, whistle
whit, white / wit / wide
white,*,ed,ting,er,est,en,ener,eness,ening, COLOR PRODUCED BY ALL COLORS OF THE LIGHT SPECTRUM, CALCIUM CARBONATE
whitle, whittle
whittle,*,ed,ling,er, SHAVE OFF SMALL PORTIONS/SLIVERS OF WOOD
whitul, whittle
whity, wit(tty)
whiz,zzes,zzed,zzing, TO STREAK BY QUICKLY AS IF BLOWN BY A STRONG WIND
who,*, TO REFER TO "IN GENERAL" WITHOUT USING A NAME/TITLE/DESCRIPTION OF (or see whoa/hue/whew/woo)
who'd, CONTRACTION OF THE WORDS "WHO HAD/ WOULD/COULD"
who'll, CONTRACTION OF THE WORDS "WHO WILL/SHALL"
who's, CONTRACTION OF THE WORDS "WHO IS/HAS" (or see whose/hose)
whoa, WORD TO GET A HORSE TO STOP (or see woo/whew/woe)
whodel, waddle / what'll
whodul, waddle / what'll
whoever, IN REFERENCE TO ANYBODY, SOMEONE WHOSE NAME/TITLE IS NOT KNOWN AT THE TIME
whole,eness,esome,lly, ENTIRE THING, ALL OF IT, WELL-ROUNDED, COMPLETE (or see hole/holy/wholly)
wholesale,ling,er, SELL WITHOUT PRICE MARK-UP
wholesome,ely,eness, COMPLETE, WELL-ROUNDED "prefixes: un"
wholly, COMPLETE IN ITS ENTIRETY (or see holy/hole/whole(y))
wholsail, wholesale
wholsel, wholesale
wholsem, wholesome
wholsum, wholesome
wholupt, wallop(ed)
wholy, wholly / whole(y)
whom, OBJECTIVE PRONOUN OF "WHO"
whomever, OBJECTIVE CASE OF "WHOEVER"
whomp,*,ped,ping, A SOUND, COMPLETE VICTORY
whoop,*,ped,ping, A TYPE OF SOUND USED IN WAR CRIES, GET A SPANKING/BEATING
whoosh,hes,hed,hing, ACTION/SOUND AS IF SWEPT UP BY THE WIND
whoper, whopper
whopper,*, GREAT/GIANT/HUGE
whore,*,ed,ring, DEROGATORY TERM FOR A PROMISCUOUS FEMALE
whorf, wharf
whorl,*,led,ling, LIKE A WHIRL/SWIRL AS IF TURNED ABOUT BY THE WIND, SPIRAL (or see whirl)
whose, BELONGS TO SOMEONE/SOMETHING IN PARTICULAR (or see who's)
whot, what / watt
whud, what / would
whudel, what'll / waddle
whudevur, whatever
whudul, what'll / waddle
whuever, whoever
whup, whoop
whurlwind, whirlwind
whut, what / would
whutel, what'll / waddle
whutever, whatever

whutul, what'll / waddle
why, A GENERAL QUESTION DESIRING AN ANSWER
wi, we / whee / why / wee
wic, witch / which / week / wick
wich, which / witch
wick,*,ked,king,ker, SLOWLY SOAK UP LIQUID, A WOVEN COTTON FOR LAMP OIL (or see wig)
wicked,dly,dness, EVIL/MALICIOUSNESS INTENT (or see wick(ed))
wicker, FURNITURE BUILT OF WOODY/ WOVEN MATERIAL
wid, wide / ride / white / with / wit / weed / we'd
wide,er,est,en,eness,ener,dth, DIMENSION OF GIRTH/ BREADTH, EXTENT/SPREAD OF (or see white/ width)
widel, whittle
wider, wither / wide(r) / white(r) / ride(r)
widin, within / wide(n)
widl, whittle
wido, widow
widow,*,wer, SPOUSE WHO LOST MATE TO DEATH
widt, width / with / wit
width,*, MEASUREMENT/DISTANCE OF ONE SIDE OF SOMETHING
widul, whittle
wiel, while / will / well / wile
wield,*,ded,ding,dable,der,dy, USE/ GIVEN TO POWER/COMMAND (or see weld/wheel(ed)/wealed/wild) "prefixes: un"
wiener, weiner / wean(er)
wif, wife / weave / we've / with
wife,ely,ives, FEMALE LEGALLY BONDED IN MARRIAGE
wifes, wives
wifs, wlves
wig,*,gged,gging, FALSE HAIR FOR THE HEAD, TO FREAK OUT/ACT NUTS, BE UNCHARACTERISTICALLY UNPREDICTABLE (or see wick)
wiged, wig(gged)
wiggle,*,ed,ling, MOVE QUICKLY FROM SIDE TO SIDE (or see wriggle)
wigul, wiggle
wik, wick / weak / week
wiked, wicked
wiker, wicker
wikur, wicker

wil, while / will / well / wile
wild,der,dest,dly, UNCONTROLLABLE, NO RESTRAINT IN ACTIONS (or see wile(d)/will(ed))
wilderness, UNTAMED/NATURAL FOREST
wildist, wild(est)
wildurnes, wilderness
wile,ed, LURE/ENTICE AWAY FROM (or see while/will)
will,*,lled,lling,llful,llfully,llfulness,llingly, llingness, DESIRE/INCLINATION TO MAKE HAPPEN, LEGAL DOCUMENT OUTLINING DIVISION OF PROPERTY AFTER DEATH (or see well/wile/ while) "prefixes: un"
willdernes, wilderness
willow,*,wy, A TREE, LIKE THE TREE
wilo, willow
wilow, willow
wilt,*,ted,ting, DROOP FROM LACK OF NOURISHMENT AS A PLANT DOES (or see welt)
wim, whim
wiman, women
wimon, women
wimp,*,ped,ping,py, LACK OF COURAGE/STRENGTH
wimpur, whimper
wimsecal, whimsical
wimsikul, whimsical
win,*,nning,nner,won,nnable, ADVANTAGE IN COMPETITION (or see when/whine/wine)
wince,*,ed,cing, TO FLINCH (or see whence)
winch,hes,hed,hing, PULL/HOIST SOMETHING BY MEANS OF A DEVICE (or see wench/wrench)
winchd, wench(ed) / winch(ed) / wrench(ed)
winchis, wench(es) / winch(es) / wrench(es)
wind,*,ded,ding,dy,dier,diest,wound, dless, AIR MOVING FASTER THAN A BREEZE,TURN SOMETHING UNTIL TIGHT/TAUT (or see went) "prefixes: en/in/re/un/up"
wine,*,ning, FRUIT/FLOWERS THAT HAVE BEEN CAREFULLY AGED/ FERMENTED (or see whine/whinny)
wined, wine(d) / whine(d) / wind
winefer, whenever
winefur, whenever

winer, win(nner) / whine(r) / weiner
winey, whine(y) / weeny
wing,*,ged,ging,gless, BIRD/INSECT/ PLANE ARMS, TO AD LIB "prefixes: under"
wini, weeny / whine(y)
wink,*,ked,king, QUICK BLINK OF ONE EYE "prefixes: un"
winor, win(nner) / whine(r) / weiner / wean(er)
winsday, wednesday
winsh, wench / winch / wrench
winshd, wench(ed) / winch(ed) / wrench(ed)
wint, went / wend / whine(d) / wind
winter,*,red,ring,ry, SEASON BETWEEN FALL/AUTUMN/ SPRING "prefixes: over"
wintre, winter / wintry
wintry,rier,riest, LIKE WINTER
wintur, winter
winur, win(nner) / whine(r) / weiner / wean(er)
winy, whine(y) / whinny
wip, whip / wipe
wipd, whip(pped) / wipe(d)
wipe,*,ed,ping,er, REMOVE CONTAMINANT/SURFACE DEBRIS/ MATERIAL TO CREATE SMOOTH PLANE/SURFACE (or see whip)
wipen, whip(pping) / wipe(ping)
wiperwil, whippoorwill
wipon, whip(pping) / wipe(ping)
wipt, whip(pped) / wipe(d)
wipun, whip(pping) / wipe(ping)
wipurwil, whippoorwill
wir, wire / were / wear / ware / where / we're / whirr / weir
wird, word / wire(d)
wire,*,ed,ring,eless,ry, METAL STRAND (or see were/whirr/weir) "prefixes: pre/re/un/under"
wiri, worry / weary
wirk, work
wirkeble, work(able)
wirkt, work(ed)
wirkuble, work(able)
wirkur, work(er)
wirl, whirl / whorl
wirld, whirl(ed) / world / whorl(ed)
wirleng, whirl(ing)
wirles, wire(less)
wirlpul, whirlpool
wirlwind, whirlwind

wirm, worm
wirnt, weren't
wirpool, whirlpool
wirs, worse / worst
wirshep, worship
wirshup, worship
wirth, worth
wirthe, worth(y)
wirthy, worth(y)
wis, wise / whiz
wisd, whiz(zzed)
wisdem, wisdom
wisdom, KNOWLEDGE GAINED BY EXPERIENCE "prefixes: un"
wisdum, wisdom
wise,er,est,ely,eness,sdom, KNOWLEDGE GAINED BY EXPERIENCE "prefixes: un"
wisel, whistle
wiserd, wizard
wises, whiz(zzes) / wise(s)
wish,hes,hed,hing,hful,hfully,hfulness, HOPE/IMAGINE FOR THE FUTURE "prefixes: un"
wishus, wish(es)
wisk, whisk
wiskd, whisk(ed)
wiske, whiskey
wisker, whisker
wiskur, whisker
wisky, whiskey
wisol, whistle / weasel
wisp,*,py, LIGHT, AIRY, OF LITTLE WEIGHT
wispe, wisp(y)
wisper, whisper
wisperd, whisper(ed)
wispur, whisper
wispurer, whisper(er)
wisteria, A FLOWERING BUSH
wistle, whistle
wisul, whistle
wisurd, wizard
wisus, whiz(zzes)
wit,*,tted,tting,tty,ttier,ttiest, QUICK IN MIND/RESPONSE (or see with/wet/white/write/wheat) "prefixes: un"
witch,hes,hing,hy,hery, TERM FOR A FEMALE WHO GIVES IMPRESSION THEY HAVE SUPER POWER (or see which)
wite, wit(tty) / white
witel, whittle

with, PREFIX INDICATING 'BACK/AWAY/AGAINST' MOST OFTEN MODIFIES THE WORD (or see width)
withaut, without
withdrau, withdraw
withdraw,*,wing,wal,wn,hdrew, PULL/MOVE BACK, RETREAT
withdro, withdraw
withdron, withdraw(n)
witheld, withheld
withen, within
wither,*,red,ring, SHRIVEL/SHRINK FROM LACK OF NOURISHMENT/MOISTURE, MEASUREMENT OF SOME QUADRUPED ANIMALS AT THE SHOULDER (or see weather/wether/whether)
withheld, PAST TENSE FOR THE WORD 'WITHHOLD', TO HOLD BACK
withhold,*,ding,held, THE ACT OF HOLDING BACK, REFRAIN FROM MAKING VISIBLE/APPARENT
within, CONTAINED, NOT VISIBLE/APPARENT
withold, withhold
withor, wither
without, LACKING, NOT HAVING
withstand,*,ding,tood, TO STAND AGAINST, TOLERATE
withstood, PAST TENSE FOR THE WORD 'WITHSTAND'
withstud, withstood
withur, wither
witle, whittle
witness,sses,ssed,ssing, HAVE KNOWINGNESS OF, HAVING SEEN
witnus, witness
witol, whittle
witul, whittle
wity, wit(tty)
wives, PLURAL WORD FOR 'WIFE', MORE THAN ONE WIFE
wiz, wise / whiz
wizard,*,dry, A PERSON WHO PARTAKES IN ACTIONS INVOLVING MYSTICAL POWER
wizd, whiz(zzed)
wizer, wise(r)
wizerd, wizard
wizest, wise(st)
wizur, wise(r)
wizurd, wizard
wo, whoa / woo / woe / whew

wobble,*,ed,ling,ly, LACKS STABILITY IN POSITION, NOT STEADY
wobul, wobble
woc, walk / woke / wok
woch, wash / watch
wochd, watch(ed)
woches, watch(es)
wochful, watch(ful)
wocht, watch(ed)
wochus, watch(es)
wod, wad / wood / would / what / wait
wodent, wouldn't
woder, water
wodercres, watercress
wodere, water(y)
woderfol, waterfall
woderkres, watercress
wodertite, watertight
wodery, water(y)
wodid, wad(dded) / wait(ed) / wade(d)
wodil, waddle / what'll
wodint, wouldn't
wodir, water
wodirfal, waterfall
wodirkres, watercress
wodirtite, watertight
wodul, waddle / what'll
wodur, water
wodurkres, watercress
wodurtite, watertight
woe,*,eful,efully,efulness, SORROW/LAMENT (or see woo/whoa)
wofel, waffle
woful, waffle
wok,*, VESSEL FOR COOKING (or see woke/walk)
woke, PAST TENSE FOR 'WAKE' (or see wok/walk)
woken, PAST TENSE FOR 'WAKE', BRING TO CONSCIOUSNESS FROM A DEEP SLEEP
wokin, woken
wokun, woken
wol, wall / wool
wold, wall(ed)/ wail(ed) / would
wolen, wool(en)
wolep, wallop
wolet, wallet
wolf,lves,fing, OF THE WILD CANINE/CANID FAMILY
wolin, wool(en)
wolip, wallop
wolipd, wallop(ed)
woliped, wallop(ed)

wolit, wallet
wolk, walk / woke
wolken, walk(ing)
wolker, walk(er) / walker
wolkur, walk(er) / walker
wolnut, walnut
wolo, wallow
wolod, wallow(ed)
wolopd, wallop(ed)
wolopt, wallop(ed)
wolres, walrus
wolrus, walrus
wolsem, wholesome
wolst, waltz(ed)
wolts, waltz
woltsd, waltz(ed)
woltz, waltz
wolup, wallop
wolupt, wallop(ed)
wolut, wallet
wolveren, wolverine
wolverine,*, ANIMAL IN THE WEASEL FAMILY NOT RELATED TO WOLVES
wolves, PLURAL FOR 'WOLF', IN THE CANID FAMILY
wolwrus, walrus
wolz, waltz
wom, womb
woman,men,nism,nless,nly,nliness, AN ADULT FEMALE
womanhood, GROWING INTO ADULT FEMALE HUMAN
womanize,*,ed,zing,er, MEN WHO DENIGRATE WOMEN
womb,*, FEMALE ORGAN THAT CREATES LIFE "prefixes: en"
women, PLURAL FOR "WOMAN"
womin, woman / women
womp, whomp
won, PAST TENSE WORD FOR 'WIN' (or see one/wan)
won't, CONTRACTION OF THE WORDS 'WILL NOT' (or see want)
wond, wand / won / wane(d) / wan(ed)
wonder,*,red,ring,rful, QUESTION, PONDER, MARVEL (or see wander)
wonderd, wander(ed) / wonder(ed)
wonderful,lly,lness, FULL OF AWE, IMPRESSED
wondurd, wander(ed) / wonder(ed)
wondurer, wander(er)
wons, once / want(s) / win(s)
wonten, wanton
wontenes, wanton(nness)

wonter, wander / wonder
wonton, wanton
wontunes, wanton(nness)
wontunle, wanton(ly)
woo,*,oed,oing,oingly,oer, PERFORM ACTS TO GAIN ATTENTION/ AFFECTION/APPROVAL FROM SOMEONE (or see whew/woe/ whoa)
wood,*,ded,den,dy,dsy,dless, FIBROUS/ NATURAL MATERIAL, STEM/BASE OF A TREE/BUSH, HEAVILY TREED/ BUSHY AREA (or see would) "prefixes: under"
woofer,*, LOUDSPEAKER IN SOUND SYSTEM
woofur, woofer
wool,*,len,ly, HAIR FROM THE FLEECE OF ANIMALS
woolvs, wolves
woom, womb
woop, whoop
woose, woozy
woosh, whoosh
woosy, woozy
woozy,zily,ziness,zier,zies, FEELING OUT OF SORTS/UNSTABLE/SLIGHTLY DRUNK
woper, whopper
wopur, whopper
wor, war / wore
worant, warrant
worbeld, warble(d)
worbild, warble(d)
worbler, warbler
worblur, warbler
worbuld, warble(d)
word,*,ded,ding,dy,dily,diness,dless, dlessly,dlessness, LETTERS ARRANGED TOGETHER TO CREATE MEANING, USING TOO MANY WORDS TO DESCRIBE (or see war(rred)/ward/where'd/wart) "prefixes: re"
worden, warden
wordon, warden
wordrob, wardrobe
wordun, warden
wore, PAST TENSE FOR THE WORD 'WEAR' (or see war)
woreir, warrior
woren, warren
worent, warrant
worented, warrant(ed)

worentes, warrant(ies)
worenty, warrant(y)
woreur, warrior
worf, wharf
worier, warrior
worin, warren
worint, warrant
worinte, warrant(y)
worinted, warrant(ed)
worinty, warrant(y)
work,*,ked,king,ker,kable,kability, kableness, PERFORM ACTIONS/ TASKS TO ACCOMPLISH A DESIRED RESULT "prefixes: over/re/un"
workuble, work(able)
worl, whirl / whorl
world,*,dly,liness, OF/BELONGS TO THIS PLANET "prefixes: un/under"
worm,*,med,ming,mer,my, AN INVERTEBRATE WHICH LIVES MOSTLY CONCEALED FROM VIEW (or see warm)
wormd, warm(ed) / worm(ed)
wormer, warm(er) / worm(er)
wormest, warm(est)
wormle, warm(ly)
wormth, warm(th)
wormur, warm(er)
wormust, warm(est)
worn, PAST TENSE FOR THE WORD 'WEAR', USED MANY TIMES (or see warn) "prefixes: un"
wornd, warn(ed)
wornt, warn(ed) / weren't
worp, warp
worpd, warp(ed)
worry,rries,rried,rying,rrisome,yingly, rrier, BE CONCERNED/ FEARFUL ABOUT SOMETHING WHICH MAY/ MAY NOT HAPPEN
worse,st,en, MORE THAN BAD, MORE TROUBLE THAN EXPECTED/ ANTICIPATED (or see worst)
worsen,*,ned,ning,st, CONTINUES TO GET WORST/ DETERIORATE
worsh, wash
worshep, worship
worship,*,pped,pping,pper, ONE WHO IDOLIZES/ADORES SOMEONE/ SOMETHING
worst, MORE EXTREME THAN WORSE, MORE TROUBLE THAN EXPECTED/ ANTICIPATED (or see worse)
wort, wart / word / ward

worth,hier,hiest,hiness,hless,hlessly,hy,hily, VALUE/QUALITY OF SOMETHING/ SOMEONE "prefixes: un"
worun, warren
worunt, warrant
worunty, warrant(y)
wory, worry
wos, was / woe(s)
wosh, wash
woshd, wash(ed)
woshepl, wash(able)
wosher, washer
woshir, washer
wosht, wash(ed)
woshuble, wash(able)
woshur, washer
wosnt, wasn't
wosp, wasp
wosy, woozy
wot, watt / what / wad
wotch, watch
wotertite, watertight
woturd, water(ed)
would, PERHAPS WILL BE DONE/ ACCOMPLISHED, POSSIBLE (or see wood)
would've, CONTRACTION OF THE WORDS 'WOULD HAVE'
wouldn't, CONTRACTION OF THE WORDS 'WOULD NOT', WILL NOT BE DONE/ ACCOMPLISHED
wound,*,ded,ding,dless, PHYSICALLY HARMED/INJURED, PAST TENSE FOR THE WORD 'WIND' "prefixes: en/un"
wount, won't
wove,en, PAST TENSE FOR THE WORD 'WEAVE' "prefixes: inter"
wownt, won't
woz, was
wozp, wasp
wozy, woozy
wra, ray / raw
wrack,*,ked,king,kful, WRECKED/ RUINED, PERTAINING TO CLOUDS (or see rack)
wrak, rack / rake / wrack / rag
wrangle,*,ed,ling,er, BE CONFRONTATIONAL/ ARGUMENTATIVE, TO ROUND UP CATTLE
wrangul, wrangle

wrap,*,pped,pping,pper, COVER/ SURROUND SOMETHING, TO PACKAGE UP (or see rap) "prefixes: en/un"
wrased, raise(d) / race(d) / erase(d)
wrath,hful,hfully, EXTREMELY ANGRY/ PUNISHING/REVENGEFUL
wreak,*,ked,king, CAUSE CONFUSION/ DAMAGE AS IF BY MEANS OF RAGE/ VENGEANCE (or see reek/wreck)
wreath,*,hless, CIRCULAR GARLAND OF VARIOUS PLANT/ORGANIC MATERIAL, CIRCULAR SHAPE, NOUN (or see wreathe)
wreathe,*,hed,hing, THE ACTION OF CIRCLING/ENCIRCLING, VERB (or see wreath) "prefixes: en"
wrech, wretch / reach
wreck,*,ked,king,ker, CRASH/ALTER/ DESTROY (or see wreak)
wrecker,*, A TRUCK THAT TOWS VEHICLES
wreek, wreak / reak
wreeth, wreath / wreathe
wregul, wriggle
wreker, wrecker
wrekur, wrecker
wren,*, A SMALL BIRD
wrench,hes,hed,hing, A HAND TOOL USED FOR TURNING/TWISTING, TWIST SOMETHING AROUND (or see winch/wench)
wrer, rear / rare / wear
wresil, wrestle
wrest,*,ted,ting, TO FORCIBLY TWIST/ WRING/REMOVE FROM GRASP/ POWER (or see wrist)
wrestle,*,ed,ling,er, FORCIBLY ATTEMPT TO MANEUVER/ MANIPULATE
wresul, wrestle
wretch,hed,hedly,hedness, POOR/ MISERABLE/UNHAPPY PERSON
wreth, wreath / wreathe
wriggle,*,ed,ling,ly, TO SQUIRM/ WRITHE/MOVE IN TWISTING/ TURNING MOTIONS (or see wiggle)
wright, PROFESSIONAL INVOLVED IN ART/HAND WORK, AN ARTISAN (or see right/rite/writ)
wrigle, wriggle
wrigul, wriggle
wrin, wren
wrinch, wrench

wring,*,ging,rung, TWIST SOMETHING AROUND TIGHTLY CREATING COMPRESSION (or see ring)
wrinkle,*,ed,ling,ly, LINES, CREASES
wrist, A JOINT THE ARM (or see wrest)
writ, WRITTEN COURT ORDER (or see write/right/rite)
write,*,tten,ting,rote,table,tability, PUT WORDS/MUSIC INTO PHYSICAL/ VISIBLE FORM (or see writ/right/ rite/wright) "prefixes: over/pre/re/ under"
writer,*, SOMEONE WHO WRITES (or see writ/right/rite/wright) "prefixes: under"
writhe,*,ed,hing, TWIST/SQUIRM EMOTIONALLY AND/OR PHYSICALLY
written, PAST TENSE FOR THE WORD WRITE "prefixes: un"
wrk, work
wrm, worm/ warm
wrom, worm / warm
wron, worn / warn
wrong,*,ged,ging,gly,gness, NOT SUITABLE/CORRECT/PROPER/ NORMAL
wrot, wrought / wrote / rote
wrote, PAST TENSE FOR THE WORD "WRITE" (or see rote/wrought/rot) "prefixes: under"
wrought, DECORATIVE METALWORK, PAST TENSE FOR THE WORD "WREAK", TWISTED WITH WORRY/ PAIN "prefixes: over"
wrout, wrought
wrudikulus, ridiculous
wrudiquelus, ridiculous
wrung, PAST TENSE FOR THE WORD "WRING" (or see rung)
wry,rier,riest,yly,yness, TWISTEDLY IRONIC, OUT OF SHAPE (or see rye)
wryth, writhe
wu, whew / woo / what
wud, would / wood / what
wudal, what'll / waddle
wudent, wouldn't
wudever, whatever
wudil, what'll / waddle
wudint, wouldn't
wudul, what'll / waddle
wue, whew / woo
wufer, woofer
wufir, woofer
wufs, wolves

wul, wool
wulen, wool(en)
wulf, wolf
wulferene, wolverine
wulin, wool(en)
wulveren, wolverine
wulviren, wolverine
wulvs, wolves
wum, womb
wumen, woman / women
wumin, woman / women
wuminhud, womanhood
wuminizer, womanize(r)
wund, wound
wunderful, wonderful
wunefur, whenever
wunevur, whenever
wup, whoop
wur, were / whirr
wurd, word / where'd
wure, worry
wuri, worry
wurk, work
wurkd, work(ed)
wurkebul, work(able)
wurker, work(er)
wurkt, work(ed)
wurl, whirl / whorl
wurld, whirl(ed) / world / whorl(ed)
wurlpool, whirlpool
wurlpul, whirlpool
wurls, whirl(s) / whorl(s)
wurlt, whirl(ed) / world / whorl(ed)
wurlwend, whirlwind
wurlwind, whirlwind
wurm, worm
wurnt, weren't
wurs, worse / worst
wursen, worsen
wurshep, worship
wurshup, worship
wurst, worst
wurth, worth
wurthe, worth(y)
wurthy, worth(y)
wury, worry
wus, was / woo(s)
wuse, woozy
wush, whoosh
wusi, woozy
wusnt, wasn't
wut, what / would / wood
wutefer, whatever
wutel, what'll / waddle

wutever, whatever
wutil, what'll / waddle
wutul, what'll / waddle
wuz, was
wuznt, wasn't
wuzy, woozy
wy, why
x, ex
x-ray,*,yed,ying, RADIATION WHICH PENETRATES PHYSICAL MASS
xagurate, exaggerate
xajurate, exaggerate
xakut, execute
xam, exam
xamen, examine
xamin, examine
xampel, example
xampul, example
xamun, examine
xanth, PREFIX INDICATING "YELLOW" MOST OFTEN MODIFIES THE WORD
xaspurate, exasperate
xaust, exhaust
xchang, exchange
xdra, extra
xdru, extra
xekute, execute
xemplify, exemplify
xempt, exempt
xen, PREFIX INDICATING "STRANGE" MOST OFTEN MODIFIES THE WORD
xeno, PREFIX INDICATING "STRANGE" MOST OFTEN MODIFIES THE WORD
xenon, A GAS
xenophobe,bia,bic, IRRATIONAL/ EXTREME HATRED/CONTEMPT FOR FOREIGN PEOPLE
xer, PREFIX INDICATING "DRY" MOST OFTEN MODIFIES THE WORD
xerafit, xerophyte
xeraphyte, xerophyte
xero, PREFIX INDICATING "DRY" MOST OFTEN MODIFIES THE WORD
xerophily,lous, SURVIVES IN DRY/HOT REGIONS
xerophyte,*,tic,tically,tism, DROUGHT/ HEAT RESISTANT PLANT
xet, exit
xhale, exhale
xibit, exhibit
xil, exile
xilene, xylene
ximplify, exemplify
xiraphyte, xerophyte

xist, exist
xit, exit
xklud, exclude
xklumashen, exclamation
xkurshen, excursion
xkuse, excuse
xkuvate, excavate
xodik, exotic
xpand, expand
xpans, expanse / expense / expand(s)
xpekt, expect
xpel, expel
xpens, expense
xpereins, experience
xperumint, experiment
xpir, expire
xplan, explain
xplod, explode
xplor, explore
xployt, exploit
xport, export
xpoz, expose
xpres, express
xpudeshin, expedition
xpurt, expert
xsalint, excellent
xsed, exceed
xsel, excel / accel / axle
xsept, except
xses, excess
xsit, excite / exit
xsploshen, explosion
xsplosive, explosive
xsulent, excellent
xsurpt, excerpt
xsursiz, exercise / exorcise
xtend, extend
xtenshen, extension
xtenuate, extenuate
xtereur, exterior
xtinkt, extinct
xtra, extra
xtradite, extradite
xtrakt, extract
xtrem, extreme
xtrordenair, extraordinaire
xtrordinery, extraordinary
xtru, extra
xturnol, external
xukute, execute
xurt, exert
xyl, PREFIX INDICATING "WOOD" MOST OFTEN MODIFIES THE WORD
xylafon, xylophone

xylagraf, xylograph
xylaphone, xylophone
xylatomy, xylotomy
xylaudomy, xylotomy
xylem, THAT WHICH FORMS WOODY FIBER/TISSUE/STEM IN PLANTS
xylene,*,lol, A CHEMICAL
xylo, PREFIX INDICATING "WOOD" MOST OFTEN MODIFIES THE WORD
xylofon, xylophone
xylograph,*,her,hy,hic,hical,hically, WOOD CARVINGS USED TO EMBOSS SOMETHING ELSE
xylophone,*,nist, MUSICAL INSTRUMENT
xylose, A CHEMICAL
xylotomy,mic,mical,mous,mist, THE ART OF CUTTING WOOD
xylum, xylem
y, why
y'all, CONTRACTION FOR THE WORDS "YOU ALL" (or see yell)
ya, yaw / ye / yea / yeah
yacht,*,ting, PLEASURE SHIP
yahoo,*, EXPRESSION OF JOY, ROWDY PEOPLE
yal, yawl / y'all / yowl / you'll
yam,*, TYPE OF POTATO
yank,*,ked,king, TO SWIFTLY JERK/PULL
yard,*,dage, ENGLISH MEASUREMENT OF DISTANCE/LENGTH, THREE FEET, AREA FOR SPECIAL USE
yareu, urea
yareul, urea(l)
yarn,*, SPUN THREADS
yarrow, A WILD HERB
yart, yard
yat, yacht
yau, yaw / ye / yea / yeah
yaul, yawl / y'all / yowl / you'll
yaupon, SHRUB HOLLY
yaurd, yard
yaw,*,wed,wing, VERTICAL ROLL/TILT ON A SHIP/VESSEL/CRAFT
yawl,*, TYPE OF BOAT (or see y'all/ yowl)
yawn,*,ned,ning, EXAGERRATED STRETCHING OF JAW WHILE DEEPLY INHALING
ye, ANOTHER EXPRESSION OF "YOU"
yea,*, VERBAL VOTE OF "YES" (or see yeah)
yeah, SAME MEANING AS "YES" (or see yea)

year,*,rly, DAYS "prefixes: bi/semi"
yearling,*, AN ANIMAL IN ITS SECOND YEAR OF LIFE
yearn,*,ned,ning, LONG FOR/WANT SOMETHING
yeast,*,ted,ting,ty, A FUNGUS THAT ACTIVATES FOOD TOWARD FERMENTATION
yeild, yield
yel, yell
yeld, yell(ed) / yield
yell,*,lled,lling, TO VOICE/VOCALIZE LOUDLY (or see yield)
yellow,*,wed,wing,wer,west, A COLOR "prefixes: non"
yelp,*,ped,ping, HIGH-PITCHED SOUND DOG MAKES ASSOCIATED WITH PAIN
yelt, yell(ed) / yield
yeoman,*,men,menly, A NAVAL TERM/ POSITION, ATTENDANT TO NOBILITY
yep, yip / yes
yepe, yippee
yer, your / you're
yeraneum, uranium
yerater, ureter
yerathan, urethane
yereik, urea(eic)
yerek, uric
yerethu, urethra
yerin, urine
yerinary, urinary
yerinate, urinate
yerolegy, urology
yerolugy, urology
yers, your(s)
yerun, urine
yerunal, urinal
yerunolegy, uranology
yes,ses, AFFIRMATIVE/CONFIRM/ APPROVE
yeseg, usage
yest, yeast
yesterday, THE DAY BEFORE TODAY
yet, EXCEPT/BUT, IN REFERENCE TO TIME
yeu, ewe / you / yew
yeuld, yield / yell(ed)
yew,*, A TREE (or see you/ewe)
yewbikwite, ubiquity
yewcaliptus, eucalyptus
yewderis, uterus
yewdirus, uterus

yewdulize, utilize
yewjuale, usual(lly)
yewkalale, ukulele
yewkulale, ukulele
yewl, yule / you'll
yewnafid, unify(fied)
yewnaform, uniform
yewnaformedy, uniform(ity)
yewnasen, unison
yewnasikul, unicycle
yewnatery, unitary
yewnaversul, universal
yewnek, unique
yewnekorn, unicorn
yewneladeral, unilateral
yewnelateral, unilateral
yewnesikul, unicycle
yewnet, unit
yewnety, unity
yewnevers, universe
yewnikorn, unicorn
yewniladeral, unilateral
yewnilateral, unilateral
yewnit, unit
yewnitary, unitary
yewnite, unite
yewnufikashen, unification
yewnusen, unison
yewnusikul, unicycle
yewnutarean, unitary(rian)
yewnuversul, universal
yewnyun, union
yewsd, use(d)
yewshwul, usual
yewtensul, utensil
yewtilutarean, utilitarian
yewtilute, utility
yewtinsul, utensil
yewtopea, utopia
yewtulize, utilize
yewturis, uterus
yield,*,ded,ding, GIVE WAY TO, GAIN/ PRODUCE "prefixes: un"
yip,*,pped,pping,pper,ppee, SOUND/ BARK FROM A DOG (or see yep)
yipe, yippee
yippee, JUBILANT SOUND OF JOY
yipy, yippee
yir, your / you're / year
yiraneum, uranium
yirathan, urethane
yirek, uric
yiren, urine
yirenary, urinary

yirenate, urinate
yirenul, urinal
yirethu, urethra
yiruter, ureter
yo, yaw / ye / yea / yeah
yoc, yoke / yolk
yocert, yogurt
yocurt, yogurt
yodel,*,led,ling,ler, FALSETTO SOUND COMING FROM THE THROAT
yoeman, yeoman
yoga, FORM OF MEDITATIVE EXERCISE
yoge, yogi
yogi,ic, TEACHES/PRACTICES THE ART OF YOGA
yogurt, FOOD WITH PUDDING TEXTURE/CONSISTENCE(CY)
yok, yoke / yolk
yoke,*,ed,king, HARNESS (or see yolk) "prefixes: un"
yokel,*, A LOCAL/COUNTRY TYPE PERSON
yokert, yogurt
yokirt, yogurt
yokurt, yogurt
yol, yawl / y'all / yowl / you'll
yolk,*, YELLOW PART OF EGG, EMBRYO (or see yoke)
yoman, yeoman
yonder, WAY OVER THERE
yoni, FEMALE GENITALIA
yor, your / you're
yord, yard
yorn, yarn
yot, yacht
you, REFERRING TO A PERSON OTHER THAN SELF (or see yew/ewe)
you'll, CONTRACTION FOR THE WORDS 'YOU WILL'
you're, CONTRACTION FOR THE WORDS 'YOU ARE' (or see your)
youbikwite, ubiquity
youdulize, utilize
youduris, uterus
youl, yule / you'll
younanemus, unanimous
younaversul, universal
younavirsity, university
youneladeral, unilateral
younelateral, unilateral
younevirsul, universal
younevursity, university
young,ger,gest,gish,gster, YOUTHFUL, EARLIER YEARS

youngster,*, YOUNG PEOPLE/CHILDREN
youniversity, university
youniversul, universal
younivurs, universe
younuvers, universe
your,*, IN REFERENCE TO SOMEONE ELSE'S POSSESSION (or see you're)
yourself,lves, MAKING REFERENCE TO SOMEONE ELSE
yous, use
yousd, use(d)
youseg, usage
youser, user
youserp, usurp
yousery, usury
yousful, useful
youshwule, usual(lly)
yousles, useless
youslus, useless
youtensul, utensil
youth,hful, YOUNG
youthful,lly,lness, OF BEING YOUNG
youtilady, utility
youtilutarean, utilitarian
youtilute, utility
youtopea, utopia
youtulize, utilize
youturis, uterus
youz, use
yowl,*,led,ling,ler, MOURNFUL CRY OF ANIMAL/PERSON (or see jowl)
yu, you/ yew/ ewe
yubikwite, ubiquity
yuderus, uterus
yuduris, uterus
yue, ewe / you / yew
yukaliptus, eucalyptus
yukulale, ukulele
yul, yule / you'll
yule, PAGAN FESTIVAL AROUND CHRISTMAS (or see you'll)
yunanemus, unanimous
yuneform, uniform
yuneladeral, unilateral
yunelateral, unilateral
yup, yip / yes
yuraneum, uranium
yuranium, uranium
yurathen, urethane
yureik, urea(eic)
yurek, uric
yuren, urine
yurenal, urinal
yurenary, urinary

yurenat, urinate
yurethu, urethra
yureu, urea
yureul, urea(l)
yurin, urine
yuritur, ureter
yurolegy, urology
yurolugy, urology
yuron, urine
yurs, your(s)
yurt,*, TENT/DOME STRUCTURE/ DWELLING
yusd, use(d)
yuseg, usage
yuser, user
yuserp, usurp
yusful, useful
yushuel, usual
yushwul, usual
yusig, usage
yusir, user
yusirp, usurp
yusiry, usury
yuslus, useless
yust, use(d)
yutopea, utopia
yutulize, utilize
yuturis, uterus
yuwl, yawl / y'all / yowl / you'll
yuze, use
yuzer, user
yuzir, user
yuzur, use
zar, czar
zderty, sturdy
zdirdy, sturdy
zdurdee, sturdy
zdurty, sturdy
zeal,lous,lously,lousness, PASSIONATE/ EXUBERANT/EAGER EMOTIONS
zealot,*, ONE WHO IS FANATICAL/GETS CARRIED AWAY BY EMOTIONS
zebra,*, AFRICAN STRIPED HORSE
zebru, zebra
zefir, zephyr
zegzag, zig-zag
zel, zeal
zeleon, zillion
zeles, zeal(ous)
zelet, zealot
zelis, zeal(ous)
zelit, zealot
zelus, zeal(ous)
zelut, zealot

zenafobia, xenophobe(bia)
zeneth, zenith
zeng, zing
zenge, zing(y)
zenith,hal, HIGHEST/FARTHEST PEAK/ POINT
zenk, zinc
zenofob, xenophobe
zenofobic, xenophobe(bic)
zenon, xenon
zenuth, zenith
zenya, zinnia
zep, zip
zephir, zephyr
zephyr, FRAGILE/GENTLE WIND/FABRIC
zepur, zipper
zerafit, xerophyte
zeraufilus, xerophily(lous)
zerconium, zirconium
zero,oes,oed,oing, NUMBER INDICATING NIL/NOTHING, TARGET IN ON
zerofele, xerophily
zerofelus, xerophily(lous)
zerofit, xerophyte
zerofule, xerophily
zerofulus, xerophily(lous)
zest,ty,tful,tfrully,tfulness, WITH ENERGY/SPICE/GUSTO
zethur, zither
zigzag,*, GO BACK AND FORTH WHILE MOVING IN SPECIFIC DIRECTION
zilafon, xylophone
zilagraf, xylograph
zilaudime, xylotomy
zilaugrafur, xylograph(er)
zilauteme, xylotomy
zilefon, xylophone
zilegraf, xylograph
zilem, xylem
zilen, xylene
zileon, zillion
zilion, zillion
ziliphone, xylophone
zillion,*, EXTREMELY HIGH NUMBER
zilodeme, xylotomy
zilograf, xylograph
zilom, xylem
zilos, xylose
ziloteme, xylotomy
zilufon, xylophone
zilugraf, xylograph
zilum, xylem
ziluphone, xylophone

zimerge, zymurgy
zimolege, zymology
zimurge, zymurgy
zinafobia, xenophobe(bia)
zinafobic, xenophobe(bic)
zinc,ced,cing,cic,coid,cous,cky,cy,cite, A METAL
zing,*,ged,ging,gy, A SPEEDY/SHRILL SOUND/ACTION WHICH HAPPENS VERY QUICKLY, FAST, SPEEDY
zinia, zinnia
zink, zinc
zinnia,*, A FLOWER
zinya, zinnia
zip,*,pped,pping,ppy,pper, FAST/SWIFT "prefixes: un"
zipd, zip(pped)
zipe, zip(ppy)
ziped, zip(pped)
ziper, zipper
zipper,*,red,ring, A CLOSING DEVICE
zipur, zipper
zirafule, xerophily
zirconium, ON THE PERIODIC TABLE OF ELEMENTS
zirkoneum, zirconium
zirofit, xerophyte
ziruphyte, xerophyte
zither,*, AN INSTRUMENT
zithur, zither
zoademy, zootomy
zoagrafe, zoography
zodeak, zodiac
zodiac,*,cal, DEPICTION OF CONSTELLATIONS AND HOW THEY RELATE TO HUMANS
zoezu, zoysia
zoisa, zoysia
zombe, zombie
zombie,*, SOMEONE WHO IS ROBOTIC/ CONTROLLED BY A NON-HUMAN FORCE
zone,*,ed,ning,nal,nate,nated,nation, A SPECIFIC AREA DESIGNATED FOR SPECIFIC PURPOSES "prefixes: bi/ inter/intra"
zoo,*,oography,oology,oometry, oomorphic,oophyte,ootomy, PLACE WHERE ANIMALS ARE AVAILABLE FOR VIEWING PUBLIC, PREFIX INDICATING 'ANIMAL' MOST OFTEN MODIFIES THE WORD
zoodeme, zootomy
zoofit, zoophyte

zoography,her,hic,hical,hically, RELATED TO THE STUDY OF ANIMALS AND THEIR BEHAVIOR
zoogrufe, zoography
zoology,gical,gically,gist, SCIENCE OF STUDYING ANIMALS AND THEIR BEHAVIOR
zoom,*,med,ming, TO DECREASE DISTANCE BETWEEN OBSERVER AND THE OBSERVED
zoometry,ric,rical,rist, SCIENCE WHICH STUDIES ANIMALS AND THEIR SIZES/ PROPORTIONS
zoomorfik, zoomorphic
zoomorphic,ism, PORTRAY/ASCRIBE ANIMALS AS IF HAVING HUMAN FEELINGS/ BEHAVIORS/ CHARACTERISTICS
zoophyte,*,tic,tical, ANIMALS THAT RESEMBLE PLANTS
zootomy,mic,mical,mist, STUDY/ DISSECTION OF THE ANATOMY OF ANIMALS
zorgem, sorghum
zorgum, sorghum
zorkum, sorghum
zoysa, zoysia
zoysia, A GRASS
zu, zoo
zuamorfik, zoomorphic
zuchene, zuchinni
zuchinni,*, A VEGETABLE
zufit, zoophyte
zukene, zuchinni
zukine, zuchinni
zum, zoom
zumd, zoom(ed)
zuografe, zoography
zuolege, zoology
zuometre, zoometry
zurconium, zirconium
zurkoneum, zirconium
zyg, PREFIX INDICATING 'UNION/PAIR' MOST OFTEN MODIFIES THE WORD
zygo, PREFIX INDICATING 'UNION/PAIR' MOST OFTEN MODIFIES THE WORD
zym, PREFIX INDICATING 'UNION/PAIR' MOST OFTEN MODIFIES THE WORD
zymerge, zymurgy
zymirgy, zymurgy
zymo, PREFIX INDICATING 'UNION/ PAIR' MOST OFTEN MODIFIES THE WORD
zymolege, zymology

zymology,gic, SCIENCE DEALING WITH FERMENTATION
zymurgy, STUDY OF THE PRINCIPLES OF FERMENTATION

www.ingramcontent.com/pod-product-compliance
Lightning Source LLC
Chambersburg PA
CBHW080242030426
42334CB00023BA/2668